Three Thousand Illustrations
for Christian Service

Three Thousand Illustrations

for

Christian Service

by

Walter B. Knight

WM. B. EERDMANS PUBLISHING COMPANY

Grand Rapids 1950 Michigan

Three Thousand Illustrations for Christian Service
by Walter B. Knight

Set up and printed, July, 1947

Third Printing, July, 1950

PRINTED IN THE UNITED STATES OF AMERICA

This volume is affectionately dedicated to my unfailingly constant wife, Alice Marie Neighbour Knight, whose painstaking effort and discrimination have entered into the compilation of this volume.

"I marvel that God made you mine,
For when He frowns, 'tis then ye shine!"

—Lanier.

Introductory Note

Was it not Spurgeon, that prince of preachers, who said on one occasion when addressing a group of embryo ministers: "Remember, the sermon is the house; the illustrations are the windows that let the light in"?

Many sermons give evidence of careful preparation, deep spiritual insight, and of earnest effort to help and bless their hearers; but unfortunately they fail to sustain the interest of the bulk of the audience who listen to them because of the fact that they are too heavy for the average mind to follow. They lack those brightening illustrations which mean so much in compelling attention and even in elucidating doctrinal positions, which are not grasped readily by those untaught in theology or who have very little acquaintance with Biblical truth.

Therefore, the importance of a book such as this now before the reader, which contains such a large number of excellent illustrations in the form of stories and poems, all carefully classified as to subjects, so that they are readily available for the preacher's use.

Needless to say, the compiler is himself sound in the faith and has only grouped together such incidents and paragraphs as would be in keeping with a thoroughly evangelical presentation. I have no hesitancy in recommending this book to all who value such helps.

H. A. IRONSIDE,
Pastor of the Moody Memorial Church,
Chicago.

PREFACE

During the formative years of young manhood, it was my privilege and pleasure to come, as a news correspondent, under the inspiration and influence of the late Drs. R. A. Torrey, A. C. Dixon, George W. Truett, L. R. Scarborough, James M. Gray, R. E. Neighbour, and J. B. Phillips — all mighty in the Scriptures, and faithful, fearless preachers of the Word.

How clear, challenging, and convincing were their messages, which were always interspersed with stirring, striking, illustrations drawn largely from their varied experiences with all classes and conditions of humankind. What light flooded our soul as these stalwart servants of the Saviour opened the windows, through which shaft of light entered on the wings of some heart-warming, soul-stirring illustration. Can we ever get beyond the power of the illustrations on soul-winning by Dr. Scarborough? Or the action-producing illustrations of Dr. Truett, so fervidly related? Or the convincing, conversion illustrations of Dr. Torrey? Never can we forget the story told by Dr. Torrey of the heroic rescue by Ed Spencer of more than a score of imperilled men and women, floundering amidst the wreckage of the "Lady Elgin." It was this gripping illustration which set aglow in my youthful heart the quenchless desire to win souls.

As a teen-year-old boy, I was soundly saved under the ministry of Dr. T. W. Callaway, whose life and preaching God used greatly to mould my young manhood, and guide my steps into the pathway of God's choosing. Not until one awakens with Christ's likeness can he fully appraise the value to my boyish heart of his enthusiasm-enkindling illustrations and stories. It was in those early years that I began to see the purpose and power of well-chosen illustrations in preaching, in teaching, and in writing. It was Moody who said that "what windows are to a home, illustrations are to a sermon."

For the past twenty-five years, I have been diligently and delightedly gleaning and gathering, from widest possible sources, the quotations, excerpts, poems, and illustrations, 3,000 of which appear in this book, the remainder of a like number to appear in a later volume of illustrations. So wide and varied has been the origin of this illustrative material that any printed acknowledgement in these brief prefatory words would be prohibitive. However, wherever sources of authorship are known to the compiler, these are indicated throughout the book. In an undertaking so vast, and extending over such a long span of years, with no thought at the outset of compiling from this illustrative material books of illustrations, some failures as relates to source or authorship have naturally crept in. For this we ask indulgence. As can be seen, however, the overwhelming majority of illustrations are from well-known and duly acknowledged sources.

All of this illustrative material is Bible-centered, Christ-exalting, God-honouring. It is, therefore, hopefully and prayerfully believed that this volume will, under God's blessings, meet a unique need, and take its place in the hearts and hands of preachers and teachers of the Word and Christian workers everywhere. At least, this is our ardent prayer and expectation.

For decades, the compiler of this volume has been a minister, a contributing writer for various religious publications, a writer of booklet-tracts, and for fifteen years, one of the editors for the young people's literature and Sunday school publications of the Union Gospel Press, Cleveland, Ohio. In my writings, as well as in preaching and teaching, we have found the contents of this (and Volume II, forthcoming) book of illustrations to be invaluable. What tools are to the builder and mechanic, this illustrative material has been to me. I have found instantly, at my finger tips, just the illustration, story, or poem needed to "clinch" any Bible truth. As through the years this illustrative material was in the process of being collected, it was arranged under a complete, alphabetized index system, with cross references, so as to make easily available what was needed on any given subject. This feature will greatly enhance the usefulness of this volume.

May God be pleased to use this illustrative material to bring illumination and inspiration to many.

WALTER BROWN KNIGHT.

CHICAGO, ILLINOIS.

CONTENTS

Three Thousand Illustrations
for Christian Service

AMBITION

The Last Word of Foch

When Marshal Foch, that great commander, came to the close of his life, those listening heard his last word, *Allons*—"Forward." He was watching his glorious army meeting the enemy, being thrown back, and then making an heroic effort to conquer. The greatest word he ever gave, the word that put spirit and power into his soldiers, was "Forward."—*The Homilope (church envelope)*.

* * *

The Best

God has His best things for the few
  Who dare to stand the test;
God has His second choice for those
  Who will not have the best.

It is not always open sin
  That risks the promised rest;
The *better* often is the foe
  That keeps us from the *best*.

There's scarcely one but vaguely wants
  In some way to be blessed;
'Tis not Thy blessing, Lord, I seek;
  I want Thy very best.

I want in this short life of mine
  As much as can be pressed
Of service true for God and man;
  Help me to be my best.

I want amid the victor throng
  To have my name confessed;
And hear my Master say at last,
  "Well done! You did your best."

Give me, O Lord, Thy highest choice,
  Let others take the rest;
Their good things have no charm for me,
  For I have got Thy Best.

—*A. B. Simpson.*

What Made Him a Tramp

Margot Asquith tells how she once met a tramp and asked him how he decided which way he would tramp, and his answer was, "I always turn my back to the wind." That was what made him a tramp. He never had the courage to breast the wind and go courageously on in its teeth, or he would have ceased to be a tramp and have become a man. Alas! many people with plenty of money in their pockets are only tramps who always turn their backs to the wind and thus lose the real joy and achievement of life. It was not so with Paul and Barnabas.—*From the Homiletic Review.*

* * *

Life is a sheet of paper white
Whereon each one of us may write
His word or two, and then comes night.
Greatly begin! Though thou hast time
But for a line, be that sublime.
Not failure, but low aim is crime.

—*Lowell*

* * *

Climb On

James T. White

"He died climbing" is the simple inscription on a monument to an Alpine guide, who perished when attempting the ascent of a peak. That record is a noble tribute to a hero. His attitude should be ours—looking upward and pressing forward. He was pressing on in the pathway of duty. Many a splendid career, intercepted at the critical juncture, might be described by the same concise record.

"He died climbing" may be said of many a young and ardent enthusiast—of Mackay, soon cut off in Uganda; of Bishop Hannington, reaching the border of the same land and martyred there; of Patterson, soon slain in Melanesia by islanders who mistook him for a slave-catching captain. Of Henry Martyn, who did not live to see any of the results of his mission; of Wycliffe, who sent forth the Bible in England but was not permitted to see the beginning of the Reformation. All these "died climbing."

"Climb on! Climb ever! Ne'er despond,
Though from each summit gained
There stretch forth ever heights beyond—
Ideals to be attained!"

—*Character Lessons.*

* * *

"In The Lord"

O, to be something, something!
Something, my Saviour, for Thee;
To show forth the wondrous power,
Of the love that could save even me.
Something—for use in Thy vineyard,
Tho' simple the service may be;
Something—Thy grace can find use for,
To win other wanderers to Thee.

O, to be something, something!
A word—or a light—or a song,—
To speak—or to shine for the Master,
Or sing,—to win lost ones from wrong.
The cup of cold water to offer,
To those who in weariness stray,—
Thy "sure word of promise" to whisper,
To those whom temptations dismay.

O, to be something, something!
Where others Thy likeness may see;
That self may be lost in service,
And our lives glorify Thee.
Ready to work or to suffer,
Whichever Thy love shall command;
Secure—whether shadow or sunshine,
They are all from Thy loving hand.

—*Ida Tremain*

* * *

The Doldrums

There is a region in the ocean near the equator where the winds are either baffling or there is a calm, sometimes lasting through several days. The sailors called this region "The Doldrums." Since there were no other kinds of vessels but sailing vessels in those days, it is readily seen how impatient the sailors would be if they had an important cargo, and were delayed by a calm. There was nothing in the world they could do but just wait until a breeze sprung up.

One can readily imagine also how these long delays got on the nerves of the sailors, especially when there was nothing for them to do but loaf about and wait for a wind. They became depressed in mind and gave way to low spirits during such times, and it was hard for them to remain patient and keep from giving way to the "blues."

It was easy therefore to transfer this name from that region in the ocean to that state of mind into which so many fall when everything does not go as they want it to. And so we must credit the sailors with giving us a name for being out of sorts and unhappy, which has now become the meaning of "The Doldrums" since there are steam vessels which are not so dependent on the winds to drive them over the ocean.

—*Gospel Herald*

* * *

The Letter Over the Door

A student of Amherst College, soon after entering, put over the door of his dormitory room the letter V. Because of it he endured all sorts of ridicule and withstood questioning. But he paid no attention to either, nor would he disclose the secret of the letter. When his four years were over, and graduation day came, that student was appointed to deliver the valedictory. Then the mystery of that letter V was revealed. It stood for valedictory.

That letter on the door held before him during his four years the ideal that he had set for himself. Not every boy puts a letter over the door of his college room or over the door of his house. But nevertheless, somewhere, if only in his mind, there is a letter that he pastes there and that holds before him an ideal.

Some put up the letter M that stands for money. Others put up F, for fame. Others put up S, which may stand either for self or for service. *It is a good idea once in a while to step outside your door and look at the letter you have put there. It may be that when you realize what it is you will want to change it.*

—*Courtesy Moody Monthly*

APOSTASY

Apostasy

Church of Christ, awake today!
Let the Spirit have His way;
"Come ye out"; "love not the world";
What though ridicule be hurled
In your face? Stand firm and true!
There's a mighty task to do.

Worldly members like to say;
"Do things in a modern way!
Put on programs! Hold the youth
As they question: 'What is truth?'"
Church of Christ, exalt the Lord!
Try all spirits by His Word.

—*Alice Louise Cary*

* * *

Couldn't Put the Fire Out!

A Denver magazine reports a disastrous fire in that city during which a large warehouse, containing thousands of tons of ice, was destroyed. The editor points out that the building actually contained thousands of gallons of a potent extinguisher—*but it was frozen!* What a picture of the apostate condition of the churches today, while sin rages throughout the country.—*Ohio Independent Baptist.*

* * *

The Ex-Convict's Disappointment

Pity poor Benjamin Ullmo, who served a twenty-six year sentence on Devil's Island, far-famed French penal colony, and undoubtedly yearned in his prison for the opportunity to return to "civilization." One day he went back to France, and after a short stay, voluntarily went back to Devil's Island. He was disappointed with what he found, and it might interest you to know what this ex-convict thought about the modern world: He was struck most with "the extraordinary spiritual collapse of the world and the decline in conscience and intelligence." That's hard criticism coming from a convict. He was less impressed with material progress and the lowering of moral standards, but astounded at the "immeasurable stupidity of present-day humanity which regards itself as so superior." Is it possible that the man from Devil's Island is near the truth?

—*The General Baptist Messenger.*

ASHAMED (See also: Confession)

A Modern Mrs. Nicodemus

"Mither," said a Scots laddie, "there's a new mon come to toon to preach. Gang and hear him." Thinking it strange to be asked by her boy, she resolved, though reluctantly, to go. How to conceal from her neighbors her going to a revival meeting was her difficulty. Nicodemus went to Jesus under cover of night; this woman took her market basket on her arm, as if she were going to make the usual daily purchases, thus screening herself from the observation and jeers of her neighbors. Day after day she appeared at the meeting with her basket. At length she was brought to know the Lord. "Ye'll not need the basket any-more," said the evangelist to her, with a significant twinkle in his eye.—*London Christian Herald.*

* * *

Ashamed, and Not Ashamed

A young convert tried to preach in the open air. He could not preach very well, but he did the best he could. Someone interrupted him and said: "Young man, you cannot preach; you ought to be ashamed of yourself!" Said the young man: "So I am, but I am not ashamed of my Lord." That is right. Do not be ashamed of Christ—of Him who bought us with His own blood. — *Christian Herald* (*London*).

A Japanese Schoolboy

A Japanese schoolboy once showed his courage in a way that puts many of us to shame. He belonged to a school in Nagasaki containing one hundred and fifty boys, and he was the only Christian among them all. He brought his luncheon to school, as he lived at a distance, and he dared to fold his hands and ask a blessing every day before he ate. He had some enemies among the boys, who went to the master of the school and accused him of "doing something in the way of magic." The master thereupon called the lad before the school and asked him what he had been doing. The little fellow spoke up bravely, explaining that he was a Christian, and that he had been thanking God and asking him to bless the food. At once the master burst into tears, putting his head down on the desk. "My boy," he said, "I, too, am a Christian; but I did not dare let men know that I was one. Now, please God, I will try to live as a Christian ought to live."—*From the late Amos R. Wells, in Christian Herald.*

* * *

Aaron Burr's "Almost."

Have you ever noticed the danger of standing on the borderland? Some of those men who became the greatest enemies of Christ were so near to becoming Christians that it is a wonder they evaded it. Take that man, Aaron Burr, who was the traitor of America, who bartered his country. He was in a Yale University revival meeting. The invitation was given for those who wished to give themselves to Christ to leave their seats and go into another room. He was moved, deeply moved by the Spirit to become a Christian and went with the other young fellows. As he passed, someone said, "Look at Aaron Burr going into the inquiry room." Burr turned and came back and said, "I was only fooling."—*From Sermon by William Evans in Good News.*

ASSURANCE

Heart Knowledge Is Power

Some years ago at a drawing-room function, one of England's leading actors was asked to recite for the pleasure of his fellow guests. He consented and asked if there was anything special that his audience would like to hear.

After a moment's pause, an old clergyman present said: "Could you, sir, recite to us the Twenty-third Psalm?"

A strange look passed over the actor's face; he paused for a moment, and then said: "I can, and I will, upon one condition; and that is that after I have recited it, you, my friend, will do the same."

"I?" said the clergyman, in surprise. "But I am not an elocutionist. However, if you wish it, I will do so."

Impressively, the great actor began the psalm. His voice and his intonation were perfect. He held his audience spellbound; and as he finished, a great burst of applause broke from the guests.

Then, as it died away, the old clergyman arose and began the psalm. His voice was not remarkable; his intonation was not faultless. When he had finished, no sound of applause broke the silence—but there was not a dry eye in the room, and many heads were bowed.

Then the actor rose to his feet again. His voice shook as he laid his hand upon the shoulder of the old clergyman and said: "I reached your eyes and ears, my friends; he reached your hearts. *The difference is just this—I know the Twenty-third Psalm, but he knows the Shepherd.*"
—*The War Cry.*

* * *

Resting on Certainties

When that great Christian and scientist, Sir Michael Faraday, was dying, some journalists questioned him as to his speculations concerning the soul and death. "Speculations!" said the dying man, in astonishment, "I know nothing about speculations; I'm resting on certainties. '*I know whom I have believed, and am persuaded that he is able to keep that which I have committed unto him against that day.*' "—*Gospel Trumpet.*

* * *

His Word Not Broken

An old Scotch lady, to whom in the bygone days of searching pastoral visitation, her minister went as she lay dying. Wishing to try her faith, he said to her; "Janet, what would you say if, after all He has done for you, God should let you perish?" She replied: "Even as He likes: if He does, He will lose more than I'll do: for I would lose my soul, but He would lose His honor, for His Word would be broken."—*Selected.*

* * *

What Persuasion

A visitor said to a poor wounded soldier, who lay dying in the hospital, "What Church are you of?"

"Of the Church of Christ," he replied.

"I mean, what persuasion are you of?"

"Persuasion!" said the dying man, as he looked Heavenward, beaming with love to the Saviour, "I am persuaded, that neither death, nor life, nor angels, nor principalities, nor powers, nor things present, nor things to come, . . . shall be able to separate us from the love of God, which is in Christ Jesus."

—*Selected.*

* * *

Assurance

Robert Bruce, of Kinnaird, after breakfast on the last day of his life, said suddenly to his daughter: — "Hold, daughter; my Master calleth me." At these words his sight, unconsciously to himself, failed, and he called for a Bible; but finding that he was sightless, he said:—"Turn up the eighth chapter of Romans, and put my finger on verse 39." "Now," he said, "is my finger on it?" They told him it was. Then he said: "God be with you my children; I have breakfasted with you, and I shall sup with the Lord Jesus Christ tonight"; and immediately he died.—*Dawn.*

"Are You Sure?"

In a humble cottage out on a jagged promontory, a fisherman lay dying. His pastor sat beside him. "Are you sure, John?" he asked the old man. Rising on his elbow, the old veteran bade him look seaward through the open window. "Are the Seven Stones still there?" he asked. "And the Twin Maidens and the Wolf Rock—are they still there?" "Yes, yes," replied his pastor, "they are still there." Lying back upon his pillow, the dying man said, reverently: "The mountains shall depart, and the hills be removed; but my kindness shall not depart from thee, neither shall the covenant of my peace be removed, saith the Lord that hath mercy on thee."—*Christian Herald.*

* * *

My Anchor Holds

"A sailor in Gloucester, Mass., had been wounded in a wreck and was brought ashore. The fever was great, and he was dying. His comrades gathered around him in a little fishing house, and the physician said: 'He won't live long.' The sailor was out of his mind until near the close. But within a few minutes of his death he looked around, and calling one comrade after another, bade them goodbye, and then sank off to sleep. Finally as it was time for the medicine again, one of the sailors rousing him, said, 'Mate, how are you now?' He looked up to the face of his friend and said, 'My anchor holds!' These were his last words. And when they called upon a friend of mine to take charge of the funeral service, how powerful was the impression made upon his hearers when he quoted the dying words; 'My anchor holds!' "—*Selected.*

* * *

Why Fear?

"I fear you are near another world," remarked a friend to an aged Christian. "I know I am," was the cheerful reply; "but, blessed be the name of the Lord, I do not fear it—I hope it!"—*D. L. Moody.*

Pay The Price

An express train started out from Chicago to the west coast. On board was the president of the road. As they rushed along in the darkness of the night the train was wrecked. The president of the road hurried to the front. The engineer was pinned beneath the engine. As the president stood looking at the prostrate form, he saw his lips move, and leaning down, he heard the dying man say, "I know whom I have believed, and am persuaded that He is able to keep that which I have committed unto Him against that day." "Jim," said the president, "I would be willing to give my life with all that I have for such a faith as that."

"Mr. President," said Jim, "that is just what it cost."—*Selected.*

* * *

"Blessed Assurance Jesus Is Mine"

"Here is a new hymn tune I have written; what does it say to you?"

Mrs. Joseph Knapp, the composer of Gospel music, asked the question one day as she and Fanny Crosby were chatting in the latter's home. While the blind hymn writer listened, Mrs. Knapp played her new tune several times on the piano. Suddenly, Fanny Crosby's face was lighted with inspiration.

"Why, that music says 'Blessed assurance, Jesus is mine!' " she answered. And that is how one of America's most beloved and beautiful hymns came to be written.

Fanny Crosby, who never could remember having seen the light of day, always has been admired for the remarkable way in which she turned her handicap into a blessing. She never permitted anyone to express sympathy for her blindness. One day a clergyman, talking with her, mentioned her affliction. The blind poetess surprised him by declaring that she was sometimes glad to be sightless.

"You see," she explained, "when I get to Heaven, the first face that shall ever gladden my sight will be that of my Saviour."

In her own account of the origin of *Blessed Assurance*, Fanny Crosby said, commenting on Mrs. Knapp's hymn tune:

"It seemed to me one of the sweetest tunes I had heard in a long time. She asked me to write a hymn for it and I felt, while bringing the words and tones together, that the air and the hymn were intended for each other. In the hundreds of times that I have since heard it sung, this feeling has been more and more confirmed."

Blessed assurance, Jesus is mine!
O what a foretaste of glory Divine!
Heir to salvation, purchase of God
Born of His Spirit, washed in His Blood.

—*Selected*

* * *

If the Lord is My Shepherd

The missionary was teaching a class of small Navajo boys to say the Twenty-third Psalm. When Bahi's turn came, he started out confidently, "The Lord is my Shepherd, I've got all I want."—*Rev. J. R. Smith.*

* * *

Spiritual Talk

Did you ever think whence came the words "papa" and "mama"? We can trace most words to an etymological source; we can find in the study of language and grammar the roots from which they came; but you can find no etymological source for "papa" and "mama." They come from the grammar of nature, the etymology of nature. When a child begins to talk, he uses the simplest consonants and the simplest vowels; and because he knows how to make but one syllable, he repeats the syllable. And so he says "papa" and "mama."

God gives us the spirit of adoption, and we cry "Abba." That is Aramaic for "papa." It is a repetition of the two simplest syllables. *The spirit of adoption comes into the child of God, and teaches him to look up into the Father's face, and say, "Papa, Papa!"*—Arthur T. Pierson, in *The Heart of the Gospel.*

He Knew The Boy

When Rudyard Kipling was a lad he went on a sea voyage with his father, Lockwood Kipling. Soon after the vessel got under way, Mr. Kipling went below, leaving Rudyard on deck. Presently there was a great commotion overhead, and one of the officers ran down and banged on Mr. Kipling's door.

"Mr. Kipling," he cried, "your boy has crawled out on the yardarm, and if he lets go, he'll drown!"

"Yes," said Mr. Kipling, glad to know nothing serious was wrong, "but he won't let go."—*Selected.*

* * *

What He had Been Living For

A writer in the *Church Union* tells this story. The writer's grandfather had an old colored workman who had been a slave, and was used to the severest kind of labor. No need for a slave-driver for him, however, as his tasks were conscientiously performed. Corporal, as the old slave was called, was of a religious turn, and believed with an unalterable firmness in the truths brought to him. Finally the time came for Corporal to leave this world. The doctor said to him: "Corporal, it is only right to tell you that you must die." "Bless you, Doctor; don't let that bother you; that's what I have been living for," said Corporal with the happiest of smiles.—*The Earnest Worker.*

* * *

His Hold, Not Ours

There is a beautiful story told of McLeod Campbell, the Scotch preacher and divine. One day a friend came to him in spiritual perplexity. "Tell me, how do you know that you have always got hold of God?" For a long minute the minister was silent, and then, with a great wistfulness in his eyes, he said: "How do I know that I have always got hold of God! I don't always know; but I do know He always has hold of me!"—*From the Christian Herald.*

* * *

"He Will Not Let Me Fall"

A climber in the Alps had come to a perilous gap in the ice where the only way to get across was to place his foot in the outstretched hand of the guide. Told to do this by the guide, the climber hesitated a moment as he looked into the gloomy depths below. Seeing the hesitation, the guide said, "Have no fear, sir, that hand never yet lost a man." And when any soul truly commits itself into the hands of Jesus Christ, that one is committed to the strong, sure keeping of hands *that never yet lost a man.—Sunday School Times.*

* * *

What The World Needs

One cold, winter afternoon the philosopher, Thomas Carlyle, was sitting before the open fire-place in his library. The door opened and the new pastor of the local church entered the room. After Carlyle and the young minister had visited for a few minutes, the young minister asked the great philosopher, "What do you think this parish needs most?" Carlyle, without any hesitancy, replied, "What this parish needs is a man who knows God otherwise than by hearsay."—*Selected.*

* * *

For We Know

"For I know whom I have believed" (II Tim. 1:12).

What wondrous blessings overflow,
When we can truly say, "I know"—
I know in whom I have believed,
I know the One I have received,
I know His Blood avails for me,
I know that I was blind, but see,
I know that my Redeemer lives,
I know the gift He freely gives,
I know He'll keep me to the end,
I know He's my unfailing Friend,
I know He's coming in the sky,
I know the time is drawing nigh.

— R. E. Neighbour, D.D.

* * *

"I'm A Poor Sinner"

Charles H. Spurgeon used to tell years ago the story of a huckster. His name was Jack and he was one of the happiest men in London. He went about singing a little verse:

I'm a poor sinner, and nothing at all,
But Jesus Christ is my All in all.

Those who knew him were astonished at his constant composure. They had a world of doubts and fears, and so they asked him why he never doubted. "Well," said he, "I cannot doubt but what I am a poor sinner, and nothing at all, for I know that and feel it every day. And why should I doubt that Jesus Christ is my All in all? For He says He is." "Oh!" said his questioner, "I have my ups and downs." "I do not," says Jack; "I can never go up, for I'm a poor sinner, and nothing at all; and I cannot go down, for Jesus Christ is my All in all."

He wanted to join the church, and they said he must tell his experience. He said, "All my experience is that I am a poor sinner and nothing at all, and Jesus Christ is my All in all." "Well," they said, "when you come before the church meeting, the minister may ask you questions." "I can't help it," said Jack, "all I know I will tell you, and that is all I know—
I'm a poor sinner, and nothing at all,
But Jesus Christ is my All in all."

He was admitted into the church, and continued with the brethren, walking in holiness; but that was still all his experience, and you could not get him beyond it. "Why," said one brother, "I sometimes feel so full of grace, I feel so advanced in sanctification, that I begin to be very happy." "I never do," said Jack, "I am a poor sinner, and nothing at all." "But then," said the other, "I go down again and think I am not saved, because I am not sanctified as I used to be." Said Jack, "I never doubt my salvation, because Jesus Christ is my All in all, and He never alters." The old huckster knew the secret of the Gospel and of true Christian experience, which is "Not I, but Christ."—*Selected.*

* * *

Not The Shady Side

An old man who had lived a long life of fellowship with and service for his Lord was asked, "You are on the shady side of seventy, I suppose?" "No," he replied, "I am on the sunny side, for I am on the side nearest glory."—*Sunday School Times.*

ATHEISM

The Goat and the Critics

Dr. Brookes of St. Louis used to tell of a backwoods railroad in the old days —just a train with a wood-burning engine, a lot of cars, a conductor, and a brakeman. The people put the freight on the flat cars and had it carried to the next station. Someone shipped a goat up the line with a tag on him indicating the station to put him off. The goat began to eat everything in sight as a goat will, and finally chewed his tag and swallowed it. The brakeman did not know where to deliver him so let him go at the end of the line. "Why didn't you put that goat off?" the conductor asked. "Well, boss," he answered, "he don't know where he's going, and I don't know; he's chewed up his tag." That is like the critics who say the Bible is a lot of myths and legends, thus making the Bible of none effect. If we have no authoritative Book from God, who knows where we are going?— *Serving and Waiting.*

* * *

Dissolved

Incidently it might be mentioned that the American Association for the Advancement of Atheism has gone into liquidation. Its members lack sufficient "consecration" for the cause to keep it going.—*Pentecostal Evangel.*

* * *

The Same God

I have noticed that many men who call themselves atheists do not carry their atheism into their speech. They freely take the name of the Lord in vain, and seem quite unaware that such profanity is really a left-handed confession of faith. When I meet such a man, who loads his language with all sorts of oaths, and yet declares his unbelief, I want to repeat to him that pithy saying of old Richard Hooker: "*What! shall we have a God to swear by and not one to pray to?*"—S. S. paper.

* * *

The Communist Who Succeeded

A Communist agitator rode into Hyde Park and after leaning his bicycle against the railings, mounted a soap box and proceeded to address the crowd. "If your family is hungry," he shouted, "raid a shop and take food for them, and don't care what anyone says. If your wife hasn't got a coat, pick the best fur coat you can see, and ignore the consequences!" After several more minutes in this strain he dismounted from his soap box, and his next words were, "Who are the scoundrels who pinched my bike?"—*The Toronto Globe.*

* * *

False Science and Manners Are Morals

I recently talked with a judge of the United States Circuit Court, who had just gone back to his alma mater for a visit, the first since his graduation. He was received as an honored guest, a famous "old grad," and was made to feel at home. He spoke a few words in the assembly, words of faith and trust. After the assembly he dropped into a science class, and was in time to hear the professor make some facetious remarks about "the old fossil who had talked in chapel." The professor's remarks were so well received by the class that he felt encouraged to go on, and he sneered at the virgin birth of Jesus Christ, called him a martyr who died for a foolish ideal, scoffed at His resurrection, and rudely jested about His return. The old judge rose in indignation to defend the Lord Jesus, and the class jeered him to silence! He said he was so amazed that he went on a tour of investigation, and found that the "faith, manners, and morals" of the student body were gone.
— *Dr. Harry Rimmer.*

"Authoritarian?"

Under the heading, "Extraordinary" Chapel Talk, the *King's Business* states that Dan Gilbert spoke at the chapel period at a great eastern university about a year ago. Attendance was compulsory. When he told the university president his subject, "God in Our Generation," the educator expressed amazement. He said, "Why, I presumed you would be speaking on some outstanding political or social issue of the day." Later he added: "While it was interesting, your address was quite out of the ordinary; in fact, rather irregular. To my knowledge, it has been at least two years since anyone dealt with the idea of God in such a way as to convey the impression that our thinking regarding Deity should be dictated by *Biblical* teachings. Generally, we regard religion as a private matter, and one man's concept of God is as good as another's. We do not think the students should be indoctrinated with 'authoritarian' principles of religion."—*Selected.*

* * *

Vain Boasts:

Here is the boast of Adolph Hitler with which the whole world was made acquainted some time ago. "Nothing will prevent me from tearing up Christianity, root and branch . . . We are not out against a hundred-to-one different kinds of Christianity, but against Christianity itself. All people who profess creeds . . . are traitors to the people. Even those Christians who really want to serve the people . . . we have to suppress. I myself am a heathen to the core." How successful Adolph Hitler has been in making good his boast may best be told by a chaplain in one of the camps of German prisoners in Tennessee, who recently wrote: "I wish you could have been present to see with what avidity these books [*Bibles*] were received by these [German] prisoners of war . . . I am here to tell you that Hitler has not succeeded in eradicating the hope of the Christian faith from the hearts of his people." It is related that once upon a time the famous atheist, Tom Paine, who wrote "The Age of Reason," asked Benjamin Franklin what he thought of the book. The only reply from Franklin was: "Tom, he who spits against the wind spits in his own face."—*Free Methodist.*

* * *

Thou Remainest

One day Voltaire said to a friend, "It took twelve ignorant fishermen to establish Christianity; I will show the world how one Frenchman can destroy it."

Setting to his task, he openly ridiculed Sir Isaac Newton. One day Newton made a prophecy based on Dan. 12:4 and Nahum 2:4 when he said, "Man will some day be able to travel at the tremendous speed of 40 miles an hour."

Voltaire replied with, "See what a fool Christianity makes of an otherwise brilliant man, such as Sir Isaac Newton! Doesn't he know that if man traveled 40 miles an hour, he would suffocate and his heart would stop?"

Twenty-five years after Voltaire died, his home was purchased by the Geneva Bible Society and became a Bible storage building, and his printing press was used to print an entire edition of the Bible—*Sunday School Times.*

* * *

Questioning God's Word

Some time ago I spoke to a great Southern audience. I pictured the atheistic drift in the educational life of America. A man sat on the front seat and followed my every word with an expression of agony I have rarely seen on a human face. When the service was over his pastor said to me, "Did you see that man who looked like the incarnation of agony? He sat in the front seat today. He is a member of my church. He is one of the truest Christians I have ever known. He is on my board. He had one daughter. She was a beautiful child. She grew up in the Sunday School and the church. She finished high school. He sent her off to a certain college. At the end of nine months she came home with her faith shattered. She laughed at God and the old-time religion. She broke the hearts of her father and mother. They wept over her. They prayed over her. It availed nothing. At last they chided her. She rushed upstairs, stood in front of a mirror, took a gun and blew out her brains."—From Bob Jones, in the *Pentecostal Evangel.*

* * *

The Ark the Skeptic Stumbled Over

A choice example of the "knowledge" of the Bible possessed by skeptics has been related. One such skeptic was at a dinner and sat next to a Bible teacher, who engaged him in conversation, and opened to him the subject of faith in Christ. The skeptic said he had once been a reader of the Bible, but that he had grown disgusted with its errors, and no longer had any use for it. The Christian asked to know the definite things that so impressed him, and received the following answer: "When I began to read the Bible, I came across the story of Noah and the ark. I am a lumberman, and it interested me. I began to figure out its dimensions and how many feet of lumber went into it. I was astonished and impressed at its size. But a few days later, I opened the Bible again, and saw that the Levites took the ark on their shoulders and carried it around in the wilderness. Such foolishness made me angry, and I have never looked inside the book again."—*Young People's Full Gospel Quarterly.*

* * *

The Modernists' Masquerade

Dr. George B. Foster in his "The Finality of the Christian Religion" says, "An intelligent man who now affirms his faith in miracles can hardly know what intellectual honesty means." Dr. Foster claims that "Jesus did not transcend the limits of the purely human." It was of this book that a Chicago daily wrote: "We are struck also with the hypocrisy and treachery of these attacks on Christianity. This is a free country and a free age, and men can say what they choose about religion, but this is not what we arraign these divinity professors for. Is there no place in which to assail Christianity but a divinity school? Is there no one to write infidel books except the professors of Christian Theology? Is a theological seminary an appropriate place for a general massacre of Christian doctrines? We are not championing Christianity or *infidelity*, but only condemning infidels masquerading as men of God and Christian teachers." — *Sunday School Times.*

* * *

Remember

Remember how Voltaire stood in Paris two hundred years ago and said that it took 12 men to originate the Christian religion but it would take but one to eliminate it, and then he dipped his pen in the ink of hatred of his heart and wrote against God's Book and Christianity. His name is forgotten but we still have the Christian religion here, and on the very spot that he uttered these words is a printing press opened and operated by a Bible society which sends Bibles to every nation in the earth. Some 50 years ago Robert Ingersol wrote on the "Mistakes of Moses." He said, "Twenty-five years after I am dead there will not be a church in the land." Ingersol has gone but the Bible is here, and churches are still here.—*Selected*

* * *

Is There No God

There is no God? Then tell me pray
Who started the sun on his golden way,
Who paints the flowers and tints the sky
From a pallette of color of secret dye?

Who is it that tells in early Spring
The flowers to waken, the birds to sing,
The ice to thaw, the river to flow,
And tells sleeping things to rise and grow?

Who is it that set the stars in their course?
Just natural law commingled with force?
Is it that which brings comfort in hours of pain
And soothes a tired body to sleep again?

The sea and the valley, the plains and the hills,
The mighty rivers, the sparkling rills;
The primrose, the holly, the goldenrod—
All of them symbols. Is there no God?

—*The War Cry.*

Why Not An Infidel

I once met a thoughtful scholar who told me he had read every book he could which assailed the religion of Jesus Christ, "And," said he, "I should have become an infidel but for three things:

"First, I am a man. I am going somewhere. Tonight I am a day nearer the grave than I was last night. I have read all such books can tell me. They shed not one solitary ray of hope or light upon the darkness. They shall not take away the Guide and leave me stone blind.

"Second, I had a mother. I saw her go down into the dark valley where I am going, and she leaned on an Unseen Arm as calmly as a child goes to sleep on its mother's breast. I know that was not a dream.

"Third, I have three motherless daughters. They have no protection but myself. I would rather kill them than leave them in this sinful world, if you blot out the teachings of the Gospel."—Bishop Whittle, in *The Christian Armour.*

* * *

God Is Not Mocked

A notorious infidel had a considerable following in a certain town. He was one of the braggart stamp, and seemed to revel in his outpourings of blasphemy against God. One day, in the height of his folly, he challenged God, if such a Being existed, to fight him in a certain wood.

The day came, and he went defiantly to the wood, stayed a certain time, and returned home again apparently all right, and no doubt jubilant of his seeming success.

But when in the wood there had alighted on his eyelid a tiny midge, which he brushed away, paying no attention to it. At night it swelled up, and blood poisoning setting in, *he died.*

"The fool hath said in his heart, There is no God." God sent one of His tiniest insects, and the boasting braggart fell before it.

Note.—This remarkable and striking incident is vouched for as strictly accurate. The place and time of its occurrence are known. It is worthy of being pondered over, especially in the fact that a long-suffering God did not strike the blasphemer dead upon the spot, but gave him four days' warning, and space for repentance.—*Faithful Words.*

* * *

The Skeptic's Dilemma

A young skeptic once said to an elderly lady, "I once believed in God, but now, since studying philosophy and mathematics I am convinced that God is but an empty word." "Well," said the lady, "it is true that I have not learned these things, but since you have, can you tell me from whence this egg comes?" "Why, of course, from a hen," was the reply. "And where does the hen come from?" "Why from an egg." Then the lady inquired, "May I ask which existed first, the hen or the egg?" "The hen, of course," rejoined the young man. "Oh, then a hen must have existed without having come from an egg?" "Oh, no, I should have said the egg was first." "Then I suppose you mean that one egg existed without having come from a hen?" The young man hesitated: "Well, you see—that is—of course, well, the hen was first!" "Very well," said she. "Who made that first hen from which all succeeding eggs and hens have come?" "What do you mean by all this?" he asked. "Simply this, I say that He who created the first egg or hen is He who created the world. You can't explain the existence even of a hen or an egg without God, and yet you wish me to believe that you can explain the existence of the whole world without Him!"—*From a sermon by W. H. Griffith Thomas.*

* * *

"Safety First"!

There is the story of an American tourist in France who went to the hotel keeper to pay his bill. The French hotel keeper said, "Don't you want a receipt?" "Oh, no," said the American, "if God wills I will be back in a week. You can give me a receipt then." "If God wills," smiled the hotel keeper, "do you still believe in God?" "Why, yes," said the American, "don't you?" "No," said the hotel keeper, "we have given that up long ago." "Oh," replied the American, "well, *on second thought I believe I'll take a receipt!"*—J. M. Vander Meulen, in *The Faith of Christendom.*

* * *

A Troublesome Question

A teacher was telling her class of girls about the time when the Lord Jesus fed the multitude with five loaves and two fishes. Said she: "And of course you will understand, children, that it does not mean that Jesus actually fed all those thousands with a few loaves and fishes. That would have been impossible. It just means that He so fed the people with His teaching that they lost all sense of bodily hunger, and went home satisfied." But an inquiring girl put this question, "But, Miss ——, what was it filled the twelve baskets of fragments left over?"—*Christian Herald.*

* * *

The Safe Path

"Have you studied Voltaire, Tom Paine, Robert Ingersol, or any of those fellows?" asked a friend of a Christian captain of a steamship.

"No," replied the captain.

"Well, you should. You can't fairly turn down their argument until you have thoroughly investigated for yourself," argued the captain's boyhood friend.

"I've been captain of this ship a long time, John," returned the captain. "The chart that was given me pointed out the deep water that would carry the ship safely into port. As a young captain I never considered it advisable to investigate the rocks; the experience I've known other chaps to have with the rocks has been sufficient warning for me.

"So, the Bible that I learned at my mother's knee, in the old Sunday School and from my old pastor, is my chart for the sea of life. This Bible brings me a knowledge of the fathomless sea of God's love and mercy, which if I cast myself upon, will carry me safely into the Heavenly port.

"Look at our classmates, John; there's poor Harry with every prospect—no finer specimen of manhood could be found anywhere—until he threw away the 'chart' (his faith in the Bible), then little by little he lost his grip on the finer things of life, dying at last in a gambling hell.

"No, John, others have tampered with the rocks of infidelity to their sorrow; the shores of time are strewn with such wrecks. I shall continue to steer my boat for the 'deep water' that has landed millions upon the Golden Shore. I shall hug to my heart the Holy Scriptures for as David said, 'In them is Thy servant warned' of danger, 'and in keeping of them there is great reward'."—*Selected*

* * *

God's Answer

There is an ancient legend of an infidel knight who openly expressed his unbelief in the reality and power of God. He determined upon an experiment to prove that there was no God. Going out into the field, fully armed for combat, he cast his glove upon the ground after the fashion of his day when one challenged another to fight. Looking up into the heavens, he cried, "God, if there be a God, I defy thee here and now to mortal combat. If thou indeed art, put forth thy power, of which thy professed, pretended priests make such boast." Waiting for an answer to his challenge, he looked up and saw a piece of parchment fluttering in the air above his head. It fell to his feet, and when he picked it up, he found inscribed upon it the words, "God is love." Overcome by this unexpected response to his challenge, he broke his sword, and, kneeling upon the fragments, he consecrated himself to the service of the God whom he had before defied.—*Sunday School Times.*

* * *

The Stars Left:

During the French Revolution Jean Bon St. Andre, the Vendean revolutionist, said to a peasant, "I will have all your steeples pulled down, that you may no longer have any object by which you may be reminded of our old superstitions."

"But," replied the peasant, "*you can't help leaving us the stars.*"—*The Chaplain*

* * *

How Atheists and Agnostics Die

Hobbes, noted infidel, said when dying: "I am taking a fearful leap into the dark!"

Mirabeau said: "Give me more laudanaum. I don't want to think of eternity!"

Edward Gibbon, noted atheist, said: "All is dark!"—*Selected.*

* * *

"There Are No Atheists In Foxholes"

"Once, during a particularly violent raid, I leaped into a fox-hole, only to find a sergeant already there. We squeezed in together. Presently I found myself praying out loud. The sergeant was praying, too. He prayed almost as loud as I did. When the attack was over, I turned to him and said, 'Sergeant, I noticed you were praying.'

"The sergeant didn't bat an eye, 'Sir,' he said, 'there are no atheists in foholes!' "—*An incident related by Col. Warren J. Clear, of the United States Army, shortly after he returned from Corregidor fortress.—From The Army Hour*

* * *

The Fool

"The fool hath said in his heart, There is no God"—Psalm 14:1.

An evangelist, E. L. Hyde, conducted some revival meetings in New Jersey, and in the course of his remarks said that he could prove to the satisfaction of any infidel within ten minutes that he was a fool. The next morning while walking, a gentleman accosted him very abruptly by saying, "Aren't you the evangelist preaching up here at the church?"

"Yes, sir."

"Well, I suppose you are a gentleman."

"I claim to be one."

"Well, I don't think you are one. Didn't you say last night that you could prove to the satisfaction of anyone within ten minutes that all infidels are fools? If you don't prove it to my satisfaction I will publish you in all the city papers as the most consummate liar that ever struck the city."

Seeing there was no possibility of reasoning with the man, Mr. Hyde said: "Where is your infidel?"

"I claim to be one," was the reply, "and I want you to know I am no fool either."

"You don't mean to say there is no reality in Christianity?"

"I do, sir. I have studied all phases of the subject, and have traveled and delivered lectures against Christianity for more than twelve years, and I am prepared to say there is nothing in it."

"You are certain there is nothing in it?"

"Yes, sir; there is nothing in it."

"Will you please tell me," said Mr. Hyde, "if a man who will lecture twelve years against nothing is not a fool, what in your judgment would constitute a fool?"

He turned away in a rage. Mr. Hyde, drawing out his watch, insisted he still had six minutes, but the infidel would not hear him, nor was Mr. Hyde published in the city papers.—Selected.

* * *

When Chaff Fights Wheat

A Russian university in Leningrad is opened to "teach atheism." Three hundred students, forty-seven of them women, will prepare themselves for "active propaganda of militant atheism." It suggests a colony of ants on a railroad right of way organizing a university to prove that there is no such thing as an engineer.—*Sunday School Times*

* * *

An Atheist Speaks

The *Lutheran News Letter* contains the following interesting item: "The French author, Lavredan, long known as an atheist, when confronted by the horrors of the World War made this gripping confession: 'I laughed at faith and thought myself wise. Finally this laughter became hollow and vain for I saw France bleeding and mourning. What would become of France if her children did not believe, if her women did not pray? Oh, a people whose fields are covered with the dead! How difficult it is to remain an atheist on this national cemetery! I cannot! I cannot! I have deceived myself and you who have read my book. It was a delusion, a giddiness, an evil dream. I see death and call for life. Hands equipped with weapons make death; folded hands bring life. France, turn back to faith! To forsake God means to be lost! I do not know whether I shall live tomorrow, but I must tell my friends, Lavredan is afraid to die an atheist. I am not afraid of hell, but the thought impresses me, God lives and you are so far from Him. Rejoice, my soul, that I have been permitted to experience the hour when, on my knees, I can say, I believe, I believe in God. I believe, I believe—that word is the main hymn of humanity. For him who does not accept it, it will soon be night.' "

—*The United Presbyterian.*

* * *

An Atheist Convinced

A great astronomer, Athanasius Kirchner, desiring to convince an atheistic friend, procured a globe of the heavens, handsomely bestarred, and placed it in his study. The friend, coming in, asked whence it came and to whom it belonged. "Shall I tell you," replied Kirchner, "that it belongs to no one; that it was never made; and that it came here by chance?" "That is impossible," said the atheist, "you are joking." "Look!" answered the astronomer, *"you instantly refuse to believe that this globe—a mere shadow of the mighty heaven it pictures —was never made, and arrived by chance. Yet the heaven it pictures you claim came without either design or Designer."* The rebuke was used of the Holy Spirit to the conviction and conversion of the hearer.—*Full Gospel Quarterly.*

Fooling Those Who were Robbed

An Illinois thief stole five hundred dollars worth of shoes, the entire stock of a store, and in addition played a trick on the dealer by leaving all the empty boxes, putting them back just where they belonged. One after another the customers arrived the next day, and the dealer pulled out box after box, only to find that each was empty. That was a unique theft, but something much like it takes place all the time in the spiritual world. *For there are many thieves of faith, writers and speakers who make it their business to destroy belief in God, in Christ, in the Church, in religion. But they always leave the boxes. They always leave the shell of what they have taken, in order to fool people into thinking that they have taken nothing at all.* But pull out the boxes, try to get any comfort and strength out of what they have left, and you will see that the theft has been complete.—*Christian Endeavor World.*

* * *

If Modernist Were Banker

Now comes a wise editor and remarks: "A century ago the attitude toward the pagan religions was that they were all false, while Christianity alone was true. Now this classification of 'true and false' is being given up by all careful students of religion, because the pagan religions teach some moral truths." Let the editor substitute coin for religion: "A century ago the attitude toward outside coins was that they were all false, while the mint coins alone were true. Now this classification of genuine and bogus is being given up by all careful students of numismatics, because all coins contain some true metal." The bank teller who reasoned that way would soon lose his position. No one says that truths in pagan religions are false, but the Christian says that the religions that contain them are spurious and powerless. —*The King's Business.*

* * *

God, The Master Mind

Some time ago there appeared in the *American Magazine* an article by a manufacturer, with the following paragraph: "It takes a girl in our factory about two days to learn to put the seventeen parts of a meat chopper together. It may be that these millions of worlds, all balanced so wonderfully in space—it may be that these just happened; it may be by a billion of years of tumbling about they finally arranged themselves. I don't know. I am merely a plain manufacturer of cultery. But this I do know: that you can shake the seventeen parts of a meat chopper around in a washtub for the next seventeen billion years and you'll never make a meat chopper!"

You cannot put one little star in motion,
You cannot shape one single forest leaf,
Nor fling a mountain up, nor sink an
 ocean,
Presumptuous pygmy, large with un-
 belief.

"The invisible things of him from the creation of the world are clearly seen, being understood by the things that are made, even his eternal power and Godhead; so that they are without excuse" (Rom. 1:20)—*Serving and Waiting.*

BACKSLIDING

The Log Jam

In the Timberlands springtime sees great quantities of logs shooting down the rivers. Sometimes a jam occurs. Then the lumberjack seeks the log which is stemming the wooden tide. When he finds that key log, he jerks it out of place, and the flow moves onward with its freight. There is such a thing as a spiritual log jam. We lose our religious enthusiasm, interest in personal devotions wanes, an hour in the Lord's house becomes a bore, the Bible becomes a silent Book. Then we must find the key log that is checking the flood of spiritual life. It may be an unforgiving spirit, or jealousy, or hypocrisy. Jerk the obstruction out of place and spiritual vitality will surge onward—*To-day.*

* * *

Time to Renew the Altar

Mr. Moody once told of an aged Christian, with many active years of faithful service to his credit. Circumstances caused him to lose out in Christian experience in a measure. After considerable mental and spiritual conflict he came to entertain the mistaken conclusion that it was the will of God for him to be lost. Then something whispered within him: "Suppose there is a hell for you, what would you, with your disposition and habits, do there?" The quick answer was, "I would set up a prayer meeting," and with the words came the light of God to show him the absurdity of it all. He put away backsliding out of his heart, and renewed the altar of the Lord.—*Sunday School Times.*

* * *

Not Sudden

There is really no such thing as a sudden fall. Oh! the last step is only the last of a series of steps. I believe there are always many steps before a child of God reaches the verge of the precipice. I believe, further, that even when the edge of the precipice is reached, very few jump over. Most of them slide down, slowly at first, and it is so easy, so gentle, so effortless, so natural, so pleasant, that, alas! alas! they seem to enjoy the sensation. It is only when the pace begins to accelerate terribly, it is only when control is slipping away, that this pleasant enjoyment gives way to anxiety and alarm.—*Selected.*

* * *

Symptoms

"The symptoms of spiritual decline," says Dr. Payson, "are like those which attend the decline of bodily health. It generally commences with the loss of appetite, and a disrelish for wholesome food, prayer, reading the Scriptures and devotional books. Whenever you perceive these symptoms be alarmed! Your spiritual health is in danger. Apply immediately to the Great Physician for a cure."—*Gospel Herald.*

BAPTISM

The Branded Maverick

Out on the cattle ranches of the West the unbranded calves that roam at large are known as "mavericks." They are claimed by the man who is first to get his brand on them at the annual round up. A little Western girl had been baptized one Sunday by the Methodist minister of the town. Her schoolmates questioned her the next day as to the meaning of the ceremony. "Well," she said, "I will just tell you. I was a little maverick out on the prairie and that man put the Jesus mark on my forehead so that when He sees me He will know that I am one of His children."—*The Evangelical Christian.*

Baptism

Baptism is a Gospel ordinance commemorating the death, burial, and resurrection of Christ. In baptism, public testimony is given to the effect that the one baptized has been crucified with Christ (Gal. 2:20); buried with Him (Rom. 6:4); and is raised with Him to walk in newness of life (Col. 3:1).—J. W. K., *in Evangelical Visitor.*

* * *

But They Were All Baptized

Unique experiences of baptism in strange places came to the Rev. (Colonel) F. F. Miles during the Great War. He was privileged to baptize converts in such varied places as the marble swimming bath of the Mena House Hotel; under the shadow of the Pyramids; in the sea at Anzac Beach, Gallipoli; in a German shell hole in the Ypres Salient; and in the Louis Prison. —*(London) Christian Herald.*

* * *

Obedience in Simple Faith

It is said that in the early days of missions in Korea a page or two of the Gospel story found its way up into a remote mountain village. The people read such of the story as was found there, believed, and accepted the message. They would establish a church group and perhaps one would come who could instruct them further, for they knew only what the few meager pages contained. As far as they were able to understand, they fulfilled the conditions until it came to baptism, and they did not know just how it should be done. They talked it over, and after prayer and discussion they went home and each took a personal, private bath in the name of the Trinity. Who would dare say that the Lord of Heaven did not accept and honor their interpretation of that symbol of a cleansed life?—*Sunday School Times.*

BIBLE

A People of the Book

John Richard Green begins his second volume of *A Short History of the English People* with these words: "No greater moral change ever passed over a nation than passed over England during the years which parted the middle of the reign of Elizabeth from the meeting of the Long Parliament. England became the people of a book, and that Book was the Bible."—*The Chaplain.*

* * *

They Could Not

In Armenia a whole village of sixty families embraced Islamism under threats of torture and death. There was only one exception—a woman aged 110 years, who refused, saying, "I am too old to deny my Lord." The fierce Turks snatched her Bible from her hands, tore it up, and burned it. She said very calmly, "You can do that, but you cannot tear the promises out of my heart."—*Life and Light.*

* * *

We search the world for truth. We cull
From graven stone and written scroll,
The good, the true, the beautiful
And all old flower-beds of the soul;
And, weary seekers of the best,
We come back laden from our quest,
To find all the sages said
Is in the Book our mothers read.

—*Gospel Herald*

* * *

Apple-Tree Bible Study

Luther said he studied his Bible as he gathered apples. First he shook the whole tree, that the ripest might fall; then he shook each limb, and when he had shaken each limb, he shook each branch, and after each branch, every twig; and then he looked under every leaf. Search the Bible as a whole, shaking the whole tree. Read it rapidly, as you would any other book. Then shake every limb—study book after book. Then shake every branch, giving attention to the chapters when they do not break the sense. Then shake each twig, by a careful study of the paragraphs and sentences. And you will be rewarded if you will look under each leaf, by searching the meaning of the words.—*The Christian Fundamentalist.*

* * *

Can Man Create Life?

An old professor of biology used to hold a little brown seed in his hand. "I know just exactly the composition of this seed. It has in it nitrogen, hydrogen, and carbon. I know the exact proportions. I can make a seed that will look exactly like it. But if I plant my seed it will come to naught; its elements will simply be absorbed in the soil. If I plant the seed God made, it will become a plant, because it contains the mysterious principle which we call the life principle." This Bible looks like other books. We cannot understand altogether its marvelous power. Planted in good ground, it shows that it has the life principle in itself; it brings forth spiritual life; it bears fruitage.—*Sunday School Times.*

* * *

How To Search The Scriptures

S—eriously (Acts 17:11; II Tim. 2:15).
E—arnestly (Josh. 1:8; Ps. 119:11).
A—nxiously (John 20:31; Ps. 119:9).
R—egularly (Acts 17:11; Ps. 1:2).
C—arefully (Luke 24:27; II Tim. 3:16, 17).
H—umbly (Luke 24:45; James 1:22).

—*The P. H. Advocate.*

* * *

Profitable Devotion

An old Scotch woman who was alone for the greater part of the day was asked, "What do you do during the day?" "Well," she said, "I get my hymn book, and I have a little hymn of praise to the Lord." Then she added, "I get my Bible and let the Lord speak to me. When I am tired of reading, and I cannot sing anymore, I just sit still and *let the Lord love me.*"—*Selected.*

* * *

The Life Plant

E. L. Langston in one of his splendid books says: "There is a strange plant in Jamaica, called the 'life plant.' It is called this because it is almost impossible to kill or destroy any portion of it. When a leaf is cut off and hung by a string, instead of shriveling up and dying like any other leaf, it sends out white threadlike roots and thus gathers moisture from the air and begins to grow new leaves. The Bible," says Mr. Langston, "is the Life Plant of the moral and spiritual world. Circulate the Bible or portions of it anywhere, and it will soon take root in the affections and heart of mankind and send out tendrils of life. In the heart of Africa, or among the aborigines of South America, or among the Eskimos of the Arctic Circle, it has the same quickening power which no climate or heathenism has the power to kill."—*The Wonderful Word.*

* * *

The Best Book of All

No fragment of any army ever survived so many battles as the Bible; no citadel ever withstood so many sieges; no rock was ever battered by so many hurricanes, and so swept by storms. And yet it stands. It has seen the rise and downfall of Daniel's four empires. Assyria bequeaths a few multilated figures for the riches of our national museum. Media and Persia like Babylon, which they conquered, have been weighed in the balance, and long ago found wanting. Greece faintly survives in its historic fame; and Rome of the Caesars has long since ceased to boast. And yet the Book that foretells all this still survives. While nations, kings, philosophers, systems, institutions have died away, the Bible engages now men's deepest thoughts, is examined by the keenest intellects, stands revered before the highest tribunals, is more read and sifted and debated, more devoutly loved and more vehemently assailed, more defended and more denied, more industriously translated and freely given to the world, more honored and more abused, than any other book the world ever saw. It survives all changes, itself unchanged; it moves all minds, yet is moved by none; it sees all things decay, itself incorruptible; it sees myriads of other books engulfed in the stream of time, yet is borne along till the mystic angel shall plant his foot upon the sea, and swear by Him that liveth forever and ever that time shall be no longer. *The Old Book Stands!—The Wonderful Word.*

The Bible

Other books tell us what men suppose; the Bible tells us what God knows. Other books tell us what other men, almost as foolish as ourselves, speculate; this Book tells us what an infinitely wise God, who made us and all things, and consequently knows all things, has inerrantly revealed. This Book makes men wise with the wisdom that is golden, the wisdom that brings eternal salvation. No one can study this Book aright, no matter how ignorant he may otherwise be, without becoming possessed of that priceless wisdom that means eternal life. No other book has the power to make us acquainted with God and with His Son, Jesus Christ, that this Book has. Oh, study the Book that brings eternal life; make it in your own experience "the implanted Word, which is able to save your souls" (James 1:21, R.V.).—*R. A. Torrey.*

* * *

"The Bible has lost hold, but nothing has arisen to take its place. That is the gravest aspect of the matter. It was the cement with which our Western communities were built and by which they were held together."—*H. G. Wells.*

* * *

They Said This About the Bible

Hundreds of illuminating and helpful passages about the Bible are scattered here and there upon the pages of Christian literature. The following are but a few of the "handfuls of purpose" which are readily found by gleaners in this field.

Christianity Depends Upon It

"We speak with gratitude of the profound influence which has been exercised on the world by Christianity. But it is to be remembered that Christianity comes to men, and is kept alive in their memories and hearts, only through the Bible—through the possession, translation, diffusion, and devout and prayerful reading, preaching, study and teaching of the written Word.

"Without the Bible to revert to, keeping the truth fresh and living, the image of the Master would long since have been blurred and distorted beyond recognition. His Gospel would have been perverted beyond recovery by corrupt human tradition. His doctrines and moral teaching, with those of His Apostles, would have been buried under a mountain load of human inventions.

"It is not, therefore, an exaggeration to say that it is the Bible which has preserved Christianity to the world."—*Rev. Robert Murdoch, B. Th., (Scotland)*

* * *

Not As Good As the Book

"I'll tell you what's the matter with you Christians,"—a high-caste Hindu gentleman was talking with the missionary—"you are not as good as your Book."

Rather a startling charge, isn't it? But scrutinize your own life carefully under the light of sacred precepts before you venture to deny its truth. If only we were as good as our Book, what a different place this world would be!

The Book is powerful. One writer declares that it has dynamite in it, so wonderful is the way in which it speaks to the hearts of men.

Once, when Dr. John Chamberlain had read to the natives of an East Indian city the first chapter of the Epistle to the Romans, an intelligent Brahman said to him: "Sir, that chapter was written by one of you missionaries about us Hindus. It describes us exactly." But we know that those inspired words were written by the Apostle Paul almost two thousand years before the first missionary went to India.

A learned Chinese student was employed to translate the New Testament into his native language. At first he worked stolidly, but after a few weeks he came to the missionary greatly agitated.

"What a wonderful Book this is," he exclaimed.

"Why so?" questioned his employer.

"Because," the Chinese replied, "it tells me so exactly about myself. It knows all that is in me. The One who made this Book must be the One who made me."

—*The Gospel Herald*

World's Oldest Bible Found

The discovery of a pile of dusty manuscripts in a Cairo bookshop, by Herman Junker, director of a German Archaeological Institute, is of more than ordinary interest. Hans Gerstinger, chief of the manuscript section of the Austrian National Library, says, "The laboriously written pages date back to the second century." The sheets do not include the entire Bible, but the Gospel of Matthew and Paul's Epistles are complete, and there are fragments of the Old Testament. In all 190 sheets were found. These Gospels, if Gersinger's estimate as to their age be correct, were actually written within 200 years of the lifetime of Christ!—Perhaps as near as 150 years.

That this is another severe blow to the critics goes without saying. In this unbelieving age God is giving more and more evidence to silence the enemy, and to give a clear light of fact for faith to feed on. There is plenty of evidence of the authenticity and genuineness of the New Testament. The incontrovertible fact is, God *has spoken.*

The believer reads with joyous assurance, "Forever, O Lord, Thy Word is settled in Heaven" (Ps. 119:89). It is comforting to know that God has magnified His Word above His Name (Ps. 138:2). *The Bible will stand.* — *The Evangelical Visitor.*

* * *

Peril of Ignoring the Bible

The frightful fall of Prince, of the Agapemone, emphasizes the fact, extraordinarily pregnant, that our Lord, in the moment that He was baptized without limit in the Holy Ghost, yet when confronted by hell, relied on the *Word.* A. A. Rees, an intimate friend of the Prince, says of the latter that he was extraordinarily devoted to God, and his private life was in harmony with what he appeared in public. He was unusually blessed in the edification of saints and the conversion of sinners long before he entered the public ministry. Few were more deeply acquainted with the Scripture, and he was a man of prayer and self-denial. But a book he read about the ministry of the Holy Spirit led him to give himself up unreservedly to the Spirit's guidance. . . As he grew in this habit of yielding absolutely to spiritual guidance, the Bible became less and less his study and he ended by neglecting it altogether. Being thus guided in every detail of his daily life, he [thought he] no longer needed the written Word; and the *total abnegation of his own judgment followed.* This complete surrender of mind and will to what he believed to be the guidance of the Holy Spirit left him a prey to the terrible delusions in which he was at last engulfed. So also his successor, J. H. Smyth-Piggott, once wholly devoted to God, yielded to an untested spirit, and is now a false Christ, awaiting, as an old man, in the "Abode of Love," his thousand years' reign as Messiah.—*The Dawn.*

* * *

Billy Sunday's Estimate of the Bible

One of the most beautiful and truthful tributes to the Bible ever written is that by Billy Sunday, voiced by him in his preachings.

"Twenty-nine years ago, with the Holy Spirit as my Guide, I entered at the portico of Genesis, walked down the corridor of the Old Testament art-galleries, where pictures of Noah, Abraham, Moses, Joseph, Isaac, Jacob and Daniel hang on the wall. I passed into the music room of the Psalms where the spirit sweeps the keyboard of nature until it seems that every reed and pipe in God's great organ responds to the harp of David the sweet singer of Israel.

"I entered the chamber of Ecclesiastes, where the voice of the preacher is heard, and into the conservatory of Sharon and the lily of the valley where sweet spices filled and perfumed my life.

"I entered the business office of Proverbs and on into the observatory of the Prophets where I saw telescopes of various sizes pointing to far off events, concentrating on the bright and morning Star which was to rise above the moonlit hills of Judea for our salvation and redemption.

"I entered the audience room of the King of kings, catching a vision written by Matthew, Mark, Luke and John. Thence into the correspondence room with Paul, Peter, James and John writing their Epistles.

"I stepped into the throne room of Revelation where tower the glittering peaks, where sits the King of kings upon His throne of glory with the healing of the nations in His hand, and I cried out:

All hail the power of Jesus' Name,
  Let angels prostrate fall
Bring forth the royal diadem
  And crown Him Lord of All."

—*The Watchman-Examiner.*

* * *

The Precious Word

A pocket Testament, dropped from an English warship in a Japanese harbor in 1854, was the beginning of an endless chain of blessing, reaching to the present day and beyond. A Japanese general, Murata, who was suspiciously watching the movements of the alien vessels, picked up the little Book. But he could not read it. A Dutch interpreter informed him that it told about God and Christ—which only increased his perplexity.

At last he secured from China a translation of the strange Book. He read and was profoundly impressed. Risking death, since the Christian religion was strictly forbidden in Japan, he and his brother came to Dr. Verbeck for baptism.

Their distinguished rank added to their influence upon others, and there are many Christians in Japan today who owe their religion to the Testament fished out of the waters of Nagasaki harbor.—*Elim Evangel.*

* * *

"Doth God Care?"

Just as Dr. Judson had finished translating the New Testament into Burmese, he was cast into prison. His wife took the precious manuscript and buried it in the ground. But, if left there it would soon decay, while to reveal its existence to its foes would surely lead to its destruction. So it was arranged that she should put it within a roll of cotton and bring it to him in the form of a pillow, so hard and poor that even the keeper of the prison did not covet it. After 7 months this pillow, so uninviting externally, so precious to him, was taken away, and then his wife redeemed it by giving him a better one in exchange. Some time after that he was hurried off to another prison, leaving everything behind him, and his old pillow was thrown into the prison yard, to be trodden under foot as worthless cotton; but after a few hours one of the native Christians discovered the roll and took it home as a relic of the prisoner, and there, long afterwards, the manuscript was found within the cotton, complete and uninjured. Surely the hand of the Lord was interposed to save from destruction the fruit of years of toil, so important to those who were to read from the Burmese Bible.—*Reformed Church Record*

* * *

Is It Our Trouble, Too?

In a certain well-known Bible school the instructor was talking to a pupil, a young man in his twenties, who had difficulty in remembering Bible verses and references. He had come to the instructor for advice. "What do you read in the morning?" asked the instructor. The student replied that, after his quiet time, he had been in the habit of reading the newspaper. "How much time do you give to the reading of the newspaper?" continued the instructor. "About an hour, I guess," answered the student, "including the time that I read it on my way to work. Then I read the evening paper for about an hour at night." "And you are asking me why it is that you cannot remember your Bible verses?" asked the instructor significantly.—*Sunday School Times.*

* * *

Lesson from a Book Worm

At one time when Mr. Spurgeon, the great evangelist, was in Scotland he came across a very old and much-worn

Bible. As he held it reverently in his hand, turning it this way and that, he observed a small hole where a worm had eaten its way from cover to cover. "Lord, make me a book worm like that," the preacher exclaimed. "From Genesis to Revelation it has gone clear through the Bible."—"*Our Boys and Girls.*"

* * *

The Living Word

We get life into us by the Word, we keep life in us by the Word: "Wherewithal shall a young man cleanse his way? by taking heed thereto according to Thy Word." We are kept from sin by the Word: "Thy Word have I hid in mine heart, that I might not sin against Thee." And we conquer sin also by the Word: "They overcame him by the Blood of the Lamb, and by the word of their testimony." We keep ourselves separate from the world by the Word: "Ye shine as lights in the world; holding forth the Word of Life." And we repulse Satan by the Word: "It is written." We are judged by the Word, condemned by the Word, commended by the Word. "The word that I have spoken, the same shall judge [you] in the last day."—*Charles A. Fox.*

* * *

The Greatest

Book even written (II Tim. 3:16, 17).
Teacher of Bible ever known (John 14:26).
Answer regarding *eternal life* (Luke 2:49).
Change within the power of God (John 1:12, 13).
Evidence of a true Christian II Cor. 5:17).
Guide to a spiritual condition (II Tim. 2:15).
Description of Christ our Lord (Rev. 1:13-17).
Understanding and object (I John 5:20).
Parable fully explained and why (Luke 8:9-15).
Power in any life today for good (Rom. 1:16).
Question to be decided by all (Acts 16:30, 31).
Mystery in the entire Bible (I Tim. 3:13).
Gift to every true believer (Rom. 6:23).
Weapon ever used for peace (Heb. 4:12).
Reward given to all for obedience (John 5:14).
Sacrifice attainable in life (Gal. 2:20).
The only sacrifice asked of believers (Rom. 12:1).
Desire of Paul's whole life (Phil. 3:10, 11).
Rule relating to all mankind (Matt. 7:12).
Assurance for true believers, I John 5:13).
Condition to insure continual happiness (Luke 10:20).

—*Church of Christ Advocate.*

* * *

Continual Preaching

At the tender age of eleven years, Dr. Kelly said, "I began the lifelong habit of carrying a New Testament, or some portion of Scripture, in my pocket." He constantly gives out portions of the New Testament, saying, "Here's my card." With the nurses of the Kelly Hospital for three mornings of the week, at seven o'clock when the night nurses are leaving duty and the other nurses are coming on duty, he meets for Bible reading and prayer. On three other mornings of the week he meets the servants of his home for Bible reading and prayer. On every morning of the week he meets with the members of his family for the same holy purpose.—*Christian Herald.*

* * *

Why Mrs. Bottome Was So Confident

At a large dinner given in New York, Mrs. Margaret Bottome, for a long time head of the King's Daughters' Circle, sat beside a German professor of science. In the course of conversation, Mrs. Bottome said, quite naturally for her:

"The Bible says so and so."

"The Bible?" remarked the professor. "You don't believe the Bible!"

"Yes, indeed I believe it," was the quick reply.

"Why, I didn't suppose that any intelligent person today believed the Bible!"

"Oh, yes," Mrs. Bottome said assuringly, *"I believe it all. You see, I know the Author!"—Morning Star.*

* * *

Just Thanking God

Lente, an Indian storekeeper of Isleta, told the missionary that he had read nearly all of the New Testament which he had given him. "I read all the time I have to spare," he added. "Ah, Lente," his white partner interrupted, "don't try to make the missionary believe you are so interested. I watch you over there in the corner. You have the book open, but you go to sleep over it . . ." "No, I am not asleep. You do not understand. You see, all my life I wondered why we did not have any of the words that Jesus spoke when He was here on earth; why someone did not write them down so we could know just what He said. But I never knew that they had been written down until Brother Burnett came. He gave me a little book. . . . I thought it could not be of much importance. But when I came to read it, I found these words, 'Jesus said.'—On and on I read, and every time I came to those words, 'Jesus said,' my heart was so happy I could hardly bear it. I had found what I had been longing for all my life—the words that Jesus spoke while on earth. . . . When I come to these words, I cannot go on. I must stop and close my eyes and pray. I must thank God that the words that Jesus said came to me before I died." Turning to his partner, he said: "No, you do not understand. I am not asleep. I am thanking God that I have in my hand to read for myself the words that Jesus said."—*From "The Word of Their Testimony," by Una Roberts Lawrence, Home Mission Board, S. B. C.*

* * *

The Treasure in the Scriptures

There is something intriguing about a treasure hunt. . . . The thought of finding real pirate gold is enough to whip any man into a frenzy. In a Massachusetts bay two fishermen discovered two buccaneer hulls and touched off a spirited hunt. The hulls are thought to have belonged to the pirates Edward Lowe or Samuel Bellamy, who preyed on shipping between 1719-1730. There was also the discovery of a casket. Investigation disclosed that an English merchantman was lost with five million English dollars for the pay of the Hessian mercenaries in America. Then, too, there was the ship that went down some eighty years ago with a half million dollars in tin. Weeks of searching have brought no gold or tin, but the hunt goes on in hope. The Bible has been a source of treasure to man for centuries. Within its pages are truths dearer than gold and more precious than fine jewels. The treasure in God's Word is at hand for anyone who will seek; the source is never expended. Frequently, in reading a familar passage we come to a truth which catches us up short; we say to ourselves, "I never knew that was there before." The real coin of living is to be found within the Bible. "The law of thy mouth is better unto me than thousands of gold and silver" (Psa. 119: 72).—*From Essex.*

* * *

Is Deuteronomy True?

A few years ago in a railroad train, a lawyer, seeing I had my Bible in my hand, asked, "Do you believe that Deuteronomy belongs to the canon of Scripture?" He had been reading infidelity and criticism of the Word of God. I answered by asking the question, "Do you believe in the resurrection of Jesus Christ from the dead?" He said, "Yes, certainly, I believe the resurrection of the God-Man to be the best authenticated fact in all history. But that has nothing to do," he said, "with my question of the inspiration of the Book of Deuteronomy." "Oh, yes, it has," was my reply. "Was Christ, as proved by the resurrection, divine and God's Son and perfect in life and teaching?" "Yes." "Then you have taken your question to the final court of appeal. Christ expounded unto them the Scriptures beginning at Moses and all the prophets, concerning himself, and called it Scripture, and endorsed it as God's Word. Deuteronomy was in it."—*Sunday School Times.*

* * *

Treasures Ready for Use

I recall a young man whom I used to meet at our Bible conferences. He was an illiterate man, but he had set his mind to the plan of getting a verse a day of the Bible. When I first met him he had been working on it for eight years. He had committed over two thousand verses of Scripture to memory. His prayer was a marvel. It was like a rich brocade of silver and gold of the Word of God, interwoven with praise, testimony, and petition. It was a marvelous thing to hear that young man, a workman in a steel mill, give his testimony for God; and yet it all came from committing a single verse of Scripture a day.—*James H. McConkey, in Christ Life.*

* * *

How Many Times Have You?

A gentleman in Bristol, in his last interview with George Muller (says Dr. Dinsdale T. Young), said, "Excuse me, but how many times have you read the Bible through?" "Well," George Muller replied, "as you ask me, I may say that I have read it through sixty-six times, and I am now going through it for the sixty-seventh time, and it gets more interesting and sweeter every time I read it." That is the testimony of all Bible lovers.—*Christian Herald.*

* * *

The Immortality of the Bible

John Clifford, D.D.

The Bible is indestructible. It cannot be holden of death. Buried a thousand times beneath the accumulated heaps of hostile criticism, it rises again to newness of life. It is absolutely insuppressible. The continuity of the Bible as a spiritual and ethical force in the life of the world is one of the outstanding marvels of history. Recall its story. Reckon up the number, the strength, the malignity of the open and avowed enemies it has encountered, whose extinction it has survived. Look at the character and power of the schools of criticism, and note the way in which they have come and gone, whilst it has kept on forever. Each had found the mystic key for its explanation. Each knew more than its predecessor. Each had the newest fact to supply, and each did its critical work; some rendering real service, others none. But the Bible abides, attracts, conquers. Add to this the greatest wonder of all, that it has lived through the inconceivably foolish and misguided behavior of its friends. No book was ever more universally loved, no book ever suffered more from its admirers. The crude interpretations of its messages, the wild theories preached in its name and backed by perversions of its texts, the absence of sense and method in the exposition of its statements, the preposterous schemes and movements undertaken for its defense, convince us that if the book had not an absolutely indestructible center it would have disappeared long ago. But God lives, and is its life, therefore it endures, and shall endure forever—*Selected*

* * *

How God Spoke to Him

A woman whose husband was a confirmed drunkard led a most miserable life until one day a colporteur came to her poor home and brought her a Bible. She found much comfort in reading it and soon came to treasure it above everything. Her husband sneered and railed at her about it. One day, when he came home half intoxicated, and found her sitting over her newly found treasure, he snatched the Bible from her, threw it into the stove, and set fire to it. "Now we shall see," said he, "what will be left of your new religion." The next day he opened the door of the stove, and taking the fire tongs, was about to stir up the cinders, which, as he thought, were all that was left of the Bible, when his eye fell upon the words: "Heaven and earth shall pass away: but my words shall not pass away." Having been thrown in closed, some pages of the Book were partly preserved, and these words stood out clear and distinct. They were like a revelation to the man; he stood convicted and awe-stricken. Soon after he was converted, and led a different life.—*Sunday School Times.*

Why People Don't Read The Bible

When Queen Elizabeth's wrinkles waxed deep and many, it is reported that an unfortunate master of the mint incurred disgrace by a too faithful likeness of her cast on the shilling; the die was broken and only one mutilated specimen is now in existence. Her maids of honor took the hint and were thenceforward careful that no fragment of looking-glass should remain in any room in the palace. In fact, The *Quarterly Review* (a magazine of the times) says the queen "had not the heart to look herself in the face for the last twenty years of her life!"

A mirror exposes wrinkles, dirt, *etc.*, that may be on the face; *so does the Word of God with the heart.* Reading the Bible shows us our sins. If we refuse to repent and change we soon get tired of seeing our "dirty faces" in God's Mirror—so we stop looking into the Mirror! How foolish! Better see the dirt, confess it, and be cleansed by the Blood of the Lamb!—*Selected.*

* * *

Unknown Riches

Several years ago an old man living in New Jersey discovered about $5,000 in a family Bible. The bank notes were scattered throughout the Book. In 1874 the aunt of this man had died, and one clause of her will was as follows:

"To my beloved nephew, Steven Marsh, I will and bequeath my family Bible, and all it contains, with the residue of my estate after my funeral expenses and just and lawful debts are paid."

The estate amounted to a few hundred dollars, which were soon spent, and for about thirty-five years his chief support had been a small pension from the Government. He lived in poverty, and all the time within his reach there was the precious Bible containing thousands of dollars, sufficient for all his wants. He passed the Bible by. His eyes rested on it, perhaps his hands handled the old leather-bound Bible, with its brass clasps, but he did not open it once. At last, while packing his trunk, to move to his son, where he intended to spend his few remaining years, he discovered the unknown riches which were in his possession. What thoughts of regret must have come to his mind. If he only had opened that Bible years ago, he then might have used the money to great advantage. Instead of it the treasure lay idle for thirty-five years. And he might have had it and enjoyed it all that time.

This is a sad story. But there is something infinitely sadder than the experience of this man. It is the neglect of the Bible by God's people. Our God has given to His people a costly treasure in His own Word. In this Book of books the riches of the wisdom and knowledge, the love and grace of God are made known. All the child of God needs spiritually is to be found on its pages; all wants are there supplied. And yet these riches, put at our disposal by a loving Father, are unknown and unused riches. Instead of being enjoyed, used, and in using them multiplied, they are neglected.

Many of God's people are dragging along in a spiritually impoverished state, when they might have all their need supplied and constantly increase in the knowledge of God. Occasionally we receive letters from aged Christians, including preachers. They tell us how they deplore the fact that they did not know certain truths thirty or forty years ago. "How different my Christian life and experience as well as my service might have been," is what an old Christian wrote to us recently. And all this time these riches were in the Bible, they might have enjoyed them. Oh, the neglected Bible! May we arise and possess our possession.—*Faithful Words.*

* * *

Helen Keller and Bible

The American Bible Society sent to Miss Helen Keller a copy of the new Braille Bible in twenty volumes. In acknowledgment she said: "I sat beside them, caressing them with loving pride. For forty years I have loved the Word of God. I feel the blessed pages under my hand with special thankfulness as a rod and a staff to keep firm my steps through the valley of the shadow of depression and world calamity. Truly the Bible—the teaching of our Saviour—is the only way out of the dark. If the wealth of things which we have possessed in abundance has not knocked on our selfish hearts and opened them to the central message of Jesus, 'Love ye one another,' perhaps these days of widespread suffering will be the pointed instrument that will 'stab (our) spirit broad awake.'"—*The Christian Advocate.*

* * *

Lightning Bugs and the Sun

I would rather trust a bunch of blind men to take a few old lanterns and a string of lightning bugs some day at high noon and go out to examine the noonday sun and analyze it by the power of the lanterns and the lighting bugs, than to trust Modernism advocates to take their own light and examine and analyze the Sun of Righteousness and the Word that reveals Him.—A newspaper editor. — *Sunday School Times.*

* * *

And It Does Just This!

A commercial traveler, who was also a Gideon, and who made a practice of reading his pocket Bible while on his railroad trips, was asked by an unbelieving fellow traveler why he spent so much time reading a book which everybody criticized so much these days. *"My main object,"* replied the Gideon drummer, *"is not to criticize the Bible, but to let it criticize me."*—Selected.

* * *

The Persistent Little Book

A Christian worker in Arizona tells of a fierce-looking cowboy who came to him asking for copies of Mark's Gospel, and who told him this story: "I went to San Francisco and threw away much money in rough revelry. I slept late after a night of dissipation. When I awoke I saw a little book on the table near my bed: the Gospel of Mark. I angrily threw it on the floor. I did the same thing the second morning. Awakening the third morning, I saw that same little book. This time I took it with me to a near-by park and began to examine it. I spent the day reading it. I heard the Son of God say to a leper, 'Be thou clean.' I heard him say to a paralytic, 'Thy sins be forgiven thee.' I heard him commend the widow for her mite. I saw him take little children in his arms and bless them. I heard him say, 'Couldst thou not watch one hour?' I saw him die. It broke my heart and changed my life. I am a different man. Now, stranger, I spend much time giving away copies of the Gospel of Mark.—*Winona Echoes.*

* * *

The Inscription in Every Bible

After a little girl had prayed about what gift would be best for her father's birthday, she felt led to buy a Bible. She wondered what to write on the flyleaf. "From Maggie" seemed too cold. "From your little daughter" would not do, either, for her father had said she was getting to be a big girl. Would "From one who loves you" do? Scarcely, for quite a lot of others loved him, too. Finally she went to her father's library. She found that one of the books had this on the flyleaf—"From the Author." Later, when her father opened his gift, and saw "From the Author," he realized that he was not acquainted with the Author of the Bible. He began to study his Bible, was converted, and became a preacher. In telling the story of his conversion, he often held up the little Bible, and told about the inscription, "From the Author." Let us then accept it, read it, believe it, confess it, and tell to others that it is a love gift for them "From the Author." — *Shortened, from "Golden Sheaves."*

* * *

Without the Bible

A certain man dreamed that he went to consult his Bible and found every page blank. In amazement he rushed to his neighbor's house, aroused him from sleep, and asked to see his Bible; but they found it also blank. In great consternation they sought other Bibles, with the same result. Then they said, "We will go to the libraries and gather the quotations from books, and remake our Bible." But when they examined all the books, they found blank spaces where any Scripture quotations had been. When the man awoke, his brow was cold, yet covered with perspiration, so great had been his agony during the dream. Oh, how dark this world would be without the Bible!—*From the King's Business.*

* * *

The Sword

Ralph C. Norton, who was the Director of Personal Work for the Chapman-Alexander Missions and Director of the Belgian Gospel Mission, was talking with some friends about the supreme work of winning men one by one, in which God has used him so wonderfully. When they noticed the almost exclusive place he gave to the Bible in personal work, one asked him: "What do you do Mr. Norton, in cases where the unsaved man does not accept the Bible as having any authority?" "Well, if I had a fine Damascus sword with a keen double-edged blade I would not sheath it in a fight just because the other man said he did not believe it would cut."—*Sunday School Times.*

* * *

Into All the World

At the annual meeting of the Bible Society, the late Dan Crawford said: "We have a Bantu proverb that says, 'You can count the number of apples on a tree, but you cannot count the number of trees in one apple.' I was working away at a difficult translation, and the Devil came to me and said, 'Drop it; it is not translatable.' I thought a while, then went back to it, and my Bible opened at Daniel 7:14, 'And there was given him . . . that all . . . languages, should serve him.' We have 440 translations. That is not enough. I went on, and succeeded." Men of every language and tribe "shall come from the east, and from the west, and from the north, and from the south, and shall sit down in the kingdom of God" (Luke 13:29).—*Sunday School Times.*

The Bible

A noted orator asked Dickens for the most pathetic story in literature, and he said it was that of the Prodigal Son. Mr. Coleridge was asked for the richest passage in literature, and he said it was the first sixteen verses of the fifth chapter of Matthew. Another asked Daniel Webster for the greatest legal digest, and he replied that it was the Sermon on the Mount. No one has equaled Moses for law, nor David for poetry, nor Isaiah for vision, nor Jesus for ethics, nor Peter for holy zeal, nor Apollos for fiery oratory, nor Paul for logic, nor John's statements of sanctified love. What a ridiculous statement that to study the Bible "marks a step backward in education!" God's Word is the very greatest of all the books, and its Author the very greatest of all teachers. We do well to stay close to its pages. It is *THE BOOK.—Selected.*

* * *

The Best Seller

The Bible remains by all odds the "best seller." It has no competitor. It is now read in 1020 languages and dialects. To meet the demand for its circulation, some thirty societies put out 36,500,000 copies in one year. The production rate of one of these publishing houses was more than 2,000 every hour. The Bible was the first Book to be printed, and it has reached an estimated output of 882,000,000 copies in these centuries of distribution.

There must indeed be something of vital worth about this world-sought Book. What a grim disappointment this popularity would be to Voltaire, who predicted that the Bible would be obsolete in a hundred years! Well may we meditate upon the secrets of the Bible's pull upon the human heart. As we do so, let every one make an honest check of his own personal attitude, as reflected in the use or disuse of the Book, the reverence or disrespect for its intrinsic worth, as shown in his daily habits.—*Gospel Herald.*

President Grant's Message

President Grant sent this message for *The Sunday School Times in* 1876: "Your favor of yesterday, asking a message from me to the children and youth of the United States . . . is this moment received. My advice to Sunday Schools, no matter what their denomination, is, 'Hold fast to the Bible as the sheet anchor of your liberties. Write its precepts in your hearts, and practice them in your lives. To the influence of this Book are we indebted for all the progress made in true civilization, and to this we must look as our guide in the future. 'Righteousness exalteth a nation: but sin is a reproach to any people.' Yours respectfully, U. S. Grant." — *Sunday School Times.*

* * *

A Very Modern Book

Dr. Dean of China had been conversing with an intelligent Chinese respecting our sacred books, assuring him that they are very old. He gave a specimen. Soon after the man came to Dr. Dean, and with a look of triumph and accusation exclaimed: "You told me your Book was very ancient; but that chapter," pointing to the first chapter of Romans, "you have written yourself since you came here and learned all about the Chinese."—*Courtesy Moody Monthly.*

* * *

A Sermon in Insurance Rates

Anyone would be foolish to contend that the mere reading of the Bible in our public schools would revolutionize the morals of a nation over night. It seems equally unwise to assert it would make no improvement in a generation. The burglary insurance rate is $12 per thousand in Boston; $22 in New York, and $27.50 in Chicago. Is there any connection between these figures and the fact that the Bible has been read daily in the public schools of Boston for sixty-five years, for twenty-two years in New York, and excluded for thirty years from the schools in Chicago?—*The Dearborn Independent.*

Which Stage is Yours?

There are three stages of Bible study: first, the cod-liver-oil stage, when you take it like medicine, because it is good for you; second, the shredded wheat biscuit stage, dry, but nourishing; third, the peaches and cream stage. Have you reached the third stage?—*Moody Monthly.*

* * *

What They Say About the Bible:

If you take out your statutes, your constitution, your family life all that is taken from the Sacred Book, what would there be left to bind society together?—*Benjamin Harrison.*

The Bible seems to me like a river of light flowing through my darkness and it has kept my hope of accomplishments bright when things seemed too difficult to overcome.—*Helen Keller.*

A whole Bible for my staff, a whole Christ for my salvation, a whole church for my fellowship, and a whole world for my parish.—*St. Augustine, Bishop of the Latin Church,* 395.

I must confess to you that the majesty of the Scriptures astonishes me; . . . if it had been the invention of men, the inventor would be greater than the greatest heroes. — *Jean Jacques Rousseau, French Savant.*

Read your Bible—make it your daily business to obey it in all you understand. To my early knowledge of the Bible I owe the best part of my taste in literature.—*John Ruskin, English Author.*

Its light is like the body of heaven in its clearness; its vastness like the bosom of the sea; its variety like scenes of nature.—*John Henry Newman, Catholic Cardinal.*

The Bible has been the Magna Charta of the poor and oppressed; down to modern times no State has had a constitution in which the interests of the people are so largely taken into account. —*Thomas Henry Huxley, English Scientist.*

The Bible is a book in comparison with which all others in my eyes are of minor importance, and which in all my perplexities and distresses has never failed to give me light and strength.—*Robert E. Lee, American Soldier and Educator.*

If we abide by the principles taught in the Bible our country will go on prospering and to prosper, but if we and our posterity neglect its instructions and authority, no man can tell how sudden a catastrophe may overwhelm us and bury our glory in profound obscurity.—*Daniel Webster, Statesman, U. S. A.*

I have known ninety-five great men of the world in my time, and of these eighty-seven were all followers of the Bible.

Talk about questions of the day, there is but one question and that is the gospel. It can and will correct anything that needs correction. My only hope for the world is in bringing the human mind into contact with Divine Revelation.

Though assailed by camp, by battery, and by mine, the Holy Scriptures are nevertheless a house builded upon a rock, and that rock impregnable.—*Wm. E. Gladstone, England's "Grand Old Man."*

Behold it upon this table. I never omit to read it, and every day with the same pleasure. . . Not only is one's mind absorbed, it is controlled, and the same can never go astray with this Book for its guide.—*Napoleon Bonaparte, Emperor of France.*

The more profoundly we study this wonderful book, and the more closely we observe its divine precepts, the better citizens we will become and the higher will be our destiny as a nation.—*Wm. McKinley, 25th President.*

Almost every man who has by his life-work added to the sum of human achievement of which the race is proud, of which our people are proud, almost every such man has based his life-work largely upon the teachings of the Bible. —*Theodore Roosevelt, 26th President.*

A man has deprived himself of the best there is in the world who has deprived himself of this (a knowledge of the Bible). . . . There are a good many problems before the American people today, and before me as President, but I expect to find the solution of those problems just in the proportion that I am faithful in the study of the Word of God.

It is very difficult indeed for a man or for a boy, who knows the Scripture, ever to get away from it. It haunts him like an old song. It follows him like the memory of his mother. *It forms a part of the warp and woof of his life.—Woodrow Wilson, 28th President.*

. . . Above all, the pure and benign light of Revelation has had a meliorating influence on mankind, and increased the blessings of society.

I now make my earnest prayer that God would be most graciously pleased to dispose us all to do justice, to love mercy, and to demean ourselves with that charity, humility, and pacific temper of mind which were the characteristics of the divine Author of our blessed religion.—*George Washington, 1st President.*

On one occasion a person asked D. L. Moody how he knew the Bible was inspired, to which the evangelist gave the brief but correct response, "Because it inspires me."

The last words of a dying bishop were, "If I had my life to live over again, I would study the Bible itself more, and about the Bible less."

* * *

A Vast Collection of Bibles

Here we are in the midst of all sorts of revolutions—political, economic, social. And J. P. Morgan lends the Pierpont Morgan collection of illuminated Bibles to the New York Library for a public exhibit. Then what occurs? Why, people stop going to regular amusements to see this greatest collection of illuminated Bibles in the world.

The Morgans have spent actually millions collecting Bibles. I should say that some are worth from $300,000 to $400,000 apiece. I saw one that took four hundred years to complete, that represented the labor, the life labor of an infinite number of monks. Surely that is worth $500,000.

In England a Bible, one of those ancient Bibles, has become a national issue. The British government has bought from Soviet Russia an illuminated Bible for several hundred thousand dollars. It is to repose in the British museum.

Labor is objecting. It is saying that the money should be given to the starving.

In the future, however, the descendants of those who suffer now will look with pride upon that treasure. And may it not be that the Russians of the future, even in a land where religion as we knew it in the past was doomed, will sigh for the lost Bible?

The United States government bought a Guttenberg Bible two years back for a quarter of a million dollars. That reposes in the Congressional library.

While the market for art treasures is narrow at the moment, I should guess that a Guttenberg Bible was a good investment. That particular Bible is likely to be worth a million dollars fifty years hence.—Leslie Eichel, *The Gideon.*

* * *

Men Don't Know More Than God

Professor Robert Dick Wilson, great linguist, a man who mastered twenty-seven languages, to throw light on it, and who devoted thirty years of his life and more to the study of questions that bear on the Word of God, said this: "I have seen the day when I have just trembled at undertaking a new investigation, that is, some point in the Bible in connection with profane history, collateral history. I have seen the day when I have just trembled for fear of what it might show"—and he was a true Christian, who wanted to believe the Bible. "But I have gotten over that," he said. "I have come now to the conviction that no man knows enough to assail the truthfulness of the Old Testament. Whenever there is sufficient documentary evidence to make an investigation, the statements of the Bible, in the original languages and texts, have stood the test."—*Sunday School Times.*

* * *

The Bible Will Stand

O God, Thy Word is true we know!
It makes men's souls with beauty glow
With radiance from above.
Help us to plant it in each heart
That none from Thee might wish to part,
But walk with Thee in love.

We know its entrance giveth light
To guide us through life's darkest night,
To light that is divine.
The hope it gives is from above,
And floods our souls with truest love,
Making us know we're Thine.

Heaven and earth shall pass away,
And yet Thy Holy Word shall stay
Until its task is done.
It is the truth, and cannot fail,
Though foulest hell doth it assail—
Its fight has long been won.

Eternal Truth, give us to know
That joy our souls may overflow,
While on Thy Word we rest.
Bestow upon us now Thy grace
That we may truly seek Thy face,
And know that we are blest.

—By William James Robinson, D.D., Kansas City, Mo.

* * *

Troublesome Scriptures

Mark Twain once said: "Most people are bothered by those passages of Scripture which they cannot understand; but as for me, I have always noticed that the passages in Scripture which trouble me most are those which I do understand."—*From the Homilope church envelope.*

* * *

A Sure Revival

A native of India, writing to a friend about a great revival they were having said, "*We are having a great rebible here.*" The Church needs to be rebibled. —*C. E. World.*

Better Than Breakfast

At a school in Japan a teacher asked the children if there were any who had not breakfasted that morning, thinking thereby to discover some needy family. A boy of nine years put up his hand. Knowing that he came from a comparatively well-to-do family, the teacher asked why he had not had breakfast. The boy replied: "In our home we do not eat till we have partaken of spiritual food. As I was late getting up this morning I had to leave for school immediately after the spiritual food, so I have not had any breakfast." The boy explained that in his home the Scripture Union daily portions were read. The teacher and the boy's schoolmates were so much impressed that about fifteen have joined the Scripture Union and are reading the Bible daily.—*From The Toronto Globe.*

* * *

The Tragedy of Bible Owners

The family or individual that does not possess a Bible is an exception in America today. A popular magazine presents a striking article on the high-pressure salesmanship that places Bibles in the homes even of illiterates in the South. Many persons feel that there is something akin to magic in mere possession of a Bible. Christians derive gratification from the fact that the Bible is still the world's "best seller," as it always has been. Yet a Chicago newspaper reports a University of Chicago professor as saying, in course of an interview, "Ignorance regarding the Bible on the part of otherwise intelligent people is one of the astounding things today." It is the tragedy of Bible owners that so many Bibles show little sign of use. In one home it was naively said, "We hide our money in the Bible, because no one ever thinks of looking there." We once found a Bible used on the floor for a doorstop! If we could get closed Bibles dusted off and really studied, many a one might say, with the prophet of old: "Thy words were found, and I did eat them; and thy word was unto me the joy and rejoicing of mine heart" (Jer. 15:16). The secular paper presenting the interview from which we have quoted, closed its account thus: "If the churches of Chicago during this year would forget their bazaars and nonessential activities, and concentrate on opening the Bible and its revealed truths to their 2,500,000 members and adherents here, there would be something akin to a spiritual rebirth before the year is out." —*The Evangelical Messenger.*

* * *

Moody's Prayer for His School

Rumor has it that when Dwight L. Moody was dedicating the first building of what later became the Moody Bible Institute, he gave the cornerstone a vigorous whack with the trowel and then made an invocation to this effect: "Lord, you know that what this old world needs more than anything else is thy Word. We pray that if the day ever comes when anything contrary to the Bible is taught here, you will wipe this school from the face of the earth."—*From "Moody Marches On,"* by Clarence Hall, in the *Christian Herald.*

* * *

A Letter in The Sea

The editor of *The Dawn* vouches for this incident, which he received from one of the persons concerned. Some years ago a steamer was wrecked. One of the crew succeeded in supporting himself upon a piece of wreckage, and the horror of his position awoke the pangs of conscience. It was a mail steamer, and hundreds of letters floated by him in the water. One, the envelope of which the water had made transparent, caught his eye: he saw a verse of Scripture, and he seized the letter. It was from a lady in England to a soldier in India. That letter brought him to Christ there and then. When he landed—for he was rescued—he found the lady from the address on the letter. She said: "I felt God tell me to write that letter to the soldier; but I confess that when I heard the mail boat had gone down, I wondered why God had done it." He said: "You may write another letter to the soldier if you wish; but *this* letter goes with me to my grave."—*The Alliance Weekly.*

Diamonds Wrapped in The Bible

An English diamond merchant packing some gems which he was sending to a trader in India, wrapped each one separately with great care. Coming to the last and costliest of them all, he used as its covering the first three chapters of the Gospel of John, tearing them, as he had done other Gospel portions, from a waste volume in his office, because the soft paper made an ideal wrapping. A Hindu, to whom this precious stone was sent, received with it what was infinitely more precious to him than the diamond which it covered—a leaf from the Book of Life, whereon he found the words: "God so loved the world, that He gave His only begotten Son, that whosoever believeth in Him should . . . have everlasting life." He was astounded. He spoke to many about his "find," and constantly inquired: "Why did I not know this before?" The Word grew in his heart, by the power of God's Spirit. "Surely," said he, "this means me—this salvation is for me." By faith he accepted it; he told others of it, until, when a European missionary went to that place, expecting to find only heathen, he found a large gathering of Indian Christians.—*Christian Victory.*

* * *

What A Testament Did

A Japanese colporteur reports that in a certain village of 430 houses he sold 400 copies of Scripture. This unusually high proportion of sales was due to the persuasion of his companion's life. Of him people said, "If Christianity is like Miyamoto's religion we would like to believe it."

And who is Miyamoto?

At the age of seventeen he was condemned to penal servitude for manslaughter. He spent more than twenty-five years in prison. One day he found himself in a certain prison with a group of discontented men who were planning a riot. Suddenly a Book fell from a shelf and struck him on the head. As he picked it up he noticed that it was open at the words, "Come unto Me." And how had a New Testament come into the prison? The governor, who was a Christian, had placed it there.

Miyamoto sought an interview with the governor in order to find out the meaning of the words, and this good man led him to Christ. He went on reading the Testament. His character changed; he was released under special Imperial amnesty. He returned to his own village and family. His faithful, hardworking life won for him the respect of the community. At one time he planned to change his place of residence, but his fellow villagers begged him to remain in order that his life might be an example to their boys. No wonder that when he accompanied the colporteur so many copies of Scripture were sold.—T. E. Ashford, *With Tongue and Pen.*

* * *

Curious Bible Facts

As all Bible lovers are eager to gain knowledge regarding the most unique Book in all the world, we have sought to tabulate several facts and statistics, curious and otherwise, regarding it. We would suggest that the following be cut out, and kept inside your Bible.

	Old Testament	New Testament	Total
Books	39	27	66
Chapters	929	260	1,189
Verses	23,214	7,959	31,173
Words	592,439	181,253	773,692
Letters	2,728,800	838,380	3,567,180
Middle Book	Proverbs	II Thesalonians	
Middle Chapter	Job 29	Romans 13, 14	
Middle Verse	II Chronicles 20:17, 18	Acts 17:17	
Shortest Chapter	Psalm 117		
Shortest Verse	I Chronicles 1:25	John 11:35	
Longest Chapter	Psalm 119	Luke 1	

The middle verse of the whole Bible is Psalm 118:8. the longest verse of the whole Bible is Esther 8:9, containing 90 words.

Ezra 7:21 contains all the letters of the alphabet, except J.

II Kings 19 and Isaiah 37 are exactly alike. Ezra 2 and Nehemiah 7 are similar.

The last two verses of II Chronicles and the opening verses of Ezra are alike.

The word "and" occurs 35,543 times in the Old Testament, and 10,684 times in the New Testament.

The word "Jehovah" occurs 6,855 times in the Bible.

The name of "God" does not occur in Esther or the Song of Solomon.

The letter *Mem* in the Hebrew text occurs 77,778 times; the letter *Vau*, 76,922 times; *Teth*, 11,052 times; *Samech* 13,580 times.

In Psalm 107 four verses are alike, 8, 15, 21, and 31.

Each verse in Psalm 136 ends alike.

The Bible was divided into chapters by Cardinal Hugo de Sancto-Caro, about 1236.

The Old Testament was divided into verses by Rabbi Mordecai Nathan, in 1661.

The New Testament was divided into verses by R. Stephens, a French printer, it is said, while on horseback.

The Septuagint, a translation into Greek, was made in Egypt 285 B.C.

The Scriptures have been translated into 1068 languages or dialects.

The first complete English translation was by Wycliffe in A.D. 1380; the first French translation in 1160; the German translation in 1460; the American translation in 1752.

The oldest manuscript of the Bible in the British Museum is the "Codex Alexandrinus"; the "Codex Vaticanus" is the oldest in the Vatican Library at Rome.

The Apocrypha has 4 books, 183 chapters, 6,081 verses, 252,185 words, and 1,063,876 letters.

There is a Bible in the library of the University of Gottingen written on 2,470 palm leaves.

Our English Bible is the combined writings of about forty men. These men were not contemporary, but lived at various times during a period of more than 1500 years. These men wrote under the most varied conditions. Some wrote in prison, some in palaces, others in caves, in deserts, by the river bank, in exile, in victory, in defeat, in success—in fact, under most every possible condition.

These men were from every walk of life. Kings, peasants, priests, fishermen, generals, shepherds, noblemen, tax-gatherers, doctors, lawyers, statesmen, and politicians are among its writers. They made use in their writings of every form of expression used by men to convey thought: prose, poetry, law, government decrees, laws, sermons, parables, pictorial symbols, even personal letters, and, most particular, prophecy. They wrote about every subject which vitally affects men: creation, the origin, working and destiny of sin, death, life, nations, governments; hell and heaven; and the being, character, and plan of God.

Such is our Bible, so majestic, exalted and marvelous in its sweep. The Old Testament ends with a curse; and the New Testament with a benediction.

Acts 26 is the finest chapter to read; Psalm 36, the most beautiful. The five most inspiring promises are John 14:1-3, 23; 6:37; Matthew 11:28; Psalm 37:4. Let us hide such within our hearts.

Isaiah 60:1 is the verse for the young convert, and Psalm 25:4 is the pillow for the head of the dying saints.

All who boast of perfection should learn Matthew 6.—*Rev. Herbert Lockyer.*

* * *

The Boat That Was Shipwrecked

Before Alexander Duff, the missionary, reached India, he was twice shipwrecked. On the very coast of India, only a few miles from the place that was to be his home, an awful storm struck the ship and wrecked it upon the shore. The first night in India he slept in a heathen temple.

He was sailing from his home for India in the "Lady Holland." He had been a great student and had won many honors in college and gathered together a library of eight hundred volumes. He loved these books very much. When the ship was wrecked, he lost all of them. Everything was gone! All gone!

When the people were safe on land, they looked like an unhappy company. From the shore the missionary watched, hoping he might see something from the wreck floating on the sea.

All of a sudden he jumped up, for he saw something very small on the water. He thought it hardly worth saving. It was washed up on the shore and when he picked it up he found it was his own Bible. He thought it was very strange that out of all his eight hundred books, only one was saved, and that one was his Bible. He thought God wished him to know that that one Book was worth more than all the other seven hundred and ninety-nine which he had lost, and that he was to make it the chief study of his life. He opened it, and there on that lonely shore he read to his friends these words from one of the Psalms:

"They that go down to the sea in ships, that do business in great waters; these see the works of the Lord, and His wonders in the deep."

When Alexander Duff began his work in India he started a school to educate the Hindu boys. In that school the Bible was taught. He loved the Bible and he wanted to teach it to others who did not know it. After a few years there were a thousand scholars, and several big school buildings. Often they sang:

"Holy, Bible! Book Divine,
Precious Treasure, thou art mine;
Mine to tell me whence I came,
Mine to tell me what I am."

—*Children's Missionary Story Sermons.*

* * *

His Word Shall Stand

Why not take God at His Word,
As you read it:
Let your confidence be stirred,
Read, then heed it.

All He says will come to pass,
So receive it;
Why should you your mind harass?
Just believe it.

Do not try one word to change,
Seek to fix it;
This, and that, to rearrange,
You will mix it.

Let each prophecy remain,
As He told it;
You may make its meaning vain,
If you mold it.

Believe it always as it is,
Don't add to it;
Ev'ry statement made, is His,
Take not from it.

Prophecy will never fail,
Why deny it;
Ev'ry sentence shall prevail,
Don't defy it.

If you cannot grasp it all,
Why dissect it ?
It must live e'en though you fall,
Don't reject it.

Time will show that God is true,
It will show it;
So, His prophecies pursue,
Then you'll know it.

Soon upon the golden shore,
You will say it:
Naught has failed, God said of yore,
You'll essay it.

—R. E. Neighbour, D.D.

* * *

Bible Bulwark

A physician, bright but critical, went to hear D. L. Moody. Although he had no thought of such a result, he was converted. When asked the reason for his change of heart, he said, "I went to hear Mr. Moody with no other idea than to have something to laugh at. I knew he was no scholar, and I felt sure I could find many flaws in his argument. But I found I could not get at the man. He stood there hiding behind the Bible, and just fired one Bible text after another at me till they went home to my heart straight as bullets from a rifle. *I tell you, Moody's power is in the way he has his Bible at the tip of his tongue.*" Jesus didn't convert the devil; He did not set out to, but He defeated his purpose, and in just the same way that Moody defeated the physician.—*Christian Instructor.*

* * *

The Pear Test

"You tell me that your book is the Word of God, but you do not prove it so." So said the owner of an orchard in North Italy to Colporteur Mariani, who offered him the Scriptures as he stood admiring the fruit trees. "What fine looking pears," said the colporteur, suddenly changing the subject; "but what a pity they are of such poor quality." "What!" exclaimed the orchard owner. "Of poor quality? It is plain that you have not tasted them. Pick one or two and try them!" The colporteur did as he was bidden, and began to eat. "Yes, you are right," he said, smacking his lips, "the pears are excellent; but, sir, you must deal with my book as I have dealt with your fruit. Taste, and you will see that the Word of God is good."—*Bible Society's Report.*

* * *

Christ on Every Page

It matters little what else we are finding in the Bible if we are not finding Him on every page. "If you read a chapter in the Old Testament and do not find Christ in it, read it again, for He is there," said Dr. D. M. Stearns in an address at a Bible conference. That one sentence was all that a certain young man heard that night, but it transformed his Bible study and his life. He is now a well-known teacher in a Bible institute, and is publishing a Bible correspondence course based on this principle of finding Christ as the key to every chapter of the Book. "I have a peculiar Bible," he said recently. "In my Bible the New Testament is printed between the lines of the Old Testament. Have you a Bible like that?"—*Sunday School Times.*

"I have never in my whole life met a man who really knew the Bible, and rejected it." The difficulty has always been an unwillingness to give it an honest trial. Our Lord Himself said, "Ye will not come unto me, that ye might have life."—*Christ Life.*

* * *

A Doctor Witnesses

Dr. Malan, of Geneva, on a trip to Paris fell into conversation with a chap who began to reason with him about Christianity. The doctor answered every argument with a quotation from the Scriptures—not venturing a single remark or application. Every quotation his companion evaded or turned aside, only to be met by another passage.

At last he turned away. "Don't you see, I don't believe your Bible. What's the use of quoting it to me?" he screamed.

But the only reply was another thrust, "If ye believe not that I am He, ye shall die in your sins."

Years afterwards Dr. Malan one day tore open a letter in an unfamiliar handwriting. "You took the Sword of the Spirit and stabbed me through and through," it read. "And every time I tried to parry the blade and get you to use your hands, and not the Heavenly steel, you simply gave me another stab. You made me feel I was not fighting you, but God."

At the close Dr. Malan recognized the name of his Paris-bound companion of years before.—*Arthur Mercer in "Problems"*

* * *

A Good Reply

A skeptic in London recently said, in speaking of the Bible, it was quite impossible in these days to believe in any book whose authority is unknown. A Christian asked him if the compiler of the multiplication table was known. "No," he answered. "Then, of course, you do not believe in it?" "Oh, yes, I believe in it because it works well." "So does the Bible," was the rejoinder, and the skeptic had no answer to make.—*Messenger.*

Chemistry in the Bible

The greatest miracle of the Bible is its chemical accuracy. The first book of the Bible says man was made out of the dust of the earth, and this is literally and scientifically true. In the dust of the earth, there are fourteen different chemical elements, and in the body of man, there are those same fourteen chemical elements.—*Dr. E. E. Slosson, a famous chemist.*

* * *

The Royal Law

The coronation of King George VI was the first to be broadcast to the world by radio. What a magnificent testimony to the Bible was heard at that point in the Westminster Abbey service when the crystal-clear voice of the Archbishop of Canterbury rang out with these words: *"Our gracious King, we present you with this Book, the most valuable thing this world affords. Here is wisdom; this is the royal law; these are the living oracles of God."—Bible Society Record.*

* * *

Saved Through Wallpaper

There is an interesting little story related concerning the incalculable good which was accomplished through the agency of a pile of Bible leaves which had been cast away as useless.

A lady on one occasion went into a cake-shop in Japan to purchase some cakes for her children. While waiting for the cakes she saw that the walls were papered with leaves from the Bible. This was so strange that she asked the old woman about it; and she told the lady that one day, passing by a book-shop, she saw a pile of papers which had been thrown away. As her shop needed papering, she thought this was just the thing and took some of the papers home, and pasted them over the walls.

One evening her grandson came in and began reading aloud from the paper on the wall. The old woman was so interested in what she heard that she listened eagerly, and got all who would to read it to her. One day a young man came who asked her if she understood it, and whether she was a Christian. She told him how much she enjoyed hearing it, but she did not understand it much; so he promised to take her to church the next day. After this she attended regularly, and became an earnest Christian. She now keeps a stock of tracts by her, and into every bag of little cakes she drops one.—*Selected.*

* * *

Never was a better reply made than that a poor Irishman gave to a Catholic priest, while he was defending himself for reading the Scriptures for himself. Said the priest, "The Bible is for priests, and not for the likes of you." "Ah! but sir," he answered, "I was reading in my Bible, 'You shall read it to your children,' and sure the priests have no children." "But, Michael," says the priest, "you cannot understand the Bible. It is not for you to understand it, my man." "Very well, yer riverence; if I cannot understand it, it will do me no harm, but what I can understand does me a heap o' good." "Mike," said the priest, "you must go to the Church, and the Church will teach you; the Church will give you the milk of the Word." "And where does the Church get it from but out of the Bible? Ah, yer riverence, I would rather keep the cow myself."—*Chapel News.*

* * *

Back to the Bible

When Henry Drummond, the great scientist and lecturer of Glasgow University, Scotland, was forty-six years of age, he was found to be dying of a mysterious disease. Weary of the jungle philosophy of evolution and tired of rattling the dried bones of dead monkeys as a means of finding the origin of life, he said to Sir William Dawson, a scientist and a devoted Christian, "I am going back to the Bible to believe it as I once did. I can no longer live in uncertainty." He did go back and his intellectual wandering and weariness were over.—*Gospel Herald.*

God's Wonderful Book

A certain Christian traveler was packing his suitcase when about to proceed on a journey, when he remarked to a friend: "There is still a little corner left open in which I desire to pack a guidebook, a lamp, a mirror, a telescope, a book of poems, a number of biographies, a bundle of old letters, a hymnbook, a sharp sword, a small library, containing thirty volumes, and all these articles must occupy a space of about three by two inches." "How are you going to manage that?" queried his friend, and the reply was: "Very easily, for the Bible contains *all these things.*"

The most wonderful, the most marvelous book in all the literature of the world is the Bible, because it is God's own Book!

God's creatures are we, proceeding through this world of sin on our short pilgrim journey, and it is therefore necessary to know one thing, or at least inquire for it, and that is *the way to heaven.* God Himself has clearly shown us the way even unto eternal life, and these directions are to be found in the Bible. This Book of God, therefore, is absolutely necessary on the pilgrim's journey as the Guide, which reveals unto fallen man the profoundest, the highest of all revelations: namely, the love, grace and mercy of the triune God.—*The Comforter.*

* * *

Where the Bible is Not Out of Date

As a converted African cannibal sat reading his Bible a European trader passed by and asked him what he was doing, "Reading the Bible," was his reply. "That Book is out of date in my country," said the trader. *"If it had been out of date here,"* said the African, *"you would have been eaten long ago."* —*Record of Christian Work.*

* * *

The Bible Is True

Young man! the Bible is true. What have these infidels to give you in its place? What has made England but the open Bible? Every nation that exalteth the Word of God is exalted, and every nation that casteth it down is cast down. Oh, let us cling close to the Bible. Of course we shall not understand it all at once. But men are not to condemn it on that account. Suppose I should send my little boy, five years old, to school tomorrow morning and when he came home in the afternoon, I would say to him, "Willie, can you read? Can you write? Can you spell? Do you understand all about algebra, geometry, Hebrew, Latin, and Greek?" "Why, papa," the little fellow would say, "how funny you talk; I have been all day trying to learn the ABC's!" Well, suppose I should reply, "If you have not finished your education, you need not go anymore." What would you say? Why, you would say I had gone mad. There would be just as much reason in that as in the way that people talk about the Bible. My friends, the men who have studied the Bible for 50 years—the wise men and the scholars, the great theologians—have never got down to the depths of it yet. There are truths there that the Church of God has been searching out the last 1800 years, but no man has fathomed the depths of that everliving stream.—*D. L. Moody.*

* * *

His Search Warrant

A Roman Catholic priest in Ireland reprimanded a peasant for reading the Bible. "But I have a search warrant to do so," replied the man. "What do you mean, sir?" said the priest in anger. "Why," answered the peasant, "Jesus said, 'Search the scriptures,' and I am doing only what he tells me to do." The argument was unanswerable—*The King's Business.*

* * *

President Coolidge and the Book

A committee from the Pocket Testament League presented former President Coolidge, while he was in office, with a copy of the New Testament. Mr. Coolidge, in receiving the Testament, said: "In this little book will be found the solution to all the problems of the world." Although Mr. Coolidge was noted for being a man of few words, the above sentence could not be improved upon very much if volumes were written or sermons preached about the problems of our troubled world and the solution of them by the wisdom of men—*Sunday School Times.*

* * *

"What Time I Am Afraid, I Will Trust"

The Rev. Bishop Taylor Smith, D.D., when speaking at Keswick, told of the "stage fright" he had when for the first time he was asked to read a lesson in church. He said: "So great it was, that I retreated into the vestry as the service was proceeding, and kneeled down, and asked that I might be helped to read that lesson. And then I came back and read it, and the lesson was from the Epistle to the Romans: 'There is therefore now no condemnation to them which are in Christ Jesus.' A few weeks afterward, the vicar told me that the church-warden had been converted through the reading of that lesson! I realized the power of God's Word as never before, and I think I can say that I have never read a lesson in church from that day to this without first reading it over, and praying over it, and having confidence that God can bless His own Word."—*Sunday School Times.*

* * *

The Bible

Born in the East and clothed in Oriental form and imagery, the Bible walks the ways of all the world with familiar feet and enters land after land to find its own everywhere. It has learned to speak in hundreds of languages to the heart of man. It comes into the palace to tell the monarch that He is a servant of the Most High, and into the cottage to assure the peasant that He is the Son of God. Children listen to its stories with wonder and delight, and wise men ponder them as parables of life. It has a word for the time of peril, a word of comfort for the time of calamity, a word of light for the hour of darkness. Its oracles are repeated in the assembly of the people, and its counsels whispered in the ear of the lonely. The wicked and the proud tremble at its warnings, but to the wounded and penitent it has a mother's voice. The wilderness and the solitary place have been made glad by it, and the fire on the earth has lit the reading of its well-worn page. It has woven itself into our dearest dreams; so that love, friendship, sympathy and devotion, memory and hope put on the beautiful garments of its treasured speech, breathing of frankincense and myrrh. No man is poor or desolate who has this treasure for his own. When the landscape darkens and the trembling pilgrim comes to the valley named of the shadow, he is not afraid to enter; he takes the rod and staff of Scripture in his hand, he says to his friends and comrade: "Good-bye, we shall meet again," and comforted by that support, he goes toward the lonely pass as one who walks through darkness into light.—*Henry Van Dyke.*

* * *

The Bible A Restraining Power

Wherever God's law is supreme, life and property are safe. Wherever the Bible is despised or discarded, neither life nor property is secure. When infidel friends were discussing their theories around the dining table one day, Voltaire said: "Hush, gentlemen, till the servants are gone. If they believed as we do, none of our lives would be safe."

The influence of the Bible in restraining sin and promoting righteousness is one of the evidences that it is a supernatural and divine revelation.—Otterbein Teacher.

* * *

Checking Criticism

We live in a day when man is criticizing God's Word. Modernism is emasculating it; modern cults are perverting it and the world is neglecting it. Dr. W. H. Griffith Thomas once said that the word "discerner" (Heb. 4:12), in the Greek, should be translated "critic,"—"a critic of the thoughts and intents of the heart," and he added, "It is the only place in the Bible where the word 'critic' is found, and you notice it is the Word criticizing us, and if we allowed the Word of God to criticize us a little more, we would criticize it a great deal less." —*Sunday School Times.*

* * *

Leper Memorizes Matthew

In a letter published in the *Bible Society Record* the story is told of K. Pong Cho, a leper, who recited the whole Gospel of Matthew. "He has not a whole finger left; his ears are twice their normal size, and his feet swollen so that he can hardly walk. He can speak only in a hoarse whisper, and he is totally blind." When he was asked what he wanted to recite, he said, "I might start with the Gospel according to Matthew." And when consent was given, off he went. "It was beyond belief . . . He sat on the floor, presently swaying to and fro as the recitation developed into a kind of song. One by one the chapters rolled by . . . It seemed almost effortless." At the close of the recitation of the 28 chapters, he was asked, "This painfully hard work— has it been worth while?" "It has given me," he answered, "a mind at peace with God. My faith has been strengthened. I have joy." "And death?" he was asked. "The matter of death is not my business. That belongs to God. I see Heaven in my mind."—*The Alliance Weekly.*

* * *

Hoover Says:

"There is no other book so varied as the Bible, nor one so full of concentrated wisdom. Whether it be of law, business, morals, or that vision which leads the imagination in the creation of constructive enterprise for the happiness of mankind, he who seeks for guidance in any of these things may look inside its covers and find illumination. The study of this Book in your Bible classes is a post-graduate course in the richest library of human experience.

"As a nation we are indebted to the Book of books for our national ideas and representative institutions. Their preservation rests in adhering to its principles."—*Ex-President Hoover.*

* * *

The Bible Made America What She Is

America rests upon four corner stones: The English Bible, the English language, the common law, and the tradition of liberty. But liberty, language, and law might have been drawn from the Bible alone. Had we brought nothing with us across the sea besides this supreme Book, we might still have been great. Without this Book, America could not have become what she is and when she loses its guidance and wisdom, she will be America no more.

Did we bring the Bible to these shores? Did it not rather bring us? The breath of ancient Prophets was in the sails that drove the tiny *Mayflower.* The hope and faith of ancient poets, kings, and lawgivers were in the hearts of those who first sang the Lord's song in this strange land. Our first dim outlines of a commonwealth in the Western world were drawn "as near as might be to that which was the glory of Israel."

From those beginnings until now the Bible has been a teacher to our best men, a rebuke to our worst, and a noble companion to us all.—*Christian Advocate.*

* * *

The Bible and "The Spirit of the Times"

It is surprising how many church members seem to think that we must adjust Bible teachings to "the spirit of the times" in which we live. Even a middle grade Sunday School scholar who has been trying to study the Bible and has had a teacher that studies his Bible rather than the spirit of the times should know that one of the outstanding characteristics is, that it at no time in its history ever adjusted itself to the spirit of the times. To the contrary, both the prophets of the Old Testament Scripture, and the apostles of the New Testament of the shed blood of Christ, everywhere and always preached a gospel that took hold of the spirit of the times in the way of rebuke and correction.

They had a gospel that had in it power to wrestle with the spirit of the times and to conquer that spirit in favor of the spirit of righteousness and godliness.

The spirit of the times may, and often does, bring into churches a dozen or more sectional meetings during each week, while it is restive under the ministrations of the pulpit for two or three times a week, even if the preaching of the gospel from the pulpit takes more than twenty-five minutes at each time.

God help us to serve our times and to love the people of our times, but God help us in spiritual things everlastingly to set our faces against the materialism and lust for pleasure, and the ignorance of the teaching of the Word of God which characterize our times. May He help us, each in his own way and place, to declare the whole gospel of God for our times whether our times shall applaud or shall not applaud.—*Western Recorder.*

* * *

The Bible

It seems as if to the feet of the sacred writers the mountains had brought all their gems, and the sea all its pearls, and the gardens all their frankincense, and the spring all its blossoms, and the harvests all their wealth, and Heaven all its glory, and eternity all it stupendous realities; and that since then poets and orators and painters had been drinking from an exhausted fountain and searching for diamonds amid realms utterly rifled and ransacked.

Oh, this Book is the hive of all sweetness, the armory of all well-tempered weapons, the tower containing the crown jewels of the universe, the lamp that kindles all other lights, the home of all majesties and splendors, the stepping-stone on which Heaven stoops to kiss the earth with its glories, the marriage ring that unites the celestial and the terrestrial, while all the clustering white-robed multitudes of the sky stand round to rejoice at the nuptials. This Book is the wreath into which are twisted all garlands, the song into which hath struck all harmonies, the river of light into which hath poured all the great tides of hallelujahs, the firmament in which all suns and moons and stars and constellations and galaxies and immensities and universes and eternities wheel and blaze and triumph.

Where is the youth with music in his soul who is not stirred by Jacob's lament, or Nathan's dirge, or Habakkuk's dithyrambic, or Paul's march of the resurrection, or John's anthem of the ten thousand times ten thousand doxology of elders on their faces, answering to the trumpet blast of archangel, with one foot on the sea and the other on the land, declaring that time shall be no longer?—*Talmage.*

* * *

A Scientist's Testimony

As a result of many years' diligent study and crucial testings, I now believe — and am sure — that the *whole Bible* is God's Word.

I am certain that Jesus Christ is the Son of God, born of the Virgin Mary. I believe that all men are by nature sinners, alienated from the life that is in God. Our Saviour shed His sacrificial blood upon the cross to pay the infinite penalty for the guilt of a lost world. I believe that he who thus receives Jesus Christ as his Saviour is "*born again*" spiritually by His Holy Spirit.

I perceive that no man can save himself by his good works or by what is called a "moral life," while such works in the new life are but the evidence and natural fruits of the hidden life of faith within. I believe that the rebellious agent — Satan, — both the cause of man's fall and of his continuance in sin, — is the prince of the kingdoms of this world, who, as the Bible announced at the very outset (Gen. 3:15) will be finally defeated and made forever impotent. As Christ first came in weakness and humility, He will return to earth in incomparable glory to reign over His kingdom through unending ages and for His return I look daily; all signs seem to herald His Approach! —*Howard A. Kelly, M.D.,LL.D., etc.*

When He Forgot to Shave

Some years ago there came to the city of Chicago a man who sold goods for a New York concern. He had been stealing money from his company until the amount totaled a few thousand dollars. The man had worked out a plan by which he thought to stifle his conscience. He would work hard all day and go out to places of amusement at night, and remain to a late hour. One day in a Chicago hotel, he was stropping an old-fashioned razor, and, looking for a piece of paper to wipe the blade on, he tore out a page from a Gideon Gible. Starting to wipe the blade, his eye caught these words, "The wages of sin is death." Conviction struck his heart, and smoothing out the page, he read, "The wages of sin is death; but the gift of God is eternal life through Jesus Christ our Lord." The startled salesman read the Bible for two hours, and then on his knees beside the bed with the Bible open in front of him, he acknowledged himself to be a sinner and in need of a Saviour. He took Christ as his Saviour, and realizing that a new life had been bestowed upon him, he wired the firm in New York that he was returning. He made a confession of the stolen money. He was not prosecuted and not even discharged, but allowed to pay back something each month out of his salary. Dr. Will H. Houghton states that the last he heard of this man he was living in New Jersey and bearing his testimony to the power of the Bible and the saving power of his Saviour, Christ Jesus. —*Condensed from Gideon Magazine.*

* * *

The Bible's Freshness

Who doubts that, times without number, particular portions of the Scriptures find their way to the human soul as if they were embassies from on high, each with its own commission of comfort, of guidance, or of warning? What crisis, what trouble, what perplexity of life, has failed, or can fail, to draw from this inexhaustible treasure-house its proper supply? What profession, what position, is not daily and hourly enriched by these words which repetition never weakens, which carry with them now, as in the days of their first utterance, the freshness of youth and immortality?—*William E. Gladstone.*

* * *

A Jew's Discovery of a Forbidden Book

On the streets of Vienna, Austria, one day, a New Testament in Hebrew was given to a brilliant young teacher in a Jewish school. He had been warned against reading this book, but once in his room he locked the door and opened the book to the first page. Before he had finished a page or two he was comparing it with the Old Testament prophecies and seeing how marvelously they were fulfilled. He was utterly captivated and could not lay it aside. Before he realized it, he discovered that he had been reading all night long! Thus, as he read, without anyone saying a word to him, he became convinced beyond any shadow of doubt that the Christ of the New Testament, and the promised Messiah of the Old Testament, were one and the same Person; and that He was the one of whom Moses and the prophets did write. He at once accepted Him as his own Messiah and Saviour. This one copy of the New Testament transformed the life of this young teacher; then the lives of a number of others to whom it was secretly passed; and then caused him to travel 5,000 miles to another continent for the purpose of winning his brother, Jacob Gartenhaus, to the Saviour.—*Sunday School Times*

* * *

Testimonies of Allied Generals

In Sydney, Australia, a group of Christian people maintain a Christian center for servicemen. Many American soldiers, as well as British, have found it to be a haven of refuge. From its headquarters at 4a Bligh Street, Sydney, an intercessory circular letter was issued in February, signed by W. Bradley, and from that letter the following striking testimonies are taken:

The late Field Marshall Sir Douglas Haig: "The Gospel of Christ is the only hope of the world."

General MacArthur: "I give thanks for God's guidance who has brought to us this success in our great crusade — His the Honor, the Power and the Glory forever."

General Sir Arthur Smith: "Christ meets every need of soldier and civilian."

General Wavell: "What the men want is a quiet place to read their Bible and turn their thoughts to God."

General Montgomery (to Staff Officers): "I read my Bible every day and I recommend you to do the same."

General Dobbie: "Christ has saved and satisfied me for forty-seven years."

* * *

He Was The Other Fellow

A shrewd worldly agnostic and a Christian clergyman dressed in a modest clerical suit, says Eli Perkins, sat at the same table in the Pullman dining car. They were waiting for the first course at the dinner, a delicious Hudson River shad. Eying his companion coldly for a moment, the agnostic remarked:

"I judge you are a clergyman, sir!"

"Yes, sir; I am in my Master's service."

"Yes, you look it. Preach out of the Bible, don't you?"

"Oh, yes; of course."

"Find a good many things in the old Book that you don't understand — eh?"

"Oh, yes; some things."

"Well, what do you do then?"

"Why, my dear friend, I simply do just as we do while eating this delicious shad. If I come to a bone I quietly lay it on one side and go on enjoying the shad, and let some fool insist on choking himself with the bones."

Then the agnostic wound up his watch and went into the smoker.—*Evangelical Messenger*.

* * *

All Inspired

It is not enough to say that Scripture is generally inspired, but every letter is inspired. A man purchased a large bill of goods of a New York merchant, giving his note in promise of payment and a well known firm in Chicago as reference. A telegram was sent to Chicago and the answer received, "Note good for any amount." The goods were delivered, and never paid for. It turned out upon inquiry that the telegram ought to have read, "Not good for any amount;" but through carelessness the word *not* was changed into *note*, and one letter made a mighty big difference to the New York merchant. Let us remember that every letter which the Holy Ghost has communicated is worthy of respectful notice. —*Selected.*

* * *

Clearer, Day by Day

Two Mongol Tartar chiefs were engaged by a missionary to assist him in preparing a translation of the Gospels into the language of their country, and they had, as a matter of course, to study the subject intently. At length the work was completed, the last correction made, and the book was closed on the table. Still they sat, serious and silent. At last the missionary inquired what was the matter, and was equally surprised and delighted to hear them both declare themselves converts to Christianity. "At home," they said, "we studied the sacred writings of the Chinese, and the more we read the more obscure they seemed; but the longer we have read the Gospel, the more simple and intelligible it became, until at last it seemed as if Jesus was talking with us."—*Sunday Companion.*

* * *

Peter's Two Swords

When Peter used his own sword in the garden of Gethsemane he succeeded only in cutting off one man's ear. But when he used the Sword of the Spirit which is the Word of God on the following Pentecost about three thousand were pricked in their hearts. Christ, who healed Malchus' ear, healed these three thousand heart-wounds also. — *Sunday School Companion.*

* * *

Inseparable Partners

These hath God married
And no man shall part,
Dust on the Bible
And drought in the heart.
—*Record of Christian Work.*

The Teaching of the Light

May every voice be hushed in me,
 Except Thy living Word;
Let every move be crushed in me
 That does not own Thee Lord;
To silence all be brought in me,
Except what Thou hast wrought in me.

Oh, let Thy kingdom come in me,
 Till Thou dost reign alone;
Let my heart be a home for Thee
 On earth, where Thou hast none;
When Thou shalt fully rest in me,
I shall be fully blest in Thee.

May everything depart from me
 That clouds the inward sight;
Implant deep in the heart of me
 Things that with Thee are right;
That truths taught by Thy light in me
May shine undimmed and bright in me.

—*by Max I. Reich, D.D.*

* * *

Bible Complete

All the good from the Saviour of the world is communicated through this Book; but for this Book we could not know right from wrong. All the things desirable to man are contained in it.—*Abraham Lincoln.*

* * *

Samuel Chadwick on the Bible

"I have worked at the Bible, prayed over the Bible, lived by the Bible for more than sixty years, and I tell you there is no book like the Bible. It is a miracle of literature, a perennial spring of wisdom, a wonder-book of surprises, a revelation of mystery, an infallible guide of conduct, and an unspeakable source of comfort... Read it for yourself. Study it according to its own directions. Believe its message. Follow its precepts. No man is uneducated who knows the Bible, and no man is wise who is ignorant of its teachings... I never go anywhere without it, and it is my chief joy."—*Free Methodist.*

* * *

I supposed I knew my Bible,
 Reading piecemeal, hit or miss,
Now a bit of John or Matthew,
 Now a snatch of Genesis;
Certain chapters of Isaiah,
 Certain Psalms (the twenty-third),
Twelfth of Romans, first of Proverbs,
 Yes, I thought I knew the Word.
But I found a thorough reading
 Was a different thing to do,
And the way was unfamiliar
 When I read the Bible through.

You who like to play at Bible,
 Dip and dabble here and there,
Just before you kneel a-weary
 And yawn out a hurried prayer;
You who treat the Crown of Writing
 As you treat no other book—
Just a paragraph disjointed,
 Just a crude, impatient look—
Try a worthier procedure,
 Try a broad and steady view—
You will kneel in very rapture
 When you read the Bible through.

—*Amos R. Wells.*

* * *

"It Is God's Voice"

"The ears of all the people were attentive unto the Book of the Law" (*Neh.* 8:3).

The Rev. Douglas Gray, a Wesleyan Methodist missionary, was translating the Gospel of Mark into Mukuni, the language of a tribe in Northern Rhodesia. One morning he went to his church and thought that, without saying anything, he would read the lesson from his notes in their language instead of using a translation in the language of the neighboring tribe as usual. The chapter was given out, and he began to read. Suddenly all seemed to sit up and start into new life. They called out, "It is God's voice; He is talking to us, He is using our language!"

A hymn was sung, and Mr. Gray was about to give out his text when the people called, some with tears streaming down their cheeks, "No, no! Let God go on talking to us. He speaks our language!" So for the rest of the service the chapter was read and reread. Mr. Gray will never forget what it meant to give the people the Word of God in their own language.—*Glad Tidings.*

Christ Throughout the Bible

Jesus Christ is the heart of the Bible. He is the Shiloh in Genesis; the I Am in Exodus; the Star and Scepter in Numbers; the Rock in Deuteronomy; the Captain of the Lord's Host in Joshua; the Redeemer in Job. He is David's Lord and Shepherd; in the Song of Songs He is the Beloved; in Isaiah He is the Wonderful, the Counsellor, the Mighty God, the everlasting Father, and the Prince of Peace. In Jeremiah He is the Lord our Righteousness; in Daniel He is the Messiah; in Zechariah He is the Branch; in Haggai He is the Desire of all Nations; in Malachi He is the Messenger of the Covenant and the Sun of Righteousness; and in the Book of Revelation He is the Alpha and the Omega and also the Morning Star.—*The American Fundamentalist.*

* * *

An Astonished Missionary

To show the need of circulating the Scriptures all over the world, the following remarkable incident will bear witness.

An American missionary was sent to Burma to make inquiries about the languages. He himself spoke Burmese, and traveled up the country for many hundred miles. One night he encamped near a small village. Here he heard prayer going on in Burmese. He listened, and to his utter atonishment heard, not the name of Buddha, or that of any idol, but the Name of our Lord Jesus Christ. He was the more surprised, for he knew that no missionary or white man had ever been to that part of the world, and so he went into the village and began to make inquiries.

He found that the head man of the village had, some years previously, been down to another village some miles distant and had brought an article of food wrapped up in a Burmese printed paper, which happened to be one single chapter of the *Word of God* with a piece torn out of the corner. He read it, and having himself sought to put sin away, he found that Saviour who is the Son of God, and who he found was able to cleanse from sin.

He now called his friends together, and read that piece of the Scriptures to them, and induced them to put away their idols. And when this missionary found them they had been for six years praying to Christ as the Saviour of sinners. This is the blessing of God upon the glorious work of spreading abroad simply and solely the truth as it is in Jesus Christ.—*Friends Witness.*

* * *

Bible Repays Study

"The Bible will richly repay study, but only if the conditions are observed which common sense dictates. It has no power of working like a charm, so that a chapter read in a couple of minutes by a preoccupied mind can do any good. The mind must rest on it and give itself time to receive impressions. It requires the whole force of our thinking and the whole of our feeling."—*Stalker.*

* * *

Military Stratagem and Bible

A Brigade Major with General Allenby's forces in Palestine during World War I was reading his Bible one night by the light of a candle, looking for the name "Michmash." His brigade had been ordered to capture a village of that name which stood on a rocky hill just across a deep valley. The name had seemed vaguely familiar.

Finally, in Samuel I, Chapter 13, he read: "And Saul, and Jonathan his son, and the people with them, abode in Gibeah of Benjamin: but the Philistines encamped in Michmash." The major went on to read how Jonathan and his armor-bearer went over to the Philistines' garrison alone one night, through a pass that had "a sharp rock on the one side, and a sharp rock on the other side: and the name of the one was Bozez, and the name of the other Seneh." They climbed the rocky hill till they came to "a half acre of land, which a yoke of oxen might plow." Then the Philistines awoke, thought they were surrounded by the armies of Saul, and "the multitude melted away."

Saul then attacked with his whole army, and "so the Lord saved Israel that day."

The major thought to himself, "This pass, those two rocky headlands and the flat piece of ground are probably still there." He woke the brigadier, and they read over the story. Scouts were sent out and found the pass, thinly held by the Turks; rocky crags were on either side — obviously Bozez and Seneh — and high up in Michmash moonlight showed a small flat piece of ground.

Then and there the general changed his plan of attack: instead of sending the whole brigade, one company alone was sent along the pass at dead of night. The few Turks met were silently dealt with; the hill was climbed; and just before dawn the company found itself on the flat bit of ground. The Turks awoke, thought they were surrounded by the armies of Allenby, and fled in disorder. Every Turk in Michmash was killed or captured that night.

And so, after thousands of years, the tactics of Saul and Jonathan were repeated with success by a British force. *—Major Vivian Gilbert, Romance of the Last Crusade (Appleton-Century).*

* * *

The Bible Lives!

Generation follows generation — yet it lives.
Nations rise and fall — yet it lives.
Kings, dictators, presidents come and go —yet it lives,
Hated, despised, cursed — yet it lives.
Doubted, suspected, criticized — yet it lives.
Condemned by atheists — yet it lives.
Scoffed at by scorners — yet it lives.
Exaggerated by fanatics — yet it lives.
Misconstrued and misstated—yet it lives.
Ranted and raved about — yet it lives.
Its inspiration denied — yet it lives.
Yet it lives—as a lamp to our feet.
Yet it lives—as a light to our path.
Yet it lives—as the gate to heaven.
Yet it lives—as a standard for childhood.
Yet it lives—as a guide for youth.
Yet it lives—as an inspiration for the matured.
Yet it lives—as a comfort for the aged.
Yet it lives—as food for the hungry.
Yet it lives—as water for the thirsty.
Yet it lives—as rest for the weary.
Yet it lives—as light for the heathen.
Yet it lives—as salvation for the sinner.
Yet it lives—as grace for the Christian.
To know it is to love it.
To love it is to accept it.
To accept it means life eternal.

—Religious Digest

* * *

Family Bible Survives Royal Chapel Bombing

When the Royal Chapel at Buckingham Palace was bombed, some beautiful and valuable things were destroyed.

But among the treasures that escaped was the king's family Bible — on the flyleaves of which are recorded the royal births, marriages, and deaths for several generations.

The secretary who found the Bible among the ruins wrote to a friend saying: "We took it as an omen of what is going to survive when this war is finally over."—*Now.*

* * *

My Bible

That grand old Book, my Bible,
With pages soiled by years,
Has been a comfort all through life
'Mid happiness and tears.

With comfort for the aged
Who near death's portal door;
And blessings for the children
Whose lives are all before.

To sinners in the natural, this
Good Book tells their fate,
And warns them to accept the Lord
Before it is too late.

There're many leaves with marks upon,
That when I'd turned away
The baby hands had scribbled up,
In part of childish play.

And if those selfsame little ones
Who've marked my Book in play,
Make this dear Book their rule through life
They''ll never go astray!

How to Use the Bible

When in sorrow, read John 14.
When men fail you, read Psalm 27.
When you have sinned, read Psalm 51.
When you worry, read Matthew 6:19-34.
Before church service, read Psalm 84.
When you are in danger, read Psalm 91.
When you have the blues, read Psalm 34.
When God seems far away, read Psalm 139.
When you are discouraged, read Isaiah 40.
If you want to be fruitful, read John 15.
When doubts come upon you, try John 7:17.
When you are lonely or fearful, read Psalm 23.
When you forget your blessings, read Psalm 103.
For Jesus' idea of a Christian, read Matthew 5.
For James' idea of religion, read James 1:19-27.
When your faith needs stirring, read Hebrews 11.
When you feel down and out, read Romans 8:31-39.
When you want courage for your task, read Joshua 1.
When the world seems bigger than God, read Psalm 90.
When you want rest and peace, read Matthew 11:25-30.
When you want Christian assurance, Romans 8:1-30.
For Paul's secret of happiness, read Col. 3:12-17.
When you leave home for labor or travel, Psalm 121.
When you grow bitter or critical, read I Corinthians 13.
When your prayers grow narrow or selfish, Psalms 67.
For Paul's idea of Christianity, read II Corinthians 5:15-19.
For Paul's rules on how to get along with men, Romans 12.
When you think of investments and returns, Mark 10:17-31.
For a great invitation and a great opportunity, Isaiah 55.
For Jesus' idea of prayer, Luke 11:1-13, Matt. 6:5-15.
For the prophet's picture of worship that counts, Isaiah 58:1-12.
For the prophet's idea of religion, Isa. 1:10-18, Mic. 6:6-8.
Why not follow Psalm 119:11 and hide some of these in your memory?—*Prof. Harris Franklin Rall.*

* * *

Secret Study

Preeminent, supreme among the helps to secret prayer I place, of course, the secret study of the holy written Word of God. Read it on your knees, at least on the knees of your spirit. Read it to reassure, to feed, to regulate, to kindle, to give to your secret prayer at once body and soul. Read it that you may hold faster your certainity of being heard. Read it that you may know with blessed definiteness whom you have believed, and what you have in Him, and how He is able to keep your deposit safe. Read it in the attitude of mind in which the Apostle read it, in which the Lord read it. Read it, not seldom, to turn it at once into prayer. — *H. G. C. Moule.*

* * *

The Scoffer Silenced

A party of American tourists were some time ago touring Palestine, amongst whom was a young man who took delight in discrediting the Word of God. Having come over the rim of mountains which encircle the sea of Galilee, and having their first view of its beautiful waters, which were very peaceful, this young man engaged in a taunting laugh as he ridiculed the idea of any fisherman who had any knowledge about a boat getting scared in a storm on such a small portion of water — as the disciples did according to Luke 8:23.

The party had scarcely reached the shore when with great suddenness a storm — even a typical Galilean one — broke upon the scene, coming down from the hills, it being so severe that within a very short time the waves were breaking over two towers situated there, and that party of tourists were taking shelter behind one of the buildings a short distance from the shore, for fear of being drenched by the spray which was given by the storm.

It is, of course, needless to say anything of the one who demonstrating his unbelief in the Bible, because he was having a taste of the very thing which he denied. Even today we find many who say the Scriptures are untrue, and all the time the Lord is showing the truth of His precious Word by the work of the excavators in Bible Lands. Oh, how this should silence those who throw discredit upon the Holy Scriptures.—*S. L., in The British Evangelist.*

* * *

She Knew Too Much Bible

A little girl, being asked by a priest to attend religious instruction, refused saying it was against her father's wishes. The priest said she should obey him, not her father. "Oh sir, we are taught in the Bible, 'Honor thy father and thy mother.'" "You have no business to read the Bible," said the priest. "But, sir, our Saviour said, 'Search the Scriptures.'" "That was said to Jews, and not to children. You don't understand it," said the priest in reply. "But Paul said to Timothy, 'From a child thou hast known the holy scriptures.'" Said the priest, "Timothy was being trained to be a bishop and he was taught by the church authorities." "No, sir," said the child, "he was taught by his mother and his grandmother." The priest turned away, saying she "knew enough of the Bible to poison a parish." —*Sunday School Times.*

* * *

"I've Translated For Myself"

A young man went home from a theological school to visit his aged grandmother. To have a bit of fun at her expense he said: "Grandmother, you know the *Bible* that you say you believe was written in Hebrew and Greek. It had to be translated by great scholars into our language. How do you know those who translated it got it right?" "Ah, Jamie, lad," she answered, "never mind the great men; I have translated a few of them promises myself."—*Overcomer.*

The Miracle Book—

An Argentine woman who had bought a Spanish Bible was so much afraid of her husband that she read it every day in his absence, as he was an enemy of religion. One night, however, she had omitted to hide the Book, and her husband saw it on the table. Without saying anything, he began to read it, and then remarked to his wife that it appeared to be a good Book; and every night when he returned home he went on reading his wife's Bible. Shortly afterward his wife suggested that they should go together to see her parents, to whom they had not spoken for about two years. They went, and asked forgiveness, and now both families are following the Lord.—*Watchman Examiner.*

* * *

"Let's Go Back to the Bible"

The *Bounty* was a British ship which set sail from England in 1787, bound for the South Seas. The idea was that those on board would spend some time among the islands, transplanting food-bearing trees, and doing other things to make some of the islands more habitable. After ten months of voyage, the *Bounty* arrived safely at its destination, and for six months officers and crew gave themselves to the duties placed upon them by their governments.

When the special task was completed, and the order came to embark again, the sailors rebelled. They had formed strong attachments for the native girls, and the climate and ease of South Sea island life was much to their liking. The result was mutiny, and the sailors placed Captain Bligh and a few loyal men adrift in an open boat. Captain Bligh, in almost miraculous fashion, survived the ordeal, was rescued, and eventually arrived home in London to tell his story. An expedition was launched to punish the mutineers, and in due time fourteen of them were captured and paid the penalty under British law.

But nine of the men had gone to a distant island. There they formed a colony. Perhaps there never has been a more degraded social life than that of this colony. They learned to distill whiskey from a native plant, and whiskey, as usual, was their ruin. Disease and murder took the lives of all the native men and all but one of the white men, Alexander Smith by name. He found himself the only man on an island, surrounded by a crowd of women and half-breed children. And then occurred something unexplainable from the human viewpoint. Alexander Smith found a Bible among the possessions of a dead sailor. The Book was new to him, and he read it, and believed it and began to live it. He wanted others to share in the benefits of this book, so he gathered the women and children around him to read to them and to teach them.

So far as the record goes, it was twenty years before a ship touched the island, and when it did a minature Utopia was found. The people were living in decency, prosperity, and peace. There was nothing of crime, disease, insanity, illiteracy, or drunkenness. How was it accomplished? By the reading and acceptance of the Bible!

Here is the reason for a return to our exhortation, "Let's Go Back to the Bible." Because the Bible and only the Bible can do what needs to be done for our nation in this threatening hour. I'm afraid it sounds too simple for some people. They are looking for the complex and the complicated. — *Courtesy Moody Monthly.*

* * *

The Quick and Powerful Word

A highwayman once stopped John Wesley and demanded his money or his life. Wesley after giving him the money, said, "Let me speak one word to you: The time may come when you will regret the course of life in which you are now engaged. Remember this: 'The Blood of Jesus Christ * * cleanseth from * * all sin.' " No more was said, and they parted. Many years afterwards, as Wesley was going out of a church in which he had been preaching, a stranger introduced himself, and asked Mr. Wesley if he remembered being way-laid at such a time. He said he recollected it. "I was that man," said the stranger, "and that single verse you quoted on that occasion was the means of a total change in my life and habits. I have long since been attending the house of God, and giving attention to His Word."

"So shall My Word be that goeth forth out of My mouth: it shall not return unto Me void, but it shall accomplish that which I please, and it shall prosper in the thing whereto I sent it."

—*Kingdom Truth.*

* * *

Neglect of the Bible

Dr. James Hamilton once related an anecdote which illustrates a vital question in the Christian life. A writer recounts it as follows: "A gallant officer was pursued by an overwhelming force, and his followers were urging him to greater speed, when he discovered that his saddle-girth was becoming loose. He cooly dismounted, repaired the girth by tightening the buckle, and then dashed away. The broken buckle would have left him on the field a prisoner; the wise delay to repair damages, sent him on in safety amid the huzzas of his comrades."

The Christian who is in such haste to get about his business in the morning that he neglects his Bible and his season of prayer, rides with a broken buckle.— C. Lee Cook.

* * *

The Bible: Effective Proof

One day a skeptic asked a highly educated and cultured Christian woman how she could prove the Bible was the Word of God, and she said to him, "How can you prove there is a sun in the sky?"

"Why," he replied, "because it warms me and I can see its light."

"And so it is with me," she said, "*the proof of this Book being the Word of God is that it warms my soul and gives it light.*"—*W. E. Biederwolf.*

* * *

Five Pounds And The Book

A wealthy old gentleman residing in London on one of his birthdays invited his servants into the house to receive presents.

"Which will you have," he asked, addressing the groom, "this Bible or a five-pound note?"

"I would take the Bible, sir, but I cannot read: so I think the money will do me more good," replied the hostler.

"And you?" he asked the gardener.

"My poor wife is so ill that I sadly need the money," responded the gardener with a bow.

"Mary, you can read," said the old man, turning to his cook, "will you have the Bible?"

"I can read, sir, but I never get time to look into a book, and the money will buy a fine dress."

Next was the chambermaid, but she had one Bible and did not want another.

Last came the errand boy. "My lad," said his kind benefactor, "will you take these five pounds and replace your shabby clothes by a new suit?"

"Thank you, sir; but my dear mother used to read to me that the Law of the Lord was better than thousands of gold and silver. I will have the good Book, if you please."

"God bless you, my boy! and may your wise choice prove riches and honor and long life unto you!" As the lad received the Bible and unclasped its covers, a bright gold piece rolled to the floor. Quickly turning its pages, he found them thickly interleaved with bank notes, while the four servants, discovering the mistake of their worldly coveteousness, hastily departed in chagrin. — *Selected.*

* * *

Jonathan Goforth's Conviction

"I believe the Bible is the Word of God because it is the holy book God uses in the conversion of men. Mr. Moody said in every case of conversion he knew of it was some portion of the Bible that the Holy Spirit used. My own experience leads me to the same conclusion. I am so convinced of this that I never speak to the unsaved in China without having my open Bible,—'the sword of the Spirit, which is the word of God.' His Word is like fire and like a hammer that breaketh the rock in pieces. In all the history of the Church of Jesus Christ there is no authentic instance of a soul being genuinely born into the Kingdom of God apart from the Bible or something derived from it. I saw a man in the province of Kwonghsi, China, who, with his whole family, was converted only through the reading of the Word. He wrote over the door of his house, 'This household belongs to the living God.' "—*The Sunday School Times.*

* * *

She Didn't Believe It!

When Dr. J. C. Massee's daughter was small, attending a school in Brooklyn, her teacher said one day "There is no doubt at all but that the moon is made of green cheese." She further explained that this was due to a "chemical reaction." Dr. Massee's daughter told her father, "I told her I didn't believe it, that it wasn't in the Bible and I'd prove it."

She then asked her daddy to help her win her point; but he told her to study her Bible and try to figure it out herself, for he was too busy to help her that evening. The next morning he had planned to help her, but she left for school without his help. All day he wondered how she got along with her teacher; so when she came home that evening he was interested to hear her explain. "I got down my Bible as you told me and found where it said that the moon was made on the fourth day and cows were not made until the sixth day. *So I asked the teacher how the moon could be made of green cheese when there wasn't any milk to make it of."—Christian Victory.*

* * *

The Spiritually Deaf

How many there are who listen to the Word of God but never let that divine instruction penetrate their souls. Sunday after Sunday they listen to instruction without reforming in any way... They put on a Sunday attitude like a Sunday suit. They are the spiritually deaf, who hear the word of God but are not influenced by it... The inspirations to kindness and mercy and justice which He sends are rejected by them; the remorse which follows their hard dealings, uncharitable words and unethical practices is disregarded; the examples of virtue around them make no impression, and the instances for chastisement of sin go unheeded. Of them the words of the prophet Zacharias were fittingly spoken: "They would not harken and they turned away their shoulders to depart; and they stopped their ears not to hear"... One cannot hear with attention two different discourses. You cannot sit at home and read a book profitably while listening attentively to a lecture coming over the radio. So, one cannot listen to the call of God and at the same time give ear to the seductions of the world... With just a little honesty, I think we can all find within us some signs of a spiritual deafness that forms the background of our confession story and a spiritual dumbness which explains our frequent stumblings into temptation.—*Rev. Francis P. Goodall.*

* * *

The Inexhaustible Book of the Ages

The distinguished archeologist and New Testament scholar, Sir William Ramsey, has written at least forty books about New Testament subjects, and his writings are simply indisputable for an understanding of the Gospel of Luke and the Book of Acts. After giving himself for one-half century to these themes, Sir William remarked at the age of eighty-five, "I should like to devote the last years of my life to a fresh study of the New Testament, which I seem only to begin to understand." Sir William Ramsay had mastered Greek and Latin literature by the time he was twenty-five, yet he did not say that he wanted to spend the last years of his life in Plato, Virgil, or Cicero, because he "only begins to understand" them, but with the inexhaustible Word of God. The thousands and thousands of commentaries and lives of Christ and works about the Bible which stand on the shelves of every "well-equipped theological library in every important language of our modern world bear testimony to the truth that the Word of God is the preeminent book of all ages. — *Dr. Wilbur Smith, in Moody Monthly.*

How Readest Thou?

A young woman, asked by her friend to explain what is meant by devotional reading of the Bible, replied:

Yesterday morning I received a letter from one to whom I had given my heart and devoted my life. I freely admit to you that I have read that letter five times, not because I did not understand it at the first reading, nor because I expected to commend myself to the author by frequent reading of his epistle. It was not with me a question of duty, but simply one of pleasure. I read it because I am devoted to the one who wrote it."

To read the Bible with the same motive is to read it devotionally, and to one who reads it in that spirit it is indeed a love letter.—United Presbyterian.

* * *

Reaction Follows Action

Many years ago there walked across the campus of Yale University a young man distressed about his religious faith. He was saying to himself, "Really, judged scientifically, there is nothing to it. The Bible is a myth."

He was on his way to the chemical laboratory. There he took his textbook and performed the experiments exactly according to formula and directions, and he secured the predicted reactions. That night in his room he said to himself, "I'll do the same thing with religion."

He took the textbook. It condemned sin. He put all sins of every kind out of his life. It commended prayer. He prayed. It commended public worship. He went to church. It commended service. He offered his services as a teacher of boys.

The reactions came. He found a faith, and Horace Bushnell went out from Yale not to become a lawyer as he had planned, but one of the best and most revered preachers of his generation.—New Century Leader.

* * *

The Bible The Key To The Heart

If I had a lock of very complicated construction, and there was only one key that would unlock it, I should feel very sure that that key was made by one who understood the construction of that lock.

So when I find that notwithstanding all the windings and mysteries of iniquity in the human heart, the Bible, and the Bible only, is adapted to it throughout, and is able to penetrate its most secret recesses, I am constrained to believe that the Bible was made by Him who "alone knoweth the hearts of the children of men."—*A. M.*

* * *

Twelve Times a Day For a Month

Many years ago I met R. A. Torrey in Baraboo, Wis. I said to him one day, "I am a complete failure as a Bible teacher and speaker, and the Bible is as dry as dust to me. I must either cease to be a Christian worker, or find a way to know and love the Bible as other Christians do. Please tell me how to study it so that it will mean something to me." Dr. Torrey replied, "Read it." I said, "I do read it." He said, "Read it some more." I replied, "How?" He answered, "Take some book and read it twelve times a day for a month." I said, "What book could I read that many times a day, working as many hours as I do?" He said, "Try Second Peter." I did. My wife and I read Second Peter three or four times in the morning, two or three times at noon, and two or three times at dinner. Soon I was talking Second Peter to every one I met. It seemed as though the stars in the heavens were singing the story of Second Peter. I read Second Peter on my knees, marking passages. Teardrops mingled with the crayon colors, and I said to my wife, "See how I have ruined this part of my Bible." "Yes," she said, "but as the pages have been getting black, your life has been getting white."—*Dr. Congdon, in Moody Monthly.*

* * *

Suppose the Bible Were Gone

A certain man dreamed that he went to consult his Bible and found every page blank. In amazement he rushed to his neighbor's house, aroused him from his sleep, and asked to see his Bible, but when he brought the Book they found it also blank. In great consternation they sought other Bibles, with the same result. Then they said: "We will go to the libraries and from great books we will gather the quotations of Scriptures, and thus remake our Bible." But when they examined all the books upon the shelves of all the libraries, they found that wherever a quotation of Scripture had been, that part of the page was blank. When the man awoke, his brow was cold, yet covered with perspiration, so great had been his agony during the dreams. Oh! how dark this world would be without the Bible! Man would be like a wrecked ship dashed into mid-ocean.—*The King's Business.*

* * *

Prove It Yourself

There is a something in each of us which makes us eager and curious to know about another person's success or failure as the case may be. This is more apparent when it is someone who is or has been well known.

There is an interesting incident which occurred in the lives of *Gilbert West* and *Lord Lyttleton.* They were both avowed skeptics, so much so that they maintained that the Bible was the biggest imposture ever foisted upon mankind. They were not content to say this, however, but purposely set out to prove it. Mr. West set out to write a book about the irregularities and impossibilities of the resurrection of Christ. Lord Lyttleton was going to make a proper laughing stock of the conversion of Paul. With a hearty good will they set to work, leaving no stone unturned which would prove the absurdity and inconsistencies of either Paul's conversion or the resurrection of Christ.

At the time and place appointed they met to gloat over their successes in their respective searches before making the results known to the world. Imagine their surprise, then, when they met each other, to discover that they had both been converted to God through their studies. Instead of finding an imposture they found the very Words of Life. Their eyes were opened and they saw that they were sinners and that it was *God's Word* they were seeking to attack. It proved itself again, however, to be "sharper than any two-edged sword, piercing even to the dividing asunder of soul and spirit, and of the joints and marrow, and is a discerner of the thoughts and intents of the heart" (Heb. 4:12).—*Gospel Herald.*

* * *

A New Tenant

In a small town of Guatemala, a woman named Mercedes Morales operated a saloon with a flourishing trade. Four years ago she was going through a bunch of old papers and came upon a sheet nearly destroyed by rats — it was a page her son had torn out of a Gospel songbook some years before. She read it, thought it must refer to angels in Heaven, and spoke to her son about it. He answered, "No, Mother, those are the believers in Jesus." "But where are they?" said she, "in Heaven?" He said, "No, right here on earth." "Well, then," replied Mercedes Morales, "I want to believe in Jesus; I want joy like that. But, see here, boy, is there anyone here in the village who can tell me more about Jesus?" The son said that there was a woman in the village who had a Bible. That very day she found this woman, borrowed her Bible, and sat up all night, reading it. Then and there her life was changed. The following day when customers came for drinks they were told, "You can't get any more liquor here because the woman who used to sell it does not live here. Today a Jesus believer lives here." She poured out the barrels of liquor, and now she keeps a little store where she sells buttons, needles, thread, and dress goods. No one comes in to her shop who does not receive a tract. When a missionary passing through the town some time later, held a meeting, seven men and one woman accepted Christ.—*Guatemala News.*

* * *

God's Book

A woman missionary in Africa saw an unknown native coming toward her. He was dressed in the customary skins and was leading a goat. He put down his spear and tied up the goat, and then said: "White lady, has God's Book arrived in our country?"

"Are you interested in God's Book?" she asked.

"Yes," replied that native; "my son brought me these pieces of paper, and has been teaching me the words, 'God so loved the world, that He gave His only begotten Son'. I heard that God's Book had arrived, and I have walked for five days, and I have brought this goat to buy God's Book."

Then she showed him a copy of the Bible and found the place where the words were printed.

"Give me that Book," he entreated, "and you may keep this goat."

Then he walked up and down, pressing the Book to his heart, and saying. **"God's Book. God's Book. He has spoken** to us in our own language."—*Apples of Gold.*

* * *

Winston Churchill Unmoved by Dr. Dryasdust

When professors with high sounding titles attempt to palm off their pernicious denials of the Holy Scriptures by labelling them: "The Findings of Science" or "The Concensus of Scholarship," some folks take them seriously and are ready to throw away their Bibles.

But Premier Winston Churchill is not in that class. Read what that rugged and eloquent individualist said:

"We reject with scorn all those learned and labored myths that Moses was but a legendary figure upon whom the priesthood and the people hung their essential social, moral and religious ordinances.

"We believe that the most scientific view, the most up-to-date and rationalistic conception, will find its fullest satisfaction in taking the Bible story literally, and in identifying one of the greatest human beings with the most decisive leap forward ever discernible in the human story.

"We remain unmoved by the tomes of Professor Gradgrind and Dr. Dryasdust. We may be sure that all these things happened just as they are set out according to Holy Writ. We may believe that they happened to people not so very different from ourselves, and that the impressions those people received were faithfully recorded and have been transmitted across the centuries with far more accuracy than many of the telegraphed accounts we read of goings on of today. In the words of a forgotten work of Mr. Gladstone, we rest with assurance upon 'THE IMPREGNABLE ROCK OF HOLY SCRIPTURE.'

"Let the men of science and learning expand their knowledge and probe with their researches every detail of the records which have been preserved to us from these dim ages. All they will do is to fortify the grand simplicity and essential accuracy of the recorded truths which have lighted so far the pilgrimage of man."—*Now.*

* * *

The Hated Mirror

A certain society in order to gain access for a missionary to some African tribes, sent down trinkets to be bartered with the natives. Among them was a package of those little hand glasses, such as ladies use.

The natives had never seen their own faces, except in the waters of some lake or stream, and the news of this wonderful instrument, by which people could see their own features, was spread abroad until the missionary was invited by tribe after tribe to visit them, with his hand glass.

It happened that away in the interior there was a princess in one of the tribes, who had been told that she was the most beautiful woman in the tribe, and that her face was the most beautiful on earth. When she heard of this instrument in which she might see what a beautiful creature she was, she sent for the missionary and bade him bring one of those mirrors.

But the truth was, the princess was the least attractive woman in the tribe. So she got the mirror, and went into the hut to take one good long delicious look at her beauty, but when she held up the glass and saw what a hideous creature she was, how ugly in every feature, she lifted her royal fist and dashed the glass to pieces, banished the missionary, and made a law that no looking-glass should ever be brought into the tribe.

Why did the princess hate the glass? She hated it because it told the truth about herself. The truth was not a pleasant one. She found that she was an ugly woman and she did not like it. Why do men slight the Bible? Because righteousness of a man is as filthiness in God's sight; that out of the heart proceed murders, lying, false witness, adulteries, and such things; that the heart is like a cage of unclean birds. And when this Book, like a mirror, reveals man to himself; when the truth is seen in that mirror, with the light of the great white throne falling upon it, then their hatred is aroused, and the Bible is smitten as the heathen princess destroyed the mirror, because it told the truth.

But she was just as ugly after she destroyed the mirror as before. And it remains true that, though man rejects the Bible and tramples it under foot he is exactly the same sinner as before, and is moving on just as steadily toward eternity and the great white throne, as before he rejected the Bible.

—*Selected*

* * *

Thy Word is like a garden, Lord,
With flowers bright and fair;
And every one who seeks may pluck
A lovely cluster there.

Thy Word is like a deep, deep mine
And jewels rich and rare
Are hidden in its mighty depths
For every searcher there.

—*Gospel Herald*

* * *

"Search The Scriptures"

A traveler tells of seeing in one of the Western states men and women engaged in picking minute gold nuggets out of the sands of a small stream, entirely unaware of the fact that a little more effort would have enabled them to uncover a rich vein of the precious metal in a near-by mountainside. Is not that the way most of us approach the riches of the Word of God? How many there are who are satisfied with bits of truth, gathered here and there through the casual reading of His message to mankind, when a more careful and diligent study would open great treasures of the Divine wisdom.

We are to "search the Scriptures," not approach them casually and haphazardly. We are to "study diligently," not merely to read without plan or purpose. Rich rewards await those whose "delight is in the Law of the Lord." The Holy Spirit is ever ready to guide and enlighten the minds and hearts of those who seek to know God's truth as it is revealed in His Word.—*Christian Observer.*

* * *

The Anvil And The Hammers

I stood one evening by the blacksmith's door
And heard the anvil ring the vesper chime,
And looking in I saw upon the floor
Old hammers worn with years of beating time.
"How many anvils have you had," said I,
"To wear and beat these hammers so?"
"Just one," the blacksmith said with twinkling eye,
"The anvil wears the hammers out, you know,"
And so methought the anvil of God's Word
For ages skeptic blows have beat upon,
And though the sound of clanging blows is heard,
The anvil is unharmed, the hammers gone.

—*Selected*

* * *

Not Well Qualified?

"In conversation with members of the pulpit committee of one of our larger churches in this state, the writer urged them to consider a man with 'Moody' background, assuring them that we could commend for their consideration some well qualified man. After some discussion the chairman stated he did not believe they would consider Moody men, and asked for the reason, he made this significant reply, 'Moody men preach only the Bible.'"—*Moody Bible Institute Bulletin.*

Smashing The Microscope

Through a microscope a native of India, was shown the germs in the water from the Ganges, and was told not to drink that water anymore. He didn't like the looks of the germs wriggling round in the water, so he took a heavy club and broke the microscope and continued to drink the water.—*Exchange.*

* * *

Bible From The Dumps

Not all hotel managers like to have Bibles in their rooms. For example, when a hotel in western Canada changed ownership, the new proprietor had all the Gideon Bibles thrown out on the dump. Later, a poor girl went to the dump hoping to find something of value that she could sell. Noticing the Books, she picked up one and took it home. Through reading it she found Christ, and this led to the formation of a Sunday School class, whose members also went to the dump and provided themselves with Bibles, so that not one copy was left unappropriated.—*Sunday School Times.*

* * *

Preferred Literature

An atheist sent a parcel of infidel literature to a young man, advising him to read it in preference to the Bible. He wrote back:

"Dear Sir: If you have anything better than the Sermon on the Mount, more beautiful than the story of the prodigal son or the Good Samaritan; or any code of morals higher than the Ten Commandments or the 'Golden Rule' of Jesus Christ; or more consoling and beautiful than the Twenty-third Psalm; or anything that will reveal to me a more loving and merciful God, or will throw more light on the future — send it along!" — *Sunday School Times.*

BURDENS

Why God's Yoke Is Easy

The superintendent of a mission school read the text, "My yoke is easy." Turning to the children she asked, "Who can tell me what a yoke is?" A little girl said, "Something they put on the necks of animals." Then she inquired, "What is the meaning of God's yoke?" All were silent for a moment, when the hand of a four-year-old child went up and she said, "God putting his arms around our necks." What could be more comforting than that?—*Rev. Mark Guy Pearse.*

* * *

"I Can Wait!"

But there are also sufferings for which there seems to be no explanation, and for which we shall have to wait to understand. A little while ago a woman, prematurely aged, drew me aside at the close of a service and said, "I came a hundred miles today to hear you preach, and to speak with you a few words, and to seek comfort from you in my distress. You have known our family many years. You knew my husband well. He was a good man, a Christian man, who lived the life he preached. Once he was happy and useful in the Lord's work. Difficulty arose in connection with his work, and blame was thrown on him. It broke his heart, and he could not bear up under it. Distressed and dazed, he staggered along for two years and then died — as I believe a martyr to his Lord. Our oldest son ceased not to grieve for his father, and within two years followed him to the grave. I gave myself to the task of educating the two girls, even going to the wash-tub to support them and keep them in school. The eldest entered Christian work and was the joy of my heart. But a little while ago she fell into terrible sin, and now it is discovered that the cause was her unbalanced mind, and she grows worse as the weeks pass. But I have comforted myself in my little girl — now fifteen — who has been my constant companion all these years. But of late she has been given to fits of *anger* and strange uncontrol, and last week, the specialist told me she has an incurable form of insanity. And one of the strange things is that in her unaccountable moments she turns against me, accusing me of mistreating and neglecting her and of being an unnatural mother. My heart is crushed, but I still believe in God, and in the goodness of God. And though I am distressed above measure, I hold fast to faith and my hope of Heaven. And when I prayed I was impressed that if I would come here today you could and would help me."

I stood for a moment silent in the presence of a grief and sorrow deeper than death. Then I said, "Sister, God sent you here to help me. The very fact that you hold fast in the midst of your many and deep griefs gives me greater courage. I shall preach the comfort of Christ to those in sorrow and distress as I never preached Him before. You have had the seventh trouble and He has not forsaken you. I shall preach a stronger Gospel because of your visit today. I cannot help you, but you have helped me." Then that strange thing happened that many a faithful pastor has witnessed. The woman's deep grief found relief in copious tears, and, between sobs, she cried, "You have said just the things I needed to hear. Your words have comforted me beyond measure. I knew God had heard my prayer and sent me to you. I shall go home this afternoon to fight further the good fight of faith, and, by His grace, to lay hold upon eternal life. I can wait to learn why so many grievous things have happened to me and my family, but I shall understand it all when I stand in His Presence. *I can wait.* I am happy and glad to wait."— *Gospel Herald.*

* * *

Do not trouble trouble
  Till trouble troubles you;
Do not look for trouble,
  Let trouble look for you.

Do not hurry worry,
  By worrying, it comes;
To flurry is to worry,
  'Twill miss you if you're "mum."

Who feareth, hath forsaken
The Heavenly Father's side;
What He hath undertaken
He surely will provide.

The very birds reprove thee
With all their happy songs;
The very flowers teach thee
That fretting is a wrong.

"Cheer up," the sparrow chirpeth,
"Thy Father feedeth me;
Think how much more He careth,
Oh! lonely child, for thee."

"Fear not," the flowers whisper;
"Since thus He hath arrayed
The buttercups and daisy,
How canst thou be afraid?"

Then do not trouble trouble
Till trouble troubles you;
You'll only double trouble,
And trouble others, too!

—*Selected.*

* * *

The Cost Of Dodging Duty

I have read of a king who placed a heavy stone in the road and hid to see who would remove it. Men of various classes came and worked their way around it, some loudly blaming the king for not keeping the highways clear, but all dodging the duty of getting it out of the way. At last a poor peasant, on his way to town with his burden of vegetables for sale, came, and contemplating the stone, laid down his load, and rolled it into the gutter. Then, turning around he spied a purse which had lain right under the stone. He opened it and found it full of gold pieces with a note from the king, saying it was for the one who should remove the stone.

Under every cross our King has hidden a blessing. We can turn back from a cross, or go around it, but we are eternal losers if we do. We cannot dodge the cross without dodging God's blessing, and we cannot refuse it without endangering our crown — He is watching. — *Selected.*

O Lord, who knowest every need of mine,
Help me to bear each cross and not repine;
Grant me fresh courage every day,
Help me to do my work alway
Without complaint.

O Lord, thou knowest well how dark the way,
Guide thou my footsteps, lest they stray;
Give me fresh faith for every hour,
Lest I should ever doubt thy power,
And make complaint!

Give me a heart, O Lord, strong to endure,
Help me to keep it simple, pure;
Make me unselfish, helpful, true,
In every act, whate'er I do.
And keep content!

Help me to do my woman's share,
Make me courageous, strong to bear
Sunshine or shadow in my life;
Sustain me in the daily strife
To keep content!

—*War Cry.*

* * *

One of Devil's Bundles

"A Christian woman who had been living a very unhappy life, and was always overwhelmed with burdens and cares of the future, came downstairs one morning telling her family that she had had a beautiful dream, and that through it God had delivered her from all her fears and worries. She said she had seen a great crowd of people passing along a broad way, and weighed down by innumerable burdens they were carrying. To and fro in the crowd a lot of imps were passing, throwing these burdens all around, and getting the people to pick up and carry them. Among others, she was carrying several of these loads of lead, and was almost worn to death. Suddenly in the crowd she saw the face of the Lord coming toward her, and she eagerly beckoned for Him to come and help her carry her burden. He looked sternly at her and refused to touch it. He said, 'I have no strength for that. I have no grace for loads like this. That is not My burden you are bearing. It is one of the devil's bundles, and all you have to do is to drop it and you will have plenty of strength for the loads that I bid you carry.' "—*Gospel Herald.*

* * *

How Carry the Package?

The late Henry Moorhouse, a noble evangelist, was once in very "trying circumstances." His little daughter, who was paralyzed, was sitting in her chair as he entered the house with a package for his wife. Going up to her and kissing her, he said, "Where is mother?" "Mother is upstairs." "Well, I have a package for her." "Let me carry the package to Mother." "Why, Minnie, dear, how can you carry the package? You cannot carry yourself." With a smile on her face, Minnie said, "Oh, no, Papa; but you give me the package, and I will carry the package, and you will carry me." Taking her up in his arms, he carried her upstairs — little Minnie and the package, too. And then "the word of the Lord came" to him that this was just his position in the work in which he was engaged. He was carrying his burden, but was not God carrying him?—*Christian Herald* (*London*).

* * *

"He giveth more grace when the burdens grow greater,
He sendeth more strength when the labors increase,
To added affliction He addeth His mercy,
To multiplied trials, His multiplied peace.

"When we have exhausted our store of endurance,
When our strength has failed ere the day is half done,
When we reach the end of our hoarded resources,
Our Father's full giving is only begun.

"His love has no limit, His grace has no measure,
His power no boundary known unto men,
For out of His infinite riches in Jesus
He giveth and giveth and giveth again."

—*Gospel Herald.*

* * *

Shut in from dale and glen,
Shut in from blooming bowers,
Shut in your lonesome den,
Through trying, weary hours.

The world goes on its way
Unmindful of your gloom;
Alone, you sit and pray,
Shut in your little room.

Yet, not shut in, alone,
The Lord is with you there,
He fills your heart with song,
He takes away your care.

Shut in, you see His face,
His wonders you explore,
You roam in realms of grace,
And pleasures evermore.

—*Selected*

* * *

Our Eyes Upon Thee

"When my heart is overwhelmed: lead me to the rock that is higher than I" (Ps. 61:2).

The end of self is the beginning of God. "When the tale of bricks is doubled, then comes Moses." That is the old Hebrew way of putting it. "Man's extremity is God's opportunity." That is the proverbial expression of it. "When my heart is overwhelmed: lead me to the Rock that is higher than I." That is David's way of expressing it. "We have no might against this company, * * neither know we what to do." No might, no light — "but our eyes are upon Thee," that was Jehoshaphat's experience of it. "Mine eyes fail with looking upward: O Lord, I am oppressed; undertake for me."

"When I had great troubles I always went to God and was wondrously carried through; but my little trials I used to try to manage myself, and often most signally failed." So Miss Havergal has expressed the experience of many a Christian. How often we ask God to help, and then begin to count up the human probabilities! God's very blessings become a hindrance to us if we look from Him to them.—*Selected.*

* * *

Loved To The End

"Casting all your care upon him: for he careth for you."—I Peter 5:7.

Christian, when thy way seems darkest,
And thine eyes with tears are dim,
Straight to God thy Father hastening,
Tell thy sorrows unto Him.
Not to human ear confiding
Thy sad tale of grief and care,
But on God thy Father resting,
Pour out all thy sorrows there.

All thy griefs by Him are ordered,
Needful is each one for thee;
All thy tears by Him are counted,
One too much there cannot be!
And if, whilst they fall so quickly,
Thou canst own His love aright,
Then each bitter tear of anguish
Precious is in Jesus' sight.

Far too well thy Saviour loves thee,
To allow thy life to be
One long calm, unbroken summer,
One unruffled stormless sea.
He would have thee fondly nestling,
Closer to His loving breast;
He would have that world seem brighter
Where alone is perfect rest.

Though His wise and loving purpose,
Clearly now thou canst not see,
Still believe, with faith unshaken,
All shall work for good to thee,
Therefore when thy way seems darkest,
And thine eyes with tears are dim,
Straight to God thy Father hastening
Tell thy sorrows unto Him.

—*Selected.*

* * *

The Blessing of Irritations

Life on earth would not be worth much if every source of irritation were removed. Yet most of us rebel against the things that irritate us, and count as heavy loss what ought to be rich gain. We are told that the oyster is wiser; that when an irritating object, like a bit of sand, gets under the "mantle" of his shell, he simply covers it with the most precious part of his being and makes of it a pearl. The irritation that it was causing is stopped by encrusting it with the pearly formation. A true pearl is therefore simply a victory over irritation. Every irritation that gets into our lives today is an opportunity for pearl culture. The more irritations the Devil flings at us, the more pearls we may have. We need only to welcome them and cover them completely with love, that most precious part of us, and the irritation will be smothered out as the pearl comes into being. What a store of pearls we may have, if we will!—*Sunday School Times.*

* * *

I'll Hide Myself in Jesus

When trials come, and storms arise;
When tempests darken earth and skies,
And everything my spirit tries,
I'll hide myself in Jesus.
When friends turn cold, and scorn to own
That I, as friend, was ever known,
And I am left to go alone,
I'll hide myself in Jesus.

Should fortune fail, and sorrows come,
And I am left without a home,
I know in Christ there's always room
To hide myself in Jesus.
Should that dear one on whom I lean
No longer by my side be seen,
Should death's dark veil e'er come between,
I'll hide myself in Jesus.

As one by one my ties are riven;
As one by one the dear ones given,
Are torn from earth, to live in Heaven,
I'll hide myself in Jesus.
While here below, on storm-tossed sea,
Where dangers ever threaten me,
It ever shall my purpose be
To hide myself in Jesus.

There is no other safe retreat
Where I may hide when tempests beat,
Here I have found a rest complete
While hiding now in Jesus.
O let me always here abide,
Safe sheltered in His wounded side,
Till I, the storms of earth outride,
Till then I'll hide in Jesus.

—*Herald of Holiness.*

The "Hardship" of Our Cross

If a person with a deadly disease were told that he could go to a hospital, and there come under the treatment of the greatest physician in the world, who had never lost a patient suffering from that disease; that all the expenses would be paid, and the treatment would be without personal suffering or risk; and he could count on being discharged with a complete and permanent cure, would such a patient say that this offer, and this experience, if he went through it, was a great hardship? Or would he look back on that hospital experience with unspeakable gratitude as the most blessed thing in his life? That is a faint and inadequate suggestion of what the cross is to the Christian.—*Sunday School Times.*

A Changed Torrent

In the Canton of Bern, in the Swiss Oberland, a mountain stream rushes in a torrent toward the valley, as if it would carry destruction to the villages below; but, leaping from the sheer precipice of nearly nine hundred feet, it is caught in the clutch of the winds, and sifted down in fine, soft spray whose benignant showering covers the fields with perpetual green. So sorrow comes, a dashing torrent, threatening to destroy us; but by the breath of God's Spirit it is changed as it falls, and pours its soft, gentle showers upon our hearts, bedewing our withering graces, and leaving rich blessings upon our whole life.—*God's Revivalist.*

CARE, GOD'S

Gipsy Smith's Christmas Dinner

It was the day before Christmas, and a little lad in a gipsy caravan asked his father what they would have for Christmas dinner. The lad's mother was dead, and the father answered, "I do not know, my dear."

The man's fiddle was hanging on the wall, and he knew that if he took his fiddle to the public house and played the money would soon be found for the Christmas dinner. This he had done in former days; but Cornelius Smith, the father of Gipsy Smith, had not played in saloons from the time he was converted. So he instantly put aside the temptation, fell on his knees, and began to pray. Said he to his children: "I do not know what we shall have for Christmas, but we will sing." The trusting father then began a Gospel song familiar in those days:

In some way or other the Lord will provide:
It may not be my way,
It may not be thy way;
And yet, in His own way,
The Lord will provide.

Then came the chorus:

Then we'll trust in the Lord,
And He will provide;
Yes, we'll trust in the Lord,
And He will provide.

A knock was heard at the door of the van while the family were still singing. There stood the Cambridge town missionary, Mr. Sykes. Said he:

"It is I, Brother Smith. God is good, is he not? I have come to tell you how the Lord will provide. In a shop in this town there are three legs of mutton, and also groceries, waiting for you and your brothers." A wheelbarrow was needed to bring home the supplies, and the three brothers (all of whom had become evangelists) never learned who furnished these things for them. But God had provided their Christmas dinners.—*Sunday School Times.*

* * *

How God Protected

My sister and I were itinerating in a lonely mountain village in Japan, and night was coming on when we started to return home. We committed ourselves into the hands of the Lord, and felt certain he would see us through. As we were about to enter a thick wood through which our road ran, we saw two Japanese men in front of us, and we felt they meant mischief, and as we cried to the Lord to stand by us, there came a great black Newfoundland dog. It stepped between my sister and me as if to protect us and then barked fiercely at the men as if to tear them to pieces and chased them away. The dog guided us directly all the remaining three miles right to our door. Then stepping inside, the dog lay all night on the floor keeping vigil. In the morning it went away as mysteriously as it appeared.—*Glad Tidings.*

* * *

God's Kind Care

God hath not promised
Skies always blue,
Flower-strewn pathways
All our lives thro';
God hath not promised
Sun without rain,
Joy without sorrow,
Peace without pain.

God hath not promised
We shall not know
Toil and temptation,
Trouble and woe;
He hath not told us
We shall not bear
Many a burden,
Many a care.

God hath not promised
Smooth roads and wide,
Swift, easy travel,
Needing no guide;
Never a mountain,
Rocky and steep,
Never a river
Turbid and deep:

But God hath promised
Strength for the day,
Rest for the labor,
Light for the way,
Grace for the trials,
Help from above,
Unfailing sympathy,
Undying love.

—*Annie Johnson Flint*

Measuring the Immeasurable

An old primitive Methodist preacher tells how, in boyhood, he used to see many people going to draw water from the village well, and he feared that the supply might fail. To find out if the water were getting less and less, one morning he descended the well steps and placed a mark on the brickwork, just above the water line. In the evening he went down again, happily to find just as much water in the well, though people had been drawing all day. A perennial spring beneath the well continually replenished the supply. So Jesus Christ, the Well-spring of salvation, supplies every believer's need. He is "a well of water springing up into everlasting life."—*Christian Herald.*

* * *

Prayer Controls Fire

The restraining hand of the Lord was felt recently in Pohang, Korea, during a terrible fire where twenty houses were burned to the ground. One of the believers from the church, and a faithful Christian from a Presbyterian church lived in that district, and the fire came right up to both of their houses and then stopped, so that they were unharmed in any way. This incident has had a remarkable effect, for not only do the Christians feel that this was the hand of the Lord, but the unsaved have also been made to say that it was the Lord, the God of the Christians!—*Oriental Missionary Standard.*

* * *

Dave Fant's Deliverance:

Along the line of the Southern Railway, between Greenville, South Carolina, and Atlanta, Georgia, there goes a limited train driven by one of the best engineers on the system, whose name is D. J. Fant. "Dave," as he is familiarly known, is not only an engine man who knows his business, but he is known far and wide as a most earnest Christian and a splendid preacher of the Gospel of Christ. Humble and consistent, prayerful and earnest, he has the confidence of all the men of the road from the president, down. It is my privilege to count this man among my closest friends in Gospel bonds.

Two miles from the town of Tocoa, Georgia, through which town this railroad runs, there is a high curved fill on the side of the mountain. Up in the hills some distance was a little summer hotel where I occasionally spent portions of the summer with my family. Fant was at that time running a fast mail train which on its south bound trip would pass this fill near 10 o'clock at night, and he said to me, "Miller, when I get to the big fill I will blow you a signal each night I go down and when you hear it you may know I am praying for you." So, many a night ere retiring I have gone out on the upper piazza of the hotel to listen for that signal, and then send up a prayer for the man at the throttle who was also remembering me at the same time.

Some time later, Fant's run was changed to a limited Pullman train passing this place in the afternoon. One day when he struck the curve at regular speed he felt instinctively that there would be a wreck, as the track workers had been engaged in repairs and had left the track in such condition tnat he knew the engine would not stay on the rails. He called to his fireman to jump for his life and he did so, rolling down the steep embankment and coming out with many bruises but fortunately no broken bones. Dave stayed at his post, and sure enough, the ponderous engine soon left the rail. As he was rounding the curve ordinarily it would have turned over to the right which would have crushed him, but after running over the ties a short distance it turned to the left, and instead of rolling down the embankment it plowed its way down, several cars plunging down behind it. Fant stepped up through the open window, and found himself standing amid blinding smoke and hissing steam, on top of the overturned cab, without a scratch of any kind. None of the sleepers were overturned, and not a passenger was hurt. The conductor from the rear car looked out when he felt the jar, and saw the engine plunging down across the curve of the fill. He afterward testified that it looked as if great cables of some kind were holding her to keep her from rolling.

Being at Spartanburg, South Carolina, at the time, and seeing an account of the wreck in a paper, I telegraphed Brother Fant at his Atlanta home, using in the message Psalm 91:11, 12;

"He shall give His angels charge over thee," etc. The same day Fant mailed me a clipping from an Atlanta daily describing the wreck, and on the margin he had written, "Psalm 91:11 and 12." In answer to prayer, God had sent His angels of deliverance.

How remarkable, and how like our God, that at the precise point where so many nights His faithful servant on this railroad engine had sent his prayers up to the throne while at the same time sending his signal out over the hills to another fellow servant, this mighty deliverance had come to him in a time of impending death!

Fant still prays and labors for his Lord, and wherever I go in my services I tell this incident of his faith and God's answer and many others are cheered and encouraged to continue to call on God.—R.V. M. in *Moody Colportage Book*. I cried — He answered.

Cleave unto Him: for He is thy life, and the length of thy days (Deut. 30:-20).—*Gospel Herald.*

* * *

In the Perils of Traffic

A morning newspaper of London recently printed a picture taken the day before, near Buckingham Palace. A policeman was holding up the busy traffic with his white-gloved hands. The busses throbbed and simmmered, the big horses in the drays champed their bits and stamped their feet. The motor vans and taxis all stood obedient; the boys on bicycles put one leg to the ground and held onto whatever was nearest to them; all the work of that busy street was stopped. All the people wondered who was coming, and many craned their necks to see if it were the king about to drive through the big gates of the palace. Then came a surprise indeed. On the empty street so carefully guarded and protected, there walked across, looking very proud and clever, a mother duck with her ten little ducklings in single file behind her! There they waddled — all the little necks on the stretch, all the little beaks atwitter, all the little eyes wide open. When they got safely across, the big policeman lowered his arm and the waves of traffic surged on once more. "That was just like Moses and the Israelites crossing the Red Sea," said a little girl showing the picture to her father, only there were no Egyptians following her!" —*The Presbyterian.*

* * *

God Holds Key

A consecrated missionary whose life was in peril, writes to a friend at home, "The days ahead of us are quite full of uncertainity, but 'God holds the key to all unknown, and I am glad.' He has given us a delightful peace of mind, and in His Father-care we are not only safe but secure."—*Gospel Herald.*

* * *

Wesley Saved From a Fire

Of course you know that John Wesley was the father of Methodism. Directly under a portrait made of him during his life is a drawing of a burning house, and beneath this are the words, "Is not this (meaning Mr. Wesley) a brand plucked from the burning?" He certainly was a brand whose spiritual flame never went out, until Wesley's own spirit left the body.

When John Wesley was but six years old, his father was awakened one night by the cry of "Fire!" from the street. He little thought that it was his own house that was on fire. But as he opened his bedroom door, he found the place full of smoke, and the roof already burned through. Calling his wife and his girls to rise and hurry for their lives, he then ran to the nursery, where the maid and the five other children were sleeping. The maid quickly caught up the youngest child, and called the others to follow her. The older ones did so, but John remained asleep.

The rest of the family escaped, some through the windows, and some through the garden door.

When they were safely outside and gathered together, John was missing, and they heard him crying in the nursery. His father dashed in and started up the stairs: but they were so badly burned that they would not bear his weight, and in his desperate agony and despair, he fell upon his knees and commended the child's soul to God. John had been awakened by the light, and had tried to get out through the door; but the fire was there. Then he climbed onto a chest that stood near a window.

There he was seen by people in the yard. There was not time to hunt for a ladder, for the roof was ready to fall in upon the child; so one man stood on the shoulders of another, and thus was able to reach the child. A moment or two later, the blazing roof fell in. When John was carried to his parents, who had supposed that he was lost in the fire, the father cried out, "Come, neighbors, let us kneel down. Let us give thanks to God, who has given me all my eight children. Let the house go; I am rich enough now." Therefore, by the goodness and mercy of God, John Wesley was saved "as a brand plucked from the burning."— Mabel P. Smith in *Light and Life Evangel.*

* * *

There is an Eye that never sleeps
 Beneath the wing of night;
There is an Ear that never shuts
 When sink the beams of light;
There is an Arm that never tires
 When human strength gives way;
There is a Love that never fails,
 When earthly loves decay.

—*Selected.*

* * *

Called by Name

He who "made the stars" named them and "he calleth them all by their names" (Ps. 147:4). This great Shepherd "calleth his own sheep by name" (John 10:3). When He called Ananias by name from Heaven, He not only gave him the name of a recently converted persecutor, but also named the street on which he was visiting, and the name of his host (Acts 9:10-12). He is not too engrossed with the affairs of the universe to call even the weakest believer by name, and to note his house and street address, and the circumstances surrounding him, and to minister to him! Hallelujah, what a Saviour!—

* * *

He Will Care For Me

There was a poor colored woman who earned her living by hard daily labor, but who was a joyous, triumphant Christian.

"Ah, Nancy," said a gloomy Christian lady to her one day, "it is well enough to be happy now; but I should think the thoughts of the future would sober you. Only suppose, for instance, you should have a spell of sickness, and be unable to work; or suppose your present employer should move away, and no one else should give you anything to do; or suppose—."

"Stop!" cried Nancy. "I never supposes. De Lawd is my Shepherd, and I knows I shall not want. And, Honey," she added, to her gloomy friend, "it's all dem supposes as is makin' you so mis'able. You better give dem all up and just trust de Lawd."

The believer is always joyful, but who ever saw a joyful supposer?

"Let me like a little sparrow
  Trust Him where I cannot see,
In the sunshine or the shadow,
  Singing He will care for me."

—*S. C. Bredbenner in Gospel Herald*

* * *

When the Enemy Stood at Attention

Three Scotch privates and a corporal had been cut off during a fierce engagement in a Belgian town one day just preceding Dunkirk. Taking refuge in the loft of an empty house they waited what seemed to be certain death. Outside they heard the Germans setting fire to buildings, looting, killing. Suddenly the corporal said, "Lads, it's time for church parade, let's hae a wee bit of service here; it may be oor last." The soldiers looked a bit astonished, but placing their rifles in a corner, they stood at attention. The corporal took a small Testament from his breast pocket and turned the pages. As he read, loud shouts came from below. Doors banged, and glass was shattered. He ended, and his grave face took on a wry smile. "I'm noo a gude hand at this job, but we must finish it off. Let us pray." The corporal stood with the Testament in his hand. The others kneeled and bowed their heads. A little haltingly and very simply he committed their way to God and asked for strength to meet their coming fate like men. Suddenly a heavy hand crashed open the door. An exultant exclamation in German was heard, and then a gasp of surprise. Not a man moved and the corporal went calmly on. After a pause he began, with great reverence, to repeat the Lord's Prayer. Hearing a click of his heels, they knew the enemy was standing at attention. A moment of suspense, the door closed, and footsteps died away. At dusk the four men ventured out, worked around the enemy's flank, and reached the British outposts in safety that night.—*The Record.*

* * *

Beside The Plow

Besides the plow He walks with me,
  And if my steps be slow,
He pauses, waiting so that He
  May lead me where I go.
I feel His presence at my side,
  His hand upon my hair,
His love sweeps boundless like the tide
  About me everywhere.

Beside the plow He walks with me,
  I cut the furrows deep,
I know His gentle eyes will see
  The harvest that I reap.
His guiding touch is on my arm,
  And well I know the care
That keeps me safe from sin and harm
  Is with me everywhere.

Beside the plow He walks with me,
  And all my troubles sweep
Away, I know that there will be
  No time to pine or weep.
My very oxen seem to feel
  The rapture in the air;
The love that lives to bless and heal
  Surrounds us everywhere.

Beside the plow He walks with me,
  And lo, the sun shines down;
The same that smiled on Galilee,
  And on a thorny crown.

God grant that when the shadows creep
Across the mountain fair
His love may still be wide and deep
About me everywhere.

—*Selected.*

* * *

Moody's Bible:

In Moody's Bible, which was in my possession all of one never-to-be-forgotten night over a half century ago, I found this notation, on the margin opposite Philippians 4:19—"The Christian's Bank Note: President of the bank—'My God'; promise to pay—'Shall supply'; the amount—'all you need'; the capital of the bank—'according to his riches in glory'; the Cashier's name—'Christ Jesus.'"

The "amount," Moody noted, was left blank in order that each one might write in the measure of his need. Fortunately Heaven's bank is always available. The Cashier is always present. The capital of the bank has never been impaired.

The Christian is to ask largely, according to his present need, and must use at once the riches provided. Christ's promises are more than beautiful sentiments to be hung upon the wall for decorative purposes. They are not intended as life-savers for use only in time of shipwreck. In the presence of such divine provision, there is no excuse for spiritual poverty.—*Dr. Harry Ironside.*

* * *

When We Forget

Many years ago a poor German immigrant woman sat with her children in the waiting room of an Eastern station. A lady passenger to a train, struck by her look of misery, stopped a moment to speak to her. She confided that her husband had been buried at sea; she was going to Iowa, and it was hard to enter a strange land alone with her babies. The stranger had but one moment. She pressed a little money into the poor creature's hand, and said: "Alone! Why, Jesus is with you! He never will leave you alone!" Ten years afterward the woman said: "That word gave me courage for all my life. When I was a child I knew Christ and loved Him. I had forgotten Him. That chance word brought me back to Him. It kept me strong and happy through all troubles."—*"All Aboard."*

* * *

On The Journey

The story is told of a young lad who one day was put on a railroad train by his father, and sent on a journey to the home of his aunt in the city. As the boy entered the train he was greatly troubled at the thought of what might happen to him while on the train and when he arrived at his destination. But he soon found that all his worrying was for nothing. No sooner had the train started than the conductor came up and spoke to him very kindly. Then the newsboy brought him apples, candy, and picture books to look at. So the time passed very pleasantly and quickly. When he arrived at the city, a cabman was at the gate to meet him and to take him safely to his aunt's home. The boy couldn't understand it. He thought it was a miracle. But as he grew older he learned that it was his father who had told the conductor to look after the boy, who gave money to the newsboy to supply his wants, and who had telegraphed ahead to a cab company to send a man to meet his boy at the train. Because his father was on the job, all his wants had been provided for.—*The Expositor.*

* * *

Had God Failed?

It seemed as though God had failed us one day,—of course, he hadn't,—when the morning mail failed to bring in sufficient money and the needs for food and other provisions were so very pressing. In the morning prayer time, at nine o'clock, the workers at Keswick had faced the need, definitely committed it to the Lord, and then with a full assurance of faith, believed that he would send the needed $30 in time to get the supplies. It was difficult to understand, and a real test, when the morning mail arrived and was found to contain only $6. Should we order the food anyway? No, that would mean indebtedness, and God *could not* fail us. We would wait. A few moments later one of the workers seemed directed to open a voluntary offering box, which during the winter months is seldom noticed or used, and drew from it a check for $25, placed there nearly a week before by a young woman, who after a few day's stay in Keswick had returned home with a new vision of her Lord.—*Sunday School Times.*

* * *

Overruling Providence

Some time ago, according to *Motor News*, a little girl was having her knowledge of safety measures tested at the safety booth of a large motor club. With out any directions from the older persons looking on, she was filling out the blanks in her scrawling childish hand when she came to the question: "Who must look out for your safety on the street?" Without an instant's hesitation she wrote, "God." "If those around the booth chuckled," says the account, "rest assured it was not irreverently. In the laugh the shadow of a tear was found. May the confidence of this little one never be confounded! She has more wisdom than we." This spirit of faith is something that all of us need. *Many of us who are older have sometimes forgotten that with all of our wisdom and our dependence upon self there is after all no real safety except as it is vouchsafed us by an all-wise Providence.—Christian Observer.*

* * *

How God Supplied Their Need

"Certainly I know Philippians 4:19 says, 'But my God shall supply all your need according to His riches in glory by Christ Jesus,' but, does it work?"

Listen, and I will tell you:

It was during the panic of 1894, a terrible blizzard was sweeping East, the thermometer registered way below zero. In a little old house on the bank of the Susquehanna river, was a mother and two young children. Two years before the father had left them, and so the mother and children were alone.

It was evening, after supper, which consisted only of crusts and heels of bread left over, spread with lard; and some black coffee. The mother and children went into the front room to try to amuse themselves and forget their troubles. The children were playing upon the floor, when the mother turned to the older boy, who was just about seven, and said: "Boys, I don't know what we will do now, we have eaten the last bit of food in the house, and my money is all gone. You have no shoes to go out." Then bursting into tears, she continued, "Besides, your father has not brought any money around, and I haven't got clothes to go out, and the snow is now about two feet deep, and it is still snowing."

"Haven't we got anything to eat at all, now mamma?" inquired the older boy.

"No, the bread-box is empty and we have nothing else in the house, except some fryings we ate on our bread." Then looking out through the window she said: "It is awful out tonight, and no one will come that we can tell about it."

"Well, mamma, let's say our prayers, maybe God will send someone around, like the stories you read to us," said the older boy.

"Well, boys, we will have prayer tonight; we haven't had prayer for a long time together, maybe God will hear us anyway," replied the mother. Then she read a passage of Scripture and all knelt in prayer. That mother told God how they were alone and everything was eaten up. She told God just how she felt, and asked Him to send some "Good Samaritan" around to help them.

"Mamma do you think someone will come tonight now?" asked the boys, after they arose from prayer.

"I don't know; maybe God will send someone around. We won't go to bed right away anyhow. We will wait, in case some one does come," she replied. Then, going to the organ, she played while the boys sang.

They had been at the organ only a short time, when there was a knock at the door. The singing stopped and all went to the door to see who it was.

The prayer was heard, and here stood the answer, knocking at the door.

"Good-evening, Mrs.——," said Mr. Evans, and stepped into the room with a basket full of groceries and provisions — bread, sugar, rice, potatoes, coffee, butter and other things that were needed. The family asked him to stay a while, but he said he had another basketful he wanted to bring, and he would have to go and get it before the store closed.

He was gone only a short time, when he returned with the other basket laden with supplies. Everybody in that little home was happy then.

"Who ever made you think of us, Mr. Evans?" asked the mother.

"Well, I don't know," replied Mr. Evans. "I was sitting in our living-room beside the fire reading the evening paper, and all at once I just thought of you, and wondered if you might be in need of coal or food. I tried to read, but could not get interested. I looked out and saw it snowing; then I thought perhaps you might be snowed in and have nothing to eat. So I put on my coat and hat, told my wife how I happened to think of you, and said I would go up to the store and get some things and take them around, so that's all that made me come; but I'm glad I came. By the way, do you have coal so you can keep warm, Mrs.——?" asked Mr. Evans.

"No, Mr. Evans, we have not had any coal for quite a while; we have been burning drift wood, and the last is in the stove now. I was just wondering what we would do now for fuel, the river is frozen over and the snow has covered all the wood that might be along the bank," the mother replied.

"Don't worry Mrs. ——, I am going to send coal around in the morning. You just let them put it in; it's paid for and you are welcome, and if you need anything else, just let me know," said Mr. Evans.

The family could hardly get done thanking him, and after he left there was another prayer of gratitude offered. God had sent the "Good Samaritan," and the blessing was enjoyed by the giver as well as by the recipients.

The mother has gone to be with the Lord. The two boys are now active Christian men, one an evangelist. They have never forgotten this experience and it has many times encouraged their faith when the days were dark. They *know* Philippians 4:19 is true.—*Gospel Herald.*

* * *

My Guard With God

I'm standing guard at sunset,
But I know I'm not alone;
There's another One who's watching
From His place upon a throne.
He's my Lord, my Great Protector,
Who once died to make men free.
He is watching, He is guarding.
He is taking care of me.

I'm standing guard at midnight
On an island in the sea,
Far from home and all my loved ones,
But my Lord is still with me;
And the Southern Cross is gleaming
In the starry sky above,
And it serves as a reminder
Of my Lord's undying love.

I'm standing guard at sunrise,
With the dawn's bright sky above,
And I know the Lord will keep me,
Watching over me in love.
Now my watch is almost over,
But His watch shall never cease—
He has given me assurance
And an everlasting peace.

This poem was sent to us by a soldier who said his "buddy" wrote it just before he was reported "missing in action."

* * *

The Royal Engineers

Dan Crawford tells of an experience he and his party had while returning to his African mission field after a furlough. A stream to be crossed was in flood, and there were no boats. Haste in getting back was important. The missionaries camped and prayed. After a time a tall tree which had battled with the river for a century, perhaps, began to totter, and then fell — clear across the stream. "The Royal Engineers of Heaven," Mr. Crawford said, "had laid a pontoon bridge for God's servants."—*Sunday School Times.*

* * *

Wilkinson's Answer

The following story is told of the Rev. John Wilkinson and the Mildmay Mission to the Jews: On one occasion two American gentlemen sat at Mr. Wilkinson's breakfast table and noted his opening of letters which brought God's supply for the day. "This is all very well so far," said one, "but what would you do, Mr. Wilkinson, if one morning the expected supply did not come?" He answered: "That can only happen, sir, when God dies."—*Christian Herald.*

* * *

I Shall Not Want—or My Shepherd

He maketh me rest in His pastures green,
This wonderful Shepherd, my Lord,
He quenches my thirst by the waters still,
When I drink from His own precious Word.

My soul He restores, though ofttimes it strays,
And chooses the path that I take,
A path of Righteousness, safe and good,
And that for His own Name's sake.

When I walk through the valley, I'll fear no ill,
Though the shadow of death will be there,
His rod shall protect me, His staff be my stay,
For I'm under His love and care.

Ofttimes among foes my table He spreads,
My head with oil He anoints,
A cup overflowing with joy He gives,
In the place that His love appoints.

His goodness and mercy shall follow me still,
And I'll dwell in His House for aye,
His promise was true that I never should want,
This Shepherd who led all the way.

—*Flora L. Osgood*

Angelic Ministry

Rev. H. L. Hastings of Boston, a very godly man, was riding on horseback through the New Hampshire mountains with £100 when he stopped his horse to readjust his stirrups. The moon shone down brightly on him and his horse. He fixed his saddle, jumped on his horse and reaching his destination delivered the money.

Several years afterward he was called to the bedside of a dying man who asked him if he remembered the experience in getting off his horse. Mr. Hastings said, "Yes." The dying man replied: "I was lying in wait for you there, and intended to kill you and take that money I knew you had; but when you got off your horse *I saw another man standing on the other side of your horse,* and I was afraid to kill two men, so I did not shoot." "Why?" Mr. Hastings exclaimed, "there was no other man with me." *"Yes, there was,"* the man replied. Before dying he asked Mr. Hastings' forgiveness, which was given him.—*The Dawn.*

* * *

"Holded"

Little Maisie was tired and fretful. Mother took her up and held her close and lovingly, and presently Maisie was rested. Mother herself was weary. A great trouble had come to her. The earth was fresh above the dear mother who had held her when she was a little girl, and to whom she had gone in later life with all her cares and troubles. She sighed above the golden head, and Maisie asked, "Mamma, don't you want to be holded?" In spite of herself the tears came, and the little one, patting her cheek, and thinking of words with which to comfort, whispered at last: "Mamma, God will hold you, won't he?" And the Mother, who had told her child how the Good Shepherd carried the little ones in his arms, was rebuked and comforted.

—*Sunday School Times.*

* * *

"Then to the Dogs"

The Turks, having tortured and slain the parents of a little Armenian girl before her eyes, turned to the child and said: "Will you renounce your faith in Jesus, and live?" She replied, "I will not." "Then to the dogs!" she was thrown into a kennel of savage and famished dogs and left there. The next morning they came and looked in, to see the little girl on her knees praying, and beside her the largest and most savage of all the dogs, snapping at every dog that ventured near, thus protecting the child. The men ran away terrified, crying out, "There is a God here; there is a God here."—*Sunday School Times.*

* * *

Whom Do We Trust Most?

A mature Christian man who has served the Lord truly and effectively for many years writes to a friend about a new work and new experiences that he is having. He says: "What a change! I think, also, that I am going to enjoy resting wholly on the Lord for daily needs. I never did it before in my life. I do not know where the rent for next month is coming from, but I am not worried at all. I am wondering why I have always slept better when some big (financial) man underwrites me, and a bit nervous when only the Lord says He will supply all my needs! Aren't Christians funny?" —*Sunday School Times.*

* * *

While the Robber Listened

The evangelist Charles Inglis records the following story told by a lady in a prayer meeting: "Some years ago my husband was traveling in Europe, and I was left alone with my maids in a large lonely house in a Western State. One evening, after our usual reading and prayer, we retired to our several rooms. As I entered my room, I happened to look into a mirror at the opposite side of the room, and was horrified to see the reflection of a man crouching behind my wardrobe. I was tempted to cry aloud for help, but knew it would be useless, and determined to put the faith in God about which we had been reading to the test. I walked as courageously as possible, though trembling in every limb, across the floor, took my Bible from the table, and sank into a chair. I began reading aloud the fifty-third chapter of Isaiah. I then kneeled and prayed aloud, telling God how we were unprotected women, and imploring Him to protect us from thieves and robbers and all evil persons. I had barely risen and sunk once more into the seat, when a hand was laid on my shoulder and a voice said: 'Do not cry out or be frightened, for you are perfectly safe. I came here to rob this house, but that chapter is one I used to hear my mother read, and your prayer reminded me of the prayers she offered. I am going now. You need fear nothing.' "—*The Dawn.*

* * *

The Lord's Prescription

A missionary found herself without means, among a heathen people, far from any source of supplies. In her distress she claimed the promise of God that He would supply her need. She was also in poor health. From a businessman in another part of China came several large boxes of Scotch oatmeal. She already had several cans of condensed milk, so with these two commodities she was obliged to sustain life for four long weeks. As time went on, it seemed to agree with her better; and by the time the four weeks had passed she felt in excellent health. In relating the experience some time later to a company of people, which included a physician, she was asked more particularly of the nature of her former illness. The physician said, "The Lord heard your prayer and supplied your need more truly than you realize. For the sickness from which you were suffering, we physicians prescribe a four weeks' diet of nothing but oatmeal gruel for our patients. The Lord prescribed it for you, and saw to it that you took the proper remedy."—*Alliance Weekly.*

* * *

His Little Girl's Answer

A young clergyman in a London church lost his wife. They had a little girl. The parishioners hoped that some relative would come to take care of her, but none appeared. Two or three years passed. One Sunday when the pews were crowded, the clergyman came up the aisle leading the child, whom he seated in the corner of the front pew. The service went on until the sermon began. In his sermon the minister spoke of the mother of Christ, and her agony of heart at the cross. Said he, "Think what a child's life is without a mother's love! Who else can tend, who can cherish, who can love, like a mother?" In the depth of his feeling, the rector's strong voice halted, as if for an aswer, and in the hush of the great congregation a little childish voice spoke out, very sweetly and clearly: "A faver would do just eve'y bit as well, Papa dear." So our Father with heart more tender than a mother's, with sympathy more pronounced than a brother's, and with love exceeding all human love combined seeks to do the greatest good to the family of mankind. Can we not, then say with Jesus — "Our Father"? —*Present Truth.*

* * *

"He Forgets Not His Own"

Does God grant special protection to His children in battle dangers? Listen to this. A group of soldiers on the Anzio bridgehead in Italy were cut off from their company by German machine gunners. When the farmhouse they were defending was directly hit, all but three of the fifteen were wounded. The officer lay in the rubble but was able to reach for his Daily Light. The text he saw proved to be, "When the enemy shall come in like a flood, the Spirit of the Lord shall lift up a standard against him" (Isa. 59:19). Happily the officer read it aloud, declaring his assurance that all of them would be rescued. True enough, in a few minutes an Allied hospital truck drove up and the entire group was helped in and carried to safety. But the strange thing about it was that German machine gunners watched the operation from their trenches only fifty yards away and never fired a shot, while a German sentry at the crossroads appeared equally indifferent. All agreed that it was nothing less than a direct intervention of God. —*Wesleyan Missionary.*

Special Providence

A sparrow had built its nest in a freight car while in the shops for repair. When the car was in order and started again into service, a nest full of young sparrows seemed about to be robbed of a mother's care. But though the car traveled several hundred miles, the mother bird would not desert her young. The sympathy of the trainmen was touched and they notified the division superintendent, who ordered the car out of commission until the little birds were able to care for themselves.

If a great railroad system can be ordered so as to protect helpless sparrows, is it hard to believe that the great Superintendent of the universe orders all things for the good of His children? —*Otterbein Teacher.*

* * *

A Wagonload of Food

A young minister and his wife were sent on to their first charge in Vermont about the year 1846. On the circuit were few members, and most of these were in poor circumstances. After a few months the minister and his wife found themselves getting short of provisions. Finally their last food had been cooked, and where to look for new support was a question which demanded immediate attention.

"The morning meal was eaten, not without anxious feelings; but this young servant of the Most High had laid his all upon the altar, and his wife also possessed much of the spirit of self-sacrifice; and they could not think that Saviour who had said to those He had called and sent out to preach in His Name: 'Lo, I am with you always', would desert them among strangers. After uniting in family prayer he sought a sanctuary in an old barn, and there committed their case to God:—his wife met her Saviour in her closet and poured out her heart before Him there.

"That morning a young married farmer, a mile or two away, was going with a number of hands to his mowing field, but as he afterward told the minister, he was obliged to stop short. He told his hired help to go on, but he must go back — he must go and carry provisions to the minister's house. He returned to the house, and telling his wife how he felt, asked her help in putting up the things he must carry. He harnessed his horse to his wagon; put up a bushel of potatoes, meat, flour, sugar, butter, etc. He was not a professor of religion. The minister's wife told me there was a good wagon-load. He drove it to the house, and found that his gifts were most thankfully received. This account was received from the minister himself, — David Y. — who died in Chelsea, Mass., in December 1875, — and subsequently from his wife, — and communicated to a correspondent of the *The Christian.*" —*Selected.*

* * *

Rolling Them Back

If any man suffer as a Christian, let him not be ashamed; but let him glorify God on this behalf. The old colored saint knew the secret when he quaintly said, "When the Lord tests me, then I always test Him. When He rolls any heavy burden on me, I just roll it back on Him." —*Alliance Weekly.*

* * *

Saved From Lions

My God hath sent His Angel, and hath shut the lions' mouths.

One day a boy in Africa was sent on a lonely track through a country full of lions. Now I should have been very frightened, wouldn't you? Well, Andrew was very frightened, but he kept saying to himself, "Heavenly Father has sent me on this journey and He will look after me."

Then suddenly what do you think happened? He turned a corner in the path, and there were two huge, tawny lions crouching on an ant hill by the side of the path waiting for him! What was he to do? If he ran back they would come bounding after him, if he went forward they would spring on him — and so what do you think poor trembling Andrew did? He knelt in the path right in front of the lions and prayed to His Heavenly Father to protect him, and then he said to himself, "I must forget my doubts and deliver this letter!"

So he got up and walked straight on past the lions! And God did just the same for Andrew as He did for Daniel — He shut those lions' mouths. Andrew walked past, and they never made one attempt to eat him; they couldn't because God was holding them back!

Now won't you also trust such a wonderful Father to keep you day by day? —*British Evangelist.*

* * *

Christ The Door

For a good many years we have wondered why Christ mixed His figures in His parable of the Good Shepherd. At one place He calls Himself the Shepherd and at another the Door. A recent book explains it beautifully. It says: "A traveler in Palestine once had a conversation with a shepherd at work near a sheepfold, who showed him the various features of the fold. Thereupon the traveler remarked: 'You say, here is the sheepfold, there are the sheep, and this is the doorway; but where is the door?' 'The door?' asked the shepherd. 'I am the door. I lie across the entrance at night. No sheep can pass out, no wolf can come in, except over my body.'" Beautiful, is it not? Christ did not mix His figures, after all. He is both the Shepherd and the Door.—*Council Fires.*

* * *

The Best Dugout

Mr. Toliver, a missionary in Szechwan, West China, met two high Government officials who are out-and-out Christians and soul-winners. One told of an air raid he, his wife, and their six-year-old daughter went through. Having no dugout, they took refuge under the dining room table. As bombs fell near by they bowed and prayed. When the danger had passed, the little girl looked up and said, "Daddy, the Lord Jesus is the best dugout, isn't He?"—*China's Millions.*

* * *

Under Observation

Some years ago I sat with a brother in a rowboat on the sheltered waters of the Erie harbor. The wind was less than a gale, and we could hear the roar of tumbling water on the unprotected shore of Presque Isle. Just as we neared the lookout tower of the life saving station, a motorboat, occupied by a lone woman, passed the tower, and headed for the white-capped waves... I wondered if she drove her boat into the threshing water to divest her mind of unhappy memories, dull the edge of sorrow, or forget a sin. As she passed the tower she called to the watchman, "I am going outside about six miles. Will you keep me under observation?"... The guard touched his cap... With a telescope pointed in her direction, the least indication of trouble would have brought a powerful motor-driven lifeboat to her rescue. Somewhere in the mystic towers of God, they know the stars by name, and note the sparrow's fall. He giveth His angels charge over some... Our Lord declared that the little children about Him were watched over by the angels.—*Sunday School Times.*

* * *

The Word that Stayed With Him

A young man who was driven out of western China during the riots, years ago, was the treasurer of our mission there, and there were others farther up than he who needed silver to pay their way out. He saw that they were cared for, and then started down the river himself. The rioters overtook him, boarded his boat, and he jumped overboard. They began to spear at him in the water. He would dart under the boat and come up on the other side, only to find another spear shot at him. Down he would go again, and up again, only to be speared at again, until his case became hopeless. Finally, he struck out for the shore, and as he stood in the face of the surrounding mob, the chief said, "Let him go," and they melted away. At Northfield, when he was asked to tell his story on Missionary Day, he said, "Some friends were curious to know what particular text of Scripture came to me when I was down under the boat. *Scripture* text? The Lord *Himself* was there!" And everyone who heard him speak knew that He, the Lord was there.—*The King's Business.*

Was It Trust?

A minister said he had heard so much about trusting God to provide support in hard times that he thought he would try it for himself. So as he was about to attend a certain convention he decided he would go and trust God for his board while there. He went, but on returning he was heard to say: "If I had not taken along money to pay my board, I don't know what I would have done."—*Sunday School Times.*

* * *

The Abiding Secret

Once talking in this strain, in a hall in Ireland, I said, "What is it to abide in Him?" It is to keep on saying, minute by minute, "For this I have Jesus." And what will He be saying with all the grace of His victory, and all the victory of His grace? "For this you have me." As I sat down and the meeting opened for testimony, the young lady presided at the piano rose and said, "I must be the first to testify, since I have now to leave the hall. While the message of the sermon was going forward, I received this telegram which reads, 'Mother is very ill; take first train home.' As I read the startling news, my heart looked up and said, 'For this I have Jesus.' Instantly a peace and strength flooded my being." We who listened saw in her face a light that never was on land or sea. She went on, "I have never traveled alone, 'For this I have Jesus.' I must take a midnight train, 'For this I have Jesus.' Then I make connection and cross the channel, 'For this I have Jesus.' Then I take my long railroad journey to the south of England. For this and all the suspense that goes with it, I have Jesus." So she left us a living illustration of the faithfulness of Jesus to them who count on him. Three or four weeks passed when a letter, a psalm of praise, came from her: "Life has become an uninterrupted psalm of victory as I see that everywhere, uninterruptedly, 'For this I have Jesus.'"—*Alliance Weekly.*

* * *

Never "All By Myself"

A Methodist minister tells a pretty story of his little girl, who, wishing to speak to him one day when he was in his study, came up the stairs, and, finding the door closed, put her small hand on the doorknob. The child's hand was too tiny to grasp the handle firmly enough to turn it. To her delight, however, the handle turned, the door opened, and she ran into the study, exclaiming: "Oh, Daddy, I have opened the door all by myself!" She was all unaware that her father, hearing her trying to open the door, had quietly got up from his chair and turned the handle from the inside. Thus God helps us when we do our best, and he makes the impossible possible. "I can do all things through Christ which strengthens me."—*Christian Herald.*

* * *

"When sorrows press and faith seems dim,
Hold fast, look up, and trust in Him
He fainteth not.

"Mid earth's confusion, strain and din.
He giveth perfect peace within;
He faileth not.

"His every word fulfilled shall be:
His unveiled glory we shall see;
He changeth not."

—*Selected*

* * *

A Remarkable Answer To Prayer

Mr. Jay Gould once left his eastern home for a trip across the continent. In the western part of Texas the train he was traveling on was halted for a few hours at a little town to make needed repairs on the engine. Mr. Gould, to pass the time, walked up the village street, and found a sale going on, and the auctioneer calling out, "Fourteen hundred and seventy-five dollars." He inquired of a man what was being sold, and was told that it was a new church that the contracting builder had a claim on for the work. Mr. Gould, to help the sale, offered fifteen hundred dollars, which the auctioneer called a few times without a raise, and the church was sold to Mr. Gould at his bid.

Three gray-haired old men standing near watched the proceedings of the transfer and, going up to Mr. Gould, not knowing who he was asked him what he intended to do with the church he had just bought.

"What is it to you what I do with it? It is mine now, to keep or to give away," said the millionaire.

One of the men said: "This is what it is to us: We three men are trustees of that church house and were sent here to see and then report what disposal was made of it; and in the church, at this present moment, the entire congregation, with the presiding elders and preachers, are down on their knees before the God of Heaven, asking Him to Divinely interfere in some way to save our church, so that it may not be lost to us. That is what it is to our people."

Jay Gould gave the people their church. —*Selected.*

* * *

The Right Kind of Religion

Some years ago in the little suburb of Rock Run, where I have my Mission Sunday School, an epidemic of chicken pox broke out. I visited one of the homes where this infantile ailment seemed to be the worst; the whole family were down with it. I danced the youngsters on my knee, carried the baby in my arms. The father had it pretty badly also, and I kneeled by his bed and prayed with him. Then lo and behold! it was discovered that our "chicken pox" was the worst form of smallpox. Rock Run Suburb was strictly quarantined, the public school closed and our chapel where we had Sunday-school was not permitted to open for almost a year. But nothing happened to me or mine. "I would have been scared to death," one young lady exclaimed. "You don't have the right kind of religion, come and join my church," I laughingly told her. "The religion of the church I belong to teaches that the Lord takes care of His own."—*Sunday School*

* * *

The Best of All

When John Wesley came to the end of his "unparalleled apostolate," as Augustine Birrell beautifully described it, with his eighty-eight years behind him and over sixty of unremitting activity and service, he was not sighing or longing for just one more year, one more of those amazing circuits of his. There was no hint of the best of his life being in the past. Not at all. Great as those triumphant years had been, these last hours of his were just as good as any. The best was right here now, and he closed it all by saying, "The best of all is, God is with us." And when Dean Stanley's devotion put up the tablet to the Wesleys in Westminster Abbey, he summed up all Wesley's life in these own words of his: "The best of all is, God is with us." And all the worst that can happen to us must be judged by that.—*Sunday School Times.*

* * *

Some Big "Ifs"—And God

A speech which Winston Churchill made behind closed doors, to representatives of the mining industry, has just been made public. In it the Prime Minister revealed more plainly than hitherto the defenseless position of Britain on land, immediately following the fall of France. We had lost all our equipment in France and could only muster two hundred field guns, some of which were brought out of museums, and less than fifty tanks. "I have often asked myself," he said, "what would have happened if Hitler had put three-quarter of a million men on board all the barges and boats, and let them stream across, taking the chance of losing three-quarters of them. There would have been a terrible shambles in this country, because we had hardly a weapon."—*Courtesy of Moody Monthly.*

* * *

Quiet Trust

An Englishman traveling through Ceylon says: "As I was dining in a home in Timcomolec I was startled to hear the hostess ask her servant to place a bowl of milk on the deerskin near her chair. I knew at once there was a cobra in the room, for they prefer milk to anything else. We also knew that a hasty movement meant death, so we sat like statues. Soon, to our amazement, a cobra uncoiled itself from my hostess' ankle and swiftly glided toward the milk, where it was quickly killed." What a triumph of self-control over the external! But if we use the same quiet trust in Christ as this woman did in the bowl of milk, when the serpent of all evil approaches us, internal triumphs over him would be more numerous than they are now.—*Record of Christian Work.*

* * *

When the Missionaries Prayed

The missionaries at a certain Chinese mission were ordered by the British legation to leave Sanyuan because of the dangers from conflicting soldiery. "Carts were ordered, and all was ready to start the next day. Then it came over the missionaries that it would be dishonoring God to go to a place of safety, leaving their flock exposed. So a prayer meeting was held, with the result that the carts were sent away and they stayed. They were kept in peace of mind, although a robber band, a thousand strong, was marching on the city and was within twelve miles. Then came a terrific downpour of rain, such as had not been known for years, scattering the robbers and making the roads impassable." It was a small scale representation of the story of Sennacherib's host.—*The Expositor.*

* * *

Another Person with Them

Three men were treading over the inhospitable mountains and treacherous glaciers of South Georgia in the Antarctic, in an attempt to rescue the rest of the South Polar party. Later, Sir Ernest Shackelton wrote in his diary: "When I look back at those days, I have no doubt that Providence guided us... During that long and racing march of thirty-six hours over the unnamed mountains and glaciers of South Georgia, it seemed to me that we were four, not three. I said nothing to my companions on this point, but afterward Worsely said to me, 'Boss, I had a curious feeling on the march that there was another person with us.' Crean confessed the same idea. One feels the dearth of human words, the roughness of mortal speech, in trying to describe things intangible, but a record of our journeys would not be complete without a reference to a subject so very near our hearts." Those who cleave to God will find that in the time of need He is ever near.—*The Upper Room.*

* * *

No Need of Counting

There is a strange tribe of natives in Africa. It is said that they never count. They know nothing of arithmetic. A gentleman asked one of them how many sheep he had. "Don't know," replied the native. "Then how do you know if one or two are missing?" The reply was striking and beautiful. "Not because the number would be less, but because of a face that I would miss."
—*Sunday School Times.*

* * *

God Is "Just the Same" in Japan

In the village of Abashiri, Japan, lived an earnest Christian man. He had an orchard of one thousand trees, and upon these depended the livelihood of himself, and his family. One morning, great was his dismay to find that his apples, which were then half grown, were being destroyed by a peculiar worm. As he walked through the orchard he observed that every tree was affected. What was he to do? He called his family together there in the orchard and they called upon God. Works were added to faith, and all through the day and until late at night, they worked, picking off the worms and destroying them; but with the pests multiplying by the thousands, it became evident that all their efforts were in vain. In desperation they turned to God for help. Weary with the long strain they lay down on their straw mats for a little sleep. Returning the next morning to their orchards to begin another strenuous day, they were startled to see hundreds of strange birds alighting in the trees. All day long the birds stayed, eating up the worms, but never injuring the trees or the leaves. This kept up for three days in succession. In the evening of the third day, as the family walked through the orchard, they found that it was entirely free of the pest. God had vindicated the faith of his children.—*The Revivalist.*

Good Night

An old shepherd was walking home one evening with a farmer friend. The couple had plodded a half mile or so downhill toward the village. The old man stopped suddenly. He said, "I forgot to say good night to the sheep. I must go back."

His friend laughed at him and went on home. But the old shepherd toiled back up the hill to the fold. There he leaned over the hurdles and said, "Good night, sheep. Good night to 'ee."

Wasn't that a nice thing for the old shepherd to do? And every boy and girl may know that every night, Jesus, the Good Shepherd, is there to say "good night" to each one. But He does not go away in the night, for He says, "Lo, I am with you alway."
—A. G. Street in *A Year of My Life.*

* * *

"More To Follow"

Rowland Hill tells a story of a hard working man who fell on evil days. Through no fault of his own he lost health, situation, and all his capital; and at last he and his family were face to face with ruin. A rich man heard of the case, and sent the distressed a note for twenty-five dollars in an envelope with these words attached, "More to follow." After a few days, the rich friend sent another note of the same amount with the same phrase, "More to follow," and for many weeks the broken family received a constant stream of bank notes always with the cheering message, "More to follow," until their ruined fortune was mended, and a measure of their prosperity restored.

So it is with God's gifts. He gives enough for the present needs and there is always the cheering assurance, "More to follow." — *British Weekly.*

* * *

A Thrilling Incident

The world of fiction hardly contains a more thrilling chapter than an incident which marked the life of the late Rev. Mr. Lee, Presbyterian minister of the village of Waterford, New York.

Mr. Lee was sitting in his study about midnight, preparing a discourse to deliver to his congregation, when he heard a noise behind him, and became conscious that someone was in the room. Mr. Lee exclaimed, "What is the matter?" and, turning round in his chair, beheld the grim face of a burglar, who was pointing a pistol at his breast. A ruffian had entered the house by a side window, supposing all the occupants were locked in slumber.

"Give me your watch and money," said he, "and make no noise or I will fire."

"You may put down your weapon. I shall make no resistance, and you are at liberty to take all the valuables I possess," was Mr. Lee's calm reply. "I will conduct you to the place where my most precious treasures are placed."

He opened the door and pointed to the cot where his two children lay slumbering in the sweet sleep of innocence and peace.

"Those," said he, "are my choicest jewels. Will you take them?"

He proceeded to say that as a minister of the Gospel he had few earthly possessions, and that his means were devoted to but one object—the education of the two motherless children. The burglar was deeply and visibly affected by these remarks. Tears filled his eyes, and he expressed the utmost sorrow at the act which he had been about to commit.

After a few remarks by Mr. Lee, the would-be criminal consented to kneel and join in prayer, and there in that lonely house, amid the silence of midnight, the offender poured forth his remorse and penitence, while the representative of religion, of peace, and good will told him to "go, and sin no more."

Such a scene has few parallels.

—*Selected*

* * *

The Living Presence of Jesus

Did you ever hear that story about the young Scottish probationer who was visiting an old lady who knew her Bible pretty well? I suppose he thought it was his duty to leave a text with her; so he said, before he left the room, "what a lovely promise that is, 'Lo, I am with you alway'!" She replied, "Hoot, mon, it's not a promise; it's just a fact!" It is not merely a promise, it is just the declaration of a glorious fact. *It is the "I Am," whose presence is such an inspiring certainty.—Selected.*

* * *

When There Is Nothing

In looking to God for deliverance of any kind, we are prone to try to discover what material He has on hand to work on in coming to our relief. Just think a moment. It is not at all necessary for you to see any help in sight, nor is it really necessary for God to have any relief on hand. He does not need anything to begin on. In the beginning God created the Heaven and the earth. What did he make them out of? Nothing, absolutely nothing. When the earth was made, what did He hang it on? Nothing. Pretty satisfactory earth to be made of nothing, eh? Remember, not a scrap of anything was used to make it. "He . . . hangeth the earth upon nothing." It hangs all right, doesn't it? Very well, then. A God who can make an earth, a sun, a moon, and stars out of nothing, and keep them hanging on nothing, can supply all your needs, whether He has anything to begin to work with or not. Wonderful, isn't it? Trust Him and He will see you through, though He has to make your supplies out of nothing.—*From a tract entitled "He Can."* (*Joakim Tract Soc.*)

* * *

No Limit in God's Partnership

A millionaire agreed to go into a business partnership with a young mechanic whom he believed would make good, and this young fellow was much elated because he thought that man's millions would be at the disposal of the business; but when the legal papers were drawn up by the millionaire's attorney they called for the word "Limited." It was the firm of "So and So, Ltd.," and the charter showed very clearly that the millionaire was responsible only to the extent of $5,000. Your Senior Partner owns all the silver and the gold and the cattle upon a thousand hills, and if you are true to Him He will tax the resources of the universe if necessary to see you through.—*Sunday School Times.*

* * *

God's Protective Care

A young soldier, back from service in South Africa, tried to get out of telling of his experiences by saying that nothing had ever happened to him; but his questioner was persistent. "Something must have happened," she declared. "Now tell me, in all your experiences in South Africa, what was it that struck you most?" "Well, ma'am," said the soldier, after some thought, *"the thing that struck me most was the number of bullets that missed me."*

So we may be struck most by the number of dangers that have threatened us, only to be diverted by God's protecting hand.—*New Century Leader.*

* * *

Father Is On Deck

"I will both lay me down in peace and sleep: for Thou, Lord, only makest me dwell in safety" (Ps. 4:8).

One night when all were quietly asleep, there arose a sudden squall of wind at sea which came sweeping against the side of a ship sailing between Liverpool and New York. The great boat was instantly thrown on her side by the force of the gale, crashing everything that was movable and awakening the passengers to the consciousness of imminent peril.

Everyone on board was alarmed with the exception of one little girl, the eight-year-old daughter of the captain. "What's the matter?" asked the child, rubbing her eyes as she was thrown out of bed. Her mother told her of the danger.

"Isn't Papa on deck?" asked the child. She was told that he was. "Then I'm going back to bed," answered the child, and dropping herself on the pillow without a fear, in a few minutes she was asleep.

Fear not the windy tempests wild,
  Thy bark they shall not wreck.
Lie down and sleep, Oh, helpless child!
  Thy Father's on the deck.
—*Gospel Herald.*

He careth for the sparrows!
  Winter's long night is o'er,
And on the budded branches
  They greet the Spring once more.

He careth for the sparrows!
  Through days of darkest dread,
His Love has kept them sheltered;
  His servants kept them fed.

He careth for the sparrows!
  How simple, then, to see,
That if His Hand keeps them from harm
  He'll do the same for me!
—*Selected.*

* * *

The Missionary's Defense

The following occurrence was related by Missionary Von Asselt, Rhenish missionary in Sumatra from 1856 *to* 1876, *on a visit to Lubeck*:

When I first went to Sumatra, in the year 1856, I was the first European missionary to go among the wild Battas, although, twenty years prior, two American missionaries had come to them with the Gospel; but they had been killed and eaten. Since then no effort had been made to bring the Gospel to these people, and, naturally, they had remained the same cruel savages.

"What it means for one to stand alone among a savage people, unable to make himself understood, not understanding a single sound of their language, but whose suspicious, hostile looks and gestures speak only a too-well-understood language — yes, it is hard for me to realize that. The first two years which I spent among the Battas, at first all alone and afterward with my wife, were so hard that it makes me shudder even now when I think of them. Often it seemed as if we were not only encompassed by hostile men, but also by hostile powers of darkness; for often an inexplicable fear would come over us, so that we had to get up at night and go on our knees to pray or read the Word of God, in order to find relief.

"After we had lived in this place for two years we moved several hours' journey inland, among a tribe somewhat civilized, who received us more kindly. There we built a small house with three rooms — a living room, a bedroom and a small reception room — and life for us became a little more easy and cheerful.

"When I had been in this new place for some months, a man came to me from the district where we had been, and whom I had known there. I was sitting on the bench in front of our house, and he sat down beside me, and for a while talked of this, that, and the other. Finally he began:

"'Now, teacher, I have yet one request.'

"'And what is that?'

"'I would like to have a look at your watchmen close at hand.'

"'What watchmen do you mean? I do not have any.'

"'I mean the watchmen whom you station around your house at night, to protect you.'

"'But I have no watchmen,' I said again; 'I have only a little herdboy and a little cook, and they would make poor watchmen.'

"Then the man looked at me incredulously, as if he wished to say: 'Oh, do not try to make me believe otherwise, for I know better.'

"Then he asked: 'May I look through your house, to see if they are hid there?'

"'Yes, certainly,' I said, laughingly; 'look through it; you will not find anybody.' So he went in and searched in every corner, even through the beds, but came to me very much disappointed.

"Then I myself began a little probing and requested him to tell me the circumstances about those watchmen of whom he spoke, and this is what he related to me:

"'When you first came to us, we were very angry with you. We did not want you to live among us; we did not trust you, and believed you had some design against us. Therefore we came together and resolved to kill you and your wife. Accordingly, we went to your house night after night; but when we came near, there stood always, close around the house, a double row of watchmen with glittering weapons, and we did not venture to attack them to get into your house. But we were not willing to abandon our plan, so we went to a professional assassin (there still was among the savage Battas at that time a special guild of assassins, who killed for hire anyone whom it was desired to get out of the way), and asked him if he would undertake to kill you and your wife. He laughed at us because of our cowardice, and said, "I fear no God, and no devil. I will get through those watchmen easily." So we came all together in the evening, and the assassin, swinging his weapon about his head, went courageously on before us. As we neared your house, we remained behind, and let him go on alone. But in a short time he came running back hastily, and said, "No, I dare not risk to go through alone; two rows of big strong men are there, very close together, shoulder to shoulder, and their weapons shine like fire." Then we gave up killing you. But now, tell me, teacher, who are these watchmen? Have you never seen them?'

"'No, I have never seen them.'

"'And your wife did not see them either?'

"'No, my wife did not see them.'

"'But yet we all have seen them; how is that?'

"Then I went in, and brought a Bible from our house, and holding it open before him, said: 'See here; this Book is the Word of our great God, in which He promises to guard and defend us, and we firmly believe that Word; therefore we need not see the watchmen; but you do not believe, therefore the great God has to show you the watchmen, in order that you may learn to believe.'"

—*Gospel Herald.*

* * *

When the "Storm Cloud" Came

In February, 1931, our district was reduced to a state of famine, and there was yet another month to wheat harvest. We had helped many, but one day when the Christians came for help we had to tell them we had nothing left. I told them that God was a prayer-hearing and prayer-answering God. They proposed to come and join in my prayer each afternoon. On the fourth day of the intercession I was called out of the meeting to see what was happening. In the north was a dark cloud approaching, and as we watched, it crossed our district and rained heavily. It was not an ordinary rain, but a deluge of little black seeds in such abundance they could be shoveled up. They asked, "What is it?" The seeds proved edible and the supply so great it sustained the people until harvest. We learned later that the storm had risen in Mongolia and wrecked the places where this grain (called Kao-Liang) was stored. The seed was carried fifteen hundred miles to drop on the district where prayer was being answered.—*The Sunday School Times.*

* * *

Returning to the Moody Bible Institute late one evening, Joseph H—, one of our pastor's course students stopped his car for a traffic light. A man climbed into the seat beside the student and thrust a gun against his side, then curtly ordered, "Drive on, and don't do anything to attract attention." Joe obeyed the gunman's order. His mind turned to the Lord, and almost unconsciously the words came from his lips, "For to me to live is Christ, and to die is gain." Now it was the bandit's turn to be startled. "What are you talking about? Are you crazy?" he asked. This gave Joe an opportunity to explain that because he was born again and Christ lived in him, he had eternal life, and that physical death would only mean continued life in glory. The stranger snorted, "Now I *know* you're crazy." But his interest was kindled and the student continued to tell the gunman about the Saviour. Suddenly the holdup man asked his driver to "pull over to the curb," then withdrew his gun, explaining that he wanted to hear more about how to gain victory over fear and death. Opening his Gospel of John, the student asked the man to read from the third chapter. As Joe explained John 3:16, the gunman suddenly stopped him and shouted joyfully, "I see it." He then confessed faith in the Lord Jesus Christ, and the two bowed their heads and prayed.—*From a leaflet published by Moody Bible Institute.*

* * *

His King's Nearness

The late Mrs. Ralph C. Norton asked the Belgian Queen's permission to tell how one soldier, who later fell in battle, found faith in God. This true story came from the chaplain, known to Mrs. Norton. The soldier had received a Gospel at the front. He read of God, but because he could not see Him, he could not believe in His reality and His omnipresence. He longed to believe. One night at the Yser, while on sentry duty, alone in the presence of danger he thought of God. If only he could believe! Soon he was aware of someone behind him. He knew he was standing there, yet he did not dare to turn his head to see. At last ever so little, he turned his head, and saw King Albert! Yes, his king was standing sentry duty with him — sharing in the very experience of his soldier. His monarch stood motionless for a long time, while the soldier prayed. Faith in God through Christ came. The presence of the king, silent yet so near, had brought him faith in the presence and personality of God.—*The Expositor.*

* * *

"They've Got God"

The Watchman-Examiner publishes an interview of the editor with Miss Homer, who recently spent fifteen months in China and Japan, representing the Church Committee for China Relief. In that interview Miss Homer told of a curious incident which happened in Chungking in May, 1939, setting forth the influence on the Chinese of Christian Generalissimo and Madame Chiang Kai-shek. In an air raid on Chungking, the cliffs, going down into the rivers on three sides of the city, became a veritable death trap to thousands. Five thousand were wounded. "Finally, toward dawn, when the fires had burned down a bit, what used to be streets were jammed with screaming, hysterical people. * * Suddenly there came a yell from the crowd, 'Look! Look over there! There's the Generalissimo and Madame Chiang!' Everybody looked, and sure enough, there they were, those two, just wandering down the street hand in hand clothes torn, faces dirty, stopping now and then to adjust a bandage or comfort someone, so stricken and near to tears they could hardly speak. Then the crowd began to mutter and then to roar. 'They haven't a bodyguard!

Where are their soldiers?' For just a moment there was a panic, and then suddenly a little coolie on the edge of the crowd yelled out, 'Oh, that's all right; they've got God!' They say that a curious quiet settled down over that crowd. They stood there — screaming stopped — perfectly silent, just watching while those two wandered off into the snow and disappeared."—*Selected.*

* * *

The Deliverance at Dunkirk

The deliverance at Dunkirk was so extraordinary that even a newspaper such as the London *Daily Telegraph* acknowledged it to have been miraculous. Writing of the "epic story" it says: "I have talked to officers and men... and all of them tell of these two phenomena. The first was the great storm which broke over Flanders on Tuesday, May 28, and the other was the great calm which settled on the English Channel during the days following.

"Officers of high rank do not hesitate to put down the deliverance of the British Expeditionary Force to the nation being at prayer on Sunday, May 26. I am told that after careful survey of the position had been made, the maximum number whom it was thought could possibly escape death or capture was 30,000. Instead of that, more than ten times the number were safely embarked. The consciousness of miraculous deliverance pervades the camps in which the troops are now housed in England... It is undoubted that there was such a calmness over the whole of the waters of the English Channel for that vital period of days as has rarely been experienced. Those who are accustomed to the Channel testify to the strangeness of this calm.

"So the two miracles made possible what seemed impossible. In the darkness of the storm and the violence of the rain, formations which were eight to twelve miles from Dunkirk were able to move up on foot to the coast with scarcely any interruption from aircraft, for aircraft were unable to operate in such turbulent conditions.

"One thing can be certain about tomorrow's thanksgiving in our churches. From none will the thanks ascend with greater sincerity or deeper fervor than from the officers and men who have seen the Hand of God, powerful to save, delivering them from the hands of a mighty foe who, humanly speaking, had them utterly at his mercy."—*Sunday School Times.*

* * *

God's All-Sufficiency

One of Spurgeon's quaint sayings was: "If there were an ant at the door of your granary begging for help, it wouldn't ruin you to give him a grain of your wheat. You are but a tiny insect at the door of God's all-sufficiency."

If a great king should issue an order that your needs should be supplied as long as you might live, you would cease to worry, for here is one who has authority and resources in plenty. How much more should the promises of the King of kings stop our worrying.

His promises are so many bonds that may be cashed in the day of the believer's need. Our only concern needs to be that our rights to the promises may be cleared up, for it is sad when one stands with the King's promises in hand and fears to face the Cashier with them.—*Living Links.*

* * *

Food From Above

Mr. He Li was very old and very poor, but a Christian. His cousin, a priest, would bring bread or meal, and Mr. Li would say, "My Heavenly Father's grace." This angered the priest, who said, "If I didn't bring you the food, you would starve, for all He would care." "But He puts it into your heart to help me." "Very well, I'll stay away and then we'll see what happens." After many days Mr. Li had not a single crumb, but while he was praying there was a strange cawing and flapping in the yard. Some crows were fighting and dropped a piece of pork and a loaf of bread. While the meat was boiling, the priest walked in, saying, "Has the Heavenly Father you talk so much about sent you food?" When he saw the meat he exclaimed, "Where in the world did you get that?" "My Heavenly Father sent it." Then the priest wanted to know more about Him, was converted, became a preacher, and died a martyr in the Boxer war.—*Sunday School Times.*

* * *

"Oh, the wonderful story of deathless love!
Each child is dear to that heart above;
He fights for me when I cannot fight,
He comforts me in the gloom of night,
He lifts the burden, for He is strong,
He stills the sigh, and awakens the song;
The burdens that bow me down He bears,
And loves and pardons because He cares."

* * *

When Burdens Become Bridges

The Rev. Charles Piggott tells how when he was on a holiday he came to the top of one of the high hills of Devonshire. His attention was attracted by an ant, which he watched carrying a long straw until it came to a crack in the rock which was like a precipice to the tiny creature. After attempting to take its burden across in several ways, the ant got to one end of the straw and pushed it in front of him over the crack till it reached the other side, crossed over on the straw, and then pulled it after him. There is no burden you and I carry faithfully but some day is going to become a bridge to carry us over.—*British Weekly.*

* * *

A Little Girl Knew Daniel's God

Mrs. Dan Crawford tells this thrilling story in a recent letter. A little girl about nine years of age had repeatedly run away from home to a Bible school nearby, only to be dragged back by her perturbed mother. But beat her as she would, away she would bolt to join the sweet singing and memorizing of Bible stories. She was put into the witch doctor's hands "to put fear upon her," but without effect. The now desperate mother determined on a last effort to rescue her child for the time-honored tribal customs. So driving her into the forest she bound her to a tree, thinking that if the spirits aided her the lion would frighten the "Jesus belief" out of her. She left her, saying, "A worthless child art thou to me — but food for lions." The dreaded black night enveloped the shivering little girl. Ah the terror of it all! But most surely the angel of the Lord must have encamped about that tree, for when at dawn a Christian lad found her he saw lion tracks encircling the spot, but noted that not one animal had come nearer than five yards. She had seen their glaring eyes but remembered what she had learned in school, that God who made the lions had made her too. Fear left her; she felt sure that God would not let the lions eat her.—*Sunday School Times.*

* * *

Charles Abel's Deliverance

At Maivara, a village near the head of Milne Bay, God intervened in the early days to save the life of Charles Abel. He had left his wife and first-born child in the mission boat while he went to try to establish a friendly contact with the villagers. He had gone only a short distance when a messenger from his wife came in haste, asking him to return, as their baby was ill. He turned back, and did not gain an entrance to this village for some years later. Then he learned that just beyond the point where the messenger had reached him, a group of hostile natives lay in wait to take his life, as others murdered his fellow missionary, James Chalmers. Today a church which they have built marks the spot where his enemies lay in wait to take his life.—*D. L. Pierson, in Kwato Mission Tidings.*

* * *

If God Does Not Forget the Oyster Shells

The river Rhine brings down annually lime enough to supply millions upon millions of oysters with shells. From the far-off Alps help comes to aid the humble oyster in the North Sea. The sun itself works for the oyster, for it lifts the vapors to the heights where they become snow. And the snow in turn becomes a glacier that grinds and pulverizes the granite into lime for oyster shells. Then the hundreds of leaping waterfalls and roaring mountain brooks fling themselves down the heights carrying that precious lime. Soon the stately Rhine, famous in story and song, flows past great cities and ancient castles, bearing the material so essential to the oysters in making their shells. And surely, if God so marvelously cares for the lowly things of His creation, oh! how much more He will care for us who are His children.—*Bible Messages.*

CHARACTER

Tests of Sanctified Character

Some of the acid tests of sanctified character will always be:

1. Can you labor on cheerfully without earthly reward?

2. Can you toil on hopefully without tangible returns?

3. Can you travel the road of frequent criticism without bitterness?

4. Can you lift and agonize and sacrifice and pray and give, way down out of sight, while others lead the procession and receive the honors? In other words, are you willing to be soil in which providential events may grow, while others fill the places of leaves and blossoms on the trees of time?—*Selected.*

* * *

A Valuable Slip

When James A. Garfield was a young man a printed slip was given him by a friend which he carefully cherished. It reads as follows: "Make few promises. Always speak the truth. Never speak evil of anyone. Keep good company or none. Drink no intoxicating liquors. Good character is above everything else. Be honest if you would be happy. When you speak to a person look into his eyes. Spend less than you earn. Live within your income. Never run into debt unless you see your way out. Good company and good conversation are the essentials of virtue. Good character can be injured only by your own acts. If evil is spoken of you, let your life refute the falsehood. If your hands cannot be employed, attend to the cultivation of your mind. Read the above carefully and thoughtfully." — *Watchman-Examiner.*

Reflecting Her Soul

A striking line was found in a story by Margaret E. Sangster. The story told of a man who was looking at a girl, but the latter was unconscious of his presence. Soon he said, softly, to another onlooker, "What a pretty soul she has!" Commenting on this, Miss Sangster made this observation: "Often we say to one another, 'What a pretty frock,' or 'What an adorable coat,' or 'What an exquisite gown!' But we seldom say, 'What a pretty soul — what a charming heart!'" Yet the inner life is the thing of highest value. Said an old and wise writer, "Keep thy heart with all diligence; for out of it are the issues of life" (Prov. 4:23). — *Sunday School Times.*

* * *

Character

Character is what a person *is* — not what he is supposed to be. It is not shaped by trifles any more than marble is sculptured by puffs of air. Only through hard struggles and stern conflicts with temptation and resolute self-mastery does this Divine principle manifest itself. The sharpness of our trials and the hardness of our lot show what we are and how long we will last.

Character is a fortune. It pays far better dividends than bank or railroad stock. In every emergency it is the man of character who is sought. Character once lost is lost forever. A shattered character may be retrieved in part, but can never be restored to its original strength and perfection. The physician may cure the body and even find a remedy for the diseased mind, but there is no power on earth that can assuage the pain of the hearts that are consumed by terrible and unavailing remorse.

The above may have been written from a nominal Christian, or perhaps only a moral, standpoint; but is there not much truth contained in its statements, and is it not because of this state of affairs that many, having made a misstep in one direction or another, throw their lives away, selling themselves (as it were) to sin and shame? But, while character once lost can never be restored to its *original* strength and no power upon *earth* can assuage the pain of hearts consumed by remorse, yet there is hope in Jesus who came from Heaven and of whom it was said, "He shall save His people from their sins." This hope lifts us even above Adamic perfection, making us new creatures, old things having passed away, and all things becoming new, having received a right spirit within us. The world ignores the sinner; Christ lifts him up.

—*A. L. Halteman*

* * *

Character

The Greek word from which our word "character" originated signified a sharp-pointed instrument or graving tool. Much of this first meaning is implied in the word as we use it, for is not character the means by which each of us makes his impression on the world? To be sure, the instrument itself is not a finished product, is a mere tool; but, like many a fine instrument, character improves with use. Our actions and reactions temper the blade, and make the edge powerful or impotent. Each must forge his own character, each must be responsible for keeping it in condition, each must be responsible for its results.—*Selected.*

* * *

Sickle, Harvester, and Ruth

The Bible, along with history, teaches us that man's natural inclination is downward. Science, on the other hand, has been reluctant to believe that its task was not to lift a rising race but a fallen one. Now comes Dr. Alexis Carrell, noted as a surgeon and author, and declares that physicians are "keenly disappointed in observing that their efforts have resulted in a larger number of healthy defectives, healthy lunatics, healthy criminals; and there is no progress of man." Science has greatly improved living and working conditions, and it is a long step from the sickle Ruth wielded in Boaz' field to the modern harvester. "But," pointedly inquires Dr. Homer McMillan, in "Other Men Labor," "have we improved upon Ruth?" —*Courtesy Moody Monthly.*

* * *

Real Beauty

A Quaker lady was once asked the secret of her beautiful complexion. She said, "I use truth for my lips; for my voice, prayer; for my eyes, pity; for my hands, charity; for my figure, uprightness; and for my heart, *love.*"—*Reginald Wallis.*

* * *

"Build it well, whate'er you do;
Build it straight and strong and true;
Build it clear and high and broad;
Build it for the eye of God."

—*Charles Daniel Brodhead.*

* * *

Honesty Is No Policy, But A Principle

A slave boy, on the auctioneer's block, was approached by a kind-hearted man who asked him: "If I buy you and take you to a beautiful home, will you be honest and truthful?" The black boy answered: "Sir, I will be honest and truthful whether you buy me or not."

—*Selected.*

* * *

Caste or Character

A high caste Indian gentleman interested in Lucknow Christian College, in India, brought his son to this school for education. He was reminded of the fact that the boy would lose caste if he came there and studied the Bible with the other students. The father, an example of the new India, promptly gave this courageous reply: "I would rather have my son lose caste and save his character, than have him save his caste and lose his character."—*New Century Leader.*

CHILDREN

Too Young?

Rose Mary was an attendant at one of the schools conducted by the Canadian Sunday School Mission. Only six years of age, it might be questioned if she was not too young to profit — so thought the teacher. On the final day opportunity was given for any who wished to accept Christ to come to the front. Rose Mary left her seat, but the teacher said, "Perhaps you don't fully understand, Rose Mary; you are so young; you better go back to your seat." And Rose Mary went back, her heart full of anguish that overflowed in tears. Questioned by the teacher as to the cause, the child who was "too little to understand" sobbed, "My parents don't want me to be a Christian, and now teacher doesn't want me to be one either." Rose Mary and "teacher" knelt together in the schoolroom, and a little child entered into life. "Simply to Thy cross I cling." One need not to be very old or very wise to do that.—*Sunday School Times.*

* * *

Blessings of a Christian Lifetime

"Suppose that Paul had been converted at seventy instead of twenty-five. There would have been no Paul in history. There was a Matthew Henry because he was converted at eleven and not at seventy; a Dr. Watts because he was converted at nine and not at sixty; a Jonathan Edwards because he was converted at eight and not at eighty; a Richard Baxter because he was converted at six and not at sixty. How much more a soul is worth that has a lifetime... before it than the soul which has nothing! Lambs are of more worth than sheep in the realm of souls as well as in the market place." — *The Presbyterian.*

* * *

The Children's Graves

An old sexton in a cemetery took special pains with the little graves. When asked why, he said, "Sir, about those larger graves I don't know who are the Lord's saints, and who are not; but you know, sir, it's different with the bairns." — *Rev. C. M. Keach in tract, "Childhood."*

* * *

Should They Be Shut Out?

A little girl nine years old greatly desired to unite with the church but was told, much to her distress, that she was too young. Soon afterward she was taken seriously ill and seemed to realize that she probably would not get well. Her pastor came to see her, and she, looking up with tear-filled eyes, said to him, "Jesus will understand, won't he?" "What do you mean, dear?" he asked. "Why, he'll know that I wanted to join the church and you wouldn't let me, won't he?" The pastor, overcome by the child's words, hurriedly called his elders together in united prayer that the little girl's life might be spared. Their prayer was granted, and as soon as she was able she was taken into the church and proved her sincerity by her faithful Christian life.—*Sunday School Times.*

* * *

A Child's Misunderstanding

Asked to receive an alms (Acts 3:3).

The minister was being entertained at the home of one of the elders. While they were at dinner the little daughter of the house said to the minister, "I, heard you preach today." "You did?" said he. "Can you tell me, then, what I preached about?" "Yes," answered the little girl. "You preached about a man who asked for arms, and got legs."
—*Selected.*

* * *

Watchers

A morning in September comes
When mothers stand to see
Mere babies faring forth to meet
A world's complexity;
They loose small hands — they bid them go —
They watch them yearningly.

So brief — so swift — the years have been
So dear — the constant care,

And now bereft — at open doors —
Stand mothers — everywhere —
Within their eyes a wistful light,
Upon their lips — a prayer.

Dear God — compassionate to all —
I pray Thee keep apart
A space of warmth and tenderness
Within Thy sheltering heart,
For women watching through their tears
An eager child depart.

A mother's need is great this hour —
Oh, come to her today
And reassure her, God, and take
The anxious care away,
Then go with every child who goes,
And stay with them, I pray.

* * *

For Children Only

"Their Size is Their Ticket," the *Chicago Daily News* captions a picture of small children entering a "tiny-tot play lot" through a low gateway shaped like a keyhole. Admittance to the lot, given to the youngsters of Oak and Sedgwick Streets by Mr. and Mrs. Charles S. Dewey, depends on the ability of the child to walk upright through the low gate. Size too, determines whether or not a person enters Heaven. When His disciples asked the Lord Jesus who was the greatest in the Kingdom of Heaven, he "called a little child unto Him, and set him in the midst of them, and said, Verily I say unto you, Except ye be converted, and become as little children, ye shall not enter into the kingdom of heaven" (Matt. 18:1-3).—*Selected.*

* * *

An old man going a lone highway,
Came at the evening cold and gray
To a chasm vast and deep and wide.
The old man crossed in the twilight dim,
The sullen stream had no fear for him.
But he paused when safe on the other side
And built a bridge to stem the tide.
"Old man," said a fellow pilgrim near,
"You are wasting your strength by building here,
Your journey will end with the closing day,
You never again will pass this way.
You've crossed the chasm deep and wide
Why build you this bridge at ev'ntide?

The builder lifted his old gray head,
"Good friend, in the path I've come," he said,
"There followeth after me today
A youth whose feet must pass this way
This chasm that's been as naught to me
To that fair-haired youth may a pitfall be;
He, too, must cross in the twilight dim
Good friend, I'm building this bridge for him."

—*Selected.*

* * *

Far-Sighted

A farmer was walking over his farm with a friend, exhibiting his crops, herds of cattle, and flocks of sheep. His friend was greatly impressed and highly pleased, especially with the splendid sheep. He had seen the same breed frequently before, but never had seen such fine specimens. With great earnestness he asked how he had succeeded in rearing such flocks. His simple answer was "*I take care of my lambs.*"—*Scottish Magazine.*

* * *

"Give me the children until they are seven and anyone may have them afterwards."—*Xavier.*

* * *

When Little Boys Pray

When little boys kneel by their beds
And fold their hands and bow their heads
And shut their eyes and start to pray
I don't think God is far away.
I think He listens with intent
To any message that is sent
By little boys who kneel at night;
I think God tries with all His might
To answer prayers that small boys make
In His Son's name, for His Son's sake.

—*Gates Hebbard.*

* * *

The Plight of Childhood

Two out of three of the children in the United States and Canada, as a whole, are in no Sunday School. In the

United States alone 27,000,000 children under the age of twelve are getting no definite Christian teaching.

Eighty per cent of the children now attending the Sunday Schools of America (some 10,000,000) are unconverted, and will never be converted until more stress is placed on child evangelism.

Eighty-five per cent of the children leave Sunday School before they reach the age of fifteen. Had the spiritual growth of our churches kept pace with the need, ways would have been found to make it impossible for this condition to exist. No adequate impact is being made on this tragic situation through our existing Christian agencies.

The proportion of unreached children becomes greater each year. God alone can meet this need. But God always works through His own people.—*Courtesy Moody Monthly.*

* * *

A pound of mischief,
An ounce of care —
A bushel of love,
And spun-gold hair —
The scales add it up
As the weights move along,
But even scales
Are sometimes wrong!

For the precious weight
Of his tiny soul,
That links him to God
And points him a goal,
Is most important
In weighing him well,
And that great worth
No scale can tell!

—*Selected.*

* * *

Does It Mean Me?

A missionary to the mountain people of the South was once laid aside temporarily from teaching on account of illness, and she wrote the following account of one of the children of her charge: "I must tell you of the little girl who lived with us, and of her practical application of a Scripture text. It was my custom to teach her from the Bible every Sunday afternoon. I had been reading from the ninth chapter of Mark, where it speaks of the child-like spirit our dear Saviour wants us to possess. She listened very attentively, and seemed especially interested when we came to the forty-first verse, 'For he shall lose his reward.' She left me a few moments, but presently came back saying, 'Won't you tell me about that verse again?' I gladly complied. Then came the question, 'Does it mean me — can I do something for Jesus?'

"That evening there came a gentle rap on my door, and to my 'Come in!' Minnie entered, bearing a glass of water. Coming near, she placed the water on a little stand by my bedside. Noticing that she stood as though she would speak, I said, 'What is it, Minnie?' She hesitated a moment, then replied, 'I was thinking of what you said about the cup of water, and I wanted to give you something else 'cause you was sick, but I didn't have anything, so I thought maybe you might like a fresh drink of water, for it's all I've got.' Indeed, my heart was touched by this poor girl's beautiful application of the lesson learned. Nor was it forgotten. Every evening during my illness came the 'fresh drink' from the hands of the little beginner, who wanted to do something for Jesus."—*American Missions.*

* * *

In the Modern Home

Everything in the modern home is controlled by switches except the children.—*Evening Tribune. Surrey, Eng.*

* * *

The Spring in the Desert

In the early fifties a party of emigrants on their way to the gold fields of California struck out on the desert for the land of promise. The trail was well defined by abandoned wagons and the bones of horses, mules and human beings. Struggling through the yielding sand, the thermometer at 120 degrees, wheels falling apart, animals dying from heat and thirst, they on the second night out halted some ten miles from "Cook's Well," with water in their kegs exhausted.

Tradition states that a little ten-year-old girl was heard praying in one of the wagons for water. It states that in her childlike faith she said: "O, good heavenly Father, I know that I have been a very naughty, naughty girl, but oh dear, I am so very thirsty, and mamma, papa and the baby all want to drink so much. Do, good God, give us water, and I will never, never be naughty again."

The gaunt, half-starved, desperate men gathered around the wagons and listened to the humble petition. One voiced the rest and said, "May God grant it!" Soon the voice of the little girl, in cheerful accent, sounded clear in the silent night:

"Oh, mother, mother, get me water; oh, I can hear it running; oh, do get some water for baby and me."

They thought her delirious from her sufferings, and suddenly a babel of sounds broke forth from the oxen and mules, all frantic and endeavoring to break loose from the wagon poles. A rustling noise called their attention to a slight depression near the wagons, and investigating the cause they found water, clear and sparkling, gushing up out of the sand.

This spring continued to flow, running due north for twenty miles, then was lost in the sand. In places it was two miles wide from four to twenty feet deep. Along this new river life arose, and there the desert blossomed as the rose. It changed the desert into God's park. Who shall say it was not an answer to the faith of a child?—*The Christian Herald.*

* * *

If in the golden streets were heard no baby laughter,
How empty Heaven would be!
And so, dear Lord, to wait till I shall follow after,
I send my Little Swan to Thee.
If in God's many mansions, no babes were ever sleeping,
What beauty Heaven would lack!
And so to wake and smile when I have ended weeping,
Your Little Swan, dear Lord, comes back. —*Selected.*

Is Strict Training the Trouble?

A good deal of nonsense is being palmed off on the community about the reaction of the child from overstrictness in parental training. When I hear a man say, "My parents brought me up so rigidly that a reaction took place in my mind and I have turned away from religion," I have sometimes asked, "Did they teach you to be honest?" "Yes." "Were they strict about it?" "Yes." "Did they teach you to tell the truth?" "Yes." "Were they strict about that?" "Yes." "Has any reaction taken place on these points?" No man learns the multiplication table from sheer love of it; but I never knew of anyone whose mind was in reaction against the multiplication table.—*John Hall, D.D.*

* * *

The Toy-Strewn House

Give me the house where the toys are strewn,
Where the dolls are asleep in the chairs,
Where the building blocks and the toy balloon
And the soldiers guard the stairs;
Let me sleep in the house where the tiny cart
With its horses rules the floors,
And rest comes into my heart,
For I am at home once more.

Give me the house with the toys about,
With the battered old train of cars,
The box of paints and the books left out
And the ship with her broken spars;
Let me step in a house at the close of day
That is littered with children's toys,
And dwell once more in the haunts of play
With the echoes of bygone noise.

Give me the house where the toys are seen,
The house where the children romp,
And I'll be happier than man has been
'Neath the gilded dome of pomp.
Let me see the litter of bright-eyed play
Strewn over the parlor floor,
And the joys I knew in a far-off day
Will gladden my heart once more.

Whoever has lived in a toy-strewn house
Though feeble he be and gray,
Will yearn, no matter how far he roam,
For the glorious disarray
Of the little house with its littered floor
That was his in the bygone days
And his heart will throb as it throbbed before
When he rests where a baby plays.
—*Selected.*

* * *

A Wrong Righted

Many years ago a company of slaves were sold by auction in a Nigerian market place. When the market was almost over, a poor little boy was placed on the auction block. He presented such a miserable appearance that the slave buyers laughed at the suggestion to bid for him. At last the boy was purchased for a roll of tobacco, and was made to walk with a gang of slaves to the coast where he was put in the hold of a ship bound for America. But the ship was captured by the British who took the slaves to Freetown in Sierra Leone and set them at liberty. The little boy was put in charge of the missionaries. Many years later there was an interesting ceremony in St. Paul's Cathedral, London. In the presence of church dignitaries, nobles, and statesmen there was consecrated the first bishop of Nigeria. It was the little boy who was sold for a roll of tobacco. Bishop Samuel Crowther did a wonderful work for God in Nigeria where his name is still revered as a true hero of the Lord Jesus Christ.
—*J. S. Hall, in the Sudan Witness.*

* * *

Girls Sold For Taxes

Here is further proof that militarism is a curse. Japan's farmers must pay 60 per cent of their earnings in taxes. The government spends annually 46 per cent of the national revenue for maintaining the army and navy. Unable to meet these demands in any other way, many Japanese country people are selling their daughters to help pay taxes! Girls of saleable age range from sixteen to twenty-three years, and prices for them run from $3.00 to $300. One farmer rejoiced when he sold his twenty-year-old daughter for Yen 1,000, but changed his tune when he learned that the broker took about 30 per cent as his commission. The National Christian Council of Japan has been concerned about the welfare of Japanese girls and steps have been taken to prevent such sales.—*Missionary Review of the World.*

* * *

But Some Never Grow Up

It was Johnny, the seven-year-old, who tired of the merry-go-round. The previous summer it had fascinated him, and he could not ride on it too often. This season a single trip had satisfied him, and he declined another. "No, thank you, Grandfather," he said, "you see, we ride and ride, but we stay under that old tent all the time. I guess when anyone gets to be seven years old they're too big to care about going and going that doesn't get anywhere."— *The Sunday Circle.*

* * *

When the "New Generation" Began

We are told that the younger generation are "progressive." Typical young people of today insist upon a new freedom, unhindered self-expression, that they may make needed contribution to the progress of the human race. A cartoon in a recent issue of *Collier's* admirably satirizes this. It is a ridiculous picture of Adam, Eve, and Cain. Cain has just killed Abel, a portion of whose body is seen lying full length on the ground. Adam is showing considerable excitement over the murder, and Eve is trying to quiet him down. Cain, smoking a cigarette, looks unconcernedly at the dead body of his brother. Under the picture are the words Eve is speaking to Adam: "Now don't take on, Adam. You simply don't understand Cain. He belongs to another generation which is solving its problems in its own way—facing the facts of life frankly, fearlessly, wide-eyed, and unashamed."—*Sunday School Times.*

A Coleridge Incident

A visitor of Coleridge argued strongly against the religious instruction of the young, and declared his own determination not to "prejudice" his children in favor of any form of religion, but to allow them at maturity to choose for themselves.

The answer of Coleridge was pertinent and sound. "Why prejudice a garden in favor of flowers and fruit? *Why not let the clods choose for themselves between cockleburs and strawberries?*"—*Presbyterian Record.*

* * *

What Are Our Schools Doing?

Steeped in doubt, a Pasadena parent, who is working his son's way through college, appeals to the Los Angeles *Times.* "Tell me, please," he requests, "your interpretation of the over-subscribed expression, a 'Christian land.'" "A 'Christian land,'" defines the editor, "is one where people support colleges to destroy the faith they have taught their children."—*The Pathfinder.*

* * *

Child Conversion

Too much stress cannot be laid upon the importance of the conversion of children, and that when they are quite young. History gives us many instances to support this thought. Here are a few:

In the first century Polycarp, a boy only nine years of age was genuinely converted. He remained a faithful Christian and when the great persecution of the second century was raging he was condemned to death. They told him that they would set him free if he would deny his loyalty to Jesus Christ to which he replied, "Eighty and six years have I served Christ; He has never done me any harm; then why should I deny His Name?"

Isaac Watts also was saved at about nine years of age. As a result of his devoted life many thousands have been lifted Heavenward through the medium of his hymns.

Jonathan Edwards, that great apostl of the New England revival was save when only seven years of age. Wha a loss to the Church it would have bee if someone — whoever that someone ha been—had not led that little boy, taugh him, encouraged him and helped t shield his young and tender life agains the powers of Satan.

Henry Ward Beecher received hi first religious impressions when he wa five years old, from an old colored serv ant. We may not know this humble unrecognized, unpraised servant but th Lord knows.

Rev. F. B. Meyer said, "If the worl is ever to be saved it must be save through childhood." I wonder who wrot the following lines:

"An angel paused in his downward fligh
With a seed of truth and love and light;
And he said, 'Where must this seed b sown
To bring most fruit when it is grown?'
The Master heard as He said and smiled,
'Go, plant it for Me in the heart of a child.'"

Suppose Paul had been converted at sixty instead of about thirty or so. How different his record would be. Matthew Henry was saved at eleven. Had he been saved at seventy we would not have his helpful commentary.

Richard Baxter was saved at six years of age. Had he been saved at sixty we would have hardly had that grand book, "A Call to the Unconverted," with that long trail of inspiration and blessing following it.

It is said that Millet, the famous painter of "The Angelus" was but a little boy when he saw his first sunset on the ocean. This made a wonderful impression upon his mind; it threw him into an ecstacy of delight. His father standing by his side noticing this in his son's expression reverently took off his cap and said to him, "It is God!" The boy never afterward failed to associate this vision with the glory of God.—*Gospel Herald.*

Too Little Children

Said a precious little laddie,
To his father one bright day,
"May I give myself to Jesus,
Let Him wash my sins away?"

"Oh, my son, but you're too little,
Wait until you older grow,
Bigger folk, 'tis true, do need Him,
But little folk are safe, you know."

Said the father to his laddie
As a storm was coming on,
"Are the sheep safely sheltered,
Safe within the fold, my son?"

"All the big ones are, my father,
But the lambs, I let them go,
For I didn't think it mattered,
Little ones are safe, you know."

Oh, my brother! Oh, my sister!
Have you too made that mistake?
Little hearts that now are yielding
May be hardened then — too late.

E'er the evil days come nigh them,
"Let the children come to me,
And forbid them not," said Jesus,
"For such shall my Kingdom be."
—*Selected.*

* * *

Prayer To Bear Pain

In a Northern hospital a little girl was to undergo a dangerous operation. She was placed upon the table and the surgeon was about to give her ether.

"Before we can make you well, we must put you to sleep."

She spoke up sweetly, and said, "Oh, if you are going to put me to sleep, I must say my prayers first."

So she got on her knees and said the child's prayer, "Now I lay me down to sleep."

Afterwards, the surgeon said, he himself prayed that night for the first time in thirty years. No one can tell what power a little child has, even on those who are older in years.—*Selected.*

* * *

Which Kingdom?

The teacher had been instructing the class about the three kingdoms of the universe, and to make it plain she said, "Everything in our schoolroom belongs to one of the three kingdoms, — our desk to the vegetable kingdom, our slates and pens to the mineral kingdom, and little Alice," she added, looking down at the child nearest her, "belongs to the animal kingdom." Alice looked up quite resentfully, and her eyes filled with tears as she answered, "Teacher, my mamma says that all little children belong to the Kingdom of Heaven." — *Christian Herald.*

* * *

Another Little Maid

Some years ago, a little Jewish girl in Russia learned large portions of the New Testament from a boy who had committed them to memory. One day upon the arrival of her father, after an absence, she ran to meet him, and said, "I do love Jesus; He loved little children." This angered the father, and he forbade her to speak on the subject again. Soon the child was stricken with scarlet fever, and the medical attendant gave no hope for her recovery. A gentile woman was called to nurse the child, as the Jews feared the fever. The woman quoted the verse of a hymn; and the father of little Deborah offered the death-bed prayer of the Jews. Then the child opened her eyes and repeated accurately the story of Jairus' daughter. When she finished her head fell back, and to all appearance she was gone. In an agony of mind the father fell down at the feet of Jesus and besought him, saying, "O Jesus, thou who didst raise up the daughter of Jairus, raise up little Deborah, and I will believe in thee as Israel's Messiah." That cry of agony was heard, and the child rose from her couch of death, and the Jewish family was converted to Christianity.—*The Illustrator.*

* * *

A Pioneer Sunday School's "Find"

About the year 1828 (possibly some years earlier) two young ladies were visiting in Wilkes-Barre, Pennsylvania, and while horseback riding saw little children playing in the road and asked them if they went to Sunday School. They had never heard of it; so the young women hunted up the mothers and asked them if the children could come if a place were found. On their ride they spied a new barn, and asked permission to have the children come there, planning to make seats themselves from new lumber that was there. The following Sunday they found quite a crowd of little boys and girls there, barefooted, bareheaded, and very dirty — all save one, a little boy about six, who was clean and who knew the Lord's Prayer. They followed up this work till they returned to Philadelphia in the fall. That was the first Sunday School in the Wyoming Valley. Thirty-five years later, one of the ladies, who had been married to a merchant named Gildersleeve, was walking in Philadelphia, when a gentleman stepped up to her and said, "Mrs. Gildersleeve, you do not know me, but I am little Johnny Hart of your Sunday School in the barn at Parsons. I am professor in a large school, have had over two thousand boys under my care, and have tried to teach every one of them the same lessons of faith in God and love to Him that you taught me in that barn." — *Sunday School World.*

* * *

A Four-Year-Old's Gospel

Four-year-old Arthur was visiting his father's place of employment and chatting with some of the employees. "Mr. Job, where's your mother?" he asked, meaning the man's wife. "She's dead, Arthur, and in Heaven — I hope," replied the man. Noticing the doubt, the child at once, responded, "Well, Jesus died to save her, so's she *could* go, anyway." Much impressed, the man related the incident to the child's father, adding, "Ah! if you and I had been taught that when we were his age we would be different men today."—*Sunday School Times.*

* * *

"I Never Heard Such Words Before"

A fourteen-year-old boy from a missionary school went to his friend's during what we call the Christmas holidays. He was in the village temple one afternoon when a feeble old man entered and passed from idol to idol, praying and offering incense sticks. The boy's heart was touched by the sight, but it would be impertinent for a boy to attempt to teach an old man. Yet, as he watched him, the tears rolled down his cheeks, and he was finally forced to go to the old man, and say: "Would you mind a boy speaking to you? I am young; you are very old." The man was not offended, and after some further conversation the lad told him the story of God's love. The man's heart was melted as he listened. "Boy," he said, "I am over sixty years of age, and I have never heard such words before." He took the lad home to dinner with him that his wife might hear the wonderful story. And these two people were led to the Saviour before they ever saw or heard of a missionary.—*Selected.*

* * *

Carpets,—or Souls?

Recently, I read of a certain evangelical pastor of a fashionable city church who started a work among slum boys. He succeeded in getting a lot of them into the church parlors for meetings, and taught them the way of salvation. Unfortunately the boys soiled the parlor carpets and upholstery. The pastor was called before the church officers to give an account of the damage done. His defense was something like this: "Brethren, when called to give an account to my Master, what shall I say? — 'Here, Lord, is the church with which thou didst entrust me. It is in good shape. The church parlor carpets and chairs are as good as new, all nice and clean. May He not say to me, 'Where are the *souls* which I sent you to win for me? Where are the boys?"—*Sunday School Times.*

* * *

Soul-Winning

Perhaps the strongest love of a Christian friend is that which impels him to speak to another of his Saviour.

Gypsy Smith says that when he was converted he immediately became anxious for the conversion of his uncle. Among gypsies it was not considered proper for children to address their elders on the subject of duty, and so the boy just prayed, and waited for God to open the way.

One day his uncle noticed a hole in his trousers, and said, "Rodney, how is it that you have worn the knees of your pants so much faster than the rest of them?" "Uncle, I have worn them out praying for you, that God would make you a Christian," and then the tears came, of course. Nothing more was said, but the uncle put his arm around the boy, and drew him close to his breast, and in a little while was bending his knees to the same Saviour.

When we wear our clothes thin in praying for others we shall not find it hard to speak to them if the opportunity occurs.—New Illustrator.

* * *

Boy Patriot Prevents Bridge Demolition

From *Time* (Sept. 25) we quote the following:

> "Near the town of Boom, in Belgium, the Germans fled across the last bridge still standing over the Rupel River. Rear guards clambered under the bridge, set dynamite charges, began to string a detonating wire to a safe distance, a minute or two away. But they had been seen. A patriot slipped out from his hiding-place in the bushes, ducked under the bridge, whittled at the wire with his pocket knife, severed it, scurried away. Moments later British patrols crossed the bridge, heard from Boom's Maquis the story of their hero. He was eleven years old."

The Bible has its child heroes too! It was a child who secured the best possible nurse for Moses when he was in dire need of one. (See Exodus 2).

It was a child who informed a field-marshal how he could be cleansed of his leprosy. (See II Kings 5).

It was a child the Lord placed in the midst of His disciples when He gave His exhortation on humility. (See Mark 9).

It was children whom the Lord called to Him and said: "Of such is the kingdom of God." (See Luke 18).

It was a child who brought the five barley loaves and two small fishes which the Lord used to feed the hungry multitude. (See John 6).

It was a child that mother and grandmother taught the Holy Scriptures which made him wise unto salvation through faith in Jesus Christ. (See II Timothy 1 and 3).

Never despise, slight nor underestimate a little child.—*Moody Monthly.*

* * *

Character by Example

"How can I bring up my son in the way he should go?" asked an anxious father.

"By going that way yourself," was the reply. Words are easily forgotten but the example of a good life is never forgotten. It behooves parents to keep their tempers under control and let love's winsome ways and wooing words adorn their lives.

There is no more effective way of making children dislike their homes and break home ties and leave home than the habit of faultfinding, wrangling, and ill-tempered argument on the part of the parents.

Peace, gentleness, love and consideration bind heart to heart, strengthen the ties of affection, and make home both interesting and attractive. Concord is essential to happiness.—*The Religious Telescope.*

* * *

Communism Among Children

The *Morning Star*, which we presume is an American publication, says: "The Communists know the importance of making disciples among the young. So, having made some converts among the teachers, they set to work to grasp the children, establishing infidel Sunday schools and scattering infidel literature. In their leading journal we read, 'The children's movement must be placed in the uppermost rank. They must be organized into clubs, taught revolutionary songs to sing in the streets, and to carry on all sorts of propaganda.' At one school there was a doormat with a figure of Christ upon it on which the children were required to wipe their muddy shoes!"

In contrast to these atheistic labors to destroy faith the people of God should renew their diligence to build up the Church in all its branches, especially in the Sunday School department and other agencies to reach the childhood of the world.—*Selected.*

* * *

How Old Ought I To Be?

"Dear Mother," said a little maid
"Please whisper it to me —
Before I am a Christian,
How old ought I to be?"

"How old ought you to be, dear child
Before you can love me?"
"I always loved you, Mother mine,
Since I was tiny wee."

"I love you now and always will,"
The little daughter said,
And on her mother's shoulder laid
Her golden, curly head.

"How old, my girlie, must you be,
Before you trust my care?"
"Oh, Mother dear, I do, I do —
I trust you everywhere."

"How old ought you to be, my child
To do the things I say?"
The little girl looked up and said
"I can do that today."

"Then you can be a Christian too.
Don't wait till you are grown.
Tell Jesus now you come to Him.
To be His very own."

Then as the little maid knelt down
And said, "Lord, if I may,
I'd like to be a Christian now,"
He answered, *"Yes, today!"*

—*Michigan Bible Club Beacon.*

* * *

A Little Girl's Question

June was a curly headed little girl of five years. She lived in a small Illinois town where her father was a pastor. Her mother frequently sent her to the Post Office for the mail. She was a bright, cheerful child, and a general favorite with the people. One day as she was on one of her trips to the Post office, an old man stopped her and asked "Little girl, where did you get those pretty curls?"

"God gave them to me," she sweetly replied.

After a few more words of conversation she looked up earnestly into the old man's face and asked, "Mister are you saved?"

He was greatly surprised and deeply impressed by this question and sorrowfully answered "No, little girl, I'm not."

"Well," answered June, "You ought to be, for you're getting to be a pretty old man." Then she ran on to fulfill her errand.

Several weeks after this the old man attended an old-fashioned revival meeting and was saved. He testified in the meeting that it was the question that the little girl had asked him, that he could not get out of his mind, and had at last brought him to Jesus.

On the way home that night from the revival, the car in which the old man was riding was struck by a train, and he was hurled into eternity. This was very sad, but how blessed it was that he had been saved just in time, and sudden death was to him sudden glory.—*Selected.*

* * *

No One to Tell About It

How true to life! Children with their parents now living little realize what it will mean to them when they can no longer tell Father and Mother of their triumphs. Somewhere we read of a boy away at school who in midterm was summoned home by the terrible news that both his parents had been killed in an auto accident. After the funeral he returned to school. At commencement, when honors were read, he received one of the most coveted. For a moment his face flushed with pride, then he put his head on his desk and sobbed. He had just remembered that he had no parents to whom to tell the good news. Someone has well said, "Fame is worthless except as an offering of homage to those whom we love."—*Sunday School Times.*

The Teacher's Prayer

My scholars all for Jesus —
This be my earnest prayer,
For they are souls immortal,
Entrusted to my care;
For each the Master careth,
I long so much for each,
Grant, Lord, the Heavenly wisdom
These wayward hearts to reach.

My girls, light-headed, thoughtless,
On trifling things intent,
These cost a priceless ransom,
On these my care be spent,
That each a willing handmaid,
Be brought to own her Lord,
"What e'er He says, to do it,"
Obedient to His Word.

My boys I want for Jesus —
My wayward wandering boys,
So full of life and mischief,
So charmed by earthly joys.
For them the Saviour suffered,
For them His life was given,
Lord, by that holy ransom,
Bring all my boys to Heaven.

Lord, be in every lesson
Bless every faltering word
My trembling lips may utter,
To bring them to the Lord.
So fleeting are the moments
Of opportunity!
O Jesus, Lord and Saviour,
Bring all my class to Thee.

—*Selected.*

* * *

"No Children"

A young army officer's wife with a small child recently tried to find a room in a crowded city near a port of embarkation. She had come quite a distance from her home, to spend the last weeks with her husband, before he was sent overseas. She knew that there was a possibility that this would be the last time she would ever see him, and she felt that she must come at any cost.

But though there were rooms for rent in the community, most of those advertised specified "no children." And wherever she went, it was the same story; no one wanted children in the house, even at the high rent asked for the rooms.

We do not know if the young woman found a room or not. Her husband later wrote a letter to the local newspaper, rebuking the landlords in general for their heartless attitude todward children. He had supposed that he was to fight to keep his country free and safe for his own children, and for the children of others. And he naturally found it difficult to understand how those who were being benefited by his sacrifice could show no kindness toward his own wife and child, whom he had been forced to leave to provide for themselves.

—*Gospel Herald.*

* * *

Better Than Little Gifts

A beautiful incident of his visit to a state convention in Minnesota is related by Mr. Ralph Wells. After one of the sessions a little girl stepped forward and presented him a small bouquet of ordinary flowers, doubtless the only one she could well procure at that season. He inquired why she gave him the bouquet. "Because I love you," the child answered. "Do you bring any little gift to Jesus?" said Mr. Wells. "Oh," said the little child, "I give myself to Him."—*Biblical Museum.*

* * *

Little Brother Hymn

If every child could see
Our Saviour's shining face,
I think that each one eagerly
Would run to His embrace.

Though black the hand, red, brown or white,
All hearts are just the same;
Each one is precious in God's sight,
Each one He calls by name.

And those who hear in every land
With loyal hearts and true,
Will grasp some little brother's hand
And lead him onward, too.

—*Alfred R. Lincoln.*

Can You Trust Him with the Children?

A man was asked if his wife was well. He replied, "Pretty well, if only it was not for worrying about the children... Oh, yes, she's a Christian! She ain't afraid but what the Lord will take care of her — but seems like she ain't got faith to believe He's to be trusted with the children."—*Sunday School Times.*

* * *

Never Too Busy for a Child

St. Francis of Assisi was once very much occupied with some important work, and he gave orders to his attendants that he must on no account be disturbed. If anyone came desiring to see him, that one must be sent away. But after giving these strict orders, he paused and said, "But if a child should come —." That is what our Father in Heaven says. Perhaps, so busy in His universe is He, when men come as philosophers or theologians and knock at the door, they are not admitted, but if a child should come — which means, if any come in the child spirit of loving trust — the door is opened instantly. If a child should come — the Father is never too busy.—*Sunday at Home.*

* * *

The Point

It is a well-known fact that children are only too quick to see the application of what is being told them. Some years ago a well-known Scottish preacher was addressing a large gathering of boys in Glasgow, and after telling them an interesting story, he said, "Now boys the moral of this is," when a young ragamuffin cried out, "Never mind the moral, sir, gi-e us another story!"—*W. H. Griffith Thomas.*

* * *

"Two-and-a-Half Conversions"

D. L. Moody is said to have once returned from a meeting with a report of "two-and-a-half conversions."

"Two adults and a child, I suppose?" queried his host.

"No, two children and an adult," said Mr. Moody. "The children gave their whole lives. The adult had only half of his left to give."—*Selected.*

A lesson from the Chinese: There are about 3,000 Chinese boys and girls in a certain area of New York city. During the past eight years there have been among them only two cases of Juvenile delinquency. A recent legislature and court investigation has discovered that Chinese percentage of delinquency is the lowest of any racial or sectional group, the ratio being almost negligible. Chinese teachers were questioned by the investigators concerning the reason for this remarkable showing. What they learned should be broadcast throughout America. It was a precept of Confucius: "The misconduct of the child is the fault of the parent."—*Selected.*

* * *

The Soul of a Child

The soul of a child is the loveliest flower
That grows in the Garden of God.
Its climb is from weakness to knowledge and power,
To the sky from the clay and the clod.

"To beauty and sweetness it grows under care,
Neglected, 'tis ragged and wild.
'Tis a plant that is tender but wondrously rare,
The sweet, wistful soul of a child.

"Be tender, O gardner, and give it its share
Of moisture, of warmth and of light,
And let it not lack for thy painstaking care
To protect it from frost and from blight.

"A glad day will come when its bloom shall unfold,
It will seem that an angel has smiled.
Reflecting its beauty and sweetness untold
In the sensitive heart of a child."
—*Selected.*

* * *

A Child's Mission

In another land lived a skilled engineer, able to command a fine salary, but morally a waster. Christians tried to help him but failed miserably. He went down and out in his own profession and

became a street car conductor. One day a woman and her little girl got on the car. While he was taking the fare the little child looked up into his face and innocently asked, "Do you love Jesus?" Two weeks later the man found out where they lived and went to see the child. With a heavy heart the mother told the street car conductor that the child had passed away a few days after she spoke to him. The man replied most sympathetically to the mother saying that the child's mission was done, for she had led him into the kingdom.
—Courtesy Moody Monthly.

* * *

His Father's Hindrance Also

A little boy, whose father was a newspaper printer, was preparing his Sunday school lesson, and came across these words, "He sought to see Jesus . . . and could not for the press." "Oh, Dad," said the little lad, "is that why you can't love Jesus, — because you are in the press?" The child's words impressed the father, and, like Zacchaeus, he ran on and followed Jesus; and better still, he found the presence of Christ a reality even in the pressroom.—*Christian Herald.*

* * *

My Opportunity

My opportunity! Dear Lord, I do not ask
That Thou shouldst give me some high work of Thine,
Some noble calling, or some wondrous task,—
Give me a little hand to hold in mine.

I do not ask that I should ever stand
Among the wise, the worthy, or the great;
I only ask that, softly, hand in hand,
A child and I may enter at Thy gate.

Give me a little child to point the way
Over the strange, sweet path that leads to Thee;
Give me a little voice to teach to pray;
Give me two shining eyes Thy face to see.

The only crown I ask, dear Lord, to wear,
Is this — that I may teach a little child
How beautiful, oh, how divinely fair
Is Thy dear face, so loving, sweet and mild!

I do not need to ask for more than this.
My opportunity! 'Tis standing at my door;
What sorrow if this blessing I should miss!
A little child! Why should I ask for more?

Who knows what future stretches out along
Those strange, far years? Dear Father, if I knew!
Who knows what sorrow, or who knows what song,
Who knows what work those little hands may do?

Who knows what word of mine may shape a thought
To turn his heart to that far heaven above?
Who knows what lesson that I may have taught,
Will turn his heart to the dear God of love?

Thou knowest, oh, Thou knowest! Unto Thee
All things are plain. Help me, Lord Christ I pray,
That I may ever helpful be,
To lead a little child along the way.

My opportunity? I need not seek it far,
It standeth at the door, and waiteth me;
Dear Lord, two trusting hands uplifted are —
A little child, my opportunity!
—Marian B. Craig.

* * *

On His Father's Ground

Colonel Fred N. Dow tells the following story to illustrate how the son of a father devoted to a great principle is likely to follow in his father's steps. Colonel Dow once visited friends at Quebec, and, while seeing the sights of the city and its surroundings, he took a public carriage to visit the Falls of Montmorency. At a halfway house on the road the driver pulled up his horse and remarked, "The carriage always stops here." "For what purpose?" asked the Colonel. "For the passengers to treat," was the reply. "But none of us drink, and we don't intend to treat." The driver had dismounted, and was waiting by the roadside. Drawing himself up to his full height, he said impressively: "I have driven this carriage now for more than thirty years, and this happened but once before. Some time ago I had for a fare a crank from Portland, Maine, by the name of Neal Dow, who said he wouldn't drink; and, what was more to the point, he said he wouldn't pay for anybody else to drink." The son found himself occupying the same ground as that on which his father had stood.—*New Century Leader.*

* * *

Contrast

Children, obey your parents in the Lord: for this is right (Eph. 6:1).

THE TWO PRAYERS

Last night my little boy confessed to me
Some childish wrong;
And kneeling at my knee
He prayed with tears:
"Dear God, make me a man
Like Daddy — wise and strong;
I know You can."

Then while he slept
I knelt beside his bed,
Confessed my sins,
And prayed with low-bowed head,
"O God, make me a child
Like my child here —
Pure, guileless,
Trusting Thee with faith sincere."

—*Sunday School Times*

* * *

The Chap at Home

To feel his little hand in mine,
So clinging and so warm,
To know he thinks me strong enough
To keep him safe from harm:
To see his simple faith in all
That I can say or do;
It sort o' shames a fellow,
But it makes him better, too;
And I'm trying hard to be the man
He fancies me to be,
Because I have this chap at home
Who thinks the world o' me.
I would not disappoint his trust
For anything on earth,
Nor let him know how little I
Just naturally am worth.
But after all, it's easier
That brighter road to climb,
With the little hands behind me
To push me all the time.
And I reckon I'm a better man
Than what I used to be
Because I have this chap at home
Who thinks the world of me.

—*Selected.*

* * *

World Friendship for Boys and Girls

In hearts too young for enmity lies the way to make men free;
When children's friendships are world wide
New ages will be glorified.
Let child love child, and strife will cease,
Disarm the hearts, for that is peace.

—*Ethel Blair Jordan.*

* * *

Beginning Early

Ere your *child* has reached the seven
Have him taught the way to Heaven;
Better still, if he would thrive,
He should know before he's five;
Best of all, if at your knee,
He knows the way before he's three.

—*Women's Missionary Magazine.*

* * *

Where Did They Come From?

"Where did all these learned men come from?" asked Queen Victoria of John Bright at a dinner table. She had found him very difficult to talk to, and the conversation had been lagging. "From babies," he replied. At this the Queen burst into laughter. The ice was broken, and from that moment there was no loss for words. It is from the same source that the future members of our church must come, and, therefore, the necessity for beginning to train the young at the earliest possible moment.—*Albert G. Mackinnon.*

Led By a Child

In a prayer meeting a man rose and said, "I have been thoughtless and impenitent till within a short time. I will tell you how it came about that I am now a disciple of Jesus.

"One Sunday morning, I was in my room. My wife had gone out and no one was with me but little Mabel. At length she came up to the sofa and began talking to me in her child-like way. 'Uncle,' she said, 'tell me something of Jesus. Mamma always does Sunday nights.'

"I was struck with the question, but evaded it. But the little one would not be put off. Again and again she came back with the same request, 'Uncle, *tell me something about Jesus.*' Finding I did not comply, she said at last, opening wide her blue eyes, 'Why, you do know about Jesus, don't you?'

"That question awakened thoughts and feelings I never had before. I could not sleep that night; the dear child's wondering words, 'You know about Jesus, don't you?' haunted me through the long, silent hours. I felt I did *not* know about Jesus, had not *wished* to know. A sense of my ignorance and guilt weighed heavily upon my soul. I was distressed for days. I read my Bible with an enquiring, anxious heart, till *at length I found the blessed Saviour* and could say in humility and faith, 'Now I know about Jesus.' "

It is possible to know about Jesus, and yet not to know Him as one's personal Saviour and Lord. It is personal faith in Him and in His atoning death and resurrection that saves. Have you this personal faith?—*Scattered Seed.*

* * *

What Rich Dividends!

A missionary lady was telling the story of her work in China. When she finished, a little girl came forward and gave her twelve pennies. "Please," she said, "I have been saving these pennies and now I want them to be missionaries to China." How happy the missionary was to receive the offering from its wholehearted giver! Months went by and finally a letter came for the little girl which read, "With your twelve pennies I bought twelve penny Gospels of John. I gave one to each of my class of Chinese girls. They read the wonderful story in their own little books, and today all twelve gave their hearts to Christ. What a splendid investment you have made in Kingdom stock!"—*The Secret Place.*

* * *

Prayer for the Children

Father, our children keep!
We know not what is coming on the earth;
Beneath the shadow of Thy heavenly wing,
O keep them, keep them, Thou who gav'st them birth.

Father, draw nearer us!
Draw firmer round us Thy protecting arm;
Oh, clasp our children closer to Thy side,
Uninjured in the day of earth's alarm.

Them in Thy chambers hide!
Oh, hide them and preserve them calm and safe,
When sin abounds and error flows abroad,
And Satan tempts, and human passions chafe.

Oh, keep them undefiled!
Unspotted from a tempting world of sin;
That, clothed in white, through the bright city gates,
They may with us in triumph enter in.

—*Horatius Bonar, D.D.*

* * *

If We Were Really Wise

I saw tomorrow marching by
On little children's feet;
Within their forms and faces read
Her prophecy complete.

I saw tomorrow look at me
From little children's eyes,
And thought how carefully we'd teach
If we were really wise.

—*Selected.*

In the Children's Ward

One Sunday evening the head nurse of a children's hospital was reading Bible stories and showing pictures to the little ones. Then they began to sing hymns, and the children asked for the "little friend hymn." The nurse played it over, and one of the newly arrived girl invalids said, "Oh, Nurse, may I sing that, please? We learned it at our Sunday school." The nurse gave her consent. Some of the children were sitting up in bed, the tiny soloist among the number, and those who were too weak or too ill tc sit up were told to hold up their hands when the chorus was reached. The evening was very quiet, and the sweet, piping voice of the little singer sounded out clearly, "I am Jesus' little friend," until at the chorus every child in the ward held up a hand at the words, "Jesus' friend, little friend, on His mercy I depend." The nurse says: "As I looked down the whole length of the ward, and saw all the thin, white hands held up, and thought what they meant, it was almost too much for me. The ward became a holy temple, as I thought I could see our Lord going from child to child, taking each by the hand, saying, 'My little friend.' "—*Christian Herald.*

CHOOSING

He Wanted to Help Me, But I Would Not Let Him

In one of the penitentiaries of the United States, there is a man serving a sentence for a crime. This man had a good mother who not only prayed for him, but did everything she could to get him to accept Christ as his Saviour. Many of his friends had gone to see him, including ministers of the Gospel, pleading with him to turn from his evil way, but his heart was hardened against all the pleadings of his friends. At last, his mother went to the Governor of the State, asking him if he could not pardon her son. So the Governor, dressed in a ministerial garb, went to this man's cell and spent a long time with him, pleading with him to turn from his evil way, accept Christ as his Saviour and start a life of freedom from sin, even though not free from the law. Not knowing that he was talking to the Governor of the State, he did as he had done before. He turned a deaf ear to all the pleadings of the Governor. Being asked by the warden if he knew who he had been talking to, he said, "No." When he was told that he had been talking to the Governor, he simply said, "*He wanted to help me, but I would not let him.*" —*Evangel Herald.*

When We Take the Back Seat

"Two men looked through prison bars; one saw mud, the other saw stars!" This is well exemplified in the history of Lot and Abram. Lot looked around with an eye to earthly advantage, and he got it, but — ! His was a downward look. What a contrast in verse 14 with its wonderful "after that"! Now God steps in, — God who had been quietly watching those two men, waiting to see what they would do; who saw the generous hearted Abram giving up his rights, letting Lot choose the best for himself. But we never lose by taking back seats! —*Courtesy Moody Monthly.*

* * *

Then came a period in the pastorate, and once more I propose to indulge in a personal reminiscence of a sacred nature. Soon after I had settled as a minister of the Church, in Stone, and success as to increasing congregations was evident, I went home one Sunday night and had to face a challenging question. I heard no articulate voice, but the question came with clarity, "*What are you going to be, a great preacher or My messenger?*" I fought the question on the assumption that I might be both. At last, however, I decided that above everything else, I desired to be the messenger of God. I declare, without hesitation, that from that day in 1900 until now I have cared nothing about reputation as a preacher. I have cared greatly about being His messenger.—*The Gospel Herald.*

* * *

Second Best

The Lord spoke to my heart one day
Saying, "Child, you need to pray—
There's special work for you to do,
Fields are white and laborers are few."

At first I did not heed the call;
The work, to me, looked very small.
So God gave another man my work
And blessed him in the task I shirked.

I saw the thing that God had done,
The precious souls another won;
So penitent I went to Him
And pled forgiveness of my sin.

He hearkened to my pleading voice,
But gave to me His second choice;
And now His will I do obey,
But oft remember yesterday.

—E. L. Burges.

* * *

His Little Girl's Startling Question

A little girl asked her father, "Do you ever pray?" He asked her, "Is it your mother or your aunt who has put you up to this?" "No, Father," said the child, "the preacher said that all good men pray." He answered, "Well, you and your mother and your aunt can go your way, and I will go mine." "Father," said the little thing with simplicity, "which way are you going?" It flashed upon him that he had chosen the way of death. He began to pray for mercy. Which way are you going?—*Light and Life Evangel.*

* * *

Do It Now

It is said if you take one of a migratory flock of birds out of the line which the God-given instinct has formed and is guiding to its distant home, and place it behind iron bars, it will beat its wings against the cage in its frantic efforts to rise and go on its journey. But let the season pass in which birds migrate, then open the cage; your bird will not go now. You may take it into your hand and toss it high into the air; it will be of no use; the instinct for motion has passed; the bird returns heavily to the same spot. So decisions for Christ may be delayed until there is no desire to be His.—*The Elim Evangel.*

* * *

A Noble Choice

Julitta, a noble lady in the third century, known to be a Christian, was despoiled of her property by one of the Roman emperor's officers. In seeking redress before the judges, her right was denied, and even protection and life, unless she would worship idols and renounce her Christian faith. Hearing the decision of the judge, she said, "Farewell, life; welcome, death: farewell, riches; welcome, poverty. All that I have, were it a thousand times more, I would rather lose than speak one wicked and blasphemous word against God my Creator. I yield thee most hearty thanks, O my God, for this gift of Thy free grace, that I can contemn and despise this frail and transitory world, esteeming Christian profession above all treasures."

Her friends urged her to change her mind, but in vain. She was condemned and led to execution. Addressing the spectators from the place of suffering, among other things, she said, "O sisters, labor after true piety and godliness. Be weary, my sisters, of a life led in darkness, and honor Christ, my God, my Redeemer, my Comforter, who is the true Light of the world. Persuade yourselves—or, rather may the Spirit of the living God persuade you—that there is a world to come, wherein the worshipers and servants of the most high God shall be crowned eternally."—*Glad Tidings.*

* * *

He came to the crossroads all alone,
With the sunrise in his face;
He had no fear of the path unknown—
He was set for an ambitious race.

The road stretched east, and the road stretched west:
The "Signboard" showed which way was the best;

But the boy turned wrong and went on
down,
And lost the race and the victor's crown,
And fell at last into an ugly snare—
By choosing the wrong at the crossroads
there.

Another boy on another day,
At the selfsame crossroads stood:
He paused a moment to choose the way
Which would lead to the greater good.

The road stretched east, and the road
stretched west,
But the "Signboard" showed him which
way was best.
And the boy turned right and went on
and on;
He won the race and the victor's crown.
And came at last to the Mansions fair—
For choosing *right* at the crossroads
there. —*Selected.*

* * *

If God Gave Me the Choice?

May God bring us all to the mind of an old writer who said, "If God gave me the choice, I should ask Him to choose for me." Apart from all personal desires or feelings, we surely agree that God's will and God's glory must be put before man's wants.—*Sunday School Times.*

* * *

Signing Away His Interest

It was in a country store one evening. A number of young men were sitting together about the stove, telling what they didn't believe and what they were not afraid to do. Finally the leader of the group remarked that, so far as he was concerned, he would be willing any time to sign away his interest in Christ for a five-dollar bill.

"What did I understand you to say?" asked an old farmer, who happened to be in the store, and who had overheard the remark.

"I said that for five dollars I would sign away all my interest in Christ, and so I will."

The old farmer, who had learned to know the human heart pretty well, drew out his leather wallet, took therefrom a five-dollar bill, and put it in the storekeeper's hand. Then calling for ink and paper, he said: "My young friend, if you will just step to the desk now and write as I direct you, the money is yours."

The young man took the pen and began:

"In the presence of these witnesses, I A—— B——, for the sum of five dollars, received, do now, once for all and forever, sign away all my interest—"

Then he dropped the pen and with a forced smile said: "I take it back. I was only fooling."

That young man did not dare to sign that paper. Why? He had an accusing conscience. He knew that there was a God. He believed in religion. He meant to be a Christian some time.

And so do others. Notwithstanding their apparent indifference, their trifling conduct, their boasting speech, they would not today for ten thousand dollars sign away, if such a thing were possible, their interest in Jesus Christ.—Congregationalist.

* * *

Letting Them Know Which Side

When General Lee was coming up the Chambersburg Road to Gettysburg, "Gettysburg Hannah" (as she was called) grabbed her poker and started down the road to meet the enemy. Nothing happened. Lee came right on, and the decisive battle was fought. After the war was over, they were having a quilting party in one of the Gettysburg homes and Hannah was there. The other women were having some fun with Hannah. Said Mrs. Bomberger, "Hannah, what in the world did you expect to do with that old poker against that great Southern army?" "Vell," said Hannah in her rich Pennsylvania Dutch (if I can spell it right), "I no expect to do nodings yet a ready, but I *left 'em know what side I vas on, ain't it!"—Sunday School Times.*

* * *

Life's Supreme Moment

A whole destiny depends upon a single choice. In the Alpine mountains of Switzerland there is a spot where you may throw a chip in one direction and it will roll on by way of the Danube to the Black Sea. Throw it in another direction and it will travel down the Rhine to the North Sea. Cast it in yet another direction and it will go by way of the Rhone into the Mediterranean. Although these three seas are so far apart, and the three chips thrown from the same point have such widely separated destinations, the ultimate destiny of each chip is determined, in the first instance, by the direction in which it is cast.

It is the same with life. One day Peter, James and John decided to throw in their lot on the side of Jesus. A young society star, too, heard the call of Christ. And with what diverse consequences! The first three found life more abundant. The other is lost to history. —T. Howard Crago.

* * *

Decision, The Open Door to Power

George Bowen, missionary to Bombay, is famed for his life of self-sacrificing love for Christ. For many years he was a skeptic. Utterly wearied with the contention of his thoughts, which like phosphoresence in the wood fascinated him, but gave no light for his path, he once exclaimed: "O God—if there is a God who notices the desires of men—I only wish that Thou wouldst make known to me Thy holy will. I will do it at any cost." From that moment his skepticism ceased.

It was the illuminating rays of God's sunrise touching the highest peak of his soul, his volition, and soon filled all the landscape of his being with light.—James M. Ludlow.

* * *

Christ's Choice for Me

Catherine S. Mozley

"So are My ways higher than your ways, and My thoughts than your thoughts" (Isaiah 55:9).

I would have chosen a sunlit path,
All strewn with roses fair,
With never a cloud to darken my way,
Nor a shade of anxious care.
But He chose for me a better way—
Not sunshine or roses sweet,
But clouds o'erhead and thorns below,
That cut and hurt my feet.
I have deep joys of another kind,
My Rose of Sharon is He:
And as for sunshine—His lovely face
Is perfect sunshine to me.

'Tis far, far better to let Him choose
The way that we should take.
If only we thus leave our life with Him,
He will guide us without mistake.
We in our blindness, would never choose
A pathway dark and rough,
And so we should never find in Him
"The God who is enough."
In disappointment, trouble, and pain,
We turn to the changeless One,
And prove how faithful, loving, and wise
Is God's beloved Son.
—*The Olive Branch.*

* * *

The Stone Inside

I was talking to a little group of boys and girls in a Sunday school in San Francisco. "How sad to know, each time you say 'No' to the Lord Jesus, your heart gets a little harder, and if you keep on saying 'No,' the heart gets harder and harder until by-and-by God calls it a heart of stone, and you persist in spurning His grace, and you will therefore die in your sins." So I was pleading with those boys and girls to give their hearts to Jesus in their early days. There was one dear little tot there, only five years old. Her mother brought her to Sunday school and then took her home. The little one was thinking of her own dear father who never went to hear the Word of God. When she got to the house she darted into her father's arms, and said, "Daddy, Daddy, feel your heart! Is it getting like stone?" He said, "What are you talking about?" She said, "Well, the man at Sunday school said if you say 'No' to Jesus you are going to get a stone inside. Oh, Daddy, I hope you haven't, for if you have, you can't be saved." The father said angrily to the mother, "What have they been telling this child, anyway?" Then the mother explained a little more fully, and when he saw the tears in his wife's eyes and felt the arms of his little girl about his neck, and heard her saying, "Oh, Daddy, don't go on saying 'No' to Jesus," he looked up and said, "Well, I think I had better settle this thing, and he got down on his knees and yielded his life to Christ. —*"Addresses on the Gospel of John,"* by H. A. Ironside.

* * *

No Time For Delay

An earnest preacher received a great surprise as he stood before his audience engaged in the delivery of a glowing message, as related by Richard Weaver. "On one occasion my son was speaking on a platform about those olden time Jews demanding that Barabbas should be released to them and Christ crucified. Standing forth he declaimed: 'Christ or Barabbas! Christ or Barabbas! Choose ye this day whom ye will have!' He did not expect an immediate response, but much to his surprise a young man in the center of the hall jumped up and enthusiatically cried out: 'Christ for me! Christ for me!' That was settling the question of salvation for eternity at once. The candidate saw, by the light and teaching of the Word and the Spirit, that there was no time for delay, and nothing to be gained by procrastination. Are there not all too many unsaved people around us with whom it would be well for them to decide just now, with all the earnestness that that young man did: *'Christ for me! Christ for me!'"—The Illustrator.*

* * *

By choosing the easy way for ourselves, we make the way harder for others.—*Selected.*

* * *

Hollywood or Christ?

A young woman had been working in one of the studios of Hollywood for several years, and she had loved the life. But one night she wandered into an evangelistic service and was brought face to face with Christ. She accepted the marvelous gift of salvation and found a new happiness and joy in living. The Lord led her to enroll in a Bible school to train for service, but Satan was not so easily defeated. He persuaded her to keep her job at the studio; he told her it would be ridiculous to leave a good job. She believed the sensible thing to do was to attend Bible school during the day and work in the studio at night. This continued for a year and a half. She had no victory in her life and she lost her vision of Christ, so finally decided to leave school. After that she spent a most miserable year living in the world. The Holy Spirit would not give her peace, so in desperation she prayed, "Lord, show me if it is Thy will that I go into definite Christian service."

She was crossing a street one day, when suddenly she heard the screeching of brakes and saw a car swerving toward her. Terrified and unable to move, she closed her eyes and waited, but nothing happened. The car had stopped just in time, the bumper touching her skirt. After recovering from the shock, she walked on, but the experience had told her one thing — God had saved her life for His service. She realized then that she must go all the way with Christ, so she resigned her job and waited upon the Lord for guidance. He did not fail, for she enrolled in the Moody Bible Institute, her life wholly yielded to Him.—*Student News Service.*

* * *

Choose Thou for Me

I dare not choose my lot;
I would not if I might;
Choose Thou for me, my God,
So shall I walk aright.

The kingdom that I seek
Is thine; so let the way
That leads to it be thine,
Else surely I might stray.

Take Thou my cup, and it
With joy or sorrow fill;
As best to Thee may seem,
Choose Thou my good and ill.

Choose Thou for me my friends,
My sickness or my health;
Choose Thou my cares for me,
My poverty or wealth.

Not mine — not mine the choice,
In things or great or small;
Be Thou my Guide, my Strength,
My Wisdom and my All!

—Horatius Bonar.

The Great Divide

Near Stephen, B.C., about 500 miles east of Vancouver and 950 miles west of Winnipeg, well over 5,000 feet above sea level, there is a scene well known to travelers, called the Great Divide.

Here will be seen a stream running north which just as it arrives within a few yards of the C.P.R. main line parts into two streams; one running eastward, eventually finding its way into the Atlantic Ocean; the other flowing off westward, at last draining into the Pacific.

This wonderful sight, where the water of the stream comes to a point where it must go one way or another, and after passing which its destination is definitely and unchangeably settled, might remind one of the dividing line in every man and woman's life when he or she is confronted with two eternal realities — when God's Holy Spirit pleads with that person to accept pardon, cleansing from sin, and peace; and when the enemy of souls is trying at the same time to keep that sinner from deciding for the Lord Jesus Christ.

The Spirit in love and mercy strives oftentimes with a sinner, but God has said in Genesis 6:3 "My Spirit shall not always strive with man." Today God wants to save you, but take heed, dear friend, lest you pass the fatal point, thus despising God's offer of salvation to you. How long, God asks, halt ye between two opinions?

There is a time, we know not when —
A place, we know not where —
That seals the destiny of men
For glory or despair.

There is a line, by us unseen,
Which crosses every path,
The hidden boundary between
God's mercy and His wrath.

—*Faithful Words.*

* * *

Poor Taste in Clothes

In the spring of 1924, I was assisting Pastor N.E. Norwood in a revival meeting at Fort Ogden, Florida. Driving along the highway, we passed a gang of convicts working the road. They were clothed in stripes; and I remarked to Pastor Norwood: "I don't like their clothes. If I had had the selection, I should have selected a different suit." "Why," he answered, "they don't select their suits, do they?" "Oh, yes!" I answered. "Well," he said, "I didn't know that. I thought the state selected their suits for them." "No," I replied, "every man selects his own suit. Those fellows knew the penalty of violating the law before they committed the acts. They made their choice; they selected their suits. And they are wearing the suits of their own selection." What suit have you selected — the black stripe suit of shame and dishonor, or the "white robe of righteousness?"—"*Wings.*"

* * *

The Higher and the Lower Paths

John Wesley

From long experience and observation, I am inclined to think that whoever finds redemption in the Blood of Jesus — whoever is justified — has the choice of walking in the higher or the lower path. I believe the Holy Spirit at that time sets before him "the more excellent way," and incites him to walk therein — to choose the narrowest path in the narrow way — to aspire after the heights and depths of holiness — after the entire image of God. But if he does not accept this offer, he insensibly declines into the lower order of Christians; he still goes on in what may be called a good way, serving God in his degree, and finds mercy in the close of life through the Blood of the Covenant.

I have frequently observed that there are two very different ranks of Christians, both of whom may be in the favor of God — a higher and a lower rank. The latter avoid all known sin, do much good, use all the means of grace, but have little of the life of God in their souls, and are much conformed to the world. The former make the Bible their whole rule, and their sole aim is the will and image of God. This they steadily and uniformly pursue, through honor and dishonor, denying themselves, and taking up their cross daily; considering one point only, "How may I attain most of the mind that was in Christ, and how may I please Him most?"—*Living Waters.*

But One Throne

When Raphael's great picture, the "Sistine Madonna," was first brought to Dresden it was displayed in the castle in the presence of the king. It was brought into the throne room, but the most favorable spot in the room was occupied by the throne itself. The king, taking in the situation, pushed the throne aside, saying, "Make room for the immortal Raphael."

There is but one throne in the human heart, and the most important question for any of us in life is to determine who is to occupy that throne. Will it be Christ or self? It cannot be both. It will not be easy to say "no" to self, to put one's foot on self, to keep self in the proper place. If we suppose it to be easy, it is because we have never seriously made the effort. To offer to God a divided allegiance means loss of spiritual power and fruitfulness in the Christian life.—*Gospel Herald.*

* * *

Bushnell's Choice

Long years ago there was a popular young professor in Yale College. There was a revival being held in the city in which the college was located. This young professor was not exactly an infidel, nor was he a Christian. He was, however, being disturbed in mind and heart by certain religious questions. He knew he was exerting a tremendous influence over his students, and that they would not be disposed to become Christians so long as he was half an infidel. What should he do, for he was grieved to see he was standing in the way of his students. He paced his room for hours with this problem on his mind. With even more concern for them than for himself he decided what to do and he expressed it in these words: "I throw myself over the line between right and wrong toward the right, and hereafter consecrate myself irrevocably, utterly, affectionately to the following of the best religious light I possess." That professor was Horace Bushnell who became one of our foremost religious thinkers, preachers, and writers.—*Gospel Herald.*

Decide You Must

When Gustavus Adolphus, king of Sweden, went over to Germany to help the Protestant princes in the cause of the Reformation, he was sorely tried by their lack of decision and lukewarmness. On meeting the ambassador of the Elector of Brandenburg, he uttered these stirring and memorable words:

"This I say unto you plainly beforehand, I will hear and know nothing of neutrality. His Highness must be friend or foe. When I come to his border he must declare himself hot or cold. The battle is between God and the devil. Will his Highness hold with God? let him stand at my side. Will he prefer to hold with the devil? then he must fight against me. *No third position will be granted him.*"—*Evangel Herald.*

* * *

Why He Surrendered

The Rev. T. E. Ruth of Sydney, Australia, relates that when just in his teens he went to a church where the curate preached on the text, "Choose you this day whom ye will serve." The sermon made him thoroughly disgusted with himself, and, annoyed with the curate, he went to another church. To his surprise, the same curate ascended the pulpit and preached the same sermon. At night he went to a third place of worship, where the preacher proved to be the same curate, and his text was, "Choose ye this day whom ye will serve." "It was too much for me," said Mr. Ruth. "That night I surrendered to the love that had sought me in three places." —*The Christian Herald.*

* * *

Destiny and God

On the summit of a hill in one of the western states of America, there is a courthouse so situated that the raindrops falling on one side of its roof descend into Lake Erie and thence, through the St. Lawrence, into the Atlantic Ocean. The drops on the other side trickle down from rivulet to river until they reach the Ohio and the Mississippi Rivers, and enter the ocean by the Gulf of Mexico. A faint breath of wind determines the destination of these raindrops for three thousand miles.

So God uses a single act to determine sometimes a human destiny for all time and for eternity.—S. S. World.

* * *

I have made my choice forever,
I will walk with Christ my Lord.
Nought from Him my soul shall sever
While I'm trusting in His Word;
I the lonely way have taken,
Rough and toilsome though it be,
And although despised, forsaken,
Jesus, I'll go through with Thee.

* * *

Join the Minority

A gentleman said to J. B. Gough as if it were a discouragement: "You are in a minority." Praying men are in a minority. Bible loving men are in a minority. Men who honor God's house and God's day are in a minority. "Follow not a multitude to do evil." Join the minority. Stand up and stand out for Jesus. Don't muddle to destruction with the majority. The Master says: "Broad is the way, that leadeth to destruction, and many there be which go in thereat."

The majority has had its way and brought mess, muddle and war. The majority has failed us. Join the minority. Come to the house of God. Take down your Bible and read it again. Keep the Lord's Day holy. Commence to pray or to pray again. Give your life and heart to Jesus Christ. Take your part in turning the nation from being a people of God-forgetters to a reverent and Godly nation. Begin now — tomorrow will be too late.—*The P. H. Advocate.*

* * *

A Minister and a Life-Termer

While preaching one day to the convicts in the penitentiary of a certain state, a minister saw in the audience a man whose face seemed familiar. At the close of the sermon he went to the convict's cell and the following conversation is reported to have ensued: "I remember you very well, sir," said the prisoner. "We were boys in the same neighborhood; we went to the same school; sat beside each other on the same bench, and then my prospects were as bright as yours. But, at the age of fourteen, you made choice of the service of God and became a Christian. I refused to come to Christ, but made choice of the world and sin. And now you are a happy and honored minister of the gospel, while I am a wretched outcast. I have served ten years in this penitentiary, and am to be a prisoner here for life."—*Florida Baptist Witness.*

CHRISTIAN EXAMPLE—INFLUENCE

(See also: Influence, 371)

We're the Only Bible

Said Robert E. Speer: "After thirty years of leadership in Christian work, it is my conclusion and conviction that the greatest missionary problem is just the failure of Christian people to live up to their profession."

God help us as sharers of the nature of God to so live that others may crave to claim His precious promises for themselves.—*The Gospel Herald.*

* * *

Practice What You Preach

It's easier to preach than to practice,
It's easier to say than to do;
Most sermons are heard by the many
But taken to heart by the few.
It's easier to cheer than to battle,
It's easier to stay than to go;
To drift you but lay down the oars
To go up the stream you must row.
—Ben L. Byer.

* * *

Stumblingblocks

He could not see Jesus for the press, we are told. The crowd was in the way. They were between him and Jesus and he was not tall enough to see over them. Their bodies obstructed his view and prevented him from seeing Jesus. I wonder if the same thing is not true today, if some who claim to know Christ are not in the way of others' seeing

Him? Our bodies may not keep anybody from seeing Jesus, but our lives can and sometimes do. People cannot see Jesus because our lives are in the way. When you hear a person of the world say, "If that is Christianity, I don't want it," some professed Christian's life has come between that person and the Saviour. Is your life and mine a stumblingblock that keeps someone else from Christ? *A blind man went about with a lantern on his arm. Someone asked him why he carried the lantern inasmuch as he was blind. He replied, "To keep other people from stumbling over me."* That is something to think about.—*The Gospel Herald.*

* * *

"On and Off"

Gypsy Smith once asked a man in an after meeting, "Are you a Christian?" "Yes." "How long have you been a Christian?" "Twenty-eight years, on and off." "More *off* than *on*, I guess," replied Gypsy Smith. I would rather be "out and out" than "on and off."

The "out and out" Christians are the only ones whose lives adorn the doctrine of Christ.—*The Gospel Herald.*

* * *

God Revealed in Human Flesh Today

"I have never seen Jesus, but I have seen Dr. Shepard," was the remark of a poor Armenian, who had seen the Christlike service of that great medical missionary to the Near East.

This utterance expresses one great Christian truth: Christ continues to reveal God through the lives of His followers.

A missionary in China once told of Jesus for the first time to a group of people in an inland town. When he had finished someone said:

"Oh, yes, we knew Him; He used to live here."

Somewhat surprised, the missionary said, "No, He lived centuries ago in another land."

The man still insisted that he had seen Jesus, saying, "Not so, He lived in this village, and we knew Him." Whereupon the crowd conducted the missionary to the village cemetery and showed him the grave of a medical missionary who had lived, served, healed and died in that community.

Christ's spirit taketh breath again
Within the lives of holy men.
Each changing age beholds afresh
Its Word of God in human flesh.

—*Missionary Review.*

* * *

Is Such a Life Possible?

A story is told of a minister who had preached a powerful message on the surrendered life; and as he made an appeal to his hearers to make the surrender, a woman sitting near another woman said: "That is excellent preaching, but I wonder if such a life is possible?" The other woman smiled back at her and said: "Well, I know the preacher lives such a life, because I happen to be his wife."

—*The Gospel Herald.*

* * *

"I've Been Watching You"

A group of women were talking together before missionary meeting started. The subject they were deeply concerned over was how they could get their husbands to come to church and really follow the Lord. An elderly woman spoke up—"I don't often tell this," she said, "but I will today because it may encourage you ladies not to give up but to pray and work on for your husbands' salvation."

"For a good many years I went to church alone. My husband was good enough to take me, but he always left me at the front door of the church and then drove home again. Sometimes I felt very concerned because he would never come in, but when I'd tell the Lord all about it He would tell me to keep on trusting and to live the Gospel before him. As I put up my husband's lunch one day I put my Sunday School paper over the top of his lunch knowing that in his lunch hour he'd read it, asking God to help him. Sure enough, at night he asked me where I had gotten that paper from and I told him it was my Sunday School paper. 'Say,' he said, 'that certainly has some good stories in it—put one in every day, will you?' So while I continued to pray and obey God He prepared my husband's heart.

"One day at the close of a Sunday service we were asked to bow our heads in prayer and an invitation was given. When I raised my head there was my husband at the front kneeling. When we got home I said to him, 'Husband, how did you happen to come in church tonight?' 'Well, wife,' he replied, 'I've been watching you for a long time now and I saw you had something that I didn't have. When I heard the singing inside something drew me into the church and I took a back seat. When the minister asked if there were any who would like to give their hearts to Jesus. I decided that I wanted your Saviour, too.'

"You can't imagine how surprised and happy I felt, ladies," she said, "but it was well worth my every effort and prayer. I have often thought what if I had gotten discouraged and given up. My husband's salvation depended on his seeing Jesus in me."

Someone is watching you and me.
Are we living the Gospel
That they might see
The spirit and message of Calvary?
—Margaret Bogart.

* * *

Preaching vs. Practicing

"Johnny, you take those marbles back to Willie Jones," said his mother. "You know I have told you about playing marbles for 'keeps'; you think you won them, but that is wrong; you go right back and give them to the boy from whom you took them."

"Yes, Mama," said Johnny dutifully, "and shall I take back the painted vase you won at Mrs. Jones's bridge party?" Cheeky boy, fresh, and needs spanking! Yes, but Johnny brought out what most of us know; *it is a whole lot easier to preach than it is to practice.*—Charles Forbes Taylor, in *Christ for Me.*

* * *

Orthopraxy

Orthopraxy is living straight. Orthodoxy is thinking straight. The two do not at all times coincide. Some think straight, but do not live straight. Others live straight, but do not think straight. Because these generalizations are true, some emphases declare that it does not matter about one's doctrine if his conduct conforms to the standards of right. But why the emphasis upon one to the neglect of the other? Why not insist upon both at the same time—correct thinking and correct living? Why the folly of substituting the one for the other? John Wesley is reported to have said, "We may be as orthodox as the devil and as wicked."—*Selected.*

* * *

The Power of Example

A great preacher closed his sermon with an earnest and eloquent Gospel appeal. Among the score or more who responded was a woman of wealth and social distinction. She asked permission to speak a few words to the audience.

"I want you to know," she said, "just why I came forward tonight. It was not because of any word spoken by the preacher. I stand here because of the influence of a little woman who sits before me. Her fingers are rough with toil; the hard work of many years has stooped her low; she is just a poor, obscure washerwoman, who has served in my home for many years. I have never known her to be impatient, speak an unkind word, or do a dishonorable deed. I know of countless little acts of unselfish love that adorn her life. Shamefacedly, let me say that I have openly sneered at her faith, and laughed at her fidelity to God. Yet when my little girl was taken away, it was this woman who caused me to look beyond the grave and shed my first tears of hope. The sweet magnetism of her life has led me to Christ. I covet the thing that has made her life so beautiful."

At the request of the minister, the little woman was led forward, her eyes streaming with glad tears, and such a shining face as one seldom sees on this earth.

"Let me introduce you," said he, "to the real preacher of the evening," and the great audience arose in silent, though not tearless, respect.

Oh, ye obscure toilers of the world, ye patient "doers of the Word," think not that no one sees; I say unto you that a great cloud of witnesses will rise up on that great day, and call you blessed! —*Watchword from First Baptist Beacon.*

* * *

What Made Him Understand

One time in Hangchow, Mrs. Paxton was, in the absence of the regular physician of the compound, called on to dress the arm of a native policeman, who, in an encounter with a thief, had had an artery severed. After dressing the arm, she told him to go to a surgeon in the morning, but to her surprise he returned to her. She told him that she would treat him only on condition that he take everything that she gave him. He consented reluctantly, and every morning as she slowly dressed his arm she told him the story of Christ's love. One day he said, "I will believe this story if I can see it written in a book so that I can read it." She gave him the Gospel of John in Chinese, but he seemed unable to understand why Christ had left His home to come to a life of trial to save sinners. At last one day he came with a shining face, and said: "Now I understand; and it is you who have made me see it. Christ gave up His Home in Heaven, and came to save us, just as you have left your beautiful home in America, and all your friends, to come here to a life of hardship to tell us how we may be saved."—*The Wonderful Word.*

* * *

Watch Him and See!

A certain evangelist sometimes uses this illustration:

Two merchants went to a revival service to listen to the preacher, a man of some reputation. These men were competitors in business, and each one knew the heart-burnings that arose in their business life. After some nights, one of them went forward as a seeker after life in Christ. The other was under a measure of conviction, but unyielding. As he saw his competitor go forward, he said within himself: "I will watch him. If he lives it one year I will believe there is really something in it, and will become a Christian myself."

For one year he watched that man and saw a complete change in his business life, social life, everyday life. At the end of the year, the watcher sought and found God and the forgiveness of sins through Christ. He then went to the merchant whose life he had watched so closely, and said: *"For one whole year I have watched you, and your life has convinced me there is something real in your Christian faith."—Presbyterian.*

* * *

A Thought-Provoking Mistake

It is said that an old colored man, in reading a well-known hymn which contains the line, "Judge not the Lord by feeble sense," mistook the word "sense" and gave this odd version: "Judge not the Lord by feeble saints." What a pity that people will judge the Lord that way!—*Christian Herald* (London).

* * *

Value in Evidence

A brick manufacturer, who was a very substantial man, advertised for a boy. A boy appeared, and he was running over with questions. "How much wages do you pay?" was the first question. "Five dollars a week and board," was the reply. "What kind of board?" said the sharp applicant for a position. "Well," said the corpulent and good-natured manufacturer, "I eat it." "Give me the job," said the boy, with a smiling glance at his prospective employer. *The brick manufacturer was a good advertisement of the food that he gave his workmen.* If you and I should ask someone to become a Christian, would he look at the gospel's results in our lives and say, "I want it"?—*S. S. Chronicle.*

* * *

How She Knew

A humble servant girl arose and went down the aisle to the front during one of Charles Haddon Spurgeon's great sermons.

"I have been converted," she said simply.

"How do you know," he asked, his keen eyes searching her face, "that you are converted?"

The little servant girl looked up at him shyly.

"I am quite sure," she replied, "because now I sweep under the rugs! I used to be careless when I did the sweeping."

Under the rugs!

Not lightly over the top or around the edges, but *under* the rugs. Christ's love had so filled her heart that she was expressing it in the best way she knew. She wasn't a great singer with a golden voice who could hold vast audiences spellbound with her music. She could paint no pictures nor write a piece of literature. But she could sweep under the rugs!

She was only a poor servant girl with toil-hardened hands who worked in other people's kitchens, but in her poverty how really rich she was! For Christ had become so close to her, so very near, that she felt He wanted her to do the very best she could—that He cared how she swept the rugs.

Can we not, all of us, then be guided by her as we go about our own daily tasks, whatever they may be? And, as we do them whole-heartedly and gloriously as "to the Lord, and not to men," let us try to be happy in our place, because He has seen fit in His great wisdom and love to put us where we are.

Each one of us is included in His eternal plan. If we are washing dishes, caring for the sick or working in an office, that is just where we can best serve Him. We belong to Him and it must be right.

She was a little servant girl
Doing her work each day,
With all her heart, because she felt
She could show her love that way.

All together now—join hands. Let's begin by sweeping under the rugs. —Beatrice Fugate in *The Friend* (Dayton).

* * *

Translation Work

A young miner was asked by a friend, "What have you got to do with the British and Foreign Bible Society?" "Oh, said George, "I am a translator. "What! You a translator?" "Yes," said George, "I'm busy translating the New Testament into my daily life."—*Bible in the World.*

* * *

A Quiet Example

A merchant, who had been a very worldly, godless man, was hopefully converted. On being asked what had been more especially the means of his conversion, he replied, "The example of one of my clerks." He went on to say that this young man was one "whose religion was in his life rather than in his tongue. When I uttered an oath he never reproved me; but I could see it deeply pained him. When I fell into a passion and behaved in a violent manner, though he spoke no word to that effect, I could see how painful the scene was to him. My respect for him led me to restrain myself in his presence, and gradually to break off both these habits. In fact, this man, though he never spoke a word to me on the subject of religion, exercised an influence for good over me, wielded by no other human being. To him, under God, I am indebted more than to any other, for the hope in which I now rejoice of eternal life through our Lord Jesus Christ."—*Bible Expositor and Illuminator.*

* * *

A Quest for the Beautiful Life

One day a Japanese rushed nervously into a preacher's study in Boston and said, "Sir, I am in search of the beautiful life, can you tell me where to find it?" "I presume," said the minister, "you want to discuss religion." "No," replied the Japanese, "I don't want to discuss religion. My own country is full of it, but it isn't what I want. You see, there is a carpenter who lives in the same boarding house where I live in Cambridge, and to me his life is beautiful. He never thinks of himself, he is always thinking of others. When we pass the dishes around the table in the boarding house he will not take anything until all the rest have been helped, and he takes the leavings. He just never seems to think of himself for a second, and to me his life is beautiful." The minister handed the Japanese a New

Testament and said, "Take that. If you find that life, then you will know the beautiful life."

Two years later that same Japanese rushed into that preacher's study and said, "Do you know me?" The minister replied, "I think I have seen you, but I can't say that I recall you." Then he reminded him, holding the Testament in his hand, of his previous visit, saying, "I have found the beautiful life, I have found Christ."

If only we can find Him, hear His voice and obey His will, re-echoing His accents of love in all of our relations with men, then we will have the life beautiful.—*Sunday School Times.*

* * *

Their Definition of Christianity

When a group of West Point cadets, some years ago, were confronted with the question, "What is Christianity?" they replied as one man, "Oscar Westover." Oscar Westover was a young man at West Point for whom life meant the Lord Jesus Christ in reality. He walked among his fellows, glad to let the Lord Jesus Christ shine out.—*Courtesy Moody Monthly.*

* * *

The Orthodox Devil

Benvenuto Cellini, when shut up in the Castle of St. Angelo, spent his time in writing comments with angelic fervor on the Pauline Epistles, but when let out he gave himself up to all kinds of wickedness. Nothing can take the place of individual righteousness. Right opinions are no substitute for right conduct. John Wesley once said, "We may be as orthodox as the Devil, and as wicked." — Courtesy *Moody Monthly.*

* * *

Among the People with Whom We Work

The president of a great manufacturing concern was talking with an employee who had made a mistake that cost the firm thousands of dollars. But he wasn't doing much talking. He was listening quietly to the younger man, and when the story was all before him, the president simply nodded as if he understood, and sent the young man back to his work, — and kept him there. The president was a great Christian gentleman, widely known for his good works; but in the works of which he was president he was best known, and best loved. How is it with those of you who have persons working for you? Do they really like you and your ways, and are they happy under your direction, or do they sometimes say when you don't hear them, "Well, if that man is a Christian, I don't want to be"? And if you are working for someone else, do you think every day whether Christ would approve of the way you do your work or not? . . . When you come to think of it, where is there a finer place in which to show a Christian spirit than among the people for whom, or with whom, we work?—*Sunday School Times.*

* * *

One Kind of Recommendation

An Irishman was being tried in a Kansas town. His was a petty offense. The judge asked if there was anyone present who would vouch for his character. "To be sure, your Honor," he declared, "there's the sheriff." The sheriff looked amazed. "Your Honor," he said, "I do not even know the man." "Your Honor," came back the Irishman as quick as a flash, "I've lived in this county for more than twelve years, and the sheriff does not know me yet. Isn't that a character for you?"—*Toronto Globe.*

* * *

The Chinese Girl's Discovery

A group of college girls were discussing, in a Bible study, the Sermon on the Mount, and were asking why Christians are like salt. All thought of course of salt's preservative qualities. Then a Chinese girl in the group suggested quietly, "Salt creates thirst." The truth went home. Christians are not only to bring joy and comfort to the lives of others, they should create thirst for the things of God. Our lives should be such that people would continually come to us and ask us to explain ourselves.—*Sunday School Times.*

Why the Boy Watched

A country clergyman, nailing up a trailing vine, observed a boy watching him for a long time with obvious interest. "Well, my young friend," he said with a smile, "are you trying to get a hint or two on gardening?" "No," said the lad, "I'm just waiting to see what a minister says when he hammers his thumb."—*Christian Evangelist.*

* * *

Her Stumblingblock

A clergyman was kneeling in church, talking with a young woman bowed there, who was seeking Christ at a time of revival. Something seemed to worry her. "What is it?" asked the minister kindly; "have you surrendered your all?" "I have tried," the woman sobbed. "What is the matter, then?" "It's the way Christian people have treated me. I am afraid I shall have to give up my place in the family where I work as a servant. The man is so cross and impatient with me." "Give it up, then. God will supply something better," said the minister; "for whom do you work?" The woman raised her bowed head. "For you, sir." "It's our June!" gasped the minister. Then it all flashed upon his mind — his quick, impatient disposition, his domineering spirit — and with a burst of tears he sought forgiveness there and then.—*The Illustrator.*

* * *

"Even the Dog Knew It"

A woman was telling in a testimony meeting about her husband's conversion. "The first thing that happened the next morning, he built the fire in the cook stove. Ever since our marriage I have brought water from a well outside the house. I had asked him many times if it could not be piped in. He always said, 'No.' Right away after he became a Christian he had a pump put in the kitchen. Then he sugested that I could have a new dress and shoes and that our meals should be simpler on Sunday so that we could go to church. The children saw the difference right away. The home was a different place. Even the dog knew it. Where ill will and selfishness had ruled, there was kindness and service for others." That is a home of blessing where God dwells. — *Baptist Leader.*

* * *

I'd rather see a sermon,
  Than hear one any day;
I'd rather one should walk with me
  Than merely show the way.
The eye's a better pupil
  And more willing than the ear;
Fine counsel is confusing
  But example's always clear.
And the best of all the preachers
  Are the ones who live their creed,
For to see good put in action
  Is what everybody needs.
I soon can learn to do it,
  If you let me see it done.
I can watch your hands in action,
  But your tongue too fast may run.
And the sermon you deliver
  May be very wise and true,
But I'd rather get my lesson
  By observing what you do,
For I might misunderstand you
  And the high advice you give;
But there's no misunderstanding
  How you act and how you live.
—*Selected.*

* * *

If There Were No Salt

We could not live without salt. An article in *This Week Magazine* tells that exceptionally strong men, working in the forge rooms of an automobile factory where the temperature was so high that the men perspired abnormally, would drop to the floor and writhe in agony without apparent cause. After prolonged study, a Harvard Laboratory staff discovered that, although the men drank cold water freely, in the hot temperature, this did not replace the salt that they had perspired out of their systems. A salt tablet with each drink of water stopped the "heat cramps." Not only do our bodies need salt, but the manufacturing world needs it. Steel, subjected to terrific strain in automobiles, is hardened by a salt water bath. The famous Carrel-Dakin antiseptic solution, which saved hundreds of thousands of lives during the World War, has as its chief ingredient chlorine, which comes from salt. Without salt cows stop giving milk and sicken and die. If salt disappeared from the earth, "the wheels of industry would eventually stop, and it would be only a matter of months before we'd all be dead." But, the scientists tell us, the supply of salt in the natural world "is practically unlimited, there being an inconceivable number of pounds in the ocean alone." We begin to see, from such facts, why the Lord Jesus said to His disciples: "Ye are the salt of the earth: but if the salt have lost his savour, wherewith shall it be salted?" —*Sunday School Times.*

* * *

Why She Wants Her Laundress

"When I die I want my laundress by my bedside." This unusual statement was made by a very wealthy Jewish woman who is seriously ill in a Chicago hospital. Her laundress is a colored woman who is enrolled in the Moody Bible Institute Evening School. The sick woman, a devout Zionist, first became interested in her colored laundress when she heard her testimony and learned that she was devoting several evenings a week to the study of the Bible and related subjects. Her interest increased considerably when she discovered that the colored woman was assigned to a practical work group of her own race to visit the Cook County Hospital for the purpose of bringing the Gospel to colored inmates. It was then that this wealthy Zionist became vitally concerned with the things of God. Although this wealthy Jewess had not yet publicly confessed her acceptance of Christ as Saviour, her life has been changed. There is evidence that the Holy Spirit is working to prepare her for the miracle of regeneration in the Lord. It is inspiring to observe the changes wrought in this woman through the sincere testimony spoken and lived by the colored laundress.—*Moody Monthly.*

* * *

Unconscious Influence of a Good Life

"The writer knew Brother S—— since three weeks following his (S——'s) conversion. It is a tragic condition that for many years following the beginning of such a splendid friendship, I was a backslider and a sinner of a bad type, what the world calls a 'regular fellow.' Undoubtedly, in answer to many prayers, I came back to Jesus Christ about fifteen months ago and immediately set to work to try to offset the years in the devil's service. God has been wondrously good to me. I want you to get this—during all the years I was away from God, I watched Brother S——'s career. Knowing from what he came, I *hoped* he would prove true, but I had my doubts. *Had he slipped back, I might have been a fullfledged 'bum' today*—I was 'sure' headed that way—or in a suicide's grave, as I had lost my self-respect. But I must in honesty pay tribute to the fact that S——'s life was an inspiration and a factor that helped me decide to come back and make a full surrender to Christ as my only hope of peace and happiness in this world and in the world to come. I have had many difficulties and obstacles to overcome, but God *has* been faithful in my case in giving me the needed grace for victory." — From a Private Letter.

* * *

"Real Christians"

In her book ,"Floods on Dry Ground," Eva Stuart Watt describes missionary work in the Belgian Congo, and says, "Even among the enemies of the Gospel there was growing a secret admiration for those whose lives were out and out for God. The term, *'Bakristu ya kweli,'* was often heard on heathen lips. It means, 'real Christians.' Far and wide they were known as men of truth, and men whose prayers got answered. One day the paramount chief had a big court case in which a Christian was charged with hiding a Mabudu prisoner. At the tribunal, the chief said to the accused, 'Tell me, did you hide that man?' 'No, Chief, I didn't.' Then, turning to his soldiers, he said, 'You liars, the lot of you! This man is a *Bakristu ya kweli!* He couldn't tell a lie.' "—*Sunday School Times.*

The Educated Man and the Coal Driver

Christian man, is your religion genuine? There was once a man in my congregation who could talk eloquently, and seemed to know the Bible from Genesis to Revelation. He could quote the poets, and a stranger would be charmed by his eloquent utterances. And yet when he had talked in a prayer meeting the life of the meeting had gone. All knew that in his life there was something unsavory, that he would drink before the bar with worldly friends, and that he was not as honest as he might be. His good grammar and fluent utterances did not make amends for the weakness of his character.

There was another man in that congregation who would sometimes come to prayer-meeting with a circle of coal dust around his hair. He was a coal cart driver, and he was now and then so hurried to get to prayer-meeting that he did not make his toilet with as much care as he ought. But the people learned ever to listen when he talked. And why? Because they knew that he lived every day for God. He would pick up a tramp on the road, give him a ride on his cart, that he might talk to him about Jesus. His religion was real. I would rather have good religion in bad grammar than bad religion in good grammar. — *A. J. Gordon.*

* * *

The World's Bible

Christ has no hands but our hands
To do His work today;
He has no feet but our feet
To lead men in His way;
He has no tongues but our tongues
To tell men how He died;
He has no help but our help
To bring them to His side.

We are the only Bible
The careless world will read;
We are the sinner's gospel,
We are the scoffer's creed;
We are the Lord's last message,
Given in deed and word;
What if the type is crooked?
What if the print is blurred?

What if our hands are busy
With other work than His?
What if our feet are walking
Where sin's allurement is?
What if our tongues are speaking
Of things His lips would spurn?
How can we hope to help Him
And hasten His return?

—Annie Johnson Flint.

(Copyright. Reprinted by permission of Evangelical Publishers, Toronto Canada.)

* * *

Old-Fashioned Things

There are some good, old-fashioned things
To which my heart in fondness clings;
Old-fashioned help in time of need
That's better far than modern greed;
Old-fashioned kindness, peace and love
That helps us on to Heav'n above;
Old-fashioned smiles and friendship warm
That help us brave life's sea and storm.

Old-fashioned greetings on the street
And shaking hands with friends we meet;
Old-fashioned honesty and truth
Among the aged and the youth;
Old-fashioned promises so stout
Until there is no room for doubt;
Old-fashioned praying in the home
And grace that keeps us as we roam.

Old-fashioned sermons filled with grace
And glory in the preacher's face;
Old-fashioned testifyings, too,
From "Amen Corners" and the pew;
Old-fashioned parents, pure of soul,
With children under good control;
Old-fashioned teachers in the school
With knowledge sound and grit to rule.

Old-fashioned manliness of heart,
Old-fashioned decency in art;
Old-fashioned books and songs inspired
That God approved and saints admired;
Old-fashioned living for the right
And truly walking in the light;
Old-fashioned praying for the lost
And winning souls at any cost.

—Walter E. Isenhour in *The Herald of Light* and *Zion's Watchman.*

Face The "If"

A woman once said to me, "If my family were not what they are! My husband is so against anything that is truly Christian; my children would all make sport of me if I attempted anything in the way of peculiar devotion to God. Oh, if you knew the circumstances!" With an impulse that I was glad of afterward, I said to her, "Never mind your husband; never mind your children; take God for your circumstances, and put Him between you and your husband; put God in between you and your children." She caught the idea, and exclaimed, "I will do it."

"Next morning," she afterward told me, "when I went down to breakfast, there was my husband—and he almost always found fault at breakfast about something. I looked at him and thought, 'It does not make any difference what he says, I have God between him and me.'"

That woman lived to be a power in her family, and when I heard last, nearly every child (there was a large family) was converted. Do not be thinking of your "if." Make a power out of your "if" for God.

* * *

The Obligation to Be Holy

Dr. Albert Barnes, the commentator, was a Presbyterian. He was never suspected of having been erratic or fanatical, but was always recognized as a man of very sober judgment, profound learning and a devout spirit. The following paragraph from his pen sets forth the grounds of our obligation to be holy, with much simplicity, clearness and force:

"A man who has been redeemed by the Blood of the Son of God should be pure. He who is attended by celestial beings, and is soon—he knows not how soon—to be translated into Heaven, should be holy. Are angels my attendants? Then I should walk worthy of my companions. Am I soon to go and dwell with angels? Then I should be pure. Are these feet soon to tread the courts of Heaven? Is my tongue soon to unite with holy beings in praising God? Are these eyes soon to look on the throne of eternal glory, and the ascended Redeemer? Then these feet and eyes and lips should be pure and holy, and I should be dead to the world and live for Heaven."
—*Michigan Chr. Advocate.*

* * *

The Face Shows

At a meeting in London of Christian policemen, one prayed, "O Lord, put something in our faces as we walk about that people in trouble may see, and so be led to seek our help." The next day a drunken man handed him an addressed envelope, asking him to call there. When he did, a man opened the door. "For God's sake, come in and pray with me! This morning I saw something in your face which told me you could help me. I had decided to end my life. I am a wretched failure." He had been a deacon, but drink had tripped him. He got back to the Lord, and is serving Him.
—*Selected.*

* * *

When Dr. H. C. Trumbull was a small boy, he and other lads hung around the dock for the unusual experience of seeing a real live missionary from the other side of the world, the famous Adoniram Judson. Suddenly the boys' eager eyes fell upon a face in the crowd that thrilled them. They at once knew it to be the great missionary. It had a light and glow that they had never seen on any other face. Every line of those features seemed transformed from within. — *Selected.*

* * *

It's Coming

A missionary in China advertised for a servant. A well-dressed lady responded. The missionary hesitated, for she wanted someone to scrub, wash, and make beds. But, yes, the lady understood, and was hired. One day the missionary observed her hiding some small object, to her evident embarrassment. Again it happened, and then the secret was out. "It's coming! The light on my face! I used to see the Christians on their way to chapel, and noticed how bright their faces were. I wanted that look for myself, and thought if I came to work for you I might get some of it. My husband tells me the light is coming, and I was looking in this little mirror to see!" Through accepting Jesus Christ as Saviour she became a bright and attractive Christian.—*Selected.*

* * *

Hopelessness of a Perfect Example

Dr. Joseph Parker, on one occasion, referred to the Unitarian conception of Jesus Christ as a great example only, and then went on to say: "We have been to hear Paderewski play. It was wonderful, superb, magnificent. Then we went home and looked at the piano. We would have sold it to the first man who would have been fool enough to buy it. That is the effect of your great examples upon us. I want not only a great example, but a great Saviour, one who can deliver me from my weakness and my sins." To follow a good example in the future will not blot out the black record of the past; we need the blood of Christ's atoning sacrifice to accomplish that. To hear a Paderewski play will not make us like a Paderewski. Could a Paderewski incarnate himself within one, he could play like himself. So the Christian life is not Christ and I, but Christ in me. We need the Christ from within to live the Christ without. — *Courtesy Moody Monthly.*

* * *

Unawares

They said: "The Master is coming
To honor the town today,
And none can tell at whose house or home
The Master will choose to stay."
And I thought, while my heart beat wildly,
What if He should come to mine?
How would I strive to entertain
And honor the guest divine!

And straight I turned to toiling
To make my home more neat;
I swept and polished and garnished,
And decked it with blossoms sweet;
I was troubled for fear the Master
Might come ere my task was done,
And I hastened and worked the faster,
And watched the hurrying sun.

But right in the midst of my duties
A woman came to my door;
She had come to tell me her sorrows,
And my comfort and aid to implore.
And I said: "I cannot listen,
Nor help you any today;
I have greater things to attend to."
And the pleader turned away.

But soon there came another—
A cripple, thin, pale and gray;
And said: "Oh, let me stop and rest
A while in your home, I pray!
I have traveled far since morning,
I am hungry and faint and weak.
My heart is full of misery,
And comfort and help I seek."

And I said: "I am grieved and sorry.
But I cannot keep you today;
I look for a great and noble guest,"
And the cripple went away.
And the day wore onward swiftly.
And my task was nearly done,
And a prayer was ever in my heart,
That the Master to me might come.

And I thought I would spring to meet Him,
And serve Him with utmost care,
When a little child stood by me,
With a face so sweet and fair;
Sweet, but with marks of teardrops,
And his clothes were tattered and old;
A finger was bruised and bleeding,
And his little bare feet were cold.

And I said: "I am sorry for you;
You're sorely in need of care;
But I cannot stop to give it,
You must hasten otherwhere."
And at the words a shadow
Swept o'er his blue-veined brow;
"Someone will feed and clothe you, dear,
But I am too busy now."

At last the day was ended,
And my toil was over and done;
My house was swept and garnished,
And I watched in the dusk alone;
Watched, but no footfall sounded,
No one paused at my gate,
No one entered my cottage door;
I could only pray and wait.

I waited till night had deepened,
And the Master had not come.
"He has entered some other door," I cried,
"And gladdened some other home!"

My labor has been for nothing,
And I bowed my head and wept;
My heart was sore with longing,
Yet in spite of all, I slept.

Then the Master stood before me,
And His face was grave and fair;
"Three times today I came to your door,
And craved your pity and care;
Three times you sent Me onward
Unhelped and uncomforted;
And the blessing you might have had was lost,
And your chance to serve has fled."
"O Lord, dear Lord, forgive me!
How could I know it was Thee?"
My very soul was shamed and bowed
In the depths of humility.
And He said: "Thy sin is pardoned,
But the blessing is lost to thee;
For comforting not the least of Mine,
Ye have failed to comfort Me."

—*Selected.*

CHRISTMAS

For Christ Has Come

If Christ had not been born,
Hearts burdened and forlorn
Must seek in vain
Peace to attain,
If Christ had not been born.

If to the Bethlehem home,
The Christ-child had not come,
Hearts now agleam
With love would seem
But drear, had not Christ come.

But now both hope and cheer,
God gives for every year;
To seeking hearts
His grace imparts
His love, for Christ has come.

—Fred Scott Shephard.

* * *

What Stopped the Firing

A day was dawning on a battlefield in Northern France, through a fog so thick that no one could see more than a few yards from the trenches. In the night the Germans had drawn back their lines a little and the French had gone forward, but between the two positions a lonely farmhouse was still standing. As the sun rose, heavy guns began to boom. But suddenly on both sides the firing ceased and there fell a strange, dead silence. For there in the green meadow, crawling on its hands and knees was a little baby. It appeared perfectly happy and contented, and the baby's laugh was heard as it clutched a dandelion. Not a shot was fired.—*Sunday School Times.*

Midnight Songs

Out on the bare Judean hills,
Far from the scenes of mirth,
The shepherds heard a midnight song
That echoed 'round the earth.

And straightway, challenged by the sound,
They left their lonely place,
And took the road to Bethlehem
To seek the young Child's face.

They came, they saw, they understood,
And knew a strange release
As, stooping down, they knelt before
The little Prince of Peace.

And now the midnight of the world
Has settled, dark and still,
And frightened hearts are crouching low—
Like shepherds on a hill.

What mean the ancient carols now?
Their glad and sweet refrain
Is lost amidst the scream of shells,
As men forget again.

And yet, in countless waiting hearts,
The light of faith still burns.
Lord, send again a midnight song
To say the Prince returns!

—Helen Frazee-Bower.

* * *

The King's Gifts

Bring Him thy precious things
And lay them at His feet;
The gold of love, the hope that springs
The unknown ways to meet.

Bring Him thy lovely things;
The joy that conquers care,
The faith that trusts and sings,
The frankincense of prayer.

Bring Him thy bitter things;
The myrrh of grief and fears,
The aching heart that stings
With pain of unshed tears.

These for thy gifts to Him;
And for His gifts to thee,
The comfort of His steadfast love,
His tender sympathy.

—*Annie Johnson Flint.*

* * *

The Little Prince's Command

The story is told that many years ago in Korea when the mission compound was just over the wall from the royal palace in Seoul, the small prince just before Christmas time climbed upon the wall, called to the lady doctor in the clinic below and asked if they would not give him a "Jesus birthday," meaning a Christmas celebration, as he was not allowed to attend the usual program in the Christian church. She promised to do so if he would supply a small tree. He ordered a tree delivered which the doctor and her nurses decorated with the usual bright baubles. At the specified time he again secretly climbed to the top of the wall, and stood while they told the Bible story, sang a few songs, and said a prayer. He asked and received the tree decorations, and the small red song book containing words without music. Later in the day, the missionaries heard a dreadful noise over the wall. Upon investigation they found that the small prince had his fat gentlemen-in-waiting lined up in a pavilion demanding that they sing. "The joyful noise is in that book, and you've got to get it out!" he commanded.—*Sunday School Times.*

* * *

"If I Had Not Come"

Bobby had read in his Bible lesson with Daddy just before bedtime the words, "If I had not come." When he (thought he) awoke Christmas morning there was no stocking or holly wreath. He went for a walk and found factories busy at work; he went to the orphanage and found only a vacant lot. Then he went to his church and found a "For Sale" sign with "If I had not come" written at the bottom. Again he found these words over a gate post of an empty lot, where he went to find a hospital. Disconsolate, he ran home and picked up his Bible, but all the last part of the Book had blank pages. He awoke, and lo, it was a dream! Do you wonder he slipped down on his knees and said, *"Oh, dear Jesus, I am so glad that You did come.* Help me to tell others about You." —*Missionary Monthly.*

* * *

What Shall I Give Him?

What shall I give Him, poor as I am?
If I were a shepherd, I would give a lamb;
If I were a wise man, I would do my part;
But such as I have I give Him,—
Give Him my heart.

—*Selected.*

* * *

Or Was This the Star?

The great astronomer Kepler discovered that in Christ's birth year there was an unusual occurrence among the planets. He found that in that year Jupiter and Saturn, which are generally in remote parts of the sky, came three times so near together that to the unassisted eye the rays of one were absorbed by the other, and their combination gave an extraordinary brilliant light, which continued for some months.

—F. B. Meyer.

* * *

What is the thought of Christmas? Giving.
What is the hope of Christmas? Living.
What is the joy of Christmas? Love.
No silver or gold is needed for giving,
If the heart is filled with Christmas love,
For the hope of the world is kindly living,
Learned from the joy of God above.

—Laura Hooker.

Still No Room

Because there was no room for them in the inn (Luke 2:7). Not long ago a professor of psychology in one of our great universities gave a word-suggestion test to his class of forty students. He instructed them to write the word "Christmas," and all the class did so. "Now," said the professor, "write after the word 'Christmas' the first thought that flashes through your mind regarding that day." When the papers were turned in, such answers were given as "tree." "holly," "mistletoe," "presents," "turkey," "holiday," "carols," and "Santa Claus," but not one had written, "the birthday of Jesus."—*War Cry.*

* * *

Lighting Up

A little boy who was telling the Christmas story to his mother, as he told of the shepherds, and the angel of the Lord, and the heavenly glory that shone round about them, said, "The shepherds were very much afraid, but the angel said to them, 'Don't be afraid, shepherds, they are only lighting up.'" So they were — lighting up this world of ours with a new light.—*Bible Teacher.*

"Unto You Is Born This Day—"

O what a Day!
Foretold in ages long since past;
By many Prophets oft forecast:
God's promises the world outlast—
O what a Day!

O what a Gift!
From God the Father up in Heav'n,
To sinful mortals Satan driv'n,
A Saviour, Christ the Lord, was giv'n—
O what a Gift!

O what a Babe!
A Child asleep on Mary's knee,
Yet true incarnate God was He,
With "goings forth" eternally—
O what a Babe!

O what a Love!
Born purposely for men to die,
To save them, bless, and glorify,
And bear them to His Home on high—
O what a Love!

What shall we Do?
E'er this glad Christmastide is gone,
Accept Him now, and love Him on,
His soulful praises e'er prolong—
This let us do.

—R. E. Neighbour, D.D.

CHURCH

The Layman Speaks
The Church Is Right!

The Church is Right!

Almost everyone has told us what is wrong with the Church. . . .

I believe the Church is right. And as a Church member I want to tell what I think is right with the Church. . . .

I think the Church is right because it has taught me about Jesus Christ and Him crucified. . . .

My Church has taught me about the Bible. . . .

My Church has given me faith. . . . It has taught me how to pray. . . .

The Church has taught me to appreciate all the good things which have been showered upon me. In my early youth I believed that food and clothing and the luxuries of life were mine because I was alive. Now I know that God has given me these things because of His love. As a man, I like to know who has been good to me. . . .

The Church has helped me find peace so I am content whatever my state may be. . . .

The Church has continually influenced my life and always in the right direction. . . .

The Church has given me friends, real friends. When all other friends forsook me because material resources had dwindled away, the Church continued to welcome me, and I believe, put just a little more warmth in their welcome than before. . . .

As I look back I see the wonderful many things it has done for others, countless thousands who have faith and hope and life today because of the Church. . . .
—Donald M. Foster, Presbyterian Elder, Trenton, New Jersey:

* * *

Keeping One's Soul Out of the Dust

Lovest thou me? There is a quiet, little man, a vendor of fruits and vegetables, who passes my door every day. One day I picked up a small notebook near the spot where his wagon stood. On the first page I was much surprised to find these words: "For his body's sake, which is the church." Throughout the book were scriptural quotations and many notations like these: "The following were absent from Bible School last Sunday, be sure to visit them." "Ask about the sick baby." "Leave fruit for the blind lady." "Speak a word of cheer to the old cripple man." "Invite the new family to church services." The next day I handed the book to the humble fruit peddler, with the query: "I wonder if you dropped this yesterday?" "Yes, indeed," was the answer. "It is my book of reminders, as I call it. I thank you." I told him I had glanced at the contents and expressed my surprise at their unusual character. "Well," he answered, pointing to the first page text, "this is my motive, my reason, for doing things, 'For his body's sake, which is the church.'" Then with an illuminating smile he added, "You see, it keeps my soul out of the dust."—*Alliance Weekly.*

* * *

A Decaying Church

There is a story of an artist who was asked to paint a picture of a decaying church. To the astonishment of many, instead of putting on the canvas an old, tottering ruin, the artist painted a stately edifice of modern grandeur. Through the open portals could be seen the richly carved pulpit, the magnificent organ, and the beautiful stained glass windows. Within the grand entrance was an offering plate of elaborate design for the offerings to missions. A cobweb was over the receptacle for foreign missions!
—*Gospel Herald.*

Church of God

Church of God, the Master calls to you,
For the fields are white with rip'ning grain;
Send forth reapers, for there's work to do,
Time is fleeting, shall He call in vain?

Church of God, awake, the call obey;
Linger not, the harvest time draws nigh;
Hasten forth, while it is called today;
Seek the precious sheaves, nor pass one by.

Church of God, to every nation go;
Preach the Word, as Jesus gave command;
May the Gospel, in its onward flow,
Cease not till it reaches every land.
—Fred Scott Shepard.

* * *

Reasons, or Excuses?

A pastor of the United Lutheran Synod of New York recently chose a unique way to show up the absurdity of most excuses for non-attendance at church. He published in his church bulletin: "WHY I DON'T GO TO THE MOVIES—Because my parents made me go when I was a boy. Because no one speaks to me when I am there. Because they always want money. Because the manager never visited me in my home. Because the people who go there never live up to what the movies teach, anyway."
—*Christian Union Herald.*

* * *

A Dictionary of Christians

To Which Group Do I Belong?

1. Pillars—Worship regularly, giving time and money.
2. Supporters—Give time and money if they like the pastor and treasurer.
3. Leaners—Use the church for funerals, baptisms and marriage, but give no time or money to support the church.
4. Working Leaners — Work but do not give money.
5. Specials—Help and give occasionally for something that appeals to them.
6. Annuals or Easter Birds — Dress up, look serious and go to church on Easter.

7. Sponges — Take all blessings and benefits, even the sacraments, but give no money to support the church.

8. Tramps—Go from church to church but support none.

9. Gossips—Talk freely about everyone except the Lord Jesus.

10. Scrappers—Take offense, criticize and fight.

11. Orphans — Are children sent by parents who do not set them an example.

12. Backsliders — "Go back and walk no more with Jesus" (John 6:66).

13. Hypocrites—Are leaners who say they are better than churchgoers.—*The Messenger.*

* * *

Which Are You Wearing Out?

They knew each other intimately. Said one, "I've been in the harness of this church for twenty-two years." "Yes," said the other, "and during that time you've worn out fifteen holding back straps and only one collar."—*Record of Christian Work.*

* * *

Imprisoned?

A ship sailing from the Orient brought a large number of caged birds. At about mid-ocean one restless bird escaped from his cage, and in an ecstasy of delight swept through the air, away and away from his prison. But after many hours he appeared again, struggling toward the ship with heavy wings, and panting and breathless, settled upon the deck. He had sought from over the boundless deep the ship again, now no longer a prison, but his dear home. So with the restless human heart that breaks away from the restraints of Christianity. If not lost on the remorseless deep he comes back again with panting heart to church, home, and God. The church is not a prison. It gives the most perfect freedom in all that is good and all that is safe.—*Sunday School Times.*

* * *

Must We Always Hold Up a Biscuit?

A sad-eyed seminarian, who is studying for the ministry, wrote the following after an experience with a certain church. "Behold! . . . The club clubbeth together and they eat. The businessmen take counsel and they eat. The church hath a social and they eat. The young people elect officers and they eat. And even when the missionary society meeteth together they eat. But this latter is in good cause, because they 'eat in remembrance' of the poor heathen who hath not to eat. Behold! Hath man's brains gone to his stomach and doth he no longer regard intellectual dainties that thou canst no longer call an assembly or get together even a 'baker's dozen' except thou hold up the baker's dainties as a bait? Be it true, that the day cometh that to get a crowd at prayer meeting the preacher must hold up a biscuit? Yea, verily, thou hast heard of the child races of the world. But, behold, it is nigh thee, even at the door. For as one calleth unto the child and saith, 'Come hither, sweet little one, and I will give thee a stick of candy,' even so must thou say to his grown-up papa and mamma, 'Assemble ye together and we will serve refreshments.' And lo, they come like sheep into a pen. Selah."—Courtesy *Moody Monthly.*

* * *

Choose a Real Measure

It tickles me to see an old sinner come in and pull out an old lame and dwarfed member of the church, lay him down and measure by him, and say, "Look here, boys, I am as long, as broad, and as good as this member of the church!" Why don't you go and pick out one of those grand old Christians? Because you would look like a rat-terrier lying beside an elephant.—Sam P. Jones.

* * *

Make Much of the Church

We believe the Spirit of God makes much of the local church during this age. Of course, salvation doesn't come by way of church membership, but there are a lot of good things which do come.

One unfortunate trend today is the drift of some real believers toward non-church membership and only intermittent attendance. There are too many fundamentalists who live on Bible conferences, or the messages of itinerant preachers or teachers. Some of them feel they have been driven to this by the Modernism of some pulpits, or by the Biblical ignorance of some preachers.

But it still remains that as far as organization goes the church is the one God-appointed organization of all of this age. You may have to change to another church, but we believe you should be in one and at work in it.

Some of us have lived long enough to see other organizations arise and attract a great deal of attention. We could mention the high days of Christian Endeavor and of the Baraca-Philathea movement, etc., and while all the leaders said they recognized the supplementary character of those organizations, many people made them substitutes for the church.

There is no substitute for the local church or assembly. Organizations, movements, and methods come and go, but the church outlives and outlasts them all.

As we look around and see the many new movements astir in orthodoxy—laymen's movements, workers with children, etc., we say, stick to the church. As far as you can, tie everything to the church, for the church is the only continuing corporate witness. — Courtesy *Moody Monthly.*

* * *

Present in the Pew

A traveler in a European village discovered a beautiful custom. At night she saw the people going to the church, each carrying a little bronze lamp. These lamps they placed in sockets by their pews. The soft light of the lamps was the only illumination for the service. If a member was absent, there was a dark space!

We do not carry lamps to church, but we do send forth light. When we are absent there is darkness in our stead. The more people at church, the greater the inspiration. Many small lamps together make a great and beautiful light.

The first Christian church in Jerusalem had no building. It had a small membership; it had no officers; it had no pastor; it had no choir or pipe organ; it had no wealth; and, most startling of all, it had no New Testament.

What made it a successful church? Just this: It had the total attendance of its membership. Pentecost was possible because they were *all* together in one place. Its results lasted because they were continuing steadfastly with one accord in the Temple.—Rev. Ralph V. Gilbert in *Southern Churchman.*

* * *

Pushers—Draggers—Pullers

In almost every church there are to be found three classes of members. The first class we will call the "pushers." They are full of energy, and really want to do something worth while. This is a commendable trait, but it can be abused. Sometimes it grows until the "pusher" is not satisfied until his finger is in every church pie. He is hurt unless he holds an office, and pities himself if the pastor does not recognize "his unusual ability and outstanding talents along every line." While people of this type are an aggressive force, and do some good, yet they mar their influence by the human element present in all their efforts.

Then there are the "draggers." Always late, never on hand at the beginning of anything—it seems to be a principle with them. If called to be a part of the program, or asked to perform some duty, they plead, "I can't. Get someone else." Now humility is a fine virtue, but this extreme attitude is nearer laziness than humility. Never have they been known to be on the progressive side of anything. Their stock argument when a progressive move is considered: "We are not able. We would better be satisfied with what we have. We have always got along without it." They have not yet caught the vision of God's aggressive plan for His children.

But we find in every church some "pullers." They must be relatives of the soldier whose first remark, when told of the enemy, was "Where are they?" This class of laymen does not hesitate at the hardest task, or the most insignificant job. Their question is, 'Where do you want me?" And if it is just to be doorkeeper, they resolve to be the best possible doorkeeper. They have a vision, not lopsided, but well balanced, and big enough to include the whole. They support the budgets, love missions, take the church paper, pray at the altar, and endorse every reasonable progressive movement in the church. "And their children shall rise up and call them blessed."

Pushers — Draggers — Pullers; which are you?—Vernon L. Wilcox in *Herald of Holiness.*

* * *

Whose Fault Is It?

Jesus was speaking of the Temple, which He called "my Father's house." Intended as a house of prayer for all people," where souls find God, it had been turned into "a den of thieves," and He fixed the responsibility: "Ye have made it." Each of us has some responsibility for his church. We make it, for better or for worse. Its morale, its friendliness, its spirituality, its attendance record is made by *us.* Protestant church attendance has been falling off? We "have made it." More losses last year than accessions? We "have made it." He, "as his custom was," went to church. He also cleansed the Temple; He remade it. The first and most obvious way of supporting a church is to be a regular attendant.—*Today.*

* * *

No Sunday Morning Sickness

Church attendance to many is merely a matter of duty, or of appearance, or for the effect it may have on their business and the like. When this is the case, churchgoing becomes a drag and a burden. It has lost its thrill and fails to fulfill its purpose.

When I was a small child, I wondered at the interest shown by my father and mother in going to church. Every service, including the prayer meeting, seemed equally important. More than once I have heard my mother say, "Oh, I can hardly wait until I get to church!" And, though we were living on a farm, it was the custom, on Wednesday afternoons, even in the harvest season, for my father to stop the main work of the day from a half hour to an hour earlier than on other days in order to do the nightly chores and get to prayer meeting on time. "On time" was his motto for all the services.

And why all this? What was there at the little country church which meant so much to them? Through constant observation, it gradually became apparent to me that to them church attendance meant more than mere performance of duty. The toils and trials of the week had worn on them physically and spiritually. This was the occasion when everything earthly was thrown off and cast aside and they met with God and felt His heavenly touch on their bodies as well as their souls. The inspiration they received at these services helped them to get through the trials and toils of the weeks and months victoriously. Where, then, would there be room for a prayer-meeting headache or Sunday morning sickness?—*The Free Methodist.*

* * *

Labels Sometimes Necessary

The word "Fundamentalist" is a new word in the religious world. It is a recent name. Names are necessary. They are symbols of ideas. It is not the best thing in the world to be nameless. There are some people who object to being branded. They say they will not carry labels. But labels are also necessary, and the absence of them may be embarrassing, as when a goat was being shipped by express with a tag of destination about his neck. Later the Negro in charge of the car was thrown into consternation because he found as he declared with wide-eyed astonishment and perplexity, "Dat goat done eat up whar he's gwine." Probably the goat was a Modernist, or a Conservative who refused to wear a label. But it bothered the Negro, and it bothers us today not to know definitely where people are going and with whom they are going. — *The King's Business.*

* * *

Why Be Quiet in Church

"I am building a church," said a small boy, playing on the floor with a set of building blocks, "and we must be very quiet." His father, eager to encourage this unexpected reverence, asked, "And why are we quiet in the church?" "Because the people are asleep!" was the immediate response. Think of the opportunities we have missed because of spiritual drowsiness! — *Courtesy Moody Monthly.*

* * *

Why Go To Church?

The old story of the British chieftain is to the point here. The Romans had invaded Britain and the chiefs of the tribes were gathered in council. Each had a different plan, and each was determined to go his own way. At last an old chieftain arose. Picking up a bunch of fagots, he handed each man a stick. "Break them!" he directed. Each broke his stick with ease.

Then he took an equal number of sticks and tied them together into a bundle. "Now try to break them!" he told them. Not even the strongest man could do it. "That," he pointed out, "is the difference between working separately and working together as one!"

What has this to do with religion? Religion is derived from the Latin word "re" and "ligo," meaning—"To bind together." That is one purpose of the church—to bind people together in fellowship and service. Jesus prayed that we might be "one."

You want happiness, contentment, and spiritual blessings. You cannot have these alone. You get them only as you help those around you to win them, too! So why not join with your neighbors in praying as well as in working for them. It is a joy to labor together in a task which will be blessed of the Lord. Remember what the Master promised: "Where two or three are gathered together in My Name, there am I in the midst of them" (Matt. 18:20).

Get the weight of a common aim, a common purpose, behind both your prayers and your work. Go to church! —*The Missionary Worker.*

* * *

It Is Startling

A church statistician says that five per cent of all church members do not exist; ten per cent of them cannot be found; twenty-five per cent never go to church; fifty per cent never contribute a cent to the work of the church; seventy-five per cent never attend the midweek prayer service; ninety per cent do not have family worship in their homes; and ninety-five per cent never try to win a lost soul to Christ. If the statement is true, it is startling.—*The Watchman-Examiner.*

* * *

What Makes the Difference

My gypsy tent, if Jesus be in it, is as grand as St. Paul's Cathedral, and St. Paul's Cathedral is nothing but a glorified quarry without Jesus! Christ makes the Temple.—*Gypsy Smith.*

* * *

The Handicap of the Church

"The great task of the church today is not (only) to get sinners into Heaven, but (also) to get saints out of bed." — The Rev. Ralph W. A. Mitchell, in "*The Evangelical Christian.*"

* * *

Recognition

A few weeks ago a certain preacher preached on the recognition of friends in Heaven, and during the following week this letter came to him: "Dear Sir, I should be very much obliged if you could make it convenient to preach to your audience on the recognition of friends on earth, as I have been coming to your building for nearly six months, and nobody has taken any notice of me yet."—*The Evangel.*

* * *

Too Much Like Hell

A young lawyer, an infidel, boasted that he was going West to locate some place where there were no churches, no Sunday schools, no Bibles. Before the year was over, he wrote to a classmate. a young minister, begging him to come out where he was and start a Sunday school and preach, and "be sure to bring plenty of Bibles," closing his letter with these words, "I have become convinced that a place without Christians and Sundays and churches and Bibles is too much like hell for any living man to stay in."—*Echoes.*

A Crying Need

Ah, how we need new churches ready to pluck out their eyes for the gospel's sake. God give us a new, a sweeping, burning, consuming zeal for Christ! We are in a wilderness way! We are dying of thirst for the wells of water springing up into eternal life! We need power! Oh, for a day at the right hand of God! Spirit of God, return! Come again to the churches Thou hast given up! Anoint once more the ministers who have lost passion! Yet again give to the young men visions! Recover Thy church ere it be too late! Restore to Thy people the joys of salvation! Renew a right spirit within them! Then shall transgressors be taught Thy way, and sinners shall be converted unto Thee.—*J. C. Massee in the Watchman-Examiner.*

* * *

O Church of Christ, awake, awake,
And arm thyself with His own power;
The hosts of sin are striving hard
To win the conflict of the hour.

O Church of Christ, thy foes are great,
The battle calls for strength divine;
Omnipotence is thy defense,
Let all its power, its strength, be thine.

Then seek through prayer the promised aid,
The arm of flesh is sure to fail,
But armed with God's eternal power,
The Church both must and shall prevail.

Then up, and to the battle's front,
Alert, and eager for the fray;
Strong in the strength of His great might,
Stand fast and watch and fight and pray. —*Selected.*

* * *

The Mission of the Church

The mission of the Church is to save the souls of men. That is its true mission. It is the only mission of the Church. That should be its only thought. The minute that any church admits a singer that does not sing to save souls; the moment a church calls a pastor who does not preach to save souls; the moment a church elects a deacon who does not work to save souls; the moment the church gives a supper or an entertainment of any kind not for the purpose of saving souls, it ceases in so much to be a Church and to fulfill the magnificent mission God gave it. Every concert, every choir service, every preaching service, every Lord's Supper, every agency that is used in the church must have the great mission plainly before its eye. We are here to save souls of dying sinners. We are here for no other purpose, and the mission of the Church being so clear, that it is the only test of a real church.—*Russell H. Conwell.*

* * *

Always a Fresh Supply

Old John was a man of God and loved his village chapel. One day he was stopped by an acquaintance, who, by the way, was an ardent angler. "I say, John," said the angler, "I have often wondered what attraction there is up at the village chapel. You go week after week to the same old chapel, see the same folks, sing the same old hymns—" "Wait a minute," interrupted John. "You fish very often at the same spot, and in the same water, do you not?" "Yes, that's true," agreed the other. John smiled, and then exclaimed: "Well, you do not, for the water you fished in yesterday has passed on to the sea; and every time I go up to the chapel the Lord has something fresh for me."—*Sunday School Times.*

* * *

Upper or Supper Room?

The early Church prayed in the upper room, the twentieth century Church cooks in the supper room.

Today the supper room has taken the place of the upper room. Play has taken the place of prayer, and feasting the place of fasting. There are more full stomachs than there are bended knees and broken hearts. There is more fire in the range in the kitchen, than there is in the pulpit. When you build a fire in the church kitchen, it often, if not altogether, puts out the fire in the pulpit.

Ice cream chills the fervor of spiritual life.

The early Christians were not cooking in the supper room the day the Holy Ghost came, they were praying in the upper room. They were not waiting on tables, they were waiting on God. They were not waiting for the fire from the stove, but for the fire from above. They were detained by the command of God, and not entertained by the cunning of men. They were all filled with the Holy Ghost, not stuffed with a stew or roast.

Oh, I would like the cooking squad put out, and the praying band put in; less ham and sham, and more heaven; less pie, and more piety; less use for the cook-book, and more use for the old Book. Put out the fire in the kitchen and build it on the altar. More love and more life, fewer dinners and get after sinners. Let us have a church full of waiters on God, a church full of servers, serving God and waiting for His Son from heaven.—*Selected.*

* * *

A Strange Family

The father had never missed church or Sunday school in twenty-three years. The mother had had a perfect record for eleven years. A son has not missed for twelve years. A daughter has been at the evening service every Sunday for eight years.

What's the matter with the family, anyway? Don't they ever have company on Sunday to keep them away from church?

Don't they ever get tired on Sunday morning.

Don't they belong to any lodges, where they get their religion, instead of at their Father's house, or to any clubs, or to anything?

Don't they ever have headaches, or colds, or nervous spells, or tired feelings, or sudden calls out of the city, or week-end parties, or business trips, or picnics, or any other trouble?

Don't they ever have a radio, so that they can get some good sermons from out-of-town preachers?

Don't they ever get a lot more good out of reading a sermon out of a book?

Don't they ever get disgusted with the social Gospel, or whatever it is that their minister preaches?

What's the matter with this family anyway, and why are they so happy and cheerful? We leave it to you to answer.
—*Southern Churchman.*

* * *

Burying Dead Church Members

A funeral for dead church members was held last Sunday in the Christian Church at Jackson, Miss., at which time the pastor, the Rev. James N. Faulconer, placed the names of fifty inactive church members in a small artificial casket. In announcing his novel theme, this alert young pastor stated that "when one ceases to function in the church program, he is dead, and it is time for his funeral." This is nothing more nor less than plain truth, no matter how much some church members may dislike it.

The workers in a beehive sting the drones to death and get rid of these lazy parasites. But drones in a congregation may refuse to work or neglect to pay and still sit in the "amen" corner and get credit for being veritable pillars of the church.

As for the carping critics who talk their heads off telling the world what is wrong with the preacher and the church, it is very seldom that these worthies are either able or willing to offer a constructive suggestion. The "holding back strap" of horse and buggy days was a necessary part of the harness, but it was the traces and the collar that carried the load. The more church members there are in Hattiesburg and South Mississippi who are pulling, the faster we will move toward the kingdom of heaven.

Here is the full list of "dead ones" as announced by Jackson's live wire, Jimmy Faulconer. As you read it, spend more time in asking whether any of the names fit you than in seeking to tag some other fellow:

The names of those read to the congregation were: John Backslider, Anna Lukewarm, Margaret Indecision, Alma Gossiper, Jim Knocker, Edith Never Help, John I. Dolittle, Henry Never Pay, FrankNon-Missionary, Harry It Can't

Be Done, Lizza Sunday Headache, Judas Iscariot, who sold the church for gain, Tom I-Know-It-All, Rachel Joy Killer, Carl Changeable, Maul I-Can't, George Sleep Late, Fritz Some Day, Mrs. I. Am Wise, Cliff Selfishness, Florence Sensuality, Arthur Appetite, Maud Hatred, Homer Temper, Stella Impatience, Robert I-Am-Busy, and the Critical Family of six who are: Harry, who thinks the preacher preaches too long; Jane, who thinks the pastor should call oftener; Ike, who thinks the church has too many calls for missionary help; Callie, who doesn't like the choir; and Glenn, who thinks there are hypocrites on the official board of the church. —*Selected.*

* * *

When Men Are Impotent

In Port Barrios on the Caribbean coast, our little congregation of believers, the only evangelical group in the town, was much harassed by opposers who finally designated a certain Sunday when, as their leader boasted, they would completely demolish the work. Many believers were praying to God in behalf of this little church which had been established under such adverse conditions. A few days after the Sunday designated a letter from one of the believers came to our mission headquarters saying, "The leader of the opposers died on Saturday night, they are scattered, and the work of God goes on." In the following years "much people was added to the Lord."—*W. R. Adell, Los Angeles, Cal.*

* * *

Hard to Pull Down

One of the Red Republicans of 1793 told a good French peasant, "We are going to pull down your churches and your steeples—all that recalls past ages, and all that brings to your mind the idea of God." "Citizen," replied the peasant, "pull down the stars, then." The Church is built upon a strong foundation—upon Christ Himself.—*The King's Business.*

* * *

Not Spiritual Pygmies

The *Congo Mission News* speaks of Mr. Lass' work among the pygmies near Maitulu. These little people have built a chapel for Christian worship, and two hundred of them gather on Sundays. The building is tiny, and a white man is likely to collide with a crossbeam, fastened as high as little arms could reach. But to this people it is a building of cathedral proportions, the biggest structural venture of their lives. Six of these pygmies have given their hearts to Christ, and it is expected that they will constitute a nucleus of an evangelistic band.—*Sunday School Times.*

* * *

Washington and the Lord's Day

George Washington's pastor said of him: "No company ever kept him away from church. I have often been at Mount Vernon on the Sabbath morning when his breakfast table was filled with guests. *But to him they furnished no pretext for neglecting God and losing the satisfaction of setting a good example.* For instead of staying at home out of fancied courtesy to them, he constantly used to invite them to accompany him."—*Otterbein Teacher.*

* * *

"In Church Where You Ought To Be"

Hoffman, the famous German chemist, once related an experience he had. In 1890 he visited Glasgow, arriving in town late Saturday night. The following morning he went to call on Sir William Thompson, afterward Lord Kelvin. The doorbell was answered by a maid, of whom Hoffman asked if Sir William were at home. "Sir, he most certainly is not." "Could you tell me where I might find him?" "You will find him in church, sir," was the reply, "where you ought to be."—*Sunday School Chronicle.*

* * *

For Safer Driving

Several summers ago the "Socony-Vacuum Tours and Detours" put it aptly: Motorist's Suggestion for Safer Driving — Much of the charm of New England lies in the village churches, whose white spires shine on the distant hilltops and rise from every village green. But if you would really penetrate one of the secrets of the region, make it your practice to pause, at half-past ten or eleven o'clock on a Sunday morning, at one of these churches, and spend an hour with the worshiping congregation. The service will be simple, perhaps bare, but the chances are that you will come out again a soul refreshed, a more courteous—and a safer—driver in Sunday traffic.—*Zion's Herald.*

* * *

What They Saw in Church

Do you see the Lord in church? The minister announces his text for the morning message. Suddenly a door is opened in the rear of the auditorium with a noisy bang and grating sound. The farmer has brought his plow to church. He sits there in deep thought, studying the plow through the remainder of the service. Another door opens. A woman has brought her sewing machine to church! She studies her sewing machine while the pastor preaches. The interruptions continue. A man is heard nailing a tin roof. Another is mending shoes. Another, underneath the balcony, seems to be back in his everyday clothes working on a damaged automobile. A young woman sits in the choir punching a typewriter. Another bends over a washing machine. That afternoon the farmer said to his wife who had a big wash to do on the morrow, "I didn't get anything out of that sermon this morning, did you?" His wife answered, "No, I didn't." Whose fault was it?—*Courtesy Moody Monthly.*

* * *

The Blunt Truth

A man once came to Spurgeon and asked that great preacher if his church was a *pure* church.

He said that he was looking for a pure church that he might belong to it.

Spurgeon said that he did not know about his own church. He *did* know that there were many good people in it; saintly people and truly Christian people; but there might possibly be a Judas among them, as there was in the company of Jesus' first Apostles; and there might be some deceivers and idolators and those who walk unruly, as there seemed to have been in the churches of Rome and Corinth and Galatia and Ephesus and Colosse and Philippi and Thessalonica, and all the others to which the New Testament Epistles were written.

On the whole he thought that his church was not the one his brother was looking for. Indeed, he did not know that there had been such a church in all history.

"But," said Spurgeon, "if you should happen to find such a church, I beg of you not to join it, for you would spoil the whole thing."—*The Christian Observer.*

* * *

The Church in Europe

They say now, "All that we have experienced becomes somewhat clearer. Earlier we did not know what it meant and why we had to suffer like this. Now it seems to be clearer that God is using this catastrophe to revive His Church."

These people and these churches are now filled with a sense of joy and exhilaration that even the horrors of the concentration camps cannot overcome, and those who suffered most have been deepened and strengthened in their spiritual life. The Church has become the conscience of the nation, frankly outspoken in its condemnation of wrong; and we now have a rich harvest of statements and declarations by the churches concerning the bases and criteria of social and national and international order. For a long time the Church had not done that. Its silence has been one of the causes of the present disorder. But now in Europe the churches have discovered that they have a message to proclaim to states and nations.—*Bible Society Record.*

* * *

Farewell, Old Church

The structure built in 1872-3 by Dwight L. Moody was known as the Chicago Avenue Church for many years. After the great evangelist's death it was renamed the Moody Church. Since 1918, when it became Institute property, it has served as The Moody Bible Institute Auditorium.

Farewell, dear church, the time has come
Our last good-by to say,
Ere thy blest walls come crumbling down
To pass from sight away.
What mighty saints have here proclaimed
The riches of God's grace!
What multitudes His love have claimed
Within this hallowed place!

And though the hand of time hath sought
To lay this temple low,
The miracles that God hath wrought
Destruction cannot know.
These walls of clay, alas, must fall,
The living Church goes on
With Him who is her life, her all,
To greater things to come.

We bid thee, then, our fond farewells,
With mingled joy and tears—
Joy that new heights to come foretells,
Grief as thy sad end nears,
And unto Him who changeth not
We lift our hearts in praise
For all that He in love hath wrought
Through glorious bygone days!

—Avis B. Christiansen. Courtesy *Moody Monthly.*

* * *

Is It Safe to Count?

Gypsy Smith once remarked that he rejoiced over figures. "I was sitting at a table with some preachers," he said, "and one, a Scotsman, said, 'How did you get on at your meeting?' I said, 'Well, so many passed through the inquiry room.' He said, 'Is it safe to count?' I said, 'Well, they counted at Pentecost, and put it down at three thousand.' He changed the subject. Later on the Scotsman said, 'Are you married, Mr. Smith?' I said, 'Yes.' 'Any family?' 'Yes.' 'How many?' he asked. I replied, 'Is it safe to count?'" When the laughter had subsided the Gypsy added: "You count your children and the Lord counts His. You made enough fuss when your first babe was born. The Church doesn't fuss half enough when sinners are converted."—*Sunday School Chronicle.*

* * *

The following motto is found in Woodland Christian Church, (for Negroes), Kansas City, Mo.; (let us make it our own!): "Wake up, sing up, preach up, pray up, pay up, stay up, and never give up, or let up, or back up, or shut up until the cause of Christ in this church and the world is built up!"—*Gospel Herald.*

* * *

"Bones in the Church"

"Last week, Sambo, our minister preached on 'Bones in de Chuch,' an' he stepped on lots of people's toes."

"Bones in de Chuch! Well, what am dey all, boss?"

"Well, now, he names five different kind o' 'bones' they be in the average chuch. He sez as how they be some members what is like the *wishbones.* They's always awishin' fer better things, but never gets down to work fer them, and pray fer them. These here wishbone members ain't much account. Then they is the *jawbone Christians.* They does altogether too much talkin'. They is the gossipin' kind what usually makes trouble fer every one. The chuch don't need jawbone Christians. Then they is the *funnybone kind,* like that there crazy bone in *your elbow* what is always *agettin' hurt.* They is the ones who is too touchy; they is always agettin' their feelin's hurt; they is too easily offended. Then they is the *drybones;* some folks calls them *'fossils.'* They is orthodox, many of them, but dead as a dodo. They is cold as an ice house."

"Say, Uncle Ezry," interrupted Sambo, "our preacher over at de colored chuch says dat an icebox chuch is O.K. fer dead chickens, but a mighty pooah place fer live ones!"

"You're right, Sambo, too many of us chuch members be dead chickens. And ef the live ones would warm things up, they'd have to soon throw out the dead ones, cause they'd spoil worse. Well, as I was a sayin', about these bones in the chuch. The last sort he mentioned wuz the *backbone* kind, and they be the spiritual support of the chuch, and he sez they be all too few of them. It sure were a good sermon."

"He doan mentioned my kind of a bone, boss."

"What kind is that?"

"Seems to be some of us is like the *tailbone* — always behind. We is behind in our donations, we am behind in our work for de Lawd; in fact, we am pretty slow all de way 'round when it comes to His work."

"Guess you're right at that, Sambo. Let's pray that they will be many more Backbone Christians." — *Christian Victory Magazine.*

* * *

Why Churches Die

The old Baptist deacon from the ranch pointed to the real reason why many churches are dying. He said something like this: "We have been milked and not fed. The preachers expect work and money from us, but they do not feed us the Word of God in return. We need to remember that there are two ends to a cow. She will not give milk unless she is fed. Our churches cannot produce unless they are fed."—*Brethren Evangelist.*

* * *

What Shall It Profit . . . If They Gain a Lawn?

Christ was never displeased at any "unusual methods" that were taken to bring men to Him. The Rev. Charles Stelzle tells the following: "In the city there is a church directly across from a large public park. On a fine Sunday night during the summer there are at least ten thousand people in the park, and about fifty people inside the church. I said to the pastor, 'Doctor, why don't you get out on your church steps with your young people, and have an outdoor service? You've got a voice strong enough to be heard two blocks away. You can attract the people by the use of the cornet, and then preach to them. You can invite them to an after meeting inside the church.' The minister was willing, and brought it before the session which was made up of twelve good men. After the question was discussed, it was decided in the negative, because as one of them put it: 'We have a lawn in front of our church, and some of the people might come over out of the park onto our grass' "! — *Sunday School Times.*

Church Attendance—What My Absence Did

It made some question the reality of Christianity.

It made some think that I was a pretender.

It made many regard my spiritual welfare and that of others as a matter of small concern.

It weakened the effect of the church service.

It made it more difficult for the preacher to preach.

It discouraged the brethren, and therefore robbed them of a blessing.

It caused others to stay away from church.

It made it harder for me to meet the temptations of the Devil.

It gave the Devil more power over lost souls.

It encouraged the habit of non-church going.—*Selected.*

* * *

The Power of the Spire

Years ago Captain Cook was cruising among the South Sea Islands. Anchoring near an island he permitted his men to go ashore. Suddenly the natives rushed down upon them, and before they could regain their boats, one of the number had been captured. Being unarmed, the men were compelled to sit in their boats helpless, while those natives killed and ate their comrade before their eyes. Twenty years later Cook was again cruising in this same part of the sea when he was overtaken by a storm and his vessel wrecked. For days they drifted upon the waves until they were driven upon this same shore. When Cook recognized the same island where his comrade had been eaten twenty years before, he urged his men to use all their strength to keep the boat out to the sea, but in spite of all their efforts, they were driven upon the rocks. Crouching for fear in the foliage and keeping a sharp watch for the savages, they sent one of the men up to the top of a little hill to spy out the land. Cautiously he went forward until he reached the top and looked over. Down there in the valley, amid a clump of trees, he saw the white finger of a spire. With great joy, he turned and began waving his arms and shouting to his companions: "Come on, come on; it's all right; there's a church over here."—*Gospel Humanizing.*

* * *

"The Faithful Few"

In every church, in every clime,
When there's some work to do,
It's very likely to be done
By just the "Faithful Few."

Many folks will help to sing,
And some are glad to talk,
But when it comes to doing things,
A lot of them will balk—

"I can't do this, I can't do that;
Excuse me, please, this time—
I'd be so glad to help you out,
But it's not in my line."

So when the leader looks about
For some who'll help to "do,"
He nearly always has to go
And ask the Faithful Few.

He knows full well they're busy, too,
And always hard at work,
Yet he is sure they'll not refuse,
Nor any duty shirk.

They never stop to make excuse
But always try to do
The very, very best they can
To smooth the way for you.

God bless, I pray, the Faithful Few,
And may their tribe increase!
They must be very precious to
The blessed Prince of Peace.
—Chester E. Shuler.

* * *

A Child's Feet

While things are pliable is the time to make them permanent. A pastor in Kansas, in a letter to the business department of the Sunday School Times, gives a striking instance of this. "On the front walk leading up to my church one can see the imprint of two baby feet, pointing toward the door. Some mother had set her baby down there when the cement was still fresh. She started him in the right direction. Early impressions are permanent. Start the child right! That was fourteen years ago, and still the impressions on the walk are as if dating from yesterday." How much better to turn the feet of a little child toward the Door that is Christ Himself, than away from that Door. — *Sunday School Times.*

* * *

Through the Tower Windows

A dignitary of the Church of England tells how once in the city of York he groped his way through a dense fog to the famous old cathedral. So murky was it that it was with difficulty he found the door. But upon pushing the door open he saw in the nave at the crossing of the transcept a circle of bright sunlight. For a moment he marveled as at a miracle. Then he understood that the tower above the light rose higher than the level of the fog outside, and there the sun shone and poured its glorious light through the tower windows into the church. Though it was no miracle, it was a mighty parable. For that is the very core and essence of a church's business, that it shall be a place that aspires to Heaven, rising far above the mist and the murk of the common day, that it may bring Heaven's light into a darkened world.—*New Outlook.*

* * *

"Not Divided We?"

It is a classical anecdote — the story of Dr. William Adams' remark at a meeting of the Pan-Presbyterian Alliance, where he saw present representatives from the Established Presbyterians, the Covenanter Presbyterians, the Seceder Presbyterians, the Cameronian Presbyterians, the Erskine Presbyterians, Associate Presbyterians, Reformed Presbyterians, United Presbyterians, and so on. Said Dr. Adams, "We have here the E.P's, the F.P's, the C.P's, the S.P's, the A.P's, the R.P's, the C. P's, theE. P's, the U.P's, and last of all the Split P's." The audience roared at the "Split P's," but on sober thought they must have grieved. Methodist, Baptists, Lutherans, and so on — all are intricately subdivided, until Protestantism itself has become a dish of split P's. There are more than one hundred different Christian denominations in the United States alone.—*Sunday School Times.*

"I Went To Church This Morning"

A Lieutenant writes his mother as follows:

"I went to church this morning. Church out here is a privilege so rare I shall never forget it. There were only about 35 present, but it wasn't the numbers. Our altar was a stand over which draped a cloth deep red... The platform was covered with a white cloth... We had a small organ about three feet high, a small hymnal and a service pamphlet which I am sending you in this letter. Behind the altar a canvass screen was set up. We were seated on the sand with no overhead shelter. I felt the presence of Almighty God like I never have before. I think partially because I felt so much in need of an assuring hand. I could not keep the tears from my eyes, and Mom, I could feel myself being cleansed of all impurities. In the Bible it speaks of washing away our sins. It was never so plain as today. If I can only stand by faith as He has by me, I shall never be afraid. You and Dad will never know what blessings you brought on us by bringing us up in the House of the Lord."—*Office of the Chief of Chaplains, Washington.*

* * *

Einstein's Confession

The magazine *Your Faith* quotes Einstein as follows: "Being a lover of freedom, when the revolution came in Germany I looked to the universities to defend it, knowing that they had always boasted of their devotion to the cause of truth; but no, the universities were immediately silenced. Then I looked to the great editors of the newspapers whose flaming editorials in days gone by had proclaimed their love of freedom; but they, like the universities, were silenced in a few short weeks. Then I looked to the individual writers who as literary guides of Germany had written much and often concerning the place of freedom in modern life; but they, too, were mute. Only the Church stood squarely across the path of Hitler's campaign for suppressing truth. I never had any great interest in the Church before, but now I feel a great affection and admiration, because the Church alone has had the courage and persistence to stand for intellectual truth and moral freedom. I am forced to confess that what I once despised I now praise unreservedly." Professor Einstein is an outstanding example of an otherwise intelligent person despising a worth-while thing... The prophet Isaiah gives prophetically the language which the remnant of Israel will use when the manifestation of the Lord Jesus Christ in glory occurs to establish his kingdom. Among other things they will say, "He is despised and rejected of men; a man of sorrows, and acquainted with grief; and we hid as it were our faces from him; he was despised, and we esteemed him not" (Isa. 53:3). —*Now.*

* * *

Only Christians

John Wesley once was much troubled in regard to the disposition of various sects, and the chances of each in reference to future happiness or punishment. A dream one night transported him in its uncertain wanderings to the gates of hell.

"Are there any Roman Catholics here?" asked thoughtful Wesley.

"Yes," was the reply.

"Any Presbyterians?"

"Yes," was again the answer.

"Any Congregationalists?"

"Yes."

"Any Methodists?" by way of a clincher, asked the pious Wesley.

"Yes," was the answer, to his great indignation.

In the mystic way of dreams, there was a sudden transition, and he stood at the gates of heaven. Improving his opportunity, he again inquired:

"Are there any Roman Catholics here?"

"No," we replied.

"Any Presbyterians?"

"No."

"Any Congregationalists?"

"No."

"Any Methodists?"

"No."

"Well, then," he asked, lost in wonder, "who are they inside?"

"Christians!" was the jubilant answer.

—*Light and Liberty.*

Don't Disturb

Sometimes I have thought that the most unappreciated man on earth is a Pullman porter who must go down that mahogany lane in early morning to awaken passengers who are in no mood to be aroused. But this business of arousing people is a thankless job whether it apply to a Pullman porter at 6 a.m. or to a minister of the Gospel at 11 a.m. Too many Christians come to church on Sunday to rest at ease in Zion, and across their faces one seems to see as upon hotel room-doors, "Please Do Not Disturb!"—*Revelation.*

* * *

Glittering Formalities

A chill winter has settled over the church. Instead of melting penitence, the tears of other days have frozen into icicles; and are hanging about the sanctuary — cold glittering formalities taking the place of that holy tenderness which pleads with God, with strong crying, and warns men night and day with tears.—*Selected.*

CIGARETTE—TOBACCO

Condemned

Tobacco, next to alcohol, is the worst possible investment a nation can make; in reality an investment in deterioration — which destroys capital and creates nothing. In the first place it robs the nation of a vast acreage of land simply to burn it up in smoke. It wastes the lives of countless thousands of good citizens, scattering all their efforts to the winds in smoke.

It is the cause of innumerable fires, destroying property estimated to run into several hundred millions of dollars annually. Tobacco is the cause of constant bickerings and bitterness between growers of the weed, and buyers, and often gives rise to feuds which results in the burning of barns, and in murders.

Its use by many creates a strong desire for alcoholic stimulants. It wastes the time and money of millions of our young men — not to mention young women. It reduces the resistance of young men so that many through this agency become a prey to tuberculosis and are less capable of resisting other diseases.

It is a direct incitant and cause of cancer of the mouth in thousands yearly.

It ruins the nerves of many young men at a time when they are about to enter into their active life in the world, making them unable to concentrate upon their work, and unfit for the responsibility of important business.

As a cause for so many fires, it imposes heavy taxes on the community by reason of the destruction of property, and increase in expense of insurance, as well as the expense of supporting the fire department.

It is particularly harmful to women who are not so able to throw off its effects on the nerves by physical exercise.

—*Dr. Howard A. Kelly.*

* * *

A Letdown

Side by side with the liquor problem comes the pernicious and disgusting cigarette habit, which has so throttled our nation that women, including mothers and high school girls, are as much addicted to the habit as men. Dr. Samuel A. Brown, dean of Bellevue Hospital, New York City, says, "Women cannot smoke moderately. It is a letdown of moral standards." George Thomason, M.D., F.H.C.S., believes "beyond question that tobacco today represents one of the greatest menaces of the human race to physical, mental, and moral stability."

In many instances, the movie industry—acknowledged as the greatest force in the world for recreation and for education — is also selling out morality in exchange for dollars. It is said that 97 per cent of released films are marked "unfit," "for adults only," "questionable," or "matter of taste."—*Courtesy Moody Monthly.*

Tobacco is Blamed For Cancer of The Mouth

Dr. Shields Warren of Harvard Medical school, in a public lecture at the Medical school building in Boston on "Cancer and New Growths," said that he never knew of a case where a woman had cancer of the mouth, although statistics have shown that of men who have had cancer of the mouth all have been smokers. He said that times had changed somewhat and he is watching with a great deal of interest to see if women in view of their present habit of smoking, will acquire this disease.— *The Youth's Evangelist.*

* * *

When a Boy Smokes Cigarettes

Magister Crane, of New York City, said: "Ninety-nine out of every hundred boys between the ages of ten and seventeen years who come before me charged with crime, have their fingers disfigured by yellow cigarette stains... When you have arraigned before you boys hopelessly deaf through excessive use of cigarettes, boys who have stolen their sisters' earnings, boys who absolutely refuse to work, who do nothing but gamble and steal, you cannot help seeing that there is some direct cause, and a great deal of this boyhood crime is, in my mind, easy to trace to the deadly cigarette. There is something in the poison of the cigarette that seems to get into the system of the boy and destroy all moral fiber."

He gives the following course of a boy who begins to smoke cigarettes: "First, cigarettes. Second, beer and liquors. Third, craps — petty gambling. Fourth, horse racing — gambling on a bigger scale. Fifth, larceny. Sixth, state prison.

Not long ago a boy in New York robbed his mother and actually beat her because she would not give him money with which to buy cigarettes. Every little while we see accounts in newspapers all over the country of all kinds of petty thefts and misdemeanors which boys commit in order to satisfy the cigarette mania.

Another New York City magistrate says: "Yesterday I had before me thirty-five boy prisoners. Thirty-three of them were confirmed cigarette smokers. Today, from a reliable source, I have made the grewsome discovery that two of the largest cigarette manufacturers soak their product in a weak solution of opium. The fact that out of thirty-five prisoners thirty-three smoked cigarettes might seem to indicate some direct connection is not hard to understand. Opium is like whiskey, — it creates an increasing appetite that grows with what it feeds upon. A growing boy who lets tobacco and opium get a hold upon his senses is never long in coming under the domination of whiskey, too. Tobacco is the boy's easiest and most direct road to whiskey. When opium is added, the young man's chance of resisting the combined forces and escaping physical, mental, and moral harm is slim, indeed."

Young men of great natural ability, everywhere some of them in high positions, are constantly losing their grip, deteriorating, dropping back, losing their ambition, their push, their stamina, and their energy, because of its deadly hold upon them. If there is anything a young man should guard as Divinely sacred, it is his ability to think clearly, forcefully, logically. — *Gospel Herald.*

* * *

Chauncey Depew's Experience With Tobacco

The late Chauncey M. Depew, who lived to the age of ninety-three, and who was daily found at his office until a few months before his death, in his ninety-third year told why he gave up smoking a half century before. When a young man, he labored under the delusion that smoking steadied his nerves, and made them more dependable. He finally made the discovery that he had been under a deception. But here are his own words:

"I used to smoke twenty cigars a day, and continued at it until I became worn out. I did not know what was the matter with me; and physicians to whom I applied did not mention tobacco. I was in the habit of smoking at my desk, and thought I derived material assistance in my work from it. After a time I found I could not do any work without tobacco. My power of concentration was greatly weakened, and I could not think well without a lighted cigar in my mouth.

"One day I bought a cigar, and was puffing it with the feeling of pleasure that is possible only to the devotee. I smoked only a few minutes, and then took it out of my mouth and looked at it. I said to it, 'My friend and bosom companion, you have been dearer to me than gold. To you I have ever been devoted, yet you are the cause of all my ills. You have played me false. The time has come when we must part.'

"I gazed sadly and longingly at the cigar, then threw it into the street. I had been convinced that tobacco was ruining me. I have never smoked from that day to this." This renunciation was not, however, without a struggle. He says, "For three months thereafter I underwent the most awful agony. I never expect to suffer more in this world or the next. I didn't go to any physician or endeavor in any way to palliate my sufferings. Possibly a physician might have given me something to soften the torture. Neither did I break my vow. I had made up my mind that I must forever abandon tobacco or I would be ruined by it.

"At the end of three months my longing for it abated. I gained twenty-five pounds in weight. I slept well for seven or eight hours every night. I have never smoked from that day to this; and while no one knows better than I the pleasures to be derived from tobacco, I am still well content to forget them, knowing their effect."—Dr. H. H. Kress.

* * *

Tobacco or Souls?

I acquired the vile tobacco habit in the public school when quite young, and grew up with it until, when I became a man I had learned to chew, smoke and dip. I would often take a chew of the strongest tobacco and at the same time smoke a cigar. I had never heard a preacher lift his voice against this vice, but quite to the contrary, the majority of them together with the laity, used it in all of its forms. I was soundly converted in an old-time Methodist revival and for weeks I enjoyed sweet communion with God, and used my tobacco every day just as I had done for many years, but one day I bought a ten-cent box of snuff, and as I started for my home in the country, I opened my box and started to take some, when something checked me and seemed to say to me, "Why do you use that filthy stuff to defile the body which God calls His home?" I could not answer for I had no excuse; it was merely a habit.

Then the Spirit said to me, "How much did you pay for that box?" I answered only 10 cents, but again He whispered, "Ten cents would buy 100 tracts, which if wisely distributed might lead at least one soul to God. Then came the question to my mind: "Which would you rather have, a soul for God or a box of snuff?" I at once saw the point; threw the box into the grass, lifted my hand to Heaven and promised God that I would never touch the filthy weed again, but would ever afterward spend my tobacco money for tracts. I knew I was bound by the dirty habit until I could not quit of myself, so I asked God to help me, and He did, for from that day nearly eighteen years ago until this hour, I have never wanted it in the least. And I have brought and distributed many thousands of tracts which I have personally enjoyed much more than the old habit, and many have been blessed thereby. Go thou and do likewise!—*Tract.*

* * *

Think of This

A teacher said the other day that ninety boys out of every hundred who fail in grammar schools and high schools smoke tobacco. He says that boys who smoke are nearly all unruly and disobedient in school. And he says again that boys who get their lessons well and stand high in grammar schools make lower marks in high school if they begin to smoke in high school. This ought to be enough to make any boy stop and think before he begins to smoke, for it shows that it not only hurts a boy's mind, but his morals also.—*The Church of God Evangel.*

Nicotine, An Enemy of Man

Nicotine is, without doubt, a declared enemy of the human organism. It always exercises its disastrous effects, whether the tobacco be smoked, chewed or inspired in the form of snuff. Its action depends upon the method and quantity employed, being manifested by vertigo, vomit, coma and violent palpitation of the heart; it not being impossible that death might ensue if the habit be continued after the development of such symptoms. Although the mild intoxication is curable (it being often sufficient to drink water, stimulants or prepared beverage), the inveterate use of tobacco produces the chronic poisoning called "tabaquismo" characterized by amnesia (loss of memory), ambliopia (diminution of visual power), stomach trouble, palpitation of the heart, and other symptoms that demonstrate abnormalities of the nervous system and blood pressure. Many ulcerations of the stomach and intestines are attributable to the use of tobacco, as well as some affections of the mouth, throat and respiratory organs, including "antracosis" or carboniferous deposit on the mucous membranes. But the point upon which we most strongly insist, in the struggle against the tobacco habit, and especially in young students, are the failure of memory and weakness of eyesight, resulting in more or less severe form in those addicted to it.—*Frank J. Fiallos, Ph.G., Honduras, Central America.*

* * *

A Simple Solution

We clip the following from Norman Dunning's Life of Samuel Chadwick, who was principal of Cliff College. "Shortly after the beginning of a certain term, a student much older than the average Cliff man knocked at the door of the principal's study. 'Sir,' he said, 'would you give me permission to have a pipe? (It is a rule at Cliff College that no student smokes.) I am not like these boys,' continued this middle-aged brother. 'I have been a smoker for twenty years. I finished my last pipe before I came through the college gates on Friday, and I have tried my best to do without tobacco since. But, sir, I can't hold out any longer. I am dying for a smoke.' The principal half turned in his chair, and swept the brother with his glance from his toes to the crown of his head. 'Is that really true, brother? Are you really dying for a smoke?' 'I am, sir,' replied the student. 'Then,' said the principal, pointing to a seat beside his desk, 'sit down in that chair and die.' He went on to explain that any man who allowed a habit to get such a hold on him that he would die if he did not give way to it, was best dead. The would-be smoker looked first at the floor and then at the ceiling and then at the floor again. 'Let us talk to God about this,' said the principal. They knelt together on the study floor. The principal prayed that God would glorify himself in this man's life. The brother rose from his knees, the craving gone. For a year, he stayed at the college, and the temptation to smoke never returned."—*Moody Church News.*

* * *

What Athletes Say About the Cigarette

The current campaign on the air offers an Aladdin's lamp to the young woman of the twentieth century. Does she want steadier nerves, a better singing voice, or more perfect form? Cigarettes are falsely offered as the unfailing answer. Does the schoolboy want to play a better football game? Smoke more cigarettes, is the urge. Do you want to be a hero? Puff cigarettes continually. A cigarette in the mouth of every man, woman, and child in the United States — that is the outrageous goal of this advertiser.

Knute Rockne, athletic director of Notre Dame University, has stated that the makers of a well-known cigarette offered him $2,000 to sign a testimonial to the effect that his athletes always used their brand because it did not hurt their wind. Look at Charles Paddock, the world's fastest sprinter, does he dare to smoke? Could he have established his long string of world records if he had poisoned his system and weakened his heart with nicotine from the cigarette? Ty Cobb, who has retired as an outstanding leader in baseball, says: "Too much cannot be said against the evils of cigarette smoking. It stupefies the brain, saps vitality, undermines one's health, and lessens the moral fiber of the man."—*Sunday School Times.*

* * *

Polluting the Blood Stream

You learned in grammar school that the lungs, mouth, the nose, and related air passages are covered by a mucous lining, comprising an area of a great many square feet over which the entire volume of the blood is spread every three minutes. You have seen what one mouthful of smoke can do to a white linen handkerchief. You must realize its similar effect upon this delicate membrane lining the respiratory system. And the blood, which comes to the lungs to be purified, absorbs these poisons instead; and carries them to the brain, the heart, and all the vital organs.

Many of you boys are looking forward to athletic success. In spite of the fact that you frequently see big, strong, husky men smoking cigarettes, have you ever stopped to think why it is that all the great athletic directors and trainers disapprove of smoking? There must be some vital reason why these men — who are not "religious cranks" or "foolish old women" trying to deprive boys of harmless pleasure — should be so firm in their opposition to smoking on the part of boys in their charge. *They are men who know the human body.* They have made it a point to learn what is necessary to put that body in the best possible condition for the strain and test of the athletic contests.—*Sunday School Times.*

* * *

What They Say:

Henry Ford: "The world of today needs men: not those whose minds and will power have been weakened or destroyed by the desire and craving for alcohol and tobacco, but instead, men with initiative and vigor, whose mentality is untainted by habits which are ofttimes uncontrollable."

Luther Burbank: "If I answered your question simply by saying I never use tobacco or alcohol in any form, and rarely ever coffee or tea, you might say that was a personal preference, and proves nothing. But I can prove to you most conclusively, that even the mild use of stimulants is incompatible with work requiring accurate and definite concentration."

Dr. J. Dixon Mann: "Tobacco smoke contains a formidable list of poisons, among which are the following: nicotine, pyridine bases, ammonia, methylammine, prussic acid, carbon monoxide, sulphuretted hydrogen, carbolic. Several of these are deadly in very small doses, so that the smoker cannot possibly escape their toxic effects."

Herbert Hoover: "There is no agency in the world that is so seriously affecting the health, education, efficiency and character of boys and girls as the cigarette habit. Nearly every delinquent boy is a cigarette smoker."

Thomas Edison: "Cigarette smoking has a violent action on the nerve centers, producing a degeneration of the cells of the brain, which is quite rapid among boys. Unlike most narcotics, this degeneration is permanent and uncontrollable."

Red Grange (greatest football player of a decade): "You cannot drink and smoke, and expect to succeed as an athlete."

Connie Mack: "We do everything in our power to discourage the use of cigarettes among our baseball boys, knowing the great harm that tobacco has done to those in the habit of using it."

Judge Crane of New York: "Cigarettes are ruining our children, endangering their lives, dwarfing their intellect and making them criminals fast. The boys who use them seem to lose all sense of right, decency and righteousness."

Judge Shaw of Michigan: "In every instance of juvenile delinquency in this court, I have found that the boys were cigarette users."

Judge Allen of North Dakota: "Every male juvenile delinquent brought before me for the last sixteen years has been a cigarette smoker."

Madame Schumann-Heink: "I want you to know that I have never smoked and I never will. I think, and I say it with all my heart, that it is a crime that you girls are poisoning your young bodies with smoking cigarettes."

Mrs. M. B. McGarvan (President, American Association of Cosmeticians): "Women smokers' faces are sharper, lips are becoming pallid, corners of the mouth sag, lips commence to protrude and develop twitching habits and the eyes acquire a blank stare."

I have toured the United States and Canada many times. Wherever I go, I observe young women and old women, without embarrassment, freely puffing on cigarettes. I have little sympathy for the old gray-haired woman who has become a tobacco fiend, but it grieves me to see a young woman with possibilities of a pleasant and happy future, throw herself into the stream of gaiety, to sink beneath the rapids of intemperance.

The average young man is not favorably impressed with the idea of a cigarette fiend for a wife. The culture of a woman is soon lost in the smoking of cigarettes. If you have begun the use of cigarettes or intoxicating drinks, stop it . . . for it will in time destroy your strength, give you much trouble and make you old when you should be young.

Speaking of Colonel Charles Lindbergh, a well-known writer says: "The flying Colonel spurned a large offer from a tobacco company for his endorsement of a popular brand of cigarettes."—*Sunday School Times.*

* * *

Luther Burbank

Luther Burbank, one of the world's best-known scientists, wrote: "You have seen pictures of military cemeteries near great battlefields. Upon every headstone is chiseled the inscription, 'Killed in action.' If one knew nothing about war, these headstones would be sufficient to impress upon him that war is deadly—that it kills.

"How much would you know about tobacco if upon the tombstone of every one killed by it were inscribed, 'Killed by tobacco'? You would know a lot more about it than you do now, but you would not know all, because tobacco does more than kill. *It half kills.* It has its victims in the cemeteries and in the streets. It is bad enough to be dead, but it is a question if it is not sometimes worse to be half dead—to be nervous, irritable, unable to sleep well. — *Sunday School Times.*

* * *

The Effects of the First Smoke

In his book, "The Cigarette as a Physician Sees It," *Dr. Daniel H. Kress,* Superintendent of the Washington Sanitarium and Hospital, Takoma Park, D. C., states in simple, forceful terms: "The best evidence of the effect of tobacco is to be seen when the first smoke is taken. Headache, nausea, and vomiting occur. But if the habit is persisted in, the body gradually builds up a 'tolerance.' This does not mean an immunity to nicotine. The nicotine continues to do its insidious work, but after a 'tolerance' is established, the disagreeable reflex test simply ceases, and the body tries to make the best of a bad situation." He continues: "Because the evil effects of tobacco are not seen by the naked eye in the smoker's heart, blood vessels, kidneys, liver, stomach, and brain day by day as he smokes a cigarette, he thinks he is 'getting by.' Tobacco kills slowly, but nevertheless surely. The smoker is committing suicide on the installment plan. The reckoning day is sure to come."

You hear frequent references to the nicotine in tobacco and its harmful effect on smokers. Perhaps you wonder just what it is and what form it takes. Dr. Kress says: "Nicotine is the poison depended upon by gardeners to kill insects and pests on plants. It is so deadly that it must be employed in a very dilute form, only a few drops to the pint of water. So virulent a poison is it that physicians have for years refrained from prescribing it. There is no antidote for tobacco poisoning, as there is for morphine poisoning, strychnine poisoning, and poisoning by some of the other drugs used in medicine." — *Sunday School Times.*

* * *

Surgeons and Smoking

It is always difficult for a layman to try to make statements in the field of other professions, particularly hard for a layman to try to speak in medical terms, so it is much better for me to quote for you the actual statements of some of the world's greatest physicians.

At a dinner given to a group of eminent surgeons not long ago at Rochester, Minn., Dr. William J. Mayo, one of the famous doctor-brothers, who was the host on this occasion, made the announcement: "Gentlemen, it is customary, as we all know, to pass around cigars after dinner; but I shall not do it. I do not smoke, and I do not approve of smoking. If you will notice, you will see that the practice is going out among the ablest surgeons, the men at the top. No surgeon can afford to smoke."—*Sunday School Times.*

* * *

The Smoker's Level

At the Grand Central Station, New York, there are two levels from which to take the trains. Over the door of the Ladies' Lounge on the upper level is this inscription: "Smoking not permitted: It is allowed in the Ladies' Lounge on the Lower Level." So, lady, if you want to smoke, you will have to — descend.—*Sunday School Times.*

* * *

Nineteen Poisons

Reading Dr. J. Dixon Mann, F.R.C.P., in the *British Medical Journal,* we learn that "tobacco contains not less than nineteen poisons, every one of which is capable of producing deadly effects. Several of these—nicotine, prussic acid, carbon monoxide, and pyridine — are deadly in small doses, so that the smoker cannot possibly escape their toxic effects." You would not recognize the names of most of the nineteen poisons he lists in his article, as they are mostly highly technical, but those above mentioned are familiar to you at least by name. For instance, carbon monoxide is the active element in ordinary gas used in your kitchen range, and is the thing that causes death when gas escapes in a closed room. It is also a frequent cause of death when persons start the engines of their automobiles in a closed garage. Dr. Kress tells us that "one gram of tobacco when smoked develops from sixty to eighty cubic centimeters of carbon monoxide."—*Sunday School Times.*

Young Women Beware

Dr. Brown, who has been with the Keely Institute, Los Angeles, California, for sixty years, is quoted as saying: "The cigarette is a greater menace to the young people of today than the open saloon ever was. Every young woman who came to us for treatment of the liquor habit was an inveterate user of cigarettes. She began her drinking after using cigarettes. If cigarettes could be prohibited in America, the liquor problem would be solved. In our institution we find that the history of every woman who comes to us for treatment could have this caption written above her name and record: Cigarettes, drink, dope!"—*The Church of God Evangel.*

* * *

Reputation

Since the World War I Sergeant Alvin C. York, the famous hero of Tennessee, has given himself to the building of the Agricultural Institute, so that the youth of his native state may have better educational advantages. Asked by Beatrice Plumb, on a recent visit, "How are the schools?" his secretary replied: "Well, of course, we need money awfully badly, but the sergeant won't compromise to get it. This week a tobacco company offered him five hundred dollars for a five-minute radio talk about his war experiences—one hundred dollars a minute! *But the sergeant doesn't smoke himself, and he doesn't believe in smoking. He said he wasn't going to sail under any false colors, and refused the offer. That's the sergeant!*"—*New Century Leader.*

* * *

How He Knew

I passed an old man on the street the other day whose pink cheeks and clear eye and steady, elastic step attracted the attention of some high school boys who were near. "He would have made a jim dandy fellow on a track team when he was young," said one of the boys. "He can outsprint some of us now," said another. "You don't say! How old is he?" "Almost sixty." "Whew! How does he keep so young, do you suppose?" "Well, he never touched tobacco or whisky, for one thing." "How do you know so much about him?" "He happens to be my father, and so I know a good deal about him, and he's just the kind of man I mean to be myself." — *Sunday School Times.*

* * *

What Tobacco Did

A little boy was very sick. The doctors said only a transfusion of blood could save him. The father offered to give the blood. The doctors tested the father's blood and found too much of a tobacco taint to make it safe for use. Someone else, *who did not use tobacco,* was chosen, and this blood was so clean that it was used, and the child's life was saved.

A merchant consulted a physician. The doctor told him he was run down with nicotine poisoning, and advised him to go to Hot Springs in Arkansas and have the nicotine sweated out of him. The man was very indignant at first, saying that he smoked only in moderation. But at last he consented to go. At the Hot Springs they gave him a hot bath to open up the pores of the skin. Then he was taken to the Turkish bathroom, a very hot, close room indeed. He was wrapped in a large, clean, white sheet from his neck to his heels; he was given cold water to drink, and a towel wet with cold water was bound around his head. Then he was placed on a couch and left there twenty minutes. How he did sweat! The sheet around him was as wet from perspiration as though it had been out in a rain. When they took the sheet off it was streaked with long stripes of tobacco stains, where the nicotine in his system had been drawn out by the perspiration and had stained the sheet.

"I was surely scared when I saw those brown streaks!" the merchant said when he told about it. It took *eighteen hot and eighteen Turkish baths* before the sheet came off from him clean of tobacco stains.—Lora S. La Mance in *The Junior Class Paper.*

* * *

When Ministers Cannot Deceive

At one of the many churches that employ the gambling game "Bingo" to rake in the shekels, a lady's purse was found during the course of the game. The priest announced the discovery and specified that the owner must identify it. A young lady stepped out and was asked to state what was within the purse. She named a number of articles and the priest asked, "And what else?" Rather shamefacedly she added, "A package of cigarettes." The priest handed her the bag, and, as she started away, stopped her to say, "I doubt whether the Virgin Mary ever smoked cigarettes." With a toss of her head, the maiden replied, "And I doubt whether the Lord Jesus Christ ever played Bingo." All of which goes to show that the churches that stoop to worldly methods of raking in the cash are not deceiving even the people who participate. — *Christian Standard.*

COMMUNION WITH GOD

The Open Door

A lady had been away from home in the afternoon, and upon her return, discovered that she had lost the key to the door.

She thought to herself, How unfortunate! and time is pressing. She went to three neighbors and borrowed as many keys, in the hope that one would fit. But not one of them would do.

Finally someone asked if she had tried the latch. She replied in a spiritless voice, "No, but I will." She did, and found that the door had been unlocked all the time, and walked in.

What a good illustration this is of the anxious soul, in his desire to approach God. He stands outside, with his mind full of doubts and fears as to his welcome. He believes there are many things in the way before he may see the Saviour, when the door is not only unlocked but stands wide open, with a cordial invitation to enter.—*Messages of Love.*

* * *

The Source of the Grace

An old violinist was poor but possessed an instrument which never failed to charm by its soothing mellowness. Played as he could play it, it never failed to awaken responsive chords in the heart. Asked to explain its charm, he would hold out his violin and tenderly caressing its graceful curves he would say: "Ah, a great deal of sunshine must have gone into this wood, and what has gone in, comes out."

How much of God's sunshine has entered into your life? How much time have you spent in the radiance of His presence?—F. T. L. in *Help and Food.*

* * *

The Quiet Time

In order to grow in grace, we must be much alone. It is not in society that the soul grows most vigorously. In one single quiet hour of prayer it will often make more progress than in days of company with others. It is in the desert that the dew falls freshest and the air is purest.—Andew Bonar.

* * *

The Quiet Hour

"In quietness and confidence shall be your strength" (Isaiah 30:15).

We need the quiet hour to keep the body in tone. A woman, weary, fretful, sick, went to her doctor. After listening to the recital of her complaints, he said, "What you need is to read your Bible more." She was inclined to resist the suggestion; but the doctor said, "Go home; read your Bible one hour each day, and in a month come back."

At the end of the month she returned. Looking in her face, he said: "You have been an obedient patient; do you think you need any other medicine?"

"No; but how did you know that was what I needed?" she replied.

Taking up his well-worn Bible, the doctor said: "If I were to omit my daily reading in this Book, I should lose my greatest source of strength and skill."

The quiet hour is good for the body.

We need the quiet hour to deepen the spiritual life.

The quiet hour should be carried into the work of the whole day by "practicing the Presence of God."—H. F. Shupe.

* * *

Better Than Being Saved

One day I saw a peddler, evidently an Irishman, selling wares from door to door. I accosted the man with the usual greetings, after which I remarked: "It's a grand thing to be saved." "Eh?" said the peddler. "It is, but I know something better than that." "Better than being saved?" I asked in astonishment. "What can you possibly know better than that?" The *companionship of the Man who saved me,*" was the unexpected and astonishing reply.—*Toronto Globe.*

* * *

Henry Drummond

Henry Drummond, speaking of the value of a little time spent alone with God, said: "Five minutes spent in the companionship of Christ every morning —aye, two minutes, if it is face to face and heart to heart—will change the whole day, will make every thought and feeling different, will enable you to do things for His sake that you would not have done for your own sake or for anyone else's sake."

Hush, my soul! Be still and listen,
Hear what the Almighty says;
Be not thou forever talking,
Silence sometimes yields more praise.

Have you never learned the lesson,
"Speech is silver? Silence—gold?"
There's a joy too deep to utter,
Joy that never can be told.

As in boundless depths of ocean,
There is stillness so profound!
That the noise of war or tempest
Never yet produced a sound.

So in soul depths, there is silence,
By no earthly music stirred,
Where the voice of the Eternal
Is the *only* voice that's heard.

Oh, 'tis joy, to sit and listen
To the still, small voice of love,
And in lowliest adoration
All our glad obedience prove.

—*The Elim Evangel.*

* * *

The Secret of Growth

An old Lancashire woman was listening to the reasons that the neighbors were giving for their minister's success. They spoke of his gifts, of his style, of his manner. "Nay," said she. "I tell you what is it. Yon man is very thick with the Almighty." The great fitness for service is in much communion. — *Bible Expositor.*

* * *

Alone With God

In silence, at the close of day,
When sun and light have gone away,
I kneel in solitude to pray,
Alone with God.

When sad, I count my every care,
And all the grief that I must bear;
Then close my eyes in peaceful prayer,
Alone with God.

When triumph brings me joy anew,
And I feel blessed in all I do,
I ne'er forget my rendezvous
Alone with God.

Through life, I always want to be
A Christian of reality,
And keep that hour so dear to me,
Alone with God.

—*David L. Diehl.*

* * *

The Most Prevalent Spiritual Disease

The worst enemy of true religion is the hustle and bustle of our times. The Christian's most persistent and deadly foe is the temptation to neglect the soul. Our worst enemy is not worldliness, but *too much care about the legitimate things of earth.* Indulgence in things positively sinful is not so destructive as spending too much time in the pursuit of things that are only secondary.

Most people's lives are too full of excitement and change to enable them to relish the more quiet but enduring joys of the intellect and the soul. They have no time to think for themselves, no patience to read good books, no taste for Bible study. Their lives are superficial, their souls are shallow.

It is no exaggeration to say that the habit of reading good religious books is in danger of disappearing. One of the reasons we are pessimistic about the future of our Church is that there is not much desire for Bible study and religious reading among the mass of young men and women in our churches.

The most prevalent disease in the body of the Church is a pernicious anemia, a serious lack of vital blood-cells, caused by refusing to partake daily of good spiritual food—such food as only the Word of God can provide. It results in spiritual weakness, listlessness, lukewarmness, and in a lack of resistance to many other kinds of spiritual ailments.

—*The Banner.*

* * *

Shut Thy Door

"Enter into thy closet, and . . . shut thy door" (Matt. 6:6).

Souls often grow lonely in a crowd, and starve in the midst of temples, worshipers and ordinances. God would have us alone with Him sometimes. Coming to church is not coming to Christ. "Enter into thy closet, and * * shut thy door." Shut out nonsense, business, care and pleasure. Shut out flatteries and frowns. Shut out strangers and acquaintances. Shut out friends and foes. Shut out this world and open the window that looks out upon the next. Give the mind rest. Give the ear quiet. Give the tongue silence. Give the heart meditation. Give the soul communion with God; look up, there are blessings waiting for you. Listen: God speaks in His stlll small voice. Ask: God waits to hear. See that your soul is at peace with God. See that no shade of sin hides from your sight the Heavenly Father's face.

Settle the question of peace, pardon and duty in secret before the Lord; then bring everything that concerns your heart and life, for time or for eternity, and lay it before the mercy seat.—H. L. Hastings.

A Quiet Heart

Oh, Lord, give me a quiet heart—
So oft my heart is filled with fear:
I need the peace Thou canst impart;
I need to feel that Thou art near.

Help me to walk by faith each day
Though shadows hide the path from view;
Give me a quiet heart, I pray,
To trust Thee as Thou bid'st me do.

I cannot see the journey's end,
I know not what lies just ahead;
But, oh, I have a Heav'nly Friend
Who knows the path my feet must tread.

So now, my heart, be still and trust,
Although thou canst not see the way;
For He who formed thee from the dust
Wilt lead thee on from day to day.

A quiet heart—a quiet heart,
From which is banished doubts and fears;
Oh, Lord, give me a quiet heart
That trusts Thee for the coming years!

—Winifred M. Nienhuis, in *Gospel Herald.*

* * *

The Power Room

The story is told of two men who were one time visiting a great factory. They were shown all the different rooms where the great machines were buzzing and making a great noise, as the wheels turned at a rapid pace. Then the guide led them to another room. Here everything was very quiet, not a sound to be heard. One of the men said, "Not much doing here." The guide smilingly replied, "But this is the most important room of all, this is where the power comes from to run the great machines. We call this the *Quiet Room* and it is the *Power Room* as well."

As I read this story I wondered where we get our power. Do we have a Quiet Room? Do we need a Quiet Room?—a Power Room? I am sure you will say, "We indeed need a Power Room, a place where we can meet the Lord and talk things over with Him." Yes, we need to tarry there, too, until we know the Lord's will and then go out to do it as best we can. Our lives will be fruitless and failures unless we *do spend* some time in the Quiet Room.—*Gospel Herald.*

* * *

Solitude

"Solitude," said Cecil, "is my great ordinance." There are Heaven-born gifts and powers in lives of which we will never be conscious until in solitude they are revealed and developed. Look at John Bunyan. Did not Bedford jail bring out the best that was in him? Look at Milton. Did not sightless eyes reveal glories he would otherwise never have seen? Look at David Livingstone. Those eight or nine years in the solitudes of Africa during his early missionary career prepared him as nothing else could have done for the remarkable series of explorations and victories that resulted in opening a continent to Christ. Or look at Paul. From a Roman dungeon he gave us his best.

Because Paul was a prisoner at Rome, what wealth of spiritual teaching, and what glimpses of the unseen and eternal are ours! There his life came to its richest fruitage. And earthly life for us will reach its highest bliss, and these Heaven-born faculties their fullest fruition, only when we are much *alone* with God.—*Selected.*

* * *

Trysting Place

Dear Lord, I want, each day that comes,
To share some part with Thee,
Where I can sit at Thy dear feet,
And hear Thee speak to me.

A place where I can turn aside,
And leave the cares of life;
Where I can get the strength I need
To banish storm and strife.

A quiet, holy, trysting-place,
Where Thou to me canst give
The very blessing that I need;
Here would I feast and live!

—Adjutant Martha Grenfell.

Alone With God

Alone with God, He speaks to me
As friend with friend;
He fills my heart with joy and peace
That has no end.
He tells me of His love for me,
And I rejoice.
Alone with God—to feel Him near;
To hear His voice!

Alone with God—the doors all shut—
I see His face;
I feel His love, so strong and true;
I know His grace.
His comfort comes, in strength'ning power,
To fill my heart.
Alone with God—how blest it is
To come apart!

Alone with God—how sweet the sound
Of His dear voice!
To seek His face—in quiet place—
This is my choice!
'Tis good to know that He is there
My need to meet;
Alone with God—His presence near—
Ah, yes, 'tis sweet!
—Sylvia R. Lockwood.

Alone With God

A minister at a camp meeting, in the course of his sermon, advised that the people, as they retired from the service, should go away and be alone with God for fifteen minutes. A brother followed the advice, and was brought into the most delightful fellowship with Jesus. The unfolding of things belonging to the Kingdom of God, even in that fifteen minutes, was rich and glorious. We would urge our readers to be *often* alone with God. If you want to be let down into eternal mysteries, into the Godhead's deepest sea, be alone with God. If you want to feel as never before the strength of the "power that worketh in us," be alone with God. Fifteen minutes in such secret fellowship is worth an age of blustering outdoor noise about religion.—*P. H. Advocate.*

* * *

The Indian's Preparation

An Indian in his prepartion for the Sabbath day services said he made his body very clean from head to foot, and then instead of laughing and chatting idly with his friends,—to use his own words,—"I sit down and think Jesus until it is time to go." How many of us "think Jesus" just before church time?
—*Home Missions Echoes.*

COMPLAINING

"The Grumble Family"

There's a family nobody likes to meet,
They live, it is said, on Complaining Street,
In the city of Never-are-Satisfied,
The river of Discontent beside.
They growl at that and they growl at this,
Whatever comes there is something amiss;
And whether their station be high or humble,
They all are known by the name of Grumble.

The weather is always too hot or cold,
Summer and winter alike they scold;
Nothing goes right with the folks you meet
Down on that gloomy Complaining Street.
They growl at the rain and they growl at the sun,
In fact their growling is never done.
And if everything pleased them, there isn't a doubt
They'd growl that they'd nothing to grumble about.

But the queerest thing is that not one of the same
Can be brought to acknowledge his family name
For never a Grumbler will own that he
Is connected with it at all, you see.
And the worst thing is that if anyone stays

Amongst them too long he will learn
their ways,
And before he dreams of the terrible
jumble
He's adopted into the family of Grumble.

So it were wisest to keep our feet
From wandering into Complaining
Street;
And never to growl, whatever we do,
Lest we be mistaken for Grumblers too,
Let us learn to walk with a smile and
song,
No matter if things do sometimes go
wrong,
And then, be our station high or humble,
We'll *never* belong to the family of
Grumble! —*East and West.*

* * *

Grumbling, Even in Plenty

Mrs. Higgins was an incurable grumbler. She grumbled at everything and everyone. But at last the vicar thought he had found something about which she could make no complaint; the old lady's crop of potatoes was the finest for miles around. "Ah, for once you must be well pleased," he said, with a beaming smile, as he met her in the village street. "Everyone's saying how splendid your potatoes are this year." The old lady glowered at him as she answered: "They're not so poor. *But where's the bad ones for the pigs?"—Sunday School Times.*

* * *

Grumble-House

Grumble-House is on the North side of Dismal street. It is surrounded by a stone wall, which fails to admit the sunlight of God's Grace. It is located near a forest which is haunted by the screech-owls of discontent. There are many rodents on the premises which spoil the fruits of the Spirit. The lamp of joy is never seen in any of its gloomy rooms. Owing to their spirit of heaviness, the inmates of Grumble-house have no garments of Praise; but are clad in the beggarly elements of the world. As they have never learned Ephesians 5:19, their only song is like the croaking of a raven; because it does not proceed from hearts overflowing with thankfulness to God for all His goodness and mercy.

I will not grumble, grunt or growl;
Or sit and mope like some old owl:
Because life's inconvenient things
Do test the strength of soaring wings;
With which to rise above the roof
Of Grumble-house; and thus give proof
That I belong to Pleasant-town;
And wear a smile, but ne'er a frown.
Thus will my aged wrinkled face
Reflect my Father's loving grace.
—*Church of Christ Advocate.*

CONFESSION

Unashamed

The verse of Scripture that converted Spurgeon from sin to the Saviour was: "Look unto Me, and be ye saved, all the ends of the earth: for I am God, and there is none else" (Isa. 45:22). Later, Spurgeon said, "I looked at Him, and He looked at me, and we became ONE forever!" From the moment of his conversion, Spurgeon began confessing the One who had saved him. "The moment I came out of that little chapel wherein I found the Saviour, I wanted to tell out my tale of joy!" Anywhere, everywhere, confess Him and His mightiness to save! —*Walter B. Knight.*

* * *

They Can't Laugh You Out

I remember when I was a little boy, how my mother would draw me to her knee and speak to me so solemnly of the importance of trusting the Lord Jesus Christ as my Saviour, and I would say, "Well, Mamma, I would like to do it, but the boys will all laugh at me." Mother used to say, "Harry, remember, they may laugh you into hell, but they can never laugh you out of it." And oh, how that used to go home to me, and it stayed with me all through the years! Yes, men may sneer and ridicule and not understand us as we come out for Christ, but after all, His is the only approval worth having. —*From "Addresses on the Gospel of John," by H. A. Ironside.*

* * *

Possible,—But Not Profitable

Two A.T.S. girls went to an Open Air Forces meeting. "I am a Christian," said one of the girls, "but I am not very open about it. Is it not possible to pray in bed?" "Possible, yes, but it is no testimony to others, is it?" The second girl added, "Well, I am not a Christian, but I am interested. There was a girl in my room who knelt at her bedside every night, and the first time I saw her do it I cried myself to sleep." Both those girls returned to barracks that night, not only trusting the Lord Jesus as Saviour, but determined to confess Him. —*In British Camps.*

* * *

Decision

Three new pupils had been received into the Argentine Mission School. I suggested that we spend a few minutes in personal testimony, intimating that each should tell when she had given herself to Jesus, and saying that I had done so myself at the age of fourteen. At that word I noticed a quick flash of intelligence pass over the face of one of the new girls, followed instantly by a very serious expression that continued until it came her turn to "take the word." I asked, "Are you a Chrstian, Deolindo?" There was a doubtful nod in response, so I varied the question. "Have you given yourself to God?" This was answered by a decidedly more positive nod. "Do you realize that Jesus is your Saviour, and that you are God's child?" All at once the black eyes flashed for joy, the whole face was transfigured, and the nod was accompanied by a soft, "Si, Senora." "Since when?" I asked, my own heart filled with gladness. "Since now," was the unequivocal answer. And from that hour she set herself definitely and joyfully to prepare herself for a life work in His service. — *Christian Endeavor World.*

* * *

Saved,—No Matter What

Abigail early learned to trust the Lord Jesus. When she was five years old her mother was taken ill, and given up to die. The child prayed for her mother's life to be spared until she had confessed Christ. The Lord answered her prayer and her mother got well. Then Satan tempted Abigail not to tell her mother she was saved. "The minute you confess Christ she will die," he whispered. So for two years her lips were closed. But one day she heard a little crossing sweeper girl singing, "I do believe, I do believe, that Jesus died for me." The girl's question, "Do you believe it?" led Abigail to the joyful confession.—*Sunday School Times.*

* * *

Three Hardest Words in English Language

Frederick the Great said: "I have just lost a great battle, and it was entirely my own fault." Bacon, in more trying circumstances, said: "I do plainly and ingenuously confess that I am guilty of corruption, and so renounce all defense; I beseech our lordship to be merciful to a broken reed." These are worthy examples for us to follow, as there is need. And never shall we be greater than when, some day, we say to God and men: "I have been mistaken," or, "I have sinned."

"Against Thee, Thee only, have I sinned" (Psalm 51:4).

David never spake greater words than these. They betokened a victory over his soul and spirit beside which all other of his victories, whether against Goliath or the nations about him, were not to be compared. Someone has said, "Next to not committing sin is confessing sin." Another has said, "The three hardest words in the English language are, 'I was mistaken,'" which in some cases may be just another way of saying, "I have sinned." Pride, self-respect, consideration of position and supposed usefulness in the world cry out against confession of any kind. But God says: "If we confess our sins"; and again, "Confess your faults one to another." It is between these opposing voices that is found the conflict; and this was the battle which David fought and won.

David's victory is the great need of the day. People have lost the sense of sin, and hence, the sense of the need of confessing sin. As a result we have atrophy of spiritual life in individuals and in organizations. The terrible result of this is, loss of power because of the loss of the presence of God in power. "If I regard iniquity in my heart, the Lord will not hear me," and this is true for the individual and the collection of individuals. David was a man after God's own heart—not in perfection, but in such soul loyalty as led to the confession of imperfection.—*Sunlight for the Young.*

* * *

Ashamed of the Truth

A girl in a fashionable home was brought to Christ, and for several years witnessed faithfully to Him. Then she was invited to stay with relatives whom she scarcely knew, and whom she had never seen; and she resolved she would not speak of her Lord, nor obtrude her religion. On the day she was to leave for home, an attractive and accomplished lady, a leader in society, while walking alone with her, suddenly said—"Where is your sister, and why didn't she come? I mean your *religious* sister: it was because I heard she was coming that I came; I am sick of my empty life, and longed to talk to a real Christian." With shame she had to confess that she had no sister.—*King's Herald.*

* * *

I Am A Thief:

Some years ago I was conducting a meeting in Stockholm. There was a young lady who wept at every meeting. One night I asked her, "Are you a Christian?" "I profess to be," she said, "but—" "Is there something especially in your life that makes you unhappy?" "Yes," she said.

The young lady finally confessed. "I am a thief; I have stolen 5,000 crowns—3,000 in one place and 2,000 in another."

"There is only one way and that is to confess," I told her.

"But I cannot. It would kill my mother to know. I would have to go to prison and that would bring my mother to her death."

"I understand, but there is only one way. If you want me to help you, I will do whatever I can."

After a few minutes she surrendered. Later I went with her and met the man from whom she had stolen 3,000 crowns. I talked about the case and this big business man turned to her and said, "How much did you take?" "Three thousand crowns." The lady was weeping and the business man was thinking. I finally interrupted the silence and said, "You have her in your hands. You can send her to prison, but you can also forgive."

After a moment the man raised his head and said to the young woman, "You need grace now. Maybe I will need grace some other day. If you can get peace in your heart, I will forgive you."

Did I need to say to that girl, "Be happy now"? No, she *was happy.*

We went to the elderly lady from whom the girl had stolen 2,000 crowns. "I am going to call the police and put you in prison," she said.

"Stop," I said, "maybe you will need grace and forgiveness some day, too." I talked to her about Jesus, His love, His marvelous salvation, and that elderly lady started to weep. "I understand it," she said, "I belonged to the Salvation Army when I was young. I will forgive everything."

Did I need to say to this girl, "Be happy and full of joy"? She almost got too much of it. *Her sins were forgiven.*

It is wonderful to get forgiveness for sin from both man and God. — *Gospel Herald.*

* * *

Which Sort of Clock Are You?

There is a strange old tower which carries a large clock face without any hands to show the hour. The clock is still good and sound. It is regularly wound up every week and has been going for many years; but either from an ancient superstition connected with it, or prophecy regarding it, the hands on the outside of the dial were long ago removed and have never been replaced. So there it stands—a clock with no outward sign whatever of its being so—a thing that might be a blessing to all the town, but an absolutely useless thing that does good to nobody!

Alas, how many Christian souls with the grace of God really within them show little or nothing of that grace to any outside eye. Let us seek grace that we may always reflect our Father's image and bring glory to Him.—*The Gospel Herald.*

Lacking Evidence

A boy said to his mother, "When I grow up I am going to be a Christian like Father. Nobody knows whether he is a Christian or not." That man was like the clock in a certain courthouse tower we used to see. It had no hands. It may have been working inside, *but how were we to know it?—Presbyterian.*

* * *

Ashamed of Jesus! that dear friend
On whom my hopes of heaven depend!
No; when I blush, be this my shame,
That I no more revere His Name.

—*Selected.*

* * *

The Most Wicked Man

Once, when Alexander Whyte was addressing a small and poor audience, he astonished them by saying that he had found out the name of the most wicked man in Edinburgh and had come to tell them. Then, bending forward, he whispered, "His name is Alexander Whyte!" He looked down into his own heart and spoke, and his word was with power.—*British Weekly.*

* * *

The Unusualness of Confession

The story is told of an Italian duke who went on board a galley ship. As he passed the crew of slaves he asked several of them what their offenses were. Every one laid the blame to someone else, saying his brother was to blame or the judge was bribed. One sturdy young fellow said: "My lord, I am justly in here. I wanted money and I stole it. No one is to blame but myself." The duke on hearing this seized him by the shoulder, saying, "You rogue! What are you doing here among so many honest men? Get you out of their company!" The young fellow was then set at liberty, while the rest were left to tug at the oars.—*Rev. C. H. Spurgeon.*

The Parlor—Not The Kitchen

"Wife, I have been converted; let us put up the family altar." So cried an American lawyer as he came into his home.

"Husband," said she, as she sought to restrain him from the action, "there are three lawyers in the parlor—perhaps we had better go into the kitchen to have prayer."

"Wife," said he in response, "I never invited the Lord Jesus into my house before, and I shall not take Him into the kitchen."

So, going into the parlor, he at once announced to the three lawyers that he had received Christ Jesus the Lord, and then asked them to join with him in prayer.

That new convert who took Christ into his parlor became the *Chief Justice of the United States Supreme Court, John McLean.* He made a clear-cut confession of Christ as his Lord and lived to witness for Him.

The Lord Jesus encourages such, as He says, "Whosoever therefore shall confess Me before men, him will I confess also before My Father which is in Heaven."

But He adds a warning word, "But whosoever shall deny Me before men, him will I also deny before My Father which is in Heaven" (Matt. 10:32, 33). —*Scattered Seed.*

* * *

How We Knew

I recollect W. E. Blackstone, author of "Jesus Is Coming" and who was converted at the age of eleven years, saying that he knew his conversion was real because he immediately went home and confessed to his mother that he had stolen a small sum of money from her pocketbook—*Sunday School Times.*

CONSCIENCE

A Sensitive Conscience

A short time ago a writer read a story in *The Sunday School Times* that made him thoughtful. A great menagerie was sold by auction. Some straw that had been used as temporary bedding for the wild beasts was bought by a man who owned a livery stable. And horses that had never seen a lion were uneasy and refused to enter the stalls where the straw was. It was an instinctive dread of an unseen enemy. *And it is possible for a conscience to be so delicately adjusted to the voice of God that when a lure which we do not certainly know to be sinful, a cunningly baited trap for the soul, is placed in our track, there shall be spiritual instinct, a divine scent, that shall make us draw back and avoid the danger.—S. S. World.*

* * *

Discharged Soldier Pays Conscience Money

The United States Treasury is $60 ahead and a former soldier's conscience is at ease, the War Department disclosed.

The unidentified ex-serviceman placed two bills—a fifty and a ten—in a plain envelope. He enclosed a one-sentence note:

> "The enclosed covers some blankets which, as I see it now, should have been turned in by me on my discharge."

Marked personal, the letter was mailed in New York to Lieut. Gen. Brehon Somervell, Commanding General, Army Service Forces. The money was forwarded by the War Department to the Treasury.

The above release from the War Department is more than interesting. It is great to have a conscience void of offense toward men. But through faith it is possible to know things are made right with God. "Therefore being justified by faith, we have peace with God through our Lord Jesus Christ" (Rom. 5:1).—*Courtesy Moody Monthly.*

Sensitiveness

Ex-Chief Bonner of the New York fire department once said that he heard the slightest tap on the bell over his bed, but the baby could cry all night without disturbing him, though his wife rarely ever heard the fire alarm, but the slightest squeak from the baby would awaken her. It is possible for us to have our hearts set to hear the messages of God so that the slightest tap on the bell of conscience will awaken us.—*From "The Bottles of Heaven," by Ridge Revilo.*

* * *

An Uneasy Conscience

What burden of fears an uneasy conscience piles on its possessor! In St. Louis a policeman used nothing more deadly than a hard stare to stop an automobile thief. While directing traffic at a street intersection, Officer Eldred Hinch, "for no particular reason," he said, glared hard at the driver of an approaching car. To his surprise the motorist pulled up alongside him and said, "Yep, I stole the car." At the station he said he came from Terre Haute. Seeing the keys in the ignition of a parked automobile there, he had suddenly decided "to take a ride," but he had a passenger with him on his ride that he had not reckoned on, his own uneasy conscience. If a policeman's eye can be so disconcerting, how will wrong-doers face the presence of the Lord, when "every eye shall see him, and they also which pierced him"? (Rev. 1:7). — *Christian Life.*

* * *

A Matter of Conscience

A minister was about to leave his own congregation for a distant city, to beg on behalf of his place of worship. Before his departure he called together the principal people connected with his charge, and said to them: "Now, I shall be asked whether we have conscientiously done all that we can for the removal of the debt. What answer am I to give? Mr. So-and-so, can you, in conscience, say that you have given all you can?" "Well, sir," was the reply, "if you come to conscience, I don't know that I can." The same question was put to a second, and third, and so on, and similar answers were returned, until the whole sum required was subscribed, and there was no longer any need for the pastor to wear out his soul in going to the city on such an errand.—*Christian Herald (London)*.

* * *

When Conscience Differed

Dr. Alexander Smellie said in an article in *The Sunday School Times*, " 'I ought' is a noble rule when the conscience has once been enlightened from above. But into what errors and excesses, foolishness and sins, the rule may plunge us when our 'ought' is opposed to Christ!" Thus a Hindu said to a British Administrator in India, "Our consciences tell us to burn our widows on the funeral pyres of their husbands." And the Englishman replied, "Our consciences tell us to hang you if you do."—*Sunday School Times.*

* * *

Convicted

The night was dark, the road a lonely one. A man named Kline, lying in wait for one whom he believed to be his enemy, and whom he decided to kill, was startled to hear the voices of several children raised in singing? The guilty conscience heard, "Jesus died for Auld Man Kline, and Jesus died for me." Terror-stricken, he fled to his home. The next time there was a Gospel meeting held he was present, and before long was able to sing with the children, "Jesus died for all mankind, and Jesus died for me."—*Sunday School Times.*

* * *

Self Respect

Before James A. Garfield became President of the United States he served for a number of years in Congress as representative of an Ohio district. One day, as he reviewed his political career, he said to some friends: "I have for many years represented a district in Congress, whose approbation I greatly desired; but, though it may sound a little egotistical to say it, I desired still more the approbation of one person, and his name is Garfield. He is the only man I am compelled to sleep with and eat with and live with and die with; *and if I do not have his approbation I should have bad companionship.*"—William R. King, in *Motives for Christian Living*, Harper & Brothers, publishers.

* * *

How To Face Christ

A man murdered another on the shores of Lake Michigan. He threw the body into the water and ran away. Three days later the body was washed up in front of the murderer's cabin. The guilty man, troubled by conscience, confessed his crime and surrendered himself to the authorities, exclaiming: "Ah, yes, I know the tides did it! The tides did it!" When the tides of memory, conscience, and reason begin to roll in on the judgment day every secret thing will be made manifest. The eyes of the Son of God will commend or condemn, according as you have acknowledged your sins here and trusted in Him as your personal Saviour, or refused to confess Him while you have clung to your sins. *Surely reason urges you to trust Christ as your Redeemer and not to wait to face Him as your Judge.*—Howard W. Ferrin, in *Unto All.*

* * *

A Modern Zacchaeus

Just a few days ago I read of two men who struck up an acquaintance while traveling on the railroad. One said to the other: "I have been to Chicago to collect some 'conscience money.' A good many years ago I made an invention; it was stolen from me by some Chicago people. I spent much money in trying to get my rights and did not get them. A week ago I received a letter from a house in Chicago, which had been manufacturing and selling my invention, saying that they had something for me. I made a trip to Chicago. When I named the amount I would take to settle the account, the gentleman who had been converted turned to the cashier and said, 'Make out the check for so much,' a sum just four times the amount I had named. The check was certified and I now have it in my pocket." — *Sunday School Times.*

* * *

To refuse to hearken to the "inner voice" when it urges obedience to the Divine will and Word is a dangerous proceeding. Well has someone written:

"Goodbye," said I to my conscience,
"Goodbye for aye and aye,"
As I pushed her from me roughly
And turned my face away;
And conscience smitten sorely
Returned not from that day.

But a time came when my spirit
Grew weary of its pace:
And I cried, "Come back, my conscience,
For I long to see thy face."
But conscience said, "I cannot,
Remorse sits in my place."
—*Selected.*

* * *

A Guilty Conscience

Some few years ago in the state of Washington a horrible murder was committed. A hitch-hiker murdered a young man who had given him a ride. The body was found, but no trace of the murderer. Several years went by; and one evening in the state of Missouri a man was coming home from work, carrying his lunch box in his hand. At the door of his home a young wife awaited him. They had been married about two years, and a little boy had been given to them. But before reaching his door, a man stepped out of the shadows, placed his hand on his shoulder, and arrested him for the murder in Washington. He immediately dropped his lunch box, saying, "I'm glad it's all over! I've lived in hell for three years." He then told how he had killed the young fellow and had carried the corpse by his side in the car for many miles looking for a convenient place to hide it. But he said, "Every time I looked at that body, I saw those dead eyes staring at me. And for three years, night and day, they have been staring at me." If a sinner could go to heaven with a burdened conscience like that, even heaven would be hell to him. But, thank God, no one will ever be in heaven with a guilty conscience. God not only forgives the repentant sinner, but He cleanses "from all unrighteousness" (1 John 1:9).—*The Gospel Herald.*

* * *

Dangerous Familiarity

A colored man had applied for a job as teamster. "Are you familiar with mules?" asked the employer. "No, sah!" replied the applicant, "for Ah knows mules too well to get familiar wid 'em." *There is great danger of our getting used to sinful practices because of their commonness.* Let us insist on keeping a conscience which will not grow dull to sin because it is prevalent. We should have convictions and follow them.—*Alliance Full Gospel Quarterly.*

* * *

Korean Boy Christians

Some boys in a mission school in Korea, when told by the Mayor that they must do obeisance before the shrines, replied: "Mr. Mayor, we do not understand just what kind of people you think we are. We have heard all your arguments before, but apart from that, do you think that after listening for two hours to what you may say we could forget the teachings we have received for the last five years? We cannot go to the shrine." Exasperated by their reply, the Mayor said, "Does not your Bible tell you to obey the laws of your country?" "Yes, your honor," was the reply, "but when our Lord Himself was faced with a question of this kind He said, 'Render to Caesar the things that are Caesar's, and to God the things that are God's,' and that is what we are trying to do now." They were thereupon sent to the police station where they were kept for twenty days and were treated as common criminals. They were told that anyone who refused to do obeisance at the shrine would not be regarded as a Japanese subject. *Sunday School Times.*

A God-Given Monitor

An Oriental story of a ring that a great magician presented to his prince sets forth beautifully the manner in which conscience works. The gift was of inestimable value, not only for the diamonds and rubies and pearls that gemmed it, but for a rare and mystic property in the metal. It sat easily enough on the finger in ordinary circumstances; but as soon as its wearer formed a bad thought, designed or committed a bad action, the ring became a monitor. Suddenly contracting, it pressed painfully on his finger, warning him of sin.

Such a ring, thank God, is not the peculiar property of kings. The poorest of us, those that wear none other, may possess and wear this inestimable jewel; for the ring of the fable is just that conscience which is the voice of God within us, that is, His law, engraven by the finger of God, not on Sinai's graven tables, but on the fleshly tablets of the heart, which enthroned as a sovereign in our bosom, commends us when we do right, and condemns us when we do wrong. Therefore, exhorted the psalmist, "harden not your heart, as in the provocation, and as in the day of temptation in the wilderness," but rather allow Christ to enter today.—Thomas Guthrie.

Conscience

Dr. David James Burrell once told this story to illustrate conscience: An Indian had bought a package of supplies at a trading post and on opening it found a silver coin inside. Something troubled him. He came back to the trading post and handed the coin to the trader. The trader laughed at his scruples, but the Indian insisted, saying: "I got a good man and a bad man in my heart. The good man say, 'It is not yours'; the bad man say, 'Nobody will know'; the good man say, 'Take it back'; the bad man say, 'Never mind'; so I think I go asleep, but the good man and the bad man talk all night and trouble me." The distressed Indian had developed a conscience. Perhaps some missionary had taught him an ideal of honesty, and his conscience sensitized his ideal so that he was compelled to return the coin in order to have peace of mind. *This is what conscience accomplishes; it brings peace of mind.—Westminster Teacher.*

CO-OPERATION

Too Late

One evening, years ago, in the Province of Alberta, Canada, a happy father and mother went out for a stroll through a near-by wheat-field with their little boy. As they wandered through the field, each thought the other held the hand of their child.

All at once they realized that the boy was not with them. They called, but there was no answer. They became more and more disturbed, then terrified, and hunted everywhere with no results.

Finally, the father went back to the village and got a searching party to assist them. Many willing helpers searched all night without avail. After many hours, someone finally suggested that they join hands and cover the entire grain-field, and not leave a single square foot uncovered in this last effort.

They joined hands and soon came across the body of the child, and a hush spread over them all, because they had found the child too late. As the group stood there in silence, with bowed heads, someone was heard to whisper: *"If we only had joined hands before it was too late!"—Selected.*

* * *

The Fanner Bees

It was a glorious night of midsummer. The old bee garden was bathed in a soft, crystalline light. At the door of a hive we stopped. There arose from the hive a sibilant note, persistent, not unlike the sound of sea-waves,—advancing,—retreating. "They are Fanner bees," whispered the old beekeeper. "It's their *job* to keep the hive sweet and fresh. They are standing with their heads lowered, toward the center of the hive. Their wings are moving so rapidly that if you saw them you would think you were looking at a gray mist. They are drawing the bad air through one side of the entrance, while the pure air is sucked in on the other side." Standing there, I felt close to one of nature's wonders, the mystery of the hive life. Presently the old beekeeper stooped to the hive, holding a lighted candle. Instantly the light was extinguished by the strong air current, those infinitesimal bee wings, moving in unison, making a draft so strong that the candle light was instantly quenched. As we stood there in the starlit garden, the old preacher said, "The Fanners—drawing out bad air, letting in the fresh. Isn't that how people who call themselves Christians ought to act?" If we had enough fanners, and if they were as keen on their jobs as those bees were on theirs, wouldn't the great hive of the world grow sweet and fresh?—*From an English Journal.*

* * *

Holy Spirit Unites

There is one thing I have noticed as I have traveled in different countries; I have never known the Spirit of the Lord to work where the people were divided. There is one thing that we must have if we are to have the Holy Spirit of God work in our midst, and that is unity.—D. L. Moody.

* * *

Two boys sat talking in leisurely conversation. One a city lad, had come to visit his friend on the farm. Said one,

"What do you say, let's go to the barn and look at the horses."

"It's O.K. with me!" the other replied, and so to the barn they went.

In the stall stood a team of beautiful black horses, which the boys petted, discussing their choices in a general way. The city lad, knowing little of the true value or marks of a good work horse, said, by way of comparison,

"I'd rather have this'n; there's not a blemish on 'im." But the other replied,

"Boy, you would not if you had to work 'im, he's the best lookin' but this one's the best horse on the farm," giving his favorite horse a big hug, "he'll pull till he's almost stretched out flat, on a hard pull, his collar does not fit any too well, but he'll pull anyhow, that's why he's got scars on his shoulders. The other'n won't come up against the collar when the pullin' gets tough. Looks do not count for much in a tight place."—*The Gospel Herald.*

* * *

Unity Not by Force

Unity was never yet brought about by force. What, then, ought we to do? We must leave alone those who do not agree with us, and wait quietly till God shall think fit to bring us together. We must learn to be thankful if sin is opposed, and the Gospel preached, and the devil's kingdom pulled down, though the work may not be done exactly in the way we like. We must praise God if souls are converted and Christ is magnified, no matter who the preacher may be and to what church he may belong. Happy are those who can say with Paul, "If Christ be preached, I rejoice; yea, and will rejoice."—Bishop Ryle.

* * *

The Value of the Individual

The story is told that once, when Sir Michael Costa was having a rehearsal with a vast array of performers and hundreds of voices, as the choir rang out with the accompanying instruments, one man who played the piccolo far up in the corner ceased to play, probably thinking that in all the din his instrument would not be missed. Suddenly the great conductor threw up his hand and all was still. Then he cried out, "Where is the piccolo?" The quick ear of the master musician missed it, and the chorus was spoiled because it failed in its part. *God expects every Christian today to do his duty.—Otterbein Teacher.*

Admiration

When Henry Ward Beecher expressed his admiration for a horse he was hiring, the liveryman responded enthusiastically, *"He'll work any place you put him and will do all that any horse can do."*

Beecher regarded the horse with greater appreciation than before and said wistfully, *"I wish he were a member of my church!"*

How we need workers like him!—Leo Polman.

* * *

Christians of Narrow Vision

Dr. H. A. Ironside told the following story at a Bible conference: A small Christian sect of an exclusive temperament was holding a convention. Outside the auditorium there was displayed the motto, "Jesus Only." A strong wind blew the first three letters away. *"Us only is too often the spirit shown by Christians of narrow vision.—Sunday School Times.*

* * *

A Lesson from a Bird

The naturalist, W. H. Hudson, tells in one of his books about a thrush and a blackbird that always came together, visiting the place where food was put for birds. The blackbird would pick up the crumbs and put them in the thrush's mouth. Then it was noticed that some trap had cut off the thrush's beak close to its head, so that it could not pick up food, and the blackbird was coming to the rescue. Can men afford to let a bird be kinder than they are? Do we not often see men take advantage of another's necessities, instead of going to their relief? How greedily men pick up bankruptcy sales at the smallest possible price, instead of at a fair price! How quickly, when a worker is losing his grip on his job, do other workers seek his place, rather than seek to encourage him to do better work! If we know anyone that cannot pick up the crumbs of life, let us pick them up for him.—*Christian Herald.*

Co-Operation

Sir Wilfred Grenfell recently gave *a striking illustration of co-operation* among religious bodies. He had amputated the infected leg of a Catholic neighbor in Labrador. Later, speaking in a Congregational Church in the United States, he asked if anyone had a leg they did not want, for artificial legs are hard to get in Labrador. At the close of the service a Methodist woman offered him a perfectly good leg, which her Presbyterian husband had used until his death. Grenfell concluded, "When I, an Episcopalian, took that Presbyterian leg given me by a Methodist woman in a Congregational church, back to Labrador, and fitted it on my Roman Catholic friend, it enabled her to walk perfectly.—*United Presbyterian.*

* * *

A Fable

Said a selfish old bee at the close of the day,
"This colony business doesn't pay.
I put my honey in that old hive
That others may eat and live and thrive,
And I do more in a day, you'll see,
Than some of the others do in three.
I toil and worry and save and hoard,
And all I get is my room and board.
It's me for a hive I can run myself,
And for me the sweets of my hard-earned pelf."

So the old Bee flew to a meadow lone,
And started a business all his own.
He gave no thought to the buzzing clan
But all intent on his selfish plan—
He lived the life of a hermit free.
"Ah, this is great," said the silly old Bee.

But the summer waned and the days grew drear,
And the lone Bee wailed as he dropped a tear,
For the varmints gobbled his little store,
And his wax played out and his heart grew sore.
So he winged his way to the old home band
And took his meals at "The Helping Hand."

Alone our work is of little worth,
Together we are the lords of earth.
So it's all for each, and each for all,
"United we stand, divided we fall."
—*The Abstainer—Cardiff.*

* * *

Prayer and Hoe

Said one man to another: "Uncle Dan, I heard that you asked the Lord for that good garden. Is that correct?" "Yes, sir, it is," proudly replied the man whose flourishing garden was his delight; "only I never pray for a good garden unless I have a hoe in my hand. I say, 'Lord, you send the sunshine and the rain, and I'll keep down these weeds.'"—*Christian Advocate.*

* * *

His Hands and Feet

God said to me, "I am going to evangelize inland China, and if you will walk with me I will do it through you." Such is the statement of the experience of Hudson Taylor.—*Association Men.*

* * *

The Finger of God

Dr. H. C. Mason tells of the man who in prayer meeting prayed earnestly that God would with His finger touch a certain man. Suddenly he stopped his prayer. A brother asked him, "Why did you change your prayer?" He replied, "Because God said to me, 'You are My finger.' So now I must go and touch the man for God."

Prayer for God's dealings with men is fundamental. If we do not wait upon Him before we go we shall be as the nine disciples who could not cast one demon out of the boy. But with the prayer must be our willingness to go at His bidding.

Some do not pray with a real care for those about who need God. Some pray but do not go. God would have us *pray and go—The Free Methodist.*

CONSECRATION

The Gift of the Jewel

Many years ago, in the reign of Queen Victoria the Good, the Punjab came under the British Crown. The young Maharajah, then a mere boy, sent an offering to his new monarch, the wonderful Koh-i-noor diamond, and it was placed, together with the other crown jewels, in the Tower of London. Several years later, the Maharajah, now a full-grown man, came to England and visited Buckingham Palace, asking to see the Queen. He was shown to the state apartments, and after making his obeisance to Her Majesty, he asked that he might see the Koh-i-noor. Greatly wondering at his request, the Queen, with her wonted courtesy, gave orders that the jewel should be sent for, and that it should be brought under armed guard from the Tower to Buckingham Palace. In due time it arrived and was carried to the state apartments, and handed to the Maharajah, while all present watched eagerly to see what he would do. Taking the priceless jewel with great reverence in his hand, he walked to the window, where he examined it carefully. Then as the onlookers still wondered, he walked back with it clasped in his hand, and knelt at the feet of the Queen. "Madam," he said, greatly moved, "I gave you this jewel when I was a child, too young to know what I was doing. I want to give it again, in the fulness of my strength, with all my heart, and affection, and gratitude, now and forever, *fully realizing all that I do."—Marching Orders.*

* * *

Her Great Privilege

It was in glad submission to the will of God that a pioneer missionary to the fierce unevangelized Indians of South America, after witnessing the martyrdom of her husband, baby daughter, and fellow missionaries, was enabled by grace to refer to this seeming tragedy as the time in which the Lord *privileged her to give Him everything.* Can you, suffering less, say as much? — *The King's Business.*

* * *

A Human Bridge

A brilliant Oxford student who went to Africa, and died after a year's work, said: "I think it is with African missions as with the building of a great bridge. You know how many stones have to be buried in the earth, all unseen, for a foundation. If Christ wants me to be one of the unseen stones, lying in an African grave, I am content, for the final result will be a Christian Africa." Such "unknown" heroes shall yet be "well known" (II Cor. 6:9) in the day of "the recompense of the Reward" (Heb. 11:26).—*Glad Tidings.*

* * *

General Booth's Secret

When I looked into his face and saw him brush back his hair from his brow, heard him speak of the trials and the conflicts and the victories, I said: "General Booth, tell me what has been the secret of your success." He hesitated a second, and I saw the tears come into his eyes and steal down his cheeks, and then he said: "I will tell you the secret. *God has had all there was of me to have.* There have been men with greater opportunities; but from the day I got the poor of London on my heart, and a vision of what Jesus Christ could do, I made up my mind that God would have all there was of William Booth. And if there is anything of power in the Salvation Army today, it is because God has had all the adoration of my heart, all the power of my will, and all the influence of my life." I learned from William Booth that *the greatness of a man's power is the measure of his surrender.*—Wilbur Chapman, D.D.

* * *

We Are Told

Ole Bull was making his way through a great American forest and he came upon a hut in which dwelt a hermit who had left his home in the city in bitterness. An old violin helped him to while away the tedious hours. At night he took down the old violin and played some simple airs. Ole Bull said, "Do you think I might play a bit?"

"I hardly think it possible; it took me years to learn. You might try, though." So the great master took the instrument, drew his bow across the strings, and instantly the room was filled with harmony. He then played "Home, Sweet Home," "Nearer, My God, to Thee," and other simple songs until the old hermit sobbed like a child. What a difference between the violin in the hands of the hermit, and in the hands of the master!

Let the idea of God take possession of a man and he will rise to heights undreamed of before.—*Gospel Banner.*

* * *

Give Christ All of Life

We have no right to offer Christ less than the whole of our lives. There can be no real dedication of self to Him that is not complete in its surrender. Was He not thinking of this truth when He laid emphasis upon the fact that the greatest of all the commandments is: "Thou shalt love the Lord thy God with all thy heart, and with all thy soul, and with all thy mind, and with all thy strength"? When we are truly His, He will altogether possess us. The whole self will be swallowed up in our zeal for Him, and all that we do will be done "as unto Him." This is one of the secrets of the lives of men like Paul and Francis of Assisi and Wickliffe and Booth and Moody—and of many other less well known to the world but not less wholly surrendered to Christ.

In this truth, too, lies the explanation of failures like those of John Mark and Demas. Those who give themselves to Christ walk with Him the whole way; those who withhold some part of self from Him ultimately find that His path and theirs diverge. The full riches of Christian experience are for those who give Christ all of life — not simply a place in their lives. And the ultimate blessing for such lives is likeness to Him.—*Christian Observer.*

Consecration

"Will you please tell me in a word," said a Christian woman to a teacher, "what your idea of consecration is?" Holding out a blank sheet of paper, the teacher replied, *"It is to sign your name at the bottom of this blank sheet of paper, and let God fill it in as He will."* James H. McConkey, in *Earnest Worker.*

* * *

William Booth's Hunger

Years ago, a plain Methodist minister fell in love with the world's unlovely. In his very own picturesque phrase, he came to where he actually hungered for hell. He pushed out into the midst of it in the East End of London. For days he stood in those seething streets, muddy with men and women. He drank it all in, and loved it because of the souls he saw.

One night he went home and said to his wife:

"Darling, I have given myself, I have given you and the children, to the service of those sick souls."

She smiled, and took his hand, and together they knelt and prayed. That was the beginning of the Salvation Army, and of the great work of Wm. Booth. —*Selected.*

* * *

"I Want You"

A touching incident has been told of a sixteen-year-old girl who was a chronic invalid and whose mother was a pleasure-loving woman who could not endure the idea of being so much with her shut-in daughter. While the mother was traveling abroad in Italy, she remembered the coming birthday of her daughter, and sent her a rare and beautiful Italian vase. The trained nurse brought it to the girl, saying that her mother had sent it so carefully that it came right on her birthday. After looking at its beauty for a moment, the girl turned to the nurse and said: "Take it away, take it away. O Mother, Mother, do not send me anything more; no books, no flowers, no vases, no pictures. Send me no more. I want you, you!"

Don't give Christ things—only things. He wants you. "Son, daughter, give Me thy heart." That daughter wanted her mother. She wanted her presence, her companionship, her love. Christ wants you. He wants you first of all. He wants your yielded heart, your confidence, your trust, your union with Him. He wants your love, prompting you to the best possibilities you have. He says, "I want you, you." Your heart fully given, He knows all else will follow.—*Selected.*

* * *

Livingstone's Dedication

When Henry M. Stanley found Livingstone, the great missionary who spent thirty years in darkest Africa, and who had been lost to the world for over two years, he wanted him to come back home to England with him, but Livingstone refused to go. Two days later he wrote in his diary, "March 19th, my birthday. My Jesus, my King, my Life, my All, I again dedicate my whole self to Thee. Accept me, and grant, O gracious Father, that ere the year is gone I may finish my work. In Jesus' name, I ask it, Amen" A year later his servants found him on his knees dead. It was said of him:

He needs no epitaph to guard a name
Which men shall prize while worthy work is known:
He lived and died for good—be this his fame;
Let marble crumble: this is Living Stone.

—Hugh T. Kerr, D.D.

* * *

Complete Consecration

Where can we find a more perfect example of complete consecration to the claims of Christ and the sweet will of God than in the story of John Wesley's mother? When her consent was asked for him to sail to Georgia, she replied in these noble words, "If I had twenty sons, I should rejoice that they were so employed, though I should never see them more." That John himself had inherited his mother's spirit of unselfish devotion to the cause of those in need, is known by the fact that during one year of his time at Oxford, out of his income of one hundred and twenty pounds, he lived on twenty-eight pounds, giving all the rest to the sick and poor.—*Teaching by Illustration.*

* * *

When Our Eyes Are on the King

The cost of discipleship very often lies in turning the eyes from the better to the best. Dr. Henry Jowett, in a sermon in the Fifth Avenue Presbyterian Church in New York City, described how, at the coronation of Edward VII, he sat in Westminster Abbey and watched the honorable assembling of princes, princesses, earls, dukes, and so on. He said: "There was much bowing and respect shown as these people of high degree entered, but when the king arrived all eyes left the people of lesser rank and were fastened on the king. "So," said Dr. Jowett, "literature, music, art, and science hold our respectful attention, but when Jesus Christ comes into our heart and our life, He must be King, and all lesser subjects must take their lesser place." — *Sunday School Times.*

* * *

I had walked life's way with an easy tread,
Had followed where pleasure and comforts led,
Until one day in a quiet place,
I met the Master face to face.

With station and wealth and rank as my goal,
Much thought for my body, and none for my soul,
I had entered to win in life's mad race,
When I met the Master face to face.

I had built my castles and built them high,
With their towers had pierced the blue of the sky,
I had sworn to rule with an iron mace,
When I met the Master face to face.

I met Him and knew Him and blushed to see
That His eyes, full of sorrow, were fixed on me;
And I faltered and fell at His feet that day,
While my castles melted and vanished away.

Melted and vanished, and in their place
Naught else did I see but the Master's face,
And I cried aloud, "Oh make me meek
To follow the steps of Thy wounded feet."

My thought is now for the souls of men,
I have lost my life to find it again,
E'er since the day in the quiet place,
I met the Master face to face.

—*Anonymous.*

* * *

God's Response to Our Surrender

A celebrated philosopher of antiquity, who was accustomed to receive large sums from his pupils in return for his instructions, was one day approached by a poor youth, who asked to be admitted as one of his disciples. "And what will you give me in return?" said the wise man. "I will give you myself," was the reply. "I accept the gift," replied the philosopher, "and engage to restore you to yourself at some future period, much more valuable than you are at present." Those who give themselves to God will become day by day more like Jesus Christ.—*Sunday School Chronicle.*

* * *

The Cost Has Been Counted

It is said that Bishop Hedding of New York once addressed a candidate for the foreign mission field as follows: "Have you considered that you will have to go away from home and friends, and be among strangers and enemies?" "I have," replied the young man. "Have you considered that you must leave your native land, with all its institutions and privileges, and be a foreigner in a strange land, where everybody will regard you with suspicion and prejudice?" "I have considered it all," said the young preacher. "Have you considered that in that land your health may fail, you may be prostrated with malarias and fevers of violence?" "Yes," again answered the young man, "and if I had a thousand lives I would give them all to Jesus. Bishop, please don't ask me any more questions, but send me, send me!"—*The Gospel Herald.*

Has He Gotten You?

God has a great many people that He hasn't gotten. Are you one of that kind? Are you all the Lord's? Has He all there is of you? "I'm so glad I am not my own," cried a young woman recently. But there are many Christian young people who need to come to a once-for-all "hands-off" their very lives, and decide that they shall henceforth be utterly and entirely the Lord's own property.

Some young folks would rather do something *for* the Lord than to belong *to* the Lord; would rather support a missionary than become a missionary — would rather give than go.

"After money for your mission school again?" said a bright, beautiful young woman to her pastor. "Well, here are five dollars—."

"No, no, I do not want money this morning," he replied smilingly, "I want you." "Me?" "Yes, I want you to come and help us save those poor children." "Down amongst those dirty, miserable people! Oh, I can't do that." "Your presence, the warmth of your love and sympathy, is worth more than all your money." God's order of giving is found among the Corinthians "who first gave their own selves unto the Lord and unto others by the will of God." First you and then yours. If God gets *us* He gets *all we have*. Has He gotten you?—*The Prairie Overcomer.*

* * *

Doves on the Wire

Just out of reach from my window stretches a wire which carries a heavy current of electricity for light and power. It is carefully insulated at every pole that supports it, and it is carried well out of common reach. If I could lean far enough out to touch it, death would be swifter than the tiger's leap or the serpent's sting—as swift as the lightning stroke.

Yet the doves light on it and take no harm. They fly from my window sill, where I sometimes feed them, to preen and rest upon it in safe content, and then fly off again to their search for food or nesting. The secret is that when they touch the full-powered wire they touch nothing else. They give themselves wholly to it. My danger would be that while I touched the wire I should also be touching the earth through the walls of my house, and the current would turn my body into a channel for escape. But they rest wholly on the wire and experience neither dread nor danger. They are one with it, and they are safe.

So would God have us seek our safety in complete self-surrender to His power and love. It is when we reach one hand to Him, while yet we keep fast hold on some forbidden thing with the other, that we are in danger.—Isaac Rankin, in *The Friend.*

* * *

What Self-Denial Is

A clergyman once said, "Do you know that Campbell Morgan came to this country, and preached one sermon that destroyed forty years of my sermons? For forty years I have been preaching on the duty of sacrifice—denying things to ourselves, giving up this and that. We practiced it in our family. We would give up butter one week and try to use the money in some way that God might bless. Another week we would give up something else, and so on. Campbell Morgan said that what we needed to give up was not things but self; and that was the only thing we had not given up in our home. We had given up everything under the sun, but self."—*Sunday School Times.*

* * *

Christ's Hands

Skilled in the use of illustrations, the Rev. Dr. J. H. Jowett, who exercised a distinguished ministry in both England and New York City, once told of the time when he went to conduct a village wedding. A great London organist was asked to play an asthmatical little organ, with but one pedal. Yet those fingers of the master-musician managed, somehow, to produce a wonderful wedding march from the defective instrument. Gypsy Smith narrating the incident said to his audience, "You let Jesus come with the fingers that painted the lily and the rosebud and the rainbow, the fingers that were nailed to the cross, and let those fingers touch the keys of your life and see what happens." *Christ transforms and glorifies life.—Sunday School Times.*

* * *

The Prior Claim

"Are the lawyers still searching for a clear title to Oakdeen?" asked John Kendricks of his friend. "Yes," responded De Costa, "they are still at it. They have traced the title back to Lord Mayor Woodroffe of England, who in 1660 took out a claim. But there is a prior claim, it seems, and I tell my wife that I should not be surprised to seeing Adam's name appearing on the title deed." "And even then," said Mr. Kendricks, "the title will not be clear; there is a prior claim." "Why, I thought Adam was the first man on this terrestrial ball!" said De Costa in surprise. "If we trace the title deeds of all estates to their origin we shall find in the most ancient of all land records this entry, 'In the beginning God created the heaven and the earth,' and across every title deed that has been executed in God's signature, 'The earth is the Lord's, and the fulness thereof; the world and they that dwell therein,'" said Kendricks. "Then, if God's signature is upon all property, where does man's claim come in?" asked De Costa. "We are at best but his tenants, and if we recognize His ownership, we are but squatters," answered Kendricks.—Courtesy *Moody Monthly.*

* * *

"Who Follows in Their Train?"

Some three years ago in the city of Toronto, I read the blazing headlines and story of the death of John and Betty Stam in the daily paper. After reading how those two dear children of God laid down their lives for the Lord and the Chinese people, in my heart I softly but earnestly said, "Lord, I give my life to Thee once more — if it be Thy will, to take the place of these two saints in that heathen land of China." Little did I realize at that time that within three years I would be sent to the very station in which John Stam labored for a summer by himself, and later, after his marriage to Betty, for another six months. My heart is indeed overjoyed because the Lord has counted me worthy to fill the very gap that the Home-going of his two children left. Do pray that I may be kept faithful to God and his work.—A farewell testimony by an outgoing missionary to China, in *China's Millions.*

* * *

"Crowned or Crucified"

I stood alone at the bar of God;
In the hush of the twilight dim,
And faced the question that pierced my heart:
"What will you do with Him?
Crown'd or crucified? Which shall it be?"
No other choice was offered to me.

I look'd on the face so marr'd with tears
That were shed in His agony;
The look in His kind eye broke my heart;
'Twas so full of love for me.
"The crown or the Cross" it seem'd to say
"For or against Me choose thou today!"

He held out His loving hands to me,
While His pleading voice said, "Obey!
Make Me thy choice, for I love thee so,"
And I could not say Him nay.
Crown'd, not crucified! this must it be;
No other way was open to me.

I knelt in tears at the feet of Christ,
In the hush of the twilight dim,
And all that I was or hoped or sought,
I surrendered unto Him.
Crown'd, not crucified! my heart shall know
No King but Christ, who loveth me so!

—Anonymous.

* * *

Dig Deeper

Somewhere we have read of a farmer who once dug a well, and to this well he brought his horses and cattle to drink. From it he drew for a long time sufficient for all the needs of his herds, but a drought came one summer and the flow of water diminished in the well and ceased to refresh these herds. Consequently, he had to drive them to surrounding springs and brooks to give them necessary water.

One day a visitor stopped at his home and talked to him about his well. He said, "Why not dig the well deeper?"

"But," declared the farmer, "the next digging must be done through a layer of rock and flint."

The visitor was persistent and said, "Even so, though it is necesary to go through flint and rock, blast the rock and just a few more feet may give you the most refreshing stream of water you can imagine."

This was done and to the farmer's amazement and joy the blast brought in a gushing stream of water, which not only filled the well but overflowed it. It was a veritable gold mine to his homestead.

Is it not true that with many of us there has been a spiritual drought, and there is no water in our well? We have dug as far as the rock, but we have never gone through the rock. Too many Christian lives are after all only superficial. Dig deeper, brethren! Let's blast a few rocks and see if there will not come a stream of water of Divine grace that will so fill our hearts and lives with the glory of His grace, that serving Him and doing His will, in fact the whole routine of Christian life and duty, will become a joy and pleasure. — Selected.

* * *

O the bitter pain and sorrow,
  That the time could ever be,
When I proudly said to Jesus,
  All of Self and none of Thee.

But He sought me, I beheld Him,
  Dying on the accursed tree,
And my feeble heart said faintly,
  Some of self and some of Thee.

Higher than the highest mountain,
  Deeper than the deepest sea,
Lord, Thy love at last has conquered,
  None of self and *ALL* OF THEE.
—Anonymous.

* * *

Who Has the Right of Way?

Are you willing to be a highway over which Jesus Christ shall come to your town and into the lives of your friends and neighbors? Right of way costs something. When President Garfield was shot, he was taken to an isolated home where he could have absolute quiet and rest in his fight for life, and a special railway was constructed to facilitate the bringing of doctors, nurses, and loved ones to his bedside. The engineers laid out the line to cross a farmer's front yard, but he refused to grant the right of way until they explained to him that it was for the President, when he exclaimed, "That is different. Why, if that railroad is for the President, you can run it right through my house." Are you willing to give Him right of way across your front yard? It may run right through some of your plans, or social engagements, or business appointments. But will you give Him the right of way—*Michigan Christian Advocate.*

* * *

An Indian's Choice

Mr. H. Carrol Whitener, director of the Pueblo Indian Mission in New Mexico, tells this story. "The first Gospel was printed in the Acoma dialect, and soon after distribution was begun a Laguna Indian sheep herder secured a copy from one of the Acomas who took it with him to his sheep tent. After returning home read it to his family and neighbors many times, but, finally, because his wife was an Acoma, the Roman priests insisted that the council compel him to desist. Out of fear, they had a mock trial, and gave him the choice of giving up his Gospel or leaving his home and family and the reservation. After thinking it over, he accepted the alternative of leaving all for Christ's sake, and did so. He is still ostracized from that reservation, but continues a fine, faithful Christian, waiting for the day when, his faith still intact, he can again be united with his wife and children. No martyrs ever bore their stripes more firmly than some of these Indians are doing today here in the U. S. A., 'the land of the free and the home of the brave,' for the sake of their faith and the precious Word."—*Sunday School Times.*

* * *

Whose Possession?

The story is told of a wealthy Englishman who had added to his valuable collection a rare violin which was coveted by Fritz Kreisler, the celebrated virtuoso. When the owner persisted in refusing to part with the instrument, Kreisler begged permission to play it just once. The opportunity was granted * * and he played as only a genius can play. He forgot himself. He poured his soul into his music.

The Englishman stood as one enchanted until the playing had ceased. He did not speak until Kreisler had tenderly returned the instrument to the antique box, with the gentleness of a mother putting her baby to bed.

"Take the violin," the Englishman burst out; "it is yours. I have no right to keep it. It ought to belong to the man who can play it as you did."

That was odd reasoning, to be sure; and yet it has something compelling about it. In a sense, ought not an instrument to belong to the master who can draw the finest music from it? And ought not your life and mine to belong to the Master who can draw the noblest harmonies from them?—A. B. Rhinow, in *The Watchman-Examiner.*

* * *

An Indian Prince's Decision

Bor Sing, heir of the Rajah of Cherry, India, was converted. He was warned that in joining the Christians he would forfeit the right to the throne of Cherry after the then ruling Prince. After the death of Rham Sing, the chiefs of the tribes met and unanimously decided that Bor Sing was not entitled to succeed him as his Christian profession stood in the way. Messenger after messenger was sent, urging him to recant, and they would all acknowledge him as king. His answer was: "Put aside my Christian profession? I can put aside my head-dress or my cloak, but as for the covenant I have made with my God I cannot for any consideration put that aside." Afterward, although impoverished by litigations, he still stood true.—*Sunday School Times.*

* * *

The Best Way

Robert Chapman of Barnstaple, a great friend of the late George Muller of Bristol, was once asked, "Would you not advise young Christians to do something for the Lord?" "No," was the reply, "I should advise them to do everything for the Lord."—*The Christian Herald.*

* * *

Only five barley loaves!
  Only two fishes small!
And shall I offer these poor gifts
  To Christ, the Lord of all?

To Him whose mighty word
  Can still the angry sea,
Can cleanse the lepers, raise the dead?
  He hath no need of me.

Yes, He hath need of thee;
  Then bring thy loaves of bread;
Behold with them, when Jesus speaks,
  The multitudes are fed.

And when thine eyes shall see
  The holy ransomed throng,
In heavenly fields, by living streams,
  By Jesus led along,

Unspeakable thy joy shall be,
  And glorious thy reward,
If, by thy barley loaves, one soul
  Has been brought home to God.

—*Otterbein Teacher.*

* * *

The Life That Abides

There were two sons in the Taylor family in England. The older one said that he must make a name for the family and he turned his face toward Parliament and honor. But Hudson Taylor, the younger, decided to give his life to the service of Christ, and so turned his face toward China. Hudson Taylor, the missionary, died beloved and known on every continent. "But," says one, "when I looked in the encyclopedia to see what the other son had done, I found the words, 'The brother of Hudson Taylor.'" Again in modern history has been lived out in our modern life the story of the talents. Build a life upon the foundation of self, and it is lost; but build it in the service of men and to the glory of God and the name by which that life is identified shall abide.—Ruth McDowell, in *C. U. Herald.*

If the Whole Nation Were Christ's

We quote a letter received from an English friend who lived through the weeks of the Nazi threat on England. In the letter he wrote: "As one man, the whole nation has handed over all its resources to the Government. We have invested the Cabinet with the right to conscript any of us for any task, to take our goods, our money, our all. Never have rich men set such little store by their wealth; never have we been so ready to lay down life itself, if only our cause may triumph." We should like to substitute the word Christ for the three words Government, Cabinet, and Cause. This is the way it would read: "As one man, the whole nation has handed over all its resources to Christ. We have invested Christ with the right to conscript any of us for any task, to take our goods, our money, our all. Never have rich men set such little store by their wealth; never have we been so ready to lay down life itself, if only Christ may triumph." —*Bulletin of the Moody Bible Institute.*

* * *

Your Best

It is said that a committee once called on Enrico Caruso, then at the zenith of his operatic fame, to ask if he would sing at a concert for the benefit of the soldiers. The chairman of the committee hurriedly said, "Of course, Mr. Caruso, as this is a charity affair, we would not expect you to do your best. Your name will draw the crowd and you can merely sing some song requiring little of strength or skill." Caruso is said to have drawn himself to full height as he said, "Caruso never does less than his best."

There are altogether too many Christians entirely willing to give God less than their best. Fag ends of time and the dregs of the purse are sufficient for Him, they think. What an awakening at the judgment seat of Christ!—Courtesy *Moody Monthly.*

* * *

"Let Me Go"

Lee Lockett, my wife and myself were in school at Baylor at the same time. Lee went as a missionary to dark Africa —he married a beautiful Christian girl a few years ago their children had to be brought back to America because of African fever—While they were out at Abilene where her people lived, one day as they were driving through a creek, the flood waters came down on them suddenly and the three children were swept away, and all three drowned. Lee and his wife got on a boat and went back across to dark Africa. Finally her health failed and she had to come back to America for her health, and now, just as she was restored to go back with him, without a word, his little engine stopped, and he woke up in heaven. She is left alone —Do you know what she is doing?—Think of this, with her three children buried yonder, her husband buried beside them, this woman, this wife and mother alone now, got everything ready to go back to give the rest of her life. She said, "Let me go"—"Let me go"—"Let me go."

That is the spirit of the cross, that's the marred life made another and better vessel.—*Florida Baptist Witness.*

* * *

"He Is All My Life"

A mother, saved from heathenism, was asked, after worship, whether she could send away her only little boy for Christian training. "He is all my life," she cried. After a struggle, she brought him to the missionary. Pointing Heavenward, she said, "Thomas, Christos." God's joy flooded her. The boy became a mighty witness for Christ.—*The Gospel Herald.*

* * *

Unconditional Determination

It is not unworthiness, but unwillingness, that alone disqualifies us from following Jesus. It is unconditional determination that He demands. D'Aubigné, the great church historian, says that when he was a student at college he was much beset by doubts and difficulties in relation to questions connected with divine truth, and it was his wont to repair to an old Christian in very humble life, whose rich experience had often served to help the young student. But at length, upon proffering some grave difficulty,

D'Aubigné received an unexpected rebuff, for his aged friend replied, "Young man, I shall not answer any more of these questions of yours. If I settle them one day, new perplexities arise the next day. The great question for you is, '*Do you mean to belong altogether to Christ?*'" That is the shortest way of setting at rest these misgivings.—*Biblical Illustrator.*

* * *

Enough to Be Miserable

Aunt Dinah described a young member of her church as having "jes' 'nough religion to make her miser'ble—too much to be happy at dances an' too little to be happy in pra'r meetin'." Alas! the type is common—a troubled spirit that halts halfway, afraid to go back and unwilling to go forward. *There is no peace in the borderland. The halfway Christian is a torment to himself and no benefit to others.—Earnest Worker.*

* * *

Members of Christ

Thou hast no tongue, O Christ, as once of old,
To tell the story of Thy love Divine,
The story still as strange, as sweet, as true;
But there's no tongue to tell it out *but mine.*

Thou hast no hands, O Christ, as once of old,
To feed the multitudes with bread Divine;
Thou hast the Living Bread, enough for all;
But there's no hand to give it out *but mine.*

Thou hast no feet, O Christ, as once of old,
To go where Thy lost sheep in desert pine;
Thy love is still as deep, as strong, as kind;
But now Thou hast no feet to go *but mine.*

And shall I use these ransomed powers of mine
For things that only minister to me?
Lord! Take my tongue, my hands, my feet, *my all;*
And let them live, and give, and go *for Thee!*

—Anonymous.

* * *

Why Harkness Couldn't

One of the State societies at Los Angeles was holding its annual reunion. Three thousand people had gathered in a beautiful grove and had partaken of a hearty lunch. The president of the society announced that a musical program would be given. Robert Harkness, the well-known Christian pianist, then rendered a few numbers of old sacred melodies with variations, which were received with enthusiasm. Then the president announced that three young ladies would perform a special dance, and asked Mr. Harkness to play for them. Much to his surprise and chagrin he received a polite negative reply. The president appeared before the throng and announced that Mr. Harkness had refused to play. Mr. Harkness arose and said, "My reason for not playing for the dance is simply that my talent is not my own. It is devoted wholly to the service of Christ."—*Grace and Truth.*

* * *

A Young Jew's Choice

At a Sunday school anniversary a boy of Jewish caste, with piercing eyes, rose and repeated, "Jesus, I my cross have taken, all to leave and follow Thee," in a voice so thrilling as to move the whole audience. Many eyes were moist, for the story of the young Jew was known. His father had told him he must either leave the Sunday school or quit home forever, and the words of the hymn showed what he had given up to follow Christ. The meeting was inspired with new life. Friends and businessmen secured him a situation by which he could earn his own living.—*Christian at Work.*

The Other Half

Several years ago I heard Dr. Glover, of the China Inland Mission, tell of a consecration meeting he had held in a certain church. Many arose in answer to the invitation to give their hearts to God for service. Seven years later he returned to the same church and in answer to another similar invitation some of the same persons stood. He then said, "Seven years ago some of you stood, saying, 'Lord, here am I,' but you must have forgotten to say, 'Send me.' "—Courtesy *Moody Monthly.*

* * *

What Part?

The new church was at last completed, and one of the officials approached the bishop of the diocese with a request to come and consecrate the building. "What part do you want me to take in the dedication service?" asked the bishop. "Take in the *whole* thing from underpinning to steeple," replied the other. That is consecration — all life's energies and resources devoted to one great purpose.—*British Weekly.*

* * *

Complete Consecration

When the soldiers of Napoleon's army were invading Russia, they came to a village from which all the inhabitants had fled except one man. He was a Russian peasant, a woodsman, and still carried his ax in his leather belt. When the French captain saw him he ordered him to be shot immediately. The soldiers fell in and leveled their guns, but the man did not seem afraid, looking fearlessly down the gun barrels. The French captain noticed this, and before the soldiers could pull their triggers, ordered them to lower their guns.

He then ordered that the peasant's life should be spared. "But," said he, "we will put a mark on him—we will brand him." So the branding iron was brought out and placed in the fire. Then it was placed upon the Russian's hand. The man saw his own flesh burn and quiver, but he did not flinch or cry out. After the iron was removed the peasant saw the letter "N" branded on his palm. "What is that?" he asked.

"This is the letter 'N' and it stands for Napoleon; you belong to Napoleon now," replied the captain.

For a moment the poor man did not know what to do or say. His pain was intense. Then an idea occurred to him. He had always been a loyal and patriotic Russian. Now was the time to show it, even in the presence of his enemies. At once he placed his burned hand on something solid. The French soldiers looked on, laughing and jeering at him. The brave man took the ax out of his belt, and swinging it high, brought it down with such might that he severed his own hand. "There," he said to the soldiers, "the hand may belong to Napoleon, but I am a Russian. If I must die, I will die a Russian."

This is the spirit needed in the church today, both among ministers and members. Our Christianity has become too soft and easy. To some people the symbol of Christianity is a rocking chair instead of a Cross. Most of us do not suffer or sacrifice enough for our faith. If we did, we would love it more. We ought to love our Lord and His cause more than any person or thing. Laymen and ministers need complete consecration to give them power to work for the Lord. This power can be had if we are willing to pay the price, the price of sacrifice and self-denial.—Rev. Joseph D. Ryan, in *The Presbyterian.*

* * *

Said Betty Stam

"Lord, I give up my own purposes and plans, all my own desires, hopes, and ambitions (whether they be fleshly or soulish), and accept Thy will for my life. I give myself, my life, my all utterly to Thee, to be Thine forever. I hand over to Thy keeping all of my friendships; all the people whom I love are to take second place in my heart. Fill me and seal me with Thy Holy Spirit. Work out Thy whole will in my life, at any cost, now and forever. To me to live is Christ. Amen. (1 Thess. 5:23, 24; Phil. 1:21.)" Nine years later, on December 8, 1934, Betty and her husband, John Stam, calmly and bravely laid down their lives for Christ when they were martyred by Chinese Communists. As Mrs.

Scott spoke of lessons of trust and faithfulness from the lives of John and Betty, she said she believed that Betty's victory over the power of the Enemy in that dark hour in 1934 had been won at Keswick in 1925. Betty was victor in the crisis because, years before, she had utterly yielded herself to the Lord Jesus Christ and trusted him to be her Victor. —*Sunday School Times.*

* * *

Indian Must Lay Down Indian

Once an Indian lived alone, hunting and trapping in the Selkirk Mountains. His family had all been killed by a band of white hunters, and he grew up a wild man. At length another trapper, a white man, came to the mountains to live. He was kind and patient, and gradually the wild boy came to trust him and love him, and slowly entered into the love of Jesus Christ, as the white man taught him. After many months of thought, one moonlit night on top of a noble peak, the young Indian dressed himself in all his heathen finery, took his friend's hand, knelt and prayed silently. Then he rose and made his confession of his new purpose, suiting the action to the word:

Indian lay down blanket,
Indian lay down pipe,
Indian lay down tomahawk,
Indian lay down Indian.

Well may all of us learn a lesson from that child of the forest. What Christ requires of us is not some modifications, more or less complete, of our old life of sin and selfishness and doubt, but that we walk with Him in entire newness of life. Indian must lay down Indian.—*Alliance Weekly.*

* * *

The Surrendered Life

Oh, the peace of full surrender!
All my joy to do His will!
Mine to trust His faithful promise;
His the promise to fulfill.

Oh, the glory and the rapture
Thus to dwell with Christ the Lord;
New delight and wisdom gaining
From the study of His Word.

Pleasure's songs no more entice me,
Nor the bugle note of Fame;
Sweeter far the holy music
Of my dear Redeemer's Name.

Oh, the glory and the rapture—
Earthly burdens pass away!
Stormy winter turns to summer;
Lonely darkness into day.

—Anonymous.

CONTENTMENT

When They Found Their Man!

A story is told of a king who was suffering from a malady and was advised by his astrologist that he would be cured if the shirt of a contented man were brought for him to wear. People went out to all parts of the kingdom after such a person, and after a long search they found a man who was really happy, but he did not possess a shirt. — *The Christian Evangelist.*

* * *

Be Yourself

Do not spend your time in longing to be somebody else, to have his place, and do his work, and expect his gifts, and speak in his way. Be yourself! God made you. Respect your own individuality. If we are to enter into and to continue in God's way for us, we must not have some little plan of our own. Two people cannot be in control of one life at one and the same moment. God has His way for you. If you have a way for yourself, then it is not under control and cannot be until you surrender your program and accept His.—*The Elim Evangel.*

Contentment

A bishop who was contented and cheerful through a long period of trial, and was asked the secret of his contentment, said: "I will tell you. I made a right use of my eyes." "Please explain." "Most willingly," was the answer:

"First, I look up to Heaven and remember that my principal business is to get there.

"Then I look down upon the earth and think about how small a place I shall occupy when I am dead and buried.

"Then I look around and see the many who are in all respects much worse off than I am.

"Then I learn where true happiness lies, where all our cares end, and how little reason I have to complain. — Selected.

* * *

If you can keep "the faith" when those about you
Are losing it and seeking something new;
If you can stand the firmer though they flout you
As being simple, and old-fashioned, too;

If you can put your hand in Christ's, and feeling
The marks of Calvary's scars upon your palm,
Can gladly say "Amen" to all His dealing,
Or change the sigh into a joyous psalm;

If you can laugh when human hopes are banished,
When castles fall and cherished prospects die,
And just keep on though earthly props have vanished,
Content to see the pattern by and by;

If you can meet abuse without complaining,
And greet your unkind critic with a smile;
If, conscious that your human love is waning,
You claim a Calvary love that knows no guile;

If you can bear the unjust imputation
Without a murmur or revengeful thought,
And even forfeit rights and reputation,
Because *His* glory is the one thing sought;

If you can give an honest commendation
To him whose work looms larger than your own,
Or scorn to speak the word of condemnation
To him who fails or reaps what he has sown;

If you can give consent to Calvary's dying,
And live again in resurrection power;
If you can claim the victory, not by *trying*,
But *resting* in His triumph every hour;

If you can be content with His provision,
Though others seem to prosper and succeed;
Nor let repining mar the Heavenly vision,
And simply trust in God for every need;

If you can let the mind of Christ possess you,
To think on "things of good report" and true,
And ever let the love of Christ obsess you,
Constraining everything you say and do;

If you can find in Him your highest treasure,
Let Him hold sway o'er heart and soul and limb:
Then *life* is yours, and blessing without measure,
And—what is more—*you'll live and reign with Him!*

—*The Christian* (London).

* * *

"She Never Said a Word, But—"

Dr. A. T. Schofield's eldest daughter was a great horsewoman, but being thrown when rough-riding got a depressed fracture of the skull upon which no surgeon would operate, and of which, after some years of great suffering, she died. "When my daughter had been ill a fortnight, her nurse came to me and said she thought I would like to know that she had become a Christian. 'Why, what were you when you came?' 'I was an atheist, Doctor.' 'I suppose your patient has been speaking to you?' 'No, she never said a word, but she is the only absolutely contented girl I ever met, and I couldn't understand it, so I asked for her secret, and now I'm a Christian.' "—Dr. A. T. Schofield.

* * *

Can you show me the way to the "Land of Content,"
Where the struggle with self is done?
Where the disappointments and vain regrets
Are gone with the evening sun?
Where pride and anger play no part,
Where only Truth can live?
Where wrongs are forgotten and blotted out,
And the best in us can live?
—*The Gospel Herald.*

* * *

Their God-Given Contentment

Mr. and Mrs. Robert Ekvall on the border of Tibet in a lonely, far-away station, told us: "We do not want a radio; we are content in our far-off field, and do not need any earthly thing to help or make it possible to go on with the work; contentment is our portion." Their friend, in a letter continues: "That is God-given, for only so could they have been content to live as they did, for the love of souls. Their front yard was anything but inviting, but it was for the good of their people who would be free to come, animals and all. Mail reached them every three weeks or so (perhaps). Just living among the wild Tibetans, with all their unclean ways and smells, their rough, ugly style of doing things, then to be "contented." *How* wonderful! Mr. and Mrs. Ekvall were college-bred and used to something so different, yet in the wilds of Tibet they were "content, restful, resourceful, and happy." What a tribute to the grace of God!—*Gospel Herald.*

* * *

An Allegory

A story is told of a king who went into his garden one morning, and found everything withered and dying. He asked an oak that stood near the gate what the trouble was. He found that it was sick of life and determined to die, because it was not tall and beautiful like the pine. The pine was out of heart because it could not bear grapes like the vine. The vine was going to throw its life away because it could not stand erect and have as fine fruit as the pomegranate.

And so on throughout the garden. Coming to a heartsease, the king found its bright face lifted up as full of cheerfulness as ever. Said the king: "Well, heartsease, I am glad to find one brave little flower in this general discouragement and dying. You don't seem one bit disheartened." "No, your majesty, I know I am of small account; but I concluded you wanted a heartsease when you planted me. If you had wanted an oak or a pine or a vine or a pomegranate, you would have set one out. So I am bound to be the best heartsease that ever I can."—Selected.

CONVERSION

The Forgotten Name

A missionary was traveling on the train and she had a long stopover in Cawnpore. Going into the station she found a woman sadhu crouched on a bench, and soon she began talking to her about God. As the missionary mentioned the name of Christ, the woman looked up happily, and with beaming countenance said, "That's it, that's His name! I had forgotten it! What you are saying is the truth! I know you are right because that's His name! Tell me again, so I won't forget." And then this pitiful soul, transformed and radiating new life from God, began to tell her story. She told of how she was wandering through the jungles, chanting her prayers and repeating the name of her god—"Ram! Ram! Ram!—" Suddenly a voice said to her, "Don't worship Ram; worship Christ," and each time she would say "Ram," the same voice would say again, "Don't worship Ram; worship Christ." She came out of the jungle wondering what it all could mean, but in the meantime she had forgotten the name. When the missionary spoke of Christ, it came to her that He is the One to be worshiped. His name is Christ! What a rejoicing, not only in that railroad station, but among the heavenly host in Glory, for this lost sinner brought into the fold!—*Independent Board Bulletin.*

* * *

The Queen's Prayer

Many years ago there lived on the Osborne House Estate an old lady, one of the late Queen's pensioners, who had a niece in a business house at Cowes. One day the niece went to her aunt's cottage to tea, and during the afternoon Her Majesty Queen Victoria walked in and remained some time, knitting and chatting with the old lady, and also had tea with them. After tea Her Majesty said, "Now I will read a few verses from the fourteenth of John." Then, looking very kindly at the young girl, she said, "I wonder whether you are a Christian, my dear?" "Oh, yes, your Majesty," replied the girl. "How do you know you are?" asked the Queen. The reply was, "Because I've been christened and confirmed." The Queen made no answer, but gently said, "Now we will have a few words of prayer." Her Majesty then prayed, and in her prayer she said, "Lord, open the eyes of this dear young girl, and show her that without a change of heart she can never become a true Christian; and show her that no outward observances can in any wise save her soul." When the girl related this incident, she remarked, "Well, I have many times sung, 'God save the Queen,' but I never dreamed that I should hear the Queen pray to God to save me." The prayer was abundantly answered about a year afterward when this girl was converted and greatly used as a soul-winner.—*The Dawn.*

* * *

George W. Truett's Conversion

May I take a little leaf out of my own poor life? When I was a young fellow, seeking Jesus, the way was all dark to me. I could not understand how to be saved. Oh, if somebody had sat down beside me when I was a lad, and told me the simple way to be saved, I think I would have walked in it! I remember one day I was alone, and for hours and hours this was my prayer: "Lord, deepen my feeling. Lord, make my eyes to be fountains of tears. Lord, fill me with remorse and misery and condemnation!" I prayed like that, supposing that if I reached a certain point of awful, deplorable remorse and regret and wretchedness of spirit, surely Jesus would then take pity on me. Why, that was not the way for me to come to Jesus. The way for me to come to Jesus was to come to Him, and say: "Lord Jesus, here I am, a sinner, and I cannot save myself. Thou hast taught it, and surely Thou knowest. I have found out in myself and by myself how weak and frail I am, how insufficient I am to save myself. Lord Jesus, Thou doest the saving, Thou sayest it, and Thou sayest: 'Come to me without delay, and I will come to you, and I will save you.' Lord, I turn from every evil way, and I give up to Jesus, that He may save me His way, and I give up right now. Dark or bright, no matter what comes, I will give up to Jesus." Oh, if I had come like that, when an interested boy, I would have found Christ, as I did find Him when my feet were turning into young manhood's morning. I did find him, when quietly one night, sitting in an audience like this, an earnest preacher pleaded that Christ must be given His own way to save the soul; that the soul, needy and helpless and unable to save itself, would make honest surrender to Christ—utter surrender. I sat back there as you sit back there before me now, and I said, "Lord, it is all as dark as it can

be. I do not see through it. I am drifting with the current. Lord, save me!"
—George W. Truett.

* * *

Dr. R. A. Torrey's Conversion

Did you ever hear Dr. R. A. Torrey, the far-famed evangelist, tell what an awful unbeliever he was when he was a young man; how he went to the deepest depths of infidelity and scouted everything—the Bible, Christ, God, heaven, hell, immortality—everything like that? His mother yearned after him, and pleaded, prayed for him. Finally, he said to his mother, "I am tired of it all, and I am going to leave and not bother you any more, and you will not see me any more!" She followed him to the door, and followed him to the gate, pleading and praying and loving and weeping, and then, she said her final word: "Son, when you come to the darkest hour of all, and everything seems lost and gone, if you will honestly call on your mother's God, you will get help!" Deeper down he went. Finally, in a hotel room, unable to sleep, wearied with his sins, and wearied with his life, he said, "I will get out of this bed, and I will take the gun there and end this farce called human life!" As he got out of his bed to do that awful thing, his mother's words came back to him: "Son, when your darkest hour of all comes, and everything seems lost, call in sincerity on your mother's God, and you will get help!" And he fell beside his bed, and said, "Oh, God of my mother, if there is such a Being, I want light, and if Thou wilt give it, no matter how, I will follow it." He had light within a few minutes, and hastened back home. Greeting him, his mother exclaimed, "Oh, my boy, I knew you were coming back. You have found the Lord. God has told me so!"—George W. Truett.

* * *

Finney's Conversion

"I suppose I *need* to be prayed for; I am conscious that I am a sinner, but I do not see that it will do any good for you to pray for me."

Charles Grandison Finney was speaking.

"You are continually asking, but you do not receive. You have been praying for the Holy Spirit to descend upon yourselves, and yet complaining of your leanness. You have prayed enough since I have attended these meetings to have prayed the Devil out of this town, if there is any virtue in your prayers. But here you are praying on and complaining still."

Thus Finney reacted when a church member asked him at prayer meeting one week if he did not wish to be prayed for. Yet the sharpness of his reply indicated that the prayers of a few young people were bringing conviction.

Finney was at this time practicing law in Adams, N. Y., and in the course of his work he found it necessary to purchase his first Bible. In the legal works which he had studied the Mosaic Code was frequently referred to as an authority for many of the principles of common law. A close examination of its contents convinced him that it was the Word of God. This constant study of the Bible deepened his convictions until one day he vowed, "I will accept Him today, or I will die in the attempt."

Alone with his Bible he sought seclusion in a near-by piece of woods. There Finney accepted Christ as his Saviour, and he returned to the village with a new heart. Back in the quiet of his law office he knelt to pray, and the Holy Ghost sent such a baptism that at last he cried out, "I shall die if these waves continue to pass over me; Lord, I cannot bear any more." — *Sunday School Times.*

* * *

Better than Seeking

There is something better than seeking God—even better than seeking Him with our whole heart. For as long as we seek we are unsatisfied; and God has something better for us than that. The Keswick Calendar gives an incident of the great Scottish scholar, Professor Duncan, known to his students as "Rabbi Duncan" because of his Oriental scholarship. A friend overheard him talking to a poor old woman, and this is what the great scholar was saying: "Now, you have promised to seek; only remember, seeking won't save you. But if you seek, you will find, and finding will save you." Finding is infinitely better than seeking. The only purpose of seeking is finding, and unless the finding comes the seeking has been a failure. —*Sunday School Times.*

* * *

Experience the Real Test

A little fellow was returning home from a store in Fife, Scotland, with a pail of honey in his hand. A gentleman who walked beside him saw him slip one finger down into the pail and then, I suppose, because his mother had told him never to wipe his sticky fingers on his blouse or trousers, it found its only logical destination. My, how good it was! After he had done this several times, the gentleman approached him and said: "See here, Sonny, what have you in that pail?" "Some honey, sir." "Honey, is it sweet?" "Yes, sir." "How sweet is your honey?" "It is very sweet, sir." "Well, I do not understand you. I asked you how sweet your honey was and you have not yet told me. How sweet is it?" "Why, it is very, *very* sweet, sir." "Well, you are a funny little fellow, I asked you how sweet your honey is, and you just tell me it is very, *very* sweet. Now, can't you tell me really how sweet your honey is?" The little fellow was impatient by this time, so he stuck his finger down in the honey, and holding it aloft, said: "Taste and see for yourself!"

A somewhat crude illustration, but *how true it is that only those who taste and see for themselves ever find how good the Lord is!*—Howard W. Ferrin, in *Unto All.*

* * *

Dr. James Gray's Conversion

When I knew the Creed, the Lord's prayer, and the Ten Commandments, at fourteen years of age, I was confirmed in the most holy faith by a bishop of my church, and was taught in the catechism that I had become "a child of God, a member of Christ, and an inheritor of the Kingdom." But I believed none of that since I was converted. That happy event took place about eight years after my confirmation. I had already turned my face towards the Christian ministry, not as a Divine calling, but a human profession, before I was really saved. My conversion was like this: I was reading a book by Rev. William Arnot, and the title was, *Laws from Heaven for Life on Earth,* a series of homilies on the Proverbs, addressed to young men. The book attracted me, though I did not care for my Bible in the quiet of my room.

One night, after an evening of excitement among worldly people, my eye fell on this sentence: "Every soul not already won to Jesus is already lost." It was an arrow of conviction to my soul. An overwhelming sense of my lost and hopeless condition fell upon me, and my soul was hanging over the abyss. I had absolutely no plea but for mercy. Daily I had said my prayers since childhood, but that night, like Saul of Tarsus, I really prayed. The blessed Saviour placed upon my lips: "God be merciful to me a sinner!" In my agony I uttered it with my face upon the floor. And God heard it. That night He lifted me up out of the miry clay and planted me upon a rock. He put a new song in my mouth, which I have been singing ever since, even salvation unto my God.—Dr. James Gray, late Dean of the Moody Institute, in *The Lamp.*

* * *

The Spirit's Different Ways

In Acts 16 we have the story of two conversions. It took an earthquake to convert the jailer, but the heart of Lydia opened like a flower to the kiss of the Sun of Righteousnesss. All down through the centuries, the Spirit of God has been at the work of conversion. Back in the third century Cyprian the Bishop of Carthage wrote to his friend Donatus: "It is a bad world, Donatus, an incredibly bad world. But I have discovered in the midst of it, a quiet and holy people,

who have learned a great secret. They have found a joy which is a thousand times better than any of the pleasures of our sinful life. They are despised and persecuted, but they care not. They are masters of their souls. They have overcome the world. These people, Donatus, are Christians—and I am one of them."
—Selected.

* * *

How a Mohammedan Found the Way of Life

A true son of the desert, wild and unkempt, doubles up his six feet of height into astonishingly small compass as he crouches on the mat. His poor brain is dulled by drugs and drinks, yet he is a mystic, a seeker after God, a search, which, alas! in the Moslem world is often carried on side by side with immoral excess.

But one bit of truth has penetrated into the dark heart: "There is only one God," he says, "therefore there can be only one Way. I must find the one Way. For years I have asked our own teachers and others to help me and no one has. Show me the one Way. He cannot have more than one."

The beautiful "I am the Way" does not touch him, and day after day he crouches before us with hungry eyes and says sadly, "Only one Way—cannot you show me that I may walk in it?"

Nothing helps, and we pray on for him. Then one day he is taught to pray:

"Lord, give me light to do Thy will,
For only, Lord, from Thee can come the Light
By which these eyes the Way of Light may see."

Next day God gives him light through the last verse of the third of John: "He that believeth on the Son [words most hard for Moslem minds] hath everlasting life: and he that believeth not the Son shall not see life; but the wrath of God abideth on him."

The Spirit Himself was teaching him that day, so very few human words were said. The puzzled weary look changes to one of rapturous joy as he breathes out, "I do believe in the Son of God."

Then like a happy child he looks up with, "I knew he *could* only have one Way."—Matilda Mary Watling, Algiers, in *The Sunday School Times*.

* * *

Spurgeon's Call

When but a lad, Spurgeon was in great distress of mind. Realizing that he had sinned against God, he prayed earnestly, and read the Scriptures, and attended places of worship, but his darkness and despair continued for many months. One Sunday morning he attended a little Primitive Methodist chapel. Owing to a severe snowstorm, the minister did not arrive, and an illiterate shoemaker tried to preach. Using as his text, "Look unto me, and be ye saved, all the ends of the earth," he exhorted his few hearers to look to Christ who was their only hope of salvation. Then observing Spurgeon under the gallery, and knowing him to be a stranger, he said: "Young man, you look very miserable. And you will always be miserable—miserable in life, and miserable in death—if you do not obey my text. But if you obey now, this moment, you will be saved." Then he shouted, "Young man, look to Jesus Christ!" Spurgeon did look, and the darkness rolled away.—From a tract entitled, *How Spurgeon Found Christ*, written by himself.

* * *

God Working with the Individual

At an open-air meeting in England, the leader appealed for testimonies. While this part of the meeting was in progress there passed by a skeptic. He would have gone right on, but at that moment the testimony of a saved drunkard reached him. He paused and listened. The converted man was telling how Jesus had wrought the miracle. The skeptic, disgusted with what he had heard, approached. He was unable to withhold a few open remarks, which were audible to all those standing around. "Spasmodic flights of imagination," he called it. He found, much to his disgust, that his remarks were not at all appreciated by the meeting or the lookers-on. No one had interfered with the man until now. God had his own special way of dealing with him. Among the listeners was a little girl about ten or eleven years old. She approached the man timidly. "If you please," she said, "*if it is only a dream, don't wake him —that's my father!*"—*S. S. Illustrator*

* * *

Aim-day-co

It is said of Miss Reside, the first woman missionary to the Kiowa Indians of Oklahoma, that after she had been with the Indians long enough for them to know what it meant to be a Christian, they gave her a new name. They called her Aim-day-co. Chief Bigtree, in explaining the name, said, "When we Kiowas see anyone on the wrong road we call out, 'Aim-day-co!' ('Turn this way.') Our sister came to us from a far land, and found us all on the wrong road, and in great danger. She stood in a new road and called to us and said, 'Turn this way,' and showed us the Jesus road. God bless Aim-day-co."—Courtesy *Moody Monthly.*

* * *

Old Betty Knew

A poor, unlettered old woman was once accosted by a skeptic: "Well, Betty, you are one of the saints, are you? Pray what sort of folks are they? What do you know about religion, eh?" "Well, well," replied the old woman, "you know, sir, I'm no scholar, so can't say much for the meaning of it; I only know I'm 'saved by grace,' and that's enough to make me happy here, and I expect to go to Heaven by and by." "Oh, that's all, is it? But surely you can tell us something nearer than that. What does being saved feel like?" "*Why, it feels to me,*" said the Spirit-taught one, "*just as if the Lord stood in my shoes, and I stood in His.*" Happy old woman! Her witness was true. — Courtesy *Moody Monthly.*

Are You Right With God?

In one of my missions a young fellow came to me, a fine character who had been put in a most prominent place in that mission. He it was who was delegated to take the hand of every inquirer and say the last word of advice and counsel. He stood it from Monday to Saturday, and on Saturday evening he said to me: "Mr. Smith, I want to see you. You don't go out on Sunday morning, do you?"

I said, "No, I rest then, unless I go to church; but I usually stay in to get a little quiet. What do you want to see me about?" I thought he wanted to see me about some special case.

He said, "About my own soul."

"Why," I said, "what is the trouble?"

He said, "I am not converted; I have never been born again."

"My brother," I said, "what does it mean?"

He said, "My parents supposed I was a Christian, and urged me to join the church, and I did so. My pastor supposed I was a Christian, and I was made a Sunday School teacher, and an officer in the church. Because they supposed and kept on supposing, nobody has ever looked me in the eye and said, 'Harry, are you right with God?'"

—Gypsy Smith

* * *

A New Name

A little girl found on the street in a basket was taken to a hospital, where she lived for a few years. The people named her, "Mary Lost." When she was still quite young, she became a Christian, trusting in Jesus as her Saviour, and He gave her a new heart and made her a new creature. Then, she wanted a new name also. She went to the superintendent of the home and said, "Please don't call me Mary Lost any more. I used to be Mary Lost, but I am no longer. Jesus has found me, and now I want to be called Mary Found."—Selected.

* * *

When a Chinese "Heart" is Broadened

A missionary is examining an old woman of seventy-three for baptism and admission to the church:

"Who is Jesus?"

"Jesus died for me."

"How did He die?"

"I don't know."

"Who were Jesus' disciples?"

"I don't remember. I can't read."

"Do you know the names of any of the Books of the Bible?"

"When one can't read . . ."

"Where did Jesus live on earth?"

Silence.

The missionary stopped. The old woman had made a very poor showing.

"This old lady is one of our most faithful Christians," said a deacon. "She always comes to our meetings, though she lives three miles away. She gives cheerfully what she can to every good cause. She used to have a terrible temper, but since she believed, she has become kind-hearted and patient. Everybody knows about it."

The missionary looked at her. Seventy-three years old. She might be gone before he could come around next year. He decided to go on with the examination.

"Who is God?"

"God is our Heavenly Grandfather."

"Where is He?"

"Wherever I go, He is there."

"Can you talk to Him?"

Her face brightened with understanding: "Yes, I can."

"When do you talk to Him?"

"Why, very often. When I am working in the fields, when I am making bread, when I feel sad, I talk to Him and my heart is broadened." She was now on familiar ground. "I talk to Him whenever I want to. Sometimes I have more to say and talk longer. Sometimes I have only one or two thoughts and talk shorter. Whatever I have in my heart, I say."—*The Missionary Review of the World.*

* * *

When the Grace of God Has Done Its Work

One night in St. Louis, Mr. Moody preached on the text, "Believe on the Lord Jesus Christ, and thou shalt be saved." A newspaper published the sermon with the heading, "How the Jailer Got Caught." A paper was taken into a jail where a burglar named Ballintyne Booth was awaiting trial. He read the headline and said, "That is good," and began reading. The sermon resulted in his conversion; and the officials saw such a change in him that when the case came to trial it was not pressed.

Booth went to New York, and back to St. Louis. One day the sheriff sent for him. He said, "I want you to be a deputy sheriff. I had you shadowed for six months, and they wrote me you were O.K." He remained a deputy sheriff for ten years, until his death. Once a preacher asked Booth to preach for him, and he asked the sheriff to be let off. The sheriff said that he was sorry but that it would be impossible as he had just levied on a jewelry store and there was a large stock of diamonds of which no inventory had been taken, and there was no one he could trust there but Booth.—*The Wonderful Word.*

* * *

Some Other Way Would Not Do

"One night when my wife was at prayer meeting I began to grow very miserable. I did not know what was the matter with me, but finally retired before my wife came home. In the morning I could eat no breakfast, and went to the office. I told my clerks they could take a holiday, and I shut myself in the office. I kept growing more and more miserable, and finally got down and asked God to forgive my sins. I did not say 'for Jesus' sake,' for I was a Unitarian, and I did not believe in the Atonement. I kept praying, 'God, forgive my sins'; but no answer came. At last in desperation I cried, 'O God, for Christ's sake, forgive my sins,' and I found peace at once." This man had no access to God until he came in the name of Christ, but when he came thus he was answered at once.—*Sunday School Times.*

* * *

A Bible in a Hotel Room

One winter morning, in the city of San Diego, California, a man turned his steps wearily from the waterfront to his hotel. He had been drinking heavily for weeks; all that seemed to be left to him were memories, and his mind was tortured with thoughts of his wife and four little children whom he had deserted. He had been a radio executive with a beautiful home, cars, servants, everything that money could provide, but now they were gone, and the little family, dragged down until they were living in a hovel, were deserted.

He had suffered a complete nervous breakdown and worst of all he had lost his voice, and for a year and a half had been hardly able to speak above a whisper. The future held no promise, and so, each waking moment, he lived over and over again the horror of it all. Such was the state of mind and soul as he opened the door of his room and flung himself into a chair.

Suddenly his gaze fell upon the Gideon Bible, and, in a distracted sort of way he picked it up and began to read. Old familiar words he had learned as a child by the checked apron of her whom he had called Mother; words of life, quick and powerful, leaped out of the pages and found their way into his heart. He fell on his knees and, spreading the Bible on a chair, made a vow that he would not leave that room, if he died of starvation, until there came into his soul a knowledge that his sins were forgiven. With a surge of joy he realized that God's promises were even for such as he.

In that hotel room he found Calvary's Cross, there he laid his burdens down, there the old man died and a new was born. From that place he walked in newness of life, and by God's grace the difficulties were straightened out between him and his wife and the little home was reunited. The "peace that passeth all understanding" loosed the taut nerves and muscles which had prevented normal speech and God gave him back his voice. Now a fine group of Christian young men are joined with him in sending out the Word of Life over the air to many thousands of listeners-in and throughout the Western States and Canada, and even in the Arctic Circle, and God is using their ministry.

"Small wonder," he says, "that there is in my heart a feeling of undying gratitude to the Christian workers who have felt the burden to place in hotel rooms the Gideon Bibles."—*The Evangelical Christian.*

* * *

Shaking Off the Dust

I remember hearing the Rev. W. V. Barratt give an account of an experience of his early days in Germany. A boy of ten or twelve, he was with his brother distributing tracts from door to door, when at one home his tract was refused and the door discourteously closed. The two boys, obeying the precept of the Lord Jesus, kicked the dust off their feet at the doorstep. Some thirty years afterward, Mr. Barratt was visiting the same part of Germany, when he was called to the bedside of a gentleman who had asked to see him. He was reminded of the incident of thirty years before, and only then learned that the gentleman, inquiring as to the meaning of the boys' singular act, had been convicted of the sin of refusing God's messenger—and had in consequence been led to seek, and find, salvation.—*Sunday School Times.*

* * *

How They Became "Sons"

A Hindu convert in India could neither read nor write, but he got others to read the Bible to him. His favorite verse was John 1:12—"As many as received him, to them gave he the power to become the sons of God." "I have received Him," said he, "so I have become a son of God." He went back to his village radiantly happy. "I have become a son of God," he cried. His life was so transformed, and his simple witness so effective, that the villagers all wanted to become "sons of God," too. He won the whole village for Christ and thousands of others besides. Why? Just because he —a poor illiterate Hindu—realized that he had indeed become "a son of God" and longed for others to become "sons" also.—From *The Happy Christian,* by An Unknown Christian.

An Indian's Explanation

It happened that a white man and a North American Indian were deeply convicted under the same sermon. The Indian was almost immediately made to rejoice in pardoning mercy, but the white man was for a long time in great distress of mind. At last he, too, found comfort in God's forgiving love. Some time afterward, on meeting his Indian brother, he thus addressed him: "How was it that I should be so long under conviction, when you found comfort so soon?" "Oh, brother," replied the Indian, "me tell you. There come along a rich prince; he promise to give you a new coat. You look at your coat, and say, 'My coat pretty good; it will do a little longer.' He then offer me a new coat. I look at my old blanket. I say, 'This good for nothing.' I fling it right away and take the new coat. Just so, brother, you try to make your old righteousness do for a little while; but I, poor Indian, had none. So I glad to receive at once the righteousness of the Lord Jesus."—*Christian Herald.*

* * *

"All Was Changed"

There was a crippled woman in China, who was the greatest spiritual power in her province. As a child she was dropped by careless hands. For many years she was bad tempered, lashing with her sharp tongue against fate and her environment. But when she became a child of God, all was changed. She became a teacher. When she was sent to her first school, there was a riot, because the people said this cripple would bring them bad luck. But when she was transferred to another school after several years, there was a greater riot, because they had never had such a teacher. No one in her city had led so many people to God.

And in the time of sorrow, God pities. Let us not forget that. I see people, ignorant people, who do not know that and I tell them this truth about God, and they are surprised. God is the God of all comfort.—*The Gospel Herald.*

True Conversion

There was in a certain village, a very mean man who sold wood to his neighbors, and who always took advantage of them by cutting his logs a few inches under the required four feet. One day the report was circulated that the woodchopper had been converted. Nobody believed the report, for they all declared that he was beyond being reached. One man, however, slipped quietly out of the grocery store where the "conversion" was being discussed and soon came running back in excitement and shouted: "It's so! He has been!" They all asked: "How do you know?" "Why, I have been over and measured the wood that he cut yesterday. It is good four feet long!" That testimony convinced the crowd. This is, to be sure, a very homely incident, but it brings out the important truth that *the person who accepts Christ must first of all become a new man—his new faith must make a difference in his life.*—Rufus M. Jones.

* * *

The Work of Grace

One of the most notoriously bad characters that ever lived in New York was Orville Gardner. He was the trainer of prize fighters and companion of all sorts of hard characters. His reputation was so thoroughly bad that he was called "Awful Gardner." He had a little boy, whom he dearly loved, and this boy died. A short time after his boy's death, he was standing in the bar of a New York saloon, surrounded by a number of his boon companions. The night was sweltering, and he stepped outside the saloon to get a little fresh air. As he stood out there and looked up between the high buildings at the sky above his head, a star was shining down upon him, and as he was looking at it, he said to himself, "I wonder where my little boy is tonight?" Then the thought came to him quick as a flash, "Wherever he is, you will never see him again unless you change your life."

Touched by the Spirit of God, he hurried from the saloon to the room where his godly mother was. He went in and asked his mother to pray for him. They spent the whole night in prayer and toward morning "Awful Gardner" had found peace and gained the victory. He was the victim of an overwhelming appetite for drink, and had in his house a jug of whiskey at the time. He did not dare to keep it and did not know what to do with it. Finally he took it down to the river, got into a boat and rowed over to an island. He set the liquor on a rock and knelt down, and as he afterward said, "Fought that jug of whiskey for a long time," and God gave him perfect deliverance. He did not dare to break it, lest the fumes set him wild. He did not dare to leave it, lest some one else get it. Finally he dug a hole and buried it. He left the island a free man. "Awful Gardiner" became a mighty preacher of the Gospel. He visited Sing Sing prison, and it was through listening to him preach that the young Irish convict, Jerry McAuley was set to thinking and praying, and resulted in his conversion, and eventually the founding of the Jerry McAuley Mission.—*Illustrator.*

* * *

Two Drunkards

Two drunkards were converted. The one said the inclination of drink was taken completely from him. He could do business in a bar room and not desire a drink. The other converted drunkard said, "Not a day has passed since my conversion that I have not wanted a drink; but God has kept me from yielding." God deals differently with his children. In one case He may remove the temptation, in another he may leave the temptation, and give grace to overcome it. Where there is daily trusting Christ to keep you out of sin, there is daily victory, no matter what your particular besetting sin may be.—*The Gospel Herald.*

* * *

Sometimes

Sometimes it all comes back to me,
When I saw Christ on Calvary;
'Twas then my sins were washed away,
Oh, what a bessed happy day;
I came believing to the Lord,
I came, accepting His blest Word;
It told how Christ had died for me,
It was a jcy to me.

Sometimes I backward look, to see
The time I came His own to be;
His own, for all I then did lay
Upon His altar, happy day:
He then, was Jesus Christ, *my Lord*
To be, to go, e'en at His Word;
It was a blest surrender hour,
With joy I felt new power.

Sometimes in mem'ry I renew,
The blest *infilling* that I knew;
The Spirit did my life invey,
That was a wondrous day;
Since then a holy walk I know,
The Spirit makes His fruit to grow,
He leads me ever on, along,
In constant joy and song.

—R. E. Neighbour, D.D.

* * *

My First Convert

How my heart leaped for joy when I heard the tidings of my first convert! I could never be satisfied with a full congregation, and the kind expressions of friends; I longed to hear that hearts had been broken, that tears had been seen streaming from the eyes of penitents. How I did rejoice, as one that findeth great spoil, over one poôr laborer's wife who confessed that she felt the guilt of sin, and had found the Saviour under my discourse one Sunday afternoon! . . . I remember well her being received into the church and her dying, and going Home. She was the first seal to my ministry and, I can assure you, a very precious one indeed. No mother was ever more full of happiness at the sight of her first-born son. Then could I have sung the song of the virgin, Mary, for my soul did magnify the Lord for remembering my low estate, and giving me the great honor to do a work for which all generations should call me blessed, for so I counted the conversion of one soul.—Charles Haddon Spurgeon.

Expecting Conversions

A young preacher went to Spurgeon to ask why he did not have conversions in his ministry.

"You do not expect to make converts after every sermon, do you?" Spurgeon asked.

The young preacher replied, "Oh, no, of course, I do not expect them after every sermon!"

"That is just the reason why you do not get them after any sermon," was Spurgeon's answer. — *The Missionary Worker.*

* * *

A Good Ending to Any Story

A writer tells of a little person of some three years who was insatiably fond of stories. When there was no one to tell them to her, she made them up herself. The invariable ending of these stories was, "And him went home to him's muvver." Bears, lions, tigers, even elephants and crocodiles passed through the most agitating and unusual adventures, but in the end they all went home to their mother. That was an astonishing bit of wisdom to be evolved by a person of three. The greatest philosophy of life has long since been stated, "When he came to himself, he said, . . . I will arise and go to my father."—*The Sunday at Home.*

* * *

How to Keep the Golden Rule

One evening the chief of the Delaware Indians was sitting by a fireside with a friend. Both were silently looking into the fire. At last his friend broke the silence by saying: "I have been thinking of a rule, delivered by the author of the Christian religion which we call the Golden Rule." "Stop," said the chief. "Don't praise it. Tell me what it is, and let me think for myself." He was informed that the rule was for one man to do to others as he would have others do to him. "That is impossible; it cannot be done," hastily replied the Indian. Silence followed. In about fifteen minutes the Indian said: "Brother, I have been thoughtful of what you told me. If the Great Spirit who made men would give him a new heart, he could do as you say, but not else."—*The Expositor.*

* * *

Not Necessarily Respectability

Would the heart of a hopeless drunkard, gambler, thief, forger, and "bum" be regarded as "good ground"? Samuel Hopkins Hadley was all that these words describe when he went to Jerry McAuley's Mission one night. Jerry put his hand on Hadley's head and said, "Brother, pray." "I can't pray," replied Hadley. "Won't you pray for me?" "All the prayers in the word won't save you unless you pray for yourself," said Jerry. Then, with a breaking heart, Hadley said, "Dear Jesus, can You help me?" From that moment until the day of his death Mr. Hadley declared he had never wanted a drink of whiskey. "That night," he said, "right on the corner of Broadway and 32nd Street, I was ordained to preach the everlasting Gospel." The seed in his case brought forth such fruit that one who knew him declared him to have been the "greatest American of his time—not measured in money and fame, but in love and likeness to Christ." "Good ground" does not necessarily refer to respectability.—*Home Department* (Baptist).

* * *

Real Conversion

There are people who say that Paul's conversion was epilepsy. Well, before the epilepsy he was a blasphemer; after the epilepsy he began to pray, and from that time forward he became a saint and a missionary and a noble warrior. Then fly abroad, thou mighty epilepsy!—Dr. Joseph Parker.

* * *

"Whomsoever a Fellow"

A messenger came to a Sunday school superintendent and said, "Hasten as quickly as you can, there is a boy wanting to see you. He is dying." The superintendent hurried to the place, and found a bright-looking lad who had been crushed by a cart. As he entered, the lad quickly said, "Didn't I hear you say the other Sunday that whomsoever a fellow comes to Jesus he would be saved?"

"Yes," replied the visitor, "I said something like that." "Well," said the boy, "then I'm saved. I have been a bad boy, but I've been thinking about that, and I have taken God at His Word, so I'm saved." After he had uttered these words, his strength seemed to fail, and not long after he passed away, his last words being, "Whomsoever a fellow comes to Jesus, He will in no wise cast out."

He did not quote the words exactly, but he had grasped the meaning of them, and believed them too (John 3:16; 6:37).—I. F., in *Sunlight for the Young.*

* * *

Two Birthdays 100 Years Apart

An old lady now in her hundred and fourth year lives in a one-room cottage at Croydon. When she was a hundred years old she was visited by a city missioner who explained John 3:16 to her. "How wonderful," she said, "and how good the Lord has been in sparing me these hundred years that I might learn the way of life!" This conversion is described in a London City Mission Magazine and ends with these words: "Born 1825; born again 1925." Surely "the longsuffering of our Lord is salvation." —*Sunday School Times.*

* * *

"I'd Open the Door"

A district visitor left a sheet almanac at a house. The central picture was a reproduction of Holman Hunt's picture "The Light of the World." Mother and son looked at it with wonder as it was placed in a prominent position on the wall of the home. The father came home for dinner and his attention was called to it by the boy. "Look, Daddy! Who is it?" The father looked at the picture, but gave no answer, though he knew. But the little fellow was not to be denied, and again came the question, "Who is it, Daddy? Tell me, Daddy." At last he blurted out, "A man, of course." "What man, Daddy? What is His name?" Compelled by the earnestness of the child, he said, "Christ." "But what is He doing, Daddy?" he asked. "Why, don't you see? He is knocking at a door," replied the father. "How long will He knock, Daddy?" came the further question. "I don't know," came the reply. Still the boy asked, "What is He knocking for?" to receive the answer, "Because He wants to go inside." "Why don't they open the door?" This question the boy repeatedly asked during the dinner, remarking, "I'd open the door. Wouldn't you, Daddy?" The father began to feel very uncomfortable, and left as soon as he could to get away from the questioning, which had aroused a tumult of thoughts in his mind and heart. Returning from work after the boy had gone to bed, he learned that even during tea the same questioning occurred. Both husband and wife confessed that the boy's questions had aroused feelings long crushed and silenced, but at last both knelt, confessed their sin of keeping the Lord outside of their hearts and lives, and received him as their Saviour.—Courtesy *Moody Monthly.*

* * *

The Weight of Past Rejections

A famous scientist tells of how, in the course of his experiments in the mountains, he used to be lowered over a precipice. He would step into the basket, and the men would lower him for his work; but whenever they lowered him, they would always test his weight to see whether they could lift him again. One day they let him down farther and farther than ever before, until all the rope at their command was exhausted. When his day's work was done, he gave the signal. When they took hold of the rope to lift him, they could not do so. They tugged and pulled and strained, but they could not manage it. So he had to wait until they got additional men to pull him up, and the scientist says that the reason they could not lift him was that they failed to take into consideration the length and weight of the rope. I know why a man of fifty years of age has a hard time to surrender. The reason is that he must always lift against his past refusals. You say, "No," and your heart is hardened; you say, "No." and your will becomes stubborn, and if you are finally lost, the responsibility is not with God.—J. Wilbur Chapman, in *The King's Business.*

* * *

Dr. H. A. Ironside's Conversion

From a very early age God began to speak to me through His Word. I doubt if I could go back to the first time when, to my recollection, I felt something of the reality of eternal things.

My father was taken from me ere his features were impressed upon my infant mind. I never have heard him spoken of other than as a man of God. He was known in Toronto (my birthplace) to many as "The Eternity Man." His Bible, marked in many places, was a precious legacy to me; and from it I learned to recite my first verse of Scripture, at the age of four. I distinctly recall learning the blessed words of Luke 19:10, "For the Son of Man is come to seek and to save that which was lost." That I was lost, and that Christ Jesus came from Heaven to save me, were the first Divine truths impressed on my young heart.

My widowed mother was, it seems to me, one of a thousand. I remember yet how I would be thrilled as she knelt with me as a child, and prayed, "O Father, keep my boy from ever desiring anything greater than to live for Thee. Save him early, and make him a devoted street-preacher, as his father was. Make him willing to suffer for Jesus' sake, to gladly endure persecution and rejection by the world that cast out Thy Son; and keep him from what would dishonor Thee." The words were not always the same, but I have heard the sentiment times without number.

To our home there often came servants of Christ—plain, godly men, who seemed to me to carry with them the atmosphere of eternity. Yet in a very real sense they were the bane of my boyhood. Their searching, "Harry, lad, are you born again yet?" or the equally impressive, "Are you certain that your soul is saved?" often brought me to a standstill; but I knew not how to reply.

California had become my home ere I was clear as to being a child of God. In Los Angeles I first began to learn the love of the world, and was impatient of restraint. Yet I had almost continual concern as to the great matter of my salvation.

I was but twelve years old when I began a Sunday School and set up to try to help the boys and girls of the neighborhood to a knowledge of the Book I had read ten times through, but which still left me without assurance of salvation.

To Timothy, Paul wrote, "From a child thou hast known the Holy Scriptures, which are able to make thee wise unto salvation, *through faith which is in Christ Jesus*" (II Tim. 3:15). It was this latter that I lacked. I had, it seemed to me, always believed, yet I dared not say I was saved. I know now that I had already believed about Jesus. I had not really believed in Him as my personal Saviour. Between the two there is all the difference that there is between being saved and lost, between an eternity in Heaven and eternal destruction.

As I have said, I was not without considerable anxiety as to my soul; and though I longed to break into the world, and was indeed guilty of much that was vile and wicked, I ever felt a restraining hand upon me, keeping me from many things that I would otherwise have gone into; and a certain religiousness became, I suppose, characteristic. Religion is not salvation.

I was nearly fourteen years old when, upon returning one day from school, I learned that a servant of Christ from Canada, well known to me, had arrived for meetings. I knew, ere I saw him, how he would greet me; for I remembered him well, and his searching questions, when I was younger. Therefore I was not surprised, but embarrassed nevertheless, when he exclaimed, "Well, Harry, lad, I'm glad to see you. Are you born again yet?"

The blood mantled my face; I hung my head, and could find no words to reply. An uncle present said, "You know, Mr. M——, he preaches himself now a bit, and conducts a Sunday school!"

"Indeed!" was the answer. "Will you get your Bible, Harry?"

I was glad to get out of the room, and so went at once for my Bible, and returned, after remaining out as long as seemed decent, hoping thereby to recover myself. Upon my re-entering the room, he said, kindly, but seriously, "Will you turn to Romans 3:19, and read it aloud?"

Slowly I read, "Now we know that what things soever the Law saith, it saith to them that are under the Law: that every mouth may be stopped, and all the world become guilty before God." I felt the application, and was at a loss for words. The evangelist went on to tell me that he too had been once a *religious* sinner, till God stopped his mouth, and then gave him a sight of Christ. The words had their effect. From that time till I was sure I was saved, I refrained from talking of these things, and I gave up my Sunday school work.

At last, on a Thursday evening in February, 1890, God spoke to me in tremendous power while out at a gay party. Some verses of Scripture I had learned months before came to me with startling clearness. Every word seemed to burn its way into my heart. I saw as never before my dreadful guilt in having so long refused to trust Christ for myself. I went back to the parlor, and tried to join with the rest in their empty follies. All seemed utterly hollow, and the tinsel was gone. The light of eternity was shining into the room, and I wondered how any could laugh with God's judgment hanging over us.

That night, when all was over, I hurried home. There, after lighting my lamp, I took my Bible, and, with it before me, I fell on my knees. I had an undefined feeling that I had better pray. The thought came, "What shall I pray for?" Clearly came back the answer, "For what God has been offering me for years. Why not then receive it, and thank Him?" My dear mother had often said, "The place to begin with God is at Romans 3. or John 3." To both these Scriptures I turned. Clearly I saw that I was a helpless sinner, but that for me Christ had died, and that salvation was offered freely to all who trusted Him. Reading John 3:16 the second time, I said, "That will do! O God, I thank Thee that Thou hast loved me, and given Thy Son for me. I trust Him *now* as my Saviour, and I rest on Thy Word, which tells me that I have everlasting life!" Then I expected to feel a thrill of joy. It did not come. I expected a sudden rush of love for Christ. It did not come either. I feared I could not really be saved with so little emotion. I read the words again. There could be no mistake. God loved the world, of whom I formed a part. God gave His Son to save all believers. I believed in Him as my Saviour. Therefore I must have everlasting life. Again, I thanked Him, and rose from my knees and began to walk by faith. God could not lie. I *knew* I must be saved!—Dr. H. A. Ironside, in *Glad Tidings.*

COURAGE

Flying Our Colors

When at a restaurant I met a gentleman whom I had met in Temperance work, and noticed that the blue ribbon which had always been most conspicuously displayed in his buttonhole at the meeting was wanting. "Where is the blue ribbon?" I asked. For reply he opened his coat and there in the buttonhole of his waistcoat was a thin—very thin—piece of blue. I asked him why he did not wear it where it could be seen, to which he replied that during business hours it subjected him to so much chaff from those whom he contacted, that he thought it better not to let it be seen. I said to him, "Did you ever hear of Admiral Nelson?" He looked surprised and said, "Yes, of course, I have; but what has Admiral Nelson to do with this question?" "You remember when Nelson was about to engage the enemy at the battle of Trafalgar he dressed himself in his full uniform, and placed all the medals and orders that he had won upon his breast. His officers remonstrated with him, saying he should take off his decorations, or at least cover them with a handkerchief, as otherwise he would become a mark for the enemy's musketry. But the gallant Admiral would have none of their advice: "I won these distinctions in the face of the enemy," he replied, "and I shall wear them in the face of the enemy." The lesson was not lost upon my hearer, I am assured. — *Bible Expositor and Illuminator.*

* * *

Courage

Staunch old Admiral Farragut of the American navy (born 1801, died 1870) —he of the true heart and the iron will —said to another officer of the navy, "Dupont, do you know why you didn't get into Charleston with your ironclads." "Oh, it was because the channel was so crooked." "No, Dupont, it was not that." "Well, the rebel fire was perfectly horrible." "Yes, but it wasn't that." "What was it, then?" *"It was because you didn't believe you could get in."* That is just the trouble with our work in winning men and building up Christ's kingdom. We don't *believe* we can succeed. And, of course. often we fail.—*S. S. Illustrator.*

* * *

God, Give Us Men

God, give us men. A time like this demands
Strong minds, great hearts, true faith and ready hands;
Men whom the lust of office does not kill;
Men whom the spoils of office cannot buy;
Men who possess opinions and a will;
Men who have honor, men who will not lie;
Men who can stand before a demagogue
And damn his treacherous flatteries without winking;
Tall men, sun-crowned, who live above the fog,
In public duty and in private thinking;
For while the rabble with their thumb-worn creeds,
Their large professions and their little deeds,
Mingle in selfish strife — lo, freedom weeps
Wrong rules the land, and waiting justice sleeps.

God, give us men: Men who serve not for selfish booty,
But real men, courageous, who flinch not at duty;
Men of dependable character; men of sterling worth;
Then wrongs will be redressed, and right will rule on earth.
God GIVE US MEN." —Selected.

* * *

The Courage of His Convictions

Weak-kneed principles always awaken contempt. Harry Shepler, a young man of whom the *Sunday School Times* tells, was in the signal service. Being ordered one morning by a sergeant to report for duty at the canteen, he refused to do so, and the sergeant threatened to report him to the officer of the day.

"All right," said Shepler, "go ahead. I did not enlist to be a bartender, but a soldier, and I will not report at the canteen."

He was duly reported to the major, who sent for him. Shepler went with trembling knees but with a steady heart, for he knew he was right. The officer said to him:

"Are you the young man who disobeyed orders this morning?"

"Yes, sir, I am."

"Why did you do it?"

"Simply because I do not believe it is right to do what I was asked to do. I enlisted to be a soldier and not a bartender."

The major arose quickly from his stool, and, extending his hand, said:

"Shepler, you are the kind of a man we want. I am glad to see a fellow who has the courage of his convictions. You are not obliged to report at the canteen."

The great need of the day is for men to have convictions founded upon the Word of God, and then be true to those convictions.—*Christian Victory.*

* * *

Loyalty Before Life

Some years ago an ocean liner was wrecked on a dangerous reef on the New England coast. The coast guard is well officered there. They went to the rescue under the captaincy of an old seaman, but with a few inexperienced young men on the crew. One of the youngsters turned a white face to the captain, saying, "Sir, the wind is offshore; and the tide is running out. We can go out, but we can never come back." All the captain said was, "*Launch the boat. We have to go out. We don't have to come back!*"—*New Century Leader.*

* * *

Which Question Was More Searching?

A story that carries its own application to Christian faithfulness has been told of a question and answer that passed between Martin Niemoeller and a chaplain who visited him in his detention: "Why are you here?" asked the chaplain. "Why are you not here?" asked Dr. Niemoeller.—*Christian Faith and Life.*

COURTESY

A Railroad Bulletin

One of the largest railroad companies in America has issued this bulletin, which is displayed conspicuously in its cars, stations, and in other public places:

Courtesy is a business asset, a gain and never a loss.

Officers and employees, above all others, should be courteous.

Use courtesy in all dealings with passengers, patrons and with one another.

Railroad men help their company by being courteous.

This railroad believes in courtesy.

Even the discourteous like to be shown courtesy.

Smooth away life's difficulties by being courteous.

You will find your value increased by courtesy.

Life is not so short but there is always time for courtesy.—Emerson.

If a railroad thus impresses courtesy upon everyone connected with it, how about a church? The manners of a Christian ought to be the best manners in the world. Are we living up to this standard? or do our rudeness and discourtesy bring reproach upon religion? —Selected.

* * *

Thomas Jefferson's Politeness

Thomas Jefferson, author of the Declaration of Independence, and his eldest grandson were one day riding in a carriage together. They met a slave who respectfully took off his hat and bowed. The President, according to his invariable custom, returned the salutation by raising his hat. The young man paid no attention to the Negro's act of civility. Mr. Jefferson, after a moment's pause, turned a reproachful eye to him and said, "Thomas, do you permit a slave to be more of a gentleman than yourself?" —*The Volunteer's Gazette.*

* * *

Be Courteous

It pays at all times to be courteous. One may not feel just like it, the circumstances may not always warrant an effort, but in the end it will pay to act the gentleman.

A friend of the writer tells of a young lawyer of brilliant prospects, who located in a Western town, and began the practice of his profession. One day soon after he had opened his law office, he was riding on the street car, when an influential business man noticed him, and thinking to introduce himself and encourage the young man, he moved across to the other side of the car, by the side of the young lawyer, and said, "What is your name?" "My name is mud," curtly answered the young man. "Oh," said the other, "excuse me for interrupting you."

The years went by and the young lawyer was successful, and finally aspired to a certain political office of prominence. The politicians said to him, "If you can secure the votes of the men working in —— mine you are sure of election." He visited the mine, asked for the superintendent, who came into his presence. With much dignity the young lawyer said, "My name is ——." "Ah," said the mine superintendent, "when did you change your name?" "Change my name?" replied the political aspirant. "I have not changed my name." "Oh, yes you have, for you told me on the street car a few years ago that your name was mud." "Oh, ah! I know—that was only a joke." "No," said the superintendent harshly, "your name is mud at this time for any favor whatever."

The election came off, and the young lawyer was defeated by just seventeen votes, and these votes were cast by the men at the mine.

Again, I say it pays to be courteous, to act the gentleman anywhere—everywhere.—C. E. Cornell.

* * *

Gentleness and Courtesy

We know many agreeable sinners, and we know of some disagreeable saints. A saint should never be disagreeable, for there is no virtue in having an ugly disposition or bad manners. Let us determine to wage unceasing warfare upon our own eccentricities, but let us determine to be patient with the eccentricities of others. Though we cannot get away from disagreeable people, we can do wonders toward reducing the numbers of disagreeable people in the world. The method is simple. Let us cultivate amiability. Let us learn to laugh. The muscles of our face are growing stiff, and as these muscles grow stiff we grow homely. After awhile we shall make the wonderful discovery that we are not meeting so many disagreeable people as formerly. It is wonderful that we can change the world by changing ourselves, but it is true nevertheless. Jesus emphasized the gentler virtues, and He exemplified them in His life. Turn the other cheek, return good for evil, give love for hatred, and soon your enemy will begin to love you. A winsome disposition can overcome many distempers. — *The Watchman-Examiner*.

COVETOUSNESS

A Speck in the Sky

A few years ago, a man in Detroit stepped out into his back yard, and looking up saw a speck in the sky. It grew larger and larger. Then he discovered it was something alive, a struggling, living mass of something slowly descending to earth. What he had first seen as a speck, had now revealed itself to be two large bald eagles in deadly combat. The huge birds were fighting in the sky over a fish. The fish had already dropped to the ground, but the birds had continued their struggle until they were bloody and exhausted. With a last wild scream, each made a fatal plunge at the other, and both birds came tumbling down to earth —dead, falling side by side, within a few feet of the man who had been witnessing the fierce battle of the sky. Greed had destroyed them.

So it may be with a life. Greed grows upon one. The selfish man finally destroys himself. Beginning as a speck, greed, if unchecked, will pull us down from the highest and noblest life just as it did those two birds of the sky. Unless we destroy greed it will destroy us.—W. G. M., in *Youth's Comrade.*

* * *

A Cure for Coveteousness

A stingy Christian was listening to a charity sermon. He was nearly deaf, and was accustomed to sit facing the congregation, right under the pulpit, with his ear-trumpet directed upward, toward the preacher. The sermon moved him considerably. At one time he said to himself, "I'll give ten dollars"; again he said, "I'll give fifteen." At the very close of the appeal, he was very much moved, and thought he would give fifty dollars.

Now the boxes were passed. As they moved along, his charity began to ooze out. He came down from fifty to twenty, to ten, to five, to zero. He concluded that he would not give anything. "Yet," said he, "this won't do—I am in a bad fix. This covetousness will be my ruin." The boxes were getting nearer and nearer. The crisis was upon him! What should he do? The box was now under his chin—all the congregation was looking. He had been holding his pocketbook in his hand during this soliloquy, which was half audible, though, in his deafness, he did not know that he was heard. In the agony of the final moment, he took his pocketbook and laid it in the box, saying to himself as he did it, "Now squirm, old natur'!"

This was victory beyond any that Alexander ever won—a victory over himself. Here is a key to the problem of covetousness. The old natur' must go under.—H. L. Hastings, in *The Expositor.*

* * *

The "Satisfied" Man

A Quaker, in order to impress a lesson upon his neighbors, put up a sign on a vacant piece of ground next to his house, which read, "I will give this lot to anyone who is really satisfied." A wealthy farmer, as he rode by, read it. Stopping, he said: "Since my Quaker friend is going to give that piece away, I may as well have it as anyone else. I am rich. I have all I need, so I am able to qualify." He went up to the door, and when the aged Friend appeared, explained why he had come. "And is thee really satisfied?" asked the owner of the lot. "I surely am," was the reply. "I have all I need, and am well satisfied." "Friend," said the other, "if thee is satisfied, what does thee want with my lot?" The question revealed the covetousness that was hidden in the heart.—*Sunday School Times.*

* * *

Strange Poverty

A Swedish writer tells of a farmer whose thoughts took living shape of gold and silver, coins, banks and barns, grains of wheat and corn, cows and pigs. These forms clouded his mind, hiding the beauty of the landscape. When he sat down to read, they settled like bees on the paper, allowing him to read only the market report and the price of cows. Just a fancy? Yes, but based on a subtle psychological fact. If we are to own money and not allow it to own us, we must have a rich soul, else we soon become victims of a strange poverty. The late Robert Horton said the greatest lesson he learned from life was that people who set their minds and hearts on money are equally disappointed whether they get it or whether they don't. It binds alike the poor who crave money and the rich who make it their god.—*Quiet Hour.*

* * *

No Union Scale Here

A faith missionary, supported by no church board, was home from China on furlough with his wife and three children. God has wonderfully blessed their ministry and remarkably supplied their needs. A large, luxurious church was having an all-day meeting of the Ladies' Missionary Society. Hard put to find a speaker, they called on this missionary's wife, who was available. Her talk proved so interesting that the ladies prolonged her message by asking questions for over two hours. The bejewelled ladies in their business meeting learned that their budget was fully met, with a surplus which they decided to apply on next year's apportionment. To the missionary, they said that they allotted 50 cents for speaker's transportation, and since she had offered to take the four chicken pies remaining from the dinner (no one else wanting them), worth 10 cents each, they would deduct 40 cents. Handing her 10 cents, they rolled away in their luxurious limousines. What does God think about the way we treat His missionaries?—*Prophecy Monthly.*

* * *

Gave Up the Dog's Life

I knew a man once who rose from poverty to riches. Poor, he was a devout servant of God, "instant in season, out of season." Rich, he gave up his life to houses, farms, banks, travel. He dropped God overboard and took up the bone in his mouth. He was deaf to all appeals of every kind to his spiritual nature. Church, the Bible, the place of prayer, all faded out of his life. For years, he enjoyed his prosperity; then his business failed. He lost everything. God took the bone out of his mouth. He gave up the dog's life and came home to God. I heard his testimony. With tears he confessed backsliding, and thanked God that he found out in time his great mistake.—S. J. Reid, D.D., in *The Watchman-Examiner*.

* * *

What He Saved and Lost

There was a shipwreck on our coast some time ago. A ship struck upon a sunken rock, and the lifeboat put out to rescue the crew. The lifeboat drew near the sinking ship, and all got in safely except the captain and the first mate. "Get aboard," said the captain to the mate. "Wait a minute, Captain," and he dived down the companion ladder to fetch something from the cabin. The captain saw the folly of the act, and jumped into the lifeboat, hoping that the mate would soon follow. To stay beside the sinking ship was dangerous, and the coxswain drew off to wait for the mate to appear. Alas; before he could do so a great wave struck the vessel; she rolled over and sank, and the unfortunate man cooped up in the cabin was drowned. A few days after, divers went out to see what could be done with the vessel, and they found the corpse of the mate in the cabin. In his hand was something tightly grasped. They brought him on deck and unclasped his clenched fist. His purse fell out. They opened it. It contained—thirty-six cents! Had that man lost his life for thirty-six cents? "Ah!" you say. "What a fool!" But what are you risking your soul for? It may be either money or pleasure, but mark you, your soul is at stake.—*The King's Business.*

* * *

When Military Despots Spoke The Truth

Once when Frederick the Great was about to declare war, he instructed his secretary to write the proclamation. The secretary began: "Whereas in the providence of God," etc., etc. "Stop that lying!" Frederick thundered. "Simply say, 'Frederick wants more land.' "—*The Earnest Worker.*

* * *

Starving with Gold

When my friend, Dr. Edwin St. John Ward, was in charge of the American Hospital in Beirut, a Syrian came to him with a weird complaint. The man had been attacked by bandits; and to save the twenty-six gold pounds he carried—his total wealth—he swallowed them. The money had so weighted his stomach that his whole digestive apparatus was thrown out of order. He could get no good of food, even if he could afford it. When Dr. Ward expressed skepticism as to the story, the man lay down and rattled the coins, and the physician could hear them clink! So he operated, and took the golden sovereigns from the man's stomach. The poor Syrian's plight, both tragic and ludicrous as it was, fairly pictured the condition of many persons. They have gold—or gold has them—but they are starving for the real food of life.—*W. T. Ellis.*

* * *

One-Eyed Religion

Dr. A. J. Gordon told of a rich miser who was afflicted with cataracts on both eyes. He applied to an eminent surgeon to remove them, and after examination was told that it could be done. "But what will it cost?" was the anxious question. "One hundred dollars for each eye," was the answer. The miser thought of his money and then of his blindness, and said, "I will have one eye restored; that will be enough to enable me to see to count my money, and I can save the expense of having the other operated on." "O Lord, open Thou mine eyes, that I may behold wondrous things out of Thy law," cries the true Christian. But the half-and-half Christian wants only one eye opened. He likes to have the minister preach conversion strongly, because he has been converted himself and believes strongly in it; but he does not like to have him preach consecration, for that implies laying himself and all his wealth on God's altar, and he is not ready for that. In other words, he deliberately chooses a one-eyed religion, that which sees Christ as Saviour, but ignores Him as Sanctifier. —*Sunday School Times.*

* * *

When They Had "Made Their Fortunes"

When the steamship *Central America* went down, several hundred miners were on board, returning to their homes and friends. They had made their fortunes, and expected much happiness in enjoying them. In the first of the horror, gold lost its attraction to them. The miners took off their treasure belts and threw them aside. Carpet bags full of shining gold dust were emptied on the floor of the cabin. One of them poured out one hundred thousand dollars worth in the cabin, and bade anyone take it who would. Greed was overmastered, and the gold found no takers. Dear friends, it is well enough to have gold, but sometimes it is a bad life preserver. Sometimes it is a heavy weight that crushes us down to hell.—D. L. Moody.

* * *

When Is a Man Rich Enough?

When I was a lad an old gentleman took the trouble to teach me some little knowledge of the world. With this view I remember he asked me one day, "When is a man rich enough?"

I replied, "When he has ten thousand dollars."

He said, "No."

"Twenty thousand?"

"No."

"A hundred thousand?"

"No."

"Five hundred thousand?" which I thought would settle the business, but he continued to say "no."

I gave up and confessed I could not tell, but begged he would inform me.

He gravely said, *"When he has a little more than he has, and that is never."—Youth's Companion.*

* * *

Greed for Gold

It is very necessary that we keep out of our hearts the greed for gold. Inevitably such greed will spoil all our finer and nobler work. The hand of the writer, the hand of the artist, the voice of the minister, the voice of the statesman will be affected by it. Leonardo da Vinci tells this finely illustrative story: "Not infrequently the lust for gold brings even the great masters down to the level of craftsmen. Thus my countryman and comrade, Perugino the Florentine, arrived at such rapidity of execution that once he replied to his wife who called him to dinner, 'Serve the soup while I paint one more saint!'" — *Watchman-Examiner.*

* * *

His Gain But Loss

A preacher was conducting a revival, and a wealthy member asked him for a private interview. Here is what the man said: "My early life was a struggle, and oftentimes I was in need of the necessities of life, but I kept struggling until I got a start. Then I gave my life up to making money. I made lots of it and have lots of it now. My family has grown up into two classes—one set gives all their thought and energy to making money and the other gives practically all their thought and time to pleasure and 'going all the gaits of society.' Not one of them cares for the church." Then he said he had been trying to find a place where he could take some time from his vast business interests and give more to the church. "But," he said, "I have so much business and so many demands made upon me that it seems I have less time than ever for spiritual things. I give largely to our church budget, more than any other member, but giving fails to satisfy me. I know I am to die, and I want something to take with me that will be with me on the other side of the grave. What am I to do? Can you tell me how to turn loose from so many demands and give more time to eternal things?" He appeared to be a very sad man in spite of all his wealth, and concluded with the statement: "I wish I had made less money and lived more for the Lord." Are you giving enough time to spiritual things to satisfy your soul? —Courtesy *Moody Monthly*.

* * *

What Are You Listening For?

Evangelist "Dick" Huston once told of two men walking along a busy New York street when one of them asked his companion if he heard a cricket. His friend laughed and replied that no one could hear a cricket with the din of trolleys, motorcars, and trucks. The other stopped, lifted up a stone, and picked up a cricket and showed it to his friend. "How could you hear it?" the incredulous friend asked. "I will show you," and taking a coin from his pocket he tossed it in the air. When the coin struck the sidewalk, several men near by put their hands to their pockets and looked to see if they had dropped any money. "You hear what you are trained to listen for," the nature lover observed. "My ears are trained to hear birds and insects and all the sounds of nature." Our Lord knew all about the many noises of earth that drown out the still small voice of God's Spirit when He warned, "He that hath ears to hear, let him hear."

Open my ears, that I may hear
Voices of truth Thou sendest clear;
And while the wave-notes fall on my ear,
Everything false will disappear.
—*Sunday School Times.*

* * *

Label Confusion

The leader of the radio devotional program, "Morning Meditations," told some time ago of a woman who, just before rationing began, laid in a large stock of canned goods, thinking she was outwitting the Government. She put them in her cellar and then went away for a month's visit; secure in her belief that her larder was well cared for. Upon her return home, she found rains had flooded the basement and every can had its label off. What confusion! Wishing to open a can of corn, she found it to be peaches; wishing pears, she opened peas. Then the speaker asked if there was confusion like that in our lives. Are we easily identified as Christians, or have the labels worn off? — *Sunday School Times.*

* * *

Sensitive Pocketbooks

Self-interest often leads men to oppose the truth. A missionary wrote: "One man was very indignant on hearing the sin and folly of idol worship exposed; the native brother who was speaking coolly replied, 'I suppose you are a maker of images?' 'Yes!' exclaimed a voice from the crowd; 'he makes and sells them for four annas apiece.' 'I thought so,' said the native brother; 'he is afraid lest any should be persuaded not to buy his images; that is the reason he is so angry with us.' This remark excited such a general laugh at the idol maker that for shame he retired from the crowd and gave us no more trouble." —Selected.

Money Getting

A millionaire in New York died. On his deathbed he gave continual expression to his remorse for what his conscience told him was an ill-spent life. "Oh!" he exclaimed, "if I could only live my years over again! If I could only be spared for a few years I would give all the wealth I have amassed in a lifetime. *It is a life devoted to money-getting that I regret.* It is this which weighs me down and makes me despair of life hereafter!" His pastor endeavored to soothe him, but he turned his face to the wall: "You have never reproved my avaricious spirit," he said to the clergyman; "you have called it a wise economy and forethought; but now I know that riches have been only a snare for my poor soul. I would give all I possess to have hope for my poor soul!" (Mk. 8:36).—*Bible Expositor and Illuminator.*

* * *

What His Money Bought

It is recorded of one of America's richest men, that before he died he said to a friend: "I don't see what good it does me—all this money that you say is mine. I can't eat it, I can't spend it, in fact, I never saw it, and never had it in my hands for a moment. I dress no better than my private secretary, and cannot eat as much as my coachman. I live in a big servants' boarding house, am bothered to death by beggars, have dyspepsia, cannot drink champagne, and most of my money is in the hands of others, who use it mainly for their own benefit." This is the testimony of one who put his treasure in "a bag with holes."—*Gospel Herald.*

* * *

Modern Idolatry

A millionaire, who had been born a poor boy, and whose money was now his idol, after showing his palatial mansion and beautiful grounds to a Quaker, said: "And the almighty dollar has done it all! What cannot money do?"

"Ah, friend," replied the Quaker, "thou remindest me of the Israelites who worshiped the golden calf, saying it brought them out of the land of Egypt. In reality, it hindered rather than helped them in their journey to the promised land, and maybe thy dollars will do the same for thee."—*Evangelical Visitor.*

* * *

Working for Arteriosclerosis

A rich man makes a confession in *Collier's*: "Sometimes it seems to me," he says, "that I have worked all these years just to gain hardening of the arteries, and a few houses I don't want to live in. I am no more at home in my garden than I am in Central Park. And one of these days I shall die and all that will be left of me will be an estate for someone to spend or quarrel over." How different his life would have been had he spent his wasted life in the service of God!—*Sunday School Times.*

CRIME

Our Cities and Salvation

The modern American city is not a wholesome place. But it is a fascinating place. Its glare and noise, its confusions and intensities, its crowds, its gayeties, its opulence, entrance and captivate our fancy and challenge our ambition. The world, the flesh, and the devil are working overtime to subjugate completely these strongholds of our nation's life. They are succeeding far too well.

The multitudes are crowding into our cities. The churches, weakened and moribund, are being crowded out of our cities. Christ is being defied and denied, and we go on our way, unheeding. Even the moral law is set at nought. The thunders of Sinai are not often heard in New York and Chicago. The Ten Commandments have as little binding force as they had in corrupt Corinth. The people of our cities are too often not only irreligious, but shallow, hard, and loose-living.

Greater, however, and far more terrible than the sin of the irreligious worldly man is the sin of the easy-going churchman, dweller in city or suburb, who cares little and does less for the redemption of the people from their iniquity. White and silent and beautiful, Jerusalem lay bathed in the sunlight of the early morning, a slumberous Oriental city. But not stone or mortar, gardens or palaces, drew tears from the eyes of the Master. Seeing Jerusalem, He saw beyond and beneath it. He saw another city sacked and despoiled and plundered, the city of the soul. Looking across to the Temple heights He saw other temples falling into ruins, the temples of human life and character. This is the vision that we need today! Who weeps with Christ over the cities of today? In what shall the cities hope if the churches fail to truly represent Christ? —*The Watchman-Examiner.*

* * *

Why America Is Criminal

Among the diabolical teachings which have flung many into the abyss of moral degeneracy, is Freudian psychology or psychoanalysis. According to Dr. Freud, self-restraint is dangerous. One must not repress his base passions else he stands in danger of becoming seriously inflicted with a neurosis that borders on insanity. Humanity is taught to follow the inclination that affords most pleasure, and to suppress conscience and inhibitions. Undermining dissipation and immorality in every form and degree are perfectly legitimate according to the teaching. Dr. Freud also intimates that adjustment could be made for most of the ills and abnormalities of mankind if self-restraint is cast aside and the baser instincts given full reign.—*Gospel Herald.*

* * *

Warden Lewis E. Lawes of Sing Sing Prison told the seventieth annual convention of the National Educational Association that "criminals springing from our schools and colleges are more brazen, more vicious and more desperate than ever before in the history of any civilized community."

Men of the world are finding out what the church has always held to be fundamental in life, that education is good in its place but nothing but the regenerating power of Jesus Christ can furnish the foundation of Christian character. —*Wesleyan Methodist.*

* * *

Crime Prevention

I have long been convinced that the "catch, convict, confine" process is not enough; that there is a missing link somewhere in our program. That link is crime prevention. . . . Obviously the most effective type of prevention is that which heads off the development of criminal careers by the prevention of juvenile demoralization.

One obvious reason why the present situation is especially critical is the changed position of the church in community life.

A hundred years ago—even fifty years ago—most children attended Sunday school regularly—although perhaps under protest!—and were there taught principles of moral and spiritual conduct which were more or less common to all denominations or sects.

Their elders—perhaps because of the absence of golf courses, automobiles and commercialized forms of amusement—attended church services, at least on Sunday, and many of them regularly on prayer-meeting and other nights. Nowadays many children never see the inside of a Sunday-school room. Many of their parents never attend the church or participate in its work in any manner. To a large extent, therefore, the church has lost the influential place it once held as an instrument of crime prevention.

What we must do, however, if we wish to prevent delinquency, and thus prevent crime, is to go out and find the probable—even the possible—delinquent child before he becomes delinquent, and do whatever is necessary to keep him from getting that way.

This is obviously a much larger order than the detection and prosecution of crime or the confinement and parole of criminals, because it must enlist the services of the home, the school, the church — the character-building organizations—and the court, the police, the entire community. — Homer S. Cummings, in *Liberty*.

* * *

Not Education, But Christ

Some time ago educators told government officials that if they would support compulsory education they would do away with war, ignorance and criminality. Since this request was granted, educators have enjoyed the golden age of privilege. But war is more universal, there is still terrible ignorance in many places on the globe, and according to J. Edgar Hoover, who knows more about American moral conditions than any other man, there are "in America three and a half times more criminals than students in our universities and colleges." Christ is the answer to our great need—not education.—*Gospel Herald.*

* * *

When John Dillinger, most notorious criminal of the '30's, was a boy in his early teens, he was taken to court for some minor charge. He was released on probation and went back to his parents and started attending a Sunday school in his little village church. However, some of the parents in the school heard that a boy with a court record was attending, went to his teacher, and said, "If John Dillinger continues to be in your class, I shall have to withdraw my son." The teacher, not knowing what to do but anxious to keep the favor of the parents, told John what had happened. He never returned and less than a score of years later was known and killed as the most dangerous criminal in the country.—*Sunday.*

* * *

Youth and Crime

That was a sad declaration recently made by a judge who said, "Of ten million arrests in the United States, eighty-five per cent of them were under twenty years of age." What is to become of a nation producing criminals at this age?

The above statement is an indictment of the home life of our country. The old-fashioned God-honoring home is almost gone. Cocktail-drinking fathers, cigarette-smoking mothers, and movie-crazed children, and you have the environment of criminal youth.

The above is also an indictment of our public schools. Another observer in speaking of our grade and high schools says, "The criminals they contribute are more brazen, more vicious, and more desperate than any other."

How long will our people sit idly by and allow our youth to go to destruction? Who cares? Who will pray in dead earnest until the moral bath of a spiritual revival cleanses our land? — Courtesy *Moody Monthly.*

* * *

J. Edgar Hoover of the Federal Bureau of Investigation recently said:

"This country is in deadly peril. We can win the war and still lose freedom for all in America. A creeping rot of moral disintegration is eating into our nation. I am not easily shocked nor easily alarmed. But today, like thousands of others, I am most shocked and alarmed. The arrests of teen-age boys and girls are staggering, and some of the crimes youngsters commit are almost unspeakable."

"Crime among youth would be practically negligible if the young people attended Sunday school regularly during their formative years. Surely no one cognizant of the true crime situation in the United States can be blind to the importance of the activities of this institution in reducing materially the army of youthful offenders and delinquents."—Selected.

* * *

Where Did He Get It?

Do you remember what Clarence Darrow said when he was defending young Leopold, the brilliant student and dastardly murderer of the Franks boy? He said, "If this boy is to blame, where did he get it? Your Honor, it is hardly fair to hang a nineteen-year-old boy for the philosophy that was taught him at the university. It does not meet my ideas of justice and fairness to visit upon his head the philosophy that has been taught by university men for twenty-five years." —*The King's Business.*

CRITICISM

The Critic

A little seed lay in the ground,
And soon began to sprout;
"Now which of all the flowers around,"
It mused, "shall I come out?

"The lily's face is fair and proud
But just a trifle cold;
The rose, I think, is rather loud,
And then, it's fashion old.

"The violet, it is very well,
But not a flower I'd choose,
Nor yet the Canterbury bell—
I never cared for blues."

And so it criticized each flower,
This supercilious seed,
Until it woke one summer hour—
And found itself a weed.

—*The Pentecostal Testimony.*

* * *

Hiding the Faults of Others

A fault in any one is an ugly thing, and no one likes to see it. The following story is told of a painter who was engaged in making a likeness of Alexander the Great. In one of his battles, Alexander had received an ugly scar on the side of his face. The artist desired to paint a great likeness of the monarch, and at the same time wished to hide the scar. It was not an easy task to accomplish. At length he hit upon a happy plan. He painted him in a reflective attitude, with his hand placed against his head and his finger covering the scar.

Christians are not without their faults—their scars. No one in this life is perfect. But we do well not to dwell upon the shortcomings of anyone. When speaking of others, we should adopt the painter's plan, and let the finger of love be placed upon the scar, concealing it from the eyes of others. —*The Boys' Friend.*

* * *

There would be less faultfinding if all faultfinders had to come from the ranks of the faultless!—Selected.

* * *

Faultfinding

We read in Matthew 12:2 where the Pharisees found fault with Jesus' disciples. They even watched to accuse Jesus Himself (Mark 3:2). A spirit of censoriousness should be prayerfully avoided. Thomas Fuller gives good advice: "Search others for their virtues, and thyself for vices." He who is critical toward himself will be charitable toward others. While he who is keen-eyed to discover the faults of others will be blind to his own.

A father scolded his little daughter until she wept because, in trying to help her mother, she fell and broke a platter. Soon he told his wife to hurry with the dinner, because he had been "a little careless" and broken his plow, and must hasten to have it mended. His carelessness in breaking the plow was more costly than his child's, in breaking the dish, but he excused himself and rebuked her.

Faultfinding is not difficult. Isaac Murray illustrates this, in his story of how a dog, hitched to a lawn mower, stopped pulling to bark at a passer-by. The boy who was guiding the mower said, "Don't mind the dog—he is just barking for an excuse to rest. It is easier to bark than to pull this mower."

It is easier to be critical than correct; easier to bark than to work; easier to burn a house than to build one; easier to hinder than to help; easier to destroy reputation than to construct character. Faultfinding is as dangerous as it is easy. Anyone can grumble, criticize or censure, like those Pharisees, but it takes a great soul to go on working faithfully and lovingly, and rise superior to it all, as Jesus did.—A. C. M., in *The Herald of Light and Zion's Watchman.*

* * *

The True Critic

We live in a day when man is criticizing God's Word. Modernism is emasculating it, modern cults are perverting it, and the world is neglecting it. Dr. W. H. Griffith Thomas once said that the word "discerner" in the Greek of Hebrews 4:12, R. V., should be translated "critic,"—"a critic of the thoughts and intents of the heart," and he added, "It is the only place in the Bible where the word 'critic' is found, and you notice it is the Word criticizing us, and if we allowed the Word of God to criticize us a little more, we would criticize it a great deal less."—*Sunday School Times.*

* * *

How Do We Take Criticism

Criticism is an acid test of humility. When we are criticized, do we first think how wrong the other person is, and try to defend ourselves? Or, are we learning that advanced lesson in the Christian life that God permits criticism, sometimes sends it, for our good? Any editor receives a large share of criticism, and both Dr. Henry Clay Trumbull and Dr. Charles Trumbull maintained that Christians should seek to profit by any truth in the criticism, even though it was not made in the right spirit. In a recent letter from one who has frequently contributed articles to the TIMES was this thoughtful statement, showing a true spirit of humility: "Criticism seems to me one of the fine things of life, for how is one to improve without it?" "He that refuseth instruction despiseth his own soul: but he that heareth reproof getteth understanding" (Prov. 15:32).—*Sunday School Times.*

Disappointed—or Surprised?

It was a beautiful prayer and I thought, "What a good kind of man you must be." But about an hour later I happened to be coming along the farm and I heard a scolding and finding fault with everybody and everything. I didn't say nothin' for a minute or two. And then I says, "You must be very much disappointed, sir." "How so, Daniel, 'disappointed'?" "I thought you were expecting to receive a very valuable present this morning, sir, and I see it hasn't come." "Present, Daniel?" And he scratched his head as much as to say, "Whatever can the man be talking about?" "You know, this morning you prayed for a Christlike spirit and the mind that was in Jesus, and the love of God shed abroad in your heart." "Oh! that's what you mean, is it?" And he spoke as if that weren't anything at all. "Now, sir, wouldn't you rather be surprised if your prayer were to be answered?" "He didn't like it very much," said Daniel, "but I delivered my testimony, and learned a lesson for myself, too."—*Sunday School Times.*

* * *

Barking Doesn't Disturb the Moon

A judge who was on circuit at a certain town was always sure of being annoyed by some sneering remarks from a conceited lawyer. After one such occasion, someone asked the judge at dinner, why he didn't come down strong on the fellow. The judge dropped his knife and fork, placed his chin on his hands, and his elbows on the table as he gave emphasis to his story: "Up in our town," he said, "there lives a widow who has a dog which, whenever the moon shines, goes out and barks and barks at it all night." Stopping short he quietly began eating again. One of the company asked, "Well, Judge, what about the dog and the moon?" "Oh, the moon kept on shining," he said. — *Sunday School Chronicle.*

Thought for the Day

There is so much good in the worst of us,
And so much bad in the best of us,
That it hardly behooves any of us
To talk about the rest of us.
—Edward Wallis Hoch.

* * *

Better Than Criticism

Wesley and a preacher of his were once invited to lunch with a gentleman after service. The itinerant was a man of very plain manners. While talking with their host's daughter, who was remarkable for her beauty and who had been profoundly impressed by Wesley's preaching, this good man noticed that she wore a number of rings. During a pause in the meal he took hold of the young lady's hand, and, raising it, called Wesley's attention to the sparkling gems. "What do you think of this, sir," said he, "for a Methodist hand?" The girl turned crimson. The question was extremely awkward for Wesley, whose aversion to all display of jewelry was so well known. With a quiet, benevolent smile, he looked up and simply said, "The hand is very beautiful." The young lady appeared at evening worship without her jewels, and became a firm and decided Christian.—*The Pilgrim Holiness Advocate.*

* * *

Horse Sense

A horse can't pull while kicking,
This fact we merely mention,
And he can't kick while pulling,
Which is our chief contention.

Let's imitate the good horse
And lead a life that's fitting;
Just pull an honest load, and then
There'll be no time for kicking.
—Selected.

* * *

Drive On

While Amanda Smith was riding in the Queen's carriage through London and was assailed by a street gamin, she simply looked at the driver and said, "Drive on!" This is the best attitude to sustain toward both the world's flatteries and hisses—drive on. When men ridicule by scoffing, and Satan hinders, drive along on your Divinely appointed way. When tasks seem difficult and the way appears almost impossible; look to God and drive on. When even friends turn cold or fall away, when your own heart would sink within you in contemplating the reign of iniquity, get out from under that juniper tree and drive on.

There is no time for falling by the way; the battle is on, the enemies of the Cross of Christ press us on every side; heresies abound; the love of many is waxing cold; Satan roars; sometimes the lowering clouds are sheeted with angry lightnings, but drive on. Yield to no discouragement. God lives. Truth will conquer. You are on the winning side. Heed not the world's praise nor censure. The years are short, the time of harvest but a brief moment, and eternity with its endless ages lies just beyond. Drive on with a steady unfailing trust in the Lord, and you will win the victor's crown.—*Christian Witness.*

* * *

Wreckers

I watched them tearing a building down,
A gang of men in a busy town;
With a ho-heave-ho and a lusty yell
They swung a beam a side wall fell.
I asked the foreman "Are these men skilled
As the men you'd hire if you had to build?"
He gave a laugh and said, "No indeed!
Just common labor is all I need;
I can easily wreck in a day or two
What builders have taken a year to do."
I thought to myself as I went my way,
Which of these rules have I tried to play?
Am I a builder who works with care,
Measuring life by the rule and square?
Am I shaping my deeds to a well-laid plan,
Patiently doing the best I can?
Or am I a wrecker who walks the town
Content with labor of tearing down?
Selected.

"But Him They Understood Not"

This was Moses, and all the time he was true to his people, and would have done anything for them, but they did not understand him! Don't you think there are lots of people we do not understand, and we misjudge them! Even Moses' motive was not understood! Spurgeon said how often he and his dear wife were misunderstood; called mean and all sorts! A visitor was at Norwood one day, and this is how it happened:

Young Charles Spurgeon asked his mother for some eggs from the dairy that Mrs. Spurgeon had. "Yes, Charles," she said, "you may have them if you pay for them!" It seemed strange to my friend! Later, rumors were circulated that Spurgeon and his wife were mean and grasping, because they sold butter, eggs and milk. But they gave no explanation, and the critics continued to criticise! The explanation came at Mrs. Spurgeon's death! There were found books containing all sales at the dairy and profits therefrom, all of which were devoted to the maintenance of two elderly widows of Welsh ministers! But the cruel critics understood not!

Let us leave it if we are not understood! God knows!

—*The Chaplain.*

All He Had—for Christ

Dwight L. Moody was once preaching to a great crowd in one of his meetings. He was putting his very soul into it as he always did. He was thinking more about the content of his message and of its effect upon the hearts of men than about the precise literary form of it. There was a certain fastidious gentleman sitting on the platform that night, and at the close of the service he went to Mr. Moody and said, "By the way, I noticed that you made eleven mistakes in grammar in your sermon tonight." "Very likely," replied Mr. Moody, "I don't doubt it for a minute. My early education was faulty. I often wish that I had received more schooling. But I am using all the grammar I know in the service of Christ. How is it with you?" We are not told what reply the man made. I hope that he went home and read a chapter in the Bible rather than another page of grammar, and then prayed for a new heart. Such as I have give I thee. That is the attitude which counts. — *New Century Leader.*

CROSS: THE BLOOD

Cross, The Blood

A very careless old man had, during a severe illness, been made to realize that he was a lost sinner. He dared not die as he was. The preacher for whom he sent became weary of visiting him, having told him all he himself knew of the way of salvation. One Sunday afternoon, however, the coachman's daughter waited on the preacher saying, "You must come once more, sir; I cannot see my father die without you." "I can tell him nothing new," said the preacher; "but I may take the sermon I have been preaching, and read it to him." The dying man lay as before in anguish, thinking of his sins, and whither they must carry him. "My friend," the preacher said, "I have come to read you the sermon I have just preached. First, I shall tell you the text: 'He was wounded for our transgressions, He was bruised for our iniquities; the chastisement of our peace was upon Him; and with His stripes we are healed." "Hold!" said the dying man, "I have it! Read no more; He was wounded for my transgressions. He suffered for me, and because He died I shall live! Thanks be unto God for His unspeakable Gift! — *Glad Tidings.*

Demons Fear It

I met an Indian gentleman who was over here to study law and languages. He went over to Paris, got in with Madame Blavatsky's set, became a theosophist, then a spiritist, and was much used as a medium. He was then converted to God. Then it was that the evil spirits distressed him. For months he was awakened by them night after night, rarely getting half an hour's consecutive sleep. Tangible hands touched him, and terrible manifestations of their presence afflicted him. He prayed to God, but got no relief. At last a voice appeared to say to him, "Mention the blood." He then spoke to them, commanding them by the precious blood of Jesus Christ to leave him. Every time he mentioned the blood they left him, and by that means he obtained complete deliverance — *Bible League Quarterly.*

* * *

From Death to Life

An old preacher was once heard preaching on a village green in England. He had lived on the American prairies, and his illustrations had a powerful fascination for my boyish ears. He told of a prairie fire and he described the way the Indians saved their wigwams from the blaze by setting fire to the dry grass immediately adjoining the settlement. "The fire cannot come," he cried, "where the fire has already been. That is why I call you to the Cross. Judgment has already fallen there and can never come again. He who takes his stand at the cross is safe evermore. He can never come into condemnation; he is passed from death unto life. He is at perfect peace in God's safety zone. — Boreham, in *Hamilton, Ontario, Canada, Bulletin.*

* * *

Sacrifice

A farmer in North Carolina once drove with two high-mettled horses into town. Stopping in front of one of the stores, he was about to enter when the horses took fright. He sprang in front of them and heroically seized the reins.

Maddened by strange noises, the horses dashed down the street, the man still clinging to the bridles. On they rushed, until the horses, wild with frenzy, rose on their haunches, and leaping upon the man all came with a crash to the earth.

When the people came and rescued the bleeding body of the man, and found him in death's last agony, a friend bending tenderly o'er him, asked: "Why did you sacrifice your life for horses and wagon?"

He gasped with his breath as his spirit departed, "Go and look in the wagon."

They turned, and there, asleep on the straw, lay his little boy.

As they laid the mangled form of the hero in his grave, no one said, "The sacrifice was too great."

"He died for you! He died for me,
His blood hath atoned for our race;
O wonderful love! He came from above
To suffer and die in our place.'

—*L. G. Broughton.*

* * *

The Nurse's Mistake

The British military hospital was full of badly wounded soldiers. A nurse was overheard to say to one of them, "You have no need to worry over your sins; anyone who gives his life for his country, as you have been willing to do, is all right." The soldier smiled faintly, but shook his head and replied: "That is a mistake! When I lay out there in the open, I knew I had done my bit. I hadn't failed my king and country; but that didn't help me to face God. I wasn't fit to die, and I knew it, and it has been an awful trouble to me every day since. But when I heard a Christian lady who visited us here pray, I saw that the Lord Jesus had been punished for all my sins, that I might go free, and peace has come into my heart. How wonderful of Him to die for one like me!" No works of righteousness we have done can save us, for our righteousnesses are but as filthy rags in the sight of the all-holy God. Let the name of Christ be all our trust.

—*Soldier's Evangel.*

Amazing words!—"He gave Himself for me,"
For me—rebellious, sinful, guilty me,
For me the Saviour bore the Cross and shame,
Rejoice my soul, and bless His sacred Name.

For me He left His glorious throne above,
For me revealed His Father's wondrous love,
For me He tabernacles here below,
For me He drank the bitter cup of woe.

For me He was reviled, despised, betrayed,
For me was scourged, condemned and crucified,
For me He hung accursed on the tree,
For,—lost, wretched, vile, unworthy me.

For me in agony He groaned and died,
For me God's righteous law He satisfied,
For me complete atonement He has made,
For me He rose triumphant from the grave.

—*The Elim Evangel.*

* * *

The Passion Flower

The passion-flower is a native of the Americas, growing wild as far north as Virginia.

It was so named by the Spanish priests who accompanied the first conquerors. In it they saw a miraculous revelation of the Crucifixion. The five anthers symbolize the wounds and the three stigmas, the nails. There are five petals and five sepals, making ten, the number of the apostles present when Christ first appeared after the Crucifixion, according to Saint John. The fringe-like corona suggests the crown of thorns, the lobed leaves are the hands of persecutors, while the tendrils are the scourges.

The commonest variety of the passion flower in this country is a low-creeping plant with three-lobed leaves, bearing a beautiful blue-and-white blossom and an ovoid fruit as large as an egg, which is edible. In some parts of South America the fruit grows to a large size, sometimes weighing eight pounds. — *The Girls' World.*

* * *

What We Need to Bring

There was once a man who went into a chemist's shop. He was a poor, untidy man, and he said, "If you please, Mister, can you give me something for a bad cold?" The chemist said, "Have you brought a prescription with you?" The man answered, "No, I ain't got no prescription with me, but I've brought my cold with me to be cured." How often sinners seeking a cure for sin try to bring their prescription to God. But he asks for nothing, save that the sinner should say, "Just as I am, without one plea, but that thy blood was shed for me." — *The Christian Herald.*

* * *

The Cross

On the stern and rockbound New England coast there lived a little brother and sister that frequently played among the rocks along the shore. One day one of them discovered a natural formation in the rocks above them that resembled a cross. After that, they took great delight in filling the crevices that shaped the cross with dry grass and sticks, and setting it on fire to see the beautiful display it made.

As the years passed, the girl remained at the old homestead, but the boy went away to seek his fortune. One stormy winter night he returned on a visit to the old home; and he told his sister he had seen signals from a ship in distress out at sea.

Neither of them knew of any way to help the distressed sailors; but presently the sister remembered the old cross in the rocks. She gathered a large armful of wood and kindlings and hastened to the spot. She filled in the crevices, as in earlier days, and then set the cross on fire.

In a short time, the light of the blaze was shining out through the storm. One of the sailors — who had been cheering his comrades on and urging them not to give up — cried out, "The cross! See the light from yonder cross! It will guide us to safety."

They manned the lifeboats and pulled toward the flaming cross. They found the faithful girl, who had remained out in the storm and cold to feed the fire, lying on the shore, frozen to death. She had given her life to direct them to the cross. — *Gospel Herald.*

* * *

Four Mysterious Words

I was brought up by pious Jewish parents in a Hungarian Roman Catholic village, where, as a boy, I saw again and again and was arrested by the sight of a crucifix and people kneeling and praying before it, and I observed at the head of the crucifix four mysterious letters I.N.R.I. I remember how often I asked myself what all this meant — the crucified figure as well as the four letters — and nobody among my own people would tell me. The riddle, and my perplexity about it, lasted until I grew up, then for the first time in my life a New Testament fell into my hands, the existence of which I knew nothing of until then. I shall never forget my surprise and sensation when reading for the first time, the story of Jesus and His crucifixion, as well as the meaning and origin of those four mysterious letters which had puzzled me so much during my boyhood. The scales fell from my eyes, and "*Iesus, Nazarenus, Rex Iudaeorum*" — Jesus of Nazareth, King of the Jews — became from that moment my King and Redeemer, separating me for His sake from my own people, ready to live and die for Him. And my case prefigures what will happen one day to Christless Israel as a whole—they will acknowledge and crown Him, and live and die for Him. Yes, Jesus Christ is *yet* to be King of the Jews! — *The Dawn*

* * *

"It Is Finished"

Professor Beare of the Presbyterian College, Montreal, points out (in *The Presbyterian Record*) that the last word of our Lord on the cross, *tetelestai* ("*it* is finished"), is properly so translated in John 19:30, yet that this word *tetelestai* is found repeatedly in tax receipts in the sense of "paid." "The word *tetelestai*, on a papyrus tax receipt, is the exact equivalent of an English rubbber stamp, 'Received Payment.' I wonder if the man of those days would not be apt to take the word on the lips of Jesus also as meaning 'It is paid,' the account is settled, the debt is wiped out, the Redeemer of mankind has paid the price of redemption." *Sunday School Times.*

* * *

'Tis midnight, and on Olives' brow
The star is dimmed that lately shone:
'Tis midnight, in the garden now,
The suffering Saviour prays alone.

'Tis midnight; and from all removed,
The Saviour wrestles lone with fears;
E'en that disciple whom He loved
Heeds not His Master's grief and tears.

'Tis midnight; and for others' guilt
The man of sorrows weeps in blood;
Yet He that hath in anguish knelt
Is not forsaken by His God.
—*William B. Tappan.*

* * *

A missionary, in the wilds of Africa, was telling the heathen the wonderful story of the Lord Jesus Christ. The people gathered in the open, on a beautiful moonlight night, in a clearing in the forest. The missionary told them, in vivid language, of the wonderful miracles and life of Christ, and finally of His death on the cross. Seated on the front row was the chief. He had listened intently to all the missionary had said. As the missionary told of how Christ was nailed to the cross, the chief jumped to his feet and said, "Stop! Take Him down from the cross; I belong there, not Him!" He realized that he was a sinner, and that Christ was the Sinless One. Yes, Jesus took our place there, and died for us. Is it not wonderful. Scripture assures us, "Christ died for our sins," "the just for the unjust, that He might bring us to God." Have you ever thanked Him for dying for you?—*Christian Victory.*

* * *

When I Survey the Wondrous Cross

Matthew Arnold, strolling home after the last Lord's Day of his life, remarked to a friend, "Those words we just sang are the finest in the English language." Mahatma Gandhi asked some missionaries who visited him during a fast to sing a hymn for him. "What hymn?" they inquired. "The hymn that expresses all that is deepest in your faith," he replied. Arnold and Gandhi were both speaking of that incomparably greatest of hymns, "When I Survey the Wondrous Cross." The whole meaning of life is contained in these lines.

When I survey the wondrous Cross
  On which the Prince of Glory died,
My richest gain I count but loss
  And pour contempt on all my pride.

Were the whole realm of nature mine,
  That were a present far too small;
Love so amazing, so Divine,
  Demands my soul, my life, my all.
—Charles G. Hamilton, in *The Witness.*

* * *

Something More Than Repentance

A clergyman, talking about death-bed conversion, said to a Christian woman, "Do you think that a death-bed repentance does away with a whole life of sin?" "No," she answered quietly, "but Calvary does."—*Sunday School Times.*

* * *

Not "Do," But "Done"

One night a young man came into a Gospel meeting earnestly inquiring, "What must I do to be saved?" "You are too late," said a friend to the anxious inquirer. "Oh, do not say that," exclaimed the young man, "for I earnestly desire salvation; I would do anything or go anywhere to obtain it." "I cannot help it," said the other; "you are too late, for your salvation was completed many hundred years ago in the person of Jesus Christ, and it is a finished work. All you have to do is simply to accept it; for you have done nothing, and can do nothing, to merit salvation. It is a free gift to all who will accept it."—*The King's Business*

* * *

Salvation—How to Obtain It

An elderly widow visited her minister to obtain his signature on a paper for claiming an allowance made by her soldier son who was on foreign service. The man of God took the opportunity of pointing out the gospel message illustrated by her action, and said: "It is not your own work that gets you the benefit of this money?" "No! it is the work of my son. It is his wish that I have it. I have only to sign and get it." "Well, it is not by your work that you get salvation. It is through the work of the Son of God on Calvary. *It is His will for you to enjoy the blessings of that work. All you have to do is put in your name and receive it."—Christian Herald.*

* * *

The Cost

A preacher had gone down into a coal mine during the noon hour to tell the miners of the glad tidings of salvation. Meeting the foreman on his way back to the shaft he asked what he thought of God's manner of saving man. "Oh, it is too cheap, I cannot believe in such a religion as that." Without an immediate reply to his remark the preacher asked, "How do you get out of this place?" "Simply by getting into the cage," was the reply. "Does it take long to get to the top?" "Oh, no; only a few seconds." "Well, that certainly is very easy and simple. Do you not need to raise yourself?" said the preacher. "Of course not," replied the miner. "As I have said, you have nothing to do but to get into the cage." "What about the people who sunk the shaft, and perfected all this arrangement? Was there much labor or expense about it?" "Yes, indeed. The shaft is a thousand feet deep, and it was sunk at great cost to the proprietors;

but it is our way out and without it we should never be able to get to the surface." "Just so; and when God's Word tells you that whosoever believeth on the Son of God hath everlasting life, you say 'Too cheap,' forgetting that God's work to bring you and others out of the pit of destruction was accomplished at a vast cost, the price being the death of His Son.—Selected.

* * *

Did you ever have the experience of someone actually bearing a punishment in your place? You yourself had done the wrong and another knowingly and lovingly took the blows for that wrong?

I shall not soon forget the story told of one of America's great men of God concerning his experience as a little lad. His mother had been very zealous to keep her home spick-and-span, and had given orders that the children were to respect her cleanliness and not to desecrate it. She was particular to give instructions concerning the whiteness of the bed linens, of which she was justly proud. Definite punishment was promised to any of the family disobeying her orders.

Little James fully understood all the orders, but like many another little lad, he loved to play in mud and dirt. One day he made mud pies after a summer rain. Tired and weary of his "toil," he trod up the stairway into his mother's bedroom and was soon fast asleep, sprawled across her snowy white linens. In due time the mother arrived. Her household rules had been broken. James was guilty of gross disobedience and must be punished. In the nick of time, an older brother, hearing the confession and sobs from his mother's room, hastened to his brother's rescue. After a bit, he was convinced that his mother was right in her determination to punish James; her household rules had been broken, and since she was always true to her promises of reward as well as of punishment, it would not be right now to overlook the boy's disobedience.

As there was only one right way to help mother to keep her word and at the same time to deliver his little brother from the punishment due him, he bent his body over the little lad's and mother laid her blows of chastisement upon the innocent older brother in James' place.

I have an Elder Brother who has done the same for me. It was Jesus, who upon Calvary's cross bore the blows of the wrath of our righteous God against my sin. "God commendeth His love toward us, in that, while we were yet sinners, Christ died for us" (Rom. 5:8).—Courtesy *Moody Monthly.*

* * *

Another Thought of Me

When George Nixon Briggs was Governor of Massachusetts three of his friends visited the Holy Land. While there, they climbed Golgotha's slope and cut from the summit a small stick to be used as a cane. On their return home, they presented it to the Governor, saying, "We wanted you to know that when we stood on Calvary we thought of you." Accepting the gift with all due courtesy and gratitude, the Governor tenderly added: "But I am still more thankful, gentlemen, that there was Another who thought of me there."

"He thought of you, He thought of me,
When hanging there in agony;
O wondrous love of you and me,
It broke His heart on Calvary!"
—*The Pentecostal Testimony.*

* * *

What Held Him to the Cross?

Not the nails, but His wondrous love for me,
Kept my Lord on the cross of Calvary,
Oh, what power could hold Him there—
All my sin and shame to bear?
Not the nails, but His wondrous love for me. —*Sunday School Times.*

* * *

"Was the Cost Too Great?"

I have recently been impressed with this question as I have been coming in contact with a man who gave himself that he might save his only and much-loved daughter from the burning flames of a tenement house. The family had retired as usual in the evening, but were suddenly awakened in the early hours after midnight to find themselves enveloped, on the fifth floor, in stifling flames and blinding smoke. All rushed for safety, which was not easily found. The daughter and one son jumped out of the window where they thought there was a fire escape; but none was there and they fell to the ground below. The girl was killed instantly and the boy died from injuries a day later. The father, mother and three other sons escaped in some way by aid of firemen, the three boys being badly burned — one dying in a couple of days.

The father, though in safety, thought his daughter was still in the flames and rushed in to rescue her. In turn he, too, was badly burned and with the boys he was rushed to the hospital. It so happened that the father was placed on the floor where I was on duty. As I looked into his most terribly swollen and burned face from time to time and saw his untold agony, my heart was strangely moved upon. His suffering was intense and as I waited upon him this question came o'er and o'er to my mind, "Was the cost too great?"

The daughter had not waited to be rescued — she took her own way — a short-cut to safety. Even while her father gave himself and endured all for her sake, she lay on the ground below—lifeless—not knowing the price that was being paid for her.

Were Calvary and Redemption worth the price that was paid? How many today are taking their own way in life—hoping that a "fire escape" may be somewhere beneath them and that they may be saved? Short-cuts will not take us to Heaven. We must go the old-fashioned road of the Cross and true repentance. "Except a man be born again, he cannot see the Kingdom of God."—Selected.

* * *

If Virtue Walked the Earth

Once, it is said, a Scottish preacher of the modern school closed a sermon with these words, "Virtue is so attractive that, if she were to become incarnate, and walk the world in human form, men would fall down and worship her." The pulpit of that church was occupied the same evening by a different type of preacher, a humble evangelical man, who loved the Gospel of a crucified Redeemer. He preached Christ crucified, and at the close of his discourse reminded the congregation of the statement made in the morning by the senior preacher, and then added, "I am very sorry to say that Virtue did once walk the world in human form, in the person of the Lord Jesus Christ, and men, instead of falling down and worshiping Him, crucified and nailed Him to a tree." —*Heart and Life Magazine.*

* * *

Bought with a Price

There is a little story that illustrates the truth of this. A small boy, it is said, made a toy sailboat. He fashioned it with loving care and finally it was ready to sail. With what pride he surveyed it —brave in its fresh red and white paint. The little boat, lifting its sails proudly to the wind, escaped from his eager fingers and swept down, down the river away from its grief-stricken owner. Though he looked long and diligently he could not find his little boat.

One day, several weeks after, he chanced to be walking down the street in town when his eye was suddenly caught by a flash of red and white in a pawnshop window. It was his own boat! The one he had made himself! He rushed into the shop and demanded that the man give him his boat. He met with a brusque refusal. The shopkeeper said that he had paid for the little boat and before the boy could have it he would have to pay the stated price. With a sad heart the little fellow walked out of the store. It would take many a day for him to secure all that money, and for his own boat! But he went to work with a will and in a shorter time than he had thought possible he had earned the needed sum. With a light step he went to the store, laid down the money on the counter, and again demanded his boat. This time he received it. As he went out of the store, down the street, with his little boat tucked under his arm, he was heard to say tenderly, "You are mine, little boat, twice mine; once because I made you, and twice because I bought you."

So do we belong to Christ; once, because He made us, and twice because He bought us.—*The Gospel Herald.*

* * *

God's Purity

A story is told of a North of England woman who hung out her week's washing, and was proud of its whiteness, till a snowstorm covered everything with its mantle of chastity. Then, seeing the garments which had been her pride an hour before shown up by a background of ineffable purity, she exclaimed in despair: "What can a poor woman do against God Almighty's snow?"

So in the white radiance of that life which is the Light of men, we are led to exclaim, "*What can any man or woman do against the purity of God Almighty's Christ?*" Truly He works, in the hearts of those who fain would serve Him best, the deepest consciousness of deviation within. — Henry Howard, in *Fast Hold on Faith.*

* * *

A Heroic Shepherd

One of the names of the Lord Jesus that is most comforting to His people is the Good Shepherd. When He used this name of Himself, He spoke of His tender care for his sheep, of the fact that He was to give His life for them, and that in His hands they would be eternally safe (John 10). Out of the horror of the present war has come a lovely picture of our Great Shepherd. Fred Mitchell, Head Shepherd, North Somerset, England, received "the Most Excellent Order of the British Empire" from the King for "brave conduct in Civil Defence." On a bitterly cold night in January incendiary bombs set fire to the sheepfold sheltering thirty-four ewes and lambs. High explosives frightened away the sheep dog. Again and again Mitchell fought his way into the burning pens, and carried out the lambs in his own arms, followed by the ewes. He took them away from the flames into an open field. At midnight he went to another part of the field "to speak words of comfort to 107 ewes due to lamb in a week." Though he had many narrow escapes and was ready to give up his life for his sheep, Mitchell did not have to do so. One wonders whether Mitchell was upheld by his trust in God through that awful night, and whether he knows how well he has illustrated Isaiah's beautiful words, "He shall gather the lambs with his arms, and carry them in his bosom, and shall gently lead those that are with young" (Isa. 40:11). Our Great Shepherd gave His life for the sheep, and because He did, all those who put their trust in Him are saved forever "through the blood of the everlasting covenant."—*Sunday School Times.*

* * *

The Badge of Freedom

Mr. E. E. Beatty, writing from Mowkung on the Tibetan frontier, mentions an interesting local custom, which he was able to use to advantage as an illustration when preaching the Gospel. He says: "A young man who resides beside us had just been released from prison after spending a week or so there for cursing a Moslem living on the other side of the compound. The sound of firecrackers attracted my attention, and on going to the front door I saw him, girdled with a crimson sash, returning from jail with his friends. I inquired the reason for this and learned that the crimson sash had been given him by the magistrate to indicate to all and sundry that the prisoner had atoned for his sin, and that he was now a free man. Next day when preaching I closed my talk with this illustration, explaining that when we trusted in the finished work of Christ, God saw us as though we were encircled by the crimson band, the shed blood of Christ, and by that same token had set us free from the condemnation of sin because it was atoned for. It was most encouraging to see how the people's faces lighted up as the illustration went home.—*China's Millions.*

* * *

What They Sing in Heaven

Some years ago, a minister was asked by a woman to go and visit her husband. He talked with him a few minutes about his physical condition and then asked about his soul. "Well," said he, "I think my chances for getting to Heaven are pretty good." The minister then said to him, "You believe that Heaven is a reality and that your soul is a reality, and that you hope soon to be happy in Heaven forever. You must have some reason for this. Will you please tell me what it is?" The man thought a moment and then responded, "Well, I've always been kind to my wife and children, and I have not intentionally wronged my fellow men."

"That's all very good," said the minister. "But what kind of place do you think Heaven is, and what do you think they do there?"

"Well," answered the man, "I think there is no sin or sorrow there. It must be a happy place, and I think they sing there a good deal."

"Yes," answered the minister, "they do sing there, and I'll read you one of the songs they sing." And opening his Bible to the first chapter of Revelation he read: "Unto Him that loved us and washed us from our sins in His own Blood."

"That is what they sing about; not what *they* have done, but what *Christ* has done. Suppose you were there, and had got there by the way you hope to get there, because you had been good to your family and had never intentionally wronged your fellow men; would you be able to join in that song about Him that loved us and washed us from our sins in His own Blood?"

The man was silent for a time, and then said, "I had never thought of that before!"

My friend, you think of your friends within the veil. You hope one day to join them. But can you sing the song that they sing? Is your faith in Him who loved you and died for you? When you enter within the veil could you join in that song unto Him that loved us and washed us from our sins in His own Blood?—From a sermon, *"Our Friends within the Veil,"* by Dr. Clarence Edward Macartney.

* * *

Where Was God

When a father received word that his son, a brilliant lad, had been killed in a railroad accident, he turned to his pastor and cried in desperation, "Tell me, sir, where was God when my son was killed?" And in that tense and terrible moment guidance was given to the counselling pastor. "My friend," he said. "God was just where He was when His own Son was killed!"—Selected.

* * *

When the King Speaks

A Swedish newspaper told this tale: On his morning's ride through Copenhagen, Denmark's king, Christian X, saw a Nazi swastika waving over a public building in violation of the terms Hitler imposed on Denmark. "Take it down!" the King ordered a German officer in front of the building. "Orders from Berlin," replied the officer. "The flag must be removed before 12 o'clock; otherwise I will send a soldier to do it," the monarch declared. "The soldier will be shot," warned the Nazi officer. "I am the soldier!" said the King. The swastika came down. When the enemy of our souls put his banner over the rebel world it was our King from Heaven who came to deal with him. The highest angels could not avail for this task (Jude 9). But the Lord spoke plainly to the enemy, went to the very heart of his citadel, becoming sin in our behalf that through death He might destroy him that had the power of death (Heb. 2:14).

There was no other good enough
To pay the price of sin;
He only could unlock the gate,
Of Heaven and let us in.
—*Revelation.*

A Startling Headline

Newspaper headlines sometimes carry a startling testimony to the truth—even when the writer does not intend it. Last autumn a noted English physiologist, Sir Joseph Barcroft, concluded a series of lectures at Yale. The New York *Herald Tribune* reported this under a headline in bold type: "Blood of Lamb Yields Clew to Chance of Life." Christian people reading this were challenged by its unusual suggestiveness, and read on to see what it was about. Sir John described his experiments with new-born lambs to ascertain the oxygen content of their blood and their prospect of living in view of this. But this exploitation of scientific news turns one's thoughts to what may reverently be called the "headline" of God's Word, which is indeed that mankind's "chance of life" is inseparably related to the Blood of the Lamb. "Only because of the "Lamb slain from the foundation of the world" has any man since Adam fell had any chance of life.—*Sunday School Times.*

* * *

Perfectly Justified

God has revealed Himself in the face of Jesus Christ. He has told out, in Divine harmony, all His attributes in the work of the cross. Sin is perfectly put away, and the believing sinner perfectly justified *"by the blood of His Cross."* When we get a view of God, as thus unfolded, we have only, like Moses, to bow our head toward the earth and worship—suited attitude for a pardoned and accepted sinner in the presence of God!—C. H. Mackintosh.

* * *

"That Red Spot"

Napoleon once took a map and, pointing to the British Isles, remarked: "Were it not for that red spot, I would have conquered the world." The Devil pointed at the cross of Christ and said: "Were it not for that red spot, I would have conquered the world." — *Sunday School Times.*

Under an Eastern sky,
Amidst a rabble's cry,
A Man went forth to die
For me.

Thorn-crowned His blessed head,
Blood-stained His every tread:
Cross-laden, on He sped
For me.

Pierced were His hands and feet;
Three hours o'er Him beat
Fierce rays of noontide heat
For me.

Thus wert Thou made all mine;
Lord, make me wholly Thine;
Grant grace and strength divine
To me.

—*Florida Baptist Witness.*

* * *

The Test

A new religion came to me
With buoyant tread and radiant smile.
And at my door asked joyously
Just to come in and talk awhile.
The jeweled hands were fair to see,
Her white robe glistened in the sun:
'Twas quite agreeable to me
To listen to her silver tongue.

She spoke of wealth and health and peace,
Of pleasure and prosperity,
Of Love Divine which fills all space—
The only great Reality.
Despite her look, her smile, her speech,
My spirit shrank — strange to remark —
As one whose fingers reach
Some cold, dead thing amid the dark.

"Give me," I cried, "O stranger guest,
Before I entertain thy plea,
An answer to this one request:
Dost come by way of Calvary?"
Swift changed her eyes from day to night,
Her smile to cold superior scorn;
She vanished from my wondering sight,
But left me neither sad nor lorn.

A shining presence filled the space,
A voice beloved spake peace to me—
A Person rare of truth and grace,
Who came by way of Calvary!

—Elizabeth Cheney, in *British Weekly.*

Saints Any Church Can Afford

The Rev. Stuart McNairn said at a meeting that at one town in Argentina the Roman Catholics built a magnificent church, but they had not been able to open it. Why? Because they could not afford to buy any saints to put in it. But yet a little way down the road, in a little mission hall, God was making saints, creating them, not out of plaster, but through the regenerating power of the blood of Christ.—*Christian Herald.*

* * *

Who Can Forgive Sins?

In R. Moffatt Gautrey's book entitled, *The Glory of Going On,* he gives this incident: "Not many months ago in an Oxfordshire village, an old saint lay dying. For over eighty years she had been on pilgrimage to Zion, until her face had grown bright with heaven's approaching glory. An Anglo-Catholic priest, under the misapprehension that none of his parishioners could find access to the celestial city unless he unlocked the gate, came to visit her. 'Madam,' he said, 'I have come to grant you absolution.' And she, in her simplicity, not knowing what the word meant, inquired, 'What is that?' 'I have come to forgive your sins,' was the reply. 'May I look at your hand?' she answered. Gazing for a moment at the hand of the priest, she said, 'Sir, you are an imposter.' 'Imposter!' the scandalized cleric protested. 'Yes, sir, an imposter. *The Man who forgives my sin has a nail print in His palm.*' "—*Indian Christian.*

* * *

A Penalty Necessary

A person once said to me: "I hate your God; your God demands blood. I don't believe in such a God. My God is merciful to all. I do not know your God."

If you will turn to Leviticus 17:11, you will find why God demands blood: "For the life of the flesh is in the blood; and I have given it to you upon the altar to make an atonement for your souls; for it is the blood that maketh an atonement for the soul."

Suppose there was a law that man should not steal, but no penalty was attached to stealing; some man would have my pocketbook before dinner. If I threatened to have him arrested, he would snap his fingers in my face. He would not fear the law, if there was no penalty. It is not the law that people are afraid of; it is the penalty attached.

Do you suppose that God has made a law without a penalty? What an absurd thing it would be! Now, the penalty for sin is death: "The soul that sinneth, it shall die." *I must die, or get somebody to die for me. If the Bible doesn't teach that, it doesn't teach anything. And that is where the atonement of Jesus Christ comes in.*—D. L. Moody.

* * *

Dishwasher with the Soul of a King

A Matanuska Valley, Alaska, dishwasher recently was awarded the Carnegie Hero Medal for unusual bravery and devotion exhibited in sticking with an exhausted friend through an Alaskan blizzard instead of pushing on to safety alone. He is Roy (Slim) Tipton, a colonist in the government's resettlement experiment in Alaska, and his bravery cost him heavily, for he lost both feet, the use of one arm, and suffered permanent disfigurement of his face, all from freezing. The man whose life he tried to save was George Martin of Seattle, who died later from exposure, but not until a rescue party had taken him and Tipton out of the Valdez glacier where they were found. If Martin had lived we presume that every little while he would have looked upon Tipton who lost both feet and an arm for him. He would have looked upon the face of Tipton, a face forever horribly marred and scarred because of love for him. Then he would not have been able to see at all for a while because of the hot tears gushing from his eyes. There are a great many marred and scarred people in this world who gave all they had to the people they loved. *And supremely there is Jesus*: "But he was wounded for our transgressions, he was bruised for our iniquities: the chastisement of our peace was upon him; and with his stripes we are healed" (Isa. 53:5).—*United Presbyterian.*

* * *

'Twas I that shed the sacred blood,
  I nailed Him to the tree;
I crucified the Christ of God,
  I joined the mockery.

Of all that shouting multitude
  I feel that I am one;
And in that din of voices rude
  I recognize my own.

Around the Cross the throng I see
  Mocking the Sufferer's groan;
Yet still my voice, it seems to be
  As if I mocked alone.

—Selected.

* * *

He Saw the Point

A minister was boarding at a certain farmhouse. The farmer was not a Christian, but his wife had been praying for him for some time, and the minister was awaiting his opportunity to make plain to him the meaning of the sacrifice of Calvary. Early one morning, the farmer beckoned to the minister to follow him out to the chicken house. There on one of the nests sat a hen with a brood of chickens peeping out from under her wings.

"Touch her, M. ——," the farmer said.

As the minister put his hand on the hen, he found that she was cold.

"Look at that wound in her head," the farmer continued. "A weasel has sucked all the blood from her body, and she never once moved for fear the little beast would get her chickens."

"Oh, ——," said he, "that was just like Christ. He endured all that suffering on the Cross. He could have moved and saved His own life, but He wouldn't, because you and I were under His wings. If He had moved, we would have been lost."

The farmer saw the point, and accepted the Lord Jesus Christ as Saviour.—*Evangelical Visitor.*

Israel Without Blood Sacrifice

"What is it that makes atonement for the soul?" asked a Jewish rabbi's son of his father. "It is the blood," answered the father, quoting Leviticus 17:11. "Then why are there no blood sacrifices in our synagogues?" persisted the boy. The old man had to confess sadly that no sacrifice could be lawfully offered except at Jerusalem. "Then," said his son, "we have no atonement." His father could offer him no help here, for the orthodox Jews have no adequate answer to such an argument. And so began the search for atoning blood which ended for the rabbi's son at the foot of the cross. No wonder that the godly pray with tears that the Temple site might be theirs. It is only by means of an answer to that prayer, so they believe, that the blood sacrifices can be restored, and thus the sins of the people adequately dealt with. But in the meantime, many are led through the mercy of God to see this need fully met by the precious blood of Christ, shed on the cross of Calvary.—*Young People's Full Gospel Quarterly.*

* * *

Christ Does not save men by His life,
  Though that was holy, sinless, pure,
Nor even by His tender love,
  Though that forever shall endure;
He does not save them by His words,
  Though they shall never pass away;
Nor by His vast creative power
  That holds the elements in sway;
He does not save them by His works,
  Though He was ever doing good—
The awful need was greater still,
  It took His *death,* His *cross,* His *blood!*

—*The Gospel Herald.*

* * *

The Price Mark

During the holiday season, when you were purchasing gifts, how often did you hear someone say, "Be sure to take off the price mark." Certainly you did not care to have the price paid for the article left visible. It was proper to erase it. The believer in the Lord Jesus Christ is not his own. He was bought with a price. The price paid was the blood of Christ. There is no way to "take off" or erase the price paid by Him for His purchased possession. The blood-bought are blood-marked. The mark of the purchase price is on you and to remain. You need not be ashamed, O Christian, of the price paid for your redemption.—*The Wonderful Word.*

* * *

Justin Martyr wrote long ago, "Many spirits are abroad in the world, and the credentials they display are splendid gifts of mind, learning, and of talent. Christian, look carefully. Ask for the *print of the nails.*" Ah, that is the test! What place has the Crucified in your thoughts?

"What think ye of Christ? is the question
To try both your state and your scheme;
You cannot be right in the rest,
Unless you think rightly of Him."
—*Watchman-Examiner.*

* * *

A Hero on an Atlantic Liner

A number of years ago an Atlantic liner left Liverpool for the city of New York. During the first part of the voyage nothing eventful happened. After being several days on the stormy ocean, one day the passengers were suddenly interrupted in their musings and conversation by a loud explosion, followed by a heavy escape of steam. Consternation seized hold of most of them, and was clearly depicted on their countenances, while the worst fears were entertained by some.

The first engineer, who was evidently much excited, appeared on deck and explained that one of the main pipes had burst, and that the escape of steam could be stopped only at the risk of the life of him who did it. Having explained the imminent peril to which all on board were exposed, he asked various ones to volunteer. No one, however, appeared to be willing to risk being scalded to death. Again the engineer besought them, but without effect. At last a stoker appeared with a sack on his head and expressed his willingness to make the attempt. Extraordinary interest was manifested as the brave fellow descended the ladder. "Would the stoker succeed in preventing an explosion?" "Would he be able to shut off the steam?" They knew that the danger was great and grave, and if he succeeded in his mission he might sacrifice his own life in endeavoring to save theirs. All ears were strained to listen, and all hearts beat with expectancy. After a lapse of time which seemed long to them, the noise ceased and the escape of steam subsided. The stoker, however, did not emerge from below. "What has become of him?" "Where is he?" "Is he alive?" "Has he escaped?" Such were some of the questions that occupied the minds of the passengers. On going below the searchers found the body of the stoker, but, alas, life was extinct. He had, in fact, been scalded to death. "What a noble fellow!" says one. Yes, indeed, he was a real hero. When the lives of others were endangered he risked his own that they might be saved. He did not positively know, when he undertook to stop the escape of steam, that his own life would be sacrificed in accomplishing it. Yet so it was. The passengers and crew doubtless felt grateful to him who in seeking to save their lives sacrificed his own.

And yet, strange to say, multitudes have not a spark of gratitude to Him who died to save them from a death ten thousand fold worse than that of this courageous stoker! The Lord Jesus saw us, in our low and lost estate, being carried resistlessly to everlasting woe. He loved us and longed to deliver us. In Divine grace and compassion He came into this world to seek and to save that which was lost. Every step of the road from Bethlehem to Calvary was well known to Him. He did not merely risk His life. The "Good Shepherd" gave His life for the sheep. "God sent not His Son into the world to condemn the world; but that the world through Him might be saved" (John 3:17).

Through faith in Christ's death for you, you may obtain eternal life and the forgiveness of your numerous and aggravated sins. "He that believeth on Me hath everlasting life" (John 6:47). — *Tract.*

* * *

Aristocratic Vipers

It is related of John Wesley that, preaching to an audience of courtiers and noblemen, he used the "generation of vipers" text, and flung denunciations right and left. "That sermon should have been preached at Newgate," said a displeased courtier to Wesley on passing out. "No," said the fearless apostle; "my text there would have been, 'Behold the Lamb of God, which taketh away the sin of the world.' "—*Sunday School Times.*

* * *

By the Nail Prints

In writing about the Rev. John Van Ess, missionary to Arabia, Jerome Beatty in his book, "Americans All Over," tells of one of Dr. Van Ess's most triumphant moments. He asked a Bible class, "If you saw a dozen similar men passing and one was Christ, how would you tell it was He?" Some said they didn't know. One thought, by the light in His face. But one Mohammedan boy said, "By the wounds in His hands." The reason for the missionary's happiness was that Mohammedans are taught to believe that Christ was not crucified; but evidently some of the Christian teachings on the subject had broken through.—*Sunday School Times.*

* * *

In the Cleft of the Rock

Years ago, while working among the Laguna Indians, we were asked to speak at a little village called Pawate. It was in the days before automobiles, and we rode in large wagons drawn by horses for some fourteen miles over rough roads until we reached this village. We had a meeting in the afternoon, and Indians from all about gathered. We started back at 4:30 or 5 o'clock because we were to have a meeting at Casa Blanca that night. We had not gone very far when we saw a terrible storm was evidently to break over us. Soon we could see that the rain was pouring down at a distance and driving rapidly toward us. I said, "We are certainly going to get soaked." Our driver replied, "I hope not. I think we can make the rock before the storm reaches us. There is a great rock ahead; and if we can make it, we will be sheltered." And so we hurried on and soon saw a vast rock rising right up from the plain, perhaps forty or fifty feet in height, covering possibly an acre or more of ground. As we drew near, we saw a great cave going right into the rock. Instead of stopping to unhitch the horses, our driver drove right into the cave, and in another minute or two the storm broke over the rock in all its fury. The storm raged outside, and one of the Indians struck up, in the Laguna tongue, "Rock of Ages, cleft for me, let me hide myself in Thee," and we realized the meaning of the poet's words, then as perhaps never before.—Rev. H. A. Ironside, in *Alliance Weekly.*

* * *

The General and the Negro

An incident which happened in Georgia some years after the Civil War is related by the *Columbia State.* A Negro man, strong and healthy, but getting gray from years, was on trial for murder. He had killed another Negro and had been lying in jail for some time awaiting his trial. The testimony against him was given by other Negroes who witnessed the killing. When the case was called for trial by the presiding judge, an old man arose, and, in a voice deep and low, but full of marked gentleness, said, "Will your honor please mark me for the defense?"

It was General Robert Toombs. His face was wrinkled with age, but it was large and strong, and the lines of intellect made deeper wrinkles than those of age. His white hair rolled back in curls from a splendid brow. His form was large and tall and straight, although his movements were slow with the years. His eyes still flashed as when he stood in the Senate Chamber at Washington. The witnesses all seemed unfriendly towards the prisoner. In his own statement he claimed that the killing was in self-defense.

General Toombs analyzed the testimony of the eye-witnesses, and then concluded thus: "Your honor, and gentlemen of the jury, a few years ago my only brother fell wounded on the battlefield of Gettysburg. He lay there bleeding to death with no friendly hand to help him. Shot and shell were sweeping the earth all about him. No friend could go near him; no surgeon dared to approach him. My brother had a body servant, a Negro, who waited on him in camp. The Negro saw his master's danger, and straight into that sheet of battle and flame and death he went. A piece of shell tore the flesh from his breast, but on he went, and, gathering my brother in his arms, the blood of the man mingling with the blood of the master, he bore him to safety and life."

Then, turning to the prisoner, he said, "Jim, open your collar." The prisoner rose and opened his shirt in front. On the breast the jury saw the long jagged scars where the shell had torn its way. "Jim's skin may be black," the General continued, "he may be a Negro, but the man who would do what he did has a soul too white ever to have killed a man except in defense of his own life." The jury agreed with him, and Jim was cleared.

What pathos must have been in the voice of that old warrior as he pleaded the cause of the Negro! "Straight into that sheet of battle and flame and death he went." Was this not what the Lord Jesus did for the sinner when there was no eye to pity? He left the Glory for the Cross, not saying, "If I perish I perish," but coming into the world to die. "Now once in the end of the world hath He appeared to put away sin by the sacrifice of Himself" (Heb. 9:26). "Greater love hath no man than this, that a man lay down his life for his friends" (John 15:13). The Negro slave risked his life for his master. The Son of God laid down His life for *you* and *me*, "while we were yet sinners" (Rom. 5:8).—*The United Evangelical.*

* * *

Morality, or the Blood?

Morality may keep you out of jail, but it takes the blood of Jesus Christ to keep you out of hell.—The Rev. C. W. Carter, in the *Syracuse Post-Standard.*

* * *

The Cleansing Pool

"Everyone who goes to Yellowstone Park goes to Handkerchief Pool. It has about it one thing you will find nowhere else. Drop your handkerchief on its surface. Down to the bottom it will descend. Then a current will draw it out of sight. But do not think you have lost your handkerchief. In a little while the honest pool will hand it back to you laundered. You have to wait only a few moments. Then your handkerchief begins to reappear. Finally it comes out into the bottom of the pool before your eyes. Take the iron rod at hand and pick it out, and then you will find that the test stain you put upon it has disappeared. You and your handkerchief have had a new experience." What a type of the divine fountain, which not only cleanses lepers, but, what is infinitely more wonderful, the hearts of sinful men.—*Challenge.*

* * *

His Grandfather's Verse

Just a boy named Joe.... lay dying on one of our far-flung battlefronts. Dying... while the guns roared, amid the machine gun's incessant rat-tat-tat. Dying... in the mud, the filth, the blood of battle. Just a boy named Joe, one of many dying soldiers, dying far from home, comfort, loved ones. As he felt his strength slowly ebbing and his spirit seeking that other land he grasped for something to cling to. He wasn't ready. Life was too busy to bother with religion. Blood, blood, oozing out slowly. His life's blood! What was that he had heard his grandfather say? The blood, the blood...oh, why couldn't he remember it? Life was ebbing faster now. He prayed his first real earnest prayer...but oh, to remember! Then his grandfather's deep, sonorous voice rang in his ears. "The blood of Jesus Christ cleanseth from all sin." That was it! Only that, but it brought peace to a dying soldier's heart. Just a boy named Joe...but he was sheltered by the atoning blood.—*Visitor.*

* * *

How to Die in Peace

Some time ago, a man from south of Morocco went to one of the missionaries to inquire the way of salvation, as he knew he had not long to live. To help him the missionaries used what is called the Wordless Book, the first page of which is black, representing sin, the second page scarlet, representing the Blood of Christ, the third page white, indicative of the cleansed conscience, and the fourth page gold, representing the glory of Heaven. This man became truly converted, and as he lay dying, his wife, an unconverted Mohammedan, went to his bedside, and realizing that he had not long to live, told him to call upon Mohammed. The man, however, refused, saying his trust was in the Lord Jesus Christ. "Well, take that little Book the missionaries gave you," said his wife, "and lay your head on the white page while you die, and tell God that your life has been as clean as that white page, and perhaps He will accept you for Heaven." But her husband said: "No, I will not do that, for it would not be true. Open the scarlet page, and let my head rest on that." So the man died with his head resting on the symbol of the Blood of Christ.—*Christian Herald.*

* * *

The Fly and the Elephant

Moody says: "Some one has said that a little fly in Noah's ark was just as safe as an elephant. It was not the elephant's size and strength that made him safe. It was the ark that saved both elephant and fly. It is not your righteousness, your good works, that will save you. Rich or poor, learned or unlearned, you can be saved only by the blood of Christ."—*Sunday School Times.*

* * *

The Perfect Sacrifice

A missionary in Africa heard a boy say: "The lack of my fifth toe on the left foot is my life. They were going to make me one of the sacrifices at So-and-so's funeral, but a sacrifice with a blemish won't do, so I got off." What a striking reminder of our perfect Sacrifice! "Your lamb shall be without blemish" (Exod. 12:5)—*Christian Herald.*

* * *

John Wilmot, Earl of Rochester, one of the most brilliant and licentious nobles of the dissolute court of Charles II., was laid aside by a fatal disease, which gave him opportunity for reflection. In the hope of breaking the monotony of the sick room, he began the reading of books and happened one day to pick up a Greek translation of the Old Testament, when his eyes fell on the fifty-third chapter of Isaiah, which he read carefully several times.

"Where did this man, Isaiah, obtain such a conception as this?" he exclaimed. "Putting aside altogether the question of the historical reality of the character he describes, how did he, or how could any human being, unaided, come by the knowledge of such a character?"

Thus he pondered, nor would the problem down night or day, until at length he was compelled to admit the Divine inspiration of the Book and ultimately to accept the Lord Jesus as his Saviour. Bishop Burnet, who knew him well, testified that if ever there were a case of real repentance on earth, that of John Wilmot, Earl of Rochester, was one.—*The Gospel Herald.*

* * *

The Print of the Nails

It may not be easy to give such marks of the Shepherd's voice as to enable the Christian to know infallibly whether the solicitations that come to him are indeed from Christ. But there are certain characteristics which always distinguish His calls. There is a story that once there came to the cell of a saintly monk one who knocked and asked for admittance. His mien was lordly and majestic. "Who art thou?" asked the saint. "I am Jesus," was the answer. There was something in the voice and manner of the visitor, however, which made the monk suspect that he was not the Holy One he claimed to be. "Where is the print of the nails?" he asked. Instantly the stranger turned and fled away. It was Satan — not Christ! Nothing is of Christ which does not bear this mark.—*Westminister Teacher.*

* * *

Anybody for Calvary

Dr. Brummitt has given a remarkable illustration from personal experience: The town in which I live has an elevated railway. One of the stations is near a great Roman Catholic burying ground, Calvary Cemetery. For many years, because in that part of the town were many more dead than living folk, the trains did not stop at the cemetery station except on request. Just after leaving the nearest station the guard would open the door and say: "Next station is Calvary. Train stops on signal only. Anybody for Calvary?" It is a parable of life's train. At all other stations every train stops. At Market Street, School Street, University Avenue, Main Street, Vanity Fair, Broadway, Church Street, Home Avenue, no special notice needed. But Calvary is "the offence of the cross," and no one stops there unless he chooses to. It is unto the Jews a stumbling-block, and unto the Greeks foolishness. But it saves those who believe. Through all eternity we shall thank God that Christ chose Calvary, "who for the joy that was set before him endured the cross, despising the shame."—*Sunday School Times.*

* * *

For Whom Did Christ Die?

Dr. Pierson once told at Keswick of a dozen shipwrecked men, laboring in heavy seas in an overloaded boat, when one of the seamen, in order to lighten the boat, deliberately sprang overboard, and the rest were saved. For which of the eleven, asked Dr. Pierson, did the sailor give his life? If Christ died for all, He died for each; for no one more than another; and for no one excepted or omitted. The sun shines for seventeen hundred millions of mankind; but I know as a fact that it shines for me, and would tomorrow morning if not another soul survived on the globe. So Christ loved me and gave Himself for me.—*Sunday School Times.*

* * *

Under Sentence of Death

A policeman brought a man to the China Inland Mission Hospital at Anshun, Kweichow, China, of which Dr. E. S. Fish has charge, to determine whether or not the man had leprosy. If he had not, he was to be a free man; if he had, he was to be taken out and shot. Dr. Fish looked at the man and could easily see that he was a leper. He then turned to the policeman and said: "He is a leper, but he need not die." Dr. Fish found a place for him and he was given attention. So the sinner (under the sentence of death) need not die, for "the Son of Man came... to give his life a ransom for many."—Dr. E. S. Fish at the China Inland Mission Annual Conference in Toronto.

* * *

How The World Treats the Lord

An illiterate fisherman and pilot gave to Mark Guy Pearse a touching chapter from his personal experience, and the application he made of it. Mr. Pearse says he passed it along to D. L. Moody, and the latter was so affected by it that he buried his face in his hands and wept.

The fisherman told how he was lying aboard his boat in Plymouth Sound when he heard a splash in the water not far off. He jumped out of his berth, for he thought he knew what it was; there was another fishing boat not far off, and the man with it was a drinking man. He rowed there in his small boat with all speed, leaning over the side and praying God for help. Presently he got hold of the other man's arm and pulled him up, and he was drunk, sure enough. He lifted him back onto his boat and put him in his berth and worked over him and rubbed him an hour or more, till he began to come to himself. Doing everything possible to make the man comfortable, he came away.

The next morning he pulled over to see how the man was. He was standing leaning over the side of his craft. To a "good morning," he returned no answer. "How are you this morning?" his rescuer said. "What's that to you?" was the surly response. "Why," said the first man, "I can't help taking an interest in you. I saved your life last night." "Get out," responded the other, and roundly cursed him for a liar.

"I turned 'round my little boat and pulled away to my craft," he said in telling Mr. Pearse. "My heart was like a thing broke. The tears ran down my cheeks. I looked up to Heaven and could hardly get out the words that choked me. 'O Lord Jesus,' I said, 'my blessed Lord Jesus, I am sorry for Thee! I know now how Thou dost feel. That is how the world is always treating Thee. I am terribly sorry for Thee, my dear Lord.' "—*The King's Business.*

* * *

The Word Defeats Islam

A paragraph in *The Moslem World* tells of a missionary having painted in Arabic on the walls of a mission building in northern Africa the words of John 3:16. Next morning there was a blank in the text. During the night some Mohammedans had come and painted out the words "his only begotten Son"—for Islam denies that the Lord Jesus is God's Son—denies indeed that God ever had a Son. Their action was symbolic. In North Africa Christianity was once supreme. What the midnight visitors did on the mission wall Mohammedanism has done in North Africa. But the missionaries who put the text up on their wall were not to be beaten. The words which the Moslems deleted were promptly restored, only to be blotted out again; again they were restored, and again blotted out; and the strange struggle went on until the Mohammedans grew weary and left the text alone. Then followed a remarkable result. The words, "his only begotten Son," had been so often painted in and painted out that they could be read more clearly than the rest; and when the bulk of the text had faded, "his only begotten Son" still stood out, vivid and insistent.—*Sunday School Times.*

* * *

A Wounded Messiah

A lady once said to a Jewish lad in Cairo, "Are you expecting your Messiah soon?"

"Yes," he replied, "we believe He will come within six years."

"Will He have wounds in His hands?" she asked, and, as he looked at her inquiringly, she continued, "Your Prophet Zechariah said of Messiah that when He comes, they shall say unto Him, 'What are these wounds in Thine hands?' Then He shall answer, 'Those with which I was wounded in the house of My friends' (Zech. 13:6). Are you expecting to see your Messiah with wounds in His hands?"

The lad left, but appeared the following morning looking greatly distressed. He said: "I could not sleep last night. All night I was asking myself, 'If He has wounds in His hands, how did He get them?' I have come to ask you if you can tell me more."

Imagine her joy to tell one who was so eager to hear the wondrous story of the Cross, where He was wounded for our transgressions.

He received Jesus the Crucified One as his Messiah and Savior and has been the means of bringing three others to Him.—*Life Line.*

* * *

The Fool's Recipe for "Some Sense"

When Mr. Alexander and I were holding our meetings in the Royal Albert

Hall in London, someone took away one of our hymn books and went through it and cut out every reference to the blood; and then sent it back to me through the mail, saying: "I have gone through your hymn book and cut out every reference to the blood. Now sing your hymns with the blood left out and there will be some sense in them." If any of you should take your Bible and go through it in that way and cut out of the New Testament and the Old Testament every passage that referred to the death of Christ, or to His atoning blood, you would have only a sadly torn and tattered Bible left, a Bible without a heart and a Gospel without saving power. The death of Jesus Christ is mentioned more than 175 times in the New Testament. Besides this there are very many prophetic and typical references to the death of Jesus Christ in the Old Testament.—Dr. R. A. Torrey, in *Sermon on the Atonement.*

* * *

It Was Finished

"Lifted up" was He to die;
"It is finished," was His cry;
Now in Heaven exalted high:
Hallelujah! what a Saviour!

It is the Father's joy to bless,
His love has found for me a dress;
A robe of spotless righteousness,
O Lamb of God, in Thee.

* * *

The Red Cross that Cannot Be Hid

A Finnish Red Cross hospital which, in accordance with International Law, must be left untouched by enemy bombers, was attacked and several were killed. The Finns made strong protests to the Soviet Government. Upon inquiry it was learned that a snowfall during the night had covered the red cross painted on the hospital roof. Apparently the flyers were justified and the matter was dropped. In reading the account one could not but think of another cross, the crimson cross of Calvary. The security of those in the hospital was short-lived. The believer, however, is assured that Christ "by his own blood . . . entered in once into the holy place (Heaven) having obtained eternal redemption for us." Nothing can obliterate or hide that precious blood. Ever visible to God, it spells peace and safety for time and eternity to all redeemed ones.—*Good News.*

* * *

Jesus Nailed to the Cross

The manner of nailing the criminal, or the victim, to the cross was simple. The cross was laid upon the ground, and the one to be crucified was stretched upon it and spiked there. The hole for the cross was previously dug. Then the cross was carried to the hole and dropped into it. This, of course, drew every nerve and muscle into tension and produced the greatest imaginable suffering.

A teacher of a class of working girls showed them a steel engraving of a famous picture of the crucifixion. Three crosses were upon the ground. Soldiers were struggling with the two thieves, and forcing them down upon the crosses, while others drove the spikes. Upon the middle cross Christ lay down quietly and extended the quivering palms to receive the spikes. As the young women looked at the picture, one cried: *"Oh, was Christ nailed there alive? I thought that He was dead before He was nailed there."* The teacher replied: *"Yes, He was nailed there alive for you."* The girl, weeping, said: *"Then I am His forever."—Alliance Weekly.*

* * *

Rebuked by a Poor Man

The French scholar, Muretus, a Protestant exile in the seventeenth century, fell seriously ill in Lombardy and was taken to a pauper hospital. Then he overheard the doctors consulting about him in Latin, not thinking that the pauper patient could understand the language of the learned. They said, "Let us try an experiment with this worthless creature." And from his bed the sick scholar startled them by murmuring in Latin, "Will you call worthless one for whom Christ did not disdain to die?"—*Christian Observer.*

DEATH (See also: Resurrection, 554)

They Die Well

In the early days of Methodism it was said of the new brand of Christians that they died well. It is the privilege of every believer to know this victory. One phase of the work of Christ is well epitomized in the second chapter of the Epistle to the Hebrews. Verses 14 and 17 tell of the incarnation and its purpose. The heart of this section says, "That through death he might destroy him that had the power of death, that is, the devil; and deliver them who through fear of death were all their lifetime subject to bondage."

One of the young men encouraged into the ministry by the late Dr. William Anderson, of Dallas, Tex., told us this. Dr. Anderson was very ill. He seemed better, but was quite prostrated. His mother was sitting in the room with him. He gently called to her, "Come over here a minute." As she approached his bed he said, "I want to tell you something. I am going to beat you to heaven." And with a smile he shut his eyes and was gone.

The fear of death is banished in the measure that our life is fixed upon the One who tasted death for every man. It is only the person who can say, "For me to live is Christ," who can with joyful anticipation say, "To die is gain." — Courtesy *Moody Monthly.*

* * *

No Fear

"What did you do to our daughter?" asked a Moslem woman, whose child had died at sixteen years of age. "We did nothing," answered the missionary. "Oh, yes, you did," persisted the mother. "She died smiling. Our people do not die like that." The girl had found Christ and believed on Him a few months before. Fear of death had gone. Hope, giving birth to joy, had replaced it. — *Gospel Herald.*

How Unbelievers Die

Death is a blessed and glorious event for the true believer in the Lord Jesus Christ, the most wonderful experience that can ever come to a child of God. The apostle Paul said, ". . . to die is gain" (Philippians 1:21). How differently most of us look on death! We think of it as some horrible monster seeking to separate us forever from those we love. Actually, for those who are in the Lord, death is but the gateway to life, a stepping-stone to Glory.

To the unbeliever death is a terrible thing. Sir Thomas Scott, on his deathbed, said, "Until this moment I thought there was neither a God nor a Hell. Now I *know* and *feel* that there are both, and I am doomed to perdition by the just judgment of the Almighty."

M. F. Rich, an atheist, cried, "I would rather lie on a stove and broil for a million years than go into eternity with the eternal horrors that hang over my soul! I have given my immortality for gold; and its weight sinks me into an endless, hopeless, helpless Hell."—Selected.

* * *

"My Bandit"

In Cincinnati I heard Miss Muriel Lester relate the story of a missionary in China whose husband was called away from home. During his absence a bandit broke into the home, seized the missionary, and was about to kill her. To her surprise she found that she was not afraid of death, and that in her heart was no hatred for her enemy. Calmly she looked into his eyes, smiled at him, took off her ring, and gave it to him. The bandit's hold loosened; he turned and walked away. He had doubtless seen not only her high courage, but the love of Jesus shining in her face. The missionary wrote a poem entitled "My Bandit," because she felt that she was debtor to him, not so much for sparing her life as for freeing her forever from the fear of death.—*Sunday School Times.*

Crossing the Bar

Sunset and evening star,
  And one clear call for me!
And may there be no moaning of the bar,
  When I put out to sea.

But such a tide as moving seems asleep,
  Too full for sound and foam,
When that which drew from out the boundless deep
  Turns again home.

Twilight and evening bell,
  And after that the dark!
And may there be no sadness of farewell
  When I embark;

For though from out our bourne of Time and Place
  The flood may bear me far,
I hope to see my Pilot face to face
  When I have crossed the bar.

—Alfred Tennyson, in *The Works of Tennyson*. By permission of The Macmillan Company, publishers.

* * *

What Took Away the Fear

I well remember how, in my native village in New England, it was customary to toll the church bell as many strokes as the departed was years old. Anxiously I would count the strokes, and, if there were seventy or eighty, I would breathe a sigh of relief, thinking I had a long time yet to live. But when there were only a few years tolled, I was seized with horror that I, too, should be claimed by dreaded death. Death and judgment were a constant source of fear to me till I realized that neither shall have any hold on a child of God; for "there is therefore now no condemnation to them which are in Christ Jesus." — *Moody's Stories*, Bible Institute Colportage Association.

* * *

When We Forget

I had graduated from college and theological seminary, but I had never seen anyone die. It was my first week in a parish. A messenger came with the word: "Father Junkins is dying, and he wants to see you, pastor." What could I do? The man reported dying was eighty-seven years of age — the outstanding Christian in the village. I started at once for his home, but I went with fear and trembling, for I had no message. I kept praying, "O God, give me a message for this dying saint." Upon entering his room, he said, "Oh, pastor, I am dying! For years I have been feasting on the promises of God, but this morning when I woke up, I could not remember one of them! What shall I do?" Then God gave me an answer which, after visiting the bedsides of scores of dying saints during forty years, I cannot improve. I said, "Father Junkins, do you think God will forget any of His promises?" I shall always remember the sweet smile that came over the face of the old saint as he looked up at me. "Praise God," he said, "that is wonderful! He'll remember them, won't He?. . . I'll just fall asleep and trust Him to remember His precious promises to me." In a few hours he had gone Home to be with the Promiser. The promises of God are wonderful. But our Lord Himself is more wonderful than His promises.—*The King's Business.*

* * *

The Presence of Christ

A dying man, being visited by his minister, complained that he could not experience the consciousness of God's presence. The minister told him to have a chair placed by his bedside, and then to think that Christ was seated in that chair and reach out his hand to clasp the hand of Christ seated in the chair. The ill man did so and found a blessed sense of the presence of Christ with him in that sick room. When the minister called a few days later, he found his friend dead, but with his hand clutching the arm of the chair in which, to him, the Christ had sat and held his hand. *Have you ever done that—put yourself into an attitude of spirit in which you willed to think and feel that Christ was by your side?*—William Evans, in *S. S. World.*

A Lesson From Childhood

One evening recently, when I was tucking my small daughter in bed, she said, "Mother, stay with me while I go to sleep." For a moment, remembering all the tasks that await me when I come home from work, I was tempted to put her off. But only for an instant; then I sat down by her and held her little soft hand in mine. And in a calm reflection, while she drifted away to dreamland, this thought — or perhaps it was a prayer — wafted its way to the Infinite: "May I so live that when life's evening shall come I can say with utter confidence to the Divine Parent—'Stay with me while I go to sleep.'"—*Mother of Two.*

* * *

Moving Time

When John Quincy Adams was eighty years of age a friend said to him,

"Well, how is John Quincy Adams?"

"Thank you," he said; "John Quincy Adams is quite well. But the house where he lives is becoming dilapidated. It is tottering. Time and the seasons have nearly destroyed it, and it is becoming quite uninhabitable. I shall have to move out soon. But John Quincy Adams is quite well, thank you."—*The Gospel Herald.*

* * *

Voltaire at the End

The Christian physician who attended the French infidel, Voltaire, during his last illness, has left a testimony concerning the departure of this poor lost soul. He wrote to a friend as follows:

"When I compare the death of a righteous man, which is like the close of a beautiful day, with that of Voltaire, I see the difference between bright, serene weather and a black thunderstorm. It was my lot that this man should die under my hands. Often did I tell him the truth. 'Yes, my friend,' he would often say to me, 'you are the only one who has given me good advice. Had I but followed it I should not be in the horrible condition in which I now am. I have swallowed nothing but smoke. I have intoxicated myself with the incense that turned my head. You can do nothing for me. Send me a mad doctor! Have compassion on me—I am mad!'

"I cannot think of it without shuddering. As soon as he saw that all the means he had employed to increase his strength, had just the opposite effect, death was constantly before his eyes. From this moment, madness took possession of his soul. He expired under the torments of the furies."—*Our Hope.*

* * *

Her Fear Forgotten

All my life I entertained a great fear of death, till one of my own children went to be with the Lord. During the funeral service the minister told the following story: "A shepherd led his flock to the banks of a swiftly flowing stream. Sheep are naturally afraid of rapidly running water. The shepherd could not induce them to cross until he picked up a little lamb and stepped with it into the river, bearing it carefully and tenderly to the opposite shore. When the mother saw where her lamb had gone, she forgot her fear and stepped into the rushing current and was soon safely on the other side. All the rest of the flock followed her leadership."—*Sunday School Times.*

* * *

Safe on the Rock

A Welsh lady, when she lay dying, was visited by her minister. He said to her, "Sister, are you sinking?" She answered him not a word, but looked at him with incredulous eye. He repeated the question, "Sister, are you sinking?" She looked at him again, as if she could not believe he would ask such a question. At last, rising a little in her bed, she said, "Sinking! Sinking! Did you ever know a sinner to sink through a Rock? If I had been standing on the sand, I might sink; but, thank God, I am on the Rock of Ages, and there is no sinking there."—*Spurgeon's Sermons.*

Nothing Between

When Samuel Rutherford was dying he said, "I am in the happiest pass to which man ever came. Christ is mine, and I am His; and there is nothing now between me and resurrection, except—Paradise."—*The King's Business.*

* * *

"And He Died"

Henry Goodear, a merchant living in London, was very much inclined to scoff at the Bible and its teaching.

One day his niece, Mary Goodear, persuaded him to go to church, "just to please her." Greatly to her grief the lesson was from the fifth chapter of Genesis. As the verses were read she could only shrink back in her place. Why had God permitted such an uninteresting list to be read this day of all others?

Mr. Goodear made no comment as he and his niece walked homewards. A little quieter, a little more thoughtful than usual, that was all. And yet, with every passing footstep, every tread of his own feet, every throb of his heart, came the refrain, *"And he died."*

Up in his own room that night went Henry Goodear, and each hour, as it struck from Big Ben, seemed to echo the words, *"And he died."*

The next morning, busy at his ledger, as usual, his pen seemed to trace the words, *"And he died."* "This will never do," thought Mr. Goodear, as he failed in a simple addition. "I must read that chapter." So, as soon as he reached home the half-forgotten family Bible was opened, and he read the words again, "All the days that Adam lived were nine hundred and thirty years: *and he died."* "All the days of Seth were nine hundred and twelve years: *and he died."* "All the days of Enos were nine hundred and five years: *and he died."*

Right to the end of the chapter read Mr. Goodear. Wicked or good, the same simple story was told of each, "He lived —*and he died."*

The Spirit of God can use the most unlikely of instruments. By this uninteresting list of facts Mr. Goodear's life was entirely changed. He was living—and he would have to die, and what then?

That very night this London merchant gave himself to the Lord, who has said, he that "believeth in Me shall never die."

I think, don't you, that we may learn something from the left-out portion, even if it seems an uninteresting list?—L. O. C., in *The Gospel Banner.*

* * *

What They Said at Death's Door

Thomas Hobbs, a skeptic who corrupted some of England's great men: "If I had the whole world, I would give it to live one day. I shall be glad to find a hole to creep out of the world at. About to take a leap into the dark!"

Dwight L. Moody, just before his home-going: "I see earth receding, Heaven is opening. God is calling!"

Thomas Paine, a noted American infidel and author: "I would give worlds if I had them, that 'The Age of Reason' had never been published. O Lord, help me! Christ, help me! O God, what have I done to suffer so much? But there is no God! But if there should be, what will become of me hereafter? Stay with me, for God's sake! Send even a child to stay with me, for it is Hell to be alone. If ever the Devil had an agent, I have been that one."

Ben Hill, Georgia's silver-tongued orator, who, with flaming eloquence, espoused the cause of liberty and justice, triumphantly said: "Almost Home."

Napoleon Bonaparte, who changed the map of Europe, the military strategist of the ages: "I die before my time, and my body will be given back to the earth. Such is the fate of him who has been called the great Napoleon. What an abyss between my deep misery and the eternal kingdom of Christ!"

Francis Voltaire, the noted French infidel. He was one of the most fertile and talented writers and strove to retard and demolish Christianity. His cry in health concerning Christ was, "Curse the wretch!" He said once, "In twenty years, Christianity will be no more. My single hand shall destroy the edifice it took twelve apostles to rear." Some years after his death, his very printing press was employed in printing New Testaments. Said he to his doctor, "I am abandoned by God and man! I will give you half of what I am worth if you will give me six months' life. Then I shall go to Hell; and you will go with me. O Christ! O Jesus Christ!"

Charles Wesley, author of over 4,000 published hymns, which hymns contributed largely to his brother's success. How different it is when he said: "I shall be satisfied with Thy likeness. Satisfied!"

John Wesley: "The best of all is, God is with us."

John Quincy Adams: "This is the last of earth. I am content!"

Jeanne d'Arc: "Yes, my voices were from God. My voices have not deceived me—Jesus!"

Francis Bacon, Lord Chancellor of England: "The sweetest life in this world is piety, virtue, and honesty."

Ludvig von Beethoven, the deaf Prussian composer: "I shall hear in Heaven."

Mrs. Catharine Booth, wife of the general of the Salvation Army: "The waters are rising, but so am I. I am not going under, but over. Do not be concerned about dying; go on living well, the dying will be right."

J. Wilkes Booth, the assassin of President Lincoln: "Useless! Useless!"

Elizabeth B. Browning, an English poetess: "We want the touch of Christ's hand upon our literature." At death's door, she said: "It is beautiful!"

John Bunyan, author of "Pilgrim's Progress": "Weep not for me, but for yourselves. I go to the Father of our Lord Jesus Christ, who no doubt will receive me, though a sinner, through the mediation of our Lord Jesus Christ; where I hope we shall ere long meet to sing the new song and remain happy forever; world without end. Amen!"

Robert Burns, the Scottish poet: "I have but a moment to speak to you, my dear. Be a good man; be virtuous; be religious. Nothing else will give you any comfort when you come to be here."

John Calvin, the French Protestant Reformer, at Geneva: "Thou, Lord, bruisest me, but I am abundantly satisfied, since it is from Thy hand."

Thomas Carlyle: "I am as good as without hope, and without fear; a sad old man gazing into the final chasm."

Karl W. von Humboldt, a German statesman, as he was gazing on the sun: "Those rays, they seem to beckon me to Heaven."

John Huss, Bohemian reformer and martyr. At the last moment the Duke of Bavaria asked him to recant, but he replied: "What I taught with my lips, I seal with my blood."

Cornelius Vanderbilt, one of the great railroad kings of America. His wealth at death was estimated to be the largest ever bequeathed to heirs in the United States. When dying he said concerning the hymn: "'Come, ye sinners, poor and needy.' Yes, yes, sing that for me. I am poor and needy."

Adoniram Judson, American missionary to Burma. He wrote, "Come, Holy Spirit, Dove Divine," and other hymns. He died at sea and his body was committed to the great deep. He said: "I go with the gladness of a boy bounding away from school. I feel so strong in Christ."

Sir Walter Raleigh, English admiral and courtier, beheaded: "It matters little how the head lies if the heart be right. Why dost thou not strike?"

Augustus M. Toplady, English minister, author of "Rock of Ages, Cleft for Me": "The Celestial City rises full in sight, the sense of interest in the covenant of grace becomes clearer and brighter. The Book of Life is opened to the eye of assurance, the Holy Spirit more feelingly applies the blood of sprinkling, and warms the soul with that robe of righteousness which Jesus wrought."

Mrs. Ann Hasseltine Judson, missionary to Burma and wife of Adoniram Judson: "Oh, the happy day will soon come when we shall meet all our friends who are now scattered—meet to part no more in our Heavenly Father's house."

Charles IX. This cruel wretch, urged on by his inhumane mother, gave the order for the massacre of the Huguenots in which 15,000 souls were slaughtered in Paris alone, and 100,000 in other sections of France, for no other reason than that they owned Christ, and not the Pope, as their master. The guilty King died bathed in blood bursting from his own veins. To his physicians he said in his last hours: "Asleep or awake, I see the mangled forms of the Huguenots passing before me. They drip with blood. They point at their open wounds. Oh! that I had spared at least the little infants at the breast! What blood! I know not where I am. How will all this end? What shall I do? I am lost forever! I know it. Oh, I have done wrong. God pardon me!"

David Strauss, outstanding representative of German rationalism, after spending years of his life trying to dispense with God: "My philosophy leaves me utterly forlorn! I feel like one caught in the merciless jaws of an automatic machine, not knowing at what time one of its great hammers may crush me!"

Lord Thomas Cromwell: "Oh, God, I prostrate myself to my deserved punishment; Lord, be merciful to Thy prostrate servant."

George Whitefield, an English evangelist, one of the most eloquent of pulpit orators. He refused to limit his ministrations to one denomination. He said: "Lord Jesus, I am weary *in* Thy work, but not *of* Thy work. If I have not yet finished my course, let me go and speak for Thee once more in the fields, seal the truth, and come home to die."

William of Normandy. When he died he ordered his body to be placed in a stone coffin, and not buried, but placed under the eaves outside of the chapel, in order, as he said, "that the drippings of the rain from the roof may wash my bones as I lie, and cleanse them from the impurity contracted in my sinful and neglected life."—Selected.

DEVIL

What About the Devil?

Men don't believe in a devil now
As their fathers used to do;
They've forced the door of the broadest creed
To let his majesty through;
There isn't a print of his cloven foot
Or a fiery dart from his bow
To be found in the earth or the air today,
For the world has voted so.

They say he doesn't go round about
As a roaring lion now,
But whom shall we hold responsible
For the everlasting row
To be held in home and church and state
To the earth's remotest bound,
If the devil by a unanimous vote
Is nowhere to be found?

Who is mixing the fatal draught
That palsies heart and brain,
And loads the bier of each passing year
With ten hundred thousand slain?
Who blights the bloom of the land today
With the fiery breath of hell,
If the devil isn't and never was?
Won't somebody rise and tell?

Who dogs the steps of the toiling saint,
And digs the pits for his feet?
Who sows the tares in the fields of time
Wherever God sows His wheat?
The devil was voted not to be,
And of course the thing is true,
But who is doing the kind of work
The devil used to do?

Won't somebody step to the front forthwith,
And make his bow and show
How the frauds and crimes of a single day
Spring up? We want to know.
The devil was fairly voted out,
And of course the devil's gone,
But simple people want to know
Who carries the business on.

—Selected (*Gem Cyclop.*, p. 175).)

What Satan Fears

One of the happiest men I ever knew was a man in Dundee, Scotland, who had fallen and broken his back when he was a boy of fifteen. He had lain on his bed for about forty years, and suffered much pain, but the grace of God was so abundant upon him, that I almost imagined that when the angels passed over Dundee, they would stop at this bedside to get refreshed. When I saw him I asked if Satan ever tempted him, thinking of God as a hard Master, and doubting His love. "Oh, yes," he said, "many times, as I see others in prosperity, Satan says, 'If God is so good, you might be rich and well.'" "What do you do when Satan tempts you?" I asked. "Ah, I just take him to Calvary and show him Christ, and His wounds, and say, 'Does He not love me?' And Satan got such a scare there hundreds of years ago, that he cannot stand it; he leaves me every time." —*Moody's Stories*, Bible Institute Colportage Association.

* * *

The Secret of Christian Victory

Griffith Thomas once told the story of a poor Negro who was a helpless slave to drink. He tried again and again to get free, and others tried to help him, but he could not get rid of his drunkenness until he was saved. When he was converted there was a wonderful change, and someone said, "So you have got the mastery of the devil at last?" "No," he said, "but I have got the Master of the devil."

Since Satan is a supernatural enemy, it takes a supernatural power to overwhelm him. Christ is that Power. Christ in the believer is not only the Hope of Glory—He is the Hope of victory.—*The Brethren Evangelist.*

* * *

The Reality of the Devil

The man who denies the existence of the evil one reveals the fact that he has not been considered a worthy foe by the prince of darkness. The great evangelist, Charles Finney, realized this truth from a deep experience of his opposition. On one occasion, after he had been preaching on the subject, a man came to him, and said: "Mr. Finney, I don't believe in the devil." The preacher looked at him keenly for a moment, and replied: "Don't you now? Well, you really resist him for a while, and you'll soon change your views." The mighty author of evil is not slow to accept the challenge that is thrown to him by a holy life.—Selected.

* * *

The Devil's Beans

Rowland Hill, a prominent preacher of former years, related this incident in one of his sermons: "The other day I was going down the street, and I saw a drove of pigs following a man. This excited my curiosity so much that I determined to follow. I did so; and to my great surprise, I saw them follow him to the slaughterhouse. I was anxious to know how this was brought about; and I said to the man, 'My friend, how did you manage to induce these pigs to follow you here?' 'Oh, did you not see?' said the man. 'I had a basket of beans under my arm; and I dropped a few as I came along and so they followed me.' 'Yes,' said the preacher, 'and I thought so it is, the devil has his basket of beans under his arm; and he drops them as he goes along; and what multitudes he induces to follow him to an everlasting slaughterhouse.'"—*Gospel Herald.*

* * *

"So What"

A young man, under the influence of drink, stood on the outside of a crowd and boasted that he would make the open-air preacher leave off preaching. He shouted: "Hi, Mister, you can go home; you needn't preach any more—the Devil's dead!" The preacher looked at the young man sternly, and replied: "The Devil's dead? Then you're an orphan!" The youth hurried away abashed, while the crowd smiled broadly. —*Christian Herald.*

Worse Than Rattlesnakes

At an experience meeting, in a mountainous region, one man expressed discouragement because after three years of discipleship he still had severe struggles with Satan. A veteran in the service replied: "It took me twenty years to get the hill back of my barn reasonably freed from rattlesnakes; and after fifty years I still meet one there occasionally. Brother, the Devil is harder to deal with than rattlesnakes.—*Adult Class Teacher* (Baptist).

* * *

Following the Leader

In a midwest packing house there is an animal that has become an "institution." For many years he has carried on. It is a goat, dubbed Judas. Regularly, unfailingly, he leads the sheep to the slaughter. They always follow the scoundrel; he delights in it. Unsuspectingly, sheep-like, they follow his prancing feet to their destruction, certain and sure, while he darts out another way to safety, again to lead fresh victims on the morrow. He has led millions to their destruction. How like "the god of this age" leading the unthinking masses, custom-bound, blinded, in the succession of the generations one along the track of the other, sheep-like, to their unspeakable doom!—*Gospel Herald.*

* * *

When Satan Approaches

A little Christian was once asked if Satan did not tempt her to do wrong things and how she kept from doing them.

The answer was: "Yes, I know he wants to get me, but when Satan knocks at the door of my heart I just say, 'Jesus, won't You go to the door?' and when Satan sees Jesus, he runs away every time."

The strongest man that ever lived is not strong enough to meet Satan alone! —*S. S. Quarterly.*

A Personal Devil

He is called in the Bible:

1. Angel of the bottomless pit (Rev. 9:11).
2. Accuser (Rev. 12:10).
3. Belial (II Cor. 6:15).
4. Adversary (I Peter 5:8).
5. Beast (Rev. 19:19).
6. Beelzebub (Matt. 12:24).
7. Deceiver (Rev. 12:9).
8. Dragon (Rev. 12:7).
9. God of this world (II Cor. 4:4).
10. Liar and murderer (John 8:44).
11. Serpent (Rev. 12:9).
12. Prince of this world (John 12:31).
13. Tempter (I Thess. 3:5).
14. Prince of the power of the air (Eph. 2:2).—Selected.

* * *

The Winner in a Game of Death

There is a wonderful picture called "The Game of Death," in which a young man is represented as playing chess with the Devil. The Devil has apparently won the game by the position of the chessmen. A noted chess player once went to see the picture, and after looking at it, he said, "I can save that fellow." He then explained how the chessmen should be moved to save the game. "That," said Dr. Stuart Holden, "is what Jesus Christ has done. He has in one move eternally checkmated death and the Devil, and snatched the prey from the mighty."—*The Sunday Circle.*

* * *

How to Overcome

There is only one way by which the tempter can be met. He laughs at our good resolutions and ridicules the pledges with which we fortify ourselves. There is only One whom he fears; One who in the hour of greatest weakness conquered him; and who has been raised far above all principality and power, that He may succor and deliver all frail and tempted souls. He conquered the prince of this world in the days of His flesh; and He is prepared to do as much again, in each of us, if only we will truly surrender ourselves to His gracious and mighty indwelling.—F. B. Meyer.

* * *

Everlasting Watchfulness

The words in Luke 4:13, "And when the devil had ended all the temptation, he departed from him for a season," should be carefully noted. They do not mean that after Satan tempts us, we are immune from his attacks for a little while. They do not mean that Satan will give us rest in order to recuperate for another siege of temptation. Nor do they mean that God will prevent Satan from tempting us for a time. The words, "he departed from him for a season," literally translated, are, "he stood off from him until a good opportunity should return" to continue the attack. When the Devil stops tempting us, it is only because he seeks to catch us unaware.—Courtesy *Moody Monthly.*

* * *

The Real Question

A little boy came to his father looking much in earnest, and asked, "Father, is Satan bigger than I am?" "Yes, my boy," said the father. "Is he bigger than you are, Father?" "Yes, my boy, he is bigger than your father," The boy looked surprised but thought again, and asked, "Is he bigger than Jesus?" "No, my boy," answered the father. "Jesus is bigger than he is." The little fellow, as he turned away, said with a smile, "Then I'm not afraid of him."—*Sunday School Banner.*

* * *

Why He Did Not Believe in a Devil

A friend of mine once asked me if I believed in a personal devil, to which I replied with some emphasis, "No!" His only answer was a lifting of eyebrows as though wondering at my heterodoxy; whereupon I proceeded to clear myself: "I most certainly believe there *is* a personal devil, but far be it from me to believe *in* him. He is a liar and the father of lies, and how he has lied about the Word of God! It has been the method of Satan from the beginning to tamper with, distort, and otherwise cast doubts upon the Word. "Yea, hath God said . . . ?" was the crafty, doubt-sowing utterance by which he deceived Eve. —Dr. E. J. Pace.

* * *

He Got Left

Clara Logan sat by a log fire telling stories of children. "A lady," she said, "was reclining on a couch in her library one night, with the light low, trying to sleep. Beside her on the table was a dish of fine fruit. As she lay there she saw her little daughter tiptoe into the room, in her long, white nightgown. The child, thinking her mother was asleep, advanced cautiously to the table, took a bunch of grapes, and stole out again, The mother was grieved at such misconduct on the part of her good little daughter, but said nothing. Five minutes passed, then back into the room again crept the child, the grapes untouched. She replaced them on the dish and as she departed her mother heard her utter, "That's the time you got left, Mr. Devil!"—Selected.

* * *

Anger

He that goes to bed angry, has the devil for his roommate—yea, for his bed fellow—nay, he lies not only in his bed, but in his bosom. The way to be angry and sin not is to be angry at nothing but sin (Ps. 27:9; Eph. 4:26).—*The Evangel.*

DISCOURAGEMENT

What Doest Thou in the Place of Discouragement?

God lives! He longs to give you courage for the battle! Are you downhearted? Look away from circumstances to God.

D. L. Moody became very much depressed at one time because he thought the Lord was not sufficiently blessing his ministry. He was cast down, and would talk discouragingly of what was being done. He was in this disheartened condition for several months. He tells that one Monday when he was in the valley of despondency he met a friend who was dwelling upon the top of the mountain. The friend was exceedingly elated over the Sunday services he had conducted. He turned to Mr. Moody and inquired what kind of a day he had on Sunday in the service of the Lord.

"Oh!" said Moody, "I had not a good one." "Much power?" "No." Then Mr. Moody inquired of his friend what he had preached about. "Oh? I preached about Noah!" "How did you get on?" inquired Mr. Moody. "Oh, grandly. Did you ever study up Noah?" Mr. Moody said he thought he knew about Noah, and that there were only a few verses about him. "Oh, if you haven't studied up Noah you ought to do it. He's a wonderful character." After they parted Mr. Moody got out his Bible and read all he could find about Noah, and while he was reading, this thought came to him: Here is this man who was a preacher of righteousness for one hundred and twenty years, and yet never had a convert outside his own family. After this Mr. Moody went to a prayer meeting and met a young man who had just come from a town in Illinois. This young man was telling joyfully of ten bright converts in his recent meeting. "Why," said Mr. Moody to himself, "what would Noah have said if he had ten converts, and yet Noah didn't get discouraged?" Then a man close to Mr. Moody rose and in a trembling manner said: "I wish you would pray for me." Then Mr. Moody said to himself, "What would Noah have given if he had heard that during those one hundred and twenty years, and yet he never heard the voice of an inquirer—not one. Still he didn't get discouraged."

The important thing is to know that we are in the will of God. God has said that His Word will not return unto Him void. Results may seem meager. Disheartening circumstances may howl around us like a storm, but God has promised to protect us and look after results. Come out of the place of discouragement! "Why art thou cast down, O my soul? and why art thou disquieted within me? hope thou in God: for I shall yet praise Him, who is the health of my countenance, and my God." — *Gospel Herald.*

* * *

Are Sinking Spells Necessary

Someone said: "If you have occasional spells of despondency, don't despair. The sun has a sinking spell every night, but it rises again next morning." But this is not accurate, as the sun does not have a sinking spell every night; it only seems to because the earth is so changeable! The sun never sinks, and the sun that God has placed in the heavens to give light and warmth to the earth is a type, according to God's Word, of the Sun of Righteousness, our Lord Jesus Christ. Despondency comes only from unbelief.—*Sunday School Times.*

* * *

Discouragement

A young woman, because of discouragement, was about to give up an important work for God. One night she dreamed that an angel took her to Heaven and showed her all the beauty and glory of it. The angel then led her to the gate of Heaven where she could look down on the world and see the hearts of men and women torn and broken by sin and careless living. She could see bright spots where the Gospel had worked but they only intensified the darkness of the picture. The awful sight struck deep into the young woman's soul. She burst into tears, and said: "Let me go back to the world quickly and tell them of Jesus! I will never be discouraged again." Then she awoke; it was only a dream, but the vision of the lost world was always clearly before her eyes, and from that time on she realized her personal responsibility in the work of spreading the Gospel.

Indeed we all need to get above the horizon, to get a sight of a lost world, and to reach the "up" of courage in Christian service.

No matter how dark the hour may be, there are still glints of God's love, and if we are faithful, our saddest experience will be changed into sunshine and victory and happiness!

God cannot do much with a discouraged soldier. Uncle Sam has little or no use for a discouraged soldier. Once the morale of an army is gone, they are almost sure to go down in defeat.—*Gospel Herald.*

* * *

The Cause of Discouragement

If you are counting on your own strength, I am not surprised at your discouragement, but "He that keepeth Israel neither slumbereth nor sleepeth." We ought to be humbled, yes, humbled to the dust, but never discouraged. A truly humble man is not discouraged; the discouraged man is not a humble man, for he has trusted to something beside God; true nothingness cannot (do that). Simple faith rises above circumstances to Christ. Does Christ love the Church less? Is He less powerful? Faith has constant unfailing confidence in Christ. I know what sorrow is, because of our failure, but discouragement I do not know.—J. N. D., in *Scripture Truth.*

* * *

Don't Be Discouraged

The owner of a lovely garden went out one morning to find a neighbor's rabbits busily nibbling the green sprouts off her plants. Facing the ruin of many hour's labor, she was angry, just as you and I might be. She was annoyed with the rabbits. She was even more annoyed with the owner, who had not penned them securely.

After a few moments she began to check her irritation. She struggled with that mental storm of hers so successfully that she not only gained calm; she saw a rainbow.

Without even mentioning the incident to the neighbor, she proceeded to repair the damages as best she could. Then she continued to tend and water the garden just as before. Three weeks later she had her reward. The plants again were covered with green sprouts, two new leaves for every one that the rabbits had eaten.—Marjorie Schuler.

* * *

When We Want to Resign

We shall not soon forget Dr. Villers' story of the great Scotch preacher, John Robertson, who, discouraged with his work, sat and meditated and prayed late into the night; and as the day dawned he cried out in the anguish of his soul, "Lord, I resign my commission," only to hear back the consoling words from the Master, "You do not have to resign your commission. I will *re*-sign it for you." And John Robertson went forth in new power from that day. The fraternity of the burning heart is one that requires and may have constant renewal at the touch of the Master.—*The Baptist.*

* * *

The Devil's Tools

It was advertised that the devil was going to put his tools up for sale. On the date of sale the tools were placed for public inspection, each being marked with its sale price. They were a treacherous lot of implements—Hatred, Envy, Jealousy, Deceit, Lying, Pride, and so on, comprised the outfit. Laid apart from the rest was a harmless-looking tool, well-worn, and priced very high.

"What is the name of this tool?" asked one of the purchasers, pointing to it.

"That is Discouragement," tersely replied the devil.

"Why have you priced it so high?"

"Because it is more useful to me than the others. I can pry open and get inside a man's heart with that, when I cannot get near him with the other tools. Once I get inside, I can make him do what I choose. It is badly worn because I use it on almost everyone, since few people know it belongs to me."

The devil's price for Discouragement was so high that it was never sold. Discouragement is still the devil's tool, and he is using it today on God's own people. —*Gospel Herald.*

* * *

Never Give Up

A discouraged man went once to President Roosevelt with the tale of his misfortunes. He could not see the way out. But the man who had himself learned to smile when everything looked dark told him a story that sent him away with a determination to put his best foot foremost, to look on the bright side, and to make and hold on to the determination to try again and yet again until everything came out right.

The story told by President Roosevelt that had such an effect on his attitude to life was concerning an incident in the life of General W. W. Duffield, once chief of the Coast and Geodetic Survey, who for twenty-five years had been working out unweariedly a book on ten-place logarithms.

"These calculations of half a lifetime filled about five thousand pages of foolscap," the man afterward said in repeating the life-giving story. "The intricate and exhaustive tables and equations were of such value and the prospect of their publication of such a constant hope to their author that he carried them about with him in an old-fashioned carpetbag.

"The scientist's obvious concern on all occasions for his carpetbag finally attracted the attention of professional thieves, who suspected that it contained a hoarded fortune in bills and bonds, Watching their opportunity, one of the criminals engaged the venerable scientist in conversation while a confederate decamped with the bag. To the thief the contents were doubtless regarded as worthless. Nothing was ever heard of the manuscript.

"It was a tragic blow to the scientist, and would have been a serious loss to mathematicians in general, had General Duffield given up. On the contrary, he did not waste a day in despair, but grimly set to work at once reproducing his tables.

"They were finally published by the government in a volume of eight hundred pages. In astronomy and in the daily calculations of actuaries in the United States Treasury and other large financial institutions it is regarded as indispensable."—*Gospel Herald.*

* * *

Barges, Ships, or Liners?

"There are three kinds of Christian workers," said someone with a very vivid imagination, "canal barges, sailing ships, and Atlantic liners." The canal barge needs to be dragged to work. Often they do wonderfully well, but on the whole one volunteer is worth three pressed men.

The sailing ship makes fine going as long as wind and tide are with them, but when things get hard, when "winds are contrary," when work is discouraging, they turn tail and sail away.

But give us the Atlantic liner type of worker, the man who can fight his way through wind and tempest, because within him there burns the hot throb of the mighty furnace of the love of Christ.—Onward.

* * *

Not Forsaken

Bishop Gobat of Jerusalem, after a long missionary journey at one time, was greatly discouraged, He felt that God had forsaken him. Finding a cave, he went into it, spending a long time in prayer, telling the Lord how forsaken he was. It was a very dark cave. After being in the dark a while, his eyes became accustomed to it. He was startled by seeing a wild animal, a hyena and her cubs, near him. It is said that there is no animal more ferocious than a hyena with cubs. But God protected him; the hyena never offered to touch him. God's hand was keeping him at the very hour in which he thought that he was forsaken. He passed out unharmed. Oh that God would open our eyes so that we might realize the fact that at times when we get the idea that we are forsaken of Him He is keeping us from unseen dangers.—*Gospel Herald.*

* * *

A Discourager

It happened at the siege of Ladysmith. A civilian was arrested, court martialed, and sentenced to a year's imprisonment. He was a discourager. He would go along the lines and say discouraging words to the men on duty. He struck no blow for the enemy—not one. He was not disloyal to his country. He was just a discourager—and that in a critical time. The fortunes of the garrison and of the town hung in the balance. The court-martial adjudged it a crime to speak disheartening words in an hour like that. And so it is. And that same thing is happening every day in the history of some poor fellow's life. What this old world needs more than all is the man who can cheer.—*Texas Christian Advocate.*

* * *

Do You Get Discouraged

Do you ever get discouraged
As you press your upward path?
Do you feel that you have failed Him,
And have merited His wrath?
Do you fear that you have stumbled,
Lost the very best God hath?

For you wanted to reign with Him,
And you've felt His Coming near;
And you longed for His approval,
When at Judgment you appear;
And you know how Israel doubted,
And your heart is filled with fear.

Listen, thou, for Christ is speaking,
Words of comfort unto you;
Grace abundantly He proffers,
Grace sent down from Heaven's blue;
He will help you, if you'll let Him,
And will surely see you through.

—R. E. Neighbour, D.D.

Where to Cast Your Net

"Did you ever notice," said the old lady, smiling into the troubled face before her, "that when the Lord told the discouraged fishermen to cast their nets again, it was right in the same old place where they had caught nothing? If we could only get off to some new place when we get discouraged, trying again would be an easier thing. If we could be somebody else, or go somewhere else, or do something else, it might not be so hard to have fresh faith and courage; but it is the same old net in the same old pond for most of us. The old temptations are to be overcome, the old faults are to be conquered, the old trials and discouragements before which we failed yesterday to be faced again today. We must win success where we are, if we win it at all, and it is the Master Himself, who, after all these toilful, disheartening failures, bids us 'try again.'"—*Sunday School Times.*

* * *

Mending Trousers

Two pastors' wives, alleges the *Western Christian Union,* were visiting together. One said: "I don't know what we shall do—my husband is so discouraged. Somehow his people do not care to hear him preach, and our salary is far behind. My husband feels so blue that he does not like to visit the people and pray with them, and so he sits around at home nearly all the time." The other sister said: "We are getting along fine. My huband spends much of his time visiting, and the people like to have him kneel and pray with them in their homes. Our congregations are always good, and our salary is paid up promptly."

While the two sisters were talking they were mending trousers. One was mending her husband's trousers at the *seat,* the other was mending her husband's trousers at the *knees.*—*Sunday School Times.*

ENCOURAGEMENT

Encouragement

(I Sam. 7:12)

When our souls are much discouraged,
By the roughness of the way
And the cross we have to carry
Seemeth heavier every day.
When some cloud that over-shadows,
Hides the Father's face from view,
Oh 'tis well to remember
He hath blessed us hitherto.

—Selected.

* * *

He Put the Stars Back

William T. Stidger tells a fine story of a discouraged young colored minister. Everything seemed to have gone wrong with this man. He had built a church for his people, for he had been a carpenter; but when it was completed his wife, who had worked by his side, died. This and other trying experiences left him broken and defeated. Then he heard, over the radio, a sermon by a well-known minister. He felt sure that man could help him, and he went to see him. He was cordially received and stayed in the minister's study for a long time, and when he came out there was a new light in his eyes. "*What a man he is,*" he said. "*When I went into his office all the stars had fallen out of my skies—but one by one he put them back again.*"—Archer Wallace, in *Leaves of Healing,* Harper Brothers, publishers.

* * *

Helping Others

D. L. Moody says, "It is very easy to preach when others are all the time praying for you." In an illustration, he says, "You have heard the story, I suppose, of the child who was rescued from the fire that was raging in a house away up in the fourth story. The child came to the window and as the flames were shooting up higher and higher, it cried out for help. A fireman started up the ladder of the fire escape to rescue the child from its dangerous position. The wind swept the flames near him, and it was getting so hot that he wavered, and it looked as if he would have to return without the child. Thousands looked on, and their hearts quaked at the thought of the child having to perish in the fire, as it must do if the fireman did not reach it. Someone in the crowd cried, 'Give him a cheer!' Cheer after cheer went up, and as the man heard them he gathered fresh courage. Up he went into the midst of the smoke and the fire, and brought down the child to safety."

In the day when rewards are given, the one who did the cheering in the service of the Lord "shall in no wise lose his reward" (Matt. 10:42).

Beloved, if you cannot do much, you can at least be among the ones that "helped every one his neighbor; and every one said to his brother, Be of good courage."

"Brother, for Christ's Kingdom sighing,
Help a little, help a little;
Help to save the millions dying,
Help just a little.

"Oh the wrongs that we may righten!
Oh the hearts that we may lighten!
Oh the skies that we may brighten!
Helping just a little."

—*Gospel Herald.*

* * *

An Authentic Lincoln Story

There is a story in regard to Lincoln that ought not to be lost to our people and nation. This story certainly has never been published in full. It is likely that the present writer is the only living person to whom it was communicated directly; at least, who remembers it sufficiently well to relate it clearly.

In council with Stanton, Secretary of War, Lincoln said, "Burnside must be removed, but I cannot find a man to take his place. He is doing no good. It seems like everything is against us. I do not know what to do, and cannot see one ray of hope." Stanton could offer no relief, and he left the council room. Lincoln walked with him to the door, and observing two women sitting in the waiting room, asked who they were. "They are two Quaker ladies who want to see you," was the reply. "Let them come next," Lincoln said, although there were others who had arrived earlier, officials on important business.

Rachel Grellet and Elizabeth L. Comstock were ushered into his presence. He received them kindly, and sat down between them. He had met them before; indeed, had given them letters to all army officers, directing that they should be allowed to go wherever they should elect under protection of the army. They had visited various camps and hospitals where, as angels of mercy, they had cheered many a soldier boy in distress, as two saintly mothers administering to their physical, as well as their spiritual needs.

I will relate the story of this visit, as told to me personally by Elizabeth L. Comstock, giving it in her own words, as nearly as I can remember:

"We were seated in the council room with Lincoln alone. We told him that we had been impressed that we ought to come to him with a message of love and cheer and encouragement. In appearance he was downcast and looked as if ready to give up. He said, 'Well, if you have any encouragement for me, please give it. I need it. Be free to say whatever is on your minds to say.' I said, 'Abraham, we believe we have a message from the Lord for thee. He has laid a great burden upon thee, and thou canst not bear it alone. It is too much for thee. He says, Be of good courage and I will be with thee. I will not leave thee nor forsake thee. Thou shalt prevail, only be of good courage. Cast all thy burdens upon Him. He is the great Burden-bearer. Nothing is too hard for Him. The destiny of this great nation is upon Him. Thy shoulders are too narrow. He invites us to cast all our cares upon Him. Do not try to carry it thyself. Look to Him. He will guide thee. He will give thee wisdom and thou shalt prevail. May it not be that God has raised thee up, like Moses, to be the great emancipator of His people? To establish the nation united and free. As He said to Joshua, only be strong and of a good courage.'

"When we had finished our message, as we believed the Lord had given it to us, we arose to go and said, 'We had better not take any more of thy precious time.' He said, 'Aren't you going to pray with me?' With one voice we said, 'We hoped thee would ask for that.' We both knelt, and he between us. We clasped our hands each in front. He reached his broad hand and clasped mine in his right, and that of Rachel in his left, and his hands trembled like a leaf in a breeze. It was a very solemn occasion, and we felt as if we were helping him to roll the burdens off his shoulders, and that Jesus was there ready to receive them. When we had ceased speaking, he said, 'Amen,' good and strong.

When we arose his countenance was so changed he looked as though he had the victory.—Geo. N. Hartley, in *The American Friend.*

* * *

When a man ain't got a cent,
And he's feelin' sort o' blue,
And the clouds hang dark and heavy
And won't let the sunshine through;
It's a great thing, O my brother,
For a fellow just to lay,
His hand upon your shoulder,
In a friendly sort o' way.

It makes a man feel curious,
It makes the tear drops start,
And you feel a sort o' flutter
In the regions round your heart.
You can't look up and meet his eyes,
You don't know what to say,
When a hand's laid on your shoulder
In a friendly sort o' way.

Oh, this world's a curious compound,
With its honey and its gall,
With its cares and bitter crosses,
But a good world after all.
And a good God must have made it;
Leastways that's what I say,
When a hand's laid on my shoulder
In a friendly sort o' way.

—James Whitcomb Riley.

Provoking Christians

Christians are urged "to provoke" one another "unto love and to good works." The word "provoke" means to arouse, incite, hearten. Is it not a most worthy ambition and privilege to awaken and inspire others to live righteously and godly in this present world?

Few are aware of how much failure is due simply to the lack of incentive and courage or the loss of spirit. When the heart goes out of a person, there is no longer any vision to quicken, to cheer, to lead. So it is Christian to hearten and provoke others unto love and good works.

Singing to the merry ring of his trowel, a bricklayer aroused Carlyle from the stupor of despondency and provoked him to rewrite the second volume of his *French Revolution* which had been destroyed in the manuscript.

A line quoted from the New Testament and a pat on the head changed the stupid, shy lad, Walter Scott, and kindled in his heart a quenchless flame. A kiss from his mother at the psychological moment made Benjamin West a painter.

Thus a seasonable word, a mother's prayer, a friendly grasp of the hand, the memory of a face, often turn out to be provoking destiny-making acts. —*Christian Observer.*

* * *

Encouragement from Jeremiah

Early in life I fell in love with Jeremiah. I began preaching rather early; much sooner than I think boys should be allowed to preach. My judgment on the matter now is not in keeping with my feelings then; I felt I had been called of God to preach. Others had the same thought, and I was invited to help in a series of revival meetings in a town some distance from my home. After the first service in which I had preached, as I left the church a very fine woman remarked, "What can he know about God? He is only a child." That woman will never know how near I came to fainting; it was the first word I had heard in opposition to my own desire. I at once decided that I should take the first train for home in the morning. I do not remember ever in my life to have felt more dejected and forlorn. My habit was to read a portion of Scripture before retiring for the night. I opened my Bible at random and my eyes espied these words: "But the Lord said unto me, Say not, I am a child: for thou shalt go to all that I shall send thee, and whatsoever I command thee thou shalt speak. Be not afraid of their faces: for I am with thee to deliver thee, saith the Lord" (Jer. 1:7, 8). I will confess I rather fell in love with Jeremiah. The train that would take me from the pulpit had not yet started. I did not run away, but had the joy of seeing many souls brought to God.—Dr. F. B. Stockdale.

* * *

Encouragement for God's People

Dr. F. B. Meyer used to say that if he had his preaching ministry to live over again he would preach more sermons of encouragement to God's people. Surely in such a day as this, whatever encouragement can be brought should not be withheld, for it is sorely needed. The Christian faith is basically optimistic because it views the changing scenes of experience in the light of the "unchangeable counsel" of the living God. Because with Him there is "no shadow of turning" we may indeed have "strong encouragement, who have fled for refuge to lay hold upon the hope set before us." —Courtesy *Moody Monthly.*

* * *

Why He "Dasn't Quit"

A young man had a class of boys in a mission Sunday school. Little fellows, they were, and their new teacher's kindness and tact and genuine interest in them had won them to him completely. After a while the young man became rather discouraged with his efforts among them. He went down early that last Sunday—he wanted to get his records all in shape — and while he sat working in the office adjoining the Sunday school room, two of his boys came in. One announced that he wasn't coming any more; teacher was going to quit, and he was going to quit, too. The other one flatly contradicted the first speaker's statement. The two continued to talk, but no argument could convince the one lad that teacher would quit. "Why," he declared, "he dasn't quit. I was the first boy in his class, and one Sunday he told us kids that God sent him to teach us, an' he said God was his boss, and he had to do wot He said. He's God's man, and he dasn't quit." And the young man didn't quit. He took the vision that was given him to heart. He caught the message of encouragement and cheer, of promise that came to him from God, through the medium of the boy who felt that teacher must make good because he was "God's man."—*Comprehensive Quarterly.*

What Changed Him

When Sir Walter Scott was a boy, he was considered a great dullard. His accustomed place in the schoolroom was the ignominious dunce corner with the high pointed paper cap of shame on his head. One evening when he was twelve or fourteen, he chanced to be in a home where famous literary guests were being entertained. The great Robert Burns was standing admiring a picture under which was written the couplet of a stanza. He inquired concerning the author. None of the great people present knew. Timidly a boy crept up to his side, whispered the name of the author, and quoted the rest of the poem. Burns was surprised and delighted. Laying his hand on the youth's head, he exclaimed, "Ah, bairnie, ye will be a great mon yet in Scotland some day!"

From that day, Walter Scott was a changed lad. One of the greatest men in the world believed that he would do great things!—*Gospel Herald.*

TREATMENT OF ENEMIES

(See also: Forgiving Others)

How Salvation Acted in Egypt

While holding meetings in Egypt among some soldiers, Rev. J. Stuart Holden asked a big sergeant in a Highland regiment, how he was brought to Christ. His answer was:

"There is a private in our company who was converted in Malta before the regiment came on to Egypt. We gave that fellow an awful time. One night he came in from sentry duty, very tired and wet, and before going to bed he got down to pray. I struck him on the side of the head with my boots, and he just went on with his prayers. Next morning I found my boots beautifully polished by the side of my bed. That was his reply to me. It just broke my heart, and I was saved that day.—*Church of Christ Advocate.*

Conquered by Love

Nearly thirty years ago, in a village in Northern Syria, Abu Dugaam was being severely persecuted because he had begun to believe in the teachings of the foreign missionaries. His father-in-law had taken his new wife away from him. The villagers had torn down his new house. Finally, when he refused again and again to give up his belief in his wonderful Book, he was led out to the edge of the village to be burned to death. He was tied to a pile of wood and was given a chance to say his "last words." Much to the surprise of the excited mob, he neither cursed nor wept. Ignorant of ancient martyrs, but with their selfsame spirit, he knelt and prayed for each of his persecutors. Either in fear or penitence, one by one the angry crowd stole quietly back to the village, leaving Abu Dugaam alone, but nearer to his God.—*The Presbyterian of the South.*

* * *

Loving a Neighbor

During a fierce engagement in the late war a British officer saw a German officer impaled on a barbed wire fence, writhing in agony. The fire was dreadful, yet he hung there unscathed. At length the Britisher said: "I can't bear to look at that poor chap any longer!" So he went out amid the hail of shell, released him, and bore him on his shoulders to the German trench. The firing ceased. While both sides waited in wonderment the German commander stepped out from the trench, took from his own bosom the iron cross, and pinned it upon the Britisher. — *Record of Christian Work.*

* * *

"Love One Another"

A Scotch Highlander, wounded in the World War, was stroking a German spiked helmet as he lay upon a cot in a London hospital. A nurse said to him, "I suppose you killed your man?" "No, indeed," was the reply. "It was like this: he lay on the field, badly wounded and bleeding, and I was in the same condition. I crawled to him and bound up his wounds; he did the same for me. I knew no German, and he knew no English; so I thanked him by just smiling. He thanked me by smiling back. By way of a token I handed him my cap, while he handed me his helmet. Then, lying side by side we suffered together in silence till we were picked up by the ambulance squad. No, I didn't kill my man."—*Christian Herald.*

* * *

Lesson from a Dog

One day Sir Walter Scott threw a rock at a stray dog intending to shoo him away. He threw the rock straighter and stronger than he intended and broke the dog's leg. Instead of the dog running away, he came limping up to Sir Walter and licked the hand that threw the rock, and Sir Walter Scott said he could never get over that as long as he lived.

That dog preached the Sermon on the Mount as few people have ever practiced it.

What the world needs is Christ reincarnated in the Christian. — *Florida Baptist Witness.*

* * *

Forgiveness

Some years ago a band of brigands attacked the homestead of a Manchurian farmer named Tung. They tied him up, burned his home, and carried off his property. Tung, who was an humble Chinese Christian, did not inform the authorities. He bore his loss, restored his home, and went on with his work. About two years afterward he met in the city one of the robber band, who, seeing that he was recognized, begged for mercy. Tung said, "I do not bear any grudge against you. Tell me about yourself." The man, hardly believing his ears, told the story of his troubles. His feet were frostbitten, he owed money at the inn, but had none left, and he was in need of food. "Well," Tung said, "go back and get some food," and he gave him some money, adding, "Go back and pay your account if you can. I will call for you tomorrow and take you to the hospital." The man, who feared that behind his generosity there must be some plot to capture him, would fain have run away in the night, but found it impossible, his feet were so bad. Next day Tung came for him in his own cart and took him to the hospital, saying to himself, "Perhaps he will learn of Jesus as I did, and will come out a different man." And he did.—*Missionary Review of the World.*

* * *

A Greenlander's Revenge

The first missionaries to Greenland had a very difficult task, as for a long time the people refused to listen to their message. But they did not work entirely without success as the following story shows:

Among the Greenlanders it was deemed a sacred duty to revenge sooner or later the murder of a father. A son about fourteen years of age was present when his father was killed. He grew up to manhood and became an active fisherman, and after a few years had passed away he resolved to seek the life of the person who had slain his father.

To secure his object he journeyed a long distance, and came at last to where the missionaries lived. As he listened to their preaching a desire rose in his mind to know more about the Lord of Heaven and earth. In the course of their instruction they told him it was the command of God that he should do no murder, but rather that he should forgive his enemies. He looked at them in silence, and went away in anger and for several days kept away from their house, while he was planning with his friends the best way to effect the intended act of revenge.

He was seen walking up and down the shore as though in great distress of mind, and when he came again to the mission house, he said, "I never felt so before. I will forgive him, and I will not forgive him. I have two hearts which speak different things."

He was told of the Saviour who forgave His enemies as He hung on the Cross. "But He was better than we are," was the reply of the Greenlander.

The death of Stephen was then read to him, when he replied, "Good teacher, my heart is so moved. I will — but give me still a little time: when I have brought the other heart to silence, and am quite changed, I will come again." He did come again; it was with a peaceful look: "Now I am happy," he said, "I hate no more; I have forgiven."

On this occasion a great many people stood around. Before them all he declared his faith in Christ, and turning to the Christians, said, "Receive me now as a believer."

He then sent his enemy this message, "I am now become a believer, and you have nothing to fear." He even invited him to his abode, received him in a friendly manner, and sent him home in safety.

The convert was invited to return the visit. He went alone and unarmed. On his return he had not gone far when he saw water in his boat. He paddled quickly to the shore and found that his enemy had cut a hole in the bottom. When he related this to the missionaries he said with a smile, "He is still afraid I shall slay him for my father's death, and has done this for that reason, but I will not harm him. I have forgiven him!" — Selected.

* * *

How God Delivered Stephen

In the course of a public debate George Holyoake asked Dr. Parker: "What did God do for the martyr Stephen when he was being stoned to death?" Dr. Parker was embarrassed for a moment; then lifting his heart to God gave a reply which he always believed was the Holy Spirit's direct gift. He said: "I believe the Almighty did far more for Stephen than at first appears. He did not send an angel to deliver him in his hour of agony. But God enabled Stephen to say, 'Lord, lay not this sin to their charge;' and when we shall see facts in their eternal values, we shall see that in working this miracle of forgiveness in the heart of Stephen, God did more than if He had sent a legion of angels."—*The Dawn.*

* * *

Cautious

On his death-bed the minister reminded the dying King Frederick William of Prussia of the need of confession of sin. "Well, is there anything more?" he said: "Better now than too late." "There is forgiveness of enemies. Your Majesty is bound to forgive all men, or how can you ask to be forgiven?" "Well, I will, I do. You, Feekin (his wife), write to your brother after I am dead that I forgave him — died in peace with him." "Better Her Majesty should write at once," suggests Roloff. "No; after I am dead," persists the son of nature; "that will be safer." — *Carlyle (condensed).*

Pastor Chen's Reward

Pastor Chen of Hwoshan tells the following: During the time that I was commissioned by the county government as a ward magistrate there was a vagrant named Li K'ai-fan who forcibly seized a small piece of ground belonging to me, for a vegetable garden for himself. I prayed about the affair for three days, after which the Holy Spirit led me to see that I should have no quarrels with worldly people, so I presented him with the parcel of ground. I took the deed to this property to his house and in the presence of witnesses made it over to him in perpetuity. Later the Reds occupied our district working secretly, and Li was made Commander-in-Chief of the surrounding countryside. All the local officials who did not make their escape were to be killed, and I, of course, was no exception. Commander Li gave secret orders that I was not to be molested and anyone passing my house was to go quietly so as not to alarm me as I was a righteous man. If I had gone to law when he seized my land it is certain that not only I but my whole family would have perished. I, being enabled to have the mind of Christ, was spared the calamity that would have resulted from seeking vengeance.—Selected.

* * *

Feeding Everybody

During the last war a Polish woman saw the Quakers feeding the starving on both sides of the conflict. Astonished by such Christian philanthropy, she said to one of them: "You are feeding everybody, aren't you? Poles, Russians, Germans — everybody, friend and foe? Well, I knew there ought to be people like that in the world, but I didn't know that there actually were." —*The Chaplain.*

* * *

A Bishop's Example

It is written in the stirring annals of the Melanesian Mission of a native boy whom Bishop John Selwyn had in training at Norfolk Island. He had been brought from one of the most barbarous of the South Sea peoples, and did not promise particularly well. One day Bishop Selwyn had occasion to rebuke him for his stubborn and refractory behavior. The boy instantly flew into a passion and struck the Bishop a cruel blow in the face. It was an unheard-of incident, and all who saw it stood aghast. The Bishop said nothing, but turned and walked quietly away. The conduct of the lad continued to be most recalcitrant, and he was at last returned to his own island as incorrigible. There he soon relapsed into all the debasements of a savage and cannibal people.

Many years afterward a missionary on that island was summoned post haste to visit a sick man. It proved to be Dr. Selwyn's old student. He was dying and desired Christian baptism. The missionary asked him by what name he would like to be known. "Call me John Selwyn," the dying man replied, "because he taught me what Christ was like when I struck him."—courtesy *Moody Monthly.*

* * *

No Retaliation

Haile Selassie has issued this appeal to his soldiers: "I charge you solemnly to receive kindly and protect those Italians who may surrender to you without arms, and not to retaliate with the cruelty which they inflicted upon our people, but to show yourselves to be honorable, humane soldiers." — *Sunday School Times.*

* * *

On Revenge

When one has done us a wrong we are tempted to feel that we must have revenge upon him else justice will not be done. However, this is not the case. The Lord has said, "Vengeance is Mine; I will repay." If one has actually wronged us we should pray for him as we are commanded to do. His need is great and his punishment will be great if he has this and other sins of which he has not repented.

And remember that whatever ill you may have suffered at his hands, you are far better off than he, for you have had your evil out of the transaction and his is yet to come. It is far better to have been wronged than to have done the wrong. Ask the Lord to put in your heart a real pity for the wrongdoer, then pray for him—*Gospel Gleaners.*

* * *

When We Are Robbed

A few days after my conversion I got a job with a New York contracting company, as a common laborer. Pay-day came. My earnings amounted to thirty-five dollars for a week, and at the close of the day I returned to the Mission very happy. Had I not reason to be happy? It was the first money in years that would not be gambled away; and I felt that now I was able to accept my responsibilities as a husband and father. I prepared to clean up a little before going to the post office (to send the money to his wife), but before I could do so that very first pay was stolen! It would be difficult even to attempt to express my feelings. It was bitter disappointment; it almost caused me to throw everything to the winds... And then an arm was placed around my shoulder. It was the superintendent of the Mission. He said, "I want you to do something for me." I am afraid I turned to him rather roughly as I asked, "Well, what is it?" He replied, "I want you to pray for the man who stole your money." His words almost took my breath away. I thought that was adding insult to injury as my thoughts were anything but to pray for the man; and yet after a few moments, I was on my knees praying for that very man whose act had caused me such bitter disappointment.—*Bible Today.*

* * *

A Startling Title

The author of the famous tract, "Come to Jesus," at one time engaged in a theological dispute. He at last sat down and wrote to some publication of his opponent, an answer, bristling with sarcasm and invective, sharp and cutting as a razor. Reading it to a friend, he asked: "What do you think of it?" "It is a masterpiece of invective," was the reply. "You fairly flay him alive. What have you decided to call it?" "I have not thought of a title. Can you suggest one?" "Well," came the response, "how would it do to call it, 'Go to the Devil,' by the author of 'Come to Jesus'?"—*The King's Business.*

* * *

Christlike

An old Puritan had many enemies because of his faithful stand in reproving sin. Many abusive letters were sent him, all of which he tied up in a packet and wrote on the cover, "Libels. Father, forgive them." And it was his ambition to say: "I do not know of any person in the world who has done me any ill office but I have done him a good one for it." And in the days of the saintly martyr Cranmer it passed into a byword in England, "Do my Lord of Canterbury an ill turn and you make him your friend forever."—R. H. Bennett.

* * *

What Took Away the Bitterness

A poor stonemason in China was robbed by a highwayman and struck on the knee. His knee became infected. After months it healed, but his leg was then doubled up and so stiff that he could not use it. While he was in a Christian hospital where his leg was gradually restored, his neighbors looted his fields and robbed his father. He was yearning to get well to take revenge on his assailant, and now he was even more impatient to get well that he might take it out on his neighbors. But gradually a change came over him, and when he went away, healed and strong, and I was telling him to forgive them as Christ had forgiven him, he said: "Don't you worry. As soon as ever I understood what Christ had done for me, all the bitterness and enmity went out of my heart, and now I don't want to hurt them any more." He took home Gospels and tracts, and came back to tell me how happy he was: all his affairs were prospering, and his family and neighbors becoming interested in the truth. He was a great, big, strong fellow who would have plunged into a lifelong feud, but for the Saviour; and he is now heaping coals of fire on the heads of his enemies by evangelizing them.—*The Earnest Worker.*

* * *

The Christian's Victory

When Richard Weaver was a pit worker, he inadvertently angered a fellower-miner. "I have a good mind to smack you on the face," the man exclaimed.

"Very well," Weaver replied, "if that will do any good, you may do it."

The man struck him. Weaver turned to him the other cheek. The man struck again. This was repeated five times; and when Weaver presented his cheek for the sixth time, the man turned away, cursing.

Weaver cried after him: "The Lord forgive thee, for I do; and the Lord save thee!"

His assailant was the first man Weaver met next morning in the pit; and, as Weaver approached, he burst into tears. "Oh, Richard," he cried, "do you really forgive me?"

Together they knelt and he rose a saved man.—*Gospel Herald.*

* * *

When Mud Brushes Off Best

A young man had been badly insulted, and, full of angry indignation, declared that he was going at once to demand an apology. "My dear boy," said Father Graham, a beloved old man of the village, "take a word of advice from an old man who loves peace. An insult is like mud; it will brush off much better when it is dry. Wait a little, till he and you are both cool, and the thing will be easily mended. If you go now it will only be to quarrel." The young man took his advice, and before the next day was done the insulting person came to beg forgiveness.—*Gospel Herald.*

FAITH

Faith

"If there should arise one utterly believing man, the history of the world might be changed!"—Selected.

* * *

"If you have any certainties, let us have them. We have doubts enough of our own!"—Goethe.

* * *

A Testimony of the "57" Varieties Man:

Henry J. Heinz, of the Fifty-seven Varieties fame, wrote his will as follows: "Looking forward to the time when my earthly career will end, I desire to set forth at the very beginning of this will, as the most important item in it, a confession of my faith in Jesus Christ as my Saviour. I also desire to bear witness to the fact that throughout my life, in which were the usual joys and sorrows, I have been wonderfully sustained by my faith in God through Jesus Christ. This legacy was left me by my consecrated mother, a woman of strong faith, and to it I attribute any success I have attained."—Selected.

* * *

What Faith Can Do

Oh, brethern, be great believers! Little faith will bring your souls to Heaven, but great faith will bring Heaven to your soul.—H. Spurgeon.

* * *

She Was Right

The old Scotch lady was right. When she was visited by a very young minister who was short on experience, she held fast to her firm assurance of her safety in Christ. "But just suppose that after all God should let you sink into hell?" said the minister. "He would lose more than I would," came the firm answer of faith. "All I would lose would be my own soul, but He would lose His good name." Yes, she was right. The security of the believer does not depend on the individual ability to hold on, but on the eternal power of our God and Saviour Jesus Christ.—*Gospel Herald.*

* * *

"I Believe"

I believe Jesus Christ to be the Son of God. The miracles which He wrought establish in my mind His personal authority, and render it proper for me to believe whatever He asserts. I believe, therefore, all His declarations, as well when He declares Himself to be the Son of God as when He declares any other proposition. And I believe there is no other way of salvation than through the merits of His atonement. —Daniel Webster.

* * *

The Reward of Faith

Faith knows that God has His moment, and in that moment everything yields to His will. Faith can wait. If she comes to a prison gate, she can stand without until God touches the bars, and it flies open. If the enemy hurls rocks from the battlement, she stands unmoved and unharmed. Faith knows some Jerichos need to be compassed fourteen times, and she carries with her the word of victory to give the final shout.—Selected.

* * *

We Don't Need Crucifixes

They tell the story of a young soldier in Italy who jumped into a fox hole just the seat-of-his-pants ahead of a bullet. Crouching and digging in a bit better, his hand touched metal, and he brought up a silver crucifix, left no doubt, by a former occupant. A moment later another leaping figure landed beside him as the shells screamed. When the soldier got a chance to look, he saw that his companion was an army chaplain. Holding out the crucifix, the soldier gasped, "Am I glad to see you! How do you work this thing?" We smile at the naive ignorance of the soldier. But isn't it wonderful to know that we don't need crucifixes, nor do we need to know "how to work" them. All we need, whether in or out of fox holes, is a personal faith in the living Christ who once died on the cross for our sins, but who is now alive forevermore.—*Christian Victory.*

* * *

Simple Faith

In the spring of 1875, Hudson Taylor, the beloved founder of the China Inland Mission, was returning to London from Brighton, where he had been attending some meetings. Waiting for his train at the station, he was accosted by a Russian nobleman who had also attended the meetings, and who, on learning that Mr. Taylor was going to London, suggested that they should find seats together.

"But I am traveling third class," said the missionary.

"My ticket admits of my doing the same," was the courteous reply.

And they seem to have found a carriage alone together, for presently Count Bobrinsky took out his pocketbook with the words, "Allow me to give you a trifle toward your work in China."

Glancing at the bank note as he received it, Mr. Taylor felt there must be some mistake—it was no less than fifty pounds.

"Did you mean to give me five pounds?" Mr. Taylor asked at once. "Please let me return this note; it is for fifty pounds."

"I cannot take it back," replied the other, no less surprised. "It was five pounds I meant to give, but God must have intended you to have fifty pounds; I cannot take it back."

Impressed with the incident, Mr. Taylor reached Pyrland Road, the London home of the Mission, to find a prayer meeting going on. A remittance was about to be sent to China, and the money in hands was short by forty-nine pounds, eleven shillings, of the sum it was felt would be required. This deficiency was not accepted as inevitable. On the contrary, it called together those who knew of it for special prayer. Forty-nine pounds, eleven shillings, was being asked for in simple faith, and there upon the office table Mr. Taylor laid his precious bank note for fifty pounds. Could it have come more directly from the Heavenly Father's hand? "Whoso is wise, and will observe these things, even they shall understand the lovingkindness of the Lord."—Selected.

* * *

The Jewish and Gentile Trains

The Jewish train came to a dead stop. A faulty engine rendered it useless, and it was to be shunted to a siding. God then requisitioned the Gentile train to fulfill His purposes. It had been in course of preparation since 606 B. C. After twenty-five hundred years the same engine trouble has developed. The times of the Gentiles are fulfilled, and the Jewish express, to which God is fitting new engines, will be on the main line once again. What is wrong with the Gentile engine? The same old Jewish fault—unbelief. "Have any of the rulers . . . believed on him?" (John 7:48). Do not many of our leaders, professors, popular preachers, bishops, and scientists deny the Christ who bought them? "The utterances of Jesus are unreliable," we are told; but the utterances of a German professor are evidently reliable! The same engine trouble. — *The Jewish Era.*

* * *

Ice in the Tropics?

A poor heathen woman became a Christian, and was remarkable for her simple faith. In accepting Christ, she took Him literally at His word. Some months after her conversion her little child fell sick. Its recovery was doubtful. Ice was needed for the little one, but in that tropical country, away from the great cities, it was not to be had. "I'm going to ask God to send ice," the mother said to the missionary. "Oh," but you can't expect that He will do that," was the quick reply. "Why not?" asked the simple-hearted believer. "He has all the power, and He loves us. You told us so. I shall ask Him, and I believe He will send it." She did ask Him, and God answered. Soon there came up a heavy thunder storm, accompanied by hail. The woman was able to gather a large bowlful of hailstones. The cold application was just what was needed, and the child recovered.—*The Illustrator.*

* * *

The One Essential

When the impotent man and the healing pool and the Master came together, there was health and hope. When the little lad and the few loaves and fishes and the Master came together, there was sufficiency and even abundance. A thirsty woman, an ancient well, and the Master, and there were streams of living water flowing into human hearts. A rugged fisherman, a broken net, and the Master, and there was discipleship, and a story to tell. Wherever a human need and a sincere faith and the Master meet, there is transformation and consecration. If we bring our lives, weak and insufficient, to the Master, He will remake us.—*The Upper Room.*

* * *

Oh, blissful lack of wisdom,
'Tis blessed not to know;
He holds me with his own right hand,
And will not let me go;
And lulls my troubled soul to rest,
In Him who loves me so.

So on I go—not knowing,
I would not if I might;
I'd rather walk in the dark with God
Than go alone in the light;
I'd rather walk by faith with Him
Than go alone by sight.—Selected.

Luther's Discovery

As I stood in that little out-of-the-way church in Rome and watched the worshipers climbing Santa Scala on their knees, I could but wish that they, too, like Martin Luther, might find freedom of soul. We recall that "as a monk, Luther had happened on a volume of the Scriptures. He knew it only as a forbidden book. He read it furtively until he came to the place where it is written, 'There is none other name under heaven given among men, whereby we must be saved.' . . . He read, 'By the deeds of the law there shall no flesh be justified. . . .' 'What the law could not do, in that it was weak through the flesh, God sending his own Son. . . .' The light began to break. He betook himself to Rome. Great were his anticipations; a sore disappointment awaited him. . . . He looked for voluntary poverty and simple piety; the air was full of ambition and political intrigue. He determined on penance by climbing . . . the Sacred Stairway, on his knees. Half way up he seemed to hear a voice saying, 'The just shall live by faith!' and the day broke. He stood erect, a believer in Christ as his only Saviour from sin."—From personal reminiscence, and from *Christ and Progress*, by Burrell.

* * *

What Does the Creator Need?

In looking to God for deliverance of any kind we are prone to try to discover what material he has on hand to work on in coming to our relief. It is so human to look for something in sight that will help the Lord out. Just think a moment, it is not at all necessary for God to have any relief on hand. He does not need anything to begin on. In the beginning God created the heavens and the earth. What did He make them out of? Nothing, absolutely nothing. When the earth was made what did He hang it on? Nothing. Pretty satisfactory earth to be made of nothing, eh? Remember not a scrap of anything was used to make it. "He . . . hangeth the earth upon nothing." It hangs all right, doesn't it? Very well, then. A God who can make an earth, a sun, a moon, and stars out of nothing, and keep them hanging on nothing, can supply all your needs whether He has anything to work with or not. Wonderful, isn't it? Trust Him and He will see you through, though He has to make your supplies out of nothing.—From the tract, *He Can.*

* * *

The Word of an Emperor

One day Emperor Napoleon's horse reared and pitched and charged, and he was about to lose control of his steed, when a big burly private, seeing his danger, dashed up and grabbed the horses reins near his mouth and settled him down. The Emperor showed his hearty appreciation by saluting and saying, "Thank you, Captain."

The private in quick response returned the salute, and enquired simply, "Of what company?"

The Emperor, highly pleased with this full faith in his sincerity, resaluted and said, "Of my bodyguard."

The captain wheeled on his horse, and riding back to the bodyguard, said, as he saluted, "Your captain!"

Returning the salute the officer in charge asked, "By whose authority?"

The captain answered, as he pointed to the Emperor, "By his," and the event was closed. *The whole transaction hinged upon faith in a man's word. Behold what a change resulted.* Yet not nearly so great as the change which takes place in our lives as we simply, sweetly trust our Crown Prince, our Captain General, our divine and omnipotent Leader, Christ Jesus. — *Canadian Baptist.*

* * *

He That Believeth

He that believeth shall not make haste
In useless hurry his strength to waste;
Who walks with God can afford to wait,
For He can never arrive too late.

He that believeth shall not delay;
Who carries the Word of the King on its
way
Keeps pace with the Pleiades' marching
tune,
And he can never arrive too soon.

He that believeth shall walk serene,
With ordered steps and leisured mien;
He dwells in the midst of eternities,
And the timeless ages of God are his.
—Annie J. Flint, in *The Church of God Evangel.*

* * *

The Faith That Honors God

A faith that will believe without encouragement from others. — Abraham (Gen. 18:9-15; Rom. 4:19, 20).

A faith that will believe without encouragement from God.—The Syrophenician woman (Matt. 15:22-28).

A faith that will believe without previous experience.—Noah (Heb. 11:7).

A faith that will believe without hurrying to prove.—The nobleman of Capernaum (John 4:47-53).

It is this calm, unswerving steadiness that marks matured faith, though many a tottering moment is apt to spoil its earlier steps while the evil heart of unbelief remains.—Selected.

* * *

Finding the Meaning

When the late Dr. John G. Paton was a missionary in the New Hebrides, he wanted to translate the Gospel of John into the native tongue. He had worked on the Gospel and found that there wasn't a word—at least he couldn't locate a word—in the native tongue which meant "believe." How could he translate the Gospel of John without a word for "believe"? If it is the key word (and it is) and if it is true that the word occurs more than ninety times (and it does), how could you translate it if you didn't have any word to correspond with it? So he laid his manuscript aside.

But one day one of the native workers who had been out over the hills in some Christian service came in to Dr. Paton's office, and sitting in one chair and putting his feet up on another, he used a native word which meant, "I am resting my whole weight on these two chairs." There was one native word which meant all this—"I am resting my whole weight upon." And Dr. Paton said, "I have my word." He translated the Gospel of John, and every time he needed a word for "believe," he put in the word which meant, "I am resting my whole weight upon."

Let us try it and see how it works. "For God so loved the world that he gave his only begotten Son, that whosoever *resteth his whole weight upon him* should not perish, but have everlasting life" (John 3:16). "But as many as received him, to them gave he power to become the sons of God, even to them that *rest their whole weight upon him*" (John 1:12). Is that it? Yes, that is it! "What must I do to be saved?" "*Rest your whole weight upon* the Lord Jesus Christ, and thou shalt be saved." Is that it? Yes, that is it!—Will H. Houghton, in *The Living Christ.*

* * *

"Help Thou Mine Unbelief"

A church of which I was at one time pastor was heavily in debt, and I made it a matter of prayer. One day a stranger called on me and said, "Mr. McNeill, I understand that you have a debt on your church that you are anxious to pay. I have heard a great deal about your work and I want to help." Then laying a blank check on my desk, he said, "Fill in the amount you require and I will return later and sign it." Then he was gone.

As I sat looking at that check I said, "Surely he doesn't realize that our debt runs into thousands of pounds. He would never give that much. He told me to make it out for the full amount, but I'll just put down half. I'm afraid he will not even sign that much."

After a little while the stranger returned, and with scarcely a glance signed the check, and left without another word. I looked at the signature; it was that of a well-known philanthropist. When I realized that he meant what he said, and could easily have paid the whole debt, I exclaimed, "Oh, man of little faith, I will never doubt again." — *The King's Business.*

* * *

When Blind Eyes Were Opened

Moody told this story at one of his meetings: One evening just before Christmas, a man was walking through the streets of an Eastern city. The store windows were all beautifully decorated, and he observed three little girls intensely interested in one of them. He discovered that the girl in the center was blind, and the others were trying to describe the beautiful things in the window. "Why," they said, "can't you see that Teddy bear and that doll? Just look at that pretty pink bow!" But the poor little girl stood with a blank expression on her face and could not appreciate the beautiful things before her. "Now," said Moody, "this is an illustration of the effort we Christians are making to arouse the unconverted to an interest and delight in spiritual things. The reason we cannot do so is because the sinner is spiritually blind," and he quoted 1 Corinthians 2:14. Moody had scarcely concluded when an infidel reporter was on the platform asking him where he had heard that story. "Oh," said Moody, "I read it in one of the daily papers. I have forgotten which one." "Then," said the infidel, "I wrote it myself, and I was the man who saw that little blind girl. I see now that *I am spiritually blind.*" That man was converted then and there.—*The Herald of Salvation.*

* * *

The Prospects

Faith in God makes great optimists. Over in Burma Judson was lying in a foul jail with thirty-two pounds of chains on his ankles, his feet bound to a bamboo pole. A fellow prisoner said, with a sneer on his face, "Dr. Judson, what about the prospect of the conversion of the heathen? His instant reply was, "The prospects are just as bright as the promises of God."—*The Presbyterian Advance.*

One Step Enough

Ten of us met in New York to sail. We were faith missionaries, with no board to take care of us. There was no home ready for us to go to as far as we knew. No one was pledged to send us money. None of these things troubled me at first. I must have been half way across the Atlantic before I began seriously to wonder where I would go when I finally reached India. But it did come to me at last and then I began to pray about it. Then God gave me a dream. I saw myself standing on a tiny little plank which was floating in a vast ocean. Absolutely nothing in front of me, or behind me, or at the sides. But, as I lifted my foot as if to step, another little board appeared just in front, ready for me to step on it. So God comforted me and seemed to be telling me that I was to trust Him for one step at a time. And so I went happily on, always finding a plank in front ready to be stepped on when needed.—From *My Life,* by Mrs. W. K. Norton, of the Pilgrim's Mission, Benares, India.

* * *

Things That Can't Be Done

Faith achieves the impossible. During the World War a lad at the front was carried back wounded very badly; but all aflame with enthusiasm, he looked up into the surgeon's face and said: "I tell you, Doc, they do things out there *that can't be done.*" That is the kind of faith that achieves.—*Sunday School Times.*

* * *

Was He a Fool?

I remember a missionary from China stating that while preaching to the bluejackets on a British man-of-war at the Port of Wei hi Wai, he was accosted at the close of his discourse by a sailor, saying, "I will not believe what you have told us until you inform me why God allowed sin to come into the world." The missionary was a blunt man and his answer came quickly. "Man," he said, "you are a fool and I will prove it. Suppose a man was on the top floor of an eleven-story building and a fire broke out in the first floor. The man heard the cries of fire but he kept on reading a book. Finally the flames burst right into his room. He rushed to the window, saw a fire escape there and firemen below. Instead of climbing down the ladder to safety he shouted down to the firemen, 'I won't come down until you tell me how the fire started in the building.' What would you think of that man?" he inquired of the sailor. "I would say he was a fool," the sailor blurted out, and by his statement he thus condemned himself.—*Gospel Herald.*

* * *

Do You Go With a Large Basket?

Madaki, the chief elder in the church, is also one of the most prosperous farmers in Kwoi, Nigeria. On a recent Sunday the following announcement was made: "Madaki wants all the women to gather at his house tomorrow morning, Pass on the news." When the women went to his house next morning, Madaki asked them to go to his farm, about three and a half miles away, to carry home his field corn. One hundred and four women and girls responded and went to the farm with their baskets, little, big, and middle-sized. Some brought back a big load, others only a few ears of grain. One took such a load that her strength failed before she got home. When all the loads had been brought in, Madaki called the women together and told them that each might keep what she had brought! There were shouts of joy and thanksgiving, but also sighs of regret. "If only I had known, I would have taken a larger basket," was the plaint of some. There were those who had refused to go, saying, "I have work enough of my own." These went to Madaki the following morning (their work seemed less important now!) and begged him to let them go and bring in a load. But he told them quietly, "The time is past; the corn was brought in yesterday." Through this kind deed Madaki not only helped many needy families, but he also preached a quiet sermon. The Christians are telling and retelling the story all over town, always adding: "That is just how it is in the Jesus way." — *Sudan Witness.*

* * *

Don't Trust This Plank

Don't watch your feelings. There is not one verse from Genesis to Revelation about being saved by feelings. When the devil sees a poor soul in agony in the waves of sin, and getting close to the Rock of Ages, he just holds out the plank of "feeling" to him, and says, "There, get on that; you feel more comfortable now, don't you?" And, while the man stands getting his breath again, out goes the plank from under him, and he is worse off than ever. Accept no refuge but the Rock of Ages.—*Glad Tidings.*

* * *

The Most Important Thing in Life

Dr. Howard A. Kelly, a great scientist and brilliant surgeon, seated in his library a few years ago, surrounded by an imposing array of books on medicine and surgery, said: *"A definite Christian faith is the one really important thing in life. I mean that literally.* It is vastly more important than my profession, than any scientific research, or than any other or all the activities of a man's life, and that from a strictly practical, common-sense point of view. The intimate experiences of life have shown me that the Bible is a living word, just as definitely God's word to me, personally. As such, the Bible is its own defense."—Courtesy *Moody Monthly.*

* * *

Better Than Faith in Prayer

Dr. McCormick, in "The Heart of Prayer," tells of a good woman whose daughter had died after a painful illness. She came to her minister and said, "I fear I have lost my faith in prayer. I used to believe that anything I asked for in the name of Christ, I would receive. When my child was sick, I besought God in an agony of desire for her recovery. I believed that God would answer my prayer. When she died I was stunned, not merely because of my grief, but because it seemed to me that God had failed me. I pray still, but the old faith in prayer is gone." This good woman was the victim of wrong teaching. She had, in a word, been led to substitute faith in prayer for faith in God. If our faith in prayer is uppermost, then any disapointment will shake that faith. But if faith in God is the great fact of life, then no matter what may be the outcome of our petitions we will still trust.—*The Presbyterian.*

* * *

Is Sight the Real Test?

After listening to a Gospel address, an infidel asked permission to speak. Permission being given he spoke as follows: "Friends, I don't believe what this man has said; I don't believe in hell; I don't believe in a judgment; I don't believe in God; for I never saw one of them." When he sat down another man arose and said: "Friends, you say there is a river not far from this place. It is untrue. You tell me there are trees and grass growing round where I am standing. That also is not true. You say there are a great number of people standing here. Again I say that is not true. There is no one here save myself. I suppose you wonder what I am talking about, but I was born blind; I never saw one of you; and while I talk it only shows that I am blind, or I would not say such things. And you," he said, turning to the infidel, "the more you talk, the more you expose your ignorance, because you are spiritually blind. Pray that your eyes may be opened.—*Prophetic News.*

* * *

What Don't You Believe?

The captain of the old ironclad Merrimac was skeptical concerning spiritual things. One day the chaplain of the Pennsylvania Soldiers' Home, where he was staying, gave him this challenge: "Read the Bible, and mark in red anything you don't believe. Begin with the Gospel of John." With a glitter in his eye the captain accepted the challenge. Whenever the chaplain would pass the room where the captain was confined because of illness, he would stop and say, "Captain, have you marked anything yet?" The old captain would only grin and remain silent. A number of days later the chaplain stepped into his room to find him dead upon his bed. His Bible was open, and the chaplain began looking through the Gospel of John for red marks. Nothing was marked in all the first chapter nor in all the second, nor in all the third until he came to the sixteenth verse. Beside this one he found these words, written in red, "I have cast my anchor in a safe harbor, thank God." —*Grace and Truth.*

* * *

I Cannot Feel Saved

Martin Luther, in one of his conflicts with the devil, was asked by the archenemy if he felt his sins forgiven. "No," said the great Reformer, "I don't feel that they are forgiven, but I know they are, because God says so in His Word." Paul did not say, "Believe in the Lord Jesus Christ, and thou shalt *feel* saved"; but, "Believe on the Lord Jesus Christ, and thou shalt *be* saved." — *Scattered Seed.*

* * *

Faith and Works

A ferryman had the word "faith" painted on one oar and the word "work" on the other. He was asked the reason for thus "naming" the oars, and replied by showing rather than by words. He laid the oar that had "work" painted on it in the bottom of the skiff, took the oar that had "faith" on it, and with both hands pulled with all his strength, and the boat went round and round, gradually floating down the stream with the current. Then he placed faith oar in the bottom of the skiff and took up work oar with both hands, with the same result, the boat gradually floating down the stream. Then he took faith oar in one hand, work oar in the other, and pulled with both together, and the skiff moved out of the current and across the stream.

It takes both faith and works to get anywhere in the Christian life. Doing is evidence that one believes.—*The Cumberland Presbyterian.*

* * *

Don't Examine Your Faith

An extract from a letter written by a minister to a brother minister whose faith was failing through illness: "Are you not making the mistake of examining your faith rather than the promises upon which that faith should rest? If you were traveling a new public highway and should approach a bridge of whose strength you were not satisfied, would you stop to examine your faith in that bridge, or dismount and examine the structure itself? Common sense would tell you to examine the *bridge*, and then, when satisfied of its strength, you would cross over with confidence. So now I beg you, dear brother, look away to the promises that were made by God whom you have served so long, and trust Him though He slay you. Remember the bridge."—*Sunday School Times.*

* * *

Are We Doing the Same?

Little Charlie said, "Mother, what is it to believe in Jesus?" "To think that He loves you, that He died for you, that He cares for you." Charlie stopped playing with his toys, and was still. His mother said, "What are you doing?" "Believing on Jesus."—*The Pentecostal Herald.*

* * *

The Faith of God

The man that is full of faith lives in two worlds, and he uses the faculties that are intended for both worlds. . . . Let me give you a very simple little parable. Three philosophers were deputed to pronounce upon the nature of a certain substance. The substance was really honey, but it was so disguised that they did not recognize it. The first philosopher said that judging from its color, he believed it to be bitter. The second philosopher said that judging from its odor, it surely was acid. The third philosopher said that, judging from its softness it must be salt. But there was a little girl, no philosopher, and she said, "I know it is sweet, because I have tasted it." There is a faculty, a spiritual faculty, of taste. "Oh, taste and see that the Lord is good." *The man that is full of faith lives in both worlds and he uses both sets of faculties—that of sense and that of faith.*—Evan H. Hopkins.

* * *

Only God's Word!

There is an easy, practical way to have faith. A minister said to an evangelist who was holding services in his church: "I have no faith in this matter, but I see it in the Word of God and I am going to act on God's Word, no matter how I feel." And the evangelist replied, "Why, that *is* faith!" The Word of God is the secret of faith. "Faith cometh by hearing, and hearing by the word of God." We do not attain or achieve faith; we simply receive it as we read God's Word. . . . Many a child of God is failing to enjoy God's richest blessings in Christ because he fails to receive the gift of faith. He looks within himself for some quality that will enable him to believe, instead of "looking unto Jesus" who is "the author and finisher of our faith." "If our faith were but more simple, we would take Him at His word."—*Sunday School Times.*

* * *

When Fording Unknown Rivers

The incident that gave Andrew Fuller his text for the famous sermon on faith preached to the Northamptonshire Association is full of illuminations. There had been heavy rain. The rivers were flooded, and at one crossing Fuller, who was riding on horseback, hesitated. A farmer watching him, shouted, "Go on, sir, you are quite safe." Fuller urged his horse into the water, but when it rose to the saddle he stopped again. "Go on, sir; all is right!" came the voice, and Fuller found in a few paces that the water shallowed. "We walk by faith, not by sight." But our walk is on solid ground, though it is hidden from us.—*Sunday School Chronicle.*

Daniel Webster's Saviour

This story is told of Daniel Webster when he was in the prime of his manhood. He was dining with a company of literary men in Boston. During the dinner the conversation turned upon the subject of Christianity. Mr. Webster frankly stated his belief in the divinity of Christ and his dependence upon the atonement of the Saviour. One said to him, "Mr. Webster, can you comprehend how Christ could be both God and man?" Mr. Webster promptly replied, *"No, sir, I cannot comprehend it. If I could comprehend Him, He would be no greater than myself. I feel that I need a superhuman Saviour."—Christian Witness.*

* * *

Why the Banker Became "Practical."

A minister tells how in his first parish a banker occasionally came to his church, and every time he came he happened to be preaching on faith. The banker said to him: "Why don't you preach on something else than faith? Why don't you get something practical?" A few days later there was a run on his bank and the minister went down to see what was going on. He found the foreign people demanding their money; they were alarmed and suspicious, and the banker was going up and down the line saying to these people: "Everything is all right. There is nothing wrong with the bank." The minister touched him on the shoulder and said, "What is the matter?" "Why," he said, "there is nothing wrong; but these people have lost faith in the bank; their confidence has been shaken. If you can say anything or do anything to restore their confidence, I wish you would do it." "What about faith? You remember when you told me to preach on something more practical than faith?" "Oh, yes," he said, "I remember it very well, and I take it all back. After all, there is nothing so fundamental to the business interests and commercial life of America as faith."—*Sunday School Times.*

The Blind Man's Confidence

A poet and an artist once examined a painting representing the healing of the two blind men of Jericho. The artist asked, "What seems to you the most remarkable thing in this painting?" The poet said, "Everything is very clear—the groupings of the individuals, the expression upon the faces, etc." The artist found the most significant touch elsewhere. He pointed to the steps of a house in a corner of the picture. "Do you see that discarded cane lying there?" "Yes," said the poet, "but what does that signify?" "The blind man who has rushed to Jesus is so sure he will be healed," said he, "that he has left his cane behind. He will need it no more and rushes to the Lord as though he could already see." Too often we hold on to canes and crutches of our own devising instead of looking only to Jesus, the Author and Finisher of our faith!—*The King's Business.*

* * *

What Is It to Believe?

There is a word in common use in Scotland—"lippen"—which Dr. Chalmers would use in conversation with anxious souls to explain the act of trusting in Jesus Christ. The word expresses the condition of a person who, entirely unable to support or protect himself, commits his interests, or life, to the safe keeping of some person or object. Thus a man crossing a chasm on a plank, "lippens" to the plank. One day the doctor visited a poor old bedridden woman who was dying. He tried to make her understand the way of salvation. But alas! it seemed all in vain. The mind he strove to enlighten had been closed so long that it appeared impossible to thrust into it a single ray of light. At last she said, "Ah! sir, I would fain do as you bid me, but I dinna ken how; how can I trust in Christ?" "O woman," was his expressive answer, in the dialect of the district, "just 'lippen' to Him." "Eh, sir," was the reply, "and is that all?" "Yes, yes," was his gratified response; just 'lippen' to Him and lean on Him, and you will never perish." To that poor dying woman the word was a light from Heaven, and it guided her to the knowledge of the Savior, and to the enjoyment of salvation through faith in Him.—*Alliance Weekly.*

* * *

Faith

There was once a good woman who was well-known among her circle for her simple faith and her great calmness in the midst of many trials. Another woman, living at a distance, hearing of her, said, "I must go and see that woman, and learn the secret of her calm, happy life." She went, and, accosting the woman, said, "Are you the woman with the great faith?" "No," was the answer, "I am not the woman with the great faith, but *I am the woman with the little faith in the great God.*"—*Sunday School Times.*

* * *

Simplicity of Faith

An elderly woman was starting on a railroad journey from a terminal out of which many trains move, although in different directions. Not having traveled much on the trains, she got confused. Afraid that she was on the wrong train, she showed her ticket to somebody in the seat immediately in front of her and said, "I want to go to Bay City, Michigan. Is this the right train?" "Yes, madam." Still, she was not quite at ease, for she thought that perhaps this fellow passenger might have got into the wrong train too; so she stepped across the aisle of the car, and showed her ticket to another person, and was again told, "Yes, madam, this is the right train." But the woman was a little uncertain still. In a few moments a man came in with the conductor's insignia on his cap; she beckoned to him, and said, "I want to go to Bay City; is this the right train?" "Yes, madam, this is the right train." And now she settled back in her seat, and was asleep before the train pulled out! *This illustrates the simplicity of taking God at His word. She did nothing but just receive the testimony of that conductor. That is all; but that is faith.*—Arthur T. Pierson.

* * *

Faith Alone

Dr. A. J. Gordon, while traveling on a train, engaged in a spirited conversation with a fellow passenger on the subject of "Faith." "I differ with you," said the man, "in that any person is admitted to Heaven because of a little bit of theological scrip called 'Faith.' I believe that when God receives one into Heaven He makes a searching inquiry as to his character rather than inspection of his faith." Presently the conductor came along and examined the tickets. When he passed, Dr. Gordon said: "Did you ever notice how a conductor looks at the ticket and takes no pains to inspect the passenger? A railway ticket, if genuine, certifies that the person presenting it has complied with the company's conditions and is entitled to transportation. So 'faith' alone, my friend, entitles one to that saving grace which produces a character well pleasing to God. 'Without faith it is impossible to please him.'"
—*Alliance Weekly.*

FAITHFULNESS, GOD'S

(See also: Care, God's)

How Faithful God Is

Charles Haddon Spurgeon, the prince of preachers, telling about his grandfather in one of his sermons, said: "He had a large family and a very small income, but he loved his Lord, and he would not have given up his preaching of the Gospel for anything, not even for an imperial crown. He has told me often how the Lord provided for him. He had a little farm to get his living upon it, and he had a cow which used to give milk for his many children, and one day when he came up to the cow it fell back with the staggers and died. Grandmother said, 'James, how will God provide for the dear children now? What shall we do for milk?' 'Mother,' he said, 'God said He would provide, and I believe He could send us fifty cows if He pleased.'

"It so happened that on that day a number of gentlemen were meeting in London, persons whom he did not know, were sitting as a committee for the distribution of money to poor ministers, and they had given it to all who had asked for it. My grandfather had never asked for any; he liked to earn his own money. He did not send in any petition or appeal. Well, after the gentlemen had distributed to all who had asked there was five pounds over, and they were considering what they should do with this balance.

"'Well,' said one, 'there is a Mr. Spurgeon down at Stambourne, in Essex, a poor minister. He stands in need of five pounds.' 'Oh,' said another, 'don't send him five pounds. I will put five to it. I know him. He is a worthy man.' 'No,' said another, 'don't send him ten pounds. I will give another five pounds if somebody else will put a fourth five to it.'

"The next morning came a letter to grandmother with ninepence to pay! Grandmother did not like to pay out ninepence for a letter, but there was twenty pounds in it; and as my grandfather opened it he said, 'Now, can't you trust God about an old cow?'"—Rev. James E. Naylor, in *The Watchman-Examiner*.

* * *

Divine Faithfulness

Dr. J. Wilbur Chapman told of a time when he had fallen into financial difficulties. He waited upon God for relief, and one day there came to his study a millionaire, who was a member of his congregation. He said, "Dr. Chapman, I believe that you are financially embarrassed. I will not tell you how the knowledge has come to me, but I ask you if it is true." Dr. Chapman bowed his head in quiet assent. The man continued, "I will not inquire the amount of your obligations, but I will ask if it would be a comfort to you to know that my fortune is behind you?" Dr. Chapman could not answer and his guest, drawing from his pocket a check book, handed it to him, saying, "The checks are signed, and you may fill in for what amount you need." Thus was abundantly answered the appeal of Dr. Chapman to his faithful God for deliverance. "Ye shall ask what ye will, and it shall be done unto you."—*Alliance Weekly.*

* * *

A Lincoln Letter

There is in the State House at Albany a letter written by Abraham Lincoln granting pardon to a deserter. This is the way that letter reads:

"Executive Mansion,
Washington, D. C.,
Oct. 4, 1864.

Upon condition that Roswell McIntyre of Co. E, Sixth Regiment of New York Cavalry, returns to his regiment and faithfully serves out his time, or until lawfully discharged, he is fully pardoned for any supposed desertion heretofore committed; this paper is his pass to his regiment.

ABRAHAM LINCOLN."

Written across the side are these words:

"Quartermaster's office, N. Y. City, Oct. 22, 1864. Transportation furnished to Baltimore, Md.

H. BROWNSON."

Down at the left this note is scribbled: "Taken from the body of R. McIntyre at the battle of Five Forks, Va., 1865."

And so the quitter came back and died like a man, with his pardon on his person. And just so may all who have forsaken Christ and His cause return, be forgiven and recommissioned. — *Gospel Herald.*

* * *

The Card Over the Mantelpiece

A woman, after suffering many losses, went to a great doctor for sympathy. After being in his study for some time, she suddenly exclaimed, "I've got it! I've got it!" The surprised doctor immediately asked what she had got. Instead of answering directly she pointed to a text over the mantelpiece, on which were the words "THOU REMAINEST," and said, "I see now that no matter how much I lose, God remains, and He is all I need."—*Gospel Gleaners.*

* * *

God's Planting Time

A preaching band in China asked a very poor farmer to join them one spring in the work. "But I haven't planted my wheat yet," he said. Even as he was making his excuse a voice within his heart seemed to say, "*Your* wheat? Nay, your Heavenly Father's wheat." He went, although his heathen neighbors scoffed and said he was very foolish not to stay and plant his crops first. Instead his days were filled with planting the incorruptible Seed in the hearts of needy souls around him and he was happy. After a time, there were enough men on the team, so he could be released for a few days to return home and plant his wheat. His heart sank within him as he saw his neighbor's fields a lovely green with the sprouting wheat, and he hadn't even planted as yet! Then the comfort of the words, "Your heavenly Father knoweth what things ye have need of," was brought home to his heart, and peace returned. The planting done, he returned to the team to sow the good Seed. For some little time there was no rain. The ground was so dry that his wheat seed did not sprout, but the green fields around him began to turn yellow, and before the drought was over a third of the crops had withered and died. Then came the refreshing rain, and his wheat took root and sprang up. When harvest season came he had a beautiful field of waving golden grain, whereas his neighbors complained bitterly of poor crops. Thus God honored His servant who was faithful to Him. Now his neighbors come to him, not in scorn, but to ask him when he is going to plant his crops, for they want to plant theirs at the same time.—From *Attacking on All Fronts* (China Inland Mission Report).

* * *

God is Faithful

Melancthon said, "If I had no care, I should have no prayer." Spurgeon said, "Sometimes God sends His love letters in black-edged envelopes." He allows us to taste the bitterness of want and the dessolation of bereavement. If you have lived many years, you have passed through the narrows. We have all been there, and it is not always easy to see the Divine control. It looks as if things have got out of hand, and somehow or other we have been forgotten. When there is no one at hand to say it to you, say to yourself, "God is faithful, who will not suffer the pain to exceed the measurement of my endurance."—Rev. John MacDeath.

* * *

Never

I heard some time ago of a young Scotch student in a university, who was rooming with an old Christian auntie who read her Bible and believed it. One day the student came home and said to her, "Auntie, you know that verse in Hebrews that you so often quote: 'I will never leave thee, nor forsake thee.' Well, I have found out today that there are five negatives in the Greek there in that verse, and it reads like this: 'I will never, never, never, never, never leave thee.'" "Oh," said the old lady, "one of them is good enough for me, laddie." Because he hath said, "I will never leave thee," we may boldly say, "I will not fear."—*The Moody Church News.*

FAITHFULNESS, OUR

Dr. Lambie's Decision

Dr. Thomas Lambie of the Sudan Interior Mission was in America in 1917, and his brother-in-law urged him to stay. He had toiled and endured enough. If he would join him in his large medical practice, in a few years this could be turned over to him for the rest of his days, an ample and attractive living. Later Dr. Lambie attended a missionary conference. The meetings were uninspiring and he was tired. "Either I dozed off and had a dream, or I actually had a waking vision,—I have never known which. But this I saw vividly in that midnight hour: a map of northeastern Africa, and from the center of which came a hand and an arm. It was stretched out toward me, pleading, beckoning,—a hideous leper hand. What! Must I clasp that hand in mine? I sought to evade it, but, compelled by some power beyond my comprehending, at last I reluctantly took it in mine. To my intense surprise I found it was not the hand of a leper but the hand of Christ, the beautiful hand of my Savious—the imprint of nails in the palm." That settled it. Dr. Lambie returned to Africa.—*Sunday School Times.*

* * *

"Faithful Unto Death"

Several years ago, when a railway train was approaching the city of Montreal, the engineer saw a large dog on the track, barking furiously. The whistle was blown, but still the dog stayed on the track. Just as the engine came upon him, he crouched down and extended himself across the track, where he was struck by the locomotive and killed. The engineer, looking toward the front of his engine, saw a piece of white cloth fluttering in the wind. He discovered that it was part of a child's dress. After backing the train he found not only the mangled body of the dog, but also the body of a little child. The child had evidently wandered along the track and had fallen asleep there, while her faithful companion, seeing the train approaching, had done his best to save her. Failing, he had covered her with his own body and died with her. He had been "faithful unto death."—*The King's Business.*

* * *

A Valuable Find

Once Fritz Kreisler found a lovely violin in a private collection. There it was, a glorious instrument but mute, and Kreisler, feeling *that intolerable,* begged the owner that it be taken out and used. To all importunity the man was deaf—only at last he granted this much: that the great violinist might play on it once. So Kreisler played. As he said himself, "I played that day as though to ransom a captive!"—Selected.

* * *

The Faithful Few

In every church, in every clime,
When there's some work to do,
It very likely will be done
By just the faithful few.

While many folks will help to sing,
And some of them will talk,
When it comes down to *doing* things,
A lot of them will balk:

"We can't do this, we can't do that,
Excuse us, please, this time—
We'd be *so glad* to help you out,
But it's not in our line."

So when the leader casts about
To find someone who'll "do,"
Although he's done it oft before,
He asks the Faithful Few.

Of course, *they're* very busy, too,
And always hard at work,
But well he knows they'll not refuse,
Nor any duty shirk.

They never stop to make excuse,
But promptly try to do
The very, very best they can
To smooth the way for you.

God bless, I pray, the faithful few,
And may their tribe increase—
They must be very precious to
The blessed Prince of Peace.
—Chester E. Shuler.

* * *

Perfect Love Casteth Out Fear

One day Bramwell Booth went to his aged father, then groping for sight, and told the old General that the doctors said they could do no more for his eyes.

"Do you mean that I am blind and must remain blind?"

"I fear it is so," said Bramwell.

"Shall I never see your face again?" asked the old man.

"No, probably not in this world."

The General moved out his hand until he felt and clasped the hand of his son. He said, "God must know best, Bramwell. *I have done what I could for God and the people with my eyes. Now I shall do what I can for God and the people without my eyes.*"—R. H. W. Shepherd.

* * *

A Rule of Life

I will try this day to live a simple, sincere and serene life, repelling promptly every thought of discontent, anxiety, discouragement, impurity, self-seeking; cultivating cheerfulness, magnanimity, charity and the habit of holy silence; exercising economy in expenditure, generosity in giving, carefulness in conversation, diligence in appointed service, fidelity in every trust, and a childlike faith in God.

In particular I will try to be faithful in those habits of prayer, work, physical exercise, eating and sleep, which I believe the Holy Spirit has shown me to be right.

That all my powers with all their
might
To God's sole glory may unite.
—George Eliot.

* * *

The Power of a Christian Life

A revival meeting was being held in a village church. Many had been saved during the meetings. At the end of the sermon one night, the preacher said, "Is the person here who most influenced you in becoming a Christian? Maybe it is your mother, your pastor, your Sunday school teacher, your neighbor. I wish you would now rise and go and shake hands with the one who most influenced you to accept Christ as your Saviour. A glorious scene followed! Pupils went to their Sunday school teachers. Some went to the Sunday school superintendent. Some went to the pastor. To the left of the preacher sat an aged woman, wearing a sunbonnet. She had never spoken in public. She was not a Sunday school teacher. She was not an officer in the church. She was only a faithful, consecrated Christian mother and wife. She was more than seventy-five years old. A long line went to where she sat. Some took her by the hand. Some placed their arms about her. They said, "Your quiet, faithful, consecrated life; your personal work and testimony for Christ, when we were in your home, led us to Christ, the Saviour!" It was the beautiful, holy life which the Christian woman had led throughout the years that had won so many to the Saviour. — *Gospel Herald.*

* * *

Modern Martyrs

Boxers, says Dr. D. J. Fleming, captured a mission school, blocked all gates but one, placed a cross in front of it, and sent in word that anyone who trampled on that cross went free, but that anyone who stepped around it would be immediately killed. The first seven students trampled on the cross, and went free. The eighth, a girl, knelt before the cross, rose, and went on to be shot. All the rest in a line of a hundred students followed her example. Thirty thousand such Chinese converts chose death in 1900 rather than deny their Master. In these present days many another Chinese has sealed his faith with his life blood. A thousand black converts in Uganda went to their deaths by fire. Can Christians deny their Christ to folk who, when they find Him, hold Him dearer than life?—*Forward.*

* * *

Here I stand

I suppose I am something like Mr. Cecil when he was a boy. His father once told him to wait in a gateway till he came back, and the father being very busy went about the city, and amid his numerous cases and engagements, forgot the boy. Night came on and at last, when the father reached home, there was a great inquiry as to where Richard was. The father said, "Dear me! I left him in the morning standing under such and such a gateway, and I told him to stay there till I came for him. I should not wonder but that he is there now." So they went, and there they found him. Such an example of simple childish faithfulness is no disgrace to emulate.—*Gospel Herald.*

* * *

Faithful Dog

If you are a passenger on the Great Northern train that passes through Forth Benton, Montana, and see a shepherd dog pacing up and down the station platform, it may be just another dog to you, according to Ed Shields of Great Falls, veteran Great Northern conductor, but to trainmen it means a lot more.

"That dog has met every train for approximately three years," Shields said recounting the story. "The dog is looking for his master—a man who came to Montana looking for relief from a dreaded disease.

"The man took a job herding sheep. The most important thing a shepherd needs is a good dog. A sheepman gave him the dog, at that time a puppy, and loaned him an older dog to teach the young fellow to watch the sheep during the day and round them up when it came time to return to the camp.

"The young dog soon learned to handle sheep without the aid of the older dog, but as time went on, disease took the life of the herder. The good people of the community saw that the body was sent back to his old home in an eastern state. The dog followed the body of his master to the Great Northern station of Fort Benton and saw it loaded on the train.

"This incident was soon forgotten by all except the faithful dog, who has remained at the station, meeting every train—day and night—in hopes that the next one will return his master to him.

"He has refused to make up with anyone and is seldom seen except at train time. After the train had departed, he crawls back under the station to patiently await the next one.

"The section foreman, taking pity on the dog, tried to coax him to come into the section house to stay but the dog refused to leave the spot where he last saw his master, and the good-natured foreman for nearly three years has been bringing food to the station and leaving it for the dog.

"Last spring when the weather warmed and the chinook melted the heavy snow, a portion of the tracks was swept away and trains had to be detoured over another line for a period of ten days. On one of these evenings the foreman asked the agent what had become of 'Old Shep,' as the dog had become known.

"'I do not know,' the agent said, 'I have not seen him for several days. I suppose he has left.'

"The first train to reach Fort Benton after the tracks had been repaired came in at night. The station agent, preparing to meet the train, stepped out on the platform, and, to his surprise, found Old Shep was there."

Shields said the agent has tried to coax Old Shep into the station but the dog refuses to do anything but crawl back into his den under the station.

Perhaps Shep is dreaming of the days he spent with his master and the sheep, and listening for the whistle of the next train that may return his master to him.

If the dumb brute, with no hope of Heaven and no fear of hell, will be so loyal to its master, how ought not we, the crown of God's creation, the recreated ones, look for the glorious Return of our blessed Lord!—David Nygren, in *Revival Dynamite.*

* * *

Adorning the Doctrine

What kind of Christians do African women make? For answer, read the brief stories of several who know the preciousness of Christ, chosen from among many similar cases mentioned in *The Drum Call.*

"In Nkolemvolan field women who confessed Christ were beaten by their husbands and cast into the streets with the warning that this would be their constant treatment if they did not forsake their belief in Christ. But these women have proved their faith and loyalty through many years. As an example, take our friend, Moaman. Through patience and prayer she has won her husband to Christ, although at first he tried her by various persecutions. When he died last September, leaving her with five children, her faith still held true. She carries on alone, her face shining with the light of inner faith and joy. Thus by her victory over old superstitions and customs associated with death and widowhood she continues to witness before her townspeople of Him who is her Lord and Master.

"Another example shows how our women suffer for their faith. This particular woman is one of many wives of a man who used to be a Christian but has left the faith. It seems to irk him that this wife with whom he went into the church has remained faithful, and he tries to persecute her and cause her to sin. These who went out from us because they were not of us, are like the evil spirit which took to himself seven other more evil spirits, and the last state of these people is worse than their first, for they verily seem possessed of the Devil and do their utmost to make others fall. One Sunday this particular woman was ordered by her husband to crack palm nuts and prepare them for market. She refused, saying that if he had asked her on Saturday she would have done it, but that she would not work on Sunday. He began to beat her. Still she refused. Her Christian friends, passing on their way to church, stopped to see what was going on. As she related the story later to her missionary friend, she said that she was given strength to endure because these friends had said to her, 'Hold out—if he kills you, die for the faith.' It must have been a bit gruesome, though she found it a source of strength. At length the husband evidently began to fear that she would die, so he left off beating her. He still takes delight in giving her the hardest work in the village, but he has never again told her to work on Sunday. She says, 'I am a slave, but I am content to suffer because I have a hope that cannot be taken away from me.'" — Courtesy *Moody Monthly.*

* * *

A Sunday School of One

A missionary of the American Sunday School Union tells a story that we like. He had organized a Sunday School in the fall of the year in his territory, a portion of the middle west, and one Sunday morning in the following winter he made his way through deep snow to the school-house to see how the work was coming along. Smoke was coming out of the chimney and the bell being rung, as he drew near. Entering the house, he found only one person, a boy of fourteen.

"Was that the last bell for Sunday School?" the missionary asked. He was told it was.

"How has the Sunday School been getting along?" he inquired.

"Oh, it was doing first rate till the bad weather came!" the boy replied, "but since then it has not been doing so well."

They chatted pleasantly by the warm fire the boy had built, and waited, but no one else came. "How many were here last Sunday?" the missionary asked.

"Just me," the boy replied.

"Well, that is not very encouraging."

"No," was the reply, "but I thought if I came and built the fire and rung the bell somebody else might come."

"How many were here two weeks ago?"

"Just me," was the laconic reply.

On further questioning, the missionary learned the boy intended to repeat the process until he was told to quit. He said he did not want to see the Sunday School go down. The incident does not record the further history of the Sunday School of just one boy, but the expression "Just me" means a little more to us since meditating on the faithfulness of the lad. Not all can be great, but all can be faithful.—*Life Line.*

Like the star,
That shines afar,
Without haste,
And without rest,
Let each man wheel with steady sway
Round the task that rules the day,
And do his best. —Goethe.

* * *

Fixed Stars

There is the account of a Negro coachman who, shortly before the Civil War, was taking his owner through a rough stretch of country. Suddenly the sky overhead was full of shooting stars. "Oh, massa, the world's caving in!" the coachman cried. But the master calmly pointed to the North Star. "That star is not shooting," he said. "See how steady it is!"

And surely these are days of shooting stars and of trouble in the earth. Nations are bewildered, groping, fighting, relying upon force.

Churches show growth in membership but too often make small demands as to character or experience. Religious leaders in whom we have placed our confidence fail us. Will none be steady? Are there none who can be depended upon to keep the way?

As certainly as there are stars which abide the same and can be used to guide the sailor toward his safe harbor, so God has some men and women who "remain faithful." These are the Abrahams and the Josephs and the Daniels of our times. They shall have their reward; *but greater than that,* they shall serve well. Timid souls will arise to call them blessed.—*The Free Methodist.*

* * *

Stand Firm

This morning I was reading a circular issued in Great Britain to all residents telling them what to do in case of invasion. The two principal slogans were 'Stand Firm' and 'Carry On.' The Devil's blitzkrieg is pushing forward aggressively today. Surely all who love the Lord should 'stand firm'—'holding fast the Faithful Word' and should 'carry on'—'holding forth the word of life.'" Beside these two texts from Titus 1:9 and Philippians 2:16, one may place two others, which, with them, are good for these perilous times: "Therefore, my beloved brethren, be ye stedfast, unmoveable, always abounding in the work of the Lord, forasmuch as ye know that your labor is not in vain in the Lord" (1 Cor. 15:58); "Wherefore take unto you the whole armour of God, that ye may be able to withstand in the evil day, and having done all, to stand" (Eph. 6:13). It is interesting that this message should come first from those in England, who have suffered so much, and then from the Philippines, now in the furnace of war, and then to us who have just entered. God's grace is as sufficient in America as it has proved to be in England and in the Islands of the Pacific—*Sunday School Times.*

* * *

Jesus, I My Cross Have Taken

When after an absence of two years from America, I returned to spend a month with my church in Chicago, I found that a young Jewish woman, a very brilliant woman in the work she had to do, had been converted during my absence. Her conversion was very genuine. She was full of love to Christ as Jews generally are when they are converted. She went to the place where she worked, a well-known house in Chicago, and commenced talking of Christ to the other employees. Some of them did not like it, and they went to the head of the firm and said, "Miss —— is constantly talking to us about Christ. We don't like it." The manager of the firm called her in and said, "We have no objection to Christianity, no objection to your being a Christian. We think it is a good thing, but you must not talk it about this establishment."

"Very well," she said, "I will not work in a place where I cannot take Christ with me, and talk for my Master." She had a family to support, an aged mother and other members of the family, and did not know where she was going—just converted from Judaism to Christianity.

But she would not give up her loyalty to her new Master. "Very well," they said, "you will have to lose your position." She said, "I will give up my position before I will be disloyal to Jesus Christ." They said, "Very well, go back to your work." She went back to her work expecting every day to receive her dismissal. At the end of the week, she received a letter from the manager. "Here is my discharge," she said as she tore it open. The head of the establishment said, "We have a place of greater responsibility than the one you now occupy and with a larger salary than you are getting. We think you are just the person for the place, and we offer it to you." They saw she could be trusted. Business men are looking for men and women whom they can trust.—R. A. Torrey.

FAMILY ALTAR (See also: Home)

Rebuilding the Family Altar

Richard Baxter was one of England's greatest ministers. In early life, he went into a large parish and a community which was composed almost entirely of rich, cultured people. He found that the congregation was cold, and all was not as he had expected it to be in the ministry. He was disappointed and disheartened. The young pastor said, "The way to save the church and this community is to establish religion in the homes of the community and to build the family altars." Thus Baxter spent three years in his visitation and in his determination to establish a family altar in every home in that community. He succeeded amazingly, and this condition in the homes was the fountainhead that filled his church to overflowing and started that magnificent ministry and life. Fundamentally, religion must involve the family relationship. You cannot even build a church altar that is an attractive center without the family altar. Baxter was right and proved it.

Now I will take you to the opposite side. Thomas Boston was likewise a great minister, but, unlike Baxter, he spent the years of his early ministry in the slums of a city among the poor people. There he discovered the same condition—the church was cold and empty. He had no influence. He was disheartened and discouraged. He said that the only way to save the church is to save the family. And he went all through that poor community and established family altars where they worshiped God in the home every day in the week. He built up the altars, and he says he spent three years doing it. And then Thomas Boston's church started to revive, and the community was filled with spiritual power and influence.—Courtland Myers.

* * *

Back of All Delinquency

Robert Murray of Boston was converted in a Billy Sunday meeting years ago. He is a master plumber. . . . Juvenile delinquency has come to his attention. He doesn't talk much about it, but he is going ahead to do something. He has refitted two rooms in his home in a poorer quarter of Brighton, Mass., and here the children play. He has put in oak floors, and bought a piano for them; also he has had dug a fifteen-by-eleven-foot pool for bathing. Heavy swings are also installed. Sixty-seven children are on his roll call. "We are laying a foundation for God in their hearts." He knows the taproot of juvenile delinquency. Wherever there is a tavern to menace the children of the community, there should be a place to help them. He hopes his center will be the beginning of "Children's Haven, Inc.," and he insists that the lack of Christian training and family prayer is back of all delinquency.—*Sunday School Times.*

* * *

Memories of Old Home:

I am back there now, on the banks of the Hudson River, in that old farmhouse, in that old kitchen, around that great fireplace—father, mother, twelve children, twice a day, the old family Bible, and the wonderful prayer lifted to God! I am remembering that old house, that old center, that marvelous influence.

Do not be surprised when I tell you that every one of those children was saved by the grace of God. Four of them became ministers of Jesus Christ, all the rest of them Sunday School teachers and God's chosen men and women. And they all found that inspiration and life at the family altar when father opened the Bible and then lifted his heart to God. That is the greatest heritage in this world.

The greatest inheritance is the influence of Christian blood and life, moral character, and spiritual uplifting power. Now if your old home gave you that, you do not need to have a dollar. My father and mother never left me a dollar, but they left me the greatest riches in the world.—Courtland Myers.

* * *

Family Worship

Rear you an altar that will last forever,
Longer than any shafts or marble dome;
Erect it there beside your own hearthfire—
The chaste, white family altar in the home.
Chisel the Word of God upon the waiting
Hearts and minds of the dear ones gathered there;
The blowing sands of time will not erase it,
Nor friction dim the imprint of your prayer.

For memory will hold those chiseled letters,
And prayer shall be imbedded in the heart.
O father, mother, rear that lasting altar,
And the children whom you love will not depart
From the way of life. The Word will last forever,
Though earth and heaven itself should pass away.
If you have not as yet begun the building
Of that eternal altar—start today.
—*Watchman-Examiner.*

* * *

Big Enough to Pray

The interesting volume of reminiscences, "Forty-two Years in the White House," by the late "Ike" Hoover, who was chief usher in the Executive Mansion for that long period of time, gives an interesting glimpse of President Harrison's term in the early nineties. "Immediately after breakfast the family would retire to the upper floor and be closeted in one of the upper rooms for a half-hour of prayer. The entire atmosphere of the household would be surcharged with religious feeling during that time. Until the ceremony had been completed, one could not go about one's daily duties without a feeling that prayer was disturbed." Benjamin Harrison was pictured by the cartoonists of the day, of the opposition, as sitting in a chair much too big for him. But he was big enough to be humble; he was big enough to pray. Could any nation have a better sense of its safety, peace, and prosperity, both temporal and spiritual, than comes with the realization that its earthly ruler joins with his own family circle, in his home, in prayer to the God to whom all earthly rulers owe their exalted position?—*Sunday School Times.*

* * *

If Every Home Were An Altar

If every *home* were an altar
Where holiest vows were paid,
And life's best gifts in sacrament
Of purest love were laid;

If every home were an altar
Where harsh or angry thought
Was cast aside for kindly one,
And true forgiveness sought;

If every home were an altar
Where hearts weighed down with care
Could find sustaining strength and grace
In sweet uplift of prayer;

Then solved would be earth's problems,
Banished sin's curse and blight;
For God's own love would radiate
From every altar light.
—*Sunday School Times.*

* * *

Not a Guest

A little girl of five had just asked grace at table. "Come, Lord Jesus, be our guest," when, suddenly turning to her mother, she said, "But, Mother, I do not want Jesus to be our guest." "Why, dear?" demanded her horrified parent. "Well, a guest is one who comes only *sometimes*," said the child. "I want Jesus to be here all the time."—*Courtesy Moody Monthly.*

* * *

The Family Altar

Charles H. Spurgeon, the Christian preacher, once said, "Family prayer is an instrument of family piety, and woe to those who allow it to cease." Another has said that the family without the prayer circle is like a family living without a roof over its head. When the storms come and the winds blow and the rains fall there is no protection. Surely when the home is without prayer there is no protection for the life from the problems and distresses which come our way.

One family gave the excuse for not having a family altar because they were too busy. A friend asked a question: "If you knew that your children would be sick through the neglect of family prayer, would you have it?"

"Of course," was the answer.

"If one child was smitten down with fever each morning that you neglected prayer, would you have prayer then?"

"Oh yes," they quickly replied. "We would surely have it then."

"And if there was a law that you should be fined five-dollars if you did not meet for prayer each day, would you have prayer then?"

"Yes."

"Well, then," said the one asking the questions, "it is surely a poor excuse when you who profess to be children of God say that you have no time or opportunity to have family prayers, if you would have them for such simple reason as you have just said."

If you do not have a family altar in your home, then heed this Scriptural exhortation to pray: "Pray without ceasing;" "Hitherto have ye asked nothing in My Name: ask, and ye shall receive, that your joy may be full." Finally in Ephesians 6:18 we read, "Praying always with all prayer and supplication . . . for all saints."—Harry Albus.

* * *

A Nation Needs Religious Homes

A few years ago in central Illinois a godly mother, who died at the age of 95 left the following testimony.

"A devoted Methodist minister came to our community during our early married life and preached the Gospel in our home. Husband and I both were converted and erected a family altar which we never permitted to be broken down. Thirteen children came to bless our home, two of which died in infancy. The other eleven were all converted before they were sixteen years of age. Three of my sons are ministers of the Gospel. Two sons became local preachers and two of my children married preachers. The rest are all Christians and are a blessing in their respective churches and communities. I attribute the success we had in rearing so large a Christian family, to our early conversion, our regular church attendance and to the family altar around which we gathered our family twice every day.
—Selected.

* * *

Family Worship

Henry Clay, the great American statesman and orator, once lodged overnight at a humble cabin in his native state of Kentucky. The family was in the habit of holding worship morning and evening, but the father trembled at the thought of doing so in the presence of a guest so distinguished. The children were becoming sleepy, and the wife by significant gestures suggested that the time for prayer had come. The man hinted to his guest that perhaps he would like to go to bed. But Mr. Clay with great politeness said that he did not feel at all sleepy, and that, unless it was intrusive, he would be happy to enjoy the society of his host longer. Of course, the man could not object. Still the matter of prayer could not be postponed without sending the children to bed contrary to their settled custom. At last, with considerable trepidation, the father told his guest that he could stay and unite in their devotions or retire at his option. Mr. Clay promptly replied that he would remain. When the wonted exercises, gone through with much fear and trembling, were over, Mr. Clay, with no little feeling, approached the man, and said: "My dear sir, never again feel the least hesitation in the discharge of your duty to God on account of the presence of man. I saw your embarrassment, and remained on purpose that you might never feel it again. Remember that every man of sense will respect the individual who is not ashamed to acknowledge his dependence upon his Maker; and he deserves only contempt who can cherish any other feelings than reverence for 'the consecrated hour of man in audience with Diety.' I would rather know that the prayers of a pious man, no matter how humble his position in life, were ascending in my behalf than to have the wildest applause of listening senators."—*Gospel Herald.*

* * *

God in the Home

Dr. Beiderwolf relates the following interesting incident: "The story is told of a little Japanese girl who studied at an American College and spent a Christmas vacation in the home of one of her classmates. She had seen much else in America, but the thing she longed most of all to see on the inside was a Christian home, and such a home this one was known to be. She had a delightful time and as she was about to leave at the end of the vacation time the mother said, 'How do you like the way we American folks live?' 'Oh,' she said, 'I love it. Your home is beautiful. But there is one thing I miss,' said the girl with a faraway look in her eyes. 'It is this that makes your home seem queer to me. You know I have been with you to your church and I have seen you worship your God there. But I have missed the God in your home. You know, in Japan, we have a god-shelf in every home, with the gods right there in the house. Do not Americans worship their God in their homes?' "

Christianity can never leaven our country unless it pervades the home life.—Selected.

* * *

Something Precious

After preaching on the *family* altar one Sunday morning, one of my deacons went home and announced at the dinner table that they were going to have family prayers. He took out a Bible and began to read. He got along all right until he started to pray. He had never prayed before in the presence of his children, who were nine and eleven years old. He tried to pray, but the prayer would not come. The little girl began to titter, and then the boy began to titter. The mother smiled, and he was a good sport and smiled too. It ended with all laughing. He did not let the children know how his heart was broken. He went to his room and got down on his face and asked God to forgive him. At the supper table that evening, he again opened his Bible and read; and then he knelt down and prayed with his children, and there was no tittering. There was a sweetness, and after prayer the little girl put her arms around her father's neck and thanked him. He had brought something precious into that home.

I heard a freshman get up in a group of young people in Montreat, N. C., and say, "I have missed something in my life. My father and mother have never read to me out of the Bible nor prayed with me." I would rather have my right hand cut off than have my child get up in front of five hundred people and say that about me.—Courtesy *Moody Monthly*.

* * *

The Nation's Center

Henry W. Grady visited Washington, D. C., and when he went back to Atlanta, Georgia, he wrote an editorial about the Capitol at Washington, described it beautifully and called it the home of the Nation, the center of American life. Some months passed, and he went back to his old home in Georgia. And then when he returned to Atlanta, he wrote another editorial, and in it he said that he made a tremendous blunder when he wrote that first editorial. He said that the center of this country is not in the United States Capitol — it is in the houses and in the cottages and in the old farm houses and in every home in this land in which there is a family altar. The Christian home is the center of American life from which all the rest of it moves and radiates. And Henry M. Grady was justified in apologizing for his mistake.—*Christian Index*.

* * *

Family Altars and Missionaries

One of the noblest of missionaries was John G. Paton. No man evidenced more heroism and sacrifice than did that kingly, wonderful soldier of the Cross. Read the biography of this devoted missionary. You will find on the first page the secret of that life of service, the one memory around which all the rest of Paton's ministry centers. That recollection is of his father with his old family Bible twice a day at the family altar, children all around him hearing the message of God, then down on their knees together. Paton says that in that old home his father's mighty religious influence made him all he was and started his missionary life and work. As you read the rest of his biography, you will find this spiritual influence in operation all through his life.—*King's Business*.

A Precious Heritage

I know two men that lived in a country home in their boyhood, and they became rich men when they went away from home. They went occasionally to visit their father and mother living in the old home. And finally the father and mother went to Heaven. The sons did not know what to do with this old home. One of them said to the other, "If you'll sell out your interest to me, I'll tear down the house and I'll build a summer home there, and let you come out to it when you want to." Accordingly they took a trip out to the old homestead to tear it down. Around that spot there swept many sacred memories.

Then these two brothers, past middle life and rich, went into the house, and looked around through it. One walked up and down in front of the old fireplace, and the other sat down. Finally one said to the other.

"You know, Bob, what I'm thinking about? I've changed my mind since I've been here. We're not going to tear down this old house. This house is going to stand here; it's not going to be torn down."

"That is a strange thing," the other brother said, "because when I was walking up and down in front of the fireplace, that is the same thing I was thinking about." He looked over at the chair in which father used to sit. "Here is the old chair that father sat in when he read the Bible when we had family worship — the chair around which we knelt as father lifted our heart to God."

They stayed there two hours to talk things over. They both got down on their knees by the old chair, repented and wept their hearts out before God. They went back, saved men and gave their money to God and lived for God.

And the old house stands. Not a single thing was moved out. It was too sacred to touch, because the family altar had stood there. It is a great thing to go back to the old house.—*Gospel Herald*.

FATHERS

The Story of the Prodigal Father

A certain man had two sons; and the younger of them said to his father, "Father, give me the portion of thy time, thy attention, and companionship, and thy counsel which falleth to me."

And he divided unto him his living in that he paid the boys' bills and sent him to a select preparatory school, and to dancing schools, and to college, and tried to believe that he was doing his full duty by the boy.

And not many days after, the father gathered all his interests and aspirations and ambitions and took his journey into a far country, into a line of stocks and bonds and securities and other things which do not interest a boy; and there he wasted his precious opportunity of being a chum to his own son.

And when he had spent the very best of his life, and had gained money but had failed to find satisfaction, there arose a mighty famine in his heart; and he began to be in want of sympathy and real companionship.

And he went and joined himself to one of the clubs of that country and they elected him chairman of the house committee and president of the club and sent him to Congress, and he would fain have satisfied himself with the husks that other men did eat, and no man gave unto him any real friendship.

But when he came to himself, he said, "How many men of my acquaintance have boys whom they understand and who understand them, who talk about their boys and associate with their boys and seem perfectly happy in the comradeship of their sons, and I perish here with heart hunger? I will arise and go to my son and will say to him, Son, I have sinned against Heaven, and in thy sight; I am no more worthy to be called thy father; make me as one of thy acquaintances."

And he arose and came to his son, but while he was yet afar off, his son saw him and was moved with astonishment, and instead of running and falling on his neck, he drew back and was ill at ease.

And the father said unto him, "Son, I have sinned against Heaven, and in thy sight! I am no more worthy to be called thy father. Forgive me now and let me be your friend."

But the son said, "Not so, I wish it were possible, but it is too late. There was a time when I wanted to know things, when I wanted companionship and counsel, but you were too busy; I got the information, and I get the companionship but I got the wrong kind; and now, alas, I am wrecked in soul and body, and there is nothing you can do for me. It is too late, too late, too late."

"The saddest words of tongue or pen,
The saddest are these: it might have been."

A boy has a right to more than food, clothes and correction; he has an undeniable right to a father.—Dr. Joplin.

* * *

Not Afraid

A devoted father came into the room where his eight-year-old was dying of an incurable disease. The child, sensing that he was not going to get well asked his father, "Daddy, am I going to die?" "Why, son, are you afraid to die?" The child looked up into the eyes of his father and replied, "Not if God is like you, Daddy!"—*Sunday School Times.*

* * *

Father Forgets

Listen, Son, I am saying this to you, as you lie asleep, one little paw crumpled under your cheek and the blond curls stickily wet on your damp forehead. I have stolen into your room, alone. Just a few minutes ago, as I sat reading my paper in the library, a hot, stifling wave of remorse swept over me. I could not resist it. Guiltily I came to your bedside.

These were the things I was thinking, son: I had been cross to you. I scolded you as you were dressing for school because you gave your face merely a dab with a towel. I took you to task for not cleaning your shoes. I called angrily when I found you had thrown some of your things on the floor.

At breakfast, I found fault, too. You spilled things. You gulped down your food. You put your elbows on the table. You spread butter too thick on your bread. And, as you started off to play and I made my train, you turned and waved a little hand and called, "Goodbye, Daddy" and I frowned, and said in reply, "Hold your shoulders back!"

Then it began all over again in the late afternoon. As I came up the hill road, I spied you, down on your knees playing marbles. There were holes in your stockings. I humiliated you before your boy friends, by making you march ahead of me back to the house. Stockings were expensive — and if you had to buy them you would be more careful! Imagine that, son, from a father! It was such stupid, silly logic.

Do you remember, later, when I was reading in the library, how you came in, softly, timidly, with a sort of hurt, hunted look in your eyes? When I glanced up, over my paper, impatient at the interruption, you hesitated at the door.

"What is it you want?" I snapped. You said nothing, but ran across, in one tempestuous plunge, and threw your arms around my neck and kissed me, again and again, and your small arms tightened with an affection that God had set blooming in your heart and which even neglect could not wither. And then you were gone, pattering up the stairs.

Well, son, it was shortly afterwards that my paper slipped from my hand and a terrible sickening fear came over me. Suddenly, I saw myself as I really was, in all my horrified selfishness, and I felt sick at heart. What had habit been doing to me? The habit of complaining, of finding fault, of reprimanding — all of these were my rewards to you for being a boy. It was not that I did not love you; it was that I expected so terribly much of youth. I was measuring you by the yardstick of my own years.

And there was so much that was good, and fine, and true in your character. You did not deserve my treatment of you, son. The little heart of you was as big as the dawn itself, over the wide hills. All this was shown by your spontaneous impluse to rush in and kiss me good-night. Nothing else matters tonight, son. I have come to your bedside in the darkness, and I have knelt here, choking with emotion, and so ashamed. It is a terrible atonement. I know you would not understand these things if I told them to you during your waking hours. Yet, I must say what I am saying. I must burn, sacrificial fires, alone here in your bedroom, and make free confession. And I have prayed God to strengthen me in my new resolve. Tomorrow I will be a real Daddy. I will chum with you and suffer when you suffer and laugh when you laugh. I will bite my tongue when impatient words come. I will keep saying, as if it were a ritual: "He is nothing but a boy — a little boy!" And I am afraid I have visualized you as a man. Yet, as I see you now, son, crumpled and weary in your cot, I see that you are still a baby. Yesterday, you were in your mother's arms, your head on her shoulder. I have asked too much, too much! My dear little boy! A penitent kneels at your infant shrine here in the moonlight. I kiss the little fingers and the damp forehead, and the yellow curls, and, if it were not for waking you, I would snatch you up and crush you to my breast. Tears came and heartache and remorse, and I think, a greater, deeper love, when you ran through the library door and wanted to kiss me!—*Gospel Herald.*

* * *

Sentence Me

The most tragic and heart-rending cry in the Old Testament is the cry of David when he received the news of the death of his foolish and traitorous son,

Absalom. A careful study of the relationship of Israel's great king with his son reveals that Absalom's errancy could in no small measure be laid at David's door. The poignancy of David's cry carries with it the sense of his own personal responsibility: "O my son Absalom, my son Absalom! would God I had died for thee, O Absalom, my son, my son!" (II Sam. 18:33).

"Sentence me!" a modern father said to the judge before whom his son stood to receive the sentence for a crime he had committed. "I have been so busy all my life making money, going through the chairs in my lodge, serving on boards and committees, I failed to concern myself with my boy. I alone am to blame." Undoubtedly, many a youth, serving a sentence in prison or reformatory, could point an accusing finger at his father who spent all his spare time on secondary matters to the neglect of his high responsibility of fatherhood.—Courtesy *Moody Monthly.*

* * *

A Father's Awakening

"One night after my fifteen-year-old boy had been sent home for insubordination to college authority for the second time, I slept but little. Then next morning after breakfast I cut a good switch and rehearsed to my boy his course of disobedience. I told him to take off his coat. He replied, 'I won't do it.' I looked him in the face and said: 'My boy, I am your father; you are my son. I promised God Almighty on my knees last night that I would control you, and I will whip you here this morning or you and I will die in this woodland. Take off your coat, sir.' He saw in my eye for the first time in his life the spirit of authority. He drew his coat in a moment, and I gave him a sound thrashing, at the conclusion of which I said, 'Now kneel down with me.' We knelt together, and I told God of my own neglect and of my boy's sinful conduct, and promised God in the hearing of my boy to be faithful to my duty the remainder of my life, and prayed God's blessing on my wayward child. When we arose, he put his arms around my neck and his head on my bosom. We wept together for a long time. Then he looked up and said, 'Father, I will never give you any more trouble.' And from that day to this I have never had a care about him. He has been the most obedient son a father ever had. He is married now, an official in the church, and no truer, nobler Christian man walks the earth than my precious son."
—*Christian Life.*

* * *

A Word to Fathers

We have read an incident of a little boy who, when he wanted a new suit of clothes, begged his mother to ask his father if he might have it. The mother suggested that the boy might ask for himself.

"I would," said the boy, "but I don't feel well enough acquainted with him."

There is a sharp reproof to the father in the reply of his son. Many a father keeps his children so at a distance from him that they never feel confidentially acquainted with him.

They feel that he is a sort of monarch in the family. They feel no familiarity with him. They fear him and respect him, and even love him some—for children cannot help loving everybody about them—but they seldom get near enough to him to feel intimate with him. They seldom go to him with their little wants and trials. They approach him through the mother.

They tell her everything. They have a highway to her heart on which they go in and out with perfect freedom. In this keeping aloof fathers are to blame. Children should not be held off. Let them come near. It is wicked to freeze up the love-fountains of little ones' hearts. Fathers do them an injury by living with them as strangers. This drives many a child away from home for the sympathy his heart craves, and often into improper society. It nurses discontent and distrust, which many a child does not outgrow in his lifetime. Open your hearts and your arms, O fathers; be free with your children; ask for their wants and trials; play with them; be father to them truly, and then they will not need a mediator between themselves and you. —*Glad Tidings.*

* * *

Too Busy

The story is told of a young man who stood at the bar of justice to be sentenced for forgery. The judge had known him from a child and known the family intimately. The boy's father was a famous legal light, having written some of the best material on the subject of "Trusts."

"Do you remember your father?" asked the judge in stern fashion, "that father whom you have disgraced?"

"Yes," said the boy, "I remember him perfectly. When I went to him for advice and companionship he often said to me, 'Run away, boy, I'm busy.' My father gave all his time to his work and little time for me. So here I am."

The great lawyer had written much about trusts, but had missed the greatest trust of all—his own son. God has laid definite responsibilities on Christian parents. What a tragedy to make the mistake the great lawyer made.—Selected.

FEAR

There are 365 "Fear Nots" in the Bible, or one for every day of the year.—Selected.

* * *

God Never Sleeps

A mother and her little four-year-old daughter were preparing to retire for the night. The child was afraid of the dark, and the mother, alone with the child, felt fearful also. When the light was out, the child caught a glimpse of the moon outside the window. "Mother," she asked, "is the moon God's light?" "Yes," said the mother. "God's light is always shining." The next question was, "Will God blow out His light and go to sleep?" And the mother replied, "No, my child. God never goes to sleep." Then out of a simplicity of a child's faith she said that which gave reassurance to the fearful mother: "Well, so long as God is awake, I am not afraid."

No wonder Jesus said, "Except ye become as little children, ye shall not enter into the kingdom of heaven." How often we allow fear—of darkness, of failure, of suffering, of death—to rob us of our sleep and of our joy in life! God's light never goes out; He is ever awake to our needs.—Selected.

We Will Not Fear

And though this world, with devils filled,
Should threaten to undo us,
We will not fear, for God has willed
His truth to triumph through us.
The prince of darkness grim—
We tremble not for him;
His rage we can endure,
For lo! his doom is sure,
One little word shall fell him.
—Martin Luther.

* * *

The Safety of Fear

Life that does not fear in this present world is abnormal life. Some false cults and philosophies would remove all fear from life; but they would make of us abnormal and useless beings. Not only "the fear of the Lord is the beginning of wisdom," and not only can we be delivered by Christ Himself from unworthy and weakening fears, but other fears also are vital to sane, useful living. The Keswick Calendar quotes a pertinent and needed comment: "We cannot live either our natural or our spiritual life without fear. A man will never be a first-rate surgeon unless he fears infection, and sterilizes his instruments. A child will never be fit to live alone until it fears to throw a lighted match into the waste basket. A man will never be a successful builder until he fears to put one rotten timber into his house, nor a successful Christian until he fears to put one rotten thought into his character. Do not go any farther unless you can say that you fear sin in all its forms."—*Sunday School Times.*

* * *

The Personal Touch

When just a small child I accompanied my father to see his mother, who lived about three miles from our home. We remained longer than we should and night overtook us. Between our home and grandmother's was a swamp and that night the frogs croaking and crickets chirping, together with the darkness and shadows of the trees, frightened me.

I inquired of my father if there were any danger of "something catching us" and he assured me there was no danger. Soon I asked the same question again and received the same answer. But my father saw I was frightened and he took me by the hand and said: "I will not allow anything to harm you." And all my fears passed away and I was ready to face the world; for my father had me by the hand.

How like our Heavenly Father is this. "Yea, though I walk through the valley of the shadow of death, I will fear no evil: for Thou art with me; Thy rod and Thy staff they comfort me" (Ps. 23:4). The poet says:

"There are days so dark that I seek in vain
For the face of my Friend Divine.
Tho' the darkness hide, He is there to guide
By the touch of His hand on mine.
. . . . .
—There is grace and power in the trying hour
In the touch of His hand on mine."
—W. B. Davidson, in The *Biblical Echo.*

* * *

Safe, Though Anxious

Recently we heard of a workman who was employed on some building project where he was working at night. Busy on the edge of the wall, several stories high, he suddenly lost his balance and fell, but managed to grasp the edge of the wall with his fingers. Desperately he clung, hoping that his plight would be discovered. He was in darkness below the level of the wall, and his cries were lost in the chatter of the riveting machines, the puffing of hoisting engines, and the myriad of other sounds arising from such a project.

Soon he felt his arms grow numb, and his fingers begin to relax against every effort of his will to hold them rigid. Frantically he tried to pray, but no miracle occurred. At last his fingers slipped from the wall, and, with a retching sob of sheer terror, he fell — about three inches to a scaffold that had been there in the darkness all the time!

How like a lot of Christians! Thinking their salvation depends on their endurance, and conscious of their weakness, they are fearful, anxious and unhappy most of the time: yet underneath, all the while, are the everlasting arms of a faithful, loving and all-powerful Saviour.—H. O. Van Gilder.

* * *

Nor Let It Be Afraid

"Let not your heart be troubled, neither let it be afraid" (John 14:27).

Though all the world be troubled,
And men's hearts faint with fear
At dangers in the distance
And dangers drawing near;
Though every help should fail them
On which their hopes are stayed,
Let not your heart be troubled,
Nor let it be afraid.

Though all the earth be troubled
And its foundations shake;
Though raging sea shall thunder
And mighty mountains quake;
Though lofty walls shall crumble
And in the dust be laid,
Let not your heart be troubled,
Nor let it be afraid.

Though all your way be troubled
And bounds and landmarks lost;
Though on the stormy billows
Your little bark is tossed;

Though all around be changing,
Here let your mind be stayed:
Let not your heart be troubled,
Nor let it be afraid.

Oh, blessed Word of Jesus!
And faithful from of old;
In which our fears may vanish,
To which our trust may hold;
You shall not be confounded,
You shall not be dismayed;
Let not your heart be troubled;
Nor let it be afraid.

—Annie Johnson Flint.

(Copyright. Reprinted by permission, Evangelical Publishers, Toronto, Canada.)

* * *

Better Than a Bear

My oldest son taught me a lesson. When he was little, before his brother came, I had to be his brother and play a bit with him. There was nothing he liked better than to play bear. We would fix up some chairs in the corner, with an opening on one side, and then I would get down on all fours, and growl. And then the little fellow would come running, tripping along as though there was nothing near. And because the bear was rather heavy and clumsy, he had difficulty in running the little fellow down. I remember the last time we ever played bear. He ran right into a corner, and there he was with his face in the corner, so excited, and the bear was right on him. These things seem so real to little folks. He was screaming in his excitement—here was the bear, his hot breath, about to grab him and devour him. Suddenly the little fellow stopped his screaming, and, running into my arms, said, "I ain't afraid, not a bit afraid. You are not a bear at all. You are my own papa." I picked him up and we walked up and down while his little heart was beating like a trip hammer, and he was just sobbing in my arms. And I said, "This will never do. We shall never play this game again." But the little fellow kept saying, "Papa, I am not afraid any more." I said, "Oh, God, that is just the way I was once. I was running away from You. I was treating You as though You were my enemy, as though the worst thing in the world would be to be brought into communion with You. I thank You for running me down."—Dr. H. A. Ironside.

* * *

Herbert Hoover- after visiting 14 nations

"Fear by nations of one another, fear by governments of their citizens, fear by citizens of their governments, and the vague fear of people everywhere that general war is upon them again. Fear of the promised massacre of civil populations from the air. Fear everywhere!"

* * *

Fear Not

Fear not! Whate'er betide you,
In all the coming days,
Your Lord will walk beside you,
In His appointed ways.

His hand will surely guide you,
When friends and helpers fail,
And His pavilion hide you,
When foes and fears assail.

Fear not! Turn backward never,
Whatever may oppose;
Look unto Jesus ever,
And in His love repose.

And when life's little story
At eventide is told,
Then, in the morn of glory,
You shall His face behold.

—H. B. Hartzler.

* * *

Nothing to Fear

A missionary was teaching a Hindu woman the so-called Lord's Prayer. When he got to the end of the first clause, "Our Father which art in Heaven," she stopped him. "If God is our Father," she said, "that is enough. There is nothing now to fear." And to one whose life was haunted by the constant dread of countless evil spirits, that was a sweet message indeed. — *Gospel Herald.*

The Secret of Fearlessness

Of all the memorials in Westminster Abbey there is not one that gives a nobler thought than that inscribed on the monument to Lord Lawrence — simply his name, with the date of his death, and these words: "He feared man so little, because he feared God so much."—*Sunday School Chronicle.*

* * *

Holy Fearlessness

Chrysostom of Constantinople, threatened and finally exiled by the Empress Eudoxia, stated in a sermon at the time of his banishment: "What can I fear? Will it be death? But you know that Christ is my life. Will it be exile? But the earth and all its fullness is the Lord's. Will it be loss of wealth? But we brought nothing into the world and can carry nothing out. Thus all the terrors of the world are contemptible in my eyes, and I smile at all its good things. Poverty I do not fear. Riches I do not sigh for. Death I do not shrink from, and life I do not desire to save only for the process of souls. And so if they banish me, I shall be like Elijah! If they throw me in the mire, like Jeremiah. If they plunge me in the sea, like the Prophet Jonah! If into the pit, like Daniel! If they stone me, it is Stephen I shall resemble! John the forerunner, if they cut off my head! Paul, if they beat me with stripes! Isaiah, if they saw me asunder." — *The Missionary Worker.*

* * *

The Doctor's Antidote for Fear

In his book entitled *Fear,* John Rathbone Oliver quotes a learned doctor who had under his observation and care a patient who was suddenly possessed with fear, and gradually grew worse. One day the physician talked to his patient:

"So far as my experience goes, the people who do not seem to be assailed and poisoned by fear are those who believe and practice the Christian religion. And by the Christian religion I do not mean a religion man-made, or man-given, but the Christian religion as it was established and delivered to twelve eyewitnesses by a Person who was both God and Man. This Person did not merely live in Palestine hundreds of years ago, going about doing good and then disappearing forever to some immeasurably distant heaven, but He is, by means of His own appointment, still present on earth, still walks with men, still has earthly habitations where He may be found, and is more intimately united with those who follow Him now than He ever was during the days of His human life in Galilee. I tell you that people who believe and practice the religion that centers around this Personality seem to have an antidote against fear." —*Gospel Herald.*

FELLOWSHIP

Blest Be the Tie

A beautiful story is told of the origin of the well-known hymn, "Blest be the tie that binds." It was written by Rev. John Fawcett, an English Baptist, who died in 1817, after he had spent nearly sixty years in the ministry. It was in 1772, after a few years in pastoral work, that he was called to London to succeed the famous Dr. Gill. His farewell sermon had been preached in his country church in Yorkshire. The wagons stood loaded with his furniture and books, and all was ready for departure. But his loving people were heartbroken. Men, women and children gathered and clung about him and his family with sad and tearful faces. Finally overwhelmed with the sorrow of those they were leaving, Dr. Fawcett and his wife sat down on one of the packing-cases and gave way to grief. "Oh, John!" cried Mrs. Fawcett at last. "I cannot bear this! I know not how to go!" "Nor I, either," returned her husband, "and we will not go. The wagons shall be unloaded, and everything put in its old place." His people were filled with intense joy and gratitude at this determination. Dr. Fawcett at once sent a letter to London explaining the case, and then resolutely returned to his work on his pitifully small salary. This hymn was written to commemorate the event. It expresses sentiments so nearly universal that it is one of our hymns immortal. — *The Watchman-Examiner*.

* * *

Japanese Soldiers and a Chinese Pastor

A group of invading Japanese cavalry was billeted in a Chinese village. On their arrival, they discovered a mud church bearing the notice, "This is a Jesus Chapel." Eight of the cavalrymen proved to be Christians, and they fairly hugged the old Chinese pastor, explaining how glad they were to find a Christian home in the place. During the time they were in the village, they attended worship, praying and singing hymns with their Christian brethren. When they left, they gave every house where they had stayed the equivalent of two dollars, as well as a large bag of oats.— *Sunday School Times*.

* * *

As we tread the narrow way,
Together sing, together pray,
What is sweeter here below
Than the fellowship we know?

Comfort for the hearts that bleed,
Sympathy in hours of need,
Kindly things that others say,
Brighten up the dreary day.

Friendship, fellowship, and love,
Blessed gifts from Heaven above.
Glad am I that in God's plan
There was fellowship for man!
—Selected.

* * *

With Thee

O Master, let me walk with Thee;
I fear to journey on alone;
The night is dark, no star I see,
The path is steep and edged with stone.

Then, Master, let me hold Thy hand,
For like a child I halt in fear;
I dread the unknown path beyond,
I dread the step before me near.

O Master, let me walk with Thee
When sorrows deep my spirit rend,
When naught but empty grief I see,
Be Thou my never-failing Friend.
And, Master, when temptations sweep
Like storms of night across my way,
My faith renew, my spirit keep,
Guide to a brighter, better day.

O Master, I would walk with Thee!
Though dark the way, what need I more?
Thy rod—Thy staff, they comfort me,
For Thou hast walked this path before.
Yea, Master, let me walk with Thee,
Then shall I reach the goal at length;
In Thee my confidence shall be,
In Thee my joy, my peace, my strength.
—Kathryn Blackburn Peck, in *Herald of Holiness*.

* * *

Christian Brotherhood in a Strange Land

A sailor, member of the Church of the Open Door in Los Angeles, states: On a South Pacific island my first night was a lonely one, and I went for a walk, wishing fervently for a Christian companion to talk with. Following three young men carrying Bibles I came to a hut where twenty or thirty men were assembled. I found that these men met here nightly to sing hymns and study the Word together. There was a chaplain who made occasional appearances in the meetings. Our "church" was the mess hall by day. Our music was an accordion—when the accordionist wasn't on watch. When he couldn't be present, we "sang the Lord's song in a strange land" without benefit of accompaniment. The order of service was not complex: we started off with a couple of hymns, then had the newcomers stand up and say "howdy"; we interspersed a few more songs with testimonies and Scripture verses. Finally the teacher, a chief yeoman, brought before us a selected chapter and we took it apart. There were soldiers at these meetings as well as sailors, and in that little room it was not "GI Joe" or "matie," but *"brother."* I don't believe anyone can truly appreciate that word as much as a man who is in a strange land thousands of miles from home, when he walks up to a total stranger and is met with a smile, an outstretched hand, and *"Welcome, brother!"* and knows that he is a Brother in Christ.—*King's Business.*

* * *

Walking Together

Walking is dull, I must sadly own; walking is dull if one walks alone: no one to talk with of what one sees,—flowers and meadows and birds and trees. Walking is fine if a comrade true, loving and eager, goes with you. Merry the chat and merry the song as the comrade spirits trudge along. The miles are short and the views are fair, and sweet and cool in the magic air, and a wondrous charm is the brotherly weather as you and your comrade walk together. And so, O Spirit divinely high, the Lord of the earth and the arching sky, Thy love bends down from infinity, and even descends to walk with me. What beautiful prospects grow around as Thou and I tread the hallowed ground! What hopes upspring and exultantly grow as Thou and I are traveling so! What strength in the body, what joy in the heart, as Thou art taking the comrade part! I am firm as iron and light as a feather when I and the Spirit are walking together!—Amos R. Wells, in *The Sunday School Times.*

* * *

One Language

A Hindu and a New Zealander met upon the deck of a missionary ship. They had been converted from their heathenism, and were brothers in Christ, but they could not speak to each other. They pointed to their Bibles, shook hands, and smiled in each other's face; but that was all. At last a happy thought occurred to the Hindu. With sudden joy, he exclaimed, *"Hallelujah!"* The New Zealander, in delight, cried out, *"Amen!"* Those two words, not found in their own heathen tongues, were to them the beginning of "one language and one speech."—*Gospel Herald.*

* * *

A Persian fable says: One day
A wanderer found a lump of clay
So redolent of sweet perfume
Its odors scented all the room.
"What art thou?" was his quick demand.
"Art thou some gem of Samarcand,
Or spikenard in this rude disguise,
Or other costly merchandise?"
"Nay: I am but a lump of clay."

"Then whence this wondrous perfume, say?"
"Friend, if the secret I disclose,
I have been dwelling with the rose."
Sweet parable! and will not those
Who love to dwell with Sharon's rose,
Distil sweet odors all around,
Though low and mean themselves are found?
Dear Lord, may we to Thee retreat,
Then shed abroad Thy fragrance sweet!

—*Gospel Herald.*

* * *

Just to Be Near

We are ever welcomed by God our Father when we are forced into His presence by our need. He invites us to make our requests known to Him; but we remember the little fellow who nestled very close to his father, who said to him, "What do you want now?" and whose answer was "Just to be near you, father." Of course his father was pleased. Is not our Father pleased when we seek His presence because of His love to us and ours to Him? — *Scripture Truth.*

* * *

No War Here!

A recent report from China states that a Japanese soldier entered a Chinese Christian church at service time. His entrance created misgiving and alarm until he stood up and said: "I am a conscript soldier, but I am a Christian.

I would worship with you"; then they welcomed him. After the service was over, the Japanese went up to the minister and asked him to sign his name in the Bible he had brought with him from Japan. He wrote in Chinese: "In Christ there is neither Jew nor Greek."—*Christian Herald,* London.

* * *

Isn't It True?

A happy Christian one day met an Irish peddler, and said to him. "It's a grand thing to be saved." "Aye," said the peddler, "it is. But I know something better than that." "Better than being saved?" asked the other. "What can you possibly know better than that?" "The companionship of the Man who has saved me," was the reply. The companionship of Jesus!—we may all have it.—Selected.

* * *

Demonstrable, Even if Inexplicable

The mystery of this union with Christ puzzles many. It is an experience which can be lived and even illustrated, but never fully explained. The old colored man had the right answer for the man who said sarcastically, "You said Christ lived in you, and now you say you are in Him. How can that possibly be?" The old Negro said thoughtfully, "See this poker? I'll put it in the fire until it turns red. Now the fire's in the poker, and the poker's in the fire."—*The King's Business.*

* * *

Finding the Fellowship

One of the greatest privileges of my life was when I traveled, some years ago, through a number of cities of the United States to get in touch with the spiritually minded people of those cities. I found there existed in those various cities a *fellowship*—that if you could get hold of one person who loved the Lord wholeheartedly, earnestly, and had an outspoken testimony for Him, it was just like the end of a ball of yarn, and by pulling on that person, so to speak, you could find another, and another, and another. They all knew one another; you could open up the whole spiritual life of a town, and find the people in the town who loved the Lord with a whole-hearted devotion. They knew one another.—*Sunday School Times.*

* * *

"This Beats Masonry"

Two brothers were on the Continent spending a holiday. One was an earnest Christian, the other an unconverted Freemason. Englishlike, they made tracks for the nearest fellow countryman, who happened to be the veteran missionary Harry Payne. The Christian and the missionary were "at home" at once, one telling how the work of God prospered in the old country, the other telling of the work of God's grace on the Continent. After some friendly intercourse, they left. Once the street was reached the Mason inquired of his brother: "I say, John, where did you meet that gentleman before?" "Never saw him before in my life," replied the Christian. "What!" exclaimed the Mason, "you never saw him before, and yet the last half hour you have been like brothers? Why, John, this beats Masonry." Yes, there is a bond above all bonds, "we being many are one . . . body (in Christ)."—*Christian Herald.*

* * *

Laddie!

Back in Kansas a young man by the name of Everett E. Berett Scott, of Chanute, heeded his country's call and left for Fort Ord, Calif., to enter into the service. Everett Scott had a dog named Laddie, a 10-year-old airedale. Of course, Laddie had to be left behind. Left behind, Laddie began to grieve for his master. He took no interest in his food, and his condition became very serious. After the master had been gone three months, Laddie was dying.

The whole nation was aroused, through the newspapers, with the story of this dog's absolute loyalty to his master. Science took a hand. He was given glucose injections and blood transfusions, and placed on an aeroplane and sent 2,000 miles through the air to join his master. Temporarily, he revived; but grief had so weakened him that he went "the way of all flesh."

What a valuable lesson a Christian can learn from Laddie. Laddie had everything a dog could want back in Chanute, Kans. His master's personal belongings surrounded him, but all this did not satisfy Laddie. He was brokenhearted. *He wanted nothing but the master himself!*

After all, can anything satisfy the heart of a true Christian but the Lord Himself? Would that all Christians loved the Master as Laddie loved his master. There were many men in Chanute that would be friends to Laddie, but Laddie was a one-man dog. May Laddie teach us the nature of a really born-again Christian. A born-again Christian is a one-man Christian. He has not a divided heart. Yes, a one-Man Christian — and *Jesus Christ is that Man! — The Brethren Missionary Herald.*

FOLLOWING CHRIST

Believers or Disciples

1. To believe is cheap and costs us nothing. But to follow Christ is costly, and He asks us first to consider the great cost.
2. I believe in Christ's work FOR me, but discipleship is the RESULT of His work IN us.
3. Believers consider themselves first, but disciples consider Christ first.
4. Believers (only) produce no perfect fruit, but disciples are known by their fruit.
5. Belief saves my soul, but discipleship glorifies Christ.
6. Believers (only) are not necessarily known as Christians, but disciples are known as Christians.
7. Believers go to heaven, but disciples are greatly rewarded there. — Selected.

* * *

They Really Meant It

One market day in their village, two Chwang tribesmen heard a colporteur preach the Gospel. Then he began to sell Gospels, promising blessing to those who not only read but obeyed the precepts contained therein. Both men purchased copies, and taking them home, they read along till they came to the statement, "If any man will come after me, let him deny himself, and take up his cross daily, and follow me." In their desire to obey the Word of God, they made two crosses of bamboo, and tied them on their backs. (The Chinese translation of the words, "Take up his cross," is "Bear his cross on his back.") They carried these crosses as they visited the market or went about the country, and then carefully hung them on the front of their houses when they were home. Seeing their earnestness of heart, God did not leave them long in the dark. Soon a Chinese worker discovered them, briefly explained the Gospel to them, and advised them to go to Liuchow for further instruction. They did so, and after a week of instruction returned to their village and began to witness for the Lord. Several months later they went back to Liuchow, requesting baptism and further instruction. We were glad to grant both their requests as they exhibited an earnestness seldom seen anywhere.—*Alliance Weekly.*

* * *

A Verse for Missionaries

A young lady leaving for the mission field was sitting by a dear friend in the home church the Sunday evening previous. Suddenly, as if moved by a strong impulse, the friend took the young missionary's Bible and turned to John 10, and underscored part of the fourth verse: "And when he putteth forth his own sheep, he goeth before them." How many times during the years that followed, in days of darkness and difficulty, that promise was a source of power and comfort. "The Lord . . . sent them . . . whither he himself would come."—*Sunday School Times.*

* * *

How the Sheep Were Rescued

During the World War some Turkish soldiers tried to drive away a flock of sheep. It was on a hillside near Jerusalem. The shepherd who was sleeping was suddenly aroused to see them being driven off. But singlehanded he could not hope to recapture his flock by force. Suddenly he had a thought. Standing up on his side of the ravine he put his hands to his mouth and gave his own peculiar call which he used each day to gather his sheep to him. And his sheep heard it. For a moment they listened, and hearing it again they turned and rushed down one side of the ravine and up the other, and it was quite impossible for the men to stop them. So the shepherd was away with them to a place of safety before the soldiers could make up their minds to pursue them.—*The King's Business.*

* * *

What Is That to Thee

Peter was told by the Lord to follow Him. Instead of responding, "Lord, by Thy grace I will," he seems to have been occupied with his fellow-disciple John. "Lord, and what shall this man do?" he inquired.

Answering him our Lord said, "What is that to thee?" And He added, making it more definitely personal, "Follow *thou* Me."

Let us not look upon others when we should be looking on our Lord.

Whatever the other man may be called to do, and whether he does it or not is not our business (though we should seek to help others by example and precept).

Our business is to follow our Lord for ourselves.—I. F., in *Scattered Seed.*

Processional Caterpillars

There is a sort of caterpillar called the "Processional Caterpillar," which walks in long lines, each one following closely the next in front. Now a certain man, Le Fabre by name, once saw a number of these marching round the moulding of a stone vase in his garden. He got some more of them and filled up the gap between the tail and the head of the procession, and watched to see what the caterpillars would do. They went on following each his neighbor in front; they walked round that vase for a week, and covered nearly a mile of distance. Don't be processional caterpillars, with your nose glued to your neighbor's back, and no thought as to where he is leading you, or whether he is worthy to be followed at all. Follow the Christ, the King.—*Sunday at Home.*

* * *

If Jesus Christ is a man,
And only a man, I say
That of all mankind I will cleave to him
And to him I will cleave alway.

But if Jesus Christ is a God,
And the only God, I swear
I will follow him through heaven and hell,
The earth, the sea, and the air.

—Selected.

* * *

"The Lamb Is My Shepherd"

"The Lamb is my Shepherd! How foolish! How can a lamb be a shepherd?" The thought was flashed into mind as we read the words. But in fact the words were not there at all. A blur in our bifocals was responsible for it. The motto on the wall proved to be the opening lines of the Twenty-third Psalm. But perplexity turned to praise as we said half aloud, "The Lamb *is* my Shepherd." The glorious Gospel had been held up before us as another new gem. The Old Testament represents the *Lord* as our Shepherd and the New Testament from the Gospels to Revelation tells of the *Lamb* who is our Shepherd. The apostles and disciples beheld the Lamb and followed him. And John in his Patmos vision tells us that "the Lamb which is in the midst of the throne shall feed them";—that is, shall be their shepherd. —A. S. Reitz, in *Moody Monthly.*

* * *

I Will Follow

I will follow Thee, my Saviour,
Wheresoe'er my lot may be,
Where Thou goest I will follow,
Yes, my Lord, I'll follow Thee.

Though the road be rough and thorny,
Trackless as the foaming sea,
Thou hast trod this way before me,
And I'll gladly follow Thee.

Though I meet with tribulation,
Sorely tempted though I be,
I remember Thou wast tempted,
And rejoice to follow Thee.
—Selected.

* * *

A Dog's Standard

A gentleman followed by a rough-looking dog got into a car in Edinburgh. The dog followed the car in the face of many obstacles. Soon after another dog came up, bent on a quarrel; afterward, another dog more determined; then a third, and a fourth. He took no notice, but continued to follow his master—only following and looking up. What a lesson he taught us! His one object was to follow his master, and this he did faithfully.—*The Christian Endeavor World.*

FORGETTING GOD

Getting Out of Range

A little boy's prayer on the night before leaving for the country unconsciously expressed a situation that is tragically real even in homes of Christian belief: "Good-bye, God, we are going to the country tomorrow." There are still modern Jonahs who feel that when they get away from familiar scenes they get out of range of God.—*Christian Herald.*

* * *

Ears Which Hear Not

In a dispatch in the press for September 30 (1939), referring to the "holy images" throughout Poland, he (the present pope) says: "So many miracles have been performed by these images that surely Christians can trust a merciful God and believe in the resurrection of Poland." Far from being a defense to a people, images are abhorred of God. In Psalm 78 the Psalmist says: "For they provoked him to anger . . . with their graven images" so that "he gave his people over also unto the sword; and was wroth with his inheritance. The fire consumed their young men.". . . How different the real Peter from the pseudo-Peters down through the centuries! After the healing of the lame man at the Temple gate, Peter ascribes to Christ and to Christ alone the miracle: "And his (Christ's) name through faith in his name hath made this man strong, whom ye see and know: yea, the faith which is by him (Christ) hath given him this perfect soundness."—Ernest Gordon, in *The Sunday School Times.*

* * *

Why the Answer Changed

A minister was passing a certain farm one day, when he noticed a fine rick of hay, just finished and ready for thatching. He said to the farmer who was standing by, "That's a very fine rick of hay. Who made it?" "I did," said the farmer. "I made it." A few weeks later the minister had occasion to pass the farm again. To his astonishment he saw that the rick, through a heavy gale, had capsized and fallen to the ground. He went to the farmer and condoled with him on his misfortune, and again asked, "Who made the rick?" "There were several of us," was the reply. That's it! When things go well, we are apt to say, "I did it"; but when they go wrong, we say, "There were several of us."—*Christian Herald.*

* * *

We Must Look to God

Social reform has failed to counteract crime, politics is unmentionably decayed, big business cannot handle our economic collapse, legislation is helpless to restore honesty and integrity, mediation is no cure for industrial strife, trade agreements between nations and international conferences have been destined to the scrap heap. To all of which may be added the unspeakable horror of Europe's predicament!

Yes, materialism has been tried and found wanting. No materialistic agency has been able to stem the tide of the present disruption. Only the Church of God fully united can save the world, a world that has reached a crucial turning point. There is no solution to our perplexity in the mechanics of man. We must look to God for salvation. Everywhere, among thinking people, the cry is, "Back to the Church!"

"Blessed is the nation whose God is the Lord." Psalm 33:12.—*The New Jersey Kiwanian.*

* * *

Depression—The Cause, The Cure

Less than one hundred years ago, Daniel Webster, one of America's greatest statesmen, uttered this solemn warning, "If we abide by the principles taught in the Bible, our country will go on prospering; but if we and our posterity neglect its instructions and authority, no man can tell how sudden a catastrophe may overwhelm us and bury all our glory in profound obscurity."

On being asked what was the chief cause of the depression, Congressman Clyde Kelly replied, "Spiritual bankruptcy. We have been worshiping the Golden Calf. The results are seen all around us." Senator Capper said, "Had there been the universal acceptation of the principals of Christian justice and charity there would be today neither economic nor spiritual depression. The world forgot Christ in the rush for money. The only god that many of us know seems to be the almighty dollar." In answer to the question, "How do you account for this state of affairs?" the Senator replied, "There are too many dust-covered Bibles, prayerless homes, deserted churches without even the semblance of a prayer meeting. There is a widespread spiritual ignorance and desecration of the Lord's Day. These form part of the religious background of the past decade."

"As a business man and as one whose privilege it is to have a part in shaping the policies of our government, I say to you that the greatest need in the world today is a wider acceptance of, and a greater devotion to, the fundamentals of Christianity."

The Bible says, "Be not deceived; God is not mocked: for whatsoever a man (or nation) soweth, that shall he also reap. For he that soweth to his flesh shall of the flesh reap corruption; but he that soweth to the Spirit shall of the Spirit reap life everlasting" (Gal. 6:7, 8).—*Gospel Herald.*

* * *

No Room for Christ

A friend says to me, "I have not time or room in my life for Christianity. If it were not so full! You don't know how hard I work from morning till night. When have I time, where have I room for Christianity in such a life as mine?"

It is as if the engine had said it had no room for the steam. It is as if the tree said it had no room for the sap. It is as if the ocean said it had no room for the tide. It is as if the man had said he had no room for his soul. It is as if the life had said it had no time to live, when it is life. It is not something add-to life; it is *life.* A man is not living without it. And for a man to say, "I am so full in life that I have no room for life," *you see immediately to what absurdity it reduces itself.* — Phillips Brooks, in *Flowers of Thought.*

A Confession from France

America should take a solemn warning from the decline of other nations. France's fall is passing into history, but reports occasionally reach this side of the ocean giving further insight into the cause of it. In opening his ninth series of Lutheran Hour broadcasts over a coast-to-coast network on October 19, Dr. Walter A. Maier of Concordia Seminary quoted a Paris editorial which said in part: "We are going to pay for sixty years of de-Christianization, falling birth rates, decline into paganism and materialism. We have worn out the patience of Providence; we have disgusted the good God Himself." Dr. Maier added that the most tragic waste in America is the far-reaching neglect of the Bible. Those who have worked in countries dominated by Romanism know that the phrase, "the good God," comes glibly from Catholic tongues, as though it referred to an idol. But this confession from Paris has a ring of sincerity and contains much truth. It is a fresh challenge to Americans to humble themselves before God, in repentance for our manifold sins, and in utter dependence upon His wisdom and power. It would be well for us as a nation if we could step down and say, like King Nebuchadnezzar: "Now I . . . praise and extol and honor the King of heaven, all whose works are truth, and his ways judgment: and those that walk in pride he is able to abase" (Dan. 4:37). — *Sunday School Times.*

* * *

After Thirty-Eight Years

At the Diamond Jubilee Thanksgiving Service of Queen Victoria in St. Paul's Cathedral in 1897, a young man of thirty-two, taken aback at the overwhelming military display and aghast that the religious and moral forces of the Empire should be so in the Background, went home and wrote:

> God of our fathers, known of old,
> Lord of our far-flung battle line,
> Beneath whose awful hand we hold
> Dominion over palm and pine;
> Lord God of hosts, be with us yet,
> Lest we forget—lest we forget!

At King George's Silver Jubilee Rudyard Kipling speaks again (London *Times*, May 7, 1935), this time on the world outlook: "Today State-controlled murder and torture, open and secret, State-engineered famine, starvation, and slavery; State-imposed godlessness, or State-prescribed paganism are commonplaces of domestic administration throughout States whose aggregate area is between one-fifth and one-fourth of the total land surface of the Eastern hemisphere."—*Sunday School Times.*

* * *

Spiritual Need

Roger Babson, the business expert and statistician to whom the business men send in hundreds of dollars so that he will keep them in touch with the progress of business, says, "I do not pose as a preacher, but let me tell you, if there is a God, He will not let us advance much further materially until we catch up spiritually.——*Gospel Herald.*

* * *

A Great Editor Comes Back to God

The Editor of the *Sunday Express*, Mr. James Douglas, gave his readers recently a brief but remarkable touch of spiritual biography, in the course of which he affirmed, "I have come back to the simple faith of my father and mother." After referring to a childhood of poverty, the diet of "stirabout and potatoes," the marvelous faith of his father and mother and "the chapter of chapters which rang like a tocsin of hope in our humble home," — the 14th chapter of John—Mr. Douglas says:

> Since those years I have sinned many sins and suffered many sorrows. I have lost my way in the thickets and deserts of doubt and argument. And in the end I have come back to the simple faith of my father and my mother. It, and it alone, suffices in the starkest agony of life.
>
> I cannot explain the hidden mystery of faith. It is too deep for words. But it is all in John 14.

"In My Father's House are many mansions: if it were not so, I would have told you. I go to prepare a place for you."

"And whither I go ye know, and the way ye know."

Thrilling words! Magical words! I hear Thomas in his perplexity asking the great question: "Lord, we know not whither Thou goest; and how can we know the way?" I hear the mystical answer which for two thousand years has held the field against all the world and all the worldlings:

"Jesus saith unto him, I am the Way, the Truth, and the Life: no man cometh unto the Father, but by Me."

"He that hath seen Me hath seen the Father. . . . I go unto the Father: for My Father is greater than I."

I have stumbled through all the wilds and wastes of theology, philosophy, psychology, and science. I have traveled from Dan to Beersheba, and I have found all knowledge and all reason barren. The sure refuge from withering cynicism and parching pessimism I find in John 14, where the trumpet of faith blows finality and security and safety and certitude.

"I am the Way, the Truth, and the Life."—*Broadcaster.*

* * *

Leaving Out God

If we study the public documents, the charters, and political compacts of long ago, we will find that God has a great place in the thoughts of those who formulated the documents. Our own Constitution was founded upon much of Bible truth. But a study of later papers, such as the treaty of Versailles, and other important pronouncements, reveals the total absence of God's name. Thus the race progresses in godlessness. —*Young People's Full Gospel Quarterly.*

* * *

Sayings of the Sages on Returning to God (selected by W. P. Wilks)

Above all things, this country needs a nation-wide revival of old-fashioned prayer meeting religion.—Richard M. Edmonds.

It is either Christ or chaos; either the kingdom of God or world revolution.—David Lloyd George.

The sum of the whole matter is this, that our civilization cannot survive materially unless it be redeemed spiritually. It can be saved only by becoming permeated with the spirit of Christ and being made free and happy by the practices which spring out of that spirit. Only thus can discontent be driven out and all the shadows lifted from the road ahead.—Woodrow Wilson.

Henceforth the majesty of God revere;
Fear Him, and you have nothing else
to fear.

—James Fordyce.

* * *

His "Forgotten" Son

The Holy Spirit wonderfully overrules mistakes when He is dealing with souls. Dealing with an anxious, inquiring woman at the close of a service, I asked if she could quote any Scripture. She gave John 3:16, but used the word "forgotten" instead of "begotten." Taking advantage of the thought of the word I asked her, "Do you know why God 'forgot' his Son?" "No." "It was because the Lord wanted to remember you. God in Heaven was willing to part with His Son for a little while that He might have you forever. He let His Son be enveloped in terrible darkness, so that He might give you a crown of light. He let him die so that he could give you eternal life. It was for you that God 'forgot' His Son." Dr. Walter L. Wilson, in *Romance of a Doctor's Visits.*

* * *

What a Modern Scientist Says:

I think the greatest discovery will be along spiritual lines. Here is a force which history clearly teaches has been the greatest power in the development of man and history, yet we have been merely playing with it, and never seriously studied it as we have the social forces. Some day people will learn that material things do not bring happiness and are of little use in making men creative. Then the scientists of the world will turn their laboratories over to the study of God and prayer and the spiritual forces, which as yet have been hardly scratched. When this day comes the world will advance more in one generation than it has in the past four generations. — Dr. Charles Steinmetz.

* * *

Getting Back to God

"People must get back to God," says Roger Babson, the great statistician. "For a long time it has been considered rather smart to be irreligious. Now people must get back to God. Above all, they should start praying. They seem to think that there is something about prayer that is not exactly red-blooded or two-fisted.

"When business worries me," says Mr. Babson, *"I think of God. If someone has been unkind to me, I think of God. If I should come face to face with disaster, I should think of God."—Boston Herald.*

* * *

"Away with Him!"

A correspondent of the *Palestine Review* writes: "One of the great attractions of Palestine is that you are with other Jews. When you go through the streets on Saturday, shops are closed; when you go on Sunday, they are open. In the bus you meet Jews; in the theater you sit next to Jews; in the café you eat with Jews; in the hospital you are with Jews. There are the marvelous nights with a million stars. There are ghosts everywhere of Abraham and Jacob, Isaiah and Jeremiah, Akiba and Bar Cochba. Every step tells a story,—Biblical, Talmudic, Medieval, Modern." But nothing of Christ! He is the great Forgotten One. And not merely forgotten. Dr. Christie writes in the *British Weekly* that "multitudes in Israel" are determined to blot out the geographical evidences of Christianity (in Palestine), and warnings have been given to "take **away your dead Christ from our land."**
—*Sunday School Times.*

* * *

Says General Dwight D. Eisenhower:

"The longer one lives close to the turmoil and sacrifice and suffering of the battlefield, the more he becomes conscious of the eternal worth of the spiritual values inherent in the Christian religion. Moreover, because this war constitutes a direct conflict between the forces of evil and those of Christian principles of human rights and dignity, every moment which increases general familiarization with those principles has a direct uplifting effect upon the soldiery and citizens of the United Nations. In **such efforts I stand ever ready to assist."**

FORGIVENESS, GOD'S

Salvation's Swift Miracle

A very godless man, noted for his profanity, was one day carrying freight up a gangplank to a big steamer. A man following him accidentally jostled him, and the blasphemer fell into the water, between the wharf and the boat. His last utterance was a horrible oath, a curse upon his comrade. He immediately disappeared. After some time he was rescued from beneath the boat, apparently drowned. Strenuous efforts put forth to resuscitate him were finally successful. With his first breath he cried out, "Praise God, I'm saved!" "Yes, you were pretty near gone," someone replied. "Oh," he said, "I don't mean saved from drowning. I mean saved inside. The Lord has taken my sins away." Then he told them when he found himself beneath the boat, he thought the end had come. In those few seconds he saw himself kneeling again at his mother's side, and heard her prayers for him. His sin, as a high mountain, rose before him, and he cried to God to save him. In the cleansing of the blood. It was for that moment he realized forgiveness, and this that he praised God with his first breath.—*Alliance Weekly.*

* * *

The Deep Sea

The ocean covers seventy-two per cent of the earth's surface to an average depth of 11,500 feet. Its greatest depths are the Sigsbee's Deep, 13,200 feet, and Nares Deep, 28,200 feet, in the Atlantic, and the Japan Trough, 29,136 feet, Tonga Deep, 30,132 feet, and Nero Deep, 31,614 feet, off the Island of Guam, in the Pacific. If Mount Everest were dropped into the Nero Deep, the water would still cover it by half a mile. If God graciously, for Christ's sake, will pardon our sins and cast them into the depths of the sea (Micah 7:18, 19), where even the penetrating rays discovered by Milliken cannot reach them, then we may rejoice in our freedom.—J. M., in *The Missionary Worker.*

* * *

Keep Him Going

A man asked an old Christian woman, "Does the Devil ever trouble you about your past sins?" She said, "Yes." "What do you do then?" "Oh, I just send him to the east." "Does he come back after that?" "Aye." "And what do you do then?" "I just send him away to the west." "And when he comes back from the west what do you do?" "Man, I just keep him going between the east and the west."—*The King's Business.*

* * *

Lord, Forgive

If I have wounded any soul today,
If I have caused one foot to go astray,
If I have walked in my own wilful way—
Good Lord, forgive!

If I have uttered idle words or vain,
If I have turned aside from want or pain,
Lest I myself should suffer through the strain—
Good Lord, forgive!

If I have been perverse, or hard, or cold,
If I have longed for shelter in thy fold,
When Thou hast given me some fort to hold—
Good Lord, forgive!

Forgive the sins I have confessed to Thee,
Forgive the secret sins I do not see,
That which I know not, Father, teach Thou me—
Help me to live.

—C. M. Battersby.

* * *

"Bundles of Benefits"

The Bishop of London calls Psalm 103 "Bundles of Benefits" and says: *"The psalmist set himself one day to count up the benefits he had received from God. He had not proceeded far when he found himself engaged in an impossible task.* He found he could not count the blessings he had received in a single day, so set himself to find a help to memory. He took these benefits which he desired not to forget, and he tied them up in bundles. He shaped the bundles into a song." The Bishop of London names five such bundles — forgiveness, healing, redemption, the coronation of love, and satisfaction. These, however, are in the first five verses and there are still others to be discovered in the following verses. —A. C. Crews, in *Westminster Teacher.*

* * *

Praying for Forgiveness

A small boy who had done something wrong, found himself amid a roomful of elders, stern-visaged in the hope that he would understand the seriousness of his offense. He looked at his nurse and his relatives one by one with a tear-stained face, and as he saw no sign of relenting the little one burst into tears and asked, "Oh, won't somebody forgive me?"

But here we have offended the great and holy God a thousandfold, and before we realized the seriousness of our crimes He sent His only-begotten Son to show us on His horrible cross how great our sins were; but even before that dreadful scene was enacted the Son tenderly advised us to return to this offended God with the word, "O my Father, forgive me."

What human tongue shall describe such mercy? Who could disdain this mercy without heaping insult to injury? —Jan Karel Van Baalen, in *The Journey of Man.*

* * *

Pardon for Nothing

A few days since, while visiting an old man who seemed anxious about salvation, I found great difficulty in making him understand that pardon is the free gift of God, through the precious Blood of Christ.

At last I said to him:

"Now, suppose I were to go to a shop and buy something for you, and pay for it, and tell you to go and fetch it: need you take any money with you?"

"No," said the old man, brightening up; "it would be paid for."

"Need you make any promise to pay at some future time?" I then asked.

"No," he replied; "I should have it for nothing."

"So," I continued, "is it with forgiveness of sins. The Lord Jesus has paid the full price of it. He has had the wrath, the pain, the punishment; yea, all that sin deserved. He bore it all. He paid the whole. Yes, bought forgiveness with His precious Blood, and now He gives it as a gift to all who bring their sins to Him."

"Yes," said the old man, as his eyes filled with tears, "I see it now; it is pardon for nothing! Pardon for nothing! Christ has bought it, and He will give it me."—*Scattered Seed.*

* * *

Not Dependent on Feelings

Someone asked Luther, "Do you feel
That you have been forgiven?"
He answered, "No, but I'm as sure
As there's a God in Heaven.
For feelings come, and feelings go,
And feelings are deceiving.
My warrant is the Word of God,
Naught else is worth believing."
—*Alliance Weekly.*

Before the King Could See Him

There was a young musician in the Royal band of Hanover. He was a remarkable lad for his age, and his superior playing won for him much praise. He liked to discourse upon martial music at the head of the troops, but when war came on and he had to lie in the trenches all night, he deserted and fled to England. Now for a soldier to desert, the penalty is death, as we are sadly aware, and it is usually inflicted when the deserter is caught. But this man was not caught. He became a great organist, but his heart was in the stars, and he was still a great astronomer. With infinite pains, he constructed a telescope, and then he scanned the heavens night after night, until one night he actually discovered a new planet. He verified the discovery, and then received the applause of the whole world. He was sent for by the King, and went to Windsor Castle. But the King was George, of Hanover, the sovereign to whom his life was forfeited for his old desertion. The King knew him, too; and what would he do? Before the King would see him he was requested to open an envelope containing a royal communication. He did so, wondering what the King was going to do with him. It was his pardon as a deserter. "Now," said King George, "we can talk, and you shall come up and live at Windsor and be Sir William Herschel." How like God in pardoning a sinner! He not only forgives him, but He honors him in making him a son of God.—Mark Guy Pearse.

* * *

A Sufficient Saviour

There was a Scotchman who had formerly been a notable character, a prize fighter and gambler. Changed by the grace of God, he became a mighty soulwinner, and on one occasion his message was being greatly blessed. Just before he arose to speak at one service, someone sent an envelope up to the platform. On opening it he found it contained a long list of sins and crimes that he had committed in that very city.

At first he felt that he must run away, but stepping boldly to the front of the platform he said, "Friends, I am accused of crimes and sins committed in this very city. I will read them to you." One after another he read these charges, and at the conclusion of each he said, "I am guilty." When he had finished the whole list, he paused for a moment and then said, "You ask how I dare come to you and speak of righteousness and truth, with a list of crimes like that against my name? I will tell you: *'This is a faithful saying, and worthy of all acceptation, that Christ Jesus came into the world to save sinners; of whom I am chief.'"—Moody Church News.*

* * *

When He Faced Death

He was found in a lowly hut, dead, with a dish-pan he had used for a desk across his knees, and in his skeleton hand the following letter, in the writing of which he was evidently engaged when death overtook him. "The sun is shining, Mother, but I feel so cold. I can still walk a little, but that's about all. There is no blood in me, because I have not eaten for so long. I haven't seen another human being for forty days now. There are some magazines here, but *the stories are so silly.* I have some cards, but *I don't care for solitaire. The only thing I worry about is if God will forgive my sins."* Thus ended the career of a young explorer at Long Rapids, Hay River, Alberta, Can. He was about to leap into the dark, so far as his eternity was concerned.—*Sunday School Times.*

* * *

As far as the east is removed from the
west,
My sins are remembered no more;
Forever my soul is at perfect rest,
My sins are remembered no more.

Forgiven, forgotten, all cleansed in the
Blood,
My sins are remembered no more;
Atoned for by Jesus in Calv'ry's flood,
My sins are remembered no more.
—Selected.

Sins Put Away

There is a minister in this hall this afternoon who remembers an early morning ride we had together in Canada not many weeks ago. He will remember well the third passenger in that car, another minister—a young man who has been successful in a few years of the pastorate, and who, working very hard —too hard—has had a physical breakdown which expresses itself in a kind of mental distress. The young man had a visit with me in my hotel room, and then the next day was a passenger in that car, riding over to the main line of the railroad for that early morning train. He brought up again the question with which he had pursued me just the day before, when I had tried to answer it two or three times. What about this inner voice that tells me, "Those sins back there—the sins of my life need to be cared for; there is something I must do about them"? He understands the gospel of God's grace, and has preached it faithfully. "Oh," he said, "I could stand it—I could stand it if it were the evil one trying to taunt me about those sins. I could stand it if I understood it to be the result of my physical condition. But the thing that tortures me is the feeling that it might be the Holy Spirit prodding me concerning the sins of my past." I had said to him the day before that the Holy Spirit would never nag, but suddenly, in the car, this thought came. I couldn't help but feel it was the Spirit's own thought. If it is true that God has put away your sins, and that you received Christ as Saviour—and you believe you did—He blotted them out of His own memory—if that is true—and you say you believe it is—then God has forgotten. If God has forgotten, how could He ever remind you? The Holy Spirit has not been reminding you of your sins. When you brought them to the foot of the Cross and left them there, you may be sure that God blotted them out.—Courtesy *Moody Monthly.*

* * *

Forgiveness Refused

The son of a Presbyterian preacher was arrested, charged with treason because he belonged to an organization which had been outlawed by the Government. He was tried, convicted, and sent to the penitentiary. His aged father, eminent for his learning and Christian character, circulated a petition and secured hundreds of signatures, urging President Grant to pardon the boy for the sake of his parents. The father took the petition to Washington, presented it to President Grant, who gave the pardon. The old man received it and hastened to the train. On his arrival at the prison, he was shown the cell where his boy was imprisoned. Standing with his hand upon the grated door he said, "John, I have good news. I have a pardon from President Grant, and you may now go home with me, and see your mother before she dies!" But the son made no response. "Do you understand me, John?" the father continued. "Here's a pardon for you." "I am sorry, Father," said the ungrateful son, "to give you pain, but I cannot accept it. I have decided not to be brought under obligation to this political administration, and I will serve out my time!" The old man's father-heart was almost broken. He fell against the grating, and would have sunk upon the floor if he had not been caught by the friendly hand of the warden. A pardon is offered you from the High Court of Heaven, a pardon written in the blood of Jesus. Will you accept it and go free, or will you reject it and continue under sin's bondage?—Dr. A. C. Dixon.

FORGIVING OTHERS

More Than Forgiveness

My father was fatally ill, and as I watched the precious life ebbing away, I was overcome with remorse at the thought that I must often have grieved that loving heart with my careless ingratitude and thoughtless disobedience. Penitently I begged his forgiveness for my wrongdoings in the past. With a look of ineffable love in his pain-dimmed eyes, he said, "I can't remember that you ever did anything wrong." I had expected instant forgiveness, but was not prepared for the full measure of pardon which I received. He could not remember my wrongs because of his great love for me. How like the Heavenly Father's love for us all! "For I will be merciful to their unrighteousness, and their sins and their iniquities will I remember no more" (Heb. 8:12).—From a personal experience, in *Sunday School Times.*

* * *

Is It Keeping Us From Christ?

One afternoon at Cleveland, after Mr. Moody had been speaking, he brought me to a lady to show her the way of life. I had been speaking to her trying this and that passage to see what was in the way of her accepting Christ, when suddenly I turned to her and said, "Is there somebody you cannot forgive?" She looked quickly at me, and said, "Who told you?" I said, "Nobody told me, and I have never seen you before tonight." That was her trouble, and that is the trouble with some of you. Someone has done you an injury, or you think he has, and you will not come to Jesus Christ because you want to cherish this bitter grudge in your heart.—Dr. R. A. Torrey, in *Revival Addresses.*

* * *

The Power of Forgiveness

A young Christian working man told me that he lost a valued tool from his tool kit and recognized it later in the kit of his fellow workman. Being the only Christian at work in the room he felt it incumbent upon him to show forgiveness. So he went to the thief and said, "I see you have one of my tools, but you can keep it if you need it." Then he went on with his work and put the incident out of his mind. During the next two weeks the thief three times tried to give the value of the tool to its rightful owner—once by offering to give him something else of equal value, again by offering his services between hours, and again by slipping money into his coat pocket. The incident closed with a lasting friendship between the two men, because, said the thief, "I couldn't stand being forgiven." — Henry and Tertius van Dyke in *Light My Candle;* Fleming H. Revell Company.

* * *

"Father, Forgive"

A hardened criminal in a Japanese prison, having nothing else to do, picked up a copy of the Bible that had been given him and opened it at the story of the trial of Jesus. He read on until he came to these words: "Father, forgive them; for they know not what they do." He stopped, "stabbed to the heart, as if pierced by a five-inch nail." This is his testimony: "Through this simple sentence I was led into the whole of Christianity."—*Gospel Herald.*

* * *

The Unforgiving Spirit

Nothing will hinder prevailing prayer more than an unforgiving spirit. A child was walking along a street and a large dog came out barking. She stood terrified. Soon a stranger came to her and said, "Come on, little girl, the dog has stopped barking." "Yes, she said, "but the bark is on the inside." She saw in the eyes of the dog an unfriendly spirit. *We Christians are too civilized today to quarrel outwardly, but is there not sometimes a bark inside — an unforgiving spirit?*—Robert P. Wilder, in *Christ and the Student World.*

* * *

"I Will Forgive, But—"

The Rev. E. L. Hamilton says: "I remember once rebuking a Christian worker for manifesting an unforgiving spirit toward another. At length she said, 'Well, I forgive her, but I never want to have anything more to do with her.' I stopped and said, 'Is *that* how you want God to forgive you? Do you want him to say He will forgive you, but He will have nothing more to do with you?' "—*The King's Business.*

* * *

What Is Forgiveness?

A little boy, being asked what forgiveness is, gave the beautiful answer: "It is the odor that flowers breathe when they are trampled upon." The Bible says: "And grieve not the Holy Spirit of God, whereby ye are sealed unto the day of redemption. Let all bitterness, and wrath, and anger, and clamour, and evil speaking, be put away from you, with all malice: and be ye kind one to another, tenderhearted *forgiving one another,* even as God for Christ's sake hath forgiven you" (Eph. 4:30-32).—Selected.

* * *

A Spiritual Mind for Spiritual Work

When Leonardo da Vinci was putting on canvas his great masterpiece which the world knows today as "The Last Supper," he became quite angry with a certain man. He lashed him with hot and bitter words and threatened the man with vengeance. But when the great painter returned to his canvas and began to paint the face of Jesus he found himself so perturbed and disquieted that he could not compose himself for the delicate work before him, and not until he had sought out the man and asked forgiveness did he find himself in possession of that inner calm which enabled him to give to the Master's face the tender and delicate expression he so well knew it must have. *The conscientious Christian with anything like a real spiritual experience knows how true it is.*—William Edward Biederwolf, in *The Man Who Said He Would.*

* * *

After 490, What?

The story has been told of two children, Dick and Dorothy, with a big brother who teased them unmercifully. One Sunday they heard the story of Peter's question: "Lord, how oft shall my brother sin against me, and I forgive him? till seven times?" Then they heard the Lord's reply, "I say not unto thee, Until seven times: but, Until seventy times seven." Dick had been working out the sum, and he exclaimed: "Look, it's four hundred and ninety times!" The children were silent for a moment, then Dorothy said: "We'll keep a book, and put in it every time we forgive him." "Yes," Dick exclaimed eagerly, "and when it's 490, let him look out!"—*Toronto Globe.*

* * *

The Politest Man

The politest man has been discovered. He was hurrying along the street one night when another man, also in haste, rushed out of a doorway, and the two collided with great force. The second man was infuriated and spoke abusive language, while the polite man, taking off his hat, said very discreetly: "My dear sir, I don't know which of us is to blame for this encounter, but I am in too great a hurry to investigate. If I ran into you, I beg your pardon; if you ran into me, don't mention it." And he tore away with redoubled speed.—*Forward.*

* * *

What Blocked the Revival

We were gathered to pray for a revival. After some hymns and prayers the meeting was thrown open. The silence of death settled upon the audience. Everyone waited. Presently a leading elder arose in a front seat, and said: "I don't think there is going to be a revival here so long as Brother Jones and I don't speak to each other." He left his pew, walked down the aisle, and found Brother Jones, and said: "Brother Jones, you and I have not spoken for five years. Let's bury the hatchet. Here's my hand." The old man returned to his pew and sat down. A sob broke from the audience, and then there was silence again. Presently I was witnessing the strangest scene of my life. For ten minutes men and women crept noiselessly about the house, squaring old scores. Then God began to visit them. Operatives in a factory near by heard what was going on, and at the lunch hour many of them came over. The pastor preached to them the simple Gospel, and within five minutes the ringleaders in sin in that community were crying to God for mercy. A revival broke out that swept over the district for three years." —*Baptist Teacher.*

* * *

Her Cure for Headache

At a women's meeting the subject of cures came up, and a newcomer was asked to give her experience. "I guess you will think it a funny cure," she replied. "Once, years ago, I had a dreadful headache. I hadn't slept a wink the night before. I was grieving about a friend who had not treated me right. I was going over and over what I would say to Mehitable some day. Then I saw a big grudge was growing up inside me. 'Now,' said I, 'suppose she really did do it. Is that any reason why you should grow a grudge?' So I began forgiving her as hard as I could, and soon I just loved her. And when I had thoroughly forgiven her my headache was gone, and I felt nice all over. After that, whenever I had a headache or pain, I practiced going away by myself and forgiving someone and it worked wonderfully." "Did you always have someone," asked the minister's wife, "to practice on?" "Deary me, no, I ran out of folks to forgive long ago, and about the same time I ran out of aches and pains, too. I haven't lost a day in bed in forty-five years." There was a pause, and Miss Everett, with shining eyes, said: "Ladies, I move a vote of thanks to dear Aunty Glen for a very inexpensive cure. And I move that we also adopt and practice it."—*Youth's Companion.*

* * *

Forgiveness

Forgiveness of those who have wronged us is very difficult but very Christlike.

It was told of Governor Stewart, a former governor of Missouri, that on one occasion he was examining a convict with a view to pardoning him. He recognized in the man a former mate of a river steamboat on which he had served as a cabin boy. The man had been notorious for his cruelty to those at work under him on the boat. In handing him his pardon, the governor said: "I want you to promise that you will never again take a stick of wood and drive a sick boy out of his berth on a stormy night, because some day that boy may be governor and you may want him to pardon you for another crime. I was that boy! Here is your pardon!"—William Chalmers Covert, in *Westminster Teacher*.

* * *

Unwilling to Contend

Misjudged by a fellow missionary, Livingstone gave up his house and garden at Mabotsa, with all the toil and money they had cost him, rather than have any scandal before the heathen, and began in a new place the labor of school and house building, and gathering the people round him. His colleague was so struck with his generosity that he said had he known his intention he never would have spoken a word against him. Parting with his garden cost him a great pang. "I do like a garden," he wrote, "but Paradise will make amends for all our privations here." — *Sunday School Times*.

* * *

How oft shalt thou forgive thy brother?
That depends:
How often has thy Lord forgiven thee?
Thy debt was great; it could not greater be,
And yet thou art forgiven and set free!

Wilt thou not then forgive thy brother
Who offends?
Or, wilt thou thrust him in the darksome jail
And cause him at thy ignominy to quail
Until he pays thee all thou dost entail?

If thou wilt not forgive thy brother,
What impends?
As thou hast done, thy Lord will do to you:
He'll punish thee till thou hast paid His due;
In all His dealings God is righteous, true.
—Selected.

Nursing Not the Cure

A man who suffered from a grievance, and who could talk of little else, was one day having a chat with a doctor. "I suppose your experience tells you it is possible to cure almost anything by careful nursing?" he asked. The doctor, who had a keen sense of humor, looked quietly at his questioner. "One thing can never be cured by nursing," he said emphatically. "What might that be?" "A grievance," said the doctor, with a laugh. —*Christian Herald*.

* * *

She Brought Her Answer

A man about thirty years old confessed Christ in a Sunday night service, and on Tuesday he came in and asked if I'd do him a favor. He said that he had to write a letter; that he didn't know how to go about it, and wanted some help. We went into the writing room, and I told him to tell me what he wanted to say, and I would try to express it for him properly. He had some trouble starting, but finally informed me that he had deserted his wife and baby daughter six months before, and had run off with another woman. He wanted his wife to forgive him, because he was a Christian now, and didn't want to die deserving her hatred. The poor fellow wept like a child as he unfolded his tale. He offered no excuses, asked for no favor, just begged for forgiveness. I somehow phrased his pitiful pleas, and we mailed it together. Two weeks later he came in accompanied by his wife and wee daughter. I never saw a happier man in all my life. When his wife got his letter she wasted no time writing; she answered it in person. . . . She said that she had prayed for her husband daily after he left her. She did not ask God to bring him back; only to save him. She got her answer, and her husband! — Harry Rimmer, in *Miracles at Morning Cheer*.

* * *

What He Got Out of It

All the workers in our Egyptian mission are proud of the answer of a young Mohammedan who became a Christian.

His former friends were baiting him, and said, "What have you got out of it?" He replied, "I can forgive."—*Christian Union Herald.*

* * *

Better Not Get Your Rights

Many years ago as a little fellow I attended a meeting in Toronto where some difficulty had come up between brethren and they did as the apostle suggests. My dear mother took me along. "Little pitchers have big ears," and I well remember how horrified I was to see men I esteemed and had been taught to respect apparently so indignant with each other. I can remember one man springing to his feet and with clenched fists saying, "I will put up with a good deal, but one thing I will not put up with, I will not allow you to put anything over on me; I will have my rights!" An old Scotsman who was rather hard of hearing leaned forward holding his ear and said, "What was that, brother? I did not get that!" "I say, I will have my rights," said the man. "But you did not mean that; did you? Your rights? If you had your rights, you would be in hell; wouldn't you? And you are forgetting—aren't you?—that Jesus did not come to get His rights; He came to get His wrongs, and He got them." I can still see that man standing there for a moment like one transfixed, and then the tears broke from his eyes and he said, "Brethren, I have been all wrong. Handle the case as you think best," and he sat down and put his face in his hands and sobbed before the Lord, and everything was settled in three minutes.—Dr. H. A. Ironside, in *Addresses on First Corinthians.*

* * *

The Heathen Father's Welcome

T. R. Stevenson, of Shanghai, says a wealthy merchant of Canton had two sons, the elder a dissipated youth who companied with thieves and gamblers, and was driven from home after wasting his share of the patrimony. Reduced to beggary, he joined a band of robbers who entered his father's house and stole his chest of money. His crime was discovered, and his father sent a trusty to tell him that on the promise of a better life he would be forgiven, and might return. The servant found him in penury, and advised him that the time to reform was now or never. He relented and went to his father's house, and was received with every mark of joy, even a banquet being prepared to celebrate the reconciliation, but the dish set before him was poisoned, and that night he died in agony. Nothing was done to call the father to account, as in Chinese law the son is the father's chattel to do with as he will. To such our missionaries are teaching the truth of Luke 15—Selected.

* * *

A Forgiving Spirit

God's infinite mercy and patience with each of us should lead us to be "kind one to another, tenderhearted, forgiving one another." If we see defects and failings in one another, it is well to remember that God sees more in us, for He looks on the heart. If He can "put up" with the shortcomings of certain of His servants, surely we ought to, for we are sinners likewise. If our love for Him grows cold, and the chilling, deadening effect of a harsh and bitter spirit spreads through our hearts, it is almost certain that we have forgotten how much He has forgiven us. The debtor who loved the most was the one to whom most had been forgiven (Luke 7:42). Thinking of His goodness in forgiving us, for Christ's sake, raises a song in the heart,—

A song of a sinner forgiven,
And a song that is music to Thee;
A song of a pilgrim to Heaven,
Yes, a song from a sinner like me!
—S. Trevor Francis.

* * *

No Will but Ill Will

A woman who had been bitten by a dog was advised by her physician to write her last wishes, as she might succumb to hydrophobia. She spent so long a time with the pencil and paper that the doctor finally remarked something about how long the will would be. "Will!" she snorted. "I'm writing a list of the people I'm going to bite!"—*The Reader's Digest.*

FREEDOM

Union and Liberty

Back of the platform of Faneuil Hall, Boston, stands a large painting of Webster's debate with Hayne, inscribed, "Union and Liberty, one and inseparable, now and forever." I was present when old General William Booth, founder of the Salvation Army, once made an address in Faneuil Hall. His peroration was dramatic. Turning to the painting, he cried, " 'Union and liberty' — union with Christ and liberty from sin—'one and inseparable, now and forever.' " The one safeguard against sin's thralldom is union with the living Christ. There is no spiritual liberty apart from this union.—*Teacher's Quarterly.*

* * *

True Freedom

Herod could incarcerate John the Baptist and finally behead him, but John was free while his captor was a slave although he was called King; Nero was the slave while Paul was God's free man shouting, "I can do all things through Christ which strengtheneth me," in a Roman prison. King James could imprison that humble tinker, John Bunyan, for preaching, on the streets of Bedford, a great spiritual emancipation; but Bunyan was free in a soul that reveled in spiritual visions and delights. Madame Guyon was imprisoned in the lonely Bastille but she sang:

"Stone walls do not a prison make
  Nor iron bars a cage;
Minds innocent and quiet take
  These for a hermitage;
When I am free within my heart
  And in my soul am free
Angels alone that soar above
  Enjoy such liberty."

This is the true freedom that lives under the compulsion of love. Brother, are you really free not only as a citizen of America but of that Heavenly Country? Or are you under the dominion of sin, compelled to give way to evil tempers and lusts—a servant of Romans 7th experience? If so move over into the 8th chapter and shout, "The law of the spirit of life in Christ Jesus hath made me free from the law of sin and death." —*Gospel Herald.*

* * *

Up From Slavery

Booker T. Washington, in his book, *Up from Slavery,* describes the scenes among the blacks on the night of the proclamation of their freedom.

"There was no sleep that night," he says. "All was excitement and expectancy. Early in the morning we were all sent for. The proclamation was read and we were told that we were free and could go when and where we pleased. . . . There was great rejoicing, followed by wild scenes of ecstasy. But," he goes on to say, "the wild rejoicing did not last long. By the time the colored people had returned to their cabins, there was a marked change in their feelings. The great responsibility of being free seemed to take possession of them. It was very much like suddenly turning a youth of ten or twelve out into the world to provide for himself. Within a few minutes the wild rejoicing ceased and a feeling of deep gloom seemed to pervade the slave quarters. Now that they were liberated, they found possession of freedom to be much more serious business than they had anticipated."—Selected.

* * *

"Oh, Missus, Is We Free?"

James H. McConkey relates a very helpful incident, bearing upon this question.

"Shortly after the Civil War a Northern woman came South to visit some friends. She stopped at a little wayside hotel for entertainment. There she was waited on by a colored woman who had been a slave. The service was careless, listless, and inattentive. As this went on, the Northern woman became nettled. Finally she burst out with: 'Auntie, is this the way you treat people who have set you free?' The woman made no reply but left the room. By and by she returned. Her whole demeanor was changed. Her figure was erect, her eyes were flashing, and her voice was full of tears as she cried out with great emotion, 'Oh, Missus, is we free? Is we really free?' The Emancipation Proclamation had really set her free. But she was as much a slave as though that document had never been issued. For she had not believed it. Her failure of faith meant failure of freedom. Multitudes of Christians are in the same plight."—*Way of Victory.*

* * *

Unconscious of Bondage

One reason many have never realized their bondage to sin may seem very paradoxical, but it is, nevertheless, very true. It is because they have never tried to get free. There is a yard where a dog is heavily chained. The dog, however, is fast asleep, and so he does not realize his bondage. Later on we may even notice the dog eating his food, still chained, but as the food is close to the kennel his chain is not irksome, and he is thus still unconscious of his bondage. But soon comes the owner of the dog, who, forgetting the chain, calls the dog. The animal springs up, eager to reach his master. What happens then? All his efforts are vain, and now for the first time he feels the irksomeness and restraint of his fetters. It is exactly similar with sin. Try to get free, and you feel your bondage.—Dr. W. H. Griffith Thomas.

* * *

A Buried Past

"The truth," Jesus said, "shall make you free" (John 8:32). On the night of the emancipation of the Jamaica slaves in 1838, a mahogany coffin was made, and a grave was dug. Into that coffin they crowded all the various relics and remnants of their previous bondage and sorrow. The whips, the torture irons, the branding irons, the coarse frocks and shirts, and great hat, fragments of the treadmill, the handcuffs—they placed in the coffin and screwed down the lid. At the stroke of midnight the coffin was lowered into its grave: and then the whole of that throng of thousands celebrated their redemption from thralldom by singing the Doxology! *It is a picture of the Christian's buried past.*—*The Dawn.*

* * *

"I wholly disapprove of what you say, but will defend to the death your right to say it."—Voltaire.

* * *

Free Prisoner

Madame Guyon wrote while in prison in France for her Saviour's sake. This cultured, refined, educated, and (until smitten with smallpox) exceedingly beautiful woman spent ten years of her life in different French prisons from 1695 to 1705. Here are her words:

"My cage confines me round;
  Abroad I cannot fly;
But though my wing is closely bound
  My heart's at liberty.
My prison walls cannot control
The flight, the freedom of the soul.
"Oh, it is good to soar
  These bolts and bars above,
To Him whose purpose I adore,
  Whose Providence I love;
And in Thy mighty will to find
The joy, the freedom of the mind."
—Selected.

* * *

Only Redeemed, or Saved?

When the British Government sent word to Jamaica that slavery was at an end, that was the act of a government speaking for a nation. Slavery in Jamaica was at an end. Every slave had the right to go free. I doubt not there were slaves who did not believe it and went on with their slavery. They did not take the government's action as inviolate. They did not accept the fact that slavery in Jamaica had been abolished; those who did believe it got rid of their shackles and were free. I am here to say that every man and every woman and every child in this church tonight is redeemed. Is every man, woman, and child in the church saved? That depends upon your attitude toward the finished work. Redemption is a work of God, but in order to have salvation the individual must exercise faith in what is accomplished.—W. Graham Scroggie, in *Grace and Truth.*

Four Freedoms

The Four Freedoms date from the Bible: Freedom of speech, Acts 4:1; Freedom of worship, Matt. 22:15; Freedom from fear, Isaiah 41:10; Freedom from want, Deut. 28:1.

FRIENDSHIP

False Friends

"False friends are like vermin that abandon a sinking vessel, or like swallows that depart at the approach of winter. True friends are like ivy that adheres to the tree in its decay. True friends are like the light of phosphorus: brightest in the dark."—Selected.

* * *

"A friend never gets in your way except when you are on the way down."—Selected.

* * *

True Friendship

"A friend loveth at all times," even when all the world forsakes you.

A friend will gladly suffer privation and want in any way possible to bring you comfort, and heartily do all he can for your happiness without expecting to receive something back again.

A friend will enter forbidden courts and king's palaces and plead with tyrants and judges; yes, and will assume the guilt of others and suffer, "the just for the unjust," that doomed victims might go free.

A friend will penetrate the raging fiery flames, will wade through the dark and cold, will dive into the deep, will ascend into the clouds, will go around the world and endure untold hardships, pain, and suffering to "rescue the perishing."

Friendship lives in the heart, grows in the mind, travels in the speech, shines out through the countenance, and pronounces God's sublime benediction to the troubled and distressed soul.

Friendship is the surety of peace, the seal of love.

"A friend is one who knows all about you and loves you just the same."

I would rather have a friend and not a penny, than all the world and not a friend.

You can trust a friend in the light or in the dark; in your presence or in your absence; at home or abroad, any time, anywhere.

The value of a friend is inestimable.

A friend does not merely happen to be; is not bought with money, or the price of wealth; is not made to be a friend by force, but is a friend for friendship's sake only.

A friend magnifies not the dross in you, but polishes the gold.

Heat and cold and darkness, height and depth, length and breadth of space, are no barriers to friendship.

The love of true friends is not easily broken, but it grows stronger with each sacrificial test.—William N. Browning, in *The Gospel Trumpet.*

* * *

True Friendship

Gold cannot buy it,
Poverty try it;
Thrift may not cheapen it,
Sorrow must deepen it;
Joy cannot lose it,
Malice abuse it;
Wit cannot choke it,
Folly provoke it;
Age can but strengthen it,
Time only lengthens it;
Death cannot sever
Friendship forever;
Heaven's the true place of it,
God is the grace of it.

—*Presbyterian Standard.*

More Than a Friend in Distress

Lord Houghton was at a party with some friends. When he left, one said of him, "I have many friends who would be kind to me in distress, but only one who would be equally kind to me in *disgrace*, and he has just left the room."—*Sunday School Times.*

* * *

Bound by a Golden Chain

A gentleman had found a place for a ragged street Arab, and was walking with him to it. He was stopped by a gentleman, who after a short conversation said, "You are not walking through the street with that dirty lad, surely?" "Why not?" said the gentleman, "he is my friend." Overhearing the first remark the lad was slinking away, but the answer made him the life-long, devoted follower of his new-found friend. Jesus deigns to call us His friends; are we as grateful to Him?—*Sunday School Times.*

* * *

The Unfailing Friend

The friendship of Jesus is lasting. Other friends may grow old and cold. It is not so with the friendship of our Saviour. Other friends may possibly misunderstand us. Jesus never. His love is the same in youth as in old age. The friendship will rather grow stronger in old age. **If you have lost what to you seemed everything, if you find yourself** friendless and alone, despised and forsaken, seek to get acquainted with this most lovely, dear and precious Friend.—M.

* * *

One there is above others,
  Oh, how He loves!
His is love beyond a brother's,
  Oh, how He loves!
Earthly friends may fail or leave us,
One day soothe, the next day grieve us;
But this Friend will ne'er deceive us:
  Oh, how He loves!
—Selected.

True Friendship

Christians need to revive the spirit of consecration that characterized Sam Davis, that Confederate spy, who was executed at Pulaski, Tenn. He was captured by the Union Army and found to possess some papers of great value to the Union Army. The officers knew that it was impossible that he was the one responsible for his having those papers. After he had been court-martialed and blindfolded before the firing squad the officer in charge said, "If you will give us the name of the man who furnished you this information, you may go free," to which Sam Davis replied, "If I had a thousand lives I would give them all before I would betray a friend." Are you a friend of Jesus—*Florida Baptist Witness.*

* * *

The Difference

Edgar A. Guest, telling of a conversation on happiness, said, "We were discussing a certain man the other day—a man rich and almost friendless. His life has been a long round of bickering and close dealing. Lawsuits have strewn his path. Friendship appearently meant nothing to him when he was busy making his fortune. Men who once tried to like him gave him up as a hopeless case. He is now old and has more money than he will ever need. To one with whom he quarreled bitterly more than twenty years ago, he said recently: 'I don't understand it. You have hundreds of friends about you, and I have almost no one outside of my own family to whom I can turn.' And the man replied simply: 'I was making *friends* years ago, while you were busy making *money.*' It's all in that one sentence. We carry into old age only the things we have thought to bring along the way."—Edgar A. Guest, in the *American Magazine.*

* * *

How to Cement Friendships

1. Take your friends as you find them —do not try to remove the motes you see in their eyes.
2. Use the Golden Rule always.

3. Do not talk about your "peeves."
4. Remember that sincere and appreciative letters establish a pathway to the heart of a friend.
5. Be a loyal, faithful friend. Remember that "none can be called deformed but unkind."
6. Remember that souls are greater than vocabularies, so try to read the overtones in the written and spoken words of your friends.
7. Cultivate a sense of humor.
8. Do not expect the impossible; a wood thrush and a yardstick have little in common.
9. Do not keep "tab" on the affairs of your friend.
10. Do not usurp your friend: be glad that he has other friends besides you.
11. Never force a confidence, nor betray one reposed in you.
12. Share your blessings with your friends.
13. Don't be supersensitive. You would not willingly hurt a friend, so give your friend credit for having the same feeling toward you.
14. Remember that to have a friend you must be one.
15. Remember that a friend is one before whom you may think aloud, who understands your silences.—*The Youth's Evangelist.*

* * *

The Neighbor Test

One day a mover's wagon came past Farmer Jones' gate. Farmer Jones was friendly to everybody, so he asked the movers where they were going. "We are moving from Johnstown to Jamestown," they told him. "Can you tell us what kind of neighbors we will find there?" "What kind did you find in Johnstown?" "The very worst kind," they said. "Gossipy, unkind, and indifferent. We were glad to move away." "You will find the same in Jamestown." The next day another mover's wagon passed, and a similar conversation took place. The second party asked what neighbors they would find in Johnstown and were asked what kind they had found in Jamestown. "The very best. So kind and considerate, it almost broke our hearts to move away." "You will find exactly the same kind in Johnstown," was the farmer's reply.—*Sunday School Times.*

* * *

How Much Room Is Needed?

"Is it true," asked a student, "that all the people in the world could live in Texas?" "Yes," replied the professor, "if they were friends." And if they were not friends even the world itself is too small.—*The Homilope* (church envelope).

* * *

His Only Request

In olden time there reigned in Persia a great monarch, Shah Abbis, who loved his people. To know them more perfectly he used to mingle with them in various disguises. One day he went as a poor man to the public baths, and there in the tiny cellar he sat beside the fireman who tended the furnace. At mealtime he shared his coarse food and talked to the lonely man as a friend. Again and again he visited him until the man grew to love him. Then one day he told him he was the Emporer, and he waited for the man to ask some gift from him. But the fireman sat gazing on him with love and wonder, and at last he spoke: "You left your palace and your glory to sit with me in this dark place, to partake of my coarse fare, to care whether my heart is glad or sorry. On others you may bestow rich presents, but to me you have given yourself; and it only remains to pray that you never withdraw the gift of your friendship."—*Letters to Light-Keepers.*

* * *

Too Many Friends

We hear a lot these days about "How to Win Friends and Influence People." A Christian should be filled with love and kindness, and should be friendly to all; but there is a serious danger of a Christian following a worldly philosophy. The revised version of Proverbs 18:24 gives us a needed warning. "He tnat maketh many friends (Heb., a man of friends) doeth it to his own destruction." The evident thought is the same as our Lord's warning, "Woe unto you, when all men shall speak well of you! for so did their fathers to the false prophets" (Luke 6:26).

He who goes about the business of making friends, disregarding his duty as a Christian to stand for truth and righteousness, doeth it to his own spiritual destruction. For example, the minister who is a jolly good fellow and who is afraid to witness to his people against their sins lest he offend them, is destroying his own usefulness as a servant of Christ. John the Baptist could have kept the friendship of Herod and his wife, had he only kept his mouth shut about their sin of living in adultry; *but John the Baptist thought more about pleasing his Lord than about making friends.* So there are two sides to this question of "making friends and influencing people." Let us make friends *without compromise,* and then our friends will be few in number but sterling in quality. Let us influence people *toward God and Christ and righteous living,* through the power of the Gospel and the Holy Spirit.—*Christian Victory.*

* * *

Preaching in Strange Ways

A missionary touring in South Africa came across a crowd of natives listening intently to the strains of a gramophone as it reproduced "What a Friend We Have in Jesus," as sung by the Swazi chiefs at King Edward's coronation. When the music ceased, the audience clamored to have the song explained, and the storekeeper, a Jew, told them the story of Jesus, whom the Christians call the Son of God. Thus in strange ways is the Gospel preached in the out-of-the-way places of the earth.

—*Christian Herald.*

* * *

A Friend

Kingsley says: "A friend is a human soul whom we can trust utterly; who knows the best and the worst of us, and who loves us in spite of all our faults; who will speak the honest truth to us; who will give us counsel and reproof in the day of prosperity and self-conceit, but who will comfort us and encourage us in the days of difficulty and sorrow."—Selected.

* * *

Friendship With Christ

It is said that Zinzendorf, when a boy, used to write little notes to the Saviour, and throw them out of the window, hoping that He would find them. Later in life, so strong was his faith in the friendship of Christ and in his own need of that friendship as a daily solace, that once, when traveling, he sent back his companion, that he might converse more freely with the Lord, with whom he spoke audibly. So do we all need friendly converse with Him, our soul's love. He alone is the world's Friend. That man never knew what it was to be familiar with God who complains of the want of friends when God is with him. Cultivate the friendship of the Lord Jesus. Carry every burden of life to His loving heart, and this you may do with confiding trustfulness.

"What a friend we have in Jesus,
All our sins and griefs to bear,
What a privilege to carry,
Everything to God in prayer."

Jesus is an understanding Friend; Jesus is a sympathizing Friend.

"He knows, He loves, He cares,
Nothing this truth can dim;
He does the very best for those
Who leave the choice with Him."

When President Edwards came to die, his last words, after bidding his relations good-bye, were, "Now, where is Jesus of Nazareth, my true and never-failing Friend?" And, so saying he fell asleep! How beautiful!—*God's Revivalist and Bible Advocate.*

"A Friend is one who steps in when the whole world steps out!"

Thorny Christians

You have all heard of Luther Burbank, who worked such wonderful changes in fruits and flowers, getting rid of their objectionable features and developing whatever is useful and beautiful; and if fruits and flowers can be so modified that they hardly seem the same thing, how foolish is it for anyone to say that he has to be blunt and tactless because he was "made that way!" If a cactus can get rid of its thorns, surely you can dispense with the traits that are likely to wound your friends!—*Sunday School Times.*

* * *

A Friend Indeed

I had heard on excellent authority that one of my people was "giving way to drink." He was a man of some standing in the church, and he was possessed of considerable wealth. I had already preached more than one temperance sermon, but these had been general messages addressed to the congregation. I was now ordered by my Master to carry the message to an individual, and tactfully to withstand him to his face because he stood condemned. How I wriggled under the commission! How I shrank from it! How I dallied with it! And, even when I had fought my way almost to the door, I lingered in the street in further fruitless loitering. But at length courage conquered fear. I faced my man, tremblingly gave him my message, and by the grace of God, he heard the voice of God and was saved from a horrible pit and the miry clay. —From "*John Henry Jowett.*" by Arthur Porritt.

* * *

The Highest Honor

At the close of the World War I the King and Queen of the besieged kingdom of Belgium sent for Herbert Hoover, who had given their people food and buoyed them with hope, and said, "We would like to honor you with the highest decorations in the kingdom." They gave him his choice, but he refused them all. His answer was: "You have stood at the gateway of civilization and held back the tide of aggression, while we have only shared with you what we had to give. For that one does not ask honors." The King and Queen said, "He is our very great friend," and they created for him a new order to which only one man belonged, and the title was, "Friend of the Belgian people." — *Sunday School Times.*

* * *

The Freedom of His Friends

If I become a friend of the Lord, what will be my privilege? Freedom. Is there any freedom like the freedom betwen two intimate friends? Do you know that the word "friend" comes from the same root as the word "free"? Do you know that "friend" is "freen," the freefolk? Folk, who have the run of the house; or, as Paul would say, "The people who enjoy the glorious liberty of the children of God." "My friends;" that is, "my free ones, with the run of the house."—Dr. J. H. Jowett.

* * *

Around the Corner

Around the corner I have a friend,
In this great city that has no end;
Yet days go by and weeks rush on,
And before I know it a year is gone,
And I never see my old friend's face,
For life is a swift and terrible race.
He knows that I like him just as well
As in the days when I rang his bell
And he rang mine; we were younger
then,
And now we are busy, tired men,
Tired with playing a foolish game,
Tired with trying to make a name.
"Tomorrow," I say, "I will call on Jim,
Just to show I am thinking of him."
But tommorrow comes and tomorrow
goes,
And the distance between us grows and
grows,
Around the corner, yet miles away—
"Here's a telegram. Jim died today."
That's what we get, and deserve in the
end—
Around the corner — a vanished friend.
—*Messenger of Peace.*

The Friendly Language

In the post office of Buenos Aires they make a specialty of languages. Great numbers of immigrants reach that enterprising city every year. They all soon visit the post office, and the government has made it a point to greet them there with someone speaking their native tongue. It is said that the other day, at the same time, a German, a Chinese, a Frenchman, two Poles, a Lithuanian, and three Englishmen, none of them able to speak or understand a word of Spanish, entered that friendly post office, and all came out feeling that they had reached another homeland. Let every Christian get the spirit of that post office in his own life. No one should be a stranger to a Christian. He should speak the language of love, which is current in every land. He should feel the sympathy which is the universal interpreter. Have we not, in these considerations, come to the heart of Pentecost? In Christ, every one of that conglomerate multitude had found a friend. In Christianity each one of them, though from a far-distant land, had reached the home of his soul.—*Christian Herald.*

GAMBLING

What Card Playing Did for a Sunday School Class

While a friend of mine was conducting a meeting one morning, a tramp came in and said, "My father and mother used to sit in this pew. It is the first church I ever attended. My father was an officer in this Church. Seven boys used to sit in this pew in the Sunday School Class. We had a great love and respect for our Sunday School teacher. Saturday afternoon she invited us to her home, entertaining with music, eatables and a look over the lesson. After a while she was anxious to please us and hold us, and she taught us the names of cards. None had ever used cards. We became enthusiastic over it, learning different games. After a while we would not give so much time to the lesson, but she let us have more time for playing cards, and would show us some more tricks. After a while we were off in the cotton gins playing cards and not going to her home. Later we failed to go to Sunday School. Cards, cigarettes, after a while drink and gambling. We all at different times left our homes. Two of those boys have been hung, three are in state's prison for life, one a vagabond like myself. No one knows where he is and if the authorities knew I was here I would be arrested and put behind the bars. All I wish is that that teacher had never taught us how to play cards."

As he stood there broken-hearted, a lady at the right and near the pulpit, dressed in mourning, arose, went to where the man was, fell on the floor with a scream, and said, "My God! I am the Sunday School teacher that did it." She fainted and we did not know but that she was dead. She revived. The woman was not seen any more in the meeting and the man never seen since.—The late J. Wilbur Chapman, D.D., in *Florida Baptist Witness.*

* * *

Gamblers' Recruiting Stations

During the twenty years I was in the game I found that about all the men and women who filled my houses and bet themselves into ruin were the product of the homes where card playing was encouraged. It is across the friendly poker table or in the bridge game that Satan puts his fiery brand on the young men and women of America. It is in so-called Christian homes that the gambling fever begins. The underworld is not trying to drag innocents down. It does not have to. The homes are turning out more recruits than they can possibly handle. They cannot be chased with an ax. They have secured their worldly wisdom at the dances, card parties, and other social diversions which feature modern social life. There is nothing in the underworld that can furnish them any surprises, and they are more likely to start a redder one of their own.—Courtesy *Moody Monthly.*

* * *

Gambling in the Church

On the front lawn of a certain Philadelphia church, as this article is being written, there are two new automobiles, backed by a huge sign urging the passers-by to take a chance on one of the cars. Each afternoon and evening a young man sits at the street curb at a table acecpting the money of hundreds of passers-by who are eager to win an automobile for only ten cents. When an organization that calls itself Christian, and claims to honor and follow the Lord Jesus Christ, sponsors such schemes for raising money, is it any wonder that the man on the street or the rank and file of young people fail to see any harm in taking a chance? And lest any of us should unduly condemn the automobile raffle it is well for us to remember the suit clubs, the bridge clubs, the bingo games, and the bank nights that are all about us. Is it possible that the one who called our country a "nation of gamblers" was not exaggerating?—John W. Lane, Jr., in *Sunday School Times.*

GIVING

Not a Sacrifice But a Joy

A rich business man and a prominent attorney were traveling around the world. They saw many impressive sights, but agreed that something they saw in Korea was most impressive of all.

One morning as they walked along a country road in Korea, they saw a boy pulling a plow which was steered by an old man. It amused the attorney so much that he insisted on taking a picture of the scene with his little pocket camera. Later he showed the picture to a missionary in the next village, remarking about the peculiar spectacle.

"Yes," said the missionary, "it seems a very strange way to plow a field, but I happen to know the boy and old man well. They are very poor. However, when the little church was built here in the village, they wanted to contribute something. They had no money. They had not grain to spare and winter was coming on, so they sold their ox and gave the money to the church building fund, and now, minus the valuable animal, they have to pull the plow themselves."

The men looked at each other for a moment, then the attorney said, "But what a stupendous sacrifice! Why did you allow it?"

"They did not feel that way about it. They regarded it as a great joy that they had an ox to give to the Lord's work."—*The Sunday School Friend.*

* * *

Credit Only for Intention

An old farmer had dropped a shilling in the kirk plate instead of a penny. Noticing his mistake he tackled the elder at the end of the service. "It wud be sacreeledge, Sandy, tae luft it oot noo." the elder said, "Weel, I'll git credit for it in Heaven," replied the farmer. "Na, na; ye'll only git credit for a penny, for that was a' ye intendit tae pit in." —*Church Business.*

* * *

Bearing the Loss

A benevolent man was planning $100 to the Lord's work, but before it was paid he suffered a disaster by a destructive hailstorm. "I met him," says the narrator, "and was again invited to call and receive his donation. While walking toward the house he said: 'I had intended to give this time $100, but in view of this calamity I shall be obliged to reduce it to $60.' I said nothing, but followed him into his dwelling. He gave me a seat and then called his wife out; and after an absence so long as to excite my wonder he returned and handed me his check for $100. Thinking it possible that it was so written by a slip of the thought, I said: "So you meant this for $100?' 'Yes,' he replied, 'my wife and I have talked it over a little and we have concluded it best to bear the loss ourselves, and not charge it to the Lord.' "—*The Illustrator.*

* * *

Better Than Bazaars!

On the day of dedication of our church, Dr. Louis S. Bauman made this statement: "If this church attempts to raise money by chicken suppers or bazaars, it can never be while I remain its pastor. Nor do we propose to worry the businessmen of the town for contributions, implying that they must give because we patronize them." A Christian lady in the audience had casually dropped in for the dedicatory services, and had intended to give a few dollars. When the offering was taken, in it were two checks from her, one in her own name for $2,500, and the other for $500 in the name of her parents. The pastor's method of raising money caused her change of mind. She also became a member of the congregation, and there have been many other contributions from her. The pastor is still wondering just how long it would have taken the women of the church to "clear" that amount working at chicken suppers and bazaars. —*Sunday School Times.*

* * *

There's No Pocket in a Shroud

Use your money while you're living,
Do not hoard it to be proud;
You can never take it with you—
There's no pocket in a shroud.

Gold can help you on no farther
Than the graveyard where you lie,
And though you are rich while living
You're a pauper when you die.

Use it then some lives to brighten,
As through life they weary plod;
Place your bank account in heaven
And grow richer toward your God.

Use it wisely, use it freely,
Do not hoard it to be proud;
You can never take it with you—
There's no pocket in a shroud.

—Selected.

* * *

All That He Had

At a meeting held near Oxford in connection with the building of a new church, a speaker made an eloquent appeal for funds, urging the audience to give all they had upon them. All were impressed, and among them was a small boy, who, when the offering was taken placed a top and five marbles in the plate. In the vestry afterward one of the stewards was inclined to ridicule the boy's offering; but the chairman said: "I will give you twenty pounds for the top, and will take the marbles to Oxford, and will get five of my friends to give five pounds each for them." He wrote out his check for twenty pounds, and in due course forwarded the other twenty-five pounds. At the stonelaying, there was placed under the principal stone the top and five marbles from the little boy who gave all he had. So a little given for Jesus' sake will be made much by Him.—*The Family Herald and Weekly Star.*

* * *

Possibilities in a Gift

When Livingstone went to Africa, a Scotch woman who had saved up thirty pounds, gave it to him with the words: "I want you to save yourself needless toil and exposure by hiring some competent body servant, who will go with you wherever you go, and share your sacrifices and dangers." With that money, Livingstone hired his faithful servant, Sebantino. In the heart of Africa, a lion threw the missionary down and crushed the bones of his left arm. But Sebantino saved Livingstone at the risk of his own life. What if the gift had not been made?—Selected.

Treasure

Believers in a momentarily returning Lord who amass treasure stultify their testimony before both God and man. George Muller, after a million and a half sterling had passed through his hands for his orphans, died with 118 pounds in the bank — his entire personal fortune. One secret of Wesley's power was his superb divorce from money. "I fling money out of my hands," he said, "as quickly as possible, lest it find a way into my heart." It is estimated that he gave away during his lifetime 30,000 pounds (an equivalent of 100,000 pounds today) derived principally from gifts, and the proceeds from the sales of his books and pamphlets; and dying, he left behind him as someone has put it, 'a library, a well-known clergyman's gown, a much abused reputation, and — the Methodist Church."—*The Dawn.*

* * *

What He Left

In a little village lived a lawyer famous for drawing up wills, in which branch of his profession he had long enjoyed a monopoly of the business of the country. On the death of a certain respected neighbor there was much speculation as to the value of the property, and the village gossip undertook to find out the facts. "I suppose you made Blank's will?" he said bluntly to the lawyer. "Yes," the lawyer answered. "Then you probably know how much he left. Would you mind telling me?" "Not at all," answered the lawyer deliberately. "He left everything he had." —*Forward.*

* * *

His Willing Gift

M. Lockert (of the McAll Mission) preached on a January evening on "Such as I have I give thee" (Acts 3:6). The audience of Parisian poor had nothing to give, — rather were they in need of everything. When the meeting was over all but one went home. This was a poor man who came forward to ask what he could give. He had nothing, absolutely nothing, except a card for a night's lodging. But this he surrendered to an older man, even poorer than himself, who was shivering on the steps of a church. Then he led him to his lodging house where he would be warm for the night while he himself went out into the snow.—*Sunday School Times.*

* * *

The Leper's Liberality

The Rev. Mr. Jones, of the Madur Mission, India, tells a story worthy to be placed alongside of that of the immortal widow. It was a time when the converts of the Mission were bringing gifts for the erection of a church building. Among them was a leper. Clad only in a rag of a loin cloth, his body emaciated from the lack of food, he brought an offering of one and one-half cents. To him it meant privation and hunger to lay that cent and a half upon the altar. But it lay there with the crimson touch of sacrifice upon it, not one and a half cents in the eyes of the Master of the Treasury, but riches of liberality. — *The Evangelical Christian.*

* * *

The Lord's Own Precedent.

A group of churches was raising a fund of $30,000 to finance missionary projects in Africa and South America. A little church whose members lost nearly all their property in a terrible dam disaster sent a check for $209. The secretary of the missionary society sponsoring the work was reproached for accepting the gift: "Doesn't it hurt your conscience to take money from people so 'hard up'?" The secretary replied, "Did the Lord tell the widow to come back and take her two mites out of the treasury box?"—*Sunday School Times.*

* * *

Where Are Our Treasures?

Two friends were talking. One told the other of a "good man" who died and left $30,000. "What a pity," said the other, "that he left it behind when he might have sent it on ahead? He is not likely now to ever hear of it again."—*Sunday School Times.*

The Church Plate

Someone dreamed that she went to church, and after the service was over, a plate was held at the door for the contribution of the people. This plate had the power of changing each person's gift into its real value in the sight of God. A gentleman put in a gold coin, which immediately turned into brass! He had given it in order to be thought well of by others. A lady put in a quarter, which turned into a penny. She could have given far more, but only gave because it was the *custom.* A little girl, coming up with her Sunday School teacher, dropped in a penny, which turned into a daisy. She had given it only to *please her teacher.* The dreamer felt sad to think that these gifts were not accepted by God. Just then a poor girl came up and dropped in her penny. It changed into gold! She was very poor and had denied herself to give it, because *she loved the Lord Jesus Christ.* This gift was well pleasing to God.—Selected.

* * *

Giving

Little girl told an older friend that she was going to give her papa a pair of slippers for his birthday. "Where will you get your money?" asked the friend. She opened her eyes wide and said, "Why, Father will give me the money." For a moment the friend was silent as he thought that the father would buy his own birthday present. And the father loved the little girl and appreciated the gift, even though he paid for it himself. *We have nothing of our own to give to God.*—Selected.

* * *

Are You Excused?

Horace Bushnell, the great new England preacher, once made an interesting list of those who might be excused from giving to God's work and for the support of Christian missions. Here it is:

They only may claim to be excused—

Who believe that men are not lost in sin and do not need a Saviour.

Who believe that Jesus made a mistake when He said to His followers: "Go into all the world, and preach the Gospel to every creature."

Who believe the Gospel is not the power of God, and that faith in Christ cannot save.

Who wish that missionaries had never come to our ancestors, and that we ourselves are still heathen.

Who believe that it is "every man for himself" in this world, and, with Cain, ask: "Am I my brother's keeper?"

Who wish to have no share in the final victory of Christ.

Who believe they are not accountable to God for the money and talents entrusted to them.

Who are prepared to accept the final judgment of Christ: "Inasmuch as ye did it not to one of the least of these, ye did it not to Me."

Do you belong to the Mission or the Omission Band?—*Truth.*

* * *

"Honor the Lord With Thy Substance"

Someone tells the story of a boy who was away from home, partly working his way through the school he attended, and who received a letter in which his father stated that the crops had been so disappointing that even the help he had been able to give him heretofore must now be withdrawn.

"I regret it very much," the father said; "but I think you will have to drop out of school. Come home and work on the farm."

The boy had only a quarter left in his pocket, and he knew that in order to get home he would have to walk most of the way, stopping at one or another place where he was known, for breakfast and supper or for a night's lodging. He lived in a part of the country where the latchstring is loose for boys who are poor and ambitious, and he had no fear as to how he should reach home. To give up his studies was a great hardship, and he could not bear to think of all the time he might have to lose before he could return to the beloved recitation rooms. The father's letter came on Saturday.

On Sunday morning the boy went to church and a collection was taken up for foreign missions. When the contribution box came around, the boy's silver quarter was dropped into it, although giving it up left him penniless. "Honor the Lord with thy substance" floated into his memory, and he obeyed the command.

The next morning as his bag was packed and he was about to start on the road for home, another letter was put into his hand. It enclosed a gift from a stranger, and the amount was large enough to tide him over the remainder of the half year. God's promise had been fulfilled to him: "Them that honor Me I will honor."—*The Christian.*

* * *

Stomach Money

Upon passing a church building a short time ago, a friend said, "There is a church which is supported by 'stomach money.'" Oyster stews, candy-pullings, ice cream socials, and suppers have become the props upon which the churches lean to get money with which to conduct the work of the Lord. Over and over again it is said, "Why, we simply couldn't raise the money for our church if we didn't have suppers!" In other words, the Lord's work would go by the board if it were not for "stomach money." Thank God, that is not true. When the people of God look to Him in faith and repudiate every worldly method with which they may be tempted to support the work and determinedly say, "We will give, give, give"—did you hear it? give, not buy—"as the Lord hath prospered us," then and then only is His cause on a scriptural financial basis.

When believers lean on "stomach money" they make a burlesque of their own faith, they humiliate God's cause before an already skeptical world, depart from the teachings of the Bible, and strip the message of salvation of its glory and power.

But the cause of Christ must be supported. Never was the need greater for financial backing in every department of God's work than at this present hour in this present evil age. The need will never be met by "stomach money." The need, however, will be met. God will lay it upon the *hearts* of His dear children. The need will be met by *heart-money.*—Clinton L. Fowler, in *Grace and Truth.*

* * *

Your Ship

Guy L. Morrill, in his book, *Stewardship Stories,* tells of a Sunday school class of boys, who for a number of weeks had studied stewardship. As they came to the end of their study of this subject, their teacher asked them to write out what they thought stewardship meant. One boy wrote this: "Stewardship means that life is a great ship, loaded with a rich cargo of many things to be delivered to many peoples in many places. God is the owner, but I am the captain of the ship." How do you think of yourself? As owner or as captain of the things you possess? Are you delivering the goods?—*Forward.*

* * *

The Things Money Cannot Buy

The late George Horace Lorimer, for many years editor of *The Saturday Evening Post,* once wrote these words: "It is a good thing to have money and the things that money can buy; but it is good, too, to check up once in a while and make sure you haven't lost the things that money can't buy."

The things that money can't buy would make a long list—here are some of them:

Money can't buy real friendship—friendship must be earned.

Money can't buy a clear conscience—square dealing is the price tag.

Money can't buy the glow of good health—right living is the secret.

* * *

Useless Money

Tightly clasping a penny in her small hand, a little girl, so we are told, entered a candy store intending to make a purchase. Laying her penny on the counter, she lingered over the different kinds of sweets temptingly displayed, and finally made a choice. Pointing one chubby finger, she said to the clerk, "I'll take that one."

"I'm afraid that's two cents," answered the clerk consolingly.

Again the child inspected the different candies and again indicated her selection.

"That one also is two cents," the clerk was forced to repeat.

Ruefully she turned away and started to leave.

"Wait," little girl," called the man behind the counter, "you've forgotten your penny."

"I don't want it," was her reply, "it won't buy anything."

The story reminded us of that prophecy of the day when our gold shall be removed from us, and men will cast their silver in the streets (Ezek. 7:17-19). *Yes, the day will come when men will become so exasperated over the uselessness of their money, that they will cast it in the streets!—Prophecy Monthly.*

* * *

How the African Gives

The African native is poor beyond words to describe—no house but a mud hut; no furniture but a reed mat; no dishes but clay pots; no clothing but a goat's hide; no food but corn meal porridge; no machines; no implements. Really you would say he has nothing that makes life comfortable and strong.

Yet he gives to God's work. At the outstation he builds the church, the schoolhouse, the pastor-teacher's house and kitchen, and a house for the missionary to live in when he visits the place. He gives of what money he can earn. He gives grain or anything else he may possess. In a recent offering one native brought a good helmet that he had bought with his hard-earned money, and which was the pride of his life.—*Missionary Voice.*

* * *

A Heart Full of Love

Dr. Grenfell tells of an old fisherman, rich in trust, who was "given to hospitality." He was seventy-three years of age, and had fed many hungry folk during the "hard" winters; and when times grew unusually hard this old man of faith brought forth twelve dirty, well-worn five-dollar bills, as a last resort. This money, his entire savings, he gave to the missionary to buy food for needy neighbors. But Dr. Grenfell remonstrated: "You are getting old, and you shouldn't cut the last plank away yet." Then the hardy fisherman of many perils answered: "He'll take care, doctor, guess I can trust Him. It wouldn't do not to have used that sixty dollars, and have sent folks away hungry, would it, doctor? *It would look as if I didn't much trust in Him."—Southern Churchman.*

* * *

"Nothing Kept Back"

Some of you remember that beautiful scene in the life of General Gordon. He had just returned from China after the distinguished Taeping campaign. He went as a poor man, and he came back as poor—lots of honor, but nothing more substantial. When leaving China, the emperor, out of gratitude for the services he had rendered the empire, presented to him a large gold medal. When Gordon reached Plymouth, and saw the first copies of the English papers, he read of the famine among the silk weavers in and around Coventry. The people were starving, some were dying, and public funds were being subscribed for the relief of the distress. Gordon had nothing but his gold medal, which was his most highly cherished possession; and yet he took the medal, erased the inscription, and then sent it anonymously to the treasurer of the Coventry relief funds: and he adds: *"After all, this is the secret of bliss—to give away your medal!" Nothing kept back, everything given!* So it must be with you!—Charles Inwood.

* * *

A Different Kind of Creditor

The local church was making a drive for funds, and two colored sisters were bearing down hard on Uncle Rastus. "I can't give nothin'," exclaimed the old Negro. "I owes nearly everybody in dis here town already." "But," said one of the collectors, "don't you think you owes de Lord somethin', too?" "I does, sister, indeed," said the old man, "but He ain't pushin' me like my other creditors is."—*Toledo Blade.*

* * *

A True Indictment

A man said to Sam Jones, the evangelist: "Mr. Jones, the church has put my assessment too high." "How much do you pay?" the evangelist inquired. "Five dollars a year." "Well," replied Mr. Jones, "how long have you been converted?" "About four years." "What did you do before you were converted?" "I was a drunkard." "How much did you spend for drink?" "About $250 a year." "How much were you worth?" "I rented land and plowed with a steer." "What have you got now?" "I have a good plantation and a span of horses." "Well," said the evangelist emphatically, "you paid the Devil $250 a year for the privilege of plowing with a steer on rented land, and now you don't want to give to God who saved you, five dollars a year for the privilege of plowing with horses on your own plantation. *You're a rascal from the crown of your head to the sole of your foot.*"—*Alliance Weekly.*

* * *

Investments

"My office is just across the street from the First Baptist Church, Dallas. A few days ago one of the big business men of the city came into my office, sat down, and looking across the street, said, 'Mr. W——, you have a good deal of money in that church building, haven't you?' 'Yes,' I replied, 'about forty thousand dollars in the whole plant.' 'Well,' said the visitor, 'if you had that money back now you would keep it, wouldn't you?' 'Well, you will let me reply by asking you a question. When that church plant was being erected you had more money than I had. I put mine into the plant and you kept yours; now we are both broke. I have my part in that church plant and many other church buildings and schools, hospitals, orphanages, missions, and other worthy investments to show for my failure. What have you to show for yours?—*who is the worst broke?*' "—*Watchman-Examiner.*

Glass and Silver

One day a certain old rich man, of miserly disposition, visited a rabbi, who took the rich man by the hand and led him to a window. "Look out there," he said. And the rich man looked out into the street. "What do you see?" asked the rabbi. "I see men, and women, and little children," answered the rich man. Again the rabbi took him by the hand, and this time led him to a mirror. "What do you see now?" "Now I see myself," the rich man replied. Then the rabbi said, "Behold—in the window there is glass, and in the mirror there is glass. But the glass of the mirror is covered with a little silver, and no sooner is the silver added than you cease to see others, but see only yourself."—Selected.

* * *

A Lesson from a Horse

Kosciusko once sent a young man named Seltner on an errand and desired him to take the horse which he himself usually rode. On his return young Seltner said that he would never ride his horse again, unless he gave his purse at the same time. Kosciusko asking what he meant, he answered: "As soon as a poor man on the road takes off his hat and asks for charity the horse immediately stands still, and will not stir till something is given the petitioner; and, as I had no money about me, I was obliged to make believe to give something to satisfy the horse."—*Biblical Encyclopedia and Museum.*

* * *

We give Thee but Thine own,
Whate'er the gift may be;
All that we have is Thine alone,
A trust, O Lord, from Thee.

* * *

May the Giver of Gifts give unto you
That which is Good and that which is True;
The Will to help and the Courage to do;
A Heart that can Sing the whole day through,
Whether the skies be gray or blue:
May the Giver of Gifts give these to you.
—Selected.

We "Can't Beat God Giving"

Captain Levy of Philadelphia was asked how he was able to give so much and still have so much left. "Oh," said he, "as I shovel out, He shovels in; and the Lord has a bigger shovel than I have."—**John Weaver Weddell, in** ***Sunday School Times.***

* * *

When We Give to the Poor

It is related of that quaint old London preacher, Rowland Hill, that he once attended a meeting in London, the special object of which was to raise money for the London poor. The speaker of the day failed to put in his appearance, and they called on Rowland Hill to speak, and make the appeal for the offering. He arose and said, "My brethren, my text today is: 'He that hath pity upon the poor lendeth unto the Lord.' And my sermon is: If you like your security—down with your cash—pass the baskets." —*The King's Business.*

* * *

Getting Our Money Changed

When a traveler enters a foreign land, one of the first things he does is to get his money changed into the currency of that land. We can take none of earth's coin to Heaven with us, but we can change it here into good works, distributing liberally, thus "laying up in store . . . a good foundation," by which we may "lay hold of eternal life." This is the exchange of currency Christ advised the young man of great possessions to make. No one of wealth is following Christ without this exchange, neither has he any foundation for the treasures of Heaven.—*Record of Christian Work.*

* * *

How to Sing a Hymn

At a meeting of a woman's missionary society the president arose and said: **"We will open our meeting by singing the beautiful consecration hymn, beginning:**

'Take my life, and let it be
Consecrated, Lord, to Thee!'

We will omit the fourth verse."

"Madam president," said a voice in the rear, "I object to omitting the fourth verse. There are two lines in that verse we should never forget:

'Take my silver and my gold,
Not a mite would I withhold!'

"If it were just the singing of it, it would not be so bad, but *we are omitting the practice of it in our church life, and funds are short everywhere."—The Pilot.*

* * *

Whose Loss Comes First?

A little boy started to Sunday-school with two nickels, one for the Lord, and one for himself. On the way to church he lost one of them. "There goes the Lord's nickel," he said. What the boy uttered concerning his loss is a reflection of the mind of many grown-ups. It is always the Lord's money that is lost. . . . Power will come upon the church that plays square with God. — *The Watchword.*

* * *

The Difference

A country squire, rich but godless, heard of the triumphant death of an aged Christian who had been associated with him in early life. "Yes, yes," said he, "you all wonder that I cannot be as quiet and happy, too. But think of the difference! He is *going* to his treasure, and I—I must *leave* all mine behind!" Treasure in Heaven is more to be desired than all the treasures of earth. — *The British Weekly.*

* * *

How to Get a Start in Life

A man in a New England town had been unemployed so long that he came to his last dollar. He laid fifty cents of it on the offering plate on Sunday. The following morning he heard there was a possibility of obtaining employment in a neighboring town. The railroad fare to the town was a dollar. It looked as if he should have kept the fifty cents he laid on the offering plate; but with the fifty cents he had he bought a ticket and rode half way to his desired destination. He stepped from the train and started to walk to the town. But God had something better for him. Before he had gone a block he learned of a factory near at hand that needed help. Within thirty minutes he had a job with a wage of five dollars more a week than he would have received had he gone to the other town. The first week's pay brought back his fifty cents tenfold. The man was W. L. Douglas, the shoe manufacturer.—*One Besetting Sin,* by Charles F. Weigle.

* * *

Stewardship

"I was born with music in my system. I knew musical scores before I knew my A B C's. It was a gift of Providence. Music is too sacred to be sold. I never look upon the money I earn as my own. It is only a fund entrusted to my care for proper disbursement. I reduce my needs to the minimum. I feel morally guilty in ordering a costly meal, as it deprives someone else of a slice of bread—some child, perhaps, of a bottle of milk. My beloved wife feels exactly about these things as I do. In all these years of my so-called success we have not built a home for ourselves. Between it and us stand all the homeless in the world."—Testimony of Fritz Kreisler, the great violinist, in *Gospel Herald.*

* * *

Small Son's Awkward Question

When the family returned from Sunday morning service, father criticized the sermon, daughter thought the choir's singing atrocious, and mother found fault with the organist's playing. But the subject had to be dropped when the small boy of the family piped up: "But it was a good show for a nickel, don't you think, Dad?"—*The Illinois Farmer.*

* * *

The Vain man says, Win gold and wear it;
The Miser says, Win gold and spare it;
The Usurer says, Win gold and lend it;
The Prodigal says, Win gold and waste it;
The Spendthrift says, Win gold and spend it;
The Thrifty man says, Win gold and save it;
The Wise man says, Win gold and use it.
—Selected.

* * *

Practical Christianity

A story is told of an old colored preacher who was exhorting his congregation to give freely to the church; he was interrupted by a deacon, who rose and said:

"Pahson, you done told us dat salvation am free — as free as the aih we breathe and as free as the watah in the rivahs. If dat am true, how come you always asking for money?"

The old preacher adjusted his spectacles and solemnly replied:

"Brothah Jones, you am right. Religion am free—salvation am free—like de aih am free and de watah am free; but *if you wants watah in youah kitchen you gotta have watah pipes, and somebody has got to pay for de plumbin'.*"—*Earnest Worker.*

* * *

He Doesn't Depend on Bridge Parties

A few years ago, a young minister was interviewed by the pulpit committee of a large church. They were anxious to call him as their pastor, and they boasted of the accomplishments of their church, and especially of their gifts to missions. The minister asked how these missionary funds were raised, and he was told that the feat was accomplished by bridge parties, which had been very successful! The candidate's reply was, "Gentlemen, I love the cause of missions, but the Lord whom I serve is not in such need of funds that He has to depend on bridge parties for the spread of the Gospel!" To what strange methods men have turned to finance the work of Christ! In the energy of the flesh, they have resorted to every possible scheme and plan. Our God is not in need of such carnal efforts.—*See.*

Practical Exposition

John Wesley heard that a man named Tommy was ill and he wrote to him: "Dear Tommy, I pray that you may soon be restored. 'Trust in the Lord, and do good; so shalt thou dwell in the land, and verily thou shalt be fed.'" With the letter Wesley enclosed a five-pound note. Replying, Tommy wrote: "Dear Mr. Wesley, I have often been struck with the beauty of the passage you quoted, but I have never seen such a useful expository note upon it." — *Sunday School Times.*

* * *

A Cablegram from Heaven

A secretary of a British Missionary Society called on a Calcutta merchant and asked him to help in the work. He drew a check for $250 and handed it to the visitor. At that moment a cablegram was brought in. The merchant read it and looked troubled. "This cablegram," said he, "tells me that one of my ships has been wrecked and the cargo lost. It makes a very large difference in my affairs. I shall have to write you another check."

The secretary understood perfectly and handed back the check for $250. The check book was still open and the merchant wrote another check and handed it to him. He read it with amazement. It was drawn for $1,000. "Haven't you made a mistake?" the secretary asked. "No," said the merchant, "I haven't made a mistake." And then, with tears in his eyes, he said, "That cablegram was a message from my Father in heaven. It read, *'Lay not up for yourselves treasures upon earth.'*" — *The King's Business.*

GOD, NO RESPECTER OF PERSONS

A Christian Solution

A certain ranch in California had been leased for several years to a fine Japanese family. Both that family and the owner of the ranch were greatly dismayed when the order came telling that the Japanese must be evacuated to the interior. The owner, badly needing help, succeeded in securing a Chinese family to replace that of the Japanese. Through some mix-up in dates, the Chinese family arrived a week before the Japanese family left. There was only one tenant house, and the owner did not know what to do. However, the problem solved itself. Both the Chinese and Japanese families were devout Christians. They decided that as brothers in Christ, they could live together in the one house and be happy. Each day they worshiped together, praying morning and evening in English. The Japanese helped the Chinese to get started with the work, and the Chinese helped the Japanese family to get packed and ready to go. When the time came to separate, each family promised to pray for the other. In a situation where prejudice and hatred might have divided Christians, the love of Christ was great enough to keep their minds and hearts in perfect peace.—Mrs. A. E. Caldwell, in *Secret Place.*

* * *

Mexican Children, Too

A Mexican child was brought to a vacation school in San Joaquin. Evidently she felt some difference between her reception and that of the other children. She heard the story of Christ blessing little children, and was impressed. Someone took her to Sunday school and there was decided objection to a Mexican child. She marched up to the superintendent and demanded, "Is it true that Jesus loves only little white children?" She was assured it was not true, and without a word of explanation she marched out and returned with four other Mexican children, saying, "I wasn't going to bring them until I knew."—*The Presbyterian Magazine.*

Goudama's Gospel

While in Fort Crampel, French Equatorial Africa, as a pioneer missionary, we came in contact with a native boy. This African never heard the story of Jesus and Him crucified until we had the privilege of relating the story to him. "God will save you Americans," said he, "but not us poor, black, Africans." "Yes, He will," came my quick reply, "for God is no respecter of persons." "Then I'll accept Jesus as my Saviour," said Goudama; and he became the most ardent, faithful Christian of the compound.—*Sunday School Times.*

* * *

Christlikeness

Two young soldiers were talking together in France. One of them was telling about his wonderful father. Pulling from his left breast pocket a package, he displayed pictures of his father and mother, gazing wistfully at them as he showed them to his companion.

"Say, Buddy," he suddenly exclaimed, "you have not spoken of your father. Got any pictures to show me what he is like?"

"No, I'm sorry, I haven't any of my father with me. Oh, hold on! Yes, I have, and I'll give you one." Putting his hand in his pocket, he pulled out a sovereign, and offered it to his wondering companion, remarking, "Here is a picture of my father. Keep it to remember me by."

The son of the king smiled into the face of his father on the coin, then sprang into the waiting lorry, and went away to another part of the sector. That is the kind of coin Christians should always have about them, *the kind that bears the express image of His person.—The Moslem World.*

* * *

King's Daughters

A lady residing in a factory town noticed that a great many working men and boys came to the Christian services, but almost no women. She determined to see what could be done for the women. Calling two of her maids who were Christians, she asked them to prepare the dining-room for a Bible meeting on the next Lord's Day. She visited among the wives and daughters of the village, and invited them to her home. She read and prayed, though they were Scandinavians and could not understand her. Then she called on her servants to pray. Through their united efforts seven persons were saved that afternoon. This was the beginning of a glorious work. Sometime afterward she was asked to go to a near-by town to inaugurate a similar work in the dining-room of a wealthy lady. She took her waitress with her and started. Reaching their destination by train they found an elegant car awaiting them. The servant girl hesitated: "I will walk," she said to her mistress. "No," was the answer; "come in the sedan with me. You are not my servant today. You are my sister. We are King's Daughters."—*The King's Business.*

* * *

At "All Souls" Church

Another piece of news will interest those who write the history of the "Christian" Church. The fashionable All Souls Episcopal Church in New York was padlocked because its rector insisted on allowing Negroes to come in to hear him preach. The respectable vestry demanded separate services for colored and whites, and padlocked the door. Bishop Manning, head of the Episcopal Church in New York, much to his credit, ordered the locks broken, entered with 200 colored people following him, and preached. All Souls seems to be the wrong name for that church, since it would refuse religious teaching to souls who happen to be locked up in black skins. The name of the church should be changed to Some Souls. — Arthur Brisbane, in the *Sunday School Times.*

* * *

In Both Ivory and Ebony

The Hon. Risden Tyler Bennet was a brilliant but eccentric Superior Court Judge in North Carolina years ago. A Negro was once tried before him at Statesville, and in closing his charge to the jury he said: "You are not to allow any prejudice to affect you because Almighty God has seen fit to carve His image in the prisoner at the bar in ebony instead of in ivory." — *Sunday School Times.*

* * *

Admitted by an "M"

The Countess of Huntingdon is reported to have said, "By the grace of God I got into the kingdom of God by an 'M.' Had the text read, 'Not *any* noble,' instead of, 'Not *many* noble,' I would have been excluded." — *Sunday School Times.*

* * *

The Gospel for Low Castes

For thirty years the work at Ongole, India, had had so little success that there was talk of its being abandoned. When John E. Clough took charge of the work the high-caste Brahmans began to show a willingness to hear more about Christianity. But when the low-caste Telugus also desired to be taught, the high-caste rebelled. "You must have nothing to do with these people," they said, "if you expect to teach our children or to receive our support." What was to be done? Clough sought help in prayer and in the reading of his Bible. His heart took courage in the passage, "But God chose the foolish things of the world, that He might put to shame them that are wise; and God chose the weak things of the world, that He might put to shame the things that are strong." While he was reading, his wife came to his study and said she had gotten her courage from the same passage of Scripture. After this incident, mission preaching to low-caste Telugus was continued with ceaseless energy. Before a year had passed ten thousand had been added to the church. The success of the work has continued to this day.—*Home Department* (Baptist publication).

* * *

Whitewashed or Washed White?

A colored mammy being disturbed by a racket in the kitchen discovered that her little pickaninny was wallowing in the flour barrel. "Land sake, Sonny," she said, "what am de matter wid you?" She listened to a tale of woe. He didn't like the white boys calling him "Nigger," so he was going to be like the white boys. His old mammy roared with laughter, and, setting him on her knee, said, "My boy, you'll never be white, even though you use all the flour in dat barrel. You is black 'cause it's in your blood. But, listen, sonny boy, what is more important, de Lord He done shed His blood at Calvary dat you and me might have our hearts washed white. Better have a black skin and a white heart, dan a white skin and a black heart. Dat flour can only whitewash you, but Jesus' blood can wash you white!" — Erling C. Olsen, in *Meditations in the Psalms.*

* * *

An Unrestricted Quota

The newspapers have told of the "alien-laden ships" that raced over the line to gain entry into the United States, four minutes after midnight of June 30, 1923, under the new quotas of the restricted immigration law. The *Philadelphia Public Ledger* told of twenty-four ocean liners, carrying eleven thousand immigrants from forty-three countries, coming in at that time, with a score of others racing across the Atlantic with other thousands of hopeful immigrants who must return to the Near East and Asia after spending the savings of a lifetime on the five-thousand-mile trip. "Scores of aliens, who leaned over the ships' rails gazing wistfully at the shores of America, are doomed to disappointment, as several quotas will be filled by noon. . . . Hope and anxiety are apparent to a marked degree on the faces that line the steamers' rails, looking toward the land of promise." One cannot but contrast this situation, with its limited quotas and the necessary disappointment awaiting many who have stopped at no sacrifice to get in, with the offer of entry into a Better Land still. Heaven is opened freely to "whosoever will" receive salvation and the gift of eternal life in Christ Jesus. — *Sunday School Times.*

But Fine Garments

A dear fellow Christian, now a famous evangelist, tells the tale of a colored man who had turned to the Lord. Giving his testimony one time he said, "My friends, you see in me only a big, black, ugly colored man; but in God's sight I'm altogether lovely, for I'm all dressed up in Jesus." This is the truth put in a quaint way.—*Our Young People's Delight.*

* * *

"I Was Born a Slave"

The scene was the Rotunda of the National Capitol Building, Washington; the chief actor was Dr. Walter Brooks, 96-year-old pastor of the Nineteenth Street Baptist Church. With suppressed emotion the venerable ex-slave stood before Borglum's statue of Lincoln and said: "I was born a slave, and saw my father, mother and sister sold on the auction block as chattels, 'to have and to hold with their assigns forever.' At fourteen I was emancipated with three million of my color, henceforth and forever free. I lay this memorial wreath at the feet of my emancipator, Abraham Lincoln." Once from that very spot one could have heard the auctioneer crying sales of human beings at the auction block near the foot of Capitol Hill.—*Gospel Herald.*

GOSPEL

Two Slums

It was once said of the ministry of F. B. Meyer, "He supported every effort to get a man out of a slum. He was more concerned, however, to get the slum out of the man." Man's first and great need is to be born again. And the Gospel of Jesus Christ is the only power that can give a man a new heart.—*Christian Victory.*

* * *

Power of the Gospel

"I have had twenty-one years experience with the natives. I have seen the semi-civilized and the uncivilized; I have lived with the Christian native, and I have lived, dined, and slept with the cannibals. For at least nine years of my life, I have lived with the savages of New Guinea . . . wherever there had been the slighest spark of civilization in the southern seas it has been because the Gospel has been preached there." — James Chalmers. (Have you seen news items of American flyers shot down at sea? and of their reception by those very natives? Many a prayer of thanks has been raised because James Chalmers and many like him carried the "Good News" there."—*Gospel Herald.*

"Preaching Doesn't Mean Much"

Ministers as well as laymen too often entertain this idea. Dr. Charles R. Brown tells of leaving his pulpit one Sunday evening rather discouraged. The attendance was unusually small. It seemed as if the sermon hadn't "gone across."

The preacher went to his study, closed the door and sat down to think of his failure. After a few moments there was a timid knock at the study entrance and a young man entered. After seating himself wearily, his arms on Dr. Brown's desk, he poured out his heart.

"I came to church tonight with a heavy load upon my heart. You know, I work at a bank several blocks from here, and for nearly six months I have been taking small amounts of money from my cage and using it to gamble with. I have been able to 'doctor' the books so far, but sooner or later the examiners will find me out. When they do, I am ruined. My wife's heart will be broken, I shall lose my position, and my life will be wrecked. You are the only man in the world to whom I have told this, and I have decided to come to you after hearing your sermon tonight. I want to find my way out of this situation with the help of Jesus Christ."

Dr. Brown knelt down and prayed earnestly with and for the young man and then told him to return in the morning. Together they went down to the bank, put the whole matter before the president, and upon a promise of the bank clerk to redeem his life from failure, an arrangement was made by which a certain amount could be taken out of his salary until the debt to the bank was paid. A young man and his family were saved by the preaching of the Gospel of Jesus Christ!

When the Gospel of Christ is preached, it can mean more than anything else in the world! The Christian church is dealing constantly with critical life situations. Let no one discount what may happen when the redeeming power of God in Christ is proclaimed to a world filled with sin-sick souls.—*Christian Advocate.*

* * *

The Gospel and Soap

A soap manufacturer and an evangelical preacher were walking along together, the former not being a Christian. The soap maker said, "The Gospel you preach has not done much good, for there is still a lot of wickedness, and thousands of wicked people." The preacher was silent awhile, and in a few moments they passed a child making mud pies in the street. He was exceedingly dirty. Then the preacher's turn came. "Soap has not done much good in the world, I see; for there is still much dirt, and ever so many dirty people!" "Oh, well," said the manufacturer, "soap is only useful when it is applied." "Exactly," replied the other, "so it is with the Gospel."—*Family Herald and Weekly Star.*

* * *

Advice from Antonescu

General Antonescu, head of the Rumanian state, issued some months ago a statement "to all the priests of all the altars of Rumania." He explained to them "with the love of a truly believing man, that the church is not only buildings, ikons, hymns, candles, bells. It is love, sacrifice, kindness to fellow men, zeal for purity of spirit. There where a pure soul is, is the altar of God. If your thoughts are not fully dedicated to the Creator, if your hearts do not really suffer for the sins of others, then the walls of the church will be cold, the pictures of the saints dead and hard, the bells will give no joyous sound, and the wax candles will be as if extinguished. The gospel of our Lord is a real thing. It was not written to be a dead letter but to be lived out. Christ died and suffered for our salvation. Only in His life can you make clear to believers the purpose of life. Preach the gospel every Sunday so that it may be heard and understood of all, and add thereto meaningful prayer. I beg you that in your daily life you exhibit an upright and earnest spirit of love, that you seek no gold, nor fall into human passion."

This is excellent advice, comments *Sunday School Times,* even though it comes from the head of a Government that is the tool of the Nazis in anti-Semitic persecution, and that has forbidden gospel evangelism by all Baptist and other evangelical churches.—*Gospel Herald.*

* * *

Transformed Lives

A well-known preacher of the United States was asked to say a few words to a gathering in an open air meeting. At the close of his address an atheist stepped up to him and challenged him to a debate, assuring him that he would bear all the expense of renting the hall and advertising. "I accept on one condition: When you bring with you fifty people who have been helped by your philosophy, I am ready. I will bring you hundreds who will testify to the transformation this Gospel has wrought in their lives." Needless to say the challenger departed somewhat chagrined.—*Gospel Herald.*

* * *

Deafness

A man said about something he wished to make clear, "Why, it is as plain as A B C!" "Yes," said a third party, "but the man you are talking to is D E F." So some of the hearers seem to turn away from the Word of God. Let us explain the Gospel as we may, if there is no desire in the heart, our plainest messages are lost. — Courtesy *Moody Monthly.*

* * *

The "Blues" or the Gospel?

In "Today in My Vineyard," the Annual Report of the Open Air Mission, an evangelist describes his part in a social evening at the Y.M.C.A. hut at Carnarvon Camp during the Great War. The man before him sang, "The Wibbly-Wobbly Blues." Then the evangelist went on the platform, lay down with his head on a rolled-up coat, and said, "Boys, this morning I visited a poor fellow who lay like this, doubled up with pneumonia. It wouldn't have been of much comfort to him if I had sung 'The Wibbly-Wobbly Blues,' would it? I gave him 'The Old, Old Story'—and now I'm going to give it to you." When they closed that night there were twenty men on their knees, seeking Christ.—*Sunday School Times.*

* * *

The Camel Rider's Call

When the caravans in the desert are in want of water, they are accustomed to send a camel with its rider some distance in advance. Then, after a time, follows another, and then at a short interval another. As soon as the first man finds water, almost before he stoops down to drink, he shouts aloud, *"Come!" The* next man hearing the call repeats it, *"Come!"* The nearest man again takes up the call, *"Come!"* until the surrounding desert echoes with the word *"Come!"*

This is the great invitation word of the Gospel, come! *come! COME!—Gospel Stories for the Young.*

* * *

The Gospel Not Too Short

Some years ago there was a great fire in Dublin. A high block of buildings was alight below, and the fire was working its way up to the top of the buildings very rapidly. A number of people were at the windows above calling out for help. The Fire Escape was heard coming in the distance, and the crowd of anxious spectators gave a cheer of hope, but imagine their dismay when it was found the Fire Escape was too short to reach the perishing.—Selected.

* * *

Any Competition for the Gospel?

The American agent for General Motors in Shanghai asked a Christian leader in China if he had much competition, in his missionary work, from the sages and philosophers of Confucianism. The Christian answered by asking the motor dealer a question, "Do you, when you try to sell a Cadillac or a LaSalle, have much competition with the Chinese merchant who sells wheelbarrows?"—*Good News.*

* * *

After Fifty Years the Gospel

A blessed work of grace has been going on in various parts of Scotland. Many have accepted God's great salvation, and rejoiced in their newly found Saviour. Among these was a Mr. Murray, an office-bearer in one of the churches, and for fifty years a professor of religion, without, however, the "one thing needful." One day as Mr. Murray was reading a Gospel paper he came across the following statement: "The Gospel brings us, not a work to do, but a word to believe about a work done." "I see it all," said he to his wife, "I have been working at the keyhole, and the door has been open all the time. My fifty years' profession goes for nothing, and I get salvation through simply accepting Christ."—*Love Wins.*

* * *

William Jennings Bryan on Preaching

"I desire my minister to preach every Sunday the simple gospel. 'The old, old story' never wearies the average congregation if it comes from a devout mind with preparation in the message. My ideal sermon is one that has an appeal to the unconverted and a spiritual uplift for the Christian. I want my minister to be abreast of the times on all new theological questions and resarch, but I do not want him to bring them into the pulpit. I have formed certain views of Christ, His gospel, and the inspiration of the Scriptures from a careful reading of the Book of books and of the Shorter Catechism, and it will not make me a better Christian or profit my spiritual life to unsettle these views by a discussion in the pulpit of new theories of Christ and the Holy Scriptures. Finally, I want my minister to act upon the belief that Christ's gospel is the sure cure for all social and political evils, and that his best method of promoting temperance, social morality, and good citizenship is to bring men into the Church. In a word, I want my minister to emphasize in his lifework the declaration of the most successful preacher, Paul: 'It pleased God by the foolishness of preaching to save them that believe.'" — Courtesy *Moody Monthly.*

* * *

Christ Not the Gospel

Many mistakenly think it is Christ Himself that is the Gospel. But this is not so. Christ, we may say reverently, has always been "Himself"; He is "the same yesterday, and today, and forever" (Heb. 13:8). But there has not always been a Gospel of salvation for lost sinners. Not what Christ *is,* but what He *did,*—that is the Gospel. As W. W. Martin has said: "Our justification is connected with the shedding of Christ's blood. We are not justified by His incarnation, wonderful though it is. We are not justified by His life and example, spotless and perfect though it is,—nay, we are rather condemned by it. We are justified solely and only by His death." So Paul tells us by inspiration: "But God commendeth His love toward us, in that, while we were yet sinners, Christ died for us" (Rom. 5:8). What Christ *did* for us, when He died in our stead for our sins and was raised again for our justification,—that is the Gospel.—*Sunday School Times.*

A Prime Minister of England Once Said:

"If I am asked what is the remedy for the deeper sorrows of the human heart, what a man should chiefly look to in progress through life as the power that is to sustain him under trials and enable him manfully to confront his afflictions, I must point to something which in a well-known hymn is called 'The old, old story,' told in an old, old Book, and taught with an old, old teaching, which is the greatest and best gift ever given to mankind."—Selected.

* * *

The Lighthouse in the Desert

Most lighthouses are on rocks and dangerous places in the water. Practically all lighthouses seem to say, Stay away from here. Danger! I know of a lighthouse that says just the opposite, for it says, Come. This lighthouse is in the middle of the Arizona Desert. There is no water to be had for over thirty miles in every direction, but just where that lighthouse stands there is a well. So there is light there at night to let thirsty people know where the well of water is. The tower in the daytime and the light at night say, Here is water. Isn't that like the Lord Jesus who in the midst of a desert would stand and cry, "If any man thirst, let him come unto Me, and drink"? Where else could you go for living water but to the Lord Jesus? The Gospel is still calling to all, "Whosoever will, let him take the water of life freely."—*Good News.*

* * *

Mistaken Kindness

Many kindhearted people, with a pitying concern for the underprivileged, have been misled by movements that undertake to save people with soap, soup, salve, social security, and scholarship. No Christian can be indifferent to the poverty, hardship, or sickness of anyone, but God's plan is that the ministering to the physical needs of the unsaved shall be an incentive to repentance. "The goodness of God leadeth . . . to repentance." Any ministration that convinces the sinner that sin is not so bad after all, any preaching that urges sinners to "cheer up" rather than repent is not God's Gospel.—B. H. Shadduck, in *Sunday School Times.*

* * *

Open Up the Old Wells

It is not a change of religion one needs, but a change of life. Down on Cape Cod, in a little provincial town, there was an old place which had well-nigh gone to decay; a man bought it, and was about to employ men to dig a new well, when an old farmer who had known the place in its glory said: "Why don't you clean out the old well? There used to be plenty of good, sweet water in it." The suggestion was a revelation. They began to work at it—dirt, stones and rubbish, clay and sand were brought out, and in a few days after the cleansing process the old well filled up again with fresh and living water. There is nothing the matter with the old truths, the precious religion of Jesus Christ which was once in the heart. The world can never outgrow the eternal truth of the eternal God. There can be no substitute for the pure water of life. Clean out the old wells and let the water flow. The wells of salvation from which our fathers drank are the wells that will satisfy us.—*Sunday School Times.*

GOSSIP (See also: Tongue, 698)

Her Praiseworthy Oddity

A company of ladies met at a minister's house. As he entered the room, he heard them speaking of an absent friend. "She's very odd!" said one. "She's very singular," said another. "Do you know she often does so and so?" said another, mentioning certain things to her discredit. The minister asked who it was. When told, he said, "Oh, yes, you are quite right. She is odd. She is singular. Why, would you believe it?" he added. "She was never known to speak ill of an absent friend!"—*Sunday School Times.*

* * *

Gossip

The word "gossip" has an interesting origin, and came to have its present meaning by a roundabout route. Originally it came from the Anglo-Saxon word "godsib," which meant "related to God." The word referred to a sponsor at one's baptism. Thus a "godsib" was a close friend who was familiar with you and knew all about you.

It didn't take long for the idea of "knowing about you" to change to "telling all about you," and the present meaning of the word "gossip" was born. —*The Friend.*

Watch Your Words

"If you knew whose feet were standing
Close beside the narrow stream;
If we knew whose eyes were closing
In the sleep that knows no dream;
We would be so kind and tender,
Lightly judge, and gently speak.
Let us act as though we knew it—
For the links so quickly break."

As long as a person is in this life, we always have the opportunity to apologize. When he is dead, that opportunity is gone forever. But even an apology often fails to undo the evil of an unkind act or word. For, as the poet also has said—

"Boys flying kites haul in their white-winged birds,
But you can't do that when you're flying *words.*"

If we always "act as though we knew it"—how kind and thoughtful we should be! The Christian, who knows his Bible and realizes the power of good and evil words and deeds, finds himself all the more responsible for the proper use of these great mediums of service —or curses. He will let no day go by without acting "as though he knew" it might be his, or another's, last day in this life.—*Gospel Herald.*

Why She Was Popular

A decent and honest old woman, who had for more than forty years earned a livelihood by taking in washing, was asked how it was she was so well liked by those who came in contact with her. She replied: "I make it a practice never to say in one house what I hear in another." — "Thou shalt not go up and down as a talebearer among thy people." —*Christian Herald.*

* * *

Where It Belonged

I once heard a very interesting story of a woman who was somewhat of a gossip in a small town. One day she was in the office of the *Daily News*, and leaned up against the wall where were several copies of back editions of the paper. It was warm, her dress was white, and some of the print came off onto the back of the dress. She did not know this, but as she walked down the street was conscious of giggling and tittering whenever folks came near her. She reached home, and there her poor little husband, who was greatly henpecked, was asked if there was anything on her back that should not be there. As she turned around he read in black print, "Daily News." He could not resist the opportunity, and meekly and mildly said, "No, ma'am, there is nothing there that does not belong there!"— *Moody Church News.*

* * *

We may get through this world, but
'twill be very slow,
If we listen to all that is said as we go,
We'll be worried and fretted and kept in
a stew,
For meddlesome tongues must have
something to do—
For people will talk, you know.

The best way to do is to always do right,
And at last you will always win out in
the fight,
Of course, you will meet all sorts of
abuse,
But don't think to stop there, it is not
any use—
For people will talk, you know.
—*The Baptist Examiner.*

Slander

"Show that man out!" we would say of a drunkard; yet, it is very questionable if his unmannerly behavior will do us as much mischief as the talebearer's insinuating story. "Call for a policeman!" we say if we see a thief at his business. Ought we to feel no indignation when we hear a gossip at his work? "Mad dog! Mad dog!" is a terrible hue and cry, but there are few curs whose bite is so dangerous as a busybody's tongue. "Fire! Fire!" is an alarming note, but the talebearer's tongue is set on fire of hell, and those who indulge it had better mend their manners, or they may find that there is fire in hell for unbridled tongues!—Spurgeon.

* * *

Three Things to Remember

Remember, three things come not back
The arrow sent upon its track.
It will not swerve, it will not stay
Its speed; it flies to wound or slay.

The spoken word so soon forgot
By thee; but it has perished not.
In other hearts, 'tis living still.
And doing work for good or ill.

And the lost opportunity,
That cometh back no more to thee;
In vain thou weepest, in vain dost yearn;
These three will nevermore return.
—*Gospel Banner.*

* * *

"Gossiping" Works Ruin

An elephant in a zoo bellowed in vicious notes to its mate in the next enclosure. The mate passed it on to a third elephant.

"They're gossiping!" shouted the keeper and rushed for the stockade, calling to his assistants. But he was not quick enough, and before the animals were subdued they had ruined a thousand dollars' worth of property and injured two men. The keeper explained what he meant by gossiping. One wanted something the others had, or was jealous of them, or felt "just plain ugly" and vented its spite by "tattling" maliciously some bit of news about the other.

"Animals gossip just like men and women," said the keeper, *"and they work just as much mischief by it in their way."—New Century Leader.*

* * *

Boys flying kites, haul in their white-winged birds.
You can't do that when you are flying words.
"Careful with fire," is good advice we know,
"Careful with words," is ten times doubly so;
Thoughts unexpressed may sometimes fall back dead,
But God Himself can't kill them when they're said. —Selected.

* * *

Scandal's Instrument

A godly minister was approached by one of his church members who wanted to repeat to him some of the wrongdoings of others. The pastor said, "Does anybody else know this but you?" "No, sir." "Have you told it to anyone else?" "No." "Then," said the good man, *"go home and hide it away at the feet of Jesus, and never speak of it again unless God leads you to speak to the man himself.* If the Lord wants to bring scandal upon His Church, let Him do it; but don't be the instrument to cause it."—*Herald of His Coming.*

* * *

Wise Sayings

Half the world delights in slander, and the other half in believing it.—French Proverb.

Slander, that worst of poisons, ever finds
An easy entrance to ignoble minds.
—Translation of Juvenal.

Ever have an eye as to what and to whom you speak concerning any man.—Horace.

Hearsay is half lies.—German Proverb.

A gossip speaks ill of all, and all of her.—*Gnomologia.*

A Hint for Knockers

The story is told of a peasant with a troubled conscience who went to a monk for advice. He said he had circulated a vile story about a friend, only to find out the story was not true. "If you want to make peace with your conscience," said the monk, "you must fill a bag with chicken down, go to every dooryard in the village, and drop in each one of them one fluffy feather." The peasant did as he was told. Then, he came back to the monk and announced he had done penance for his folly. "Not yet," replied the monk. "Take your bag to the rounds again and gather up every feather that you have dropped." "But the wind must have blown them all away," said the peasant. "Yes, my son," said the monk, "and so it is with gossip. Words are easily dropped, but no matter how hard you try, you can never get them back again."

"And the tongue is a fire, a world of iniquity. . . The tongue can no man tame; it is an unruly evil, full of deadly poison (James 3:6, 8).—Selected.

* * *

Gossip Town

Have you ever heard of Gossip Town,
On the shore of Falsehood Bay,
Where old Dame Rumor with rustling gown
Is going the livelong day?

It isn't far to Gossip Town,
For people who want to go,
The Idleness Train will take you down
In just an hour or so.

The Thoughtless Road is a popular route,
And most folks start that way,
But it's steep down grade; if you don't look out,
You'll land in Falsehood Bay.

You glide through the Valley of Vicious Folk,
And into the Tunnel of Hate;
Then crossing the Add-to-Bridge, you walk
Right into the city gate.

The principal street is called They-say,
And I've Heard is the public well;
The breezes that blow from Falsehood Bay
Are laden with Don't-You-Tell.

In the midst of the town is Tell-tale Park,
You're never quite safe while there,
Its owner is Madame Suspicious Remark,
Who lives on the street Don't Care.

Just back of the park is Slander Row—
'Twas there that Good Name died,
Pierced by a dart from Jealousy's bow,
In the hands of Envious Pride.

From Gossip Town, Peace long since fled,
But Trouble, Grief and Woe,
And Sorrow and Care you'll meet instead,
If you ever chance to go.

—Selected.

* * *

Roasted Neighbor

Dr. VanDyke once pictured evil-speaking in the following brief, pointed paragraph: "Cannibalism," he said, "is dying out among the barbarous tribes, but it still survives among the most highly civilized peoples. You might find yourself in some difficulty if you invited a company of friends to a feast in which the principal dish was a well-roasted neighbor. Everybody would refuse with horror. But if you wish to serve up somebody's character at a social entertainment, or pick the bones of somebody's reputation in a quiet corner, you will find ready guests and almost incredible appetites."—Courtesy *Moody Monthly.*

* * *

Three Gates of Gold

If you are tempted to reveal
A tale someone to you has told
About another, let it pass,
Before you speak, three gates of gold.

Three narrow gates: First, "Is it true?"
Then "Is it needful?" In your mind
Give truthful answer. And the next
Is last and narrowest—"Is it kind?"

And if to reach your lips at last
It passes through these gateways three,
Then you may tell the tale, nor fear
What the result of speech may be.

—*The Methodist Protestant.*

GRACE

"My Grace is Sufficient for Thee" (II Corinthians 12:9)

Booth-Tucker preached in Chicago one day, and out from the throng a burdened toiler came and said to him, before all the audience, "You can talk like that about how Christ is dear to you, and helps you; but if your wife was dead, as my wife is, and you had some babies crying for their mother who would never come back, you could not say what you are saying."

A little later Booth-Tucker lost his noble wife in a railway wreck, and the body was brought to Chicago and carried to the Salvation Army barracks for the funeral service. After others had conducted the funeral service he stood there by the casket, looked down into the face of the silent wife and mother, and said, "The other day when I was here, a man said, I could not say Christ was sufficient, if my wife were dead, and my children were crying for their mother. If that man is here, tell him that Christ *is* sufficient. My heart is all broken, my heart is all crushed, my heart is all bleeding, but there is a song in my heart and Christ put it there; and if that man is here, I tell him that, though my wife is gone and my children are motherless, Christ comforts me today." That man was there, and down the aisle he came, and fell down beside the casket, and said, "Verily, if Christ can help us like that, I will surrender to Him."

"He giveth *more* grace when burdens grow greater,
He sendeth *more* strength when the labors increase;
To added affliction, *He* addeth His mercy,
To multiplied trials, *His* multiplied peace.
When we have exhausted *our* store of endurance;
When *our* strength has failed ere the day is half done;
When we reach the end of *our* hoarded resources;
Our Father's *full* giving is *only* begun.
His love has *no* limit, His grace knows *no* measure,
His power *no* boundary known unto men;
For out of His infinite riches in Jesus
He giveth and giveth and giveth again." —Selected.

* * *

"Saved by Grace"—Kept by His Power

Two brethren who differed on the question of the believer's safety in Christ were discussing the question, and one said to the other:

"I tell you a child of God is safe only so long as he stays in the lifeboat. He may jump out, and if he jumps out he is lost."

To this the other replied, saying: "You remind me of an incident in my own life. I took my little son out with me in a boat. I realized, as he did not, the danger of his falling or even jumping, into the water. So I sat with him all the time, and all the time I held him fast, so he could neither fall out, nor jump out, of the boat."

"But," said the first speaker, "he could have wriggled out of his coat and got away in spite of you."

"Oh," said the other, "you misunderstood me if you supposed I was holding his coat; I was holding him."—*Christian Courier.*

* * *

Grace Instead of Justice

"Would you be my loyal subject if I should exercise grace instead of justice and forgive your crime?" said Queen Elizabeth to her would-be assassin. "That, madam, would be no grace at all, to found your grace on the condition of my merit. "Then I pardon you unconditionally," said the Queen. "That," replied the proud French woman as she clasped the Queen's feet, "that is queenly grace, and now I am your slave for life."—*Gospel Herald.*

* * *

God knows the way of the righteous,
Even though it be dark and drear;
He knows when we're tired and weary,
Our burdens too heavy to bear;
We ask, as the shadows lengthen,
"Lord, lift Thou this burden of care!"
And often His voice replieth:
"My child, I placed it for you there!
With grace that is all-sufficient,
That you might grow stronger in Me,
So trust, weary child, your Father,
He knoweth and careth for thee!"
—*Gospel Herald.*

* * *

Grace Can't Be Bought

When Clara Barton was engaged in Red Cross work in Cuba, during the Spanish-American War, Col. Theodore Roosevelt came to her desiring to buy some delicacies for the sick and wounded men under his command. His request was refused. Roosevelt was troubled; he loved his men, and was ready to pay for the supplies out of his own pocket. "How can I get these things?" he asked. "I must have proper food for my sick men." "Just ask for them, Colonel," said the surgeon in charge of the Red Cross headquarters. "Oh," said the Colonel, "then I do ask for them." And he got them at once; but *you notice that he got them through grace, and not through purchase.—Onward.*

* * *

The Bird with a Broken Wing

(*Written by a Rescued Girl*)

It lay by the dusty roadside where the people came and went,
But none looked down on the panting bird whose life was nearly spent.

One woman did, but she hurried on with a sigh of helpless pain,
For she said, "Poor bird with a broken wing, you can never fly again."

It fluttered in anguish all day till the sun was set,
And night came down in silence on the slopes of Olivet,
But the Master who lay on the sod that night 'neath the tress and the open sky,
Could not sleep for the sound that pierced His heart, of the dying birdling's cry.

As the glory of the morning was touching the eastern hills,
He came to where the weary bird lay cold, and faint and still.
He bent His head in compassion over the shattered thing,
It was bruised, and broken, and dying; it could never soar or sing.
He drew it from the tangled grass with a hand of healing power,
And said, "You shall soar and sing for Me as bird never sang before."

He lifted it high on His blessed palm and it spread its wings to fly,
And filled the blue Judæan sky with a flood of melody
Which echoed over hill and plain with such triumphant strain
That men stood still to drink their fill and turned to drink again.

Then with wings that were strong and tireless as an eagle's on its way,
It mounted up to the Throne of God past the gates of earthly day,
And sang its songs of liberty while angels stood in amaze,
And took up the song as it swept along, and all Heaven rang with its praise.

The song of the bird with the broken wing is the song my heart is singing:
The story of His matchless grace through all my life is ringing,
Up out of the tangle of sin and shame His love hath lifted my soul,
And the healing touch of the Son of God hath freed me and made me whole. —*Way of Faith.*

Free Grace

Rev. James Caughey tells of a minister who lay dying in Scotland. A brother minister called to see him, and inquired, "Well, my brother, what are you doing?" "Doing?" answered the dying servant of God. "Doing? I will tell you: I am gathering together all my prayers and sermons, all my good deeds and bad deeds, and *am going to throw them all overboard together, and swim to glory on the plank of free grace!*" — Albert Midlane.

* * *

Sufficient Grace on Time

"My grace is sufficient" (II Cor. 12: 9).

The Christian's repose is grounded upon this fact that his source of supply will never give out. God's grace, for every need of every man, is boundless and limitless. It is made available to the believer in the oft-proven promise: "My God shall supply all your need according to His riches in Glory by Christ Jesus." Again the believer is encouraged to "come boldly unto the throne of grace, that we may obtain mercy, and find grace to help in time of need." Dr. G. Campbell Morgan gives a very inspiring and helpful paragraph on this last text. He says, "I am never tired of pointing out that the Greek phrase translated, 'in time of need,' is a colloquialism, of which the 'nick of time' is the exact equivalent. 'That ye may have grace to help in the *nick of time.* Grace just when and where I need it. You are attacked by temptation, and at the moment of assault you look to Him, and the grace is there to help in 'the nick of time.'

"No postponement of your petition until the evening hour of prayer; but there, man, there in the city street with the flaming temptation in front of you, turn to Christ within you, with a cry for help, and the grace will be there in the 'nick of time.' "—*The Missionary Worker.*

* * *

Drink Deep!

A little boy, one of seven children, met with an accident, and was taken to the hospital. He came from a lowly home where hunger was seldom quite satisfied. The glass of milk was only part full, or, if full, shared by two of the children. After the lad was made comfortable as possible in his hospital bed, a nurse brought him a large glass of milk. He looked at it longingly and then, with the memory of many experiences of sharing with the other children, said, "How deep shall I drink?" The nurse with her eyes shining and a lump in her throat said, "Drink it all." Oh, hungry and thirsty soul, how deep shall you drink of the love and goodness of God? There is no limit! Drink it all, drink it again and again! The supply is inexhaustible.—*Upper Room.*

* * *

Sufficient Grace

"My grace is sufficient for thee." (II Cor. 12:9).

My grace is sufficient, O lost one!
Thy soul to redeem from its woe,
To give you a perfect salvation,
To keep you wherever you go.

My grace is sufficient, O weak one!
The bondage of sin to remove;
My strength is made perfect in weakness,
Then seek for this strength from above.

My grace is sufficient, O tried one!
To meet every testing and need;
Whatever may be the requirement,
My grace is sufficient indeed.

My grace is sufficient, O dear one!
Yes, even for death's trying hour;
This foe I have met and have vanquished;
No need, then, to fear its dread power.
—Fred Scott Shepard.

* * *

Enough of Something

An old incident comes to me of a wee lad taken to the seashore from a tenement house in New York. He knew nothing of the country life, had few friends and none of the comforts of life. When the ladies took him to the beach, he stood with his feet deep in the sand and his eyes fastened on the ocean. He had never seen the ocean before.

"What are you thinking of?" they asked.

"Oh," said he, "I am thinking how nice it is to see enough of something."—*Gospel Herald.*

* * *

Day by Day

A man can no more take a supply of grace for the future than he can eat enough today to last him for the next six months, or take sufficient air into his lungs to sustain life for a week to come. We must draw upon God's boundless stores for grace from day to day, as we need it.—D. L. Moody.

* * *

"Self-Made" Men

Speaking of salvation by grace, Mr. Moody has said: "It is well that man cannot save himself; for if a man could only work his own way to Heaven, you would never hear the last of it. Why, if a man happens to get a little ahead of his fellows and scrapes a few thousands of dollars together, you'll hear him boast of being a self-made man. I've heard so much of this sort of talk that I am sick and tired of the whole business; and I am glad that through all eternity in Heaven we will never hear anyone bragging of how he worked his way to get there."—*Mid-Continent.*

* * *

"Dip It Up"

We are often in the position of a ship I read of years ago, which was in distress on the high seas because her supply of fresh water had run out. The crew was liable to die the most horrible of deaths by thirst, and that with water all around him. When hope was almost given up, they sighted a ship in the far distance. At once they hoisted signals of distress. The only answer they got was, "Dip it up." What heartless mockery to tell people to dip up buckets of salt water! They signalled again, but the same answer came back. In despair, they lowered a bucket. Imagine their amazement and their joy when the water proved to be fresh, living water. There was, in reality, no miracle or mystery. They thought they were on the high seas, whereas, in fact, they were at the mouth of the mighty River Amazon.

Are we not often in the same case as that? Life all around seems dead and dull and dry. We feel inclined to throw things up in despair. Yet all the time infinite resources of a good and loving God are around us. We need to draw on Him.—The Bishop of Stafford.

GROWTH

A True "Spiritual"

There is a Negro "spiritual" that is sung very beautifully by that fine Christian Negro radio chorus, "Wings Over Jordan," on Sunday morning, and a line that is repeated in it over and over again is this: "I mus' keep a'movering along." Truly this is God's "must" for all His children. The challenging invitation and command of His Word is, "Let us go on unto perfection."—*Sunday School Times.*

* * *

Motion Without Progress

Rowland Hill once visited a home and saw a child riding a rocking-horse. After watching the little boy for some time, he wittily remarked, "He reminds me of some Christians. There is plenty of motion but no progress."—*Gospel Herald.*

* * *

Church Babies

It is astonishing how many people there are in the churches who have to be nursed. Instead of being spiritually strong men and women, they are mere babes and have to be cared for. Through their infirmity the church, instead of being a workshop, becomes a nursery—a hospital. Paul said, "When I was a child, I spoke as a child, I thought as a child, I understood as a child; but when I became a man I put away childish things." But many who profess to be matured believers are still playing with spiritual doll-rags.

Spiritual babes, instead of doing work, make work for others. The difference between a child and a man is that the man works and the child makes work for others. Most churches of today are full of babies. They do not help; they hinder. Many have not learned to walk, but they have learned to talk. Some of these church babies are a whining set, and the church finds itself under constraint of running a nursery for many of them. The preacher must spend much of his time cradle-rocking to keep them from whining.

Some of these babies are thirty, forty and fifty years old. Did you ever see a gray-headed baby? I have. Many of them. They never get out of spiritual babyhood. They have never cut their teeth. Permanently dwarfed in spiritual infancy! What a pity! Instead of eating meat, they must in mid-life and beyond be nursed from the bottle.

The reason why so many are not strong men and women in Christ Jesus is because they do not eat the proper food. We are to grow in grace and in knowledge of our Lord and Saviour Jesus Christ. We cannot grow in grace by feasting on sinful pleasures. We must have God's Word. Many are drinking milk who ought to be eating meat.

It is no disgrace to be a baby. But we must not remain babies. Religion is a growing in holiness; a development into the image of Christ Jesus. Therefore, I say, "Quit you like men, be strong."—E. H. Henderson, in *Western Recorder.*

The Fern that Couldn't Grow

Every member of a family was puzzled over the mystery of a fern that would not grow. Sulking, seemingly, the plant refused to put out new stems. That there might be no injury from transplanting, it had been taken up carefully, and sheltered until it should have been well rooted. Everything in the way of plant food had been provided, but there it stood, no larger than when brought to the house, an awkward, ugly thing, in a mockingly large flowerpot. Then arrived a guest who was a horticulturist. He forced a wire down into the earth about the fern's roots, and diagnosed the trouble at once. The plant had been set in stiff clay, and this had become packed hard. Reset in loose soil, the fern grew luxuriously. Even the flower of God's own planting cannot find root in a heart chocked by the cares and riches and pleasures of this life.—*Methodist Times.*

* * *

We are building every day,
In a good or evil way,
And the structure as it grows,
Will our inmost self disclose.

Till in every arch and line,
All our faults and failings shine;
It may grow a castle grand,
Or a wreck upon the sand.

Do you ask what building this,
That can show both pain and bliss,
That can be both dark and fair?
Lo! its name is character.

Build it well whate'er you do,
Build it straight and strong and true,
Build it clean and high and broad,
Build it for the eye of God.

—Selected.

* * *

Are We Really Growing?

I was once urging upon a company of Christians the duty and privilege of an immediate and definite step into the "land of promise," when a lady of great intelligence interrupted me with what she evidently felt to be complete rebuttal of all I had been saying, by exclaiming, "Ah! but, Mrs. Smith, I believe in *growing* in grace." "How long have you been growing?" I asked. "About twenty-five years," was her answer. "And how much more unworldly and devoted to the Lord are you now than when your Christian life began?" I continued. "Alas!" was her reply. "I fear I am not nearly so much so." With this answer, her eyes were opened to see that, at all events, her way of growing, had not been successful, but quite the reverse. The trouble with her was simply this: she was trying to grow *into* grace, instead of *in* it.—*Sunday School Times.*

* * *

Growth in Trouble

Ten thousand saints are ready to testify that their periods of most rapid and unmistakable spiritual growth have been their periods of trouble. The winter accomplishes more than the summer for the soul's development and advance. The valley of weeping is a well of living waters, and the barren heights a dewy and pleasant field. And grace prepares trial — the grace of our Saviour, our Leader, our Lover. He has been in the cold and frost before us, and He will take care that our winter is not nearly so keen as His. His made His heart bleed; it slew Him outright; ours, through His wise and tender tuition, will instruct us, brace us, ripen us into His own likeness.—Alexander Smellie.

* * *

Unconscious Progress

There is progress in a Christian's life when he may not seem to be going ahead—like a canal boat in a lock, when it stands still but is rising all the time.—D. L. Moody, in *Windows.*

* * *

Tree or Post?

Plant a tree and it begins to grow; set a post and it begins to decay. Which are you, a tree or a post?—*The Moody Bible Institute Monthly.*

Still Growing

At Hampton Court Palace, in England, one of the most famous grapevines in the world is trained over a high-arched trellis under a glass roof. It has been growing there for one hundred and sixty years, and last year it ripened six hundred fine clusters of delicious grapes. It has the best of expert care, and shows no sign of dying.—*Girls' World.*

* * *

Standing Won't Do

Someone asked a Scripture Reader in the British Army, "Do these young converts *stand?*" "No," he replied, "they go on."—Heard in a meeting addressed by Mr. H. G. Howell (The King's Body Guard).

* * *

His Next

Plutarch said of the Roman consul Coriolanus: "He was always trying to excel himself." The same secret of excellence is possessed by the sculptor, St. Gaudens. A Chicago reporter said to him, when a piece of his work was unveiled in that city, "I suppose, Mr. St. Gaudens, you consider this statue your masterpiece?" "Indeed, I do not," was the quick reply, "my next statue is always my masterpiece."—Selected.

* * *

Unseen Progress

God never places us in any position where we cannot grow. When we are not sending branches upward we may be sending roots downward. When everything seems failure we may be making the best kind of progress.—E. Prentiss.

* * *

We are all blind until we see
 That in the human plan,
Nothing is worth the building
 That does not build the man.

Why build these cities glorious
 If man unbuilded goes?
In vain we build the world
 Unless the builder also grows.
—Selected.

The Only Name He Could Write

Mrs. Booth used to tell a beautiful story of a man whose saintly life left its permanent and gracious impress upon her own. He seemed to grow in grace and charm and all nobleness with every day that he lived. At last he could speak of nothing but the glories of his Saviour, and his face was radiant with awe and affection whenever he mentioned that holy name. It chanced that, as he was dying, a document was discovered that imperatively required his signature. He held the pen for one brief moment, wrote, and fell back upon the pillows dead. And on the paper he had written, not his own name, but the Name that is above every name. Within sight of the things within the veil, that seemed to be the only name that mattered.—*Sunday at Home.*

* * *

The Power of New Life

A lady, who desired to lead a Christian life, felt that there was one thing in her life that she could not give up. When she consulted her pastor, he said: "Have you noticed that there are always a few dead leaves clinging to the old oak trees after all the other leaves have fallen? The strong blasts of winter fail to tear them off. Spring comes, and still they cling persistently. The days are calm, bright, and balmy. Presently one by one they drop off. What unseen power so quietly, but so surely, severs them? The new life rising in the tree gradually causes them to drop off. And so with us,—as the new life in Christ permeates our being, we find that we can give up for Him what before was so hard to renounce." — *Sunday School Times.*

* * *

Where Are Your Roots

In the midst of the vineyard there was one grapevine that was poor and sickly looking. This weak vine stood out, all the more through contrast, from the rest of the vineyard of strong and flourishing vines. Year after year the vine was sickly. Finally the owner started to dig the ground to find the reason why. He found an abandoned well which had been covered over with a circle of wood and shallow earth thrown on top. The vine had very long roots dangling in the thin air of the well. Perhaps your soul is like that. You have not been fast rooted in the foundation and are getting no nourishment from the Word of God. You will be a sickly Christian, bearing no fruit, unless you get your roots firmly established in Him.—*Revelation.*

* * *

"My Rule for Christian Living"

Dr. J. Wilbur Chapman had this which he called "My rule for Christian living": "The rule that governs my life is this: anything that dims my vision of Christ, or takes away my taste for Bible study, or cramps my prayer life, or makes Christian work difficult, is wrong for me, and I must, as a Christian, turn away from it." This simple rule may help you find a safe road for your feet along life's road.—*Watchman-Examiner.*

* * *

Why No Progress?

A gentleman was walking on the parade at Llandudno, and was watching a pretty little vessel with its white sail shining in the sunlight. "How is it that ship does not seem to be moving?" he said to a seaman standing by. "Her sails are spread and there's plenty of breeze, but she seems to make no progress." "She's anchored," replied the sailor. That's just how it is with many of us on our heavenward journey, but we make no progress at all because we are anchored to something here on earth—some sin indulged in, or some worldliness we will not give up.—*Home Messenger.*

* * *

Still upward be thine onward course:
For this I pray today;
Still upward as the years go by
And seasons pass away.

Still upward in this coming year—
Thy path is all untried;
Still upward may'st thou journey on,
Close by thy Saviour's side.

Still upward e'en though sorrow come,
And trials crush thine heart;
Still upward till in Heaven you wake
With Christ to walk apart.

Still upward till the day shall break,
And shadows all have flown;
Still upward till in Heaven you wake
And stand before the throne.

—Selected.

* * *

Is It Our Excuse, Too?

Billy Sunday is credited with the story of a Negro convert whom he stopped one day and asked the question: "If you were walking along the road and saw a low branch and on that branch a nice fat chicken, what would you do?" "Please don't ask me dat question," begged the Negro. When Mr. Sunday insisted upon an answer, the Negro replied: "Well, Mr. Sunday, you know Ah's only an infant in de Kingdom." It is to be feared there are many infants in the Kingdom who are not young in years, but who have failed to grow because they have not made use of the means of grace.—*The King's Business.*

* * *

Brother Jones' Testimony?

One of our evangelists in the earlier days was accustomed to tell a story of an old farmer who, in the prayer meetings of his church, was wont, in describing his Christian experience, to use the phrase, "Well, I'm not making much progress, but I'm established." One springtime, when the farmer was getting out some logs, his wagon sank in the mud in a soft place in the road and he could not get out. As he sat on top of the logs reviewing the situation, a neighbor who had never accepted the principle of the old man's religious experience came along and greeted him: "Well, Brother Jones, I see you are not making much progress, but you're established."

To be stuck on the road is not a very satisfactory type of establishment, but it is not uncommon.—Robert E. Speer.

* * *

A Faith that Holds

The following extended quotation is lifted from a recent issue of *Zion's Herald* and should come to all—both old and young—as a heart-warming example of the working of a genuine Christian faith in time of need:

"In a certain home an old man and an old woman were sick. They could neither of them get well. One was upstairs and the other was downstairs. And they were my own father and mother. We children got together and planned to take Mother up to call on Father before they were obliged to say the final good-bye on earth. So we made a chair out of our hands the way we used to do at school and took Mother up to see Father. Then we stepped out and left them alone. You can imagine how I felt—my father and mother together for the last time on earth.

"After they had been together as long as I thought they ought, I stepped in, and this is what I saw. Father sat there in his old armchair as he had sat so many times before, and mother stood over him stroking his hair and raining tears down upon him—the faces of the two were transfigured, and Mother was speaking in a low musical tone, and this is what she was saying, 'It gets brighter and brighter and brighter.'

"I had thought it would be a hard time for them and thought they would be talking about sickness, death, and the sad little cemetery on the hill. Instead they were holding a class meeting together."—*Religious Telescope.*

* * *

Nothing Left of Self

Dr. Talbot of the Church of the Open Door in Los Angeles was telling . . . of a daddy and a little boy walking down a street in Chicago past the place where a skyscraper was being constructed. Glancing up they saw the men at work on a high story. Said the little boy: "Daddy, what are those little boys doing up there so high?" "Those are not little boys; those are grown men." "But why do they look so small?" "Because they are so high." "Then, Daddy, when they get to Heaven, there won't be anything left of them, will there?" How true it is that the nearer we come to Christ, the smaller we ourselves become! —Henry Wingblade, in the *Standard.*

* * *

A Dangerous Place to Sleep

One night a small boy fell out of bed. The next day at breakfast he volunteered this explanation: "I know why I fell out of bed last night. I went to sleep too near where I got in." A dangerous place for sleeping! Yet many of us have fallen out of our place in God's plan . . . for the same reason. We think that when we accept Christ . . . we need to do nothing more about it. Or we believe we can follow Christ afar off—as long-distance disciples. . . . Spiritual reserves come only as men keep in touch with God.—*Secret Place.*

* * *

The Important Beginning

One of the greatest mistakes is trying to build people up in the Christian life before they are in it. If a baby is to grow satisfactorily it must be well born, and if we are to grow in grace we must be born again. There was a baby in New York that was fed on elephant's milk and it grew one hundred pounds in a few weeks,—but then, it was a baby elephant to begin with. A human baby would not have grown the same, even if it were fed on elephant's milk. And just so you can feed a man, woman, or child on the best food for a child of God, but he will not grow like a child of God unless he is a child of God to begin with. So to grow in grace we must first be in grace.—*The King's Business.*

GUIDANCE

Who Is the Architect?

An architect complains that many of his clients come and ask him to design a house for them, only to let him very speedily discover that they have already designed it all for themselves. What they really want is his sanction of the plan and the satisfaction of seeing him draw on paper what they have fully in mind. It is in very much the same fashion that we often go to the great Architect with our lives. *We ask Him for wisdom and guidance, but we have already planned how we will build our fortunes and shape our course and it is not His way we are seeking, but His approval of our way.—Mississippi Visitor.*

* * *

Why Fuss and Fear?

"He that believeth shall not make haste,"—or, more literally, "shall not get into a fuss." He shall not get into a panic. He shall not fetch his fears either from his yesterdays or his tomorrows. Concerning his yesterdays faith says, "Thou hast beset me behind." Concerning his tomorrows—"Thou hast beset me... before." Concerning the immediate day faith says, "Thou hast . . . laid thine hand upon me." That is enough; just to feel the presence of his guiding hand."—Selected.

* * *

The King Knows

During the first evacuation of children from bomb-torn areas of London, a train was leaving packed with children. Many of them had never been on a train, and most of them had never been in the country. The parents of a small boy and girl had just said good-bye to their precious children and left them standing on the platform. The little girl began to cry, and said she was afraid because she did not know where she was going. Her little brother, brushing his own tears away, put an arm around her in an effort to comfort her, and said, "I do not know where we are going either, but the king knows." Are not many of us like the little girl, fearful because we do not know where we are going in this distracted world of ours? We do not know, but our King knows! The emergencies and problems of our day will be calmly faced, if in our quiet moment we have met God and put our trust in Him.—*Day by Day.*

* * *

God's Leading in a Flight of Birds

Out on the sea the prow of Columbus' ship was pointed straight for Delaware Bay, when a flock of birds was observed flying southwest. Pinzon persuaded Columbus to change the course of his ship and sail after the birds. And so Columbus landed on that little island of the West Indies instead of in the mouth of Delaware Bay. Some men see in this nothing but a flight of birds. But the Christian historian sees in it the guiding hand of God. Columbus took possession of San Salvador in the name of Ferdinand and Isabella, for Spain. Spanish misrule has cursed every nation upon which its mildewed hand has been laid. God by this act saved America from this blight, saved America to be blessed with English Protestantism. — Elmer Ellsworth Helms, in *God in History.*

* * *

He Is My Guide

I see my way as birds their trackless way.
I shall arrive,—what time, what circuit first,
I ask not; but unless God sends His hail
Or blinding fire-balls, sleet or stifling snow,
In some time, His good time, I shall arrive:
He guides me and the bird. In His good time.
—Robert Browning.

* * *

Worth Following

There is a pleasing story of how the father of Matthew Henry the commentator won his bride. He was a Presbyterian minister, she an only daughter, and the heiress of a considerable fortune. Her father objected. "You see," he said to his daughter, "he may be a perfect gentleman, a brilliant scholar, and an excellent preacher; but he is a stranger, and we do not even know where he comes from!" "True," replied the girl, with all the acumen and insight that her great son afterward displayed, "but we know where he is going, and I should like to go with him." Do others have confidence in us because they know we are led of God?—*Sunday School Chronicle.*

* * *

Held by the Hand

Mr. Sankey told the story of his little boy.

It was in Scotland, in the winter. For the first time the little fellow had on an overcoat in which there were pockets. With his father the boy was walking in a somewhat slippery place. The father said to him, "My boy, you had better let me take your hand." But the boy's hands were deep in the pockets of the coat, and so he kept them there until a rather bad fall on the ice showed him that his father's advice was good. The tumble brought down his pride somewhat and he said, "I will take your hand," and he reached up and took hold of his father's hand in his somewhat feeble grasp. Then another slip and his hand was unable to keep its hold on the father's and down he went on the ice.

Then it was that humbled in spirit he said as he raised his hand, "*You* may take it now."

And so it was that the father's strong hand held the child up when the slippery places came.

Happy is the believer who knows that he is in the mighty hand of the Saviour, and that He has undertaken to bear "His own" all the way home to His glory. It is He, the Son of God, the Lord of glory, who says, "My sheep . . . shall never perish, neither shall any man pluck them out of My hand. My Father, which gave them Me, is greater than all; and no man is able to pluck them out of My Father's hand. I and My Father are one" (John 10:27-30).—*Scattered Seed.*

The Guiding Hand

When Stanley was about to cross Africa for the first time, many of the strong men of his party burst into tears as they set out. They were not cowardly, but they were overcome by the thought of the terrific hardships which they knew lay before them.

Every human life is a journey as difficult and perilous; and we might well shrink from it, had we no Guide. What absolute madness it is to set out alone!

I have read the story of a conceited young captain who would not wait off the shore for a pilot to come on board, to take him through the narrows of the harbor. "I am my own pilot," was the proud reply to all remonstrances, and he promised to be in the harbor by daybreak. He was cast ashore, dead, amid the fragments of his wrecked vessel. Such has been the fate of many a man who would be his own pilot amid the rocks and shoals of life.

When travelers climb dangerous places in the Alps, they are fastened to their guide. They have become a part of him. They may slip and fail, but he will not. So may we be bound to our omnipotent Guide; and, thus united with wisdom and security, we may travel through life without a tremor of fear. — Amos R. Wells, in *The S. S. Banner.*

* * *

"The Dove Man"

There is a guide in the deserts of Arabia who is said never to lose his way. He carries in his breast a homing-pigeon with a very fine cord attached to one leg. When in any doubt as to which path to take the guide throws the bird in the air. The pigeon quickly strains at the cord to fly in the direction of home and so leads his master unerringly. They call that guide "The dove man." The Holy Spirit, the heavenly Dove, is willing and able to lead us if we will only allow him to do so.—"Unknown Christian," in *This Is the Way.*

* * *

Only the Ransomed Knew

A yacht was cruising among the isles of Scotland, when a gale caught the craft off a perilous leeshore. The skipper made for the harbor leagues away. Through the darkness the yacht went plunging on her course. At length she swung into smooth water, and they dropped anchor, and, turning into their berths, went peacefully to sleep. In the morning the owner came on deck and surveyed the scene,—a little haven girt about by dark purple mountains. Looking toward the entrance, he saw a narrow channel with sharp rocks jutting here and there, all awash with boiling surf. Turning to the old skipper, he exclaimed, "Did we pass those in the darkness?" This is a parable of life. We know something of the goodness and mercy which have followed us all our days, but we shall never realize fully the debt we owe to the unseen Guide until we are safely within the harbor.—*British Weekly.*

* * *

Lead Me On

I cannot see, Lord, take my hand,
And guide me through the night;
When Thou art near, I do not fear,
For all Thy mercies oft appear
To point me to Thy glory land
Of light.

I do not know what I shall be
Within the pearly gates;
I only know that I shall go
Where Living Waters ever flow,
And where eternal joy for me
Awaits.
—R. E. Neighbour, D.D.

* * *

He Knows the Way

A convert in Africa made this remark, "The trail is hard and tangled, but there is a Man ahead of us." Jesus Christ always goes before us. He is ever in front. He bids us follow. "All the way my Saviour leads."—*Christian Endeavor.*

* * *

A Perilous Plank

"We were on shipboard," relates a captain's wife, "lying in a Southern harbor. We were obliged, first to make our way ashore. The waves were rolling heavily. I became frightened at the thought of attempting it, when one came to me, saying, 'Do not be afraid: I will take care of you.'

"He bore a peculiarly shaped dark lantern, only a single ray of light being emitted from a small circular opening. 'Now,' said he, 'take my hand; hold fast, do not fear. Do not look about you, or on either side of you, only on that little spot lighted by my lantern, and place your footsteps firmly right there.'

"I heard the rushing of the waters, and was still conscious of fear; but by looking steadily only where the light fell, and planting my footsteps just there, not turning either to the right or the left, clasping firmly the strong hand, the danger was overcome, and the shore reached in safety.

"The next day my kind guide said, 'Would you like to see the way by which you came last night? Then he showed me where our vessel had been lying, and the very narrow plank by which we had reached the shore. He knew that had I turned either to the right or left I should, in all probability, have lost my balance and gone over into those dark waters; but by holding fast and treading just where the light fell all danger would be averted."

The believer often comes to some dark passage, or encounters some severe trial, which so overshadows the way that he fears to go forward lest he fall. But when he clasps the hand of his Heavenly Father, he is led gently over the rough and dangerous places and landed safely in some secure spot. The storms may rage and angry waves threaten to engulf, but if we keep our eyes on Jesus we shall outride the storms, and have an abundant entrance into the heaven of eternal rest.—*Words of Life.*

* * *

Do We "Inquire" Thus?

An old Scotch woman who tramped about selling goods was in the habit of tossing a stick into the air when she came to a crossroad and taking whichever direction the stick pointed. One day she was seen tossing it several times. On being questioned, she said the road to the right looked so drear-like that she tossed the stick till it pointed to the left, that looking a nicer way. We go to God for guidance, but if His way seems dull we choose a brighter one, forgetting that He sees the end as well as the beginning. —*Sunday School Chronicle.*

* * *

The Walk of Faith

I cannot see the way I go;
  I go not knowing why;
But this I know, each step is set
  By Him who is Most High;
And so I gladly tread His path,
  Nor fear whate'er betide,
Assured that when I win His smile,
  I shall be satisfied.
    —Sue M. Voorhees.

* * *

In God's Good Time

The late Dr. Jowett said that he was once in a most pitiful perplexity, and consulted Dr. Berry of Wolverhampton. "What would you do if you were in my place?" he entreated. "I don't know, Jowett, I am not there, and you are not there yet. When have you to act?" "On Friday," Dr. Jowett replied. "Then," answered Berry, "you will find your way perfectly clear on Friday. The Lord will not fail you." And surely enough, on Friday all was plain. Give God time, and even when the knife flashes in the air the ram will be seen caught in the thicket. Give God time, and even when Pharaoh's host is on Israel's heels, a path through the waters will be suddenly open. Give God time, and when the bed of the brook is dry, Elijah shall hear the guiding voice.—F. W. Boreham, in *Alliance Weekly.*

* * *

"Oh Lead Thou Me"

Perhaps across the ocean wild
  His loving hand again may lead,
It may be *here* some suffering child
  My ministry may need.

Ah! Blessed Lord, still, still with Thee,
  If far to go or home to stay,
My soul cries out, Oh lead Thou me
  In Thine own wondrous way.
    —Lillian Washer.

* * *

A Short Sermon

The guide was taking some tourists through Mammoth Cave. When they reached "The Cathedral," he mounted a rock called "The Pulpit," and said he would preach a sermon. It was short. All he said was, "Keep close to your guide." The tourists soon found it was a good sermon for if one did not keep close to the guide he would be lost in the midst of pits, precipices, and defiles. It is hard to find one's way through Mammoth Cave without a guide; it is harder to find one's way through the world without the lamp of God's Word. A good motto for Christians is, "Keep your eye on the Lamp."—*Our Pentecostal Boys and Girls.*

* * *

And God Made the Bees!

Here is a little bee that organizes a city, that builds ten thousand cells for honey, twelve thousands cells for larvæ, a holy of holies for the mother queen; a little bee that observes the increasing heat, and, when the wax may melt and the honey be lost, organizes the swarm into squads, puts sentinels at the entrances, glues the feet down, and then, with flying wings, creates a system of ventilation to cool the honey, that makes an electric fan look tawdry—a little honey bee that will include twenty square miles in the field over whose flowers it has oversight. But if a tiny brain in a bee performs such wonders, who are you, that you should question the guidance of God? Lift up your eyes and behold the hand that supports these stars, without pillars, the God who guides the planets without collision!—*Beams of Light.*

HABIT

Grooving a Channel in the Brain

The power of habit is a matter of common observation. The philosophy of it is perhaps not quite so well known. On this point a true word was uttered by Dr. George Thomas Dowling in a sermon published in the *Churchman.* "Habit," said he, "grooves a channel in our brains. That is the secret of manual dexterity; of intellectual concentration; and of most of moral righteousness. And every day we persist in any given course, whether good or evil, that channel becomes deeper. And it never alters its own direction. If that is changed it must be changed from without; it must be changed by you." And always we need the help of a higher power to break the fetters of sinful habit which hold us back and bind us down.—*The Chaplain.*

* * *

"The Molecules Are Counting . . ."

"The hell to be endured hereafter, of which theology tells," says the psychologist, William James, "is no worse than the hell we make for ourselves in this world by habitually fashioning our characters in the wrong way. Could the young but realize how soon they will become mere walking bundles of habits, they would give more heed to the conduct while in the plastic state. We are spinning our own fates, good or evil, and never to be undone. Every smallest stroke of virtue or of vice leaves its ever so little scar.

"The drunken Rip Van Winkle, in Jefferson's play, excuses himself for every fresh dereliction by saying, 'I won't count this time!' Well! he may not count it, and a kind Heaven may not count it; but it is being counted none the less. Deep down among the nerve-cells and fibres the molecules are counting it, registering and storing it up to be used against him when the next temptation comes. Nothing we ever do is, in strict scientific literalness, wiped out." — Selected.

* * *

Delusive

A young man who thinks that he can lead a reckless and profligate life until he becomes a middle-aged man, and then repent and make a good and steady citizen, is deluded by the devil. He thinks that people are fools, destitute of memory. He concludes that if he repents everybody will forget that he was a dissipated wretch. This is not the case; people remember your bad deeds and forget your good ones. Besides it is no easy thing to break up in middle age bad habits that have been formed in youth. When a horse contracts the habit of balking, he generally retains it through life. He will often perform well enough until the wheels get into a deep hole, and then he stops and holds back. Just so it is with the boys who contract bad habits. They will sometime leave off their bad tricks, and do well until they get into a tight place, and then they return to the old habit. Of those who contract the bad habit of drunkenness, hardly one in every hundred dies a sober man. The only way to break up a bad habit is to never contract it. The only way to prevent drunkenness is never to drink.—*Standard.*

HEAVEN

The Dawn Needs No Lamps

Professor George Jackson, in his excellent book on the Rev. S. F. Collier, of Manchester, tells the following. A man whose youth and early manhood had been spent in evil ways, and who was converted to God, was one night giving his testimony. He had met an old drinking pal during the week who chaffed him for turning pious. "I'll tell you what," I said to him, "you know what I am"—he was a lamplighter—"when I goes round turning out the lights, I looks back, and all the road over which I've been walking is all darkness; and that's what my past is like. I look on in front and there's a long row of twinkling lights to guide me, and that's what the future is since I found Jesus." "Yes," says my friend, "but by-and-by you get to the last light, and turn it out, and where are you then?" "Then," says I, "why, when the last lamp goes out it's dawn, and there ain't no need for lamps when the morning comes."—*Sunday School Times.*

* * *

Home

A traveling evangelist related the following: I picked up a railroad timetable in a hotel writing room where men were smoking and spinning yarns. The map showed only one road and its connections. It seemed to cover all the many states. Up in an open space, far away from the city where we were, some man had written "Home." Some discouraged commercial traveler, sick, disgusted, worn out, traced those fond letters and located the dear place where his loved ones awaited his coming. How much it meant to him—one of a large class of men for whom little sympathy is felt! Going to my room I took out my Bible. There was only one "through-line" apparent. All branches converged at the cross of Calvary. Through trains starting now. Home is where Jesus is. An open place,—a prepared place,—safe, blessed, eternal. Are you going Home? —*Good News.*

Spiritual Sight Needed

A little boy was born blind. At last an operation was performed; the light was let in slowly. Then one day his mother led him out of doors and uncovered his eyes, and for the first time he saw the sky and the earth. "Mother," he cried, "why did you not tell me it was so beautiful?" She burst into tears as she said, "I tried to tell you, dear, but you could not understand me." So it is when we try to tell what is in Christ. *Unless the spiritual sight is opened by the Holy Spirit, one cannot understand.*—J. W. Ham, in *Good News for All Men.*

* * *

Mistaken Builders

The angels from their thrones on high
Look down on us with wondering eye,
That when we are but passing guests
We build such strong and solid nests,
But where we think to dwell for aye
We scarce take heed a stone to lay.
—*The Sunday School Times.*

* * *

God's Telegram

I read the other day that a father in Watford last year was greatly troubled about his son who had gone wrong and was ill and despondent. The boy wrote to his father tremblingly and fearfully, as if to ask whether there was any hope. The father sent a telegram to him, and the telegram consisted of one word; and the word was "Home," and it was signed "Father." The Gospel of our Lord Jesus Christ is God's telegram to the sinful world, summed up in one word, "Home," and signed by one name, "Father."—Dr. R. F. Horton, in the *Free Churchman.*

* * *

The "Way to Heaven" Was What He Needed

"Fine sermon, wasn't it?" asked one of Farmer Peter's friends, referring to a scholarly discourse with which the congregation had been favored that morning by a city preacher. "Maybe," returned Farmer Peter. "Why," persisted the first speaker, "that man knows more about the Bible, and has made a deeper study of Biblical history and geography than almost any other minister in the country." "Has he now" inquired Farmer Peter mildly. "Well, then, I reckon that the trouble must have been with me. You see, I'd calc'lated I should hear somethin' about the way to Heaven, and I only learned the way from Jerusalem to Jericho."—*Sunday School Times.*

* * *

Better Than This

The Rev. G. C. Macgregor once related how an old Aberdeen preacher was comforted by a little personal incident. He had always feared death, and was powerless to comfort others facing it. Toward the end of his life he moved to another house. Yet when the furniture had all gone, the old preacher lingered in the home where his children had been born and where his sermons had been prepared. At last his servant came to him and said, "Sir, everything's gone; and the new house is better than this one. Come away." It preached to him a lesson that he never forgot. God has prepared for His children a home much better than this,—"an house not made with hands, eternal in the heavens."—*Sunday at Home.*

* * *

The Language of Heaven

An old writer has said that "they who would enjoy Heaven must have some experimental acquaintance with the language of its inhabitants." In the case of many it would seem that they are intending to enjoy Heaven without the slightest attempt to learn the language of Canaan. There, for instance, is a man who tells you he intends to be in Heaven some day; but he has no wish whatever to talk on Heavenly subjects. He enjoys the world and the things of the world. His heart is set upon earthly things. Yet he tells you he has a hope of Heaven. Vain, delusive hope! They that are on their way to Heaven are cultivating an experimental acquaintance with the language and ways of a Heavenly people. Let me ask, is this the case with you?—Tract.

* * *

Do You Own Such a Wonderful Home?

"Next Sunday you are to talk about Heaven. I am interested in that land, because I have held a clear title to a bit of property there for over fifty-five years. I did not buy it. It was given to me without money and without price. But the donor purchased it for me at tremendous sacrifice. . . . It is not a vacant lot. For more than half a century I have been sending materials out of which the greatest architect and builder of the universe has been building a home for me, which will never need to be remodeled nor repaired because it will suit me perfectly, individually, and will never grow old. Termites can never undermine its foundations for they rest upon the Rock of ages. Fire cannot destroy it. Floods cannot wash it away. . . . I hope to hear your sermon . . . but I have no assurance that I shall be able to do so. My ticket to Heaven has no date marked for the journey—no return coupon—and no permit for baggage. Yes, I am ready to go, and I may not be here while you are talking next Sunday evening, but I shall meet you there some day." — Excerpts from a letter to Dr. Charles E. Fuller, published in *The Sunday School Times.*

* * *

Heaven

A little Negro boy, when on his deathbed, was visited by a missionary to whom he spoke of the happiness he felt and the longing desire he had to be with Jesus.

"I am going to Heaven soon and then I shall see Jesus and be with Him forever," said the little fellow.

"But," rejoined the missionary, "if Jesus were to leave Heaven, what would you do?"

"I would follow Him."

"But suppose," said the missionary, "Jesus went to hell; what would you do then?"

In an instant, with an intelligent look and a smile on his countenance, he replied: "Ah, massa, there is no hell where Jesus is. The presence of Jesus is Heaven."—Selected.

* * *

A Prepared Welcome

The Rev. George H. Sherer of Beirut, Syria, says: "A traveler in the desert, longing for a stopping place, may meet a native lad who tells him that there are tents and hospitality farther on. It is a place where he can stop, and the courtesy of the desert demands that the minimum length of the sojourn be at least three days. Then, after the lad has told the traveler of the stopping place, he likely will mount his horse and ride on, saying, 'I will go and prepare a place for you.'" This word from the East throws a flood of light on the saying of our Lord as He spoke of the mansions in His Father's house. — *Presbyterian of the South.*

* * *

The Immunities of Heaven

Bhagubai Tode is the barefooted pastor of a barefooted congregation in Manubai. His subject was "Heaven," and he was trying to make his people appreciate the prospect of a home in such a blissful land. Knowing, as he did, the many unpleasant things in the lot of his humble people, he majored on the things that are not in Heaven. At the climax, he said, "And there will be no thorns up there." Instinctively the people glanced down at their unprotected feet which had known so many cruel wounds, and then they turned back to the preacher with a better interest than ever before. They heard Heaven mentioned in terms they could understand and appreciate.

The tired housekeeper murmurs, "There'll be no scrubbing there." The weary plowman looks up from his toil and says, "There'll be no grubbing there." The defeated candidate sighs, "There'll be no snubbing there."

Indeed who is there that does not find his own special thorns in the full list of Heaven's immunities? No sorrow, no tears, no sickness, no dying, no sin, no sighing, no slander, and no more sea! What is there that makes your lot less pleasant? Well, it will not be in Heaven.

No wonder they can leave the gates of Heaven open by day and by night and yet no one ever goes out. God grant that you and I may be among those who wash their robes and make them white in the Blood of the Lamb and enter through the gates into the City; for then we shall rest under the shade of the Tree of Life and know no grief or sorrow forever, and in the midst of that unmingled bliss all we have ever known of suffering or sacrifice here will be forgotten. Heaven is my Home.—J. B. Chapman, D.D., in *Herald of Holiness.*

* * *

"A Great Longing"

A consignment of sheep had been sent from Scotland to Australia. The ship contained not only the sheep but a supply of hay for their food. Just before reaching Australia, the sheep refused to eat. At the same time a dense fog covered the waters and for two days the ship was obliged to stop. The sheep paid no attention to their food and the owner feared that he was about to lose them. Then the fog lifted and before them were the green fields of Australia. The sheep had smelled the succulent pasture in the land not far distant, and it made them lose all appetite for the dried hay.

Aged sheep of God who read these lines, I wonder if it isn't that way with you. The pasturage of this earthly life eventually loses its appeal and in your heart is a great longing for the green fields on the farther Shore.—Benedicte, in *The United Presbyterian.*

* * *

The Sweetest Verse in the Bible

A young Christian, at the deathbed of an aged saint, said to him, "Shall I read to you the sweetest verse in the Bible?" "Yes," was the reply. The young man read the verse in John 14: "In My Father's House are many mansions: if it were not so, I would have told you. I go to prepare a place for you." "No," said the dying saint, "that is not the sweetest verse. Read on." The young man read on: "And if I go and prepare a place for you, I will come again, and receive you unto Myself; that where I am, there ye may be also." "That is the sweetest," said the dying man. "It is not the mansions—it is *Himself* I want."—*Messenger of Peace.*

* * *

What Kind of Entrance?

In a vision I saw a couple approaching the end of the journey of life. In front of them was a dark, narrow chasm, a grave, their guide called it. On this side of it was a great scrap heap marked "junk." Just on the other side of this chasm was a gate of glistening pearl. Reluctantly and sadly the couple approached. He was lugging along many bonds and deeds and a bag of gold. She had an accumulation of silks and laces, and clasped her jewel case tightly to her heart. "What is that stuff to which you are holding on so tightly?" asked the guide. "Stuff?" they said, "this is the fine wealth of earth. We have spent our lives accumulating this." "Well," said the guide, "that sort of stuff does not pass up here; just throw it all on that junk pile there." "Oh! surely not our gold and jewels!" exclaimed the couple. Quietly the guide answered, "As for the gold, our streets are paved with that, and as for those few tiny jewels, we use that kind for the foundation of our city. What we value up here is souls."

And so the couple passed in, "saved as if by fire," with that which represented all their life effort lying outside on the scrap heap. Then I understood the meaning of Rev. 18:17: "For in one hour so great riches is come to nought."

Just then another couple approached the end of the journey. They came with less reluctance and with a much lighter load. With no sign of regret they laid on the scrap heap the things of earth they would no longer need. Their eyes were turned, with eager expectancy, toward the gates of pearl and the Treasury City beyond. I saw the gates swing open and heard the joy bells of heaven begin to ring. Amazed and joyfully bewildered, they stood amidst the crowd at the gate, waiting and watching for them, and singing, "Welcome Home." Some whom they had never seen before took them by the hand and said, "Next to the dear Saviour, you are our best friends." Then were the newcomers amazed, and said, "How can this be, since we have never even known each other before?" And some made answer, "Why, we were in far-away heathen lands, but messengers came to us bringing the good news of salvation, and that is why we are here; and since we came God has looked over His account books and told us that you sent the messengers to us. So, since it was announced in the city this morning that you were coming, this crowd of those whom you won to Him have been assembling to greet you!" And then, with hearts aglow with joy more rapturous than earth can know, they thought back to the times down in the little earthly home when, after talking it over, they had invested the money they could spare that year in missions; and so he had worn the old overcoat another winter and she had freshened up last season's hat and done without the new shoes a bit longer. And then, oh! then, the Saviour's own face beamed upon them, and He was saying, "Well done, good and faithful servant; thou hast been faithful over a few things, I will make thee ruler over many things!" And then I understood the meaning of "an abundant entrance!"—*Baptist S. S. Board.*

* * *

In the Poor House—But a King's Daughter

While a student, I preached in the town of Geneseo, New York. One of my appointments was the Sunday service at the County Farm. There was in the institution at that time a brave little old lady who had once lived in an atmosphere of culture and security. But misfortune came her way and she was spending her sunset years in the County

Home. . . . While I was chaplain at the institution, the doctors told her she was fatally sick and was not far from the end of the trail. So she sent for me and said, "I have just one request. When it is over, I want somebody to sing at the last service, 'I'm the Child of a King.'" I shall never forget the day we laid her to rest. . . . All was drab and drear and disconsolate, and then a transfiguration took place. A deep, rich contralto voice was singing over the pine box: "I'm the child of a King! I'm the child of a King!" And she was! She was the child of a King, and had moved out of a poor house into her Father's house of "many mansions."—From a tract published by the Christian Publishing Society.

* * *

Nearing Home

The story is told of an old Omaha chief who had ruled his tribe with wisdom and justice for many years, now blind, and the victim of an incurable disease, and quietly awaiting death.

"Why are you content?" asked an officer. "Pain and old age are not good things." The aged chief was silent a while before answering, according to the Indian habit when a grave question is discussed, and then said:

"The fish that is spawned here in this little creek will go down the Mississippi to the great gulf, but in the spring it will find its way back—back to its native waters.

"The bird that builds its nest on the tree near my wigwam in the summer, leaves it when winter is coming and travels thousands of miles to the southward; but in the spring it will come back across mountains to that very nest.

"How do such creatures know the way? They have no map, no guide. The Great Spirit puts something in their hearts to draw them back to their homes. And He has not forgotten to put something in each man's heart that draws him, draws him all his life long, up to his Home. I am coming near to mine. Shall I not be glad?"—*Herald of Light.*

I'll Keep Dreaming Still

If I am dreaming, let me still dream on
For thou hast given me an even song.
If Heaven and eternal bliss aren't real,
Don't rob me of the peace I feel.

You say I am deceived, there is no God,
Who loves and cares for men of mortal sod;
Yet, in His presence, I have all delight,
And all my darkness, He has turned to light.

You have no hope, no peace, no joy like mine,
You have no One on whom you may recline;
My Christ, my God, you want to take away,
What would you give me, in their stead, I pray?

So, if I'm dreaming, I'll keep dreaming still
And seek to serve Him with a hearty will;
Then in the future, in the vaulted sky,
We'll find who did the dreaming, you or I?

—R. E. Neighbour, D.D.

* * *

Ever New

"The holy Jerusalem, descending out of Heaven from God, having the glory of God: and her light was like unto a stone most precious, even like a jasper stone, clear as crystal" (Rev. 21:10, 11).

Many people suppose that we shall see Heaven the first day we get there. You canot see London in two weeks. You cannot see Rome in six weeks. You cannot see Venice in a month. You cannot see the great City of the New Jerusalem in a day. No; it will take all eternity to see Heaven, to count the towers, to examine the trophies, to gaze upon the thrones, to see the hierarchies. Ages on ages roll, and yet, Heaven is new. The streets new! The Temple new! The joy new! The song new!—T. DeWitt Talmage.

There or Here?

"Poor R—; I understand that poor R— did not leave much property," said a friend commiseratingly of one who had just died, as he drove home with the minister from the cemetery. "Too bad! He worked hard and made money, but he was too tenderhearted. I think every beggar in town must have known him." The minister listened politely. "I suppose what you say is right about his having no property, but I imagine, from what I have known of his life, that he must have considerable property to go to."—*Forward.*

* * *

The New Song

There was a Wesleyan preacher in England, Peter Mackenzie, full of native humor, a most godly man. He was once preaching from the text: "And they sang a new song," and he said: "Yes, there will be singing in Heaven, and when I get there I want to have David with his harp, and Paul, and Peter, and other saints gather around for a sing. And I will announce a hymn from the Weslyan Hymnal; let us sing hymn No. 749—

'My God, my Father, while I stray—'

But someone will say, 'That won't do. You are in Heaven, Peter; there's no straying here.' And I will say, Yes, that's so. Let us sing No. 651—

'Though waves and storms go o'er my head,
'Though friends be gone and hopes be dead—'

But another saint will interrupt, 'Peter, you forget you are in Heaven now; there are no storms here.' Well, I will try again—No. 536—

'Into a world of ruffians sent—'

'Peter! Peter!' someone will say, 'we will put you out unless you stop giving out inappropriate hymns.' I will ask,—What can we sing? And they will say: 'Sing the new song, the song of Moses and the Lamb.' "—*Moody's Anecdotes.*

* * *

What Will It Be

A little girl was walking with her father one night under the starry sky. Looking up, she said, "Father, I have been thinking that if the wrong side of Heaven is so beautiful, what will the right side be?"—*Christian Endeavor World.*

* * *

Longing for Heaven

John Wesley, a classical scholar with a virile mind, gave himself fully to God and consecrated all his powers to His service. Though possessed of a scholar's love for books, he spent most of his life in the saddle and in the active duties of a most strenuous life. With a passionate love for art, especially for music and architecture, he turned away from their charms to blow the gospel trumpet with all his might. With a more than ordinary longing for the sweets and comforts of human love, he rose above disappointments which would have crushed ordinary men, forgot his "inly-bleeding heart" (his own expression), and gave himself unreservedly to the work of binding up the broken-hearted. Visiting the beautiful grounds of an English nobleman, he said, *"I, too, have a relish for these things; but there is another world."*—*Sunday School Times.*

HELL

Bob Ingersoll's Choice

At a meeting of Henry A. Newell, D.D., and Robert G. Ingersoll on a railroad train, the following conversation took place: "Mr. Ingersoll," said Newell, "you are a gifted man. Why do you use your talents to war against God?" "I do it for money," was Ingersoll's frank reply. "You can't take your money with you when you die, Ingersoll." "No, but it's handy while I'm here." "There's a curse on money earned that way, Mr. Ingersoll." "Maybe, but it pays my bills." "Where do you expect to go when you die, Bob Ingersoll?" "I expect to go to hell." "Then you acknowledge there is a hell?" "That's what you claim, isn't it?" "Not my claim, it is what God's Word says, Mr. Ingersoll." "I know the Bible says so." "Wouldn't you prefer to go to Heaven?" "No. I would not be happy in Heaven. I am going to hell." "In spite of all your sins, Bob Ingersoll, you can still be saved if you repent, pray, and believe." "But I don't want to be saved. I prefer to live my own life, die my own death, and take whatever consequences follow." — William A. Corey, in *Sunday School Times*.

* * *

Worse Than Hell on Earth

One day a man sauntering down Clark Street, in Chicago, and playing with a dollar bill in his hand, had it snatched away from him by a thief who ran rapidly ahead toward the river, not perceiving that the drawbridge was open. Of course, he plunged into the river's slime. One might have thought this were punishment enough for stealing only a dollar. But no; when rescued by the police, and again on terra firma, there stood his victim beside him accusing him to the officer, who put him into jail. The fall into the water was the result of his folly, but the imprisonment in jail the punishment of his crime. Men suffer on earth as a result of their wrongdoing, but they have yet to meet their Judge, if they are out of Christ, and to answer before Him for their sin. Hell may now be in their bosom, but, alas, the day is coming when their bosom will be in hell! —Dr. James M. Gray.

* * *

Where Hell Is

A young man converted during special evangelistic meetings held in a mining village, desirous of doing something for God, bought some tracts.

He was distributing these one day when he met some of his old companions, who derided him as he spoke to them of Jesus.

"Here," said one of his companions, "can you tell me where hell is?"

After a moment's hesitation, the young man looked up and said: "Yes, it's at the end of a Christless life."—Selected.

* * *

A Question

On a recent afternoon a crowd of people stood in the bitter cold on the edge of the Tottenville mud flats on Staten Island, and for three hours watched while four men fought for their lives in the black mud at low tide. The men are surveyors for a drilling company. They had taken a dory from Perth Amboy and were headed for the Anchor Light. The boat became stuck on the mud flats. They worked feverishly to get the craft moved, and finding their efforts ineffectual, cried for help. A crowd gathered, but nobody dared go to them over the sticky mud. It seemed like suicide to try to reach land, but it was certain death from freezing to sit till the tide came in. One man jumped over, and sank in the mud to his waist. He pulled himself out by the arms and threw himself forward. The others followed. It took them an hour to make a hundred feet. They were suffering from terror as well as cold. At last the leader got within reach of a rope thrown out; eventually they were all pulled to firm ground, almost unconscious. No one thinks of calling these neighbors crazy—but what would be said of a similar crowd standing in the bitter cold three hours to save four men from sinking into the lake of fire? —*Serving-and-Waiting*.

* * *

A Welcome in Hell

After a bitter legal battle, Asa Keyes, former district attorney of Los Angeles, was convicted of bribery and conspiracy to obstruct the ends of justice, and was sentenced to serve a term in San Quentin prison. When the news of Keyes' conviction and sentence reached the prison, it is reported that the prisoners laughed "long and sardonically." The explanation of this sardonic laughter is that some two thousand convicts are in San Quentin because they were prosecuted by Mr. Keyes during his long term as district attorney. The warden at San Quentin put Mr. Keyes in a cell separated from all the other prisoners. He was not allowed to mingle with them and for exercise was taken into a separate ward. All this special care for the purpose of keeping the other convicts from killing him. Hell will be something like this—I mean with respect to the feeling of its occupants toward one another. We do not know whether there will be "sardonic laughter" in hell, but we do know there will be the "gnashing of teeth." For this we have the word of the Lord.—*Brethren Evangelist.*

* * *

Leaving the Ministry

A man in retiring from the ministry gave, among others, two reasons for his action. He said: "I believe that the world is going to be made better, not by religious spasm or revival, but by education." Jesus taught that men are saved not by education, but by regeneration. "Marvel not that I said unto thee, Ye must be born again." Was it not Francis Bacon who suggested that to educate a bad man is to make of him a clever devil? We believe in education, but not in education as a substitute for regeneration. We rejoice that the first work of the Holy Spirit, who came in obedience to the promise of Christ and to represent Him, was a great revival in which brokenhearted men sought and accepted the Saviour. These men who would substitute education for regeneration are false prophets, and we are glad that at least one of them has had the courage to decline to be supported by a church, the doctrines of which he does not believe.

Another reason given by this retiring minister is the following: "Because I do not care a snap of the finger about keeping men out of hell and getting them into heaven, but I do care tremendously about making this earth more like heaven and less like hell." Here is another perversion of truth. All sensible men believe that we ought to make this world a fit habitat for saved men and women, that we ought to drain it, cleanse it, purify it to the extent of our ability. We ought to close its saloons, its brothels, its gambling hells. We ought to see to it that the rich do not opress the poor, and that the strong do not make slaves of the weak. But a man who does not care whether his congregation goes to hell or not seems to limit his gospel of social service. We wonder that sensible men make such fools of themselves in carrying their doctrines to extremes. — *The Watchman-Examiner.*

* * *

Which Door?

George Whitefield, while preaching once on the text, "The door was shut," had two flippant young men in his congregation. One was heard to say to the other in mirth, "What if the door be shut? Another will open!" Mr. Whitefield said later in the sermon, "It is possible that there may be someone here who is careless and trifling, and says: 'What matter if the door be shut? Another will open!'" The two young men looked at each other in alarm. Mr. Whitefield proceeded: "Yes, another door will open. It will be the door to the bottomless pit—the door to hell!"—*Sunday School Times.*

* * *

Separated Forever

All through life, ever since they were classmates at college, Senator Toombs of Georgia and George Pierce were fast friends.

The senator was an unconverted man, and lived a godless life. He had, however, married an earnest Christian woman, whom he regarded with feeling akin to veneration.

One day, while visiting at his lovely home, Pierce opened a conversation with his friend on this wise:

"Something's going to happen after a while that will go mighty hard with you, Toombs."

"What's that?" asked the senator.

"You and your much-loved wife will be separated. She's going to Heaven and you will go to hell."

"No, that can't be."

"Yes, it can be; and it *will* be unless you receive the Lord Jesus Christ as your Saviour. You will be separated from her forever."

Toombs was silent for a few minutes, and then said, "George, I can't stand that. I could never stand such a thing."

That conversation resulted in the senator's conversion. As a guilty sinner he knelt at the Saviour's feet, entreated Him for pardon, and henceforward walked hand in hand with his wife as a companion of her Christian life.

It is a terrible thought that amongst the readers of these lines there may be two sisters, or two brothers, or two dear friends (it may be husband and wife), who are traveling down the stream of life side by side, but who are going to be separated for all eternity because one has been saved through the Blood of Christ, and the other still spurns Him and slights His gracious call.—*The Lamp.*

* * *

The Hereafter

"I'm tired of all this preaching about the hereafter," said an impatient young voice. "I'm living now, and I mean to have a good time. The hereafter isn't here yet!" But her more thoughtful companion replied, "No—only the first part of it; but I shouldn't wonder if the 'here' had a good deal to do with shaping the 'after.' "—*Forward.*

* * *

A Miner's Rebuke

A person who by birth, wealth, and education should have been a gentleman, but was not, went to see a coal mine.

The miner who took him down was a Christian, and was much pained by the profane language of the visitor. As they they descended the shaft, they felt it getting hotter and hotter; and at last the heat became so great that the visitor said, "Dear me! It's terribly hot! I wonder how far it is to hell?"

"I don't know the exact distance, sir," replied the Christian miner gravely, "but if one link of the chain gives way, you'll be there in a short time."

The plain miner was the means of rousing the profane man to a sense of his perilous condition.

In the case of every unconverted man, there is only a step—a breath—between him and death, and after that the judgment.—Selected.

* * *

No Hell in This Life

During the bombing of London a certain district came in for very severe bombardment and whole streets were demolished with considerable loss of life. Visiting the people with the Gospel literature after one of these nights of terror the Open Air Mission evangelist encountered an old skeptic. "Oh!" he exclaimed, "this bombing is hell, isn't it? Absolute hell!" "No," replied the evangelist. "And I'll give you three reasons why it is not hell. First I am a Christian and there are no Christians in hell. Second, there is a public house round the corner and there are no public houses in hell. Third, here I am proclaiming the Gospel, and there is no Gospel in hell." . . . Four weeks later the evangelist was proclaiming the Gospel in Hyde Park. When he made the appeal for decision who should be the first man to come forward to decide for Christ, but this old skeptic.—*In Britain's Camps.*

* * *

Beware of the Crowd

"Don't trouble yourself about me, sir. I'll slip into Heaven with the crowd some day," said a careless sinner to a Christian who was urging upon him the necessity of conversion, before it might be too late. The Christian replied, "My friend, you have mistaken the place—the crowd is on the way to hell; therefore, if you slip in with the crowd, you will slip into hell. Scripture says 'for wide is the gate, and broad is the way, that leadeth to destruction, and many there be which go in thereat; because strait is the gate, and narrow is the way, which leadeth unto life, and few there be that find it' " (Matt. 7:13, 14). He had not thought of that. Have you?—*Good News.*

You Are Responsible

Several years ago I heard a Baptist preacher tell the story of the greatest single tragedy that ever occurred in Texas. It was an explosion that killed four hundred school children and their teachers in the New London school house. The school was dismissing for the day when a streak of lightning coming from the ground instead of from the skies, the great building was blown to ashes, and lives of teachers, boys and girls were snuffed out in a flash. One family had five children (all they had) in the explosion. Scores of families lost three or four, their little bodies were so mangled that identification of many was impossible. A gloom of deep, dark sorrow swept over our state and the nation. The government sent secret service men to investigate the cause. They labored for days. One of the investigators was questioning a lady, the wife of a man who had worked on the construction of the building. She said:

"My husband told me before this tragedy happened that he knew there was faulty construction in the gas line under the building."

"What?" said the inspector. She repeated her statement. Then the inspector asked:

"Did your husband know that the construction of the gas line was faulty?"

"Yes," she answered.

"Did he report it to anyone?"

"No."

"Then your husband is a criminal," he said.

My friend, Christian people know there is a Hell and that lost people are doomed to go there unless some saved person leads them to Christ. Are you concerned for the lost? Are you picturing to them the doom that awaits them? If not, you are just as responsible for their doom as that man who knew of the faulty construction in the gas line, was for the death of those children.—*Florida Baptist Witness.*

* * *

Two Ways of Presenting Hell

It was a one-man church, and candidates for the pulpit were being heard. An applicant came and preached on the text, "The wicked shall be turned into hell." The rich man turned thumbs down on him. This preacher was followed by another, who by a strange coincidence used the same text. The rich man said, "He'll do; call him." Folks were amazed. "Why, he used the same text as the other minister," they said. "True," replied the rich man, "he preached that the wicked would be turned into hell, all right, but he was, oh, so sorry; but the other man was glad of it."—*Sunday School Times.*

HOLY SPIRIT

He Did Not Come Alone

Dr. A. J. Gordon tells of a Welsh preacher who, having been scheduled to preach one night, asked to be allowed to withdraw for a time before the service. He remained in seclusion so long that the good man of the house sent his servant to request him to come and meet the waiting congregation. As she came near the room she heard what seemed to be an indication of conversation between two parties, and though in subdued tone of voice, she caught the words, "I will not go unless You go with me." Without interfering, she returned and reported, "He will come all right, and the Other will come, too." And sure enough, when he came, the Other One came along, and with such power that it proved a wonderful service in which many found newness of life. It is both our privilege and duty thus to allow the Holy Spirit to work along with us as we endeavor to teach others about the Lord Jesus Christ.—*Christian Union Herald.*

Don't Ask for What You Have!

Dr. Fisher once wrote to his friend Lord Eldon, asking him for a special favor. Lord Eldon answered: "Dear Fisher, I cannot today give you the preferment for which you ask. I remain your sincere friend, Eldon. Turn over." Then on the other side he wrote, "I gave it to you yesterday." Our heavenly Father similarly answers His children when they ask Him for the indwelling or baptism of the Holy Spirit. "What? know ye not that your body is the temple of the Holy Ghost which is in you?" (I Cor. 6:19). "For by one Spirit are we all baptized into one body" (I Cor. 12:13). —*Sunday School Times.*

* * *

The Deflected Compass

I was interesting my boy David with a magnetic compass, and I showed him that the needle always pointed to the north. Then I played a joke on him. I had a magnet in my pocket, and I slipped my hand in and drew it out, very carefully conceiling it. Then I began to draw my hand over the compass and make the little needle go here, there, and everywhere. David said, "What has gone wrong with it? Why, it is pointing south!" I said, "If you wait a minute perhaps we can make it point east." That is what some people do with the guidance they receive of the Holy Spirit. They make the compass point anywhere they want it to go, because they have a magnet in their hand. — *Pentecostal Evangel.*

* * *

His Spirit

A young artist was trying to copy Raphael's "Madonna and Child," one of the most beautiful pictures in all the world. He went to Florence and gazed on it, then got his easel. Sitting down in front of it he began to copy it. As he looked at it his picture became a thing of beauty, too. But suppose that, instead of only copying, the spirit of Raphael could have come upon that young man: what a difference it would have made! When we come to the Lord Jesus He gives us His Holy Spirit to help us live as He would have us live, and the more the Holy Spirit controls our lives, the more like Him we grow. Do come to Him now, if you have never come, and ask Him to give you His Holy Spirit.—*Intermediate Young People.*

* * *

The Easier Way

There are two ways of traveling on the Continent. In the first, you do everything for yourself. You obtain your ticket, look after your luggage, get your seat in the carriage, ask at least three porters whether you are right; and if you have an imperfect knowledge of the language, you have perpetually an uneasy sense that perhaps you are wrong. . . . There is another method of foreign travel. You employ a Tourist Agency, which obtains your tickets, sees to your comfort, gives you precise directions, provides you, where necessary, with a conductor, and at every terminus waits to greet you. . . . And in this we have an apt illustration of the easier way of traveling to Heaven. . . . Be at rest in the indwelling and inworking of the Holy Spirit. Only see that He is not grieved, and He will see to all else.—F. B. Meyer, in the *King's Business.*

* * *

Cleansed by Fire

There are some deeply-established uncleannesses for which the action of water is not sufficiently stringent. In many cases of contagious disease, if we are to rid ourselves of every vestige of corruption, there are many things which must be burned. The germs of the contagion could not be washed away. They must be consumed away. Fire is our most effective purifying minister, a powerful and relentless enemy of disease. In 1665 London was in the grip of that terrible plague, the horrors of which may still be felt through the pages of Pepys and De Foe. The disease germs were hiding and breeding and multiplying everywhere. In the following year the Great Fire broke out, and the plague-smitten city was possessed by the spirit of burning. London was literally baptized with fire, which sought out the most secret haunts of the contagion, and in the fiery baptism the evil genius of corruption gave place to the sweet and friendly genius of health.—Dr. J. H. Jowett.

* * *

The Secret of His Eloquence

When Bishop Simpson preached years ago in Memorial Hall, London, he preached quietly and with very little gesticulation, but with such power that the whole assembly, as if moved by an irresistible impulse, arose at the climax of his message, then after a second or two sank into the seats. A professor of elocution was there. A friend who knew that he had come to criticize, asked him, after the service, how he liked the bishop's elocution. "Elocution!" he said. "That man doesn't need elocution. He's got the Holy Ghost." That was the secret back of the attracting power of Jesus Christ, and it tells the story of every great preacher whom God has used in the drawing of souls to himself. —*The King's Business.*

* * *

Strong Enough to Bear the Load

In England, some of our bridges have a red diamond-shaped symbol at either end. It is a warning to those who would cross that the bridge is limited as to the weight it can take. If, therefore, a lorry driver comes with a ten-ton wagon to a bridge which cannot take more than five tons, he must make a detour and find another bridge that is strong enough to bear the load. Some Christians have that diamond-shaped symbol against them, too. God has had to put a warning: "This believer, very energetic, cannot stand the strain of injustice." Hence, when God would use us He cannot, and He must needs find another. Is this the reason you have not fulfilled the purpose God has for you? Is this the reason you are put aside? And do you feel it to be an impossibility for you to be patient, to suffer unjustly, to forgive in the spirit of Christ? Are you crying out, like Mary, "How shall this be?" Then hear the answer of that angelic voice: "The Holy Ghost."—*The King's Business.*

* * *

He Came for the Wrong Spirit

"I have come a hundred miles," said a minister, "to get some of Mr. Moody's spirit." "You don't want my spirit," was the reply. "What you want is the Spirit of God."—*Young People's Standard.*

* * *

"Skinning the Wire"

I was in Washington some time ago. riding on a street car. It was one of those cars with an underground trolley. I observed that the motorman could easily make the car go slowly or make it go fast. When we would come to a cross street I noticed that by a touch of the handle the car would almost stop, and yet would not quite stop, but just go creeping along like a snail. Then all at once the motorman would touch the handle again, and the car would go almost at a rate of a mile a minute. And I got curious to know how the thing was done. I said to myself, "I can't see how it is that if he touches that wire at all he does not get all the power that there is in the power house," and so I ventured to go out on the platform and ask him.

"Why," he said, "when I squeeze this handle I open the mouth that grips the trolley. When I want to go slow, I open the mouth that grips the trolley, and it just touches it. When I want it to go fast it turns loose and grips the trolley, and gets all the power in the power house. We call the first 'skinning the wire.' "

I said to myself, I have got two thousand members in my church that are just "skinning the wire." They never have done anything but "skin the wire." And you know that just about nine-tenths of our churches—and I say this with intense sadness in my heart—nine-tenths of the churches in this country are skinning the wire."

But there is the power house; all the power of heaven is there, and it is at our disposal, if we will only grip the wire with the trolley of faith. The trouble is our faith is so weak that it just "skins the wire."—L. G. Broughton, in *Earnest Worker.*

* * *

Too Late

One evening when Mr. Alexander and I were in Brighton, England, one of the workers went out from the afternoon meeting to a restaurant for his evening meal. His attention was drawn toward the man who waited upon him, and there came to his heart a strong impression that he should speak to that waiter about his soul, but that seemed to him such an unusual thing to do that he kept putting it off. When the meal was ended and the bill paid, he stepped out of the restaurant, but had such a feeling that he should speak to that waiter, that he decided to wait outside until the waiter came out. In a little while the proprietor came out and asked him why he was waiting. He replied that he was waiting to speak with the man who had waited on him at the table. The proprietor replied, "You will never speak to that man again. After waiting upon you he went to his room and shot himself." Oh, men and women, there are opportunities open to every one of us tonight that will be gone, and gone forever, before another day dawns. The time is short!—R. A. Torrey.

* * *

Depending on God's Spirit

Sometimes quarrymen find a very hard kind of rock. They pick little grooves for the iron wedges, and then with great sledge hammers drive these little wedges into the hard rock. Sometimes this fails to split the rock. Then they go at it in another way. The iron wedges are removed from the grooves. Then little wooden ones of a very hard fiber are selected. These sharp-edged, well-made wooden wedges are put in the grooves tightly and water is kept in the grooves. The damp wood swells. The granite heart of the rock cannot stand against this new pressure.

It takes longer than the iron wedges and sledge, but after a while the rock yields and lies split wide open. The water works on the wood, and that in turn on the stone. The iron wedges sometimes fail, but the wood and water never fail. It seems to be a part of our make-up to make plans, and count on the plans. Planning does much. We do not want to plan less, but learn to depend more in our planning on the soft, noiseless, but resisting power of the Holy Spirit.—S. D. Gordon.

* * *

Proof That He Lives

When Nansen started on his Arctic expedition he took with him a carrier pigeon, strong and fleet of wing. After two years—two years in the desolation of the Arctic regions—he one day wrote a tiny little message and tied it under the pigeon's wing, and let it loose to travel two thousand miles to Norway; and oh! what miles! what desolation! not a living creature! ice, ice, snow and death. But he took the trembling little bird and flung her from the ship, up into the icy cold. Three circles she made, and then, straight as an arrow she shot south; one thousand miles over ice, one thousand miles over the frozen wastes of ocean, and at last dropped into the lap of the explorer's wife. She knew, by the arrival of the bird, that it was all right in the dark night of the north.

So with the coming of the Holy Spirit, the heavenly Dove, *the disciples knew that Christ was alive, for His coming and His manifest working were proofs of it.—Joyful News Magazine.*

* * *

An Experience Too Common

Charles M. Alexander said that there was once a meeting of intense power going on down in Tennessee, and one of the variety of disciples who blow hot and blow cold, who are revived at each annual revival meeting and who backslid in the interim, was praying in the assembly with a great burst of emotion.

There was present an old woman who knew him well, who read correctly his character, and had witnessed his many revivals and backslidings. So when he suddenly burst into prayer for the fulness of the Holy Spirit to be given him, the old woman emphatically cried, "Don't you do it, Lord — he leaks!" How sad a commentary! In the same sense, the most of us "leak" — we fail to retain the bestowed blessing.—Courtesy *Moody Monthly.*

* * *

A Guest, but Limited

In her book entitled "Life on the Highest Plane," Miss Ruth Paxton relates an experience that illustrates how many Christians today are grieving this Heavenly Guest. She tells of visiting a college to conduct evangelistic meetings, and being entertained in a home where the guest room was over the kitchen and approached by an outside stairway. Later when an occasion arose which made it desirable for her to enter another section of the house she found every other door fast locked. Seized with a strange sense of loneliness, she returned to the one room which was hers to occupy, and poured her heart out in prayer. God very effectively used the occasion to illustrate to her and to the thousands who have been helped by her ministry how he himself has in many cases been admitted to some little guest chamber and been forced to stay there when all the while he longed to enter every room and share all experiences. One may well ask himself the question, As a believer in the Lord Jesus Christ, have I fully understood that the Holy Spirit of God has taken up His abode in me? Am I letting Him mean all that He will to me? —*Baptist Young People's Union Quarterly.*

* * *

Wait for His Decision

Many years agone, the throne of Russia was once occupied by two boy princes. They sat side by side and gave their decisions on the gravest questions; their judgments were so wise and just, that men marveled that princes so young and inexperienced could know so much of statecraft, or speak with such discretion on questions so difficult. But the secret was that close behind the throne where they sat, hidden by a thin veil, was the Princess Sophia. She heard the cases brought to them, and gave the decisions which they pronounced. Those boys referred everything to her, and waited until she whispered to them the wise answer they delivered. So "the word of Christ should dwell" in our heart. (Col. 3:16). It is unseen but only a thin veil conceals it. We are to refer every matter to the Holy Spirit and wait for His decision. Then what He bids us do we are to do. Thus Christ "brings into captivity every thought," every feeling and affection (II Cor. 10:5; Gal. 5:24). He will settle every point of duty. He will mold our business methods. He will sit as the invisible umpire in all questions of pleasure, of profit, of ambition or leadership. "The Word is nigh thee" (Rom. 10:8).—*The Illustrator.*

* * *

"Slow of Speech"

Moses complains that he is slow of speech and of a slow tongue. God does not promise a new tongue, but that He will be with him and train his tongue. Listen to him forty years after in the Moab plain, as with brain fired and tongued loosened and trained he gives that series of farewell talks fairly burning with eloquence. Students of oratory can find no nobler specimen than Deuteronomy furnishes. The unmatured powers lying dormant had been aroused to full growth by the indwelling Spirit of God. —S. D. Gordon.

* * *

God's Way of Blessing

Are you compassed with needs at this very moment, and almost overwhelmed with difficulties, trials, and emergencies? These are all Divinely provided vessels for the Holy Spirit to fill, and if you but rightly understood their meaning, they would become opportunities for receiving new blessings and deliverances which you can get in no other way.

Bring these vessels to God. Hold them steadily before Him in faith and prayer. Keep still, and stop your own restless working until He begins to work. Do nothing that He does not Himself command you to do. Give Him a chance to work, and He will surely do so; and the very trials that threatened to overcome you with discouragement and disaster will become God's opportunity for the revelation of His grace and glory in your life, as you have never known Him before—Selected.

* * *

Touching God

An inert substance or a living body may become so surcharged and transformed with another force foreign to itself, that when we touch it we feel only the foreign force which fills it. Galvanize a pail of water, and then put your hand into it. You touch the water, but you feel only the electricity which pervades it. Take a bar of iron and put it into the fire. Soon the fire enters it, and takes possession of every atom of which it is composed. If you touch it while red-hot you will scarcely feel the iron, but you will certainly feel the fire. So it is with a man when he is filled with God. Come near to him and touch him, and as you touch the man you feel God.—Dr. F. E. Marsh.

* * *

Reverence for God's Dwelling-Place

Louis T. Talbot addressed his morning congregation in the Church of the Open Door, Los Angeles, Calif., in these searching words: "We have a large company here. Many of you are strangers to me; nevertheless, I can say with absolute certainity that no one of you will pull out a cigarette, light it, and smoke it in this room. And yet the New Testament teaches us that it is not any earthly structure that is the temple of God, for today the Holy Spirit dwells in the bodies of believers, born-again ones. It is right that we shouid have reverence for the place of worship, but why should men and women have less fear of desecrating the true temple of God?"— *The King's Business.*

* * *

Protection from Within

"Unless there is within us that which is above us, we shall soon yield to that which is about us."—*Upper Room.*

* * *

His Temple

Dr. James M. Gray in a service one evening expounded Romans 12:1. Leaning over the pulpit, he said, "Have you noticed that this verse does not tell us to whom we should give our bodies? It is not the Lord Jesus who asks it. He has His own body. It is not the Father who asks for it. He remains upon His throne. Another has come to earth without a body. God could have made a body for Him as He did for Jesus, but He did not do so. God gives you the privilege and the indescribable honor of presenting your bodies to the Holy Spirit, to be His dwelling-place on earth. If you have been washed in the Blood of the Lamb, then yours is a holy body, washed whiter than snow, and will be accepted by the Spirit when you give it. Will you do so now?" *Gospel Herald.*

* * *

The Holy Spirit Knows

Dr. Walter L. Wilson in his book *Miracles in a Doctor's Life*, tells of an interesting answer which Mr. Samuel Levermore of London made. He had told his sister about the call of God to serve as a missionary in France, whereupon she replied, "Sammy, you will be wasting your time: to find a troubled soul in France would be like looking for a needle in a haystack." "Yes," answered Mr. Levermore, "that is quite true, but you must remember, sister, that the Holy Spirit knows where the needle is, and He will direct me to it."

Burning, But Not Burned

What a sermon there is in a wick! Sit down beside it, and ask how it dares hope that it can supply light for hours and hours to come. "Will you not soon burn to an end, you wick of a lamp?" "No, I do not fear it, since the light does not burn me, though it burns on me. I only bear to it the oil which saturates my texture. I am but the ladder up which it climbs. It is not I, but the oil that is in me, that furnishes the light."—*The Daily Devotional Commentary.*

* * *

The Fulness of the Spirit

Paul sets before all Christians both the privilege and the duty of being filled with the Spirit. It must please the Adversary if he can lure God's people into thinking that such a blessing is not for everyone. Those who knew Captain Reginald Wallis remember his cheerfulness, his winsomeness, and the loving insistence with which he proclaimed the glorious Gospel of salvation from the penalty and power of sin. Quoting Captain Wallis, the Keswick Calender recently contained this message: "The Apostle Paul commands the Ephesian Christians to 'be filled with the Spirit.' Yes, it is a command as well as a privilege. This is not some special blessing which God has reserved for certain of His children only. He has no favorites. I am so thankful that there is no such thing as a spiritual aristocracy, a number of believers for whom God reserves this peculiar blessing of fullness of life. Rather is this God's norm for every one of his children." As we yield ourselves unreservedly to God, and believe His Word, we may know "righteousness, and peace, and joy in the Holy Ghost" (Rom. 14:17), and the glorious ninefold fruit of the Spirit which today is so sorely needed in the Church.—*Sunday School Times.*

* * *

"The Comforter"

A missionary in Africa is quoted in "The Bible in the World," the organ of the British and Foreign Bible Society, as seeking for three years for the proper word in which to translate the word "Comforter," using in the interim the word which embraced the filial comfort of the mother for the child. One day in the court of an African village he heard frequently during the proceedings the name of "Nsenga-Mukwashi." He asked the old chief, after court closed, if there were someone there by the name of "Nsenga-Mukwashi." The chief explained that it was the title of a man, whose duties were to interest himself "in all my people and stand by them when they are in trouble." On that particular day he had met and brought to court an old woman who had been ill-treated. He had "to spread the matter and to plead her cause. He is the comforting advocate," said the chief.

The light of a great truth flashed upon the missionary; the right word had come to him. Jesus said, "If I go not away, the Nsenga-Mukwashi will not come to you." "If any man sin, we have a Nsenga-Mukwashi with the Father." The translatability of the Bible into any tongue is one of its greatest miracles.—*The Alliance Weekly.*

* * *

Joined to the Main

Someone wrote congratulating the Rev. Archibald Brown upon his devoted and successful work for Christ, and asked the secret of it. "The answer is very simple," said he. "Fifty years ago Archibald Brown was joined up to the main, and the tap has been running ever since. Let us open the inner cells of our being to God's Holy Spirit.—*This Is the Way*, by an Unknown Christian.

* * *

We Need God

If we do not have the Spirit of God, it were better to shut the churches, to nail up the doors, to put a black cross on them and say, "God, have mercy on us."

If you ministers have not the Spirit of God, you had better not preach and you people had better stay at home.

I think I speak not too strongly when I say that a church in the land without the Spirit of God is rather a curse than a blessing. If you have not the Spirit of God, Christian worker, remember that you stand in somebody else's way; you are as a tree bearing no fruit standing where a fruitful tree might grow.—Charles H. Spurgeon.

HOME

Cheating Ourselves

Dr. J. Wilbur Chapman tells the story of a philanthropist who bade a contractor, who had been very unfortunate, build him a dwelling, and gave him authority to choose the material and to govern every part of its construction. At last the house was finished, but the contractor had felt that this was an opportunity for him to recover some of his lost fortune, and had put into it the poorest material and the faultiest of work. When the house was finished the philanthropist said, "This house is for you and your family, and you can live in it as long as you please. It is yours forever," and then the poor man realized that he had built a house in which he himself must live. He thought he was cheating the other man, but he had really been cheating himself. That is the way we are cheated when we fail in doing our duty concerning our own homes. No man, or woman, or child ever robs the home life of any good thing which ought to be there without cheating themselves just as this contractor did. They must live there, and many people find home a cruel, heartless place because they themselves have failed in their duty.—Rev. R. Cameron.

* * *

A Fine Tribute to American Christian Homes

"I have not been able to find a single and useful institution which has not been founded by either an intensely religious man or by the son of a praying father or a praying mother. I have made this statement before the Chambers of Commerce of all the largest cities of the country, and have asked them to bring forward a case that is an exception to this rule. Thus far, I have not heard of a single one."—Roger Babson.

* * *

The Meaning of Home

Why is it that "there's no place like home?" A personal friend of the beloved Bible teacher Dr. C. I. Scofield invited him to spend a night in the former's home. In his letter of reply Dr. Scofield wrote: "I like to be able to think of people who deeply interest me in their homes. Downtown we are all pretty much alike, but at home we are just ourselves. That is the very sweetest thing said of those in Christ who have 'fallen on sleep'—'at home with the Lord.' For 'at home' we are at ease; we throw off care; we are understood, and loved, and welcome." There is the answer to our question. And if Heaven is our home, how true it is that there's no place like home! Christ does not intend that we shall be satisfied with anything less than Heaven as our dwelling place; for it is He in His personal presence there who will make it both Heaven and home.—*Sunday School Times.*

* * *

Does Christ Abide in Our Home?

A minister of a colored church was hearing the experiences of his people at a class meeting. One woman spoke of the preciousness of her religion and the comfort and happiness she found in it. "That is delightful," said the pastor, "but how about the practical side? Does it make you kind in the home, cheerful, sweet and loving?" The pastor felt someone tugging at his coat tails and a man whispered, "Press dem questions, pastor! Press dem questions! Dat's my wife!"—"The Christlike Christian," by an Unknown Christian.

* * *

Battlements for the Christian Home

When thou buildest a new house, then thou shalt make a battlement for thy roof, that thou bring not blood upon thine house, if any man fall from thence" (Deut. 22:8).

The Oriental home had a flat roof where family and friends were accustomed to assemble. For the protection of every man, woman, and child, God commanded that whosoever built a new home should provide battlements on the sides of the roof. The householder was solemenly instructed to see to it that these retaining walls were erected in order to avoid accident and possible loss of life — "that thou bring not blood upon thine house." God is concerned, my brother, about the kind of home you build. As a parent, you are responsible not only for the physical safety but also for the spiritual protection of every member of your household.—*Watchman Examiner.*

* * *

Life at Home

A pastor who was commending religion to a boy expressed the hope that he would give his heart to Christ in his youth. "Religion is a continual joy," said he. "Look at your sister, Sarah. How much that dear girl enjoys her religion!" "Yes," replied the boy, "Sarah may enjoy her religion, but nobody else in the house does." The ideal Christian life in the home will make religion enjoyable to all its inmates.—*Record of Christion work.*

* * *

"Good-bye, proud world! I'm going home;
Thou'rt not my friend, and I'm not thine.
Long through the weary crowds I roam,
A river-ark on the ocean brine.
Long I've been tossed like the driven foam
And now, proud world, I'm going home.

"Good-bye to Flattery's fawning face;
To Grandeur, with his wise grimace;
To upstart Wealth's averted eye;
To supple Office, low and high;
To crowded halls, to court and street;
To frozen hearts and hasting feet;
To those who go and those who come;
Good-bye proud world! I'm going home.

"I am going to my own hearthstone,
Bosomed in yon green hill alone—
A secret nook in a pleasant land,
Whose groves the frolic fairies planned,
Where arches green, the livelong day,
Echo the blackbird's roundelay,
And vulgar feet have never trod,—
A spot that is scared to thought and God.

"O, when I am safe in my sylvan home,
I tread on the pride of Greece and Rome;
And when I am stretched beneath the pines
Where the evening star so holy shines,
I laugh at the lore and the pride of man,
At the sophist schools, and the learned clan,
For what are they all, in their high conceit
When man in the bush with God may meet?"

—Ralph Waldo Emerson.

* * *

The Homing Instinct

"Taken from its hive, the bee knows its way home and makes a 'bee line' back. An eel travels down the Rhine to the sea and keeps right on till she reaches the Azores, lays her eggs, and dies. Her progeny return to the Rhine and the process is repeated. Terns were carried in a hooded cage from their nesting grounds off the coast of Florida to Galveston, released, and in less than a week returned... Salmon... leave the sea, enter fresh waters, and ascend far inland, deposit their eggs and die. . . .

Young salmon return to the briny deep, grow up, and then find their way up the very same river to pay their debt to their kind and to nature... In the spiritual nature of man there is that homing instinct. Something within says, 'Not here, not here, but back to God.' Have you returned?"—*Evangelical Beacon.*

* * *

Home

A roof to keep out rain; four walls to keep out wind; floors to keep out cold; yes, but home is more than that. It is the laugh of a baby, the song of a mother, the strength of a father. Warmth of loving hearts, light from happy eyes, kindness, loyalty, comradeship. Home is first school and first church for young ones; where they learn what is right, what is good, and what is kind; where they go for comfort when they are hurt and sick; where joy is shared and sorrow eased; where fathers and mothers are respected and loved; where children are wanted; where the simplest food is good enough for kings, because it is earned; where money is not so important as loving-kindness; where even the teakettle sings from happiness. That is home — God bless it! — Madame Schumann-Heink.

* * *

"Home, Sweet Home"

The author of "Home Sweet Home," John Howard Payne, a genial-hearted, kind little man, was walking with a friend in the great city of London, and pointing to one of the aristocratic streets in Mayfair, where wealth and luxury had the windows closed and curtained lest the least warmth and light should go out, or the smallest air of cold winter come in, where isolated exclusive English comfort was guarded by a practical dragon of gold, he, this tiny man with a big heart, said: "Under those windows I composed the song of 'Home Sweet Home,' as I wandered about without food, or a semblance of shelter I could call my own. Many a night since I wrote those words that issued out of my heart by absolute want of a home have I passed and repassed in this locality, and heard a sweet voice coming from within these gilded, fur-lined, comfortable walls in the depth of a dim, cold London winter warbling 'Home, Sweet Home,' while I, the author of them, knew no bed to call my own."—Selected.

* * *

The Home Atmosphere

"Home is where the heart is,
In dwellings great or small;
And a home lighted by love
Is the dearest home of all."
—Mabel Beals.

* * *

Like a Drink of Water

A Christian woman writes in a recent letter to a friend from whose home had been sent greetings and remembrance: "Isn't a Christian home a real sanctuary of love and rest? The very atmosphere of such a home flowed through your letter to me as I read it and was refreshed — as if I really had had a drink of 'water from the well of Bethlehem.'" Christian *homes* can indeed give a "drink of water" to thirsty souls whenever they enter; the very atmosphere sheds abroad love and peace and joy and blessing; and how desperately the world needs all these today! The early Christians must have had such homes when they had entered upon the wonder and the joy of "that life that is Christ," for we read that "day by day, continuing stedfastly with one accord in the temple, and breaking bread at home, they took their food with gladness and singleness of heart, praising God, and having favor with all the people." The secret of the Christian home goes deep; it means not only that Christ is at home there, but also that Christ is the Home of those who live there. Their home is Christian because Christ is their Home. —*Sunday School Times.*

* * *

The Most Wonderful Thing in America

A young Chinese student, a graduate of one of America's finest medical schools, was a dinner guest in a Christian home in America. In fact, he had been invited frequently to spend an evening with the family, for his interesting conversation and flashing wit made him a favorite with all. "Doctor Tong," said his host that day, "you are soon to leave us and return to China. You have undoubtedly seen many interesting things in America. Would you then tell us, what is the thing that has impressed you most?" The young Chinaman answered without a second of hesitancy, and there was a look of deep seriousness on his face as he spoke. With a gesture that included the family circle about the table, he said, "This is the most wonderful thing I have seen in America In my country we have nothing like it." The young man had seen the great American cities, the great engineering projects, the famous universities, and the inspiring churches, but the most wonderful thing to him was the sight of an Amercian family. Woe unto the nation that despoils its homes!—*Christian Witness.*

* * *

"That Is What I Want"

The pastor of a certain church in Manchester, England, was fairly besieged by a certain woman with requests to pray for her husband. They would nearly succeed in winning the huband when this woman would fly into a violent temper and upset everything. Her husband would say, "Well, Mary if that is religion, I don't want it." Finally the pastor told her that the fault was hers; that she must overcome her temper, and the Lord would give her grace to do it. In her shame and despair she took the matter to the Lord, and he gave her the victory. The time for spring cleaning came. She had just gotten a new lamp hung in the hall and a new carpet laid when John came home, carrying something on his shoulder, not knowing about the new lamp, and there was a clattering and a breaking up of things. He expected a row, but instead a quiet woman looked over the stairs and said, "Never mind, husband; it's all right; we can get a new lamp." And he said, "Mary, what's the matter?" "Oh, my dear," she said, "I have trusted the Lord Jesus to cure me of my temper." He said, "Well, if He has cured you, come right down and pray for me, for that is what I want." And the pastor says he was converted that day.—*The King's Business.*

* * *

The Christian Home— "The Blossom of Which Heaven is the Fruit."

* * *

A Christian Home

How happy you are if you live in a Christian home. What a blessing it is to have a Christian father and mother who will teach you the Bible, and who will live for Jesus before you. Richard Cecil was a great Christian man. He tells of how he found the Saviour. He says that when he was a boy he tried to be an unbeliever. But there was one thing he could not forget, and that was his mother's faith in God and love for God. Richard Cecil's father was a sinner. He drank, and he was often unkind to Richard and his little brother, and to his mother. At such times, the mother would take Richard and his little brother to a spot under a hillside, and, kneeling there, she would pray to God, and ask God's care for her children. The mother died before long. She was killed by her husband's harshness and the hardness of her life. When Richard reached twenty-one years of age, he was an hardened, sinful young man. One day he found himself near his boyhood home. He felt drawn to go and take another look at the little place under the hill, where his mother often went to pray. It was just as he had left it. Even the grass looked as if no foot had touched it since his mother had died. Richard sat down. He heard again his mother's voice, pleading again with God for her boys. His heart was crushed as he thought of his sinful ways, and of his refusals to come to the Lord Jesus. He fell on his knees, with the tears running down the cheeks. He did not leave that spot under the hill until he had found the Saviour! He said,

"My mother's prayers came back. I stand today the loving witness of a mother's faithfulness, of a prayer-hearing God!"

We will never forget our Christian father and mother, our Christian home! The Evangelistic Singer, F. A. Mills, is well known in central New York State. Some time ago, his mother died. She had been a wonderful Christian mother. At her funeral Mr. Mills sang with deep feeling:

> "O mother, when I think of thee,
> 'Tis but a step to Calvary,
> Thy gentle hand upon my brow,
> Is leading me to Jesus *now!*"

All children from Christian homes can sing this song!—*Gospel Herald.*

* * *

"What Is a Home?"

Recently a London magazine sent out 1,000 inquiries on the question: "What is home?" Out of 800 replies received, seven gems were selected as follows:

1. Home—A world of strife shut out, a world of love shut in.
2. Home—The place where the small are great and the great are small.
3. Home—The father's kingdom, the mother's world and the child's paradise.
4. Home—The place where we grumble the most and are treated the best.
5. Home—The center of our affections round which our heart's best wishes twine.
6. Home—The place where our stomach gets three square meals daily and our hearts a thousand.
7. Home—The only place on earth where the faults and the failings of humanity are hidden under the sweet mantle of charity.—*The Covenanter Witness.*

Youth and the Family Altar

"What does it mean to you to have had a Christian home?" The question was put to a student of the Bible Institute of Los Angeles, a young man whose parents are missionaries.

"Why," he said, "it means everything; that's why I'm here. In our home in China, family worship was a normal part of every day's activities. There was nothing spectacular about it. In fact, I cannot remember anything of oustanding influence that occurred at our family altar. But that wholesome home atmosphere and the constant realization of God's presence have helped me to put God first."

Another student, the eldest daughter in a family of four children, is an accepted candidate for missionary service in Africa. "In our home," she said, "we usually sing at worship time--the old hymns, with their depth of meaning. My parents feel that music is one of the strongest ties for binding together the members of a family. When Father reads the Word, each of us follows the reading in his or her own Bible, and every one has a part in the worship. The younger children select and read Scripture verses that become their own prayers. I was saved when I was nine. The influences of my Christian home have molded my life, and they will extend soon, the Lord willing, to Africa." — *The King's Business.*

* * *

For a Happy Home

Patience, forbearance, kindness, forgiveness—these are essentials in every household; and they can come only through much prayer and supplication at the throne of grace.—Judge C. C. Featherstone.

HONESTY

Dangerous Twisted Standards

In a Sunday school class the lesson was about lying. A young girl put this proposition to her teacher, "My mother is 'old-fashioned' and thinks it is wrong to dance, so when I want to go to a dance I tell her that I am going to stay with a girl friend. Is it wrong to tell that kind of lie?" The teacher replied, "No, if your mother is such a 'back number' as that, it is all right to lie to her." Another child in the class, reporting the incident to his parents, was removed from that Sunday school, and sent to a sound one.—*The Voice.*

* * *

An Arctic Test

Sir Ernest Shackleton was once asked to tell of his most terrible moment of which many may be so described in the Arctic. But his worst was spent one night in an emergency hut. He and his fellows lying there; he rather apart from the rest. They had given out the ration of the last remaining biscuits. There was nothing more to divide. Every man thought the other man was asleep. He sensed a stealthy movement and saw one of the men turning from side to side to see how his comrades were faring. He made up his mind that all were asleep and then stretched over the next man and drew his biscut bag to himself and removed the biscuit. Shackleton lived through an eternity of suspense. He would not have trusted his life in the hands of that man. Was he turning out a thief and under terribly tragic circumstances? Stealing a man's last biscuit! Then Shackleton sensed another movement. He saw the man open his own box, take the biscuit out of his own bag and put it in his comrade's and return the man's biscuit and stealthily put the bag back at his comrade's side. Shackleton said, "I dare not tell you that man's name. I felt that that act was a secret between himself and God."—Adapted from *The Life of Faith.*

What Followed

A young man, arrested for swindling his employer out of $30,000.00, sat alone in a criminal's cell out of which daylight had faded. Cowering on his hard bed, he pictured himself with the world outside full of light and comfort. The question came to him sharply, "How came you here?"

Was it really for the stealing of this great sum?

Yes, and no.

Looking back twenty years he saw himself as a schoolboy, ten years old. He remembered his Uncle John—such a queer, kind, forgetful old man. That very morning his uncle had sent him to pay a bill at the country store and there were seventy-two cents left, and Uncle John did not ask for it. When they met at noon this boy, now in prison, stood there under the beautiful blue sky, and a great temptation came. He said to himself, "Shall I give it back to him, or shall I wait till he asks for it? If he never asks for it that is his lookout. If he does, why, I can get it together again."

He never gave back the money.

A theft of $30,000.00 brought this young man to prison; but when a boy he turned that way when he sold his honesty of seventy-two cents.

That night he sat disgraced, an open criminal, in his chilly cell.

Uncle John was dead long ago. The old home was desolate, his mother broken-hearted. The prisoner knew that what brought him there was not the man's deed, but the boy's.

Had the ten-year-old-boy been true to his honor, life now would have been different. One little cheating was the first of many until his character was eaten out, could bear no test, and he wrecked his manliness and life.—*Budget.*

* * *

Honest Abe

President Lincoln was not only known as "Honest Abe"; he was also known as one who loved the truth. One day he was visited by a gentleman who was in the habit of making promises without keeping them. He coaxed one of the Lincoln boys to sit in his lap by promising to give him the charm he wore on his watch-chain. The child climbed into his lap. Finally the gentleman arose to go, when Mr. Lincoln said to him, "Are you going to keep your promise to my boy?" "What promise?" said the visitor. "You said you would give him that charm." "Oh, I could not," said the visitor. "It is not only valuable, but I prize it as an heirloom." "Give it to him!" said Mr. Lincoln sternly. "I would not want him to know I entertained one who had no regard for his word." The gentleman colored, undid the charm and handed it to the boy, and went away with a lesson which he was not likely soon to forget. —Mabel Reynolds Makepeace.

* * *

Slapped in the Face for Years

A man said, "For years when I have bowed down in private prayer a certain incident in my life has been slapping me in the face." The speaker was a man above eighty years of age. He was a man of wealth. He had given thousands to missions and the cause of education. He was a liberal man. But there was a little sand on the journal, which caused a slight friction. This is his story as related with his own lips. "Years ago I bought some hay from a neighbor. It was weighed and I gave the man the totals. Before the account was settled the man died. I went to the administrator and asked if he had any account against me, and he found nothing and I gave the claim no further attention. The matter has put a shadow on my life for years and has hindered and impeded my spiritual progress. Tomorrow morning first thing I am going to the widow and settle the account in full. Best of all, he did it. A new light broke over his face. The controversy was over. He had liberty again. His testimony rang clear and true. That which had been slapping him in the face was gone.—*The King's Business.*

Three Will Know

A Chinese convert, newly brought to the faith, was being tempted by one of his countrymen to cheat. Upon his refusal, his tempter asked why. "Because three will know that I cheated," replied the native Christian. "You will know, and I will know, and Heaven will know." And this applies to all lands. "All things are naked and open to the eyes of Him with whom we have to do."—Selected.

* * *

She Believed in Spite of Herself

An old lady who is wholly consecrated to the Lord's service is rather poor in worldly goods, but rich in spiritual things. She is only a washerwoman, but she gets up early and works late at night in order to be able to devote time in the Lord's service through visitation and winning souls for her Master. Sometimes she is engaged by a wealthy family to look after their house during their holidays. One day the lady made the remark, "Mrs. J——, I don't believe much in this doctrine of holiness that you profess and are so fond of talking about." "Well," said the old Christian, "you know, madam, that before I came into your service you used to send everything of value that could be removed to a place of safety, but since I have been in charge you have left even your most valuable property under my care. Oh, yes, madam, you believe in my holiness."—*Christian Herald.*

* * *

It Costs to Be Honest

She was a little woman and must have been approaching her three score and ten. I saw her talking to a clerk in a Christian book store. While I looked at a new book, I could not help but overhear the conversation.

The day before she had purchased a devotional booklet for 10 cents and wanted to buy another for a friend. The clerk told her the price was 20 cents. There was some question about the price so it was verified by another clerk. When she started to pay, the little lady insisted on paying the extra dime on the booklet she bought the day before. The clerk said it would not be necessary, but the little lady insisted that it was the honest thing to do.

"It always pays to be honest," observed a man standing near-by.

"No, it costs to be honest! It just cost me a dime," the little lady replied. "God is honest—and I try to be like Him."

The little lady turned and walked out. *The whole store seemed to light up a bit because she had been there.—Baptist Messenger.*

* * *

An Honest Book

An interesting story is told about a certain English nobleman. He has an heirloom which he prizes highly. It is an old brass-bound, leather-covered ledger, and it belonged to the founder of his family. What makes it so precious is not so much its antiquity and quaintness and personal association, as the following prayer which appears as its first entry: "O Lord, keep me and this book honest." This is a prayer that every man may well adopt for himself.—*Gospel Gleaners.*

* * *

A Few Cents

In a little country store in Illinois, there was a tall, ugly country boy serving as a clerk. One day an old woman came into the store to buy some goods. She handed the clerk a bill, and he took the money due him and gave the change back to her. That night when he balanced his cash book, he found he had a few cents more than he should have had. He went back in his mind over all his sales of the day, and he remembered how much change he had given the old lady that morning. He had failed to give her as much as he should have done. Those few pennies belonged to her. He put on his hat, closed the store, and walked several miles to return the pennies to the old woman. This country boy was Abraham Lincoln, who, as you know, later became President of our United States.

"Dare to be honest, good, and sincere;
Dare to be upright, and you never need fear.
Dare to be brave in the cause of the right,
Dare with the enemy ever to fight.
Dare to be loving and patient each day;
Dare to speak the truth, whatever you say.
Dare to be gentle and orderly, too;
Dare to shun evil, whatever you do.
Dare to speak kindly, and ever be true;
Dare to do right, and you'll find your way through."—*Gospel Herald.*

* * *

Truthful

In the home of a pious farmer there hung the well-known motto: "But as for me and my house, we will serve the Lord." The motto meant something in that house, for the farmer prayed daily that he and all might truly serve the Lord. The last clause fitted all the house save the oldest son, who persistently refused to accept Christ. One day the father and son were alone in the room where the motto hung. The father said, "My dear Henry, I cannot and will not be a liar any longer. You, who belong to my house, do not want to serve the Lord. Therefore I must add the words 'except Henry.' It hurts me to do it, but I must be true." The thought so impressed the boy that he gave himself to Christ.—*Examiner.*

* * *

Honesty in Small Things

In a certain bank there was a trust department in which four young men and one older man were employed. It was decided by the directors that they would promote the older employee and also promote one of the younger men to have charge of the trust department after the older gentleman was removed to his new position. After considering the merits of each of the men, a certain one of the four younger men was selected for the new position and to receive a substantial increase in salary. It was decided to notify him of the promotion that afternoon at four o'clock.

At the noon hour the young man went to a cafeteria for lunch. One of the directors was behind him in the line with several other customers in between them. The director saw the young man select his food including a small piece of butter. The butter he flipped on his plate and threw some food on top of it to hide it from the cashier. In this way he lied to the cashier about what was on his plate.

That afternoon the directors met to notify the young man that they had intended giving him the promotion, but that because of what had been seen in the cafeteria they must discharge him. They felt that they could not have one who would lie and steal as the head of their trust department.

"Honesty is the best policy" both in natural things and in spiritual things.—Selected.

* * *

Things That "Sink" Us

A personal friend of that quaint and original Methodist preacher, Peter Mackenzie, was telling me a story about him the other day. Some years before his death he was in a railway accident, the effects of which seemed likely to end his singularly useful public life. When he was a little better, a trusted friend and adviser urged him to make a claim for damages. After a time he consented, and fixed the amount of compensation to be asked for. His friend strongly protested that the amount was not half of what he ought to ask, and less than half of what he could get. Mr. Mackenzie refused to put it higher. "It is enough," he held; then, looking his friend solemnly in the face, he said in his own characteristic way: "Eh, mon, but I shall have to cross the Jordan one day, cross the Jordan; and if I have a sixpence then that was badly gotten, it will sink me, it will sink me!"—*The Wonderful Word.*

His Fellow Soldiers Trusted Him

Dr. Will H. Houghton tells of a soldier who ultimately was made a Christian believer through seeing his companions make fun of another soldier who was a believer in Christ. The thing that impressed him was the fact that, though they made fun of this man, they left their money in his possession for safekeeping.—*Sunday School Times.*

* * *

Let's Be Honest

A member of the editorial staff of *The Christian Advocate* was seated in a dining car the other evening. His companion at the table was a clear-eyed, attractive youth in a private's uniform. Having eaten a simple meal, he was presented with a blank form of some kind and informed by the waiter that he was entitled to a discount if he were "on government business." The boy fumbled the slip for a minute or two, read it carefully, and finally handed it back, saying, "I don't think I'm entitled to this. I'm not on government business. I'm going home to see my mother."

We have nothing whatever to do with the selection of medals for acts of bravery, or services of distinction. But we would like to nominate that boy for some kind of merit badge.—*The Christian Advocate.*

* * *

Honesty in Small Things

When Grover Cleveland was a boy, he insisted upon returning the egg that a neighbor's hen daily laid on the Cleveland side of the fence. Thus he began to give proof of the honesty that marked him as a man and as President of the United States.

Honesty in little things leads to honesty in matters of great importance. There are times when a fellow feels that it will do no harm to cheat a little. "No one will notice," he thinks. But even if no one else notices, the boy himself knows, and that compromise with dishonesty paves the way for still more crooked dealings.

The boy who has the ambition to win true success will be honest in every detail. He cannot afford to make any exception.—*Pioneer*.

* * *

Important Sewing

Dr. Laws of Livingstonia, that great missionary, says that his life was once saved from a lion because the canvas of his tent was well sewed. He found afterward that it had been sewed by a girl in Greenock. That girl sewing canvas tents in Scotland little knew that away in Africa a great man's life depended on the character of her stitches. — F. C. Hoggarth.

* * *

The Old Adage

"Honesty is the best policy," is the old adage. It may be open to question, for we should be honest even if our honesty should not prove to be a profitable policy. However, we are glad that this good, old-fashioned virtue is still in existence even though we sometimes think those who practice it are getting fewer and fewer.

Recently in a public eating house we were pleased to note a man who was a stranger to us calling attention to the fact that the cashier had given him too much change. It was not a great act, for the person was only doing what he ought to have done, but it brought a warm feeling to our hearts. Let us labor to keep alive that fine principle of Christian honesty, for God has said in His Word, "Provide things honest in the sight of all men" (Rom. 12:17).—*Christian Monitor*.

* * *

Caught by His "Generosity"

It is said that a Covington grocer once met his match. He purchased a table castor for one dollar. Then he marked it with a tag inscribed "$14" and gave it to a Methodist minister whose church his family attended. The next day the minister brought the castor back to the grocer and said to him, "I am far too poor to display on my table so valuable a castor as this, and if you have no objection I should like to return it and take $14 worth of groceries for my family in its stead." The merchant could do nothing but comply.—*Earnest Worker*.

HOPE

Bernard Shaw's Hopelessness

The witty, brilliant, sophisticated Irish essayist and lecturer, Bernard Shaw, sums up the hopelessness of his own barren life and philosophy in the epigram: "There are two tragedies in life. One is not to get your heart's desire. The other is to get it." But Shaw is talking about the desire of the heart of the natural man, who knows not God nor Christ, and whose life is only death. He speaks truly when he says that, when such a man has got his heart's desire, he finds it only disappointment, empty and unsatisfying. That is why so many today, both old people and young people, having won their heart's desires, commit suicide.—*Sunday School Times*.

Sperondeo

On a train we met a young man who was a junior in college. With his father and mother he had left Sicily to establish a new home in our own land. Having settled in Southern Illinois, they had gone to work in a coal mine. Shortly afterward a mine explosion killed his father, and he himself was maimed for life by the loss of his left arm and right hand. During his hospital stay, he and his mother became so profoundly impressed with the Christian character of the institution that they decided upon two epoch-making events. First, they joined the church, and next, they legally changed their names. The old name they never mention anymore. The new name sent the lad to college where he earned his bachelor and master degrees, resulting in a professorship in an American college. The name chosen is his constant inspiration: "Giovanni Sperondeo." The first is simply the Italian "John," but the second grips us. "Sperondeo"—"my hope is in God." How uplifting to write such a name: "My hope is in God!"—*Christian Herald.*

* * *

"Better to hope, though the clouds hang low,
And keep the eyes still lifted;
For the sweet, blue skies will soon peep through,
When the ominous clouds are rifted.
There was never a night without a day,
Nor an evening without a morning;
And the darkest hour, as the proverb goes,
Is the hour before the dawning!"
—Selected.

* * *

Hopeless

It was Sir Thomas Lipton of England, the multimillionaire, who shortly before dying, said: "I'd give up every trophy in my collection for the one I haven't got" — that is a hope of Heaven and eternal life. He was well-known as a winner in both English and American boat races.

Another high railway official when dying confessed: "I have lived too much for secondary things in life — not the main thing!" Eternal life may be had for the taking, by faith, in the new birth, through the death of Christ, because of the resurrection of Christ, and because of the love and the abundant grace of God!—*Gospel Herald.*

* * *

"An' de Good Lawd Know My Name"

I jes' don' know ef de kohn'll grow,
But I plans hit jes' de same;
I jes' don' know ef de wind'll blow,
But I watch an' pray, an' I reap an' sow,
An' de sun he rise, an' de ribber flow,
An' de good Lawd know my name.

I jes' can't tell ef de cotton sell,
But I toils on jes' de same;
De birds they build where de spring sap swell,
An' dey know enough for a rainy spell,
An' dat's lots more than they gwine to tell.—
And de good Lawd know my name.

So I watch an' pray as I goes my way,
An' I toils on jes de same;
De rose is sweet, but de rose can't stay,
But I'm mighty glad when it blooms my way;
De night fall dark, but de Lawd send day,
An' de good Lawd know my name.
—Frank L. Stanton.

HUMAN BODY

Wonderfully Made

In the human body there are about two hundred and sixty-three bones. The muscles are about five hundred in number. The length of the alimentary canal is about thirty-two feet. The amount of blood in an adult averages 30 pounds, or fully one-fifth of the entire weight.

The heart is six inches in length and four inches in diameter and beats seenty times a minute, 4200 an hour, 100,800 a day, 36,792,000 a year, 2,565,440,000 in three-score and ten years, and at each beat two and a half ounces of blood are thrown out of it, one hundred and seventy-five ounces a minute, six hundred and fifty-six pounds an hour, seven and three-fourths tons a day. All the blood in the body passes through the heart in three minutes. This little organ by its ceaseless industry, pumps each day what is equal to lifting one hundred and twenty-two tons one foot high, or one ton one hundred and twenty-two feet high.

The lungs will contain about one gallon of air at their usual degree of inflation. We breathe on an average 1200 times an hour, inhale six hundred gallons of air, or 24,000 a day. The aggregate surface of the air cells of the lungs exceeds 20,000 square inches, an area very nearly equal to the floor of a room twelve feet square.

The average weight of the brain of an adult male is three pounds and eight ounces, of a female two pounds and four ounces. The nerves are all connected with it, directly or by the spinal marrow. These nerves, together with their branches and minute ramifications, probably exceed 10,000,000 in number, forming a body-guard out-numbering by far the greatest army ever marshaled!

The skin is composed of three layers, and varies from one-fourth to one-eighth of an inch in thickness. The atmospheric pressure being about fourteen pounds to the square inch, a person of medium size is subjected to a pressure of 40,000 lbs. Each square inch of skin contains 35,000 sweating tubes or perspiratory pores, each of which may be likened to a little drain pipe one-fourth of an inch long, making an aggregate length of the entire surface of the body of 201,166 feet, or a tile ditch for draining the body almost forty miles long.

Man is marvelously made. Who is eager to investigate the curious and wonderful works of Omnipotent Wisdom, let him not wander the wide world around to seek them, but examine himself.—Selected.

What Makes a Man?

Two or three young men who were once visiting Washington went into the National Museum. On one of the cabinets was a label with these words: "The body of a man, weighing one hundred and fifty-four pounds." "Where is the man?" asked one of the young men. No one answered him. In the cabinet were two jars of water and other jars in which were phosphate of lime, carbonate of lime, potassium, sodium, and other chemicals. Another section held a row of clear glass jars filled with gasses—hydrogen, oxygen, and nitrogen. The materials in those cabinets were given in exact proportion as combined in an ordinary man. After looking at the assortment for some time in silence, one of the young men said: "And that is what I am made of? That is all that goes to make me?"

"That is all," said a bystander as he smiled and walked on.

But the young man did not smile. "If that is all that is needed," said one, "so much lime, so much gas, so much water, we should be exactly alike. There is something more which they cannot put into cabinets."

"Yes," said another under his breath, "that which is added by God, who puts into these senseless elements that which makes a living soul." They passed on in silence, their souls and their God suddenly becoming real before those cabinets filled with all the material essentials for the making of a man. — *The Youth's Companion.*

HUMILITY

Be Clothed With Humility

The highest lesson a believer has to learn is humility. Oh, that every Christian who seeks to advance in a holy life may remember this well! There may be intense consecration and fervent zeal and heavenly experience, and yet, if it is not prevented by very special dealings of the Lord, there may be an unconscious self-exaltation with it all. Let us learn the lesson—the highest lesson in the holy life is the deepest humility; and let us remember that it comes not of itself, but only as it is made a matter of special dealing on the part of our faithful Lord and His faithful servant.

Humility isn't thinking meanly of oneself—it isn't thinking of self at all. The truly humble man does not know he is humble: Moses wist not that the skin of his face shone.—Andrew Murray.

* * *

Dr. Carey's Saviour

Among those who visited Dr. Carey, the missionary, in his last illness was Alexander Duff, the Scotch missionary.

On one occasion he spent some time talking chiefly about Carey's missionary life, until the dying man whispered, "Pray." Duff knelt down and prayed and then said "Goodbye."

As he passed from the room, he thought he heard a feeble voice pronouncing his name, and turning, found that he was recalled. He stepped back accordingly, and this is what he heard, spoken with gracious solemnity: "Mr. Duff, you have been speaking about Dr. Carey! Dr. Carey! When I am gone say nothing about Dr. Carey — speak about Dr. Carey's *Saviour*."

Duff went away rebuked and awed, with a lesson in his heart that he never forgot.—*Scattered Seed.*

* * *

"I Will Go as a Servant"

Robert Morrison, the noted missionary to China wrote to his friends in England, asking for an assistant. In response a young man from the country offered himself. After an interview, the members of the board decided that though he was an earnest Christian he was too rough and unpolished and they gave him this decision: "We do not think you fit to be a missionary, but if you would like to go out as a servant to the missionary, we will send you."

After hearing this answer, he said, "Well, sir, if the gentlemen don't think me fit to be a missionary, I will go as a servant. I am willing to be a hewer of wood and a drawer of water or do anything to help the cause of my Heavenly Master."

He was sent out as a servant, but he soon became a missionary and turned out to be Dr. Milne, one of the best missionaries that ever went to that country.—Selected.

* * *

The Humility of True Greatness

A party of English tourists visited the house where Beethoven, the great composer, had spent the last years of his life. The caretaker (who was something of a hero worshiper) led them at length into a certain room, and, reverently lifting the cover, said, "And this was Beethoven's piano." A young lady of the party at once took possession of the music stool and began to play one of Beethoven's sonatas. The custodian stood by, stern and silent. At last the young lady swung round on her stool, and said, "I suppose a great many people who come here like to play on Beethoven's piano?" "Well, Miss, Paderewski was here last summer, and some of his friends wanted him to play, but he said, 'No, I am not worthy.' "—*Sunday School Chronicle.*

* * *

Think Little of Yourself

Suffer a fellow pilgrim and fellow lalorer, who has known a little of Shechem's trouble and Bethel's joy, to leave you one result of his brief experience. Distrust yourself, your plans, your efforts, and your successes; habitually think little of yourself before God; and above all things, avoid listening to the meed of praise which even your fellow Christians will pour into your ears. And if you fail in this, better, far better, relinquish the service which is accompanied with apparent external successes, than carry about a soul dwarfed in its affection and communings, and which has exchanged to its immense loss in time, a low place before God for a high one before men. To the Christian *"vox populi"* is never *"vox Dei."*—*The Witness* (London).

* * *

Lower Yet

I used to think that God's gifts were on shelves one above the other; and that the taller we grew in Christian character the easier we could reach them. I now find that God's gifts are on shelves one beneath the other; and that *it is not a question of growing taller but of stooping lower; and that we have to go down, always down, to get His best gifts.*—F. B. Meyer, in *Alliance Weekly.*

* * *

A Good Blocking Back

It was one of those bad nights. The team had lost that day. Coach Tuss McLaughry, in the privacy of his home, was indulging in an old and familiar lament. "What I need is a good blocking back," he muttered. "If I'd had one we could have saved that game." The youngster, ready for bed, looked up at his father gravely. "When I grow up, I'll be a blocking back, Pop," he said. Then, as it seemed essential to know, he asked, "What *is* a blocking back, Pop?" Tuss grinned at the youngster, but there was still a trace of grimness behind the grin. "He's the fellow," he said, "who does the job and lets somebody else get the glory. Now, run along to bed." Fifteen years later John McLaughry is captain of the Brown Varsity team, and one of the best blocking backs. He seldom makes a touchdown — but he sets the stage for every one of them. "Never mind the glory."—*This Week Magazine.*

* * *

The Lowly Spirit

Every missionary should cultivate a lowly spirit. It will prevent pride and thoughts of self in prosperity, as well as discouragement when there is little visible result of his labor. No one is so much in need of a lowly spirit as servants of the Lord. It is one of the first and last qualifications for service.

It is related of Francis Xavier, that as he was preaching in one of the cities of Japan, a man went up to him as if he had something to say to him privately. Xavier leaned his head near to hear what he had to say, and the scorner spit upon the face of the devoted missionary. Xavier, without a word or the least sign of annoyance, took out his pocket handkerchief, wiped his face and went on with his important message as if nothing had happened. The scorn of the audience was turned to admiration. "The most learned doctor of the city, who happened to be present, said to himself that a law which taught men such virtue, inspired them with such courage, and gave them such complete mastery over themselves, could not but be from God. Afterwards he desired baptism, and his example was followed by others. So effectually did the meekness of the missionary promote the success of the work."

"Learn of Me"; Jesus said, "for I am meek and lowly in heart."

"Though the Lord be high, yet hath He respect unto the lowly," and "He giveth grace unto the lowly."

Dear coworkers, let Christ be your Example, love your motive, and humility your covering.—D. B. Rote.

* * *

Dr. Meyer's Humility

The last letter that I received from him (Dr. F. B. Meyer) was written March 9, 1929, in his own hand, just a few weeks before the end of his earthly life. It is thoroughly characteristic of him: "I am now eighty-two and in a nursing-home but hope to be out again in two or three weeks. I want to tell you what the Spirit of God has been showing me lately: that I have acquired a reputation for sanctity from the facility with which I have discussed on the inner secrets of life hidden with God. I see how easily this may grow upon me. I haven't said this to anyone, I have only just caught sight of it. But it makes one want to creep into Heaven unnoticed. Believe in my love. Let us have a hundred years' quiet talk beneath 'the Trees of Healing.' " How humble and sincere was this saint of God up to the very end! A. T. Robertson, in *From the Bible Today.*

* * *

New Testament Subtraction

Recently we heard Lucky Baldwin pray. His real name is Christopher Balfe. He is a redeemed sinner whose rough life has been saved and is being used of God in prison work. What a contrast to the religious attitude of the worldly wise was Lucky's prayer: "O Lord, I was nothin' and I am nothin', and nothin' from nothin' leaves nothin'. So Christ is everything." — Courtesy *Moody Monthly.*

* * *

The Sexton's Diagnosis

James McDougall, a young Scotchman, a candidate for the ministry, was on his way to the pulpit to preach his trial sermon. James had worked hard on that sermon, and he felt that it was a good one. He knew he had a good voice, and he was confident of making an excellent impression. As he walked up the aisle and mounted the high pulpit steps, the pride in his face and walk was evident to everybody in the church. Old Robin Malair, the sexton, shook his grizzled head, "I hae me doots o' yon laddie," he said to himself. James McDougall made a miserable failure in the pulpit that day. And when his wretchedly delivered sermon was done he walked slowly down the pulpit steps, head bowed and heart humbled. "Ay, laddie," mused old Robin, "if ye had gone up as ye came doon, ye'd hae come doon as ye went up!"—*The Evangelical Christian.*

* * *

Bishop Moule's Humility

It is not surprising to find those who walk humbly with God, humble before their fellows. Dr. G. Scroggie says, "I stayed with Handley Moule, Bishop of Durham, at Lochlan Castle. I never saw more wonderful unselfishness and humility. General William Booth stayed overnight, and when he got home from the meeting the Bishop put him in the easiest chair in the drawing room and knelt down and took off General Booth's shoes, carried them away, and got his slippers. And all was done so naturally—no pride, no selfishness, no desire to maintain his dignity, though he did not lose any of it by getting on his knees."—*Evangelical Christian.*

No Crowding Here

A young minister was preaching a sermon on Christ washing the disciples' feet, and in the midst of it he said, "Do you know, friends, we are all fighting for the top in the church, but there are so few fighting for the towel." This was a crude way of saying that there are very few willing to be the last, the lowest, and the least in the body of Christ.—*Gospel Herald.*

* * *

God Chooses the "Weak" and "Foolish"

When someone asked Saint Francis of Assisi why and how he could accomplish so much, he replied: "This may be why. The Lord looked down from Heaven upon the earth and said, 'Where can I find the weakest, the littlest, the meanest man on the face of the earth?' Then He saw me and said, 'Now I've found him, and I will work through him. He won't be proud of it. He'll see that I am only using him because of his littleness and insignificance.' "—*Christian Herald.*

* * *

Humility

A man can counterfeit love, he can counterfeit faith, he can counterfeit hope and all the other graces, but it is very difficult to counterfeit humility. You soon detect mock humility. They have a saying among the Arabs that as the tares and the wheat grow they show which God has blessed. The ears that God has blessed bow their heads and acknowledge every grain, and the more fruitful they are the lower their heads are bowed. The tares lift up their heads erect, high above the wheat, but they are only fruitful of evil.

If we only get down low enough, God will use us to His glory.—D. L. Moody.

* * *

The Loveliest Virtue

Humility is the Christian's loveliest virtue and his crowning grace. Once it was a stigma; today it is a compliment.

Christ took the hateful word and made it honorable. Dr. Jowett tells a story of Joseph Parker: "Why did Jesus choose Judas?" Dr. Parker was once asked. "I do not know," replied the doctor, "but I have a harder question: *why did he choose me?*"—*Sunday School Times.*

Why God Chooses Us

Hudson Taylor, the great missionary leader, once said, when someone asked him how he was chosen for the work in China, that God chose a little man so that men might see what a great God we have.—*Sunday School Times.*

HYPOCRISY

Not Clocks Only

A good story is told of old Thomas K. Beecher, who could not bear deceit in any form. Finding that a clock in his church was habitually too fast or too slow, he hung a placard on the wall above it, reading in large letters: "Don't blame my hands — the trouble lies deeper." That is where the trouble lies with us when our hands do wrong, or our feet, or our lips, or even our thoughts. The trouble lies so deep that only God's miracle power can deal with it. Sin indeed goes deep; but Christ goes deeper. — *Christian Witness.*

* * *

Nothing to Conceal

A sweet little six-year-old girl looked up suddenly at her mother and said, "Mother, I think Jesus was the only one who ever dared to live his inside out!" The mother was fairly dazed by the little one's thought. Well she might be. It carried one of the profoundest thoughts suggested by lifelong study of that divine character. But here it was out of the mouth of almost a babe. She had heard His story. She had seen that He was so pure in all His soul that there was nothing there that He needed to conceal from anybody. Was not He the only one in all the history of mankind of whom that could be truly said?—*Onward.*

* * *

Counterfeit vs. Genuine Dollars

I saw about a peck of counterfeit dollars once. Did I go to the window and throw away all my good dollars? No. Yet many reject Christianity because there are hypocrites or counterfeit Christians.—W. E. Biederwolf.

* * *

Judas Trees

On certain sections of the earth there grows a tree which has been named the Judas Tree, because of its deceitfulness. This tree, it is said, has most beautiful crimson blossoms. These appear before the leaves. Their flaming beauty attracts innumerable insects. The busy bee, ever on the lookout for honey, is drawn to the flowers. But every insect, and every bee, that alights upon the blossoms imbibes a tatal opiate, and drops dead from among the crimson blossoms to the earth. Beneath the Judas Tree the earth is strewed with its victims.

How marvelously this tree illustrates the deceitfulness and the danger of sin! The poisonous insect and the useful bee, alike, were enticed and met a similar fate — death. So it is with sin. Even with the best of intentions, one may meet disaster by approaching sin; and only the wisdom of the Holy Spirit can discern, sometimes, between the good and the evil, true and false, in these last days.

We need not only to pray for guidance, for strength, but for wisdom to discern these deceitful "Judas trees" which Satan has planted all about us. *Gospel Herald.*

* * *

Heart Belief Necessary

There is a story of a Nova Scotia sailor who has the Lord's Prayer tattooed on his back. He says that his dying mother asked him never to part with the back cover of a family Bible, on which the Lord's Prayer was printed in letters of gold. For many years he carried this cover on all his cruises; but one day, having a tussle with a sailor, he lost it overboard. Bad luck pursued him after that; and finally a companion who had heard him lament the loss of the talisman suggested his having the prayer tattooed on his back. He did this, though he suffered very much during the process.

Alas! there are many who are making the mistake of this poor, ignorant, superstitious sailor. *There are multitudes who are putting their religion on the outside rather than on the inside.—John and His Friends.*

* * *

God's Interest in Obscurities

Dr. Robert E. Speer tells the story of an old sculptor who was cutting a figure that was to stand in a niche in the wall so that its back would never be seen. Yet he was working with the same painstaking care on the back as on the front. Someone asked, "Why are you working on the back of that figure? No one will see it." "Ah," replied the sculptor, "God will always be looking upon it." "I am not so sure," continues Dr. Speer, "that it is not on the obscurities of our lives that God looks far more than on what we regard as our real life upon which men look. What He looks at after all is what is back of the life."—Courtesy *Moody Monthly.*

* * *

Unseen, But—

Saul has done everything except the most important thing of all — obey God's commands. A captain of a ship crossed the deck in a hurry, seemingly very much perplexed. A lady stopped him and asked what the trouble was. "The fact is, madam," he said, "our rudder's broken." "Oh, I shouldn't worry about that," she replied: "being under water all the time, no one will notice it."—*Youth's Companion.*

The Bat's Mistake

Aesop speaks in one of his fables about a time when the beasts and the fowl were engaged in war. The bat tried to belong to both parties. When the birds were victorious, he would wing around telling that he was a bird; when the beasts won a fight, he would walk around them assuring that he was a beast. But soon his hypocrisy was discovered and he was rejected by both the beasts and the birds. He had to hide himself, and now only by night can he appear openly. One is our Master, even Christ. Serve Him! — *Sunday School Times.*

* * *

Only Tattooed?

A man met with a severe accident and was taken to the hospital. When the doctor was examining his injuries, he noticed that the name of Jesus was beautifully tattooed across the man's breast. A nurse, standing by, said, "I wonder if it is deeper than the skin." Our religion, if it is to be fruitful, must be sincere — deeper than the skin; it must reach the heart.—*Christian Herald.*

* * *

The Cathode Ray

The General Electric Company uses every year more than one and a half million sapphires for bearings in meters and other delicate apparatus, and it becomes necessary to detect synthetic gems and separate them from the natural ones. For this purpose a cathode ray tube has been developed by a member of their research staff. If, in a dark room, the rays from this tube are thrown for a few seconds on a tray of stones, they all glow, and when the rays are turned off, the artificial sapphires continue to glow and may be picked out of the tray, while the natural sapphires cannot be seen. Diamonds, under these rays, turn brown if they are artificial, but remain unchanged if natural. So let every one of us be certain that whatever is unreal in his life and character will be disclosed by the analysis of Heaven.—*Christian Herald.*

Rusting at Anchor

A man while touring near Alexandria noticed two Turkish warships lying at anchor, and proceeded to take a picture of them. The captain of the vessel on which the tourist was traveling noticed his interest in the warships and said to him with a smile, "Yes, they look formidable enough, but they are perfectly harmless. They were anchored there eight years ago, and haven't turned a wheel since." Christians sometimes sing that glorious old hymn, "I've Anchored in Jesus." Is it not possible to be safe and yet never turn a wheel for Him?—*Sunday School Times.*

* * *

As Good as Others Think You Are

It is related of Saint Francis of Assisi that he one day met a peasant who asked him, "Art thou Francis?" And Francis acknowledged his name, it may have been with something of pride; for it was a name far-famed for piety and good deeds. But the peasant uttered this warning:

"Take heed that thou be as good as men believe thee."

It was a startling admonition, and might have seemed superfluous, for Francis was a saint, and he who warned him a peasant. But Francis was good enough and sensible enough to know that a wise word had been spoken, and he took the warning to his heart.

It would be well for every man reputed to be good if someone should thus admonish him. He to whom men look up has great need of humility. For if he fall, many will be caused to stumble by his fall.—*The Youth's Evangelist.*

* * *

Strange Fire

A Los Angeles Jewish newspaper says: At a district meeting of Sisterhoods recently held, one of the speakers, a rabbi's wife, rose to "do her stuff." While on her feet, and before launching forth on her message, she took a long puff of the cigarette between her lips, inhaled the smoke, blew it through her nose, dipped the burning end of the delicate and dainty weed in what of coffee remained in the demi-tasse, and lifting her eyes and voice on high, said: "The first and most important duty of a Sisterhood is to deepen the religious life of the congregation. The Sisterhood must be chiefly concerned with the spiritual side of the congregation's life." Sisterhoods, spirituality, and cigarettes are a strange combination. I can't imagine Sarah, Rebecca, Rachel, Leah, Hannah, Deborah, smoking cigarettes *le shame shoma yim* ("to the glory of God"). Cigarattes and spirituality suggest to me the sons of Aaron bringing strange fire to the altar of God.—*Israel's Advocate.*

* * *

Highest and Lowest

Ananias wished to have the credit of a complete sacrifice, and yet kept back part of it for himself — "professing cream and practicing skim milk," as someone has said. The *Register and Leader* of Des Moines contains this item: "Wu Ting Fang, when he came to leave America, observed in his shrewd Chinese way that Americans profess higher ideals and fall farther short of realizing them than any other people in the world."—Selected.

* * *

Bats and Swallows

A traveler in Borneo tells of finding there a great cave which was occupied in the day-time by the bats, and at night by the swallows. As he watched the mouth of the cave about sunset, the first column of bats appeared, and wheeled away down the valley in a long coil, winding over the treetops in a wonderfully close and regular order. These were followed in less than a minute's time by another column, and in forty minutes, forty-seven distinct columns were counted, each about six hundred feet long by ten feet thick. It was estimated that over half a million bats flew out of the cave in less than three-quarters of an hour. As the last bats flew away, the swallows appeared in enormous numbers and for a long time there was a ceaseless whirr of wings. Soon after dawn the next morning, the bats returned, and literally rained into the cave, while the swallows passed out in a counter current. Some people try to live a double life like that. To the outer world, they try to make it appear that they are as innocent as swallows, while underneath the bats hold revel.—Louis Albert Banks.

INFLUENCE (See also: Christian Example)

President Wilson's Tribute

President Woodrow Wilson told this story:

"I was in a very plebeian place. I was in a barber shop, sitting in a chair, when I became aware that a personality had entered the room. A man had come quietly in upon the same errand as myself, and sat in the chair next to me. Every word he uttered, though it was not in the least didactic, showed a personal interest in the man who was serving him; and before I got through with what was being done for me, I was aware that I had attended an evangelistic service, because Mr. Moody was in the next chair. I purposely lingered in the room after he had left and noted the singular effect his visit had upon the barbers in that shop. They talked in undertones. They did not know his name, but they knew that something had elevated their thoughts. And I felt that I left that place as I should have left a place of worship."

Asked to verify the truth of that incident, President Wilson did so, and added:

"My admiration and esteem for Mr. Moody were very deep indeed."—*Sunday School Times.*

* * *

Niemoller and the Atheist

Here is an interesting item about the conscientious German pastor who would not bow to Hitler, and for that reason was confined in a concentration camp.

"It is reported that the concentration camp commander at Sachenhausen, where Martin Niemoller is being held, is determined to make an atheist of his famous prisoner, and to this end placed a communist atheist in the cell next to him, with permission for them to talk. He also arranged for these two men to take their daily half hour walk at the same time and in the same yard. The atheist was a very intellectual person, skilled in argument. He had been promised all sorts of 'favors' if he could make Niemoller lose his faith. Each prisoner enjoyed presenting his own viewpoint. This lasted four days. On the fifth day, the atheist begged Niemoller to lend him his Bible, a Book that now assumed a new meaning to him. The very same day the atheist was moved to another cell." — *The News Chronicle.*

* * *

You Tell on Yourself

You tell on yourself by the friends you seek,
By the very manner in which you speak,
By the way you employ your leisure time,
By the use you make of dollar and dime.

You tell what you are by the things you wear,
By the spirit in which your burdens bear,
By the kind of things at which you laugh,
By the records you play on the phonograph.

You tell what you are by the way you walk,
By the things of which you delight to talk,
By the manner in which you bear defeat,
By so simple a thing as how you eat.

By the books you choose from the well-filled shelf:
In these ways and more, you tell on yourself;
So there's really no particle of sense
In an effort to keep up false pretense.
—*The Lighted Pathway.*

* * *

Life More Than Words

A man's life is always more forcible than his speech; when men take stock of him they reckon his deeds as pounds and his words as pence. If his life and his doctrine disagree the mass of lookers-on accept his practice and reject his preaching.—C. H. Spurgeon, in the *Keswick Calendar.*

* * *

Influence Is the Effluence of Affluence

There came over the air a few nights ago a radio voice telling the story of a young woman who went to the superintendent of her Sunday School and said: "I can't do a thing with my class of boys. I don't seem to have a bit of influence over them." And what could a mere man do in face of a determined young woman? He let her resign. Later one of her boys was in a group where the discussion turned upon the credibility of the story of Jonah and the big fish. With challenge burning in his speech he said: "I'll bet if you heard my Sunday School teacher tell it, you would have believed!" Someone who was present caught fire from that declaration and told the young woman. She called up her superintendent and said: "I want my class of boys back; I did not know until now what influence I have over them." And what could a mere man do in face of a determined young woman? She got her class back! *Influence is the effluence of affluence — the outflow of the wealth of a convinced personality intensely in earnest.*—John R. Riebe.

The Light of the World

A high-caste Hindu in Jamaica watched a lady misisonary living on the opposite side of the road for twelve months, unknown to her. At the end of the year he became a Christian, and is now an elder in the Friends' Meeting of his town, for, as he said, if Christianity can make anyone live as that lady lives it must be the true religion. One slip or one word amiss, he added, would have left him a Hindu. The terrible thing is that if our light be hid, it is hid *"in them that are perishing."*—W. P. Clark.

* * *

A Servant Like His Master

That is a beautiful testimony which a Glasgow blacksmith gave concerning the saintly Dr. Norman McLeod: "He never came into my shop without talking to me as if he had been a blacksmith all his life; but he never went away without leaving Christ in my heart."—*United Presbyterian.*

* * *

An Obstacle Removed

The story is told of a well-known Welsh preacher who went to deliver the address at the funeral of a pious and venerable village minister in South Wales. Hundreds of miners assembled in silence around the grave, and these were the first words that fell upon their ears: "My brethren, the greatest obstacle on your road to hell has been removed."—*Sunday School Times.*

* * *

How an Indian Saw Christ

A Navajo Indian woman who had been healed of a terrible ailment by a missionary doctor, was so impressed by the love he manifested that she said, "If Jesus is anything like the doctor, I can trust Him forever." There is no danger of loving too much, for Christ has set the limit. — "As I have loved you."—*Sunday School Chronicle.*

To Be Near

There is a story of a young artist in the studio of a great painter at Rome many years ago. He had much talent, and his friends urged him to establish an independent studio of his own, and predicted for him wealth, success and fame. But he said: "No, I have found my master. I want to paint like Raphael, and to do that I must be near him so that I may study his method and catch his spirit and listen to his instructions. I have no other ambition than to be like him."

This is the Christian ideal also, to be near Christ that we may be like Him, finding greatness in service with Him who came not to be ministered unto but to minister.—*Homiletic Review.*

* * *

The Gospel of the Face

It is said of Fenelon that his communion with God was such that his face shone. Lord Peterborough, a skeptic, was once compelled to spend a night with him at an inn. In the morning he hurried away saying, "If I spend another night with that man, I shall be a Christian in spite of myself."

Fenelon's manner, voice, and face reflected so perfectly the glory of Christ that he was irresistibly attractive to even the worldliest men and women.—*Earnest Worker.*

* * *

The Light Carries Far

Lady Hasie tells how she came one night to a Chinese village without a decent inn, and how her muleteer went out to find a house for her. Christian homes are always cleaner than others, and Christians always willing to help. Then a village elder came, "I understand you are asking for a Christian in this village. We have none. I am very sorry." "Where does the nearest Christian live?" 'The nearest Christian lives five days' journey from here." My father said when I told him this story, "Yes, and they knew *where* he was." Five days' journey and his light shone. How far this little light throws its beams!—*Sunday School Times.*

* * *

Deteriorating Influences

Munkacsy, the great Hungarian painter, had a mania for using bitumen in his paints, a thing that other artists use with caution. It accounts for the richness of his dark tones. But his old age saw with sorrow the sad effects of the excessive use of bitumen in his mixture. It now appears that his great picture, Milton Dictating Paradise Lost, hanging in the Public Library in New York City, is gradually to fade into obscurity.

Men who are lacking in moral vision often learn too late the sad influences of inferior ingredients in character.—William Chalmers Covert, in *Westminster Teacher.*

* * *

Connected lives

An interesting study would be that of connected lives. Pick up a few links from a certain chain. Dr. Chambers attributed the prompting of his grand career to William Wilberforce! Wilberforce confessed his similar indebtedness to Philip Doddridge; Doddridge was the reverent disciple of Richard Baxter; Baxter of Dr. Bunney. Or this: Adoniram Judson credited Claudius Buchanan with being his missionary prompter; Buchanan thanked the Lord for the influence upon him of John Newton; and Newton was converted by the thought of "mother's God."—James M. Ludlow.

* * *

I would be true, for there are those who trust me;
I would be pure, for there are those who care;
I would be strong, for there is much to suffer;
I would be brave, for there is much to dare.
I would be friend of all — the foe, the friendless;
I would be giving, and forget the gift;

I would be humble, for I know my weakness;
I would look up, and laugh, and love, and lift. Amen.

—Howard A. Walter.

* * *

A Holy Countenance

Mr. R. M. McCheyne was one of those saints, in the last century, whose face was sometimes lit up with such a hallowed expression that *souls were saved,* so attracted were they to the indescribable beauty of holiness manifested on his countenance.—*Gospel Herald.*

* * *

Bible Faces

Mr. George Goodman tells of an old woman who, while riding in a tramcar one day, got into conversation with a gentleman passenger. After some minutes she asked him:

"Sir, are you a Minister of Religion?"

"No," was the reply, "but why do you ask?"

"Because, sir, you have a Bible face." —*Happy Greetings,* 1941.

* * *

Christ Himself Had Been There

Thomas Cook, the great English evangelist, was about to conduct a mission in a certain town. Great preparations were being made in the home where he was to be the honored guest. One of the maids of this home came into the butcher's shop to make a purchase. The clerk noticing she was a bit put out, asked the reason. "Oh, you would think that the Lord Jesus Christ Himself was coming to stay with us there is such a fuss being made." Mr. Cook came stayed, and went. A day or two after he had gone she found herself once more in the same shop. Looking at the clerk she said, "You remember I told you about the fuss being made and that you might think the Lord Jesus Christ was coming to our house." "I do," said the salesman. "Well," said the girl, "He's been."—*The Threshold.*

Why They Wanted to Touch Stevens

A ship was going into action in the Jutland battle. Aboard that ship worked one, Stevens by name, a real true Christian, whom all loved and revered for himself alone. Now it happened, that to get to his appointed place, each man had to pass the spot where Stevens stood, and, as they realized this, the men passed the word softly down from one to another, "Touch Stevens, touch Stevens." And so with ready response every man and every lad as he passed along touched the man whom they felt and knew to be in touch with God and Christ and things eternal. How much Stevens counted in that time of need because his life rang true!—*United Methodist.*

* * *

Minus People and Plus People

An English essayist once divided the human race into two classes — "minus people" and "plus people." "The minus people," he said, "are those who leave us poorer, and the plus those who leave us richer." The one group is characterized by selfishness and fault-finding and other traits that detract from human happiness; the other group by generosity and appreciation and love. In such a classification there can be but one choice for the Christian who would follow his Master's example. *We can give no more effective witness for Him than to live in such a way that others shall be richer in spirit because their lives have been touched by ours.—Christian Observer.*

* * *

Unknown Influence

A story is told of a young woman who was a great lover of flowers. She set out a rare vine at the base of a stone wall. It grew vigorously but did not blossom. Day after day she cultivated and watered it and tried in every way to coax it to bloom. One morning as, disappointed, she stood before the plant, her invalid neighbor, whose lot adjoined her own, called to her and said;

"You cannot imagine how I have been enjoying the blooms on that vine you planted."

The owner looked on the other side of the wall and there was a mass of bloom. The vine had crept through the crevices and bloomed on the other side. Poor girl! She thought that her plant was a failure when all the time it was proving a blessing to one who sorely needed it. The invalid was enriched and blessed in every way because of the faithful efforts of that girl in cultivating a single vine, even though she could not see results.

How important it is, then, that we seek to create the right kind of influence. The way we live, worship, act and play, may count for more than we think. A mother whose sons all became sailors, attributed their decision to a picture of a great sailing vessel which hung over the fireplace where they spent their childhood.—*The Pentecostal Testimony.*

* * *

Babe Ruth's Tribute

The following testimony to the useful life of an old minister was given by "Babe" Ruth, the famous baseball player: "Most of the people who have really counted in my life were not famous. Nobody ever heard of them, except those who knew and loved them. I knew an old minister once. His hair was white, his face shone. I have written my name on thousands and thousands of baseballs in my life. The old minister wrote his name on just a few simple hearts. How I envy him! He was not trying to please his own immortal soul. So fame never came to him. I am listed as a famous home-runner, yet beside that obscure minister, who was so good and so wise, I never got to first base."—*Sunday School Times.*

* * *

A Walking Sermon

St. Francis of Assisi once said to a brother monk, "Let us go to town and preach." They went to town. They walked out one street, walked back another street, and returned. Then the brother said to St. Francis, "I thought you said we were going to town to preach." Said St. Francis, "We were preaching. As we walked along the street people saw us, noted our demeanor, thought of our lives. Some impulse from our souls touched them. We were preaching all the way." It was a wise answer. Christian people cannot guard too well the sermons that they preach as they go about town. These are the only sermons that many people hear.—*Gospel Herald.*

* * *

She Magnified Jesus

On a recent Sunday, Henry Burnett, of Macon, Georgia, was a guest in the home of a friend whose little girl had just come in from her first Sunday School lesson. On seeing the enthusiasm of the child for the Sunday School Mr. Burnett asked, "What did you do at Sunday School this morning?" "We sang a song," she said, "in a big room and then we went into a small room where a lady talked." "Who was she?" asked Mr. Burnett. "I don't know her name," she said, "but she must be the mother of Jesus, for she talked about Him all the time." A little child leads us here. The teacher's name meant little or nothing to the little girl, but what she said about Jesus so impressed her that she saw a close kinship between the teacher and Jesus.—*Christian Index.*

* * *

Influence of a Christlike Life

After finding David Livingstone at Ujiji, Central Africa, and spending four months with him there, Henry M. Stanley said: "I went to Africa as prejudiced as the biggest atheist in London. But there came a long time for reflection. I saw this solitary old man there and asked myself, 'How on earth does he stay here? What is it that inspires him?' For months after we met I found myself wondering at the old man carrying out all that was said in the Bible—'Leave all things and follow Me.' But little by little my sympathy was aroused; *seeing* his piety, his gentleness, his zeal, his earnestness, and how he went about his business, I was converted by him, although he had not tried to do it."—J. R. R.

* * *

Pervasive

Once in the Bureau of Standards in Washington, a tiny tube containing less than two-thousandths of an ounce of radium was accidentally dropped on a hardwood floor and broken. With a camel's hair brush they swept up the radium. Then they washed the floor to get the rest of it. But enough remained to render another washing necessary, this time with acidulated water, and still another with soda water, and a fourth time with hydrant water. Each washing yielded about four hundred dollars worth of radium. Finally a carpenter came and scraped the floor. Three years later the shavings were burned, and the ashes found to be strong in radium. It is almost impossible to get rid of human influence for good or bad exerted.—*Forward.*

* * *

The Gospel They Could Read

Some years ago a young American student named Wray was accepted as a foreign missionary. He was thoroughly good, but of small intellectual capacities, and found it more than difficult to master the language. The native people found it impossible to understand him when he spoke to them. But though they could not understand his talk, they could his walk. One day when, according to their custom, they were seated on the ground around one of their teachers, the question was asked, "What is it to be a Christian?" Not one of them could answer, but finally one of them pointed to where the young missionary was seated, and replied, "It is to live as Mr. Wray lives!" They could not read the Gospel according to Matthew or Mark or Luke or John, but they could read the Gospel according to Wray.—*Methodist Recorder.*

* * *

World Knows Us

Our lives must be incarnations of the Gospel, epistles of life and truth and love. The highest evidence of Christianity, and its strongest recommendation to the world, are lives that are unmistakably Christlike. A serious condemnation of Christian living was expressed by a Buddhist, who was in search of truth and light, when he said, "I want to believe in Christ, but I have never seen Him in those who profess to follow Him." Dr. J. Stuart Holden once expressed his opinion that "the reason why the world does not know God is because it knows us so well."—Selected.

* * *

You are writing a gospel, a chapter each day,
By deeds that you do, by words that you say,
Men read what you write, whether faithless or true,
Say, what is the gospel according to you? —Selected.

* * *

Andrew Murray's Own Family

Andrew Murray evidently lived a holy life before his children. Eleven of his children grew to adult life. Five of the six sons became ministers of the Gospel, and four of the daughters became minister's wives. Even the second generation made a good showing! Ten grandsons became ministers and thirteen became missionaries! That gave evidence of an unusual prayer power and devotion of life to the Lord, on the part of Andrew Murray.—*Christian Victory.*

JEALOUSY

Overcoming Jealousy

Have you gained the victory over the foes within you? There is jealousy. Would you overcome that? If you are jealous of anyone, do him some good turn. There is a fable of an eagle that was jealous of another that could outfly him. He saw a sportsman one day, and said to him, "I wish you would bring down that eagle." The sportsman replied that he would if he only had some feathers to put into his arrow. So the eagle pulled one out of his wing. The arrow was shot, but didn't quite reach the rival eagle; it was flying too high. The envious eagle kept pulling out more feathers until he lost so many that he couldn't fly, and then the sportsman turned around and killed him. My friend, *if you are jealous, the only man you can hurt is yourself.*—D. L. Moody.

JESUS

A Plain Question

Many years ago when Lord Tennyson was Poet Laureate, he was walking one day with a friend in his garden talking on subjects of public interest of that time. The poet's friend was a believer in the Lord Jesus, and sought as opportunities offered to testify for Him. Pausing for a moment in their conversation, he took the poet by the arm and quietly asked, "What do you think of Jesus Christ?" Tennyson pointed to a flower blooming in all its beauty by the pathway and said, "As the sun is to that flower, so Jesus Christ is to me."—*Gospel Herald.*

* * *

A Description of Christ

During the public ministry of Jesus Christ upon the earth, the following description of His person was sent by Publius Lentulus, President of Judæa, to the Senate of Rome. It is from an ancient manuscript:

"There lives a man of singular character, whose name is Jesus Christ, in Judæa. The barbarians esteem Him as a prophet, but His own followers adore Him as the immediate offspring of the immortal God. He is endowed with such unparalleled virtue as to call the dead from their graves, and to heal every kind of disease with a word or touch. This Person is tall and elegantly shaped; His aspect is amiable and reverent; His hair flows into those beautiful shades which no united color can match, falling into graceful curves below His ears, agreeably couching upon His shoulders, and parting on His head like the head of a Nazarite. His forehead is smooth and large; His cheeks without either spot, save that of a lovely red; His nose is smooth and formed with exquisite symmetry; His beard is thick and of a color suitable to the hair of His head, reaching a little below the chin, and parted in the middle like a fork. He rebukes with majesty, commands with mildness, and invites with the most tender and persuasive language; His whole address, in deed or word being elegantly graceful and characteristic of so exalted a being. No man has ever seen Him laugh, but many have seen Him weep, and so persuasive are His tears that the multitude cannot withhold theirs from joining in sympathy with His. He is very temperate, modest and wise, and in short, whatever this phenomenon may turn out in the end, He seems at present from His excellent bearing and Divine perfection, in every way surpassing the children of men."—*The Sword and the Trowel.*

* * *

How He Shared Our Infirmities

He who is the Bread of Life began His ministry hungering. He who is the Water of Life ended His ministry thirsting. Christ hungered as man, and fed the hungry as God. He was weary, and yet He is our rest. He paid tribute, and yet He is the King. He was called a devil, and cast out devils. . . . He prayed, and yet He hears prayer. He wept, and He dries our tears. He was sold for thirty pieces of silver, and redeems the world. He was led as a lamb to the slaughter, and is the Good Shepherd. He died, and gave His life, and by dying destroys death.—*The Christian.*

* * *

What Jesus Is to These

To the artist He is the One Altogether Lovely.

To the architect He is the Chief Corner Stone.

To the baker He is the Living Bread.

To the banker He is the Hidden Treasure.

To the biologist He is the Life.

To the builder He is the Sure Foundation.

To the doctor He is the Great Physician.

To the educator He is the Great Teacher.

To the farmer He is the Lord of the Harvest.

To the florist He is the Rose of Sharon and the Lily of the Valley.

To the geologist He is the Rock of Ages.

To the jurist He is the Righteous Judge, the Judge of all men.

To the jeweler He is the Pearl of Great Price.

To the lawyer He is the Counselor, the Lawgiver, the Advocate.

To the horticulturist He is the True Vine.

To the newspaper man He is the Good Tidings of Great Joy.

To the oculist He is the Light of the World.

To the philanthropist He is the unspeakable Gift.

To the philosopher He is the Wisdom of God.

To the preacher He is the Word of God.

To the sculptor He is the Living Stone.

To the servant He is the Good Master.

To the statesman He is the Desire of All Nations.

To the student He is the Incarnate Truth.

To the theologian He is the Author and Finisher of Our Faith.

To the traveler He is the New and Living Way.

To the toiler He is the Giver of Rest.

To the sinner He is the Lamb of God that taketh away the sin of the world.

To the Christian He is the Son of the Living God, the Saviour, the Redeemer and Lord.—Selected.

* * *

"What Manner of Man?"

When the first missionaries went to Japan, a young Japanese who wanted to learn English was given the Gospel of John to translate into his native tongue. In a short time he became very restless and agitated. At last he burst out with the question, "Who is this Man about whom I have been reading, this Jesus? You call him a man, but He must be God."—*Arnold's Commentary.*

* * *

The Name That Comforts

About forty years ago a Mrs. L— was visiting a place in New Zealand called Kuripapanga. One day a cart drove up to the door of the accomodation house, being driven by a Maori woman who was taking an invalid son to the hospital some forty miles away. She had not gone far before she turned and drove quickly back to the house. The people found that her son had died and the woman was so overcome with grief that they could not prevail upon her to leave the body. Mrs. L— came in from a walk soon after and was told about the woman. She went up into the cart and almost at once the woman came down and went into the house and sat talking quietly for some time, and then got up and getting up into her cart took up the reins and drove off with her eyes dried and her face calm and restful. When asked how it was that she had been able to get the woman to come away from her son, Mrs. L— said that she had asked her, "Do you know Jesus?" The woman looked into her face and smiled and at once came away. It was the power of the Name comforting the woman's soul. And she came away to talk about that name and its sweetness. "In the name of Jesus."—*Sunday School Times.*

* * *

What Christ Is to the World

1. The world's Creator (John 1:1-3).
2. The world's Example (Matt. 16:24).
3. The world's Teacher (Matt. 7:28, 29).
4. The world's Master (John 13:13).
5. The world's Saviour (Luke 19:10).
6. The world's Lord (Rom. 10:12).
7. The world's King (Rev. 11:15).
8. The world's Light (John 8:12).
9. The world's Life (John 14).
100. The world's Love (John 3:16).

—Selected.

* * *

The Divine and Human Nature of Jesus

In my earlier days—and yet I was old enough to be a lecturer in the Andover Theological Seminary—I wanted a new way of teaching my students the doctrine of Christ. I thought I would tell them to get a sheet of paper and divide it into three columns. In the first column they were to write every passage where Christ is spoken of as God-man; in the second column all the passages where Christ is spoken of as God alone; and in the third, all the passages where He is spoken of as man alone. I went to work. I think I have the paper now. It is badly balanced. The first column and the secind column filled right up, but as to the third column, *I never found a passage speaking of Christ as man alone.* Do you remember any such passage?—Alexander McKenzie.

* * *

Why She Claimed Christ

A good old Swedish woman took her pastor severely to task one morning because he had declared in his sermon that Jesus was a Jew and spoke Aramaic. She said he was wrong, that Jesus was a Swede and spoke Swedish! The pastor condescendingly said, "My dear sister, you may have some difficulty proving that." "None at all; I have the proof right here," said the woman as she produced her Swedish Bible and showed him that the words of Jesus were all in Swedish! How glad I am that she thought Jesus was a member of her race, and that I think of Him as a member of my race! It is a compliment to the Son of God.—Dr. William Ward Ayer, in *Moody Monthly.*

* * *

Trial of Jesus—From a Lawyer's Standpoint

No other literature bears the historic scrutiny as well as the New Testament biographies. If the Gospel historians be not worthy of belief we are without rational faith in secular annals of the human race.

All the forms of law were outraged and trampled under foot in the proceedings, errors so monstrous and proceedings so flagrant, many have doubted the existence of a trial. The arrest was illegal—his private examination illegal—before Annas or Caiaphas—his indictment illegal, in form, proceedings of the Sanhedrin against him illegal—because conducted at night before offering of sacrifice and on a day preceding Jewish Sabbath, trial illegal because within one day, the execution of condemnation illegal because founded on uncorroborated confession of Himself.—*The Lamp.*

* * *

Leonardo da Vinci took a friend to criticize his masterpiece of the "Last Supper," and the remark of the friend was, "The most striking thing in the picture is the cup!" The artist took his brush and wiped out the cup, as he said, "Nothing in my painting shall attract more attention than the face of my Master!"—Selected.

The Changeless Rock

There is an old saying of Samuel Rutherford's, "Believe God's love and power more than you believe your own feelings and experiences. Your Rock is Christ, and it is not the *Rock* which ebbs and flows, but your *sea*."—*The Dawn.*

* * *

Hopelessly Handicapped?

Some years ago the late Mr. Gokhals, in conversation with Dr. Hume, after speaking of Christ with the deepest reverence, remarked: "But the Lord Jesus Christ is hopelessly handicapped by His connection with the West." To which Dr. Hume replied, "For nineteen centuries the Lord Jesus Christ has been handicapeed by His connection with His followers; but *hopelessly*, never!"—*Sunday School Times.*

* * *

Resident

Near the royal residence at Osborne, in the Isle of Wight, were some almshouses. While visiting an old lady in one of these, a gentleman asked her, "Does Queen Victoria ever visit you here?" "Oh, yes," was the answer, "Her Majesty comes to see me." "And does the King of kings visit you here?" asked the visitor. "No, sir," said the old lady. "He doesn't visit, He lives here."—*Christian Herald.*

* * *

All Blessings in Christ

Every blessing you need is treasured up in Christ. Young or old, rich or poor, may now obtain the blessings of forgiveness, justification, and eternal life "without money and without price," without groans and sighs, "good works," or religious observances. — Alexander Marshall.

* * *

Without Beginning or End

One day a six-year-old lad came to his mother with this question: "Mother, who made God?" Instantly the mother's face expressed astonishment and chagrin. Presently she said curtly, "What an awful question to ask. You had better run along and play." In that same country community another lad approached his mother, and asked, "Did God make Himself?" His mother presently left her work and breathed a silent prayer. Taking off her wedding ring, she gave it to her son and asked, "Where does this ring begin and where does it end?" Before long the boy answered, "There is no starting place and stopping place to a ring." The mother remarked, "Just so is God. There is no beginning and no end to God. He always has been and always will be."—*Gospel Herald.*

* * *

She Saw Only Mozart's Physique

The young lady to whom Mozart was first engaged to be married became discontented with her choice when she saw more of the world, and gave up the composer. She thought him too small in stature. When the world had begun to recognize his greatness, she explained her refusal of him by saying: "I knew nothing of the greatness of his genius. I saw only a little man." Isaiah speaks of the rejection of Christ by the world in much the same way. These are his words: "He hath no form nor comeliness; and when we shall see him, there is no beauty that we should desire him. He is despised and rejected of men." But oh! how disappointed will those same men be, when they shall see him in His beauty!—*The Expositor.*

* * *

A Rabbi Silenced

A Jewish soldier had been attending services where he heard much of the character and teaching of the Lord Jesus Christ. He went to his Rabbi and said, "Rabbi, the Christians say that the Christ has already come, while we claim He is yet to come." "Yes," assented the Rabbi. "Well," asked the young soldier, "When our Christ comes, *what will he have on Jesus Christ?*" What could the Rabbi say?—Selected.

Who It Was They "Pierced"

Dr. A. J. Gordon relates the comments of the Hebrew Christian scholar, Rabinowitz, on the first and last letters of the Hebrew alphabet. "Do you know what questioning and controversies the Jews have kept up over Zechariah 12:10, 'They shall look upon me whom they have pierced'? They will not admit that it is Jehovah whom they have pierced. Hence the dispute about the 'whom.' But this word 'whom' is in the original simply the first and last letters of the Hebrew alphabet, *aleph* and *tav.* Do you wonder that I was filled with awe and astonishment when I opened to Revelation 1:7, 8, and there read, 'Behold, he cometh with clouds; and every eye shall see him, and they also which pierced him'; and then read on and heard the glorified Lord saying, 'I am Alpha and Omega.' The Lord Jesus seemed to say to me, 'Do you doubt who it is "whom" you pierced? I am the Aleph and Tav of Zechariah 12:10, the Alpha and Omega, Jehovah the Almighty.'" The One who was "pierced" is in both passages Alpha and Omega or Aleph and Tav.—Courtesy *Moody Monthly.*

* * *

The Shamrock Heckler

A street preacher in London was preaching to a crowd that had gathered around him. It was at the time of the Shamrock races, and everyone was talking of the event. A ruffian on the edge of the crowd thought he would have a little fun, so he called in, "Mr. Preacher! What do you know about the Shamrock?" The preacher never paused, but went right on. A second time the disturber called in, "I say, Mr. Preacher, what do you know about the Shamrock?" Still the preacher paid no heed, but preached right on. Finally the third time, not to be silenced, the ruffian called again, "Mr. Preacher! I'm asking you what you know about the Shamrock!" This time the preacher paused. The crowd became very still. Pointing upward with one hand, he said, so clearly and distinctly that every one could hear him, "On Christ, the solid Rock, I stand; all other rocks are — sham rocks!"—*Young People's Delight.*

* * *

Text and Sermon

In the World War a chaplain was ready to preach to a regiment just back from the front trenches. As they drew up in the field under the open sky which was the church for that day, rain began to fall on the weary men. The chaplain stepped forward to preach. "My text," he began, "is: 'What think ye of Christ?'" He paused. "My sermon," he continued, "is: 'What think ye of Christ?' The parade is dismissed."—Henry and Tertius Van Dyke, in the *Syracuse Post-Standard.*

* * *

Channing Wasn't Sure

Many years ago at an assemblage of ministers, the late Drs. Mason and Channing were present. The latter was strongly suspected — rather more than suspected—of Unitarian tendencies, and some degree of confident challenging had already taken place. "Dr. C.," said Dr. M. to him, "may I ask how long you have been in the ministry?" "Eleven years," was the reply. "May I ask you once again, sir, what are your views of the Lord Jesus Christ?" There was a little hesitation and flush, and the reply, "I have pondered the subject deeply, but have not exactly made up my mind." Lifting up both hands in holy amazement, and with deep emotion, Dr. M. ejaculated: "What! eleven years a preacher of the Gospel, and not to know what to think of Jesus Christ!"—*Sunday School Times.*

* * *

Our Need of a Mediator

I remember vividly an experience with Mr. Moody, that brought rich blessing to me, and many others, when I was but a lad, 11 years old. Moody was visiting my father. He had left his satchel and umbrella at the home of the elder Mr. McCormick, and he asked me if I would walk over and get them for him. I was more than glad to go. On the way home, while carrying the satchel on the end of the umbrella (and I had the umbrella poised over my shoulder) I stumbled and broke the umbrella! I was greatly disturbed by the accident, and felt so guilty I knew not what to do. I was afraid. Finally I thought, "I will tell mother; she can tell father, and father can tell Mr. Moody." Crushed with the burden, I hurried home and told mother. She, of course, was sympathetic, and told father; and father broke the news to Mr. Moody. "So you broke my umbrella," said Mr. Moody (rather sternly, I thought); "come here a minute." Fearfully I went to him. He said, "When you broke my umbrella, you became frightened and ashamed, didn't you? Then you thought. if I tell mother or father, *they* can go between me and Mr. Moody and straighten things up. Now that your father has straightened things up, you can come to me. Now, my lad, that is the way it is with *all* of us; we are sinners—afraid of God. But God has provided a Mediator—Someone to go between us and Him—and it is Jesus. You must come to God through Jesus. He died for us, and is the Way to God. I am glad this happened; I am going to tell my audiences about this, and turn them to Christ, our Mediator!" And he did.—*Gospel Herald.*

* * *

Can We Believe in the Virgin Birth?

A Christian Jew and a non-Christian Jew were conversing about the Virgin Birth. "If I should tell you that a child had been born in this city without a father, would you believe it?" said the non-Christian. "Yes," replied the Christian, "if he should live as Jesus lived."—Anon.

* * *

A Chinese Christian Explains

A Chinese Christian was explaining to those around him that "Jesus is the invisible God, and God is the visible Jesus." This was a unique way of saying, "He that hath seen me hath seen the Father," and "I and the Father are one." God is unseeable, unhearable, unknowable, and untouchable, except in Christ. —*Sunday School Times.*

JEW

Count Zinzendorf

It is told of Count Zinzendorf that one morning he met a Jew, Rabbi Abraham. The pious Count stretched out his hand and said, "Gray hairs are a crown of glory. I can see from your head and the expression of your eyes that you have much experience both of heart and life. In the Name of the God of Abraham, Isaac, and Jacob, let us be friends."

The old man had never heard such words from a Christian before. He had usually been saluted by the words, "Be gone, Jew!" He was struck dumb with wonder. His lips trembled, his voice failed, tears ran down his wrinkled cheeks upon his flowing beard.

"Enough, father," said the Count, "we understand each other." And from that moment on the two were friends. The count went to see him in his dirty home and ate black bread at his table. One morning before dawn, as the two walked out, old Abraham said, "My heart is longing for the dawn. I am sick, and yet I know not what is the matter with me. I am looking for something and yet I know not what I seek. I am like one who is chased, yet I see no enemy except the one within me, my old evil heart." And then Count Zinzendorf opened his lips and declared the Gospel of Christ. He painted a picture of love on the Cross, and how that love came down from Heaven. He painted in glowing colors how Christ met and died for corrupted humanity, that men might become like God.

As the old man wept and wrung his hands, the two were ascending a hill where stood a lonely church. As the sun rose, and its rays fell on the golden cross on the church spire, the cross glittered brightly in the light of Heaven.

"See there, Abraham," said Zinzendorf, "a sign from Heaven for you! Believe on Him whose blood was shed by your fathers, that God's purpose of mercy might be fulfilled, that you might be free from all sin and find in Him all your salvation."

"So be it," said old Abraham, as a new light flashed on his soul.

O God, give us Zinzendorfs today—men who will love the Jews and love them into the Christian faith!—*The Women's Missionary Magazine.*

* * *

Proof of Faith

Frederick the Great once asked a clergyman for a proof of his faith and the forthcoming reply was well placed and well spoken, "The Jew, Your Majesty." The Jew is the great monument to the truth of God's Word.—*Gospel Herald.*

* * *

Awakenings Among the Jews

Are the Jews really showing increased interest in the Gospel? Their acute suffering in the last few years has forced them to realize their own helplessness and the uncertainty of worldly possessions, and many are turning with more sympathy toward Jesus of Nazareth and the New Testament. George T. B. Davis, who is conducting a campaign to supply Testaments to Jews in America, Europe, and Palestine, writes of his work among Jews in Florida: "Mrs. Davis and I have been giving Palestine lectures in Florida. In one city the rabbi invited me to show the pictures of Palestine in the synagogue, and he was the first to request a copy of the Prophecy New Testament. In Miami Beach, which teems with Jewish people during the winter season, we gave three lectures on Palestine. About 900 Jews attended the meeting and, to our amazement and delight, some 500 Jews—over fifty per cent of those present—requested copies of the once-despised New Testament. Reports from abroad indicate the same unprecedented interest in the Word of God and the Gospel. In Shanghai six Jewish refugees accepted Christ at one service. In the Argentine crowds of Jews listen to the Gospel, and not a few are openly confessing their faith in Jesus as their Saviour and Messiah." This is encouraging news. Like a ray of light in an angry sky at dawn, it may be one more herald of the rising of the Sun of Righteousness. At least, as Mr. Davis himself often says, we can "thank God and take courage."—*Sunday School Times.*

* * *

A People Who Have Lost God

Wrote Rabbi Freehof, in *American Hebrew*: "Today, throughout the world, many noble thinkers, philosophers, psychologists, and scientists are groping their way through darkness toward some vision of the infinite Presence. Who shall perform this function of guiding the perplexed in modern Jewish life? Who shall rediscover our lost God?"

Centuries ago Jehovah said "I will go and return to My place, till they acknowledge their offence, and seek My face." Nineteen hundred years ago Jesus came to be the Light of the world. Israel rejected Him, and how shall they see God except in His face?—*Pentecostal Evangel.*

* * *

The Jew and the Word

Mr. Reichart, a missionary to the Jews in Cairo, undertook to be the depository of the Bible Society. In his depot one day he had a visit from a small party of Arabian Jews. They had heard somehow of the shop in Cairo and they came for Hebrew Old Testaments. Mr. Reichart very gladly supplied them, but before he fastened down the box, with earnest prayer and without a word to man, he put in a Hebrew New Testament, hidden with the old. They went away, like Joseph's brethren, and then in a year or two there came the same or like men back again, and they brought a letter. This letter declared how highly they valued the beautiful copies of the Law, Prophets, and Psalms, and also how surprised they were to find another book in holy tongue, about which they had never known. The Person of whom it spoke had never crossed their knowledge before, and as they read of Him in the holy words of the book, enclosed with their Scriptures, with one mind they had come to the conclusion that He was Israel's Messiah.—*New Century Leader.*

* * *

Lord Rothschild's Unfinished House

Some years ago a writer said: "People who pass Lord Rothschild's mansion in Piccadilly often notice that the end of one of the cornices is unfinished. One is likely to ask, 'Could not the richest man in the world afford to pay for that cornice? Or is the lack simply due to carelessness?' The explanation is very simple, yet suggestive. Lord Rothschild is an orthodox Jew, and every pious Jew's house, tradition says, must have some part unfinished to bear testimony to the world that its occupant is only, like Abraham, a pilgrim and stranger on the earth. The incomplete cornice on the mansion seems to say to all who hurry by in the streets, bent on amassing worldly wealth, or going with the crowd in the paths of folly: 'This is not Lord Rothschild's home; he is traveling to eternity.' "—*Christian Herald* (London).

* * *

Disavowing the Jew

Pity the Jew hater! . . . One who has heart disease must not use digitalis, the medical use of which was discovered by the Jew, Ludwig Traube. If he has a toothache he will not use cocaine, or he will be benefiting by the work of a Jew, Carl Koller. Typhoid must not be treated, or he will have to benefit by the discoveries of the Jews, Widal and Weil. If he has diabetes he must not use insulin, because its invention was made possible by the research work of the Jew, Minkowsky. If he has a headache he must shun pyramidon and antipyrin (Spiro and Filehne). Anti-Semites who have convulsions must put up with them, for it was a Jew, Oscar Liebreich, who thought of chloralhydrate. . . . Anti-Semitic doctors must jettison all discoveries and improvements by the Nobel prizemen, Pulitzer, Barany, and Otto Warburg; the dermatologists, Jadassohn, Bruno Block, Unna; the neurologists Mendel, Oppenheim, Kronecker, Benedikt; the lung specialist Fraenkel, the surgeon Israel; and the anatomist Henle; and others."—*Sunday School Times.*

* * *

When Jews Are Persecuted

Pobjendonostow, a persecutor of the Jews in Russia, once asked a Jew what he thought would be the result of the persecutions if they continued. The answer was: "The result will be a feast." The Jew illustrated it from history. Pharaoh desired to destroy the Jews, but the result was the Passover. Haman desired to destroy the Jews, but the result was the Purim. Antiochus Epiphanes desired to destroy the Jews, but the result was the feast of the Dedication of the Temple. Shall the present trial of the Jews be a feast of reconciliation between Israel and their Eternal King Jesus, the Son of David, and the Son of God?—*Dansk Missionblad.*

* * *

Israel may be blind, but Israel still *believes.* And he who believes shall some day *see. Listen to* "The Cry of the Jew":

"There is no Face in pity bent
When by the way I fall,
No anxious, loving Shepherd comes
In answer to my call;
There are no tender eyes to seek,
No gentle arms to hold,
No nail-pierced hands to take me up
And bring me to the fold.

"And when on naked, bleeding feet
To Calvary I go,
And stagger, crush'd, beneath the cross,
There's none to heed or know;
There's none to lift the cruel weight,
There's none to even share—
O Thou who climbed the Hill before,
Look down and help me bear!"

—"A JEW."

A Changed Attitude

"What a wonderful change has come in the attitude of the Jew toward the Lord Jesus! One can hardly believe it when one remembers their former contempt and hatred," says Joseph Lewek in the *Alliance Weekly*. "And this has taken place within a very few years, gradually and almost imperceptibly. Now, instead of as formerly, when a Jew heard the name of Jesus he would spit and pronounce the curse, 'May His name and memory be blotted out,' he may be heard to speak of our Lord Jesus very respectfully. Jesus is admired of them; he is called by many of them 'the greatest teacher,' 'the greatest prophet' Israel ever had. Rabbis use His words as texts for their sermons, and the New Testament, formerly a forbidden book, is eagerly read by them. It is even used as a textbook in some of their seminaries and teachers' institutes."—*Gospel Herald.*

* * *

Nothing Jewish Wanted

"Nothing Jewish in my house!" These were the words of a wealthy gentleman who was entertaining a well-known clergyman. Said he, "I have such a hatred for the Jew that I will have nothing Jewish in my house."

The clergyman guest quietly arose and took a beautifully bound Bible from the table and a New Testament from the bookcase and placed them before the fireplace. He then proceeded to take down some paintings from the wall. He removed one picture of Paul preaching at Athens and another of the crucifixion.

The gentleman was greatly surprised and asked, "What are you doing? Why such liberties in my house?"

To this the clergyman replied, "You just said that you would not have anything Jewish in your house. I was beginning to help you to take away the many Jewish things you happen to have in this room. Shall I throw them into the fire?"

"Stop! Stop!" cried the gentleman. "May God forgive me. I have never thought of it in that light. Little did I know how greatly indebted I was to things Jewish."—*Jewish Missionary Intelligencer.*

* * *

A Rabbi Speaks

Recently, I saw a statement by Rabbi Wise which read, "For eighteen hundred years, certainly most of the time, Jews have not been given an opportunity to know what Christianity is, least of all to understand who Jesus was and what the Christ means. The very ignorance of the Jew, touching Jesus, condemns not the Jew but Christendom."—Courtesy *Moody Monthly.*

* * *

A Modern Jew's Prayer

Recently in one of the orthodox synagogues of Brooklyn during certain days of repentance and prayer, Jews were seen lying on their faces before God, crying to Him for protection upon their persecuted brethren, especially in Russia. One elderly Jew lifted up his hands toward heaven and in an agony of soul, cried out: "Oh that Thou wouldst rend the heavens and come down. . . . Lord," he said, "send Messiah, and should Jesus of the Gentiles be the one, grant us a sign that we may be sure that it is really so, and forgive our guilt toward Him."—*The Watchman Examiner* (Baptist).

* * *

Stick Out Your Tongue, Please

Leon Tucker tells of traveling on a train in the West and of speaking to a Jewish man about the homeland. The Jew went on to say that he was perfectly satisfied here in the United States. His home was here, his business was here, his family had been born here. He was not interested in Jerusalem. Tucker said to him: "Stretch out your right hand, will you, please?" The Jew stuck out his right hand and Tucker looked at it and then said: "Stick out your tongue, please."

The Jew said, "Are you trying to make a fool out of me?"

Tucker said: "No, but I would like to see your tongue." The Jew stuck out his tongue. Tucker looked at it, and quoted from Psalm 137:5, 6: "If I forget thee, O Jerusalem, let my right hand forget her cunning. If I do not remember thee, let my tongue cleave to the roof of my mouth; if I prefer not Jerusalem above my chief joy."

That Jew bowed his head and, with tears on his cheek, said: "My God, I was never so rebuked in my life."—*The Prophetic News and Israel's Watchman.*

* * *

Israel's "Annihilation"

I was looking at an inscription in the museum in Cairo, one of the most beautiful museums in the world. In it is a stone about ten or twelve feet high, and five to six feet wide, polished on both sides, with an inscription on one side made in the days of Rameses the Second. That carries us back about 1,400 years B.C., and on the stone in a very proud way, his victories are related. The inscription ends with these words, "Israel is annihilated: Israel will have no posterity." But that proud Pharaoh did not know Jehovah, and did not know the everlasting command of Jehovah that His people were to remain and be His witnesses throughout the ages; witnesses of His sovereignty and mercy.—*Jewish Era.*

* * *

A Rabbi's Opinion

Said Rabbi Gross, a Jewish teacher of Brooklyn, to his people: "I, Rabbi of Israel, think we should accept Jesus. I think we should teach Jesus to children much as we teach them about Abraham, Moses, Jeremiah and the rest of the great teachers and prophets. Jesus, as we all know, was a Jew. He preached divine love. He was a gift of love."—Selected.

* * *

An Arab Dislike

The *Courier* publishes an interesting comment from a Palestine missionary to the effect that the Arab dislikes to buy the Bible because it promises to give their land to the Jew, and they say the promise to Abraham still holds good. They are right concerning the promise, but their refusal to buy and read the Bible will not prevent the fulfillment of its prophecies.—*Prophecy.*

* * *

The Repository of Faith—Israel Survives

There is a bit of the old temple wall still left to the Jews in Jerusalem. Thither the grief-worn sons of sorrow have made pilgrimage week after week, year after year, generation after generation, thankful to "the Eternal" for even the privilege of bending their weary bodies toward the wall, washing the cold gray stones with their tears and kissing them with fervent lips. Over and over, they sob the prayer that their fathers before them have prayed:

"Have pity, O Eternal! upon Thy people and do not let Thine inheritance become a reproach or the nations hold sway over them. . . . Do not forsake us, O Eternal our God, be not far from us, for our lives are oppressed by reason of the sword and captivity, pestilence and plague. Oh, do Thou deliver us from all kinds of sorrow and grief, for in Thee we hope!"—*Gospel Herald.*

* * *

The Dead Sea

So fabulous as to be almost unbelievable is the value of the mineral salts in and about the Dead Sea, as that value is being estimated by chemists that are supposed to know. As soon as Jerusalem was captured in 1917 by General Allenby, a British geologist began to investigate the riches of the Dead Sea. Scientists have in hand a detailed report of the various minerals, and also the extent and the value of them. We are now informed that in that desolate spot there lies embedded from twelve hundred billions to thirteen hundred billions of dollars worth of recoverable salts. We are told that there is two hundred and sixty million dollars worth of bromine, so useful for medical purposes; of potash there is seventy billions of dollars worth; and of magnesium chloride eight hundred and twenty-five billions of dollars worth, and vast values of other minerals. We are told that the wealth that lies embossed on the earth at that point is worth more than all the known gold that has been dug from the bowels of all the earth. What these minerals may mean to the world, especially in that prophetic day when we are told that the deserts are to blossom as a rose, is indicated in the fact that they are already making the gardens in the neighborhood of the sea itself productive almost beyond the wildest dreams of men.

In a recent editorial in the Los Angeles *Times* we were assured that "gardens of workers on the banks (of the Dead Sea) grow beans two feet long and radishes as big as a policeman's shillalah —and oranges that weigh a pound." Little wonder that the most recent edition of the Encyclopedia Britannica assures us that "the future of this, the most interesting of all seas, will be watched with interest whilst modern enterprise takes a hesitating step towards the fulfillment of Ezekiel's prophetic vision."—*Sunday School Times.*

JOY

Cheerfulness

"Cheerfulness is something that can be cultivated and it is the duty of all Christians to show to the world by their happy, cheerful lives that Christianity is the most worthwhile thing in the whole world!"—Selected.

* * *

R. L. Stevenson said, "When a happy man comes into a room it is as if another candle had been lighted!" When the spirit of gladness and thankfulness rules the heart, light springs up to dispel the darkness and gloom.

* * *

"Mr. Glory-Face"

Adoniram Judson went as a missionary to Burma. He so burned with the desire to preach the gospel before he had learned the language that he walked up to a Burman and embraced him. The man went home and reported that he had seen an angel. The living Christ was so radiant in Mr. Judson's countenance that men called him "Mr. Glory-Face." When Christian workers really come to know the love God has given unto them, the Christian gospel will become irresistible.—*Westminster Teacher.*

Do We Glorify God?

One day recently, a lady was crossing a certain London station, when an old man stopped her, and said: "Excuse me, ma'am, but I want to thank you for something." "Thank *me!*" exclaimed the lady. "Yes'm. I used to be ticket collector at ———, and whenever you used to go by you allays give me a cheerful smile and a 'good mornin',' and you don't know what a difference it made to me. Wet or fine, it was allays the same, and I thinks to meself, 'Wonder where she gets her smile from; one cannot be allays happy, yet she seems to,' and I know'd that there smile must come from *inside* somehow. Then one mornin' you comes by and you had a little Bible in yer hand, and I says to meself, 'P'r'aps that's where she got her smile from.' So as I went home that night I bought a Bible, and I've been readin' it, and I've found Christ, and now I can smile too, and I want to thank yer."—*The Way of Faith.*

* * *

The Heavenly Joy

Some years ago my husband was conducting a series of meetings in a large country church in Virginia. He preached a sermon on the Prodigal Son, and I never saw so many young men accept the Lord in one service. They did not look as if they were prodigals, but fine, clean young men. However, God had used the sermon to help them to realize their need of a Saviour. As each one came forward, his mother would give a little shout of joy. I had heard shouting before, but never shouting that seemed to well up from the joy in the heart of each mother over the son who had been lost but was found again. This was the only shouting that ever moved me to tears, and I think I saw that day a faint picture of the joy in heaven over one sinner that repenteth.—Selected.

* * *

Singing in the Rain

A saintly woman suffering for weary months in painful illness said to her pastor: "I have such a lovely robin that sings outside my window. In the early morning, as I lie here, he serenades me." Then, as a smile brightened her thin features, she added, "I love him, because he sings in the rain." That is the most beautiful thing about the robin. When the storm has silenced almost every other songbird, the robin sings on—sings in the rain. That is the way the Christion who is with Christ may do. Anybody can sing in the sunshine; you and I should sing on when clouds pour out their rains, for Christ is with us. We should sing in the rain.—J. R. Miller, D.D.

* * *

A Question Never Asked

A Brahman of distinction in Western India embraced the Gospel and was baptized. By this act he lost possession of his houses, his fields, his wells, his wife, and his children. Such was the inexorable law of caste. On being asked how he bore his sorrows, he replied, "Ay, I am often asked that, but I am never asked how I bear my joys, for I have joys within with which a stranger intermeddles not. The Lord Jesus sought me and found me, a poor strayed sheep in the jungles, and He brought me to His fold and He will never leave me."—*Journal of Missions.*

Show Your Joy

Joyfulness is characteristic of the soul that lives in communion with God, and that soul unconsciously will persuade others to *"taste and see that the Lord is good,"* and that *"blessed is the man that trusteth in Him."*

Parents sometimes make the mistake of talking too much to their children about salvation, and showing too little joy and pleasantness around them.

No grouty, sullen Christian has any influence in the home, or in the church. How can the world that is bent on seeking pleasure be persuaded to accept anything that will not add to their happiness?—*Gospel Herald.*

* * *

A Smile

A smile costs nothing, but gives much. It enriches those who receive, without making poorer those who give. It takes but a moment, but the memory of it sometimes lasts forever. None is so rich or mighty that he can get along without it, and none is so poor but that he can be made rich by it. A smile creates happiness in the home, fosters good will in business, and is the countersign of friendship. It brings rest to the weary, cheer to the discouraged, sunshine to the sad, and it is nature's antidote for trouble. Yet it cannot be bought, begged, borrowed, or stolen, for it is something that is of no value to anyone until it is given away. Some people are too tired to give you a smile. Give them one of yours, as none needs a smile so much as he who has no more to give. — Selected.

* * *

Why Their Singing Was Beautiful

I remember once visiting a mission station in Egypt, and we were asked to listen to the singing of the converts. It is true they sang "tremendously," but seeing that, as a people, they had no ear for music and each seemed to sing a different discord, the effect was appalling! Yet after they had finished, the missionary came to me with shining eyes and said, "Didn't they sing beautifully!" And in spite of the tingling in my ears

I said, "Yes, they sang beautifully!" You see, that missionary had given her life for those precious converts. And up in Heaven is One who gave his life for me and for you, and so He delights in our singing, however unmusical and quavering.—Dr. Northcote Deck.

* * *

The Cheerful Heart

Whether the world be bright or dark
  Depends on how we take it.
Much of the misery we know
  Is just because we make it.
If on the windows of the soul
  We let self's cobwebs gather,
We may be sure all through our lives
  We'll see much cloudy weather.
A cheerful heart and willing hands
  To do kind deeds for others
Will make the people whom we meet
  All seem like friends and brothers.
Just try it, you who think the world
  By joy and hope forsaken,
And I am sure that you will find
  That you have been mistaken.
—Selected.

* * *

Something—or Someone—to Sing About

In a log church in the hills of West Virginia, I have heard the singing of a congregation of men and women, poorly clad, overworked, and perhaps undernourished. Tears flowed and shouts interfered with the singing as they sang such songs as: "Oh, happy day, that fixed my choice on Thee my Saviour and my God." They had a preacher but once a month, and it seemed that God loaned them enough Heaven to fill them to overflowing. I rejoiced with them and thanked God that people who had no paper on their walls or carpet on their floors could have ninety minutes of ecstasy once a month, which is far more than some churchgoers have in a lifetime.—B. H. Shadduck, in *The Sunday School Times.*

* * *

"Let It Be Praise"

A friend of mine was recently summoned to the bedside of his aged mother. More than eighty years of age, she was stricken with what they feared would prove her fatal illness. While her children were gathered in the room her pastor came; and as he was about to lead them in prayer, he turned to the aged saint and asked her what selection of Scripture he should read. She said: *"Make your own selection, but let it be of praise."* The weakness of old age was on her, and the pain of sickness, but there was no gloom. It was light at eventide. "Let it be of praise."—James I. Vance, in *Earnest Worker.*

* * *

The Great Face-Changer

It takes more than food and clothes to put joy in the heart and a smile upon the face. Our Lord Jesus Christ is the great face-changer of the ages.

Marcus Dodds, the famous globe trotter, once said as nearly as we can quote from memory:

"I have been in every land on which the sun shines and never have I anywhere seen a single happy hopeful face among women where the Gospel of Jesus Christ has not been preached." —*The Brethren Missionary Herald.*

* * *

Is Your Flag Flying?

Principal Rainy, of whom a child once remarked that she believed he went to Heaven every night because he was so happy every day, once used a fine metaphor about a Christian's joy. "Joy," he said, "is the flag which is flown from the castle of the heart when the King is in residence there."—*British Weekly.*

* * *

The Influence of a Song

In one of his best-known poems Browning tells the story of a young girl who had a single holiday in the year from her work in the silk mills of Asolo. On that day she went singing through the town in sheer gladness of heart. Four times over, we are told, her words and music were carried through open doors and windows to souls that were in need of them. They moved to repentance two people who had been living in sin. They made an artist ashamed of his anger; they acted as a check on an anarchist who was determined to assassinate the king. Yet, in the end, Pippa wondered if she had been of any use. We know that her song had challenged the darkness in lives of which she knew nothing.—*The Regular Baptist Call.*

* * *

The Poor Coolie's Treasure

Into a mission chapel in Pekin, where a prayer service was being held, a poor coolie came and kneeled. He was so ignorant and stupid that it seemed he could not understand even the simple Gospel message. While others were rejoicing, he continued pleading the name of Jesus, which was all the prayer he knew. Soon he arose with a happy face, stammering out, "I am nothing but a poor stupid coolie. I have no money, and no learning, but in my heart's center I have an unable-to-speak-it-out joy." What a wonderful joy that must be, such indeed as the world cannot give.—*Christian Herald.*

* * *

The Evangelism of Joy

A bigoted Chinese who never could be induced to attend a Christian service went to a missionary and said, "I want to hear about your religion. I never have heard the words of it, but I have heard the laughter in your house and in the houses of my countrymen who have embraced your faith. And if you have anything that makes people so joyous I want it." One great need in all lands is for more glad Christians—*Record of Christian Work.*

* * *

Gift of Laughter

After a hard day's work in serious discussions, Theodore Cuyler and Charles H. Spurgeon went out into the country together for a holiday. They roamed the fields in high spirits like boys let loose from school, chatting and laughing and free from care. Dr. Cuyler had just told a story at which Pastor Spurgeon laughed uproariously. Then suddenly he turned to Dr. Cuyler and exclaimed:

"Theodore, let's kneel down and thank God for laughter!"

And there, on the green carpet of grass, under the trees, two of the world's greatest men knelt and thanked the dear Lord for the bright and joyous gift of laughter.

There is no antagonism between prayer and laughter. One is conclusive of spiritual health, the other of physical health. —*S. S. World.*

* * *

Father's Preference

Bishop William Burt when asked how he acquired the habit of good cheer is said to have stated that the remark of a child he once overheard taught him to grumble and complain as little as possible. "While I was studying at Wilbraham Academy I spent a few days with this child's father, a good man but a chronic growler. We were all sitting in the front room when the question of food arose. The little girl told cleverly what each member of the family liked best. Finally it came to the father's turn to be described 'What do I like, Nancy?' he asked laughingly. 'You?' said the little one slowly. 'Well, you like mostly everything we haven't got.'" Grumbling is one of the hardest things for the wife to bear and causes great unhappiness.—Selected.

* * *

Comfort in a Cloud

Dr. Robert Collyer, of Yorkshire, Eng., who came to America as a blacksmith, and settled in a little town in Pennsylvania, was always looking on the bright side of life. "A dear, good old lady taught me to look for the silver lining." said the doctor. "How did she teach you?" I asked. "By example," said the doctor, benignly. "She was a very poor woman, and overwhelmed with troubles. Still she was always cheerful. One day

I said: 'Mary, you must have some very dark days; they must overcome you with clouds sometimes. 'Yes,' she replied, 'but then I often find there's comfort in a cloud.' 'Comfort in a cloud Mary?' 'Yes,' she said, 'when I am very low, I go to the window; and if I see a heavy cloud I think, "A cloud received Him out of their sight," and I look up and see the cloud sure enough, and then I think — Well, that may be the cloud that hides Him; and so you see, there's comfort in a cloud.' "—Robert Collyer.

* * *

The Miracle in Martyrdom

A Christian in Central Russia wrote the following: "After our commune was closed, I spent some time in the place where God's servants have to stay... (that is, in prison). And yet, I assure you, that during that time in my heart it was as though I were living in the Garden of Eden. . . . Scarcely a single night passed when I did not rise from my bed and thank God. And what was that which moved me to praise Him? Why, the consciousness of His wonderful presence... The only thing for me to do is to get upon my knees, and praise God for His faithful and unfailing presence with us."—*Sunday School Times.*

* * *

Joy from God

When Haydn was once asked how it was that his church music was always so cheerful, the great composer made a most appropriate and beautiful reply. "I cannot," said he, "make it otherwise; I write according to the thoughts I feel. When I think upon God my heart is so full of joy that the notes dance and leap, as it were, from my pen; and since God has given me a cheerful heart, it will be pardoned me that I serve Him with a cheerful spirit." There is one thing which Christ's followers can do, and that is to keep themselves in the delightful atmosphere of His love. It is our fault and our shame if we spend so many days in the chilling fogs or under the heavy clouds of unbelief, or in the contaminating atmosphere of conformity to the world. "Is it always foggy here on the banks of Newfoundland?" inquired a passenger of an old sea captain. "How should I know, madam? I don't live here."—*Gospel Herald.*

* * *

Alexander's Lesson from Moody

Charles Alexander, when a student at Moody Bible Institute, got to wondering whether it was right for an earnest Christian to be so gay. He tells of the way in which Moody, gathering students around him for a confidential talk, noticed that many of us were wearing long faces. "I am quite sure I was one of them, for I had been studying that sentence in the New Testament where it says that every idle word shall be accounted for. I had usually been of a lively disposition, trying to cheer the fellow who was downhearted, but when I began to study that verse I thought I was wrong. I had been trying to get my face so that no smile would ever come upon it. In one of these sane morning talks, Mr. Moody spoke about that verse. Looking up with such a bright, happy look, he said, 'Young men, do not think that the teaching of this verse means that you shall go around with a long face, and never have a happy word for anyone. A cheerful word is not an idle one.'" From that time onward, Alexander enjoyed the perfect freedom which makes for unrestrained delight of service.—Charles M. Alexander, a *Romance of Song and Soul-Winning."*

* * *

Within

I stood a little while ago in the fine old ruin of Middleham Castle. I passed beyond the outer shell and beyond the inner defenses into the keep, and there in the innermost sanctum of the venerable pile, was the old well. The castle was independent of outside supplies. If it were beseiged it had resources of water at its own heart. The changing seasons made no difference to the gracious supply. That is the purpose of the

Master in placing the "well" within us. He wants to make us independent of external circumstances.—Dr. J. H. Jowett.

* * *

Happiness

If we could bury our dead woes we would be a lot happier. How prone we are to remember the things which are of no value and which make us sad. I wish I could always remember that if one thing goes wrong, another might go right. If we would sing to a hopeful tune it would help us and those whom we contact. One of old said, "Smile and the world smiles with you."

Happiness does not depend on the riches of the world. Happiness depends on planting a live seed of kindness in the heart of someone else and causing this seed to grow by repeating kind deeds. Happiness is just about another name for doing for others and then watching the glory vines of joy grow about their faces.

What pleasure would it be to throw pepper into the face of a person? Would it not afford more pleasure to hand them a sweet-smelling perfume? It is up to the individual to choose his way, and he should choose the way to make him happy and bring lasting joy.

The person who is happy is the person who manifests a Christian attitude. Such a person would look for the good points of his neighbor and use his tongue to speak words of praise. This person need not tell his neighbors that he has religion, as his neighbors will find that out. A small boy played a harp in my presence for a long time and then turned to me and said, "I have a harp." He had already told me so by playing it. So it is if we are the right kind of Christians: We will tell others by sounding the harp of praise.—*Messenger of Peace.*

* * *

Joy Midst Suffering

A western captain as he lay on the battlefield of Shiloh, suffered greatly from a fatal gunshot through both thighs, and from thirst. He said, "The stars shone out clear and beautiful above the dark field; and I began to think of that great God who had given His Son to die a death of agony for me; and that He was up there — up above the scene of suffering above those glorious stars; and I felt that I was going home to meet Him and praise Him there; and I felt that I ought to praise God, even wounded and on the battlefield. I could not help singing that beautiful hymn: 'When I can read my title clear, to mansions in the skies.' And there was a Christian brother in the brush near me. I could not see him, but I could hear him. He took up the strain; and beyond him another and another caught it up, all over the battlefield of Shiloh. That night the echo was resounding; and we made the field of battle ring with the hymns of praise to God."—*Anon.*

GOD'S JUDGMENT

Fearful Awakening

Any of our readers who have been to London years ago, will remember that close by the great dome of St. Paul's there used to stand the somber heavy stone building called Newgate prison. Some few years ago it was pulled down to make room for a new and less gloomy building.

The old building carried with it many a solemn and fearful memory which is perhaps better forgotten, but one story may serve as a sad picture of the sinner's state.

The last execution that took place there was of a poor woman who had been sentenced to death for an awful deed.

Her last night was spent in the cell alloted to those condemned to die, and early next morning she was to suffer at seven o'clock.

When six o'clock came the warders went into the cell and found her quietly sleeping and smiling as she lay unconsciously so near her death. They had not the heart to wake her, so terrible would be the awakening. So they left her for another half-hour.

Again they came, but still she slept, dreaming, as they learned afterwards, of the early days of her childhood when she lived in a village home peacefully and happily — of father and mother, of brothers and sisters, of innocent days in the field gathering buttercups or daisies, or roaming the quiet lanes in the still evenings of summer days.

The female warders stood with tears upon their cheeks as they looked upon so sad a sight. What an awakening it must be!

And indeed it was; for when, compelled by their duty, they shook the sleeping form lightly, it was to bring her back to the fearful consciousness of her sin and shame and ruin.

Then there was a bitter, piercing cry, never to be forgotten by those who heard it.

There will one day be such an awakening for every sinner, when the reality of condemnation, judgment, and eternity are seen and realized.

In the Book of Revelation we are told that some in that day will call to the rocks and the mountains to fall upon them and cover them from the wrath of the Lamb (*Rev.* 6:16, 17).

Oh, sinner, flee to Christ today, while salvation is offered and impending wrath is withheld!

"For God so loved the world, that He gave His only begotten Son, that whosoever believeth in Him should not perish, but have everlasting life." "He that believeth not the Son shall not see life; but the wrath of God abideth on him" (*John* 3:16, 36).—*Faithful Words.*

* * *

Silenced

William Hague Wood turned infidel recently. He attended a revival meeting several nights at High Shoals and ran an opposition meeting outside the church. He made mighty addresses and declared that the preachers were talking nonsense. He said they were frauds and were deceiving the people. On Sunday his tongue was paralyzed while he was making a speech ridiculing the church. This frightened his hearers, who broke for the church. At night Wood attended the meeting and handed up the following note to the preacher in charge: "I now believe that there is a hell and that I am doomed for it. Pray for me." There was a great sensation in the congregation and in less than five minutes the altar would not accomodate half the mourners.—*Pentecostal Evangel.*

* * *

Changed Faces

Some years ago when modern chemistry was in its infancy, a fashionable audience assembled in Paris for an experimental lecture on chemistry. When they came out into the open they greeted one another with exclamations of dismay. The faces of most of the women had been ludicrously transformed. Their cheeks, lips, and in some cases the entire surface of exposed skin had turned into varying shades of blue, yellow, or violet. The chemical effects of the gases set free during the lecture had touched everyone who had used any cosmetics. When the white light of God's presence shall shine upon the hearts of men, everything that has been hidden shall become open, and the naked things shall be manifest.—*Revelation.*

* * *

The Judgment

A young minister was confronted — as the congregation expected — with an able young skeptic, Burt Olney. At the close of the first service Olney said, "You did well, but you know, I don't believe in the infallibility of the Bible."

"*It is appointed unto men once to die, but after this the judgment,*" was the young man's calm assertion.

"I can prove to you there is no such thing as a judgment after death," declared the skeptic.

"But men do die," the young pastor declared, "for *it is appointed unto men once to die, but after this the judgment.*"

"But that's no argument," the skeptic protested, "let's get down to business and discuss this matter in regular argument form."

The pastor shook his head. "I am here to preach the Word of God, and not to argue over it."

Olney, annoyed, turned away with the remark ,"I don't believe you know enough about the Bible to argue about it."

"Perhaps you are right," was the calm rejoinder, "but please remember this — *'It is appointed unto men once to die, but after this the judgment.'* "

The very tree toads Olney heard on the way home sang the verse, and the stream he crossed, and the frogs seemed to croak, "Judg-ment, judg-ment, judgment."

The next morning he called at the parsonage. "I've come to see you about the verse of Scripture you gave me last night," he said. "I've spent a terrible night with those words burning their way into me. I can't get rid of them. Tell me what I must do to be saved. I've got to get rid of this torture."

When he left, he was a child of God through faith in the finished work of Christ.—*The Pilot.*

* * *

What Then?

When the great, busy plants of our cities
Shall have turned out their last finished work,
When the merchants have sold their last order
And dismissed every last tired clerk,
When our banks have raked in their last dollar
And have paid out their last dividend,
When the Judge of the earth wants a hearing
And asks for a balance — WHAT THEN?

When the choir has sung its last anthem
And the preacher has voiced his last prayer,
And the people have heard their last sermon
And the sound has died out in the air,
When the Bible lies closed on the altar
And the pews are all empty of men,
When each one stands facing his record,
And the great Book is opened—WHAT THEN?

When the actors have played their last drama,
And the mimic has made his last fun,
When the movie has flashed its last picture
And the billboard displayed its last run,
When the crowd seeking pleasure has vanished
And gone out in the darkness again,
When the trumpet of ages has sounded
And we stand before HIM—WHAT THEN?

When the bugle-calls sinks into silence
And the long marching columns stand still,
When the captain repeats his last orders
And they've captured the last fort and hill;
When the flag has been hauled from the masthead,
All the wounded afield have checked in,
And the world that rejected its Saviour
Is asked for a reason--WHAT THEN?

—J. W. Green.

* * *

Another Lesson in Swift Judgment

Mr. George Whale, the chairman of the Rationalist Press Association, fell dead last night after a ruthless attack on the dogmas of the Christian religion. "The light," he said, "from some providential spirit or Holy Ghost is said to have guided the Church for some nineteen hundred years. It has not come, and when it does come I venture to suggest it will not have the dazzling effect of the light that fell on the apostle on his way to Damascus — the light that left him dazzled for the rest of his life." Two hundred and seventeen guests present greeted his words with appreciative laughter. In a few moments there were only hushed whispers and awe-stricken faces. It was seen that Mr. Whale had collapsed in his chair, and in the instant silence his strangled breathing was the only sound. Doctors rushed to his side, and he was carried from the room dying. The dinner was to have been followed by dancing, and at the moment Mr. Whale was being carried from the banqueting hall the orchestra could be heard tuning up their instruments in the next room. It was announced that the dance would be abandoned. Women in evening frocks and men who were about to partner them in fox-trots stood about awkwardly. Although it was not officially announced that Mr. Whale was dead, the news spread from one group to another until the whole gathering slowly dispersed.—From the London *Daily Express*, May 5, 1925, and quoted in *The Dawn*, June, 1925, where the item is reproduced verbatim from the *Daily Express*.

* * *

A Blasphemer Judged

A few months after the baptism of several persons, a wicked young man took a sheep to the same place in the stream, and with fearful oaths swore he could baptize as well as the preacher. The shore of the stream was a very gradual slope, so there was no apprehension of danger from deep water. Three of his comrades stood on the shore and witnessed his blasphemous performance. Taking the sheep in, and holding it by its fore feet, he pronounced the formula of baptism, and as he leaned over to immerse the sheep, the animal struck him with its hind feet, knocking him into deep water where he was drowned, while his comrades stood looking on. When asked why they did not try to save him, they were perfectly helpless and could not stir. Let not the tongue be given to blasphemy.—Selected.

* * *

The World's Food Shortage

Says the *Christian Herald:* "A recent gathering in London of agricultural experts discussed the problem of the growing loss of fertility in the soil of the world which threatens a very serious food shortage. Every year in all but a few countries, the lack of strength in the soil is becoming more apparent, and deserts are spreading in all the five continents where once were tracts of fertile land. The value of food lost to the world every year by soil erosion cannot be estimated, but must run into many millions of dollars." In Psalm 107:33, 34 we read that God "turneth . . . a fruitful land into barrenness, for the wickedness of them that dwell therein." — *Pentecostal Evangel.*

* * *

Jesus, the Righteous Judge

A criminal who had once been before the courts was scheduled to appear once more. He rejoiced when he heard that an attorney who had defended him on previous occasions was now the trial judge. His attitude changed, however, when the judge stated, "When I was an attorney I defended you, but I am no longer an attorney. It is not my business now to defend, but to judge. I shall hear the evidence, and then I must deal with you in keeping with the oath I have taken in the office of judge."

Jesus came once to this earth as Saviour. He is even now at the right hand of God as our Intercessor, our Advocate with the Father. But the day is coming when He will return as Judge. As Judge He must perform His duty in keeping with the nature of His office. — *Open Windows.*

* * *

Others' Sins

During a revival a young man said frankly that he did not wish to be a Christian. When asked for his reason, he replied, "Several years ago I was in a man's kitchen. He finding me there, swore at me and kicked me out. He was a professing Christian, and from that time I decided never to have anything to do with religion. And I never have to this day." The young man was asked to write down his reason in full and sign it. Then it was handed back to him with the words, "Take this, and when you are asked for your excuse on the day of judgment, hand this up." The young man saw his folly and came to Christ that night.

Are you letting the sins of others keep you from giving your heart to Jesus? Don't be so foolish—for it will not stand the test of the judgment day.—*The Dawn.*

* * *

Why They Were Safe

A minister, while crossing the Bay of Biscay, became greatly alarmed as he beheld what he thought was an approaching hurricane. Trembling, he addressed himself to one of the sailors: "Do you think she will be able to go through it?" "Through what?" inquired the sailor. "That awful hurricane that is coming down upon us." The old sailor smiled and said: "That storm will never touch us. It has passed us already." So, in regard to the believer, judgment as to the penalty of our sins is past. We were tried, condemned, and executed in the person of our Surety, Jesus Christ.—*The King's Business.*

* * *

When God Strikes

A Christian physician was once obliged to take refuge from an approaching storm in a grocery store which also contained a grog shop. Two drunken men were present, and as the lightning flashed, they poured forth such a volley of fearful oaths that finally the storekeeper said, "Gentlemen, I am no Christian, but I want to say that your awful cursing is too much for me. God will strike you dead right here with a stroke of lightning if you do not hush your blasphemous oaths." The leader of the two rolled up his sleeves, went to the door, cursed God, and defied Him. At that moment a blinding flash of lightning descended with a flame of fire. Quickly the light was gone and only smoke remained. In a moment that, too, had disappeared, and there lay God's defier in a heap, just as an empty garment when let loose would fall. The physician helped to lay the man out, and he said he did not believe there was a bone two inches long left unbroken in his body.—*Sunday School Times.*

* * *

When God Was Defied

Let the *Evangelical Christian* record the story of the quake that totally destroyed the flourishing and extraordinarily beautiful city of Messina, Italy. In the early morning of December 28, 1908, the tremblor struck, and 84,000 human beings died. We read: "Only a few hours before that devastating earthquake which laid Messina and the surrounding districts in ruins, the unspeakably wicked and irreligious condition of some of the inhabitants was expressed in a series of violent resolutions which were passed against all religious principles, while the journal *Il Telefono,* printed in Messina, actually published in its Christmas number an abominable parody, daring the Almighty to make Himself known by sending an earthquake! And in three days the earthquake came!"—Louis S. Baumann, D.D., in the *Sunday School Times.*

JUSTICE

Justice

However the battle is ended,
  Though proudly the victor comes;
With fluttering flags, and prancing nags,
  And echoing roll of drums.
Still history proclaims the motto,
  In letters of shining light:
"No question is ever settled
  Until it is settled right."

Though the heel of the strong oppressor
  May grind the weak to the dust;
And the voice of fame with loud acclaim
  May call him great and just.
Let those who applaud take warning,
  And keep this motto in sight:
"No question is ever settled
  Until it is settled right."

—Selected.

KINDNESS

The Second Mile

It is not Christian to do all that is expected of us. Unbelievers often do that. Christianity does more than that. A man in a hospital, just after a severe operation, asked his nurse to turn his pillow. She at once rearranged two pillows, and made him much more comfortable. As minute after minute and hour after hour dragged on, he noticed that whenever he asked the nurse for anything, she always did more than he asked: did it instantly and cheerily. Finally he asked her if she remembered what the Lord said about "going the second mile," and told her how gratefully he had noticed that she always went that second mile. And it meant so much, to a weak, suffering patient lying there in helplessness.—*Sunday School Times.*

* * *

If I Had Known

If I had known in the morning
How wearily all the day
The word unkind
Would trouble my mind
I said when you went away,
I had been more careful, darling,
Nor given you needless pain,
But we vex "our own"
With look and tone
We may never take back again.

For though in the quiet evening
You may give me the kiss of peace,
Yet it might be
That never for me
The pain of the heart shall cease.
How many go forth in the morning
That never come home at night!
And hearts have broken
For harsh words spoken
That sorrow can ne'er set right.

We have careful thought for the stranger,
And smiles for the sometime guest;
But oft for "our own"
The bitter tone,
Though we love "our own" the best.
Ah, lips with the curve impatient!
Ah, brow with that look of scorn!
'Twere a cruel fate
Were the night too late
To undo the work of morn.

—Selected.

* * *

What "Loving-Kindness" Means

Mother asked her six-year-old what loving-kindness meant. "Well," he said, "when I ask you for a piece of bread and butter and you give it to me, that's kindness, but *when you put jam on it, that's loving-kindness.*" — *Chicago Tribune.*

* * *

What Did You Do?

Did you give him a lift? He's a poor needy man,
And bearing about all the burden he can.
Did you give him a smile? He was downcast and blue,
But a smile would have helped him to battle it through.
Did you give him a hand? He was slipping down hill,
And the world, so I fancied, was making him ill.
Did you give him a word? Did you show him the road?
Or did you just let him go on with his load?

Did you help him along? He's a sinner like you,
But the grasp of your hand might have carried him through.
Did you bid him good cheer? Just a word and a smile
Were what he most needed that last weary mile.
Do you know what he bore in that burden of cares
That is every man's load and that sympathy shares?
Did you try to find out what he needed from *you?*
Or did you just leave him to battle it through?

Do you know that it means to be losing
the fight,
When a lift, just in time, might set
everything right?
Do you know what it means—just the
clasp of a hand,
When a man's borne about all a man
ought to stand?
Did you ask what it was—why the quivering lip,
And the glistening tears down the pale
cheek that slip?
Were you brother of his when the time
came to be?
Did you offer to help him, or didn't you
see?

Don't you know it's the part of a Christian man
To find out what the grief is and help
where you can?
Did you stop when he asked you to give
him a lift?
Or were you so busy that you left him
to shift?
Ah, I know that what you say may really
be true,
But the test of your life is: *What did
you do?* —Selected.

* * *

Birds Are Friends

Did you know that little birds have their friends just as you do? If a robin is in trouble, other robins will hurry to her side; so will orioles, chickadees and many others. Suppose a mother robin is killed while she is out hunting food for her babies. Do the little birds starve? No, indeed, they do not. The other birds feed the orphan babies as well as their own.

One time a little bird was caught in a tree and could not get out. When he was found and helped out by a kind man, he was as fat as he could be. This shows us that the other birds fed him.

When birds are crippled or blind or cannot fly, they are cared for by other birds in the community. So you see birds are friendly little creatures, and love one another and care for one another much the same as the Lord has told people to do.—Selected.

"Only One of His Followers"

The little lame boy hurried to the passenger gate of the railway station as fast as his crutches and basket of fruit and candy would permit. As the passengers rushed through the gate, a young man accidentally hit the basket, knocking oranges and apples in every direction. He stopped only long enough to scold the boy for being in his way. Another young man who was passing by saw the boy's distress and began picking up his fruit. As he placed it in the basket, he put a silver dollar in his hand. With a "Better luck next time" and a smile, he went his way. "Hey, Mister," called the little boy, "are you Jesus?" "No," answered his friend, "I'm only one of His followers." . . . The people whose lives we touch need to see Jesus in your life and mine. . . . Many will not understand His love unless they see it in our deeds.—*Secret Place.*

* * *

An Infidel Answered

Mr. Charles Bradlaugh, a celebrated infidel lecturer in the last century, at one time M.P. for Northampton, a man of great talents prostituted to the attacking of the Christian faith, delivered a scathing attack on Christianity in a well-known London hall. At its close he dared any man to answer him.

The Chairman replied, "No one here is likely to try, Mr. Bradlaugh. We are all of your way of thinking."

However, a gasfitter arose and said, "You all know me. I have been a member of this club for five years. Some months ago I lost my work, and I was ill, and to make matters worse my wife was ill. Not one of you came near me, though my illness was known here. But someone came, and his wife nursed us and provided for us, otherwise neither my wife nor I would have been alive today. That man was a city missionary, whom I had driven away from my door with threats. When I was well enough to think, I asked him why he had been so kind to us, and he told me he had done it for the love of Christ. I say that a religion which will bring a man to the bedside of one who has hated him and cursed him, is a good thing for this life."

Such an incident as this can be multiplied a thousand times. Infidelity does not like deathbeds. It is a fair weather negation that crumbles into dust when the storms of life are heavy, especially when the shadows of eternal night settle on the soul.—*Gospel Herald.*

* * *

In a Crowded Elevator

The elevator man was gruff, and in his estimation the little, frail old lady who got on last made one passenger too many in his car. "Take the next car," he commanded gruffly. "Take the next car!" slipping his hand in front of her. But the little old lady, frightened in the crowd, seemed deaf to his remark and unconscious that anything was required of her. A young lady from the middle of the car worked her way out to make one passenger less. The aged woman, happy at being able to find room, did not notice that anything had been done for her. The elevator man did not appear to notice. Nobody thanked the girl, as, pressed for time in her busy day, she stood looking a little wistfully after the ascending car, thinking perhaps that it was merely a sacrifice of time that counted for little. But doubtless every heart in that car, as it went up, was beating with some better impulse because of that little kindness so unobtrusively done.—*Sunday School Banner.*

* * *

Little Kindnesses

You gave on the way a pleasant smile,
And thought no more about it;
It cheered a life that was sad the while,
That might have been wrecked without it;
And so for the smile and its fruitage fair
You'll reap a crown sometime — somewhere.

You spoke one day a cheering word,
And passed to other duties;
It warmed a heart, new promise stirred,
And painted a life with beauties.
And so for the word and its silent prayer
You'll reap a palm sometime — somewhere.

You lent a hand to a fallen one,
A lift in kindness given;
It saved a soul when help was none,
And won a heart for Heaven;
And so for the help you proffered there
You'll reap a joy sometime—somewhere.
—Selected.

Her "Good Morning"

It was a chilly day, and the wind blew cold on that particular corner.

The blind man had sold very few papers that morning. He sighed.

The wind blew colder. The hurrying crowds surged by, but no one spoke, and then, at his elbow, a sweet, young voice said suddenly, "Good morning."

The man turned his sightless eyes in the direction of the speaker. "Who is it?" he said quickly.

The young girl in the plain hat and modest suit, who had stopped to speak to him was silent a moment.

"It is I — Marjory Dean," she said gently. "I work in the Hampton Studio in the Graham Block. I thought I'd stop and say 'Good morning' to you."

The blind man nodded. He no longer felt the cold wind that had so chilled him. He forgot his own helplessness and the fact that he had sold so few papers.

Out of the darkness that shadowed him, a sweet voice had spoken. His loneliness was gone. The world was a friendly place, after all. Someone had stopped to say, "Good morning." He smiled.

"I'm so glad you did," he said softly.
—Selected.

* * *

A Prime Minister's Lesson

A French Prime Minister once sent for an eminent surgeon to perform upon him a serious operation. Said the Prime Minister: "You will not, of course, treat me in the same rough manner as you would treat your poor miserable wretches at the hospital." "Sir," replied the surgeon with dignity, "every one of those poor miserable wretches, as your Eminence is pleased to call them, is a Prime Minister in my eyes!"—*The King's Business.*

* * *

If we knew what hearts are aching for
the comforts we might bring,
If we knew what souls are yearning for
the sunshine we could fling,
If we knew what feet are weary walking
pathways roughly laid,
We would quickly hasten forward
stretching forth our hands to aid.
—Selected.

* * *

Bouquets or Wreaths?

God make me kind!
So many hearts are breaking
And many more are aching
To hear the tender word.
God make me kind!
For I myself am learning,
My own sad heart is yearning
For some sweet word to heal its hurt,
O Lord, do make me kind!

God make me kind!
So many hearts are needing
The balm to stop the bleeding
That my kind words can bring.
God make me kind!
For I am also seeking
The cure in someone's keeping
They should impart to my sick heart,
O Lord, do make me kind!

God make me kind!
So many hearts are lonely
Are asking for this only—
The kind and tender word.
God make me kind!
To all who mutely ask it
Before they fill the casket,
Or bouquets may be wreaths some day.
O Lord, do make me kind!
—Rev. Duncan McNeill, Chicago, Ill.

* * *

Not According to Worth

A good man died recently, and his fellow townsmen gathered to show their respect and affection at his grave. Among all the kind words spoken, none was quite so eloquent as one sobbing tribute that came from the town's ne'er-do-well, a poor old man whose youth and riper manhood had been the usual sad story of drink and dissipation. "He had a hand out for everybody!" was his grateful testimony. "Didn't stop to ask whether you seemed worth saving—he give ye your chance anyhow!" That is God's way with the world—a hand for everybody, and "your chance anyhow."—*Baptist Leader.*

* * *

The Kind Word

"I wonder how Vera Brooking ever got such a fine disposition?" said Eva. "She never seems to say a thing that hurts anyone or makes any trouble."

"I think she does it by watching," said Erie. "She told me once that she had had a terrible habit of saying sharp, unkind things. One day she hurt someone terribly, and after that she decided to overcome the habit of saying sharp things.

"Every night after that she used to ask herself if she had said anything harsh or unkind to anyone that day. If she had, she made herself write an apology. Now she has the reputation for saying kind things."

Let's keep a strict watch on our words Why not learn Psalm 19:14, and make it a prayer?—*Queen's Gardens.*

* * *

Worth a Bucket of Water

One hot August day, two half-starved horses, drawing an immigrant wagon with a drunken driver, a sick woman, and four children, stopped at a cabin on a Kansas prairie. "Any water?" the driver asked of a sweet young girl at the door. There was but one bucket of water in the well, which was going dry, and her parents were even then away seeking more water, but Rachel carried that to the wagon, and the half-famished group soon emptied it. "Remember, child," said the sick woman gratefully, "'Inasmuch as ye have done it unto one of the least.'" They drove on. Years passed, and Rachel, grown to be a woman, secured a well-known temperance speaker to lecture in her town. "I love Kansas," he began, "for on its plains I made my first temperance pledge." Then he related the above. When he told of the girl who gave them water, and how his father threw away the whisky bottle as a thank offering, and he himself promised his mother to join the cold water army, Rachel could only bow her head to hide the glad tears.—*The Illustrator.*

* * *

No Regret

I have wept in the night
For the shortness of sight,
That to somebody's need made me blind;
But I never have yet
Felt a twinge of regret,
For being a little too kind.
—*Christian Herald.*

* * *

Compassion

Abraham Lincoln during the Civil War frequently visited the hospitals and addressed cheering words to the wounded warriors. On one occasion he found a young fellow whose legs had been amputated, and who was evidently sinking rapidly. "Is there anything I can do for you?" asked Lincoln. "You might write a letter to my mother," was the faint reply. The President wrote at the youth's dictation: "My dearest mother: I have been shot bad, but am bearing up. I tried to do my duty. They tell me I cannot recover. God bless you and Father; kiss Mary and John for me." At the end were these words as postscript: "Written by Abraham Lincoln." When the boy perused the epistle and saw these added words, he looked with astonishment at the visitor and asked, "Are you our President?" "Yes," was the quiet answer, "and now that you know that, is there anything else I can do for you?" Feebly the lad said, "I guess you might hold my hand, and see me through." So, sitting down at the bedside, the tall, gaunt man with a heart as tender as a woman's held the soldier's hand through the livelong night till it grew cold and rigid. Is it not a precious truth that Christ, the greatest of all kings, in our affliction is afflicted, and that He can be "touched with the feeling of our infirmities"?—*The Illustrator.*

* * *

Ideal Service

A minister in London, England, called one day to see a street-crossing sweeper in his parish who was ill. Upon asking him whether anyone had called to see him, the sweeper replied: "Yes, Mr. Gladstone called." "Which Mr. Gladstone?" asked the minister. "Mr. William Gladstone!" replied the poor sick man. "How came he to see you?"

"Well," answered the sweeper, "he always had a nice word for me when he passed my crossing, and when I was not there, he missed me. He asked the man who had taken my place where I was, and when he was told, he put it down on paper, so he called to see me." "And what did he do?" asked the minister. "He read the Bible and prayed with me." Now that is what I call sitting on top of the world; taking Jesus as Saviour and Lord, and giving to mankind the blessing of Christian life.—*Gospel Herald.*

* * *

The Transferred Burden

A story is told of a certain British regiment in India which was called upon to undergo "Kitchener's Test," i.e., to march a certain number of miles along a sandy track in a specified time without one man falling out. After covering a part of the distance a young recruit marching by the side of an "old timer" named Bill, said to him: "Bill, I can't stick it." The heat was terrific and the lad was well-nigh overcome. Bill, seeing it, said: "Here, give me your rifle." After another two miles, Bill noticing again the lad's distress, took over another part of his equipment, and before they had gone all the way he was carrying the remainder of the boy's kit. At the command "Halt" every man was in his place and the honor of the regiment saved. Unload all your burdens upon Him (your Friend) for He careth for you.—*Jamaica Wesleyan Record.*

When Arab Met Jew

A short time ago a friend wrote me of an interesting experience that a traveling friend had reported to her. A member of her party, traveling in Palestine, was being driven by an Arab chauffeur. On the way there was a man—a Jew—who was having serious car trouble. The Arab stopped and tried to help with the car, but they did not have the parts for repair. So the Jew was invited to get into the Arab's car and ride to a garage for help. After the man had been left at the garage and the party was on its way again, surprise was expressed at the Arab's kind treatment of the Jew. "I did not know that Arabs were so friendly to Jews," the traveler said. The Arab answered, "Oh, but I am a Christian." —*Junior Life* (Richmond, Va.).

* * *

"But the Hands Are Different"

Rev. Ira Gillett, missionary to Portuguese East Africa, tells the story of a group of natives who made a long journey and walked past a government hospital to come to the mission hospital for treatment. When asked why they had walked the extra distance to reach the mission hospital when the same medicines were available at the government institution, they replied, *"The medicines may be the same, but the hands are different."*—*Upper Room.*

* * *

Kindness Stopped a Tragedy

A gentleman of Sedalia, Missouri, had occasion to go to a neighboring town in the caboose of a fast freight. A fellow passenger was a carpenter loaded with a heavy bag of tools. Somehow this man stumbled over a tub of grease of some sort, which had melted in the heat, and spilled it over the clean caboose floor. He was trying to mop it up with some old sacks when the conductor came in. The carpenter was trying to apologize, but the hot-tempered conductor flew into a rage and for fully five minutes heaped upon him such a torrent of abuse as made the listener's blood run cold. At the next station the man was getting off, and noticing that he looked white and sick, the Sedalia man offered to help him off with his load of tools. The other gave him a peculiar look but said nothing, which he construed as consent, and helped him off. Six years later a man stopped him on the street, asking if he remembered him. He did not, until the man mentioned the incident. "You did a most wonderful service for me that day," he said. "It was only a little act, but it saved me from being a murderer, for I had fully decided to bury my hammer in that conductor's head. Your kind words, breaking so unexpectedly on my dark feelings, caused me to keep back the mad impulse, and I am a free man today. God bless you! I shall never forget it." His heart was too full for reply, but as they clasped hands the tears stood in the eyes of both.—Condensed from the *Sunday School Times.*

* * *

"The Green Atrocity"

Several years ago there was built, across from our house, a house which my husband dubbed "the green atrocity." It was a poorly-built, small-town tenement, painted an unpleasant shade of green, and designed to house four or more poor families. Not only that, but it stood between us and a view of our beloved Rocky Mountains. The house was soon filled with Mexican families who had come to town after the beet harvest was finished in the fall. For days I could think of nothing except the fact that I resented that house being there. Then one day the realization came to me: "You believe in the Christian Friendliness program of your church, and here is a laboratory at your door in which you can experiment in being the friendly neighbor, if you but will." I am not sure that I said the exact words, "Here am I, Lord; send me," but I did go over to visit my neighbors. Our family received more than we gave, and some of the friendships formed with our unwanted neighbors have continued through the years. So the "green atrocity" was really a golden opportunity knocking at my door and saying, "Come over and find out who is your neighbor."—Lula Pulliam Colwell, in the *Secret Place.*

* * *

Kindness to a Great Physician

Dr. Howard A. Kelly is a renowned physician, surgeon, naturalist, and a humble Christian. On one of his frequent "naturalist" journeys, when he became thirsty he stopped at a farmhouse for a glass of water. A little girl came to the door, and when he asked for a glass of water she sweetly said: "I will give you a glass of milk if you wish." He drank the cool, refreshing milk heartily. On departing he said to her: "Now if you or any member of your family ever need treatment, come to my hospital, and I will treat you for nothing." The girl was thrilled at the thought of his kindness. Years later this girl's mother found it necessary to go to a hospital, and she went to Dr. Kelly's where she received personal attention. When she was ready to leave, the doctor made out a big bill for his service. At the bottom he wrote, "Paid for in full with one glass of milk."—*Watchman-Examiner.*

* * *

A Negro's Friend

The kind of helpfulness we can show to people of other races is illustrated by the following incident. One night a Negro was walking down Forty-second Street, New York, from the depot to his hotel carrying a heavy suitcase in one hand and a heavier valise in the other. Suddenly a hand was laid upon the valise and a pleasant face of a young man looked into that of the Negro as he said: "Pretty heavy, brother; suppose you let me take one; I'm going your way." The Negro protested, but the man already had the valise, and for several blocks they walked on together, talking like cronies. "And that," said Booker T. Washington long afterward, "was the first time I ever saw Theodore Roosevelt."—*Arnold's Commentary.*

GOD'S LAW

Law and Grace

The Law came by Moses—Grace and truth came by Jesus Christ.

The Law says: This do, and thou shalt live.—Grace says: Live, and then thou shalt do.

The Law says: Pay me that thou owest.—Grace says: I frankly forgive thee all.

The Law says: The wages of sin is death.—Grace says: The gift of God is eternal life.

The Law says: The soul that sinneth, it shall die.—Grace says: Whosoever believeth on Jesus, though he were dead, yet shall he live; and whosoever liveth and believeth on Him shall never die.

The Law pronounces condemnation and death.—Grace proclaims justification and life.

The Law says: Make you a new heart and a new spirit.—Grace says: A new heart will I give you, and a new spirit will I put within you.

The Law says: Cursed is every one that continueth not in all things which are written in the Book of the Law to do them.—Grace says: Blessed is the man whose iniquities are forgiven, whose sin is covered; blessed is the man to whom God will not impute sin.

The Law says: Thou shalt love the Lord thy God with all thy heart, and with all thy mind, and with all thy strength.—Grace says: Herein is love, not that we loved God, but that He first loved us, and gave His Son to be the propitiation for our sins.

The Law speaks of what man must do for God.—Grace tells of what Christ has done for man.

The Law addresses man as part of the old creation.—Grace makes a man a member of the new creation.

The Law bears on a nature prone to disobedience.—Grace creates a nature inclined to obedience.

The Law demands obedience by the terrors of the Law.—Grace beseeches men by the mercies of God.

The Law demands holiness. — Grace gives holiness.

The Law says: Condemn him.—Grace says: Embrace him.

The Law speaks of priestly sacrifices offered year by year continually, which could never make the comers thereunto perfect. — Grace says: But this Man, after He had offered one sacrifice for sins forever; by one offering hath perfected forever them that are sanctified.

The Law declares that as many as have sinned in the Law, shall be judged by the Law.—Grace brings eternal peace to the troubled soul of every child of God, and proclaims God's Truth in defiance of the accusations of the calumniator. He that heareth My Word, and believeth on Him that sent Me, hath everlasting life, and shall not come into judgment (condemnation), but is passed out of death unto life.

"By grace are ye saved."—*The Evangel.*

* * *

Nearly Perfect Will Not Do

Has any man ever kept God's whole law? A newspaper reporter announces a modest claimant to this. The Philadelphia *Public Ledger* some time ago contained a news dispatch from a Western city reading, in part, as follows: "The 'perfect man' has been found. . . . He was testifying as a witness in disbarment proceedings. . . . 'I neither smoke, chew, drink, nor swear,' —— testified. 'I never have broken a moral law or a law of God.' . . . 'You admit, then, that you are a perfect man?' asked the defense counsel. 'I do,' answered ——, 'as nearly perfect as a man can be.' " A newspaper item like this is amusing, as it is intended to be. But it goes deeper than that. Doubtless there are others who actually believe they have kept the law of God. Of course, when this man admitted that he was only "as nearly perfect as a man can be," he admitted that he was a lost soul. For not "near perfection" but absolute perfection is the only standard that can satisfy the righteous requirements of a righteous and holy God. And God's Word tells us that "all have sinned, and come short of the glory of God." The consequence? "The wages of sin is death." Yet there has been one Man who never broke the law of God. That Man is the Son of God, Christ Jesus. He kept the whole law for all of us, and then He bore the lawbreaking sins of us all, offering His own perfect righteousness if we will take this in Himself as a gift. — *Sunday School Times.*

LIGHT

"Mind the Light"

The other day I read the story, told by a brother minister, of the lighthouse keeper on Robbins' Reef off the rocky shore of New England. Jacob Walker, after years of faithful service of minding the light, caught a cold one stormy night and rapidly grew worse and died. His wife buried his body on the hillside above the shore, on the mainland, in plain view of the lighthouse upon the reef. Then she applied for and received the appointment as the keeper of the light. For twenty years she carried on alone, and then a New York City reporter went out to get her story. In the course of the interview she told him this: "Every evening I stand in the door of the lighthouse and look across the water to the hillside where my husband sleeps. . . . I always seem to hear his voice saying, as he often said when he was alive, 'Mind the light! Mind the light! Mind the light!'" Across the troubled waters and the crashing breakers of our time there comes another voice to us, a voice from that "green hill far away, without a city wall," a voice out of the blackness of earth's darkest day to us in the darkness and evil of our day. And the message of the Son of God is the same, "Mind the light! Mind the light! Mind the light!" And, God helping us, as Christian patriots, we will!—*Christian Observer.*

* * *

Sharing the Light

A gentleman was walking one day in the east end of the city of Glasgow. The streets were so narrow, and the houses so high, that little direct sunshine ever reached the houses on one side. The gentleman noticed a ragged, barefooted boy trying, with a small piece of mirror, to catch the sun's rays and direct them to a certain spot on one of the houses opposite. He became interested in the boy's earnest efforts. "What are you trying to do, laddie?" he asked. "Do you see yon window up there?" the boy replied. "Well, my wee brother had an accident two years ago, and is always lying on his back in yon room, and it is on the wrong side to get the sunshine, so I always try to catch the light in this wee glass and shine it into his room."—*The Homiletic Review.*

* * *

Keep the Light Burning

On the coast of Norway is a lighthouse where a keeper lived with his two children. One day he went to the distant shore for provisions. A storm arose, and he was unable to return. The time for lighting the lamp came, and Mary, the elder child, said to her little brother, "We must light the lamp, Willie." "How can we?" asked Willie. "We ain't big enough." But the two children climbed the long, narrow stairs to the tower where the lamp was kept. Mary pulled up a chair and tried to reach the lamp in the great reflector; it was too high. Groping down the stairs, she ascended again with a small oil lamp in her hand. "I can hold this up," she said to her little brother. She climbed on the chair again, but still the reflector was just beyond her reach. "Get down," said Willie; "I know what we can do." She jumped down, and he stretched his little body across the chair. "Stand on me," he said. And she stood on the little fellow as he lay across the chair. She raised the lamp high, and its light shone far out across the water. Holding it first with one hand, then with the other, to rest her little arms, she called down to her brother, "Does it hurt you, Willie?" "Of course it hurts," he called back, "but keep the light burning." Are we keeping the light of God's love burning in the world even though it hurts? Are we holding it up so that all nations may see its beams afar?—*The S. S. Banner.*

* * *

Little Jane Understood

At church little Jane had listened to a sermon on "Let Your Light Shine." The only part she remembered was the text, but she didn't understand what it meant until her mother explained, "It means being good, obedient, and cheerful." In the afternoon there was trouble in the nursery, and Jane excused herself for being naughty by saying, "I've blowed myself out."—*Church Business.*

* * *

Even a Small Light Better Than None

I cannot forget the confusion into which I saw a conceited young fellow thrown once when he turned to an old minister and, as if challenging discussion, said, "I am told you believe in the inspiration of the whole Bible." The good man replied quietly, "Oh, yes, my friend, what do you believe in?" A little laugh covered the defeat, but he continued, "But you certainly know what the great scholars say about it?" When again the calm answer met him, "Somewhat; but what do they say about your soul?" Now the inquirer grew restive. "They say you are leading men along with a farthing taper in your lantern." To this the aged preacher only said, "Do they say men would see any better if we would let them put the taper out?"—*Sabbath Reading.*

* * *

Like Some Religious Lanterns

One night a motorist was run down by a train at a grade crossing. The old signal man in charge of the crossing had to appear in court. After a severe cross-examination, he was still unshaken. He said he had waved his lantern frantically, but all to no avail. The following day the superintendent of the line called him into his office. "You did wonderfully well yesterday, Tom," he said. "I was afraid at first that you might waver." "No, sir," replied Tom, "but I was afraid that old lawyer was going to ask me whether or not my lantern was lit!" —*Sunday School Times.*

* * *

The Power of Light

A modern scientific discovery is of thrilling interest. The so-called death ray with which the French army experimented consists of a light of tremendous candle-power, a beam of which striking the eye causes a temporary paralysis. Troops advancing would be mowed into unconsciousness, later to recover in captivity. What an illustration of the power of light! "Let there be light: and there was light." M. de Christmas, inventor of this ray, believes that cities can be protected by a curtain of light which airmen could not face. "God is light, and in him is no darkness at all." What a symbol, this curtain of light, of the protecting care of God! — *Sunday School Times.*

* * *

Keeping the Torch Lit

Among the ancient Greeks the runner that won the race was not the man who crossed the line in the shortest time, but the man who crossed it in the least time with his torch still burning. We are so busy with life's activities that we are in danger of allowing the torch of our spiritual life to become extinguished. It was when Moses paused in his going that he heard the voice of God.—*Doran's Ministers' Manual.*

* * *

Good Society

"Your new religion has spoiled you, Mary. You will never shine in good society now," said a worldly lady to her niece, who had been brought to decision for Christ a few months before, and who was manifesting the new life in a walk becoming the Gospel of Christ. "I am seeking grace to shine as a light for God in the midst of a dark and evil world, aunt, and I'll get into good society very soon—the society of saints and angels—in my Father's House on high," was the answer she gave. Yes, Christ spoils those who receive Him as Saviour and Lord, for the world's "society." There was no room in "society" for Christ, nor will there be for His followers.—*The Milk of the Word.*

* * *

Where Is Your Light Hanging Out?

The story is told of a little girl who was shivering her way along a main street in one of our great cities. Seeing the beautiful lights of a church building and hearing the music coming from within, she went in and warmed herself as she listened. The preacher's text was, "I am the light of the world." At the close of the service, she went to the minister and said, "Did you say you are the light of the world, sir?" The minister replied, "No, dear child. Christ is the light of the world, and I am one of the lights." The little lass looked at him for a moment, and then solemnly said, "Well, sir, I wish you would come down and hang out in our alley, 'cause it's awful dark down there!" Christians are, indeed, as the Master said, "the light of the world." As one of those lights, are *you* "hanging out" in some dark alley?—*Biblical Research Monthly.*

From One Light to the Next

During a great storm a physician in a small town was called to go some seven or eight miles into the country to visit a sick child. It was evening and the snow was falling so rapidly that it soon blotted out the road and left him in a sore danger of losing his way. Reaching a farmhouse he telephoned to the next one beyond, asking them to hang out a lantern. They did so, and sent the word on to their next neighbor, who in turn sped the message, and so the doctor with his horse and buggy was enabled to drive forward through the storm, making his way from light to light until he reached the home where he was so sorely needed. Is not that a picture of the Christian life? We can each throw a light upon that part of the road that runs by our own door to make sure that no one shall miss the way because our light is not burning.—*Christian Age.*

* * *

Let Your Light Shine

"I was sitting in the gloamin' and a man passed the window. He was a lamplighter. He pushed his pole into the lamp and lighted it. Then he went to another and another. Now I couldn't see him. But I knew where he was by the lights as they broke out down the street, until he had left a beautiful avenue of light."

"Now I couldn't see him." No, but his light could be seen. And that was the important thing. It was the lamplighter's business to light the lamps, not to make himself seen. What matters it, if people take little notice of you? The important thing is to make them take notice of your light. You do not need to seek to be seen of men, but you do need to shine that men may see. "Let your light so shine that men may see your good works"—not you.

"But I knew where he was by the lights as they broke out down the street." *Can people tell where you are by the light you kindle? Can they tell what you stand for?—Evangelical Christian.*

What You Are Here For

We stopped at a garage just at dusk one evening. Something about the engine needed attention. A mechanic examined into the trouble while a helper stood by, directing the beams of a powerful flashlight into the recesses under the hood. Something attracted the helper's attention. He turned away and in doing so inadvertently turned off the light. The mechanic looked up, and with good-humored impatience exclaimed: "Shine your light! What are you here for anyway?" Something to think about in that sentence.—*Gospel Herald.*

* * *

Entertaining Royalty

Two young people were walking along a path in the Catskill Mountains. Their conversation had turned to a mutual acquaintance. The young man said, "She has what I call a radiant personality." "That's right," agreed the young woman. "How do you account for it?" They walked along for a few moments, and then, pointing across the river, he said: "See that wonderful old castle? You know, when I was a small boy, my playmates and I loved to sit on the bank and look across at it. We could tell what was going on there by the number of lights that were burning. If only the family were present, just a few lights would be seen. When guests were entertained, there would be many lights, and the palace became truly beautiful. Once a member of a royal family visited there, and you should have seen the lights! I have seldom seen such brilliance." The young couple's discussion wandered back to their acquaintance. "I think the only way her radiant personality can be explained is that she is constantly entertaining a Royal Guest," suggested the young lady. He agreed.—*Secret Place.*

* * *

The Swiftness of Shining

Talking doesn't compare with living. Suppose you were about to enter Heaven, and stopped to make a few remarks to the people on earth. Suppose at the same moment a sunbeam were leaving the sun, and that your words and the ray of light had the same distance to reach the earth. In eight minutes the people on earth would see that sunbeam; but your voice would not reach them for 1,936 minutes, because sound is so much slower than light. Yet there are so many people who would rather talk than shine!—*Sunday School Times.*

* * *

"The Path of the Just"

A little boy walked along a country lane one dark night, with his father, and carried the lantern. The black silence all about frightened him. He said, "Father, this light reaches such a little way, I am afraid." His father answered, "True, my boy, but if you walk on, the light will shine to the end of your journey." There are night times in the Christian's experience when God gives His followers only enough light to take the next step. And that is all that is needed. We may be sure of one thing,—the light will never go out. If we walk on, it will shine to the end of the journey.—*Sunday School Times.*

* * *

Light That Is Life

Light often points the way to life in both the spiritual and physical realms. A striking illustration of this was seen in a dispatch from George Weller, "somewhere in Australia" (*Evening Bulletin,* Phila.), describing a thrilling incident of the battle of the Java Sea. A destroyer had been torpedoed, and 116 men were struggling for their lives in the oil-burdened waters, swimming about and clinging to rafts. Their cries for help were answered by return cries from three cruisers, "but only some unknown, friendly hand aboard the *Houston* had the quickness of mind to throw them the illuminated life preserver. It was the light attached to it that guided a British destroyer to their rescue." "Regulation American Navy life belts, with a floating light attached, tossed overboard from the cruiser *Houston,*" were the means that saved the lives of these men. They not only supported them in the dark, troubled waters, but led to their final safety. What a vivid picture of the grace and mercy of our Lord Jesus Christ! "In Him was life; and the life was the light of men. . . . And the light shineth in darkness; and the darkness comprehended it not" (John 1:4, 5). He is the light of the world, and He gives life to all who believe in Him. He, with His almighty power, upholds His own amid the troubles of this world, and when their earthly voyage is done, He gathers them safely to Himself in Heaven. — *Sunday School Times.*

* * *

I want to be a little light,
That glistens clean and true,
I want to show forth Jesus
In everything I do.

I don't like smoky lamps, Lord,
Or candles dim and slow;
I don't like flickering, hazy lights
That do not shine and glow.

Thou hast told me in Thy Word,
To let my light so shine,
That those who look into my face
Will know that I am Thine.

—Selected.

LORD'S DAY

Is the Lord's Day Lost Time?

A citizen of the Southwest, hearing his preacher say that a man can do more work in six days than in seven, went to him and said: "I have proved that. When I came West I led the company. When Sunday came I turned my horses out to graze, and got out my Bible to read. The rest asked, 'Why are you not going to travel today?' My answer was,

'I did not leave my religion in the old state. My teams and my family need the rest.' The company moved on, and I did not overtake them the first week until Thursday. The second week I overtook them on Tuesday. After that they never overtook me, and I reached my destination two weeks ahead of all the others, my family well, my teams in good condition, and my wagons sound. The others lost horses; members of their family got sick, and their wagons broke down." The hero was seventy when the story was told; he had always kept the Sabbath, and had seldom missed church.—*Sunday School Times.*

* * *

God's Settlement (Deuteronomy 5:12)

A farmer once wrote to an editor: "Dear Sir: I have been trying an experiment. I have a field of corn which I plowed on Sunday. I planted it on Sunday. I cultivated it on Sunday. I cut and hauled it to the barn on Sunday. And I find that I have more corn to the acre than has been gathered by any of my neighbors this October."

The farmer sent the letter, sure that the editor could have no answer to the sneer implied in it. But imagine his feelings when in the next issue of the paper, he read his own letter in print, and at the end of it this one sentence: "God does not make full settlement in October."—*Home Missions.*

* * *

Pharisaism

A devout Scottish minister has told of a house at which he stopped and spent the Sabbath, when he was in northern Scotland. The day was rainy and close, and he finally suggested to the woman of the house that the window of the little parlor might be raised to admit some fresh air. "Mon," replied the old woman, with stern disapproval showing plainly on her rugged face, "dinna ye ken that ye can hae no fresh air in this house on the Sabbath?"—*The Youth's Companion.*

A Runner Who Honored God.

It is told of Eric Liddell, who won the four hundred meters race at the Olympic games in Paris, that when he found his race was to be run on the Lord's Day he refused to compete, saying, "I object to Sunday sports in toto," and thus counted himself out. The sporting press of Europe derided him; he was gibed and criticized on all sides, even by the papers of his own country. But the stand taken by such a noted athlete had its effect, and the race was not run until later in the week. He says: "I remember that when I was about to run in the finals the trainer handed me a little note. I opened it and read the words, 'Them that honor Me will I honor.' It was God's promise. He helped me, and I won." And the public that had condemned him changed its opinion and gave him great applause.—*Youth's Companion.*

* * *

Why the Dusty Shoes?

A good many years ago I was a student of Monmouth College, Monmouth, Ill. On a hot, sultry Sabbath afternoon in September (as I remember), a number of us went down to the Y.M.C.A. rooms to hear an adress by a young man, announced as the president of Knox College, at Galesburg, Ill., sixteen miles away. The speaker was sitting on the platform when we arrived and appeared to be an ordinary looking fellow, not very well dressed, and his shoes evidently not recently shined. On being introduced to the handful of Monmouth students who had gathered to hear him, he expressed his appreciation of the privilege of speaking to the boys and explained his personal appearance as due to the fact that not wanting to violate his own or any other one's principles of Sabbath keeping, he had therefore walked over. A walk of sixteen miles on a hot, disagreeable Sabbath afternoon to speak to twenty-five or thirty students from a rival school! Apart from the above remarks, which are, of course, not verbatim, I do not remember a single thing he said, but I have *never* forgotten the sacrificial thing he did. The speaker was the famous educator, Dr. John H. Finley, later president of the University of New York and now Associate Editor of the *New York Times*.

* * *

Robbing God

A Chinese preacher, speaking of robbing God, used this illustration: "It came to pass that a man went to market with a string of seven coins. Seeing a beggar who asked for alms, he gave the poor man six of the coins and kept one for himself. The beggar, instead of being thankful, followed the good man and stole the seventh coin also. What an abominable wretch! Yes, and would you, to whom God has given six days, steal the seventh also?"—*The Presbyterian.*

* * *

Sunday—Then and Now

Seventy-five years ago, de Toqueville, a French statesman, visited these shores. The most impressive thing to him was the way the people observed Sunday. Writing about it he said: "I never saw the like. I went over to America and I found a people who on one day every week closed the gateways of their traffic, left the hammer unusued upon their anvil, drew chains across the streets where the churches were and where worship was going on,—a whole people resting and worshiping God." One wonders what de Toqueville would write now of the conditions in a great portion of our land today.—*Sunday School Times.*

* * *

Her Own Day

A little princess' recovery from a dangerous illness was the occasion of setting apart a special day of quiet thanksgiving by the king, in which none of the peasants were to stir from their homes. Slipping unobserved from the castle with a basket under her arm, the little princess went among the peasants, distributing her gifts among the needy. A strange guard halted her, and in a gruff voice said, "Don't you know this is the special thanksgiving day, when no one is allowed on the streets?" She turned in childish glee, exclaiming, "Yes, but I am the princess, and this is my day."—*Sunday School Chronicle.*

* * *

A Parable

A parable tells of seven brothers who lived together. Six worked and the seventh cared for the house, having the meals ready and the house bright for his brothers in the evening. But the six said the seventh must work, too. So in the evening they returned home and found the house dark and no meal prepared. Then they saw how foolish they had been, and quickly restored the old way. Sunday is a day among the seven which provides light, comfort and good for the others. If it is driven out to work, the other days will miss its blessing.—Selected.

* * *

Value of Worship

Friend and foe of the Church have sensed the value of worship. Emerson said: "Religious worship is the most important single function of any people." Voltaire said: "I despair of destroying religion while millions meet together for worship on the first day of each week."

"The Church and the Lord's Day are of vital necessity in the development of the religious life. Without these the whole community would soon become a pagan community, where all spiritual life would disappear and a godless materialism would triumph. Property and life would not be safe if the Lord's Day and the Church were blotted out. Nothing could be more vital to the advance of pure religion than the nourishing of the spirit of worship." — Dr. Charles L. Goodell.

* * *

"Let Glasgow Flourish"

Christian people generally, will approve the decision of the Administration Committee of the Glasgow Exhibition to keep it closed on the Lord's Day. There will, of course, always be those who protest against the decision and see in it nothing but the action of narrow-minded bigots. "The opening of the Empire Exhibition at Glasgow on the Lord's Day would be an unwise and retrograde step," states a protest against the proposal to open the exhibition on Sunday afternoons and evenings, signed by eminent members of the Church of Scotland. The decision is in keeping with the best traditions of Scotland and of Glasgow itself. The words we have placed as the title for this editorial constitute the motto of the city. The exhibition will lose nothing by remaining faithful to the Word and closing its gates on Sunday.—*The Evangel.*

* * *

Better than "Back to Nature"

A friend of Lord Napier said, "I do not see any harm in a man's spending a few hours at work in his flower garden on Sunday. It seems to me that he might gain great good from it." His lordship replied, "Yes, but when a man begins in his flower garden he is likely to end in his potato patch." The cravings of man's threefold nature which assert themselves on Sunday are not for nature but for God. And blessed is the man who uses the day to get back to God instead of back to nature. — Courtesy *Moody Monthly.*

* * *

Morbus Sundayitis

There is a disease that is worse and more deadly than smallpox. It is diagnosed by the spiritual as "Morbus Sundayitis." It is a disease which afflicts most church people. The symptoms vary but never affect the appetite. It never lasts more than twenty-four hours. No physician is ever called. It always proves fatal to the soul. It is very prevalent and destroys thousands every year. The attack comes upon them suddenly every Sunday morning.

No symptoms are evidenced on Saturday night. The attack comes about nine o'clock Sunday morning. Usually the sufferer has enjoyed a very good night's sleep, eats a hearty breakfast, but about church time the attack comes upon him with sudden severity. It continues until morning services are over and then seems to abate long enough for him to eat a large dinner. In the afternoon the sufferer seems to be much better and often goes out for a motor ride, game of golf or some other form of exercise.

Morbus Sundayitis never seems to affect the eyes, for the patient seems to be able to thoroughly enjoy the Sunday paper. About supper time he gets another attack that seems to last until church services are over. On Monday he awakes refreshed and does not have another attack until the following Sunday.

Remedy: one large dose, "Awake, thou that sleepest, and arise from the dead, and Christ shall give thee light" (Eph. 5:14).—*Evangelical Christian.*

* * *

Sunday Breaking

A story is told of the early days of Queen Victoria's reign which illustrates the tenacity with which she held to obediance to what she believed to be the Divine requirement.

Late one Saturday night one of the ministers arrived at Windsor. "I have brought down for your majesty's inspection," said he, "some documents of great importance. But as I shall be obliged to trouble you to examine them in detail, I will not encroach upon the time of your majesty tonight, but will request your attention tomorrow morning."

"Tomorrow morning!" repeated the queen; "tomorrow will be Sunday, my lord."

"True, your majesty, but the business of the state will not admit of delay."

"I am aware of that," replied the queen, "and as your lordship could not have arrived earlier at the palace tonight I will, if the papers are of such pressing importance, attend to their contents tomorrow morning after Divine service." Next morning the queen and the court went to church, and so did the noble lord, and the subject of the sermon was, "The rest day: its duties and obligations." After the service the queen inquired, "How did your lordship like the sermon?"

"Very well, indeed, your majesty," was the answer of the nobleman.

"Well, then," said the queen, "I will not conceal from you that last night I sent the clergyman the text from which he preached. I hope we shall all be improved by the sermon." It is needless to add that the state papers went over till Monday morning.—Selected.

* * *

Six Working Days Enough

Sidney Cooper, R.A., was once asked. "Do you paint on Sundays?" "No," said he, "if I can't get my living in six days, I should not manage it in seven."—H. O. Mackay.

* * *

Whose Spirit Was He In?

Speaking in London, Canon Ottley told the following story as illustrating some folks' idea of keeping the Sabbath. A Scotsman, one Sunday, went into his back yard to mend a barrow. The loud banging which accompanied the driving of the nails brought his wife to the door. "Donald, Donald," she cried, "what are ye about on the Sabbath?" "I tell ye, I must mend the barrow. I want to use it," answered her husband. "Ye must not," was her reply. "What'll the neighbor's say? *Or if ye do, ye must use screws. It's the Lord's Day."—Sunday School Chronicle.*

* * *

There's Only One Way to Rear a Family

Nurture them in the chastening and admonition of the Lord.

Dwight Hillis conducted the funeral of a beautiful girl who had been killed in an automobile accident on the Lord's Day, while out for pleasure. As the father bade goodbye to the loved form, he turned to his friends and said in a choking voice: "We have spent our Sunday playing golf or automobiling. Our children have followed our example and have outstripped us. My son has disgraced me, my daughter is dead. I tell you there is only one way to rear a family, and that is in the Sunday School and the church. I know what I am talking about."—*United Presbyterian.*

* * *

Misunderstanding the Lord's Day

"In one of the English coal mines there is what the miners call a Sunday-stone. Water charged with lime trickles through the rocks, and, as it falls, makes a deposit of pure white limestone. All the week, when the miners are at work, the dust flying about gets mixed with the lime in the water, and the stone is coal-black in color. But when the Sabbath comes, and the whirring coal dust settles, then the clean limewater drips upon the stone leaving it, as it trickles off, pure white. Regularly each week the stone shows a streak of white marking the miners' day of rest. God's day ought to be kept holy, so that each tired soul may forget the week's dark hours, and in the act of true worship find sins washed away." This incident is given here to show what mistaken ideas Christian people may have about the Lord's Day. What an unspeakably low, unscriptural thought that we must necessarily get dirtied up with sin during the week, and then once a week get clean again!—*Sunday School Times.*

* * *

From the Sufferer's Viewpoint

George M. Mackie, in an article in the *Sunday School Times,* told the following: Some time ago when studying this incident (Mark 3:1-5) in the Hebrew New Testament with a class of Jewish schoolboys, I asked them what they thought about Christ's action. One boy said that as the man's infirmity had likely been of long standing, he could easily have waited one day more. Another said it would have saved trouble if Jesus had deferred the cure until the next day. A third maintained that there had been no infringement of the Sabbath law because the act of healing had not involved any manual operation. Finally the discussion was broken up by the question of a blind boy of the class—What would you have preferred if you had had the withered hand?—*The King's Business.*

* * *

A Jew's Challenge to Christians

"I love your English Sunday, your Christian Sabbath, and should be very sorry to see it pass away. If a Jew may be pardoned for making this suggestion to Christians, let me say this: If you sacrifice the Sunday you have been brought up to respect, you will lose something you will be sorry for the whole of your lives." This was the comment made in the Council Chamber at Middlesbrough by Mr. Jules Reubens, a local member, who is a cinema proprietor. Mr. Reubens was speaking against a resolution for Sunday opening of picture houses. — *Christian Herald* (London).

* * *

When Kings Defy God

There is a story told in Benjamin Franklin's autobiography of a clergyman who was ordered to read the proclamation issued by Charles I, bidding the people to return to sports on Sundays. To the congregation's amazement and horror, he did read the Royal edict in church, which many clergy had refused to do. But he followed it with the words, "Remember the sabbath day, to keep it holy," and added, "Brethren, I have laid before you the commandment of your king and the commandment of your God. I leave it to you to judge which of the two ought rather to be observed." — *Christian Herald.*

* * *

A Hindu's Observation

During the last war an Indian maharaja, conversing with an American, asked him: "Do you know why God is punishing the Christians by letting them fight and destroy each other as they are?" Answering his own question he then said: "If I paid as little attention to my religion as most Christians paid to theirs, I would expect God to punish me." Then the Hindu prince explained that though less than one per cent of the officials in his employ were British, yet for their sake he kept all his offices closed on Sunday, and had built two Christian churches, that they might have both time and place for worship. But he went on to say that services were held only about once in three months. "What do they do on Sunday?" he asked. "They go hunting, boating, tennising, racing, playing cards. If you ask me why God is punishing the Christian nations, I think that there you have the answer." There is a Hindu for you on the subject of the Christian and the Lord's Day.—*Sunday School Times.*

* * *

"The Sinners' Parade"

Two young men, seated in the early morning train on Monday, were speaking of how tired they were, more than on Saturday night. One related having driven to the shore in his new car, and said, "Never again for me!" "Have trouble?" the other asked. "No, but you know what that road is like on Sunday. At the height of the home-coming traffic there is a line of cars end to end, mile after mile, all the way across the state to the ferries—'the sinners' parade,' someone near me in a jam called it jeeringly. That phrase stuck in my mind. Of course they were not all sinners — no doubt there were preachers, church workers, and doctors on their various errands. Let's be charitable. But I can't get away from the thought of the noise, the dust, the un-Sabbath-like gayety and worldliness of the crowds, the many disabled cars and the one accident when several were seriously hurt. Don't think I am a coward," he continued, "that I am afraid of getting hurt physically. I can take my chances with the rest. But I am afraid of hurts that go deeper. I'm afraid to parade with the sinners when I ought to be in church with the saints." —*Youth's Companion.*

LORD'S SUPPER

No "Communion" Here

The writer witnessed several women seated in front of her in a large church take the bread as it was passed, then reach for their compacts and, regarding their mirrors, touch up their complexion, add rouge to their lips, then replace the compact to reach the Communion wine being extended toward them! — Mrs. Ralph Norton, in *Moody Monthly.*

* * *

The Lord's Supper (1 Corinthians 11:26)

The Lord's table is like a great bridge, spanning the entire interval of the Church's history on earth. One end of it rests on the shame of the cross, the other is planted in the glory of the kingdom. This feast sustains a threefold relationship to the Christian:

It is the Reminder of our Past Justification.

It is the Source of our Present Sustenance in the new life.

It is the Pledge of our Future Blessedness and Glory.

1. It is a Table of Remembrance (v. 24).
2. It is a Table of Obedience—Take, eat, . . . drink ye all of it" (v. 24).
3. It is a Table of Self-examination (v. 28).
4. It is a Table of Communion (I Cor. 10:16).
5. It is a Table of Thanksgiving (v. 24).
6. It is a Table of Confession (v. 26).
7. It is a Table of Expectation—"Till he come" (v. 26c).
8. It is a Table of Hope for Israel also (Rom. 11:26).—George C. Needham.

* * *

The Lord's Supper in a Concentration Camp

Aatami Kuortti, a Lutheran pastor in Russia, was sentenced to ten years of hard labor in a concentration camp because of his refusal to become a spy for the government. A very large proportion of the prisoners were Christians, whose only offense was their Christian faith. One of the Finnish believers received a package from home, a little bread and a few apples. The first thing he thought of was that it would be possible now to celebrate the Lord's Supper. He proposed this to Pastor Kuortti. The pastor thought it impossible. "The guards would certainly interfere." "But it is all arranged," said Kajada. "I have already crushed the apple juice in a mug and the crusts will serve as communion bread. We can have the holy ordinance in the corner where my brother and I have our place, and the Russians if they see us will think we are drinking tea." "I gladly fell in with the proposal of the brethren. After repetition of Scripture, I blessed the bread and the mug of apple juice, and we ate the Lord's Holy Communion. The altar was but a dirty plank, and the pastor, as well as his flock, was in rags, yet we realized the presence of Christ."—*Sunday School Times.*

* * *

Why We Should Partake

The quaint Scottish saint, "Rabbi" Duncan, was minister of a Perthshire parish. On one Communion Sunday, he observed a woman, troubled by lack of "assurance," passing the cup untasted. He stepped down, took the cup, and handed it back to her, saying in broad Doric: "Tak' it, woman, tak' it; it's for sinners." — David Smith, in *British Weekly.*

* * *

"Nothing But the Blood"

Communion even for the cannibals (Luke 22:19). John G. Paton, missionary to the New Hebrides, in describing the first Communion service on the Island of Aniwa, says: "The whole service occupied nearly three hours. The Islanders looked on with a wonder whose unwonted silence was almost painful to bear. Many were led to inquire carefully about everything they saw, so new and strange. For the first time the Dorcas Street Sabbath School Teachers' gift from South Melbourne Presbyterian Church was put to use—a new communion service of silver. They gave it in faith that we would require it, and in such we received it. And now the day had come and gone! For three years we had toiled and prayed and taught for this. At the moment when I put the bread and wine into those dark hands, once stained with the blood of cannibalism but now stretched out to receive and partake the emblems and seals of the Redeemer's love, I had a foretaste of the joy of glory that well-nigh broke my heart to pieces. I shall never taste a deeper bliss till I gaze on the glorified face of Jesus Himself" (This wonderful service occurred on October 24, 1869).—From the Story of John G. Paton.

* * *

A Bible Instead of Cutlass or Gun

A Nigerian missionary arrived at a Communion service in which four towns were combining, and heard an African addressing the crowded church in a preparatory meeting as follows: "I cannot tell you the gladness that is in my heart today. As I walked along the path with the other members from my town I saw that each man held in his hand his Testament and his hymn-book. No man carried a cutlass or a gun. No man walked with fear; every man with faith in you. And yet it is but four years ago that no man from my town would have walked through your town without a cutlass in his hand, and even then he would not have walked alone. Nor would any man from your town have come unarmed through ours. What is the reason for this difference? At that time we worshiped the same gods as you did. Today we worship the same God as you do, but the God we worship today is the God of peace. We have learned that He is our Father, and that we are brothers." — Bishop of Croydon.

* * *

The Real Absence

A speaker, in commenting on the words of the institution of the Lord's Supper — "This do in remembrance of me," calls attention to *the fact that here there is a real absence and not a "real presence"*; that we are to recall Christ's former presence and await His coming ("till He come"). — *Sunday School Times.*

* * *

Whom She Needed

A lady was lying dangerously ill. A clergyman had been sent for, and he gave her the sacrament, but it failed to give her peace. After the minister had left, the sufferer turned to the occupant of the bed nearest her own, and said sadly, "I thought it would have done me more good." The other, an earnest Christian lady, quickly replied, "Ah, you don't want *it;* you want *Him!"* — *The King's Business.*

LOST

Lost

James W——, British financier and reputed millionaire; who had owned a yacht and racing stud; entertained royalty, and had made as much as three million dollars in one day, died by his own hand, practically a ruined man.

Before he brought his life to a close he wrote a letter which was published in the British press, and laid bare the truth without any false coloring, of what this world really is.

He had tasted all that this life could give and now records his verdict in the truest sermon ever preached by mortal man. Hear what he says:

"On the last day of my life, before my eyes, my brain unwinds the film of the past. In quick succession episode after episode unwinds, *and I can now judge that life today is nothing but a human cauldron of greed, lust and power.* Gone are the nice feelings and contentment, and in their place is a roaring, hectic existence."

He draws aside the curtain and shows us the world in its true character. "I have known," he says, "to have all you desire, and to have thousands waiting to eat out of your hand. . . . From this it must be agreed," he adds, "that I am entitled to an opinion on life."

And what is that opinion? The opinion of the man who owned towns and had everything that the world could give! *Wealth cannot satisfy.*

"Gone are the nice feelings and contentment." He knew that "money is the universal provider of everything but happiness; and a passport to everywhere but heaven." Bishop Ryle said, "Riches are uncertain comforts, but certain cares."

"What shall it profit a man, if he shall gain the whole world, and lose his own soul?" (Mark 8:36).

"To lose your health is much,
To lose your wealth is more,
To lose your soul is such a loss,
That nothing can restore."
—*Gospel Herald.*

* * *

Their Loss If Unacquainted

Privates Henry Pauch and Steve Obeda, inducted at Fort Sheridan, Ill., came to Camp Wolters, Texas, in the same troop movement. For two months they were in the same platoon and slept in bunks not far apart. Then they swapped addresses. One lived at 2553 South Troy Street, Chicago, and the other at 2541, same street, same city. They were close neighbors, but strangers, for thirteen years—then got acquainted so far from home. But there is a stranger case of strangership than theirs—one which should provoke tears, not smiles.

We tread God's earth and breathe His air, yet multitudes are total strangers to Him. One might remain a stranger to his neighbor and not suffer any great loss, though neighborliness carries its own reward. But it is impossible to remain a stranger to our Lord and not suffer eternal loss.—Now.

Unheeded Warning

A tourist in Scotland some years ago, unacquainted with the nature of the coast, wandered along a path, which is only safe at low tide. Delighted with the seascape, he watched with admiration the huge waves breaking on the shore, and gazed with awe at the precipitous rocks towering above him, and so entranced was he with his surroundings, he did not notice that the sea was gradually encroaching on his pathway.

A native, observing from the lofty cliffs this stranger, evidently unaware of danger, descended as far as he was able with safety, and drew his attention by a loud "hulloo," and said: "If you pass this spot, you lose your last chance. The tide is rising, already the beach you have traveled is covered, and the waters are nearing the foot of the cliffs before you. By this path alone can you escape."

The warning went unheeded, for the tourist thought he was able to make the turn in the road before the sea reached the cliff, but he misjudged the distance, and soon saw with alarm the danger of his position. He turned back, but alas! the sea had already cut off his way of escape. He looked at the cliffs, which were inaccessible, the waters were at his feet. He sought higher ground, but to no purpose. At last a projecting rock was seen. He reached it but the relentless waves came on. They reached him inch by inch, until they reached his neck. He uttered one despairing cry for help, but none was near. The waters covered this victim of self-confidence. He neglected the warning and perished.

"There is a time we know not when,
A point we know not where,
That marks the destiny of men
For glory or despair."
—*Gospel Herald.*

* * *

Tragic—But Not the End

She was a young woman. She loved her husband. He died. She was lonely and disconsolate. She hired an airplane and placed in the fuel tank enough gasoline to take her far into the air and to sea. When the gas was consumed she would plunge into the sea and that would end her sad and lonely life. No one could trace her or find her. This must not be called suicide—this she insisted. It was just her way out; it was her exit. The newspapers and columnists commented on this tragic flight into what they called the "unknown." But there is no "unknown" to God, to whom all things are known (Psa. 139:7-12) Her body is in the sea, but this does not mean extinction, for the sea will give up its dead (Rev. 20:13). This woman who flew to the sea by way of the air did not find her husband. On the other hand, the Christian will enjoy reunion, and will be "caught up . . . to meet the Lord in the air" (I Thes. 4:17). What the crazed mind of humankind needs is the Word of the Lord; all else is helpless.—*The Wonderful Word.*

* * *

Why Be Lost?

When the *Squalus* crew realized they had taken their last dive and that they were lying helpless at the bottom of the Atlantic Ocean 240 feet below the surface, they sent up smoke flares and a buoy. Would one of the sister ships find them, and if so could they be rescued? Their help must come from above, and in agonizing silence they waited.

Within an hour after that fatal dive the submarine Sculpin set out in search. In a few hours the red smudge was found, then the buoy. But 24 hours passed before actual rescue work could be started. A giant 10-ton diving bell dipped and rose again and again, each time taking several men alive from those awful depths, until all 33 men who were alive in the submarine had been rescued.

When that huge diving bell came for the Squalus crew not one sailor refused to be rescued, but *all gladly accepted the way to safety.* Will you not *today* accept God's way of salvation for you?—*Good News Tract.*

* * *

Voltaire's Valedictory

It is reported that the brilliant, witty Frenchman Voltaire, who scorned the light of divine truth, when death was in prospect, exclaimed, "Now for a fearful leap in the dark." — *Sunday School Times.*

* * *

The Derelict

Buffeted by temperamental winds—tossed by angry waves — the derelict ship moves across the waters of the midnight sea. No steady hand at the wheel determines her course . . . no compass points her port. She is only a battered hulk, biding her time upon the waves until the elements send her at last to the burial ground of forgotten ships.

Once a useful vessel bearing her cargo, fulfilling her intended destiny—now only a broken wreck drifting to her inevitable doom!

Saddest of all dramas enacted upon the seas is that of the derelict. There is nothing beautiful about her. Forlorn she seems, somehow, with her ragged sails tossed to the mercy of the winds.

No longer is she fulfilling the purpose for which she was made. Never again will her helm swerve gently to the promptings of the wheel as she glides gracefully toward an appointed port. The sound of voices—the pull of the ropes—all these are only vague hints of yesterdays which she will never know again.

What is her story?

Perhaps a fever raged, taking one by one the members of her crew until now that battered hulk carries in its cabins a cargo of grim skeletons. Perhaps a storm threatened, and the men, unable longer to manage her in the raging seas, took to the lifeboats.

We do not know . . . for ghost ships cannot speak. But this we do know . . . she is only a Derelict!

Tomorrow she may be gone—"unwept, unhonored, and unsung." No one will mark her end . . . no one will miss her. And with her, into the graves of the sea, will go the memories of windy capes and tortuous channels. The winds that made her wise will play a ghastly requiem over the waves which claim her, and then there will be only the stretchless sea again. The derelict will be forgotten . . . forever.

Even as the sea's saddest tale is woven about the derelict ship adrift upon her bosom, so the saddest story written in the great Book of Life is that of the Derelict Soul.

How often we pass them as we journey over the sea of life—ships that pass in the night—haunted souls attempting to guide their broken barques over waters which can only be safely navigated under the guidance of the Master Pilot. Souls which sway to the will of every wind which blows and every wave that tries their slender spars . . . the Derelict Souls of Life! How pitiful they are! And how needlessly so!—*War Cry!*

* * *

Preparation of Life's End

Life must be lived for its end. If we are to end it gloriously, we must live it worthily. Human fear leads many to hide death from their thoughts. This is neither sound sense nor realistic behavior. Refusing to think of it does not make death any the less potent. Only a fool lives in this kind of bluff. In the Middle Ages, when noblemen employed fools, or jesters, to amuse them, a certain man gave his valuable cane to his fool and told him that when he could find a greater fool he should bring it back to him. In due time the nobleman came to die and said farewell to his jester. "Where is your Lordship going?" asked the fool. "I am going to another world," was the reply. "And when shall you return?" "Oh, I am never to return." "No!" said the fool; "then has your Lordship made any preparation for the journey?" "Alas, I have not." "Then take back your cane," said the man, "for never could there be folly so great as that!" Exactly!—*Gospel Herald.*

* * *

Stained With Human Blood

Dr. George W. Truett tells of a funeral he was asked to conduct of a sixteen-year-old girl. Seeking information that would help him in his ministry of comfort, the mother told him: "Dr. Truett, she was our only child." "Yes, but you sorrow not as others that have no hope," said the minister. But the mother answered, "That is where the trouble is, we have no such hope. Our daughter was not a Christian."

The mother wept bitterly while she continued her story. "While it is true that her father and I were both members of the church even before she was born, it is also true that our darling girl lying in that casket, never heard either of us pray. She was not converted, and we fear that she is lost and her blood will be upon us." Then she became hysterical in the thought of a lost daughter.

Relating the incident later, Dr. Truett asked, "Who would dare say that her blood would not be upon them?" Father and mother both professing Christians, but had never prayed in their home! May God have mercy on children coming from such homes!—*The Elim Evangel.*

* * *

Taking Good Care of the Clothes

Someone has illustrated the value of a soul with a modern parable in this striking manner. A householder took a trip into a far country and left with his servant a child and the child's clothes. After a while he returned and the servant said to him: "Sir, here are all the child's clothes. They are in excllent condition—clean and mended and pressed. But as for the child, I do not know where it is." So in the last day some will say: "Lord, here is my body—I have neglected nothing that belongs to it. It is strong and well and beautiful. But as for my soul, I have lost it."—*The Presbyterian.*

* * *

Striking Contrasts

THE UNBELIEVER

1. Dead in sin (Eph. 2:1).
2. Under God's wrath (Eph. 2:3).
3. Without God (Eph. 2:12).
4. Under condemnation (John 3:16).
5. Blinded by Satan (II Cor. 4:4)
6. A child of Satan (John 8:44).
7. Eternally lost (John 3:36).

8. Certain of hell (Rev. 21:8).
9. Awaiting judgment (Heb. 9:27).
10. Solemnly warned (Rev. 20:15).

THE BELIEVER

1. Dead to sin (I Peter 2:24).
2. Saved from wrath (Rom. 5:9).
3. Near to God (Eph. 2:13).
4. Free from judgment (John 5:24).
5. No longer blind (II Cor. 3:16).
6. A child of God (Gal. 3:26).
7. Eternally saved (John 3:16).
8. Certain of heaven (II Tim. 4:18).
9. Awaiting glory (Titus 2:13).
10. Gloriously assured (I Pet. 1:3-5).

* * *

The signs of the times are making an impression on those who have hitherto been little inclined to observe them. The president of Union Theological Seminary, Dr. Coffin, declared in Carnegie Hall that "we live in a world which is falling to pieces internationally, racially, and industrially." Dr. Edmund Chaffee at the same meeting said: "A great sense of failure has come to all of us. God Himself has convicted us of sin. We have been glibly saying for years that this was a lost world, but the terrible truth of this statement has never been driven home to us. Now we know civilization for what it is,—spiritually hollow, cruel, blind, literally sliding toward hell. Unless Christ's Gospel is preached quickly, fearlessly, passionately, ours is a lost world. Even now it may be too late."—*Sunday School Times.*

* * *

The Spurned Invitation

God invites you to the greatest happiness that can come to man in this world, and you say, "Excuse me." He invites you to a happy reunion with the loved ones whose faces faded away in the gloom of the grave, and you say "Excuse me." He invites you to a life of the noblest service any man can live, and you say, "Excuse me." And yet He has borne with you in patience and in love. Sometime He will take you at your word and say, "You are excused." and shut you out forever from His mercy and pardon.—W. E. Biederwolf.

* * *

Who Does the Finding?

Yam Sing came from China to California and was brought to know the grace of our Lord Jesus Christ. When examined before baptism concerning his experience of faith, someone asked him how he found Jesus. *"I no find Jesus at all; He find me,"* was the answer from the converted man, an answer which was more than satisfactory to the questioner, and which showed that he had learned something of the love of Him who came to "seek and to save that which was lost."—*S. S. Advocate.*

* * *

An Awful Vision

"I saw a Punjab brother convulsed and sobbing as if his heart would break. I went up to him, and said, 'The Blood of Jesus Christ cleanseth us from all sin.' A smile lit up his face, 'Thank God, Sahib,' he cried, 'but, oh! what an awful vision I have had! Thousands of souls in this land of India being carried away by the dark river of sin! They are in Hell now! Oh, to snatch them from the fire before it is too late!"—Selected.

* * *

I'm Not Going That Way

Dr. J. Wilbur Chapman once told of a prodigal son who came home for his Christian mother's funeral. Beside the casket stood his father and sister. When the prodigal boy was urged to stop weeping and leave, the father said, "We'll see Mother again." The boy answered, "Yes, Dad, you and sister shall see her again, I know, but I shall not, for I'm not going that way."

"Sad, sad, that bitter wail;
Almost—but lost!"

Where will you spend eternity?—Courtesy *Moody Monthly.*

Lost in Sight of Home

When the ill-fated ship, the Royal Charter, went down long years ago, it had toured the waters of the world, and had on board a distinguished company of passengers. They were to land finally on their return voyage in Liverpool. Great preparation was being made to welcome them. And yet, on that last night, just a few hours before they reached Liverpool, the ship caught fire, and sank to the depths of the sea, nearly all of the passengers drowning with the sinking ship. Only a few escaped to tell the terrible story. All Liverpool was agog with interest to welcome the people, not knowing of the sinking of the ship. Then, the few survivors came to shore, and told the awful story to the people. Then, the story had to be carried to the homes in Liverpool. Dr. W. M. Taylor was commissioned to carry the story of the sinking ship to one of his families, and tell wife and children that husband and father would never come back to his earthly home. The wife greeted him joyously at the door. "Oh, you have come at the right time! Husband is to be here in a few minutes!" And then she started back. Said she, "What on earth is it, Dr. Taylor? What has happened? Do not keep me in suspense." Taking her hand in his, he said, "Little woman, I am the bearer of evil tidings. The ship has gone down, just a little distance from the shore, and your husband is drowned there with the rest!" Her face turned pale with the whiteness of snow. She uttered one piercing cry and fell unconscious at his feet. This was her cry, "Oh, God, he got so near home, and yet will never come!"—George W. Truett.

LOVE FOR CHRIST

"I Love Him Too"

An old countryman, visiting London for the first time in his life, went into one of the great picture galleries to look around. Presently he came to a wonderful painting of the Lord Jesus Christ hanging upon the Cross. He stopped before it, and as he gazed at the picture a great love for the One who hung there flooded his heart. "Bless Him!'" he said, aloud. "I love Him! I love Him!"

Others in the gallery heard the old man's words, and seeing the tears trickling down his old furrowed cheeks, as he stood beside the picture, hat in hand, forgetful of all else, were touched, and stopped before the picture, too. Presently a stranger drew near to the old countryman, and grasping his hand, said: "I love Him, too, brother."

Seeing what had taken place, a third stepped forward, saying: "So do I." Then a fourth joined them, and a fifth, until there stood before the picture of the Saviour a little knot of men, perfect strangers to one another, but drawn together by the love of the Lord Jesus.—*Gospel Herald.*

* * *

They Loved Him Utterly

A celebrated Japanese statesman once said, "We do not worship our emperor, we love him utterly. The commander before Port Arthur one day called for volunteers to cut the barbed wire entanglements. 'You will never come back,' he said. 'Nor can you carry a gun. You will take your place and cut one or two wires and fall dead. Another will take your place and cut one or two wires more. But you will know that upon your dead bodies the armies of your emperor will march to victory." Whole regiments volunteered for these 'sure death' parties. If your Christians loved your God as we love our emperor, they would have long since taken the world for Him."—*Herald of Light.*

Love Fertilizes the Life

Dr. Watson (Ian Maclaren) tells of once hearing a plain sermon in a little country church. It was a layman, a farmer, who preached, but Dr. Watson said he never heard so impressive an ending to any sermon as he heard that day. After a fervent presentation of the gospel, the preacher said with great earnestness: "My friends, why is it that I go on preaching to you week by week? It is just this, because I can't eat my bread alone." That is the Master's burden. He cannot bear to be alone in His joy. *There is no surer test of love for Christ than the longing to have others love Him.—Southern Churchman.*

* * *

Anything for His Son's Sake

A very wealthy man lost his wife when his only child was very young. Then there came into his home a housekeeper to take care of that boy. The boy lived until he was of age, and then he died. The man had no other relatives; and he died heartbroken soon after the boy died. He had no one to leave his enormous wealth to, and there was a question about what would become of his possessions. They could find no will. It looked as if it would all pass over to the state. At last it was taken over by the state, and they held a sale to dispose of his personal effects, at the mansion where he had lived. The old housekeeper who had brought up that boy from infancy, not having any money of her own, being just as poor as when she began to work for this wealthy man and keep house for him, went to the sale. There was only one thing she wanted. She couldn't buy the furniture; she couldn't buy the expensive rugs, but there was a picture on a wall in that house, a picture of the boy. She loved that boy. He had been to her a son, although she held no relationship to him. When the picture came to be sold, nobody else wanted it, and she bought it just for a few cents, and took it home. It had been hanging on the wall for some time, and she thought she would clean it, take the back out, take the glass out, and polish it. But when she took it apart, some important looking papers fell out. They were given to a lawyer, who said to the woman, "I guess you have fallen on your feet this time. This man has left all his wealth to the one who loved his son enough to buy that picture." God will do anything for those who love His Son.—From a pamphlet issued by Pastor Edward Drew of Paterson, N. J.

* * *

True Love For Him

There is such a danger of our being so occupied with the things that are coming more than with Him who is to come; there is such scope in the study of coming events for imagination and reason and human ingenuity, that nothing but deeply humble waiting on God can save us from mistaking the interest and pleasure of intellectual study for the true love of Him and His appearing.—Andrew Murray.

* * *

Loving Service

Cripple Tom said, "To know Him is to love Him and to love Him is to serve Him. It wouldn't be loving without." Another has said, "Love must long, must serve, must sacrifice. Love ignores criticism. Loves sees God in everything and simply obeys. Oh! love is indeed an energizer, and finds opportunities for service unnoticed by others."—*Gospel Herald.*

* * *

Money Well Spent

Joseph T. Larsen in one of his tracts tells of a minister who went to Philadelphia from Massachusetts. He later called up his wife at a cost of $1.35 just to tell her how much he loved her. The wife was bewildered, wondering if he was sick. But, no, he simply wanted to tell her that he loved her still and to the extent that he could not wait until he came home. Do you ever tell God how much you love Him? Does He ever see you go to any expense to prove it?—*Finest of the Wheat.*

Loving the Unseen

"Papa, do you love Jesus?" asked little Emily of her father, who did not care for anything religious.

"Jesus is dead, my dear, long, long ago. He was crucified, and that was the end of Him."

"But Jesus rose again, and did what no other man could do. And if Jesus was not living now, we could not be living either, as He gives us life and everything else, Papa."

"But how can I love whom I have never seen, Emily? Tell me that, my dear."

Emily at first did not know what to reply, and her father looked pleased to know that he had puzzled her. At length she said, "Papa, how old was I when Mama died?"

"Only six months, my child."

"Then I can't say that I ever saw her for I don't remember her at all. But you have always tried to make me love her by telling me how good and kind she was; and I do love her, although I have never seen her that I can remember."

By this time the tears were running down the father's cheeks and kissing Emily, he said, "God has spoken to me by you, my dear, and now you must pray for me, and ask God to give me a new heart, with which I shall love Jesus." And the prayer was soon answered.—*Sent of God.*

* * *

A Child's Love

One night, as a little girl knelt for her good-night prayer time, her mother, as mothers sometimes do, suggested things for her little daughter to pray about, and to give thanks for. "Won't you ask the Lord Jesus to help you to love Him more?" said the mother. The child lifted her head, and there was a puzzled look in her clear eyes. "What is it, dear?" asked her mother. "Did you say for me to ask Him to help me to love Him more?" came the question. "Yes, my darling." "But how *can* I love Him more, Mummie? I am just crazy about Him now."—*Junior King's Business.*

Learning to Love Christ

A man thus described his conversion to Mark Guy Pearse: "I never professed to be a Christian or anything like that; but one morning as I was going down to my business, I was thinking of those words, 'Simon, son of Jonas, lovest thou me?' and wished with all my heart that I could answer them as Peter did. I felt very sad that I could not. Then this thought came to me, 'Well, if I cannot say so much as Peter, perhaps I could turn it around a little and find something easier.' So I began to think there was one thing I could not say. I could not say, 'Lord, Thou knowest that I do *not* love Thee,' and I found some comfort in that. At last I grew bold enough to look up and say, 'Lord, Thou knowest all things. Thou knowest that I *want* to love Thee.' *Then I began to think of His great love for me; I thought of His life, of His words, of His Cross, and almost before I knew what I was doing, I looked up and said, 'Thou knowest that I DO love Thee.'* " And at that moment the consciousness of forgiveness and a new life came into his heart.—Tilestone F. Chambers.

* * *

Lovest Thou Me?

Lovest thou Me? I left My all,
My kingly crown, My heavenly hall,
For Bethlehem, for Calvary—
I left it all for love of thee—
Lovest thou Me?

Lovest thou Me? Behold the blood,
Blood of the sinless Son of God!
Go, gaze on Calvary's crimson tide!
Behold My hands, My feet, My side—
Lovest thou Me?

Lovest thou Me? For thee I died—
God for the sinner crucified!
O Soul, what thinkest thou of Me?
What hast thou done with Calvary?
Lovest thou Me?

—Selected.

* * *

How Much Did He Love Her?

A young man spent an entire evening telling a girl how much he loved her. He said that he couldn't live without her; that he'd go to the ends of the earth for her; yes, go through fire for her, or die for her. But when leaving he said, "I'll see you tomorrow night—if it doesn't rain." How often we say we love God, yet deny it by our actions. John said, "Let us not love in word, neither in tongue; but in deed and in truth."—Ruby Barrow Oldfield, in the *Secret Place.*

* * *

A True Story of Two Lovers' Pact

A painful dilemma was solved by a young school teacher in New Mexico in 1889. Her school was at a town called Chama. There she met a young business man with whom she became acquainted. They grew attached to each other and in the summer the young man began to talk of marriage. The school teacher wanted her father's consent to the union, so at the first opportunity she paid a visit to his ranch at Alamosa. It was arranged that, after a few days her lover should follow her and learn the result of her application to her father. The girl's mission was not successful. Her father knew nothing of the young man's character or position, but was "against him on general principles." His opposition continued in spite of argument and coaxing, and was still firm when the lover appeared. The daughter happened to see the young man aproaching the ranch, and told her father. "He shall not come into my house," said the old man resolutely. Finding that pleading was of no avail, the girl considered for a minute, and then seized her father in her arms and hugged him again and again, affectionately kissing him. Then she released him with a tearful good-bye caress, and ran from the house to meet her lover. She told him the situation, and then mounting to his side in the wagon, they drove to Santa Fé where they were married. Evidently it cost her a struggle to leave her father for her lover, and doubtless her husband loved her all the more for the proof she therein gave him of the depths of her love. Such love,—stronger than all rival claims, the Lord Jesus requires of all who would be His followers.—Selected.

* * *

Knowing Christ Intimately

Mr. Glenny, the founder of the North Africa Mission, was once away upon the Yorkshire moors, and he was told there was a very godly old shepherd who would be minding the sheep out on those moors, and Mr. Glenny said, "I would like to meet that man." They said, "You will find him. Just roam over the moors, and you will come across him all right." One morning Mr. Glenny started out, and there among the sheep he found this old shepherd. He walked up to him and said, "Brother, may I shake hands with you? I hear you love the Lord Jesus." I do not feel that it is irreverent if I give you that shepherd's reply in the words he used. He said, "Yes, sir, I love the Lord Jesus, and me an' Him's very thick." Could you say that? Are you on terms like that with the Lord Jesus?—*Gospel Herald.*

LOVE FOR OTHERS

Loving the Unlovely

A poor, degraded woman was being led from the police court. She was dirty, full of sin, and sobbing with hopeless distress. A Christian woman saw her, and moved by the compassion of Christ, swept up to her and kissed her. She had never been noticed or shown love by a clean woman for years. It broke her heart. She was soon released and nursed back to health in the Christian woman's home. That Christian worker moved into a new experience in Christ, as a compassion for the unlovely possessed her.—*The Pentecostal Testimony.*

Why He Did Not Pray

A deacon living in a Berkshire town was requested to give his prayers in behalf of a poor man with a large family who had broken his leg. "I can't stop now to pray," said the deacon (who was picking and barreling his early apples for the city market), "but you can go down into the cellar and get some corned beef, salt pork, potatoes, and butter; that's the best I can do." — *Sunday School Chronicle.*

* * *

He Was No Burden

An American who was walking down the streets of a Chinese city was greatly interested in the children, many of whom were carrying smaller children upon their backs, and managing at the same time to play their games, says a writer in the *Youth's Companion.*

"It is too bad," the American sympathetically said to one little fellow, "that you have to carry such a heavy burden!"

"He's no burden," came the quick reply; "he's my brother."

"Well, you are chivalrous to say so!" said the man, and he gave the boy some money.

When the American reached home he said to his family: "A little Chinese boy has taught me the fullest meaning of the words, 'Bear ye one another's burdens, and so fulfil the law of Christ.'" He recounted his interview, and added: "If a little Chinese boy can carry and care for his brother and refuse to consider him as a burden, surely we ought not to think it a burden to carry our little brothers, the weak and the needy ones, who look to us for help. Let us rejoice as we carry one, and say, by our actions, 'He's no burden; he's my brother.'" — *Rescue Journal.*

* * *

Love Wins!

A storm swept the ocean just off the coast of Scotland. Far out in the black trough of the angry waters a ship had gone to pieces. The life-boat set out from shore in the face of what seemed almost certain disaster, but it came back with all the ship's crew except one. To have taken another in would have meant the sinking of the boat. As they came to shore the leader said, "There's another man! We need volunteers for his rescue. These men are exhausted."

Among those stepping forward was a fine-looking young Scotchman in the very prime of his life. His white-haired mother came and put her arms about him and said, "Don't go, John; years ago your father perished in the storm at sea. You know that just last year your brother William went to sea and never came back, and I guess he, too, must have gone down. John, you are the only one left, and if you should perish what would I do? Don't go, John; your mother begs you to stay."

He took her arms from about his neck and said, "Mother, I must go; a man is in peril and I would feel like a coward not to go. God will take care of us." He printed a kiss on her cheek and sprang into the boat. Every minute the fury of the storm increased. The elements seemed to vie with each other to see which one could do the worst. Down into the trough and up over the waves they went. A whole hour they were gone, and finally in dim outline they were seen beating their way back. As they came within hailing distance someone from the shore cried, "Have you found the man?" And standing in the bow of the boat John shouted back, "Yes, we've saved him, and *tell my dear old mother it's brother William!*" — William Edward Biederwolf, in *Frozen Assets.*

* * *

"Nobody Loves Me"

A little four-year-old African girl had been sold as a slave. She had never known what love was. Even her name, Keodi, meant "Nobody loves me!"

When she grew to be about ten years old, her body became covered with ugly sores. The natives turned her out and would have nothing to do with her. But some kind missionaries took Keodi in and cleaned her up, cared for her sores, and put clothes on her.

At first she could not believe any one loved her. She went about saying, "I am only Keodi; nobody loves me." The missionaries told her that Jesus loved her, and tried to teach her what love meant. Then she looked down at her dress, clean body and bandaged sores, and said, "Is this love?" They told her that it was.

Yes love is shown by kindness and giving. God showed His great love to us by giving His dear and only Son to die for us. Jesus showed His love for us by giving His life for us. He did not only *say* He loved us, but He *showed* His love by suffering in our place. Should we not then give Him our whole lives? Then we can love Him, too.—*Gospel Chimes.*

* * *

A Modern Beloved Physician

Dr. Richard F. Brown is a Canadian medical missionary who, when his station was taken by the Japanese, started traveling through the provinces of Shensi and Shansi, traveling a thousand miles on foot. He has ministered to all sorts and conditions from the foremost leaders of Communist China to humble peasants, soldiers, and civilians—Chinese and Japanese without distinction. At times he has walked thirty miles a day, working along the road from dawn to dusk. In one district alone, within a radius of three miles, were 1,400 sick and wounded and neither doctors nor supplies. "It was trying to be awakened every morning by the sick and wounded pulling at your bedclothes, but you get used to it." It was to Dr. Brown that Chuh Teh, the Communist general, expressed his gratitude for the help rendered China by medical missionaries, declaring his wish to co-operate with them. — *Sunday School Times.*

* * *

Testing Your Love for God

In an engine-room it is impossible to look into the great boiler and see how much water it contains. But running up beside it is a tiny glass tube, which serves as a gauge. As the water stands in the little tube, so it stands in the great boiler. When the tube is half full, the boiler is half full; when the tube is empty, the boiler is empty. Do you ask, "How do I know I love God? I believe I love Him, but I want to know." Look at the gauge. *Your love for your brother is the measure of your love for God.—S. S. Chronicle.*

* * *

A Beautiful Picture

First Corinthians 13:4-8 gives us a beautiful picture of the sanctified or consecrated life. I am quoting Moffatt's translation as follows—

"Love is very patient, very kind. Love knows no jealousy; love makes no parade, gives itself no airs, is never rude, never selfish, never irritated, never resentful; love is never glad when others go wrong, love is gladdened by goodness, always slow to expose, always eager to believe the best, always hopeful, always patient."—*The United Evangelical.*

* * *

Those who bring sunshine to the lives of others cannot keep it from themselves.—J. M. Barrie.

* * *

Help Poor Jim

Two freight trains on the Philadelphia and Erie railroad came into collision. Christian Dean was the faithful engineer on one of the trains. Both he and his fireman were fastened beneath the wreck of the locomotive. Dean was held by one of his legs close by the fire box of the engine. His fireman was nearly buried under the pieces of the wreck. When they were discovered, Dean had managed to reach his tool-box, and was making every effort to get the fireman out. When he saw the men had come to help them, Dean said to them, "Help poor Jim! Never mind me." The fireman was taken out as soon as possible—but unconscious. Then Dean was taken out, and it was found that during the time he had been working to relieve his friend, the fire was burning his own leg to a crisp. He was literally roasted from his knee down, and afterward it had to be cut off. And yet this noble fellow was unmindful of his own suffering in trying to relieve the suffering of his fellow-worker. He was a *generous friend* indeed.—*Gospel Herald.*

* * *

Give It to Him

A miner worked very hard every day in the mines for a living. The overseer of the mine said to him one day, "Thomas, I've got an easier berth for you, where there is not much hard work, and where you will get better wages. Will you accept it?" Most men would have jumped at such an offer. But what did this noble fellow do? He said to the overseer: "Captain, there's our poor brother Tregony: he has a sickly body, and not able to do hard work as I can. I am afraid his work will shorten his life and then what will his poor family do? Won't you please let him have this easier berth? I can go on working as I have done." The overseer was wonderfully pleased with Thomas's generous spirit. He was a faithful friend.—*Gospel Herald.*

* * *

He Sat Beside Him

A criminal under sentence of death was waiting the day of execution. A minister attended him. All efforts to lead him to repentance seemed unavailing. Going home, he met a man who was known all over the district for his life and good works. The conversation turned upon the criminal. The minister requested the elder to go and see him. He did so, and sitting beside the criminal, he took his hand in his, and said, with much fervor and simplicity, "Wasn't it great love in God to send His Son into the world to die for sinners like you and me?" In a moment, the fountain of the man's heart was broken up and he wept bitter tears, and afterward said, "When the minister spoke to me, it seemed like one standing far above me, but when that good man came in and sat down by my side, and classed himself with me, and said, 'Wasn't it great love in God to send His Son into the world to die for sinners like you and me?' I couldn't stand it any longer."—*The Presbyterian.*

* * *

A Mother Bird's Love—And How Much More!

How little even Christians really understand God's great love for us! Last spring, when they were trimming trees on our street, one day just a little before lunch time the men cut off a limb in which was a bird's nest with four baby birds in it. The little birds were killed in the fall; soon the mother bird came, and she flew over and back again and again, calling, calling, calling in her effort to find her babies. Soon the men sat down on the grass near the tree and ate their lunch, and still that little mother bird kept flying over their heads and calling. Finally something dropped with a thud almost at the feet of one of the men. He stooped and picked it up, and it was that little broken-hearted mother bird *dead.* Dear Christians, if that is the love and yearning in a little mother bird's heart, how God's great heart must yearn for His lost and straying children! Not only for those who have tasted His love and then wandered, but for the *last* and *least* soul on this old earth.—*Sunday School Times.*

* * *

Others

Lord, help me to live from day to day
In such a self-forgetful way
That even when I kneel to pray
  My prayers will be for others.

Help me in all the work I do
To ever be sincere and true
And know that all I do for You
  Must needs be done for others.

Let "self" be crucified and slain
And buried deep; and all in vain
May efforts be to rise again
  Unless to live for others.

And when my work on earth is done,
And my new work in heaven's begun,
May I forget the crown I've won
While thinking still of others.

Others, Lord, yes others!
Let this my motto be.
Help me to live for others,
That I may live like Thee.
—C. D. Meigs.

* * *

Unselfishness

Bishop Thoburn was one of the world's greatest missionaries, and served over fifty years in India and the Far East. But the world does not know so well that his brother stayed at home and worked and saved to send him through school, and to get him ready for his life work. That brother, like Peter's brother Andrew, did not become famous. He stayed back on the farm and made his brother famous, as Andrew helped Peter, who became the great leader. *If they could not do great things, they could help others close to them to do them.—Pilgrim Sunday School Quarterly.*

* * *

When Catherine Booth Died

One night I read an account of the scenes around Catherine Booth as she lay in her coffin at Congress Hall: how the poorest of the poor felt she was specially theirs in death as in life; how ministers and members of Parliament and half-starved children of the slums were alike eager for a last look upon the face they loved. Roughs passed her weeping. Lost girls turned from her side and begged to be taken to some home where they could begin a new life. "That woman lived for me," a poor drunkard cried in anguish. They drew him aside; and down on his knees, he accepted pardon and promised that her God should be his. Three men knelt together one night at the head of the coffin and poured out their penitence to God and went out of the hall saved. Another said, "I've come sixty miles to see her again. She was the means of saving my two boys." What a thrilling testimony to one who had the "qualities of a Christian"—*The King's Business.*

Love—In Poetry or Prose?

A young woman who fancied herself a poetess, and who had her own ideas about love, once came with her poems to the editorial office of a New York magazine. The editor asked her what she wanted. She told him that she had some poems that she would like to have published in his magazine. "About what?" asked the editor. "All about love," she replied. "Well, what is love?" asked the editor. "Tell me." "Love," replied the young woman, casting her eyes heavenward, "is gazing upon a lily pond at night, by the shimmering moonbeams, when the lilies are in full bloom, and—" "Stop, stop, stop," cried the editor, curtly interrupting her, "you are all wrong—very, very wrong. I will tell you what love is: It is getting up cheerfully out of a warm bed on a cold winter morning, at two o'clock, to fill hot-water bottles for ailing children. That's real love. I'm sorry, but I don't think we can use your poems."—*Christian Union Herald.*

* * *

Beating the Law Courts

You have probably heard of the man who bought a farm and soon after met his nearest neighbor. "Have you bought this place?" asked the neighbor. "Yes." "Well, you've bought a lawsuit." "How is that?" "Well, sir, I claim your fence down there is ten feet on my side of the line, and I'm going to take the matter to court and prove it." But the newcomer said, "Oh, no, you needn't do that. If the fence is on your side of the line, we will just take it up and move it." For a moment the other man was nonplused. Then he said, "Do you mean that?" "Why, yes, of course I do," was the answer. "Then," said the man who a moment before had been so pugnacious. "by George, that fence stays just where it is!" Christian brotherly love had made a friend and accomplished what no trial before the highest court in the land could have brought about.—*Church Management.*

"My Fee Will Be—"

Rev. Louis H. Evans, in *The Presbyterian Survey*, describes a few hours spent in the operating room of a medical missionary:

When he had finished, I stepped to his side. Gazing at his face, which was streaming wet from his exertions, and pale with the pallor that comes from keen anxiety and intense strain, I asked him: "Doctor, how can you stand it? Surely every day is not like this?"

He merely smiled.

"How much money would you have received in the States for an operation like this?"

"Oh, about six hundred dollars."

"How much will you receive for this one?"

A strange light blazed into his tired eyes. I shall never forget his reply of that moment. "My fee," replied the missionary physician, "*my fee will be this man's gratitude—and there can be no richer reward than that.*"

Some men's soul's are too big to be contained within their breasts; they overflow in deeds of sympathy and toil and love.—*Earnest Worker.*

* * *

Zwemer's Sermon Illustrated

After Dr. Samuel M. Zwemer had spoken very simply about the Lord Jesus Christ to the people in the waiting room of a mission hospital in Arabia, a Bedouin who had come five hundred miles to be treated said to him: "I understand all you told us, because I have seen that sort of man myself." And then he told this story: "He was a strange man. When people hurt him he did not seek revenge. He looked after the sick, the prisoners, those in trouble. He even treated Negro slave boys kindly. He seemed to think one man as good as another. He used to take long trips in the broiling sun to help somebody. He was just what you said." Dr. Zwemer had been telling about the love of Christ—its length and breadth and depth and height. The Bedouin had seen Dr. Zwemer's brother, Peter Zwemer, who had opened Christian work at Muscat in 1893 and had not lived many years to see the results. "By this shall all men know that ye are my disciples" (John 13:35).—*Bible Expositor and Illuminator.*

* * *

The Bond of Brotherhood

E. W. Caswell tells this story: "One of two brothers fighting in the same company in France, fell in battle. The one who escaped asked permission of his officer to go and bring his brother in. 'He is probably dead,' said the officer, 'and there is no use in risking your life to bring in his body.' But after further pleading the officer consented. Just as the soldier reached the lines with his brother on his shoulders, the wounded man died. 'There, you see,' replied the officer, 'you have risked your life for nothing.' 'No,' replied Tom, 'I did what he expected of me and I have my reward. When I crept up to him, and took him in my arms, he said, "*Tom, I knew you would come. I just felt sure you would come.*" ' "—Ruth McDowell, in *New Century Leader.*

* * *

The Saviour's Sorrow

By way of illustrating the feelings of our blessed Lord on the night of His trial, when He was hurt more by Peter's denial than by the taunts and slaps of the Roman soldiers, Dr. P. W. Philpott tells the story of a father he once knew.

A fine Scotch Christian and successful business man had a son; a splendid, well educated and respected young fellow who was arrested for embezzlement. At the trial, where he was found guilty, the youth appeared unconcerned and nonchalant until the judge told him to stand for sentence, whereupon he looked over the lawyer's table and saw that his father too was standing. The once erect head and straight shoulders of an honest man were now bowed low with sorrow and shame as he stood to receive, as though it were himself, his son's condemnation. The son looked and wept bitterly.

Thus it was that *Peter recognized in Jesus' look the sorrow caused only by one who is deeply loved.* Peter saw and wept bitterly.—R. G. D.

* * *

The Tie of Love

One day, one of the gigantic eagles of Scotland carried away a sleeping infant. The whole village pursued it, but the eagle soon perched itself upon a lofty crag and everyone despaired of the child's life.

A sailor tried to climb the ascent, but he was obliged to give up the attempt. A robust Highlander, accustomed to hill climbing, tried but was forced to return. At last a poor peasant woman came forward and putting her feet on one shelf of the rock, then a second, then a third, she rose to the very top of the cliff. While the hearts of those below were trembling, she came down step by step, until amid the shouts of the villagers, she stood at the bottom of the rock with the child on her bosom.

Why did that woman succeed when the strong sailor and the practiced Highlander failed. Why? Because between her and the babe there was a tie; that woman was the mother of the babe. Let there be that tie of love of Christ and to souls in your hearts, and greater wonders will be accomplished.—*The King's Business.*

* * *

Sam Hadley's Strange Invitation

Sam Hadley of the Water Street Mission in New York once said, in telling of the kind of people that the mission was trying to help, "We don't want anyone here who is welcome anywhere else." If the Lord Jesus had come to save those of us who were so good that we were worth saving on that account, how many of us would be in fellowship with Him today? God sent His Son to die for us "while we were yet sinners." — Philip Howard, in *The King's Business.*

A Father's Love

In a home in Manchester, Eng., there was a wayward son and brother. The mother was dead and the father and the family were heart-stricken with grief over the boy. Time and time again, they had coaxed, reprimanded, and threatened, all to no avail. One Christmas morning the boy came home after a dreadful debauch. The brothers and sisters were shocked, disgraced, and out of all patience. For a long time pressure was being brought upon the father to have the boy driven from home. This night the distracted father appealed to the impatient family. After consulting each one, he found the universal verdict to be expulsion. The father then turned to his liquor-drugged son and said: "Henry, your sisters say you should be put out of the house, your brothers say you should be put out"; then going over to the boy he said: "My son, I shall never put you out of the home." This loving word of his father woke up his soul. He reformed and became converted, and was none other than the Rev. Henry Moorehouse of Manchester. — C. H. Spurgeon, in *Cameos,* by H. Weigle.

* * *

"Because They Love a Fellow"

Mr. Moody tells of a little street urchin in Chicago who went many, many blocks across the frozen streets of the great city, passing church and Sunday school after church and Sunday school to the church served by Mr. Moody. A Sunday school teacher stopped him one morning and said, "Where are you going?" He said, "To Mr. Moody's Sunday school." He said, "Why, that is many, many blocks away. Come into my class in this Sunday school nearby." The boy said, "No." The teacher persisted and finally asked the boy why he went so far through the cold across the city to Mr. Moody's Sunday school. He said, "Because they love a fellow over there!" Lost souls are looking for love; they are longing for love; and if they find it not in our hearts and the atmosphere we create in our churches and Sunday schools, then they will go limping down to hell without it!—L. R. Scarborough, in *A Search for Souls.*

* * *

Freezing to Death

A man was making his way over the mountains through a terrible snow storm. He gradually got weaker and weaker, until at last he stumbled and fell. He said to himself, "This is the end. I shall never be found!" He was too weak to rise, but as he fell his hand struck the body of another man who had fallen in the same place. This first man was unconscious, and the man who had just fallen rose to his knees, and, bending over the prostrate form, began to chafe his hands and to rub his face, until by and by the man's eyes opened. He had saved another's life, but he had also saved himself, for the exercise had kept the life in his own body. And when you have a passion for souls, when you go seeking the lost, when you lift the burdens of others, your own vision of Jesus is clearer, your own hope of eternity is stronger, your own assurance of salvation is greater.—J. Wilbur Chapman.

* * *

Love Won

One of the most heart-moving conversions that I have ever known, I witnessed in my city, during the holiday period in mid-winter. There reached me the message that a little Sunday school boy in one of our mission Sunday schools had been accidentally shot by his little neighbor friend. I hurried to the humble home as fast as I could go. I found the unconscious little fellow in the hands of two skillful doctors. Said they, "He will not live. The shot is unto death." I went back the next day and the boy's father was in the stupor of a terrible drunk. I went back the next day, and the father was sobering up. He would walk the floor as tears fell from his face, while he looked on that little suffering boy, nine or ten years of age. Bending over his boy, he would say, "My little man is better, and he will soon be well!" The little face was clouded as he feebly whispered, saying, "No, papa; I will not get well." And then the father protested, as he said, "You will get well, and I will be a good man and change my ways!" The little fellow's face was clouded, and he kept trying to say something, and I reached for the man to bend over to catch it, and this is what we did catch, after awhile: "When I am gone, papa, I want you to remember that I loved you, even if you did get drunk!" That sentence broke the father's heart. He left that room, unable to tarry any longer. A few minutes later, I found him lying prone upon his face, there upon the ground, behind the little cottage, sobbing with brokenness of heart. Said he, "Sir, after my child loves me like that, oughtn't I to straighten up and be the right kind of man?" I said, "I have a story ten thousand times sweeter than that to tell you. God's' only begotten Son loved you well enough to come down from heaven and die for you, Himself the just, for the unjust, that He might bring you to God. Won't you yield your wasting, sinful life to Him, and let Him save you?" Then and there he made the great surrender. You should slip into one of our prayer meetings, when the men and women talk about what Christ has done for them, and one of the most appealing and powerful testimonies you would hear is the testimony of this harness workman, as he stands up, with tears on his face, to tell you that love brought him home when everything else had failed. They criticized him; they scolded him; they railed at him; they pelted him with harsh words because he drank. Then a little boy said, "Papa, I love you, even if you do get drunk," and love won the day when everything else failed! — George W. Truett.

* * *

Which Is Greatest?

Charles G. Trumbull, in reading the thirteenth chapter of I Corinthians to a company, read the last verse as follows: "And now abideth Fundamentalism, premillennialism, and love; but the greatest of these is love." Some of us need the lesson taught by such a rendering.—*Sunday School Times.*

* * *

Love's Persistence

A young woman who had left home because her father was a drunkard, afterward became a Christian, and announced her intention of returning and doing what she could to reclaim him.

"But what will you do when he finds fault with all your efforts to please him?" someone asked.

"Try a little harder," she answered with a soft light in her eyes.

"Yes, but when he is unreasonable and unkind you will be tempted to lose your temper, and answer him angrily. What will you do then?"

"Pray a little harder," came the answer with a fearless ring in the words.

The discourager had one more arrow: "Suppose he should strike you, as he did before. What could you do but leave him again?"

"Love him a little harder," said the young Christian steadily.

Her splendid perseverance conquered. Through love and prayer and patient effort, her father was not only reclaimed from his besetting sin, but proved Christ's power to save.—*New Illustrator.*

GOD'S LOVE

Why God Watches Us

The biographer of Bishop Watts, Ditchfield, relates that when a child he was one day in the house of a very old woman, who asked him to read a framed text, "Thou God seest me." Then she said, "When you are older, people will tell you that God is always watching you to see when you do wrong, in order to punish you. I do not want you to think of it in that way, but I want you to take the text home, and to remember all your life that God loves you so much He cannot take his eyes off you."—*Sunday School Times.*

* * *

Love's Seeming Cruelty

Sometimes love has to be cruel to be kind. Years ago, in the days before stagecoaches had been superseded by railways, a mother and her infant were the only passengers in a coach in western Montana during a bitter winter. The woman had not provided against such intense cold, and although she could protect her baby, her own life became endangered. The driver quickened the pace of his team, hoping to reach warmth and refuge before her condition became serious, but the fatal drowsiness stole over her, and when no answers to his inquiries were returned, he stopped and got down from his box. The woman's head was swaying from side to side. He took the baby from her and bestowed it as comfortably as he could in a furry bundle under the shelter of the seat; then, seizing the mother roughly by the arm, he dragged her upon the frozen ground. His violence partly awakened her; but when he banged the door and sprang on his box and drove on, leaving her in the road, she came fully to her senses and began to scream as she ran madly after him, calling, "My baby, oh, my baby." The horror of her loss and the violence of the exercise to which she was forced saved her. When her blood was in healthy circulation, the driver pulled up his horses, and allowed her to resume her place with her unharmed child.—*Methodist Recorder.*

* * *

"My God, how endless is Thy love!
Thy gifts are every evening new;
And morning mercies from above
Gently distil like early dew.

"I yield my powers to Thy command,
To Thee I consecrate my days;
Perpetual blessings from Thy hand
Demand perpetual songs of praise."
—Rev. Isaac Watts.

The Father's Love

In one of Dr. J. Wilbur Chapman's meetings a man rose to give the following remarkable testimony: "I got off at the Pennsylvania depot one day as a tramp, and for a year I begged on the streets for a living. One day I touched a man on the shoulder and said, 'Mister, please give me a dime.' As soon as I saw his face, I recognized my old father. 'Father, don't you know me?' I asked. Throwing his arms around me, he cried, 'I have found you, I have found you, I have found you; all I have is yours.' Men, think of it, that I, a tramp, stood begging my father for ten cents, when for eighteen years he had been looking for me, to give me all he was worth."

Such is the love of the heavenly Father for His sinning children.—Sunday School Chronicle.

* * *

Deeper Than That

That Christ may make His home in your hearts through your faith; that you may be so deeply rooted and so firmly grounded in love, that you may be able to comprehend with all the saints what is "the breadth," "the length," "the depth," and "the height," and may know the love of Christ which transcends all knowing, so that you may be filled with all the "plentitude" of God (Eph. 3:17-19).

When Nansen the explorer tried to measure the depth of the ocean in the far North he used a long measuring line, and when he discovered he had not touched bottom wrote in his record; "Deeper than that." The next day he tried a longer line only to write again; "Deeper than that." Several times he tried until finally he fastened all his lines together and let them down, but his last record was like the first, "deeper than that." He left without knowing the depth of the ocean at that point except that it was deeper than so many thousand feet.

Thus may we try to know the love that transcends all knowing. We know what a young child's love may be, or that of growing son or daughter, or of brother and sister, or of husband and wife, or of parents for their children, or of a patriot for his country, or of a Christian for his God. But in each case the measuring line will be too short. We may even add all these measurements together and still we cannot measure fully this love of Christ. We may have relative knowledge only. We must say it is "Deeper than that." "God so loved!" A young convert has said:

"To write the love of God
Would drain the ocean dry,
Nor could the scroll
Contain the whole
Though stretched from sky to sky."
—*The Watchman-Examiner.*

* * *

From the island of Ambrym we hear of a beautiful word, the native word for love. Literally translated it means: "The heart keeps calling, calling for me;" and "love of God" in the native Ambrym language is, "the heart callings of God." —British and Foreign Bible Society.

* * *

"He Loves You Too Much"

An atheist, blaspheming in a certain market-place, challenged God to show His power by striking him dead within five minutes. The five minutes elapsed, and following the tense delay, the man spoke to his audience, saying, "What did I tell you?" An old lady standing by said, "Sir, have you any children?" "Why?" "Well," said the lady, "If one of your children handed you a knife and said, 'Kill me, Daddy,' would you do it?" "Why, no," replied the astonished man, "I love them too much." "That is exactly why God did not strike you dead," said the lady, "He loves you too much."—*Moody Monthly.*

* * *

"One there is above all others—
Oh, how He loves!
His is love beyond a brother's—
Oh, how He loves!

Earthly friends may fail or leave us,
One day soothe, the next day grieve us,
But this Friend will ne'er deceive us—
Oh, how He loves!

"Joy and peace it is to know Him—
Oh, how He loves!
Think, oh, think how much we owe Him
Oh, how He loves!
With His precious Blood He bought us,
In the wilderness He sought us,
To His loved ones safely brought us—
Oh, how He loves!"
—*The Messenger of Peace.*

* * *

"Could we with ink the ocean fill,
And were the skies of parchment made;
Were ev'ry stalk on earth a quill,
And ev'ry man a scribe by trade;
To write the love of God above
Would drain the ocean dry;
Nor could the scroll contain the whole,
Though stretched from sky to sky."
—Song.

* * *

The Love of God

The love of God is an ocean, and no line can sound its depths. It is a sky of unknown dimensions, and no flying machine can reach its heights. It is a continent of unexplored distance, and no tape can measure its length. It is a width of unsurpassed country, and no survey can find its boundry. It is a mine of wealth, and no delving of man can estimate or exhaust its riches. It is a pole of attraction, which no explorer can discover, and the love of God is a forest of beauty, and no botanist can find and describe its variety and glory.—Selected.

* * *

Something Better than Our Love for Christ

A good man was very ill, and his friends came to comfort him. They remembered his good deeds, and how he had always cared for the lambs of Christ's flock. One prayed, "Lord, thou knowest how he loves Thee." "Ah, my friends," said the sick man, "do not say that. When Mary and Martha went to Jesus, their message was not, 'Lord, he who loveth Thee is sick,' but, 'He whom Thou lovest.' It is not my imperfect love to Him that gives me comfort, but His perfect love to me." — *Christian Herald.*

* * *

How God Loves and Gives

Peter Mackenzie, a Methodist preacher of a generation ago, living in England, preached an early sermon from John 3:16. Gipsy Smith tells us that the preacher said, after announcing the text: "There are two striking things in my text: When God loves He loves a world. When He gives, He gives his Son." Such is the boundless love of the eternal Father of mankind. — *Sunday School Times.*

* * *

Ironside's Boyhood Lesson

I remember, when I was a boy, going to a missionary meeting. A missionary was there from Africa, and was showing us a whole lot of curious things, and then he said, "Now, boys, I want to tell you the kind of Gospel we preach to the people of Africa. How many good boys have we here?" A lot of us thought we were good, but our mothers were there, and so not one of us dared hold up his hand. "Well," said he, "not one good boy here; then I have the same message for you that we have for the heathen in Africa; God loves naughty boys. "My," I thought, "he is getting all mixed up," for you see I had heard people say, "If you are good God will love you." But, dear friends, that is not true. God is not waiting for you to be good so He can love you; God loves sinners. "God commendeth his love toward us, in that, while we were yet sinners, Christ died for us."—H. A. Ironside.

* * *

Love through the Dark

A father and little daughter buried the mother of the home. They were broken-hearted when they returned to the old home after the funeral, and things were so different. The little daughter was placed in her bed for the night as usual. The father retired, but could not sleep. After a while the little daughter said, "Papa, it is so dark." And then, after a while the little child said, "Papa, you love through the dark, don't you?" Away in the dark hours of the night the father looked up into the face of Jesus and said, "Jesus, thou dost love though it is dark." Jesus loves His children, and no night is so dark that He does not see us.—*Sunday School Times.*

* * *

How Much Does God Love?

"Fond parents often say to a little child: 'How much do you love me?' The answer is usually a kiss and a hug. If you put the same question to our heavenly Father, the answer is—the cross. . . . We can glimpse the sufferings of Christ in the Garden and on Calvary; but who can picture the sorrows of the Father in Heaven in that last hour?"—*The Boston Transcript.*

* * *

The Love of God

How deep is it?

"Thou hast in love to my soul delivered it out of the pit of corruption" (Isa. 38:17).

"He brought me up also out of an horrible pit" (Psa. 40:2).

How high is it?

"But... God hath raised us up together and made us sit together in heavenly places in Christ Jesus" (Eph. 2:6).

What is its length and breadth?

"He hath chosen us in him before the foundation of the world" (Eph. 1:4). "That in the ages to come he might show the exceeding riches of his grace in kindness toward us in Christ Jesus" (Eph. 2:7).

—Selected.

Why Are We Saved?

Some years ago I was lecturing in Western Pennsylvania. In one home where I was entertained was a dear little four-year-old whom I delighted to tease. One day I asked her, "Are you worth anything?" She said, "No." And I asked, "What's the use of keeping you, then?" The little face grew dark and puzzled while she felt for an answer. Then she blurted out, "Oh, I tell you why: Mama *loves* me." And not an angel under the broad heavens could have given a better answer. Love, divine love alone, makes us worth saving.—Thomas Chalmers, in *King's Business.*

* * *

The Father's Love and Ours

A gentleman of some wealth and high social position was taken ill. Being much troubled about the little love he found in his heart for God, he complained bitterly to one of his brethren. This is how he was answered:—

"When I leave you I shall go to my home, and the first thing I expect to do is to call my baby. I expect to place her on my knee and look down into her sweet eyes and listen to her charming prattle and, tired as I am, her presence will rest me, for I love that child with unutterable tenderness. But the fact is, she loves me little.

"If my heart were breaking, it would not disturb her sleep. If my body were racked with excruciating pain it would not interrupt her play. If I were dead, she would be amused in watching my pale face and closed eyes. If any friends came to remove the corpse to the place of burial, she would probably clap her hands in glee, and in two or three days totally forget her father.

"Besides this, she has never brought me a penny, but has been a constant expense on my hands ever since she was born. Yet, though I am not rich, there is not money enough in the world to buy my baby. How is it? Does she love me or do I love her? Do I withhold my love until I know she loves me? Am I waiting for her to do something worthy of my love before extending it to her?"

"Oh, I see it!" said the sick man, while the tears ran down his cheeks, "I see it clearly. It is not my love to God, but God's love to me I should be thinking about. And I do love Him now as I never loved Him before."

We think of our littleness, when we should remember our Father's almightiness. We bewail our weak love, when we should be grateful for our Father's great love. "Herein is love, not that we loved God, but that He loved us."—Selected.

* * *

Afraid of God's Love

One morning I wanted to feed the birds. It was gray and cold, and the ground was covered with snow. I stepped out on the porch, and flung them handfuls of crumbs, and called to them. No, there they sat, cold hungry, and afraid. They did not trust me. As I sat and watched and waited, it seemed to me I could get God's viewpoint more clearly than ever before. He offers, plans, watches, waits, hopes, longs for all things for our good. But he has to watch and wait as I did for my timid friends.—Aline V. Trumbull, in the *Sunday School Times.*

* * *

A Father's Love

A steamer was wrecked on Lake Pontchartrain, on which were a father, mother, and their six children. The father was a stalwart man and a good swimmer, and resolved to get them all safely to land or perish in the attempt. He told his children not to be afraid, that he would come for them. He then jumped overboard, and his wife after him. Taking her by the hair, he drew her along through the breakers and landed her safely on shore. Then he plunged into the mad waves, and went back to the ship for his children. One by one he brought them to shore. Only one remained upon the vessel. The devoted father had not strength to stand up when the last was brought in. Friends expostulated with him against the further exposure of his life. He said, "Jimmie's aboard, and I promised to come for him." Then he floated back to the ship, and just as it was about to go down, he called to Jimmie to jump into the water. He had strength only to seize his boy, to fold his arms about him, and press him to his bosom, and, thus enfolded, they sank together, to rise no more. Such is the love of a father. "As the Father hath loved me, even so have I loved you."—*The New Illustrator.*

* * *

John's Attar of Roses

I read of a minister who was invited to go and see a garden of roses. The garden was an extensive one, covering broad acres. There was nothing but roses: roses of every fragrance, roses of every color. When he was leaving the garden the owner presented him with a little phial, a bottle containing what he called attar of roses. As far as fragrance was concerned, that little bottle contained the garden in miniature, and in its tiny globe he had the sweetness of all those broad acres. Now, the Apostle John, who leaned on the bosom of Christ, who knew Him better than any of the disciples, gives us the attar of roses, so far as this subject is concerned. He takes all the words of the Lord Jesus Christ; he presses them; he distills them, and gives us in one simple sentence the essence, the quintessence, of them all: "God is love."—Dr. Crawford Johnson.

* * *

The Love of Christ

How broad is His love? Oh, as broad as man's trespass,
As wide as the need of the world can be;
And yet to the need of one soul it can narrow,
He came to the world and He came to me.

How long is His love? Without end or beginning,
Eternal as Christ and His life it must be,
For to everlasting as from everlasting
He loveth the world and He loveth me.

How deep is His love? Oh, as deep as man's sinning,
As low as the uttermost vileness can be;
In the fathomless gulf of the Father's forsaking,
He died for the world and He died for me.

How high is His love? It is high as the heavens,
As high as the throne of His glory must be;
And yet from that height He has stooped to redeem us,
He "so" loved the world and He "so" loved me.

How great is His love? Oh, it passes all knowledge,
No man's comprehension, its measure can be;
It filleth the world, yet each heart may contain it,
He "so" loved the world and He "so" loved me.

—Annie Johnson Flint.

* * *

Think About His Love

A little maiden once came to Mark Guy Pearse in great distress because, as she said, she could not love Jesus Christ. She did want to love Him, but somehow she couldn't. So the genial minister said to her, "Well, my little woman, don't keep thinking about your love to Jesus, but just keep on saying, '*Jesus loves me.*' Say it to yourself over and over again; and come and see me tomorrow." The little girl did as she was told, and when she came to see Mr. Pearse the next day there was no need to tell him of the change that had taken place. Her face was radiant. The love of God had been shed abroad in her heart by the Holy Spirit which had been given to her.—*Christian Herald.*

MERCY

A Rainbow About the Throne

Sir Edward Burne-Jones was once walking over the downs with a party of friends during a summer shower. A rainbow glowed gloriously in the sky. "Let me see! I forgot what makes a rainbow?" cried one of the party. "The Lord set His bow in the cloud," replied Sir Edward gravely. And then, after a pause, "There are other reasons given in the books." It is the Lord who created the rainbow, as He made all else in nature. He has invested the rainbow with the singularity of being the symbol of His mercy. The occasion when this was done was after the Flood.

John's vision recorded in Revelation 4 declares that he saw the thrown of God and states "there was a rainbow round about the throne." To see the throne without the rainbow would be no comfort. The throne is the symbol and assurance of God's holiness and sovereignty. The rainbow round about the throne is the symbol and assurance of the efficacious provisions of grace and love through Jesus Christ our Lord. It is the beautiful reminder that on these grounds God, in the execution of His holy justice, will remember mercy. It is the presence of the rainbow that draws us to the throne.—*The Watchman-Examiner.*

* * *

"As Thou Wilt"

Christ's mercy, like water in a vase, takes the shape of the vessel that holds it. On the one hand, His grace is infinite, and "is given to every one of us according to the measure of the gift of Christ," with no limitation but His own unlimited fullness; on the other hand, the amount we practically receive from the inexhaustible store is determined by the measure and the purity and the intensity of our faith.

On His part there is no limit but infinity; on our side the limit is our capacity, and our capacity is settled by our desire. His Word to us ever is, "Be it unto thee even as thou wilt."—Dr. Alexander Maclaren.

* * *

Life and Light

Our life is like the dial of a clock. The hands are God's hands, passing over and over again—the short Hand of Discipline and the long Hand of Mercy. Slowly and surely the Hand of Discipline must pass, and God speaks at each strike; but over and over passes the Hand of Mercy, showering down sixtyfold of blessing for each stroke of discipline or trial; and both hands are fastened to one secure point—the great, unchanging Heart of a God of Love.—Selected.

* * *

An Earthly King's Judgment

Richard III went out at twilight to reconnoiter; he found a sentinel fast asleep at the outpost. The king promptly stabbed him in the heart, and left upon his breast a paper with the stern inscription, "I found him asleep and I left him so." What a contrast to the patience and tenderness of the Lord with His sleeping disciples—and with all of us!—*Sunday School Times.*

* * *

The Undeserving

A mother sought the pardon of her son from the first Napoleon. The emperor said it was his second offense, and justice demanded his death. "I don't ask for justice," demanded his mother, "I plead for mercy." "But," said the emperor, "he does not deserve mercy." "Sire," cried the mother, "it would not be mercy if he deserved it, and mercy is all I ask for." "Well, then," said the emperor, "I will have mercy." And her son was saved.—*Good Company.*

* * *

The Mercy Seat

There is a place of sweet repose,
From ev'ry tide of stormy woes,
A calm, steadfast retreat;
A shelter from the wind that blows.
And where it is, the Christian knows—
'Tis at the mercy seat.

A place where joys of life abound,
Where we may hear the soothing sound
Of Jesus' voice so sweet,
We know, because of grace redound,
A closer walk with God is found
While at the mercy seat.

Because of prayer when day is done,
Or at the early rise of sun,
We suffer no defeat;
Whene'er we pray through with the Son,
How many are the vic'tries won
Around the mercy seat.

—John Caldwell Craig.

* * *

The Judge Paid

In the town of Wishaw there lived an earnest Christian man who became a magistrate. One morning there appeared before him in the court a friend of his youth, who had strayed from the paths of righteousness and had committed an offense against the law of the land. Those who knew the relationship between the two men expected the magistrate to deal with the man mercifully, and they were very much surprised when they heard that the sentence was a heavy fine. But they were more surprised when the magistrate went to the officer of the court, and took from his own pocket the money to pay the fine. He did his duty as a magistrate, and upheld the law, but he also showed something of the mercy of God for his friend when he paid the penalty for his friend. There is little wonder that the law-breaker was broken-hearted in his repentance. Jesus gave Himself for you. Have you given yourself to Him?—*Peniel Herald.*

MIRACLES

Transformed Lives

Out in that yard of yours in the springtime, you clean up the ashes that have been accumulating during the winter season. Piles of ashes out there in the yard grow through the winter, and then in the spring you hire someone to come and cart them away. Ashes are from coal—coal that has been burned and consumed. Coal is carbon, and that beautiful, shining white stone in the engagement ring on your hand, lady, is carbon also. The diamond the king wears in his crown and the ashes out there in the yard are made of the same stuff!

Down in the state prison are some cinders of men, clinkers, burned out, only the ashes of life left. Down in some sections of the city are the women of the streets, burned out, clinkers, cinders, only the ashes of life are left. But the gospel is the good news that Jesus Christ can take the carbon (clinkers, if you will) and transmute it into a diamond, a gem for His own crown, made out of the ashes of sin.

A little girl made a strange misquotation of a verse but she told the truth when she said, "Christ Jesus came into the world to save cinders." Yes, He did! *He takes the clinkers, the cinders, the ashes, the burned-out, hopeless lives, and makes them glorious and new.*—Will H. Houghton, in *The Living Christ.*

* * *

We Can't—But He Can

One Sunday afternoon my wife and I were taking a short walk when we were overtaken by a storm. We took shelter in a neighboring church where we found a special service for Sunday school scholars in progress. The vicar was catechizing the children, and asked: "What is a miracle?" A little girl put up her hand and replied, "Something we can't do, but Jesus can." The minister seemed surprised at this original answer, and pressed for a response in "more dignified English." Several chimed out the set answer he wanted, "A parable in action," and he seemed well satisfied. It left me cold, however, for I was still thinking of the little child's definition, "Something we can't do, but Jesus can."—*Christian Herald.*

* * *

A Nut for the Infidel to Crack

"If the Son therefore shall make you free, ye shall be free indeed."

In the days of Joseph Parker, an infidel lecturer in a mining town in the north of England gave an address in which he thought he had demolished all the arguments for the Bible, Christ and Christianity. He concluded by saying: "Now I hope I have succeeded in explaining to you that the existence of Jesus Christ is a myth."

As he finished speaking, a miner, who had entered in his grimy clothes, stood up and said, "Sir, I'm only a working man, and I don't know what you mean by the word 'myth.' But can you explain me? Three years ago I had a miserable home; I neglected my wife and children; I cursed and swore; I drank up all my wages. Then someone came along and showed me the love of God and of His Son Jesus Christ. And now all is different. We have a happy home; I love my wife and children; I feel better in every way; and I have given up the drink. A new power has taken possession of me since Christ came into my life. Sir"—and his face was all aglow—"can you explain me?"

The lecturer had no explanation to give, but that working man sent people home feeling that the Bible was still the Word of God and that Jesus was anything but a myth, and that the Gospel was "the power of God unto salvation to everyone that believeth."—*The King's Business.*

* * *

A Miracle

I was eating a piece of watermelon some months ago and was struck with its beauty. I took some of the seeds and weighed them and found that it would require some 5,000 seeds to weigh a pound. And then I applied mathematics to a forty-pound melon. One of these seeds, put into the ground, when warmed by the sun and moistened by the rain goes to work; it gathers from somewhere two hundred thousand times its own weight and, forcing this raw material through a tiny stem, constructs a watermelon. It covers the outside with a coating of green; inside of the green it puts a layer of white, and within the white a core of red, and all through the red it scatters seeds, each one capable of continuing the work of reproduction. I cannot explain the watermelon, but I eat it and enjoy it. Everything that grows tells a like story of infinite power. Why should I deny that a divine hand fed a multitude with a few loaves and fishes when I see hundreds of millions fed every year by a hand which converts the seeds scattered over the field into an abundant harvest? We know that food can be multiplied in a few months' time. Shall we deny the power of the Creator to eliminate the element of time, when we have gone so far in eliminating the element of space? — William Jennings Bryan.

MISSIONS AND MISSIONARIES

A New Version of "The Ninety and Nine"

There are ninety and nine that safely lie
In the shelter of the fold:
But millions are left outside to die,
For the ninety and nine are cold,—
Away in sin's delusive snare,
Hastening to death and dark despair,
Hastening to death, and none to care,—
For the ninety and nine are cold.

"Lord, Thou hast here Thy well-fed sheep;
Are they not enough for Thee?"
But the Shepherd made answer, "Millions sleep
On the brink of eternity,—
And these My sheep within the fold
Care not for the dying in sin's stronghold,
Care not for the dying outside the fold,
On the brink of eternity."

But none of the ransomed ever knew
How the heart of the Shepherd did yearn;
Nor the travail of soul that He passed through
For His sheep without concern.
For no other way had He to reach
The millions of earth His way to teach,
The millions of earth except through each
Of His sheep without concern.

"Lord, whence are those marks in hands and side,
And whence the scars of Thy feet?"
"They were made for those for whom I died,
Both saved and wandering sheep."
"Lord, when wilt Thou come to claim Thine own?"
"Not till the wandering the way are shown,
Not till the wandering My Word have known,
My wandering, dying sheep."

Ah, ninety and nine, dost thou hear His voice?
Forth then to the work so great;
Beyond life's span there is no choice
For those outside the gate.
If they're brought at all, it must be now—
Then, ninety and nine, don't question how,
Oh, sheep of Mine, go quickly thou,
Else for them—and you—too late.

But all through the churches, apostate-riven,
And up from the world's rough steep,
There'll arise a glad cry to the gates of heaven,
"Rejoice, I am finding My sheep!"
And the angels shall echo around the throne,
"Rejoice, for the dying the way are shown!
Rejoice, for the Shepherd brings back His own,
His wandering, perishing sheep!"

—Thomas E. Stephens.

Slow Messengers

"You are angry," said a Negro fellow-traveler to Dan Crawford, at the end of a fifteen-mile trek in the tall grass of Central Africa. "Why do you say so?" "Because you are silent," was the reply. "Tell me more about it." "In our language," answered the black man, "we say that if a man is silent, he is angry. This is why we know God is angry—because He is silent. God is silent" The intrepid missionary was cut to the heart. He opened his pocket Testament and read to the man the first verse of the Epistle to the Hebrews. Much more, he went to work at translating the New Testament into the language of his Central African brother, and in building schoolhouses in which the people might be taught to read the Word which God had spoken in Jesus Christ nearly two thousand years before. God was not silent. But the messengers to whom He had committed His Good News had been slow to tell it as He had bidden them, unto the ends of the earth.—*Vision and Power.*

* * *

83 a Minute

At a certain mission church (says the Rev. W. W. Martin) I had put over the clock these words: "83 a minute." At last a deputation came to me and said, "Will you kindly take that down? It haunts us." They knew that it meant that eighty-three souls a minute were passing into eternity — into the dark — who had never heard of Jesus Christ. Are you quite happy about it?—*Christian Herald* (London).

* * *

No Need to Revive Them

Mrs. Howard Taylor tells how Pastor Hsi taught his fellow villagers that there is no other God but God. Suspicious of him when he became a Christian, their respect for him grew as they noted his upright life, and when they required an official to collect the taxes, take care of the temple, and so on, they decided that he, a scholar and no longer an opium smoker, was the man. Before accepting, he made two stipulations: that he should have nothing to do with the temple sacrifices, but should pray only to the true God; and that no one in the village should, during his term, worship the gods in the temple or bring gifts to them. The temple must be closed for a year. Finally the citizens agreed, and Hsi prayed to the true God that the village might prosper. At the close of the year it was found that the affairs of the village had never been more prosperous, and Hsi was re-elected. For three whole years the temple was closed. When congratulated on the service he had rendered, he smilingly replied that perhaps the village had been saved some needless expense, adding: "By this time the idols must be quite starved to death. Spare yourselves now any effort to revive them."—*Sunday School Times.*

* * *

Why the Airmen Thanked God for Missionaries

Stanley W. Tefft, 25 years old, an aerial gunner from Toledo, Ohio, disclosed that Christian natives on a South Pacific island had won to Christ seven Navy airmen who had been shot down in combat with the Japanese. He said the natives had received the Gospel of Christ from American missionaries before the war. The gunner, at the Naval Air Station at Alameda, Calif., recuperating from wounds, said that with two companions, Lieut. Edward Peck and Radioman Jeff Scott, he reached the island on a raft after two and a half days at sea. Four others also were there. For the next 87 days they hid on the Japanese-occupied island, watched over by the natives, whose first act was to give them a Bible. Tefft said, "Every night the natives would gather round us, and we took turns reading the Bible. They sang songs which we knew. You can tell the world that I am now a devout Christian." Others may criticize missionary endeavor, but these airmen are praising God that America ever sent missionaries to the islands of the South Pacific.—*Now.*

The Unchurched in the U.S.A.

1900	41,000,000
1910	50,000,000
1920	52,000,000
1930	66,000,000
1940	67,000,000
1950	? ? ?

PRAY — WORK — WIN

—Selected.

* * *

Divine Orders

Dr. Robert P. Wilder, the founder, and for many years the dynamic head of the Student Volunteer Movement, once said: "When I was working in India, I went to a place near Poona. On Saturday night, when I entered the hotel dining-room, I found seated at the same table with me a naval officer, an infantry major and his wife, and a sergeant major and his wife. When the conversation started, the naval officer said:

"'Why don't these missionaries stay at home, and mind their own business? You can get all the converts you want at a rupee a head.'

"I replied, 'Suppose you were ordered to take your battleship to Constantinople tomorrow, and I was to ask you why you didn't stay here and mind your own business; that there was no sense in going to Constantinople.'

"The man's eyes flashed fire as he said, 'I would tell you to mind your own business. If we are ordered to go, we must go, even if every ship is sunk, and every sailor killed.'

"I said to him, 'Quite right, my friend; and I have marching orders from the Divine Government to go and preach the Gospel to every creature, and the primary question is whether I am going to obey the last command of my Lord.'"—Selected.

* * *

Business Rebukes Missions

I sat in a missionary convention. A great Christian merchant arose and said: "I stood on the edge of one of the great Chinese provinces. I asked of my guide, 'How many men are there beyond us who have never heard the name of Jesus Christ? Thirty million.' 'But,' he said, 'we must go back. We are already in dangerous territory here. We must go back.' As I stood aside to bow my head and lift my heart in prayer for that great body of men and women without the message of the living Christ, I heard the creaking of one of the unspeakable Chinese wagons, and, as I turned, there passed the miserable vehicle drawn by a weather-beaten camel, driven by a weazened coolie, and loaded with cans of Standard Oil, while underneath there hung a crate of lamps marked "Made in Connecticut, U. S. A." We could send them lights for their homes, but we had not sent them light for their hearts.—*The Exchange.*

* * *

The "Reversed" Version

A missionary candidate was engaged in colportage work in the home land ere leaving for the foreign field. He called at a farm and was met at the door by an old lady. "May I sell you a Bible, madam?" he asked.

"My! Bless you!" she replied, "we have more Bibles now in this house than we use. We have the Old Testament Bible, the New Testament Bible, the Holy Bible, and besides we have the Reversed Version Bible also."

"True," thought the missionary, "it is this last mentioned Bible that is evidently read by most Christians. The Reversed Version! When the Word says 'GO' they all with one accord stay at home. When it says 'GIVE' and 'SEND' the Gospel to all the world, they all seem to think it says, 'Enough to do at home.'"—*Alliance Tidings.*

* * *

What Missionaries Have Done

Missionaries have translated the Bible into about seven-tenths of the world's speech.

Missionaries have done more than any one class to bring peace among savage tribes.

All the museums of the world have been enriched by the examples of the plants, animals, and products of distant countries collected by missionaries.

Missionaries were the first to give any information about the far interior of Africa. They have given the world more accurate geographical knowledge of that land than all other classes combined.

It is to missionary efforts that all South Sea literature is due; there is not a single case on record of the reduction to writing of a Polynesian language by another than a Christian worker.

The missionaries have expanded the world's commerce. The trade with the Fiji Islands in one year is more than the entire amount spent in fifty years in Christianizing them.—*The United Evangelical.*

* * *

Disproportionate Evangelism

A Chinese Christian asked Archdeacon Moule how many clergymen there were in England. Archdeacon Moule asked how many he thought there were. "It is a little island," the Chinese replied; "perhaps there are a thousand." "There are more than twenty thousand," he was told. "Then," said he, "you can easily spare a thousand for China."—*The King's Business.*

* * *

When Their Ships Went Out

A rich man was down at the river front waiting the departure of an ocean liner. He was joined by an acquaintance, who said to him, "You seem to be much pleased about something."

"Yes," said the man, "I do feel unusually good today. Do you see that vessel at anchor in the North River? Well, I have on that vessel ten thousand dollars worth of equipment for a hospital in China, and I just came down to see the vessel safely off."

"Well, that is interesting, and I am glad you made that gift," said the friend.

"But, you know, I also have a gift on that ship. My only daughter is on that vessel, going to China to give her life as a missionary."

The wealthy man looked touchingly into the eyes of his friend and exclaimed, "My dear brother, I feel as though I have given nothing as I think of what this sacrifice means to you."—Dr. John Roach Straton.

* * *

"Theology" or "Christ" the Need

A Japanese worker visiting a seminary in Tennessee said to a promising student, "Brother, you have finished college; we need you in Japan. Why don't you go?"

The student explained that he had to take his seminary course and must study theology before he became a missionary.

The Japanese gave an answer which applies not only to Japan but to our own land: "Brother, Japan can do without theology, but sadly needs Jesus Christ."

The best preacher said, "I determined . . ." (I Cor. 2:2).—*The Pilot.*

* * *

"The Greatest Adventure in the World"

I have often said that missionaries are the happiest people in the world. I believe I laughed more during the two years, which I spent among missionaries, than in any other two years of my life. I also believe that the chief reason for their happiness is the blessed conviction that they are placing their lives at the point of greatest need, just where the Saviour would have them placed. I am reminded of this by a paragraph in a letter written by Miss Ida McLean Black, when she was preparing to return to her work in our African Mission. Writes Miss Black:

"I cannot tell you how happy I am to be going back. All the rapture and ecstasy of the first trip—plus. A dear and intimate friend asked me if I really wanted to go back; if I still found anything interesting in those 'degraded black folk.' They are a lovable, friendly heathen people, friends, people without Christ or hope in the world. Seeing those 'degraded black folk' transformed, recreated, made new creatures in Christ Jesus, is the greatest adventure in the world. I have already attained a peace and joy in life which I never knew existed.'—Rev. E. G. Smith, in *Southern Churchman.*

Waiting!

They are waiting everywhere,
Where the fields of earth are fair,
Where the rivers nobly run,
Where the blossoms seek the sun,
Where the hills rise high and grand,
Looking proudly o'er the land—
Waiting! Waiting!

They are waiting in the wild,
Wicked, weary and defiled.
And the Saviour's healing word,
They have never, never heard;
Ever hungry and unfed
Left without the living bread—
Waiting! Waiting!

—Selected.

* * *

No Other Plan

It was said of Christ that after His resurrection, when He went to heaven in victory and power, the whole angelic host came out to welcome Him. The Archangel, the head of the parade, was the spokesman. He said, "Lord, You have finished the redemptive work on the cross. Is it enough to save the world?" The Lord answered with a note of victory, the same loud cry which came from the cross, "It is finished." And He concluded by saying, "I came not to condemn the world, but that the world might be saved. I shed my blood for the ransom of many." That is the plan of salvation. He gave His live that sinners might be saved.

The Archangel seemed to be satisfied with the answer, but another question came up as to how the world might know of this Gospel, to which the Lord answered, "I have told My disciples, 'Go ye into all the world and preach the gospel to every creature.'" But the Archangel queried again, "The world does not know. Suppose your disciples become busy with their own work and Peter goes back to fishing or Levi goes back to the customs office and they forget to preach the Gospel. What will you do?" There was a pause. The Lord looked straight into the face of the Archangel and said with determination, "They must, for I have no other plan."—Selected.

"Come and Help"

Hark! what mean those lamentations
Rolling sadly through the sky?
'Tis the cry of heathen nations—
"Come and help us or we die!"
Hear the heathen's sad complaining
Christians! hear their pleading cry:
And the love of Christ constraining,
Haste the gospel, ere they die.

—Cawood.

* * *

She Paid the Way

In a Southern hospital a Christian woman lay dying. Her broken sentences revealed her deep concern for Africa's lost millions. Heartbroken to see the restlessness of his beloved mother, the son brought to her bedside a student graduate of a Baptist school in Africa. The African bent tenderly over the bed and said: "I would not be here today had it not been for Miss E——. I would be a heathen, savage sinful man in the bush of Africa. But instead I am a Christian, a minister of Jesus Christ, studying here in America now that I may return to preach and teach for my Master. But all these blessings are the results of Miss E——'s coming to Africa—and she came because you paid her way. I have come to thank you." She smiled and fell into a quiet sleep. When she awoke she said: "I dreamed I was in Heaven. I saw my missionary—I saw all the scores and scores whom she has won to Christ. They came singing praises and love to me,—I felt so humble! I told them that I had not won them to Christ, but they insisted that I had because I paid the salary of Miss E——, who told them the way." She asked her son to promise to pay the salary of a missionary in Africa as long as he lived; then she smiled and slipped away.—*Baptist Young People's Union Quarterly.*

* * *

The Postman's Confidence

A postman was telling me what a sense of security he felt in his work of delivering the mail. "Why," said he, "all the resources of the Government are pledged to support me in carrying on my work. If I have only one small post card in my bag, no man dares molest me in its delivery. All the Federal police powers of the United States, including the Army and Navy, would be thrown into action if necessary to secure the safe delivery of that post card." And that led me to think how confidently you and I may set forth with our life, our personality, our equipment, such as it is, to deliver the flaming truth of the Gospel. The Word of our Lord is just as much for us today as it was for the disciples, when he said: "All power is given unto me in heaven and in earth. Go . . . and, lo, I am with you alway, even unto the end."—*Sunday School Times.*

* * *

Aliens Carrying the Gospel

It was a Jew who brought the Gospel to Rome; a Roman who took it to France; a Frenchman who took it to Scandinavia; a Scandinavian who took it to Scotland; a Scotsman who evangelized Ireland, and an Irishman in turn made the missionary conquest of Scotland. No people ever received the Gospel except at the hands of an alien.—*The Other Sheep.*

* * *

A Heavenly Investment

In Gloucester, Eng., there is an old-fashioned garden and orchard, in one corner of which is a little tombstone. On it are these words:

DEC. 21, 1869

Here lies Tidman's missionary hen,
Her contributions, four pounds, ten;
Although she is dead, the work goes on,
As she has left seven daughters and a son
To carry on the work that she begun.
So be it.

A man called Tidman lived in a village near by. He longed to do something for the London Missionary Society. His money was scarce; but he decided one of his hens should belong to the Society, and all the eggs she laid should be sold and the money given. Before she died the money amounted to four pounds ten shillings — about twenty-three dollars. But that was not all. She sat on eight of her eggs. They were hatched. These, too, belonged to the Society, and in time brought in a large amount of money. When the hen died the old man had her body embalmed, and buried it in the garden, and erected a little monument. He thought many others would be inclined to do something similar, so that the hen would still be helping the Society.—*The King's Business.*

* * *

Missionary Training and Evangelism

When the late Dr. F. B. Meyer was asked at the end of his tour in India to define India's need, he said, "Were I a young man again I would go to India, find twelve young men, live with them, pray with them, teach them the Bible, inspire them, and send them out to evangelize India." "And what would you do then?" *"I would find twelve more,"* was the reply.—Selected.

* * *

Should Christianity Help Buddhism?

Professor Kenneth Saunders of the Congregational seminary at Berkeley, Cal., would have "thoughtful Buddhists and thoughtful Christians come together frequently, as they did at Honolulu, for conference, and find out the religious bases and the moral ideals which they hold in common. Why should the Christion Church," he continues, "hesitate to help in training teachers for Buddhist Sunday-schools, and secretaries for the Young Men's Buddhist Association? . . . To help Buddhists return to the historic Buddha is a task which Christian scholarship may well attempt." He commends the common life of Buddhists, Taoists, and Christians in a Brotherhood of Religious Friends which is now going on in a Chinese temple. "Among such, the spirit of Christ may surely find free course and be glorified, and already in the great concepts of Logos, Tao, and Dhara they are finding common ground, as also in the central doctrine of salvation by faith." The object of faith, be it understood, may be either Buddha or Christ.—*Sunday School Times.*

A Contrast

Sometimes we try to contrast the lives that are sinful, and those given up to God. Again we tell of death-bed scenes and try to describe the passing of those that go into eternity unprepared to meet God, and of those who have "abundant entrance" into the glory world, From the *Missionary Review of the World* we quote the following to show how richly missionary work pays:

Says the *Missionary Review* writer: "One of the most pitiful things that I saw in Africa was a great strong man dying with fever, clutching his spear in his hand, raving in his delirium, fearful the evil spirits would take him before he was dead. His three wives were disfiguring their bodies with clay and ashes, making all kinds of incantations to their gods, screaming in the agony of fear at the approach of death—what a horrible, unspeakably sad thing for this man to go out into the darkness with no hope other than this spear clutched frantically in his dying hand. How different was the death of Ngo Ntoto! This man had been a native pastor for his own people. His life was an inspiration to hundreds of others, both black and white, and when his time came to reap the reward of his labors he gathered his family about him for prayers and then asked them to sing. His wife stood holding one hand, and on the other side of his little bamboo bed stood his stalwart son holding the other. They sang "Nearer, My God, to Thee," and as the song was nearing the end, he closed his eyes and was heard to say, "M'bolo, Jesus, Zambe, M'bolo," which is the Bulu salutation saying, "Good morning, Jesus, Master, good morning."—*Glad Tidings.*

* * *

Why China Needs Christ

A native Christian leader of China visited this country a few years ago. One Sunday he spoke in a modernistic church in California. At the conclusion of the message, a young college student propounded this question: "Why should we export Christianity to China when you have Confucianism in your country?" "There are three reasons," was the rejoinder. "First of all, Confucius was a teacher, and Christ is a Saviour. China needs a Saviour more than she needs a teacher. In the second place, Confucius is dead, and Christ is alive. China needs a living Saviour. In the third place, Confucius is some day going to stand before Christ to be judged by Him. China needs to know Christ as Saviour before she meets Him as Judge." —*The King's Business.*

* * *

A Secret About Norway

It is said that Norway, with a total population of three millions, which is not nearly so large as the city of Chicago alone, has 550 foreign missionaries.

Since the World War, Norway has been free from much of the turmoil which has so disrupted the other nations of the earth. Of course some will tell us that this is because Norway is so situated geographically as not to be in the line of conflict. With all due regard to this reason, we are of the opinion that God has blessed Norway spiritually and governmentally to a great extent because of the interest which the people of the nation have in the Gospel. Certainly 550 missionaries from a small country which has never been known especially for its wealth is a record worthy of commendation.—*Brethren Evangelist.*

* * *

Missionary Equipment

A life yielded to God and controlled by His Spirit;

A restful trust in God for the supply of all needs;

A sympathetic spirit, and a willingness to take a lowly place;

Tact in dealing with men, and an adaptability toward circumstances;

Zeal in service and steadfastness in discouragement;

Love for communion with God and for the study of His Word;

Some blessing in the Lord's work at home, a healthy body and a vigorous mind.—Rosalind Goforth.

When She Could Read the Name

A lady missionary in the West Indies had a class of Negro women, and among them an old Negress of seventy-two, who was eager to learn to read. Asked why, she replied: "That I may be able to read the Great Word. Perhaps I may be sick and have the fever, and Missy have plenty to do, and I live eight miles off. Den, if I can read the Great Word, it will tell of Jesus and comfort me." At length she succeeded in spelling out the name, "Lord." A sudden awe seemed to strike her. "Missy," she said, "that is the Great Massa's name?" "Yes," was the reply. Letting go of the book she stood up, and clasping her hands, lifted up her eyes full of tears, saying: "Lord, Massa! Great Massa! I can read your Great Name!" More of this spirit is wanted in our enlightened land.—*Christian Herald* (London).

* * *

Heroic Appeal of Missions

Dr. Clifford, of London, tells of an English college which was visited by a minister seeking volunteers for a mission field in India. He assured the young men that the work was not difficult, that they would live in a pleasant society, have good homes, and enjoy the services of plenty of servants. Nobody offered to go. But a little while later another mission worker came to the same school seeking men to go out to the Congo. The places that he wanted to fill were vacancies left in the forces by death. The recruiting officer said bluntly to the students, "It will most likely mean certain death to some of you too." *Immediately six men volunteered for service.—Herald and Presbyter.*

* * *

Made Extra Salty

Down at the sea they gather great quantities of fish, and by virtue of salt and lots of it, too, they are enabled to feed the world. Some of the fish are made extra salty. These I was told go to the far countries where it is hot. And this is exactly what we church folks do also. We select for our missionaries these "extra salty" ones. They are the sort that can keep sweet and palatable under India's heat and Africa's fevers.—*Sunday School Times.*

* * *

Brainerd:

"Oh, that I were a flame of fire in my Master's cause!"

Brainerd had such intense compassion for souls, and was so earnest for their salvation that he said, "I cared not where or how I lived, or what hardships I went through, so that I could but gain souls to Christ. While I was asleep, I dreamed of these things, and when I awoke the first thing I thought of was this great work. All my desire was for the conversion of the heathen, and all my hope was in God."

* * *

Fool, If Necessary, for Christ's Sake

John Wesley made a noble reply to an unbeliever who twitted him when he was about to leave England to work as a missionary among Negroes in Georgia. This man said, "You want nothing; have a good provision for life, and prospect of preferment; and must you leave it all to fight windmills—to convert savages in America?" Wesley answered calmly, "Sir, if the Bible be not true, I am a fool and a madman as you can conceive; but if it is true, I am sober-minded. For He hath declared, 'There is no man that hath left house, or parents, or brethren, . . . for the kingdom of God's sake, who shall not receive manifold more in this present time, and in the world to come life everlasting.' "—*Christian Victory.*

* * *

How Young Cyrus Hamlin Settled It

When Cyrus Hamlin was ten years old, his mother gave him seven cents to celebrate a great holiday. The money was for gingerbread, buns, etc. "Perhaps, Cyrus," said she, "you will put a cent or two into the missionary box at Mrs. Farrar's." As he trudged along, he began to ask: "Shall I put in one cent or two? I wish she had not said one *or* two." He decided on two. Then conscience said: "What, five cents for your stomach and two for the heathen! Five for gingerbread and two for souls!" So he said, "Four for gingerbread and three for souls." But presently he felt it must be three for gingerbread and four for souls. When he came to the box he dumped in the whole seven, to have no more bother about it. When he went home, hungry as a bear, he explained to his mother his unreasonable hunger. And, smiling through tears, she gave him an overflowing bowl of bread and milk. And he pathetically asks: *What is the meaning of my Mother's tears?"*—*Sunday School Times.*

* * *

Sayings of Missionaries

Carey: "Expect great things from God, attempt great things for God."

Judson: "The prospects are as bright as the promises of God."

Neesima: "Let us advance on our knees."

Livingstone: "I will go anywhere provided it is forward."

Henry Martyn: "Now let me burn out for God."

Alexander Duff: "We are only playing at missions."—Selected.

* * *

Unpalatable

A missionary fell into the hands of cannibals. "Going to eat me, I presume?" asked the missionary. The chief grunted. "Don't do it," he advised, "you won't like me." Thereupon the missionary took out a knife, sliced a piece from the calf of his leg and handed it to him. "Try this and see for yourself." The chief took one bite and choked. The missionary worked on the island for fifty years. He had a cork leg!—*Sunday.*

* * *

Has God's Book Arrived?

A lady missionary in Africa saw an unknown native coming toward her. He was dressed in the customary skins, and was leading a goat. He put down his spear and tied up the goat, and then said:

"White lady, has God's Book arrived in our country?"

"Are you interested in God's Book" she inquired.

"Yes," replied the native. "My son brought me these pieces of paper, and he has been teaching me the words, 'God so loved the world, that He gave His only begotten Son.' I heard that God's Book had arrived, and I have walked for five days, and brought this goat to buy God's Book."

She then showed him a copy of the Bible and found the place where the words were printed.

"Give me that Book," he entreated, "and you can keep this goat."

Then he walked up and down before her, pressing the Book to his heart, saying:

"God's Book. He has spoken to us in our own language!"

He returned to his own village with God's Book—a section where no missionary was.—*Apples of Gold.*

* * *

They "First Gave Their Own Selves"

In *Christ Life*, the Rev. L. L. Legters, Field Secretary of the Pioneer Mission Agency, writes of one of his visits to Central America: "On the first visit, the late Howard B. Dinwiddie and I were with a group of Indians. About seventy had come together from various parts of Guatemala to have a oonference. At the close of the evening I asked them, 'How many of you will put yourselves in the hands of the Lord Jesus, you who know Him, and will say, "God, I go to carry the Gospel to my people"?' Sixty of those seventy stood and said, 'I give myself.' Then we took up a collection. Not any of them were earning more than six pesos, which are worth ten cents, but we took up the collection, and when we counted it there were a hundred and twenty pesos in the collection box and there were sixteen of the young men whom we could send out two by two. Some said, 'We can give two days'; some said, 'Five days,' and the longest was 'thirty days.' . . . Three months afterward I passed through a town where two of these men had preached, and I found there three families and ten believers who had accepted the Lord Jesus when these two workers visited them."—*Sunday School Times.*

* * *

Fruit from Faithful Service

Back in Vella La Vella, when we were holding front-line positions, we had two dozen native workers with us. It amazed me to see these black people holding prayer meeting every night, singing, in their native tongue, the songs we all know, giving thanks to God for their blessings and praying for the American soldiers to be victorious and drive the Japanese from their land. Someone has done a grand job here, and I heard so many of the boys say that since they know where the money collected for missions went they would not be so close whenever the plate is passed again for missions back home. Many a night, as I stood listening to them, I felt the pull of God, and my heart filled my throat, and tears were brought to my eyes. It seemed queer that the natives could hold prayer meetings, while the Army had provided none for the soldiers at a time when God was our only refuge. The missionaries have really done a job over here, and can never get enough credit for their work. They are usually the last to leave a Jap-infested area. They go out the back door as the Japs come in the front.—*World Outlook.*

* * *

When God Is at the Center?

I recall that day standing on the threshold of a little home of a village in Lanarkshire, Scotland. It was a very small and humble home where one day years ago a family arose early to bid farewell to a son. After a frugal meal of porridge and bread a young man named David read the 121st Psalm, offered a prayer, and trudged over a muddy road to Glasgow, where he took ship for Africa. The years passed, and David Livingstone, out of that humble home, was found dead on his knees by his handmade cot in a little hut of the long grass country of Illala. The natives of the village carried his body 1,200 miles over river and mountain and through jungles of an enemy country until one day it was lowered in the tomb in Westminster Abbey. Last summer I stood before that grave and I wondered by what process one could argue from a birth so humble to a grave so glorious. Then I remembered what David Livingstone had written across his life, "I put no value on anything I possess save in terms of the Kingdom of God." It was the creative force of the gospel of God . . . which made all that change in his life, sending him from a cradle so ordinary to a tomb so resplendent. When a man believes in God, clear to the hilt, with all his heart, there comes to him a power which no temptation can imperil, which no experience can impeach; he will write as if an angel directed his hand; he will sing as if the invisible choirs warbled in his soul. When God stands at the center of life man can change anything. When men see God in the heart of the universe all men will matter and all souls will have a place.—Dr. Joseph R. Sizoo.

* * *

A Worthy Name

It is said that when Andrew Fuller went into his native town to collect for the cause of missions, one of his old acquaintances said, "Well, Andrew, I'll give five pounds, seeing it's you." "No," said Mr. Fuller, "I can't take anything for this cause seeing it's me," and handed the money back. The man felt reproved, but in a moment he said, "Andrew, you are right; *here are ten pounds, seeing it's for the Lord Jesus Christ."—Biblical Illustrator.*

* * *

How Much Do You Wear?

A missionary at home on furlough was invited to a dinner at a great summer resort, where he met many women of prominence and position.

After dinner he went to his room and wrote a letter to his wife. He said:

"Dear Wife: I've had dinner at the great Hotel ——. The company was wonderful. I saw strange things today. Many women were present. There were some who wore, to my certain knowledge, one church, forty cottage organs, and twenty libraries."

In his great longing for money to provide the gospel for hungering millions, he could not refrain from estimating the silks, satins and diamonds of the guests at the dinner in terms of his people's need.

If God sends us money to send to perishing millions the good news of a Saviour from sin, and we spend it in needless luxuries, what does He think of it? —Selected.

* * *

Fruit Out of Failure

A missionary in Urfa, Mesopotamia, labored thirteen years before he baptized a single convert. Everything was discouraging, even hopeless, to human appearance. Then came an epidemic of cholera. People fled in panic, deserting the sick and the dying. The missionary, forgetful of self, waited upon the sufferers, tenderly and tirelessly. The living and the dying blessed his name. Worn and weary he at last himself fell a victim to the disease. All the survivors carried his body reverently and sorrowfully to a little grove outside the city walls. It now seemed that the work of the missionary was at an end. A successor was appointed, however, and he was met nine miles away by a large company and conducted to Urfa with honors. Large numbers turned to Christ, and a substantial house of worship was built and dedicated to the memory of "The man who died for us." The "corn of wheat" had fallen into the ground, and precious was the harvest.—*Baptist Teacher.*

* * *

In Clover

"Foreign missionaries are the biggest humbug on earth," was the sneering remark made by a business man to his pastor. "The missionary lives knee-deep in clover." This statement was repeated to a missionary at home on furlough after his first eight years of service in the interior of China. "I wish that man could see our clover," he replied. "I should like to take him with me on one of our itinerating trips. I should like to have him for a companion just one night at a Chinese wayside inn. I would have him sleep with me on the filthy excuse for a bed, and with me fight the vermin which abound there." Then, as if fearful that his words might be interpreted as a complaint, he added, with flashing eye: "But how I wish I could go back to it all tomorrow! Did your friend say knee-deep in clover? He was wrong! The missionary is soul-deep in clover, for God is with him, and his soul is so full of peace that he understands the message of Paul to the Colossians, 'Now I rejoice in my sufferings for your sake.' Yes, I wish I could go back tomorrow."—*Forward.*

* * *

Fully Following

A lad was hurrying along a London street to meet another boy for a Sunday evening on the street. On his way he met the wife of the master who was teaching him a trade. "Where are you going?" she asked. When he told her she said, "That would be a wrong way to spend the sabbath. Come to chapel with me." The lad went. The minister talked about these words of Jesus, "What is a man profited if he shall gain the whole world and lose his own soul?" It came like a loud knock to the heart of the lad. He opened and let the Saviour into his life. Jesus led him to go to the South Sea Islands with the Good News. He lost his earthly life there, fully following Jesus, but Williams the brave missionary gained eternal life.—*Gospel Herald.*

* * *

The Same Thing That Christ Did

One of our Bible women, a young widow, has been very eager to lead her father to Christ. He has been bitterly anti-Christian. She visited him and told him of the air raids and dangers at one of our cities. He remarked, "I suppose the missionary has fled to a safer place." "Oh, no," said his daughter, "the missionary with some Chinese Christians is down by the railroad station, the most dangerous spot in the city, giving out tea and hot water to our thirsty soldiers as they go to the front." "Why," said he, "they must be doing the same sort of thing that Jesus Christ did when He was on earth." *To think that any pagan could see in anything that you or I do something to remind him of the living Christ! Could you ask for a greater reward than that?*—*Christian Observer.*

* * *

Protected in China

It was a tragic night in a Chinese city. The bandits had come, and dangers surrrounded the mission compound which sheltered some hundreds of women and children. On the previous night the missionary, Miss Monsen, had been laid low with a very bad attack of malaria, and now the tempter harassed her with questions such as these: "What will you do when the looters come here? When firing begins on this compound, what about those promises you have been trusting?" Miss Monsen turned to the great Conqueror of the hosts of darkness, and prayed, "Lord, I have been teaching these people all these years that Thy promises are true, and if they fail now, my mouth shall be forever closed; I must go home." All that next night she was up among the frightened refugees, encouraging them to pray and trust God to deliver them. Awful things were happening all around, but the mission compound was untouched! In the morning people from three different neighboring families asked, "Who were those four people, three sitting and one standing, quietly watching from the top of your house all night long?" When told that no one was on the housetop, they refused to believe it, saying, "We saw them with our own eyes!" They were told that God still has His angel guardians to protect His children in their hour of need, and greatest danger.—*Life and Light Evangel.*

No Interest

"I have no interest in missions," exclaimed a petulant young lady.

"No, dear," said her aunt, "you can hardy expect to.

"It is just like getting interest at the bank; you have to put in a little something first; and the more you put in—in time, or money, or prayer—the more the interest grows.

"But something you must put in, or you will never have any interest."—*Spirit of Missions.*

* * *

Judson the Missionary

Adoniram Judson, one of the first missionaries in Burma, never for a moment faltered in his purpose. The prospects, he said, were "as bright as the promises of God." He was willing to wait seven years for his first convert, and when friends at home grew impatient, he wrote, "Give us twenty-five or thirty years more, and then inquire again." He lived to baptize many scores of Burmese; to know of thousands of converts throughout the country; to translate the whole Bible into Burmese, and then, as he sought a little rest and some relief from his sufferings, he fell asleep on the open sea, and rests beneath the waters that cast their spray against the rocky coast of his boyhood home in New England and lave the tropical shores of Burma.—H. B. M., in *The Y. C. Companion.*

* * *

In a Witch Doctor's House

The town of Andravola in Madagascar had been for generations the home of evil and superstition. In heathen prayer, the ancestors and spirits of Andravola were called upon for help in time of need. A hard place, its spiritual bars were iron, and its gates brass. But God had His own plan. A soundly converted Negro was appointed as pastor to a neighboring town. He was a true shepherd of souls, and started in to visit. Then came Raza! A young Malagasi bride, who trilled Christian hymns from morning until night. Women and girls began at length to pick them up, and gradually but surely the opposition of years gave way. They consented to "the praying." They must now have a leader; and perforce they chose the only man in their town who could read—*the witch doctor!* He must therefore read the Bible at public worship, explain the teaching, and lead in prayer! That was August, 1928. His house was full of charms and aids to sorcery — "heaps and heaps of them." But the Gospel is the power of God unto salvation. In June, 1930, all the unholy arts had gone, the inner wall was down, the place cleaned and whitewashed. The one-time witch doctor had given his house to be a sanctuary for the worship of the Lord.—*World Dominion Quarterly.*

* * *

No Diluted Christianity

Sir Monier-Williams was for more than forty years a diligent student of the religions of India. This eminent Christian scholar gave the following advice to missionaries: "Be fair; be charitable; be Christ-like; but let there be no mistake. Let it be made absolutely clear that Christianity cannot, must not, be watered down to suit the palate of the Hindu, Parsee, Confucianist, Buddhist or Mohammedan, and that whosoever wishes to pass from the false religions to the true can never hope to do so by the rickety planks of compromise."—*Lutheran Women's Work.*

* * *

Must They Longer Wait?

A fine old Chinese, whose home is far inland, learning that a missionary was in his province, set out on a two day's journey to find him. He walked from daylight until dusk, and then away on into the night. Finding a tree by the roadside, he fell asleep beneath its friendly branches, renewing his journey in the early morning. He walked all day, and at nightfall was rewarded by finding the missionary, to whom he told the following story:

"We of our village have long lived with darkness in our hearts, but we hear that you have come to tell us about a God who can bring light on us. Come home with me. It is but a two days' journey across yon mountain. We are poor. My neighbors are poor, but all have promised to share with you their rice. We will give you a bed on which to rest, and will keep you warm. Away beyond us are villages, not just one, or two, or ten, but hundreds. They, too, bid you come."

The missionary, with anguish in his heart, and with tears in his eyes, had to reply: "I cannot go now; my body is broken and sick, and I am having to be invalided home." The old Chinese turned away with deep sadness to go back again into the darkness, to wait—still wait.

Must they perish eternally, these children of darkness, for want of workers to tell them the story of Jesus and His love?—Selected.

* * *

A Costly Experiment

Said a minister to his young people: "I want you to spend fifteen minutes every day praying for missions; but I warn you, it will be a very costly experiment." "Costly?" they asked in surprise. "Yes, costly," he answered. When Carey began to pray for the conversion of the world, it cost him himself, and it cost those who prayed with him very much. Brainerd prayed for the dark-skinned savages, and, after two years of blessed work, it cost him his life. Two students in Mr. Moody's summer school began to pray the Lord to send forth more laborers in His harvest, and lo! it is going to cost our country five thousand young men and women who have, in answer to their prayer, pledged themselves to the work. You will find that you cannot pray for this work and withhold your labor, or your money, or your life itself." —Selected.

* * *

The Need of India

Speaking to the Association for the Re-emphasis of New Testament Missions, Miss Mayo described the Hindu religion as at the root of practically every social, economic, and political evil of India. "The mutual sharing philosophy will never be advocated by one who has looked beneath the deep misery of this people. There is no earthly good in sending missionaries to India with a religious message that merely sprays the leaves and trims the branches of this tree. The tree must be dug up and its roots destroyed. Its place must be taken by a new and all-powerful growth. It is a great waste to send out men (as missionaries) who do not know what they believe. You cannot kindle a fire with a glow worm."—*Sunday School Times.*

* * *

A Real Prayer for Missions

With how much real earnestness do we pray for the sending forth of laborers? A Christian layman at a missionary convention prayed earnestly, "O Lord, send laborers into Thy harvest field." Then as the Spirit carried him along he prayed, "O Lord, send someone from our state convention into Thy harvest field." He paused a moment and then continued, "O Lord, send someone from our church into Thy harvest field." Again there was a pause, longer this time, and an inward struggle seemed to be taking place. At length he prayed, "I have a daughter, just one daughter. O Lord, if it be pleasing to Thee, send her into Thy harvest field." *That was real prayer for missions.*—Selected.

* * *

Better Than an Impressive Presence

A man had gone to hear the great missionary, Hudson Taylor. He was dismayed when the famous missionary rose to speak. Here was a man of small stature, not remarkable in appearance, and, when he began to speak, revealing a thin, high-pitched voice with little natural appeal. But before very long the disappointed auditor found himself in the presence of God; the little missionary had introduced him into the "heavenly places."—*Sunday School Times.*

* * *

Beautiful Feet

Dr. Northcote Deck relates that once, when he was climbing a hill in the Solomon Islands, accompanied by a faithful native, to visit some inland villages, it suddenly began to pour rain, as it does only in the tropics. The whole hillside became an expanse of thick muddy water rushing down the slopes. When the storm had abated, and Dr. Deck continued his journey, he drew his follower's attention to the thick mud which had absolutely plastered him from his hips to the soles of his boots. "And the Lord calls these beautiful," he said, holding up his mud-covered legs. "How beautiful upon the mountains are the feet of him that bringeth good tidings" (Isa. 52:7).—*Christian Herald.*

* * *

Better Stay Home

A recent visitor to China reports that the intelligent Chinese declare: "No, you missionaries do not shoot our people in Shanghai and other places, but you come here to tell us that ours are false religions: yet you bring your sacred book which you yourselves tell is a false book." Again, an Oriental is quoted as declaring: "You ask me to give up what I do believe and accept what you do not believe." The missionary with question marks in his mind would do well to stay at home.—*The King's Business.*

MOTHERS

Sayings About Mother

"Give our boys better mothers, and they will give those mothers better sons." —Thomas H. Nelson.

"An ounce of mother is worth a pound of clergy."—Selected.

"Are the Children All In?"

There were six boys and two girls in the family, so her life was a busy one in the home. She was just as busy at the church, teaching a class, superintending the school, and active in all the social life of the church. And through all her work there rang out an infectious laugh that chased the shadows from other lives. She is now in the glory land. But the other day her life was brought back to me afresh as I visited the home of a daughter. She was recalling with pleasure the olden days, and one thing that made a deep impression on her, and was told with evident pride, was that no matter what time of night the children came in her mother was always sitting up waiting for them. She would not go to bed until the last one was in. Sometimes the boys tried to play a joke on her by taking off their shoes and sneaking up the stairs in their stocking feet, but they would hear a voice saying, "Is that you, Bill?" or, "Is that you, Walt?" No matter how tired after a day's work, she would wait until every child was in. That waiting mother is a picture of deep concern for the children, and her unspoken thought was, "Are the children all in?" I rather imagine our generation needs a revival of motherhood like that.—Courtesy *Moody Monthly.*

* * *

Are All the Children in?

I think ofttimes as the night draws nigh
Of an old house on the hill,
Of a yard all wide and blossom-starred
Where the children played at will.
And when the night at last came down,
Hushing the merry din,
Mother would look around and ask,
"Are all the children in?"

'Tis many and many a year since then,
And the old house on the hill
No longer echoes to childish feet,
And the yard is still, so still.
But I see it all, as the shadows creep,
And though many the years have been
Since then, I can hear my mother ask,
"Are all the children in?"

I wonder if when the shadows fall
On the last short, earthly day,
When we say good-bye to the world outside,
All tired with our childish play,
When we step out into that Other Land
Where Mother so long has been,
Will we hear her ask, just as of old,
"Are all the children in?"
—Florence Jones Hadley, The Pathfinder

No Occupation

She rises up at break of day,
And through her task she races,
She cooks the meal as best she may,
And scrubs the children's faces;
While schoolbooks, lunches, ribbons, too,
All need consideration.
And yet the census man insists
She has "no occupation."

When breakfast dishes are all done,
She bakes a pudding, maybe;
She cleans the rooms up, one by one,
With one eye watching baby;
The mending pile she then attacks,
By way of variation.
And yet the census man insists
She has "no occupation."

She irons for a little while,
Then presses pants for daddy;
She welcomes with a cheery smile
Returning lass and laddie.
A hearty dinner next she cooks
(No time for relaxation).
And yet the census man insists
She has "no occupation."

For lessons that the children learn,
The evening scarce is ample;
To "mother dear" they always turn
For help with each example.
In grammar and geography
She finds her relaxation.
And yet the census man insists
She has "no occupation."
—Selected.

* * *

Memory of Motherhood

The heaven that lies about us in our infancy is Motherhood, and no matter how exalted or how depraved we may become, we are always attended by the grace of a mother's love. Nor does that vision splendid ever fade into the light of common day. Every great man has glorified a great mother.

In the tragedy of Calvary it is beautiful to see the Master looking down upon his mother in tenderest solicitude, telling her to comfort His best-loved disciple, and him to comfort her.

On this day let each of us honor the hallowed memory of his mother, wearing in token thereof the floral symbol of purity. Of their blessings we may have had great stores, but of that most precious influence there was but one.—James Whitcomb Riley.

* * *

Thomas Carlyle's Love and Longing

When Thomas Carlyle lay dying, he was asked if there was anything he wanted. Turning his face to the wall, the granite of his Scotch heart broke up, and the old man sobbed, "I want ma mither!"—Brengle's *Ancient Prophets.*

* * *

Her "Concern" for Mother

A young girl went out in the suburbs to spend the day with friends. She looked so sweet and cool in her dainty dimity—it was an oppressively warm day—that her friends were almost inclined to be envious. "Mamma is not at all well lately. No, thank you; I don't need a fan; I am quite comfortable. I feel quite worried about Mamma." "Why didn't you bring her with you? This country air would do her a world of good." "She is ironing today. Mamma has such big ironings, especially in the summer. Then, as you know, I am going to the seashore soon, and Mamma is busy sewing for me. I have several dresses to be made, besides numerous other frills and furbelows." While she proceeded enthusiastically to describe the fashions, her friends were busy with their thoughts. And there is no need to point a moral to this true little tale.—*The Illustrator.*

* * *

Apples and Boys

Bishop William Alfred Quayle used to tell of a circuit rider who brought home four apples, a rare fruit on the almost orchardless frontier. When the preacher's wife had given one apple to each of her three boys, she placed the one meant for her on the mantle. After the boys had eaten their apples their mother saw them observing hers, whereupon she cut it into three pieces for them. The boys returned to the cabin porch and as they munched the fruit they discussed how strange it was that their mother did not care for apples. But when one of the sons was an old man he explained to the bishop that he had come to understand that it was not because his mother did not like apples, but that she liked little boys better.—*Gospel Herald.*

* * *

John Wanamaker's Mother

When he was advancing in years, and when he had time from the cares of the great store that he had built, and from his many public duties, John Wanamaker wrote of his mother: "My first love was my mother, and my first home was on her breast. My first bed was upon her bosom. Leaning my arms upon her knees, I learned my first prayers. A bright lamp she lit in my soul, that never dies down nor goes out, though the winds and waves of fourscore years have swept over me. Sitting in my mother's old armchair which she loved because her firstborn son gave it to her forty years ago, I am writing this in the evening twilight. With the darkness falling I seem to lose myself in a flood of memories, and to feel that the arms of the chair have loosed themselves to become my very own mother's arms around me again, drawing me to her bosom, the happiest place on earth, just as she used to do in the days and nights long gone by. I feel the touch of her little hand on my brow, and I hear her voice as she smooths my hair and calls me her boy, her very own boy."—*The Presbyterian.*

* * *

Mother Love

During a forest fire on one of the government forest reserves a ranger came upon a bear cub with severely burnt feet and body. The youngster was whimpering painfully, and so the forester put it into his automobile and made it fast with a rope. When he started on his way, however, he discovered that the mother bear had appeared and was following in hot pursuit! Moreover, since the road ran uphill, she was gaining!

The ranger decided to throw the cub overboard, but his attempts to untie the knots were futile. He glanced back; the mother bear was close behind. And just then with a mighty effort she threw herself upon the back of the car, while the forester dived over the side. He regained his feet in time to see the automobile continuing its journey with a happy family reunited. Later he found it at the side of the road. Everything was intact except the side of the seat to which the cub had been tied; the old bear had torn it out to release her offspring.

There is nothing human so irresistible or so unselfish as mother love. — *New Century Leader.*

* * *

Fervent Prayer

Once, in North Africa, there was a mother named Monica, who had prayed through the years for her wayward son. Ere he left for Italy she prayed through the night that he might not go, but with the light of morning the ship sailed. Later on the son wrote: "That night I stole away and she was left behind in weeping and prayer. And what, O Lord, was she with so many tears asking of Thee but that Thou wouldst not suffer me to sail? But Thou, in the depth of Thy counsels, knowing the main point of her desire, regardest not what she then asked, that Thou mightest accomplish the greater thing for which she was ever imploring Thee." Yet, though long delayed, the mother's prayers were answered. *And her boy became Saint Augustine.*—Herbert Lockyer, in *The Presbyterian.*

* * *

Taught to Die

A young girl lay upon her bed with what proved to be a fatal sickness. She was the only child, the idol of her parents, her every whim had been gratified. The doctor was called and after examining his young patient he whispered into the mother's ear. The message was heard by the sick girl. Calling her mother she said, "Mother, you have taught me how to dance, how to dress well, how to comport myself in the world, but one thing you have failed to teach me and that is how to die."—*Watchman Examiner.*

* * *

The Greatest Preacher

Dr. G. Campbell Morgan has four sons and they are all preachers. Someone once came into the drawing-room when all the family was there. They thought they would see what Howard, one of the sons, was made of and they asked him this question: "Howard, who is the greatest preacher in your family?" Howard had a great admiration for his father, and he looked straight across at him, and then, without a moment's hesitation, he answered, "Mother." — *War Cry.*

* * *

A Daughter's Denial

An elderly woman was speaking with pride and gratitude of her young married daughter and said to a friend, "I've been such a burden to her." Quickly the friend replied: "Mothers are never that." The words came instantly and spontaneously, without any affectation or effort to "say something," for this friend had had an invalid mother for many years, and had lavished her life in caring for her, with true love and with gratitude that she had this privilege.—*The Sunday Circle.*

* * *

No one knows of the work it makes
To keep the home together;
Nobody knows the steps it takes,
Nobody knows but Mother.
Nobody knows the lessons taught
Of loving one another;
Nobody knows the patience sought,
Nobody knows but Mother.
—Selected.

* * *

Showing Love for Mother

"I love you, Mother," said little John;
Then, forgetting his work, his cap went on
And he was off to the garden swing
And she had the wood and water to bring.

"I love you, Mother," said rosy Nell;
"I love you more than tongue can tell."
Then she teased and pouted half the day,
Till her mother was glad when she went
to play.

"I love you, Mother," said little Nan;
"Today I'll help you all I can;
My doll and playthings I know will
keep!"
Then she rocked the baby fast asleep.

Then, stepping softly, she brought the
broom,
And swept the floor and tidied the room;
Busy and happy all day was she,
Helpful and good as a child could be.

"I love you, Mother," again they said,
Three little children going to bed.
How do you think the mother guessed
Which of them really loved her best?

—*Olive Plants.*

* * *

Always Welcome

Moody used to tell the story of a Scotch girl who wandered away from God and from her father's instruction and her mother's counsel, and went deeply into sin. One night in a wild frenzy in the city of Edinburgh, she concluded that she would commit suicide, but before doing so she could go out and look once more on the home where she was born and spent her youth. When in the middle of the night she came into the neighborhood again, and finally up to the mother's gate, it was dark, and so she lifted the latch and stole in. As she walked up the path she came to the door of the cottage. To her surprise she found the door wide open. In fear lest some harm might have come to the old mother, she called, and mother answered. The girl said, "Mother, I found the door open." And the old Scotch mother got up and came down and said, "Maggie, it is many a long day since you went away, but always the prayer has been in my heart, 'Lord, send her home.' And I said, 'Whether she come by night or day, I want her to see an open door and know she is welcome.'"

And that night the girl was clasped in her mother's arms of love and forgiveness, and it all suggested the divine love and the possibility of divine pardon. So by the open door of mother's cottage she found her way back to the open door of Christ, the way into divine love and pardon and cleansing. Yes, the door is open, inviting, appealing, entreating, enticing, welcoming, wooing and, thank God, winning.

"There is a gate that stands ajar,
And through its portals gleaming,
A radiance from the Cross afar,
The Saviour's love revealing.

"Oh, depth of mercy! can it be
That gate was left ajar for me?
For me . . . for me?
Was left ajar for me?"

—*Gospel Herald.*

* * *

His Mother's Argument

Dr. Breckenridge once said to his mother: "Ma, I think you ruled us with too rigid a rod in our boyhood. It would have been better if you had used gentler methods!" The old lady straightened herself up, and said, "Well William, when you have raised up three such good preachers as I have, you can talk." —*Sunday School Times.*

* * *

Precious Memories

Dwight L. Moody once wrote of his boyhood:

"Dad died when mother was forty-one. What a struggle she had with us; six besides myself, and then the twins were born after father's death. Only three books in the place, and yet they were enough—the family Bible, the catechism, and a book of family devotions. How the spruce log fire sparkled as we sat on the mat on the cold Sunday nights when church was impossible. I can hear mother now, solemnly adjuring us to walk in the ways of God, as she read from the big Bible to us. After father died, mother wept herself to sleep every night, sister said, and yet we younger ones who slept soundly in our blissful innocence, knew it not. She was always cheerful to us. Brave old mum! Her motto was, 'Give others the sunshine, tell Jesus the rest.' "—*Christianity Today.*

* * *

Mother's Prayer

I cannot tell you how much I owe to the solemn words of my good mother. It was the custom on Sunday evenings while we were yet little children for her to stay at home with us, and then we sat around the table and read verse after verse and she explained the Scriptures to us. After that was done there came a time of pleading and the question was asked how long it would be before we would think about our state, how long before we would seek the Lord.

Then came a mother's prayer, and some of the words of our mother's prayer we shall never forget even when our hair is gray. — Charles Haddon Spurgeon.

* * *

Like a hope divine in this troubled world
Is the thought of a Mother's care . . .
No payment is asked for its giving,
No selfishness prompts its prayer.
Shared, it increases in richness,
Divided, 'tis full in each part.
For God has hidden a love like His own
In the depths of the Mother heart!
—*War Cry.*

* * *

Hope Hangs a Star

Hope hangs a star over every cradle. It is given to mothers to plant the angel in men.

When Richard Cecil was a youth, he tried his utmost to be an infidel; but there was one argument he could never answer; it was the beautiful, eloquent Christian life of his mother. That held him fast.

Dr. Newman Hall had a similar experience. Against all the solicitations and seductions of infidelity there stood the holy life of his mother. He could not get away from that.—Selected.

Mother's Reward

Down in the mountains of Georgia lived a poor widow. She had a few acres of ground where she raised berries and one thing and another and made a little money keeping chickens and selling eggs. She also took in washing and did other humble work for a living. God gave her a bright son. He, too, surpassed everyone in the district school. The mother worked hard to get the money to send him to Emory College. The son worked hard to get himself through the college. He graduated with high honors and won a gold medal for special excellence in study. When it came time for him to graduate he went up to the mountain home for his mother, and said, "Mother, you must come down and see me graduate." "No," said his mother, "I have nothing fit to wear, and you would be ashamed of your poor old mother before all those grand people." "Ashamed of you!" he said, with eyes filled with filial love. "Ashamed of you, Mother, never! I owe everything I am to you and you must come down. What is more, I will not graduate unless you come." Finally she yielded. He brought her to the town. When the graduating day came she went to the commencement exercises in her plain calico dress with her neat but faded shawl and simple mountain bonnet. He tried to take her down the middle aisle where the richest people of the town, friends of the graduating class, sat, but this she refused and insisted on sitting way off under the gallery. The son went up on the platform and delivered his graduating address. He was handed his diploma and received his medal. No sooner had he received the gold medal than he walked down from the platform and away to where his mother sat off under the gallery and pinned the gold medal on her faded shawl and said, "Mother, that belongs to you; you earned it!"—R. A. Torrey.

* * *

"Who ran to help me when I fell,
And would some pretty story tell;
Or kiss the place to make it well?
MY MOTHER!"
—Selected.

Remarkable Mothers

There lived at one time in England a remarkable woman. She had nineteen children. Their infant life was regulated by method. Their sleep was meted out by rule. Each child on its fifth birthday began to have regular lessons. The mother was herself the teacher of all the children, younger and older. She had marvelous ability, wonderful patience, and her success in the training and education of her children has won for her an unquestionable place among great mothers—Susannah Wesley, mother of John and Charles Wesley, we might add, Mother of Methodism.

There is Monica, mother of Augustine, who when her son wandered far astray from her early teaching, never lost faith that God would bring him back, and by her love and prayers dragged him from the mire and set him among princes.

Benjamin West said that a kiss from his mother made him a painter.

D. L. Moody said all that he ever accomplished in life was due to his mother.

Daniel Webster ascribed his masterful use of English to his mother's teaching.

Thomas Carlyle's strongest personal passion all through his life was his love for his mother. Disagreeable he often was to others, but to her always tender and considerate.

Eugene Field was a child of six years when his mother died, but he said, "I have carried the memory of her gentle voice and soothing touch all through life."

Robert Moffatt testified that it was his mother's influence that led him to become a missionary.

John Randolph said, "I would have been an atheist but for the recollection of kneeling at my mother's side while she taught me to say—'Our Father.'"

Wm. Lloyd Garrison ascribed all his merits to his mother's teaching.

We recall Cowper's lines to his mother's picture, and Eliza Cook's beautiful poem to her mother, and Kipling's "Mother o' Mine."

The great, the famous can leave on record their tribute to their mother and many others of us who have walked life's common paths can say with them—

"Over our hearts in days that are flown,
No love like mother-love ever has shown;
And though many a summer the grass has grown green,
Blossomed and faded our faces between,
Yet with strong yearning and passionate pain
Long we at times for our mothers again."

—*Christian Union Herald.*

* * *

In a Parent's Heart

A very pretty story is told by Mr. Stuart Robertson in his delightful book of "Talks to Children." A little girl was sitting on her mother's knee. She was very fond of her mother. She called her, her "very own mother," and like one who was rejoicing over very precious treasures she was touching, one after the other, the features of her mother's face with her little fingers—her mother's lips, her eyes, her cheeks, her hair. After a while she said, "Mummy, can I see your heart?" The mother said, "I don't know about that, but you can look into my eyes, and see if you can see anything." The child climbed up and peered in; and then she cried out gleefully, "I can see your heart, Mummy, and there is a wee girl away in there, and it's me!"—*Sunday School Times.*

NATURE

The Wonderful Heavens

Dr. Edwin P. Hubble, of Mount Wilson Observatory, says that scrutiny at Mount Wilson of the observable part of universe with the world's largest telescope, whose range is 500,000,000 light years, showed uniform arrangement of stellar systems, with no void and no indication of a super-system of nebulae. A light year is an astronomical measurement approximating 6,000,000,000,000 miles.

"The observable region of space," says Dr. Hubble, "is a vast sphere, perhaps 1,000,000,000,000 light years in diameter. Throughout the sphere are scattered 100,000,000 nebulae—stellar systems—in various stages of their history.

"The nebulae are distributed singly, in groups, and, occasionally, in great clusters but, when large volumes of space are compared, the tendency to cluster averages out. To the very limits of the telescope, the large-scale distribution of the nebulae is approximately uniform. They are scattered at average intervals of 2,000,000 light years or perhaps 200 times their mean diameters. The pattern might be represented by tennis balls, fifty feet apart."

Let us remember that light travels at the rate of 186,000 miles a second. And here they speak of a billion light years. And in this space which staggers the human brain, this space with its mysteries unsolvable, there are billions of luminous bodies which we call stars. Listen: "Lift up your eyes on high, and behold, who hath created these, that bringeth out their host by number; He calleth them all by names by the greatness of His might, for that He is strong in power, not one faileth" (Isa. 40:26). What a wonderful God we have! What a wonderful thing that He who created all came down to this little bit of earth to die for us! What a wonderful Lord to trust and to serve. And what a day it will be when we pass through the heavens to meet Him in yonder glory! Hallelujah!—Selected.

* * *

I Saw God Wash the World

I saw God wash the world last night
With His sweet showers on high,
And then, when morning came, I saw
Him hang it out to dry.

He washed each tiny blade of grass
And every trembling tree;
He flung His showers against the hill,
And swept the billowing sea.

The white rose is a cleaner white,
The red rose is more red,
Since God washed every fragrant face
And put them all to bed.

There's not a bird; there is not a bee
That wings along the way,
But is a cleaner bird and bee
Than it was yesterday.

I saw God wash the world last night,
Ah, would He had washed me
As clean of all my dust and dirt,
As that old white birch tree.
—Wm. L. Stidger.

* * *

At Dawn

One has but to awaken a little before sunrise, if living in the country or a city suburb at this season, to hear a wonderful orchestra. One or two birds will pipe forth their morning call, then others join them, and still others, till the full orchestra is pouring out its symphony of praise, each member seeming to vie with another in trills and roulades that any human singer might well envy. The robin's joyous song, the oriole's liquid trill, and the nervous little house wren with its shrill piccolo obligato. How wonderfully God has equipped these little songsters, and how joyously they usher in the new-born day!

But alas, how few hear them! Again, what a difference it would make if we did but stop and listen as God thus speaks to us in hope and promise for the day.

I suppose many of us have at some time visited Niagara Falls. We were impressed with its grandeur and mighty roar. But did you know that that mighty roar was majestic harmony?

Some years ago a famous organist visited Niagara. "Listening to it for the first time he thought he detected a musical note. Anxious to put it to the proof, he went to Goat Island, where he could get its full diapason. Thence he went to Luna Island, and finally to the island of the Three Sisters. At each place the predominant note was clearly recognizable. It was the chord of G of the thirty-two foot pipe of the organ only four octaves lower.

"He tested it theoretically and practically. He found that the seventh note, the interval of the tenth was of a power and clearness entirely out of proportion to the harmonies usually heard in the organ.

"'Were the tone of Niagara a mere noise,' he said, 'this seventh note would be either weak or confused, or absent altogether. The beat is just once per second.'

"He was quite certain that the musical tone of the falls is clear, definite and unapproachable in its majestic perfection."

Oh, if we did but stop to listen, what might we not hear? And if we would "once stop to look at it," what a difference it would make!"—Selected.

* * *

Nature Worshipers

"Can't I worship in the green fields?" piously asks the Sunday hiker. "You can," was the answer, "but you don't." Nature never, of itself, leads to God. **The African savage sits at his cannibal** feast, surrounded by natural scenery which surpasses in splendor and glory anything we in England have ever seen. Nature has not led him to God.—*Why Sunday?*

* * *

The Master's Touch

If the Master deigns to touch with divine power the cold and pulseless heart of the buried acorn, causing it to burst forth into a new life, will He leave neglected in the earth the soul of man, made in the image of his Creator? If He stoops to give to the rosebush, whose withered blossoms float upon the autumn breeze, the sweet assurance of another springtime, will He refuse words of hope to the sons of men when the frosts of winter come?

If matter, mute and inanimate, though changed by the forces of Nature into a multitude of forms, can never die, will the imperial spirit of man alone suffer annihilation, after it has made a brief visit, like a royal guest, to this tenement of clay? No; I am as sure that there is another life as I am that I live today.

Some time ago while in Cairo, I was shown a few grains of wheat that had slumbered for more than 3,000 years in an Egyptian tomb. As I gazed upon those grains of wheat, this thought came into my mind, that if one of them had been planted upon the banks of the Nile the next year after it was grown, and all of its lineal descendants had been harvested and planted from that day to this, its progeny would be sufficiently numerous to feed the teeming millions of this world.

There is an unbroken chain of life that connects the earliest grain with the one which we now sow and reap. If there is an invisible something in a grain of wheat which enables it, when warmed by the sunshine and nurtured by the rain, to discard its old body, and build out of the earth and air a new one so much like the old that you cannot tell the one from the other, and transmit its own likeness through 3,000 generations, I need not fear that my soul will have the power to clothe itself with a new body, suited to another existence, when this earthly frame has crumbled into dust.—Wm. Jennings Bryan.

* * *

For Comfort, Not for Food

A city missionary visited a poor old woman in a city attic, whose scanty pittance was scarcely sufficient for her bare subsistence. He observed in a broken teapot that stood on the window a strawberry plant growing. He remarked from time to time how it continued to grow, and with what care it was watched and tended. "Your plant flourishes nicely; you will soon have strawberries on it." "Oh, sir, it is not for the sake of fruit I prize it, but I am too poor to keep any living creature, and it is a great comfort to have that plant living, for I know it can only live by the power of God, and as I see it live and grow day by day it tells me God is near." In like manner the rainbow reminds us of God's faithfulness.—*Thinker*.

* * *

A Wayside Flower

A lily by the wayside grew,
All alone;
And beamed in radiance on the few
Who passed the weary path along,
Dejected, sore, with ne'er a song
To cheer them.

It breathed its fragrance in the air,
This flower,
And gave the sunshine odor rare;
It led a pilgrim in surprise
To lift his vision to the skies
Above him.

And thus it lived its tranquil life
In silence.
It heeded not earth's stress and strife—
Just breathed forth purity awhile,
Then loosed its petals with a smile,
And vanished.
—Frank Wilford.

* * *

The Season I Love Best

I love the Springtime with its leaves
And grass of dainty green
And flowers bursting all around
Of every shade and sheen.

I love the summer with its weight
Of ripened fruit and grain,
Its sighing winds and singing birds,
And silvery falling rain.

I love the Autumn with its wreath
Of rainbow tinted hills,
And Jack Frost hiding in the grass
And by the flowing rills.

But when King Winter comes along
And wraps the earth with snow—
The other seasons—I forget—
Because I love it so.
—Alice Montgomery Barr.

* * *

A Time to Listen

Be still, and know that I am God.—Psalm 46:10.

When suddenly upon your sight
There bursts some marvel of God's hand—
A towering peak all glistening white,
Or canyon vast; or when you stand
Beside a lake with shadows deep,
Or in a grove of His big trees,
One moment listening silence keep;
God speaks to us from such as these
—Florence Aiken Banks.

* * *

God's Beauty Amid Man's Wreckage

With a lavish hand the divine Artist still decks earth and sky and sea in gorgeous colors. In keeping with His promise to Noah, He has sent another springtime and summer to this troubled world. Knowing our frame, He provides relief from the sad scenes and thoughts of war. A letter received a year ago from a little land that has been devasted by war for the second time in our generation contains a triumphant note of true Christian thankfulness. "Some of the small parks of Brussels," wrote Dr. Vansteenberghe, co-director of the Belgian Gospel Mission, "are ravishing at this time with their trees in bloom. In spite of the carnage that goes on around us the work of God in nature continues. We had much encouragement in that. I love to look at the little flowers which cast a note of joy into the grass plots and the parks. They bloom, spreading their beauty without care for the evil times that we are now experiencing. I ask for myself that grace of being able to spread abroad the sweet savor of Christ without being troubled by events."—*Sunday School Times.*

* * *

The Father's Handiwork

When Dr. Bonnell asked if exploring the uncharted spaces did not give him a feeling of loneliness and insignificance, the astronomer replied very reverently: "No, there is nothing insignificant about man. Wherever I turn this telescope, I can trace my Heavenly Father's handiwork."—Selected.

NEGLECT

Can You Name Me?

I never was guilty of wrong action but on my account lives have been lost, trains have been wrecked, ships have gone down at sea, cities have burned, battles have been lost and governments have failed.

I never struck a blow nor spoke an unkind word, but because of me homes have been broken up, friends have grown cold, the laughter of children has ceased, wives have shed bitter tears, brothers and sisters have forgotten, and fathers and mothers have gone broken-hearted to their graves.

I have intended no evil, but because of me talent and genius have come to naught, courtesy and kindness have failed, and the promise of success and happiness has yielded sorrow and disaster.

I have no color except black, no sound but just my silence, no cause for being myself, no progeny except grief and disaster. You may not on the instant call me by name, but surely you are personally acquainted with me. I am *Neglect.*—T. M. Olson.

* * *

"The Land of Pretty Soon"

"I know a land where the streets are paved
With things we meant to achieve;
Walled with money we meant to have saved,
And the pleasures for which we grieve,
Kind words unspoken, promises broken,
And many a coveted boon
Are gathered there in that land somewhere,
The Land of Pretty Soon.

"There uncut jewels of possible fame
Are lying about in the dust,
And many a noble and lofty aim
Are covered with mold and rust.
And, oh, this place, while it seems so near,
Is farther away than the moon;
Though purpose is fair, we'll not get there—
To the Land of Pretty Soon.

"The road that leads to that mystic land
Is strewn with pitiful wrecks,
The ships that sailed for its shining strand
Bear skeletons on their decks.
It's farther at noon than it was at dawn,
And farther at night than noon;
Oh, let us beware of that land down there—
The Land of Pretty Soon."

"How shall we escape, if we neglect so great salvation?"—Selected.

The Consequences of Neglect

In a certain asylum there is a white-haired man who has been an inmate for twenty-five years. He spends his days repeating these words, "Too late, too late!" During one of the visiting days at the institution, these strange words attracted the attention of one of the visitors. When the attendant of the ward was asked about the history of the man, this was the story: Years ago, the poor fellow had been the keeper of the signal station on one of the great eastern railroads.

One day he forgot to give the right of way to one of the fast trains. Seeing some beautiful flowers growing along the highway nearby he went to pick them. While engaged in this pleasant task, the train was heard approaching in the distance. On and on it came with rapid pace. Suddenly he realized that the train did not have the right of way. In a vainless effort he tried to correct his mistake, but it was too late! "Too late, too late!" he cried in anguish, as he covered his eyes as the helpless passengers were carried to a speedy death. *How little we realize the destruction caused by human neglect!—Youth's Companion.*

* * *

Lenin's Ghastly Collapse

Capt. Francis McCullagh, an eyewitness of the trial of the Roman priests in Moscow, says: "On the night after the Archbishop and his companions were paraded in a motor-lorry through the streets of Moscow, the terrible leader of the Reds gazed in horror on one more terrible than himself, on a dread, nocturnal visitor, who having passed swiftly through the triple guards and the bolted doors, had halted at his bedside and laid an icy hand on the proud and formidable brain. From that day Lenin was a living corpse." Percival Phillips gives the rumor than ran through all Russia on Lenin's death (*Daily Mail*, Feb. 1, 1924): "The once all-powerful Dictator of Red Russia spent his last days of activity crawling on all fours like a beast around the room in his carefully-guarded retreat at Gorky, apologizing to the furniture for his misdeeds —the memory of which remained amid the ruins of his mind — and shouting repeatedly, 'God save Russia and kill the Jews!' " — D. M. Panton, in *The Dawn.*

* * *

Far Worse Than Hunger

One of the incidents of the great Chinese famine of 1906-1907, was a visit I made to the refugee camp outside the walls of Chinkiang. Mrs. Paxton was taking simple medicine to the suffers; and as we made the rounds of the miserable straw mat shelters, within which the starving people hungered on the cold ground, she turned to me with a startled expression and said, "Do you know what most of them are saying? They complain of lack of appetite." These famine victims were not hungry — because they were starving. They had passed the stage of desire for food. That picture portrays many a soul's state. It has lost interest in or longing for spiritual satisfactions because it is starving.—*Christian Herald.*

* * *

A Triumph of Satan: A Parable

Luther says in one of his sermons, "The Devil held a great anniversary at which his emissaries were convened to report the results of their several missions. 'I let loose the wild beasts of the desert,' said one, 'on a caravan of Christians, and their bones are now bleaching on the sands.' 'What of that?' said the Devil. 'Their souls were all saved.' 'I drove the east wind.' said another, 'against a ship freighted with Christians, and they were all drowned.' 'What of that?' said the Devil. 'Their souls were all saved.' 'For ten years I tried to get a single Christian asleep,' said a third, 'and I succeeded, and left him so.' Then the Devil shouted," continues Luther, "*and the night stars of hell sang for joy.*"—*Biblical Treasury.*

* * *

In What Part of the Train Are You?

"Many people are on Salvation Train; but a lot of them are traveling in the sleeper."—*Christian Victory.*

Playing Safe!

A motorist once stopped for water at a dilapidated house in the South where a barefooted man, leaning against a rickety fence, was gazing meditatively across a field that had grown up to weeds. "How is your cotton this year?" asked the motorist. "Well, sir," replied the man, "I ain't got no cotton. I didn't plant none 'cause I was afraid the boll weevil might be bad." "How is your corn?" "Well, I didn't plant no corn neither, for I didn't know if we'd git rain," he replied. The motorist hesitated, "How are your sweet potatoes?" he asked at last, "Well, now, Stranger," the man replied, "you see, it's just this way: I didn't plant no sweet pertaters 'cause I was afraid the bugs might take them. No, sir, I didn't plant nothin' I just played safe."—*Youth's Companion.*

* * *

Miss Meant-To

Miss Meant-To has a comrade
And her name is Didn't-Do.
Have you ever chanced to meet them
Did they ever call on you?
These two girls now live together
In the house of Never-Win,
And I'm told that it is haunted
By the ghost of Might-Have-Been.
—Selected.

* * *

Unused

There is a story told of Paganinni's famous violin, which was left to his native city of Genoa on condition it should not be played upon. It was a most unfortunate policy, for as a result "this magic violin, which might have thrilled the world for hundreds of years to come... is becoming worm-eaten in its grand glass case, and will soon be a little bit of worthless dust." — *Gospel Herald.*

* * *

The Things We Leave Undone

Sometimes we may put too much stress on the things we do, without taking into consideration that we will be judged as much by the things that we leave undone. I think it was Margaret Sangster who reminded us, "It isn't the thing you do, dear, but the thing you leave undone, that gives you a bit of a heartache, at the setting of the sun." The kind word we might have spoken, the letter we might have written, the friendly deed that would have helped another over a rough place; all these undone things are apt to make us miserable and at the same time rob others of that which would have meant so much to them.

We must bear in mind the Master's condemnation, "Inasmuch as ye did it not to one of the least of these, ye did it not to Me" (*Matt.* 25:45).

On the other hand, how sweet it is to know what He also said, "Inasmuch as ye have done it unto one of the least of these My brethren, ye have done it unto Me" (*Matt.* 25:40). What a delightful thought to know that every kind deed we do for any of Christ's brethren is in His sight as if we did it unto Him. How it should encourage us in helping others. And how it saddens us to know that the things we failed to do for others we failed to do for Him.

If all our good intentions were put into practice, how much happier and better this world would be. If all the kind words we say about people after they have left this world were only said while they were here, how it would have brightened their pathway and sweetened life for them.

A pathetic incident was related in the papers recently concerning a man who was found dead in a gas filled room. He had become despondent because he could not get work and was behind in his room rent. A letter unopened outside his door contained a gift of money, which if it had arrived sooner might have given him encouragement to live. "Do It Now" is a good motto to keep in mind provided the thing we are contemplating is right; for very often if we do not do it at once we may not do it at all. The old saying, "Strike while the iron is hot" is another good motto, for if the iron is allowed to cool, the striking is of no effect.

Someone has defined "Duty" as doing a thing when it ought to be done. I know a lad who left home to go out into the world. He was a good lad and fond of his mother, but he grew careless about writing. He moved without letting his family know his address, then one day his conscience began to bother him, so he sat down and wrote to his mother. Alas, the letter came too late, for his mother had gone to her Heavenly Home a short time before it arrived!

It would be a good thing if we prayed each morning for strength and guidance so that we would leave nothing undone that we ought to do, nor do that which is grievous to our Lord.—*Gospel Herald.*

* * *

"Do It Now"

"If with pleasure you are viewing,
Any work a man is doing;
If you like him, or you love him,
Tell him now!
Don't withhold your approbation,
Till the parson makes oration,
And he lies with snowy lilies o'er his brow.
For no matter how you shout it,
He won't really care about it,
He won't know how many teardrops you have shed,
If you think some praise is due him,
Now's the time to ease it to him,
For he cannot read his tombstone when he's dead!

"More than fame and more than money.
Is the comment kind and sunny,
And the hearty warm approval of a friend,
For it gives to life a savour,
And it makes you truer, braver,
And it gives you hope and courage 'til the end.
If he earns your praise bestow it,
If you love him let him know it,
Let the words of true encouragement be said,
Do not wait 'til life is over.
And he is underneath the clover,
For he cannot read his tombstone when he's dead!"

—Selected.

NEW YEAR

Ring Out the Old, Ring In the New

Ring out, wild bells, to the wild sky,
The flying clouds, the frosty light;
The year is dying in the night;
Ring out, wild bells, and let him die.

Ring out the old, ring in the new,
Ring, happy bells, across the snow;
The year is going, let him go;
Ring out the false, ring in the true.

Ring out the grief that saps the mind,
For those that here we see no more;
Ring out the feud of rich and poor,
Ring in redress to all mankind.

Ring out a slowly dying cause,
And ancient forms of party strife;
Ring in the nobler modes of life,
With sweeter manners, purer laws.

Ring out the want, the care, the sin,
The faithless coldness of the times:
Ring out, ring out my mournful rhymes,
But ring the fuller minstrel in.

Ring out false pride in place and blood,
The civic slander and the spite;
Ring in the love of truth and right,
Ring in the common love of good.

Ring out old shapes of foul disease ;
Ring out the narrowing lust of gold;
Ring out the thousand wars of old,
Ring in the thousand years of peace.

Ring in the valiant man and free,
The larger heart, the kindlier hand:
Ring out the darkness of the land.
Ring in the Christ that is to be.

—Alfred Tennyson in *The Works of Tennyson*. By permission of the Macmillan Co., publishers.

* * *

New Year's Wishes

A pearl-strewn pathway of untold gladness,
Flecked by no gloom, by no weary sadness—
Such be the year to thee!
A crystal rivulet, sunlight flinging,
Awakening blossoms, and joyously singing
Its own calm melody.
A symphony soft, and sweet, and low,
Like the gentlest music the angels know
In their moments of deep joy;
'Mid earth's wild clamor thy spirit telling
Of beauty and holiness, upward swelling,
And mingling with the sky.

Blessings unspoken this year be thine!
Each day in its rainbow flight entwine
New gems in thy joy-wreathed crown;
May each in the smile of Him be bright,
Who is changeless Love and unfading Light,
Till the glory seem to thy tranced sight
As Heaven to earth come down.

—Frances Ridley Havergal.

* * *

New Year's Wishes

What shall I wish thee? Treasures of earth?
Songs in the springtime, pleasure and mirth?
Flowers on thy pathway, skies ever clear?
Would this insure thee a happy New Year?

What shall I wish thee? What can be found
Bringing thee sunshine all the year round?
Where is the treasure, lasting and dear,
That shall insure thee a happy New Year?

Faith that increaseth, walking in light;
Hope that aboundeth, happy and bright;
Love that is perfect, casting out fear;
These shall insure thee a happy New Year.

Peace in the Saviour, rest at His feet,
Smile on His countenance, radiant and sweet.
Joy in His presence, Christ ever near!
This will insure thee a happy New Year.

—Frances Ridley Havergal.

* * *

The Coming Year

Another year is dawning!
Dear Master let it be,
In working or in waiting

Another year with Thee.
Another year in leaning,
Upon Thy loving breast,
Of ever-deepening trustfulness;
Of quiet, happy rest.

Another year of mercies,
Of faithfulness and grace;
Another year of gladness,
In the shining of Thy face;
Another year of progress,
Another year of praise,
Another year of proving
Thy presence "all the days."

Another year of service,
Of witness for Thy love;
Another year of training
For holier works above.
Another year is dawning!
Dear Master let it be
On earth, or else in heaven,
Another year for Thee.
—Frances Ridley Havergal.

* * *

I know not what awaits me
As dawns another year;
The path untrod I cannot see,
Yet knows my heart no fear!
I know not whether long or short
My pilgrimage may be!
I'll daily praise my *God* in song
For all *His* love for me.
With joy I greet the year—
It cannot bring me ill
Since *Christ my Lord* is ever near,
My soul with peace to fill. Amen!
—Sister Tillie Albright.

* * *

Thou Remainest

Thou remainest. Jesus, Master,
Thou art evermore the same:
Yesterday, today, forever,
Changeless as Thy peerless Name.

Thou remainest. Changing seasons,
Speak to us of fleeting days:
Faithful Thou to endless ages,
Worthy, too, of ceaseless praise.

Thou remainest. Earthly treasures,
Lose their charm and fade away:
Thine are riches everlasting,
Blessings which shall ne'er decay.

Thou remainest. Though the warfare
Fiercely rages. hotter grows,
Thou wilt hide in Thy pavilion,
From the rage of bitter foes.

Thou remainest. Deepening shadows
Of sin's ever darkening night,
Wait to usher in the dawning
Of the morn, eternal, bright.

Thou remainest. Ceaseless Lover,
Ever gracious, wise and true;
Make us holy, keep us faithful,
Living here Thy will to do.
—A. Gardner.

* * *

The New Year

Upon the threshold of the year we stand,
Holding Thy hand;
The year holds mysteries and vague surprise
To meet our eyes;
What will its passing moments bring,
To weep, or sing?

We fear to take one step without Thy care
And presence there;
But all is clear to Thine all-seeing gaze,
Counting the days
From dawn of time, till ages cease to be-
Eternity!

Upon the threshold of the year we stand,
Holding Thy hand;
Thou wilt walk step by step along the way
With us each day;
So whether joy or woe shall come this year,
We shall not fear!
—Homera Homer-Dixon.

* * *

The Old Year and the New

"Into the silent places
The Old Year goes tonight,
Bearing old pain, old sadness,
Old care and old delight.
Mistakes, and fears and failures,
The things that could not last,
But naught that e'er was truly ours
Goes with him to the past.

"Out of the silent places,
The young year comes tonight,
Bringing new pain, new sadness,
New care and new delight;
Go forth to meet him bravely,
The New Year all untried,
The things the old year left behind us-
Faith, Hope, and Love abide."
—Annie Johnson Flint.

* * *

He came to my desk with quivering lip,
The lesson was done.
"Have you a new leaf for me, dear Teacher?
I have spoiled this one!"
I took his leaf, all soiled and blotted
And gave him a new one, all unspotted,
Then into his tired heart I smiled:
"Do better now, my Child!"

I went to the throne, with trembling heart.
The year was done.
"Have you a new year for me, dear Master?
I have spoiled this one!"
He took my year, all soiled and blotted
And gave me a new one, all unspotted,
Then, into my tired heart he smiled:
"Do better now, my Child!"
—Selected.

* * *

The Year Before Us

Standing at the portal
Of the opening year,
Words of comfort meet us,
Hushing every fear:
I, the Lord, am with thee,
Be thou not afraid!
I will keep and strengthen,
Be thou not dismayed!
Resting on His promise,
What have we to fear?
God is all-sufficient
For the coming year.
—Frances Ridley Havergal.

Backward, Forward, Upward

I don't look back; God knows the fruitless efforts,
The wasted hours, the sinning, the regrets;
I leave them all with him who blots the record,
And mercifully forgives, and then forgets.

I don't look forward; God sees all the future,
The road that, short or long, will lead me home,
And He will face with me its every trial
And bear for me the burdens that may come.

But I look up—into the face of Jesus,
For there my heart can rest, my fears are stilled;
And there is joy and love, and light for darkness,
And perfect peace and every hope fulfilled.
—*Annie Johnson Flint.*

* * *

The Important Direction

One stormy night a boat could make no headway, and while the captain was struggling to get into port, a nervous passenger said to him: "Do you think we shall get in all right?" He replied: "This is a leaky old boat, and we may go down; and the boilers are not in very good condition, so we may go up. But, whatever happens, we are going on."—*Sunday School Times.*

* * *

Wishes for the New Year

BLESSINGS in abundance,
STRENGTH for every way,
COURAGE for each trial,
GLADNESS for each day.

FAITH in heaven's guidance,
HOPE that's firm and true,
May the Lord the Saviour
Give these gifts to you.
—Selected.

Hitherto and Henceforward

Hitherto the Lord has helped us
Since we've walked the heavenly way;
Filled our cup to overflowing
With His joy from day to day;
Cheered us by His constant presence,
Blessed with mercies daily new;
Let us raise our Ebenezer,
All His promises are true!

Hitherto the Lord has helped us
When our way was rough and steep;
Safely led us o'er the mountain,
Sometimes through the waters deep;
Yet He gives us strength for weakness;
Thus with confidence we say,
"Let us raise our Ebenezer;
He has led us all the way."

Hitherto the Lord has helped us
When on Him we have relied;
Food for soul and food for body,
Not a need but He supplied.
There are times when faith has wavered,
Doubts and fears our peace assailed;
Still we raise our Ebenezer,
Never has His promise failed.

Hitherto the Lord has helped us
Can we doubt Him? Dare we fear
Though from earthly help we're severed,
Facing now another year?
While our future paths are clouded,
Faith tonight o'er doubt prevails,
Let us raise our Ebenezer,
For His promise never fails.

—Courtesy *Moody Monthly.*

OBEDIENCE

The Cost of Obedience

Pierre Barlot was a gunner in the fort of Mont Valerin during the Prussian siege of Paris. One day he was standing by his gun when General Noel, the commander, came up and leveled his glass at the Sevres bridge. "Gunner," he said, "do you see the Sevres bridge over there?" "Yes, sir." "And that little shanty in a thicket of shrubs to the left?" "I see it, sir," said Pierre, turning pale. "It's a nest of Prussians; try it with a shell, my man." Pierre turned paler still. He sighted his piece deliberately, carefully, then fired it. "Well hit, my man, well hit!" exclaimed the general. But as he looked at Pierre he was surprised to see a great tear running down the gunner's cheek. "What's the matter, man?" "Pardon me, General," said Pierre, "it was my house — everything I had in the world."—*The Sunday-School Chronicle.*

* * *

Obedience

Somewhere I have read a little story of a child in a woodland camp whose father sent him with a letter to the village, pointing out a trail over which the lad had never gone before. "All right, father, but I don't see how that path will ever reach the town," said the boy. "Do you see the trail as far as the big tree down there?" answered the man. "Oh, yes, I see that far." "Well, when you get there by the tree you'll see the trail a little farther ahead, and so on until you get within sight of the houses of the village." *There is in our pilgrimage of faith an element of sheer faith, not seeing.—Sunday School Times,* Frederick Robertson (Brighton).

* * *

The Karen's Reminder

A Karen convert in Burmah who was taken to America, was asked to address a meeting upon their obligation to send out missionaries. After a moment of thought he asked with a good deal of meaning, "Has not Christ told you to do it?" "Oh, yes," was the reply, "but we wish you to remind them of their duty." "Oh, no," said the Karen, "if they will not mind Jesus Christ, they will not mind me!"—*The Biblical Illustrator.*

* * *

Obedience

James T. White has said that perhaps the most effective illustration of obedience is the reply of the mother of George Washington made at the banquet given to the allied officers after the surrender of Lord Cornwallis. A distinguished French officer asked Washington's mother how she managed to rear such a splendid son. She replied, "I taught him to obey.—*S. S. World.*

* * *

True Surrender

The late Rev. J. H. Jowett said he saw seventy Salvation Army officers receive their commission for foreign service. Not one of them had any idea where the command would send him — whether to Africa, or India, or Brazil, or to a crowded city in Japan. When each man received his commission, he welcomed it with a salute.—*Christian Herald.*

* * *

Very Busy, But—

When I was a boy on the farm, my father once told me to do a certain thing one day that I really did not like to do. He went to town, and I noticed that our barn door needed paint. I knew where there was a can of red paint and a new brush. I tried my hand at painting that door. I did a good job, but when my father came home, well—I do not need to tell you about it! It was not a precious memory! I performed a service, but I did not do the thing that my father left for me to do. So with the Christian: he will be rewarded, not for doing the thing that he wants to do, but for doing the thing that Christ left him here to do — to fulfill the great commission. — *The King's Business.*

* * *

He Knows What Is Best

A Persian legend runs that a certain king needed a faithful servant, and two men were candidates for the office. He took both at fixed wages, and his first order was to fill a basket with water from a neighboring well, saying that he would come in the evening and see their work. After putting in one or two bucketfuls, one man said, "What is the good of doing this useless work? As soon as we put the water in one side it runs out the other." The other answered, "But we have our wages, haven't we? The use is the master's business, not ours." "I am not going to do such fool's work," replied the other. Throwing down his bucket, he went away. The other man continued until he had exhausted the well; looking down into it he saw something shining—a diamond ring. "Now I see the use of pouring water into a basket," he cried. "If the bucket had brought up the ring before the well was emptied, it would have been found in the basket. Our work was not useless." Christians must believe that their divine Master knows what is best, and obey His commands, and in due time they will know and understand. — *Christian Herald.*

* * *

"Let God"

Some few years ago a university student was listening to a Bible reading on the first chapter of Genesis. The speaker described God in His work of turning chaos into cosmos, and he played on the word "let"—"And God said, Let there be light; and there was light," and urged his hearers to "let God." This young man went home with the Word of God ringing in his ears and he could not get rid of them. He carved them out in wooden letters, threaded them on a string and hung them in his dressing room. "*Let God!*" But how could he "let God"? It meant so much. And then one morning in desperation he banged his bathroom door as he went out, saying, "I cannot let God." When he came back the "d" from his legend was missing and it read, "Let go." And he saw his difficulty. He saw the thing to which he was clinging, which kept him from blessing, and he "let go" and "let God." --Courtesy *Moody Monthly.*

* * *

Trained Ears

What trained ears a captain needs! To hear the different signals in a fog and so to know his position. To hear and read an echo. A ship was in a fog on one of the Canadian lakes. The captain's face suddenly became tense, then perplexed. He rang for slowed engines, then for reversed engines. The whistle shrieked, but no answer came. "There's something dead ahead," he declared, "I get an echo from something." Just then the fog lifted a little, and not ten feet from the bow was a huge steel scow which had broken loose from harbor and drifted. A landman said he had heard no echo. The captain chuckled. "It's a matter of an educated hearing. God gave us ears, but we don't always train them."—Sunday School Times.

* * *

The Reason

"Who is the best girl in your school?" I asked a group of schoolgirls.

"Lucy Jones," was the quick reply.

"What makes her the best?" I asked.

"She recites the best," answered one.

"She is always ready and never keeps the class waiting," said another.

"She never gets excused," said a third.

"She's never late," said a fourth.

"She keeps all the rules," said a fifth.

"And something else," said one who had not spoken before.

"Ah, what is that?" I asked.

"Mother says she loves and willingly obeys God and her parents," she answered.

Yes, that's it. Lucy was working for Jesus by setting a good example.—*Story World.*

* * *

Obedience

It is said that a tradesman once advertised for a boy to assist in his shop. A few hours after the morning paper was circulating his office was thronged with all kinds of boys; and, not knowing which to choose, he advertised again, as follows: "Wanted, to assist in a shop, a boy who obeys his mother." In response to this, there were only two boys who ventured to apply for the situation. *This would still be a good test very likely.—Gospel Herald.*

Are We Obeying?

S. D. Gordon, in his *Quiet Talks on Power*, says that a prominent clergyman in New England tells this experience: "In the house of his pastoral work he was called upon to conduct the funeral service of a young woman who had died quite unexpectedly. As he entered the house he met the minister in charge of the mission church where the family attended, and asked him, 'Was Mary a Christian?' To his surprise a pained look came into the young man's face as he replied, 'Three weeks ago I had a strong impulse to speak to her, but I did not; and I do not know.' A moment later he met the girl's Sunday school teacher and asked her the same question. Quickly the tears came as she said, 'Two weeks ago, Doctor, a voice seemed to say to me, "Speak to Mary," and I knew what it meant, and I intended to, but I did not, and I do not know.' Deeply moved by these unexpected answers, a few minutes later he met the girl's mother, and thinking doubtless to give her an opportunity to speak a word that would bring comfort to her own heart, he said quietly, 'Was Mary a Christian girl?' The tears came quick and hot to the mother's eyes as she sobbed out, 'One week ago a voice came to me saying, "Speak to Mary," and I thought of it, but I did not do it at the time, and you know how unexpectedly she went away, and I do not know.'"—*The King's Business.*

* * *

God's Loving Plans

God's forehandedness is one of the wonders of His providence. At a Victorious Life Conference at Keswick, N. J., the Rev. L. L. Legters told the story of Sam, a slave who, as soon as one piece of work was done returned at once to his master's doorstep in order that he might always be ready for his master's bidding, just as we should be waiting for instructions from our Lord and Master. At some previous meeting of Mr. Legters, a girl who had been impressed with this illustration prayed, "O Lord, make me just like Sam"; and the next morning as she awakened with her resolution to be a bondslave of Jesus Christ still flaming in her, the day verse in her Scripture calendar was: "Blessed is the man that heareth me, watching daily at my gates, waiting at the posts of my doors" (Prov. 8:34). Upon hearing this incident of the confirmation of purpose through a Scripture calendar, related at this Conference, a young woman missionary, home from China on furlough, told Mr. Legters of a similar experience. Her name is Mary, and, on the day she first set sail for China her Scripture calendar day verse was, "Mary hath chosen that good part, which shall not be taken away from her." In order to encourage our hearts and to assure us of His care and guidance, God, in fulfilling Romans 8:28, "All things work together for good to them that love God," even takes a hand in the printing of Scripture calendars!—*Sunday School Times.*

* * *

"Ear Is Only"

"For a long time we were looking for a word for obedience—a virtue that the natives never practiced," related a missionary. "One day as I went home from the village my dog stayed behind. I whistled, and he came running after me at top speed. An old native man by the roadside said with admiration, *'Mui adem delegau ge'*; literally, 'Dog yours, ear is only,' that is, 'Your dog is all ear' (obedient). I got hold of that expression at once and found I had a beautiful word for obedience. Let us be 'all ear' to our Lord."—*Christian Herald* (London).

* * *

Are We As Obedient?

There is in the Catskill Mountains a memorial to a noble dog, cut in the rock. The creature was so attached and obedient to his master that when the latter happened to point a friend to something just beyond a precipice, the dog took it for an order and leaped over to his death. Be as promptly obedient to Him who will never mislead you. — *Sunday School Chronicle.*

* * *

When We Follow Instructions

An illustration of how God is able to guide aright comes to us in the daily press of January 15, 1944. An aviation cadet, on a practice flight, temporarily stricken blind, in panic radioed that message to his control officer. This officer radioed back, "Follow my instructions implicitly." After keeping the blinded cadet circling the landing field until the whole field was cleared and an ambulance had arrived, the control officer radioed, "Now lose altitude." "Now bank sharply." "You're coming onto tne field now." The cadet brought his plane to a perfect landing, was saved, and later his sight was restored.—*Independent Board* (for Presbyterian Foreign Missions) *Bulletin.*

* * *

Knowing Is Not Doing

Through United Press comes the report that termites have eaten through a large stack of pamphlets entitled, *Control of Termites*, in the mailing room of the University of California at Berkeley. Maintenance men made the discovery. One would naturally expect that university buildings would be free of termites, because at such a center of higher education so much is known of termites and the destruction they cause. But it is one thing to have in a pamphlet the information concerning the control of termites, and quite another thing to make a practical application of that information! On speaking to His disciples on one occasion, the Lord Jesus said regarding the things He taught them, *"If ye know these things, happy are ye if ye do them"* (John 13:7).—*Now.*

OLD AGE

About Getting Old

"Let it be our unceasing prayer that as we grow older we may not grow colder in the ways of God," said good George Muller. Some do. The enthusiasm of their earlier years flees away, and they become jaded in their affections, stale in their thoughts, indifferent toward everything. The sense of wonder is gone and they have no longer any interest. All things are full of weariness—all is vanity and vexation of spirit. They have given up the idea of going any further or learning anything more. "What do you do all day, Uncle Jimmy?" "I just sit and think, and sit and think—sometimes I just sit," answered Uncle Jimmy. That's getting *old*, in the bad sense of the word—ceasing to live before we die. God has something better than that for His saints.

That same George Muller above quoted, lived up into the late nineties—always bright, full of interest, hopeful, joyful. In his last years he would often stop in the midst of his conversation to exclaim, 'Oh, I am so happy!" And it was not a mannerism nor was it feigned. "As we advance in years," he had written long before, "let us not decline in spiritual power; but let us see to it that an increase of spiritual vigor and energy be found in us, that our last days may be our best days. . . . Let the remaining days of our earthly pilgrimage be spent in an ever-increasing, earnest consecration to God." So indeed it was with him. And so it should be with all God's people. "The devil has no happy old men," it has been said. But those who are the Lord's, increase in faith and joy.—R. H. B., in *The Word and Work.*

* * *

Old Men's Achievement

The Earl of Halsburg when ninety years old prepared to celebrate the century mark by giving England a revised edition of their law amounting to twenty volumes. The great artist, Titian, painted one of his greatest pictures, The Battle of Lepanto, when he was 98. Von Moltke was in active service at 88. Goethe finished "Faust" when 82. Six months later he died. The astronomer Galileo was 73 years of age when he made some of his greatest discoveries. Socrates began to study music at the age of 80. Cato influenced the world more after he was 80 years of age than during all his previous life. Ludovico, at the great age of 115, wrote the memoirs of his own times.—*Sunday School Times.*

* * *

Consolation in Old Age

"I am on the bright side of seventy," said an aged man of God; "the bright side, because nearer to everlasting glory."

"Nature fails," said another, "but I am happy."

"My work is done," said the Countess of Huntingdon, when eighty-four years old: "I have nothing to do but to go to my Father."

"Eighty and six years," was Polycarp's answer when required to deny the truth, "have I served my Saviour, and He hath never done me any harm; and shall I deny Him now?"—*The United Evangelical.*

* * *

Indian Summer

Someone has well said that of all the seasons of the year in our American climate, there is none so tender, so beautiful, so weird and unearthly, so fascinating and perfect as Indian summer.

After the buds, blossoms, heat, and harvests of summer; after the autumn of fruits and frosts, when the forests are mantled in crimson, fire, and gold; when chill winds and vagrant snow warn of the approach of ice-mantled winter, then some invisible hand seizes the galloping steeds of the seasons and reins them up suddenly for a few days, while earth, air and sky weave around the weather-beaten brow of the year the golden crown of Indian summer. The sun pours down a soft and dreamy golden light;

the sky is robed with a delicate, purplish gauze that seems to float everywhere; the air is balmy and caressing. There is a bewitching charm in the unearthly spell that has been cast upon nature.

"November leads us through her dreary straits
To find the halcyon Indian summer days,
Where, sitting in a dreamy, solemn haze,
We catch the glimmer of the jasper gates,
And hear the echo of the celestial praise."

And so God designs old age to be the Indian summer of life—the gentlest, the tenderest, the most beautiful of all of life's seasons, for He says, "And even to your old age I am he; and even to hoar hairs I will carry you; I have made and I will bear; even I will carry and deliver you." God's special care and love for old age marks it as the Indian summer of earth's pilgrimage. — *Baltimore Southern Methodist.*

* * *

Dr. Goforth Testifies

Extracts from a letter written by Dr. Jonathan Goforth to his children on February 10, 1934, his seventy-fifth birthday:

"I have attained to my seventy-fifth birthday. In all sincerity I can say, 'It is but by the grace of God I am just what I am.' My conversion at eighteen was so complete that ever onward I could say, 'I am crucified with Christ.'

"Then came that never-to-be-forgotten Sunday when I read the Memoirs of Robert Murray McCheyne. The call of God to preach the Gospel of His Son was so definite and so resistless that I could not but yield, and all thoughts of being a politician forever departed from my mind.

"Two years later, in old Knox Church, Ingersoll, I heard Dr. McKay of Formosa plead the claims of the heathen. From that hour I was a foreign missionary Firty-three years have passed, but by the grace of God, 'I (have) not been disobedient unto the Heavenly Vision.' At seventy-five I feel the same resistless urge to seek the 'other' sheep for whom the Saviour died.

"True, the loss of my sight is a great handicap. But the Lord has seen our special need and has sent to us an unusual young Chinese man to meet this need. In five months he has been with us, he and I together have read the New Testament three times. We have just finished the last chapter of Revelation today. This makes the sixty-sixth time I have read the New Testament in Chinese since the (then) New Version came out twenty-three years ago. Consequently it has become so familiar I can readily detect any mispronouncing of a word on Mr. Kao's part. Tomorrow we commence reading the Old Testament, going over each chapter five times.

"When I was five years of age, my mother started me memorizing Scripture. I owe so very much to that early impulse to memorize the Word. My great text has been, 'Search the Scriptures; . . . they are they which testify of Me.' I more and more realize the whole Bible has but one theme and that theme is the Lord Jesus Christ. Consequently no matter how many times one may read the Bible it never grows old. I have never known the New Testament to seem so fresh as while reading it this last time.

"In early years two lines made a deep impression on me. They came to be my impelling motto:

'Slacken not pace yet at inlet or island;
Straight for the haven steer, straight for the Highland.'

But the crowning motto of my life has even been that of the great Apostle, 'Forgetting the things which are behind, and stretching forward to the things which are before, I press on toward the goal unto the prize of the high calling of God in Christ Jesus."

"You must not wonder at me even at seventy-five, eager to remain here in the high places of the Field, for the opportunities of service were never greater, and the outlook for a great harvest never brighter than now." — (Furnished by Miss Rose A. Huston.)—*The Covenanter Witness.*

Old Age

Sometimes the sun seems to hang for half an hour in the horizon, only just to show how glorious it can be. The day is done, for the fervor of shining is over, and the sun hangs golden in the west, making everything look unspeakably beautiful, with the rich effulgence which it sheds on every side. So God seems to let some people, when their duty in this world is done, hang in the west, that men may look on them and see how beautiful they are.—H. W. Beecher.

* * *

Treasures for Old Age

After all, when the chimney corner years come, it will not be our adventures in business, where we fought a tough fight and won by crushing the enemy, but the adventures in friendship and neighborliness that will count most with us. . . The little letters we write to friends, the clusters of flowers with which we enrich their lives, the almost insignificant acts of kindness and love—these are the treasures we lay up to warm our hearts with when old age creeps in and beckons youth away.—Thomas Dreier.

* * *

Growing Old

A little more tired at close of day;
A little less anxious to have our way;
A little less ready to scold and blame;
A little more care for a brother's name:
And so we are nearing the journey's end,
Where time and eternity meet and blend.

A little less care for bonds and gold;
A little more rest than in days of old;
A broader view and a saner mind,
And a little more love for all mankind.
A little more careful of what we say:
And so we are faring a-down the way.

A little more leisure to sit and dream;
A little more real the things unseen;
A little bit near to those ahead,
With visions of those long loved and dead:
And so we are going where all must go,
To the place the living may never know.

A little more laughter, a few more tears,
And we shall have told our increasing years;
The book is closed and the prayers are said,
And we are a part of the countless dead.
Except that translation may take us home
And we cease forever on earth to roam.
Thrice happy, then, if some soul can say,
"I live because he has passed my way."
—Selected.

* * *

Not Growing Old

This frail old shell in which I dwell
Is growing old, I know full well—
But I am not the shell.

What if my hair is turning grey?
Grey hairs are honorable, they say.
What if my eyesight's growing dim?
I still can see to follow Him
Who sacrificed His life for me,
Upon the Cross of Calvary.

Why should I care if Time's old plow
Has left its furrows on my brow?
Another house, not made with hand,
Awaits me in the Glory Land.

What though my tongue refuse to talk?
What though I falter in my walk?
I still can tread the Narrow Way,
I still can watch, and praise, and pray

My hearing may not be as keen
As in the past it may have been,
Still, I can hear my Saviour say
In whispers soft, "This is the way."

The outward man, do what I can
To lengthen out his life's short span,
Shall perish and return to dust
As everything in nature must.

The inward man, the Scriptures say,
Is growing stronger every day.
Then how can I be growing old
When safe within my Saviour's fold?

Ere long my soul shall fly away,
And leave this tenement of clay,
This robe of flesh I'll drop, and rise
To seize the "everlasting prize"—
I'll meet you on the Streets of Gold,
And prove that I'm not growing old.
—John E. Roberts.

Fruit in Old Age

"Lo, I am this day fourscore and five years old" (Josh. 14:10).

God dealt justly and liberally with this old saint. . . . At the age of eighty-five he met the challenge of the hardest task of his life! Forty years of wilderness life had not dimmed his vision, lessened his faith, dulled his youthful zeal, nor diminished his physical powers. This is the heritage of those who wholly follow the Lord. Old age is no bar to the power of God. "They shall bring forth fruit in old age" is the promise to those who wholly follow the Lord.

Dr. McConnell built a great church in the City of Atlanta at the age of seventy. J. Hudson Taylor, at seventy, was vigorously pushing into new territory, opening new fields to the Gospel and praying out new bands of missionaries to Inland China. George Mueller at ninety was still expanding and enlarging a work that not only housed 1,500 orphans, but was publishing religious literature and sending out missionaries to half a dozen mission fields.

In his old age Caleb went up to the stronghold of the Anakim, and dislodged them from their fortress and took possession of their cities. "Let us go up at once, . . . for we are well able to overcome it," is the victorious cry of a triumphant faith, and its reward is to reign in the place it has wrested from the hand of its fiercest enemies.—*Christ-Life.*

* * *

Old Age—God's Crown of Glory

When Polycarp was given the alternative of denying Christ or suffering martyrdom, the aged saint replied: "Eighty and six years I have served my Saviour and He hath never done me any harm; and shall I deny Him now?" What heroism is this! What faith!—*Christian Witness.*

* * *

When I Am Old

Lord, keep me sweet when I grow old,
And things in life seem hard to bear,
When I feel sad and all alone,
And people do not seem to care.

Oh, keep me sweet when time has caused
This body, which is not so strong,
To droop beneath its load of years,
And suffering and pain have come.

And keep me sweet when I have grown
To worry so, at din and noise;
And help me smile, the while I watch,
The noisy play of girls and boys.

Help me remember how that I,
When I was younger than today,
And full of life and health and joy,
Would romp and shout in happy play.

Help me to train my heart each day,
That it will only sweetness hold;
And as the days and years roll on,
May I keep sweet, as I grow old.

Oh, keep me sweet, and let me look
Beyond the frets that life must hold,
To see the glad *eternal* joys;
Yes, keep me sweet, in growing old.
—Mrs. J. A. Hazard.

OPPORTUNITY

The Road of Opportunity

When the Children of Israel crossed into Canaan, it was on the Jericho road that they wrought that miraculous capture of Jericho by encompassing the city day by day as they had been directed. It was on the Jericho road that Zacchæus climbed up into the sycamore tree to see Jesus as He passed by, which resulted in having Him in his home and heart. It was on the Jericho road that the sons of the prophets were working on their building and the head of a borrowed ax fell into the water, and was rescued by a miracle by the prophet. It was on the Jericho road that two blind men called to Jesus as He was passing, and had their sight restored. It was on the Jericho road that a certain man was going from Jerusalem to Jericho and became in need of help. The Jericho road is the road of opportunity, and it runs by your home, and your shop, and your office, and there is always "a certain man" there.—*Sunday School Times.*

* * *

Opportunity

They do me wrong who say I come no more,
When once I knock and fail to find you in;
For every day I stand without your door
And bid you wake and rise to fight and win.

Wail not for precious chances passed away,
Weep not for golden ages on the wane;
Each night I burn the records of the day,
At sunrise every soul is born again!

Laugh like a boy at splendors that have sped,
To vanquished joys be blind and deaf and dumb;
My judgments seal the dead past with its dead,
But never binds a moment yet to come.

Though deep in mire, wrong not your hands to weep;
I lend my arm to all who say, "I can."
No shame-faced outcast ever sank so deep,
But might yet rise again and be a man.

Dost thou behold thy lost youth all aghast?
Dost reel with righteous retribution's blow?
Then turn from blotted archives of the past,
And find the future's pages white as snow.

Art thou a mourner? rise thee from thy spell;
Art thou a sinner? sins may be forgiven;
Each morn I give thee wings to fly from hell,
Each night a star to guide thy feet to heaven."

—Walter Malone.

* * *

Lost Opportunity

Opportunity is a small word with a great meaning. *Lost* is a smaller word with as great a meaning. Put the two together, and they spell *tragedy.*

Opportunity is not a tangible thing — something that can be lost and found again. Once lost, it is gone forever! Another opportunity may present itself, but what if it should not? And if it should have we learned the lesson well enough in the school of experience to take advantage of it when it comes?

There was once a young lady to whom God had been marvelously good. She had a good home, Christian parents, and every opportunity for an education. God had even given her a special talent which she neither appreciated nor tried to cultivate.

Finally, she received a very clear and definite call to missions. But did she obey God? She did not. She was not even grateful to Him.

As life went on, the responsibilities of womanhood fell heavily upon her shoulders. God gave her another chance, and mercifully saved her soul. But there is now no opportunity in her busy life to forge ahead for Jesus as she might have done in the freedom of young womanhood. Her education is incomplete; the talent she should have used for God lies buried, and home ties hold her close.

She is grateful now, and thankful to have God's second best, happy to do the little things she can for Him, but how profound a regret she feels for willfully turning aside from His *first* plan for her!

If only folk could realize in their youth the value of the quickly passing years. It has been truly said that:

"There is a tide in the affairs of men
Which, taken at the flood, leads on to fortune;
Omitted, all the voyage of their life
Is bound in shallows and in miseries."

—*Wesleyan Methodist.*

"This world is but the vestible of an immortal life; and every chord of our lives touches on some other chord, which will vibrate in eternity. Stern task-master's opportunity is bald behind and must be grasped by the forelocks. This world is full of tragic 'might-have-beens,' No remorse, no regret, no self-accusation will avail one jot when the time for plowing is past. We cannot stick the share into the ground when we should be wielding the cycle. 'Too late' are the saddest of all human words, and unless our lives are filled each moment with the task that is apportioned to us, then through all eternity we must ever regret lost opportunity."—Ian Maclaren.

Recognizing Opportunity

A neighbor knocked at the lazy man's door and told him of a position he could get by going after it. "Um," said the man, "it appears that considerable effort will be involved." "Oh, yes," said the neighbor, "you will pass many sleepless nights and toilsome days, but it is good pay, and a chance for advancement." "Um," said the man, "and who are you?" "I am called Opportunity." "Um! *You call yourself Opportunity, but you look like Hard Work to me!"* And he slammed the door!—*New Success.*

PARENTAL RESPONSIBILITY

The Little One's Challenge

The wife of a prominent lawyer who had been under deep conviction for several days gave the following account of her conversation at our prayer meeting. "Last evening my little girl came to me and said, 'Mamma, are you a Christian?' 'No, Fannie, I am not.' She turned and went away, and as she walked off I heard her say, 'Well, if Mamma isn't a Christian, I don't want to be one.' And I tell you it went right to my heart, and I then gave myself to Christ."—*Sunday School Times.*

Swindled

I have the feeling that the modern girl is being swindled. She is trading modesty for recklessness; chastity for sophistication; freedom for danger; womanliness for daring; and charm for cosmetics.

Perhaps I am a Puritan. But America owes more to the Puritans than to all the white lights, cabarets, and jazz bands in the world.

I am wondering what would have happened if Abraham Lincoln's mother had had an ambition to be a flapper, or if Theodore Roosevelt had started out to be a shiek. Boys will be boys, but they will also be men.—*Religious Telescope.*

A "Desirable" Parent

A newspaper comments on a questionnaire recently sent to 369 high school boys and 415 girls, who were asked to check a list of ten desirable qualities in a father. The quality receiving the second largest vote was, "Respecting his children's opinions." Others were: "Never nagging his children about what they do; making plenty of money; being prominent in social life; owning a good-looking car."

The Scriptures, with their unfailing accuracy, predict what we are seeing today as a fact of the end of the age, that "perilous times shall come" when "men (meaning mankind, including young and old) shall be lovers of their own selves... boasters, proud... disobedient to parents."—*Sunday School Times.*

* * *

Parental Responsibility

"The best safeguard for the young generation is a good example by the older generation."—Selected.

* * *

The Forgotten Instructions

Two proud young parents were showing the minister their firstborn. Very thoughtfully the young mother said, "I don't know whether I know enough about Baby to raise him or not." The young husband laughed, "She says that about Baby because she didn't get a book of instructions with him." He was thinking of the books of instruction that had come with the sewing machine, the electric sweeper, and the refrigerator when they bought their household furniture some fifteen months before. Of course he was mistaken. There is a book of instructions with each baby given to the home. God's Book, the Bible, is the book of instructions that should be studied as never before when a little child comes. —*United Presbyterian.*

* * *

"T'was a sheep not a lamb, that went astray
In the parable Jesus told.
'Twas a grown-up sheep that wandered away
From the ninety and nine in the fold.
And out on the hilltops and out in the cold,
'Twas a sheep that the Good Shepherd sought.
And back to the flock, and back to the fold,
'Twas a sheep that the Good Shepherd brought!

"Now, why should the sheep be so carefully fed
And cared for still today?
Because there is danger if they go wrong
They will lead the lambs astray,
For the lambs will follow the sheep, you know,
Wherever they wander, wherever they go!

"If the sheep go wrong, it will not be long
Till the lambs are as wrong as they;
So, still with the sheep we must earnestly plead,
For the sake of the lambs today.
If the lambs are lost, what a terrible cost
Some sheep will have to pay!"
—*Gospel Herald.*

The Sins of the Parents Visited Upon the Children

Of our present-day crime-breeding conditions the most culpable of all is the unthinking American parent. Certainly here is a field in which pioneering is to be done. Here is an opportunity for the bravery necessary to tell the silly, soft-brained, indulgent parent who prates of the independence of youth, that he or she is nothing more nor less than a moral coward.

It takes courage indeed to stand perhaps with some good friend and point out the defects in parenthood by which this person is breeding in his or her child a lack of respect, first for parental law, for family tradition, and finally for the statutes of the land which should govern us all.

Yet this must be done; for in the breakdown of the American home there has been a steady lessening of parental supervision, of parental understanding, of parental courage, and an increase of parental laziness whereby the sins of these parents are being visited upon the children, and the children are paying for those sins of omission by committing 17 per cent of all the crime committed in America.—J. Edgar Hoover, in the *Lutheran Witness.*

* * *

Start Them Right

Only a few weeks ago, a fine Christian woman who has known the Lord only seven years, the widow of a millionaire, said to me, "Pray for my boy; pray for my girl; they have no interest in the things of God. I can never get them to hear the Word of God. They are courteous and polite if I bring a servant of the Lord to my home, but they will allow no one to say a word to them, and they will not read the Bible."

And then she added, "The worst of it is that they are what they are because I brought them up that way. Until seven years ago, I lived the life that they are living; I led them in the path they are now going. A Bible was never opened in my home until my husband died, and left me a broken-hearted woman, surrounded with all the luxuries he had given me, and I was crying out for something that could help me. Christ came to me, but it was too late to turn my children's steps in the right way. They are treading the path on which I started them."—*Gospel Herald.*

* * *

Angels and Needles

Centuries ago idle men discussed the question, How many angels can stand on the point of a needle? A faithful pastor in Scotland returning home one night saw the mother of seven children, herself a widow, mending the clothes of her bairns. "I know now," he said to his wife as he came in out of the dark, "I know now how many angels can be supported on the point of a needle," and then he told what he had seen.—Louis Albert Banks, in *"Hero Tales."*

* * *

Is Overstrictness the Trouble?

A good deal of nonsense is being palmed off on the community about the reaction of the child from overstrictness in parental training. When I hear a man say, "My parents brought me up so rigidly that a reaction took place in my mind and I have turned away from religion," I have sometimes asked, "Did they teach you to be honest?" "Yes." "Were they strict about it?" "Yes." "Did they teach you to tell the truth?" "Yes." "Were they strict about that?" "Yes." "Has any reaction taken place on these points?" No man learns the multiplication table from sheer love of it; but I never knew of anyone whose mind was in reaction against the multiplication table.—John Hall, D.D.

* * *

The Secret of Perfect Attendance

A young girl was being introduced to the Sunday morning congregation not long ago on the occasion of having won an award for perfect attendance at church school for seven years. As she was receiving her congratulations, and the audience was applauding her fine record, the pastor came forward and said: "Mary, before you go, I want to ask you a question or two. What kind of family have you grown up in? Didn't they ever have any company on Sunday? Has your family never gone on a picnic on the Lord's Day? Has there never been a time when your mother was 'just worn out' and your father had to stay at home because it was the only day they ever had together? Didn't it ever happen that something went wrong with the car so that you couldn't get it started? How has it happened that your parents never kept you home from church school?" The girl did not get the satire in the preacher's questions, and replied, "Why, they always wanted me to be in church school, and they planned it so I could get there." That was the secret.—*Church School Journal.*

* * *

Saved from the "Hell Club"

A widowed mother in Edinburgh had lain on her face all night long, crying, *"Oh, God, my boy! Save him! I plead the Blood!"* During the same night the boy, a medical student in the University and a member of the *"Hell Club,"* was assisting in a mock celebration of the Lord's Supper. He took up a glass of wine and held it up and said, "The Blood of our Lord Jesus Christ!" Then, trembling and pale, he put it down and seized his hat and fled from the place. It had seemed to turn to literal blood, and as he walked he knew not where at every step he moaned, *"I am guilty of the Blood of Christ!"* At dawn he came home and went to his room, and his mother heard him crying there and praying for mercy, and went in and threw her arms about his neck, saying, "You are really praying, my son?"

As the sun came up over the hills that morning, a mother's prayers were answered, and her son was saved. He went to his classes and asked leave to testify to the students of his experience; then he was excused for the day that he might go out on the streets and witness.

One day at a conference a man was called upon to pray. He said, "We praise Thee, O God, for the Son of Thy love—for Jesus who died, and has now gone above!" It was William P. Mackey, once the president of the Hell Club, who breathed this prayer which became a hymn, and who became a minister of the Gospel.—Selected.

* * *

"There"

"There are little eyes upon you,
And they're watching night and day;
There are little ears that quickly
Take in every word you say;
There are little hands all eager
To do everything you do,
And a little boy who's dreaming
Of the day he'll be like you.
You're the little fellow's idol,
You're the wisest of the wise;
In his little mind about you
No suspicions ever rise;
He believes in you devoutly;
Holds that all you say and do,
He will say and do in your way
When he's grown up just like you.
There's a wide-eyed little fellow
Who believes you're always right,
And his ears are always open,
And he watches day and night.
You are setting an example
Every day in all you do,
For the little boy who's waiting
To grow up to be like you."
—*Gospel Herald*

PATIENCE

Give God Time

The late Dr. Jowett said that he was once in a most pitiful perplexity, and consulted Dr. Berry, of Wolverhampton. "What would you do if you were in my place?" he entreated. "I don't know, Jowett. I am not there, and you are not there yet. When have you to act?" "On Friday," Dr. Jowett replied. "Then," answered Berry, "you will find your way perfectly clear on Friday. The Lord will not fail you." And surely enough, on Friday all was plain.

One of the greatest and wisest of all Queen Victoria's diplomats has left it on record that it became an inveterate habit of his mind never to allow any opinion on any subject to crystalize until it became necessary to arrive at a practical decision.

Give God time, and even when the knife flashes in the air, the ram will be seen caught in the thicket.

Give God time, and even when Pharaoh's host is on Israel's heels, a path through the waters will be suddenly opened.

Give God time, and when the bed of the brook is dry, Elijah shall hear the guiding voice.—*The Alliance Weekly.*

Waiting on the Lord

"*Wait, I say, on the Lord*" (*Ps.* 27:14)
Wait on the Lord, thou contrite one,
In penitence draw near;
He will His pard'ning grace bestow;
Your cry for mercy hear.
(*James* 4:8).

Wait on the Lord, thou tempted one,
Beset by hosts of sin;
Sufficient will his grace be found
The victory to win.
(*II Cor.* 12:9).

Wait on the Lord, thou weary one,
When cares of life oppress;
In Him find ev'ry need supplied;
In Him find quietness.
(*Ps.* 84:10).

Wait on the Lord, thou saddened one.
That grief and sorrow knows;
He shares the measure of your need;
His heart with love o'erflows.
(*Ps.* 103:13).

Wait on the Lord: In confidence
And expectation wait;
His promises are ever sure;
His mercy truly great.
—Fred Scott Shepard.

Our Only Opportunity Now

"Beloved, have you ever thought that some day you will never have anything to try you, or anybody to vex you again? There will be no opportunity in that happy Realm to learn or to show the spirit of patience, forbearance, and long-suffering. If you are ever to practice these things it must be now."—Dr. A. B. Simpson.

* * *

Wanamaker's Patience

The following incident was recorded in the life of John Wanamaker. One of the executives in the Philadelphia store recalls that one day, when he was a cash boy, he mustered up courage to go into Wanamaker's office to show him a new and cheap way to wrap small packages that he thought he had discovered. President Wanamaker was sitting at his top desk, and the boy timidly passed to him a sample package he had wrapped. As he did so his sleeve caught on the ink well and upset it. The horrified boy stood rooted to the spot. Wanamaker said: "Now I am going to show you something. If you attack a pool of ink with the edge of a blotter, instead of stamping the blotter flat down on it, it is astonishing how quickly it disappears." The devotion of a lifetime of able service was thus won in a minute by this fine display of patience.—*Sunday School Times.*

* * *

Two Helpful Bears

There lived an old couple who quarreled frequently. The whole village knew about it, and when, at last, they ceased their quarreling, questions were asked as to how it all came about. "Two bears did it," said the wife. "Two bears?" exclaimed a neighbor, "we thought two bears caused all the trouble." "Ah!" said the husband, "but these are two new bears which we found in the Bible. We have learned to love "*Bear* ye one another's burdens," and "*Forbearing* one another in love."—*Christian Advocate.*

A Day at a Time

A doctor was once asked by a patient who had met with a serious accident, "Doctor, how long shall I have to lie here?" The answer, "Only a day at a time," taught the patient a precious lesson. It was the same lesson God had recorded for His people of all ages, long before: The day's portion in its day. Faithful for one short day, long years take care of themselves.—Andrew Murray.

* * *

Wait!

God's delays are not denials;
He has heard your prayer;
He knows all about your trials,
Knows your every care.

God's delays are not denials;
Help is on the way;
He is watching o'er life's dials,
Bringing forth the day.

God's delays are not denials;
You will find Him true,
Working through the hardest trials
What is best for you!

—*The Believer's Magazine.*

* * *

Patience That Can Run

George Matherson said: "To run with patience is a very difficult thing. Running is apt to suggest the absence of patience, the eagerness to reach the goal We commonly associate patience with lying down. We think of it as the angel that guards the couch of the invalid Yet I do not think the invalid's patience the hardest to achieve.

"There is a patience which I believe to be harder — the patience that can run. To lie down in the time of grief, to be quiet under the stroke of adverse fortune, implies a great strength; but I know of something that implies a strength greater still:

"It is the power to work under a stroke; to have a great weight at your heart and still to run; to have a deep anguish in your spirit and still perform the daily task. It is a Christlike thing!

"The hard thing is that most of us are called to exercise our patience, not in bed, but in the street."—*Gospel Herald.*

"Waiting"

"Waiting! Yes, patiently waiting!
Till next steps made plain shall be;
To hear, with the inner hearing,
The Voice that will call for me.

"Waiting! Yes, quietly waiting!
No need for an anxious dread;
Shall He not assuredly guide me,
Who giveth me daily bread?

"Waiting! Yes, hopefully waiting!
With hope that need not grow dim;
The Master is pledged to guide me,
And my eyes are unto Him.

"Waiting! Expectantly waiting!
Perhaps it may be to-day
The Master will quickly open
The gate to my future way.

"Waiting! Yes, trustfully waiting!
I know, though I've waited long,
That, while He withholds His purpose,
His waiting cannot be wrong."

—*Gospel Herald.*

* * *

Interpretations of Love

Patience is Love on the anvil, bearing blow after blow of suffering.

Zeal is Love in the harvest field, never tiring of toil.

Meekness is Love in company when it vaunteth not itself.

Perseverance is Love on a journey, pressing on with unflagging step toward the end.

Joy is Love making its own sunshine where others see nothing but gloom.

Power is Love driving the soul's chariot wheels over all opposition.—Selected.

"Wait, patiently wait,
God is never late;
The budding plans are in thy Father's holding,
And only wait His Divine unfolding;
Then wait, patiently wait."

—Selected.

* * *

When to Do Nothing

There are times when doing nothing is better than doing anything. Those are the times when only God can do what is needed. True faith trusts Him then, and Him alone, to do the miracle. Moses and Jehoshaphat knew this secret; they knew the same Lord, and the same divine grace. As the pursuing Egyptians trapped the helpless Israelites at the Red Sea, Moses said: "Fear ye not, stand still, and see the salvation of the Lord. . . . The Lord shall fight for you, and ye shall hold your peace" (Exod. 14). As the Moabites and Ammonites, a vast multitude, closed in on Judah, King Jehoshaphat said to the helpless people: "Be not afraid nor dismayed by reason of this great multitude; for the battle is not your's, but God's. . . . Ye shall not need to fight in this battle: set yourselves, stand ye still, and see the salvation of the Lord" (II Chron. 20). So the Psalmist gives us God's word: "Be still, and know that I am God" (Psa. 46:10). When God alone can win the victory, faith lets God do it all. It is better to trust than to try. — *Sunday School Times.*

* * *

Wait for the Mud to Dry

Father Graham was an old-fashioned gentleman, beloved by everyone, and his influence in the little town was great, so good and active was he.

A young man of the village had been badly insulted and came to Father Graham full of angry indignation, declaring that he was going at once to demand an apology.

"My dear boy," Father Graham said, "take a word of advice from an old man who loves peace. An insult is like mud; it will brush off much better when it is dry. Wait a little, till he and you are both cool, and the thing will be easily mended. If you go now it will only be to quarrel."

It is pleasant to be able to add that the young man took his advice, and before the next day was gone the insulting person came to beg forgiveness.—*Our Young Covenanters.*

True Greatness

Once there was a woman who did a big washing. She hung her clothes on a line. The line broke and all the wash came down. She did her washing over again and spread it on the grass to dry. A dog with muddy feet came along and walked all over the nice, clean, white clothes. The woman did not get angry nor lose her temper. She said: "Ain't it queer he didn't miss nothing?"

That was true greatness. But only people who do washings know it.—Christian Union Herald.

PATRIOTISM—CITIZENSHIP

"Just today we chanced to meet,
Down upon the crowded street;
And I wondered whence he came,
Where was once his nation's name?
So I asked him, 'Tell me true,
Are you Pole or Russian Jew?
English, Irish, German, Prussian,
French, Italian, Scotch, or Russian?
Belgian, Spanish, French Moravian,
Dutch, Greek, or Scandinavian?'
Then he raised his head on high,
And he gave me his reply:
'What I was is naught to me,
In this land of liberty,
In my heart and man to man,
I am just AMERICAN!'"

—Selected.

* * *

Benjamin's Franklin's Motion

In 1778, at the meeting of the Constitutional Convention in Philadelphia, Benjamin Franklin made the motion to those assembled that the Convention should not proceed without an opening prayer each day. Said he:

"I have lived for a long time, and the longer I live the more convincing proof I see of this truth, that God governs in the affairs of men. If a sparrow cannot fall to the ground without His notice, is it probable that an empire can rise without His aid? We have been assured in the Sacred Writings that 'Except the Lord build the house, they labour in vain that built it.' I firmly believe this, and I also believe that without His concurring aid we shall proceed in this political building no better than the builders of Babel."

Prayer was the foundation stone in our country's beginning. There should be more national prayer today. — *Our Hope.*

Christ's Attitude Toward His Country

1. Loved His country, "His own country" (Matt. 13:54, 57).
2. Kept its laws, refusing to be made a king, or to start a political revolution (John 6:15; and at the Triumphal Entry, Mark 11:1-11).
3. Recognized right of taxation (Mark 12:17), and paid taxes (the temple tax, Matt. 17:24-27).
4. Loyal to national institutions: temple, synagogue, etc.
5. Recognized first claim of His country (Matt. 10:6; Luke 24:47).
6. Warned it of its perils (Matt. 23 37-39).
7. Rebuked its officials (Matt. 23:1-36).
8. Wept over its sins and impending doom (Luke 19:41-44).

Jesus Christ was a model citizen.—W. Beatty Jennings, in *Earnest Worker.*

* * *

The First Is Religion

In his message to the Seventy-sixth Congress, President Roosevelt introduced a passage which has been noted by commentators as a most remarkable element in a presidential address. A similar statement is not recalled for many years. President Roosevelt said: "Storms from abroad directly challenge three institutions indispensable to Americans now as always. The first is religion, and is the source of the other two—democracy and international good faith. Religion, by teaching man his relationship to God. gives the individual a sense of his own dignity and teaches him to respect himself by respecting his neighbors. Where freedom of religion has been attacked, the attack has come from sources opposed to democracy. Where democracy has been overthrown, the spirit of free worship has disappeared, and where religion and democracy have vanished, good faith and reason in international affairs have given way to strident ambition and brute force. Any ordering of society which relegates religion, democracy, and good faith among nations to the background, can find no place within it for the ideals of the Prince of Peace. The United States rejects such an ordering and retains its ancient faith."—Selected.

* * *

What America Needs

"What America needs more than railway extension, western irrigation, a low tariff, a bigger cotton crop, and a larger wheat crop is a revival of religion, the kind that our fathers and mothers used to have; a religion that counted it good business to take time for family worship each morning right in the middle of the harvest, a religion that made men quit work a half hour earlier on Wednesday so the whole family could get ready to go to prayer meeting." — *Wall Street Journal.*

* * *

True Then—True Now

"Our civilization cannot survive materially unless it be redeemed spiritually. It can be saved only by becoming permeated with the spirit of Christ and being made free and happy by the practices which spring out of the spirit. Only thus can discontent be driven out and all the shadows lifted from the road ahead." —President Woodrow Wilson.

* * *

Lincoln's Plea

A visitor to the White House during the days of the Civil War said: "I had been spending three weeks in the White House with Mr. Lincoln as his guest. One night—it was just after the battle of Bull Run—I was restless and could not sleep. It was coming near to the dawn of the day, when I heard low tones proceeding from a private room where the President slept. The door was partly open. Instinctively I walked in, and there I saw a sight which I shall never forget. It was the President kneeling before an open Bible. The light was turned low in the room. His back was toward me. I shall never forget his tones so piteous and so sorrowful. 'O Thou God, that heard Solomon in the night when he prayed and cried for wisdom, hear me! I cannot lead this people, I cannot guide the affairs of this nation without Thy help. I am poor and weak and sinful. O God, thou didst hear Solomon when he cried for wisdom—hear me and save this nation.' God heard, and He answered him then and there. Will He not answer today?"—*Christian Beacon.*

* * *

In God We Trust

The familiar motto, "In God We Trust," which appears on most of our coins, has a somewhat odd and interesting history. Its appearance there is due directly to a Maryland farmer who, in November, 1861, wrote to the then Secretary of the Treasury stating that since we claim to be a God-fearing, Christian people, we might at least make some recognition of the Deity on our coinage.

Secretary of the Treasury, Salmon P. Chase, refered the letter to James Pollock, Director of the Mint, for serious consideration. Pollock enthusiastically endorsed the suggestion and immediately two mottoes, "Our Country, Our God," and "God Our Trust," were proposed.

Chase had the matter presented to the Congress at their next session, which was in 1862, but nothing was done about it. Again the following year it was brought up, but still nothing was done.

Our country, at this time, was being racked by civil war. The national spirit was slowly ebbing, a crisis was nearing. Realizing this, Chase made one last appeal in 1864. The motto, "God Our Trust," he offered as his chief argument. "It is taken from our national hymn, *The Star-Spangled Banner*," he said, "and is a sentiment familiar to every citizen of our country; it has thrilled millions of American freemen. The time is propitious. Now in this time of national peril, our strength and salvation must be of God."

Secretary Chase won his plea. The Congress authorized the coining of a two-cent piece upon which was to be stamped the motto, "In God We Trust," in place of the old "E Pluribus Unum." The following year, on March 3, 1865, the Director of the Mint was further authorized to place the new motto on all gold and silver coins, thus fulfilling the words of Francis Scott Key in his poem, *The Star Spangled Banner:*

"Then conquer we must, when our cause it is just,
And this be our motto, 'In God is our trust.'"

—Courtesy *Moody Monthly.*

* * *

A well-known, cruel and powerful ruler demanded things that would hinder advance of Christ's cause through much of the world. A well-known missionary told him that he and Christians would not yield to his desires in that they were accountable to the King of kings, whose desires must have precedence over every earthly ruler. The ruler was subdued in spirit and his opposition overcome. — *Gospel Herald.*

* * *

Then, too, sail on, O Ship of State,
Sail on, O union, strong and great,
Humanity with all her fears,
With all the hope of future years,
Is hanging breathless on thy fate.
Stand thou for righteousness, people so blest,
Lend thou the victory, greatest and blest,
Lead on so grand and free
Nation of Destiny,
For as goes America so goes the world.

—Longfellow.

* * *

The Liberty Bell

There are some things about the liberty bell it would be well to cut out and paste in your scrapbook:

July 8, 1776, the bell was rung for the proclamation of the Declaration of Independence.

On October 4, 1781, the bell rang out for the surrender of Cornwallis.

April 16, 1783, it rang out for the proclamation of peace.

September 29, 1824, it rang to welcome Lafayette to the Hall of Independence.

July 4, 1826, it ushered in the year of Jubilee, the fiftieth anniversary of the Republic.

July 4, 1826, it tolled the death of Thomas Jefferson and John Adams.

July 4, 1831, is the last recorded ringing of this famous bell to commemorate the day of independence.

February 22, 1932, it rang to commemorate the birthday of Washington.

In the same year it tolled the death of the last survivor of the Declaration, Charles Carroll, of Carrolton.

July 2, 1834, it tolled once more. Lafayette was dead.

July 8, 1835, while being tolled for the death of Chief Justice John Marshall, a crack was developed, starting from the rim and inclining in a right-hand direction towards the crown.

Its voice is silent, but its deeds will ring in the hearts of all patriotic people so long as the name of liberty shall last. —Selected.

PEACE

The World's Peace Plans

Recent attempts toward peace have been in the direction of disarmament. Why the move to disarm has thus far largely failed is explained in a clever parable by Winston Churchill: Once upon a time all the animals in the zoo decided they would disarm, and they arranged to hold a conference to decide the matter. The rhinoceros said that the use of teeth in war was barbarous and horrible, and ought strictly to be prohibited by general consent. Horns, which were mainly defensive weapons, would, of course, have to be allowed. The buffalo, stag, and porcupine said they would vote with the rhino, but the lion and the tiger took a different view. They defended teeth, and even claws, as honorable weapons. Then the bear spoke. He proposed that both teeth and horns should be banned. It would be quite enough if animals would be allowed to give each other a good hug when they quarreled. No one could object to that. It was so fraternal and would be a great step toward peace. However, all the other animals were offended with the bear, and they fell into a perfect panic. — *New Century Leader.*

* * *

Christ's Legacy—Peace and Joy

"Peace I leave with you, my peace I give unto you; not as the world giveth, give I unto you. Let not your heart be troubled, neither let it be afraid" (John 14:27).

Did you ever think that when Christ was dying on the cross he made a will? Perhaps you have thought that no one ever remembered you in a will. If you are in the kingdom Christ remembered you in His will. He willed His body to Joseph of Arimathea; He willed His Mother to John, the son of Zebedee; and He willed His spirit back to His Father. But to His disciples He said: "My peace, I leave that with you; that is My legacy. My joy, I give that to you."

"My joy," think of it! "My peace"—not our peace, but His peace!

They say that a man cannot make a will now that lawyers cannot break, and drive a four-in-hand right straight through it. I will challenge them to break Christ's will. Let them try it. No judge or jury can set that aside. Christ rose to execute His own will. If He had left us a lot of gold, thieves would have stolen it in the first century; but He left His peace and His joy for every true believer, and no power on earth can take it from him who trusts. — D. L. Moody.

His Calm and Peaceful Life

A Cambridge undergraduate was much impressed with a preacher who had an arresting message and a lovely face, with a calm and peaceful expression. "I should suppose," said the university man, "that preacher spends most of his time in prayer and preparation in his study, apart from the din and noise of ordinary life." Smiling rather knowingly, the older friend said, "Would you like to meet him?" The young man said he would, and they arranged to meet on a Monday morning outside of St. Paul's Cathedral. Pushing his way through the swinging doors of a large London countinghouse, the old friend introduced his young companion to the man with the beautiful message and calm countenance, sitting at his desk immersed in business. "My young friend is very anxious about your occupation," said the older man. "My occupation, my boy? My occupation is to wait for His Son from Heaven, and meanwhile I make buttons." — *Evangelical Christian.*

* * *

The Peace of Ryswick

On a house near Durham there is a Latin inscription to the effect that it was built "in the year 1697 of the peace of the Gospel, and in the first year of the peace of Ryswick." The latter is almost forgotten now, but, as Macaulay points out, it was considered most vital and permanent at the time; trade revived, the army was disbanded, and a happier era inaugurated. All in vain. The treaty proved ere long to be an idle basis of peace. For only the peace of the Gospel abides.—*Sunday at Home.*

* * *

Rest of a Soul

A woman lay dying. A minister sat beside her and tried to break the news as gently as he could. He said, "They think your time is short." "Yes," she said, "I know it." "Have you made your peace with God." "No," she replied, "I haven't made my peace with God." "Then you are not afraid to die?" "No." "Do you realize that in a few hours you must meet God?" "Yes." "And you have not made your peace with God?" "No, and I'm not going to."

There was a strange light of perfect peace in the woman's eyes, and the minister realized that there was something back of it all. He said, "What do you mean?" She said, "Listen! I know I am dying, yet I have no fear of meeting God. I am resting in the peace which Jesus Christ made in his atoning death upon the cross, and I don't have to make my peace with God for I am resting in the peace which Jesus Christ has already made."—*Evangelical Visitor.*

* * *

Only One Man Could Cover It

It makes a great deal of difference by whom our sin is covered. The trusted agent of a large firm had, in time of unusual expense, run past his allowance, and had taken company funds for a wrong use. He became distressed for fear he would be discovered and regarded as a criminal. Thinking to gain advice he disclosed his trouble to a fellow agent, who responded, "Oh, don't worry, I can cover that up for you!" "But you're not the man to cover it up," he replied, and he went straight to the head of the firm and explained everything to him. "You've made a serious mistake," said the man, "but I'll cover the discrepancy for you this time," and he wrote a check for the amount. "Ah, if you cover it, I am all right!" said the relieved man. When *God* forgives a man his sin, he finds a peace which he had never known before. — *The Christian Life Missionary.*

* * *

The Sign on the Door

Many, many years ago, when the city of Cincinnati was just a little frontier town, a wild rumor of Red Indian bands on the warpath was brought to the settlers, and many of them fled to a neighboring fort for safety. For it was different from Pennsylvania, where William Penn, the great Quaker leader, had made peace with the Indians, and saved the homes of the Friends from the perils which surrounded people who had not dealt justly with the savages, and so feared their revenge.

But there was one man who did not go to the fort, for he belonged to the people of Pennsylvania. It was George Fox, who said that he strove to live "in the power of that Spirit which takes away the occasion of all war." It seemed to this Friend right, that, like Penn, he and his family should trust in the better way of peace and good will. So they stayed on in their little log hut, and did not get any guns or other weapons ready to defend themselves if the savage Indians came; but they often prayed together, and gave themselves into the keeping of that God who said, "I will never fail thee, nor forsake thee."

In those days the fastening of a door was often a heavy wooden latch, which was raised from the outside by a thong made of deer skin. This latch string was pulled inside when there was no admittance. To say "the latch string is out" meant that visitors were welcome. And so it generally was in the home of which we are telling.

But one night, when they were going to bed, the Friend drew in his latch string! After this was done his wife could not sleep; and at last she told him how uneasy it made her feel. It did not seem as if they were really trusting in the way of love and good will. He was beginning to feel that way, too, so he got up and put the string out again.

Then, before long, they heard the Indians coming, and the hut was surrounded. There was a Babel of wild cries and savage war-whoops as the Indians tried the door. But then they grew quiet, and presently began to steal away.

The Friend and his family rose and crept to the window to watch. On the edge of the forest they had stopped, sitting down to hold a council, as Indians do, talking things over together. Perhaps the pioneers' heart began to sink, as they thought, "Suppose they all come back again!" "Suppose they have only been waiting to decide whether to kill us or to take us prisoners!" They had heard such awful stories of the Indians.

But soon a tall chief in war-paint left the rest and came slowly back to the cabin. He carried in his hand a long white feather and he reached up and fastened this at the top of the door. Then in a few minutes all the Indians were gone!

There the white feather hung for a long time, and the summer suns shone on it, and it swayed about in the winter winds which swept across the prairie, but they never took it down. For a friendly Indian, who spoke English, had told them that it meant, "This is the house of a man of Peace. Do no harm." He had heard that the band of Indians felt sure that any man who would leave his door open to the stranger and welcome all who came was not a man to be harmed.—*Gospel Herald.*

* * *

The Leper's Sure Hope

Lady Hosie of England, on a visit to China, visited the Leper Hospital at Hangchow. She had photographed a group of lepers, when down the stairs was helped an elderly woman in a most pitiable condition; her sightless eyes, without their lids, were covered by a woolen mutch. A cry was raised that Chang Ma had missed having her picture taken, so the visitor prepared to take another with her in the midst. As she was focussing her camera, that worst leper of all started to sing, "There Is a Happy Land," and suddenly instead of poor lepers the visitor was seeing them as "saints in glory . . . , bright, bright as day." She was taken to see one who was dying, and wondered what she could say to him. Steadying her voice, she called to him with the politeness that China teaches, "Elder Brother, art thou at peace?" And from that frame, almost unrecognizable as human, with an affected tongue and from a lipless mouth, came a voice, cracked yet steadfast, "Yes, at peace, at peace. And I shall soon see my Lord."—*The Sunday School Visitor.*

The Peace of God

There is what is called the "cushion of the sea." Down beneath the surface that is agitated with storms, and driven about with high winds, there is a part of the sea that is never stirred. When we dredge the bottom and bring up the remains of animal and vegetable life, we find that they give evidence of not having been disturbed for hundreds of years. *The peace of God is that eternal calm which lies far too deep down in the praying soul to be reached by any external disturbance.*—A. T. Pierson.

* * *

Peace Found in Him

From very ancient times the hearts of men have longed for peace. Not merely that there shall be no more war, though that too; but more particularly peace of mind and heart. In the early days of Israel we have the benediction, "The Lord lift up His countenance upon thee, and give thee peace." The Sanskrit invocations end with, "Peace, Peace, Peace." The Mohammedan greeting is, as of old, "Peace be upon thee."

Where can we secure this peace that men have longed for through many centuries? The answer is given us in the words of the Master: "Peace I leave with you, My peace I give unto you. . . . These things have I spoken unto you, that in Me ye might have peace." The peace that brings calm to the soul, even amid the storms that sweep over every life, is to be found in Him. It can be found nowhere else.—*Christian Observer.*

* * *

The Spring Within

In some old castles are found deep wells meant to supply the garrison in time of siege. An aqueduct bringing water from without would be at the mercy of the enemy. But the foe has no power over the well inside. The peace the world seeks depends on one's surroundings, and in time of trouble its source is cut off; but the peace of Christ is a spring inside.—*The King's Business.*

PEACEMAKERS

How to Live in Peace

The Chinese have a proverb which says, "If you talk with a soft voice, you do not need a thick stick." If any man desires to live peaceably, this proverb shows the way. The fighting man seldom lacks antagonists. If we carry the big stick, it is sure to be flourished, and it means that other big sticks will appear, with no end of a row in prospect. The man who persists in carrying a gun is sure to pull it sooner or later.

But the soft word has no recoil. It never seems to challenge the other fellow to a fight. In fact, it makes him rather ashamed of his fiery speech and combative attitude. Miles Standish was willing to fight, and he had plenty of chances; William Penn would not fight, and the Indians who fought Standish so fiercely had no quarrel at all with Penn. War begets war: peace produces peace.

If you want to make friends with a cross dog, don't stir him up with a stick —Selected.

* * *

The Two Goats

"Blessed are the peacemakers."

Philip Henry often would quote Luther's story of the two goats that met upon a narrow bridge over a deep water. "They could not go back; they durst not fight. After a short parley, one of them lay down and let the other go over him, and thus no harm is done. The moral," he would say, "is easy: Be content if thy person be trod upon for peace's sake. Thy person, I say, not thy conscience." —*The Elim Evangel.*

* * *

The Peacemaker

"Mama, dear, I was a peacemaker today," said a little girl as she snuggled up to her mother in the evening. "How was that?" asked the mother, "*I heard something, and I didn't tell it,*" was the reply. "*Blessed are the peacemakers.*" —*The King's Business.*

Abraham Lincoln's Advice to a Client

Yes, we can doubtless gain your case for you; we can set a whole neighborhood at loggerheads; we can distress a widowed mother and her six fatherless children, and thereby get for you six hundred dollars to which you seem to have a legal claim, but which rightfully belongs, it appears to me, as much to the woman and her children as it does to you. You must remember, however, that some things legally right are not morally right. We shall not take your case, but we will give you a little advice for which we will charge you nothing. You seem to be a sprightly, energetic man. We would advise you to try your hand at making six hundred dollars in some other way.—*Watchman-Examiner.*

* * *

The Best System of Self-Defense

"Do you think it would be wrong for me to learn the noble art of self-defense?" a religiously inclined young man inquired of his pastor. "Certainly not," answered the minister. "I learned it in youth myself, and I have found it of great value during my life." "Indeed, sir! Did you learn the old English system or the Sullivan system?" "I learned neither," said the minister. "I learned the Solomon system." "The Solomon system?" answered the young man. "Yes; you will find it in the first verse of the fifteenth chapter of Proverbs: 'A soft answer turneth away wrath.' It is the best system of self-defense of which I know!" It would be well if more would know this way of self-defense.—*Youth's Counselor.*

* * *

Keep Cool

Some boys were playing baseball. Joe Harding said angrily, "You did." "No, I did not," quickly replied Frank Talbot. "I say you did; and if you say you didn't, that is the same as calling me a liar. And nobody shall call me a liar." Joe was a splendid looking fellow, the envy of all the boys; for he was the best ballplayer in the school. But he had a quick temper, and it was easy for him to fight when he was angry. "He always manages to keep cool when Frank is around," said Tom. "Frank is his match; so we will never see that fight," he added sneeringly. Everybody rushed up to where the boys were, as soon as they saw there was going to be a fight. But what! Frank a coward? not going to fight? There he stood, with his hands at his side, saying as Joe rushed at him, "I never called a boy a liar," but Joe struck him a blow in the face, which sent him reeling. He recovered himself in time to take another blow, then another and another, merely saying, "I did not call you a liar." "Shame to hit a fellow that will not hit back," called some big boys; and they caught Joe and held him. There stood Frank, his face all bruised and bleeding.

"Why on earth didn't you fight him? you are his match." "No, I am trying to be a Christian," replied Frank. "I do not think it is right to fight." "You are a fool, that's what you are," said big Tom. "Are you going to let your face be battered in this way?" "I can't help that; I have made up my mind never to fight as long as I live." That evening, in Frank's room, you might have seen a sight, that none would have thought possible. Joe kneeling to Frank, begging pardon for what he had done.

"Why, Joe, get up this instant; of course it's all right between us," and Frank lifted Joe up by the hand. "I can never forgive myself for striking you as I did."

"Joe is conquered for once," said the boys at supper. "I always said Frank was his match," replied big Tom, "but I didn't think he was going to take that way to conquer him." Joe never struck a boy after that. Soon it came to be a disgrace to fight in that school. Love is better than revenge any time.—*Gospel Herald.*

PERSECUTION

The Cost of Believing

Among our converts in Poland is a woman who has showed much faithfulness to the Lord Jesus Christ in spite of the hostility of her family. Her two daughters and her son, angry when they learned that their mother attended evangelical meetings, decided that they would prevent her from going in the future. One day, therefore, when she was about to go out to a meeting her daughters pushed her back into the corridor. One caught her by the hair, the other held her fast, and the son came and stood in front of her with an ax while he demanded her promise that she would not attend any more.

She trembled with fear at the threatening look on her son's face as he stood there brandishing the ax, but desiring to be faithful to her Saviour, she exclaimed, "I love the Lord Jesus."

Then she burst into tears and from weakness sank to the floor. The son dropped the ax and left her.

For about a year she was obliged to remain at home. Her children sometimes refused to give her anything to eat. In answer to prayer one of the daughters came under the conviction of sin and soon made it possible for her mother to go to the meetings once more. The mother's joy was increased when the daughter came with her and before a crowded congregation confessed her wrongdoing and sought God's forgiveness.—*European Christian Missions.*

* * *

A Coolie's Lesson on Persecution

A lovely story is told by Mrs. R. J. Richardson, a missionary refugee from China. When traveling with two little children, she was examined by a Japanese soldier whose rude handling of her person provoked her protest. This was answered by a harsh slap on her face, which stunned her mentally and physically. She was finally released and got into her ricksha and drove off. "As we passed through a little lane, seeing nobody in sight, I gave vent to my feelings and began to sob. I could not help it. When the ricksha coolie heard me crying, he turned around and said, 'Don't cry, lady. Blessed are those that are persecuted for righteousness' sake.' This humble servant of the Lord, a perfect stranger to me, was being used of the Lord to bring me a message of comfort and to give me a thought that would overcome all feeling of resentment."—*Religious Survey in The Sunday School Times.*

* * *

How He Took Persecution

Pastor J. H. Crowell, when about sixteen, shipped on a sailing vessel, where he was the only Christian, in a crew of twelve. Before leaving his mother he promised to meet her three times a day at the throne of grace. So regularly he went below and prayed aloud. He thought he must. They threw wood at him and poured buckets of water over him, but could not put out the fire in his soul. Then they tied him to the mast and laid thirty-nine stripes on his back. Still he prayed. They tied a rope around his body and threw him overboard. He swam as best he could, and when he took hold of the side of the ship they pushed him off with a pole. At last his strength gave way, and, supposing they meant to kill him, he prayed that God would forgive them, and called out: "Send my body to my mother and tell her that I died for Jesus." He was then pulled on deck unconscious, but after some time came to. Conviction began to seize the sailors. Before night two of them were gloriously converted. Inside of a week every one on board, including the captain, was blessedly saved. — *Sunday School Times.*

* * *

One Knew from Experience

An English judge in India heard that a certain native, who formerly was a wealthy owner of an indigo farm, had confessed Christ, and was cast out of all his possessions. "Let him come to me," said the judge, "and if he is a true Christian, he will not mind working as the attendant-bearer of my little son." So Nordubur came. One evening at household prayers, the judge read from the English New Testament, "Every one that hath forsaken houses, or brethren, . . .or wife, or children, or lands, for my name's sake, shall receive an hundredfold." He thought a moment, and said, "Now, none of us has done this except one—Nordubur." He looked straight at the bearer and asked: "Will you tell us? Does this verse speak the truth?" Quietly Nordubur spoke. "I have not *much* possessions now," he confessed, "but I do have a new peace and joy. Christ says He gives a hundredfold. I know He gives a thousandfold."—*Secret Place.*

* * *

His Scripture

A young man who was driven out of western China during the riots, years ago, was the treasurer of our mission there, and there were others farther up than he who needed silver to pay their way out. He saw that they were cared for, and then started down the river himself. The rioters overtook him, boarded his boat, and he jumped overboard. They began to spear at him in the water. He would dart under the boat and come up on the other side, only to find another spear shot at him. Down he would go again, and up again, until his case became hopeless. Finally he struck out for the shore, and as he stood in the face of the surrounding mob, the chief said, "Let him go," and they melted away. When he was asked to tell his story at Northfield on Missionary Day, he said, "Some friends have been curious to know what particular text of Scripture came to me when I was down under that boat. Scripture text? The Lord Himself was there." And every one who heard him speak knew that the Lord was there indeed.—*Sunday School Times.*

* * *

Not Worthy

Some years ago, when Japan was taking over Korea, and was bitterly persecuting many of the leading Christians by carrying them off to Japanese jails, believers who were not arrested felt that by this very fact they were somehow lacking in their Christianity. A native Methodist pastor went to a missionary with the complaint: "Maksa, there must be something wrong in our Methodist church. I fear we are lacking in faith. There are thirty-seven Presbyterians in jail, and only one Methodist. I fear the Lord does not count us worthy to suffer persecution." — *Sunday School Times.*

* * *

Persecution's Blessing

The work among Jewish refugees in Shanghai, in which the Christian Alliance is engaged, is bearing fruit. From eighty to a hundred Jews attend these meetings, and recently nineteen men and eleven women were baptized, all wearing white Chinese gowns. Some of them were men of fine education, with good homes and good incomes in their European countries, and all say that if it had not been for the persecution they never would have found Christ. One brother still limps as a result of the bayonet stabs in the leg which were given him in Germany.—*Sunday School Times.*

* * *

"A persecuted church has a repelling power as well as an attracting power. The great awakenings of the past have not been begun by the gathering in of the many, but by the deeper consecration of the few."—Vance Havner.

God's Way in Persecution

During a time of persecution in Korea, a young church member was accused by police and put in jail as a suspect. He was placed in a cell by himself and he grieved because he was restrained from speaking of Christ to the other prisoners. Soon he was banished to one of the neighboring islands. When he was released after the breakdown of the accusation, he said with shining face, "Just think, I have been longing for a chance to speak of Christ, and was mourning because I could not speak in jail. *Then God sent me off to an unevangelized island, where there was plenty of work to do, and the government paid my fare.*"—*King's Highway.*

* * *

Recognizing the Road

A Spirit-filled worker connected with the Africa Inland Mission was giving his testimony, after returning from a very dangerous service in the first World War. He said that if someone sent him on a journey and told him the road to take, warning him that at a certain point he would come to a dangerous crossing of the river, at another point to a forest infested with wild beasts, he would come to that dangerous river crossing and the other dangers with the satisfaction of *knowing that he was on the right road.* So he told them that the Lord had predicted that Christians would have tribulation, and when the tribulations came he knew he was on the right road.—*Sunday School Times.*

PERSEVERANCE

Remember This

When Abraham Lincoln was a young man he ran for legislature in Illinois, and was badly swamped. He next entered business, failed, and spent seventeen years of his life paying up the debts of a worthless partner. He was in love with a beautiful young woman to whom he became engaged—then she died. Later he married a woman who was a constant burden to him. Entering politics again, he ran for Congress, and again was badly defeated. He then tried to get an appointment in the United States land office, but failed. He became a candidate for the United States Senate, and was badly defeated. In 1856 he became a candidate for the Vice Presidency and was once more defeated. In 1856 he was defeated by Douglass.

One failure after another—bad failures —great setbacks. In the face of all this he eventually became one of the greatest men in America, whose memory is honored throughout the world. When you contemplate the effect of a series of setbacks like this, doesn't it make you feel rather small to become discouraged? —Waneta Grimes Holt, in *The Junior Class Paper.*

* * *

If You Want Him as Much as—

If we want God as much as the astronomer Herschel wanted the distant stars, with such sincerity that he would sit all night on a balcony in the wintry winds with an awkward telescope; if we want Him as much as Edison wanted an electric filament, so that he would experiment with six hundred different substances that he might get his radiant light—if we hunger like that for God, we will not complain about difficulty; we will quit arguing and postponing and begin this very hour to seek Him!—Robert M. Bartlett.

* * *

Bruce and the Spider

A long time ago, Robert Bruce, the king of Scotland, was forced to hide from his enemies. He found refuge in a cave deep in the forest. He was downhearted and discouraged. He had tried to save Scotland from her enemies, but he had lost every battle. His soldiers had been killed or hurt or forced to hide.

"It is of no use to fight any more," he said. "Our enemies are too strong for us."

Just then he saw a spider weaving a web. She was trying to spin the web between two rocks. She had fastened one end of her thread to a rock and was trying to swing herself across, but each time she failed to reach the rock.

Bruce sat watching her for a long time. He wondered how long she would keep on trying. The spider tried and failed seven times. "You are a brave and patient spider," thought the king. "If you try once more and succeed, I, too, will fight again."

The spider swung herself once more on her thin thread. This time she reached the other rocks and fastened her thread.

"Thanks for the lesson you have taught me, little spider," said Bruce. "I will try once more to free Scotland from her enemies."

So King Robert went forth again at the head of his army. He and his men fought as they had never fought before. Bruce won the battle and his country was freed.—Selected.

* * *

When in a Tight Place

When you get into a tight place and everything goes against you until it seems you cannot hold on a minute longer, never give up then, for that is just the place and time when the tide will turn.—Harriet Beecher Stowe.

* * *

Try Him Once More

Some years ago in a manufacturing town of Scotland, a young lady applied to the superintendent of a Sunday School for a class. At his suggestion she gathered a class of poor boys. The superintendent told them to come to his house during the week, and he would get them each a new suit of clothes. They came and were nicely fitted out.

The worst and most unpromising boy in the class was a lad named Bob. After two or three Sundays he was missing, and the teacher went to hunt him up. She found that his new clothes were torn and dirty, but she invited him back to the school, and he came.

The superintendent gave him a second new suit, but, after attending once or twice, Robert again absented himself. Once more she sought him out, only to find that the second suit had gone the way of the first.

"I am utterly discouraged about Bob," she said, when she reported the case to the superintendent, "and must give him up."

"Please don't do that," the superintendent answered; "I cannot but hope there is something good in Bob. Try him once more. I'll give him a third suit if he'll promise to attend regularly."

Bob did promise and received his third new suit. He attended regularly after that, and got interested in the school. He became an earnest and persevering seeker after Jesus. He found Him. He joined the church. He was made a teacher. He studied for the ministry.

The end of the account is that that discouraged boy—that forlorn, ragged, runaway Bob—became the Rev. Robert Morrison, the great missionary to China, who translated the Bible into the Chinese language, and by so doing opened the Kingdom of Heaven to the teeming millions of that vast country.—*Church of Scotland's Children's Review.*

* * *

Forward

A way to ensure success is to press forward, and never look back. When the late Dr. F. B. Meyer was in his seventeenth year he decided that he would go into the ministry, and told his mother of his decision. She suggested that such a step would involve sacrifice in his prospects, but hinted also that if he regretted the step taken later, he would be able to leave the ministry. The boy, looking straight at his mother, said, "Never! That would be putting my hand to the plow and looking back." That lad never looked back, but, as you all know, did marvelous work for his Master in this and in other lands. Who knows but that probably his success in life can be traced back to that day when he said "Never," and meant it?—*Intermediate Young People.*

* * *

I Won't

I want to let go, but I won't let go,
There are battles to fight,
By day and by night
For God and the right,
And I'll never let go.

I want to let go, but I won't let go,
I'm sick 'tis true;
Worried and blue,
And worn through and through,
But I won't let go.

I want to let go, but I won't let go,
I will never yield;
What, lie down on the field
And surrender my shield?
No! I'll never let go.

I want to let go, but I won't let go,
May this be my song,
'Mid legions of wrong;
Oh, God, keep me strong,
That I may never let go.

—Selected.

* * *

Hold On! Wait!

A young convert told of his experience in the first World War. He was in the "Lost Battalion." We were cut off from our main army and all around us were Germans. Our food and water gave out, and every once in a while a German would come to say "Surrender." Only one shell was left, and we decided to use it as a signal. At night we turned the cannon straight up, put in the shell, and prayed and pulled the trigger. How we hoped the Americans would see it. Next morning an airplane dropped us canteens of water and bread and a note saying, "Hold on! We are coming!" This continued for several days. Then we heard cannons roaring. Soon our army came and took us to our own lines. We Christians are being asked to surrender to the world in these last days, but God sends us this message, "Hold on! I am coming!"—In *The Latter Rain Evangel*, by N. C. Baskin, adapted.

* * *

"I Hanged On"

Mr. Addison Raws of Keswick, N. J., was crossing a crowded street in Philadelphia. He had hold of the hand of his little boy, and the latter lost his footing. Mr. Raws just held him up until they were across. "I hanged on, Daddy," he said, as they reached the far side of the street. Yes, he had. But his father had first "hanged" onto him.—*Christ Life.*

Keep a Goin'

If you strike a thorn or rose,
If it hails or if it snows,
Keep a goin'.
'Tain't no use to sit and whine
When the fish ain't on your line;
Bait your hook and keep a tryin';
Keep a goin'.

When the weather kills your crop,
When the rain will never stop,
Keep a goin'.
S'pose you're out o' every dime,
Gettin' broke ain't any crime,
Tell the world you're feelin' fine—
Keep a goin'.

When it looks like all is up,
Drain the weariness from the cup,
Keep a goin'.
See the wild birds on the wing,
Hear the bells that sweetly ring,
When you feel like sighin', sing—
Keep a goin'.
—F. L. S., in *Evangelical Christian.*

* * *

The Sticker

Oh, it's easy to be a starter, lad
But are you a sticker, too?
'Tis fun, sometimes, to begin a thing,
But harder to see it through.

If you failed sometimes when you did your best,
Don't take it too much to heart;
Just try it again in a different way,
For it all depends how you start.

And sometimes a failure is best, dear lad,
To keep you from being too sure;
Success that is built on defeat, you know,
Will oftentimes longest endure.

'Tis the sticker who wins in the battle of life,
While the quitter is laid on the shelf;
You are never defeated, remember this,
Until you lose faith in yourself.

Oh, it's easy to be a starter, lad,
But are you a sticker, too?
You may think it a game to begin a task:
Are *you* game to see it through?
—Selected.

Not Far Enough

Professor Drummond saw at a fair a glass model of a famous mine. The owner drove a tunnel a mile long through the strata he thought contained gold, spent one hundred thousand dollars on it, and in a year and a half had failed to find the gold. Another company drove the tunnel a yard further and struck the ore. So the gold of life may be but a short distance off. There are countless failures in life due to not going far enough. Keep on—the reward may lie but a yard ahead.—Exchange in *The Sunday School Banner.*

* * *

Victory Over Disaster and Loss

When William Carey had succeeded in establishing his pioneer missionary work in India, his supporters in England sent him an assistant, a Mr. Ward, who was a printer by trade. Soon they were turning out printed portions of the Bible for distribution among the natives. Carey spent many years learning the language and wrote grammars and dictionaries for the use of his successors.

One day while Carey was away from his station, a disastrous fire broke out and completely destroyed the building, the presses, many printed Bibles and, worst of all, the manuscripts, grammars and dictionaries on which Carey had spent so much time.

When Mr. Carey returned, his servants told him of the loss. Without a word of despair or anger he knelt down and thanked God that he had the strength to do the work all over again. He started immediately, not wasting a moment in idle despair and before his death he duplicated his first achievements and produced far better work than he had done formerly.

Thousands, in this world, have lost all—including the very house over their head—and many who know the Lord have gone on, in faith, seeking to serve *Him* in and through it all. When sudden disaster and loss come to God's people, *He* again proves His all-sufficiency. Having *Him,* all else is as refuse. Let us be wholly occupied with *Him* and His glories.—*Christian Victory.*

Perseverance

In 1935, in Oklahoma, young Manning Duncan was ordained to the ministry. In the examination he was asked, "If you were to preach ten years and see no results, what would you do?" He answered, "*I would preach ten years more.*"

That answer was of God. Human standards demand immediate, visible results. How far are modern standards from those of the Bible! And what the results!—Courtesy *Moody Monthly.*

POWER

Spiritual Power Needed

The early Church had little machinery, but they had power. A young woman, a member of my church, worked in a large umbrella factory (in Philadelphia), at that time considered the largest umbrella factory in the world. She said to me one day, in a discouraged manner, "Pastor, I'll have to hunt another job." "What's the matter?" I asked her, "have they discharged you?" "No, they haven't discharged me." "Well, hasn't your factory enough orders to keep going all the time?" "No, not that at all. They have more orders than they can fill; but they haven't enough electricity to keep all the machines going at once, and my machine has to lie idle part of the week, and I lose so much time and pay. The trouble with the factory is, they have more machinery than power."

Let us not forget that the finest machinery made is useless without power, and it is God's power which is ESSENTIAL *to the carrying out of the Great Commission.*—L. S. Bauman, in *Adult Quarterly.*

* * *

Moody's Testimony

"I remember two holy women who used to come to my meetings. It was delightful to see them in the congregation. When I began to preach, I could tell by the expression on their faces that they were praying for me. At the close of the Sunday evening service they would say to me, 'We have been praying for you.'

"I said, 'Why don't you pray for the people?'

"They answered, 'You need power.'

"'I need power?' I said to myself. 'Why, I thought I had power.' I had a large Sunday school and the largest congregation in Chicago. There were some conversions at the time. I was, in a sense, satisfied. But right along these two godly women kept praying for me, and their earnest talk about being 'anointed for special service' set me to thinking.

"I asked them to come and talk with me, and we got down on our knees. They poured out their hearts that I might receive the anointing from the Holy Spirit, and there came a great hunger into my soul. I did not know what it was. I began to pray as I never did before. I really felt that I did not want to live if I could not have this power for service. The hunger increased. I was praying all the time that God would fill me with His Holy Spirit.

"Well, one day in the city of New York—oh, what a day! I cannot describe it; I seldom refer to it; it is almost too sacred an experience to name. Paul had an experience of which he never spoke for fourteen years. I can only say that God revealed Himself to me, and I had such an experience of His love that I asked Him to stay His hand.

"I went to preaching again. The sermons were not different; I did not present any new truths; and yet hundreds were converted. I would not now be placed back where I was before that blessed experience if you gave me all Glasgow,—it would be as the small dust of the balance.

"If we are full of the Spirit, anointed, our words will reach the hearts of the people—we need the filling always, and if we are filled with the Spirit, there will be no room for Satan or self. If we are filled with the Spirit and full of power, one day's work is better than a year's without. It is the work of the Holy Spirit to get the secrets of eternity and reveal them unto us. My work is to preach, and the Holy Spirit convinces of sin."—D. L. Moody.

* * *

Little Strength Needed for Noise

We read the other day of a man who had rigged up a dynamo-battery system to operate an electric light for his room. After a while the light "flickered and faded." A friend was called in, and after examination he told him that his plant would never again run a light, but it might run a call bell. It wasn't strong enough to make a light, but it could make a noise. This needs no enlargement. We have all seen samples of religion that weren't strong enough to make a light but that could make any amount of noise.—*From Herald and Presbyter.*

* * *

The Filling with the Fulness

W. B. Anderson of India uttered a warning at a convention, against the theoretical knowledge of spiritual things: "Perhaps we never miss the morning devotional hour. We have whole passages of the Bible at our tongue's end. We have read widely in systems of theology. We have constructed a great system of truth for ourselves. We know all about the theory of prayer. We have become sure of these things with a certain knowledge." Yet, as the speaker declared, this may all be only a phantom with which we deceive ourselves. We may be spiritually powerless in the midst of this accumulated knowledge. For spiritual power consists not in mere knowledge, but comes only through the presence of a Person, Jesus Christ. *Only as we yield to Christ and draw continually upon Him will He fill us and flow out from us in the fulness of the power of God.* — *Sunday School Times.*

* * *

God's "Majority"

When Saladin beheld the sword of Richard, the lion-hearted, he marveled that a weapon so ordinary could have wrought such mighty deeds. The brave Englishman bared his arm and said, "*It was not the sword that did these things: it was the arm of Richard.*" It was the arm of God that fought against the Midian host. What mattered it to God whether Gideon's army numbered one hundred thousand or one thousand or one? One with God is a majority. Anyhow, God *measures* men; never *counts* them.—W. E. Biederwolf, in *The Man Nobody Missed.*

* * *

Where Are You Weak?

A minister, calling on an old Negress, found her bending over the washtub, scrubbing with all her might, "Aunt Dinah," said he, "don't you get very tired doing that hard work?" "Oh, yes, massa," she replied, "I hasn't got much strength, but I ask the Lord, and He gives me the spirit of washin'."—*Sunday School Times.*

* * *

Conspicuous by Its Absence

An old colored minister was praying earnestly for unction. A white minister, who heard him, asked, "What is unction?" "Brudder," he replied, "I dunno whut it is, but I knows when it ain't!" —*Christ Life.*

* * *

What They Overlooked

The friends of Mary Slessor, missionary in Africa, were amazed when they saw that she, a weak woman, had been able to mold savage chiefs to her will. One of the chiefs explained, "You have evidently forgotten to take into account the woman's God."—*Westminster Quarterly.*

* * *

"Twisted Together"

Our word strength comes from a word signifying twisted together. "The Lord is the strength of my life." "God is the strength of my heart." Then my life is twisted together with the Lord. God and my soul are two strands twisted together with one that is infinite, the weakest shall not fail.—*Gospel Herald,*

Better than Will Power

Strong will power is no guarantee of getting a thing done. The trouble with our common worship of will power is that we leave out of account another factor that is even stronger. It is like the predicament of an old darkey who, wrestling with a balky mule, was asked, "Why, Sambo, where's your will power?" "My will power's all right," came the reply, "but you ought to come out here and see this yer animal's won't power." There is in all of us a "won't power" that is more powerful than the strongest will power any human being ever had. It's name is sin. Will power crumbles like a piece of tissue paper in a flame when, unaided, it confronts some real sin-desire of our life. And when will power has done its feeble most, and failed, then Christ has His opportunity. —*Sunday School Times.*

* * *

The Log Jam

In the Timberlands springtime sees great quantities of logs shooting down the rivers. Sometimes a jam occurs. Then the lumberjack seeks the log which is stemming the wooden tide. When he finds that key log, he jerks it out of place, and the flood moves onward with its freight. There is such a thing as a spiritual log jam. We lose our religious enthusiasm, interest in personal devotions wanes, an hour in the Lord's house becomes a bore, the Bible becomes a silent Book. Then we must find the key log that is checking the flood of spiritual life. It may be an unforgiving spirit, or jealousy, or hypocrisy. Jerk the obstruction out of place and spiritual vitality will surge onward.—*To-Day.*

* * *

Unused Power

The following instance was frequently cited by A. J. Gordon: An American with an English gentleman was viewing the Niagara whirlpool rapids, when he said to his friend: "Come, and I'll show you the greatest unused power in the world." Then he took him to the foot of Niagara Falls. "There," he said, "is the greatest unused power in the world." "Ah, no, my brother, not so," was the reply. "The greatest unused power in the world is the Holy Spirit of the Living God."—*Christian Endeavor World.*

* * *

Where Hudson Taylor's Power Lay

When I first met Mr. Hudson Taylor, in London in 1887, I expected to see a man with a black beard and a full round voice. Instead, I found him a little man, with a blonde beard and a quiet and gentle voice. I immediately concluded that his power was not in his personality, but rather in God. As the years of my acquaintance lengthened out, this conclusion was increasingly confirmed. To the end of his life he won great victories with God and over men; but the secret was always communion with his Father in Heaven.—Henry W. Frost, in *China's Millions.*

* * *

Accomplishing the Impossible

On a slope of the Alps mountains lived a little hunchback, himself an ardent admirer of the beauties about him, but unable to join the climbers. His daily business was to minister to those passing in the little matters related to their long and arduous endeavor. But one day a famous mountain guide said to him, "How would you like to climb the mountain yourself?" The face of the poor misshapen man beamed. "I should like it very much," he said, "but of course I can't do it." "Let's try it," said the guide; and on the summit the grateful man kneeled down to pour out his soul in gratitude. He did his best; his leader did the rest. It was so with these common men and women we study. They were of the earth, but God came to them and they did the unearthy. — *Christian Standard.*

* * *

Why Fulness Doesn't Last

Most of us fit the description of the old woman quoted by Charles M. Alexander at Northfield. Down in Tennessee, Alexander said, there was once a meeting of intense power, and one of the variety of disciples who blew hot and cold who was revived at each annual revival and who backslid in the interim, was praying in the assembly with a great burst of emotion. There was present an old woman who knew him well, who read correctly his character, and had witnessed his many revivals and backslidings. So when he suddenly burst into prayer for the fulness of the Holy Spirit to be given him, the old woman emphatically cried: "Don't you do it, Lord. He leaks!" — Courtesy *Moody Monthly*.

* * *

Unconscious of the Power

W. P. Nicholson, the Irish evangelist, went for special electrical treatment to a practitioner in Edinburgh. He was asked to sit in a chair, while the doctor sat down and began to read the daily paper. After waiting some time Mr. Nicholson asked that the treatment might begin. "You are being treated now," was the answer. He said he felt nothing at all. Then the physician took a board with several electric lamps on it, and placed it against his breast. Instantly the lamps glowed with light. The doctor said, "Mr. Nicholson, there is enough power passing through your body to run the tram car on the street. You do not feel it because you are insulated." Mr. Nicholson said afterward, when narrating this experience: "My friends, you may have all the power of almighty God passing through you, and yet be unconscious of it because there is no special call for its use. But let the need come, and the power will be manifested, for it is there."—*Alliance Weekly*.

* * *

Form Without Power

Some years ago, the captain of a Greenland whaling vessel found himself at night surrounded by icebergs and "lay-to" till the morning, expecting every moment to be ground to pieces. As the morning dawned, he sighted a ship at no great distance. Getting into a boat with some of his men, he carefully picked his way through the lanes of open ice towards the mysterious-looking craft. Coming alongside, he hailed the vessel with a loud "Ship ahoy!" But there was no response. He looked through the porthole and saw a man, evidently the captain, sitting at a table as if writing in a log-book. He again hailed the vessel, but the figure moved not. It was dead and frozen! On examination, the sailors were found, some frozen among the hammocks, others in the cabin. From the last entry in the log-book, it appeared the vessel had been drifting the Arctic seas for thirteen years—a floating sepulchre, manned by a frozen crew. And there are souls today who have refused the divine offer of life, forsaken the centers where they were warmed with hallowed influences, and drifted into the chilling regions of Arctic darkness and frost. Many of these have certain appearances of Christian life, and a name to live, but are dead!—*Christian Journal*.

PRAYER

When We Are Ciphers

A certain theological seminary, in its early days, was often in need of money. Once, in a time of great financial stress, three members of the board of managers met to talk over the situation. They were all deeply disheartened. "Is there no one to help us?" asked one. "No one," echoed the second dismally. Finally the third man spoke. He was a man of great faith and piety, and he had been in earnest prayer. "Gentlemen," he said, "by your own confessions you can do nothing, and I can do nothing. In other words, in this matter we are just about three ciphers. But Jesus Christ is certainly One. Now if we put one before three ciphers, we become a thousand, do we not? I propose that we put Him first, get down on our knees, and ask Him to show us the way."

The suggestion was followed, new courage was implanted, and the difficulty was promptly met. — *Westminster Adult Quarterly.*

* * *

A Boy's Prayer

A little heathen boy who had just learned the alphabet, was one Sunday morning seen out on the hillside, with his hands clasped together and his eyes closed. He was repeating the letters of the alphabet over and over. The missionary drew near, and asked him what it meant. He replied, "I was praying." "But why," replied the questioner, "did you repeat the alphabet?" "Well," he said, *"I felt that I must pray, and as I knew no prayer, I just said the letters of the alphabet, knowing that the great God would put them into words for me."—Canadian Epworth Era.*

* * *

An Answered Prayer

One day a lady was giving her little nephew some lessons. He was generally a good, attentive child, but on this occasion he could not fix his mind on his work. Suddenly he said, "Auntie, may I kneel down and ask God to help me find my marble?" His aunt having given her consent, the little boy knelt by his chair, closed his eyes, and prayed silently. Then he rose and went on with his lessons contentedly. Next day, almost afraid of asking the question, lest the child had not found his toy, and so might lose his simple faith, the lady said to him, "Well, dear, have you found your marble?" "No, auntie," was the reply; "but God has made me not want to." God does not always answer our prayers in the way we wish or expect; but if we are sincere in our appeal to him, He will take from us the desire for what is contrary to His will and give us faith to leave all to His holy will.—*Grace and Truth.*

* * *

Why Prayer Is Different

I shall never forget what the late Dr. A. C. Dixon of Spurgeon's Tabernacle once said when speaking upon this theme of prayer. I cannot quote him verbatim, but the substance was this: "When we rely upon organization, we get what organization can do, when we rely upon education, we get what education can do; when we rely upon eloquence, we get what eloquence can do; and so on. Nor am I disposed to undervalue any of these things in their proper place. "But," he added impressively, "when we rely upon prayer, we get what God can do."—*The European Harvest Field.*

* * *

Pray All Night

Do we want souls saved? Do we want revival? Do we want refreshing from the Lord? Dig the trench of persistent prayer and it is ours. When John Livingstone preached at Shotts in days past, many people were amazed, for under one sermon on one occasion five hundred souls publicly acknowledged Christ as their personal Saviour. When they inquired into the matter, they found that the previous night several hundred had prayed all night, that God's Spirit would rest upon the preacher in such power that a backslidden church and community might find out that God still had power to quicken believers and save lost souls. The wonder revival at Yale University in the past generation came after many of the students had spent weeks of prayer to God that old Yale might be shaken with a heaven-sent, Holy Ghost, prayed-down revival.—Courtesy *Moody Monthly.*

* * *

The Secret of England

Mr. E. P. Brown, M.P., has just revealed the fact that a Thursday prayer meeting has been held in the House of Commons without a break since William IV. Such action in high places is the secret of England.—*The Dawn.*

* * *

Prayer Ends a Church Feud

I was once in a church where there was a deadly feud between certain members and officers, and it was so bitter that the opposing parties would not even sit on the same side of the prayer-meeting room. After eighteen months of strenuous endeavors to heal the sore and get the contention out of the way, I said to the Lord, "Thou hast put me here, and Thou art bound by Thy promise to stand by me. Now I have sought to remedy this difficulty, and I cannot, and I find this conflict facing me every way, and these antagonists have arrayed themselves against each other like hostile forces; now, Lord, either heal the breach, or remove out of the way the real offenders." *From the day I offered that prayer not one of those offenders ever darkened that church door.*—Arthur T. Pierson.

* * *

Living As We Pray

A man prayed fervently every morning at family worship for the poor in the community, but he was never known to give anything to the poor. One morning at the conclusion of family worship, after the usual prayer had been offered for the poor and destitute, his little son said, "Father, I wish I had your corn-crib."

"Why, my son?" asked the father.

"Why, because then I would answer your prayer myself."—Selected.

* * *

The Blacksmith Knocked

In Ohio, one Saturday evening, a blacksmith sat down to his supper. He was supporting a girl in a mission school in India. On his plate had been placed a letter just received from India. He began to read, but soon said, "Wife, I must pray." The letter in question told that this girl was not only resisting Christ for herself, but was standing seriously in the way of others accepting Him. Unless a change should come very shortly in the girl, the missionary wrote, they would be obliged, for the sake of the other girls, to send her from the school altogether. The blacksmith entered into his closet and prayed. Saturday night in Ohio is Sunday morning in India. On that Sunday morning the missionary gathered with her class of girls in Sunday school as usual. The lesson, however, had not proceeded far until this incorrigible girl leaped from her seat, flung herself in tears at the feet of the missionary, and wept her way to the Saviour. The other girls were deeply moved. One by one they followed her example, and salvation came to the whole class that morning. Vital energy had been put forth by prayer in Ohio, and, as a result, great things came to pass in India. — Dr. Robert Glover, in *Gospel Herald.*

* * *

What Prayer Changes

Perhaps you have a motto in your home which reads: "Prayer changes things" and no doubt you can testify of many occasions when prayer most certainly did change "things." But I am inclined to believe that very frequently "things" do not change one iota. Rather, prayer changes *us* to such an extent that we gloriously triumph over "things," whether they be a disagreeable environment or an unpleasant task, or perhaps a fiery inexplicable trial. Praise God, His all-sufficient grace is able to make us completely oblivious to all of these "things," and our triumphing over them is a more glorious victory, and brings more glory to God, than their removal could ever accomplish. — *Gospel Herald.*

* * *

Seven Prayers Answered

A godly mother of six children had come into great stress. Their last loaf of bread had been eaten at the evening meal. Next morning, without a morsel of food in the house, the trustful mother set the table with seven plates, and, gathering the children about her, said: "Now, children, we must ask God to supply our need." As she finished her petition for help one cried out, "There is the baker at the door." On entering, he said, "I was stalled in the snow this morning and stopped here to get warm. Do you need any bread this morning?" "Yes," said the mother, "but we have no money to buy any." "What? Do you mean to say you have no bread for these children?" "Not a morsel," said the mother. "Well, you shall soon have some," and going out quickly to his wagon he returned with seven loaves of bread and laid one at each plate. One of the little children cried out, "Mamma, *I* prayed for bread, and God heard *me*, and sent *me* bread." "And *me!*" "And *me!*" chorused the rest of the children. Each felt that God had answered him personally. And was it not true?—*Prayer*, by James H. McConkey.

* * *

Her Case Seemed Hopeless

Ask God for deliverance when danger is near. In the flood at Pueblo, Colorado, a few years ago, a woman was trapped in an overturned railroad car. Unable to get out, and the water rising until it was up to her neck, and holding a child in her arms, her case seemed hopeless. The frightened child said, "Mother, what shall we do?" Mother said, "Pray, dear." While Mother cried unto God in her heart, the child prayed, "Jesus, I trust You; Jesus, I trust You." She said this many times. From that moment the waters began to recede.—*Gospel Herald.*

* * *

Father, hear us as we pray;
Guard and keep us day by day;
Help us feel Thy loving care,
Ev'ry day and ev'rywhere.

Help us to be good and true,
Jesus' work on earth to do;
All we have with others share,
Ev'ry day and ev'rywhere.
Ida F. Leyda.

* * *

Prayer Changes Things

On an Atlantic steamer one time our old captain announced to us at the supper table:

"We have a radiogram from the ship ahead of us, saying that they are in the worst storm of the season. By midnight we will be in the midst of the storm. I will don my woolens and stay on the bridge this night."

We spent the hours in our cabin in prayer, for the boat was reeling to and fro like a drunken man, mounting up to the heavens and going down again to the depths. Our souls were melted because of trouble. As we cried unto the Lord He brought us out of our distress, and made the storm a calm so that the waves were stilled. When the captain came to the breakfast table he said to four missionaries:

"The strangest thing has happened that I have known in my forty-eight years at sea. Last night we were scheduled for the worst storm of the season; at midnight the stars came out—and in the morning the sun rose clear."—*The Crusader.*

* * *

There Is a Place

There is a place where thou canst touch the eyes
Of blinded men to instant perfect sight;
There is a place where thou canst say, "Arise,"
To dying captives, bound in chains of night;
There is a place where thou canst reach the store
Of hoarded gold and free it for the Lord;
There is a place—upon some distant shore—
Where thou canst send the worker or the Word—
There is a place where heaven's resistless power
Responsive moves to thine insistent plea;
There is a place—a silent, trusting hour—
Where God Himself descends and fights for thee.
Where is the blessed place—dost thou ask where?
O Soul, it is the secret place of prayer.
—Selected.

* * *

Before the Little Girl's Operation

Mary, aged nine, was taken sick and grew rapidly worse; with her father and the family physician she was taken to a city hospital. When examined, the surgeon said an operation was necessary to save her life. Her mother was sick at home; her father was not a Christian. The surgeon said to the girl: "My dear, a light operation is necessary, and before I perform that, I must put you to sleep." The nurse removed her clothing, put on her little white nightdress, and the child said, "I am ready, but if I am going to sleep, I must first say my prayers." The surgeon said, "Do just as you please, my dear." Then she knelt down, clasped her tiny hands, and prayed: "O Jesus, you know where I am, and that Mamma is sick at home. Bless dear Papa, my Sunday school teacher, this surgeon, and all for Jesus' sake." It was too much for the father. He begged to be excused, went to his room, and falling on his knees, surrendered to God, and became an earnest Christian. The great surgeon said, "I had not prayed for thirty years, but that night I went to my knees and begged for mercy." The child rapidly recovered. — *Sunday School Times.*

* * *

"When They Prayed"

A father and son were taking a long journey and must stay overnight in a country home. As they carried a fair amount of money with them, they had a certain fear. These people were strangers, but they had to have a place to stay, so the father and son decided that they would change off sitting up, lest the people in whose home they were abiding should seek to rob them. The father went to bed first and was soon fast asleep. After a while the father was awakened by the son's coming to bed, too.

"Why, son," said the father, "are you tired already? I thought that you were going to sit up the first part of the night and I the last."

"Well, father," said the son very quietly, "we don't have to sit up and watch in this house. While I was sitting here I heard the old man tell his wife that he thought they would read a few verses in the Bible and have prayer as usual. He read Romans, 13th chapter, I heard him say it was. I wish I could remember all that is in it, but I can't, so I'll read it some time, for a I never knew that there was so much in one chapter. The only verse that I remember is that '*love worketh no ill to his neighbor*' and then the old couple *prayed.* Such prayers I have never heard before! They asked God to help them to be a help and blessing to others and, do you know, they asked God to bless the strangers too. I can't be afraid that they will harm us after hearing their prayer. I wish that you could have heard it."

"You are right, son. People who make prayer a part of their lives will harm no one"; and then father and son slept peacefully, for they were not afraid.—*Gospel Herald.*

* * *

"Pray Without Ceasing"

Old Betty was asked the meaning of "Pray without ceasing." "Well, it just means what it says," said she. "When I wash my face in the morning, I pray God that many sinners may be washed in the blood of Christ during the day. When I put on my clothes, I pray God to clothe me with Christ and with humility. When I take up the broom, I think of the woman who swept the house for the lost piece of silver, and I pray God to sweep the world and to save lost sinners. When I brush the grate and it begins to brighten up, I pray to the Lord to brighten my soul." And thus Betty went on mentioning the things that gave her an opportunity of approaching God in prayer.—Selected.

* * *

Prayer Plus

It is recorded of D. L. Moody that, upon one of his journeys across the Atlantic there was a fire in the hold of the ship. The crew and some volunteers stood in line to pass buckets of water. A friend said to Moody, "Mr. Moody, let us go to the other end of the ship and engage in prayer." The common-sense evangelist replied, "Not so, sir; we stand right here and pass buckets and pray hard all the time." How like Moody this was! He believed that prayer and work were the two hands of the one person; that they should never be separated.—*Christian Herald* (London).

Pray First

There is a motto which reads: "You can do more than pray AFTER you have prayed, but you cannot do more than pray UNTIL you have prayed." — *The King's Business.*

* * *

An Unselfish Prayer

A little twelve-year-old girl, Marian Richardson, won first place in the 1938 National Spelling Bee at Washington, D. C. She was not only a leader in spelling, but a leader in prayer and Christian principles. After winning the honor of the National Speller, she was asked if she had prayed that God would help her win. She replied: "I prayed, but prayed that the best speller would win." It was an impressive lesson for the minister who asked, as well as to all of us who heard her answer.—From a real life experience, in *Sunday School Times.*

* * *

Death of a Prayer Meeting

Death was caused by serious neglect on the part of careless Christians, and unless the Lord raises it up in answer to the prayers of a few exercised saints, the funeral will take place shortly. The remains will be taken to the Judgment Bar of God, where HE will hold an inquest, having all the facts relative to the wicked neglect of those who forsook the Prayer Meeting, causing such a sad and untimely death.—Selected.

* * *

My Prayer

Jesus, Saviour, hear my prayer;
Keep me in Thy tender care;
Never let me go astray,
Watch Thou o'er me every day.

I am just a little child—
Saviour, keep me undefiled—
Pure and clean in heart and mind,
Loving, merciful, and kind.

Help me, now, and every day
As I walk along life's way
Always to obey Thee, Lord,
And to love Thy Holy Word.

Keep me—not for self alone,
But that I might be Thine own—
Thine for service all my days,
And to sing Thy worthy praise. Amen.
—N. E. Schrock.

* * *

Where to Find the Bravest Men

It is related of Lord Clyde, states the Rev. E. J. Hardy, chaplain to the forces, that on one occasion he asked his officers to pick him the bravest men from his small army before Delhi, to form the forlorn hope in a desperate attack. It was on a Sunday evening. "There is a prayer-meeting going on now in the camp," said the officers. "If you go there you will find all the bravest men."—*The Christian Age.*

* * *

Praying—But

"Yes, we're praying for a revival," said a godly woman, "but we don't expect it. And others are praying for it, but I don't know of anyone who expects it."—*The King's Business.*

* * *

Prayed for Twenty Years

"If God be for us, who can be against us?" (Rom. 8:31). God is for us when our lives are right with Him. God does not require big channels, but insists upon clean channels through which to bless. A woman prayed twenty years for her husband's salvation. The very opposite took place. Her life was spiritually changed. Shortly her husband gave evidence of salvation and home life changed. Blessing prayed for was hindered for twenty years by wrong living. Blessing came within a few days when prayer was watered with Biblical living.—*Gospel Herald.*

* * *

No Time Lost Looking Up

There is an old church in Europe in which may be seen a picture of a plowman who has left his plow and turned aside to pray. But while he prays an angel is going on with his plowing for him. The moments that we spend "looking up" are not lost time. We work the better and the more effectively for them when we return to our ordinary duties. Your plowing, whatever it is, will not suffer by your taking some moments every day to direct your prayer unto God and to "look up." "My voice shalt thou hear in the morning, O Lord; in the morning will I direct my prayer unto thee."—*Triumphs of Faith.*

* * *

Are We Ahead of Time?

Peter McKenzie, the famous Methodist preacher, was noted for the replies he often made to those who favored him with remarks on spiritual matters. "My prayers are not answered," complained a Christian to him one day. "Oh," replied Peter, "possibly that's because your prayers are like some promissory notes—presented before they are due." Do not cease to pray.—*The King's Business.*

* * *

Pray Much

John Welsh, worthy son-in-law of John Knox, thought the day ill-spent if he did not spend several hours in prayer. His wife complained when she found him on the floor praying. He replied, "I have the souls of 3,000 people to answer for, and I know not how it is with many of them." Dr. A. Judson spent several hours a day in prayer. He impressed the empire of Burma for Christ. John Elios, a Welsh preacher, had 2,500 professions of Christ when he preached after spending a night in prayer.—Selected.

* * *

Answered, But Not as Expected

James McConkey says that one summer when he was ill he spent the summer on the shores of the Great Lakes. Sailing was the only recreation possible. One day when sailing in the midst of the bay, the wind suddenly died out. His boat was utterly becalmed with not a breath of air astir. The hot rays of the August sun beat down mercilessly upon his weak body. He had come out with a stiff breeze, and naturally he began to pray for a breeze to take him back. For an hour he prayed, but no breeze came. Then he espied a boat coming toward him. An old fisherman, realizing that Mr. McConkey would be helpless out in the bay with no wind, came out to row the sailboat to harbor. Then Mr. McConkey says he learned his lesson. *His real need had been for deliverance, and while God had denied the words of his petition, He provided for his need.—Sunday School Times.*

* * *

General Dobbie's Testimony

A personal testimony closed an address by Lieut.-Gen. Sir William Dobbie when he spoke to an audience that crowded the largest hall available in Manchester, England, January 9, 1943, on "The Hand of God in Malta." Said the *Methodist Recorder*, London: "Finally General Dobbie spoke of a lifetime's experience of the friendship of Christ. 'Forget all I've said,' he concluded (he had been speaking especially of answers to prayer, 'but that Jesus Christ is a Saviour and a Lord. . . . He has taken away my sin and He will take away yours; and that is what I am here to say to this great meeting this afternoon.' "—*Sunday School Times.*

* * *

Praying Aright

A number of years ago the football team of Center College, Kentucky, was called "The Praying Colonels." The team that particular year had won the Conference championship and had defeated Harvard. Football coaches all over the country were interested in knowing how the team prayed. "Did the players ask to win by a certain score, or just what course did they follow?" The answer was this: "We do not pray to win by a certain score, but ask that we may live clean lives, to be given wisdom to play a clean game, without any mistakes. To play honestly and fearlessly, free from prejudices, hatred and ill-temper."

God can answer our prayers only as we are willing to do our part in the fulfilling of the answer.—Literary Digest.

* * *

A New Argument

Billy Sunday told of an old infidel blacksmith who had boasted that he could meet any argument that a Christian could make. An old deacon heard this boast and he and his wife spent the night till three o'clock praying for him. That morning the deacon went over to see him. As he entered the shop where the infidel was at work, he said, "My wife and I prayed for you until three o'clock this morning." Then his eyes filled with tears and he turned away and left him standing there at the forge. When the deacon arrived back home he said to his wife: "I've made an old fool of myself; it was all for nothing. When I saw him I just broke down and couldn't talk to him." In the meantime the infidel went home. He said to his wife: "I heard a new argument this morning; that old deacon drove in to see me and told me that he and his wife had prayed for us until three o'clock this morning. Then he sobbed and went away." And the infidel said to his wife: "Let's hitch up and go over and see him. I'd like to talk to him." It was only a few moments until he was on his knees with the old deacon, confessing his sin. — *Sunday School Times.*

* * *

"Unanswered Yet"

The story is told that Dr. Patton once met a pious friend with a troubled face, who said: "Doctor, you are just the man I have been wanting to see. I wish to ask you a question." "Well," said the Doctor, "what is it that is troubling you today?" "We read that God is good, just, merciful and kind," said the friend. "That is what we preach," replied Dr. Patton. "The Bible further says, 'Ask and ye shall receive, seek and ye shall find, knock and it shall be opened unto you.'" "Correctly quoted," said the Doctor. "Again," added his friend, "the good Book says, 'Not one jot or tittle of my Word shall fail.'" "Very true," said the Doctor. "Now," said the anxious friend, "if all that I have quoted is correct and the Bible be true, I want to ask you how it is, Doctor, that I have been praying to God for the last thirty years that He will do certain things for me, and so far as I know, not a single thing that I have asked for has been granted. Pray tell me why I have not received answers to my prayers?" The Doctor, turning and looking his questioner straight in the face replied: "My friend, did it ever occur to you that you were *presenting bills to God and asking payment for the same before they were due?*"—Selected.

* * *

"Just a whispered prayer,
And the load of care
From the burdened heart is lifted;
And a gleam of light,
Makes the pathway bright,
For the heavy clouds are rifted.

"Do not travel on in darkness,
When you may walk in sunshine fair.
You can find the light,
And the pathway bright,
By the aid of a whispered prayer."

—*Gospel Herald.*

* * *

"God Forbid That I Should Sin, in Ceasing to Pray for You" (I Sam. 12:23)

The shades of night come swiftly down
On sad hearts everywhere,
So for the troubled ones of earth,
Oh, breathe an earnest prayer!
And may they turn to Him above
Who all their heart doth know—
For only He can speak the words,
His comfort to bestow.

For I've been in life's darkest night,
And only He was there;
And only He knew how to keep
My sad heart from despair.
But while I slept for very grief,
I heard His voice once more—
Oh let us pray for all who weep!
He'll broken hearts restore.

—*Gospel Herald.*

The General's View of It

An officer once complained to General Stonewall Jackson that some soldiers were making a noise in their tent. "What are they doing?" asked the General. "They are praying now, but they have been singing," was the reply. "And is that a crime?" the General demanded. "The article of war orders punishment for any unusual noise," was the reply. "God forbid that praying should be an unusual noise in this camp," replied General Jackson.—*Wesleyan Methodist.*

* * *

Prayer Links to God

The main function of prayer is linking us to God in fellowship and preparing us to grow for further participation in His plan. Someone may ask if it is not futile to pray for that which is predetermined as a part of the plan of God. We can but answer that Christ thus prayed. In John 10 He made a certain and definite promise concerning the safety and keeping of the believer (vs. 27-29). Yet in John 17 He prayed seven times for the believers, that they might all be kept, though He had said that they would be.—Selected.

* * *

True Prayer

It is said that during the great battle of Waterloo when the fate of all Europe hung in the balance, the issue of the fight turned upon one point. On an eminence on the battlefield stood a farm house called Quatre Bras. Napoleon, looking over the field of battle, issued orders to take and hold that center at any cost. The Duke of Wellington was equally keen to perceive its value. It was the strategic point on the battlefield. But the strategic point is always the storm center, and throughout that fateful day, that farm house was the scene of shock upon shock. It was captured and re-captured many times. Neither side spared men or munitions in their determination to hold it, knowing that ultimate victory on the whole battle line rested with the one who held Quatre Bras. It is even so in the great conflict against the powers of darkness. He who wins in the prayer closet, wins everywhere. The one and only weapon that Satan dreads is true prayer.—*Gospel Herald.*

* * *

One Cry in a Thousand

Dr. Forsythe told the story of a friend of his who was taken over a sheep farm in Australia at the time of shearing, and how the guide took one little lamb from a pen and placed it in a huge enclosure with some thousands of sheep, where the noise of the bleating sheep and the shouting of the shearers was deafening. The lamb remained still for a moment, then it cried, and its cry was answered by the mother at the other end of the enclosure, along which the lamb walked to its mother, who came to meet it. "Do not imagine that you are beyond the reach of God," said the doctor. "He sees you as if there was no other child in the whole world."—*Sunday School Times.*

* * *

When God Spoke to Locusts

A plague of locusts had come to a Chinese village. The people surrounded their fields with small flags used in the worship of a god who would destroy locusts. One Chinese Christian refused to pray to the locust god, though his neighbors urged him. "No," he said stoutly, "that god cannot hear. My God can hear. I pray to Him," and earnestly he besought the Lord to save His little field from destruction. And the Lord did. This poor man cried and the Lord delivered him." The locusts destroyed every green thing round about, but never touched his field. — *The Presbyterian.*

* * *

Hanging Prayers on Stars

A few weeks ago a Christian father was bidding farewell to his son who was about to set out upon the high seas in defense of his country. In that solemn and intimate parting the father said, "My son, when you are out on the high seas and night comes on, I want you to look up into the sky. You will see the same stars that I am looking at, and know that on every star Dad is hanging a prayer."

A few days ago the father received a letter from the boy, and in it were these words, "Dad, tonight I lay upon the deck until late. It seemed to me I never saw so many beautiful stars. Then I remembered what you said. Good-night, Dad, I shall continue to look at the stars."—*The Lighted Pathway.*

* * *

Swift Communication

A mighty vessel was in mid-ocean when a lady passenger was taken desperately ill. The ship's surgeon was called and did everything in his power to relieve the woman's sufferings, but to no avail. When the first paroxysm of pain had ceased she said that her trouble seemed like the return of the symptoms of a former malady, one that her family physician always was very successful in combatting.

As rapidly as possible the wireless apparatus, with which the vessel was equipped, got into communication with the port of New York, which in turn used the long distance telephone to consult the family physician up-state. In a surprisingly short time his prescription was received through the air by radiogram.

As marvelous as is the working of wireless telegraphy, the simple prayer of one of God's dear children is more powerful. Hundreds of years before such modern communication was thought of, the Psalmist said, "The righteous cry, and the Lord heareth, and delivereth them out of all their troubles."

The Great Physician has said, "Call upon Me in the day of trouble: I will deliver thee" (Ps. 50:15). Do we forget God's promises, or do we not trust Him? —Alan Pressly Wilson, in *Light and Life Evangel.*

* * *

On Praying Ground

Do you ever make it impossible to pray prevailingly? A Christian man in a place of large responsibility was talking with a friend about a serious disagreement that had arisen between the institution of which he was the head and another man who had been connected with it, but whose relationship to the work had now been severed. This man had written sharp letters, and his letters had been answered in Christian quietness and courtesy. The friend commented on the unusual tone of the letters that had gone in response to the angry accusations. "But," said the friend who had written the letters that were marked by the fruit of the Spirit, "I must keep on praying ground." And he did! He realized that if he replied to the heated un-Christian letters in kind, he would be off praying ground, and not able to pray the matter through with any assurance that God was hearing, leading, and answering. Not only in letter writing, but in many other things in every-day life, it is easy to get off praying ground. Have we kept on praying ground today? —Selected.

* * *

Coming to God

"That He might bring us to God." Years ago on the stone coping that ran around the White House sat an old man. Threadbare clothes covered with dust made him a marked figure, and tears were on his face. A little boy rolling a hoop stopped and asked what was the matter. The bent form lifted, and the sad tale was poured out to the child. His son in the Army of the Potomac had been arrested for desertion and condemned. The guards had not permitted the man to pass to President Lincoln. "I can take you to the President," said the boy. "You?" "Yes, he is my father. He lets me come in any time." Thus it was the old man found the way to Lincoln, and thus gained pardon for his son. Thus it is that through Jesus Christ, the Son, we have access to God the Father. —Selected.

* * *

"Praying Always"

PRAY, when the morning breaketh;
PRAY, when the sun is high;
PRAY, when the shadows falling

PRAY, when the darkness deepens;
PRAY, in the silent night;
PRAY, when the shadows fleeing
Break into morning light.

PRAY, for the sorrow-laden;
PRAY, for the tempted soul;
PRAY, for the saint, the faithful,
Pressing toward the goal.
PRAY, for the missionaries
Toiling beyond the deep;
PRAY, for the heathen millions,
Over them pray and weep.

PRAY, that the Truth triumphant
Over the wrong may win;
PRAY, for the reign of power
Crushing the monster Sin.
PRAY, for the Bridegroom's coming;
Surely 'twill not be long.
Prayer, then shall turn to shouting
And to the victor's song.

—Belle Staples.

* * *

Exceptional Help

A gentleman at a summer resort had the misfortune, while roaming in the woods, to lose a very small part of a very valuable camera. He reported his loss to a lad of sixteen years who was choring there and offered a reward of two dollars for the return of the lost piece. The youth entered his small sleeping apartment, closed the door and prayed to the Lord that he might be successful in his efforts. He was soon away through the "trackless waste." In a short time the camera was once more complete. The owner, surprised and delighted, presented the reward, of which the lad would take but half. Questioned later as to his reason for this he replied, "That man did not know of the help that I had."—*Sunday School Times.*

* * *

Two Vital Prayers

There are two famous prayers, apparently contradictory. The first is Augustine's anguished cry, "Lord, save me from that evil man—myself." The second is the well known prayer of an early Wesleyan preacher, James Spence: "Lord, save me from that good man—James Spence." I confess that I do not know which of the two is the greater, or betrays the deeper insight. They are both typically Christian prayers; there are moments in our experience when each must be offered.—Dr. James Black, in *The Christian World.*

* * *

The Response to Need

Prof. E. P. Gulliver says this of the Holly engine: "As we stood by the steam gauge we observed constant and considerable changes in the amount of steam produced. As there was no cause in or about the engine itself, we asked for an explanation. 'That,' said the engineer, 'is done by the people in the city. As they open their faucets to draw water, the draft upon our fires is increased. As they close them it is diminished. The smallest child can change the movements of our engine according to his will. *It was the design of its maker to adjust it so that it would respond perfectly to the needs of the people, be they great or small.*' How much more will God's heart respond to every prayer of His creatures!" — *Sunday-School Journal.*

* * *

When God Spoke to Fire

Some years ago a Nova Scotia town was burning. An old retired minister entered the church, and knelt to pray for its safety. The oncoming sea of fire was very near. His friends entreated him to leave, but the old servant of God prayed on. Then a strange thing happened. The great sea of flames parted in two streams. When it had passed the church and the few surrounding buildings the two streams of fire came together again, and completed their work of destruction and desolation. But the man of God was still on his knees in the church.—*Christian Herald.*

* * *

Not Possibility, But Reality

A Christian woman was in financial need. She had been talking a good deal to the Lord about it. Her income that month had been thirty dollars. She is a warm personal friend of the *Times* staff, and she says she quoted to the Lord, one day, from a clipping she had in her Bible, made long ago from the *Times*: "We seldom pray with real confidence for anything, to the realization of which we cannot imagine a way." She began praying for the impossible, asking the Lord for thirty dollars more. The next morning the mail brought her a certain envelope, and she writes the Editor about it as follows: "I opened the envelope when my husband and I were at breakfast, and my eyes began to feel queer, so that I had to wink fast, and there was a big lump in my throat." The envelope contained a check for $32.84. "And instantly there was a little prayer in my heart, 'O dear heavenly Father, I just can't thank you enough!' Why, it just seemed as if the Lord were standing right by my table!" Yes — but why say, "as if the Lord were"? For the Lord *was!* And He had been standing right alongside when she had asked Him for the impossible. — *Sunday School Times.*

* * *

Then, Let Us Pray

The day was long, the burden I had borne
Seemed heavier than I could longer bear;
And then it lifted—but I did not know
Someone had knelt in prayer.

Had taken me to God that very hour,
And asked the easing of the load, and He
In infinite compassion, had stooped down
And lifted the burden from me.

We cannot tell how often as we pray
For some bewildered one, hurt and distressed,
The answer comes, but many times these hearts
Find sudden peace and rest.

Someone had prayed, and faith, a lifted hand
Reached up to God, and He reached down that day.
So many, many hearts have need of prayer—
Then, let us, let us pray.

—Selected.

* * *

Please Stop the Rain

The tin-roofed tabernacle in Waterloo, Iowa, roared under a driving rain when Charles Fuller stepped up to the microphone to pray, "Lord, if you don't stop the rain the Old Fashioned Revival Hour will not be able to go out over the air. For Jesus' sake, please stop the rain!" Within three minutes the rain stopped abruptly and the program was broadcast without interference. But five minutes after the service was over a downpour drenched the homegoing crowds.—*Sunday.*

* * *

When a Pilot Prayed

A bomber pilot was very explicit to me about his experience. "When the ack-ack hit us," he said, "both engines conked out, and we headed for the sea. I began to pray. Well, that was the last I knew until I came to in the water. I was in bad shape. My leg was gone below the knee, the water was red all around, and I knew I'd bleed to death in a few minutes. Then something nudged me. Believe it or not, it was a piece of plyboard with the plane's first-aid kit on it. I got the tourniquet out of it, and my co-pilot helped me to get the thing on and stop the bleeding. Another plane came along and dropped a life raft, and four hours later we were picked up by a rescue launch. If you don't call that a miracle, I'd like to know what is. God had something to do with that, mister." —*The Reader's Digest.*

* * *

Believing Prayer

A very worldly man was an object of special prayer with his wife. Her little daughter became a Christian, and very soon entered into sympathy with her mother and joined her in prayer that her father might be converted. Her faith was remarkably simple. She read the promises given in the Scriptures to the prayer of faith. "I believe," said she to her mother, "father will be converted." One evening he did not return home at his usual hour. An hour passed, two hours, her mother became anxious, then alarmed. The little girl said, "Why, mother, he is going to come home a Christian tonight. I have prayed that he might. The mother smiled at what she thought was her child's ignorant simplicity. The hour grew late.

Still he came not. The mother said, "I must sit up for him." The child replied, "Why, he is all safe, Mother. We ought to trust God and go to bed." She went to bed. When the father came home at midnight he told his wife how he had found the Saviour, and later, when they stood in cheerful joy looking upon the sleeping face of their little daughter, she awakened and, seeing them, before either could speak, with glad cry exclaimed, "There, Mamma, did he not come home a Christian?"—Selected.

* * *

When God Substitutes

I remember years ago living in a town where I could never buy anything to fit me. I used to send away occasionally to a certain big store for what I needed, and they would send me printed order forms. At the bottom of the forms were some such words as these: "If we have not the article you order in stock, may we substitute?" Once I said, "Yes," and they wrote, "We are sorry we have not in stock the article you ordered, but we are substituting. . ." and they sent me something that was worth double the price I paid. They made it a rule, if they could not supply the article ordered, to substitute with one of a much better quality. Ever after that I printed it out boldly so they would understand it — Y E S. When we pray to God, we had better put on the order form that we are quite willing to let Him substitute, for every time He does He sends us something far better, "exceeding abundantly above all that we ask or think."—*Gospel Witness.*

The Only Safe Place

Several weeks ago I heard a sermon by a young minister who used an illustration which interested me very much and which seems applicable to the present war situation. The illustration was this: A guide was taking a party of tourists up a very high mountain to see an unusually fine view. The mountain was so very high, that the wind blew constantly so hard that it was not safe to stand upright on the summit, and he told the party they must kneel in order to enjoy the view safely. All the party followed his suggestion except one man who was so impressed with the magnificient view that he tried to stand upright, but the guide put his hand on his shoulder and said, "To your knees, sir! It's the only safe way." Many of us would like to be in the front line, but let us remember, "They also serve who only stand and wait." And let us put it this way: Who only kneel and pray.—*Florida Baptist Witness.*

* * *

A Moment in the Morning

A moment in the morning, ere the cares
of day begin.
Ere the heart's wide door is open for the
world to enter in;
Ah, then, alone with Jesus in the silence
of the morn,
In heavenly, sweet communion let your
duty day be born.
In the quietude that blesses with a prelude of repose,
Let your soul be soothed and softened,
as the dew revives the rose.

A moment in the morning take your
Bible in your hand,
And catch a glimpse of glory from the
peaceful Promised Land;
It will linger still before you when you
seek the busy mart,
And, like flowers of hope, will blossom
into beauty in your heart;
The precious words, like jewels, will
glisten all the day
With a rare, effulgent glory that will
brighten all the way.

—Selected.

Pray More—Talk Less

There was a church in the city of Hartford, Connecticut, that had a very brilliant man for its pastor, but he was not sound in doctrine. There were three godly men in that church who realized that their pastor was not speaking the truth. But they did not go around among the congregation stirring up dissatisfaction with the pastor. They convenanted together to meet every Saturday night to pray long into the night for their minister. So Saturday after Saturday they met in earnest and protracted prayer: then Sunday morning they would go to church and sit in their places and watch for an answer to their prayers. One Sunday morning when the minister rose to speak, he was just as brilliant and just as gifted as ever, but it soon became evident that God had transformed his ideas and transformed the man, and Dr. Theo Cuyler is authority for the statement that God sent to the city of Hartford the greatest revival that city ever had, through that minister who was transformed by the prayers of his members. Oh, if we would talk less to one another against our ministers, and more to God in their behalf, we would have far better ministers than we have now.—Selected.

* * *

"Have Peace With One Another"

A missionary in West Africa tells the following very pleasing and instructive incident: "In visiting a sick communicant and his wife (who was formerly a student in a Bible school) I asked if they prayed together, read a part of the Scriptures (the woman can read), constantly attended public worship, and lived in peace with their neighbors. All these questions were answered in the affirmative. I then asked if they lived in peace together. The man answered, 'Sometimes I say a word my wife no like, or my wife talk, or do what I no like; but when we want to quarrel, we shake hands together, shut the door, and go to prayer; and so we get peace again.' "—Selected.

Prego

The "Unknown Christian" of England says: "I have just returned from Italy. I asked an Italian why the people replied 'Prego' when I said 'Gracia' (thank you) for some favor. 'O,' said he, 'it means, Your prayer is answered, and I'll do the same again.' " This is a beautiful expression of graciousness and love on the part of the one who has been asked to do something for another. And the Italian word 'Prego" beautifully expresses God's attitude and response when any of His children ask Him for something He knows it is best for them to have. Let us remember, as we pray how continuously and joyously our heavenly Father answers us with that word "Prego"—"Your prayer is answered, and I'll do the same again."—*Sunday School Times.*

* * *

The King's Bounty

A skillful surgeon recently undertook the responsibility of performing a serious operation on the eyes of an Eastern monarch which proved highly successful. After the king's recovery the problem of presenting his account puzzled the doctor, for he was dubious as to what figure would correctly estimate the value of the result achieved; as in Eastern countries it is a serious wrong to charge the king more or less than the actual value. Taking a blank billhead the doctor wrote across it, "The king can do no wrong," and respectfully submitted it to the monarch. His answer was a letter enclosing a sum far beyond his highest hopes. When we know not what to pray for, let us leave it to our Heavenly King, who doeth all things well.—*Christian Herald.*

* * *

And Paul Was a Pharisee

"See," said an evangelist to a penitent who was slow in taking comfort, "See how even the publican was accepted when he cried for mercy!" "Ah," said the other, "but I have been a greater sinner than a publican; I have been a Pharisee." "Well," was the answer, "since God was so glad to hear a publican say, 'God, be merciful to me a sinner!' how glad would He be to hear a Pharisee say so!"—*Christian Herald.*

* * *

There's a holy, high vocation
  Needing workers everywhere;
'Tis the highest form of service,
  'Tis the ministry of prayer.

Do you long to see the millions,
  Who are perishing today,
Snatched as brands plucked from the burning?
  Do you long, yet seldom pray?

Come and join the intercessors!
  Laurels, then, some day you'll wear;
For there is no higher service
  Than the ministry of prayer.
—Selected.

* * *

Prayer Is Practical

The following is taken from an incident recorded by Dr. H. Clay Trumbull, for years Editor of THE SUNDAY SCHOOL TIMES. A friend of his was away from home. The wife and children with an invalid friend of the wife, were alone in the house. In the dead of night the wife was awakened by hearing the window bolt thrown back. She realized that a burglar or an intruder was forcing an entrance. What should she do? It was about the time that Professor Huxley had been lecturing and writing on the folly of expecting direct answers to prayer. She thought of this, but it was immediately followed with the thought, "God can help me now, and I will pray to Him." So the following prayer was fervently uttered: "Lord, send me a policeman to our rescue." Pistol shots were heard in the yard. Running to the window, she saw a man slipping away in the darkness, and, a little later, a policeman called for admission to the house. On being admitted, he said he had passed the house and saw nothing out of the way, but, after passing, something told him to return and look again.—*Arnold's Commentary.*

It Worked Both Ways

At sixteen I joined the church. After that I read a few verses from the Bible each night and morning and prayed for strength to live a Christian life. After a year or so I began to suspect I was not making good, although I did not bring reproach on my profession. When I entered college I didn't let it be known that I was a church member. One afternoon the fellow I roomed with had a fall in the gymnasium. He was carried to our room more dead than alive. The blood gushed from his nose and mouth, and the physician we summond was not assuring. I shall never forget the terror in my roommate's eyes as he wispered, "Wilson, I—wish you'd pray for me." We were alone, and I kneeled down and said something aloud to God about helping my friend. I was surprised to see the change in him and still more in myself. That faltering prayer opened to me the whole wide vista of intercession. I saw that my Christian faith had languished because I had never prayed enough for others. A Christian must needs be an intercessor.—*Youth's Companion.*

* * *

A Mighty Answer

A plain seaman stood on watch on the bridge of a U.S. battleship several hundred miles out on the Atlantic when a wireless was handed to him. "Little Donald passed away yesterday. Funeral Wednesday afternoon. Can you come? Mary." The seaman forgot his watch. He saw the smiling face of his baby boy as he had left him three months before. His only boy—his hope. Then he broke, and the captain found him sobbing. "What's the matter, my lad?" The seaman stood at attention and handed the captain the message. "Where do you live?" "Cleveland, Ohio, Sir." The captain did some rapid figuring and in a moment the wireless of the big battleship began sputtering out messages to her sister ships in the vicinity. "Full steam ahead" was the order. Soon a gray form appeared — a faster ship; the seaman was quickly transferred. The second battleship raced 200 hundred miles until a torpedo-boat destroyer came up which had also received the wireless, and into it the seaman descended. Then full steam ahead for the nearest port—a waiting taxi—the train which left in four minutes for Cleveland, and the next afternoon, one hour before the funeral, the seaman-father stood looking down on his little boy, with the mother and wife in his arms. Three battleships somewhere on the Atlantic had felt the impulse of his fatherhood. And shall not God hear his own elect who cry day and night unto him? I tell you, yes. Sailor-friend of mine, tossed on the high seas of life, the Captain waits for your message.—*Camel's Nose.*

* * *

Didn't Need Explaining

"And how do you explain it?" asked one who had heard an old saint tell of a wonderful answer to prayer. "I don't," she answered simply, "it does not need explaining. I just took the Lord at His word and He took me at mine."—*Sunday School Times.*

* * *

Seek

Pray for my soul! More things are wrought by prayer
Than this world dreams of. Wherefore let thy voice
Rise like a fountain for me night and day.
For what are men better than sheep or goats
That nourish a blind life within the brain,
If, knowing God, they lift not hands in prayer
Both for themselves and those who call them friend?
For so the whole round world is every-way
Bound by gold chains about the feet of God.

—Alfred Tennyson.

A Revelation from God

In conversation with Prof. S. F. B. Morse, the inventor of the telegraph, Rev. George W. Hervey asked him this question:

"Professor Morse, when you were making your experiments yonder in your rooms in the university, did you ever come to a stand, not knowing what to do next?"

"Oh, yes; more than once."

"And at such times, what did you do next?"

"I may answer you in confidence, sir," said the professor, "but it is a matter of which the public knows nothing. *I prayed for more light.*"

"And the light generally came?"

"Yes. And may I tell you that when flattering honors came to me from America and Europe on account of the invention which bears my name, I never felt I deserved them. I had made a valuable application of electricity, not because I was superior to the other men, but solely because God, who meant it for mankind, must reveal it to someone, and was pleased to reveal it to me."

In view of these facts, *it is not surprising that the inventor's first message was, "What hath God wrought!"*—Selected.

* * *

A Jew's Prayer Answered

Some years ago a little Jewish girl in Russia learned large portions of the New Testament from a boy who had committed them to memory. One day upon the arrival of her father, aften an absence, she ran to meet him, and said, "I do love Jesus; He loved little children." This angered the father, and he forbade her to speak on that subject again. Soon the child was stricken with scarlet fever, and the medical attendant gave no hope of her recovery. A Gentile woman was called to nurse the child, as the Jews feared the fever. The woman quoted the verse of a hymn, and the father offered the death-bed prayer of the Jews. Then the child opened her eyes, and repeated accurately the story of Jairus' daughter. When she finished, her head fell back, and to all appearances she was gone. In an agony of mind the father fell down at the feet of Jesus and besought Him, saying, "O Jesus, Thou who didst raise up the daughter of Jairus, raise little Deborah, and I will believe in Thee as Israel's Messiah!" That cry of agony was heard, and the child rose from her couch of death, and that Jewish family was converted to Christianity.—*The Illustrator.*

* * *

Another Mother's Faith

Dr. Thomas N. Carter, the ex-convict, tells a thrilling story of the faith of his mother who followed him with her prayers for many years until she listened to him preach the gospel in answer to her prayer. On one occasion, while he was in prison, his mother received a telegram from the prison stating that her son was dead, and asked what she wanted done with his body. His mother was stunned at receipt of the telegram for a few minutes, then retired to her prayer closet after instructing others in the house not to disturb her. She got her Bible and opening it, spread it before her, with the telegram beside it. "Oh, God," she began, "I have believed the promise you gave me in your Word, that I would live to see Tom saved and preach the Gospel, and now a telegram comes saying he is dead. Lord, which is true, this telegram or your Word?" When she rose from her knees, having won the victory, she wired the prison: "There must be some mistake. My boy is not dead." And there *was* a mistake. Tom Carter lived and was recently in our church preaching, with his mother seated on the platform.—*Sunday School Times.*

* * *

If Two of You

Jonathan said to his armor-bearer, "There is no restraint to the Lord to save by many or by few." The two of them started a movement that led to the discomfiture of a whole army. Finney tells of a blacksmith who was so wrought up over conditions in his community that he locked the shop door and spent the afternoon in prayer. A great revival started the very next Sunday, and people dated their deep conviction of sin from the very hour the old man was praying in his shop.

When Finney was conducting a revival in a certain place, a young woman came from a neighboring town and asked him to go there and preach. "Her utterance was choked with deep feeling." Mr. Finney told her he did not see how he could go, but he looked up the place and found that it was a moral waste, cursed by a minister who had changed to infidelity. The young woman came the next Sunday, and appeared greatly affected; too much so to converse, for she could not control her feeling. The evangelist consented to go the next Sunday P.M., and after his arrival at her home he heard her praying in a room above. He remained in the home overnight, and heard her praying and weeping nearly all night. She pleaded with him to come again, and "at the third service the Spirit of God was poured out on the congregation." A spirit of prayer came powerfully upon Mr. Finney, as it had upon this young woman. The spirit of prayer spread, and the revival that followed was so powerful that "nearly all the principal inhabitants of the town were gathered into the church, and the town was morally renovated." This great spiritual movement was started by the young woman's prayers.

Where can we find anyone interested enough to pray like that today? Finney was noted for his wonderful life of prayer, and for his dependence on the leading of the Holy Spirit. Cannot we learn a lesson from him, who says, "I find myself better or worse as I pray more or less"? Do we care enough about others to pray for them in a way which will mean an intensity of desire for them to find God?—Rev. Homer F. Yale, in *Gospel Herald.*

* * *

Pray One for Another

I cannot tell why there should come to me
A thought of someone miles and miles away,

In swift insistence on the memory,
Unless a need there be that I should pray.

Too hurried oft are we to spare the thought
For days together, of some friends away;
Perhaps God does it for us, and we ought
To read His signal as a call to pray.

Perhaps, just then, my friend has fiercer fight,
And more appalling weakness, and decay
Of courage, darkness, some lost sense of right—
And so, in case he needs my prayer, I pray.

Friend, do the same for me. If I intrude
Unasked upon you, on some crowded day,
Give me a moment's prayer as interlude;
Be very sure I need it, therefore pray.
—Marianne Farningham.

* * *

Is Prayer Impractical?

The *Living Church* tells of how a missionary doctor saved the life of a famous Arctic explorer (Stefansson). It was a case of double pneumonia, and the explorer had to be brought in fifty miles to the hospital. When he had recovered and was going on, he said to the doctor, "Money cannot repay what you have done for me. You have saved my life. But I should like to make one criticism. You would accomplish more if you did not spend so much time in religious work, and in prayer." Then the doctor replied, "If it had not been for prayer, I should not be here; this hospital would not have been here, and you would be lying dead in the snow."—*Bible Expositor and Illuminator.*

* * *

Not Noticed

Said a pastor, "I abandoned my prayer meeting long ago." "How did your church officers like that?" "Oh, they did not find it out for more than a year."—*Church Business.*

If We Only Pray

Sir John Kirk, the founder of the Ragged School Union, once said to a friend, "If you can only get people to *pray* for the work, there will be no difficulty about getting them to *pay* for it."—*Sunday School Times.*

* * *

Prayer Changes You

There was an old gentleman who was remarkable for his gentleness. When a young man he was known to have a violent temper. He was asked how he managed to overcome his temper. His answer was a short but wise one. He said it was—"By praying to God and speaking low." When persons are angry they raise their voices and speak loud. To overcome anger and learn the lesson of gentleness, we must—"pray to God and speak low."—*Gospel Herald.*

* * *

Not a Strong Preacher

A young preacher had just settled in his first pastorate in Philadelphia, when he was visited one evening by one of the laymen of his church. The man said bluntly to him, "You are not a strong preacher. In the usual order of things you will fail here, but a little group of us have agreed to gather every Sunday morning to pray for you!" The young man saw that group of people grow to more than one thousand praying weekly for their pastor. The minister was *J. Wilbur Chapman,* who grew to be one of the greatest preachers America has ever known.—Selected.

* * *

How Brainerd Prayed

No sublimer story has been recorded in earthly annals than that of David Brainerd. No miracle attests, with diviner force, the truth of Christianity than the life and work of this godly man. Alone in the savage wilds of America, struggling day and night with a mortal disease, unschooled in the care of souls, having access to the Indians for a large portion of time only through the bungling medium of a pagan interpreter, with the Word of God in his heart and in his hand, his soul fired with the divine flame, a place and time to pour out his heart and soul to God in prayer, he fully established the worship of God and secured great results. After spending a whole week in prayer he spoke with such power that countless numbers of the Indians were led to yield their lives to God. The Indians were changed from the lowest besotments of heathenism, to pure, devout, intelligent Christians.

Brainerd lived a life of holiness and prayer: by day and by night he prayed. Before preaching and after preaching he prayed. Riding through the interminable solitudes of the forest he prayed. On his bed of straw he prayed. Morning, noon, and night he communed with God. Little wonder he had such power—God was with him mightily because he lived in the presence of God.—*Gospel Herald.*

* * *

A Little Talk With Jesus

A little talk with Jesus, how it smooths the rugged road,
How it cheers and helps me onward, when I faint beneath my load.
When my heart is crushed with sorrow, and my eyes with tears are dim,
There's naught can yield me comfort, like a little talk with Him.

I tell Him I am weary, and I fain would be at rest,
That I'm daily, hourly longing for a home upon His breast,
And He answers me so sweetly in tones of tenderest love,
"I'm coming soon to take thee to My happy home above."

Ah! this is what I'm wanting, His lovely face to see,
And I'm not afraid to say it,I know He's wanting me.
He gave His life a ransom to make me all His own,
And He can't forget His promise, to me His purchased one.

I know the way is dreary to yonder far-off clime,
But a little talk with Jesus well occupies my time,
And yet the more I know Him, and all His grace explore,
It only sets me longing to know Him more and more.

I often feel impatient, and mourn His long delay,
I never can be settled while He remains away.
We shall not long be parted, for I know He'll quickly come,
And we shall dwell together in that happy, happy home.

So I'll wait a little longer, till His appointed time,
And glory in the knowledge that such a hope is mine.
Then in my Father's dwelling, where many mansions be,
I'll sweetly talk with Jesus, and He shall talk with me!

—*The Missionary Worker.*

* * *

The Guard of Prayer

The morning is the gate of the day,
But ere you enter there,
See that you set to guard it well
The sentinel of Prayer.

So shall God's grace your steps attend,
But nothing else pass through
Save what can give the countersign:
The Father's will for you.

When you have reached the end of day,
Where night and sleep await,
Set there the sentinel again,
To guard the evening Gate.

So shall no fear disturb your rest,
No danger and no care;
For only peace and pardon pass
The watchful guard of prayer.

—Anonymous.

* * *

Prayer Changes Things

Once a little old Christian lady, who rented half of a double house, was praying loudly to God for her needs; she had not a meal for a mouse. Now the man from whom she rented, was an infidel, brazen and hard. He heard her praying, and said to himself, "Now, I'll play my trump card. I'll show this foolish old lady up, and prove beyond a shadow of a doubt, that her God is less than nothing, and only man can help out."

So he left his eavesdropping position and went down to the grocery store. "Give me a loaf of bread," he said, "you'd laugh if you knew what for." So he went back home with a chuckle, as he thought how he'd have a good time. "This is going to be really funny," thought he; "and it only cost me a dime."

On reaching his house he climbed to the roof, and listening down through the fireplace flue, he heard the little old lady thank God that her prayer had broken through. He heard her praise God for the substance of faith, and for the manna that comes from above; for salvation and all of the blessing, and for Calvary's Cross and His love.

The infidel laughed as he leaned over the flue and let the loaf fall down at her feet. He heard her break out with a queer little cry; he listened, and heard her repeat, "Thank you, Lord; I knew You wouldn't fail me. Oh, you do supply all my needs. And now, Lord, save the man next door, in spite of his infamous creeds."

With a sneer on his face he climbed to the ground and went around to her door. Now he'd make her feel cheap, and have a good laugh—the laugh he paid a dime for! He knocked and listened; she called out, "Come in," and he opened and went inside. "Thank You, Lord," she said, as she arose from her knees, with the infidel there by her side.

Then the man spoke up. "You poor, foolish thing, to really believe that God hears and answers prayer. Why, I'm the one who brought you that loaf. I just dropped it down the fireplace there."

"Well, praise the Lord!" cried the little old lady. "God gave you the dime and you spent it. He answered my prayer, and gave me the loaf, if it was by the devil, He sent it."—Selected.

The Great Need to Cry

A young lieutenant "in the United States Army on some far-off battle front" writes to his sister in Pennsylvania: "Prayer is going to win this war. Not guns alone. Fervent, agonizing prayer. . . . Pray, Sis. Pray as you never prayed before. *Tell everyone to pray.* Tell all America to go to its knees. Before each decisive victory anywhere over here, sometimes for hours, sometimes for days, there has been a feeling of people praying from far away. The feeling is so strong that you can hear it. One of the most stubborn of the men said, in the stillness of the night, 'Did you hear anything? Sounded like people praying from some distant place. . . .' Again I plead, *Tell America to pray.* This war will not end until nations and people have paid in blood and tears for thrusting God out of their hearts and countries. And tell them to send Bibles, and *more* Bibles. . . . And you complacent, bridge-playing, cocktail-drinking mother, why didn't you teach your son about God instead of handing him a cigarette, and a dance program? Get to your knees and ask God to forgive your sins. And then pray for the Army. Pray, pray, pray. . . . Only repentance for sins can stop the shelling, the killing, and the murdering. . . . So tell them to keep on praying." — *Waynesbury* (Pa.) *Republican.*

* * *

And What of Today?

When the Constitutional Convention was in session, a skeptical tendency appeared. Benjamin Franklin, then in his eighty-third year, prepared and read a speech as follows: "When we were in great peril we had daily prayers in this room for the protection and guidance of Almighty God. I have lived a long time, and the longer I live the more convincing proof I have that God governs in the affairs of men. If a sparrow cannot fall to the earth without His knowledge, is it possible for a nation to rise without His aid? To that kind Providence we owe this happy privilege of consulting in peace on the means of establishing our future national felicity. Have we now forgotten that powerful Friend; or have we no longer need of His assistance?"—*Christian Faith and Life.*

* * *

Ling Wei's Answer to Prayer

The new Chinese evangelist was very homely but the Lord, looking into his heart, saw there a burning love for Him and a desire for the salvation of his people.

His mother was not a Christian and often persecuted him. One night on his return home she met him at the door and told him that he could not go to church on the morrow and threatened him with all kinds of punishment if he opposed her.

Poor Ling Wei was in great trouble. He went to his room and lay down on his hard mat at the floor. "What shall I do?" he moaned. "My teacher will think I have gone back to my idols if I do not go to church."

Just then the door opened and Cheng, his friend in the Jesus faith, entered. "Why, what is the matter, Ling Wei?" he whispered. "You look so sad, I came for help and I find you weeping."

"My heart is indeed very sad," Ling Wei answered. "When I came home my mother told me I must give up the Jesus religion. And she has hidden my clothes so I cannot go to church tomorrow."

"A Chinese boy or man must mind his parents," said his friend, "but we can pray—get help from our Jesus. Let us pray to Him."

The two friends threw themselves on their faces and prayed to the God who hears the prayers of white and yellow alike.

The night passed away. The early morning light found them still weeping and calling to God to save the poor heathen mother.

Suddenly the door was opened and Ling Wei's mother stood in the doorway.

"Oh, my dream! My dream!" she cried. "The True God you talk to told me in a dream to let you alone or He would punish me. Here are your clothes. Dress and go to church. I will hinder you no more."

When the two friends entered the mission that day their hearts were very happy.—Selected.

* * *

A Chinese Stephen's Prayer

Two pastors of Bishop Roots' diocese were imprisoned, after having been badly beaten. Release, they were told, would come when they renounced their faith. It happened that the day on which they were imprisoned was, in the Episcopal Church calendar, sacred to the memory of St. Stephen. So the two Chinese pastors stood up in the midst of their fellow prisoners and preached the story of Stephen. "We need men like Stephen in China," said the prisoners; and together the whole company knelt and prayed that God would send more Stephens to the aid of China.—*The American Missionary.*

* * *

A Child's Prayer

One November day, in England, a clergyman was telling his two boys, one five and the other eight years of age, about a lady, formerly their governess, who had gone as a missionary from their home to far-off Ceylon, that she might carry the blessed news of Jesus Christ's love into a land where very few had heard of Him, and fewer still had learned to love Him.

He told of some of the hardships which she had to undergo; of the roof which let the rain through during the long wet season, of the spiders and creeping insects which infested the house, and of the poisonous snakes and reptiles which made it unsafe even to venture out of doors.

To the older boys the adventurous nature of the calling appealed most, but to little Fred the thought of poisonous snakes brought fear and sadness, and that night as he knelt before his bed for his evening prayers, the father heard him say, "God bless my dear father and mother, and make me good, for Jesus' sake." Then in a voice which quivered with earnestness, he added, "And, oh, dear God, take care of my Miss Price, and please do keep her safe from the snakes."

Then the little boy went to bed, and the clergyman, with moist eyes, went to his evening service and preached on "The Power of Prayer" with more earnestness because of the petition he had heard.

But there is another part of the story, and that we take from a narrative by Katherine E. Morgan in *Medical Missions.*

Far away in Ceylon, the missionary was wending her way to a house that she called home. Her arms were full of books, and she looked as if she had just come from her little Tamil children. She seemed tired, and yet she had that look of brightness and joy characteristic of her.

Near her house she thought of the dear ones in the homeland, and for a moment longed for a glimpse of them and for the opportunity of joining them once more in the Sunday evening worship of that cozy little vicarage, with its two little occupants.

But she was brought back to her present surroundings by a sudden and unexpected danger; right across her path, to her dismay, she saw one of the small but very venomous snakes of that district — its neck and head raised and arched, its eyes gleaming with a malignant fire, ready with lightning stroke to spring upon her with its awful fangs. To escape seemed impossible, and for one terrible moment she was riveted to the spot in mortal dread. Then, to her inexpressible relief and utter astonishment, the snake seemed suddenly to change its mind, and turning around in the opposite direction, it deliberately and noiselessly resumed its way among the long, thick grass.

With a cry of thankfulness, the tired worker reached her home as fast as her trembling limbs would carry her, and going on her knees, she poured out her heart to God who had saved her from such a terrible death.

Mail day came, and among her little pile of letters was one from her English pastor. As she read it, she felt cheered to know that she had become their missionary, greater interest had been stirred up in the parish, and more zeal manifested in the work which was so dear to her heart. But the postscript at the end of the letter thrilled her as she read it—

"Little Fred never forgets to pray for you. Two Sundays ago I was telling the children of your life of danger and hardships, and the dear little fellow was so upset to think that his 'dear Miss Price' was in danger of anything, that he prayed so earnestly, of his own accord, that God would take care of you, and keep you from the snakes! He prayed for this with such simple faith, and with such a natural and eager expectancy for an answer, that he quite put me to shame."

The missionary read this over and over again, and her eyes were dim as she laid the letter down. Yes, it was that Sunday! Now she understood; and with new meaning she read the text hanging over her couch, "Before they call, I will answer; and while they are yet speaking, I will hear" (Isa. 65:24).—*Prairie Pastor.*

* * *

"You Can't Defeat that Prayer"

A lawyer came to his client and said he could not prosecute a certain claim. "I stepped into the little hall, and through a crack in the door I saw on the bed an old woman. She said: 'Come, Father, now begin. I'm all ready.' Down on his knees by her side went the old white-haired man. First he reminded God that they were still His submissive children, and that whatever He saw fit to bring upon them they would accept. It would be hard for them to be homeless in their old age. How different it would have been if at least one of the boys had been spared. Then he quoted several promises assuring the safety of those who put their trust in God. Last of all he prayed for God's blessing on those who were demanding justice." "Afraid to defeat the old man's prayer?" asked the client. Said the lawyer, "You *couldn't* defeat that prayer! My mother used to sing, 'God moves in a mysterious way.'" "Well, my mother used to sing that, too," said the client. "You can call in the morning and tell Mother and him that the claim has been met."—*Alliance Weekly.*

* * *

Selfwill

The following incident may be familiar to some, but warnings need to be repeated.

"A minister, praying over a child apparently dying, said, 'If it be Thy will, spare.' The poor mother's soul yearning for her beloved, exclaimed, 'It *must* be His will: I cannot bear *ifs.*' The minister stopped.

"Contrary to expectation, the child recovered. But the mother, after almost suffering martyrdom by him while a stripling, lived to see him *hanged* before he was two and twenty."—*Gospel Banner.*

* * *

Expectant Prayers

A beautiful little book, *Expectation Corners,* tells us of a king who prepared a city for some of his poor subjects. Not far from them were large storehouses, where everything they could need was supplied if they but sent in their requests. But on one condition — they should be on the outlook for the answer, so that when the king's messengers came with the answers to their petitions, they should always be found waiting and ready to receive them. The sad story is told of one desponding one who never expected to get what he asked, because he was too unworthy. One day he was taken to the king's storehouses, and there, to his amazement, he saw, with his address on them, all the packages that had been made up for him, and sent. There was the garment of praise, and the oil of joy, and the eye-salve, and so much more. They had been to his door, but found it closed. He was not on the outlook. From that time on, he learned the lesson Micah would teach us: "I will look to the Lord; I will wait for the God of my salvation; my God will hear me!"—Andrew Murray.

* * *

"Why Are Not My Boys Saved?"

It was in a country place in the home of a deacon. Three children had been born to the family, two of them boys who had come to the years of accountability. The preacher who held the meeting was stopping in this home. One afternoon, when the fires of evangelism had been burning, the mother in this home said to the preacher, "Why are not my boys saved? The children of other homes are being converted by the score. My boys are interested, but I see no tears; I see no evidence of conviction. Tell me why." The preacher said, "Can you stand a little plain talk?" The mother said, "I can." Said the preacher, "Your boys are dry-eyed and unconcerned because their mother is. Did you ever take either of them aside and teach him and pray with him and for him about his salvation?" The mother answered, "Never." "Have you spent sleepless nights weeping over their lost condition?" The mother, sobbing, said, "Never." The preacher said, "The boys are unsaved because the mother has no burden for them!" That night was a momentous night in that home. Next morning, at the breakfast table, with sad and tearful face, the mother refused to eat, saying, "All night long I walked the floor and prayed for my boys. My boys," she said, "are on my heart and I cannot live unless they are saved!" Both boys that very day were born again into God's family. Said the boys, "Mother, I heard you when you prayed for me last night, we are saved now in answer to your prayers!"—L. R. Scarborough.

PREACHERS—PREACHING

The Principal's Criticism

Years ago it was the custom in a certain theological college for the student who had preached in sermon class to go into the Principal's room next morning for a quiet talk on the sermon. On one such occasion the revered and saintly old Principal said to the young man before him: "It was a good sermon you gave us yesterday; the truth you dealt with was well arranged and well presented. But your sermon had one omission, a grave one. There was no word in it for a poor sinner like me."—The Rev. A. E. J. Cosson, in the *United Methodist Magazine.*

* * *

The Sermon Lincoln Enjoyed

Abraham Lincoln put it rather strongly but effectively nevertheless, when he said: "I do not care for cut and dried sermons. When I hear a man preach I like to see him act as if he were fighting bumble bees!"—Selected.

* * *

Why Moody Used Stories

Of course, there were those who criticized his constant use of "stories." "People," Moody once said, "don't seem to understand why I use these stories. It is to touch the heart, and while it is soft, to send right in the arrow of truth." With pathos and tender feeling he would use his simple illustrations and touching stories with a great disregard of all secondary considerations of any kind whatever. His most moving appeals, his gentle persuasiveness, his most passionate declamations, his most direct home-thrusts, his reference to people and places, were all used for the highest ends. Happily, many of Moody's unique stories have been preserved for us in his book on *Anecdotes.*—Selected.

* * *

Unconverted Preacher

It would be a great mercy if every converted person would positively refuse to listen twice to any minister who denies the inspiration of the Bible, or to give a penny to a church or missionary society that gave the right hand of fellowship to men of this type.—*Sunday.*

* * *

More Interest in Antichrist than Christ

Dr. A. C. Gaebelein is credited with saying, "I find many people whose consuming passion is to know more and more about the Antichrist." Others of us have met these people, too. If it is advertised that Christ is to be presented to the congregation, the hearing may be small, but if the preacher is to identify the Antichrist, there may be hardly room in the building. Which may mean that people would rather hear a man tell what he does not know than speak of what he understands. But this may mean also that too few people realize that one's first responsibility is to get Christ for himself and then bring Him into the lives of others.—*The Free Methodist.*

* * *

Eliminating the Ministry

Woodrow Wilson spoke these words of preachers and they are worthy of the careful consideration of every one of us: "When I hear some of the things which young men say to men by way of putting the arguments to themselves for going into the ministry, I think they are talking of another profession. Their motive is to do something.

"You do not have to be anything in particular to be a lawyer, and I know. You do not have to be anything in particular, except a kind-hearted man perhaps, to be a physician. You do not have to be anything, nor undergo any strong spiritual change, in order to be a merchant. The only profession which consists in being something is the ministry of our Lord and Saviour—and it does not consist of anything else.

"And that conception of the ministry which rubs all the marks off and mixes him in the crowd so that you cannot pick him out, is a process of eliminating the ministry itself."—*Word and Way.*

The Sight that Blinds

The apostle Paul was perhaps one of the greatest travelers of his day. He visited many lands, and saw many new scenes in different countries. When he returned he wrote a good deal; his epistles were widely read by the early churches. And yet, in all the writings of the apostle, there is not one line that is descriptive of the scenery of the countries through which he passed; not a line telling of the wonders of the architecture of his day; not a line describing the customs of the people. Is not this singular? There is a reason for it. The apostle was blind. As he traveled about he was blind to all else but one thing. On the way to Damascus, when he met the Lord Jesus, he was blinded by the vision of His great glory, and from that time he could see nothing but Him and tell of nothing but His Gospel. —The Rev. R. A. Jaffray, in *The Sunday School Times.*

* * *

Pastoral Success

Requisites for pastoral success are the following: "The strength of an ox, the daring of a lion, the industry of a beaver, the versatility of a chameleon, the vision of an eagle, the disposition of an angel, the loyalty of an apostle, the heroism of a martyr, the faithfulness of a prophet, the tenderness of a shepherd, the fervency of an evangelist, and the devotion of a mother."

That is rather a formidable picture in its demands, and yet it is not going too far to say that many or most of these qualifications are found in many true Christian ministers, and have been since the time of the apostles. One could go through the whole list of "requisites" and find Scripture authority for each. The kaleidoscopic description brings to mind such Scripture passages as these:

"Be strong in the Lord, and in the power of his might."

"Having done all, to stand."

"Be ye steadfast, unmoveable."

"Be strong and of a good courage, fear not, nor be afraid." — *Sunday School Times.*

Points for Preachers

An exchange has the following story: A minister preached on I Corinthians 13:1. The reporter for the daily paper, strangely enough, got it right, but the linotype operator, in setting the word "charity," made the mistake of using an "l" instead of an "h," and the proofreader overlooked it. So the minister was reported in the morning paper as having preached from the following text: "Though I speak with the tongues of men and of angels, and have not *clarity,* I am become as sounding brass, or a tinkling cymbal." Commenting on the story the editor says: "As it appears in print it was not New Testament truth, but it was truth, nevertheless. The people want the preacher to be luminous rather than voluminous, and the preacher who is without clarity will soon be without a congregation."—Courtesy *Moody Monthly.*

* * *

A Millionaire's Reflection

One of the most influential men in Great Britain is Lord Beaverbrook, who owns the *London Daily Express* and a number of other daily papers. He is the son of a preacher. He made a fortune in Canada and then went to England, where he has forged ahead and made money and a name for himself. Some years ago he was elevated to the peerage. Recently he wrote, "The evangelist is the man who has the greatest opportunity for doing good and if I were in a position to influence the life of a sincere young man today I would say to him, 'Rather choose to be an evangelist than a cabinet minister or a millionaire.' When I was a young man I pitied my father for being a poor man and a humble preacher of the Word. Now that I am old I envy him, his life, and career." —Selected.

* * *

Fear Sin

Give me one hundred preachers who fear nothing but sin and desire nothing but God, and I care not a straw whether they be clergymen or laymen; such alone will shake the gates of hell and set up the kingdom of heaven on earth. God does nothing but in answer to prayer.—John Wesley.

* * *

Preach for God's Glory

When the great "Welsh Revival" was in progress some years ago its human leader, Evan Roberts, on one occasion suddenly and quietly left the service, simply because the curiosity and expectancy concerning him was very distasteful to his consecrated soul. Then a godly young woman arose and exclaimed, "Whom are you after, Evan Roberts or Jesus?" And the meeting proved more than ordinarily successful because only the glory of God was sought. Verily our constant aim should be "that God in all things may be glorified through Jesus Christ."—*Gospel Herald.*

* * *

Everything But God's Word

An Ohio church called a pastor who qualified on nine points beyond all other candidates, being "selected on a strictly scientific basis." Some of these points included: "Spirituality—but this doesn't mean belief in the virgin birth, or any of the other dogmas of the old church, such as Jonah and the whale." If candidates professed belief in any such ideas they were marked off on the first point. Other points were Intellectuality, Scholarliness, Adaptability, Poise, Personality, Tolerance and Sympathy, Vision, Appeal to Youth. The minister, according to these qualifications, should "enjoy the same things a college professor does," have a good "stage appearance," his shoes should always be shined and his suit pressed; he should have a tolerance for all religious sects. The minister chosen "scored ninety-three per cent out of a possible one hundred, outstripping the other candidates by a large majority." It is a relief to turn from this to Paul's word to ministers: "I charge thee . . . preach the word."—*Sunday School Times.*

"One Damning Defect"

At the close of a service a preacher was accosted by one of his hearers who, after conceding that the sermon possessed certain commendable features, added, "But it had one damning defect!" The startled minister, having inquired what this defect was, received the following reply, "'I am a Jew, I have only recently been born again. Up to that time I attended the synagogue. But there was really nothing in your sermon that I could not have heard in the synagogue, nothing that a Jewish rabbi might not have preached." "That," said the preacher, in after years, "was the greatest lesson in homiletics I was ever taught."—*Sunday School Times.*

* * *

Spurgeon on "Adverbs"

Spurgeon once said, "That the pastor who would be a blessing must preach the Gospel, and preach it with adverbs in his mind — earnestly, interestingly, fully." The Gospel should be preached Scripturally as Christ did (John 3:14-18), preached simply as Paul did (I Cor. 15: 1-4), preached earnestly as Peter did (Acts 2:14-40), preached lovingly as John did (I John 4:9-14), preached earnestly as Philip did (Acts 8:35-40), preached effectively as the woman did (John 4:42), preached passionately as the Apostle did, that is, in the power of the Spirit (I Peter 1:12), and preached practically by a consistent life as the Thessalonians did (I Thess. 1:7-10).—*Gospel Herald.*

* * *

With Christ at His Elbow

We must preach what has passed through the crucible of our own experience. We shall never produce conviction in others until truth is a burning conviction in our own souls. Bunyan says, "I preached what I did feel, what I smartingly did feel." When David Hume, the philosopher, had listened to John Brown, of Haddington, he remarked: "That's the man for me; he means what he says, he preaches as if Christ were at his elbow."—*United Methodist.*

Better Than Loving to Preach

When the Rev. George Pentecost had finished a discourse in the city of Edinburgh, Horatio Bonar put his hand upon his shoulder and said, "You love to preach to men, don't you?" And Dr. Pentecost answered, "Yes." And Mr. Bonar said, "Do you love the men you preach to?" That was Christian preaching in the days of Jesus Christ. "When he saw the multitudes, he was moved with compassion on them."—George Dowling.

* * *

He held a lamp each livelong day
So low that none could miss the way,
And yet so high to bring in sight
That picture fair, of Christ, the Light;
That gazing up, the lamp between
The hand that held it was not seen.

He held the pitcher, stooping low,
To lips of little ones below,
Then raised it to the weary saint
And bade him drink when sick and faint;
They drank, the pitcher thus between,
The hand that held it scarce was seen.

He blew the trumpet soft and clear
That trembling sinners need not fear:
And then with louder note and bold
To storm the walls of Satan's hold;
The trumpet coming thus between,
The hand that held it was not seen.

But when the Captain says, "Well done,
Thou good and faithful servant, come!
Lay down the pitcher and the lamp,
Lay down the trumpet, leave the camp!"
The weary hand will then be seen
Clasped in His pierced ones between.
—Selected.

* * *

Chalmers' Regret

When Dr. Chalmers was a guest in the house of a nobleman, among the gentlemen present was an old highland chieftain who kept his eyes fixed on Dr. Chalmers and listened to his conversation with intense interest. The subject was pauperism, and its causes and cure. At night the Doctor, whose room was near the chieftain's, heard a heavy groan, and on hastening to him, found him dying of apoplexy. As the company stood around, Dr. Chalmers, the very picture of distress, said tremulously: "Never before did I see the meaning of that text, 'Preach the word; be instant in season, out of season." Had I known what was to happen I would not have dwelt upon this evening's topic. I would have preached Jesus Christ and Him crucified. You would have thought it out of season, but ah! it would have been in season, both as respects Him and as it respects you."—*The Dawn.*

* * *

Preachers Without a Message

There was a young preacher, fresh from college, who went to the front during the first World War. He announced to the soldiers that he would let them choose as to whether he would preach or just tell them some funny stories. A tall, blunt-speaking fellow arose and said, "If you have come three thousand miles to talk to a bunch of soldiers some of whom are going into eternity within three days, and you don't know whether to preach to them or tell some funny stories, I suspect you had just better go ahead and tell something funny." What a condemnation on a preacher of the Gospel!—*Herald of Holiness.*

* * *

A Happy Meeting

Robert Moffat, the missionary to Africa, on one of his visits to his native country, had been engaged in a missionary service in the North of England, and was invited to stop for the night in the home of a friend. Here he met an aged minister named Caldwell. In the course of the conversation Moffat adverted to his mother, for whom he entertained the most devout regard.

Mr. Caldwell, whom Moffat did not know, not even his name, mentioned that he perceived that he was a Scotchman.

"Yes," said the missionary, "the scenes of my boyhood and youth in my native land are very dear to my memory. I often think of them when far away among the heathen. I often think of my excellent mother leading me when a little fellow to the old meeting house to hear an excellent minister whose name was Caldwell." He then spoke with enthusiasm of his mother, of the minister, and of the impressions he had received then and there.

The venerable listener rose up, with tears coursing down his cheeks, and exclaimed: "Can it be? Are you little Bobbie Moffat? Is Moffat the missionary, the little fellow whom his mother used to lead to my meeting house in Falkirk when I was a minister there many years ago?"

The mutual recognition, the embrace, the rapture, may be better conceived than described. The venerable Caldwell had not till then identified the little boy with the man who had done so much for Africa.

May there not be many surprises in store for workers when they enter into their rest in Heaven? We are favored even now to enjoy some instances of this happy nature; but what will be the unfolding of the pages of our life history in the perfect light of eternity? Christian worker, faint not, even in the darkest hour of discouragement. The wintry days and stormy nights will soon pass away; and then eternal peace and rest. —*Gospel Herald.*

* * *

Treated Like a Minister

"You look very much like a minister," said an English gentleman to Woodrow Wilson many years ago. "Have you ever been taken for one?" "No," was the reply, "but I have been treated like one." "And how was that?" "Well," said Mr. Wilson, "there was a time when I waited six months for my salary." *Christian Herald.*

* * *

The Tragic Omission

Jesus Christ, the Son of God and the sinner's Friend, should be the theme of every sermon. No other theme will so meet and minister to human needs.

It is said that on one occasion three people went into church to get help. The first was a business man who had failed and was contemplating suicide. The second was a youth of extravagant tastes who, finding his wages insufficient, was planning to steal from his employer. The third was a young woman of gay habits and conduct who had been tempted from the path of virtue. The choir arose and sang an anthem about building the walls of Zion. The minister addressed an eloquent prayer to the Lord, and then preached a sermon on the theme, "Is Mars Inhabited?" and thus the hungry souls that needed bread received stones.

The man committed suicide, the boy stole and landed in the penitentiary, and the woman went home to a life of shame. —*Westminster Teacher's Quarterly.*

* * *

Must We Sin?

A certain preacher closed his sermon with the declaration that "no man can live without sin." "No one," said he, "can keep the commandments. I break them all myself, every day and hour." He called upon a staunch old saint to close with prayer. The brother prayed about as follows: "O Lord, have mercy on us! Thou hast said: 'Thou shalt have no other gods before me, Remember the Sabbath day to keep it holy,' and 'Thou shalt not bear false witness;' and here is a preacher who says he breaks them all every day and hour. Thou hast said, 'Thou shalt not steal,' 'Thou shalt not commit adultery,' and Thou shalt not kill,' and here is a preacher who says he breaks every commandment every day and every hour. Lord have mercy on us, and send us a better preacher. Amen!" —*The Pentecostal Herald.*

* * *

That Blessed Sameness

When Spurgeon was criticized for a sameness in his messages, he admitted, "Perhaps they are right. It is true that no matter where I take my text, whether it be in the Old Testament or the New, I immediately hit across country to Jesus Christ, and preach Him and His saving grace."—Courtesy *Moody Monthly.*

Safe Hiding—For Foxes

The St. Louis *Globe-Democrat* declared that Bishop Chandler of Atlanta, apropos of worldly parsons, said a while ago: "There was a worldly parson of this type in Philadelphia — a great fox hunter — whom a Spruce Street Quaker took in hand. 'Friend,' said the Quaker, 'I understand thee's clever at fox-catching.' 'I have few equals and no superiors at that sport,' the parson complacently replied. 'Nevertheless, friend,' said the Quaker, 'if I were a fox I would hide where thee would never find me.' 'Where would you hide?' asked the parson, with a frown. 'Friend,' said the Quaker, 'I would hide in thy study.' "—courtesy *Moody Monthly.*

* * *

Preaching that Costs

A clergyman once told his bishop that he could preach and think nothing of it, and the prelate replied that the parishioners were of the same opinion. Work done easily, service which costs nothing, will have little come of it... Begin the day by pleading with God for men, and then go forth to plead with men for God.—C. H. Spurgeon.

* * *

How to Preach the Gospel

II Thessalonians 2:1-12.
With boldness (vs. 1, 2).
With sincerity (vs. 3, 4).
With honesty of purpose (vs. 5, 6).
With gentleness and affectionate desire (vs. 7, 8).
With labor and pain (vs. 9).
With the power of a godly example (vs. 19).
With the aim of producing a holy life (vs. 11, 12).

—John C. Page.

* * *

The Book She Needed

A special minister came to preach at the Mission Anniversary. The relater of the incident was, after the afternoon's service, wending his way homeward with old Mary Howarth. "Well, Mary," he said, "how have you enjoyed him this afternoon?" "None so grand," she answered. "I took the wrong book with me." He looked at the Bible under her arm and saw it was the large-print Bible she always carried to church, and so he said, "No, you didn't; it's your regular Bible you've got." "Ay," she said, "I know that, but it was the dictionary I needed this afternoon."—*Sunday School Times.*

* * *

Why Honored

An Indian sweeper who was a Christian used to attract great crowds as he preached the Gospel. One day a passer-by said scornfully: "Why do people gather so respectfully to listen to a sweeper?" "When the Saviour was riding to Jerusalem on an ass," replied the man. "people spread their garments beneath the feet of the ass. Not for the ass's sake, but because the King of kings was riding on it. When Christ got down from the ass, nobody cared any more about it. It was honored just as long as the King of kings was using it."—*Presbyterian Advance.*

* * *

"Do and Die"

It is related of the late Dr. Hinson, of Portland, Oregon, that two or three years ago, after undergoing an operation by which a large portion of his stomach was removed, he was warned by the surgeons that he must not preach anymore.

"Not preach anymore," said he; "and why not?"

"Because," replied the physician, "your physical condition will not permit it."

"Do you mean that if I preach I shall die?"

"Yes; that is precisely what will happen."

"Well, how long might I live if I stop preaching?"

"You might live for many years."

"And how long might I live if I preach?"

"You would probably die very soon."

"Well, then," decided the patient, "I'll preach and die."

The following is a quotation from the words of Dr. W. B. Hinson. Speaking from the pulpit a year after the commencement of the illness from which he ultimately died.

"I remember a year ago when a man in this city said, 'You have got to go to your death.' I walked out to where I live, five miles out of this city, and I looked across at that mountain that I love, and I looked at the river in which I rejoice, and I looked at the stately trees that are always God's own poetry to my soul. Then in the evening I looked up into the great sky where God was lighting His lamps, and I said, 'I may not see you many more times, but Mountain, I shall be alive when you are gone; and River, I shall be alive when you cease running toward the sea; and Stars, I shall be alive when you have fallen from your sockets in the great down-pulling of the material universe!'" This is the confidence of one who knew the Saviour. Is it yours?—Selected.

* * *

Preaching

On a certain occasion Gladstone said: "One thing I have against the clergy both of the country and in the towns. I think they are not severe enough on congregations. They do not sufficiently lay upon the souls and consciences of their hearers their moral obligations, and probe their hearts and bring up their whole lives and actions to the bar of conscience. The class of sermons which I think are most needed, are of the class which once offended Lord Melbourne. He was seen coming from church in the country in a great fume. Finding a friend, he exclaimed, 'It is too bad I have always been a supporter of the church, and I have always upheld the clergy, but it is really too bad to have to listen to a sermon like that we have heard this morning. Why, the preacher actually insisted upon applying religion to a man's private life!' But that is the kind of preaching which I like best, the kind of preaching which men need most, but it is, also, the kind of which they get the least."—Selected.

Undue Self-Depreciation

When John Knox was called to be a preacher in the Church of Saint Andrews, he was so embarrassed that, after an attempt to speak to the congregation, he burst into tears, rushed out, and shut himself up in his chamber. He determined never to appear again in the pulpit. Yet he afterwards became a powerful preacher, fearing not to face kings or queens.

It is a good thing for a man not to be too sure of himself, but undue self-depreciation is not to be commended. Isaiah's "Here am I; send me" is much better.—A. C. Crews, in *Westminster Teacher.*

* * *

The Bishop's "Wisdom"

A certain British bishop, hearing a young preacher in his first church, said to the young man that his method of preaching was not getting results. The bishop volunteered to preach a sermon to show how it ought to be done. He took as text: "The fool hath saith in his heart, There is no God." When he had finished, a humble parishioner was asked by the beaming bishop how he liked the sermon. "It was very fine," said the parishioner, "but somehow, in spite of all you said, I still believe there do be a God." And the bishop did no worse than many of the rest of us — trying to be impressive with big words and only covering up our meaning.—Newark, Ohio, *Advocate.*

* * *

"Preach Jesus"

The officials of a certain church were not satisfied with the sermons their new young minister had been preaching. One Sunday morning they placed a little slip of paper on the pulpit Bible where the minister would not fail to notice it when he ascended the platform. When he discovered the note he picked it up and read these two significant words: "*Preach Jesus.*"—*Gospel Herald.*

A Time to Shout

The construction boss was surveying the work on a tall building from his place on the street. Looking up he saw two men about to venture out on some unsupported timbers. Immediately he began to shout to them; "Get back there! Don't step on that timber. Hey, you fellows, haven't you any sense?" The man's great bellowing voice attracted the attention of a police officer several blocks away, who came running to the spot. "Here!" he called, "Can't you give orders without making all that noise? What are you doing, anyway?" "Just trying to keep some idiots up there from breaking their necks," was the reply. "What'd you want me to do, sing 'em to sleep?"—*The Lookout.*

* * *

Pity the Preacher

A Texas paper comments as follows: "The preacher has a great time. If his hair is gray he is too old; if he is a young man he hasn't had experience enough; if he has ten children he has too many; if he has none he is not setting a good example. If his wife sings in the choir, she is presuming; if she doesn't she isn't interested in her husband's work. If a preacher reads from notes he is a bore; if he speaks extemporaneously he isn't deep enough. If he stays at home in his study he does not mix enough with his people; if he is seen around on the streets he ought to be home getting out a good sermon. If he calls at the homes of the wealthy, he is an aristocrat; if he calls on the poor family, then he is playing to the grandstand. Whatever he does, some one could have told him to do better."

So pity the poor preacher.—The United Evangelical.

* * *

To Dying Men

It is said of a famous preacher that he always preached "as a dying man to dying men." It is such preaching that is always effective. A minister visiting a penitentiary one Saturday, was invited by the Christian warden to speak to the inmates the next day. That evening the minister felt impressed to go to the penitentiary and learn the details regarding the service. Noting two chairs draped in black in the main assembly room he inquired as to the reason. Said the warden, "These two chairs are draped for death. Your sermon will be the last these men will ever hear." You can realize that Browning and Emerson figured very little in the sermon that was delivered on that occasion. There are chairs in most audiences draped for death.—*The Toronto Globe.*

* * *

Man-Centered Preaching

A layman who had been long from home, on his return made it his business to take his little girl to church with him regularly, that she might learn the way of Christ. After attending various churches he said that he seldom heard the name of Christ as Saviour proclaimed, and his little girl several times asked him, "When is the preacher going to tell about Jesus?"—courtesy *Moody Monthly.*

* * *

"That Gives Me Peace"

Sainted Bishop Whipple of Minnesota sat by the sick bedside of a cultured, old judge in the Southland, talking in his scholarly way. At last the judge politely said, "Pardon me; but you know I'm facing the real things. Won't you talk to me like you'd talk to my black boy Jim?"

And the Bishop said quietly, "You're a sinner, like me. Jesus died for our sins. Trust Him as a little child." And the judge said, "Thank you, Bishop, I can get hold of that. That gives me peace."

When one faces the real things of life, or beyond, it's touch with the Man of the Calvary Hill that gives peace. —S. D. Gordon.

* * *

Ministers' Wives

A quiet observer sees many wise things,
And that's why this writer so frequently
sings:

He notes that since preachers have arduous lives,
God saves the best girls for ministers' wives.
She keeps down expenses and pays up their dues,
And cheers up her husband when he has the blues.
She tends her own babies and some others, too,
And nurses and cheers many sick women **through.**

She's here and she's there, all over the town,
With a bright, sunny smile and never a frown;
She coaxes wild fellows to slacken their pace,
Reform their habits and better the race,
Persuades the girls inclined to be flirts
To cover their necks and lengthen their skirts;
She's kind to the poor and nurses the sick,
And people say, "She's a regular brick!"

Her husband comes first in all of her plans,
Although she's a sister to every good man;
She tells him his sermon's a little too long,
And that Johnson's new clerk has been going wrong;
Her home is a refuge for all the oppressed,
And come when they may, they find her well dressed.
All classes declare she has blessed their lives,
And say that none equal these ministers' wives.

Don't pity your preacher, but pay him his dues,
And heed what he says and bury bad news;
Some day a great sorrow may come to your home,
And then you will find you are glad he has come.
And, if in your house some dear one should die,
He'll point the way plainly to Jesus on high;
His tender devotion, his prayer and his love
Will seem like a blessing from heaven above.

In public and private, you'll find him the same,
The friend of all classes, of whatever name;
He tries to be helpful, but sometimes he fails;
When he points out men's sins, he's often assailed.
Be fair in your judgment, be honest, sincere,
And no one will come to your heart quite so near;
If preachers are blessings, sometimes in disguise,
Remember it's due to these ministers' wives.

—Howard W. Pope.

* * *

Why Some Sermons Fail

Methodist layman visited a great city church in Ohio during a business trip. After the service he congratulated the minister on his service and sermon. "But," said the manufacturer, "if you were my salesman I'd discharge you. You got my attention by your appearance, voice and manner; your prayer, reading and logical discourse aroused my interest; you warmed my heart with a desire for what you preached; and then — and *then you stopped, without asking me to do something about it.* In business, *the important thing is to get them to sign on the dotted line."—Record of Christian Work.*

* * *

Our Pastor

Who is it calls when we are ill
With cheerful words and right good will,
And lingers gently then to pray
And soothe our care and fear away?
Our Pastor!

Who is it comes when sorrow falls,
When death of friends our heart appalls,
And tells us of the mansions fair
And that sweet home, "just over there"?
Our Pastor!

Who is it shares our happiest hours,
When life is crowned with wedding flowers,
And to the scene lends added grace
By reverent voice and kindly face?
Our Pastor!

Who is it that on Sabbath day
Points us to heaven, and leads the way,
And brings a message from the Word,
Until our hearts within are stirred?
Our Pastor!

For whom then shall we daily pray
And ask for him God's grace alway,
And wish for him a glad New Year,
With new-born souls his heart to cheer?
Our Pastor!

—Lena G. Browne, Pasadena, Calif.

* * *

A Radio Parable

To modernize the parable of the sower into a form that is not nearly as beautiful, we might say: "Behold, a broadcaster was speaking forth the words of eternal life. Some, as soon as he began, turned off the radio. Others listened, but when they found that to understand him would require real mental effort, and to apply him to life would require sacrifice, they, too, turned off the radio, or shifted to another wave length. Some kept their radio on until the whole speech was finished, but in the meantime they looked over the evening paper and commented now and then upon the sporting news and the market reports, so that at the end they had really no deep understanding of what was said. Others listened intently, meditated on what they had heard, applied it to life, and were transformed."—*Christian Advocate.*

* * *

Enough Said

A minister was annoyed by people talking and giggling during the service. He paused, looked at the disturbers, and said: "Some years ago as I was preaching a young man who sat before me was constantly laughing, talking and making uncouth grimaces. I paused and administered a severe rebuke. After the close of the services a gentleman said to me: 'Sir, you made a great mistake. That young man is an idiot.' Since then I have been afraid to reprove those who misbehave in chapel lest I should repeat that mistake and reprove another idiot."

During the rest of the service there was good order.—*Watchman-Examiner.*

* * *

"No Good to Anybody"

A certain minister is said to have been unable to say, "No," to any request that came to him. He was invited to speak for other ministers, and at clubs and banquets and other gatherings, until his own church had but a small fraction of his time, and his home was neglected. One day, while walking alone by a lake, he met a man who was about to drown a small dog. "What's wrong with the dog?" he inquired. "Well, you see," said the man, "When Gipsy was a pup, he was all right. But he has grown to be a regular nuisance. We are always losing him. He follows everyone. And a dog that follows everybody is no good to anybody." The last sentence struck the minister like a blow. He begged for the dog and took him home, saying, "Gyp, you and I will learn faithfulness together!" And then and there began a new era in his life and usefulness.—*Sunday School Times.*

* * *

Dead In Earnest

Moody was the most earnest evangelist I ever heard. He had no mannerisms, very few gestures, and seldom raised his voice to a shout; but his deep and unaffected piety, his apposite figures of speech, his humor, his solid common sense, his thrilling earnestness, made him amazingly effective. He did great good, and as he hated hysteria and sensationalism, he never did any harm. He was a man of genius. In later years I got to know him intimately, both at his school at Northfield and during his visits to Yale; it was impossible to talk with him without feeling his sincerity and his knowledge of human nature. . . . When I was an undergraduate, he preached one Sunday at Yale. Attendance was compulsory and the attention to the average sermon was not very keen; and most sermons were no longer than twenty minutes. Mr. Moody preached for one hour, and held the breathless attention of the students.—Wm. Lyon Phelps of Yale.

* * *

"Answer a Fool—"

Beau Nash objected to Wesley's preaching in the city of Bath, alleging that "it frightened people out of their wits." "Sir," inquired the great evangelist, "did you ever hear me preach?" "No," was the reply. "How, then, can you judge of what you never heard?" "*By common report.*" "Sir," came Wesley's crushing rejoinder, "is not your name Nash? *I dare not judge of you by common report.*"—*Torch Bearer.*

* * *

"Give Them Their Letters at Once"

When Henry Ward Beecher was yet a young man in the ministry, he was faced with the demand of a prominent member of his church to put the soft pedal on the slavery question. He was told if he did not keep quiet he would lose six of his most prominent families. He answered, "Give me their names now, please, that I may give them their letters at once!"

He rightly judged that such families who tried to hog-tie the true testimony of the preacher were better out of the church than in.—*Christian Victory.*

* * *

"Wrong Stuff" for the Sick

In a school examination the examiner put the question, "What is false doctrine?" Up went a little boy's hand, and there came the answer, "It's when the doctor gives the wrong stuff to the people who are sick." False doctrine (doctorin') indeed! Reports of sermons that we see in the press, and that we hear from some preachers, show that there are pulpit doctors who are giving the "wrong stuff" to sin-sick souls.—*Sunday School Times.*

Fact or Fiction?

A minister asked Macready, the actor, "Why do you draw out crowds to see you act while no one comes to hear me preach?" and received the answer, "I act my fiction as though it were fact; you preach your facts as though they were fiction!" Nowhere is it easier to play with the gospel than in the ministry. With a pleasing personality, a gift of eloquence,a fine moral character and plenty of business sense, one can take the gospel for a football and make a great many goals. *But preaching is no game, and woe unto him who plays at it, whether he pipe or whether he mourn!*—Vance Havner, in *Revelation.*

* * *

Why the Sermon Went Home

Once, after a certain Philadelphia minister had completed the service, as he was leaving the pulpit, he was met by an old colored man, a former slave. The tears were rolling down his cheeks, and he said: "Oh, Massa Allen! dat was a heap good sermon yo' gave us today. I understood ev'ry word. Yo' preached just as if yo' was one of us niggers." The minister was delighted with the compliment. It was one of the best he had ever received.—*Christian Herald.*

* * *

He Knew What to Expect

A preacher friend told us of this experience: He recently met a prominent citizen of his community whom he had noticed in attendance at his church on several occasions. At this meeting he questioned him as to his church membership, by way of introducing a more important question. The man responded: "Oh, I belong to Dr. Blank's church. When I want to hear about Dumbarton Oaks I go to my own church. When I want to hear about God I go to yours." Enough said.—Courtesy *Moody Monthly.*

* * *

What They Missed

A brilliant young preacher went to his first church, full of pride, learning, and forensic ability. His congregation had a certain pride, too, in this newly acquired product of the theological seminary, with two degrees after his name and many ohs! and ahs! after his breathless perorations. But they missed something. One day when the young man entered his pulpit, crammed with reason and rhetoric, he saw a note pinned on his pulpit sofa, bearing the legend, "Sir, we would see Jesus." The fire died on the altar of learning that day. Ere he returned to the pulpit again he had built another altar, and above it was a form like unto the Son of man, and they who came to be thrilled, remained to pray. On a later Sunday the young minister found another note pinned on the pulpit sofa, which read, "Then were the disciples glad when they saw the Lord."—*Revival Pulpit.*

* * *

"I love those that thunder out the Word," said Whitefield. "The Christian world is in a deep sleep. Nothing but a loud voice can awaken them out of it."

* * *

"Nothing is more indecent that a dead preacher speaking to dead sinners the living truth of the living God."—Baxter.

Popular Preaching

Amaziah's attitude toward the message of Amos (Amos 7:12, 13) reminds us much of the lines of Charlotte Perkins Gilman:

Preach about the other man, Preacher!
 The man we all can see!
The man of oaths, the man of strife,
The man who drinks and beats his wife,
Who helps his mates to fret and shirk
When all they need is to keep at work—
Preach about the other man, Preacher!
 Not about me!

—*Sunday School Times.*

* * *

The Best Source of Instruction

It is related that one of his hearers once asked, "How is it that Mr. Bramwell always has something that is new to tell us when he preaches?" "Why," said the person interrogated, "you see, Brother Bramwell lives so near the gates of Heaven that he hears a great many things that we don't get near enough to hear anything about."—C. H. Spurgeon.

PRIDE

His "Trumpet"

Humorous incidents happen even on the mission field. I think that it was in an African village that a native Christian went to the village merchant to purchase a pair of shoes. He was fitted out with a suitable pair, and went away happy. Some weeks later he brought the shoes back. "Did they not fit? Were they not good?" asked the merchant. "Yes." "Then why are you returning them?" "Because they don't have any squeak." It appeared that the man wanted a pair of shoes that would squeak as he walked up the aisle of the church. He wanted something that would draw attention to himself. That type of Christian is as old as the church.—*Christian Union Herald.*

Safe Righteousness

A man may with utter sincerity trust in his own life as sufficient to justify him before God, but he has no conception of how searching is the judgment storm that is coming. The builder of the first Eddystone Lighthouse was so enamored of his designs and workmanship that he said, "I wish nothing better than to be in my building in a storm." He was; *and neither he nor the lighthouse was ever heard of again.* There is only one righteousness which will stand the hurricane of judgment. A London clergyman, called to the garret of a dying man, found him plunged into anxiety over the mystery of a torn text. A stray leaf from a torn Testament had caught his eye. It was part of Romans 3. He read the portrait of the sinner, and recognized it as his own; but as he read on—"But now the righteousness of God without the law is"—the leaf was torn off. "Is *what?*" cried the dying man. What worlds on worlds hang on the answer! Withheld, refused, withdrawn, forgotten, cancelled? *The rest ofthe verse he drank in as life to the soul*—"is manifested."—*The Dawn.*

* * *

When Self Gets in the Way

"Some of us are so full of ourselves," says a writer in the *Canadian Baptist,* "and our busy servings, that we cannot see Christ in all His beauty. Some years ago, when I was away on a preaching appointment, my wife and little daughter stayed at the home of a friend. On the bedroom wall, just over the head of the bed in which they slept, there was a picture of the Lord Jesus, which was reflected in the large mirror of the dressing table standing in the bay of the bedroom window. When my little daughter woke on her first morning there, she saw the picture reflected in the mirror while she still lay in bed, and exclaimed, 'Oh, Mummy, I can see Jesus through the mirror!' Then she quickly kneeled up to take a better look, but in so doing brought her own body between the picture and the mirror, so that instead of seeing the picture of Jesus reflected, she now saw herself. So she lay down again, and again she saw the picture of Jesus. She was up and down several times after that with her eyes fixed on the mirror. Then she said, 'Mummy, when I can't see myself, I can see Jesus; but every time I see myself, I don't see Him.' How true it is that when self fills the vision we do not see Jesus!"—*Sunday School Times.*

* * *

No Place for Pride

Two ladies at Shanghai once got to talking about Mr. Taylor, wondering if he was ever tempted to be proud. One of the ladies went and asked Mrs. Taylor. She did not know. But Mrs. Taylor went and asked Mr. Taylor. He was surprised and inquired, "Proud about what?" Mrs. Taylor replied, "Why, about the things you have done." Then immediately came this beautiful answer, "I never knew I had done anything." And Mr. Taylor was right; he never had done anything, for it was God who had wrought in and through him. Only, there was this difference between this man of God and some other persons: he knew it, and others do not. As it was with Mr. Taylor, so should it be with us. When we have done all, greatly and grandly, then let us say, "We are but unprofitable servants," and so give the glory of our successful service to God, to Him alone —*China's Millions.*

* * *

Why She Went to Church

A milliner says that one day a woman came into the store, and wanted the trimming on her new hat changed, saying it had been trimmed on the wrong side. "But," said the saleslady, "the trimming is on the left side. That is where it ought to be." "It doesn't make any difference where it ought to be, . . . it's got to be on the church side." "Church side!" gasped the astonished girl. "Yes, I sit next to the wall. I want it on the other side so the whole congregation can see it." And that hat applies to many other things, in men as well as women, that distract from true worship. —*Sunday School Times.*

* * *

Letting Her Down

A girl went to a Catholic priest and confessed that she had incurred the sin of vanity. "What makes you think that?" asked the priest. "Because every morning, when I look into the mirror," she replied, "I think how beautiful I am." "Never fear," said the priest, "that isn't sin—that's just a mistake." Some fancy they have attained sinless perfection, but the mirror of the Word of God should be sufficient to show them that it is a mistake. The nearer men come to Christ, the more they feel how immeasurably short they fall of the beauty of holiness found in Him.—*Sunday School Times.*

Expensive Chandeliers Not the Secret

I recollect a little town where there was a chapel, the people connected with which thought that if they could only buy a chandelier that was on sale, they would cut out all the other chapels entirely, and everybody would feel that they were made weighty and respectable people, and that the place would be filled with people to see the chandelier. I believe for a time it was, but its light grew dim, and they found that was not the way in which the light of the kingdom of God was to be spread.—C. H. Spurgeon.

* * *

Pride Is a Weed

Plants grow only in certain soils, or at certain heights, or under certain lines of latitude. Unlike these, pride is a weed that, springing up in every heart, grows at all elevations—as well in the humblest as in the highest stations of life; and under every system of religion, the true as well as the false.—*Gospel Herald.*

* * *

His Boy's Admiring Question

I have heard of a boy whose father was forever teling of his exploits at Bull Run, and Gettysburg, and Cold Harbor, who listened one day while the sire waxed eloquent afresh over the same tales. When he concluded, the astonished admiring son said, "Father, did anyone help you put down the rebellion?" Mark Guy Pearse said, "My faith in perfection is very weak when I look at others; it is extinguished altogether when I look at myself."—*Sunday School Times.*

* * *

Set Aside

A recent account tells of an Australian who discovered a pearl perfect in shape, in color, and almost an inch in diameter, but which, though practically invaluable, could not be sold, for it was too large to be used as a ring setting, and few other pearls could be found to match so that it might be part of a necklace.

Thus it is with the proud and haughty Christian: he may have more than ordinary ability; be well versed in God's Word and possess fine personality; but pride, selfishness, vitriolic condemnations of others, unmannerliness and boasting, will render his otherwise invaluable services valueless, and he is set aside, while God uses a more humble, obedient servant, though perhaps one with less ability, to perform his work.—R. G. D.

* * *

Goethe's Needless Distress

One afternoon Goethe and Beethoven walked out together in the Carlsbad Valley to talk at ease. Everywhere, as they walked, passers-by saluted them, pointed them out, and bowed with ostentatious deference. "Isn't it maddening?" exclaimed Goethe. "I simply can't escape this homage." "Don't be too much distressed by it," said Beethoven; "it is just possible that some of it may be for me." —*Christian Faith and Life.*

* * *

Clemenceau's Own Epitaph

The world is always reissuing Ecclesiastes in italics. M. Clemenceau, one of the half dozen giants of World War I, passing the grave he had had dug for himself, said to his secretary: "Take a look at it. There, in a nutshell, is all you can say about me—a hole in the ground and a great deal of noise about nothing." The most exalted sinner dies without God *and without hope.* — *The Dawn.*

* * *

Our Greatest Hindrance

Spiritual pride is a great hindrance to spiritual growth. When the saintly James Harvey was a young curate, he frequently talked with a wise old plowman named Clayton. One day the subject under discussion was this: "What is the greatest impediment to spiritual growth and happiness?" The curate said: "Surely to renounce our sinful self." "No," said the plowman, "the greatest difficulty is to renounce our righteous self."—*Sunday School Times.*

Chief Justice Hughes' Interest

"But" is a little word, but my, what a big word it is! Some years ago, when Chief Justice Charles E. Hughes of the United States Supreme Court was the United States delegate to the Pan-American conference at Havana, an interpreter was whispering into Mr. Hughes' ear the flowery introduction by a local orator. Mr. Hughes stopped his aide, saying, "Don't bother about interpreting anything until he says 'but.' Give me everything after that." — *Buffalo Evening News.*

* * *

The Wrong Measure

A little boy came running to his mother, shouting, "Mother, I am nine feet high!" His mother said, "Don't talk such nonsense." He answered, "I really am nine feet high." She said, "What makes you think so?" "Because I measured myself." "How did you measure yourself?" "I took off my shoe and measured myself with that. It is just the same size as my foot, and I really am nine feet." "Oh, I understand now." said his mother, "but, Sonny, your measure was not the right one. You may be nine feet high measured by your shoe, but you are not that tall measured by a twelve-inch ruler." The Bible says that people, "measuring themselves by themselves . . . are not wise."—*Sunday School Times.*

* * *

Ancestor Worship

Sir Thomas Overbury once remarked, "The man who has nothing to boast of but his ancestors is like a potato—the only good belonging to him is underground."—*Sunday School Chronicle.*

* * *

The Highbrows

A highbrow is a man who is educated above his intelligence, and tells you things you already know in language that you cannot understand. — *The Watchman-Examiner.*

Inflating Pride

Up in the mountains of North Carolina, lived a farmer who had a poor farm with thin soil, where he worked hard, but was barely able to make a living for himself, wife and son. The son, however, was a remarkably bright boy, and easily surpassed all the other boys in the district school. One day, the father said to the mother, "Our son is a natural born scholar, and if he is only a poor farmer's son, he shall have as good an education as a millionaire's son." The father and mother economized and raked and scraped and got enough together to send the boy off to college. The boy did well at college, and every little while sent a letter home, telling how well he was doing in his classes. "Mother, these letters are all right," said the father. "They do cheer my old heart, but letters are not enough. My heart is lonely for the boy and I must see him. I cannot wait. I must see him!" Loading up his old farm wagon that afternoon, he got up before sunrise next morning and started for the college town. It was a long, tedious journey, but it did not seem long to the farmer, for he was going to see his boy! Every hour of his dreary journey, as he drew near the college town, his heart grew lighter and happier. "In a little while now, I'll see my boy. Won't he be surprised! Won't he be glad!" As he drove up the hill towards the college, who should he see coming down the sidewalk but his boy with two gay young college companions. "There he comes! There he comes!" said the old man. He jumped off the wagon and ran to meet his son, who had not seen him. "My son," he cried. His son was surpised, but was not glad. He was ashamed of his father in his plain old homespun clothes before his gay college companions. "There must be some mistake, sir," he said. "I am not your son; you are not my father. I do not know you. There must be some mistake, sir!" He might as well have driven a dagger into his father's heart. I am told that the father went home with a broken heart to die.—R. A. Torrey.

PROCRASTINATION

Too Late

A bright boy heard and was deeply impressed by the text, "My son, give Me thine heart." But Satan whispered, *"Time enough yet,"* and he put it off. Ten years later a brilliant college student heard the same text under the circumstances which seemed to make that the time of his salvation. Again the tempter whispered, *"Time enough yet."* Twenty years later a statesman listened to the same text from the lips of an aged bishop, and felt it was a message to him. This time the tempter said, *"Visit foreign countries before you decide."* A traveler in Paris was stricken with cholera. But his greatest suffering was agony of soul because he was not prepared to die. His last words were, *"Too late."* The boy, the college student, the statesman, the traveler were all one.—*Dawn.*

* * *

The Sun Dial's Question

A boy sat bneath the tall Gothic towers of Beverly Minster in Yorkshire. The great question of giving his heart to the Saviour had been troubling him. "Put it off a little while. There is plenty of time," whispered the tempter. "No, decide at once for Christ," urged that other Voice. Thus the conflict went on through the long bright summer afternoon. It was decided at length as the boy lifted his eyes to the spot where the ancient sun dial on the Minster wall marked the progress of the day. He did not dwell so much on the shadow on the plate as on the words inscribed as a motto, "Now, or when?" "When," he thought, "when shall I give my heart to God?—Now or when?" For a moment he paused and looked up once more at the sundial on which the shadow was rapidly declining. "Now!" he said aloud, and jumping up, ran home. That was the moment of decision in the life of one whose devoted labors and saintly life are still remembered by many. — Canon Jackson of Leeds, in the *Church Army Gazette.*

Don't Wait

On the church calendar of St. Peter's Vicarage, the church of the well-known British Keswick speaker, the Rev. J. Russell Howden, is this striking sentence: "Those people who expect salvation at the eleventh hour often die at 10:30." Postponement is perilous in spiritual matters.—*Sunday School Times.*

* * *

The Time to Get Ready

There is an old fable that once upon a time a wild boar of the jungle was whetting his tusks against the trunk of a tree. A fox passing by asked him why he did this, seeing that neither hunter nor hound was near. "True," said the boar, "but *when that danger does arise I shall have something else to do than to sharpen my weapon."*—*Earnest Worker.*

* * *

Mrs. Tsan's Zeal

"Why, Mrs. Tsan, where did you come from?" exclaimed the missionary as the woman entered.

"Oh, Miss Kan, I'm so tired. I'm so tired! I've walked fifteen miles today" (her feet were bound and encased in shoes not more than three inches long, and she carried a child huddled in her coat), "because I heard that you were going to the city soon, and I have not learned the Lord's Prayer yet."

"But why did you not wait till I came back again?"

"Who knows whether I shall be living when you come again? I want to learn it now."

"But you can't learn it tonight, and I am going to Peking tomorrow morning."

"I must learn it tonight. I will learn it tonight! I'll learn it right now; you begin."

And so the missionary began, and the woman repeated it after her, nor would she go to bed nor allow the missionary to retire until she could repeat the prayer from beginning to end.

This is a true story told by Dr. Isaac T. Headland, and "Miss Kan" is Mrs. Headland.—*Tarbell's Teachers' Guide.*

One Month Too Late

At a prayer meeting in a country neighborhood in Western Washington a young man appeared to be much convicted. An earnest worker in the meeting went to him and lovingly pleaded with him to seek the Lord. He hesitated, but finally said, "No, I will attend to that matter when I am through hauling logs; I have one month to work yet." Four weeks from that day he and a young friend went bathing in Lake Tacoma. He was using profane language while undressing. Plunging into the lake, he swam into the deep, cold water. He was taken with a cramp, screamed wildly for help, then sank to the bottom. He was one month too late!—*Gospel Herald.*

* * *

Danger in Delay

An Indian native told a missionary that he believed on Jesus Christ and meant to give Him his love some day.

A native helper turned and said: "If you and I were walking through the jungles and came face to face with a tiger, if I placed myself in front, and said, 'Run, brother, for your life!' would you love me?"

"Yes, surely!"

"When? Some day?"

The native saw the point and said: "I will give myself to Him now, and you must baptize me tomorrow."—*Presbyterian Syndicated Calendar.*

* * *

Tonight or Never

At the close of a meeting held in a mining district in England, a stalwart miner, in deep anxiety of soul, walked up to the preacher to inquire what he had to do to be saved. God's Word, through the power of the Holy Spirit, had touched his heart, and he had made the awful discovery that he was a lost sinner on the way to everlasting perdition.

The preacher unfolded to him the way of salvation. He showed him, from Scripture, that Christ came into the world "to seek and to save that which was lost"; how He of His own free will gave His life a ransom for us, so that God's righteous sentence of death as to the wages of sin having been borne by our Divine Substitute, all who simply believe on Him—all who rest on His finished work — are saved. All seemed dark to the miner. The burden of unforgiven sin pressed heavily upon him. As the hours passed, the preacher urged him to turn from self and sin, and "behold the Lamb of God, which taketh away the sin of the world." No impression appeared to be made, and as it was now 11 o'clock the preacher told the miner it was time to go home, suggesting that he should return to the chapel on the following evening.

With an agonizing look the poor fellow replied, "No, I won't leave; it must be settled tonight or never!"

They remained together. Hours passed and the anxious inquirer did not lay hold of the soul-saving truth; but as the clock struck three, the light of the glorious Gospel suddenly burst upon him. He saw and believed the glorious fact that the work of Christ on the Cross had satisfied the justice of God on account of his sins, and joy and peace filled his heart. Rising from his seat, and clasping his hands together, he exclaimed, "It's settled now, Christ is mine!"

He thanked the servant of God who had been the instrument of leading him to the Saviour, and soon afterwards went to his work in the coalpit, happy and rejoicing, because a saved man.

In the course of the day a sudden crash was heard by those in the neighborhood of the pit. Part of the roofing of the mine had fallen in, burying a number of men beneath it.

As quickly as possible willing hands set to work to excavate the earth in order to rescue those who were underneath. After working for some time they heard a sound, and digging with renewed energy in the direction whence it proceeded, they reached the converted miner. Life was not quite gone, for he was speaking. Eagerly they listened, and the words they caught were these: "Thank God, it was settled last night." They were the last words he uttered. When taken out life was extinct. The happy, redeemed spirit had "departed to be with Christ." Little did the miner think how solemnly true the memorable words which he had uttered the preceding night were to prove in his own case: "It must be settled tonight or never."—*Gospel Herald.*

* * *

" 'Tis Always Now"

'Tis always NOW, tomorrow never comes.
Where'er we go, or be, it is today;
Yet, e'en "today" not long with us will stay,
'Tis here, then gone; how quickly NOW succumbs!

What thou wouldst do, do quickly! do it now;
Wouldst thou be saved? Do not procrastinate;
Now is thy time; beware, ere 'tis too late,
While yet 'tis day, thy faith in Christ avow.

Wouldst thou the gospel story tell to someone lost?
Or wouldst thou go to lands which lie afar,
And preach the gospel, be a guiding-star?
Now is the time to go; count not the cost.

—R. E. Neighbour.

* * *

Without Remedy

One day my telephone rang and a lady asked me to come down and visit her husband, who was very, very sick, and unsaved. I went and stood by the bed—the man had double pneumonia—and I said, "Old boy, I am sorry you are so sick." After a while, as the Lord helped me, I talked of the Lord Jesus, and the man said, "Here and now I receive Him; and I will tell you what I will do; if the Lord will restore me, I will forsake my sin, and I will come down and be baptized."

In a few days I went again to see him, and he was out of danger. On the third visit I found him sitting on the woodpile watching his chickens — he loved good horses and fine chickens. I said, "You will soon be ready to come to church." He replied, "Brother Neighbour, I am going to keep my promise and unite with your church and be baptized a week from next Sunday."

A couple of weeks went by and he did not come. One day I saw him on the street riding a beautiful black steed. I hailed him and said, "Wait a minute, old boy. I thought you were coming on to live for Christ." He said, "Oh, Brother, I will come!" But he did not.

Then one day I met a grocery-man, a member of our church, and he said, "We are going to have a sudden death in this city." I said, "Who do you think is going to die?" He said, "The man that promised you all sorts of things when he was dying. The Word of God says, 'He, that being often reproved hardeneth his neck, shall suddenly be destroyed, and that without remedy.' "

I do not believe a week passed until I heard that man's wife, over the telephone, say, "Oh, Brother Neighbour, come! B. is dead! He was at a banquet at the hotel and he fell over dead." I think that was the saddest funeral I ever attended.—R. E. Neighbour.

* * *

A Week Too Late

God forbid that any of you should, at the last, have the dismay of the woman Dr. Talmage used to tell about. One night she could not sleep because of her soul's anxiety about the future without Christ. She got up and wrote in her diary: "One year from now. I will attend to the matter of my soul." She retired, but she could not sleep. So she arose again, and wrote a better promise in her diary: "One month from now I will attend to the matter of my soul." She retired again but found no sleep; and arose again and wrote: "Next week I will attend to the matter of my soul." Then she slept soundly. The next day she went into scenes of gaiety. The following day she was sick, and the middle of the next week she died. Delirium lifted from her mind just long enough for her to say: "I am a week too late. I am lost!" To be a week too late, or even an hour too late, is to be forever lost! May God Almighty, by His grace, keep us from the awful experience of a ruined soul! Abner promised a kingdom, but could not insure his life for one day. Haman plumed himself upon the prospect of the queen's banqet, but was hanged like a dog before night.—*Gospel Herald.*

* * *

Deadly Indecision

I sat one day by the far-away shores of the Great Lakes listening to a tragic story from the lips of a white-haired fisherman. Years before, he said, when the village was but a hamlet the mail was carried from the distant shore of the bay to the fishing village by an Indian and his son-in-law. One bitter day in mid-winter they set out from the south shore for the long trip across the Great Lake. All day they traveled on the ice, skirting the frozen shore of the bay. As night came on they pitched their tent and went ashore for firewood. Gathering what they needed they started back from the mainland toward camp. Just as they stepped upon the ice it broke loose from its moorings and began to drift out from the shore. The boy, quick-witted and alert, immediately dropped his bundle of wood and leaped across the crevice in the ice. The father-in-law hesitated a moment and in that moment the gap widened too much to over-leap. He paused in hesitation, for the waters were black and forbidding in their deadly chill. The boy shouted to the older man to leap in and swim to shore, as that was his only chance for life. But the old man still delayed. Then the lad began to cry out in earnest entreaty for his father-in-law to leap, as it was his only chance to be saved from a dreadful death. The older man seemed paralyzed with fear and indecision. He began to call out farewell messages for his wife and children across the watery waste now rapidly widening as the wind kept drifting the great ice-floe out into the darkness. The last the boy saw him he was standing with outstretched arms drifting to death in the bitter cold and darkness of the night. He perished a victim of deadly indecision. "How shall we escape, if we neglect so great salvation?"—James H. McConkey.

* * *

Our Most Dangerous Enemy

Said J. L. Ralston: "Our most dangerous enemy on this side of the Atlantic is *the idea that we have plenty of time.*" This is equally true in the matter of preparedness for eternity — as well as for our country! Because we know not when we may lose the use of our faculties, because we have no lease of our lives, because we know not when the Lord Jesus will come again, and because the Word commands it, we should act *NOW.—Now.*

* * *

Coming! Coming!

The turnpike stood on a quiet country road, and, especially at night, the traffic was not very great. So the old turnpike man used to shut his gate when darkness descended on wood and moor, and retire to bed.

One night, when the rain was falling, and neither stars nor moon dispelled the blackness in which trees and road and heather disappeared, a horseman cautiously approached the gate, dismounted, and knocked for the turnpike keeper.

"Gate! gate!" he cried.

"Coming!" replied the old man.

Out there in the pitiless rain and the silence and the gloom the horseman remembered his cosy home, and became impatient to be gone. So he knocked again.

"Gate! gate!" he cried.

"Coming! coming!" repeated the voice.

After another long delay, during which he felt the rain penetrating his clothes, he again banged at the door.

"Gate! gate!" he cried more impatiently.

"Coming! coming!" was the reply.

But still the turnpike man did not appear, and the horseman became quite angry.

He opened the door, and, putting in his head, demanded—

"Why do you say, 'Coming, coming,' this twenty minutes, and yet you never appear?"

"Who is there?" asked the old man in a sleepy voice. "Oh! I ask your pardon, sir, but I get so used to hearing 'em knock, that I answers, 'Coming, coming,' in my sleep, then I takes no more notice."

How many there are who have become so accustomed to the sound of the Gospel that they hear without listening, and without understanding! How many have said, again and again, when they have heard God's call, "Coming, coming," and have never meant it at all!—*Glad Tidings.*

PROPHECY

Prophecy Fulfilled Under Our Eyes

Most ministers and Bible teachers give small attention today to the study and exposition of predictive prophecy. Even the large bulk of space given in the Scriptures to prophetical writings would seem to suggest a different course. But it is still more embarrassing to consider that such neglect seems to ignore teachings to which the Spirit of God gives large prominence and emphasis.

Our attention has been directed to a particular instance of prophecy which was uttered sixteen centuries B.C. and the fulfillment of which has transpired within the last few years. The prophecy relates to the future of Zebulun, one of the twelve tribes, and what should happen in their tribal allotment in Palestine. It was uttered by Jacob in his blessing to the tribes, and later by Moses, as follows:

"Zebulun shall dwell at the haven of the sea; and he shall be for a haven of ships; and his borders shall be unto Zidon" (Gen. 49:13).

"And of Zebulun he said, Rejoice, Zebulun, in thy coming out . . . they shall call the peoples unto the mountain; there shall they offer sacrifices of righteousness, for they shall suck the abundance of the seas and the hidden treasures of the sands" (Deut. 33:18, 19).

For nearly 3,600 years since the prophecy was uttered no port of consequence was ever builded on the coast of Zebulun. But in October, 1933, the British High Commissioner of Palestine opened at Haifa a magnificent new harbor, which is actually under the shadow of Carmel. This he did in preparation for the opening of the pipeline that has been laid to convey the oil from the great oil wells of Iraq, 1,100 miles eastward, westward to the coast.

The line is now being operated and it is declared that more than 4,000,000 tons of oil annually will be delivered to the sea at Haifa for transport. Not only will this make Zebulun increasingly "a haven for ships," but the commercial development of the land itself calls for the harbor.

Jaffa (old-time Joppa) was more suitably situated in relation to Jerusalem. But "all this was done that it might be fulfilled which was spoken by the prophet, Zebulun shall . . . be a haven for ships." Little did those in authority know when they builded the harbor of Haifa that they were the instruments of God, fulfilling what the prophet had predicted more than 3,600 years ago.—Courtesy *Moody Monthly.*

* * *

The Infallible Bible-Barometer

In September, 1938, a man who lived on Long Island was able one day to satisfy a life-long ambition by purchasing for himself a very fine barometer. When the instrument arrived at his home, he was extremely disappointed to find that the indicating needle appeared to be stuck, pointing to the sector marked "*Hurricane.*" After shaking the barometer very vigorously several times, its new owner sat down and wrote a scorching letter to the store from which he had purchased the instrument, and on the following morning, on his way to his office in New York, he mailed the letter. That evening he returned to Long Island, to find not only the barometer missing, but his house also. The barometer's needle had been right—there was a hurricane! . . . Yet how many Christians there are who seem to regard the clear fingers of prophecy in the Word of God with like indifference and disdain! —E. Schuyler English, in *Our Hope.*

* * *

The Scoffer and Prophecy

A short time ago I worked with a college fellow, a very efficient man and capable of doing his work with an accuracy and speed that few men possess. It apparently came natural to him; therefore he expected the men under him to do as well as he. We didn't always do it, but one of the men was quite slow, unusually so at times, and during the course of a day's work this supervisor would gloat over this certain fellow, or any of us for that matter, and invariably he would start or end up by saying, "You're slower than the second coming of Christ." Little did this man know that he was fulfilling the words of prophecy written nineteen hundred years ago when Peter, speaking of the Lord's coming, said: "Knowing this first, that there shall come in the last days scoffers, walking after their own lusts, and saying, Where is the promise of his coming?" (II Pet. 3:3, 4). Do not be deceived by the space of years, but remember, "The day of the Lord will come as a thief in the night" (II Pet. 3:10). —*Faithful Words.*

* * *

Daniel Saw It

The *Saturday Evening Post* carries a short note from Washington, D. C. Its information is very interesting: "The American Humane Society estimates that there are not fewer than 330,000 American families who wander almost continuously from region to region without fixed addresses." Daniel saw that coming. In speaking of this day, Daniel said that "many should run to and fro." There it is. Home life is surely fading from the scene in America as well as the rest of the world.—*The Church of God Evangel.*

* * *

Mount of Olives in Prophecy

During recent years, earthquakes have severely damaged buildings on the famous Mount of Olives. But the greatest earthquake of all is yet future, and will take place exactly as predicted by the prophet Zechariah. The geological formation of the soil of the Mount of Olives is all set for the coming event. It only awaits God's appointed moment to act. Professor Bailey Willis, the seismological expert of Leland Stanford University, made this striking statement before the British Association for the Advancement of Science: "The region around Jerusalem is a region of potential earthquake danger. A 'fault line,' along which an earth slippage may occur at any time, passes directly through the Mount of Olives."—Selected.

* * *

Pre-Written History

In all ages God has pre-announced certain things which He purposed to do. These announcements are termed prophecies. Prophecy is history pre-written. It is as credible as any Word that God hath spoken. The Bible is filled with prophecies. Almost all the sixty-six Books contain some prophecy; but sixteen Books of the Old Testament and one of the New Testament are wholly prophetic in character. In all, nearly one-fourth of the Bible was predictive when it was written. It is most reasonable to conclude, since every Bible prediction concerning the past has been fulfilled, in minutest detail, that we may expect all the remaining prophecies to be just as literally fulfilled.—Selected.

* * *

If We Believe the Living Word

A few years ago, in a railroad train, a lawyer, seeing I had a Bible in my hand, asked, "Surely you don't believe that Deuteronomy belongs to the canon of Scripture?" I answered by asking the question, "Do you believe in the resurrection of Jesus Christ from the dead?" He said, "Yes, certainly, I believe the resurrection of the God-Man to be the most authenticated fact in all history. But that has nothing to do," he said, "with my question of the inspiration of the Book of Deuteronomy." "Oh, yes, it has," was my reply. "Was Christ, as proved by the resurrection, divine and God's Son and perfect in life and teaching?" "Yes." "Then you must take your question to the final court of appeal. Christ expounded unto his disciples the Scriptures, beginning at Moses and all the prophets concerning Himself, and called it Scripture, and endorsed it as God's Word. Deuteronomy was in it."—*Sunday School Times.*

* * *

The Bible in Prophecy

Fulfilled prophecies of Holy Scripture provide testimony to prove that God lives and reigns. Indeed, the Bible literally abounds with predictions concerning men and nations—predictions that have been so exactly fulfilled that they bear upon them the stamp of Divine inspiration.

Certainly the Prophets could not have forseen the future themselves; that is beyond the power of any man. Even with the latest scientific instruments, it is not possible to foretell the nature of the weather more than a day ahead—much less the fate of empires. Ability to describe the future with accuracy demands supernatural vision; and a sequence of predictions fulfilled to the letter provides, without question, the strongest possible evidence of the existence of God and His guidance and control in the affairs of men.

More than a century before Nineveh was sacked and burned by Nebuchadnezzar, while Assyria was still the greatest power in the world, and men thought it would never be overthrown, Nahum the prophet wrote: Nineveh shall be "empty, and void, and waste" (Nah. 2:10).

While Babylon was in its prime and all the world marveled at its wealth and might, Jeremiah dared to fortell its doom in these striking words: "Babylon shall become heaps . . . without an inhabitant" (Jer. 51:37).

In the days of Tyre's supremacy in the Mediterranean, when her island fortress still proudly defied the world, and her ships ruled the waves, God declared through Ezekiel: "They shall destroy the walls of Tyrus, like the top of a rock. It shall be a place for the spreading of nets in the midst of the sea" (Ezek. 26:4, 5).

While Egypt was still a power to be reckoned with in world affairs, the same prophet announced: "It shall be the basest of the kingdoms; neither shall it exalt itself any more above the nations" (Ezek. 29:15).

Of the beautiful Temple that was standing in Jerusalem in the days of our Lord, He Himself foretold: "There shall not be left here one stone upon another, that shall not be thrown down" (Matt. 24:2).

As for the city itself, He said: "Jerusalem shall be trodden down of the Gentiles, until the times of the Gentiles be fulfilled" (Luke 21:24).

A glance over history demonstrates how every word of these predictions has come true. The site of Nineveh is a sandy waste. All that remains of Babylon is a heap in the desert. Fishermen today spread their nets on the rocks where Tyre once stood. Certainly Egypt has never again exalted itself above the nations. As for Herod's Temple, it was thrown down within forty years of the prophecy; and to this day Gentiles still rule in Jerusalem.

No wonder H. L. Hastings once wrote: "So long as Babylon is in heaps; so long as Nineveh lies empty, void, and waste; so long as Egypt is the basest of kingdoms; so long as Tyre is a place for the spreading of nets in the midst of the sea; so long as Israel is scattered among all nations; so long as Jerusalem is trodden under foot of the Gentiles; so long as the great empires of the world march on in their predicted course—so long we have proof that one Omniscient Mind dictated the predictions of that Book, and 'prophecy came not in old time by the will of man.'"

There is a God. Blessed assurance! He is infinite in power and can predict! By far the greater number of prophecies have to do with the Second Coming of Christ. What confidence and glorious expectation fill the heart when it is known that all the prophecies pertaining to the past have been fulfilled to the ultimate detail. Their fulfillment seals our assurance that those pertaining to the most stupendous event of all — Christ's Coming in power and glory—will likewise come to pass.—Selected.

* * *

Many Locks, One Key

Dr. A. W. Hare once said: "If you saw a half-dozen doors with as many locks to them, so new and strange that not a locksmith in the country could make a key to fit any one of them, and if a man then came with a key which fitted all these different locks and opened all the six doors, could you doubt that his was the right key? This is just the kind of proof which the prophecies afford of the truth and divinity of Christ. The weight of this proof rests on two simple facts: One is that the prophecies were written many hundreds of years before the birth of Christ. The other is that Jesus died the death related in the New Testament. Jesus is the true key for the prophetic lock; and the prophets who foretold all these things *hundreds of years before* must assuredly have spoken, as Peter says, 'not by the will of man: but . . . as they were moved by the Holy Ghost.' Where—outside of the Bible—shall we find propheices of this kind?"—*The King's Business.*

* * *

The Gospel of the Old Testament

Daniel Rose, head of the Jewish department of the Bible Institute of Los Angeles, dealing with one of his Jewish friends, said, "I want to read you a portion of the Bible, and when I have finished I want you to tell me what part of the Bible I have been reading." He agreed, and opening my Bible I began to read from Isaiah's prophecy beginning at the 13th verse of chapter 52 and reading through chapter 53, which marvelous passage has been called by some the 'Gospel of the Old Testament.' When I had finished, I asked this friend from what part of the Bible I had been reading. Without hesitation he replied: 'From the New Testament.' 'And to whom does the passage refer?' Again, without the slightest hesitation the answer came back: 'It refers to Jesus of Nazareth.' With my Bible still open to the page I had been reading, I showed my friend that I had not been reading from the New Testament, but from the Old Testament. 'But,' I said, 'your second reply is correct, for this Old Testament passage does refer to Jesus Christ, and this Jesus Christ is our true Messiah.'" Since that day Mr. Rose has repeated this procedure with many others, leading them to Jesus Christ.—*Prophecy.*

PURPOSE

The Power of Purpose

From the *Reader's Digest* we have the following:

"One morning I watched a couple of cowpunchers going out to bring in a wild steer from his range in the mountains. They took along one of those shaggy little gray donkeys—a burro. Now a big three-year-old steer that's been running loose in the timber is a tough customer to handle. But those cowboys had the technique. They got a rope on the steer and then they tied him neck and neck, right up close, to the burro.

"When they let go, that burro had a bad time. The steer threw him all over the place. He banged him against trees, rocks, into bushes. Time after time they both went down. But there was one great difference between the burro and the steer. The burro had an idea. He wanted to go home. And no matter how often the steer threw him, every time the burro got to his feet he took a step nearer the corral. This went on and on. After about a week the burro showed up at ranch headquarters. He had with him the tamest and sorriest looking steer you ever saw. (Arthur Kudner, in *The Atlantic Monthly*)."

If one were expected to point out the morals in this story he might observe that much beef, brains, gifts, or education amount to little unless there is some worth-while and well-established purpose in control of the large resources.

Then, of course, that burro, lacking much in size and weight, put all he had in one direction and kept on doing it. And as surely as you live, some men and women who have been, figuratively speaking, no bigger than the burro, have obtained their own purposes and the purposes of God in their lives because of what pull they had always in one direction.

So it is not so much your size but your eternally determined direction that counts.—*The Free Methodist.*

* * *

Daniel's Backbone

Recently a speaker recalled a story of Spurgeon's concerning a class of boys who were having a Scripture lesson on Daniel. One of the boys was asked to read some verses aloud, and presently he came to verse three in chapter six, which reads ". . . because an excellent spirit was in him" but by mistake the boy rendered it ". . . because an excellent *spine* was in him." It was undoubtedly bad reading, but *it was excellent theology, for Daniel was a man of real backbone"—strong, courageous.—New Century Leader.*

* * *

Boys Who Had a Plan

Jonathan Edwards, the great minister and educator, when eighteen said, "If there could be one man in the world at one time who was pleasing to God, I would want to be that man." He became one of the world's greatest men, whose influence is still felt.

Spurgeon decided when a small boy to become a preacher. Time did not change his decision. His sermons, both spoken and translated into other languages, reached the entire Christian world.

Judson's ideal as a boy and young man was to become famous as an actor. He became famous and one of the world's greatest men, but in quite a different work. He became a pioneer missionary to Burma.

Livingstone cherished a desire in his teens to go to China as a medical missionary; he studied and planned to that effect, but Providence saw to it that he was to plant the Cross in the heart of Africa.

James A. Garfield, when a boy said, "I intend first of all to make a man of myself," and his resolve never failed. It was always his ambition to do a little better than others.

Would that young men and boys of today would consider the way their lives are to go and decide to climb to the higher and safer level. In the little poem of John Oxenham there is wonderful advice to all:

"But to every man there openeth
A way, and ways, and a way,
And the high soul climbs the high way,
And the low soul gropes the low;
And in between, on the misty flats,
The rest drift to and fro;
But to every man there openeth
A high way and a low,
And every man decideth
The way his soul shall go."
—*The Junior's Friend.*

* * *

An Exhortation

"The work is solemn — therefore do not trifle; the work is difficult—therefore do not relax; the opportunity is brief—therefore do not delay; the path is narrow—therefore do not wander; the prize is glorious—therefore do not faint."—D. M. Panton, in *The Presbyterian.*

* * *

Driftwood

Away up on a Canadian hillside grew a tree that had weathered the storms for many and many a long year. But the time came when it had to be felled, and put to some definite use, and with the last clean cut of an axe in the hands of a lumberjack it came to the ground. It was rolled down to the river, but later, in the "drive" it floated down stream not to the sawmill, where it would have been utilized for a specific purpose, but past the mill, on and on until it finally reached the ocean. Here the storm-tossed waves lashed it with others of its kind, until the mass became a water-logged unit, and a menace to navigation. One dark, foggy morning, the look-out on a ship plying to a distant port gave the signal "danger ahead." Engines were reversed, speed was reduced, and with every member of the crew at his post the captain rushed to the bridge for observation. One look at the thing that lay on the surface of the water was sufficient to cause him to turn away with an expression of disgust on his face as he exclaimed, "Only driftwood! Full speed ahead!" Alas, there are many living today without any definite purpose, simply floating down the stream and out toward the angry sea of dissatisfaction and unrest, there to become "driftwood." —*Gospel Herald.*

* * *

Willing to Wash Windows

A neat, rather prepossessing young man applied to John Wanamaker for a job a number of years ago, in Philadelphia, and when told that there was no job for him, said, "I am willing to do anything."

Thinking to get rid of him, Mr. Wanamaker said, "The only job I have is a job of washing windows." "I will take it," said the young man. He washed those windows as they had never been washed. In time he became the manager of the great store.

When this manager died, after twenty-five years of splendid service, Mr. Wanamaker said, "I am willing to pay as high as one hundred thousand dollars a year for a manager who can fill the place of the one I lost."

What the Church needs is men and women who are willing to "wash windows" for the sake of the Kingdom.—*Canadian Churchman.*

* * *

Instability

As to lack of faith and practice in prayer, James uses a simile which is ludicrously striking—the wave, literally, "The surge of the sea, driven with the wind and tossed." There are two motions when the sea is tempestuous: undulation, up and down; fluctuation, to and fro. Both are referred to—"driven with the wind," fluctuation; "tossed," undulation. The peculiarity of the wave is that it stays nowhere; and so the double-souled man is unstable in all his ways. If he is impelled forward, he falls back; if he is lifted up, he sinks down again. If he believes one moment, he distrusts the next; if he gets a little ahead, he cannot hold on to any advantage. Unstable as water, he cannot excel.—A. T. Pierson.

* * *

One ship sails East,
And another West,
By the selfsame winds that blow;
'Tis the set of the sails,
And not the gales,
That tells the way to go.

Like the winds of the sea
Are the waves of Time,
As we voyage along through life;
'Tis the set of the soul
That determines the goal,
And not the calm or the strife!
—Selected.

* * *

David Livingstone said,

"I will set no value upon anything I have or may possess except in relation to the kingdom of Christ. If anything will advance the interests of that kingdom it shall be given away or kept according as to whether the giving or keeping it will promote the glory of Him to whom I owe all my hopes for time and eternity."—*Gospel Herald.*

READY

What the Flags Meant

In one of the Western cities an old sea captain who had crossed the Pacific at least fifty times resigned his position, and being an earnest Christian he devoted all of his time to helping others. He especially gave his efforts to help sailors. He came into the hospital one day and the matron in charge said, "Captain, at the last cot yonder is an old sailor, and he is not long for this world." He marched down between the cots, and as he came nearer he saw around the cot a number of little flags, as if the sailor had gone back to the days of his childhood and had decorated his cot with the flags of many colors. He found the old sailor had served him in the old days, and he said, "Man, what do these mean?" The sailor said, "Captain, have you forgotten how to use the signals? Don't you know how to read flags?" "I am a bit rusty," replied the captain; "if I had the book I could read." "Well, Captain, if you have forgotten I will tell you what the flags say. They say this: 'The ship is all ready to sail,' and 'She is waiting orders,' Captain," said he, "I know Christ; one day He will come for me."—J. Wilbur Chapman.

* * *

Ready

Ready to leave behind
  Fortune, and friends, and fame,
To preach in the uttermost parts
  Salvation through Thy Name.
    Ready to yield my all
    And go where my Lord shall call!

Ready to stay? Oh, Lord!
  Surely 'tis not Thy will
For one so eager to go,
  To linger, patient and still?
Ready to stay behind
  And watch the rest go on;
To hold the fort at home,
  And see that these are won?
    Lord, it is hard to stay
    When you long to be on your way!

Still, the harvest field at home
  Is as ripe as that abroad,
And the man who lives next door
  Is hungering after God.
And perhaps He can use me more
  When He calls me at last to go,
For the lessons of grace I learned
  In the days when I served Him so,
    Ready to go or stay—
    Lord Jesus, have Thy way!

—Barbara Elden Comet.

* * *

No Time to Get Ready?

God is very merciful, but He is just and righteous as well. When men disregard warning and entreaty, then law steps in. I remember when I was living some years ago in Burnley in Lancashire, a woman told her husband, who had always kept aloof from things religious, about a man whom they both knew very well, and who had just died very suddenly. The man remarked, "What a terrible thing to be called away like that without any chance of getting ready!" And the woman could not help replying: "Without any chance of getting ready! Why, he has had fifty-four years of chances!"—*Sunday Circle.*

* * *

Are You Ready?

The matter of being ready is of such supreme importance that our Lord has not left us without kindly admonition, and as willingness to serve naturally leads to preparedness for service, how vitally important it is that we consider what He has to say on being ready.

1. Ready to give the gospel (Rom. 1:15).
2. Ready for every good work (Titus 3:1).
3. Ready to distribute (I Tim. 6:18).
4. Ready to give an answer (I Pet. 3:15).
5. Ready to go where the Lord leads (Luke 22:33).
6. Ready to feed the flock (I Pet. 5:2).

7. Ready to die for the Lord Jesus (Acts 21:13).

8. Ready to be offered (II Tim. 4:6).

9. Ready for His coming (Matt. 24: 44; 25:10).

10. Ready also in receiving the Word and searching the Scriptures daily to see whether these things are so (Acts 17: 11).—J. T. Bougher.

* * *

Ready

Robert Hardy had a dream, and in that dream he thought he was to live only seven days. If you had only seven days to live, how would you live them? How did Robert Hardy begin? He began to study. He began to get ready. He did all in his power each day. He came to the seventh day, and he neared the end of the day. But all at once it was made known to him that he wasn't going to die. He looked around and he was glad, but he said, "Some seven days will be my last seven," and he lived every day as though he were in his last. You will be in your last seven days, some day. Maybe you are there now.—Scoville.

Ready

Ready to take from the Master's hand
All things—both good and ill;
Willing in highest place to stand,
Or lowliest nook to fill;
Ready to follow the Saviour's call
Though your heart would rather stay;
Ready to offer to Him your all—
To go with Him all the way;
Ready to serve—though you "were not asked,"
Willing to step aside;

Scorning no small or lowly task;
Fearing nothing but pride;
Ready to suffer the taunts of men
And give in exchange a prayer,
Ready to stand for Jesus, when
No glory is offered there;
Ready to pray, and ready to love,
Ready to serve and give;
Ready to honor the Lord above
Each moment that you live.

Blessed indeed each ready soul
To His dear service true;
Under the blessed Lord's control
We learn of Him through you!

Esther M. Peterson.

REPENTANCE

Real Repentance and Faith

Congo News tells of a very old woman who was being examined recently by the native pastor for baptism, and showed by her testimony that she fully understood the plan of salvation. When the day for baptism arrived, the old lady hesitated at the church door and said that she must go and fetch something from her house. When she came back, she walked right to the front of the church, laid a small fetish on the ground, and then quietly took her place with the other women. Serious looks were on every face, for they all knew that the "medicine" she had put there was "lightning medicine," the last that any of them is willing to give up. Her father had been killed by lightning years before, and never had she been without her fetish to protect her from the same fate. Having found Jesus as her Lord and Saviour, she was willing to trust Him for all.—*Alliance Weekly.*

* * *

The Difference Between Penance and Repentance

Repentance, which was the burden of the Baptist's message, involves the sense of sin, sorrow for sin, and severance from sin by the grace and power of God. He who repents realizes that he is a sinner, regrets his sin, and resolves to forsake it. Remember: "He that lacks time to mourn lacks time to mend." A clergyman found the children reading the Douay version of the Testament, and on noticing a passage in the chapter which was translated "Do penance," where the English version rendered the same word by "Repent," he asked them if they knew the difference between penance and repentance. A short silence followed, and then a little girl asked, "Is it not this . . . : *Judas did penance,* and went and hanged himself; Peter repented, and wept bitterly?" — *The Teacher.*

* * *

His Fall Brought Humiliation

Bishop John Jewel (one of the English Protestant leaders expelled from Oxford in the reign of Mary, 1553-1558), being by the violence of Popish inquisitors, assaulted on a sudden to *subscribe,* he took a pen in his hand, and said smiling: "Have you a mind to see how well I can write?" and thereupon underwrit their opinions. Jewel, however, by his cowardly compliance, made his foes no fewer without, and one the more—a guilty conscience, within him. His life being waylaid for, with great difficulty he got over into Germany. Arriving at Frankfort, by the advice of some friends, he made a solemn and affecting recantation of his subscription, in a full congregation of English Protestants, on a Sunday morning, after having preached a most tender, penitential sermon. Said he: "It was my abject and cowardly mind, and faint heart that made my weak hand commit this wickedness." He bitterly bewailed his fall; and with sighs and tears supplicated the forgiveness of the God whose truth he had denied, and of the Church of Christ, which he had so grievously offended. The congregation was melted to tears, and all embraced him as a brother in Christ; yea, as an angel of God. Whoever seriously considers the high parts (talents) of Mr. Jewel will conclude, that his *fall* was necessary for his *humiliation.*—T. Fuller.

Thus was the penitent Peter restored from his *denial,* while Judas, the traitor, persistently impenitent, "went to his own place."—*Gospel Herald.*

* * *

"Except Ye Repent"

By his frequent spasms of violent coughing, a tall emaciated patient drew attention to himself in the prison ward of Bellevue Hospital in New York City. He had been a policeman and only a few years had passed since he was happily married. He had acquired the bad habit of going home nights in an intoxicated condition. One night his mother-in-law met him at the entrance to the house. "Drunk again," she ejaculated and began to chide him sharply. Then without a moment's hesitation, he drew his gun, fired and killed her. He was arrested, charged with homicide and held for trial in the city prison. There he developed tuberculosis and that resulted in his transfer to the prison ward of a municipal hospital.

Over and over in a mournful and disconsolate tone of voice, he could be heard asking the question, "Why did I pull that gun?" Gospel messengers pled with him, to call upon the Son of God who said, "Him that cometh to Me I will in no wise cast out" (John 6:37). They assured him that Jesus was able and willing to save, but he spurned them and the offer of full and free salvation through the atoning Blood of Jesus Christ. He was never brought before an earthly judge because he died before the prosecuting attorney was ready to present his case for trial before a jury. He was summoned to appear before the court from which there is no appeal. His final words before he departed this world were the frequently muttered question, "Why-did-I-pull-that-gun?" — The late Ernest A. Eggers, in *Gospel Herald.*

* * *

Repentance

If there is no repentance, there can be no pardon. Some years ago a murderer was sentenced to death in the United States. The murderer's brother, to whom the State was deeply indebted for former services, besought the governor of the State for his brother's pardon. The pardon was granted, and the man visited his brother with the pardon in his pocket. "What would you do," he said to him, "if you received a pardon?" "The first thing I would do," he answered, is to track down the judge who sentenced me, and murder him; and the next thing I would do is to track down the chief witness, and murder *him." The brother rose, and left the prison with the pardon in his pocket.—The Dawn.*

* * *

Dead Trees

One day a man who had a Christian wife, but who himself was opposed to Christianity, left home for the woods to fell trees. As he glanced around before commencing, he noticed one tree dead and dry, with its leafless branches extending into the air, and he said to himself, "That tree will I cut down, for it is dead and dry, and fit only to be burned." The moment he arrived at that conclusion the question flashed into his mind, "Am I not a dead tree, fit only to burn?" He tried his utmost to banish this unpleasant thought, but it was an arrow from the quiver of the Almighty. He approached the tree and struck a few blows with the ax, but still the thought rankled in his heart, "Will God ever say of me, 'Cut it down; why cumbereth it the ground'?" He plied his ax with increasing vigor, but every blow seemed to deepen the conviction of his own spiritual deadness and awful destiny. Eventually these thoughts became so unbearable that he shouldered his ax, returned home, and went directly to his room. There he fell upon his knees before God, and with a penitent and broken heart sought forgiveness through Christ.—*The Dawn.*

* * *

Real Repentance

Perhaps the quaintest letter in the whole White House collection is one which came from a child, addressed to President Cleveland, written in September, 1895. This is what it says: "To His Majesty President Cleveland. Dear President: I am in a dreadful state of mind, and I thought I would write and tell you all. About two years ago—as near as I can remember, it is two years —I used two postage stamps that had been used before on letters; perhaps more than two stamps, but I can only remember of doing it twice. I did not realize what I had done until lately. My mind is constantly turned on that subject, and I think of it night and day. Now, dear President, will you please forgive me, and I will promise you I will never do it again. Enclosed find cost of three stamps, and please forgive me, for I was then but thirteen years old, for I am heartily sorry for what I have done. From one of your subjects." — *The King's Business.*

RESPONSIBILITY

Burdened for Lost

A consecrated Sunday school teacher came to her pastor. She taught a class of young college boys. Twenty-four of them were unsaved. She sat speechless and sobbing before the pastor. "What is the matter?" asked the pastor. She exclaimed, "My boys, twenty-four of them, are standing on my heart like the weight of a lost world. I did not sleep any last night. I cannot eat. I must have them or I cannot live!" Prayer followed, prayer immersed in tears. In less than two weeks, every one of those twenty-four boys gave glowing, personal testimonies about the saving power of the Lord Jesus!—L. R. Scarborough.

Personal Accountability

Daniel Webster, the great statesman of other years, was once asked, "Mr. Webster, what is the most sobering, searching thought that ever entered your mind?" Without hesitancy, the staunch statesman replied, "My personal accountability to God!"—Selected.

* * *

Personal Responsibility

A temptation against which every Christian who occupies a place of trust should be on his guard is the temptation to minimize his individual responsibility—to lose himself in numbers. It is this attitude that is responsible for much of the disappointment in the church. An Arab sheik once gave a banquet for his son, and invited his friends to share his hospitality. His one request was that each guest bring a small skin of wine as his contribution to the feast. On the appointed day when the skins were emptied, it was found, to the mortification of host and guest alike, that all contained water. Each guest had reasoned that, since everyone else would bring wine, he might be able to make a substitution and not be detected.—Selected.

* * *

Responsibility

"Yours must be a very responsible position," said a traveler to a switchman who had charge of the switches where five lines converge. "Yes," was the reply, "but it is as nothing compared to yours as a Christian."—*Christian Herald.*

* * *

Response-ability

Dr. W. H. Griffith Thomas once interpreted responsibility to some friends as made up of two words, "response," "ability." "Man's response and God's ability." Charles H. Spurgeon once remarked to a young minister who complained of the smallness of his congregations, "*They are as large perhaps as you will want to give an account for in the day of judgment.*"—Selected.

REST

Just let me rest in Thee, O Lord,
  Nor strive, nor fret, nor strain
Against the burden of the days
  That bring me tears and pain.

Let me remember that Thy Hand
  Can lighten every load.
And in Thy presence, I shall be
  Safe on life's darkest road.

For Thou hast said that Thou art near
  To all who need Thine aid.
Then, foolish mortal that I am,
  Why should I be afraid?

—Selected.

* * *

Why They Waited

A story is told of an exploring party in Africa which had employed a group of native carriers to go with them into the interior. Being in a hurry to reach their objective, the party was pushed relentlessly for several days. Finally the natives just sat down and would go no farther. Asked what was the matter, the superstitious natives replied, "We are waiting for our souls to catch up with our bodies." A lot of Christians who have run away from God in their hurry and rush for worldly things need to stop and catch up on spiritual things. —From a radio message by Dr. F. William May, Salina, Kans.

* * *

A Perfect Resting Place

Now, published by R. G. LeTourneau, Inc., tells of a woman in Cedar Rapids, Iowa, who was injured. Some $20,321 was found about the mattress of her bed. When told about the amount, the woman, who died later, said: "Is that all? I thought there would be $25,000." *Now,* in commenting, says: "Does not this incident reveal the fact that even if one were wealthy enough to lie on a money-stuffed mattress, it would be an unsatisfactory resting place? *The only perfect place of rest is on the finished work of Christ.*"—*Watchman-Examiner.*

* * *

Not Breaking

In a Sunday night service at the Marble Collegiate Church, New York City, Bishop Leonard concluded with this moving appeal. He said that during the recent floods at Johnstown, Pa., a rumor

had gone forth that the great dam was giving way again. Quickly, the valley was filled with excitement and fear. Swiftly, too, the report came to the ears of the architect who had built the work. He exclaimed: "It is untrue. The dam is not giving way. I built it and know every bit of material and workmanship put into its construction. It will bear any pressure of water that can be put upon it." Leaping into his car he drove up the valley from which others were fleeing. He parked his car at the very base of the dam, and, standing on the running board, he cried: "The dam will hold. It is not breaking." Said the Bishop: "This bewildered age needs men and women with just such faith in Jesus Christ. He will never fail. He is sufficient for all time and for eternity."
—*New York Christian Advocate.*

* * *

Better Than Rest-Stones

India has many boy merchants, and for their use, as they journey, the charitable have placed rest-stones along the roads. A woman missionary once passed a weary little fellow as he reclined against one of these stones, and quoted Matthew 11:28 to him: "Come unto me, all ye that labor and are heavy laden, and I will give you rest." The lad was invited to the mission school, and there he learned to love Jesus. His face lighted up as he heard the verse beginning, "The Lord is my rock." "That is better than any resting-stone," he said. "It keeps one rested all the time."

* * *

Healed of the Fever

A woman awoke one morning and viewed the day's work ahead — meals, children to get ready for school, a dainty luncheon to prepare for a group of women who were coming—and she became anxious. Her husband in departing, said, "Hadn't you better take a rest, dear? You are feverish." When all were gone she took her Bible, and read, "He touched her hand, and the fever left her." She saw that was just what she needed, so she knelt and asked him for it. She arose, went about her work quietly, prepared a simple luncheon instead of the elaborate one. At the close of the meeting, she told the women of her experience, thus giving a testimony for the Master. When her husband returned, he said: "I see you took my advice, and took a rest; the fever is gone." — Selected.

* * *

God's Rest

(Matthew 11:28, 29; I Peter 5:7)

I heard the voice of Jesus say,
"Come unto Me and rest:
Oh, weary one, bowed down with care,
Come, lean upon My breast.
There is no load I cannot bear;
Nor burden that I will not share,
So cast on Me thine every care;
Come unto Me and rest.

"All ye that labor come to Me
And I will give you rest.
Though heavy laden you may be,
Come, lean upon My breast."
He spoke to me so tenderly,
"Come, take My yoke and learn of Me:
My burden shall rest light on thee
And I will give you rest."

Heavy laden, tired with care,
I came to Him for rest:
There I laid my burden down
And leaned upon His breast.
He gave me strength from day to day;
He guided me along life's way,
And now my soul must ever say,
"Praise God! He gave me rest!"
—Sylvia Ratcliffe Lockwood,
in *Gospel Herald.*

* * *

A Little Child's Understanding

Matthew 11:28 was the text of the preacher one night. He was a true and warmhearted man, and as he drew near the close of his address, his heart was so full of Christ that his lips could not express what he felt, and wanted to say. All he could say was, "'Come unto Me'—what does it mean? 'Come unto Me'—what does it mean?" Again and again he repeated, "What does it mean? What does it mean?" All at once, a little girl, sitting on a front seat, timidly rose and, childlike, held out her hand. "Well," said the kindly preacher, "what does it mean, dear child?" "Please, sir, it means that He wants me," was the touching reply. The preacher sat down. Both he and the people felt no more need be said. Hearts became tender, eyes became wet with tears, and afterwards one and another said, "The wisest and most able among us could not have given a truer and sweeter exposition of the text. "Come unto Me" means that "He wants me."—*Christian Life Missionary.*

RESTITUTION

Two Infidel Neighbors

Two infidel neighbors lived among the hills of New England. One of them heard the Gospel, was convicted of his sins and believed unto eternal life. Soon after he went to his infidel neighbor's home and said, "I have come to talk to you; I have been converted."

"Yes," sneered the other, "I heard that you had been down to the meeting, and had gone forward for prayers. I was surprised, for I thought you were as sensible a man as any in town."

"Well," said the first, "I have a duty to do to you. I haven't slept much for two nights for thinking of it. I have four sheep in my flock that belong to you. They came two years ago with your mark on them and I took them and marked them with my mark. You inquired around, but could not find them. They are in my field now, with their increase, and I want to settle with you if you are willing, or you can settle with me by the law if you will."

The other infidel was amazed, and told his neighbor that he could keep the sheep only please go away. He trembled at the thought that something had got hold of his old friend which he did not understand. He repeated, "You may keep the sheep, if you will only go away."

"No," said the Christian, "I must settle this matter up, and cannot rest until I do. You must tell me how much."

"Well," replied the other, "pay me the worth of the sheep when they went to you, and six percent interest, and please go away and let me alone."

The Christian laid down the amount and then doubled it. He went his way, leaving his old friend's heart heavily loaded. The full result of that scene is only known to God. But today that other infidel is going to the house of God.—A. S. Burrows, in *John Three Sixteen.*

* * *

Repentance and Restitution

A little boy had broken the glass of a street lamp and was greatly disturbed. "What shall I do?" he asked his father in trepidation. "Do?" cried his father, "tell the lamplighter about it, ask him what you must pay, then go and settle like a man." This very practical way of dealing with the matter was not what the boy was looking for, and he whimperingly replied, "I—I—thought that all I had to do was to ask God to forgive me." Be sure God will freely forgive us, when in obedience to His Word we turn our steps into the way of righteousness. —C. F. Goss.

* * *

Repentance and Restitution

There is something more in this abandonment than the desertion of an old road. We cannot turn from that road as though nothing had been accomplished in it. A certain life has been lived and certain damage has been done. What about the damage? Colonel Robert G. Ingersoll, in a lecture that is now forgotten, put this challenge in an indictment of the Christian doctrine of forgiveness: "If I rob Mr. X and God forgives me, how will that help Mr. X?" Yes, but God won't. No man can leave that road where ruin has been wrought and turn away as though nothing has been done. *The abandoning of the old road must be accompanied by the rectifying of the old wrong. So far as restitution is possible, it is part of our forsaking the old life.* Here, then, is where repentance begins.—J. H. Jowett.

* * *

What God's Word Did

"Arriving at a house," writes one of the Bible Society's Italian colporteurs, as reported in *The Life of Faith,* "I knocked at the door. *'Aventi,'* called a voice from within. I did so, and found myself in the presence of a woman who, dusting a chair, invited me to sit down. She seemed a little embarrassed, then turning suddenly, said, "What is the price of a New Testament?" "Two lira, Signora." She handed me the coin, and I was going to give her the book, when she refused it with a gesture. "We have one," she said; "my son stole it from you a few days ago, but the reading of it brought him to see his sin. So he told me about it and asked me to pay you and apologize."—*Alliance Weekly.*

Let Scoffers Laugh This Off

There are some people who scoff at religion and get apparent pleasure out of the habit. They will never understand the following letter, received by the War Department from an unnamed man living in Colorado:

"While in the service during 1918-20, I stole equipment and clothing to the amount (as near as I can tell) of about $50.00.

"Since that time God has wonderfully saved me and I am going back over my tracks and make every wrong right that I possibly can.

"Enclosed find check for same and by His grace I hope nothing of its kind will have to be repeated."

Here is positive testimony of the force that comes into human lives when the individual accepts God and begins to serve Him. It will take more than the cynic's smile to convince most of us that the ex-soldier has been fooled by an old-time, worn-out myth.

He has found something valuable in his life, worth more than money. Can many of the scoffing tribe truthfully say as much?—*Middleburg Independent.*

RESURRECTION (See also: Death)

"Jesus Defeated Death"

An aged verger of Winchester Cathedral never tired of standing on the Cathedral roof and relating the story of how the news of Wellington's victory over Napoleon reached England. News of the history-making battle came by a sailing vessel to the south coast, and by semaphore was wig-wagged overland toward London. Atop Winchester Cathedral the semaphore began to spell out the eagerly awaited message: "W-e-l-l-i-n-g-t-o-n — D-e-f-e-a-t-e-d —," and then a dense fog settled oppressively over the land! The semaphore could no longer be seen, and thus the sad, heartbreaking news of the incomplete message went on to London, whelming the country in gloom and despair: "Wellington Defeated!"

But, ere long, the fog lifted, and again the signaling semaphore atop the Cathedral became visible, spelling out the complete message of the battle. "W-e-l-l-i-n-g-t-o-n — D-e-f-e-a-t-e-d — t-h-e — E-n-e-m-y!" Now the message was all the more glorious because of the preceding gloom. Like the spread of a prairie fire, the joyful news spread across the land, and lifted the spirits of the people onto a plane of gratitude and jubilant praise: *"Wellington Defeated the Enemy!"*

In the long years ago, on a hill lone and gray, situated without the city's gate, the sinless Son of God gave Himself willingly in a vicarious death upon His cruel cross for the sin of the world. The prophet Amos had predicted an interesting thing about the awesome scene in these words: "And it shall come to pass in that day, saith the Lord God, that I will cause the sun to go down at noon, and I will darken the earth in the clear day" (Amos 8:9). His prophecy was literally fulfilled, for Luke tells us: "And it was about the sixth hour (noon), and there was a darkness over all the earth until the ninth hour. And the sun was darkened and the veil of the temple was rent in the midst" (Luke 23:44, 45). As that dense darkness enshrouded the land, obscuring from the gaze of man the open shame to which the Sufferer on the central cross was being submitted, "Jesus cried with a loud voice," and then He said, "Father, into thy hands I commend my spirit" (Luke 23:46). As He thus died, the darkness deepened for His fearful followers. To them Calvary meant but one thing: "J-E-S-U-S — D-E-F-E-A-T-E-D." Placing His limp, lifeless body in the borrowed tomb of Joseph of Arimathæa, the persistent thought of their troubled hearts reiterated its hopeless message: "Jesus Defeated!"

During the three days of His entombment, all hell was vibrant with ghoulish glee, for the prince of darkness, Satan, had apparently triumphed over the Sun of righteousness. Did ever a darkness so deep envelop the hearts of God's children as the darkness which whelmed the souls of Jesus' disciples while His body lay in the tomb? We think not! Listen to their dismal dirge: "We trusted that it had been he which should have redeemed Israel: and beside all this, today is the third day since these things were done" (Luke 24:21). How unbelieving and undiscerning were His followers: "For as yet they knew not the scripture, that he must rise again from the dead" (John 20:9)! Betimes, the Saviour had foretold His death and resurrection: "After three days I will rise again" (Matt. 27:63); but they either misunderstood or disbelieved what He said.

The three dreary days dragged to their close, then suddenly the darkness lifted. The white radiance of a Lord's day morning flooded an Eastern garden, as the gladsome, gloom-dispelling news spread: "J-E-S-U-S — D-E-F-E-A-T-E-D — D-E-A-T-H!"—In, "*Because He Lives,*" by Walter Brown Knight.

The Light Left Behind

A small boy from a non-Christian home had been brought into the Sunday school. His mother was not only unsaved, but she had a morbid fear of death. After her little boy became interested in the Sunday school he begged her to come to church with him, but she persistently refused his entreaties because she was afraid that the preacher might say something about death or dying. On Easter Sunday the teacher noticed the lad's rapt attention while she told the beautiful story of the risen Christ. The child hastened home with a shining face, and exclaimed, "Oh, Mother, you needn't be afraid of dying any more, for *Jesus went through the grave and left a light behind Him!*" Gradually the fear in her heart melted under the influence of her son's words about "the light behind Him." Early one evening she had put him to bed and heard him pray as he did nightly that God would make her a Christian, "and do it right quick!" he added. Later that evening a neighbor persuaded the mother to go to church. The Heaven-sent message brought conviction, and that night her little boy's prayer was answered!—*Sunday School Times.*

* * *

Christ, a Living Saviour

A missionary in Turkey wished to teach to a group of people the truth of the resurrection of Christ. He said: "I am traveling, and have reached a place where the road branches off in two ways; I look for a guide, and find two men: one dead, and the other alive. Which of the two must I ask for direction, the dead or the living?" "Oh, the living," cried the people. "Then," said the missionary, "why send me to Mohammed, who is dead, instead of to *Christ, who is alive!*"—*Christian Endeavor World.*

* * *

Not Afraid—Home Is Just Beyond

I read once of a little girl whose home was near a cemetery, and in order to go to the store, she had to follow a path that led through the cemetery. But this little girl never seemed to have any sense of fear, even when she returned through the cemetery at dusk. Someone said to her, "Aren't you afraid to go through the cemetery?" "Oh, no," she replied, "I'm not afraid, for my home is just beyond."

Are you afraid of the cemetery?

Not if you are a Christian, and know that your Home is just beyond. — *The Biblical Echo.*

* * *

Do You Really Know It?

Reichel was conducting the final rehearsal of his great choir for the production of the "Messiah." The chorus had sung through to the point where the soprano solo takes up the refrain, "I know that my Redeemer liveth." The soloist's technique was perfect— she had faultless breathing, accurate note placing, flawless enunciation. After the final note all eyes were fixed on Reichel to catch his look of approval. Instead he silenced the orchestra, walked up to the singer with sorrowful eyes, and said, "My daughter, do you really know that your Redeemer liveth? Do you?" "Why, yes," she answered, flushing, "I think I do." "Then sing it!" cried Reichel. "Tell it to me so that I will know, and all who hear you will know that you know the joy and power of it." Then he motioned the orchestra to play again. This time she sang the truth as she knew it and had experienced it in her own soul, and all who heard wept under the spell of it. The old master approached her with tear-dimmed eyes, and said, "You do know, for you have told me."—*The Presbyterian of the South.*

* * *

Items a Skeptic Could Not Skip

One of the many interesting incidents that come out of the annals of old England is that of the conversion of two great men who were skeptics.

One was the eminent Gilbert West. The other was Lord Littleton, famous English jurist and a light in the literary world.

They were agreed that Christianity should be destroyed, but they further agreed that in order to destroy it two things were necessary.

They must disprove the resurrection of Jesus and explain the conversion of Saul in a way that met the demands of skepticism. There was a task for each of these master minds, and each accepted his task.

West assumed the task of getting rid of the resurrection and Littleton would dispose of the Scripture that had its setting on the Damascus road. They took ample time, a year or more, and then came together to compare notes.

When they met both were Christians, each confessing to his conversion as a result of his own research. The resurrection fact withstood the test of unfriendly, but honest investigation, as did also that of Saul's conversion. Both facts still stand.

There are so many things — tremendous realities—that cannot be explained without them.—*Religious Telescope.*

* * *

We'll Meet Again

Easter not only proclaims victory over death, it also predicts union after death. Which of these transports is the greater I dare not say; but they need not be discriminated between for they both belong to the Christian. We shall awake on the resurrection morning, not isolated, but in the company of our dear ones; not like one flower blooming in a lonely Spring, but a myriad of flowers bursting into each other's sight upon a bank together. Dr. J. R. Miller relates this incident. A father and son had been shipwrecked. Together they clung to the rigging until the son was washed off. The father was rescued in the morning in an unconscious state. Several hours later he awoke in a fisherman's hut, where he was lying in a soft, warm bed. In an agony he remembered his boy. But as he turned his head he saw his son lying beside him.

One by one we are being swept away with the billows of time. Some storm will carry the last and stoutest heart of us away. But when we awake beyond the raging of the sea we shall be together again. When our eyes open in the Heavenly morning, near by us, in the bowers of Paradise, we shall see those "whom we have loved long since, and lost awhile."—*The Evangelical Christian.*

* * *

Believe His Word

Mary wept because the Lord was no longer in the tomb. Ah, she should have wept if He had been there. Had He remained in the grave, we would have been without a Saviour. Does it not show that we often weep senselessly? Jacob said, "All these things are against me," when in reality they were working together for the most wonderful blessing. Mary's unbelief was responsible for her tears. Had not the Lord told her and the others repeatedly, that He was to rise from the dead the third day? Oh, how much sorrow we bring upon ourselves because we do not believe His word.—A. V. R.

* * *

Saying and Doing

A man was once conversing with a Brahmin priest, and he asked:

"Could *you* say, 'I am the resurrection and the life?' "

"Yes," replied the priest, "I could say that."

"*But could you make anyone believe it?*"

Christ proved His superiority right there. His character and His actions were back of His words. He exhibited His divine power to silence His enemies. —D. L. Moody.

* * *

After the battle of Inkerman, in the Crimean War, some soldiers, gathering up the dead for burial and the wounded for the hospital, came upon the body of a young man, who had drawn himself, being fatally wounded, to the shade of a tree, and was lying with his head upon his arm as if asleep. As they picked him up they heard something tear, and looking more closely they saw an open Bible upon which he had placed his bloody fingers, and the congealed blood had carried with the finger a portion of the leaf. Scanning the leaf closely, one of them read aloud the words: "I am the Resurrection, and the Life," and with that text upon the finger of the dead Christian, they buried him. Dying, he was really beginning to live. With his finger upon the promise that Christ was the Life, he passed from the land of the dying, to the land of the living, from struggle to conquest, from darkness into light, from pain to peace.—*Gospel Herald.*

* * *

The Blessing of His Absence

Oh, the anguish of Mary, the depth of despair,
When she came to the tomb and the Lord was not there!
As she desolate stood with her balm and her myrrh,
And His winding sheet only was waiting for her!

Oh, the blackness of death, oh, life's utter despair,
Had she come to the tomb and the Lord had been there,
Lying wrapped in the sheet with the balm and the myrrh,
And no risen Redeemer had waited for her!

—From *The Evangelical*, by Marion Douglas.

* * *

Ingersoll Nonplused

It is said that the late Robert G. Ingersoll, well known infidel, used to tell this story: "I was never nonplused but once. I was lecturing one night and took occasion to show that the resurrection of Lazarus was probably a planned affair to bolster the waning fortunes of Jesus. Lazarus was to take sick and die. The girls were to bury him and send for Jesus. Lazarus was to feign death till Jesus should come and say, 'Lazarus, come forth.' To emphasize the situation I said, 'Can anyone here tell me why Jesus said, "*Lazarus*, come forth"?'

Down by the door a pale-faced, white-haired man arose and with a shrill voice said, 'Yes, sir, I can tell you! If my Lord had not said, "Lazarus," he would have the whole graveyard of Bethany coming out to him!' " — *Sunday School Times.*

* * *

Proof of the Resurrection

To me, the central point is the Resurrection of Christ, which I believe. Firstly, because it is testified by men who had every opportunity of seeing and knowing, and whose veracity was tested by the most tremendous trials, both of energy and endurance, during long lives. Secondly, because of the marvelous effect it had upon the world. As a moral phenomenon, the spread and mastery of Christianity is without a parallel. I can no more believe that colossal moral effects lasting for two thousand years can be without a cause than I can believe that the various motions of the magnet are without a cause, though I cannot wholly explain them. To anyone who believes the Resurrection of Christ, the rest presents little difficulty. No one who has that belief will doubt that those who were commissioned by Him to speak — Paul, Peter, Mark, John — carried a Divine message.—The late Marquess of Salisbury, in the *Dawn.*

* * *

Not Dead!

At the funeral of Dr. A. J. Gordon in Boston, Dr. A. T. Pierson said that the telegram announcing his death came at three o'clock in the morning, and, being unable to sleep, he read the New Testament through from Matthew to Revelation to see what it said about death. And he noticed that after the resurrection of Jesus the apostles seldom used the word death to express the close of a Christian's life, but "sleep," "at home in the Lord," or "depart," "loose the moorings," as of a vessel about to set out on the sea.

What a comfort to the Christian to think of the loved ones as being "asleep in Christ," instead of having ceased to be.—Harry H. Crawford.

"Dying together" with Jesus,
This is the end of strife!
"Buried together" with Jesus,
This is the gate of life!
"Quickened together" with Jesus,
By the touch of God's mighty breath;
"Risen together" with Jesus,
Where is thy sting, O death?"

—Selected.

* * *

More Important than Knowing Where

A traveler in Switzerland, uncertain of his way, asked a small lad by the wayside where Kaudersteg was, and received, so he remarks, the most significant answer ever given him. "I do not know, sir," said the boy, "where Kaudersteg is, but there is the road to it." There are a great many things I cannot tell you about the life to come, but I know where lies the road. As I know Christ, the hope of glory, I have the certain assurance of immortality.—*Sunday School Times.*

* * *

Victory by Death

I had a bed of asters last summer that reached clear across my garden in the country. Oh, how gaily they bloomed! They were planted late. On the sides were yet fresh blossoming flowers, while the tops had gone to seed. Early frost came, and I found one day that the long line of radiant beauty was seared, and I said, "Ah! the season is too much for them; they have perished." I disliked to go and look at the bed, it looked so like a graveyard of flowers.

But, four or five weeks ago one of my men called my attention to the fact that along the whole line of that bed there were asters coming up in the greatest abundance; and I looked, and behold, for every plant that I thought the winter had destroyed, there were fifty plants that it had planted.

What did those frosts and surly winds do? They caught my flowers, they slew them, they cast them to the ground, they trod with snowy feet upon them, and they said, leaving their work, "This is the end of you!" And the next spring there were for every root, fifty witnesses to rise up and say, "By death we live." And as it is in the floral tribe, so it is in God's kingdom. *By death came everlasting life.—Streams in the Desert.*

* * *

Our Lord's Loving Purpose

"The other day," writes Dr. Gray, in the January *Moody Bulletin*, "I read of a traveler in Portugal who saw a fisherman's wife at the waterside holding an infant child by the hand. They were opposite a deep and dangerous spot, and the mother was leading the boy toward the brink. When the ripples of the water wet his feet he was alarmed and clung to her. But with soft and affectionate caresses she led him there again and again, until at length, emboldened by her encouragement, he toddled down alone. The traveler trembled at the risk and uttered an exclamation, for a few feet farther the water deepened dangerously. But there was no real cause for alarm. The mother's eye was on the boy and her hand was ready to catch him before he went too far. 'What are you doing?' the traveler asked. 'Drawing out his fear,' the woman answered. Ah, dear friends," says Dr. Gray, "there is a tenderer, surer Hand that guides our earthly way, 'drawing out our fear.'" **So Christ, by an oft reiteration of the** worst that lay before Him led His disciples to the very brink of the abyss itself and pointed to them the hope of the resurrection.—*Sunday School Times.*

* * *

What Was It that Set Us Free

If you lay imprisoned in some great fortress, and one who loved you went forth to try to rescue you, and fell and died fighting, you would cherish the memory of your friend's valiant effort on your behalf, but you would still remain in chains, undelivered. So it would have been with those whom Christ came to save if He had not risen; those for whom He gave His life would have been undelivered. But Christ has conquered death and holds in His hands the keys of the grave.—Dr. J. R. Miller.

What saith the empty tomb to me
This hallowed Easter morn?
It speaks of life and victory,
And glorious hope new-born.

It tells of One who hung in shame
Upon a cross of woe,
That all who call upon His name
Eternal life might know.

It tells me He hath risen indeed,
And at the Father's throne
Now daily stands to intercede
For His redeemed, His own.

It tells me that because He lives,
I too shall never die;
And everlasting hope it gives
Of joy with Him on high.

It tells me death is overthrown—
Yea, 'tis a conquered foe,
For Christ the way of life hath shown
Through Calvary's cross of woe.

What saith the empty tomb today?
It saith, "The Lord hath risen,
Dispelling evermore the gloom
Of death's foreboding prison."

It saith, "Look unto Him and live,
For He hath power to save;
Life everlasting He doth give,
And vict'ry o'er the grave!"
—Avis B. Christiansen.

* * *

Dr. Meyer Going Home

Surely never was a more touching letter written than this by Dr. F. B. Meyer when he knew that his time on earth was now very short. It was to Pastor D. J. Findlay, of Glasgow.

"MY DEAR F. AND WIFE,—To my surprise I have just been told that my days and hours are numbered. It may be that before this reaches you I shall have gone into the Palace. Don't trouble to write. We shall meet in the morning.—With much love, yours affectionately.

F. B. MEYER.

—*Pathway of Blessing.*

* * *

"The Place Where God Is"

"Doctor, I want you to get me well by Sunday!" said a dear little lad not yet five years old, stricken suddenly with a fatal disease. "Why, my boy?" asked the kind doctor. "Well, you know, teacher showed us the tabernacle last Sunday. We saw all the outside, but there was a curtain, and teacher said the priest went in behind it to speak to God, and she is going to show us about it next Sunday. Oh, Doctor, shan't I be able to go? I do so want to see inside where God was." The doctor had walked to the window while Charlie was speaking, but now came back, and laying a caressing hand on the child's feverish brow he said softly, "Next Sunday, dear, you may see the place where God is." Next Sunday he had passed away—the little white crib was empty. Little Charlie had passed from earth to "the place where God is." —*The Life Line.*

* * *

The Note of Triumph

That useful and beloved Jewish-Christian, the Rev. Joseph S. Flacks, who passed to glory recently, mailed on the very day of his death the following post card message to friends:

TRIUMPHANT THROUGH GRACE

This is to announce: I moved out of the old mud house (II Cor. 5:1); arrived in Glory-land instantly, in charge of the angelic escort (Luke 16:22); absent from the body, *at home* with the Lord (II Cor. 5:6).

I find, as foretold (Psa. 16:11), "in thy presence *fulness of joy . . . pleasures* for evermore!"

Will look for YOU on *the way up* at the redemption of the body (Rom. 8:23). Till then *look up.*

J. S. FLACKS.

—*Sunday School Times.*

* * *

"You'll Get Me Back"

From the pen of a missionary writer comes this beautiful story. A faithful missionary in distant Korea sat by the bedside of his dying wife. For fifteen years they had toiled together in the Gospel of Jesus Christ. And now her summons had come. The heartbroken husband sat waiting for the end. She knew what the parting meant to him. She realized the keenness of his suffering. So, with her last thought an unselfish one for him, she left him this last message of eternal comfort, "Do not grieve for me, my dear. You'll get me back; you'll get me back." A month passed and the grief-stricken husband sat by the same bedside watching the spirit of their only child, a little four-year-old boy, take its flight to the same Lord to whom the darling mother had gone. Again the father's heart was crushed. Again he faced a parting which meant untold anguish to him. But the little fellow had the same message as his mother for the sorrowing father. "Don't cry, daddy," said he. "Don't cry. Daddy, I see a great, shining light. It's coming nearer, daddy, it's coming nearer. And daddy, it's mudder; it's mudder! And I want to go, I want to go. But don't cry, daddy, don't cry. You'll get me back; you'll get me back!" A few days later the stricken father was riding in the funeral train behind the body of his dead boy. From behind the curtains of the chair in which he was being borne by the natives he heard the voice of a woman weeping. Presently the voice of another Korean woman spoke up and said, "Why are you weeping?" The sorrowing woman answered, "I am weeping for the foreigner who has lost his little boy." "Don't weep for the foreigner; weep for yourself, woman," came the answer. "You have lost a little girl, and you will never get her back. I have lost a little boy, and I shall never get him back. But let me tell you something. These foreigners have a strange way of getting back their dead!" And then as the stricken father laid the white lily upon the coffin of his little one, he bowed his head before his Lord and gave himself anew to Him to preach to these heathen people that blessed Gospel of Jesus Christ which would give back their dead to all who believe in Him as Saviour and Lord of the glory that is one day to come with Him. For he knew that if death came he would go to them, but if resurrection first, they would come to him.—*Gospel Herald.*

No Good-Bye Needed

A Christian mill owner was fatally hurt one day. With wonderful serenity he proceeded to the tasks a dying man must do. A lawyer was summoned and a settlement of his business was made, then his wife and children were brought in. There was a most affectionate leave-taking. Then came his aged father whose face reflected his steadfast faith. "Father," said the son tenderly, "it is hardly worth while saying good-bye to you." Kneeling by his son the patriarch prayed with the simple fervency of a great soul. Then he took the hand of his son, already entering the shadows. "No, Aleck," he said comfortingly, "it is hardly worth while for us to say good-bye."—*Christian Herald.*

* * *

A Voice from the Other World

I knew a young man who was an infidel. He told me that he did not sympathize with my belief in God; he did not even believe in a future state. He said, "When I die I am going to dust, and that will be the end of me." He had a Christian mother, who had long prayed for him. One day he came home from his office about noon and said, "Mother, I feel fatigued; I think I will lie down till lunch is ready"; so he lay down and fell asleep. At one o'clock she spoke to him and said, "We are ready to sit down at the table." but she could not waken him. She shook him violently, but she could not rouse him. He was in a comatose state, and there was no perceptible pulse. He sank lower and lower until his breathing also was scarcely perceptible. They sent at once for a physician, who came in, examined his pulse, listened to his heart, made a thorough examination, but said, "I can do nothing for him; you will just be compelled to leave him as he is. He may come out of it, and he may not." He went away. About five o'clock in the afternoon, as they were sitting around him, simply watching the last rays of flickering life, he opened his eyes, looked around, saw his mother, and stretched out his hand to her. He said, "Mother, what you taught me is all true; there is a future life. I have been treading along the verge of another world, and been looking over into that other world. Mother, it is all true!" He shut his eyes and died.

God allowed him to come back from the other world just long enough to assure that mother who had trained him in the true faith, that he saw at the last his error and abandoned his infidelity, and then he passed away. — Arthur T. Pierson.

* * *

When Death Must Yield

A radio preacher, speaking recently of God's resurrection power, spoke this word of comfort: "You may be taken to the Potter's Field. But never fear; if you are a saint of God, the trumpet will locate you." And it will not be a long, difficult hunt for God, for "in a moment, in the twinkling of an eye, at the last trump: for the trumpet shall sound, and the dead shall be raised incorruptible, and we (who are living when the Lord comes) shall be changed." Thank God for the locating trumpet! Better still, thank God for the Lord who seeks and saves that which is lost, even the dead bodies of those whose souls have been with Him. — *Sunday School Times.*

* * *

An Easter Poem

Should saints fear death since Christ arose
And took away its sting and woes,
And broke its sway and power?
Can death bear off on pinioned wing,
The spirit of the saints will sing?
Or, can it knowledge take away,
And leave them in oblivion's sway
For e'en one passing hour?
Nay, death can only ope the door
That points the way to Heaven's shore,
To glory and to power.

But, o'er our bodies which decay
Does death hold unremittent sway
Forever and forever?
Nay, disembodied though we be,
Our bodies shall from dust be free;
The sun goes down to rise again,

The parched ground revives with rain,
And shall we rise, no, never?
Lo, Jesus rose, we too shall rise
And raptured mount the vaulted skies
Where naught from Him shall sever.
—R. E. Neighbour, D.D.

* * *

Lasting Longer than the Cross

In walking through the Continental section of our great picture galleries, how rarely do we see a picture of the risen, radiant Son of God. On One occasion Michelangelo turned upon his fellow artists in a spirit of great indignation and said: "Why do you keep filling gallery after gallery with endless pictures of the one ever-reiterated theme, of Christ in weakness, Christ upon the cross, Christ dying, most of all Christ hanging dead? Why do you concentrate upon that pasing episode, as if that were the last word and the final scene, as if the curtain dropped upon that hour of disaster and defeat? At worst, that only lasted a few hours. But to the end of unending eternity, *Christ is alive: Christ rules and reigns and triumphs*." Romanists and Anglo-Catholics need a similar rebuke in our own day. In revealing Himself to John on the Isle of Patmos, our glorified and exalted Lord said: "Fear not; I am the first and the last: I am he that liveth, and was dead; and, behold, I am alive forevermore."—*Sunday School Times.*

* * *

The Christian Doctor's Message

The doctor was a strong, sunny nature who carried good cheer into his patients' homes and still had enough for the frail little wife who needed all the vigor of his personality to sustain her. When the doctor suddenly passed away friends said, "It will kill her!" But the life of faith in God that they two had shared together did not fail her. By the doorway of the living room she fastened the card that he had sometimes left, in short absences, on his office door: GONE OUT—BACK SOON. Those who came with consolation went away, themselves consoled by that brief message.—Condensed from the *Youth's Companion.*

"He Will Yet Deliver Us" (II Cor. 1:10)

Beneath Westminster Abbey is an old crypt which for centuries was used as the burial place of the early kings. It is related that one day, some years ago, a visitor who had wandered into this vault was locked in. He did not notice as the doors swung together. The janitors were busy, and no one heard the muffled voice which began to cry from the crypt, or the muffled blows which began to beat upon its oaken door. The afternoon passed away. What that imprisoned man suffered as it gradually grew upon him that he was buried alive, who can know?

At the usual hour the janitor made his evening round before closing the building for the night. The entombed man heard him as his footsteps came near, then retreated, came near again then, finally receding, grew fainter and fainter, and died away at length in the distance. What imagination can conceive his agony! He redoubled his cries. He dashed his body wildly against the solid door. In vain.

Now he thought he heard the distant entrance doors creak on their hinges, and the key pushed into the great iron lock. In a moment more the vast tomb would be closed for the night. Fortunately, before turning the key, the janitor paused a moment and listened. He thought he heard dull blows faint and far away—a sound as of stifled, agonizing cries. He listened more intently. A horrible thought suggested itself to his mind: "Someone is locked into the crypt." He hastened to the place, threw open the heavy oaken door, and held his lantern up to see. The buried man had fallen senseless upon the stone floor. He was rescued just in time to save his reason.

Were it not for the resurrection of Jesus Christ, we had all been like that poor imprisoned man, helplessly and hopelessly beating our wounded fists and raising our hopeless cries against the bolted door of the living tomb.—Watchword and Truth.

More Beyond

If the grave had ended all with the Lord Jesus, there would be utterly nothing beyond death for the children of God. Before Columbus discovered the New World, the coat of arms of Spain bore the motto: "Ne Plus Ultra," which means, "There is nothing beyond." The three-mile limit of their shore line was the limit of their utmost horizon and furthest possibilities. But Columbus envisioned undiscovered world's beyond, and braved the terrors of the then unknown and uncharted sea. With his discoveries, the "Ne" was dropped from the Spanish coat of arms, leaving the "Plus Ultra"—'There Is More Beyond!"

Before the Lord Jesus Christ came into the world and brought life and immortality to light, the grave was the utmost limit of all human hopes and expectations. "Ne Plus Ultra" was the motto of human kind, until Jesus divested death of its sting and turned the radiance of an endless life upon the valley of the shadow of death, so that now there shines from the portals of death the hope-inspiring words: "Plus Ultra" —"THERE IS MORE BEYOND!" How much more, only the unfolding æons of an immeasurable eternity can bring before our wondering eyes: "Eye hath not seen, nor ear heard, neither have entered into the heart of man, the things which God hath prepared for them that love him" (I Cor. 2:9).—*Because He Lives*."—By Walter Brown Knight.

* * *

"All Clear"

When a Christian passes into the presence of his Lord, he no longer sees "through a glass darkly; but . . . face to face" (I Cor. 13:12). Much that we cannot understand down here will become "all clear" when we reach our heavenly Home. These two words have become very familiar in this present war, as they are used to describe the signal that marks the end of an air raid. A remarkable incident is given by Mrs. Spencer Johnson in this summer's *Life and Liberty*. "A friend of many years has been called Home. At the hour of her death, there was an air raid overhead. Her sister was near to her, waiting to hear the 'All Clear' to sound. The invalid was sinking fast, and had not been able to speak. Quietly she opened her eyes, looking happy and restful, and said in a clear strong voice: 'That's the All Clear,' as its welcomed sound was heard. Then she passed away. Was it not a fresh vision of the power of the blood of Jesus, and the clear way to Glory as she fell asleep in His arms?" We too may take comfort from this striking coincidence of two events which were undoubtedly providentially joined together. Christ has opened for us "a new and living way" (Heb. 10:20), and there will be no more misunderstanding nor darkness, nor sin, nor sorrow in His presence.—Selected.

* * *

The True Andrew Jackson

We have heard much of "Jackson Day Dinners," and appeals have been made, in the name of "true Democracy," to the memory of Andrew Jackson, the seventh President of the United States. Would that our President and other leaders in our Government would take a leaf from Andrew Jackson's Christian faith, who wrote this as his own epitaph: "I have prepared an humble depository for my mortal body beside that wherein lies my beloved wife, where, without any pomp or parade, I have requested, when my God calls me to sleep with my fathers, to be laid; for both of us there to remain until the last trumpet sounds to call the dead to judgment, when we, I hope, shall rise together, clothed with that heavenly body promised to all who believe in our glorious Redeemer who died for us that we might live, and by whose atonement I hope for a blessed immortality."—*Sunday School Times*.

* * *

They Were Never There

When Fricourt on the Somme was taken by the Allies in July, 1916, the village cemetery was found to have been heaved and shattered to bits as by an earthquake. Afterwards, when the Germans went right back to the "Hindenburg line," the peasants came trickling up to their village and sought out the cemetery; but the cemetery was no longer there. They lamented and said, "Where are our dead?" A priest of theirs was standing by, and he said to them, "Children, our departed were never there!" Then they wept afresh, but now with joy as of a new discovery, and they were much comforted. It took the thundering earthquake wrought by monstrous shells to open their minds to this shining Christian truth. And yet this revealing earthquake had taken place 1,900 years ago for all to know and see. —Dr. A. Boyd Scott, in the *British Weekly*.

* * *

Better Than a Dead Bone

When in South Africa I heard a colored Christian give an address. This is an illustration he used: "When a heathen is dying, the witch doctors put in his hand a dead bone as a passport into the world beyond. But we do not grasp a dead bone as we pass through the veil. We grasp the hand of the living Lord." —Rev. H. Lees.

* * *

The Master's Touch

The famous clock in Strasburg Cathedral had a mechanism so complicated that it seemed to the ignorant and superstitious almost a work of superhuman skill. The abused and offended maker, while as yet unpaid for his work, came one day and touched its secret springs, and it stopped. All the patience and ingenuity of a nation's mechanics and artisans failed to restore its disordered mechanism and set it in motion. Afterward, when his grievances were redressed, that maker came again, touched the inner springs, and set it again in motion, and all its multiplied parts revolved again obedient to his will. When thus by a touch, he suspended and restored those marvelous movements, he gave to any doubting mind proof that he was the maker, and certainly the master, of that clock. And when Jesus of Nazareth brings to a stop the mechanism of nature, makes its mighty wheels turn back, or in any way arrests its grand movement—more than all, when He cannot only stop, but start again, the mysterious clock of human life — He gives to an honest mind overwhelming proof that He is God. For a malignant power might arrest or destroy, but only God could reconstruct and restore.—A. T. Pierson.

* * *

The Price Accepted

In the market squares of the Orient, merchants display their articles for sale. The purchaser lays down the price beside something that he desires. The moment the merchant lifts the price, the sale is made. The act is an indication that the price lifted has been accepted. At the cross, Christ laid down His life. On the third day, God lifted the price. Thus it is that we can say in the words of another, "When Christ was crucified, the law was magnified, justice was satisfied, sin was nullified, God was glorified, and the sinner was justified."—*The King's Business.*

* * *

Christ Has Risen!

Tomb, thou shalt hold Him no longer;
Death is strong, but life is stronger;
Stronger than the dark, the light;
Stronger than the wrong, the right;
Faith and hope triumphant say,
Christ will rise on Easter Day.

While the patient earth lies waking,
Till the morning shall be breaking,
Shivering 'neath the burden dread
Of her Master cold and dead,
Hark! she hears the angels say,
Christ will rise on Easter Day.

And when sunrise smites the mountains,
Pouring light from heavenly fountains,
Then the earth blooms out to greet
Once again the blessed feet;
And the countless voices say,
Christ has risen on Easter Day.

—Phillips Brooks, reprinted from *Moody Monthly.*

Where the Road Stopped

An old Indian chief was told of the Saviour, but he said: "The Jesus road is good, but I have followed the old Indian road all my life, and I will follow it to the end." A year later he was on the border of the shadow of death. As he was seeking a pathway through the darkness, he said to the missionary: "Can I turn to the Jesus road now? My road stops here. It has no path through the valley."—*The King's Business.*

* * *

The Watchword—Lutanda

Dan Crawford used to tell how, when his Africans were on the march and night was coming on, they would lie down to sleep. But before dropping off to sleep there would pass from group to group about the fires the watchword *Lutanda* ("Morning Star"). It was a laconic agreement to be up and ready to move when the morning star appeared. To Mr. Crawford it was ever a parable for those who lay down in their last sleep with heart and mind fixed on Him who is the Bright and Morning Star, and who will awaken the sleeping to resurrection life and glory. — *The King's Business.*

* * *

Her Easter Picture

In an art school a prize was offered to the one who should draw the most beautiful Easter card. Every girl's heart and brain was busy, except one, and she never again would be well and strong. All day she must sit and press her patient face against the one bright window and watch her classmates go to and from school. At her side was a rose bush that had blossomed many times but now its branches were slowly withering. On the other side was a lily just showing a pure white bud. Easter was drawing near and all the other girls had finished their drawings but she could think of nothing but her sufferings.

One day she saw an ugly caterpillar crawling on the withered rose bush and said to her nurse, "I am just like that poor, tired caterpillar that can only crawl around and lie in the sun." The nurse tried to comfort her by telling how the ugly worm made a gorgeous butterfly. Not long after, one bright sunny morning the sick girl cried out in great delight: "Look at that beautiful creature on my lily. Where did it come from? Someone must have opened the window!" There on the open lily rested an exquisite butterfly. On the dry sand of the rose pot lay only a little hairy skeleton. The caterpillar had left his old shell at last and risen into the new life and glory of a butterfly. Suddenly the sick girl exclaimed, "I've got my Easter picture!" Pencils and colors were quickly brought and her eager fingers painted in one corner of a card, the rose bush and ugly caterpillar; in the other a pure white lily and the beautiful butterfly. Her picture was sent in with the others. When Easter morning dawned, the teacher held a beautiful card before the class and told them the prize had been given to the little sufferer whose patient face had so often looked out on them from between the lily and the rose. As her name was read, every scholar clapped their hands in wonder and joy. —*Gospel Herald.*

* * *

The Declining Years

When Dr. Rees preached last in North Wales, a friend said to him, "You are whitening fast, Dr. Rees." The old gentleman did not say anything then, but when he got into the pulpit, he said, "There is a wee white flower that comes at this season of the year. Sometimes it comes up through the snow and frost, but we are all glad to see the snowdrop, because it proclaims that winter is over and the summer is at hand. A friend has reminded me that I am whitening fast. But heed not that, brother; it is to me *a proof that my winter will soon be over; that I shall have done presently with the cold east winds and the frosts of earth, and that my summer, my eternal summer is at hand.*"—*United Methodist.*

The headstone over a little mound in a cemetery bears just these words: "Freddy!" as if someone called, and underneath, "Yes, Father!" as if someone answered.—*Sunday at Home.*

* * *

Known of Him

"He calleth his own sheep by name." John 10:3.

"Mary!" just one word;
'Twas all He need employ
To turn a woman's sorrowing heart
Into a well of joy.

She thought He was the gardener;
"Master!" she answered now.
His voice, her name—it was enough;
She asked not, "Is it Thou?"

In my great hour of trial
The Saviour oft appears;
He makes no long, impressive speech
To scatter all my fears.

He gently speaks my name.
Enough! What need I more,
Than to be known and loved of Him
Whom Heaven and earth adore?

Men know not Jesus lives,
In unbelief they dwell;
And as to Mary then, so now,
He bids us, "Go—and tell."

REVIVAL

"Successful" Method

Due to report of successful revivals by Gipsy Smith, a certain preacher approached the noted evangelist to ascertain the secret of his success. He was asked to explain the best method to start a revival. The answer was: "Brother, go back home, lock yourself up in a private room. Take a piece of chalk and mark a circle on the floor, get down on your knees inside the circle, pray God to start a revival inside this circle. *When this prayer is answered, the revival will be on.*"—C. A. Curry, in *Western Recorder.*

* * *

Where Is the Revival?

During the revival which some years ago swept through the land of Wales, and whose power that principality feels to this day, a friend of mine went down from London to take part in some of its services. He got out at a country station and asked the policeman standing in the village square, "Where is the Welsh revival?" The man in blue drew himself up to his full height, patted his chest, and said: "The Welsh revival, sir, is under these buttons!"—*Sunday School Times.*

Revival

In a certain town there had been no revival for many years. The church was nearly run out. The people were unconverted. Spiritual desolation reigned. There lived in the town an old blacksmith, who stammered so greatly in his speech that it was painful to hear him speak. At work in his shop his mind became greatly exercised about the church; his agony was so great he locked the door and spent the afternoon in prayer. He prevailed with God. He then obtained the reluctant consent of his pastor to appoint a meeting, but with no hope on the preacher's part of any attendance. But the room was more than filled. All was silent for a time until one sinner broke out in tears and begged, if anyone could pray, to pray for him. Others followed, and it was found that persons from every quarter of the town were under deep conviction—all dating their conviction from the hour the old man was praying in his shop. A powerful revival followed. The stammering man prevailed and, as a prince, had power with God.—*Gospel Banner.*

A Prayer in Song

John Newton, who lived in a dark day, in common with faithful ministers and their people, was praying for the reappearance of revival. He wrote to a friend: "A revival is wanted here with us as it is with you, and some of us are praying and also singing for a revival. The song we are singing will be found on the reverse side of my letter." This was their revival song:

Saviour, visit Thy plantation,
Send, oh send, a gracious rain;
All will come to desolation
Unless Thou dost bless again.

Break the tempter's fatal power,
Turn the stony hearts to flesh,
And begin this very hour
To revive Thy work afresh.

Once, O Lord, Thy garden flourished;
Every part looked gay and green;
Then Thy Word our spirits nourished:
Happy seasons we have seen.

But a drought has since succeeded,
And a sad decline we see:
Lord, Thy help is greatly needed:
Help can only come from Thee.

Let our mutual love be fervent:
Make us prevalent in prayer;
Let each one esteemed Thy servant
Shun the world's bewitching snare.

—*Sunday School Times.*

* * *

Spiritual Leaders Needed

Roger W. Babson declares, "Today the nation is in another unemployment pocket. As Whitefield pulled us out following 1730; as Finney saved the day following 1810; as Moody reshaped America beginning 1858; and as a score of national evangelists restored confidence following 1898, so the nation is awaiting such spiritual leaders today."
—Selected.

* * *

Roosevelt Said:

"We still remain true to the faith of our fathers who established religious liberty when the nation began," the President said. "We must remember, too, that our forebears in every generation, and wherever they established their homes, made prompt and generous provision for the institutions of religion. We must continue their steadfast reliance upon the providence of God.

"I have said and I repeat to this solemn eucharistic congress that no greater blessing could come to our land today than a revival of the spirit of religion. I doubt if there is any problem in the world today — social, political, or economic—that would not find happy solution if approached in the spirit of the Sermon on the Mount."—Franklin D. Roosevelt.

* * *

A Needed Kind of Revival

A native of India, writing to a friend about a great revival they were having, said, "We are having a great rebible here." The Church needs to be rebibled.
—*C. E. World.*

REWARDS

Degrees in Heaven

A lady was bringing her plants into the house in the autumn. Some had hardly grown at all—they had made no progress and produced no bloom. They had just lived, and that was about all. Others had done well—grown strong and beautiful, and repaid her care by abundant blossoms. The former were taken in and saved from perishing, but had obscure places, with little regard or use —just saved and that was all—while those which had used their powers and opportunities were taken to grace the parlors and windows of the house, and given missions of beauty and power. So it is with people in God's garden and house, some are just saved, "so as by fire"; they "hardly enter in." But those who live lives of loving service to God and humanity have an abundant entrance into the joy of the Lord.—Selected.

* * *

"Let No Man Take Thy Crown"

Have you become discouraged? Have you allowed something to keep you from being what you know you should be? Have you allowed depression or disaster to make you lose heart and to slacken your effort? If so, remember the Word of the Lord: "That no man take thy crown." Be diligent; in season and out of season. Be faithful in the face of storm, as well as in times of sunshine, for if there is "no battle, there will be no victory; no cross, no crown."—Henry J. Westermeyer, in *Christian Observer.*

* * *

Bennie Locke's Railroad Run

Bennie Locke, an engine driver who has done fifty-seven years of service on the Lakawanna Railroad, and has never received a demerit mark from his superior officers, had the habit, during the greater part of his service, of removing his cap on entering his engine and uttering a prayer for God's protection on each day's run. One experience he thus describes: "Number Six was twenty-five minutes late out of Scranton one day, and I had my little prayer as usual when I stepped into the cab. After I had asked for the safety of our train, I said, 'Lord, help me to bring her in on time.' It was a stiff climb up the Pocono Mountains for the first part of the trip, and it never seems so steep as when you are late. I couldn't gain a second on the way up but after we dipped over the summit, things began to break just right for me. It was a beautiful day, with air perfectly clear, and we almost flew down the mountain. I just held her steady and let her go. At last the old train shed at Hoboken loomed ahead, and, as we pulled into the station I looked at my watch and we were just on the dot. As I stood wiping the sweat from my face there was a tap of a cane on the outside of my cab and on looking out I saw the president of the road, all smiles, and he said to me, 'A good run, sir! A very good run!' That meant more to me than anything that could have happened in this world. And, brother, when I make my last run, and pull into the Great Terminal, if I can just hear Him say, 'A good run, sir! A very good run!' the toil and the struggle down here won't matter." — *Sunday School Times.*

* * *

Andrew Bonar's Answer

When Andrew Bonar made his first and only visit to America, they gave him a farewell meeting in New York. Several men eulogized him, and one man in closing said, "Think of the 'crown of righteousness,' which is laid up for Andrew Bonar, 'which the Lord, the righteous judge,' shall give him in that day." Dear old Andrew Bonar walked to the front of the platform and held up his hands toward Heaven and completed Paul's saying to Timothy: "and not to me only, but unto all them also that love His appearing."—James M. Gray, in the *Sunday School Times.*

* * *

The Joy Set Before Us

It will make the toils of the road and all the renunciation and willing sacrifices of life seem nothing to have some such words of commendation from the lips of our glorious Saviour, and to hear Him say to one who has sought to be faithful at all cost: "Well done! You were never popular on earth, and nobody knew about you. The life you laid down for Me in that Central African village, or in that crowded Chinese city, or lived to My glory in the uninspiring sphere of home duty seemed to be wasted and its sacrifices to be worthless by those who knew it; but 'thy love to Me was wonderful.' Men said you made mistakes and were narrow-minded; men thought that you were a fanatic and a fool and called you so; men crucified you as they crucified Me; but '*thy love to Me was wonderful.*' "—*Northfield Calendar.*

After the Cross the Crown

When all around seems dark and drear,
The heart with lonely grief bowed down,
No earthly friend to soothe or cheer,
There's One who lends a listening ear
And says, "My child, give Me thy fear:
After the cross the crown."

When hope lies dead, and not one ray
Of sunshine lights the world's dark frown;
When sorrow's tear, like ocean's spray,
Will from thy burdened heart find way:
In accents tender hear Him say,
"After the cross the crown."

Poor tossed one, weep no more, but leave
At His dear feet thy burden down;
Thy Father speaks, no longer grieve;
Rejoice in Him, His Word believe;
Earth's night is brief; thou'lt soon receive
After the cross thy crown.

—Isa L. Christenson, in *Herald of Holiness.*

* * *

God Doesn't Give Half Crowns

A minister in England was preaching to a crowd of people in a street meeting. A rough man, driving past, shouted, "Well, governor, you'll be getting a half crown for that job." Instantly, the minister replied, "No, my man, you are wrong. The Lord Jesus Christ, my Master, never gives half crowns. He gives whole crowns to those who serve Him."—*Gospel Herald.*

* * *

"Well Done!"

A short time ago, one of our blind soldiers was playing the piano in the convalescent ward of a London hospital. Presently some visitors entered the room, but he was used to such interruptions, and played on, filling the long ward with lovely melody. When the music ceased, a gentleman walked over to the piano and said, "Well done, my friend!" The surprised soldier, thinking it was one of his comrades, swung round on his stool, and with a smile said, "And who are you?" Quick as a flash, and as startling, came the reply, "Your King!" In an instant the man was on his feet with his hand at salute, his whole being instinct with pleasure at the honor accorded him by the royal word of praise. —*The Sunday Strand.*

* * *

When We Haven't Much to Show

There is a very human story told of a commercial traveler who presented himself before his chief after finishing his round. Taking the very small batch of orders in his hand, the manager looked at the man and said, "And is this all you've done?" In reply the man looked steadily at his employer and said, "No, sir, it isn't all I've done, but I'm afraid it is all I can show." In our work for God it is often when we toil hardest that we can show the least tangible result. But if there has been the earnest endeavor to serve Christ, we may be sure that He knows all about it, and will reward us accordingly.—*United Methodist.*

* * *

God's Hundredfold

Mrs. Amanda Smith said, "When God does anything, He does it handsome." "So," said J. Hudson Taylor, "God's hundredfold is a very liberal one. He has given me a thousand fathers and mothers, sisters and brothers, friends and homes—everything that I ever left for Him. What a household is the household of faith! What a family is that of which God has made us members! Why, all the choice and the noble, and all the beautiful and the good, the grand and the faithful are ours. We are allied to them all. We are all one in Christ Jesus."—*The King's Business.*

* * *

Is a Sunday School Worth While?

Two men met upon a steamer during a Scotch excursion and talked of many things, among others of Sabbath schools. "To tell the truth," said one of them, "I am not very enthusiastic about that kind of work. I was a teacher for many years, and, after all, I seem to have done no good." "Well, I do believe in Sabbath school work," said the other. "As a lad I received life-long influences for good in my old class." And he named the school with which he had once been connected. "Were you there?" asked the other. "That is where I taught. Were you there in my time? My name is George Brown." "And I was your scholar. I remember you now," said the younger man. "I owe everything to you." There, side by side, stood the teacher who believed that he had done nothing, and the man he had influenced for life.—*The Presbyterian.*

* * *

Russian Guard

The story is told of the suffering in Russia many years ago; how the Christians were persecuted and imprisoned: Some gave up Christianity and their faith in Christ and were freed. Others chose to suffer, "not accepting deliverance." The story went on to tell of seventy who had been imprisoned for a long time, underfed, and at last taken out, thinly clad, one cold winter night, to a lake of ice where they were left to die.

A Russian guard was in charge of them. He was warmly clad, and properly fed and did not mind the cold. However he seemed to see the prisoners fall one by one on the ice, and as one fell it seemed as if the heavens opened and an angel appeared with a golden crown. Then another would fall and another angel appeared with another golden crown.

It seemed as if they had nearly all fallen, and the Russian guard, thinking he must be in a trance or a dream, aroused himself and found all had fallen save one.

That one called to him, and said: "Oh, sir, save my life, I'm dying! I'll not be a Christian, anything, only save my life."

"Quick," said the Russian guard, "change clothes with me." And he stepped out on the ice. He had seen that there was one more angel and one more golden crown.—Courtesy *Moody Monthly.*

* * *

"Cast the bread upon the waters,
Ye who have a scant supply;
Angel eyes will watch above it,
You will find it by and by.
He who in His righteous balance,
Doth each human action weigh;
Will your sacrifice remember,
Will your loving deeds repay."
—Selected.

RICHES

Property Not Subject to Taxation

A tax collector one day came to a poor minister in order to assess the value of his property and to determine the amount of his taxes.

"I am a rich man," said the minister.

The official quickly sharpened his pencil and asked intently, "Well, what do you own?"

The pastor replied, "I am the possessor of a Saviour who earned for me everlasting life and who has prepared a place for me in the Eternal City."

"What else?"

"I have a brave, pious wife, and Solomon says, 'Who can find a virtuous woman? for her price is far above rubies.' "

"What else?"

"Healthy and obedient children."

"What else?"

"A merry heart which enables me to pass through life joyfully."

"What else?"

"That is all," replied the minister.

The official closed his book, took his hat and said, "*You are indeed a rich man, sir, but your property is not subject to taxation.*"—*The King's Business.*

"Rich Toward God"

These words are found in connection with the parable of the rich fool, whose folly illustrates that of every person who "layeth up treasure for himself and is not rich toward God."

There are four classes of people when it comes to the matter of possessions. (1) Those who are rich in this world's goods and poor toward God. (2) Those who are poor in this world and rich toward God. (3) Others are poor in both this world and the next. (4) Some have considerable amount of this world's goods, but because they hold them with a loose hand they are rich in the next world, too. But this latter class are not very numerous. Only a few can possess much of the materials of earth without attaching their hearts here, too. "Where your treasure is, there will your heart be also." — Roy L. Hollenback, in *Gospel Herald.*

* * *

The Power of a Gold Piece

A man once visited Robert Hall to make exception to some statement which the preacher had made in his sermon. It was evident that the man was in the grip and bondage of the love of money. When Hall had gauged the man's character he took a half-sovereign out of his pocket, and, opening the Bible, pointed to the word "God." "Can you see that?" said Robert Hall. "Certainly," replied the man. Then the preacher took the half-sovereign and placed it over the word. "Can you see it now?" he asked. The man immediately understood the symbol, and through it was led into the light. Gold hid God. Money blocked the vision. Love of money shut out the face of the Father.—*The Sunday Circle.*

* * *

James W——, British financier and reputed millionaire, who had owned a yacht and racing stud, entertained royalty, and had made as much as three million dollars in one day, died by his own hand, practically a ruined man.

Before he brought his life to a close he wrote a letter which was published in the British press, and laid bare the truth without any false coloring, of what this world really is.

He had tasted all that this life could give and now records his verdict in the truest sermon ever preached by mortal man. Hear what he says:

"On the last day of my life, before my eyes, my brain unwinds the film of the past. In quick succession episode after episode unwinds, *and I can now judge that life today is nothing but a caldron of greed, lust, and power.* Gone are the nice feelings and contentment, and in their place is a roaring hectic existence."

He draws aside the curtain and shows us the world in its true character. "I have known," he says, "to have all you desire and to have thousands waiting to eat out of your hand. From this it must be agreed," he adds, "that I am entitled to an opinion on life."—*Gospel Herald.*

* * *

What Agassiz Could Not Afford to Do

The great Agassiz was devoting time and talent to a poorly paid but absorbing line of scientific study, when he received a message from a college president offering him what seemed a munificent sum to come and deliver a course of lectures on Natural History. His characteristic reply was rather startling, but might well be stamped on the hearts of all God's stewards: "I cannot afford to waste time making money."—Courtesy *Moody Monthly.*

* * *

"Died Rich"

Many years ago John Somethingorother, a gold prospector, at last believed himself rich. But he was starving amid the shifting dunes of Death Valley, Cal. On a scrap of paper John scribbled, "Died rich." Then hugging a small bowlder of mica, whose pyrites, resembling gold, apparently had deceived him, John passed away. Recently a party of motor tourists discovered the skeleton. An old miner's pick lay near by. A rusty watch was also found—but was not running.—*Pathfinder.*

True Wealth

"How does it feel to be a millionaire?" George M. Pullman was asked.

"I have never thought of that," replied the maker of Pullman cars and owner of Pullman city; "but, now that you mention it, I believe that I am no better off—certainly not happier, than when I did not have a dollar to my name, and had to work from daylight till dark. I wore a good suit of clothes then, and I only wear one suit now. I relished three meals a day then a good deal more than I do three meals a day now. I had fewer cares, I slept better, and may add generally, that I believe I was far happier in those days than I have been many times since I became a millionaire."

True wealth is found in the knowledge of Christ and of His great salvation and in the possession of the real abiding riches which He bestows on all who believe in Him.

The heart can never be satisfied with anything of the world, and the world passes away.—*Scattered Seed.*

* * *

Sending Treasures Home

I once had friends who were traveling abroad for several years. They intended to build a home on their return, and the dream of the home that was to be went with them in all their journeying. When they could secure a beautiful picture, statue, or vase, they purchased it, and sent it home to await their coming. Rare and curious treasure which would afterward be linked with happy memories they forwarded for their future enjoyment. I love to think that we are doing the same for our heavenly Home in these pilgrimage days on earth. The kindly deed that made a rare picture in somebody's life, the little sacrifice that blossomed into joy, the helpful friendship,—all these we shall find again; and the patience we have gained, the "song in the night" that we have learned, whatever of beauty, tenderness, faith, or love we can put into other lives or our own will be among our treasures in Heaven! —*Forward.*

* * *

His Great Danger

As a Christian man was passing out of a church he met an old acquaintance whom he had not seen for several years. In their brief interview he said to his acquaintance, "I understand you are in great danger." It was said seriously, and was heard with surprise. The friend addressed was not aware of any danger and eagerly inquired what was meant. The answer was, "I have been informed that you are getting rich." — *Sunday School Times.*

* * *

A Man's Back

G. F. Watts' famous picture illustrating "For he had great possessions" is familiar to every one. The artist gave this account of the rich young ruler: "I am doing a man's back—little else but his back—to explain, 'He went away sorrowful; for he had great possessions.' Fancy a man turning his back on Christ rather than give away his goods. They say his back looks sorry. I don't know. It is what I meant to express."—*Quiver.*

ROMANS 8:28

"And we know that ALL things work together for good to them that love God, to them who are the called according to His purpose!"

* * *

Some Day We'll See

"Why did my precious baby die? We could have cared for her properly and would have trained her in a godly life." "Why did this financial disaster overtake me? I've tried honestly to be God's steward. I've lost all!" Why? Why? Why? Such questions are not presumptuous. God made us mental and moral beings. We are taught that this is a moral universe. But these questions may not be answered on earth. Does that mean that they will never be answered? No! There will be a time when we shall have explanation and judgment. We shall say: "I see it now, Lord. Thy loving-kindness is great. 'Blessed be the name of the Lord'!"—*To-Day.*

* * *

Blessed Disappointment

When Lord Clive, as a young man, in the spirit of adventure set out from his British home for India, the ship upon which he sailed was caught in a terrific storm, and continuous adverse gales drove it far off the course, until it finally limped into a South American harbor. There he had to remain for many months before being able to get passage to India. But during the long wait he acquired the Portuguese language which qualified him when he did reach India to take an important position with the East India Company, ultimately resulting in his being appointed by the crown as Governor General of India. Do not deplore upsets; they may be God's messengers.—*Sunday School Times.*

* * *

"No Mistake of God's"

"I have heard that this physician [who unwittingly caused her blindness] never ceased expressing his regret at the occurrence; and that it was one of the sorrows of his life. But if I could meet him now, I would say, 'Thank you, thank you, over and over again, for making me blind.' . . . Although it may have been a blunder on the physician's part, it was no mistake on God's. I verily believe it was His intention that I should live my days in physical darkness, so as to be better prepared to sing His praises and incite others so to do."—From Fanny Crosby's Life Story by Herself.

* * *

Whichever way the wind doth blow,
Some heart is glad to have it so;
Then blow it east or blow it west,
The wind that blows, that wind is best.
My little craft sails not alone;
A thousand fleets from every zone
Are out upon a thousand seas;
And what for me was favoring breeze
Might dash another, with the shock
Of doom, upon some hidden rock.
And so I do not care to pray
For winds to waft me on my way,
But leave it to a Higher Will
To stay or speed me; trusting still
That all is well, and sure that He
Who launched my bark will sail with me
Through storm and calm, and will not fail
Whatever breezes may prevail,
To land me, every peril past,
Within His sheltering Haven at last.
—Caroline Atwater Mason.

* * *

Had He Lost All?

A young businessman who had been severely tested, and whose heart was again and again tempted to rebellion during the process of trial to which he was submitted, came to a Christian worker. His motherless babes, two and five years old, clung one to either hand. Though still in his early thirties, his hair was snow white from the hours of anguish through which he had passed. An income of twenty thousand dollars a year was gone. His capital was swept away. His home was gone; his car for sale. Stripped of everything but the two loved children, the big, broad-shouldered young father, towering over six feet, in the strength of a capable manhood, looked steadily at the worker, and said, "In looking back upon my sufferings, I find that God makes no mistakes."—*Sunday School Times.*

* * *

"Nevertheless Afterward"

There must be light beyond this darkness,
God's sun has never failed to rise;
The blackest night has had its ending
When morning brought its glad surprise.
The tears that fell those hours of waiting
Are changed to sparkling gems of dew;
All dazzling in the sun's bright shining,—
God's rainbow in its richest hue.
—Selected.

Brought Home by Trials

A boy made a boat and went off to sail it. Presently it got beyond his reach, and he appealed to a big boy, asking him to get it back for him. Saying nothing, the big boy picked up stones, and seemed to be throwing them at the boat. The little chap thought he would never get his boat back, and that the big boy was annoying him. But presently he noticed that instead of hitting the boat, each stone went beyond it, and made a little wave, which moved the boat a little nearer to the shore. Every throw of the stones was planned, and at last the toy was brought within reach, and the little boy was happy in the possession of his treasure. Sometimes things in our life seem disagreeable. But wait awhile, and we shall see that each trial has brought us nearer to God.—Courtesy *Moody Monthly.*

* * *

Knowing the Code

Four men were standing in a telegraph office while a message was being received. Three of them heard merely a succession of taps. The other surprised his companions by repeating the message aloud. He knew the code, and to him every tap or group of taps meant a letter. Pharaoh's kine and ears of corn were fantastic and meaningless pictures to all but the man to whom God gave the key. It is the same today. We cannot puzzle out the problem of life by ourselves; without God all is dark, mysterious, incomprehensible. But our Father holds the key, and He will give all needful light to those who trust in Him.—*Sunday School Times.*

* * *

Why the "Lamb" Was Taken

A few years ago a wealthy lady and gentleman were both made very happy by the birth of a little daughter whom they loved greatly. To their great sorrow, however, the child sickened and died. The mother nearly lost her reason, while the father bore the grief silently.

So concerned was the father about his wife that he consulted a doctor. The doctor advised him to give his wife a complete change. He did so, taking her to the East.

One day, after a walk, the two noticed a shepherd leading his flock. Coming to a brook which he wished the sheep to cross, the sheep refused to do so; whereupon he picked up a lamb, jumped the stream with it, placing it about fifty yards on the other side.

Presently the lamb began to bleat for its mother. Its mother, hearing the call, raised her head, and jumping over the stream, ran to the lamb. The other sheep, seeing this, followed. Thus the shepherd was able to lead all his sheep safely home.

"I see," said the mother of the dead child. "The Lord has taken my lamb to enable me to meet it on the other side." —*Peniel Herald.*

* * *

No Accidents

Down in Georgia in a rural section of the country, a good man of God was holding a revival meeting. There was a Negro nurse who attended these meetings. She was very poor, but had one great ambition, and that was to own enough uniforms to have a clean one every day without having to wash several times a week. After a period of hard work and much saving, her ambition was realized. In her clothes closet hung a row of beautiful white uniforms. One day while at work, word came that her cabin was on fire. She was rushed to her home only to find what had been her home was now a pile of ashes. She walked to the pile of ashes and allowed her eyes to stray in the direction of what had been the clothes closet that held her precious uniforms. This Negro Christian woman lifted her eyes toward Heaven and remarked: "I is not only a Christian, I is a consecrated Christian, and nothing much can happen to a consecrated Christian." Praise the Lord!—Selected.

God's Purpose

A young man was trying to establish himself as a peach grower. He had worked for years, and invested his all in a peach orchard, which at last bloomed bounteously—and then came a frost. He didn't go to church the next Sunday, nor the next, nor the next. His minister went to hunt him up, and inquired the reason. The discouraged young fellow exclaimed: "No, and what is more, I'm not coming any more. Do you think I can worship a God who loves me so little that He will let a frost kill all my peaches?"

The old minister looked at him a moment in silence, and then replied kindly: "Young man, God loves you better than He does your peaches. He knows that, while peaches do better without frosts, it is impossible to grow the best men without frosts. His object is to grow men, not peaches."—Selected.

* * *

The Use of Affliction

God never permits affliction without a wise purpose. When Dr. Moon, of Brighton, England, was at the height of all his mental powers and acquisitions, he became blind. At first there was a constant rebellion against God. "What are all my acquisitions, what are all my powers worth now, when I am shut up here and the whole world shut out?"

But Dr. Moon began to ask himself if it were possible that he might help the blind to read the Word of God. While his own eyes were sightless, he invented the Moon system of alphabet. This has gone into twenty different countries, and has assimilated itself to the languages of those countries. From three to four million blind people all over the world are reading the Bible in their native tongue because Dr. Moon became blind. Trouble was sent in order that Dr. Moon might help other people out of trouble.—*The Dawn.*

* * *

All Things for Our Good

A sincere, pious old Southern Negro was asked to speak at the funeral of a little child. He was talking on the text, "All things work together for good to them that love God." He said in substance: "Brethren, we can't take one of God's dealings by itself. We got to put them all together. He don't say His dealings work by themselves. He says dey work together for good. You hear dat brass band? Take all dem horns sep'rate—be mighty poor music. De high tenor horn makes shrill music by itself. It takes all de horns togedder to make de music. Dis life is like de notes ob de big bass horn. Dere's no music here. But let us wait in faith till God brings in de odder instruments, and den dere will be music. Dis is de bass horn ob death, a solemn sound. We will wait for de horn ob de resurrection, for de horn ob de ascension, for de angelic horn. When all de horns in God's great band ob providence get togedder, den dere will be music in Heaven."—*The Elim Evangel.*

* * *

Glad to Be a Leper

Peking missionaries were astounded when an old man once rose and said: "I am glad I am a leper! For if I had not been a leper, I would never have come to this mission hospital; if I had not come to this hospital, I never would have learned to know Jesus. *And I had rather be a leper with Christ than to be free from leprosy without Him.*"—*Christian Life.*

* * *

Some Day

Sometimes such shadows overhang our path
We cry we cannot walk in light so dim.
O child of God, fear not, the way is safe
Through deepest darkness if we walk with Him.

Sometimes our spent and burdened souls have cried,
"Of what avail this anguish and this pain?"
Oh, sweet and tender mystery of God,
There is no travail of the soul in vain!

Some day,—"At evening time there shall be light."
Somewhere these aching hearts will understand:

Our pain was the refining of our gold,
Our darkness but the shadow of His hand!

When our sight
Is made perfect in His grace,
In the light
Of the glory of His face
All will be plain!
—Martha Snell Nicholson, in *Gospel Herald.*

* * *

No Clouds, No Showers

"We know that all things work together for good to them that love God" (Rom. 8:28).

We are often comforted by the words of others who have experienced the loving-kindness of our God, but if we are able to bear witness to it we must experience it for ourselves.

And old saint was speaking of God's great goodness so joyously that it seemed as though she had never known a trial. "But have you never had any clouds?" she was asked, "Clouds?" she replied; "why of course, else where would all the showers have come from that have refreshed and blessed me so?"

No clouds, no showers; no trials, no refuge; no labor, no "well done." But all is in His hands, who tempers all, balances all, and has nothing but our present and eternal good in view.—*Scripture Truth.*

* * *

Trials Turned to Triumphs

There is a mission in Japan which has a meeting place built by the stones that were thrown at the Christians in years gone by. A mob rushed upon the company and stoned them away; and when the time of peace came the Christians picked up the stones, and worked them into the building. "All things work together for good" (Rom. 8:28).—*Glad Tidings.*

* * *

Shadows of the Almighty

"There are ferns in the garden of the soul as well as flowers. The flowers grow best in the sunshine; the ferns grow best in the shade.

"There is the fern of Patience, and the fern of Longsuffering, and the fern of Meekness. And the great Gardener of the soul delights in ferns, and purposes to save them from destruction by the garish day.

"And so He takes us into the shade—the shade of disappointment, or the shade of sorrow, or the shade of sickness and pain. But it is a very blessed shadow, for it is the 'Shadow of the Almighty.' And here the ferns flourish and the cloudy day makes the garden beautiful."—J. H. Jowett.

* * *

Our Plimsoll Line

God knows our frame, and does not place upon us more than we can bear. It is due to the efforts of Samuel Plimsoll (1824-1888), British reformer, that the Merchant Shipping Act of 1876 was passed, requiring all ships to bear a mark known as the Plimsoll line and indicating the maximum load line. By this act the Board of Trade of England was empowered to detain any vessel deemed unsafe, and the amount of cargo was restricted, thus making the long and perilous ocean voyages of those days much safer. The Plimsoll mark, with its gradations and figures, may be seen on the bow of ships near the water line as they lie at anchor. In God's sight, each of us has a similar mark. The burdens and responsibilities He gives us may seem unbearable, but He knows our limit; His everlasting arms are underneath, and by His grace we can bear them without sinking.—*Sunday School Times.*

* * *

"I Know Him"

In China a faithful little Chinese woman was afflicted with a malady which caused almost unbearable pain. After some weeks of the most intense suffering she finally recovered, but after a few months the same malady again fastened itself upon her. She almost felt that she could not enter the days and weeks ahead, knowing what they held of pain and suffering.

One Sunday afternoon a group of us went to call on her and before leaving we sang several Gospel songs and had prayer. When we opened our eyes she looked up at us and with tears streaming down her cheeks and in the midst of the most acute pain, said, "I don't know *why*, but I know *Him*." She knew that the hand which permitted it was a hand of love, therefore she gladly accepted anything which that hand should allow. —*Gospel Herald.*

* * *

Enlargements

It is well when we can say with the Psalmist: "In pressure thou hast enlarged me" (Ps. 4:1, J. N. D. Trans.). Naturally pressure would *diminish* one, but God can use it to *enlarge* His saints. The way we are exalted and enlarged is not in our circumstances here, but in the knowledge of Christ.—Selected.

* * *

"The Weaver"

Some years ago when I was a pastor in Minneapolis, Minnesota, I had in my congregation a woman who spent the last ten years of her life upon a sickbed. She scarcely knew a day without pain, and yet she gave herself to the giving of thanks to God for the very testing through which she was passing. After her triumphant death, her husband found the following poem in her Bible. The title is "The Weaver."

"My life is but a weaving
Between my Lord and me:
I cannot choose the colors;
He worketh steadily.
Ofttimes He weaveth sorrow,
And I in foolish pride
Forget He sees the upper,
And I, the under side.

"Not till the loom is silent
And the shuttles cease to fly,
Shall God unroll the canvas
And explain the reason why
The dark threads are as needful
In the Weaver's skillful hand
And the threads of gold and silver
In the pattern He has planned.

"He knows, He loves, He cares;
Nothing this truth can dim.
He gives His very best to those
Who leave the choice with Him."

* * *

The Master Weaver

Are the threads of your life all tangled?
Have the plans that you dreamed gone astray
Do the bright tones clash with each other,
And the dark ones cloud most of the way?

Remember the Master Weaver
Can straighten the tangled strands,
And weave anew the pattern
If you place the threads in His hands.

The dark days and the bright ones
Will be woven with infinite skill,
For both joy and sorrow are needed
His perfect plan to fulfill.

Some day you will see the upper side,
In its matchless symmetry,
His plan, with the threads all blended
In an exquisite harmony.

—Lillian M. Weeks, in *Sunday School Times.*

* * *

We read the story of a young woman, a sincere and beautiful woman, who had consecrated herself to the work of Christian missions and was to go out to India. But before she went, an accident disabled her mother, and the journey had to be postponed. For three years she ministered to her mother, until the mother died, leaving as her last request that before going to India, the daughter should go and visit her sick sister in the far West. She went, intending to sail for India immediately on her return. But she found the sister dying of a lingering illness and without proper attention. Once more she waited until the end came. Again her face was turned eastward when the sister's husband suddenly died, and five orphan children, all of them young, had no soul on earth to care for them but herself. "No more projects for going to the heathen," she wrote to a friend; "this lonely household is my mission." She was greatly disappointed, but cheerfully submitted to the will of God, and set herself, with loving devotion, to a mother's task. Fifteen years she devoted to them. In her forty-fifth year, God showed her the key to the mystery of her unanswered prayers, and revealed to her why He had held her back from India, as she laid her hand, in blessing, on the heads of three of these young people whom she had mothered, ere they sailed as missionaries to the land whither, twenty years before, she had consecrated her life to go. Her broken plan had been replaced by a larger and a better one. She could not go, but three went in her stead: a three hundred per cent interest for twenty years.—Louis Albert Banks.

SACRIFICE

Why He Traveled Third Class

My dear old friend, Evangelist James McKendrick, I found down among the third-class passengers, just recovering from a serious operation. When asked why he was traveling third-class, he replied: "Because there is no fourth-class." He and his good wife live in the most frugal manner in order to have the more to give to the Lord's cause. What he saved in passage money, I have it on good authority (though he wouldn't tell it), he gave to foreign missions.—E. J. Pace's *Travel Letter.*

* * *

Can't Stop Love

In an overcrowded tenement in the city slums the cry "fire, fire" is heard, and the fire engines come thundering down the street. From every doorway, from every fire escape, from every window, eager, excited streams of humanity tumble out on to the pavement. The flames mount higher. The smoke belches from the broken windows, and the open doors. "Stand back," demands the fire marshal, as a little woman with drawn features and tender eyes rushes toward him to say that her child is on the third story of the burning building. "But it's impossible for anyone to venture there now. No fireman can attempt it." Then, before the marshal can grasp her, she has shot by him. She rushes toward the burning building and disappears through the smoke filled door. *They found her* afterwards among the ashes, her charred hand resting on the face of the child she had died in a vain attempt to save.—*Florida Baptist Witness.*

* * *

Himself He Cannot Save

One of the most glorious things said of Jesus was said in derision by His enemies: "He saved others; Himself He cannot save." It is always so. On Dr. Adam Clarke's tomb in London is carved the figure of a candle expiring in its socket with the words underneath, "In giving light to others, I myself have been consumed." Shortly after the death of Phillips Brooks, his oldest brother said to Dr. McVicker, "Phillips might have saved himself, and so prolonged his life. Others do; but he was always giving himself to any who wanted him." Dr. McVickar answered, "Yes, indeed! He might have saved himself, but in doing so he would not have been Phillips Brooks. The glory of his life was that he did not save himself." That is the path to Glory for us as well.—Selected.

* * *

Ready for Either

An ancient medal has upon it the device of a bullock standing midway between a plow and an altar, and under it this inscription, "Ready for Either." —Gospel Herald.

Declining Demotion

A well-known missionary to Turkey was offered a consulship in one of the chief Turkish cities at a princely salary. "Why in the world did you not accept such a chance?" asked a young man in amazement. "Well," was the quiet reply, "I declined to step down from an ambassadorship to a consulship." — *The Friend of Russia.*

* * *

The Spirit of Sacrifice

An excellent story is told of an old Southern slave who had refused his freedom and lived with his master until the last.

Through the years he had carefully saved up money enough to buy a railroad ticket back to Georgia, when his master should be needing him no longer. One morning, as the Georgia train was pulling out of Washington, the old Negro with a very black face and white hair came rushing down the platform and barely caught the last car. His shoes were covered with dust, and his appearance showed signs of a long tramp. Going from one end of the car to the other, he found no empty seat, so he stood up against the door, wearily shifting from one foot to the other. A young man saw he was tired, and courteously said, "Take my seat, Uncle."

Very soon the conductor came along, calling loudly, "Tickets! Tickets!" As he reached a lady in the seat behind the ex-slave, she said, "Oh, sir! I have no ticket, but you must not put me off. Last year," she went on, "the doctors said my husband had tuberculosis, and that his only chance of recovery was to go South. So we sold a few things, and got money enough to send him to Georgia. Yesterday I got a telegram saying he was dying; and, oh! I must go to him, and I have no money. You won't put me off."

The kind-hearted conductor was touched, but told her, "Rules are rules. Your story touches me deeply, madam, but if I do not put you off, I will lose my job. Tickets! Tickets!" The old negro looked up and said, "I speck, Conductor, you will have to put me off."

The conductor spoke gruffly. "You old nigger! What do you mean? This woman has some excuse, but you — if it were not for the time, I would stop the train and put you off on the roadside. Get off at the next stop!"

"Yes, sir!" weakly said the tired old man.

As the train slowed down, he pulled his Georgia ticket out of his pocket, bought with the savings of years, that the pull of his birthplace so strong in the negro race might be satisfied. When the train stopped he rose up, stepped to the lady's seat, and with splendid courtesy bowed like a courier of the old school, and said, "Dere's your ticket to Georgia, mam," and going down the steps of the car, started on his long tramp to Georgia — touched by the spirit of sacrifice.—*Gospel Herald.*

* * *

The Sure Reward

Garibaldi, the great Italian reformer of a past generation, in a fiery speech, urged some thousands of Italy's young men to fight for the freedom of their homeland. One timid young fellow approached him, asking, "If I fight, Sir, what will be my reward?" Swift as a lightning flash came the uncompromising answer, "Wounds, scars and perhaps death. But remember, that through your bruises Italy will be free." "Then," said the young man, "I will follow to the death." Are you not willing to endure the scars in order to liberate souls? —*The C. U. Herald.*

* * *

He Came to Die

A little frail old man entered the Oakland (Calif.) Red Cross Blood Donor Center. He stood patiently in line waiting his turn at the reception desk. He was immaculately dressed, hands clean and freshly manicured, hair carefully combed, and his necktie bright and new. And he was smiling. As he told the receptionist he was eighty years old, she smiled, too. "I'm sorry," she said, "but you are too old to give a pint of blood." The man's face fell, and when he turned away, convinced at last they could not accept what he came there to give, he said quietly: "I was not going to tell you this if you had accepted me. I knew I would not survive a blood donation. I dressed for my funeral. I should have died happy, knowing my death might mean life for some boy somewhere far from home." Blood to be used in such a noble adventure must meet all the requirements of medical science. The Lord Jesus — the antitype of the old sacrifices — was of acceptable age as well as character, for He was in the prime of life and the vigor of manhood. He met every requirement of divine justice. The Lord Jesus also came prepared to die, and He did die for us; and it is impossible to gauge the infinite happiness of the risen Christ, knowing as He does that His death means life to all who are far from the heavenly Home, if they put their faith in Him.—*Now.*

* * *

Have You Counted the Cost?

Two young soldiers were talking about the service of Christ. One of them said:

"I cannot tell you all that the Lord Jesus is to me, or what He has done for me. I do wish you would enlist in His army!"

"I am thinking about it," answered the other young man, "but it means giving up several things — in fact, I am counting the cost."

A Christian officer, just passing, heard the last remark, and laying his hand on the shoulder of the young soldier, said:

"Young man, you talk of counting the cost of following Christ, but have you ever counted the cost of not following Him?"

For days that question exercised the mind of that young man, and he found no rest till he trusted the Lord Jesus Christ, the Saviour of sinners, whose faithful soldier he has been for twenty-seven years.—T., in *Scattered Seed.*

Jimmy Was Ready

Five-year-old Mary was obliged to undergo an operation, and lost so much blood that it was necessary to resort to blood transfusion. The blood of thirteen-year-old Brother Jimmy was found by test to match exactly the little patient's. "Will you give your sister some of your blood, Jim?" asked the doctor. Jimmy set his teeth. "Yes, sir, if she needs it." He was prepared for the transfusion. In the midst of the drawing of the blood, the doctor observed Jimmy growing paler and paler. "Are you ill, Jim?" he asked. "No, sir, but I'm wondering just when I'll die." "Die?" gasped the doctor. "Do you think people give their lives when they give a little blood?" "Yes, sir," replied Jimmy. "And you were giving your life for Mary's?" "Yes, sir," replied Jimmy. Can you tell me of a finer heroism than this? — Amos R. Wells, in *Christian Herald.*

* * *

"I Must Tell"

Missionary labor and personal work are the outstanding demonstrations of love. As in the case of the patient in one of our hospitals in India, who inquired of the doctor how long she would live. When he said. "Three months if you stay in the hospital," she wanted to know how long if she did not stay. The answer was, "Two or three weeks, and you will suffer much." Whereupon she said, "I am going home, I must tell my people about Jesus." And she went and she did it. That was sheer foolishness from the point of view of those who are selfish, but it was a real illustration of what a mighty love for God and for our neighbors the Holy Spirit supplies. —*Gospel Herald.*

* * *

"Second Mile" Nursing

It is not Christian to do all that is expected of us. Unbelievers often do that. Christianity does more than that. A man in a hospital, just after a severe operation, asked his nurse to turn his pillow. She at once rearranged two pillows, and made him much more comfortable. As minute after minute and hour after hour dragged on, he noticed that whenever he asked this nurse for anything, she always did more than he asked: did it instantly and cheerily. Finally he asked her if she remembered what the Lord said about going "the second mile," and told her how gratefully he had noticed that she always went that second mile. And it meant, oh, so much, to a weak, suffering patient lying there in helplessness! This man had learned a new lesson from his nurse; all unconsciously she was showing him the meaning of that grace of God that does "exceeding abundantly above all that we ask or think."—*Sunday School Times.*

* * *

Cost Not Counted

An old low caste woman in India was once asked the price of a temple in the process of building. She turned to the missionary in surprise and said, "Why, we don't know! It is for our god. We don't count the cost!" We should certainly do as much for our Christ as the heathen do for their gods. Real love finds joy in sacrifice as well as in service. —Courtesy *Moody Monthly.*

* * *

A High Salary or Heavenly Reward?

Recently the Standard Oil Company wanted two extra men, and out of the twenty who applied Mr. Li was one of the two chosen. He was housemaster in a boys' boarding school of the China Inland Mission. His wages were to be double what he was earning in the school. Mr. Li prayed much about the matter. He accepted the position, but when he found he would have to work on Sunday he gave it up. Then the manager offered him three times higher wages than he had as a teacher and gave him his Sundays free. He returned to the office but *became* very unhappy, and in the evening after praying with the head teacher of the school he wrote the following letter in English: "I am sorry I cannot come and work for your company. I have decided to work for God, and win the boys to Jesus Christ. I beg you a thousand pardons." The manager said to one of his friends: "I thought I did well to engage a Christian, but I see they put Jesus first and business second."—*China's Millions.*

* * *

The Making of a Missionary

John saw some ragged boys and invited them to Sunday school. One said that he would go, but he had no coat. John gave him his coat and went in, with him, without one. Years afterward a teacher of a Bible class told the story. A man said, "I was that boy, and Dr. John G. Paton, the now famous missionary, gave me his coat.—*The Pentecostal Herald.*

* * *

The Lepers' Way

On the night of March 16 ruffians set fire to the church in Soonchun Leper Colony, Korea. In vain were efforts to stay the flames. The lepers were heartbroken. To repair the damage will cost $1,250. This sum the lepers have pledged themselves to raise by going without dinner every Sunday for two years.—*Missionary Review of the World.*

SALVATION

"Help Him Up"

It is said that the Duke of Norfolk, once tipsy, hiccoughed to a drunken friend in the gutter: "My dear fellow, I can't help you out, but I'll do better, I'll lie down by your side."

The only way to help a man out of sin is to be on the solid rock (Christ Jesus) above him, and help him up to that Rock. Don't get down in the gutter with him!—*Christian Victory.*

He First Gives Us His Nature

In Egypt a Christian worker was trying to show the way of salvation to a young soldier who supposed he could become a Christian by "being good." Finally the truth dawned on him that God was offering him a gift, and he exclaimed: "I see it now! God does not expect me to live His life without first giving me His nature."—*The Dawn.*

* * *

"Are You Saved?"

Four years after the "Titanic" went down, a young Sotchman rose in a meeting in Hamilton, Can., and said, "I am a survivor of the 'Titanic.' When I was drifting alone on a spar on that awful night, the tide brought Mr. John Harper, of Glasgow, also on a piece of wreck, near me. 'Man,' he said, 'are you saved?' 'No,' I said, 'I am not.' He replied, 'Believe on the Lord Jesus Christ, and thou shalt be saved.' The waves bore him away; but, strange to say, they brought him back a little nearer, and he said, 'Are you saved now?' 'No,' I said, 'I cannot honestly say that I am.' He said again, 'Believe on the Lord Jesus Christ, and thou shalt be saved.' Shortly afterwards, he went down, and there, alone in the night, and with two miles of water under me, I believed. I am John Harper's last convert."—Selected.

* * *

"Have It Charged"

Once, in a Sunday School, a visitor was asked to take charge of the Primary Class for that session, the regular teacher being absent.

The stranger accepted, and, on entering the room, learned that the lesson was from the 55th chapter of Isaiah.

The beautiful first verse was read aloud, namely:

"Ho, every one that thirsteth, come ye to the waters, and he that hath no money; come ye, buy, and eat; yea, come, buy wine and milk without money and without price."

The leader thought this text might be intelligently taught to senior pupils, but could "wee bairns" be made to understand how to buy "without money"? The invitation seemed so difficult to explain to little folks, that the teacher just silently prayed for light upon the subject.

Immediately, another beautiful verse came into his mind, namely, "A little child shall lead them"; and believing God meant that perhaps one of the little scholars could better explain what Isaiah's text was intended to teach, the class listened carefully while he read the first verse once more.

When asked to say what they thought the Prophet meant by inviting people to "buy . . . without money," a little girl, only six years old, promptly answered:

"Please, sir! have it charged."

"Jesus paid it all,
All to Him I owe,
Sin had left a crimson stain,
He washed it white as snow."

Jesus asks us to place the purchase price to His account.—*Gospel Herald.*

* * *

Things Unchanged, But—

A young girl who was dissatisfied with her home life, and was always talking of her grievances and showing her discontent in voice, look, and manner surprised a friend one day by her quick step, bright smile, and happy voice. "How are things at home?" asked the friend, thinking that some good news had made the change. "Oh, everything is just the same, but I am different," was the reply. The grace of God will make us new creatures in Christ Jesus.—*Christian Witness.*

* * *

The Greater Honor

The story is told of Dean Stanley, who offered to take two soldiers around Westminster Abbey, seeing they had come too late for the official guide to conduct them through the historic shrine. Dean Stanley explained all he knew about the noble people whose names were inscribed on the walls and tablets, and in brass letters on the floor. As the soldiers were about to pass out of the gates, the saintly Dean said, "Now, lads, you may never do anything great enough for your country to keep your names in remembrance carved here in Westminster, but I can tell you of a greater honor than that of having your name in this old Abbey, that is, of having it written in the Lamb's Book of Life."—Selected.

* * *

Salvation, Not Reformation

A party of friends went to pay a visit to an old parish church which was of great interest. They applied for admission, and the sexton gave them the key, saying: "You can unlock the door and go in, and I will come to you directly." They went to the door, put the key in the lock, and tried to open it, but they could not turn the key. They turned and twisted, but to no effect, and had just given up in despair when the sexton arrived. "We cannot make this lock shoot," said one of the party. "I beg your pardon," said the sexton, "for giving you so much trouble. I quite forgot to tell you that the door is not locked at all. All you need to do is just to lift the latch and walk in."

A great many are like them. They try by their own efforts to unlock the door of salvation, but all their efforts are a waste of time. Our Lord and Saviour Jesus Christ long ago unlocked the door, and all we need to do is just to lift the latch and by faith walk in. — *Sunday Circle.*

* * *

Accepting the Gift

Well I remember my futile attempts to begin the Christian life. One Sunday morning I made up my mind to be a Christian, and never doubted that I knew what to do. I must leave off this evil thing, I thought—and already evil things had place in my life—I must do this good thing, I must read my Bible more, and pray more, and repent, and weep if possible. That evidently was the proper way. So I began. On Sunday I prospered well, and on Monday and Tuesday, I almost succeeded, but on Wednesday and Thursday I made some serious slips, and gave it up in despair on Friday and Saturday. But that was the less matter, for I began again the next Sunday. In my self-confidence I thought I knew where I had gone wrong, and that I could guard against the danger. So I read my Bible more diligently, and prayed with increasing devotion, prayed until sometimes I fell asleep on my knees beside the bed. I watched more carefully and imagined I repented more deeply. Often I wept and hid the tears.

Then came the wonderful Sunday afternoon when the new minister was to give his first address to the Sunday school. He said many things, no doubt, but I can only remember one sentence, and that was the living word for me: "All you have to do to be saved is to take God's gift, and say, 'Thank You.'" Here was a new and great light. Hitherto I had been trying to get God to take my gift, and trying to make it great enough to be worthy of His acceptance; and; lo! it was I who had to take, and it was His to give. Simply and quietly that Sunday afternoon my heart turned to God, and I took the gift for which I have been trying to say "Thank You" ever since. I have not yet learned to say it well, but I keep on trying to say it better, and some day, by infinite grace, I believe I shall have learned to say it perfectly.—W. Y. Fullerton.

* * *

Sincerity Does Not Save

"We do not think it matters much what religion a man professes, so long as he is sincere." This is a fearful mistake. Let us test your sincerity of such a notion. Your child is taken very ill, you need a doctor, you start to run for him. You know the name of the street he lives in, but you do not know where it is situated. Never mind that, you keep on running. "Stop, friend, stop!" cries a neighbor, "you're running the wrong way." "Never mind! I am sincere, look how hard I am running." But you never reach the doctor, and your child dies. Sincerity on the wrong road means traveling faster to eternal destruction. — Courtesy *Moody Monthly.*

The Opening

Mr. Walter Scott was once speaking about the veil of the Temple being rent in twain from the top to the bottom, when a man at the back stood up and asked, "How big was that hole?" "It was big enough to let any sinner pass through," immediately replied Mr. Scott. Thank God, it's true; "the new and living way" is free to all sinners.—John W. Ham.

* * *

A Horse Trainer's Testimony

A testimony heard in the "White Chapel," London, England: "Nearly forty years ago I drifted into a mission one cold night. The city was engulfed in one of those old-fashioned London fogs. I was partly intoxicated, and in my wanderings I heard the strain of familiar music as the people were singing, 'Jesus, Lover of my Soul.' The minister preached on Christ's triumphant entry into Jerusalem, astride a Syrian colt on which no man had ever sat (an untrained Syrian colt). I was intensely interested. I knew Syrian colts. I was in the employ of a nobleman, as a trainer, who was a lover of Syrian colts. I trained over a score of such animals, and of all the vicious, stubborn, deceitful beasts that ever lived, a Syrian colt excelled in disposition. Just when you thought you had him well in hand, you would find him poking his heels into your back; and when I realized that here was an untrained Syrian colt, carrying the Lord Jesus into Jerusalem, with people singing and waving palms enough to scare any colt (Syrian or otherwise), I said to myself, 'Jesus Christ was a great jockey.' And when the minister called for converts, I said to myself, 'Well, if Jesus Christ could do that with an untrained Syrian colt, what could He do with me?' and I went to the altar and was saved. My prayer that night was this: 'Lord, I'm willing to be an ass, yes, the foal of an ass, if I can serve You; ride me, as You did that Syrian colt, and may every ride be a triumphant entrance into the heart and life of another man.' "—*The Gideon.*

Christ, the Only Way

A man, wont to trust in his own merit for salvation, dreamed one night that he was occupied with the task of constructing a ladder which was to reach from earth to heaven. Whenever the dreamer did a good deed the ladder went up higher, and occasionally when an extra good act was performed, the progress toward the skies was correspondingly accelerated. So in course of years the ladder passed out of sight of the earth, clear up into the clouds. But at last when the competent builder was about to step off the topmost round onto the floor of heaven, a voice cried, "He that climbeth up some other way is a thief and a robber!" Down came the ladder with a crash. The startled dreamer awoke. He had learned his lesson. He saw that he must get salvation from Jesus Christ, for his own self-righteousness, inadequate to fulfill the whole law of God, availed not. *There is only one way of sure entrance to the fold of God, and that is by the atoning merit of Him who said, "I am the door!"* — *Zion's Herald*

* * *

No "Chance" at All

An airman, pretty badly smashed up, was brought back from "Somewhere in France" to a hospital, "Somewhere in the north of England." After the doctor had patched him up as best he could, he turned to the airman in the next bed. "Say, mate, can you help a fellow with a bit of religion?" he asked. "Sorry, chum," the man replied, "I'm afraid I can't, but you'll be all right; a lady visits here on Thursdays with Gospels and tracts; she'll put you right!" "Well, I may not be here on Thursday," he said. "Can't you do anything?" Presently he turned again to the fellow in the next bed. "I've been thinking. I don't know if it's a bit out of the Bible or part of a hymn, but some words keep running through my mind: 'Jesus said, Suffer the children to come unto me, for of such is the kingdom of heaven.' " "Yes, that's in the Bible, all right, mate." "Well, if Jesus Christ wanted the children to come to Him, do you think He'd have me, for I know I jolly well need Him? Anyway, I'm going to ask Him!" He pulled the sheet up over his head; that sheet never came down again! "Him that cometh unto me, I will in no wise cast out. . . . Come unto me, all ye." I was telling that story to a group of airmen at Kingston, Ontario, when one U.T. pilot in training camp came to me afterward and asked, "Reverend, do you think that fellow had any chance?" I replied, "No! He'd no chance at all; he'd an absolute certainty!"—*Prairie Pastor.*

* * *

It Keeps You Sane

Because occasionally an insane person incoherently dwells on religious questions, unthinking persons jump to the conclusion that often religion is responsible for mental unbalance. Someone wrote Dr. A. B. Richardson, superintendent of an insane asylum in Ohio, for information, perhaps expecting to get confirmation of the notion that religion and insanity are closely related.

Dr. Richardson's answer is worth quoting: "You have asked me an easy question. I have tested that matter *thoroughly.* There are only two patients in the hospital whose insanity has any relation to religion, and I think from their predisposition to insanity, that they would probably have become insane on some other subject if they had not on religion.

"Now, if you had asked me how many people in Ohio *are kept by religion from insanity,* you would have given me a question hard to answer, for *they are a multitude.*

"The good cheer, bright hopes, rich consolations, good tempers, regular habits and glad songs of religion are such an antidote for the causes of insanity, that thousands of people in Ohio are preserved from insanity by them. But for the beneficial influence of religion, Ohio would have to double the capacity of her hopsitals in order to accomodate her insane patients."—*Fellowship News.*

"Science Cannot Explain This"

It was frequently the custom of a certain philanthropist to visit the New York Rescue Mission at night. On one occasion he took with him a well-known physician, head of the psychiatric department of one of the great New York City hospitals. Arrived at the mission, they listened together to the testimony of one converted man after another. When the season allowed for such volunteer speeches had passed, Mr. John Wyburn, superintendent of the mission, asked the visiting physician if he would like to say a word. Dr. G—— is then reported to have risen to his feet and addressed the assembled company in the following fashion:

"Tonight I have been given an opportunity to observe something I did not know existed anywhere. It has been my privilege to listen to the testimony of men who were glad to witness to what Christ has done for them. I know nothing about that, but I confess *I cannot otherwise explain what has taken place in their lives.* A few of these men I recognize. As drunkards, and even as dope fiends, some of them have come under my observation at the hospital. Had I been asked about and given a thought to their probable fate, I should have said that very likely they were in the 'potter's field.' Here they are, alive, well-dressed, delivered, and in their right minds. I do not know how the miracle has been wrought, but of one thing I am confident—nothing in science can account for this change in them. That kind of Gospel is worth preaching to *any*one, *any*where."

The doctor spoke truly. That kind of Gospel is worth preaching. That kind of *Saviour* is infinitely worth preaching. He saves to the uttermost. As someone has aptly said, He stoops to the "*guttermost*" and saves to the uttermost.—*Gospel Herald.*

* * *

"He Is Able"

"Since His power is so glorious" God one day could make a dying drunkard, an artist. As he stumbled out of a saloon, the saloon keeper had said, "I am afraid you are a goner, Bill." And he thought he was, too, for as he staggered along the street, he could see the cars going by, but could not hear them. He could walk down the sidewalk, but he could not feel it. He must have been almost at the point of dropping on the street as he went along. Then crawling up a stairway into his studio he closed the door. He knew all hope was gone. He knew he had tried every possible way to break the drink habit, every way to get help out of those who might be able to help him. As he closed the door, he knew that he had just a few hours to live. Then one ray of hope drifted into that darkened heart—his mother's God. Dropping down on his knees in front of his chair in front of the easel where he painted pictures, he cried out, "Oh, God, if You will save me from this terrible death and take out of my life this awful curse, You can do what You will with me for the rest of my days." He confessed the awfulness of his sin, believed the Saviour his mother had told him about was the only One who could meet his need. That man was my father. No, not that man, but the one who arose from his knees was my father! I never knew my father except as one of the most wonderful men I have ever met, one whose heart was so great that it reached out to the man in the lost condition, one who actually burned out his life for the Lord and died at the age of fifty-two mainly because he poured out his heart so continuously night and day for the lost. That dying drunkard cried out to the only One who had power to meet his need and arose three hours later and for twenty-six years before his death never again touched any of the drink, never again gambled, never again did any of those things that had characterized his life before.—*Gospel Herald.*

* * *

A Chapter for Christians

A young converted Jewess, daughter of a New York rabbi, tells this story: "My father taught me to read the Bible in Hebrew when a young child. We began at Genesis. When we came to Isaiah he skipped the fifty-third chapter. I asked him why. He said it was not necessary for Jews to read that chapter. I became more curious. I asked him who it was for, and he said Christians. I asked him what the Christian Bible was doing in our Bible. He became very angry and told me to keep quiet. He said again it was not necessary to read it. I wondered why God would put unnecessary things in the Bible. I copied the fifty-third chapter on paper and carried it in my stocking for two years until I came to America—the free country. I looked at it at night and every chance I could without being seen. I took better care of that paper than people do of money. Through reading this wonderful chapter I was led to accept Christ as my Saviour. I was walking in New York one day and heard a lady reading this chapter. She explained that it referred to Jesus Christ. It satisfied me completely.—*Sunday School Times.*

* * *

Not Unless We Take Him

Dr. Walter L. Wilson tells of using John 3:16 to help a boy receive Christ. He quoted the verse and stressed the word "gave." Showing the lad that Christ was God's gift, he asked, "Does the giving of a gift make it yours?" The boy replied, "You must take it if it is to become yours." "True," said the doctor, "and so Christ must be taken as God's gift, if He is to become yours. I am a doctor," he went on, "but I am not your doctor, am I?" "No," said the lad. "Why not?" asked the doctor. "Because we never took you as our doctor," replied the boy. "Very well, then, Jesus Christ is a Saviour, but He is not your Saviour unless you take Him. Will you do so now?" With bowed head, the boy told the Lord Jesus that he would take Him as his Saviour then and there.—*Sunday School Times.*

* * *

Why God Chose the Outcast

"I am by birth," said a converted Hindu, when addressing a number of his countrymen, "of an insignificant and contemptible caste, so low, that if a Brahman should chance to touch me he must go and bathe in the Ganges for the purpose of purification; and yet God has been pleased to call me, not merely to a knowledge of the Gospel but to the high office of teaching it to others. My friends, do you know the reason of God's conduct? It is this: if God had selected one of you learned Brahmans, and made you the preacher, when you were successful in making converts, bystanders would have said it was the amazing learning of the Brahman and his great weight of character that were the cause; but now, when anyone is convinced by my instrumentality, no one thinks of ascribing any praise to me. And God, as is His due, has all the glory." — *Sunday School Chronicle.*

* * *

Better Than Working a Miracle

We may not work a miracle
In any given place,
But we can be a miracle
Of God's redeeming grace.

The call to work a miracle
May be for one short day;
The gift to be a miracle
Shall never pass away.
—*Sunday School Times.*

* * *

Unlimited Resources

One of our Exchanges quotes this true testimony: "A few nights ago I was walking along a street near the Chicago river when a hold-up man suddenly stepped up in front of me and demanded my money. I had spent my last cent that morning for breakfast so of course the robber found no money on me, but in my purse he found this check, which I always carry, on the 'Bank of Jesus.' Because it was dark, the man could not see what the check was; so he asked me if it were good. Seeing an opportunity to witness for the Lord, I replied that if he had the proper endorsement he would be a wealthy man. Then going to the street light, I explained the check to him and told him that if he would let the blood of Jesus cover his sin, that he would have access to the resources in Jesus' bank. At first he was angry, then he was greatly convicted, and kneeling with me behind a signboard he accepted Jesus as his Saviour. He was filled with joy. Then throwing his gun in the river he took me to a restaurant and gave me a much-needed meal. The next morning I found a good job and am more than sure that the resources of Jesus' bank are unlimited. There is enough for all—enough for me and enough for my new friend, the ex-hold-up man."—J. R., in *The Dawn.*

* * *

"Beauty for Ashes!"

A missionary teacher of Tokyo tells of a Japanese woman who asked her if only beautiful girls were received into her school to be educated. "No," was the reply, "we take all the girls who come to us." "But," continued the woman, "all your girls seem to be very beautiful." "We teach them the value of their souls in God's sight," explained the teacher, "and this makes their faces lovely." "Well," said the woman, "I don't want my daughter to become a Christian, but *I would like to send her to your school to get that look in her face."—Christian Herald.*

* * *

Old Betty Knew

A poor, unlettered old woman was once accosted by a skeptic: "Well, Betty, so you are one of the saints, are you? Pray what sort of folks are they? What do you know about religion, eh?" "Well, well," replied the old woman, "you know, sir, I'm no scholar, so can't say much for the meaning of it. I only know I'm 'saved by grace,' and that's enough to make me happy here, and I expect to go to Heaven by and by." "Oh, that's all, is it? But surely you can tell me something nearer than that. What does being saved feel like?" "*Why, it feels to me,*" said the Spirit-taught one, "*just as if the Lord stood in my shoes, and I stood in His.*" Happy old woman! Her witness was true.—Courtesy *Moody Monthly.*

It Needs to Be Melted and Remade

Human nature is too bad to be improved, too dilapidated to be repaired. Here is a cracked bell. How again to restore it? By one of two methods. The first is to repair the bell, to encompass it with hoops. Nevertheless, you can easily discern the crack of the bell in the crack of the sound. The only effectual way is to remelt the bell and recast it; then it will ring clear and sonorous. Human nature is a bell, suspended high in the steeple of creation, to ring forth the praise of the Creator. But in the fall in Eden the bell cracked. How again to restore it? By one of two ways. One is to surround it with outward laws and regulations. This is the method adopted by philosophy, as embodied in practical statesmanship, and without doubt there is marked improvement in the sound. Nevertheless the crack in the metal shows itself in the crack of the tone. The best way is to remelt it, recast it, remold it; and this is God's method in the Gospel. He remelts our being, refashions us, makes us new creatures in Christ Jesus; and by and by we should sound for His praises in a nobler, sweeter strain than we ever did before.—Courtesy *Moody Monthly.*

* * *

Better Than a Covering

The snow lay white over all the earth, hiding every scar and sign of death. "It is a symbol of purity," said a man, and he prayed, "O Lord, as Thou hast covered the earth with whiteness, cover my soul with purity." But the sun shone on the morrow, and the snow melted away. The brown bareness of the dead earth, with all its waste and defilement, showed through again. So he who had prayed to be covered with purity, amended his prayer, and his petition became, "Create in me a clean heart, O God." Purity is not a covering — it is a new life within.—*Sunday Companion.*

* * *

No Renovation Possible

No better illustration of the new birth can be found than that given by Dr. Charles G. Trumbull in his book, *What Is the Gospel?* He pictures a man whose arteries had been opened and whose blood had poured out from his body, lying dead in the gutter. He points out how utterly futile it would be to step up to such a man and tell him to do something to help himself. No amount of "setting up" exercises, however carefully worked out, could possibly stimulate him into action. Before he can do anything at all for himself he must first be brought to life. God must first do something for him, and it is that act of God that we call the new birth, or salvation, or regeneration, or conversion.—John W. Lane, Jr., in the *Sunday School Times.*

* * *

Hope for the Devil's Castaways

The good news of salvation is for all. George Whitefield, standing in his tabernacle in London, and with a multitude gathered about him, cried out: "The Lord Jesus will take the devil's castaways!" Two poor abandoned wretches standing outside in the street heard him, as his silvery voice rang out on the air. Looking into each other's faces, they said: "That means you and me." They wept and rejoiced. They drew near and looked in at the door, at the face of the earnest messenger, the tears streaming from his eyes as he pleaded with the people to give their hearts to God. One of them wrote him a little note and sent it to him.

Later that day, as he sat at the table of Lady Huntington, who was his special friend, someone present said: "Mr. Whitefield, did you not go too far today when you said that the Lord would take the devil's castaways?"

Taking the note from his pocket, he gave it to the lady and said: "Will you read the note aloud?"

She read: "Mr. Whitefield, two poor, lost women stood outside your tabernacle today and heard you say that the Lord would take the devil's castaways. We seized upon this as our last hope, and we write you this to tell you that we rejoice now in believing in Him, and from this good hour we shall endeavor to serve Him who has done so much for us."—*The Elim Evangel.*

A Great Preacher on a Great Theme

Said D. L. Moody: "I was twenty years old before I ever heard a sermon on regeneration. I was always told to be good, but you might as well tell a black man to be white without telling him how. You might tell a slave to be free, but that would not make him free; but He frees us.

We are a bad lot, the whole of us, by nature. It is astonishing how the devil blinds us and makes us think we are so naturally good. Don't talk to me about people being naturally good and angelic. We are naturally bad, the whole of us. The first man born of a woman was a murderer. Sin leaped into the world full grown, and the whole race has been bad all the way down.

I have heard of reform, reform, until I am tired and sick of the whole thing. It is regeneration by the power of the Holy Ghost that we need."—*The Church Militant.*

* * *

How They Inherited Eternal Life

In Cayuga, Guatemala, a group of five women, who had heard a little of the Gospel, were gathered in a room awaiting the arrival of a lady missionary whom they had asked to come to their village and tell them how they could accept the Lord and be saved. The missionary was unable to go, but they were so desirous of obtaining salvation that they decided to do what is done in the meeting of the *evangelicos,* where one rises, or raises the hand, or both, as a first step in accepting Jesus. So the five women rose, raised their hands and repeated together, "I accept the Lord Jesus Christ as my personal Saviour." He whom they accepted met them and filled their hearts with joy, and they knew that His presence was better than that of a missionary. They were the first Christians in their town.—W. R. Adell, Los Angeles, Cal.

* * *

The Water Mill

A man in Ireland, convicted of sin, was on the point of "believing" when the Devil raised the oft-repeated objection: "If you believe, it won't last. What about tomorrow?" The worker dealing with him pointed to a water mill near by. "What turns that wheel today?" "The stream." "What will turn it tomorrow?" "The stream." "And the days after?" "The stream." The anxious one was led to see that there was abundant grace to save, keep, and meet all needs. "Wherefore he is able . . . to save . . . to the uttermost" (Heb. 7:25) — "The same yesterday, and today, and forever."—*Christian Herald* (London).

* * *

"They Cried"

"They cried, and their cry came up unto God by reason of their bondage." The late President Theodore Roosevelt, when a colonel in the army, visited the reservation of the Navajo Indians. In conversation with a Christian missionary, the colonel asked, "Do you think if we were to provide these Indians with better living conditions, better housing, clothes, and the like, that you could more easily reach them with the Gospel?" The missionary replied, "Suppose, Colonel, that when the prodigal son was in the far country someone had given him a good home, a new suit of clothes, and a bank account: how soon would he have returned to the father's house?" Colonel Roosevelt pondered a moment, and then snappily answered, "Never!"—*Sunday School Times.*

* * *

The Secret a Bandit Learned

A colporteur reports: "On my way from D—, to a village situated among high mountains, I had to go by a solitary road. I suddenly saw a man holding a big knife in his hand and approaching me, apparently with the intention of robbing or killing me. I said: 'Why do you do this, my friend. I do not mind if I die, as I am sure to be received into eternal places. But, oh, how I pity you! In what a wretched state you will be, with your conscience whipping you, and the Government following you! Above all, you will be cast into the furnace of eternal fire of hell!' He said: 'You are the first person I ever saw who stood before death with a smile on his face. There must be a secret to this. What is it?' Reading from John 11, I knelt down and prayed earnestly for him. He began to confess the sins of his life. 'For twenty-seven years,' he said, 'I have been leading a lawless life. This dagger has pierced nine breasts. . . . Can God forgive me all these sins?' 'Yes, certainly, if you will repent,' I answered. The man continued: 'I would like to buy your Bible, but I do not have your money. Will you accept this dagger in exchange for it?' 'I will take the knife as a sign of your repentance,' I replied. He then refused the two dollars I offered him, saying, 'I prefer to go without money, and to trust the God who spoke to me through you and saved me.' " — *Bible Society Record.*

* * *

Everything Except Human Nature

The *Literary Digest* quotes a quip from the St. Joseph *News Press:* "Man has now conquered almost every dangerous thing in nature except human nature." It was Christ who announced, almost two thousand years ago, "That which is born of the flesh is flesh; . . . Marvel not that I said unto thee, Ye must be born again."—*Revelation.*

* * *

The Inward Man a New Creature

Dr. Lawes of New Guinea describes how he has seen and heard in New Guinea former canibals at the prayer meeting. "I have heard savages pray," he says, "men with tattooed marks on their chests to indicate that they were murderers, that their spears had tasted blood. I have heard them pouring out their hearts in prayer to God, as children holding converse with their Father, and I know that they have been taught by the Spirit of God." The outward marks remain. Once they were the man's pride and glory; now he would give all he has to remove them. Though they can never be removed, though the outward man remains the same, the inward man is a new creature, known and understood of God. The Lord who looks upon the heart finds there the soul of a son.—*London Sunday School Times.*

* * *

"Without Price"

Dr. Norman Harrison once dealt with a nurse who did not seem to comprehend salvation as a gift, so he put it this way, "I will give you a gem worth ten thousand dollars. But you say, 'Excuse me, Dr. Harrison, I have only fifty dollars.' But you misunderstand, I am giving you the gem. It is yours for the taking." Then, that she might appreciate how service follows salvation, he asked if she would be willing to care for his child following the reception of the valuable gem. Of course, she would. This is where works come in. They follow the gift of salvation. — Courtesy *Moody Monthly.*

* * *

The Physician's Solution

A workman had trouble with his eyes. He went to see a doctor who said: "There are two cataracts growing over your eyes, and your only hope of recovery is to go to Dr. ——. I would advise you to go at once, and take plenty of money with you, for the fee will be heavy." The man had twenty pounds in the bank, which he had been saving for a "rainy" day. That day had come. He drew it out and went to see the specialist. After examining his eyes, the specialist remarked: "I am not sure that you can pay the fee. I never accept less than one hundred guineas." "Then I must go blind and remain so, for I have only twenty pounds," said the man. But the great doctor replied: "You cannot come up to my terms, and I cannot come down to yours, but there is another way open to us—I can perform the operation gratis, and that is what I am willing to do." So fallen man cannot come up to the conditions laid down for him in the divine law, and God cannot in His righteousness and holiness set aside the law and accept even the best that man could give. There was another way open; God found a way through the Lord Jesus Christ to pay the penalty of man's sin and give him the free gift of salvation through faith in His Son.—Courtesy *Moody Monthly*.

* * *

And when in heavenly glory
My ransomed soul shall be,
From sin and all pollution
Forever, ever free,
I'll cast my crown before Him,
And loud His grace extol,—
"Thou hast Thyself redeemed me;
Yes, Thou hast done it all."
—Selected.

* * *

Wolves

Remember Boswell's remark to Dr. Johnson: "Don't you think, sir, that man is naturally good?" "No," was the answer, "no more than a wolf." — Selected.

* * *

Saved to the Uttermost

A noted English preacher, after preaching a sermon one Sunday evening on "The Sufficiency of Christ," was followed into the vestry by a plain workingman, who said, "Did you finish your sermon just now?"

The preacher answered, "Yes, I think so; I meant to finish."

"No," said the other man, earnestly. "I think there was something you did not say, and it is a part which I never like to have left out."

The preacher was now most interested, and said, "What is it?"

"Why," he said, "years ago I was brought to Christ, and a terrible total I took to Him, and placed it down at the Cross, and I thought all was right; but it was not. The next morning my skies were gray. The next day I was down in the Valley of Humiliation, fighting with Apollyon, and he won. My temptation was drink. I fell, and I fell again, till everybody ceased to believe in me, and I ceased to believe in myself and held myself in contempt. But at last in desperation, I raised my hands to Heaven, and said, 'Lord Jesus, I claim Thy promise, and I claim Thy power.' Look at me tonight; for five years He has kept me as I am, and I am willing to praise Him. The next time you stand up to declare the truth in His Name, preach, I beseech you, that Christ is able to save to the uttermost."—Selected.

* * *

A Soldier's Gift

In the annual report of the Open Air Mission, a British soldier writes: "I gave my heart to Jesus at Halton Park Mission Hut twenty years ago last February. I forget all about the sermon, but I still remember the last hymn—'Alas! and aid my Saviour bleed.' And when we came to the last verse,

"But drops of grief can ne'er repay
The debt of love I owe:
Here, Lord, I give myself away,
'Tis all that I can do.—

the missioner asked all who could sing that in sincerity and truth to stand up while the others remained seated. I stood up, and my heart went with the words, and I was born again. And I am glad to tell you that I am still rejoicing in Him, my Saviour and Friend." — *Sunday School Times*.

* * *

The Drink of Death—or Life

A missionary in India had been speaking about the "Water of Life," and pointed to a fountain close by where people were drinking and filling their pots. A Moslem bystander said, "Your religion may be compared to a little stream of water, but Islam is like a great sea." "Yes," replied the missionary, "but there is just this difference: men drink sea water and die of thirst, while they drink of the living water and live."—Selected.

* * *

Righteousness, More Than Morality

A young artist had wrought long upon an angel statue and concealed himself that he might hear what the master Michelangelo would say about it. The master looked upon it awhile, with breathless suspense, and the young artist waited, expecting his verdict. He heard Michelangelo say, *"It lacks only one thing."* So nearly broken-hearted did the young sculptor become that he could neither eat nor sleep until a friend of his in deep concern for him, made his way to Michelangelo's studio and inquired what it was the statue lacked. The great artist said, *"Man, it lacks only life; with life it would be as perfect as God Himself could make it."*

Many cannot see the difference between a man's morality and a Christian's righteousness. Why a moral man should not simply grow better and better until he is good enough to enter the kingdom of God, they say they cannot see. A man's morality is the mere outward adornment of the flesh; a Christian's righteousness is the fruit of an indwelling Spirit — the Spirit of Christ.—W. E. Biederwolf, in *The Man Who Said He Would.*

* * *

The Mercy of God's Justice

In reply to a question as to how she expected to be saved an old saint replied, "Through the justice of God." The questioning cleric corrected, "You mean through the mercy of God, do you not?" But the maturer scholar in God's school persisted: "Through the justice of God. 'He is faithful and just to forgive us our sins.'" *Sunday School Times.*

* * *

Mink Coats or Spiritual Garments

Columnist E. V. Durling is amazed at the eagerness of women to wear mink coats. He says: "It is understandable that a woman would enjoy and be thrilled at wearing a mink coat. But why is the desire to wear such a garment so intense that women place it among their outstanding ambitions? The things a woman will agree to do to own or even be allowed to wear a mink coat are astonishing. A New Jersey woman, finding it impossible to get a maid in the normal way, added to her advertisement: 'Maid can wear my mink coat on her day off.' She received over 600 answers, and now has the most efficient maid she ever had." Our amazement is somewhat different. We marvel that more women, as well as men, do not allow the Lord to clothe them with the "garments of salvation" and the "robe of righteousness" (Isa. 61:10). Costly as are mink coats, they cannot compare in value with that of these spiritual garments!—*Now.*

* * *

A Chinese Nicodemus

A missionary couple to a far interior town of China were up early on Christmas morning. The day promised to be full of opportunities for Christ, through them. In China it is the custom to celebrate any special occasion by paying respect to friends with a call. To make a visit to anyone in the name of Christmas was to make a greater impression for Christ than almost anything they could do. While they were checking the list of those they must visit, a call came from outside. The gatekeeper soon announced the name of a "gentry" whom the missionaries had been trying to win for years. With a sigh, the missionary wife said: "I wonder what your Nicodemus wants so early in the morning?" "My Christmas greetings in the name of Christ!" said the missionary. The Chinese merely waved his hand slightly toward the open gate. "A very humble remembrance of this great day." The missionary's eyes fell on a new insignia over his gateway. He recognized his name, and above it, John 3:16. Instead of thanking him, the missionary asked eagerly, "Can this mean—?" "Yes, I believe." This Christmas gift was his token of belief and love. Later the missionary said to his wife: "Our Nicodemus has claimed the very love message, the heart of the whole matter, that Jesus gave His Nicodemus. He has hung it over our gate as a token of his belief and as a message for all who pass this way."—*Teacher.*

* * *

"Christ Crucified, the Power of God"

Chundra Lela, an orphaned Hindu girl, made four successive journeys to the cardinal points of India in her quest for soul-satisfaction. Each involved great personal suffering. And when the weary years of wandering failed, she entered upon a most severe course of penance, sitting all the hours of the hot day exposed to the burning rays of an Indian sun, surrounded by fires. In the chilly hours of the winter nights, she half submerged herself in water, all the time wearily counting the beads upon a chain until the morning sun appeared over the horizon. Finally, through the simple words of a Gospel message, falling from the lips of a faithful missionary, she was led to believe, and in consequence discarded her idols and every heathen practice in her life. "Christ crucified" is "the power of God" to save from sin.—*Gospel Herald.*

* * *

"What Must I Do?"

"The inner question of men's hearts for centuries has been, 'What must I do to be saved?' Some think by attainment; God says by atonement. Some declare by character; God says by the Cross. Some maintain by courage; God says by Christ. Some assert by trying; God says by trusting. Christ's answer is crystal clear: 'Ye must be born again.' "—Selected.

* * *

The Love That Saves

Norman McLoed tells of a highland mother, a widow, who attempted to take her baby across the mountains in a snowstorm, to the home of relatives. They found her frozen body, stripped. Her dying hands had wrapped the baby in her clothing and placed it in a nook where it was sheltered. The son of the minister who conducted the mother's funeral was preaching years later and told the story to illustrate God's love. A stranger was in the church that morning. Several days later, the preacher was summoned to the bedside of the stranger, who was dying. "I am that baby you told about," he said. "I never forgot my mother's love, but I never saw the love of God in giving Jesus for me until I heard that story. God led you that morning."—*Sentinel.*

Saved from the Fire

Dr. W. Leon Tucker tells of a great street demonstration in New York in which twelve thousand people marched. In the procession were three sight-seeing motor cars packed full of men, women, and children. In one was a judge of the Court of Appeals, and in the last one was a ragged street boy. On the sides of the cars it said, "These people have all been saved from burning buildings by the New York firemen." Then back of the cars marched the men who had saved them, wearing their medals, while hundreds of thousands of people cheered them. Think of the eternal joy that will thrill the hearts of those who, following their Lord and disregarding the consequences, have spent their lives "pulling men out of the fire."—*The Elim Evangel.*

* * *

Salvation and Clothing

There came a day in my father's little mission church in Swaziland a tiny, round-eyed boy, wearing nothing but a bit of skin about his waist. After the service he disappeared. The next Sunday he appeared again, clad this time in patched, baggy trousers. Again he disappeared after the service. The third Sunday he arrived wearing a shirt as well as the trousers, and my father, managing to catch him before he escaped, asked if he would like to come to the mission school. The little lad shook his head solemnly to this, and also to the question: "Won't you believe in Jesus?" The next Sunday, added to his other garments was a pair of large broken boots, and a man's collar securely pinned around his tiny neck. At the end of the service he approached my father and said: "Peter ready now. Peter coming to school. Peter believes Jesus."—*Christian Herald.*

* * *

New Light for a Desperate Husband

In the Charlotte Division a number of business and professional men, both white and colored, became interested in placing Gospel portions in parked cars, each portion bearing the name and address of the sponsor. One of these portions was left in a taxicab. Several days later a young man came to Secretary Tross' office. With tears in his eyes, he took the Gospel from his pocket and said: "See this little book?" It is not a checkbook, and you see it is not a revolver; but it saved my life and the life of my family. When this book was thrown into the taxi in which I sat waiting for the driver, I had a gun in one pocket, and a bottle of whiskey in the other. I was through with everything and everybody. It was wholesale murder for my family, and suicide for me; but when I opened this book, the first thing I read was this: 'Come unto me, all ye that labor and are heavy laden, and I will give you rest.' A new light came to me. I see things differently now and I am solving all my problems. I thank you for what I found in that car."—*Bible Society Record.*

* * *

Reform Does Not Rectify the Heart

The scene is laid in a sawmill. Here is a crooked log. The heart in the middle of it is crooked. The owner looking at it says to the sawyer, "I want you to run down that side, and then this side, and then the others." After doing that he has a straight stick. But the heart of that stick is just as crooked as it was before it was sawed.

Here is a man who says, "I have been in the habit of swearing; I will saw that off. I have been in the habit of lying; I will saw that off. I have been in the habit of cheating; I will saw that off. I have been in the habit of staying out late nights; I will saw that off." He saws off the four sides, but his heart is just as sinful as ever. *Exterior change will not do; interior renovation by the indwelling Christ is necessary.*—A. T. Howell.

* * *

Dr. Kelly's Christian Rose

Dr. Howard A. Kelly of Baltimore, Md., is never seen unless he is wearing in his lapel a beautiful pink rose. It carries a sermon, and here it is. It is a kind of badge of friendship and admiration, which is given to him regularly by a friend little known to many people. His acquaintances, or a stranger, will remark to him, "That's a lovely rose Dr. Kelly." "Yes, it is," he replies, "because it's a Christian rose." "But why is it a Christian rose?" Then, he turns back his lapel, and displays the little water bottle he manufactured himself, which holds the stem of the rose, keeping it sweet and fresh, and replies to his questioner, "You see, this is a Christian rose, because it has a hidden source of life and beauty."—*Christian Herald.*

* * *

Neglecting the "Up-and-Outs"

Until eight years ago I didn't know there was anything in me that was valuable. I only thought about dollars and cents. I am not going up and down the country to get the shekels. God saved me when I had a million and a half dollars' worth of masonry work in Washington, D. C. He called out a business man, but I had a soul that was worth more than all the buildings I could possibly erect. There is such a thing as being "up and out." Not many people are going after that class. Folks usually concentrate on those who are "down and out." There are many today who, so far as material things are concerned, have everything they think they need, yet they are poor and naked and miserable because they have not yet been born again. You would never have heard of men in a Christian club if it had not been for this marvelous born-again experience in my life.

You can cultivate the soil for vegetable life, but unless you sow the seed there will be no results. The same principle applies in human life. A giver of life as well as a receiver is required. This is equally true in the spiritual realm. There has to be a Giver and He is still giving. That agency is the Holy Spirit. This Word of God is the Seed, and the minute a heart is opened to Him, God drops into it the Seed, and that person is born into the family of God. He gave the best He had in Heaven to save my soul.—*Gospel Herald.*

Poor Food—and Pure Food

Did you ever notice what the unconverted man lives on? In Hosea he feeds on the east wind: not very satisfying. In Proverbs he feeds on foolishness: not very substantial. In Luke 15 he feeds on husks; and in Isaiah on ashes. Come and feed on the Bread of Life, sinner, and "if any man eat of this bread, he shall live forever." — *The King's Business.*

* * *

Testifying Without Words

In a mission station there was a convert who could hear and read, but not speak. He was proposed for baptism, but the pastor and brethren hesitated, feeling it impossible to gain from his speechless lips adequate proof that he was sincere and ready for church membership. He was brought before the church, however, and asked this question: "What is the ground of your belief that there is salvation for you in Christ?" He instantly arose and proceeded to answer by signs. He put his hands on his breast with a gesture of loathing, then stepped forward and looked down as into a pit, from which he shrank back in terror; drawing near again, he seemed to see something just beyond; then he made the sign of the cross — Jesus was there! Again he looked into the pit and smiled, then pointed to Heaven with a smile of ecstasy. Jesus had died for his sins, and was risen forever to make intercession for him.—*Indian Witness.*

* * *

A World Question of Today

The famous publicist, H. G. Wells, writes in an issue of *Pearsons*:

"The world is now a very tragic and anxious world and the desire for a peace of mind and a courage such as only deep and pure convictions can supply has never been so pure and so widespread. More people are asking today, and asking with a new intensity: 'What must I do to be saved?' The trouble with the Christian churches is that they give a confused, unconvincing, and unsatisfying answer."

Whatever criticisms befall Mr. Wells' grievous indictment of the church, it must be admitted that a "confused, unconvincing, and unsatisfying" answer *is* being given in many places to the exceedingly important and personal question, "What must I do to be saved?" But however much the "Christian churches" may be charged with "darkening counsel by words without knowledge," there is a BOOK which gives a clear, convincing, and satisfying answer. That Book is the Bible.

If it is true as Mr. Wells says: "More people are asking today, and asking with a new intensity: 'What must I do to be saved?' " it is due them to hear the original answer to the question. That answer is recorded in Acts 16:31, *"Believe on the Lord Jesus Christ, and thou shalt be saved."*—Tract.

* * *

Scenery Doesn't Cure

You might as well try to cure smallpox by scenery as to save the world by improvement of environment.—*Christian Observer.*

* * *

Kill the Spider

An old deacon who used to pray every Wednesday night at prayer meeting, always concluded his prayer the same way: "And, Lord, clean all the cobwebs out of my life." I think you know what he was talking about. The cobwebs—those things that ought not to have been there but had gathered during the week. Well, it got too much for one fellow in the prayer meeting, and he heard the old deacon one time too often. So when the old man made that prayer, the fellow jumped to his feet and shouted, "Lord, Lord, don't do it! Don't do it! Kill the spider!" Beloved, that's what needs to happen.—*Gospel Herald.*

* * *

How Can Man Keep the Golden Rule?

One evening the chief of the Delaware Indians was sitting by a fireside with a friend. Both were silently looking into the fire. At last his friend broke the silence by saying: "I have been thinking of a rule delivered by the Author of the Christian religion, which we call the Golden Rule." "Stop," said the chief, "don't praise it; tell me what it is, and let me think for myself." He was told that the rule was for one man to do to another as he would have the other do to him. "That's impossible; it cannot be done," hastily replied the Indian. Silence followed. In about fifteen minutes the Indian said: "Brother, I have been thoughtful of what you told me. If the Great Spirit who made man would give him a new heart, he could do as you say, but not else."—*Book of Bible Stories.*

* * *

The Difference

Walter Lippman, the newspaperman, in concluding his imaginary dialogue between a Modernist and a Fundamentalist, makes the Modernist ask that the question be discussed without heat. But the Fundamentalist says, "Has it ever occurred to you that this advice is easier for you to follow than for me?" "How so?" asked the Modernist. "Because for me an eternal plan of salvation is at stake. For you there is nothing at stake but a few tentative opinions, none of which means anything to your happiness. Your request that I should be tolerant and amiable is, therefore, a suggestion that I submit the foundation of my life to the destructive efforts of your skepticism, your indifference, and your good nature. You ask me to smile and to commit suicide."—*Heart and Life.*

* * *

When a Duxbury, Mass., man refused to pay one-cent postage due on a letter, it was returned to the Plymouth dead-letter office. Postmaster Wm. Goodwin disclosed that when the letter was opened, it contained a $450 check. It will be returned to the sender in Boston. Kindly reserve your criticism of the man who refused to pay one cent for a check-laden letter until you have answered this question: "Have I received the message on which nothing is due and which offers me that which money cannot buy and works cannot secure: Eternal Life?" Here is the message: "For God so loved the world, that He gave His only begotten Son, that whosoever believeth in Him should not perish, but have everlasting life" (John 3:16). Is that priceless message but a dead letter to you, to be sent back to the sender, the Lord Jesus Christ?—*Now.*

* * *

Japanese Police Advise Well

Unsaved men often see the advantages of salvation. The Christ-rejecting world is not wholly blind to the beauties of Christ. A letter from the Japan Evangelistic Band, bringing "Hallelujah News from Japan," tells of a Japanese who was saved some time ago and then who fell back into his old ways and took to drinking again. He found this to be bottomless quicksand that was rapidly engulfing him. "Called to the police station, he was told that he was no trouble to them while attending the Christian church (he had a prison record), and was advised by the police to go back to his Christian experience!" That was good advice, even if it came from those who were not taking it to themselves. The backslidden Japanese Christian "is not yet fully back but is on the way." Let us pray that he may speedily come back all the way, and that believers in Christian lands who have turned away from the Lord will heed the sound counsel of the Japanese police.—*Sunday School Times.*

* * *

The Cultured Pig

When Henry Moorhouse was a boy, on a certain occasion he was walking with his father through the streets of Manchester, England. His attention was suddenly called to a man standing before the door of a building, and crying aloud, "Walk in, ladies and gentlemen, and see the great American pig." Having his curiosity aroused, he paid his penny, and entered the building. There sure enough was a wonderful pig, performing feats and giving evidence of an intelligence probably never a pig exhibited before.

At the command of his master he would pick out from the alphabet lying upon the floor, the letters, "G-o-o-d P-i-g." He would also walk about upon his hind legs and shake hands with those who paid him a visit. Moreover he had been washed and scrubbed until he was perfectly clean, and he was dressed in a beautiful garment. Of course he excited the highest admiration, and no one could deny that he was well educated, and well behaved in every respect. But notwithstanding his remarkable culture, and his attractive appearance, he was still a pig; better off perhaps than most other pigs, and yet after all, only a pig, and a pig he would remain however advanced his learning.

There is no error, amid the perils of these last days, more dangerous, as there is none more shallow and silly, than the notion taught by many, that culture is the way of salvation.—*Gospel Herald.*

SECURITY

Still Safer

Some years ago at the great Keswick Convention in England, a brother said to the Rev. George Silwood, "Is it not blessed to be safe in the arms of Jesus?" "Yes," said Brother Silwood, "*but I am safer than that.*" "Why," said his friend in astonishment, "how could you be safer than in the arms of Jesus?" "Why, I am as safe as an arm of Jesus," said the preacher; nor did he over-emphasize this great and glorious fact, "for we are members of His body, of His flesh, and of His bones" (Eph. 5:30). P. W. Philpott, in *Moody Church News.*

* * *

Kept

The *Sunday School Times* told, not long ago, about a drunkard, very conscious of his weakness and helplessness, who was urged to "Sign the Pledge and keep it." "But," cried the distressed man, "I do not want something to keep; I need something to keep me!" Soon after that, thank God, he found the Lord Jesus as his Saviour, of whom it is written, "He is able to keep."—*Gospel Herald.*"

* * *

How to Stand

Who can stand alone? A minister traveling on a Continental train was the sole occupant of a compartment, save for a young man reading a newspaper. The youth was also a Christian, but so weak was his faith, and so many were his temptations, that he told the minister he did not think he would be able to stand life a week longer. The minister took from his pocket a Bible and a penknife, and said, "See, I will make this penknife stand up on the cover of this Bible, in spite of the rocking of the train." The young man, thinking this was some conjuring trick, watched the proceeding with interest, saying, "I am afraid that it will not be very easy to do that, sir." "But," said the minister, "I am doing it." "Oh, but you are holding it," retorted his fellow passenger. "Why, of course! Did you ever hear of a penknife standing up on its end without being held up?" "I see; you mean that I cannot stand unless Christ holds me. Thank you for reminding me."—*Sunday School Times.*

* * *

"Enclosed in His Name"

When David, without any outside armor, stood before the giant Goliath who "had an helmet of brass" and "a coat of mail" and his weapons, David faced him confidently, saying: "Thou comest to me with a sword, and with a spear, and with a shield: but I come to thee in the Name of the Lord of hosts (i.e., 'enclosed as in a tower in the Name of the Lord'), the God of the armies of

Israel, whom thou hast defied." David in that "strong tower" was safe, as Goliath, in his armor, was not.

To come "in the Name of the Lord Jesus Christ" is not merely saying His Name over, but it is being enclosed in His Name, and representing that which His Name represents.—H. Clay Trumbull.

* * *

The Secret of Holding On

Mr. Addison Raws of Keswick, N.J., was crossing a crowded street in Philadelphia. He had hold of the hand of his little boy, and the latter lost his footing. Mr. Raws just held him up until they were across. "I hanged on, Daddy," he said as they reached the far side of the street. Yes, he had. But his father had first "hanged" on to him.—*Christ Life.*

* * *

Comfort in the Dark

That wonderful Scotch preacher, John McNeill, when a lad lived in the country. He worked away from home all week and came home Saturday nights. Not far from his home there was a dark piece of woods. In the old country the darkness can be felt, and John, walking home, would enter that ravine with its dense darkness and thick woods, and fear would get hold of him. Wicked men had hidden there, and robbed and murdered people. On a particular Saturday night the darkness was fearful. Did you ever hear a voice in the darkness? It sounds like thunder. All at once, on this particular night, a voice rang out. He said, "My heart stood still for a moment in terror." Then the voice said, "Is that you, John?" It was his father. Oh, the joy of it! His father slipped up to his side and threw his arm around him. He knew his boy's feelings, walking through the dark, and had come to meet him, and the rest of the way the boy snuggled up close to the big, strong father, feeling perfectly safe. Nothing will ever make you feel real comfortable *in* the dark but a great Presence. —The Rev. Joseph Hogue, in *Moody Church News.*

A Mark of Ownership

If you have a book which you do not wish to lose you write your name in it. The shepherd brands his name upon his sheep, and every one knows they are his. "From henceforth let no man trouble me," wrote Paul, "for I bear in my body the marks of the Lord Jesus." And we read in Revelation 22:4 of those who serve the Lord, "My name shall be in their foreheads." The Good Shepherd knows His own sheep by name, and no one can pluck them out of His hand.—*Sunday at Home.*

* * *

Another Lion Was There

A little lad was once asked by his father why he thought the lions could not touch Daniel, and he made answer "Because the Lion of the Tribe of Judah was with him."—*Sunday School Times.*

* * *

Kept

Kept every day from morn to night,
We know His promises are sure.
Kept by His truth, His power and might
No jot shall fail, while words endure.

Kept all the way from youth to age,
Thus far the Lord hath sheltered me.
Kept from the fangs of Satan's rage,
Safely we'll cross life's troubled sea.

Kept all these years by God's own hand,
To Him be praise and homage given.
Kept by His grace we'll hope to stand.
At evening time, in sight of Heaven.

Kept from the power of hell and sin,
Home of the pure in heart we'll see.
Kept by His love we'll here begin
The life that fills eternity.

—Selected.

* * *

Safer Than a Good Record

One day I met an old Negro and asked him how long he had been serving the Lord. "Fifty years," he replied. "Well, uncle," I said, "after keeping the faith for so long, you must feel pretty confident of holding out to the end!" "Ah, massa," he replied, "it's only a question of whether de Lord can hold on, and I reckon I can trust Him."—*Sunday Circle.*

SECOND COMING OF CHRIST

"He Said He Would"

A life insurance leaflet contains the following: A father and a girl of ten years, both good swimmers, entered the waters of the Atlantic at a New Jersey seashore resort a few summers ago. When some distance from shore they became separated, and the father realized they were being carried out to sea by the tide. He called out to his daughter: "Mary, I am going to shore for help. If you get tired, turn on your back; you can float all day on your back. I'll come back for you." Before long many searchers in boats were scurrying over the face of the water hunting for one small girl, while hundreds of people to whom the news had spread waited anxiously on shore. It was four hours before they found her, far from land. She was calmly floating on her back and not at all frightened. Cheers and tears of joy and relief greeted the rescuers with their precious burden as they came to land. The child took it calmly. She said, "He said he would come for me, and that I could float all day, so I swam and floated, because I knew he would come." May such faith in our Heavenly Father sustain us in those hours in which we must swim and float and wait.—*Gospel Chimes.*

* * *

He Promised

Someone has imagined the convalescent traveler able to sit in the doorway of the inn, earnestly looking up the road, waiting for the return of his deliverer. He could say, "He promised to come again. I know he will keep his word. I want to be waiting and watching for him when he returns." Is not this the attitude in which every redeemed sinner should be found—daily waiting for "the *coming of our Lord* Jesus Christ, and... our gathering together unto him?" (II Thess. 2:1).—*Sunday School Quarterly.*

* * *

A Little Girl's Example

A little girl had been listening while her mother's friends had been speaking about the near return of the Lord. After some hours she was missed. She was found looking out of a window at the top of the house. Asked what she was doing, she said, "Oh, Mother, I heard you say Jesus might come today, and I wanted to be the first to see Him. See! I washed myself and put on a clean pinny."—*Sunday School Times.*

* * *

Today? Tonight?

At night as Dr. Horatius Bonar retired to rest, his last action ere he laid down to sleep was to draw aside the curtain and looking up into the starry heavens, say: *"Perhaps tonight, Lord?"* In the morning, as he arose, his first movement was to raise the blind, and looking out upon the gray dawn, remark: *"Perhaps today, Lord?" — The Dawn.*

* * *

Watchman, Tell Us of the Night

Watchman, tell us of the night,
What its signs of promise are;
Trav'ler, o'er yon mountains height
See that glory-beaming star!
Watchman, does its beauteous ray
Aught of hope or joy foretell?
Trav'ler, yes; it brings the day,
Promised day of Israel.

Watchman, tell us of the night;
Higher yet the star ascends;
Trav'ler, blessedness and light,
Peace and truth its course portends:
Watchman, will its beams alone
Gild the spot that gave them birth?
Trav'ler, ages are its own,
See, it bursts o'er all the earth.

Watchman, tell us of the night,
For the morning seems to dawn;
Trav'ler, darkness takes its flight,
Doubt and terror are withdrawn:
Watchman, let thy wandering cease.
Hie, thee to thy quiet home!
Trav'ler, lo, the Prince of Peace,
Lo, the Son of God is come!
—John Bowring.

The Only Solution a Dictator

The Rev. D. M. Panton tells of a story of the late Dr. John Kelman that, when he was ministering in New York City, he asked one of his church members the question, "What is your solution of the present world unrest?" "His answer," Dr. Kelman said, "amazed me. It was, 'A Dictator.'" "But," argued the great preacher, "your Dictator would have to be a superman — one with perfect understanding of civic and economic problems, and with genius to meet the opposition and resolve the fears of those who doubted and opposed him." "I know it," was the quiet answer; "but we are looking for such a Man, and we have Him in view. His name is — Jesus." Commented Dr. Kelman, "The thrill of that answer will never leave me."—*Alliance Weekly.*

* * *

Perhaps Today

O Blessed Hope! Perhaps today—
A moment more, and then—away!
Caught up in clouds to be with Him,
Beyond the reach of conflicts grim,
Of disappointments, pain and tears.
O Blessed Hope! The rapture nears!
Today, Perhaps! We hail the dawn,
Of Heaven's glad, eternal morn;
Above earth's turmoil, strife and fear,
Christ's, "Lo I come!" His children hear.
All things declare the time's at hand!—
God's schedule will mature as planned.
—Annie Lind-Woodworth.

* * *

The Rim of the Sunrise

We are told that there is a town in the extreme north of Norway where, about January 18, in each year, the people climb a hill in order that they may see the sun rise after months of night. Nothing more than a little rim is seen at first; but the people are satisfied, because they know that tomorrow, and throughout the days to come, the sun will shine in all his strength. We are seeing, as it were, that small rim. The Sun of Righteousness will soon bring in the dawn of a new and brighter day. We cannot fix a date, but we can say in full assurance, "The coming of the Lord draweth nigh." (Jas. 5:8).—*Jewish Hope.*

* * *

Not Even an Angel Will Do

A noted preacher was invited to preach away from home one weekend. Arriving at the station he stood with his suitcase waiting for someone to claim him. A motor drew up, and the driver asked, "Are you Mr. Brown?" "Yes," he answered, whereupon his luggage was placed in the car which was immediately driven away. He was wondering what to do next, when another and more handsome car drew up to his side. "Mr. Brown, I think?" observed the gentleman who was driving. "Yes. But someone else has just asked me that and gone off with my luggage!" "Oh, that was a servant of mine. I sent him for your luggage, but I've come for you myself." The Lord Himself will come for His people. Even an angel would not do. Let us yield ourselves to His Holy Spirit that we may be ready at the Lord's appearing. — *Christian Herald (London).*

* * *

Not Ready for the Prince

While the last Prince of Wales was on a visit to the Midlands, he went into a certain workingman's home. Next day, the workingman told his mates sadly: "I never expected him, nor did my wife. The house was untidy, and I hadn't washed. We shall never forgive ourselves. If we had known he was coming, we should have been ready for him." *The Prince of Peace is coming* again, in power, to this earth of ours, and we know not the day or the hour. The one question for all is, "Are we ready to meet Him?"—*Intermediate Young People*

* * *

A Vision

The sun was sinking in the West,
A glory cloud swept o'er its crest,
Then as it passed beyond my view
It sent a message from the blue:

'Tis but a little while, and then,
I will be coming back again;
I'll come to drive the night away,
E'en at the breaking of the day.

So Christ has said, I'll come to earth
To bring it life and light and mirth;
Thus while the night rules on, in fear,
I know God's day is drawing near;
I know its gloom will pass away
And there will dawn God's blessed day;
When wars and famines will be o'er,
We'll reign with Him whom we adore.
—R. E. Neighbour, D.D.

* * *

A Warning

A young girl, who was very anxious about her soul, occupied the same room as a young Christian. As she began to arouse herself at early dawn she looked for her companion, but she was gone. She remembered that they retired together on the previous evening, but now her place was vacant, and she knew not whither her friend had gone. She thought of the words of the preacher on the previous afternoon, "One taken and the other left." She stayed not to dress, but went into the next room to awaken her companions, and as she went from room to room she saw that all who loved the Lord Jesus were missing and the unsaved ones were left. She knew not what to do; some slept on in indifference, but the anxious one searched the house, and at last found the little prayer meeting, and with mingled joy and sorrow she exclaimed, "I will not leave you again until I know that I am safe if the Lord does come." — *Sunday School Times.*

* * *

"Messiah Is Coming Soon"

William Bernard writes as follows:

"While in Java we called on a Chinese lady who held a good position. She told us that not very long before, she heard the sound of an unfamiliar voice while in her own home one day. No speaker was visible, but the message was clear and unmistakable. It was in her own language — 'Messiah is coming!' At heart she was a Christian; however the name 'Messiah' she had never heard before. Surmizing that she was being advised that a visitor was coming to call on her, she began to think of the entertainment of the coming guest. Again, however, she heard the voice, this time saying, 'Messiah is coming soon.' Perplexed, she went to a Christian friend and asked who Messiah was. She was informed that the Messiah was Jesus Christ. Thus God gave to this Chinese lady in her own home in that far-away island the second advent message, 'Messiah is coming soon.' "—Selected.

* * *

Half-Way Flying

Dr. Dinsdale T. Young once said: "A wonderful spiritual enrichment came into my life and ministry because I realized the great New Testament revelation of the personal return of our Lord. Dr. Andrew Bonar told a story of a plain man in one of the Scottish Presbyterian country kirks who had learned this precious doctrine. The man spent a Sunday in Edinburgh, to play the part of a sermon taster. When he returned to his village, the people asked him how he liked the Edinburgh preachers. His reply was: 'They all fly on one wing. They all preach the first coming of Christ, but they do not preach his second coming.' Nothing recovers evangelical fervor and rekindles missionary passion, and gives a yearning for entire sanctification, like a realization of the great fact that 'He comes,' and that He may come at any moment."—*Christian Age.*

* * *

In the glow of early morning,
  In the solem hush of night;
Down from Heaven's open portals,
  Steals a messenger of light.
Whisp'ring sweetly to my spirit,
  While the hosts of Heaven sing,
'Tis the wondrous thrilling Story,
  Christ is coming—Christ my King.

Oft methinks I hear His footsteps,
  Stealing down the paths of time,
And the future dark with shadows,
  Brightens with this Hope sublime;
Sound the soul-inspiring anthem,
  Angel hosts, your harps attune;
Earth's long night is almost over,
  Christ is coming—coming soon.
—Gospel Herald.

* * *

"Hustling to Get the Chores Done"

In a recent issue of the *Christian Witness* appeared a selected article under the above subject in which a story was told of a query put to Mr. W. E. Blackstone, author of the book, *Jesus Is Coming,* as to whether he was still looking for the Lord. He said, "I'm looking for the Lord every day, but I'm hustling to get the chores done before He gets here."

What a glorious truth is hidden here for all the Lord's dear children! If you do not believe He is coming so soon as do others, yet you likely do not have any time to waste to get all your "chores" done. Those of us who believe His Coming is imminent, how busy we should be with life's chores! We will do well to get most of them done!—*The C. H. and H. Banner.*

* * *

Why Dr. Stratton Quit Smoking

The late Dr. John Roach Stratton, valiant defender of the faith, gave this testimony: "I wish to bear my own personal testimony that I did not overcome the habit of smoking until the truth of the return of our Lord came home clearly to my mind and heart. When I did thus believe that Jesus Christ is surely coming back to this world again, even as He plainly promised, and that His coming for His church—the redeemed—may be at any moment, I found grace to throw pipes and cigars away completely, never to take them up again. I did not want Jesus to come back and find me with a breath that was offensive, or presenting the sorry spectacle of a preacher with a pipe or cigar in the corner of his mouth!"—*Sunday School Times.*

The Morning Star

I awoke and the night was passing,
  And over the hills there shone
A star all alone in its beauty
  When the other stars were gone.

For a glory was filling the heavens
  That came before the day,
And the gloom and the stars together
  Faded and passed away.

Only the star of the morning
  Glowed in the crimson sky;
It was like a clear voice singing,
  "Rejoice, for the sun is nigh."

Oh, children, a star is shining
  Into the hearts of men;
It is Christ with a voice of singing,
  "Rejoice, for I come again.

"For the long long night is passing,
  And there cometh the golden day.
I come to My own who love Me,
  To take them all away."

It may be today, or tomorrow;
  Soon it will surely be;
Then past are the tears and sorrow,—
  "Then Home forever with Me."
—*The Prayer Room,* Memphis, Tenn.

* * *

The Jews' Expectancy Today

Mr. Mark Kagan, speaking at one of the Advent Testimony meetings, said that when on a visit to Palestine he and some other Christians gathered together in an upper room within the city wall of Jerusalem, to remember Christ's sacrifice and death. After the meeting was over, he and another friend went to the Mount of Olives; and as they passed along they caught up a Jew who said that he also was going to the Mount of Olives. "We orthodox Jews," he said, "as we watch the things that are happening in the world, cannot come to any other conclusion than that the Messiah's coming must be near at hand. On that day His feet will stand on the Mount of Olives, and I am going there every day that I may be ready to give Him a welcome." Seeing that Israel is making such preparations for His coming, what is the Church doing?—*Christian Herald.*

Quite Suddenly

"In a moment, in the twinkling of an eye, . . . we shall be changed" (I Cor. 15:52).

Quite suddenly—it may be at the turning of a lane,
Where I stand to watch a skylark soar from out the swelling grain,
That the trump of God shall thrill me, with its call so loud and clear,
And I'm called away to meet Him, whom of all I hold most dear.

Quite suddenly—it may be as I tread the busy street,
Strong to endure life's stress and strain, its every call to meet,
That through the roar of traffic, a trumpet, silvery clear,
Shall stir my startled senses, and proclaim His coming near.

Quite suddenly—it may be as I lie in dreamless sleep—
God's gift to many a sorrowing heart, with no more tears to weep—
That a call shall break my slumber, and a Voice sound in my ear,
"Rise up, My love, and come away, behold the Bridegroom's here."
—*The Evangelical Christian.*

* * *

We Have the Score

Dr. Guinness had spoken on "The Imminent Return of the Lord Jesus." And he used the following illustration to show how he knew that the coming was near. He had heard "The Messiah" with great delight the previous evening. Now if a man had asked him after the performance had proceeded a couple of hours, how long he thought it would continue, he would have answered, "About five minutes." "But," the man might have expostulated, "how can that be? It is in full swing, has been going on for two hours, and I see no reason why it should not continue for two hours longer. How do you know it will be over in five minutes?" "Then," said Dr. Guinness, "I should have answered him, 'Because I have the score. Don't you remember that beautiful solo?' And he would have said, 'Yes.' 'And that chorus?' 'Yes.' And then I should have said to him, 'And I know it will soon be over because I have the score and they are singing the last chorus.'" It is a wonderful thing to "have the score," so you may follow events that lead to the advent. Perhaps soon the present will be past and God's new day will dawn. *We are near His coming. How near we do not know, but one thing we do know, it cannot be long!*
—Courtesy *Moody Monthly.*

* * *

The Unbalanced Clock

Movers left a clock, without its pendulum, sitting in the living room. The seconds ticked on in a frenzied manner. Without the pendulum all the intricate mechanism rattled on in a blind precipitation. Here is a picture of the world today. God has created all things to move in proper balance, but men refuse the Lord Jesus Christ who is God's Providence. Men talk about Providence as though it were a force. God says it is a Person—Christ, and that He "upholdeth all things by the word of His power" (Heb. 1:3). Nothing will move with perfection until He comes again.—*Revelation.*

* * *

Earthquakes

The frightful earthquake by which the city of Quetta in India was wiped out with the loss of 60,000 human lives and many million dollars' worth of property, calls attention to the fact that since the beginning of the twentieth century more than 250,000 lives have been snuffed out through earthquakes. Scientists who study the earth's crust and record the seismic disturbances tell us that earthquakes felt simultaneously in many places, particularly around the Mediterranean and in Great Britain, are forerunners of a far greater earthquake which might be also universal. In this case they agree with what was written in the Old Testament 2,500 years ago.
—*Just a Word.*

A Triumphant Termination

A lady visitor to the great Exhibition at Paris was stricken with a malady which almost took away the power of speech. Weaker and weaker she grew and the end gradually drew near. One word only escaped her lips, and that word was, "Bring — bring — bring —." Flowers, fruits, dainties, treasures from the Exhibition, were brought, but she still uttered the word, "Bring—." Bewildered and wondering, the watchers noticed the dawning of the Glory. At last the cloud was lifted from the memory, and in a clear and deliberate voice she exclaimed, "Bring forth the royal diadem, and crown Him Lord of all." Then she quietly laid her head upon the pillow and fell asleep. The uttermost longings of her soul were satisfied as she passed in "to see the King in His beauty."—Selected.

* * *

"The Lord Is Coming"

Many years ago a first cousin of the late Queen Victoria became a converted man and crossed the sea to preach the Gospel; he spent much of his time in Canada, in large cities, and in the back woods, among farmers, in the lumber camps, everywhere, in fact. One Sunday morning on his way to celebrate the Lord's Supper he passed a Christian's house, and saw the man at his woodpile, industriously chopping wood to cook the Sunday dinner. Knowing the man to be a backslider, one who had once been a faithful witness for his Saviour, Lord Cecil stopped and shouted to him, "The Lord is coming, brother, the Lord is coming!" He said no more nor was there need for more. These words, that reminder of the return of the Lord was enough; the words entered his heart as he had been sending the keen edge of the axe into the heart of the wood he was cutting; his conscience smote him, and the reminder from God's servant that the coming of the Lord was imminent so wrought upon his soul that it resulted in his happy restoration to the lost communion with his God and renewal of fellowship with his brethren in Christ. And what led to it? The thought of his Saviour's coming again.—*Gospel Herald.*

* * *

Signs Are Multiplying

Walter Lippman, that brilliant Jewish journalist and essayist, wrote two years ago in his column, "Today and Tomorrow" (New York *Herald-Tribune*, March 2, 1935): "The signs are multiplying that the stage is set for an event of world-wide importance and of unpredictable consequences." Nineteen centuries ago the Lord described this "setting of the stage" for the end of the age, an event of world-wide importance—but the consequences were not "unpredictable" to the Lord. He told us plainly that these things would happen, and what the result would be.—*Sunday School Times.*

* * *

There Will Be Disgraced Christians When Jesus Comes

Some time ago I was holding a meeting in a small town in the Middle West. While there I heard of a young man who in the past had been upheld as a model young man in the community. In all his activities in the community he seemed to be on the side of righteousness, and was a popular member of the local church. One morning the newspaper of the neighboring city told of a gambling raid staged by the police department of that city the night before, and to the utter astonishment of the readers in that small community, among the names of those caught in the place of gambling was the name of this model young man. A fine young man at home, he was secretly indulging in unlawful practices. It is hard to describe the result of the discovery. When the young man finally came home, he refused to leave the house for several days. He was disgraced and beaten by the sudden revelation, and went about some time with his head down.

In First John 2:28 we read: "And now, little children, abide in Him; that when He shall appear, we may have confindence and not be ashamed before Him at His coming." The original of "not be ashamed" is "not stand disgraced." Many Christians, who are now regarded as fine believers, are going to stand disgraced before the Lord when the secrets will be revealed and it will be seen that secretly they indulged in things and practices displeasing to the Saviour who bought them with His own blood.—*The Brethren Missionary Herald.*

* * *

Why He Left

Dr. J. C. Massee has told how when a young man he was persuaded to attend a theater much against his will. After being seated, he quickly got up. "What are you doing?" asked his friends. "I'm getting up," he replied. "But where are you going?" they urged. "I'm going out," said he. "But you just came in." "I know it, and I'm going out. See here," added Dr. Massee, "I'm a Christian; I believe the Bible, and my Bible tells me that Jesus, my Lord, is coming back to this earth, and that He may come at any time, and *I don't want Him to catch me here.*"—*Sunday School Times.*

* * *

Behold the Sun

I have read that near the North Pole, the night lasting for months and months, when the people expect the day is about to dawn, some messengers go up on the highest point to watch; and when they see the first streak of day they put on their brightest possible apparel, and embrace each other, and cry, "Behold the sun!" and the cry goes through the land, "Behold the sun!" Some of you have been trudging on in the darkness of sin. It has been a long and wearisome night for your soul; but now I cry, "Behold the Sun of righteousness rising with healing in His wings." "The dayspring from on high hath visited us, to give light to them that sit in darkness." Behold the sun! Behold the sun! Would God that every blinded eye might now see it! — Dr. Talmage, in the *Biblical Illustrator.*

How They Showed Their Faith

Lord Shackleton once went to search for the South Pole. He had to turn back, leaving some of his men on Elephant Island amid the ice and snow. He promised to come back for them. He finally reached South Georgia, where he secured another ship and supplies; and then went back to get his men. He tried to reach Elephant Island, but failed time after time. Suddenly one day there appeared an open place through the ice leading to the island! Quickly he ran his men through the open place, got his men on board the ship, and came out again, just before the ice crashed together. It was all done in half an hour. When the excitement was partly over, he asked one of the men who had been on the island, "How did it happen that you were all packed and ready for my coming? You were standing on the shore ready to leave at a moment's notice." The man replied, "Sir, you said that you would come back for us, and we never gave up hope. Whenever the sea was partly clear of ice, we rolled up our sleeping bags and packed our things, saying, 'Maybe Shackleton will come today.' We were always ready for your coming." Even so, let us be ready for the coming of Christ.—*Gospel Herald.*

* * *

If you knew that the Lord would come tonight:
Is there something you ought to do today?
Then, do it now!
Is there some debt you ought to pay today?
Then, do it now!
Is there some quarrel you ought to make up?
Then, do it now!
Is there a sinner you ought to warn?
Then, do it now!
He is coming. Perhaps tonight.—*Gospel Herald.*

* * *

What "Be Ye Ready" Means

A man visiting a certain school gave out that he would give a prize to the pupil whose desk he found in the best order when he returned. "But when will you return?" some of them asked.

"That I cannot tell," was the answer.

A little girl, who had been noted for her disorderly habits, announced that she meant to win the prize.

"You!" her schoolmates jeered. "Why, your desk is always out of order."

"Oh, but I mean to clean it the first of every week."

"But suppose he should come at the end of the week?" someone asked.

"Then I will clean it every morning.

"But he may come at the end of the day."

For a moment the little girl was silent. "I know what I'll do," she said decidedly; "I'll just keep it clean."

So it must be with the Lord's servants who would be ready to receive a prize at His coming. It may be at midnight, at cockcrowing, or in the morning. The exhortation is not "Get ye ready," but "Be ye ready."—Mattie M. Boteler.

SELF-CONTROL

A Recipe for a Bad Temper

Some people have quite a time with that temper! Something goes contrary to their selfish plan—someone says what does not fit in with their thinking—or something annoys them and they fly into a fit of temper, often doing and saying things which cause their heads to hang in shame.

I was traveling in a train and sitting beside a man, when one of his friends, in a gesture of fun, played an innocent, but foolish prank on him. It annoyed him so that he flew into a temper. Then when he cooled down, he said, "My, I wish I did not do that." What was wrong? He was a sincere Christian and loved his Lord, but he had failed to develop an inner power over passion and temper. He had never discovered that Christ could do more than blot out sin, that He could and would enter the very heart and life, and take control by His indwelling presence.

A certain woman who was most faithful in attendance at church, and who manifested a beautiful spirit at all times, lived under most trying circumstances. She was asked, "How is it that you are never out of temper? Is it that you do not feel the injustice, the annoyances?" "I feel them as much as anyone else," she replied, "but they do not hurt me." She was then asked, "Have you some special recipe?" "Yes," she replied. "for vexations caused by people I apply affection. For those caused by circumstances, I apply prayer. And over every wound that bleeds and burns, I murmur the words, 'Thy will be done.' "—*The Pentecostal Testimony.*

* * *

First Laws

A number of ministers were once dining together after an ordination, and when one of them seemed unduly attentive to the good things before him, he met with the approval of the host who said, "That's right! To take care of self is the first law of nature." "Yes, sir," said an old minister sitting by in reply, "but to deny self is the first law of grace!" Self-control or temperance in all things is God's law for all men.—*Sunday School Evangel.*

* * *

Christian Restraint

The story is told of a young minister who was going home late one evening from the church. He entered a crowded car, with his Bible under his arm, and at once there began some sneering remarks from some rough fellows. These remarks kept up, and when the young minister left the car, to the amusement of his companions, one youth said: "Say, mister, how far is it to heaven?" Many a Christian under the circumstances would have kept quiet or have resented the insult; but the minister, with a quiet dignity, and with all gentleness, replied: "It is only a step; will you take it now?" *This reply and the influence of the young minister keeping his temper under provoking circumstances were later the means of bringing that young man to Christ.—Earnest Worker.*

* * *

When Her Husband Was Angry

Not long ago a Hindu woman was converted chiefly by hearing the Word of God read. She suffered very much persecution from her husband. One day a missionary asked her, "When your husband is angry and persecutes you, what do you do?" She replied: "Well, sir, I cook his food better; when he complains I sweep the floor cleaner; and when he speaks unkindly I answer him mildly. I try, sir, to show him that when I became a Christian I became a better wife and a better mother." The consequences of this was that, while the husband could withstand all the preaching of the missionary, he could not stand the practical preaching of his wife, and gave his heart to God.—*Evangelical Visitor.*

* * *

The Soft Answer

Once a man came to our house red with wrath. He was boiling over with rage. He had, or supposed he had, a grievance to complain of. My father listened to him with great attention and perfect quietness until he had got it all out, and then he said to him in a soft and low tone, "Well, I suppose you only want what is just and right?" The man said. "Yes," but went on to state the case over again. Very gently father said to him, "If you have been misinformed, I presume you would be perfectly willing to know what the truth is?" He said he would. Then father very quietly and gently made a statement on the other side, and when he was through the man got up and said, "Forgive me, doctor, forgive me." Father had beaten him by his quiet, gentle way.

I saw it and it gave me an insight into the power of self-control. It was a striking illustration of the passage, *"He that ruleth his spirit* [*is better*] *than he that taketh a city."*—Henry Ward Beecher.

Am I a Ruler

A merchant falsely accused an innocent Quaker. When the latter called to try to explain, the merchant called to the servant to inform the Quaker that he was not at home.

Calmly the old Quaker looked up the stairway and said something to this effect, "God put thee in a better mind, friend."

This meek reply disturbed the merchant so much that he later apologized and inquired how he could bear such abuse as he had been receiving.

The old Quaker then told how he had observed that one in a passion always spoke loud and so he by God's help made an effort to use a moderate voice.

I'm sure this Quaker had learned the verse that tells us that he that can rule his spirit is better than he that can conquer a city.—*Gospel Herald.*

* * *

Roots of Bitterness

Have you ever considered your heart as a parcel of ground? Years ago our forefathers came to this country and "homesteaded" certain portions of land which belonged to the government. This was virgin soil. Much of it had to be cleared of woods and brush before it could be cultivated. It took long, arduous months of work before the land was cleared and crops rewarded the homesteader. But with patience and perseverance much was accomplished and the pioneer was the proud possessor of fertile fields and brought him rich return for his labor.

In clearing the land in the days of the pioneers the task of cutting the trees and removing the thickets and underbrush covering the land was but a small portion of the work involved, for this could quite quickly be accomplished by burning the wood. The difficult part of the work was the removing of the roots and stumps and stones which were underneath the surface of the ground but which must needfully be removed before the work was complete and before cultivation could be undertaken. If this was not done within a short time the area would be covered with a second growth, as difficult to remove as the first. Hebrews 12:15 says: "Looking diligently lest any man fail of the grace of God; lest any *root of bitterness* springing up, trouble you, and thereby many be defiled." It is these hidden things in our lives, the "roots of bitterness" which need to be eradicated completely.—*Gospel Herald.*

* * *

Treatment of Insults

Sir Walter Raleigh, a man of known courage and honor, being very injuriously treated by a hot-headed, rash youth, who proceeded to challenge him, and, on his refusal, spit in his face, and that, too, in public, the knight, taking out his handkerchief with great calmness, made him only this reply: "Young man, if I could as easily wipe your blood from my conscience as I can this injury from my face, I would at this moment take away your life." The youth, with a strong sense of his improper behavior, fell on his knees, and begged forgiveness.—*Biblical Encyclopedia.*

* * *

The Missionary's Triumph

Samuel Stokes, an American missionary, walked through the Punjab, carrying only a water-bottle and blanket, trusting wholly to native hospitality. In one village he was given a particularly hostile reception. The headmen of the village sat in chairs in a circle, smoking, leaving him the whole evening sitting on the floor. When he asked if he might nurse their sick and teach them, they hurled horrible insults at him; but he made no reply. Then they gave him stale crusts in a filthy bowl. He thanked them courteously, and ate. For two days this lasted. On the third day, the headman laid his turban at Stokes' feet as a token of respect. He explained that they had heard that Jesus' disciples were commanded to love their enemies, and had decided to put him to the test. The result had amazed them. Now they brought him their choicest food, and were eager to hear his teaching. If he had lost his temper, he would have lost his chance.—*Gospel Herald.*

Quietly Trusting

A traveler in Ceylon tells the following story: "As I was dining in a home I was startled to hear the hostess ask her servant to place a bowl of milk on the deer skin beside her chair. I knew at once that there was a cobra in the room, for they prefer milk to anything else. We also knew that a hasty movement meant death, so we sat like statues. Soon, to our amazement, a cobra uncoiled from my hostess' ankle and swiftly glided toward the milk, where it was quickly killed." What a triumph of self-control over the external! But if we use the same quiet trust in Christ as this woman did in the bowl of milk, when the serpent of all evil approaches us, internal triumphs over him would be more numerous than they are now.—*Record of Christian Work.*

* * *

Christy Mathewson's Lesson in Obedience

Obedience is necessary in playing a straight game. Christy Mathewson was a much loved ball player, but he had trouble with one of the rules—obedience. Manager McGraw required that at the end of every day's practice all extra players must run around the ball field twice before climbing into the bus to go home. On this particular day all who were supposed to run around the bases started except Mathewson. Go ahead, Matty, take the run with those fellows, and we'll all go home," said the manager. "I've worked hard enough today," replied Mathewson. "Just the same you've got to go," said McGraw. Matty sat there on the bench. "We don't move a foot till Matty runs," said the manager. His teammates urged, but there he sat for over half an hour. Finally he arose, stood at first base as if struggling with himself, then ran the bases twice and jumped into the bus. He said, "That was the most important lesson I ever had. I had to win in the fight over myself, and I did it."—*Presbyterian.*

Lincoln's Worst Enemy

When Abraham Lincoln was candidate for the Presidency, someone asked him what he thought of the prospect. With characteristic humor he answered, "I do not fear Breckinridge, for he is of the South, and the North will not support him; I do not much fear Douglas, for the South is against him. But there is a man named Lincoln I see in the papers, of whom I am very much afraid. If I am defeated, it will be by that man."—*Gospel Herald.*

* * *

The Path of Sanity

How is the path of sanity and steadfastness to be found? How is one to learn to be sober and gentle, and self-controlled? The great secret, I am firmly convinced, and I beg for earnest consideration of it, is to keep nearer to God than to Christians. One can stand almost anything if one dwells in the secret place of the Most High. Our Lord could face all the contradictions of sinners and the unbelief of His own family in Nazareth because He dwelt not there, but in the bosom of His Father.—Dr. A. T. Scho-

* * *

Things to Keep in Mind

The Value of—

A clock is in its reputation for accuracy.

A wrench is in its ability to adjust a problem.

A car is in its ability to perform well on the upgrade.

A stamp is in its ability to stick to the end of the journey.

A pair of scissors is in its ability to cooperate.

A tack is in its head that will not let it go too far.

A man is in his ability to combine all these virtues.—Courtesy *Moody Monthly.*

SELFISHNESS

Me-Sickness

The French speak of a disease which they call *La Maladie du moi*, or "Me-sickness." The disciples were troubled with that disease; they were too much concerned with themselves. Despite all the strides science has made, it has offered no vaccine to combat this deadly ailment. The only remedy that has ever been effective was that offered by the Great Physician. His love engenders selflessness for selfishness in the heart of man, and "Me-sickness" vanishes as does the morning mist before the sun's healing rays.—*Sunday School Times.*

* * *

She Did Not Try

It was in Chicago years ago. A terrible fire had raged. The Iroquois theater burned. Many were trampled to death as a maddened crowd fought for the exit.

One of those who got out was a young lady. She was borne along in the stampede, passing over many who had fallen. When on her way home she was nervous and agitated. To such an extent was this evidenced that a fellow traveler at length spoke to her desiring to be of help if it were possible. The story of the disaster and of her escape from the terrible fire was told.

"Certainly you ought to feel thankful that you escaped such a frightful death."

"Yes! I know I ought to be thankful, but oh, I didn't save anyone!"

"Yes! dear, but you were perfectly excusable in acting for yourself under such intense excitement."

"Yes! but I didn't even try to help anyone."

A bitter lament. Probably the girl could not have aided any if she had tried. But she had not tried. This was her source of sorrow.

Are we seeking to succor souls? The perishing are about us on every side. Shall we be satisfied with being saved ourselves and not care for those around us?—*Scattered Seed.*

I looked upon a sea and lo 'twas dead,
Although by Hermon's snow and Jordan fed.
How came a fate so dire? The tale soon told—
All that it got it kept and fast did hold.
All tributary streams found here their grave
Because that sea received but never gave.
O sea that's dead, teach me to know and feel
That selfish grasp my doom shall seal.
And help me, Lord, myself, my best to give,
That I may others bless, and like Thee live.

—*Gospel Herald.*

* * *

Recipe for Misery

If you wish to be miserable, think about yourself; about what you want, what you like; what respect people ought to pay you; and then to you nothing will be pure. You will spoil everything you touch; you will make misery for yourself out of everything good; you will be as wrethced as you choose.—Chas. Kingsley.

* * *

Profitable Emptying

It has been my experience that when you really come to the Lord, He never sends you away empty unless you come to Him stuffed full of yourself.—*Prophecy Monthly.*

* * *

Tommy's Indignation

Somewhere I read this dialogue: Father—"I should think, Tommy, that you might find some boy to play with you. Now, what's the matter with Johnny Jenkins and the little Drake boy?" Tommy, contemptuously—"Pooh! Why, they're a whole year younger than I am. I couldn't play with them." Father—"Well, there's Jack Spear and Willie Hanson. Won't they do?" Tommy, wistfully—"Yes, but they're a year older than I am, so the mean things won't play with me."—*Earnest Worker.*

The Boy Who Dropped Out

The boys of a junior high school were going to organize their basket ball team. All wanted to be the captain. The argument became heated, only one boy, Robert, was willing to give up to someone else. He took the ball and entered the gym, and practiced throwing for the goal, while the other boys argued in the hall. After a half hour their coach appeared upon the scene and saw the situation. He said, "Well, we will settle it this way, each boy take ten throws for the basket, and the one who makes it the greater number of times is captain." "O. K.," they all had to agree. Robert came out on top and was appointed captain.—*Sunday School Times.*

* * *

The Lost Letters

Dr. H. A. Ironside told the following story at a Bible conference: A small Christian sect of an exclusive temperament was holding a convention. Outside the auditorium there was displayed the motto, "Jesus Only." A strong wind blew the first three letters away. "Us Only" is too often the spirit shown by Christians of narrow vision. — *Sunday School Times.*

* * *

Things That Count

Not what we have, but what we use,
Not what we see, but what we choose—
These are the things that mar or bless
The sum of human happiness.

The things near by, not things afar,
Not what we seem, but what we are—
These are the things that make or break,
That give the heart its joy or ache.

Not what seems fair, but what is true,
Not what we dream, but good we do—
These are the things, that shine like gems,
Like stars in fortune's diadems.

Not as we take, but as we give,
Not as we pray, but as we live—
These are the things that make for peace,
Both now and after time shall cease.

—Selected.

Selfish Ambition

I wanted to walk in the beaten path
That was trod by the feet of men.
I wanted to thrive by the sweat of my brow,
And rove in the valley of gain.
But the Master said,
" 'Twas not thus I walked, nor lived;
If so, I lived in vain."

I wanted to live with a selfish will.
My logic was surely sane;
No thought had I for a hungry world
Nor for those who suffered pain.
But the Master said,
" 'Twas not thus I loved, nor gave;
If so, I gave in vain."

I wanted to climb to a lofty height,
To be known by the fame of men.
No care had I for the souls of men,
Nor for death at the end of the lane.
But the Master said,
" 'Twas not thus I lived, nor died;
If so, I died in vain."

And so my all to Him I gave
In consecration deep. For me
He loved and lived and gave
And died. Then self died out of me.
—Zech Ford Bond, in *Western Recorder*.

* * *

A Very Small Parcel

J. Stuart Holden once said: "We sometimes speak of men and women—even Christian men and women—being wrapped up in themselves, and when a man is wrapped up in himself, he makes a very small parcel. When he has shrunk to that size so that he can be wrapped up in himself, there is not much to wrap up." Selfishness shrivels the soul and the effect is like a boomerang. There is a parable in India of the Selfish Fool, to whom a rice field was bequeathed. The first season the irrigation water covered his field and made it fruitful, then flowed on to his neighbor's fields, bringing fertility everywhere. But the next season the Selfish Fool said in his heart, "This water is wealth, it is liquid harvest. I was a fool to let this treasure escape to my neighbor's land. He robbed his neighbor—and he spoiled his own crop; for the irrigation water brought blessing while it flowed, but when it became stagnant it bred a marsh. Paul's injunction applies to me today, "Look not every man on his own things, but every man on the things of others."—*Gospel Herald*.

* * *

Safety First—But Whose?

This article is being written on a westbound train. On its steps and elsewhere is the oft-seen reminder, "Safety First!" An unselfish soul had the following reaction to such a sign: "Safety first may be good for a railroad crossing but its mighty bad for a human life." Miss Margaret Slattery once told of a visit to the home of a childhood friend who had grown very rich. She said that as she looked beyond the roses in his conservatory she saw a poor woman searching for coal in the snow and that, while she wanted her friend to have abundant joys, she longed also for the essentials for others.—*Gospel Herald*.

* * *

Disturbing the Sunday Peace

A generation ago, it was a rare U. S. town that grew up without at least one church in its midst. Even the smallest settlements could support churches of two or three Protestant denominations. Today the trend, observable particularly in new TVA towns in the South, and in such Government developments as Greenbelt in Maryland, is toward Community churches, one to a locality. Away out in front of this trend last week marched a suburb of Richmond, Va.. named Hampton Gardens. As an inducement to the congregation to move to Hampton Gardens, Mrs. William Smith Morton had offered her house and lot, worth $100,000 to St. Giles Presbyterian Church of Richmond. Other residents promptly got up a petition declaring they would not welcome a church because "the peace and quiet of the locality would be disturbed . . . clustering of a large number of cars on Sunday would constitute a traffic inconvenience and hazard." To preserve their Sabbath peace, the Hampton Gardens Association thereupon voted, 51 to 7, against allowing St. Giles or any other church to build there.—*Time.*

* * *

A Suggestive Sign

In a city that he visited during one of his many journeys preaching the Word of God, Dr. A. C. Gaebelein noticed a sign in a small tailoring and dyeing establishment which read:

I LIVE TO DYE, I DYE TO LIVE
THE MORE I DYE THE MORE I LIVE
THE MORE I LIVE THE MORE I DYE

Read these words aloud, and you will hear a great spiritual truth. The more there is death to self, that much more fully is the Lord Jesus Christ able to live His life in us. "I am crucified with Christ: nevertheless I live; yet not I, but Christ liveth in me" (Gal. 2:20). This kind of living is possible to every believer by full appropriation of all that is his in Christ. "Likewise reckon ye also yourselves to be dead indeed unto sin, but alive unto God through Jesus Christ our Lord" (Rom. 6:11).—*Revelation.*

* * *

Working in the Light

Michael Angelo, we are told, carried a lighted candle in the front of his cap when at work on his matchless pieces of sculpture that his work might not be hindered even by his own shadow. His work in marble endures, but not eternally. The humblest life at work in carving out its present and future has a task even more difficult than Angelo's creations, for we must stand or fall with it throughout eternity. Have we the true light bearing down upon the work? The light of God's Word has illuminated millions of human lives as they toiled away in the making of a life, and we cannot do better than to bring it daily into use in our tasks.—Selected.

* * *

Selfishness Blights

"Selfishness seeks more than its own. It cheats, it robs, it murders, to get what belongs to others. How desolate and desolating is a selfish life! It blights and ruins wherever it rules."—Selected.

* * *

A Common Malady

A Springfield neighbor of Lincoln's was drawn to his door one day by the sound of the crying of children. He saw Lincoln passing by with his two sons, both crying lustily. "What is the matter with the boys?" asked the man. "Just what is the matter with the whole world!" answered Lincoln. "I have three walnuts, and each boy wants two." Surely, this spirit is still abroad today.—*London Christian Herald.*

SERVICE

"I Have Done So Little"

One time Ian MacLaren went to a certain house and saw an old Scotch woman standing in her kitchen, weeping. She wiped her eyes with the corner of her apron, and when the minister asked her what was the matter, she confessed, "I have done so little." She further said, "I am so miserable and unhappy." "Why?" "Because I have done so little for Jesus. When I was just a wee girl the Lord spoke to my heart and I did so much want to live for Him." "Well, haven't you?" asked the minister. "Yes, I have lived for Him, but I have done so little. I want to be of some use in His service." "What have you done?" "I will tell you. I have washed dishes, cooked three meals a day, taken care of the children, mopped the floor, and mended the clothes. That is all I have done all my life, and I wanted to do something for Jesus." The preacher, sitting back in the armchair, looked at her and smiled. "Where are your boys?" he inquired. She had four sons and had named them after Bible characters. "Oh, my boys? You know where Mark is. You ordained him yourself before he went to China. Why are you asking? There he is preaching for the Lord." "Where is Luke?" questioned the minister. "Luke? He went out from your own church. Didn't you send him out? I had a letter from him the other day." And then she became happy and excited as she continued, "A revival has broken out on the mission station, and he said they were having a wonderful time in the service of the Lord!" "Where is Matthew?" "He is with his brother in China. And isn't it fine that the two boys can be working together? I am so happy about that. And John came to me the other night—he is my baby and is only nineteen, but he is a great boy. He said, 'Mother, I have been praying and, tonight in my room, the Lord spoke to my heart, and what do you suppose He told me? I have to go to my brother in Africa! But don't you cry, Mother. The Lord told me I was to stay here and look after you until you go Home to Glory.'" The minister looked at her: "And you say your life has been wasted in mopping floors, darning socks, washing dishes, and doing the trivial tasks. I'd like to have your mansion when we are called home! It will be very near the throne!"—Selected.

* * *

Divine Paradoxes

The way to be master is to be servant;
The way to get up is to get down;
The way to receive is to give;
The way to be rich is to be poor;
The way to be wise is to be a fool;
The way to be exalted is to abase yourself;
The way to live is to die.

—*Sunday School Times.*

* * *

Disease or Service

"Goiter was common in Savoy, and the government took notice of it to the extent that young men afflicted with it were excused from military service. It was found that iodine lozenges would prevent goiter, and they were given free to the people. But the mothers of the boys in Savoy used to hide these lozenges, preferring the terrible mark of goiter to having their sons drafted for military service. There is many a man who would rather be marked by sin than to be absolutely at the disposal of Christ and drafted for His service." —*Record of Christian Work.*

* * *

Clara Barton's Fears

"People say that I must have been born brave. Why, I seem to remember nothing but terrors in my early days. I was a shrinking bundle of fears—fears of thunder, fears of strange faces, fears of my strange self." Such is Clara Barton's confession of her girlhood. It speaks volumes for her that she was able to overcome these fears so as to become the "angel of the battlefield." She managed the rebellious drivers of the army wagons which carried her supplies of food, bandages, and medicine. She ministered to thousands of wounded on the firing-line amid such scenes of blood and carnage as made veteran surgeons and soldiers pale at the very sight. She was in Fredericksburg when "every street was a firing line and every house a hospital." General Patrick caught sight of her and thought her a refugee. "Do you want protection?" asked the General chivalrously. "I believe I am the best protected woman in the United States," answered Miss Barton with a smile.—*Young People's Delight.*

* * *

Why Not Happy Now?

That farsighted man of a past generation, Theodore Cuyler, never gave a more telling message than when he said: "We hope to be happy in Heaven; why not now? Why parse the word 'Heaven' in the future tense? The unselfish service of Christ and of our fellow creatures is the beginning of paradise; the more we do for him here, the more we shall have of Him up there. Open your ear to every call of duty; open every door and window of your soul to the instreaming light and love of Jesus, and your joy shall be full." — *Christian Endeavor World.*

* * *

She Did What She Could

At a mission hall in London, a wealthy lady, who was unfortunately deaf, made good use of her riches by providing for the poor some excellent Gospel services. On one occasion a celebrated preacher said to her, "And what part do you take in this noble work?" "Oh," she an-answered, "I smile them in, and I smile them out again." Soon after this the preacher saw the good result of her sympathy as a crowd of working men entered the hall and looked delighted to get a smile from her. The Bread of Life and the Water of Life cannot be recommended to people by those who look as if that food and drink disagreed with them. —Henry Pickering.

* * *

"Before and After" the Cross

"Before my conversion I worked toward the Cross, but since then I have worked from the Cross; *then I worked to be saved, now I work because I am saved.*"—Dwight L. Moody.

* * *

Life's Richest Reward

A young woman in New York held what was considered a splendid position in a school attended by children from wealthy homes. Suddenly she gave it up and went to teach in one of the most squalid districts on the East Side.

"These East Side kiddies have so little," she explained. "School is the one bright spot in their lives. I feel almost like a fairy godmother when in their midst. The children in my other school had everything. They even were conveyed to the schoolroom door by nurses and chauffeurs. There was no 'kick' in it for me."

Such confessions as this prove that Jesus was right when He stressed the fact that the joy that comes from helping others is the richest reward one can experience in life.—Selected.

* * *

His Will Not Labor

A trained nurse was asked if she did not grow weary of her work. She replied: "Yes, when I have to attend rich patients who might hire someone else to wait on them; then my head aches and my hands are heavy. But give me my basket of foods and medicines, and let me go among the poor who can pay me only with their eyes, and I can imagine no greater happiness. Heaven! There I ask the Lord of Paradise to give me at least August vacation that I may spend dog days in the slums. I am sure He will, for did not the Christ find it His meat to do the will of His Father in just such places?"—Courtesy *Moody Monthly.*

* * *

Service Costs

A woman who was interested in Christian work in London wrote me once and said, "I have a meeting I want you to come to speak to. It is only a small meeting and will take nothing out of you." I answered, "I cannot come, and it would be of no use if I did come. *If it takes nothing out of me it will do nobody any good.*" It is service that costs, and a cheap religion is not worth preaching.—Gipsy Smith, in *The Evangelical Christian.*

* * *

Helping Jesus

A medical student was in the operating room waiting to watch a great surgeon's work. The surgeon's assistant failed to come and the surgeon called this student to help him. "How proud I was," he said, "to help this great man save a life." Jesus has called us to help Him save others, and we should be proud of the honor, glad that we can help to save others to everlasting life. A great minister said that he praised God for the honor and privilege of helping to save the world. We have only to obey His command and trust Him to help us do this work for Him.—*Gospel Herald.*

God's Call Is Clear

God's service call is clear, definite, personal, and authoritative. It assures that the omnipotent, omniscient and sufficient Caller will assist the one called in unchanging faithfulness. It assures that response is possible. It is dependent upon the obedience of the one called. A chisel is a lifeless piece of steel, but controlled by the hand of the sculptor, it can aid in producing wondrous statuary. Who can estimate the blessing caused mankind because of yielded obedience to Christ's call by Peter, James, John, Paul, Luther, Livingstone, Carey, Hudson Taylor, Moody and a host of others? Who can estimate the catastrophe to all concerned had they not obeyed?

God's service calls test faith. God's sufficient grace is always available for the task, despite any sense of unworthiness or inability upon the part of the servant. Ann Hasseltine, considered by many the most popular young woman in New England, married Adoniram Judson against advice of many well-meaning friends. Fourteen days later they sailed for Burma. Her suffering and heroism with her husband is history. They labored six years without a visible convert. When Judson died, there were 63 churches and 7,000 Christians in Burma. —*Gospel Herald.*

* * *

Off and On

Those who bless the Lord only when all goes well with them are much like the man of whom it was said, "He served the Lord off and on for forty years." "Off and on" thanksgiving is a poor kind.—*Christian Herald.*

* * *

Five Qualifications

There are certain qualifications we must have if we would be used of God. These qualifications do not include great learning, genius, riches, executive ability, and other similar assets that many of us will never have. Paul has told us, by inspiration, just what they are. D. L. Moody is quoted in the Keswick Calendar as follows: "Paul sums up five things that God uses: 'the weak things,' 'the foolish things,' 'the base things,' 'the despised things,' and 'the things which are not.' When we are ready to lay down our strength and our weakness before the Lord, He can use us."—*Sunday School Times.*

* * *

First Things

Someone asked John Wanamaker: "How do you get time to run a Sunday school for four thousand scholars, in addition to the business of your stores, your work as Postmaster-General, and other obligations?" Instantly Mr. Wanamaker replied: "Why, the Sunday school is my business! All other things are just *things.* Forty-five years ago I decided that God's promise was sure: 'Seek ye first the kingdom of God, and His righteousness; and all these *things* shall be added unto you.' "—*The King's Business.*

* * *

A Thankful Dedication

O Master, let me walk with Thee
In lowly paths of service free;
Tell me the secret; help me bear
The strain of toil, the fret of care.

Help me the slow of heart to move
By some clear, winning word of love;
Teach me the wayward feet to stay,
And guide them in the homeward way.

Teach me Thy patience; still with Thee
In closer, dearer company.
In work that keeps faith sweet and strong,
In trust that triumphs over wrong.

In hope that sends a shining ray
Far down the future's broadening way;
In peace that only Thou can'st give,
With Thee, O Master, let me live.
—Washington Gladden.

* * *

The Individual in Christian Service

The work of God in the world is given out as piece-work among His children. No servant of God is too young, or too poor, or to ungifted, or too obscure to be a fellow-laborer with Him. Sir Michael Costa was once rehearsing with a large orchestra and hundreds of voices. Amidst the thunder of the organ, and the roll of the drums, the player on the piccolo said to himself: "In all this din, my little instrument doesn't matter," and he ceased to play. Suddenly the great conductor threw up his arms, and all was still. "Where is the piccolo?" he cried. God listens for our share in His orchestra, and it is as if He said: "What is in thine hand, Abel?" and Abel replies, "Nothing, O God, but a wee lamb." Yet the smoke of that sacrifice has been a sweet savor for thousands of years. Or to Moses, and he replies: "Nothing but a rod, O God," but that rod swallows the serpents of hell. Or to Dorcas, and she answers: "Only a needle, Lord," but those garments have been the heavenly pattern for holy women ever since.—*The Dawn.*

"I've Done Refusin'"

"I've done refusin'." These were the words of an aged Christian who had been unexpectedly asked by his pastor to lead the special meeting for the evening. In commencing the service, he stated that he had not expected to take charge of the meeting, and so was unprepared to make remarks on the topic before them. "But," said he, "I have made up my mind that when I am asked to do anything in Christian work by one whom I have confidence in, if he thinks that it is my duty, even if I do not feel that I am prepared, I will try to do it. I've done refusin'." No better opening for the prayer meeting that night was needed. What better keynote could be found? What a difference would be seen in our social meetings and every branch of church work if only each professing Christian could say, 'I've done refusin'." —*The Congregationalist.*

SIN

Sin and Salvation

Sir John Simpson, the Scotch surgeon, was once approached by a young man, who asked him what he regarded as his greatest discovery. The simple reply of this eminent scientist was, "My greatest discovery is that I am a sinner, and that Jesus is a great Saviour."

This generation seems to have lost the true sense of sin. Indeed, many individuals say there is no such thing as sin. Others admit the reality of it, but confine it to those acts which are commonly regarded as disgraceful and heinous. By this reasoning they confine sin to a small group.—William James Robinson, D.D., in *Gospel Herald.*

* * *

The Pressure of Need

If we have a conviction of sin, we will feel the pressure of need. Sin is not a theological abstraction. It is the evil of the world brought home to our door. It is the lust of the world that brings men to ruin. It is the lowered moral standard that threatens our youth. It is the greed for power and money that fills the economic world with rackets. It is the impatience with discipline that breaks up our homes. Sin crouches at the door of democracy to weaken it. Sin is as real as flu or cancer, the corrupting influence which poisons the very air. We face the sickness of soul which sin has created.

The world we face is lost. Men are lost when they don't know where they are or where they are going or what they are here for. They are lost when the moral compass does not operate and when the price tags are so mixed that they can't tell where life's values really are. We should not be surprised if people stay away from special meetings. Why should they come? They are lost. They don't know God or the Father's house. The Son of Man came to seek the lost, not to have them seek Him.—*Gospel Herald.*

Shall We Change the Label?

Dr. J. Wilbur Chapman tells of a distinguished Methodist minister of Australia who preached on sin. One of his church officers afterward came to see and talk with him in his study. He said to the minister: "Dr. Howard, we don't want you to talk so plainly as you do about sin, because if our boys and girls hear you talking so much about sin they will more easily become sinners. Call it a mistake if you will, but do not speak so plainly about sin." The minister took down a small bottle and showed it to the visitor. It was a bottle of strychnine and was marked, "Poison." He said: "I see what you want me to do. You want me to change the label. Suppose I take off this label of 'Poison' and put on some mild label, such as 'Essence of Pepperment,' don't you see what happens? *The milder you make the label, the more dangerous you make the poison.*"—W. S. Bowden.

* * *

In the Coffin

In Waterbury, Conn., a few months ago a Negro evangelist exhorted a wailing audience, with fists milling, to clean living. In front of the platform in the African Methodist Church a casket was piled high with flowers. The evangelist told of the horrors of hell, and there were not a few hysterical cries from his listeners. The newspaper announcement said that the service was to be a funeral. Over the coffin the evangelist chanted no eulogy. The dead man had committed every sin. He was wicked, and therefore he would go into eternal torment. When the sermon was finished, the audience was invited to file past the casket and take one look at this horrible sinner. Each man and woman peered into the casket. The casket was empty. A mirror in the bottom reflected the face of every person who stared.—*Defender.*

* * *

The Apple with a Wormhole

You have many times seen an apple with a wormhole in it. But did you know whether the worm began to bore the hole in the apple from the inside or from the outside? Many would say from the outside; but the scientist will agree with the common observer who declares that the worm began on the inside. As a matter of fact, they tell us that the egg was laid in the blossom and that the worm was hatched in the heart of the apple, whence he bored his way out.

And that is precisely the way the worm of sin starts work in the human life. He begins in the heart and bores his way out. We know it is true that out of the heart are the issues of life. Nor must we ever forget that the heart must be sound or the life will be mutilated.—Selected.

* * *

Do You Ever Feel the Burden?

As an Indian evangelist was preaching, a flippant youth interrupted him. "You tell me about the burden of sin. I feel none. How heavy is it? Eighty pounds? Ten pounds?" The preacher answered: "Tell me, if you laid four hundred pounds' weight on a corpse, would it feel the load?" "No, because it is dead," replied the youth. The preacher said: "That spirit, too, is dead which feels no load of sin."—*The King's Business.*

* * *

None Guilty

Paul J. Loizeaux said: "Oh, how hard it is to find sinners! If only I could find one, I have a marvelous message for him." Of course he meant sinners who know themselves to be sinners, and such sinners that there is no hope for them but in the Saviour. To be a sinner is one thing. To know it is another. But whether we know it or not, God knows our sinnership, and knows if we go on without His saving help we must perish. But to deliver us from perishing He gave us His Son. That is the twofold reason then for this gift of gifts, God's great love and man's great need.—*Sunday School Times.*

What Kind of Sinners

The church of which Mr. Samuel Colgate, the great American business man, was a member, entered into an agreement to make special prayer for the conversion of sinners. For some days they prayed earnestly. One day applicants for church-membership were invited to present themselves. A woman came forward. Heart-broken, she told her story of what a sinner she had been, and how God had forgiven her for Christ's sake, and she wished to slip into a corner of the church and have the fellowship of God's people as she made the start for Heaven. The silence was oppressive. Then a member arose and moved that action on the application be postponed. Mr. Colgate arose and said in substance: "I guess we made a blunder when we asked the Lord to save sinners. We did not specify what kind. I think we had better all ask God to forgive us for not specifying what kind of sinners we want saved. He probably did not understand what we wanted." They all saw the point. The woman was received into fellowship.—*The Elim Evangel.*

* * *

When Danger Approaches

Major Whittle tells of a soldier who was posted in a forest to watch for the approach of Indians. It was a position of peculiar danger, three different men having been surprised and killed at this post without having time to fire a shot. The soldier was left with strict orders to observe the utmost vigilance. In a short time an object moving among the trees at some distance caught his eye. He watched it, with gun ready. As it came a little nearer, he saw it to be a wild hog. Another came in sight. He satisfied himself it *was* a wild hog rooting under the leaves. Presently in another direction the leaves were rustled, and a third wild hog appeared. Being now used to them, he paid but little attention. The movements of the last animal, however, in which was a slight awkwardness, made him think possibly an Indian might be approaching covered in a hog's skin. If it was an Indian, the safest thing was to shoot; if not, there would be no harm. He raised his rifle and fired. With a bound and a yell, an Indian leaped to his feet and fell back dead. The man had saved his life and prevented the surprise of the garrison by his watchfulness. So the child of God must be ever on the alert against the approaches of the evil one. Draw the Word of God upon every object that approaches you in this dark world of sin.—*The Illustrator.*

* * *

The Secret Working of Sin

Judas was unsuspected to the last. *A secret sin works insidiously, but with quiet power. Its hidden ravages are awful, and the outward revelation of their result and existence may be contemporaneous.* Until that revelation was made, probably no one ever suspected the presence in the man of anything but a few venial faults which were as mere excrescenses on a robust character, though these growths were something rude. Often a large fungus will start from a tree, and in some mysterious manner will sap the lifepower on the spot on which it grows. They were like the fungus. When the fungus falls in the autumn, it leaves scarcely a trace of its presence, the tree being apparently as healthy as before the advent of the parasite. But the whole character of the wood has been changed by the strange power of the fungus, being soft and cork-like to the touch. Perhaps the parasite may fall in the autumn, and the tree may show no symptoms of decay; but at the first tempest it may have to encounter, the trunk snaps off at the spot where the fungus has been, and the extent of the injury is at once disclosed. As long as any portion of that tree retains life, it will continue to throw out these destructive fungi; and even when a mere stump is left in the ground, the fungi will push themselves out in profusion.—*Scientific Illustrations and Symbols.*

* * *

Sin's Wages Not Reduced

There is no incident that more forcefully illustrates sin's ruin than that connected with the painting of Leonardo Da Vinci's great masterpiece, "The Last Supper." Long and in vain had the artist sought for a model for his Christ. "I must find a young man of pure life," he declared, "before I can get that look on the face I want." At length, his attention was called to a young man who sang in the choir of one of the old churches of Rome, Pietro Bandinelli by name. He was not only a young man of beautiful countenance, but his life was as beautiful as his face. The moment he looked upon this pure, sweet countenance the artist cried out for joy, "At last I have found the face I wanted!" So Pietro Bandinelli sat as the model for his picture of Christ. Years passed on, and still the great painting, "The Last Supper," was not finished. The eleven faithful apostles had all been sketched on the canvas, and the artist was hunting for a model for his Judas. "I must find a man whose face has hardened and distorted," he said; "a debased man, his features stamped with the ravages only wicked living and a wicked heart can show." Thus he wandered long in search of his Judas, until one day in the streets of Rome he came upon a wretched creature, a beggar in rags, with a face of such hard, villainous stamp that even the artist was repulsed. But he knew that at last he had found his Judas. So it came about that the beggar, with the repulsive countenance, sat as a model for Judas. As he was dismissing him, Da Vinci said, "I have not yet asked your name, but I will now." "Pietro Bandinelli," replied the man, looking at him unflinchingly. "I also sat to you as the model for your Christ!" Astonished, overwhelmed by this startling declaration, Da Vinci would not at first believe it, but the proof was at hand, and he had finally to admit that Pietro Bandinelli, he whose fair, sweet face had been the inspiration for his great masterpiece, the face of Christ, had now become so disfigured by the sins of a lifetime that no trace was left of that marvelous beauty which before had been the admiration of men! "Sin when it is finished bringeth forth death!"—J. Wilbur Chapman.

The Parables

The parables of judgment in the teachings of Christ are aimed at sins of omission, as if He saw that there our peril lay. The foolish virgins did not stone the wedding procession or steal the refreshments or insult the bride—they neglected the duty of having oil in their lamps and were therefore excluded from the feast. The man with one talent did not use it for any evil purpose—he did not use it at all, and stood therefore condemned. The men on the left hand in the great judgment scene were not accused of robbing the poor or mistreating the sick or the imprisoned. Inasmuch as they did it not to the least of the needy, they failed of acceptance with Him. The way to perdition is paved with moral neglect.—Charles R. Brown, in *The Watchman-Examiner.*

* * *

Rescue by Robber

The winter of 1874 was a very severe one in Palestine. Snow lay in the streets and on the flat roofs to a depth of several feet, and by its weight many houses were crushed. On the eighth of February a terrible storm raged in Gaza, and during the night a robber entered a house and ransacked the lower apartments, laying his plunder ready to carry away. Then he entered the sleeping apartment occupied by the father and mother. A baby sleeping showed signs of waking, and fearing lest he should be betrayed, he carried it down near the door. The child began to cry, and awakened the mother, who proceeded to its cradle; not finding it there she called the father, who hearing the cries said, "It is crying out of doors. How can that be?" Both of them ran outside, and no sooner had they got out than the roof fell in. The robber was found beneath the ruins with the stolen wealth in his possession.—J. R. Miller's Year Book, in the *Sunday School Times.*

* * *

Sin

A man in the open country watched from a distance an American eagle mount into the sky upon its mighty wings. It was a magnificent sight; but soon it appeared that something was wrong. The king of birds did not continue to rise in the sky with the same power and speed. His flight at first seemed hampered, then came to a stop. until at least the great bird fell down at the wanderer's feet.

Looking closely, the man saw that the eagle was dead. Searching still more closely, he observed that a small weasel had dug its claws into the abdomen of the splendid bird, had soared upward with it into the sky, and had drained the eagle of his life-blood while the latter tried to escape. *Sin is like that.*—Jan Karel Van Baalen, in *The Journey of Man.*

* * *

Blushing

French doctors are trying to find a cure for blushing. According to the Bible, inability to blush, says *The Gospel Minister*, is an evidence of crime. This is what is written in Jeremiah 8:12, "Were they ashamed when they had committed abomination? nay, they were not at all ashamed, neither could they blush: therefore shall they fall among them that fall: in the time of their visitation they shall be cast down."—*Gospel Herald.*

* * *

It Would Rejoice God's Heart

"See," said an evangelist to a penitent who was slow in taking comfort—"see how even a publican was accepted when he cried for mercy!" "Ah," said the other, "but I have been a greater sinner than a publican; I have been a Pharisee!" "Well," was the answer, "since God was so glad to hear a publican say, 'God be merciful to me a sinner,' how glad would He be to hear a Pharisee say so!" God used these words to bring comfort, light, and salvation to the man's heart.—*Christian Herald.*

* * *

Lions Are Never Tamed

Said a lion tamer: "There is no such thing in the world as a tamed lion. A lion may be on his good behavior today and a whirlwind of ferocity tomorrow. He may eat out of your hand, or permit you to place your head in his mouth today. But tomorrow he will rend you limb from limb if the fury takes him. The biggest giant that ever lived takes his life in his hands when he enters the cage of the tamest lion. The blood thirst is there and sometime it will flame out." There is a whole sermon in that and many a man who has kept his body under by sheer force of will for a score of years finds at the end of that period that he has not tamed, but only checked, the power of sin within him. What he needs is not an animal trainer, but some power to create in him a wholly new life.—*Pacific Presbyterian.*

* * *

Why Not Everything?

A story has been written by Frederick Hall about that lad who played such an important role in the miracle of the loaves and fishes. It tells how the boy reported that exciting incident to his mother when he returned home that evening at sunset. When, with eyes still big with the wonder of it all, he had told how his five barley loaves and two dried fishes had increased in the Master's hands until the vast crowd had been fed to a sufficiency, he added, "I wonder, Mother, if it would be that way with everything you gave Him?"—*Sunday School Times.*

* * *

Would We Prize the Knife?

Spurgeon says , "If I had a dear brother who had been murdered, what would you think of me if I valued the knife which had been crimsoned with his blood? If I made a friend of the murderer, and daily consorted with the assassin who drove the dagger into my brother's heart, surely I, too, must be an accomplice in the crime. Sin murdered Christ; will you be a friend to it? Sin pierced the heart of the incarnate God, can you love it?—*Senior B.Y.P.U. Quarterly.*

How Sin Works

A vivid illustration of sin and how it works, is an old story of the Middle Ages. During that time there lived a smith who boasted that he could break any chains, except those forged by himself. He committed some act which displeased the noble whom he served, and he was punished by being condemned to the dungeon. On the way to the dungeon, he boasted that he would soon be out again as he was sure he could break any chain put upon him. When he was chained, he immediately started to look for the flaw in the links which would set him free, but he found his own mark on the links, and knew he was hopelessly bound by his own handiwork, and could not escape because of his own chain.

So many sins start so small and so innocently, and we are certain we can break these self-forged chains at will, but they grow strong until we cannot break them, and it is we ourselves who have made our chains for all evil comes from within, existing in the mind first.—*Gospel Herald.*

* * *

The Only Fitness Needed

An aged saint told the writer that as a young girl, aroused and anxious about her spiritual condition, she picked up from the pavement a page from a hymn book and read this verse:

Let not conscience make you linger
Nor of fitness fondly dream;
All the fitness He requireth
Is to feel your need of Him.

She saw, *believed,* and was saved on the spot.—*The King's Business.*

* * *

"Did You Ever Steal a Watermelon?"

A juvenile judge some years ago had a very unusual experience during the course of one of his trials. An elderly man who owned a watermelon patch had caught a boy stealing his melons, and had him arrested. When the time came for the trial the man made his complaint to the court, after which the judge turned to the boy and said, "Son, what do you have to say for yourself?" The boy looked up at the judge with questioning eyes, and answered, "Judge, did you ever steal a watermelon when you was a kid?" The judge was somewhat startled at the turn of events, dropped his head into his hand for a few moments of thought, and finally responded with, "No cross examination of the court allowed. The case is dismissed." The judge was "on the spot," as we commonly say!—Norman M. Sorenson, B.A., in *Gospel Herald.*

* * *

When Sin Is Not Noticed

How often we commit one sin in order to hide another, or to drive another from our thoughts! One is reminded of the owner of an old car who said to his companion, "You don't notice that knock in the engine so much now, do you?" "No," was the reply; "how did you manage it?" "Oh, I just loosened one of the mud guards."—*Christian Herald.*

* * *

How Sin Ruins

A relief lifeboat was built at London many years ago. While the workmen were busy over it, one man lost his hammer. Whether he knew it or not, it was nailed up in the bottom of the boat. Perhaps if he found it out, he thought that the only harm done was the loss of one hammer. But the boat was put to service, and every time it rocked on the waves the hammer was tossed to and fro. Little by little it wore for itself a planking and keel down to the very track, until it had worn through the copper plating, before it was found out. Only that plate of copper kept the vessel from sinking.

It seemed a very little thing in the start, but see what mischief it wrought. So it is with a *"little" sin in the heart.* It may break through all the restraints that surround us, and but for God's great mercy, sink our souls in endless ruin.—*Sunday School Times.*

"He Found No Place for Repentance"

A remarkable instance of the penalty of success is reported by persons living near Jamestown, N. Y. For many years a colony of American eagles had made its home near the shores of Chautauqua Lake. They had not been molested and had grown bolder in their depredations.

Not long since one of them was noticed hovering over the lake, and its graceful flight was watched by several persons. Suddenly it darted with lightning rapidity toward the water, catching in its talons a muskellunge two feet or more in length, and weighing probably ten pounds. There was a clash and splashing of fins and feathers, but slowly the bird rose in the air with its captive dangling and wriggling below. When at a height of about 1,000 feet the bird, still clinging to the fish, began to sink slowly toward the lake again gaining speed as it descended, and finally fell with a splash in the water. Later, the bird and fish were found together dead.

The eagle had evidently found the fish too heavy to carry, but had been unable to drop it, owing to its claws being so firmly imbedded in the flesh that it could not release its hold, and as its strength gave way it sank into the water whence it had sought its prey, and was drowned. The very tenacity with which the eagle grasped its prize prevented it losing it when it wished to do so.

It is often so with men who discover when too late that some eagerly coveted prize is proving fatal to them.—Watchword and Truth.

* * *

Proper Approach to God

One of Murray McCheyne's elders was in deep darkness and distress for a few weeks, but one Sunday after the pastor's faithful preaching he found his way to the Lord. At the close of the service, he told Mr. McCheyne, who knew of his spiritual concern, that he had found the Lord. When he was asked to explain how this happy change had come about, he said, "I have been making a great mistake. I have always been coming to the Lord as something better than I was, and going to the wrong door to ask admittance; but this afternoon I went round to the sinner's door, and for the first time cried, like the publican, 'Lord, be merciful to me a sinner'; and, oh, sir, I received such a welcome from the Saviour!" *Are any of you like the self-righteous Pharisee?—Otterbein Teacher.*

* * *

The Wages of Sin

S. D. Gordon says that there are seven simple facts that everyone ought to know about sin: The first is that "sin earns wages." The second, "sin pays wages." The third, "sin insists on paying. You may be quite willing to let the account go, but sin always insists on paying." Fourth, "sin pays its wages in kind. Sin against the body brings results in the body. Sin in the mental life brings results there. Sin in contact with other people brings a chain of results affecting those others. It is terribly true that 'no man sinneth to himself.' Sin is the most selfish of acts. It influences to some extent everyone whom we touch." Fifth, "sin pays in installments." Sixth, "sin pays in full, unless the blood of Jesus washes away the stain." Seventh, "sin is self-executive, it pays its own bills. Sin has bound up in itself all the terrific consequences that ever come." *"The logical result of sin is death; death to the body, death to the mind, death to the soul!"—Earnest Worker.*

* * *

Spelling Sin

Someone in speaking to an audience of young people about sin described the word very effectively as follows: It contains three letters, he said. The first of these is S, and that stands for Serpent,—who brought sin into the world. The last letter is N, and that stands for Nothing,—for sin is emptiness; there is nothing worth while in it. But between its beginning and its ending is a great big capital letter I. It is because of the I in me that I am sinful. The I is my sinful human nature; it is hopelessly bad; calling it "the flesh," the Holy Spirit says of it that it is enmity against God, is not subject to the law of God, and cannot be. So the only safe thing to do with this heart-center of sin in our lives, the I, is to put it to death; let it be crucified with Christ, so that it is no longer "I" that live, but Christ liveth in me. Not until that miracle is wrought,—the death of self and its replacement by Christ,—are we safe from sin. But that very miracle we may have any instant that we will take it by faith.—*Sunday School Times.*

* * *

The Telescope

One day the astronomer Mitchell was engaged in making some observations on the sun, and, as it descended toward the horizon, just as it was setting, there came into the rays of the great telescope the top of a hill seven miles away. On the top of that hill were a large number of apple trees, and in one of them were two boys stealing apples. One was getting the apples, and the other was watching to make certain that nobody saw them, feeling certain that they were undiscovered. But there sat Professor Mitchell, seven miles away, with the great eye of the telescope directed fully upon them, seeing every movement they made as plainly as if he had been under the tree. Often it is thus with men. Because they do not see the eye that watches with sleepless vigilance, they think they are not seen.—*The King's Business.*

* * *

Who Else Was There?

If Christ had declined to associate with sinners, He would have had a lonely time on earth.—D. L. Moody.

* * *

Heart Trouble

I think of a New York lawyer who said several years ago that he would be a Christian if he could believe that Jesus Christ arose from the dead. He had a minister friend who said, "I will be glad to give you the evidence of this fact." His friend submitted it to him. He took it home. A week or ten days passed. He came back to his minister friend, and as he turned the manuscript over to him, this is what he said: "I believe now beyond all reasonable doubt from the historical evidence of credible witnesses that Jesus Christ rose from the dead." And he added, "But I am no more a Christian now than I was when I took the evidence from you ten days ago." Then, speaking in a lower tone, he said, "I have found out that the chief trouble is not with my head, but with my heart." —*Gospel Herald.*

* * *

"Tiger," the Bandit Leader

Pastor Gih of Bethel Mission, Shanghai, China, was evangelizing in bitter cold weather. He began preaching in a dead Christian church. He was told that he need not have come all the way from Shanghai to preach on sin, and as he was leaving the hall a giant of a man told him openly that he would beat him up if he preached on sin again. For three nights Pastor Gih preached on the same subject, to ever-increasing crowds. He was still threatened. The next night Miss Grace Hwang preached. She says: "I went to my knees and asked that the Holy Spirit would give me the message. All I could think of was 'sin.'" Many desperate men were in the crowded church. Suddenly a horrible cry of despair rang through the church, and the giant, known throughout the entire Province as "Tiger," the bandit leader, fell on his knees in the aisle, crying, "O God, my sin! my sin!" Pastor Gih led him to Christ. He confessed sins of the most terrible character. The day following was intensely cold, but the converted bandit started at daylight to talk with his old father whom he had at various times attempted to kill. The father forgave him, and at the evening meeting the giant was back to give his testimony. He still corresponds with Pastor Gih, and is rejoicing in his new life. — *Sunday School Times.*

A Snow Story

It was winter-time, and the freshly fallen snow had clothed the whole face of the country in a beautiful white robe.

Crossing a field with her milk can in hand was a little girl. She was on her way to the farmhouse to buy some milk. About the middle of the field she stopped and took three looks.

She looked around: all was pure and white, the hedges, the trees, the ground, the houses, all were covered with snow.

She looked within; she thought of her sins, of how many wrong words she had spoken and of how many wrong things she had done; she felt she was black with sin and not at all like the snow around her.

She looked up; she turned to the Saviour of sinners, and from the field rose the cry, "Lord, wash me, and I shall be whiter than snow."

Would the Lord hear that cry? Indeed He would! He answered it at once and gave that little girl to know that His precious Blood cleansed her from all sin, and that she was whiter than snow in His sight.—Selected.

* * *

Building Our Prison

At one time many convicts were employed in building high walls around the prison grounds at Portland. Soldiers posted above them with loaded guns watched them at their work. Every brick laid rendered their escape more impossible, and yet they themselves were laying them. So each sin committed makes it harder to refrain from further sin, more difficult to turn back. — *Sunday School Times.*

* * *

Slow to Learn

An incident of unusual interest occurred recently at Niagara Falls. A large army of geese, on their annual southern flight, settled down on the waters of the upper Niagara River. The leading ganders brought their followers to rest there, but several minutes later the strong current swept flock after flock to the crest of the Horseshoe Falls, where the mighty roar and swift water gave the geese an alarm of danger. Only by frantic flapping of wings were they able to rise up and save themselves from the strong current at this point.

But the strange part of this whole procedure was that the geese, instead of learning by a few experiences that the Niagara River was a hazardous place to settle down, repeated these exhausting maneuvers continuously. They would ride down the current to the Falls, then rise and fly back, circle around and alight on the river again, and with each rotation the flocks were diminished as weaker birds were swept over to death and injury on the lower river.

Finally game officials, fearing complete destruction of the birds, permitted hunters to shoot into the flocks, on the theory that the noise of guns would drive the geese to resume their flight southward. Whether or not this strategy effected the result is uncertain, but a few hours after daybreak, when wildly honking ganders took the lead, flock upon flock arose from the upper river to pursue their journey to warmer climes and quieter waters. Some hundreds of geese perished in their weakened condition by being carried over the falls, or from the shots of hunters.—*Gospel Herald.*

* * *

No Prescription, But—

There was once a man who went into a chemist's shop. He was a poor, untidy man, and he said, "If you please, mister, have you got anything for a bad cold?" The chemist, who was an eminently respectable chemist, said, "Have you brought your prescription with you?" The man answered, "No, I ain't got no prescription with me, but I've brought my cold with me." How often sinners seeking a cure for sin try to bring their "prescriptions" to God! But he asks for nothing save that the sinner should say: "Just as I am, without one plea, but that thy blood was shed for me."—*Christian Herald.*

When God Looks

There is no darkness intense enough to hide your sin from the eye of God. I went into a doctor's office to see the wonders of the X-ray machine. He made ready and handed me a strange lens and I looked upon the bones of my friend though covered with a veil of flesh. The tacks in the soles of his shoes seemed to hang in space; the bones of his foot were plainly seen; but when I turned my attention to the vertebrae I saw the ribs standing like grim specters, and when I reached the region of the heart I saw the dim outline of a living, moving organ which meant life and action. I trembled as I thought: Man has discovered a ray that reveals the vitals of a man in action; his heart is open for observation under that light. But the Lord God reads the sins of the heart. For the first time I understood the words "God looketh upon the heart." — *Sunday School Times.*

SINGING

A Songful Religion

Christianity is the only religion that abounds in song. Atheism is songless; agnosticism has nothing to sing about; the various forms of idolatry are not tuneful; but Judaism said, "O come, let us sing unto the Lord;" and when Christ came, the angels greeted His birth with praise, and since then Christian song has gained in fulness and strength of voice with each century.—Selected.

* * *

He Sang a Hymn

Within the quiet upper room,
All furnished and prepared,
The Master and His little band
The sacred feast had shared.

Three years and more He had healed the sick
And bade the weak be strong;
Now as He reached His night of woe
His voice was raised in song.

The cross He knew was close at hand,
Just hid by shadows dim;
(The shades of dark Gethsemane)
But first—HE SANG A HYMN.

No lofty peal of organ tones
Through frescoed arches rang,
In silent awe the angels heard
The hymn that Jesus sang.

O Christ, who sang that hymn of praise
In sight of shame and woe,
Then bore the cross in agony
That we God's love might know,

Fill all our hearts with grateful love
When grief or pain shall come;
Give us to sing Thy praise on earth,
And richer praise—at Home.

—Mary L. Stanger.

* * *

John Wesley on Church Singing

In the year 1742 John Wesley gave these five rules on singing in church:

1. *Sing all.* See that you join with the congregation as frequently as you can. Let not a slight degree of weakness or weariness hinder you. If it is a cross to you, take it up and you will find a blessing.
2. *Sing lustily and with a good courage.* Beware of singing as if you were half asleep; but lift up your voice with strength.
3. *Sing modestly.* Do not bawl so as to be heard above or distinct from the rest of the congregation; but strive to unite your voices together so as to make one clear, melodious sound.
4. *Sing in time.* Whatever time is sung, be sure to keep with it. Do not run before nor stay behind it.
5. Above all, *sing spiritually.* Have an eye to God in every word you sing. In order to do this, attend strictly to the

sense of what you sing and see that your heart is not carried away with the sound but offered to God continually—courtesy *Moody Monthly.*

* * *

When the Little Boy Sang

"I wish I could sing; I think I'd feel weller then!" said a little seven-year-old lad in Bellevue Hospital while a surgeon was examining him to find out what injuries he had sustained in a fall into a twelve-foot-deep excavation. "All right, laddie; you can sing if you will sing something nice," said the kindhearted Dr. McLean. The little fellow began to sing in a high, clear soprano, "Nearer, My God, to Thee." As the childish notes rang out, nurses, doctors and attendants from various parts of the hospital began to steal in until there were fully a hundred people in the room. "Well, I guess you are right, little man," said the doctor as he finished his examination; "I can't find any broken bones." "I guess it was the singin' that fixed me," replied the boy. "I always sing when I feel bad." If we grown-ups would do as this little boy did—sing when we "feel bad," no matter what our loss or misfortune or trouble—we would certainly "feel weller."—*The S. S. Banner.*

* * *

"Poor, Wretched, Blind"

John B. Gough was once placed in a pew with a man so repulsive that he moved to the farther end of the pew, according to Amos R. Wells. The congregation began to sing Charlotte Elliot's hymn, "Just as I am, without one plea." The man joined in the singing so heartily that Mr. Gough moved up nearer, though the man's singing was "positively awful." At the end of one of the stanzas, while the organ was playing the interlude, the man leaned toward Mr. Gough and whispered, "Won't you please give me the first line of the next verse?" Mr. Gough replied: "Just as I am, poor, wretched, blind." The man replied: "That's it; and I am blind—God help me; and I am a paralytic." The man, in his pitiful condition, tried with his twitching lips to make music of the glorious words. Mr. Gough then thought that never in his life had he heard music so beautiful as the blundering singing of that hymn by the paralytic.—*Sunday School Times.*

* * *

In Gypsy Tents

Soon after his own conversion Cornelius Smith, father of Gipsy Rodney Smith, succeeded in winning his two brothers to Christ. From that time, the three gave themselves earnestly to evangelistic work. One of the first hymns they learned and the one they were all fond of singing was:

Gentle Jesus, meek and mild,
Look upon a little child.

And Gipsy (Rodney) Smith says: "After all, they were only children, felt themselves children always, and possessed all their days a truly childlike spirit." The three brothers were fond of music, and enjoyed singing with their parents.

One Sunday morning, about two months after their conversion, the three brothers set out to visit their father and mother. When they were within hearing distance of the place where their parents were camping, they began to sing, "Gentle Jesus, meek and mild."

Their mother recognized their voices, and said, "Why, bless me, if them's not my boys coming!" Then, turning to her husband, she said, "Jim, come out of the tent and see if these ain't my boys!"

The three stalwart fellows marched forward, singing their favorite hymn.

"What in the world is the matter with you?" said the aged mother.

"Oh, Mother," said Gipsy Smith's father, "we have found Jesus; we are converted."

Their father began to walk around the tent, saying, "My boys have come home to teach me what I ought to have taught them!"

The result of that visit was that both the father and the mother of the men, at the age of seventy, found the Saviour; and for five years they lived to testify to the grace of God.—*Sunday School Times.*

* * *

A Hard-Bitten Agnostic

One summer evening late in the last century a hard-bitten agnostic sat on the banks of the Connecticut River in Massachusetts. Dusk had settled in a blue haze on the mountains across the river. Dimly he glimpsed the lights of the church on a rise just above the village of Northfield. He smiled cynically. Then drifting across the still water there came the faint sound of a voice singing.

There were ninety and nine that safely
lay
In the shelter of the fold,
But one was out on the hills away.
Far off from the gates of gold—
Away on the mountains wild and bare,
Away from the tender Shepherd's care.

The man listened. What a voice it was! The beauty of it fascinated him, but the words—He shrugged off the first two verses, but the third caught him. That voice—its earnestness, its pleading. As the last note died away the man bent his head and accepted the Shepherd as his Saviour and Lord.

On another day an inveterate criminal slouched against the wall of his cell in a Belfast prison. Suddenly through the barred windows came the sound of music —then a voice singing the well-known "Hold the Fort." Coming from a church at the other end of the block, the voice was faint, but it filled the narrow room. And its tender compassion touched the heart of the hardened criminal. Half way through the song he dropped to his knees and before that voice ceased he had believed and was saved. He died a tireless church worker.—*Sunday School Times.*

* * *

Saved by Song

On board the ill-fated steamer *Seawanhaka* was one of the Fisk University singers. Before leaving the burning steamer and committing himself to the merciless waves, he carefully fastened upon himself and wife life-preservers. Someone cruelly dragged away that of the wife, leaving her without hope, except as she could cling to her husband. This she did, placing her hands firmly on his shoulders and resting there until her strength becoming exhausted, she said, "I can hold no longer!" "Try a little longer," was the response of the weary and agonized husband; "let us sing 'Rock of Ages.'" And as those sweet strains floated over those troubled waters, reaching the ears of the sinking and dying, little did they know, those sweet singers of Israel, whom they comforted.

But lo! as they sang, one after another of those exhausted imperiled ones were seen raising their heads above the waves, joining with a last effort in this sweet, dying, pleading prayer:

"Rock of ages, cleft for me,
Let me hide myself in Thee."

With the song seemed to come strength; another and yet another was encouraged to renewed effort. Soon in the distance a boat was seen approaching! Singing still, they tried, and soon with superhuman strength laid hold of the life boat. This is no fiction; it was related by the singer himself, who said he "believed Toplady's sweet 'Rock of Ages' saved many another besides himself and wife."—*Western.*

* * *

Swearing Johnny's New Song

At a memorial meeting held for Jerry McAuley at the Water Street Mission, New York City, where the reformed man had helped many others to accept Christ, General Clinton B. Fisk said that one night, when in a seaman's mission meeting in Liverpool, a sailor with a shining face arose to give a testimony. Many were startled when he began by saying, "I found Christ over there in America." This man was known as "Swearing Johnny" before his conversion. Said he, "When we were paid off, I took my money to the saloons, and pretty soon I was again drunk. I went out into the street, and the snow was beating against my face. As I passed along the street I heard singing, and stopped to listen. I heard them sing,

> I am so glad that Jesus loves me,
> Jesus loves even me.

" 'I'll go in and see about that,' I said to myself. I went in, and there saw that wonderful man, Jerry McAuley, and *he* led me to Christ."

"Yes," said his wife, "and it's been nothing but Jerry McAuley and 'Jesus loves me' ever since Johnny's ship came home."

The song which that sinning sailor heard was written by one of America's sweet singers, P. P. Bliss. Often it has made its appeal to the heart of those who have heard the words:

> I am so glad that our Father in heav'n
> Tells of His love in the Book He has giv'n;
> Wonderful things in the Bible I see,
> This is the dearest, that Jesus loves me.
> —*Sunday School Times.*

* * *

Two Remarkable Days

At the age of sixteen Augustus Toplady was taken by his widowed mother to Wexford, Ireland.

In the district a simple servant of God—James Morris—was preaching the Gospel in an old barn. This was an uncommon place for such a matter. The youthful Augustus was prompted by curiosity to attend one of the services. It proved to be a turning point in his life.

The preacher in deep earnestness spoke upon the text he had chosen: "But now in Christ Jesus ye who sometimes were far off are made nigh by the blood of Christ" (Eph. 2:13). The Word preached was mixed with faith. The youth heard and believed. Writing about the occurrence he said, "Under that sermon I was brought nigh by the Blood of Christ. Strange that I who had so long sat under the means of grace in England, should be brought nigh by the Blood of Christ in an obscure part of Ireland, amidst a handful of God's people met together in a barn in and under the ministry of one who could hardly spell his own name. I shall remember that day to all eternity."

Ten years later Augustus Toplady had become a preacher. He was out for a walk in the hills at Burrington Combe, Somerset, when he was overtaken by a thunder storm of unusual severity. Where should he hide? Looking about him he espied some huge overhanging rocks, which seemed to have been tossed about in some volcanic upheaval. These leaning one against another formed a secure shelter. To this he fled. From his refuge he watched the storm as it fell in severity upon the whole countryside.

His thoughts turned to the barren Irish barn. The rough and rugged preacher in his earnestness was once again in view: the peace-giving passage from the Word of God: the value of the precious Blood of Christ which had been shed that the sinner might have a place of refuge from the storm of judgment. All this came before him as he wended his way back to his home. When there he wrote the result of his meditation. It was the well-known hymn, perhaps the best known of all:

> "Rock of ages, cleft for me,
> Let me hide myself in Thee;
> Let the water and the Blood,
> From Thy riven side which flowed,
> Be of sin the double cure,
> Cleanse me from its guilt and power."
> —*Gospel Herald.*

* * *

The "Glory Song"

"I've got a song that's going to live!" declared Charles Gabriel, a Gospel song writer, to a Chicago publisher. The two men were bicycle riding, during the summer of 1900. The song to which Gabriel referred was *Oh That Will Be Glory*, or as it is best known, *The Glory Song.*

He was right. It enjoyed a remarkable popularity, but the author received only ten dollars for all the publishing rights to his splendid song.

Perhaps the *Glory Song* would not have been nearly so well known had it not been for Charles M. Alexander, the Gospel singer, who traveled all over the English speaking world, singing it.

"I remember quite well the first time I saw this song in looking over a new songbook," said Alexander. "I just glanced at it, and then said to myself, 'That man has wasted a page, for I do not believe that song will be sung much.' "

Alexander heard the song sung in a large Sunday School convention several months later by the audience, and it had the same effect on him it has on all who hear this remarkable hymn.

"It took such a hold of me that I could think of nothing else for days thereafter. I got my friends to sing it. Then I began to teach it to large audiences, and soon whole towns were ringing with the melody."

The singer went to Australia on a tour. Everywhere he sang the *Glory Song*, it took the audience by storm. He had leaflets with the *Glory Song* printed on them and an invitation to the meetings. These were scattered far and wide.

The story is told of a lady who, after returning home from the service, had a pair of shoes which needed mending. She sent them to the shoemaker, but before wrapping the paper around them, she slipped in a copy of the *Glory Song*.

When she returned for the shoes next day, the man was nailing a new sole on a shoe before him, and there were tears in his eyes.

"What is the matter?" the woman asked.

"That *Glory Song* you put into the bundle. Last night my family and I gathered around the old organ while we sang it. We saw the invitation to hear Torrey and Alexander at the Town Hall, and I went last night. I sent my wife and children this afternoon, and I am praying that God will save them."—E. H. Jordan, in *Gospel Herald*.

* * *

The Story of a Great Song

"Jesus, Lover of My Soul" was written by Charles Wesley, a brother of John Wesley. The story of its origin is like this: A dreadful storm was raging on the sea, filling the hearts of all those on the shore with dread. Through the dim morning light a ship could be seen helplessly floundering off-shore. The passengers were trying to reach the land, but many were being drowned in the tempest. Charles Wesley, aroused by the noise of the storm, opened his casement window to watch the struggle. Suddenly a tiny bird, frightened and pursued by a large hawk, flew through the open window into his bosom, where it found protection.

Under the inspiration of this incident, he wrote the song. Note the words in connection with this dramatic happening:

"Jesus, lover of my soul,
Let me to Thy bosom fly,
While the nearer waters roll,
While the tempest still is high.
Hide me, O my Saviour, hide,
Till the storm of life be past;
Safe into the haven guide—
Oh, receive my soul at last."

—*God's Revivalist and Bible Advocate.*

* * *

Seven Hymns for Service Men

The fact that in the *Song and Service Book for Ship and Field* Fanny J. Crosby leads all other authors in the number of hymns contributed is sufficient reason for reviewing her life. She was born in Putnam County, N. Y., in 1820, and when six weeks old she was blinded by a careless physician. The brave and cheerful manner in which she accepted her misfortune is reflected in her explanation that "the merciful God has put His hand over my eyes."

At the age of fifteen she entered the New York School for the Blind. She had been scribbling verse since she was eight, and was soon recognized as the "poet laureate" of the school. When William Cullen Bryant, Horace Greeley and other notables paid visits she was selected to welcome them with garlands of verse. Twice when the students visited Washington, D. C., she recited poetic greetings to joint sessions of Congress. For her the muse sang as also it had for Homer and Milton in their blindness, and by 1858 she had published three volumes of verse.

"There's Music in the Air," "Proud World, Goodbye," and other of her offerings were set to music by George F. Root and became best sellers in the field of sheet music. In 1864 she dedicated her talent to hymn writing. The times were favorable with William B. Bradbury, Philip Phillips, H. R. Palmer, Hubert P. Main, W. H. Doane, Robert Lowry, George C. Stebbins and other composers in search of religious verse. Camp meetings, singing schools and hymn festivals were running at full capacity, and even in city churches worshipers had not yet muted their vocal chords and transferred praise to the choir. Many preachers were songsters and thought it no indecorum in public worship to produce a tuning-fork and lead their congregations in making a "joyful noise unto the Lord." Those were the days when congregational singing *was* congregational singing, and everyone enjoyed the heart-warming and inspiring hymn-sings.

For such a receptive public Miss Crosby penned some 5,000 devotional pieces of which probably the best were not always selected by the composers. But the fact that such selections as "Praise Him; Praise Him," "Jesus Is Tenderly Calling," "I Am Thine, O Lord," "Blessed Assurance," "All the Way My Saviour Leads Me," "Nearer the Cross" and numerous others have retained their popularity through three generations, is proof enough of the enduring appeal of her songs.

Fanny Crosby was no religious recluse. She was a witty, spirited and accomplished woman who played pranks on General Winfield Scott and showed her spunk when she was reprimanded for allowing Grover Cleveland, a clerk in the school from a New Jersey manse, to copy her poems.

On February 12, 1915, she departed for "The Tuneful City" which was her name for heaven.—Jacob Simpson Payton, in *The Chaplain.*

Let Them Know Where the Well Is

In one part of India the maharajah has proclaimed to all who go forth to draw water from a well in any part of his country must go with a song on their lips—and go singing all the way. The reason for this command is that a man was found dying of thirst within a few yards of a well. *He did not know the well was there.* He never recovered consciousness. And now, if you hear songs on the lips of one walking through the jungle today, you know that there is a well near by.—From *"The Unknown God by One Who Loves Him."*

* * *

A Singer's Witness

A young Christian traveler found himself in a commercial room one night, where, the party being large and merry, it was proposed that each man should sing a song. Many of the usual character on such occasions were sung. It came the turn of our young friend, who excused himself on the ground that he knew no songs they would care to hear. In derision, one present asked him if he could not sing one of Sankey's hymns, and several declared they would join in the chorus. He decided to take them at the word, and with a silent prayer he chose one of the well-known hymns, and sang it as he had perhaps never sung before. All present joined in the chorus. Before its close there were moist eyes and troubled hearts, and several gathered round him thanking him for the song. When he retired, he had not been long in his room when he heard a knock at the door. He opened it to a young traveler who was in deep trouble. The song had brought back to memory the songs his deceased mother had sung. He knew his life was not right, and the inquiry was on his lips, "What must I do to be saved?" He was pointed to Christ. Scarcely had he left when there was another knock; this time an older man whom the song had reminded of a lost joy and peace. He was a backslider, The singer had the joy of pointing him also to the Saviour, and though it was nearly two o'clock before he could lie down, it was with heartfelt gratitude to Him who had honored his personal testimony for Christ.—*The Illustrator.*

* * *

Their Hymn, Facing Massacre

I once heard Dr. Usher of the American Board tell of the experience undergone by the staff of an Armenian mission at the time of the last devilish massacre. The workers gathered in one room in a silent waiting. They felt their coronation day had come. The women dressed in white, for any hour they would be seeing the Bridegroom! Outside the compound wall was the frantic, crazy horde of Turks, shouting in one breath the praise of Allah and the doom of the Christians. But, said the doctor, in spite of the frenzy without, there was an unearthly calm within. None feared, no one complained. In fact, one broke out in song, a hymn in which all joined. The crucifixion cry was drowned out by singing saints, and here was the paean they sang:

"Peace, perfect peace, our future
all unknown,
But Jesus we know, and He is
on the throne.'

The music died, the mob dispersed, the peace of God reigned without, within. Only the Spirit of God works such miracles.—*The Christian Standard.*

* * *

A Little Love Offering fo' De Lawd

An old Negro arose one morning with his heart full of love for his Lord. "De Lawd done so much fo' me I wisht I could do a little mite fo' Him today," he said to himself.

At the close of the day as he was returning on the street car to his humble home, he thought over the day. He had done his work faithfully and well. "But dat wasn't fo' de Lawd. Dat was fo' wages. Don't t'ink I'se done anyt'ing special for de Lawd all day."

Soon the car stopped. Several passengers got off, and a tired-looking high school girl got on, her arms laden with books. She sank into a seat and looked at the books.

"All these to be looked over, and extracts read for the coming literary event. Oh, for one day of rest!" she sighed. "If it were just myself, I would stop right here; but I cannot. I have been chosen by the school and I cannot fail. Oh, but I'm tired!"

Just then the old Negro looked about him. There was only one other person on the car.

"I don't believe dat pooty little gal would care if I'd sing a little," he said to himself. So on he began softly:

"Swing low, sweet chariot"—

The tired girl listened.

"Comin' for' to carry me home."

The melody of his voice, and the thought of the swinging chariot was restful. The old man finished the song, then began:

"Sweet hour of prayer, sweet hour of
prayer,
That calls me from a world of care."

"That is the trouble," said the tired girl. "I have been neglecting the hour of prayer. I thought I was too busy, but I will neglect it no longer."

In a few minutes she rang the bell. But on her way to the door, she stopped and said to the old saint, "Your songs have helped me greatly. I thank you."—Selected.

* * *

No Singing for Infidelity

Christianity came into the world on the wings of song. Infidelity never sings. Unbelief has no music, no anthems, no hymns, oratorios, or symphonies. When Robert Ingersoll died, the printed notice of his funeral said, "There will be no singing."—Hugh Thomson Kerr.

Paganism Has No Doxologies

"Do the heathen get no comport whatever from their religion?" a missionary was asked.

"Yes," he replied, "the same kind of comfort you get out of a narcotic."

Buddhism, Brahmanism, Taoism, Confucianism, Mohammedanism are opiate religions.

Christianity, on the contrary, wakes up the soul with a new life. "The fruit of the Spirit is . . . joy," and must find outlet in singing.—*Missionary Review of the World.*

SMALL THINGS

Famous Sayings:

"Little is much if God is in it!"

"He who is a Christian in small things is not a small Christian!"

* * *

Only a Little Thing

It was only a tiny seed,
Carelessly brushed aside;
But it grew in time to a noxious weed,
And spread its poison wide.

It was only a little leak,
So small you could hardly see;
But the rising waters found the break,
And wrecked the great levee.

It was only a single spark,
Dropped by a passing train;
But the dead leaves caught, and swift and dark
Was its work on wood and plain.

It was only a thoughtless word,
Scarcely meant to be unkind;
But it pierced as a dart to the heart that heard,
And left its sting behind.

It may seem a trifle at most,
The things that we do or say,
And yet it may be that at fearful cost
We may wish it undone some day.

—Mrs. M. P. Handy, in *The Friend* (Dayton).

* * *

"Only a Boy"—and God

In Scotland many years ago, a faithful minister was waited upon one day by one of his deacons, who seemed to be under a great burden. "I came early to meet you," he said. "I have something on my conscience to tell you. There must be something wrong with your preaching and work; there has been only one person added to the church in a whole year, and he is only a boy." The old minister went into the pulpit that day with a grieved and heavy heart. He lingered in the church to pray, after the rest had gone. He wished to be alone. He had labored hard for years, only to be told at last that his labor was no longer blessed. At last he became conscious that he was not alone, as he supposed. It was "only a boy." "Well, Robert," said the minister, "what is it?" "Do you think if I were willing to work hard for an education I could ever become a preacher?—A preacher?—Perhaps a missionary?" There was a long pause. Tears filled the eyes of the old minister. At length he said, "This heals the ache in my heart, Robert. I see the divine hand now. Yes, I think you will become a preacher." That boy was Robert Moffat. He was "only a boy," but the measure of the old minister's reward will be found in the gathered fruitage of the labors of Robert Moffat, the great African missionary.—*The Sunday School Teacher.*

* * *

The Greatness of Small Things

The tiny snowflake flutters as it falls. It seems so insignificant and helpless; it cannot defy even a child.

But it is a different matter when it unites with countless millions of other snowflakes. First, they cover the ground with a beautiful mantle of white. Then they pile higher and higher. The wind gathers them into huge drifts. Man stands helpless on the highway as the little flakes call out in unison: "You shall not pass!" The mighty railroad engine speeds along, but again the small, white messengers say: "You, too, must stop!"

In Minneapolis, we went to the information booth at the Great Northern. When will the train leave for Sioux Falls? "There will be no train tonight," came the courteous reply. "All roads are blocked in all directions." Thirty hours later, a train did bring us to Sioux Falls. When does the train leave for Madison? "There will be no trains. All railroads and roads are blocked in all directions." But finally we did manage to ride the caboose of a freight over different roads until we reached home. Why all the difficulty and delay? *Simply because the tiny snowflake had become the mighty snowflake.*—Lester A. Pierson, in *Lutheran Herald.*

* * *

What One Cent Did

It is said a lady was filling a box for India when a child brought her a cent with which she bought a tract and put it in the box. It was at length given to a Burmese chief and led him to Christ. The chief told the story of his new God and his great happiness to his friends. They also believed and cast away their idols. A church was built there, a missionary was sent, and 1500 converted from heathenism was the result of that little seed.—*Gospel Herald* (Scottdale).

* * *

Little Things Count

We should mind little things—little courtesies in life, little matters of personal appearance, little extravagances, little minutes of wasted time, little details in our work.

And it seems that a thing cannot be too small to command our attention.

The first hint Newton had leading to his most important optical discoveries was derived from a child's soap bubble.

The art of printing was suggested by a man cutting letters in the bark of a tree.

The telescope was the outcome of a boy's amusement with two glasses in his father's shop.

Goodyear neglected his skillet until it was red hot and the accident guided him to the manufacture of vulcanized rubber.

The web of a spider suggested to Captain Brown the idea of a suspension bridge.

Henry Ford's idea about a perfect watch plant gave him a plan for his giant motor industry.

J. L. Kraft's idea to put cheese in a sanitary package was the start of his enormous business.

Watching a spider weave its web gave Robert Bruce the courage to try again.

Little things. Every one a little thing. Yet how important they proved to be to the man who had the wit to correlate these little things with the idea in his head.—*Church and Home.*

* * *

Too Small?

"Father, where shall I work today?"
  And my love flowed warm and free.
Then He pointed me out a tiny spot,
  And said, "Tend that for me."
I answered quickly, "Oh, no, not that.
  Why, no one would ever see,
No matter how well my work was done.
  Not that little place for me."
And the word He spoke, it was not stern,
  He answered me tenderly,
'Ah, little one, search that heart of thine.
  Art thou working for them or Me?
Nazareth was a little place,
  And so was Galilee."

—*Sunday School Times.*

* * *

Size Not Always Strength

A Japanese visitor to New York City remarked that he thought the policemen were too heavy to be effective. He weighed only 110 pounds, but every pound had been developed. He stepped into police headquarters and astonished the picked athletes of the force. With bare hands he overcame with ease their very best men. Let small men and small enterprises take heart. Size is not the measure of strength.—*Christian Herald.*

Little Things

A stamp is just a little thing
  Of very little worth,
And yet 'twill take a letter all
  The way across the earth!
A smile is just a little thing,
  But you will find this true:
To give it brings much happiness
  To others, and to you.
  —Charles Mish, in *The Water Lily.*

* * *

Little Things

It was a little thing to do,
  Just a few words he spoke—
And yet they were the magic wand
  That slumb'ring hope awoke.

It was a priceless thing he gave,
  And yet had nothing cost—
The smile that gave a burdened soul
  The courage it had lost.

It was a handclasp, warm, sincere,
  Just that, and yet a spark
From it had caused to leap aflame
  Bright tapers in the dark.
    —Edward D. Garner.

* * *

The Floating Ice Palace

What is the mystery of that mighty mass which has the strength to rip open the steel walls of a giant ocean liner as easily as a tin opener rips off a tin lid? It is one of the wonders of God's creation, compared with which the greatest things made by man are feeble. It begins as gentle snow, but year after year this slowly forms a glacier, and a hundred years may pass before the soft snowflakes grow to mighty icebergs. Single icebergs have shown a weight of two thousand million tons, equal to the weight of over three hundred and thirty Great Pyramids. There are records of huge icebergs which towered 1,500 feet above the sea, almost three times the height of the Washington Monument.

"What is man compared with his Creator?" asked a scientist in giving a lecture on icebergs. And this great God who created the icebergs loves us and has planned a beautiful life for us if we will give Him our lives. Will you do it?—*Our Pentecostal Boys and Girls.*

* * *

Little Foxes

Not long ago there was a wreck on the Southern Pacific. Investigation showed that a track, supposed to be solid, had been undermined by a squirrel, the hole had left a place for water to gather, the roadbed had become soft. Along came a heavy train and it was plunged to destruction; all because of a trifle, the vagrant meandering of a mite. It is not given to all to deal directly with big things, but the one who deals with small things has a mission as important. It is in his power to bring about a wreck; the wreck of himself or of somebody else. "That which is least" (Luke 16:10).—*Tacoma Ledger.*

* * *

Never Great, But—

There was an actor, Charles Brookfield by name, who was mistakenly reported to be dead and so had the unusual opportunity of reading his own obituary notices. One of them in particular he always remembered. It ran like this: *"Never a great actor, he was invaluable in small parts."—Gospel Herald.*

* * *

Be Faithful

The beginnings of unfaithfulness are always the little things that we think will make no difference. No one was ever called of God to a high position who did not lay the foundation of that call in courageous faithfulness to the small details of life. But whether our position be high or low, it is required of a steward that he be faithful.—Selected.

SORROW, SUFFERING, CHASTENING

From Inez Edwards, in "The Tennessee Smilo Club News":

"They whisper, 'She's a shut-in,'
As they pass my cottage door,
Where daily, by my window,
I've sat twenty years or more.
My feet are lame, I cannot walk,
I've been that way since birth;
I'll never travel 'round and see
The wonders of this earth.
They whisper, 'What a pity
She should be afflicted so!
She just sits there in her wheel chair,
Never has a chance to go!'
They wonder how I bear it,
And perhaps you wonder, too?
Well, it really is no secret,
And a simple reason, too.
It's because I have a Promise
That was given long ago,
By another One who suffered
Greater pain than I can know.
And He's building me a mansion,
In a Land more wondrous far
Than the majesty of oceans,
Than the lofty mountains are.
And I know when I shall go there,
The very first thing I'll do,
Is exchange these withered feet of clay
For others straight and new!
Then, up and down the Golden Streets,
On limbs so fine and strong,
I'll wend my way 'mid angels fair,
And lift my voice in song!"

—*Gospel Herald.*

* * *

Behind the clouds the sunlight lurks
To quicken the rain-drenched sod . . .
Behind life's darkest events rules the power
Of a light-renewing God.

So bless the travail of gloom-filled hours,
For joy oft is wrought in pain . . .
And what if the day be dark? Thank God
That the sun must shine again!

—Ian MacLennan.

The Darkness Reveals

As only the darkness of the night can reveal to us the beauty of the stars, so it is only in the dark hour of sorrow that there is revealed unto us in fullest measure the peace that Christ is able to give. In the time of happiness and prosperity our consciousness of our need of Him grows dim, but when troubles enshroud us like a cloud we learn that the more heavily we lean upon Him the more surely is His strength apparent in our weakness. He is adequate to meet our every need, however great that need may be; and no matter how heavy laden our hearts are, He is able when we come to Him to give us rest.—*Christian Observer.*

* * *

Testings for the Christian

If we are really Christians, we must expect severe tests. A soldier in the East Indies, a stalwart man who had been a prize fighter, was a terror to his regiment. He was converted, and the lion became a lamb. Two months afterward in the mess-room some of those who had been afraid of him before, began to ridicule him. One of them threw a basin of hot soup over him. The whole company gazed in breathless silence, expecting that the offender would be murdered. But after he had torn open his waistcoat and wiped his scalded breast, he turned around and said, "This is what I expected when I became a Christian!"—*The Elim Evangel.*

* * *

Night Perfumes

Most of us have noticed how fragrant the air is at night. Passing through a garden or a field of clover the very atmosphere seems to be laden with delightful perfumes. Scientists now tell us that certain varieties of roses are from thirty to forty per cent more fragrant at night than in the day, and that other varieties of flowers show an almost equally large percentage.

But it is not the flowers alone that give out their heaviest fragrance in the darkness. It is true of human lives also. It takes the night of sorrow to call forth their sweetest fragrance. *Patience, sympathy, love, forgiveness—these and other rare perfumes are exhaled most freely when the skies are overcast and the way is hard to our feet.* Many a one who has gone to the sick chamber to impart a word of encouragement or hope has testified that he has brought away infinitely more than he has given.—Selected.

* * *

The Sunless Valley

If we never find our path dipping down into the sunless valley, we may seriously question whether we have not missed our way to the Celestial City. The road to the Mount of Ascension invariably passes through the shadowed Garden of Gethsemane, and over the steep ascent of Calvary, and then down into the Garden of the grave.—F. B. Meyer.

* * *

Why Sit?

"He shall sit as a refiner and purifier of silver." "Why *sit?*" we ask. "It is such delicate work I do not dare to stand," says the refiner. He never overdoes. He loves us too much to underdo. "I wish I had never been made," said a character in one of Marriot's books. "You are not made yet," was the answer, "and you are quarreling with the process." "How do you know when the metal is done?" we ask the refiner, and he tells us, "When I can see my face in it." Refining fire, go through my heart and all my sin consume!—*Gospel Herald.*

* * *

God was better to me than all my hopes,
  Better than all my fears;
For He made a bridge of my broken
    sighs,
  And a rainbow of my tears.
—Selected.

In the Dark Room

Some of you have stood within a dark room, and developed a film. You have seen the gradual strengthening of the image on the little strip of celluloid, until at last the picture stood forth clearly.

You know a little about photography. You know how the picture was obtained, by focusing the camera on the object you wanted to photograph, and upon no other object. You know how the camera maker, and you yourself as you held the camera, made sure that light should enter that camera and impinge on the film from no other object but the one you wanted to photograph.

You and I must think of our life as a kind of photograph, which, the closer it is seen and the more it is developed, shows the image of what we want to be. If it is to show the image of a Christlike character, then our whole being must be aimed at that. Everything else must be ruthlessly excluded. That is the price we must pay.—Ronald W. Thomson.

* * *

Recognizing the Road

A Spirit-filled worker connected with the African Inland Mission was giving his testimony after returning from a very dangerous service in the World War. He said that if someone sent him on a journey and told him the road to take, warning him that at a certain point he would come to a dangerous crossing of the river, at another point to a forest infested with wild beasts, he would come to that dangerous river crossing with the satisfaction of knowing that he was on the right road. So he told them that the Lord had predicted that Christians would have tribulation, and when the tribulations came he knew he was on the right road. — *Sunday School Times.*

* * *

The Final Design

J. Stuart Holden tells of a visit he once made to a factory in the north of England, where costly China was being made. The thing which interested him most was the painting of the finished product. "It had been through many different processes," he said, "and was taken to the studio for the artists to complete. I saw the pattern being put on in various colors, and noticed that a great deal of black was being put on. On asking why, I was told, 'It is black now, but it will be gold when it comes out of the fire.' "

Is not this just as in our lives? What is put on black we do not recognize as gold at the time; and the thing which is gilding our lives—or is intended to do so —is very often put on in darkness and blackness.—Alliance Weekly.

* * *

The Physician's Assurance

"Extraordinary afflictions," said Matthew Henry, "are not always the punishment of extraordinary sins, but sometimes the trial of extraordinary graces." Sometimes we are helped by being hurt. A skilled physician about to perform a delicate operation on the ear said reassuringly to the patient, "I may hurt you, but I will not injure you." How often the Great Physician speaks to us that same message if we would only listen!—*Sunday School Times.*

* * *

Taken Aside by Jesus

Taken aside by Jesus,
To feel the touch of His hand;
To rest awhile in the shadow
Of the Rock in a weary land.

Taken aside by Jesus,
In the loneliness dark and drear;
Where no other comfort can reach me
Than His voice to my heart so dear.

Taken aside by Jesus,
To be quite alone with Him;
To hear His wonderful tones of love,
'Mid the silence and shadows dim.

Taken aside by Jesus—
Shall I shrink from the desert place,
When I hear as I never heard before,
And see Him face to face?
—*Gospel Herald.*

A Test of Faith

An exchange tells the story of a man who was invited by an artist to come to his house, to see a picture which he had just finished. When the visitor arrived, he was shown into a home which was pitch dark, and there he was left for a quarter of an hour alone. He expressed surprise, when the artist came to him, at the reception which had been given him.

"Surprised, were you?" said the artist. "Well I know if you came to the studio with the glare of the street in your eyes, you would never be able to appreciate the fine coloring of my picture. Therefore I left you in the dark till the glare had worn away from your eyes."

Is not that the secret of many an hour in which God leaves His children in the darkness? When we are dazzled by the pleasures and successes of this present life—we cannot see the things that are unseen, and an interval is necessary in the darkness until the glare has worn away from our eyes. — *The Alliance Weekly.*

* * *

Shadows

I cannot think that God has meant
For shadows to be fearsome things,
Else He would not have given us
The shadow of His wings.
Nor would His tall trees by the way
Trace out a cool sweet place
Where weary travelers may pause
To find His soothing grace.
Nor would the shadows of the night
Enfold us in that tranquil rest
That falls upon the sleeping babe
Rocked on its mother's breast.
And though the shadows over life
May seem to creep apace,
Behind the darkest one of them
Is His assuring face!
—Mrs. Claude Allen McKay.

* * *

Hymns in Suffering

It is said of Charlotte Elliott, the author of the "Invalid's Hymn Book," that though she lived to enter her eighty-second year, she never knew a well day.

Her sweet hymns were the outpouring of a heart that knew what it was to suffer. Like so many other bards, she "learned in suffering what she taught in song." —*Expositor's Minister's Annual*, 1929.

* * *

The Chastisement of Love

A week ago the newspapers carried the story of a father and mother, who, finding their little girl had taken and eaten something from a cupboard, began to shake and slap the child. When the child became tired and sleepy, they did not let up, but continued their shaking and slapping for four hours. What cruel punishment for such a little offense! No! It was compelled by love. The child had swallowed ten sleeping tablets and the doctor said the only hope of saving the child's life was in keeping it awake. *We do not always understand the path through which He leads us, but we may be certain His chastisement is always born of love.*—A. D. Hill.

* * *

Tuning

Even as a harp loses its tone, so the Lord's people often get out of tune.

When this happens it is necessary that they should be tuned afresh, and for this the strings have to be tightened. The Lord has to bring pressure to bear when tuning His own, so that they may not give out an uncertain and unmusical sound. Sometimes the tuning process is a very painful one for our spirits and our feeble bodies.

It is most interesting to observe a musician tuning his harp, resting it as he does so upon his shoulder. So in our own case *while the Lord may have to tighten the strings very forcibly, we can praise Him for His support during the tuning process; and when we are tuned, we can again praise Him for the pressure which makes us more like Himself,* so that others may hear sweet melody, and see the graces of Christ in us.—Selected.

The Son Not Exempt

All the saints must go to the proving house. God had one Son without sin, but he never had a son without trial.—*Sunday School Times.*

* * *

The Song of the Martyrs

Many Japanese converts died in the terrible persecution of Christians in Japan in the 16th century. On one occasion a nobleman of the highest rank, his wife and their six young children, with upwards of forty other Christians, were sent to the stake. It was a dark night before fire was set to their several piles; but as soon as the smoke had cleared away the martyrs were seen amid the bright flames in which they stood, with eyes fixed on Heaven, their forms motionless and erect as though they had been chiseled out in stone. In very horror the spectators were silent, and the hush of death was upon the midnight air when suddenly from out of that fiery furnace a flood of melody was poured—men and women and children singing the praises of the Living God as sweetly and with notes as true as though the red and thirsty flames had been but the dews of Heaven upon their brows. The sighs and prayers of the Christian watchers, which could no longer be repressed, the shouts and execrations of the soldiers and executioners, soon mingled with this death-song. The music of that marvelous choir died gradually away; the sudden failing of each gladsome voice, the silent sinking of each upright form telling that another and yet another had yielded to his doom.—*The Dawn.*

* * *

Remember the Love of God

A few years ago there was found in an African mine, the most magnicent diamond in the world's history. It was presented to the king of England to blaze in his crown of state. The king sent it to Amsterdam to be cut. It was put in the hands of an expert lapidary. And what do you suppose he did with it? He took this gem of priceless value.

He cut a notch in it. Then he struck it a hard blow with his instrument and, lo, the superb jewel lay in his hands cleft in twain. What recklessness! What wastefulness! Not so. For days and weeks that blow had been studied and planned. Drawings and models had been made of the gem. Its quality, its defects, its lines of cleavage had all been studied with minutest care. The man to whom it was committed was one of the most skillful lapidaries in the world.

Do you say that blow was a mistake? Nay, it was the climax of the lapidary's skill. When he struck that blow, he did the one thing which would bring that gem to its most perfect shapeliness, radiance and jeweled splendor. That blow which seemed to ruin the superb precious stone was in fact its perfect redemption. For from these two halves were wrought the two magnificent gems which the skilled eye of the lapidary saw hidden in the rough, uncut stone as it came from the mines.

You are the most priceless jewel in the world to God. And He is the most skilled lapidary in the universe. Some day you are to blaze in the diadem of the King.—James H. McConkey.

* * *

Against a Thorn

Once I heard a song of sweetness
  As it cleft the morning air,
Sounding in its blest completeness,
  Like a tender pleading prayer;
And I sought to find the singer,
  Whence the wondrous song was born,
And I found a bird, sore wounded,
  Pinioned by an ugly thorn.

I have seen a soul of sadness
  While its wings with pain were furled,
Giving hope and cheer and gladness
  That should bless a weeping world;
And I knew that life of sweetness,
  Was of pain and sorrow borne,
And a stricken soul was singing
  With its heart against a thorn.

Ye are told of One who loves you,
  Of a Saviour crucified,
Ye are told of nails that pinioned,
  And a spear that pierced His side;
Ye are told of cruel scourging,
  Of a Saviour bearing scorn,
And He died for your salvation,
  With His brow against a thorn.

Ye are not above the Master!
  Will you breathe a sweet refrain?
And His grace will be sufficient,
  When your heart is pierced with pain;
Will you live to bless His loved ones,
  Tho' your life be bruised and torn,
Like a bird that sang so sweetly
  With its heart against a thorn?

—*The Sunshine News.*

* * *

Be Careful with that Thorn

The pearl oyster sometimes receives into its tiny shell a sharp and irritating grain of sand. The most natural thing would be to throw it out. But this would only rasp and irritate its sensitive flesh, and produce pain, disease, and death. Instead of this, it throws out an exquisite crystalline fluid with which it covers and smothers the rude obstruction, and makes it free from all friction and annoyance, until gradually the rough grain of sand turns into a beautiful pearl.

Be careful what you do with that thorn that was given you, or you may miss the most precious experience of your life.

The Lord Jesus can meet the most trying circumstances of your life with His love, and grace, and comfort.—*Gospel Herald.*

* * *

A Changed Torrent

In the Canton of Bern, in the Swiss Oberland, a mountain stream rushes in a torrent toward the valley, as if it would carry destruction to the villages below; but, leaping from the sheer precipice of nearly nine hundred feet, it is caught in the clutch of the winds, and sifted down in fine, soft spray whose benignant showering covers the fields with perpetual green. So sorrow comes, a dashing torrent, threatening to destroy us; but by the breath of God's Spirit it is changed as it falls, and pours its soft, gentle showers upon our hearts, bedewing our withering graces, and leaving rich blessings upon our whole life.—*God's Revivalist.*

* * *

Whom God Chooseth

When God wants to drill a man,
And thrill a man,
And skill a man,
When God wants to mold a man
To play the noblest part;
When he yearns with all His heart
To create so great and bold a man
That all the world shall be amazed,
Watch His methods, watch His ways!
How He ruthlessly perfects
Whom He royally elects!
How He hammers him and hurts him,
And with mighty blows converts him
Into trial shapes of clay which
Only God understands;
While his tortured heart is crying
And he lifts beseeching hands!
How He bends but never breaks
When His good He undertakes;
How He uses whom He chooses,
And with every purpose fuses him;
By every act induces him
To try His splendor out—
God knows what He's about!

—Selected.

* * *

The Refiner's Fire

Late in the last century a great fire gained the upper hand in Virginia's famous jungle, the Dismal Swamp. Careless hunters caused it. The fire gained rapid headway, the undergrowth and frost-bitten shrubbery being devoured by the greedy flames. Clouds of dense smoke covered the horizon. So wide-sweeping was the fiery storm that hundreds of animals, bear, fox, deer, and multitudes of smaller animals were driven out of the jungle to be slaughtered by eager hunters. So it is in a great Holy Spirit revival. The fire of the Spirit drives out into the open areas of conscience all the hidden sins of the heart. The Spirit drives them out so that they can be destroyed by the redeeming grace of Christ.—*The Watchman-Examiner.*

* * *

How to Press through Trial

Do not keep your eye on the trial, or difficulty, in order to see what God will do for you; but keep your eye on Him to see what is coming, as though there were no difficulty at all. The trials and difficulties are, I might say,always preparatory to some step in advance. And if the eye be kept on Him, you will be ready for the onward step, whereas if the eye be only on the trials, though there will be a sense of mercy, in the way He makes a way of escape out of them, there will not be, as with Jehovah-jireh, "In the Mount of the Lord it shall be seen," and a great blessing from the trials!—*Latin American Evangelist.*

* * *

"Why All this Pain?"

A lady was once summering in Switzerland, and in her mountain walks she came upon a sheep-fold. She stood and watched very interestedly, for there was one poor sheep lying there moaning and looking very sick. She saw his leg was broken, and, full of pity, asked how it had happened.

"I broke it myself," said the shepherd sadly.

She was even more pitiful, for she thought it must have been an accident.

"No," said the shepherd, "it was done on purpose; it was the only way. That sheep will follow me afterwards, when I've nursed it and got it better, and it will always come at my call then. But before it wouldn't; it was always wandering off into dangerous places, and it wouldn't let me take care of it along with the rest, and wouldn't even come when I called. It would have got killed certainly if I hadn't done that."

Yes, sometimes we poor human sheep will have all our own way, will stray into dangerous paths until the Good Shepherd Himself has to send sorrow and pain to us, so that at last we will hear His voice and follow Him.—*Living Streams.*

The Lining

There's never a cloud so thick, so black,
That it has not a priceless lining;
But the lining is never found outside,
'Tis inside the light is shining.
You must pass through the dark to reach the light;
It is there ever waiting your finding;
In the cloud that's the darkest, the blackest outside,
God has set His most precious lining.
—Sue Miriam Voorhees.

* * *

The Blow that Saves

Once in a while one reads a story in the papers with a real lesson attached. So it is with the account of how "Slim" saved his friend from death. Let the man who was saved tell it in his own words. He works for a power company; he and his gang repair the lines, set new poles, and so on. "Sometimes new poles are green, and water-soaked, and will conduct electricity. A short time ago my gang was sent to replace a pole that had been badly burned. The new pole to be set up was wet and green, the street was wet, and overhead was a high line carrying 33,000 volts. We were hoisting the new pole up through the wires to a place where it could be dropped in the hole dug for it. I had thoughtlessly seized the butt end of the new pole as it swung clear of the ground and was guiding it into place when suddenly one of the boys made a run for me and knocked me sprawling. I arose from the sloppy street, wet, muddy, and ready for fight. . . . He pointed aloft to where I saw the new pole had hit the lower high-line wire. I also saw instantly that had he not taken such a quick action in knocking me clear of the pole, I would have been a 'goner.'" Does God not often strike down sinners, as He did Paul on the road to Damascus, that He might get them to listen to His voice and so be—come saved from the wrath to come? God often must knock us away from our foolishness to keep us from permanently injuring ourselves.—*Gospel Herald.*

I walked a mile with Pleasure,
She chattered all the way,
But left me none the wiser,
For all she had to say.

I walked a mile with Sorrow,
And not a word said she;
But, oh, the things I learned from her,
When Sorrow walked with me!
—Robert B. Hamilton.

* * *

Perfect Through Suffering

God never would send you the darkness,
If He felt you could bear the light;
But you would not cling to His guiding hand,
If the way were always bright;
And you would not care to walk by faith,
Could you always walk by sight.

'Tis true He has many an anguish
For your sorrowful heart to bear.
And many a cruel thorn-crown
For your tired head to wear;
He knows how few would reach glory at all
If pain did not guide them there.

So He sends you the blinding darkness,
And the furnace of seven-fold heat;
'Tis the only way, believe me,
To keep you close to His feet,
For 'tis always so easy to wander
When our lives are glad and sweet.

Then nestle your hand in your Father's
And sing if you can, as you go;
Your song may cheer someone behind you
Whose courage is sinking low;
And, well if your lips do quiver—
God will love you better, so.
—Selected.

* * *

Praise for Thorns

We do not understand that we are to give thanks for evil in itself, but we may offer praise for the overruling of it for good. Again, many things that we regard as misfortunes are blessings. Trials and crosses are often among the greatest blessings in disguise, for it is only through such disciplinary processes that the character is perfected. When we consider that the disagreeable is indispensable enrichment and strengthening of character, we see that we should offer thanks for this phase of experience, as well as the agreeable. What a change would be wrought in our lives if we thus acted.

George Matheson, the well-known blind preacher of Scotland, now with the Lord, says: "My God, I have never thanked Thee for my 'thorn'! I have thanked Thee a thousand times for my roses, but never once for my 'thorn'; I have been looking forward to a world where I shall get compensation for my cross, but I have never thought of my cross as itself a present glory. Teach me the glory of my cross; teach me the value of my 'thorn.' Show me that I have climbed to Thee by the path of pain. Show me that my tears have made my rainbow." — *Pittsburgh Christian Advocate.*

* * *

Trouble Tells

Dr. W. M. Taylor in his book, *David, King of Israel,* says: "Traveling once on a train, among my fellow passengers was a little child who romped and was at home with everybody. Had anyone looked at her while she was frolicking thus, he would not have been able to tell to whom she belonged—she seemed to be the property of everyone. But soon the engine gave a loud shriek as we plunged into a dark tunnel, and in a moment the child flew like a bird to nestle herself in a lady's lap. I knew then who was her mother. So in the day of prosperity the good man may go hither and thither and there may not be very much to tell whose he is; but let him be sent through some dark tunnel of affliction and you will see at once to whom he belongs."—*Christian Beacon.*

* * *

"I Will Not Leave Thee"

God is with us in our sorrows. There is no pang that rends the heart, I might almost say, not one which disturbs the body, but what Jesus Christ has been with us in it all.

Feel you the sorrows of poverty? He "hath not where to lay His head."

Do you endure the grief of bereavement? Jesus wept at the tomb of Lazarus.

Have you been slandered for righteousness' sake, and has it vexed your spirit? He said, "Reproach hath broken My heart."

Have you been betrayed? Do not forget that He, too, had His familiar friend who sold Him for the price of a slave.

On what stormy seas have you been tossed which have not roared about His boat? Never glen of adversity so dark, so deep, apparently so pathless, but what in stooping down you may discover the footprints of the Crucified One.

In the fires and in the rivers, in the cold night and under the burning sun, He cries, "I am with thee: be not dismayed; for I am both thy Companion and thy God."—Spurgeon.

SOUL WINNING — PERSONAL WORK

"Lord, lay some soul upon my heart,
And love that soul through me;
And may I nobly do my part,
To win that soul to Thee."
—David Johnson.

* * *

Talking Business

A pastor was passing a big department store, and followed a sudden impulse to go in and talk to the proprietor on the subject of his salvation. Finding him, he said: "Mr. T., I've talked beds and carpets and bookcases with you, but I've never talked my business with you. Would you give me a few minutes to do so?"

Being led to the private office, the minister took out his New Testament and showed him passage after passage which brought before that business man his duty to accept Jesus Christ. Finally the tears began to roll down his cheeks, and he said to the pastor: "I'm seventy years of age. I was born in this city, and more than a hundred ministers, and more than five hundred church officers have known me as you have, to do business with, but in all these years you are the only man who ever spoke to me about my soul."—Selected.

* * *

Taking His Commands Seriously

A young Chinese man was converted in Atlanta, Ga. His godly teacher gave him a copy of the New Testament and said: "You are now a Christian and you must read the Christian's guide book and follow its teachings." He took this instruction seriously, and began at the first chapter and read straight through. When he came to John's Gospel, the story of the two disciples who followed Jesus and then went out and found their brothers and brought them to Christ gripped his heart. In far-away China he had a father, mother, brother and sister, and he felt that it was his duty to bring them to Christ. He wrote letters telling them about his new-found joy, but he could not make them understand. He must go and *bring* them to Jesus. He worked hard and saved his money and went back to China. After many weeks he won his loved ones to Christ. Again he worked and saved his money until he could come back to America, his adopted home, where he had found Christ.—From *Taking Christ Seriously*, by J. B. Lawrence.

* * *

Suppose

Suppose someone were to offer me a thousand dollars for every soul I might earnestly try to lead to Christ, would I endeavor to lead any more souls to Him than I am endeavoring to do now? Is it possible that I would attempt to do for money, even at the risk of blunders or ridicule, what I hesitate or shrink from doing now in obedience to God's command? Is my love of money stronger than my love of God or souls?—From the tract *Suppose*, published by the Great Commission Prayer League.

How Five Soul-Winners Did It

A business man in Wales spoke to his office boy about his soul, and from that word a work began that won his entire office force to Christ.

A merchant in England determined that no day should pass without his speaking to someone about Christ; in one year he had led scores to the Master.

An invalid Christian woman in Australia, for thirty years unable to put her foot to the floor, by means of her pen and prayer led forty people to Christ in a single year.

A Christian gentleman spoke to his servant while they were walking together; the boy became a Christian and later a minister of the Gospel.

A Sunday School teacher took one of her class of boys for a walk on Sunday afternoon when the session of the school was over; she told him of her concern that he should become a Christian, and had the joy of seeing him take his stand for Christ.—Selected.

* * *

So It Was of Old

A missionary on his return from Africa was asked how many of the natives in his district had been brought to the knowledge of Christ as Saviour. He replied, "Fifty." "And how many of these are preachers?" "Fifty," was again his answer. So it was in the days of old (Acts 8:4 ; so it should be to-day (Mark 16:15).—*Glad Tidings.*

* * *

The Italian Ambassador's Appreciation

Senator Dolliver's father lived with him in Washington, D. C. As the father was returning from class meeting he met the Italian Ambassador descending the steps, and preached Christ to him. The grandchildren were shocked at the familiarity of the aged man. When the grandfather died, the Ambassador sent flowers and asked the privilege of sitting with the family, saying, "He was the only person who thought enough of me to speak to me about my soul."—*Sunday School Times.*

Changed by a Dream

I heard once of a man who dreamed that he swept into Heaven, and he was there in the Glory World, and oh, he was so delighted to think that he had at last made Heaven, that he got there. And all at once one came and said, "Come, I want to show you something." And he took him to the battlements and he said, "Look down yonder. What do you see?" "I see a very dark world." "Look, and see if you know it." "Why, yes," he said, "that is the world I have come from." "What do you see?" "Why, men are blindfolded there; many of them are going over a precipice." "Well, will you stay here and enjoy Heaven, or will you go back to earth and spend a little time longer telling those men about this world?" He was a worker who had been discouraged. He awoke from his sleep and said, "I have never wished myself dead since!"—D. L. Moody.

* * *

An Infidel's Sermon to a Preacher

Never shall I forget the remark of a learned, legal friend who was at one time somewhat skeptical in his views. Said he,

"Did I believe as you do, that the masses of our race are perishing in sin, I could have no rest. I would fly to tell them of salvation. I would labor day and night. I would speak it with all the pathos I could summon. I would warn and expostulate and entreat my fellow men to turn unto Christ and receive salvation at His hands. I am astonished at the manner in which the majority of you ministers tell your message. Why do you not act as if you believed your own words? You have not the earnestness in preaching that we lawyers have in pleading. If we were as tame as you are, we would never carry a single suit."

A decade of years has passed away since that remark was made. I bless God that it was addressed to me. It put a fire into my bones which I hope will burn as long as I live. God preached a stirring sermon to me that day by the mouth of that infidel lawyer.—*The Gospel Banner.*

They Counted the Cost

Every week the Moody Bible Institute sends out bus loads of young people to different sections of the city to hold gospel meetings. Hundreds of people would never hear the gospel if it were not for these groups who go out on the street corners and testify for Christ. Let us join one of these groups, and share the actual experiences.

First, we meet with the group for a half hour of prayer. Then the bus is loaded, and we are off.

Someone starts a chorus and all join in. We ride around several blocks looking for a desirable corner. One is selected, the organ is set up, and the students gather in a semicircle. Hymns are sung and testimonies given. One passerby stops and listens, then others hesitate and stop. Soon a crowd has gathered. A lull seems to go over the crowd as one by one the young people tell of what Christ has done for them. A gospel message is given by one of the men students. The crowd listens attentively. As he brings the message to a close, he tells the audience that if any of them would like to know more about this Jesus, to come up to one of the students when the meeting is over.

One of the young women sings,

"Have you counted the cost
If your soul should be lost,
Though you gain the whole world for your own?"

Men, women, and children come to the front. Each student is surrounded. Eager listeners desire to know more about Jesus. Thirty-eight souls are brought to Him that night.

The students' faces were lighted with joy as they returned to the Institute. There is no joy to be compared with the joy of winning a soul to Christ.—*Student News Service.*

* * *

Better than Joseph's Robe

A very little girl attended a meeting, and heard about "the best robe." When she went home she said to her father, a policeman, "Father, have you got on the best robe?" He replied, "What do you mean, child?" "Father, have you got on the robe of salvation?" The father looked very perplexed, and, turning to his wife, said, 'What does the child mean?" The child said, "The preacher told us that Jesus Christ had made a garment for us, and that God gives it to every one who asks for it; and he told us that if any of us wanted it, to hold up our hands, and I held up my hand, and now I have got it on." "How do you know that, child?" "Why," she said, 'of course I know. Jesus said so. He told us that He would give it to us. I asked Him, so I have on the best robe.' That night, before she went to bed, she said to her mother, "Have I been naughty today?" "No, my child; you have been very good." "Mother, I did one naughty thing — I slapped Polly (her sister), and when I did that I made an ugly spot on my best robe; but the preacher told us that if we got any stains on our best robe, we were to ask Jesus to wash them away; so I knelt down and said, Please, Jesus, wash my best robe, and make it clean again.' "—*Christian Herald.*

* * *

Early Led to Jesus Christ

An only boy lay tossing on his sick-bed; he was very ill, and all that medical skill and a mother's tender nursing could do were powerless to arrest the disease. The mother sitting by was waiting to hear the father's footsteps, for it was close on the hour that brought him home. She wanted to meet him and tell him what the doctor had said to her when he came out of the sick room that day. Soon she heard the familiar sound of the latchkey in the door, and, softly leaving the room, she went to break the news to the anxious father. When he heard the doctor's verdict, that the boy could not live out the day, the shadow on his face deepened; with an effort he said, "God's will be done." Ascending the stairs he entered the room where the boy lay. As he bent over the child and kissed his fevered cheek, the sick boy opened his eyes, and asked, "Father, am I very ill?" "Yes, Frank, my boy," answered the father. "Shall I die?" added the boy. "Yes, we think you will, dear, before tonight." He lay silent a moment, and then he said, 'Then I shall spend tonight with Jesus." "Yes, Frank, dear," answered the father, turning away with the tears streaming down his face. "Don't cry, father," said Frank, "directly I get to Heaven I shall go straight to Jesus and tell Him that ever since I can remember you have tried to lead me to Him."—*Gospel Herald.*

* * *

"Love Your Enemies"

"Will you kindly send to me, for approval, the Fundamentals of Christian Faith Course? I wish to assure myself that it will be suitable for a young convert."

This is quoted from a letter recently received at the Correspondence School of the Moody Bible Institute, from one of the institute donors. The four textbooks were sent, and in a few days a letter was received from the inquirer which enclosed a check to cover the course, stating that the textbooks had been sent to a recently converted young man, and asking that the Correspondence School forward all necessary materials to him.

The woman who had written presented a most interesting story concerning the young man. He had been walking the broad path of life; the Devil had him in hand, and had led him to be a thief. He had broken into this woman's house and robbed it. He was caught, brought up for trial, convicted, and sent to Joliet prison. In time the woman visited him in prison. There she showed him, through the guidance of the Holy Spirit, the way of salvation. She made plain that if he would place his trust in the Lord Jesus Christ, he would be saved. The Holy Spirit used the message, and the prisoner accepted Christ as his own personal Saviour.—*Student News Service.*

* * *

Whose Boy Is in Danger

Dr. Cortland Meyers, of Brooklyn, relates the following story, as told by a ship's surgeon:

"On our last trip a boy fell overboard from the deck. I didn't know who he was, and the crew hastened to save him. They brought him on board the ship, took off his outer garments, turned him over a few times and worked his hands and feet. When they had done all that they knew how to do, I came up to be of assistance, and they said he was dead and beyond help. I turned away, as I said to them, 'I think you have done all you could,' but just then a sudden impulse told me I ought to go over and see what I could do. I went over and looked down into the boy's face and discovered it was my boy. Well, you may believe I didn't think the last thing had been done. I pulled off my coat and bent over that boy; I blew in his nostrils and breathed into his mouth; I turned him over and over; and simply begged God to bring him back to life, and for four hours I worked until, just at sunset, I began to see the least flutter of breath that told me he lived. Oh, I will never see another boy drown without taking off my coat the first instant and going to him and trying to save him as if I knew he were my own boy."

Are we as much interested in trying to save boys who are exposed to the curse of drink, the cigarette curse, and the social evil as if they were our own boys?

Are we concerned for the salvation from sin of those who are lost and away from God?

Are we doing all within our power to save them? Whose boy is in danger?—Selected.

* * *

Let Your Light Shine

Rev. J. Hudson Taylor tells the story of a Chinese pastor meeting a young convert and asking him if it were true that he had known the Lord for three months. The reply was, "Yes, it is blessedly true." The pastor then asked him, "How many have you won to Jesus?" "Oh," said the convert, "I am only a learner and never possessed a whole New Testament until yesterday." "Do you use candles in your home?" asked the pastor, "Yes." "Do you expect the candle to begin to shine only when it is burned half way down?" "No, as soon as it is lighted," said the convert. The young man saw the point and went to work immediately. Within six months he led several to the light. The Gospel messenger cannot save anyone, but he can prepare the way for Jesus to come into the heart and do the saving work.—Selected.

* * *

If we work upon marble, it will perish.
If we work upon brass, time will efface it.
If we rear temples, they will crumble to dust.
But if we work upon immortal souls, and embue them with just principles, the fear of God, and the love of their fellow men, we engrave on those tablets that which will brighten all eternity.

—Daniel Webster.

* * *

A Fisher of Men

A commercial traveler, named Rigby, was compelled to spend a weekend every quarter in Edinburgh. He always worshipped in Dr. Alexander Whyte's church and always tried to persuade some other visitor to accompany him. On one occasion, having taken a Roman Catholic traveler there who thereby accepted Christ, he called on Dr. Whyte to tell him of the conversion. The doctor then asked his name, and on being told that it was Rigby, he exclaimed: "Why, you are the man I've been looking for for years!" He then went to his study and returned with a bundle of letters from which he read such extracts as these: "I was spending a weekend in Edinburgh some weeks ago, and a fellow-commercial named Rigby invited me to accompany him to St. George's. The message of that service changed my life." "I am a young man, and the other day I came to hear you preach at the invitation of a man called Rigby, and in that service I decided to dedicate my life to Christ." Dr. Whyte went on to say that twelve of the letters were from young men, of whom four had since entered the ministry.—*Record of Christian Work*

Soul Saving Service

In the graveyard of a Baptist church located a short distance from Barnegat Island off the South Jersey coast, are the graves of a captain and twelve sailors. They all perished one night in a severe storm, when they tried swimming ashore from their ship, which struck a sandbar, less than three hundred feet from the beach and was pounded to pieces by the raging waves.

William A. Newell, who lived only a short distance away from where this happened was an eyewitness of this tragic event. He was sorely distressed and heavily burdened, because of his inability to offer any assistance. On many occasions he declared to his neighbors, "They could have been saved if a determined effort had been made from shore, to rescue them." There were those who told him to forget it. Seven years later, Mr. Newell was elected to Congress where promptly he introduced a bill for the establishment of a Life Saving Service. The usual thing happened, it died in committee.

"Introduce that bill again this coming session of Congress. I am interested and will help you," said Abraham Lincoln who served as a member of Congress at that time, to the sponsor of the Life Saving Service. John Quincy Adams, who occupied a seat behind Mr. Newell, assured him of his support. It was attached as an amendment to the Lighthouse Bill and became a law, making provision for lifeboats, rockets and other equipment and devices for the preservation of life and property along the New Jersey coast. In course of time, this life service was extended and today, there are hundreds of rescue stations manned by thousands of life-savers, at a cost of millions of dollars. Mr. Newell won the approval and admiration of the voters of New Jersey and subsequently was elected governor of his State.—*Gospel Herald.*

* * *

"Just Brass"

Howard W. Pope, in the *American Messenger, says*: "When Major D. W. Whittle was in business, before he gave all his time to Christian work, a woman came into his office one day and said: "Major Whittle, my husband was greatly impressed with the services last night, and he promised me that he would come down and see you this morning. Did he come?' 'Yes,' said the major. 'Well, what did he say?' 'Why, he just asked the price of brass, and talked around a little.' 'Oh!' said the wife, 'that was just an excuse for his coming; but what did you say to him?' 'I am sorry to say,' said the major, 'that all I talked about was *just brass, too.*' 'That was a lesson to me,' said the major, 'which I can never forget.' *And it may be that all of us can learn a lesson from his mistake.*"

* * *

"That Makes No Matter"

A writer in one of the Methodist papers recalls a story concerning the late Dr. Rigg, a well-known Methodist preacher of half a century ago. In the early days of the Salvation Army the good doctor was approached by a devoted lassie, who asked, "Are you saved?" "Go away!" was the reply. "No, I can't go away," replied the girl. "Are you saved?" "My good girl," replied the incensed doctor, "I would have you know that I am President of the Wesleyan Conference." "That makes no matter," was her response; "there's hope even for the vilest!"—*Christian Herald.*

* * *

"My Boy Is Gone and He Knew Christ"

"To your charge, sir, I am committing my boy."

Thus spoke a rough-looking, lumberjack father to the young pastor, in an Ontario lumber town. Burdened for his salvation, he had brought his eldest son into the hospital across miles of deep snow that Lord's day. He was incurable, about thirty years of age, red-haired, and utterly cross-grained in spirit. When told of his anxious father's promise to pray as we sought to be God's messenger, he resented it. He would not have God's message of Calvary. Two months went by as we visited him faithfully.

One day we were oppressed by the feeling that this soured man was slipping into eternity. That day his room was crowded and we could not speak. But we vowed to God we would go again and speak if the whole hospital were around his bed. Fortunately he was alone. We drew up a chair, pulled out our pocket Bible, and told him we literally *must* make "the way of life" plain, which we did using Isaiah 53:6; John 1:12; 6:37, etc. We clinched it with Dr. Torrey's illustration that represents the sinner's black load of sin by a book upon his one hand; then transferring this load to Christ, represented by the other hand, thus saying, "The Lord hath laid on him the iniquity of us all." Praying then, we lifted him in faith to God, and left him. All the while he was gritting his teeth in antagonism to the whole business.

Several days later the Christian nurse met us as we ascended the staircase to the ward. "Mr. R., your parishioner went home this morning, and died resting in Christ. None other spoke to him." I said, "Thank God, we got him through." This fact that interceding father knew, and no human voice told him. "My boy is gone, and he knew Christ," were his first words as he stood before our door that same evening, footsore and weary. His wrestling in intercession was rewarded.

"Ye also helping together by prayer for us." is a twofold factor in the conversion of perhaps every soul, the conjoining of forces. And hence let us not be too proud of supposedly personal results. "The day" will declare these things, and the spokesman and the intercessor will rejoice together.—Rev. W. F. Roadhouse, Toronto, Can.

* * *

Two Ways of Catching

A story is told of a Sunday school teacher who told her pupils the story of Peter, who was told by our Lord that he was henceforth to be a fisher of men. After the lesson was given the children were asked the question: "Who catch men nowadays?" One child quickly answered: "Policemen." The teacher then explained the difference between soul winners and policemen. Policemen catch men to bring them before a judge. Soul winners catch men to bring them before a Saviour.—*Christian Herald, London.*

* * *

To Rescue Only One

A traveler says: "On the Aktsch glacier I saw a beautiful sight, the parable of our Lord reacted to the letter. One day we were making our way with ice ax and alpenstock down the glacier, when we observed a flock of sheep following their shepherd over the intricate windings of the crevasses and so passing from the pastures on the one side to the pastures on the other side of the glacier. The flock had numbered 200 all told; but on the way one sheep was lost. One of the shepherds, in his German *patois*, appealed to us if we had seen it. Fortunately, one of the party had a field glass. With its aid we discovered the lost sheep far up, amid a tangle of brushwood, on the rocky mountainside. It was beautiful to see how the shepherd, without a word, left his 199 sheep on the glacier waste (knowing that they would stand there perfectly still and safe), and went clambering back after the lost sheep until he found it."—*Sunday School Chronicle.*

* * *

The Ant's Evangelism

The story is related of a gentleman who laid a piece of sweetmeat on the table, and then picked up an ant and placed it on the sweetmeat. He was astonished to see the little creature rapidly descend by one of the legs of the table and seek his fellows. They appeared to understand the news. He then at once turned back, followed by a long train of his fellow citizens, and conducted them to the prize. Are there not many who know the sweetness of the Gospel, who might learn a lesson from this ant? If we have tasted and seen that the Lord is good let us do what we can to lead others into like blessing—Selected.

Gospel Singing

Returning home late one night through the deserted streets of a Syrian city, I noticed a man going about the streets singing out repeatedly the same call. Here and there a window was opened while some curious one asked a question, then as the window closed, the man hurried on, ever repeating the same earnest call. Not understanding the Arabic language, I inquired what the man was doing. "Why, he is singing for a little child," was the reply. "Singing for a little child? What do you mean?" I asked. "It means that a child is lost and the police are 'singing' all through the streets of the city, trying to find the child and restore it to its father." Many of God's children are lost. Are you out "singing" for them? Have you joined the search? Or are you only casually interested, lulled, and comforted by the thought that the lost ones are none of yours?—Rose A. Huston, Sterling, Kans.

* * *

A Rather Important Lack

A college professor, being ferried across a stream, asked the boatman, "Do you understand philosophy?" "No, never heard of it." "Then one-quarter of your life is gone. Do you understand geology?" "No." "Then one-half of your life is gone. Do you understand astronomy?" "No." "Then three-quarters of your life is gone." Presently the boat tipped over and both fell into the water. "Can you swim?" asked the boatman. "No." "Then the whole of your life is gone!"—Courtesy *Moody Monthly.*

* * *

What Are Christians "For"

A Christian woman who was engaged in work for the poor and degraded was once spoken to by one who was well acquainted with both the worker and those whom she sought to reach.

"It does seem wonderful to me that you can do such work," her friend said. "You sit beside these people, and talk with them in a way that I do not think you would if you knew about them, just what they are, and from what places they come."

Her answer was, "Well, I suppose they are dreadful people. But, if the Lord Jesus were now on earth, are they not the very people He would strive to teach? Would He feel Himself too good to go among them? And am I better than my Master?"

A poor, illiterate person, who stood listening to this conversation, said with great earnestness and simplicity, "*Why, I always thought that was what Christians were for.*" The objector was silenced, and what wonder? Is not that what Christians are for?—Courtesy of *Moody Monthly.*

* * *

Soul-Winning

Are you seeking out the lost ones
Whom the Saviour died to win?
Are you showing them the Fountain
That can wash away their sin?
Are you looking by the wayside
For the weary ones who fall?
Do you win them to the Master
Who has promised rest to all!
—Selected.

* * *

Better Than a New Assignment

A policeman in Birmingham, becoming a Christian, was so greatly troubled by the sights and sounds and sin among which he worked, that for a long time he and his wife prayed: "Lord, take me out of the police service. Give me some other work." No answer came, and no other work was opened to him. At last he said to his wife: "I think we have been making a great mistake. We have been praying that I may be taken out of the force, and I begin to think He has put me there to work. Now I am just going to pray that He will let me serve Him where I am." This was the beginning of a life of marvelous usefulness. His influence over the men was so great that he was promoted to be the head of detectives. He was instrumental in the salvation of many criminals. The place where God has put you is the place where you can do the best service for Him.—Courtesy *Moody Monthly.*

An Invalid Shames Us

Are we willing to go as an invalid in Melbourne went? This man is blind. Every joint in his body is immovable. His jaw is locked so that his front teeth had to be removed to insert the spout of his drinking cup. His whole body is as stiff as a log of wood, but his mind is full of vigor, and his heart is full of the grace of service. For twenty-nine years he has lain thus, fed only on liquid foods. For twenty-two years he has been blind. Is it possible that such a one as he could do anything to help others? Listen. Seventeen blind children are supported by his efforts in India; ten in China; a blind Bible woman in Korea; a blind boy in the Sudan; a blind boy in Fiji; a blind Bible woman in Jaffa. Three hundred pounds a year is received in answer to prayer by that faithful, sightless, silent, paralyzed disciple in that little shut-in room in Melbourne. If Christ could use this man to bless and help so many, how may He not use us if we will only surrender our all to Him?—*The Evangelical Friend.*

* * *

"Better Tell Sister"

"Hadn't I better tell sister about Jesus?" abruptly asked a boy of ten of a guest in the home. The sister, some years younger, was in an upper room asleep, and the boy had been telling of his admiration for her. The guest, thinking to draw out the boy, asked why he should tell his sister. This was the boy's reply: "Father never told me, Mother didn't, and my teachers at school never said anything, and I wouldn't have given my heart to Jesus but for what you told us in Sunday school last Sunday. Maybe nobody will tell sister; don't you think I'd better?" The Lord Jesus did not promise to make His disciples eloquent orators, clever logicians, or effective preachers. But He did promise them, if they would follow Him, that He would make them "fishers of men."—*Sunday School Times.*

Andrew's Good Example

"He first findeth his own brother Simon, and saith unto him, We have found the Messias, which is, being interpreted, the Christ" (*John* 1:41).

"What did you preach about on Sunday?" was the question asked of a city pastor one day.

"I preached about Andrew," was the reply, "and, do you know, I found him a most interesting character!"

"What was there about him that was remarkable?"

"Well, I do not suppose you would call him a great man, but the significant thing about him was that every time he is mentioned in Scripture he was introducing someone to Jesus."

This was certainly a beautiful occupation, and yet it does not call for any wonderful talents. It is work that any one of us can do.—*Presbyterian Standard.*

* * *

"My Best—My Dead Level Best"

In the other years, in Northwestern University, a group of students organized themselves into a life-saving organization, whose purpose was to go to the rescue of drowning people on Lake Michigan. Early one bleak November morning, urgent word came to the life-saving group that the Lady Elgin, with its human cargo, had been caught in the jaws of a violent storm, and was rapidly going to pieces. The college youths hurried to the scene of the wreck. In the life-saving group was a cleancut, athletic youth by the name of Ed Spencer. Hurriedly, Ed threw off superfluous garments, tied a rope about his waist, and threw himself into the choppy, chilly waters of Lake Michigan! Swimming out to the wrecked vessel, he signalled to be pulled to shore, until he had rescued a seventh, an eighth, a ninth, and a tenth person! Utterly exhausted, he went and stood by the fire of logs that cold bleak morning, blue, pinched, trembling, and hardly able to stand. As he stood there, he lifted his eyes again toward the scene of the Lady Elgin. There he saw men, women, and children struggling in the water. Said he, "Boys, I'm going in again!" "No, no, Ed," they implored, "it is utterly vain to try; you have used up all your strength; you could not save anybody. For you to try again in your spent condition would be suicidal!" Said Ed, "But they are going down — perishing — and I will try again!" Into those bleak, blue waters he lept, and brought to safety an eleventh, a twelfth, a thirteenth, a fourteenth, and a fifteenth person. He could scarcely get to the fire on the beach. As he stood there, he saw a spar rising and falling upon the waves. Seeing a man's head above the spar, he said, "Boys, there's a man trying to save himself. He watched the spar as it drifted toward the point. He knew that to drift around that point meant certain death. Said he, "Boys, I'm going to help that man!" "No, no, Ed, you can't help him. Your strength is gone." "But, I'll try anyway," said he. Into the waters he sprang. He rescued his man, and was then carried to his room in a delirious condition. As the delirium lifted from his mind intermittently, he would ask, "Did I do my best, my dead level best?" "Why, Ed," came the reply, "you saved sixteen!" Replied Ed wearily, "Yes, I know that, but did I do my best, my dead level best?" Though he rescued so many his only thought was of the men, women, and children who perished that bleak November morning. Throughout that night, he would mumble but one thing: "Oh, if I could only have saved just one more!"

Friends, in this momentous, fateful hour, let the ruling passion of each one be to do his best, his dead level best for God, for country, and for others. It was His best, His dead level best, which the Saviour did for you and me when He gave willingly His life upon His cruel cross that we, through faith in His Name, should have life eternal: "Greater love hath no man than this, that a Man lay down His life for His Friends" (John 15:13); "For God so loved the world, that He gave His only begotten Son, that whosoever believeth in Him should not perish, but have everlasting life" (John 3:16).—Dr. R. A. Torrey.

Hardships Welcomed

"I cared not where or how I lived, or what hardships I went through, so that I could but gain souls to Christ. While I was asleep I dreamed of these things, and when I awoke the first thing I thought of was this great work. All my desire was for the conversion of the heathen, and all my hope was in God" —Brainerd.

* * *

Why the Dog Looked Sad

A preacher of the Gospel, traveling in the Alps, was greatly interested in the St. Bernard dogs. One day the dogs were sent out in a storm to seek travelers who might be lost. One dog returned in the late afternoon, wearied from fighting his way through the drifts. The dog went to his kennel, lay down in a corner, and acted thoroughly despondent despite the effort of the master to encourage him. Was he sick? No, said the master, the dog was not sick in body, but in heart. He had failed to find anybody to help, and had come back ashamed. Oh, does that apply to us individually as bearers of good news?—*Gospel Herald.*

* * *

What Would Happen If All Did Their Share?

The Record of Christian Work tells of a missionary physician in one of China's hospitals who cured a man of cataract. A few weeks later, forty-eight blind men from one of China's interior provinces, each holding on to a rope held in the hands of the man who was cured, came to the hospital. Thus in a chain, they had walked two hundred and fifty miles to the doctor, and nearly all were cured.

Does not this give a picture of our share in the missionary enterprise? The first blind man came to the physician, put his trust in him, received his sight, and then went out to lead others to the same power that had blessed him. If we have come to Christ and by faith have received Him and the eternal life He offers, our part will be to lead others to Him.—*Sunday School Times.*

Burdened for Lost

"A Punjab brother convulsed and sobbing as if his heart would break. I went up to him and put my arms about him, and said, 'The Blood of Jesus Christ cleanseth us from all sin.' A smile lit up his face. 'Thank God, Sahib,' he cried, 'but, oh! what an awful vision I have had thousands of souls in this land of India being carried away by the dark river of sin! They are in Hell now! Oh, to snatch them from the fire before it is *too late!*"—*Accountability.*

* * *

The Best Doctoring

There is an American medical missionary in a foreign field who is more interested in the spiritual health of his patients than in their physical health, while at the same time he is greatly used as a physician and surgeon. Difficult, even baffling, physical cases are brought to his hospital, and, by keeping in touch with the latest medical and surgical research in America, he has been able to restore health in a wonderful way. But the fact in which he most rejoices is, as he wrote in a letter home last year, "The more the patients come in the more the Gospel goes out."—*Sunday School Times.*

* * *

What Fishing Means

If you are going to be fishers of men, you must go where men are. I wonder if our churches have not made a mistake when they settle down in a comfortable church and put a sign outside, "Welcome." Suppose I went down to the stream and stood on the bank with my rod, line, and bait in my hand, and said, "Come on, little fish, I have a lovely line, and the nicest worm on my hook; come right out of the water and help yourself." How many fish would I get? —*Sunday School Times.*

The Man by the Road

If I were the man by the side of the road
Who watches the world go by,
I'd stop every man with a frown on his face
And ask him the reason why,
I'd stop every one with sad, weary eyes
And find out what made him so;
I'd point out to each the Christ on the Cross
And help him His love to know.

If I lived in a house by the side of the road
And tried for the friendship of man,
I'd tell him of Christ, the wonderful One,
Who gave us salvation's plan.
I'd show him the road to Heaven's gate,
The way that the Saviour trod,
If I were the man by the side of the road,
I'd try to lead someone to God.

I do not live by the side of the road,
Where the race of man passes on,
But I meet them each day on the path of life,
Those wanderers far from home.
You don't have to live in a house by the road
To scatter the sunshine of love.
But wherever you live, if a man ask the way,
Just point him to Heaven above.

You don't have to live in a house by the road
To offer your friendship to man.
A kindly word and a cheerful smile,
A friendly clasp of the hand,
A word of love to a sinsick soul
Helps lighten the heavy load
And makes you a friend of all mankind
If you are the man by the road.

—Selected.

* * *

Sometimes Talking Tells

"From the time I was twenty-five until I was sixty-one no one ever spoke to me personally on the subject of religion. I lived opposite a church which I attended quite regularly; I had Christian neighbors; I lived near my pastor, and saw him almost every day, and yet for thirty-six years no one ever spoke to me about my soul. I doubt if I should ever have been converted, had not some crusaders come into the town and led me to Christ."

The neglect of Christians to speak to the unsaved is a great occasion of skepticism. Said a lady to a friend of mine, "I will tell you why I am a doubter. I was in a sewing society last week. Forty ladies were present and every one a church member except myself. We were there three hours. We talked of everything, even down to crazy patchwork, but not a word about Jesus. Do you suppose I can believe that He is precious to them, when they never say anything about Him? I cannot do it."—*Gospel Church Calendar.*

* * *

Hustle to Save Souls

A motorcycle patrolman paced a parson through the streets of Cambridge, hailed him to the curb, and gave him a ticket for speeding. "Officer," explained the speeder, "you have to hustle if you're going to save souls." The cop tore up the ticket.—Selected.

* * *

A Chinese Woman's Testimony

A Christian blind woman became concerned regarding a blind friend who had never head the Gospel. She took a journey of two days over high mountains to bring her the good news of salvation. The friend was saved, and in answer to prayer her blind eyes were opened. Within an hour after her healing the whole city knew that she could see. All day she received visitors, to whom she testified about Christ. Later she learned to read, and the Lord has greatly used her in the women's evangelistic band. As a result of her work, there is now a self-supporting church of a hundred members. Other remarkable healings are on record, enough to assure to any reasonable person the certainity of miracle.—Letter from Madame Chiang Kai-shek, concerning work of China Inland Mission, quoted in *Sunday School Times.*

Heart Cries of Soul Winners

Give me Scotland or I die!—John Knox.

If my eternal salvation depended on winning a thousand souls to Christ within the next ten years, I would not attempt to do it from the pulpit. I would come right down and go after souls.—Bishop Jesse Peck.

Young man, young woman, make the most of your life. Go after souls. Go after them the best way you know, but go after them. Do not listen to those who warn you that you will offend and drive away by your persistence. Go after souls. Go after them by public and private testimony. Go after them by service and by prayer. But go after them. Go after them with love and a burdened heart. Go after them by kind deeds. Go after them by song and praise. Go after them when they are bereaved and in sorrow. Go after them when they are especially favored of God and men. But go after them. This soul-winning life is your life — make the most of it—J. B. Chapman.

One of Wesley's biographers said, "He was out of breath pursuing souls." Whitefield's cenotaph has carved upon it a blazing heart. The seal on Adam Clarke's grave is a candle burned down to its socket, and underneath are the words, "In living for others, I am burned away."—F. A. Daw, *The Free Methodist*

* * *

Personal Contact Wins

Dr. Cortland Myers one Sunday morning spoke to a young man who stood in the vestibule of Tremont Temple. He said to the youth, "I hope you are a Christian." To Dr. Myers' amazement the young man replied, "No, I am not a Christian; but I know you, and I have heard you preach for seven years." Dr. Myers then took him aside, and they had a heart-to-heart talk. What seven years of preaching Sunday after Sunday had failed to do, was accomplished in a few minutes.—Courtesy of *Moody Monthly.*

Responsibility for Others

A company of reapers are seated beneath the shade taking their noontide repast. They see a solitary figure crossing the field with slow and irregular steps. He carries a staff before him, and now and then trips and stumbles on the unseen surface. They percieve that he is blind. He is out of the path, too, and has no guide. A little way off in the direction he is following is a precipice, looking sheer down a hundred feet. He moves on toward the brow, piloted with his staff! Nearer and nearer he draws all unconscious of what is before him.

They who watch him are silent and unmoved; no voice is lifted up, no hand is stretched out. They see him pacing steadily to the awful verge. His staff meeting no obstacle, slips from his hand into the abyss. He takes a step forward and stoops to recover it; still no warning from the reapers. His foot overhangs vacancy; his bending form leans from the brink. A wild cry and he is gone! What have they done? Nothing. They did not put out his eyes; they did not lead him to the precipice; they did not push him down; they have done nothing; they have only neglected to do; and yet his blood shall be required at their hands.

We are not responsible for the sins of others, but God will not hold us guiltless if we fail to warn them according to His commands.—*Sunday School Journal.*

* * *

In the Same Way

An old man, so the story runs, once lost a banknote in his barn. Said he to himself: "That note certainly is in the barn somewhere, and I will search for it until I find it." After long and patient seeking, he found the note and returned to the house and related the circumstance to his wife. A few weeks later, having been awakened to a sense of his spiritual state, he asked his wife, "What must I do to become a Christian?" She replied, "You must seek Christ as you sought the bank note — until you find Him." And he did so.—*Pentecostal Herald.*

Simple Words Blessed

Illustrating the ease with which souls can sometimes be won, Bishop C. C. McCabe (U. S. A.) tells how when paying a cabman he grasped his hand and said: "I hope to meet you in Glory." He had often done the same before, but this time the arrow went home.

About midnight the man came back to the house, and insisted on seeing the bishop, although he had retired, assuring the host that the bishop would see him, which was the case. When they met tears were on his cheeks. He said: "If I am to meet you in Glory, I have got to turn round. I have come to ask you to pray for me." And what a privilege it was to point him to Jesus!—*Pathway of Blessing.*

* * *

An Old Indian's Record

On one of my trips to Guatemala, Mr. Burgess asked me whether I would give a few Indian men special lessons in soul-winning. Just imagine trying to teach this man when you hear the story. Anselmo was sitting on the fourth seat back. While speaking I turned to this old man and said, "Tell me, Anselmo, how many have you led to Jesus this year?" (This was about the twelfth of February.) The old man's face fell. He said, "Ah, Senor, very few." I said, "Tell me how many." He said, "There are not more than thirty, Senor." Early in July of that year, I received a letter from this old man, and it contained a list of 144 whom he had led to Christ before the first of July. That would be a life work for most Christians in America.—*Christ Life.*

* * *

When Heinz Was Rebuked

Everyone knows of Heinz, of the "fifty-seven varieties," but few know of his zeal as a soul-winner. At a revival meeting one day, the minister turned to him and said, "*You are a Christian man; why aren't you up and at it?*" He went home in anger, and went to bed, but could not sleep. *At four o'clock in the morning he prayed that God would make him a power in His work, and then went to sleep.* At the next meeting of bank presidents which he attended shortly afterward, he turned to the man next to him and spoke to him of the Christian life. His friend looked at him in amazement and said, "I've wondered many times why you never spoke to me about it if you really believed in Christ." That man was the first of 267 *souls* which Heinz won to Christ after that time. — *The King's Business.*

* * *

Wasps and Men

Huber, the great naturalist, tells us that if a single wasp discovers a deposit of honey or other food, he will return to his nest, and impart the good news to his companions, who will sally forth in great numbers to partake of the fare which has been discovered for them. Shall we who have found honey in the rock Christ Jesus, be less considerate of our fellow men than wasps are of their fellow insects? Ought we not rather, like the Samaritan woman, to hasten to tell the good news? Common humanity should prevent one of us from concealing the great discovery which grace has enabled us to make.—Charles Haddon Spurgeon.

* * *

How a Chinese Found God

One evening an elderly Chinese said to the great missionary, Hudson Taylor, "Are you a foreigner?" "Yes, I am an Englishman." "Are there books in that bag on the table?" "Yes, there are." "Are you a teacher of a foreign religion?" "Yes; of the Jesus religion." The Chinese then told Taylor that for many years he had been a seeker after truth but could find no religion that could take the burden of guilt from his soul. A few nights before he had had a vision of a man in white who had told him to go into Hangchow, that there he would find a foreigner sitting in an inn with a bag of books on the table before him; that he had visited inn after inn that day, but had found no such person. Finally, he had heard of this inn in the suburbs, and as a last hope had entered it. The missionary then preached the Gospel to him and gave him a New Testament. Two days later he visited his home and found that he had destroyed all his idols and was rejoicing in Jesus Christ as Saviour. Hudson Taylor parted from the man, adoring God, not only for His power to save, but also for His marvelous and miraculous way of leading souls to the messenger and the message of the Gospel.—From a sermon by Dr. C. E. Macartney.

* * *

The Personal Touch

A Sunday school teacher mailed successively ten cards to a girl who had been absent. When the last one was posted, the teacher met the girl's mother on the street, who said, "You need not mail Mary any more cards."

"Why?" asked the astonished teacher.

"We buried her last week!"

Who can foretell the difference if the hand used to write a card had reached a little farther to ring a door bell.—*Alliance Weekly.*

* * *

Why He Was Saved

In a Southern city a pastor was working on a sermon one afternoon. A sudden impulse came to speak to a young man in his place of business. Immediately he went downtown and in a few minutes led that young man to the Lord. Later, when the young man went jubilantly home, he found all except his father at the supper table. Walking into the living room he saw his father, and joyously said, "Dad, I was saved a little while ago." The father looked up with tears in his eyes, and said, "Son, twenty-four hours ago I became so troubled about your salvation that I vowed before God neither to eat nor drink, but only to pray until you were saved, but I told no one of my purpose." In desperate need the father had cried from the depth of his heart, and God heard him. Is anything too hard for God?—Courtesy *Moody Monthly.*

His Opportunities to Witness

In Shanghai it is a common sight to see four or five coolies pulling a cart, often heavily laden. They get on very well on the level, but when they need to go up over the bridges they often find it very difficult to pull the cart up. As I crossed a bridge one morning I saw a well-dressed Chinaman go to the assistance of a cart that was stuck. In answer to a question he said: "That is my work; whenever I see them unable to pull their loads I help them and then I have a chance for a few moments to preach the Gospel to them. I tell them, 'It is because I am a Christian that I help you.'"—*Sunday School Times.*

* * *

The Undelivered Message

A poor wayward boy died of cold and hunger in a western city, and his parents' hearts were broken, because a message from his father, forgiving him and entreating him to come home, failed to reach him. The boy was down-and-out. He had reached his row's end. At first rebellious and determined never to return, he soon grew weary of his folly and confided to a chance acquaintance that he would go back on account of his mother, but he was sure his father would drive him away, and it was no use.

At that very moment there was a message from his father, posted in Jim Goodheart's Mission in the Denver slums, telling him to come home and all would be forgiven. But the boy never saw it, and he died in his rags and in his misery—died for the want of food and warmth and love—all of which were awaiting him in abundance in his father's house not very far away.

There is a message in your hand for your generation, a message so big and so important that Jesus died on the Cross that it might be delivered. If you are a Christian, if you are a professed disciple of the Lord Jesus Christ, that message is in your hands. Are you delivering it?—Wade C. Smith, in *Sunday School Times.*

"Edified—for What?"

A minister called his elders together and told them that because no souls were being saved he would tender his resignation. A deacon urged him not to do so, because people were being edified. The minister said, "Edified for what?" adding, "Brother, do you believe that through you a soul was ever saved?" The frank reply was, "No." The same was admitted by the other men present. The next day the man who had been the first to say, "No," spoke to his confidential clerk. He said, "Bob, Bob, you are not a Christian, and I, an elder, have never spoken to you about your soul. I want that we kneel here and give ourselves to Christ: I for consecration, and you for salvation." The clerk became a Christian. Before the week was over the elders who had met with their minister had won thirty men to Christ.—*Adult Bible Teacher.*

* * *

Workmen Needing to be Ashamed

One evening a certain group of young people asked me to speak to them on church work. I called a young lady to the front, and asked her to sit down, and then called up another young lady to tell her how to be saved. It was a heartbreak. Both of them had been in the church for I don't know how long. The second girl started the conversation: "You're a stranger in our city, aren't you?" "Yes," her friend replied, "we just moved here from Oklahoma." "Have you ever gone to church?" she continued. "No," was the answer. "Then we should like you to come to our church. We have a fine young people's group, and we play games and sing." "That is enough, sister," I interrupted at this point, "you may go back to your seat." There wasn't a drop of life in her. I tried out four of these young folks, but not one of them had a drop of water to give to this poor sinner. They talked about their church, their society, and their good times, but said nothing about the Lord Jesus. Beloved, let us quit playing, and be out-and-out for Christ.—From *A Sure Remedy,* by Dr. Walter L. Wilson.

He Knew What He Would Be Doing

When the Japanese invaded Malaya, no one knew of the fate of the missionaries. A member of one society having workers there was asked if he knew what a certain missionary was doing. The reply was, "We don't know where he is, but we know what he is doing; he will be converting the Japanese."—*Christian Laymen and Tomorrow's World.*

* * *

While the Preachers Talked

Not long ago three preachers and a Christian layman were riding together on a train. They chatted about the things of the Lord, and were enjoying real fellowship. When the matter of personal work came up, the clergymen frankly admitted to each other that it was never easy for them to approach another individual about Jesus Christ. While they were discussing the probable reason for this difficulty, the laymen left them and sat down beside a soldier farther down the aisle, engaging him immediately in conversation that led toward the presentation of the Gospel. Is it any wonder that there were three very red faces, and that one of the three said with evident feeling: "May the Lord forgive us. We three preachers sit here talking about soul-winning, and he goes and does it."—Courtesy *Moody Monthly.*

* * *

Just One Soul

Value just one soul, for one may be many. Andrew brought Simon — just one. But that one was many, for under God Simon brought 3,000 in one day. Joel Stratton, a waiter in a restaurant, brought John Gough to Christ — just one. And Gough brought many to Christ. Ezra Kimball, a Sunday School teacher, brought Moody to Christ—just one man. But that one was many, for Moody rocked two continents toward God. But why say more? Just one digit is valuable in the multiplication table and one letter in the alphabet—far more valuable is the conviction of the value of just one soul in God's sight.—R. G. Lee.

Winning the Lost

The noted preacher, Charles H. Spurgeon, once said: "Even if I were utterly selfish, and had no care for anything but my own happiness, I would choose if I might, under God, to be a soul-winner; for never did I know perfect, overflowing, unutterable happiness of the purest and most ennobling order till I first heard of one who had sought and found the Saviour through my means. No young mother ever rejoiced over her firstborn child, no warrior was so exultant over a hard-won victory."

* * *

One Person at a Time

Dr. H. C. Trumbull, in his excellent book, *Individual Work for Individuals,* says: "I have been for more than twenty-five years an editor of a religious periodical that has a circulation of more than a hundred thousand a week during much of the time. Meanwhile, I have published more than thirty volumes. Yet, looking back upon my work during all these years, I can see more direct result of good through my individual efforts with individuals than I can through all of my spoken words to thousands upon thousands of persons in religious assemblies, or all my written words." *"Reaching one person at a time is the best way of reaching all the world in time."—Earnest Worker.*

* * *

At Your Own Door

A rescue missionary was lecturing where he was unaccustomed to speak. He said that every Christian, however poor or busy, could do personal work for Christ, if willing. After the lecture a woman said: "What can I do? I am a poor widow with five children to support. How can I find time to go to anyone about Christ?" "Does the milkman call at your house?" "Of course." "Does the baker?" "Yes." "Does the butcher?" "Yes," was the curt reply, and the woman turned away. Two years after, the man of God spoke in the same place.

After the service a woman said, "I am the person who was vexed with you when you asked whether the milkman and butcher and baker visited me. But I went home to pray. God showed me my duty. Through my humble efforts five persons have been led to the Saviour, and they all are consistent working members of the church." — *Home Study Quarterly.*

* * *

He Helped Someone

I do not know how soon 'twill be
Ere I will cross life's darkest sea;
But when on earth my life shall end
I hope in Heaven to meet a friend
That I did help, by act or word,
To follow Christ, the Risen Lord.
No greater joy to man can come
Than just to know he's helped someone.
—*Gospel Herald.*

* * *

How They Became "Sons"

A Hindu convert in India could neither read nor write, but he got others to read the Bible to him. His favorite verse was John 1:12—"As many as received him, to them gave he the power to become the sons of God." "I have received him," said he, "so I have become a son of God." He went back to his village radiantly happy. "I have become a son of God," he cried. His life was so transformed, and his simple witness so effective, that the villagers all wanted to become "sons of God," too. He won the whole village for Christ and thousands of others besides. Why? Just because he—a poor, illiterate Hindu—realized that he had indeed become "a son of God" and longed for others to become "sons" also.—From *The Happy Christian,* by An Unknown Christian.

* * *

Have We Done This?

A poor seamstress was troubled because she had never won anybody to Christ. She determined to speak to the milkman next morning. Before daylight she was up waiting for him to come. Opening the door she greeted him and said, "Do you know Jesus Christ?" Dropping his pails he said, "Little woman, why do you talk to me like this? For two nights I have been unable to sleep, and the burden of it all is that I am not a Christian. I am in the darkness. If you know how to find the light tell me." So she told him how she had been saved, and he was saved that morning.—Selected.

* * *

In a Stable

A London city missionary, during his visiting, went into a stable and began to talk to a jockey about the salvation of his soul. "This is no place to talk religion, so there's an end of it!" exclaimed the jockey. "Oh, no, that's not the end of it; it's only the beginning," said the missionary. "Christianity began in a stable. Jesus Christ was born in a stable, and you can be born again in one." He then talked to the man until he kneeled in prayer and accepted the Saviour.—*Christian Herald.*

* * *

His Greatest Experience

A few years ago a young man in Indianapolis was heard to say that he had intellectual difficulties about the faith of the Christian. A prominent layman of the city heard of this and got his address. That evening he went to his boarding house and in his hall bedroom sat down to talk about the Gospel with that man. One difficulty after another faded away. At last he got on his knees by the young man and prayed for him. Then he turned to him and asked: "Won't you surrender to Christ, now and here?" And the young man said, "I will." That layman went to his pastor and told the story, and said: "I have had many thrilling experiences, but that one outranks them all." The man who stayed in that hall bedroom with a strange young man till one o'clock in the morning was Benjamin Harrison, ex-President of the United States.—*Earnest Worker.*

"I Wish Some One Would Look for Me"

Between the hours of ten and twelve, for many nights, a poor woman might have been seen making her way through the streets of London. A year had passed since her only daughter had left home, and entered service in the great city. There she became acquainted with gay companions, and she was now living a life of open sin. The mother learned that her daughter might be seen every night in a certain part of the town. After many nights of watching, she was about to despair, when she saw a figure closely resembling that of her daughter. She eagerly approached, and was about to stretch out her arms to embrace it, when the light of a lamp showed that it was not her child. In an agony of grief, she exclaimed: "Ah! it is not she! I was looking for my daughter; but, no, you are not my child!" The poor girl burst into tears, saying: "I have no mother — I wish I had; I wish I had someone who would look for me. I wish someone would look for me!"

Alas! there are multitudes who in the bitterness of their souls cry out: "I wish someone would look for me!" Fatherless, motherless, homeless, Christless, they tread their darkened courses, and in the anguish of their stricken spirits cry out: "No man careth for my soul!" Thanks be to God, there is One who is higher than all, whose tender mercies fail not, and who looks with pitying eye on those upon whom others look with hate and scorn. And let us follow the example of Him whose mission here was to seek the ruined, and to save those that are lost. — *Christian Herald.*

SOWING AND REAPING

"We sow a thought and reap an act;
We sow an act and reap a habit;
We sow a habit and reap a character;
We sow a character and reap a destiny."

—Selected.

* * *

Seeds for God's Harvest

It is said of an English traveler that he so loved the wild flowers that grew at the sides of the lanes and in the fields of England, that when he went abroad he would fill his pockets with the seeds and scatter them broadcast. *Almost every day we live there are opportunities for sowing the seed of God in some heart; it may be some simple word, some kindly act. Just a line in a letter we write, or a text we quote, and the seed is sown and some life is blessed.*— A. Lindsey Clegg, in *Youth with a Capital Y.*

* * *

Reaping

Many years ago, ill health compelled the two missionaries stationed at Efulan to return to America, leaving but six believers, for the station had only been open a short time. They dared not hope they would find any Christians on their return two years later, for how could six recent converts stand alone in an African village? They found, however, that the small group had met several times every week for prayer and Bible study and had witnessed so faithfully for Christ that all the neighboring villages knew that they were "Jesus men." Is it any wonder, then, that the church grew into a great congregation and that, on the 25th anniversary of its organization, 7000 people assembled for a communion service in which the sacrament was celebrated by three African ministers — the bread and wine distributed by 24 native elders?—Selected.

* * *

His Present Occupation

Notwithstanding many "wets" declare that Prohibition does not prohibit, hundreds of prisons throughout the United States contain evidence to the contrary. "Whatsoever a man soweth, that shall he also reap." In a certain State in the Union a millionaire was engaged in the bootlegging business, thinking it an easy way to increase his wealth. He now undoubtedly believes the verse quoted above, for he is at the present time serving a long term in prison. A friend who called on him within the prison walls found him working, sitting cross-legged, with a big needle and a ball of twine, sewing burlap bags. The friend, not knowing what else to say, remarked, "Sewing, eh?" Looking up with an ill-natured smile, the man replied, "No: I'm reaping."—*The Boy's World.*

* * *

The Harvest

A man asked his servant to sow barley. The servant sowed oats. The master asked why he sowed oats. The servant replied, "I hoped to grow barley." The master said, "What a foolish idea! Who ever heard the like!" The servant replied, "You yourself constantly sow seeds of evil, and yet expect to reap the fruits of virtue." God says to Christians, "Whatsoever a man soweth, that shall he also reap" (Gal. 6:7).—*Gospel Herald.*

* * *

"The Sower"

A Sower one day went forth to sow;
His seed was the word of life,
The field that He sowed was the world of men
Where the briars of sin grow rife.

What seed by the wayside chanced to fall
The birds of the air devoured,
And that which fell in the barren soil
In the heat of the day expired.

'Mid thorns and tares some grew for a time,
Tho' weakened, and warped, and lean,
But harvest time found them withered and dead
For fruitless their growing had been.

But the seed that fell in the fertile soil
Bore fruit, some an hundred fold;
And the heart of the Master sang for joy
As He garnered His sheaves of gold.
In your heart, my friend, the seed is sown;
Oh, what will the harvest be,
A blackened field at the harvest time,
Or the joys of eternity?

Oh, think, dear friend, of the harvest time—
It may be tonight for you—
Will you yield your heart to the Master's call?
The Saviour—is speaking—to you!
—James G. Arcus, Courtesy *Moody Monthly.*

* * *

Life's Mirror

There are loyal hearts, there are spirits brave;
There are souls that are pure and true;
Then give to others the best you have,
And the best will come back to you.

Give love, and love to your life will flow,
A strength in your inmost need;
Have faith, and other hearts will show
Their faith in your word and deed.

Give truth, and your gifts will be paid in kind,
And honor will honor meet;
And a kindly smile will surely find,
A smile that is just as sweet.

Give a helping hand to those in need,
And a harvest of golden grain
You'll reap some day from the love-sown seed,
If you sowed in the Master's Name.

For life is the mirror of king and slave—
'Tis just what we are and do;
Then give to others the best you have,
And the best will come back to you.
(Luke 6:38).
—*The Gospel for the Youth.*

* * *

A Share in Sowing

Mr. Spurgeon tells of a visit he made to a public house in Nottingham, to see the landlord's wife who was dying, and found her rejoicing in the Saviour's love. He asked her how she found Christ. *"Reading that,"* she replied. Mr. Spurgeon looked at the paper and discovered that it was part of an American newspaper containing an extract from a sermon preached in London. He asked where she found the paper, and she said it was wrapped round a parcel sent from Australia.

Think how that message of salvation was ordained to travel from London to America, then to Australia, and then back to England, on a piece of paper to a needy soul in Nottingham.

Yes, think of the blessing that piece of paper contained though the sender may not have had any purpose in view, and then think of the blessing the tracts and papers must be that are sown and watered with tears in behalf of needy souls by the publishers and the distributors.

"Sown in the darkness, or sown in the light,
Sown in our weakness, or sown in our might;
Gathered in time or eternity,
Sure, ah, sure will the harvest be."

No one is too weak nor too insufficient to have a share in the sowing. Loving hearts and willing hands are all that is required.

* * *

A Splendid Inheritance

A young man lay on a hospital cot, recovering from an operation which had been a most serious one. His surgeon—a renowned and skillful operator—was paying his daily visit. He had been making some inquiries about the young man's family, for certain points in the case greatly interested him, and he had wished to know of the inheritance that lay back of this young man. In answer to a question, the patient said, "Oh, yes, my folks are all religious—all the family way back—" adding carelessly, "I don't take much stock in that sort of thing myself."

"You have inherited stock in it, young man, and very valuable stock," answered the Christian physician. "Do you know why you are recovering so rapidy from your accident—why the bones knit and the wounds heal so rapidly? It is because those ancestors of yours have bequeathed to you good clean blood and a sound constitution—the physical makeup of those who have kept God's laws. He is a God of justice, and the heritage of those that fear His Name is a precious and priceless one in many ways. I wouldn't speak lightly of such a birthright. The responsibility is upon you to pass on an equally desirable one to your children."—*The Illustrator.*

* * *

Life A Boomerang

People get back in this world just about what they give. If we think the world is hard on us, the probability is that the hardness is in ourselves, and that it is the echo of our own speeches that we hear, the rebound of our own smitings that we feel, the reflection of our own ugliness of disposition and temper that we see, the harvest of our own sowing that we gather into our bosoms. If we are untrue to anyone, it is quite likely that some day somebody will be untrue to us. If we are unjust to another, there is little doubt that sometime someone will deal unjustly with us.—J. R. Miller.

* * *

Slightly Soiled

Two theological students were walking along an "old clothes" street in the Whitechapel district of London. Suddenly one exclaimed: "What a splendid text for a sermon to young men!" pointing to a suit of clothes that hung swaying in the breeze at the side of a window. "Slightly soiled, Greatly Reduced in Price." "That's it exactly," he went on. "We young people get soiled so slightly, just seeing a vulgar show in a theater, just reading a coarse book, just allowing ourselves a little indulgence in dishonest or lustful thoughts, just slightly soiled, and lo! when the time comes for our manhood to be appraised, we are 'greatly reduced in price.' *Our charm, our strength is gone. The consecration of youth is gone. We are just part and parcel of the general, shop-soiled stock."—Congregationalist.*

* * *

What Are You?

A story is told of two Scotchmen who emigrated to California. They wanted to have in their new home some reminder of their homeland. One took with him a *thistle,* the national emblem. The other took a swarm of *honeybees.*

Years passed by. Fields for a long distance are cursed with the thistle, which the farmer cannot get rid of. But the forests and fields are laden with the sweetness of honey.

Little did those two men think of what would grow out of their selections, either for good or for evil.

Is it not so always? The seemingly insignificant acts mean much to future generations. We are a *burden* or *blessing* to others through the little things of life, which are fuller of help or hindrance than we often think.

Beginnings count; we can control beginnings. We can make them what we will. Thoughtlessness may bring trouble to many. Thoughtfulness may bring untold good.—*The Friend* (Dayton).

* * *

A Bitter Reaping

He was a tenant farmer. From time to time he renewed his lease. He had worked long hours, year after year, and had made the farm a model of its kind. One day the agent mentioned to him that the owner would require the farm for his son, who was about to be married. The farmer was greatly upset, and made a number of offers in hopes that his terms would affect the owner's decision. It was in vain. The day drew near when he had to vacate the home, and then he did something he had decided upon in weeks of angry brooding. He gathered seeds of all the pests of the farmer, and when it was dark, moved up and down over that fertile, clean soil, casting into it this rubbish. Next morning, bright and early, the agent rode up to the door, and informed him that the owner's plan had fallen through and he would be glad to renew the lease. He did not understand the farmer's "My God, what a fool I've been!"—*War Cry.*

* * *

Oh, scatter seeds of loving deeds
  Along the fertile field;
For grain will grow from what you sow,
  And fruitful harvest yield.

Though sown in tears through weary years,
  The seed will surely live;
Though great the cost it is not lost,
  For God will fruitage give.

The harvest-home of God will come:
  And after toil and care,
With joy untold your sheaves of gold
  Will all be garnered there.
  —By Sonny Captain Benibo, native missionary of Nigeria, West Africa.

SYMPATHY

Sympathy

D. L. Moody gives the following experience, which is a good illustration of sympathy.

I want to tell you how I got up a sympathy with a family in Chicago, while I was living there. I attended the funerals of a good many children. I got hardened to it like a doctor, and could go to them without sympathy. One of my little Sunday School scholars was drowned, and word was sent by the mother that she wanted to see me. I went. The husband was a drunkard, and was then in the corner drunk. I had my little girl with me then. She was about four years old. When we got outside she asked:

"Suppose we were poor, Pa, and I had to go down to the river after sticks, and should fall in and get drowned, and you had no money to bury me, would you be sorry, Papa?" And then she looked up into my eyes with an expression I had never before seen, and asked, "Did you feel bad for that mother?" I clasped her to my heart and kissed her, and my sympathy was aroused.

My friends, if you want to get in sympathy with people, in order to help them and do them good, you must consider how you would feel in their place. Let us work for the Master along the lines of sincere compassion for the unfortunate and depraved.—*Biblical Illustrator.*

* * *

What a Little Girl Needed

I believe it was Pastor Dolman whom I heard tell of how he was sitting at his desk one day when he heard the door creak, and then suddenly there was a sharp cry of pain. Looking up he saw his little daughter who had started to enter the room when her little fingers had caught in the door. He jumped and calling the mother said, "You better come and look after this little girl." The mother came and taking the child said tenderly, "Does it hurt so dreadfully?" "Oh, it hurts," said the child, "but the worst is that Daddy didn't even say, 'Oh!' How we like someone who says, "Oh!" someone who sighs for us, weeps with us, feels with us in our troubles; and you remember what is said of our Lord, "In all their affliction he was afflicted."—H. A. Ironside.

* * *

The Warmth of the Hand

"Don't forget that the warmth of the hand will increase the diameter of the shaft," is one of the "Don'ts" published in a little book for mechanics. *If the touch of the human hand can move cold iron or steel, what may we not expect when it touches the hand of another human being? — Record of Christian Work.*

* * *

Compassion

There is nothing that wins in personal work like a compassionate love. Colonel Clarke, founder of the Pacific Garden Mission, had the tenderest heart. I would go down in the early days, and five or six hundred men would be there sometimes. The greatest preachers in Chicago would go down, and couldn't hold them five minutes. When Colonel Clarke spoke, those men would sit quietly and drink in the Word. He loved them and they knew it. One night he was weeping, and he said to himself, "The idea of you, a 250-pounder, weeping so." He checked back his tears, and he lost his power. Then he went to God and said, "O God, give me back my tears," and he gave him back his power. —R. A. Torrey, in *Moody Monthly.*

* * *

If We Knew—

If we knew but half the troubles
That our neighbor has to bear;
If we knew what caused those furrows
On his brow, and kept them there—
We should surely try to cheer him
In some kindly, helpful way,
And there'd be a lot more sunshine
In the lives of both, today.

If we realized all heartaches
That a friendly word or smile
Would alleviate and banish,
We should "go the second mile"
To be of helpful service
To our fellow men, each day,
And life's path would seem much brighter
To the folks who pass our way.

If we knew whose feet were standing
Close beside the narrow stream;
If we knew whose eyes would close soon
In the sleep that has no dream;
Then perhaps we'd be more tender,
Lighter judge, more kindly speak—
Oh, why not act as though we knew it—
For life's cords so quickly break!
—Chester E. Shuler.

* * *

Someone Near

The late S. D. Gordon wrote of a devout Christian mother who was always teaching her daughter lessons of faith and trust, especially telling her that she need never be afraid at any time because

God was always near. One summer evening she tucked her little girl in bed after her prayers, put out the light, and went downstairs. Then an electrical storm came rolling out of the west with vivid flashes of lightning and a reverberating roar of thunder. Suddenly there was a simultaneous blinding flash and a deafening crash, and when the echoes died away, mother heard the little girl calling desperately, "Mama! Mama! Come and get me." The mother found her little girl in tears and trembling. After she had soothed her somewhat, she thought it might be an opportune time to teach a spiritual lesson, and said, "My little girl, has mother not taught you many times that you need never be afraid, that God is always near, and nothing can harm you?" The little one put her arms around her mother's neck and said, "Yes, mama. I know that God is always near, but when the lightning and the thunder are so awful I want someone near me what's got skin on 'em."—Courtesy *Moody Monthly.*

* * *

"That's Me"

Sitting down in the orphanage grounds upon one of the seats, I was talking with one of our brother trustees, when a little fellow, we should think about eight years of age, left the other boys who were playing around us, and came deliberately up to us.

He opened fire upon us thus, "Please, Mr. Spurgeon, I want to come and sit down on that seat between you two gentlemen."

"Come along, Bob, and tell us what you want."

"Please, Mr. Spurgeon, suppose there was a little boy who had no father, who lived in an orphanage with a lot of other little boys who had no fathers, and suppose those little boys had mothers and aunts who comed once a month, and brought them apples and oranges, and gave them pennies, and suppose this little boy had no mother and no aunts and so nobody ever came to bring him nice things, don't you think somebody ought to give him a penny? 'Cause, Mr Spurgeon, that's me."

Somebody felt something wet in his eye, and Bob got a sixpence, and went off in a great state of delight. Poor little soul, he had seized the opportunity to pour out a bitterness which had rankled in his little heart, and had made him miserable when the monthly visiting day came round, and, as he said, "Nobody ever came to bring him nice things."—*Gospel Herald.*

* * *

Is He Deserving?

It always irritates me when, on asking some good person to help a distressed brother, I am met with the silly inquiry: "Is it a deserving case?" As a rule, it certainly is not. The man who is down and out has been just an average sort of fellow, and has helped considerably to bring his troubles on himself. But am I a deserving case? Is anybody a deserving case? The mother cares for her child, not because it is a supernaturally good child, but because the helpless mite happens to be hers, to love and live for. We have got to love all sorts of tricky and unpleasant people simply because of the eternal mystery and miracle that Jesus loved them enough to die for them.
—*F. A. Atkins.*

* * *

If We Only Understood

Ah! we judge each other harshly,
Knowing not life's hidden force;
Knowing not the fount of action
Is less turbid at its source;
Seeing not amid the evil
All the golden grains of good;
And we'd love each other better,
If we only understood.

Could we but draw back the curtains
That suround each other's lives,
See the naked heart and spirit,
Know what spur the action gives,
Often we should find it better,
Purer than we judge we should,
We should love each other better
If we only understood.

Could we judge all deeds by motives,
  See the good and bad within,
Often we should love the sinner
  All the while we loathe the sin;
Could we know the powers working
  To o'erthrow integrity,
We should judge each other's errors
  With more patient charity.
—Selected.

* * *

Understood

Understood by Christ the Saviour;
  Understood when trials come;
Understood if we should waver,
  Understood when vict'ry's won.

Understood when we are weary;
  Understood when we are sad;
Understood when we are fearful;
  Understood when we are bad.

Understood by our big Brother;
  Understood e'en though we fail;
Understood in all our weakness;
  Understood though others rail.

Understood by Christ our Saviour;
  Understood! 'tis all we need;
Understood by Him who loves us—
  Understood by Christ indeed.
E. M. Svacha.

* * *

"No, Me No Go"

This pretty little story is told of a spelling class in China. The youngest of the children had by hard study contrived to keep his place so long that he seemed to claim it by right of possession. Growing self-confident, he missed a word, which was immediately spelled by the boy standing next him. The face of the victor expressed the triumph he felt, yet he made no move towards taking the place, and when urged to do so, firmly refused, saying, "No, me no go; me not make Ah Fun's heart solly."

That little act implied great self-denial, yet it was done so thoughtfully and kindly that spontaneously came the quick remark, "He do all same as Jesus." After being saved by the Lord Jesus, the next thing is, to "follow in His steps." and keep longing for His appearing.—L. W., in *Boys and Girls.*

All Head

A traveler called his companion's attention to a firm's peculiar name. It was "Head and Hart." The companion remarked: "Poor Hart has died and left Head alone." This often occurs in Christian life, worship, and service—all head and no heart.—*Sunday School Superintendent.*

* * *

Have We No Compassion?

Compassion for the lost must show forth in everyone who has received it. Every unsaved one is lost—lost in the most fearful sense of that term—helpless, hopeless, peaceless, joyless, godless, and deceived, defiled, despoiled, enslaved, damned, and doomed by sin. The life of the heathen is characterized by spiritual uncertainty, ignorance, superstition, idolatry, selfishness, cruelty, unchastity, impurity, deceit. The dark picture in Romans 1:29-31 is only too true. A lady missionary with her porters had crossed a swollen stream. They sat down on the bank to rest a bit. An African mother with her dearly loved baby on her back essayed to cross over. The swift waters were too much for her and she and her baby perished. The porters saw them drowning but made no effort to save them but laughed instead. Are there others who belong to that class?—*Inland Africa.*

* * *

The Pity that Helps

There is a pity that exhausts itself in tears, but does little besides. It sees things are not right, but makes no effort to make them right. It talks about them and laments over them, but goes no further. There is another kind of pity. It is the kind that has eyes and heart to sympathize, and it also has hands to help. It quickly sees that weeping, even to the point of exhaustion, if it ends there, is not adequate in a world like ours. If all the energies bound up in tears and shed over calamities of one sort and another could be coined into bread and clothing and medicine and

Bibles, both those who give and those who would receive would be better off.

What the world needs today is not fewer tears of sympathy, but the more general application of a real helpful ministry, such as each of us can render. We have not done our best until we have gone with the resolute purpose of taking some of the chill and the sting and the fever out of the lives of the people who are walking in a hard way.—*The Prospector.*

* * *

Our Lord's Touch

Some rude children in Madagascar were one day calling out, "A leper, a leper," to a poor woman who had lost all her fingers and toes by the dread disease. A missionary lady who was near-by put her hand on the woman's shoulder, and asked her to sit down on the grass by her. The woman fell sobbing, overcome by emotion, and cried out, "A human hand has touched me. For seven years no one has touched me." The missionary says that at that moment it flashed across her mind why it is recorded in the Gospels that Jesus touched the leper. That is just what others would not do. It was the touch of sympathy as well as of healing power. —*Sunday School Chronicle.*

TEMPERANCE — ALCOHOL

The Saloon

The saloon is sometimes called a bar;
That's true;
A bar to heaven, a door to hell,
Whoever named it, named it well.
A bar to manliness and wealth,
A door to want and broken health,
A bar to honor, pride and fame;
A door to grief and sin and shame,
A bar to hope, a bar to prayer;
A door to darkness and despair,
A bar to honored, useful life;
A door to brawling, senseless strife.
A bar to all that's true and brave;
A door to every drunkard's grave.
A bar to joys that home imparts,
A door to tears and aching hearts.
A bar to heaven, a door to hell,
Whoever named it, named it well.

—Written by a life-time prisoner in Joliet Prison.

* * *

Says Evangeline Booth:

"Drink has shed more blood, hung more crepe, sold more homes, plunged more people into bankruptcy, armed more villains, slain more children, snapped more wedding rings, defiled more innocence, blinded more eyes, dethroned more reason, wrecked more manhood, dishonored more womanhood, broken more hearts, blasted more lives, driven more to suicide and dug more graves than any other scourge that has cursed the world."—*War Cry.*

* * *

His Reasons

A lawyer was speaking at a large gathering with a great display of learning in opposition to prohibition. An old farmer who had been listening quietly, shut up his knife with a snap and said: "I may not understand all the points of this question, but I have seven good reasons for voting for prohibition." "What are they?" asked the lawyer. "Four sons and three daughters," was the reply.—*Christian Herald.*

* * *

What Pershing and Lloyd George Think of Drink

General Pershing said: "Banish the entire liquor industry from the United States; close every saloon, every brewery; suppress drinking by severe punishment to the drinker, and if necessary, death to the seller, or maker, or both, as traitors, and the nation will suddenly find itself amazed at its efficiency, and startled at the increase in its labor supply. I shall not go slow on prohibition, for I know what is the greatest foe to my men, greater even than the bullets of the enemy."

Lloyd George said: "Drink during the World War used up as much tonnage as the Germans have sunk with all their submarines; it killed more men than have been killed by the German submarines. Drink destroyed more food than all the submarines put together."—*United Presbyterian.*

* * *

The Man She Married

A speaker at a temperance meeting told how drink had once caused the downfall of a brave soldier. In the course of the sad story he said: "Sometimes after a debauch the man would be repentant, humble. He would promise his wife to do better. But, alas! the years taught her the barrenness of all such promises. One night when he was getting to be an old man—a prematurely old man, thin-limbed, stoop-shouldered, with red-rimmed eyes—he said to his wife, sadly: 'You're a clever woman, Jenny; a courageous, active, good woman. You should have married a better man than I am, dear.' She looked at him, and thinking of what he had been, she answered in a quiet voice: 'I did, James.'"—*Sunday at Home.*

* * *

Do You Know Me?

I am the greatest criminal in history.

I have killed more men than have fallen in all the wars of the world.

I have turned men into brutes.

I have made millions of homes unhappy.

I have transformed many ambitious youths into hopeless parasites.

I make smooth the downward path for countless millions.

I destroy the weak and weaken the strong.

I make the wise man a fool and trample the fool in his folly.

I ensnare the innocent.

The abandoned wife knows me; the hungry children know me.

I have ruined millions and shall try to ruin more.

I am Alcohol.—H. W. Gibson.

* * *

It's the Brain that Counts

The noted surgeon, Dr. Charles Mayo, in addressing a large convention of boys, said in part:

"You can get along with a wooden leg, but you can't get along with a wooden head. The physical value of man is not so much. Man as analyzed in our laboratories is worth about ninety-eight cents. Seven bars of soap, lime enough to whitewash a chicken coop, phosphorus enough to cover the heads of a thousand matches, is not so much, you see.

"It is the brain that counts, but in order that your brain may be kept clear you must keep your body fit and well. That cannot be done if one drinks liquor.

"A man who has to drag around a habit that is a danger and a menace to society ought to go off to the woods and live alone. We do not tolerate the obvious use of morphine or cocaine or opium and we should not tolerate intoxicating liquor because I tell you these things are what break down the command of the individual over his own life and his own destiny.

"Through alcoholic stimulation a man loses his co-ordination. That is why liquor is no advantage to the brain. You hear people tell how they had their wits quickened for the first half-hour by liquor but they don't tell you how later their body could not act in co-ordination with their brain."

* * *

Barnum's Prefix

P. T. Barnum was a temperance advocate. Once when he was giving an address, a man in the gallery howled: "How does alcohol affect us, externally or internally?" "Eternally," flashed back Barnum.—*Sunday School Times.*

A Noted Physician's Reason

Giving evidence before the British Royal Licensing Commission, Dr. C. C. Weeks, noted British physician, was asked the reasons why he became a teetotaler. He replied: "My reasons, I am afraid, were entirely selfish. There wasn't much altruism about it. I was a young doctor, and I saw round me what was doing. The doctor whose practice I took killed himself with drink. All round me men were drinking, and I made a rule that during the day I would never drink with my patients. I found that without it I was a better cricketer and a safer catch. The thing that finally put it over was when I was called in consultation by another doctor. He was in evening dress, and had been out to dinner. He wasn't drunk, but he met me with that fatuous grin which is associated with drinking—and upstairs there was a tragedy. He had made a profound error of judgment in a woman at her hour of confinement. As I drove home I said to myself, 'This might happen to me,' and that night I made up my mind that I would not take any more alcohol."
—*Queensland Prohibitionist.*

* * *

The Lord Our Keeper

A man who was a confirmed and hopeless drunkard, being about to go to the Fishing Banks with a fisherman, proposed, before they started, to "take a drink." "No," said the fisherman; "I don't drink." "Don't you drink anything?" "No; I don't drink anything." "Why not?" "Because I am a Christian." "What!" said the man, "does Christ keep you from drinking?" "Yes," answered the fisherman, "Christ keeps me from drinking." The poor inebriate was struck by the reply. He thought, "There is help that I didn't think of." He went home, and knelt down and said, "O Lord Jesus, keep me from drinking." His appetite for liquor suddenly left him. He was delivered.—*The Monthly Visitor.*

A Breaker of Hearts

In one of our cities not long ago a mother asked her pastor to come to see her. When he reached the home he found the mother with her children waiting for him. She was the wife of a man who was to be executed the following day for murder. And she said, "I am wondering if you would intercede and get my husband's body that we might bring him home, and have a little service here. And would you mind conducting that service for me?" The preacher did so. The next morning at the mother's request he went to her home and awaited the dread hour with them. Finally the hands on the clock pointed to noon, and there was just a sob. It was only a little while until a plain black wagon came down the street. It backed up to the front door, and the officers came in carrying a plain unpainted box. They placed it upon two chairs and hurried away. The preacher unfastened the lid and lifted it. The boy came and looked into the casket, then the mother came and stood there with her little ones. And as she stood and stroked the father's brow, she said to the preacher, "Father was such a good man when he didn't drink."—*Sunday School Times.*

* * *

Why He Differed with the Minister

At a church meeting a discussion on temperance was taking place, and an influential clergyman arose and made a vehement argument in favor of wine. When he had resumed his seat, a layman arose, and said: "Mr. Moderator, it is not my purpose to answer the learned argument you have listened to. My arguments are more humble. I knew a father who at great inconvenience educated his son at college. The son was dissipated, but reformed and remained steady for several years. One day he was invited to dine with a neighboring clergyman. He was offered wine, but refused until he was ridiculed. That he could not stand, so he drank, and has long since found a drunkard's grave. I am that father, and it was at the table of the clergyman who has just taken his seat that my son took the fatal glass of wine."—*The Northern Messenger.*

He Stood the Test

A young man from Virginia was transferred, apparently for no reason, to the New York office of his firm. He and his wife took rooms in Brooklyn, and the first Sunday went to a Baptist church there, remaining for Sunday school. A few weeks later, the wife told her teacher she was afraid her husband would not be able to keep his position, that the salesmen had to take their customers out for meals, and were not only *supposed* to buy liquor for them, but the heads of the firm *insisted* upon it, which he had flatly refused to do, saying that he didn't drink himself and would not give it to others. The salesman told him he would not last long if he took that stand. The teacher said how glad the woman should be to have a husband like that, and to give him every encouragement. One Sunday later, the wife told the teacher that her husband was to attend a conference the next day and they knew it meant only one thing—dismissal. Monday evening the wife telephoned her teacher, and she was greatly excited, for her husband had been given a big promotion, and they were to go back to Virginia. It seems that the firm, sensing ability and character, had sent him to New York, deliberately to test him, for this position called for a strong character and one who could withstand temptation, and he had stood the test. Of course the salesmen did not know it, but the heads of the firm did.—*Sunday School Times*.

* * *

The Better Soldier

"The soldier who abstains altogether is the best man. He can accomplish more, can march better, and is a better soldier than the man who drinks even moderately. Mentally and physically he is better. Brandy is the worst poison of all. Next to it comes beer. Each limits the capacity and lowers the mind, body, and soul. Strong drink tires and only increases thirst."—Count von Haeseler, one time commander of the German Sixteenth Army Corps.

"Alcohol should be regarded as a fifth column," says Dr. Chavasse, Bishop of Rochester, "the enemy within our gates, sabotaging armament output and sapping morale."—*Sunday School Times*.

* * *

Uncle Sam Ought to Know

Jim—"Too bad, ain't it, that Repeal ain't balanced the budget, nor reduced taxes, nor pushed off the bootlegger, nor chased off unemployment, nor brought true temperance, nor nothin'?"

Joe—"Yes, but Uncle Sam orter ha' known by observation that nobuddy ain't never pulled theirself outa trouble with a corkscrew!"—*Evangelistic Echoes*.

* * *

The Stealth of Sin

A remarkable story was recently told in the daily press. An oyster fisherman, on opening the shell of an oyster, discovered within a fish, three and a half inches long, alive and weakly struggling. The oyster, however, was not to be found. The fisherman was quite convinced that the fish had entered the open shell, and had been trapped by its closing. Once inside, however, it proceeded to devour the oyster, but being unable to open the shell, would have died in it.

Certain forms of sin enter the life through the door of a careless will. Once thus inside, their eviction is most difficult, and they speedily make themselves master of the premises, eventually destroying the whole life. Such also is the liquor traffic rapidly becoming in the United States. Permitted to enter through the door of repeal, it is gaining wider and wider control in individual lives. Permitted to remain, the results are certain in the lowering of moral ideals, the introduction of even more criminal savagery than has yet been seen in the "public enemies" of the state, and the destruction of multitudes of lives.—*Alliance Weekly*.

* * *

Clothing Someone's Daughter

"Papa, will you please give me a half crown for my new hat?" asked a schoolgirl of her father one morning. "No,

May; I can't spare the money." The refusal came from the parent in a curt, indifferent tone. The disappointed girl went to school. The Father started for his place of business. On his way he met a friend, and invited him into a tavern for a drink. And the man who could not spare his daughter half a crown for a hat laid that sum on the counter, which just paid for the drinks. Just then the saloonkeeper's daughter entered, and said, "Papa, I want half a crown for my new hat." "All right," said the dealer, and, taking up the coin from the counter, handed it to the girl, who departed smiling. May's father was dazed, walked out alone, and said to himself, "To think I should have brought my money here for the rum seller's daughter to buy a hat with, after refusing it to my own daughter! I'll never drink another drop!"—*The King's Business.*

* * *

When Applied to Eggs

Clarence Darrow and Clarence True Wilson were debating. Said Darrow, "I bought some grape juice and put it away for a month and God turned it into wine." Wilson replied, "How about eggs? Nature in time will do the same thing to them. But I don't insist on eating them addled because it was nature that fixed them that way; and I don't argue my right to put them on the market." Darrow had no answer. — *The King's Business.*

* * *

Condemnation on the Face

An officer wearing the insignia of a colonel's rank called to see President Lincoln. Lincoln listened with sympathy to the man, for he knew that he had a record for gallantry, but he also knew that the lines on the officer's face told their own story of long and unrestrained indulgence. He rose up, and, as was his habit when deeply moved, he grasped the officer's hand in both of his own and said, "Colonel, I know your story, but you carry your condemnation in your face." The President afterward said. *"I dared not restore this man to his rank and give him charge of one thousand men, when he puts an enemy into his mouth to steal away his brains."—Christian Herald.*

* * *

When Business, Not Conscience, Voted

Did you ever sit at a table with strangers and overhear their conversation? These two women gave the liquor trade all that was coming to it. The younger one remarked that she couldn't understand the actions of her sister Helen's husband, John. As we remember, her exact words were: "'You know . . . it seems to me that he makes more 'spiritual' talks than anybody in the church, except the preacher." Then she told about an auto accident she and her sister's husband John had experienced a few days before when a drunken driver had smashed into them. She said: "I couldn't help tell my 'spiritual' brother-in-law that that is what he voted for when he voted—for the re-legalization of the traffic—to help his business."—*National Voice.*

* * *

The Greater Weapon

A company of people stood looking at an immense brass-mouthed gun. A gentleman said, "It is perfect and beautiful; but was there ever such a whole sure weapon of death?" "Yes, a distillery," said a lady aloud; and no one said a word more; they knew that every barrel of liquor scatters broadcast woe and want, shame and sorrow, disease and death.—*New Illustrator.*

* * *

A Squadron Leader Speaks Up

A "squadron leader" in the British Air Force, engaged daily in long distance reconnaissance flights and moral conflict with enemy 'planes, has borne the following striking testimony to the value of temperance: "I am not an abstainer," he said, "but in common with others on this job I must be a T. T. (total abstainer) if I am to be and do my best. The smallest quantity of alcohol is sufficient to affect adversely the powers of the eye, brain and hand that must be at their highest state of efficiency if we are to cope confidently and successfully with the enemy with whom, at any moment, we may be engaged in a life or death struggle thousands of feet in the air. What applies to alcoholic liquor applies also, in measure, to the use of tobacco and many of our men have given up smoking "for the duration."—From the *London Daily Mail* of January 21, 1940.

* * *

Cooked Brains

Ironical indeed was the appearance of a huge billboard recently displayed in the business district of Los Angeles, Calif. A huge portrait of a shrewd businessman appeared beside a slogan that, interpreted in one way, implied that real brains required a certain brand of whiskies. Behind the top portion of the head, electric lights flashed on and off at intervals, illuminating the area where the brain would be. The effect of the heat from the lights, however, gradually baked the paint on the forehead of the man in the picture. By daylight there could be seen a sharp alteration in the appearance of the forehead that had been "baked" by the repeated heat to which it had been exposed. The brain had been *cooked.* What a tragic symbol of what happens to the brain of many a man who yields to liquor propaganda!—*The King's Business.*

* * *

I Am Dry, Bone-Dry

Because I have known unborn babies to be cursed through booze; little children to starve because of booze; young people to be stunted for life through booze; gifted women to become imbecile through booze; leaders in industry to become beggars in the street because of booze; wedding rings to be sold for booze; every article of furniture to be pawned for booze; fortunes to be squandered for booze; girls to become prostitutes through booze; boys to become criminals through booze; women to be hanged because of booze; men to go to the electric chair because of booze; because of all the foregoing I am bone-dry.

Because I have never known booze to contribute to the happiness of a single child, or to the mental ability of a single young person, or to the moral uplift of a single middle-aged person, or to the comfort and blessedness of a single old person, I am bone-dry.

Why shouldn't I be bone-dry? — Guy Edward Mark.

* * *

What Criminals Say

Among many persons of some general intelligence, a notion prevails that fermented liquors rarely excite to crime. Such is not the judgment of those practically conversant with our criminal courts; such is far from the testimony of criminals themselves.—Cora Frances Stoddard.

* * *

What Is Intoxicating?

Dr. George O. Higley, Professor of Chemistry, Ohio Wesleyan University, says that drinking 3 per cent beer by volume, often results in hilarity, followed by surly behavior, with a loss of self-control, and often self-respect, the drinker's actions becoming careless and even immoral; that a larger dose of the same liquor might cause quarrelsomeness; fear, jealousy, and hatred might be aroused, without cause, so that crimes are committed; and that the subject showing any of these departures from normal condition is "intoxicated" in the proper meaning of the term, even though he does not stagger and is not "drunk" in the popular meaning of that term. It was, therefore, Dr. Higley's opinion that "a court may very properly hold as intoxicating not only whiskey, brandy, and gin, but also beer, even if it contains alcohol to the amount of only 3 per cent by volume."—*Sunday School Times.*

* * *

Gas and Booze Don't Mix

Five gallons of gas and a pint of gin—
And all they found was a mess of tin.

Might As Well Have What Was Left

When she married a fine young man and had a beautiful home, the young wife said, "This is heavenly." But the young man began to drink, and she suffered untold abuses and privations. A few years later he, her husband, was brought home a corpse, killed in a drunken brawl. After the funeral the saloonkeeper sent her notice that her home and all she had was his in settlement of her husband's drink bill. As she tried to break her last crust of bread into a saucer for her two children, she broke down and cried, the tears falling into the saucer. She poured these tears into a bottle and sent it to the seller of booze with a note which said, "These tears represent my love, my home, my husband, my hopes, my all. Take them, too. It is all I've got."—Selected.

* * *

Conviction Needed

A brewer was addressing a farmer's convention, laying stress upon how much grain the brewer's and distillers bought from the farmers. At the height of his flight of oratory he cried: "What would you farmers do with your surplus corn if we did not buy it?" A great hush came over the gathering; there seemed to be no answer to that startling question. But a little woman arose in the back of the hall and suggested.: "Well, we might make it up into cornstarch to stiffen the men's backbones."—*Otterbein Teacher.*

* * *

Do You Want a "Following"?

In the early career of Miss Francis E. Willard, when the W.C.T.U. was yet in its infancy, the question came up as to whether the name "Christian" should be a part of the title of the organization. Some thought that by omitting the word "Christian" the organization would command a larger following. This, no doubt, was all true enough. Miss Willard was then at the beginning of her career. She took the floor and said, "If I understand correctly the purpose of this organization, is not to get a following, but to set up a standard." Her argument won.

The Christian is to set a standard and present God's Truth, and not worry about a following.—Victory Magazine.

* * *

Why He Lived Through It

A bishop, while laboring in the capital of Argentine, was suddenly stricken with appendicitis. One of the best surgeons in the southern hemisphere was called. After a careful diagnosis, he said, "Your only hope is a surgical operation; but a man of your age ordinarily has only one chance in a hundred for recovery. Have you ever used alcoholic liquors? Have you ever used tobacco in any form?" The bishop replied that he had never used either. The operation was a success. The blood of the patient was so pure that the wound healed like the flesh of a child. Later the surgeon said to the bishop, "You are a walking temperance lesson."—*From Teachers Quarterly.*

* * *

A Burglar Married a Drinking Woman

A burglar married an alcoholic woman. In the first generation, their children included one murderer, one burglar, one sneak thief, one common drunkard and four abandoned women; in the second generation, two murderers, four burglars, six sneak thieves, two drunkards, and six abandoned women; in the third generation, five drunkards, six burglars, ten sneak thieves, eleven idiots, and twelve women of bad character; 74 defective descendants in all.—*Sunday School Times.*

* * *

A Surgeon's Success

At a banquet in New York, during the visit of Dr. Lorenz, the great Austrian surgeon, he was reported by the newspapers to have said: "I cannot say that I am a temperance agitator, but I am a surgeon. My success depends upon my brain being clear, my muscles firm, and my nerves steady. No one can take alcoholic liquors without blunting these physical powers, which I must keep always on edge. As a surgeon, I must not drink."—*The Lighted Pathway.*

Moderate Drinking

"The trouble with moderate drinking, so the scientists tell us, is that most of us cannot constrain our drinking habits," says John Nuveen, Jr., in a most helpful and readable pamphlet, "John Barleycorn, Esquire," published by The American Business Men's Research Foundation, Chicago. "The difficulty is that alcohol gradually weakens the brain tissues which exercise control. The situation is apparently not unlike our experience with the automobile. If, in violation of the advice of automotive engineers, we race up to every stop light and jam on the brokes, we eventually wear them down to the point where they do not hold, and we start slipping beyond the lights. Similarly our brain controls are apt to lose their effectiveness if called upon too frequently to resist demands for increased consumption which are characteristic of habit-forming drugs."—*Sunday School Times.*

* * *

What He Had Tried

Judge Ben B. Lindsey was lunching one day — it was a very hot day — when a politician paused beside his table. "Judge," said he, "I see you are drinking coffee. That is a heating drink. In this weather you want to drink iced drinks, sharp, iced drinks. Did you ever try gin and ginger ale?" "No," said the judge, smiling, "but I have tried several fellows who have."—*Classmate.*

* * *

Not Mere Patching

A certain preacher was pressing home the question of the Lord at Bethesda, "Wilt thou be made whole?" Suddenly he leaned forward and said, "Remember, men, it's not patched up, but made whole." "That's it, that's just it, and all of it," responded a man, who rose and said, "I patched for years, but the patches fell off or made bigger holes. I had become a hard drinker. I lost my position. I sobered up and got another position, failed again and again. Still I patched, and still I fell. At last my wife and children went away to her parents. One wet, cold, windy night, as I sat half asleep in the doorway of an empty house, a Bible woman asked me to come to a mission. There the Lord Jesus found me. He didn't patch; He just made me whole. And now we are all together and happy again."—*Milk of the Word.*

* * *

Farragut's Choice

In giving an account of his early life, Admiral Farragut said: "My father went down in behalf of the United States Government, to put an end to Aaron Burr's rebellion. I was a cabin boy, and went along with him. . . . I knew all the wickedness there was at that time abroad. One day my father cleared everybody out of the cabin except myself, and locked the door. He said, 'David, what are you going to do? What are you going to be?' 'Well, Father,' I said, 'I am going to follow the sea.' 'Follow the sea, and be a poor, miserable, drunken sailor . . . ?' 'Oh, no, Father, I will not be that; I will tread the quarter-deck and command, as you do.' 'No, David,' my father said, 'a person who has your principles and your bad habits will never tread the quarter-deck or command.' My father went out and shut the door after him, and I said then: 'I will change; I will never swear again; I will never drink again; I will never gamble again'; and, gentlemen, by the help of God, I have kept those three vows to this time. I, soon after that, became a Christion, and that decided my future for time and for eternity."—*Teacher.*

* * *

Poison!

Dr. De Lancy Carter says:"Beer contains alcohol to the extent of from 3 to 5 percent... Therefore, in small or large amounts, bear . . . contains alcohol.

"Alcohol is a narcotic, a poison, and an abnormal drug, the quantity matters not; the gradual accumulation of this poison has been found to be destructive to man, inasmuch as it destroys that moral, mental, and physical standard so necessary to the good of mankind."—*Union Signal.*

* * *

Just Less Ashamed

The great Canadian physician, Sir William Osler, was lecturing one day on alcohol. "Is it true," asked a student, "that alcohol makes people able to do things better?" "No," replied Sir William, "*it just makes them less ashamed of doing them badly.*"— *From Moody Monthly.*

* * *

What Each Got Out of It

From a bushel of corn the distiller got four gallons of whiskey, which retailed at	$16.80
The farmer got	.25
The U. S. Government got	4.40
The railroad got	1.00
The manufacturer got	4.00
The drayman got	.15
The retailer got	7.00
The consumer got	Drunk
The wife got	Hunger
The children got	Rags
The politician got	Office

—*The Southern Farmer*

* * *

His Business Wouldn't Permit

A man in a covered wagon, driving through a Western town, stopped and hailed a man on the street. "Hey, any saloons in this town?" he asked. "Yes, four," was the answer. "Giddap," said the stranger, moving on. "I can't locate here; I've got three boys in this wagon." "Stop a minute," yelled the stranger, "what's your business?" "My business is to save these boys," came back the answer, as he disappeared round a bend in the road.—*Kansas City Star.*

* * *

Burbank on Wine

A visitor, being shown a new grape by Burbank, asked if he had ever improved the wine grape, to which Burbank replied: "This is not a wine grape. The continued use of wine destroys the finer qualities of both mind and body. Tell the children that I have never produced a superior wine grape and that if I ever do produce one, it shall be at once destroyed. No wine plant will ever be sent into the world from my plant school."—Luther Burbank on Temperance, *Journal of Character training.*

* * *

Starvation of the Brain

Dr. T. D. Crothers, in *American Medicine,* N. Y., says: "Science has proved beyond question that the action of alcohol is an anesthetic and depressant, and its continuous use is followed by sensory and motor impairments, and also poisoning and starvation of the brain and nervous system, hence sanity and responsibility are not possible. . .The fact of excessive use of alcohol should be accepted as evidence of mental impairment and inability to control acts and conduct."—*Sunday School Times.*

* * *

The Dangers of "Moderation"

The moderate use of fermented drinks carries with it the danger of immoderate use. The light exhilaration of the brain produced by alcohol is a pleasant sensation which, once experienced, leads to a desire for its repetition. Precisely there lies the danger, for this light mental exaltation, not very dangerous in itself, is after all the first stage of drunkenness, and that stage overstepped, the man drawn on by an unobserved decline, passes quickly from occasional intoxication to habitual drunkenness.—Dr. Bergeron, Member of the French Academy of Medicine.

* * *

A Physician Speaks Out

And again, Dr. J. H. Kellogg, of the famous Battle Creek Sanitarium, and member of the Michigan State Board of Health, says emphatically:

"Alcohol never, under any condition, increases the vital energy of the body, but on the contrary, decreases it in a marked and uniform manner through its poisonous influence upon the living cells.

"Alcohol is never a tonic or a stimulant. It is always a narcotic interfering with bodily functions and lessening the nerve tonic and vital energy.

"Alcohol diminishes, never increases the energy of the heart and hence is detrimental rather than beneficial in cases of shock, collapse, fainting, etc.

"Alcohol increases liability to infectious diseases and prevents the development of immunity.

"Alcohol does not aid digestion, but actually hinders it."—*Gospel Herald.*

* * *

Guilty As Charged

Why has there been persistent throughout the centuries this long opposition to alcohol as a beverage? Because there is something in beverage alcohol which is inimical to human welfare — to high civilization.

It is a dehydrating, protoplasmic poison, a habitforming narcotic drug, a noxious commodity. It develops a consuming thirst, which allures and enslaves, and at length bestializes and disintegrates.

Because the liquor business is nefarious and devastating it has been subject to regulation by civilized nations for thousands of years, even as far back as the code of Hammurabi, king of Babylon and law-giver, 2300 years before Christ.

The liquor traffic is utterly lawless, mendacious, sinister and repugnant. The Eighteenth Ammendment is repealed, but nature never repeals. Its implacable penalties are unrelenting and pitiless, no pardons, no reprieves; it is inescapable. Like the avaricious Shylock it claims "the pound of flesh," equally exacting. It is " denominated in the bond."—Bishop Charles Locke.

* * *

Hell Let Loose

Last summer in A—, I saw the name Helfenstein over a saloon. A man was walking along the street, and when he saw the name, being uneducated he spelled out the strange word as follows: H-e-l—hell; f-e-n-s-t—fenced; e-i-n—in; hell fenced in. "Well, well," said he, "that's a good name for a saloon." The story is true, but the name for the saloon is not hell-fenced-in, but, rather, hell-let-loose. If the saloon was confined to its own four walls we might not object so strenuously; but it lets hell loose on our streets and in our homes.—*Sunday School Times.*

* * *

Night's Driving Casualties

We are killing now on our highways and streets about one hundred persons a day, and injuring one hundred every hour. In proportion to traffic volume the period from midnight to 6 a.m. is the most dangerous. In this period occurred 17.3 per cent of all the accidents, although only 5.1 per cent of the day's traffic was using the streets. There is only one thing which explains the high percentage of accidents from midnight to 6 a.m., and that is Drink.—Dr. Clarence E. Macartney.

* * *

How the Brewer Puts It Over

Let me call attention to another distressing fact in connection with the war. Fine, upstanding, moral and Christian boys were betrayed by the authorities while in uniform. Here is a statement made by the brewers themselves, "One of the finest things that could have happened to the brewing industry was the insistence for high-ranking army officers to make beer available at army camps. Here is a chance for the brewers to cultivate a taste for beer in millions of young men who will eventually constitute the largest beer consuming section of our population."—*Sunday School Times.*

* * *

Tragic Evidence

The body of a young suicide was discovered in Louisville, and in one of the pockets was found this note: "I have done this myself. Don't tell anyone. It is all through drink." The printing of this letter in the public press drew two hundred and forty-six letters from two hundred and forty-six families, each of whom had a prodigal son who, it was feared, might be the suicide.—*The Evangelical Christian.*

* * *

Is This a Change of Heart?

A daily newspaper carried an ad which on first glance was quite astounding. A large space — a third of the page — was taken by a liquor manufacturer. And here was the message of the ad in large type: "We who make whiskey say: 'Drinking and driving do not mix.'"

This is exactly true, but how dare the industry admit such a thing? Why not make some of the claims of their cigarette chums, "Whiskey will improve your driving." "Not a wreck in a tankful." "For smooth roads and no stop lights, take three drinks of whiskey before starting." The possibilities are alluring!

Their difficulty is that the particular type of poison in which they deal is instantaneous in action. The liquor business runs almost without restraint today and it doesn't want to arouse the public conscience. So the manufacturers frankly declare in their ad, "It is very much to our self-interest to see that the privilege of drinking is not abused."

The ad closes with this exhortation, "Think before you drink! Don't drink before you drive!" But if they really think, they will never drink. Your only chance to exist as an industry is in building appetites which rob men of their abilities, including the ability to think. "Don't drink before you drive," say you. No, nor after!

However, as an industry you should recognize that another potential threat is the drunken pedestrian. We saw one topple over on the street car tracks at seven a.m. yesterday. If going without whiskey is good for the driver, it is also good for the walker. Go on with your reform, Mr. Whiskey Manufacturer, until you can get every person who drives and every one who walks to give up drinking and you will earn the thanks of many children who cannot eat because father drinks.

We are afraid, however, that this ad does not indicate a change of heart.—Courtesy *Moody Monthly.*

* * *

A Former Governor's Views on Liquor

"I am not a fanatic on the liquor question, but I continue to regard liquor as Public Enemy No. 1," declared Gov. Clyde R. Hoey, in his inaugural address as Governor of North Carolina.

"I have not changed either my opinion or position on this question," he said, "and I do not believe any solution has been found for this vexing problem. Personally, I cannot subscribe to the doctrine that the way to advance the cause of temperance and decrease drinking it to provide all the liquor you want and make it easily obtainable and readily accessible. You will never build a great state or a great country upon profits derived from the sale of liquor."

* * *

A Sermon in Rhyme

Someone in France received from the United States a poem, and sent it to the editor of the *British Weekly.* Here it is:

One evening in October
When I was far from sober,
And dragging home a load with manly pride,
My poor feet began to stutter,
So I lay down in the gutter,
And a pig came by and parked right by my side.

Then I warbled: "It's fair weather
When good fellows get together."
When a lady passing by was heard to say:
"You can tell a man who boozes
By the company he chooses."
Then the pig got up and slowly walked away!

—*Sunday School Times.*

Twenty-Five Minutes

Life insurance companies are not governed by sentiment. They are coldly calculating.

The insurance business with them is a business and nothing more. Expectancy of life is the center of their interest, and they have reduced their calculations on expectancy to an exact science.

They have made this amazing discovery — that every drink of liquor a man or woman takes reduces his expectancy of life by twenty-five minutes.

That is the result of a survey made by Dr. Arthur Hunter, actuary of the New York Life Insurance Co., after studying the records of sixty life insurance companies involving over two million persons.—*National Voice.*

* * *

Yes, It Warms One!

A patient was arguing with his doctor on the necessity of taking a stimulant. "But, Doctor, I must have some stimulant; I am cold, and it warms me." "Precisely," came the reply. "See here. this stick is cold," taking a stick of wood from the box beside the fire. "Now it is warm, but is the stick benefited?" The man watched the wood first send out little puffs of smoke and then burst into flame, and replied, "Of course not; it's burning." And so are you when you warm yourself with alcohol; you are literally burning up the delicate tissues of your stomach and brain.—*Sunday School Times.*

* * *

Why Lincoln Refused to Smoke or Drink

One day Abraham Lincoln was riding in a stage coach, as they rode in those days, in company with a Kentucky colonel. After riding a number of miles together the colonel took a bottle of whiskey out of his pocket and said, "Mr. Lincoln, won't you take a drink with me?"

"No, Colonel, thank you," replied Mr. Lincoln, "I never drink whiskey."

They rode along together for a number of miles more, visiting very pleasantly, when the gentleman from Kentucky reached into his pocket and brought out some cigars, saying, "Now, Mr. Lincoln, if you won't take a drink with me, won't you take a smoke with me? For here are some of Kentucky's finest cigars."

"Now, Colonel," said Mr. Lincoln. "you are such a fine, agreeable man to travel with maybe I ought to take a smoke with you. But before I do so. let me tell you a story, an experience I had when a boy."

"My mother called me to her bed one day, when I was about nine years old. She was sick — very sick — and she said to me, 'Abey, the doctor tells me that I am not going to get well. I want you to promise me before I go that you will never use whiskey nor tobacco as long as you live.' And I promised my mother I never would. And up to this hour, Colonel, I have kept that promise. Now would you advise me to break that promise to my angel mother and take a smoke with you?"

The Colonel put his hand on Mr. Lincoln's shoulder and said with a voice trembling with emotion: "No, Mr. Lincoln, I wouldn't have you do it for the world. It was one of the best promises you ever made. I would give a thousand dollars today if I had made my mother a promise like that and had kept it as you have done."

There is scarcely a man or woman in this country today but what believes that Abraham Lincoln's keeping his promise to his mother helped to make him the great and good and loved man that he was.—*The Dry Legion.*

* * *

The Beer Bottle Had to Go

Ethel Hubler tells about a family—father, mother, son Tommy—being invited to the home of a relative for dinner. On the dining table was a bottle of beer, placed there by the grandfather who thought he had to have "something to pep him up a little." As Tommy, nine years old, was known to regularly ask the blessing at meals, the host called upon him to voice their thanks.

Tommy was on the spot. He had never "said grace" over a beer bottle before, and he was troubled. All bowed their heads, including Tommy, but his lips uttered not a sound. Presently he raised his head, looked earnestly to his mother, and with tears in his eyes, said: "Mom, I just can't ask God to bless us with that beer bottle sittin' there."

One would have thought granddad was only in his teens from the way he quickly jumped up, grabbed the beer bottle, and made for the back door. When he returned Tommy asked the blessing, and the meal was eaten in a regular camp meeting way. "A little child shall lead."—*Cumberland Presbyterian.*

* * *

Can You Save Your Captain?

On a stormy night a middle-aged man staggered into the Bowery Mission. He was intoxicated, his face unwashed and unshaven, and his clothes soiled and torn. He sank into a seat, and, gazing around, seemed to wonder what kind of a place he had come into. "Rescue the perishing" and other Gospel hymns were sung and seemed to interest him, and to recall some memory of his youth long since forgotten. As the leader of the meeting told the simple story of the Gospel, and how the Lord had come to seek and to save lost sinners, the man listened eagerly.

The leader in his younger days had been a soldier and had seen hard and active service. In the course of his remarks he mentioned several incidents which had occurred in his experience during the war, and he gave the name of the company in which he served. At the close of the meeting the man eagerly staggered up to the leader and in a broken voice said to him:

"When were you in that company you spoke of?"

"Why, all through the war," said the leader.

"Do you remember the battle of———?"

"Perfectly."

"Do you remember the name of the captain of your company at that time?"

"Yes, his name was—— ——."

"You are right! I am that man. I was your captain. Look at me today, and see what a wreck I am. Can you save your old captain? I have lost everything I had in the world through drink, and I don't know where to go."

He was saved that night, and was soon helped by some of his former friends to get back his old position. He often told the story of how a soldier saved his captain, and how much he loved the words of "Rescue the perishing."—*Gospel Herald.*

* * *

Our Major Problem

There is much that might be said about the social havoc that is being wrought by alcohol. It is bad enough that a man pays 25 cents for a drink, but even worse, that he gives 25 minutes of his life for each indulgence. But the liquor industry covers that up under a mask of festivity, making booze look like a desirable adjunct to congenial and successful living. It does not picture the bleary eye and the babbling tongue of the drinker, nor does it present the broken-hearted mother, the devastated home, the ragged children, and the empty cupboard. Liquor is one of America's major problems. — Courtesy *Moody Monthly.*

* * *

An exact copy of the business card of J. J. McMurtrey, Dealer in Whiskies, Wines, Beer and Cigars, "The Temple Bar Saloon," Flagstaff, Arizona:

Friends and Neighbors: I am grateful for past favors and having supplied my store with a fine line of choice wines and liquors, allow me to inform you that I shall continue to make drunkards, paupers, and beggars, for the sober, industrious, respectable part of the community to support. My whiskies will excite riot, robbery, and bloodshed.

They will diminish your comforts, increase your expenses, and shorten life. I shall confidently recommend them as sure to multiply fatal accidents, and incurable diseases. They will deprive some of life, others of reason, some of character, and all of peace. They will make fathers fiends, mothers widows, children orphans, and all poor. I will train your sons in infidelity, dissipation, ignorance, lewdness and every other vice. I will corrupt the ministers of religion, obstruct the Gospel, defile the church, and cause as much temporal and eternal death as I can. I will thus "accommodate the public," it may be at the loss of my never-dying soul, but I have a family to support—the business pays, and the public encourage it.

I have paid my license and the traffic is lawful, and if I don't sell it somebody else will. I know the Bible says, "Thou shalt not kill," "No drunkard shall enter the kingdom of heaven," and I do not expect the drunkard-maker to fare any better, but I want an easy living and I have resolved to gather the wages of iniquity and fatten on the ruin of my kind. I shall therefore carry on my business with energy and do my best to diminish the wealth of the nation and endanger the safety of the State. As my business flourishes in proportion to your sensuality and ignorance, I will do my best to prevent moral purity and intellectual growth.

Should you doubt my ability, I refer you to the pawnshops, the poor house, the police court, the hospital, the penitentiary, and the gallows, where you will find many of my best customers have gone. A sight of them will convince you that I do what I say. Allow me to inform you that you are fools, and I am an honest saloonkeeper.—J. J. McMurtrey.

* * *

When Savages Are Saved

Dr. J. G. Paton said that the savage inhabitants of the New Hebrides cultivate a plant from which is made intoxicating drinks. But as soon as they accept Christianity they dig *up the roots*, bring them together, and burn them in a great fire. They all become, as a matter of course, total abstainers.—*Sunday School Chronicle.*

Clean Blood

Doctor Mayo, late chief of staff of Mayo clinic, one of the best and most widely known and highly respected physicians in the world, stood like a rock for the best things in life, "he dared to be different."

Here follows some of Dr. Mayo's sayings: "The majority of doctors and pharmacologists agree that alcohol is not a stimulant but a habit-forming narcotic poison in the same class with morphine, codeine, heroin, etc. Three drinkers out of ten become addicts. We doctors," he said, "must begin to promote temperance."

Dr. Mayo once asked a very prominent brewer why brewers did not find one-half per cent alcohol or "near beer" profitable. The brewer answered, "There is not enough alcohol in 'near beer' to produce the thirst that would lead people to drink more. It takes two per cent to three per cent alcoholic content to do that." Alcohol in the blood slows down the white corpuscles which are the body "policemen," making a person more susceptible to disease.

Good clean, clear, healthy blood safeguards humanity in a good many ways. Good clean healthy blood (no alcohol) would mean a lot less accidents, less money wasted. Any item which drains money from a community drains everyone's pocketbook.—Mary Kimberly in *The United Evangelical.*

* * *

The One He Wanted

A businessman once wanted somebody to fill a most important position, one of great responsibility, so he advertised and got a large number of applications. From these he picked twenty men, and asked them to be at a certain place on a certain day. On that day he went and found the twenty men there. "Well, men," he said, "before we get on with the business, I think we may as well have a little drink. Come on," and he set off toward a licensed hotel near by. The men quickly followed, all except one who lagged behind. "Hi, hurry up! Aren't you coming for a drink?" the employer shouted. "No thanks," said the man, "I'm a total abstainer." "Good for you," said the employer, "you're the man I want for this job!" and he turned and left the other men all tremendously surprised and disappointed.—*Gospel Herald.*

* * *

When a Fortune Is Bad News

In New York City there is an institution known as "The Stock Market." It is famous as a place where "lambs" are attracted for the "shearing." As I write I have been trying to get a job for a man I know. His father at one time was very well-to-do and had retired with a competency and was a good friend of mine. Then in some way this friend got into Wall Street. One day he said to me, "Bill, do you have any Anaconda Copper Stock?" "No," I replied. "Why?" "Well," he said, "I've just cleaned up some $250,000 in it." I said to my brother later. "Ellis, I have some bad news concerning our friend Charlie Brown." "What is it?" "He has just cleaned up a quarter of a million in the stock market." "That doesn't sound like bad news to me. Why do you think so?" "Ellis, it will be his first drink of whisky." And it was. Some few months later he said to me, "Bill, I am all wiped out. I do not have a dollar to my name." The "lamb shearers" over in New York had done for him what they had done for thousands of others. My whilom rich friend has died, and here I am trying to find a job for his boy.—*Sunday School Times.*

* * *

Standing for a Principle

A small boy went with his father to an evening business men's dinner. The father took him with the apology that he had to do so, because they were together at a hotel and far from home and he had no one with whom to leave him. When all were seated at the table, the waiter began to fill the glasses, and the little boy saw with dismay that the big men about him were accepting the sparkling beverage that fell with a musical tinkle from the crystal pitchers into the dainty glasses. Father was busy talking with his neighbor on the other side. When the waiter got as far as Jack, he smiled down at the boy and bent over to serve him. Gathering up his courage, Jack hastily reversed his glasses, and, with evident fear that if all these fine-looking gentlemen could be persuaded to drink the wicked stuff, of which mother had told him such sad tales, father also might be tempted, he stretched over to his father's plate and put his glasses, too, out of business. This done, he said, in a clear, childish treble, that reached every ear, "Father and I don't drink." A general smile went round. Men remembered little lads in their own homes, whom they hoped to see grow up as true and sturdy as Jack, and one after another they followed Jack's example. No one at that end of the table took liquor. —*United Presbyterian.*

* * *

A Lesson from Luigi

There is a story that Luigi, an Italian nobleman of the Middle Ages, was at forty told by the doctors that he could not possibly live another year.

However, he died at one hundred and four, and a writer in a recent magazine tells how those extra sixty-four years were added to his life: "Not doctors—he had nothing to do with them. Not medicine. Not exercise. Luigi simply stopped eating. He made a careful study of himself to discover just how little food he could eat and still feel well. Out of this study he soon learned the valuable truth that 'most men dig their graves with their teeth.' Most men die because they have so loaded their bodies with excess food that their organs of elimination have broken under the strain. Most men are tired because they are self-poisoned with too much food. All this Luigi discovered and wrote in a book called the 'Temperate Life.'"

* * *

Alcohol is a depressant, habit-forming narcotic drug.

Alcohol is a protoplasmic poison.

Alcohol is drunk to get the drug effect, and whenever it is so taken in whatever amount it exerts to some degree its depressant and toxic effects.

Alcohol causes disease; psychosis, multiple neuritis, gastritis, cirrhosis of the liver.

Alcohol causes death; from acute and chronic poisoning.

Alcohol reduces resistance to infection.

Alcohol diminishes likelihood of recovery from acute infections, such as pneumonia.

Alcohol increases liability to accidents, and delays recovery.—Dr. Haven Emerson, Columbia University.

* * *

Alcohol and Heredity

The tendency to discredit alcohol damage in heredity has been seen in recent literature on alcohol for which reason, the following statement, taken from a book by two leading authorities ("Alcohol Explored," by Haggard and Jellinek; Doubleday, Doran and Company), is of added interest. Although they credit the unfavorable environment produced by the inebriate parent as a greater source of danger than heredity, they nevertheless say: "The fact that a craving for alcohol itself as a substance is not inherited and that use of alcohol in particular as an intoxicant is due to environmental influence, does not, however, exclude the possibility that heredity may play a part in the development of inebriety. This possibility is strongly supported by the fact that some 60 per cent of all inebriates studied have been found to have parents or grandparents who were inebriate."—*Sunday School Times.*

* * *

Liquor Is a Stimulant

It stimulates idleness.

It stimulates profanity.

It stimulates the animal, and strangles the human.

It stimulates the coarse and smothers the fine.

It stimulates insanity.

It stimulates self-destruction.

It stimulates accident.

It stimulates failure.—*Heart and Life.*

His Reason for Prohibition

Some years ago in a village of western New York, on election morning, the recognized village toper went to the polls. He asked for a Prohibition ballot, and a liquor seller got him one, supposing a joke was on hand. Folding it as best he could with trembling hands, the blear-eyed, bloated, ragged, unkempt man went to the ballot box and registered his wish. Then they began to scoff and sneer at the drunkard who had cast his temperance vote. "A pretty temperance voter you are," said one. "Why, if there was a bottle of whisky yonder there at the top of the Liberty Pole and if you could have the whisky by climbing it at the risk of your life, you know you'd climb." And then the drunkard straightened himself and answered, "Know it! Oh, yes, I know it. And I know another thing, gentlemen; if the whisky wasn't there I wouldn't climb." —*Young Canada.*

* * *

"There is no disease in the world for which alcohol is a cure. . . . It does undeniably cause thousands of cases of disease. . . . Its use is ruinous to the kidneys, liver, heart, and smaller blood vessels, and gives rise to that most common fatality, high blood pressure.

"All this has been proven by innumerable tests. Two men may play tennis or chess equally well. Give one of them a single glass of beer and he will be easily defeated by the one who abstains."—Dr. Howard A. Kelly.

* * *

Are We Locking up the Wrong Person?

A story is told of a woman who stood near the magistrate who was hearing a case against her husband. Somehow the pathetic face of the woman touched the judge, and he said to her, "I am sorry, but I must lock up your husband." "Your Honor," she returned, "wouldn't it be better for me and the children if you locked up the saloon and let my husband go to work?"—*Christian Endeavor World.*

The Wife

Once upon a time we thought that any woman who went into a barroom was a good woman to stay away from. But that's old-fashioned now, when women follow their husbands through the swinging doors. Says Martin Nelson, secretary of the Keeley Institute at Dwight, Illinois:

"Repeal returned drinking to the barroom and the wives followed their husbands there. Today public complacency about women drinking at bars is making the problem of the woman inebriate tragically serious."

Mr. Nelson should know: *seventy-four per cent of the patients at Keeley are housewives.*

* * *

Best Wishes to a Newspaper Chain

In a day when the only question of the poorest as well as the richest seems to be one of financial gain, it is refreshing to know a business organization which refuses to barter its conscience.

Having heard that Frank E. Gannett, president of the Gannett Newspapers, had refused to accept liquor advertising, we investigated, and we are glad to give you the story in Mr. Gannett's own words over his own signature:

"It is true that our nineteen newspapers do not accept any advertising for alcoholic beverages, not even beer. Last year we might have added a million dollars to our revenue if we had not had this policy in force. We try to make papers that are fit for the home, and we are sure the great majority of our readers don't want their children reading liquor advertising in their favorite home newspaper."

Thank you, Mr. Gannett. We congratulate you on such costly courage, and we wish you and your papers a deserved prosperity. America needs much at this hour men who live by conviction rather than convenience. — Courtesy *Moody Monthly.*

* * *

A President's Promise

But motor accidents increase, liquor-contributed juvenile delinquency grows, drinking among women and children at the open bar becomes a public scandal, and the number of saloon equivalents, open drinking places in America, reaches the appalling all-time record of nearly five hundred thousand. In spite of the inaugural promise of the President of the United States when he said, "The saloon must not return. By no possibility, at any time or under any conditions, at any place, or under any circumstances, shall that institution, the saloon, or its equivalent be allowed to return to American life," — in spite of these solemn and measured words, "happy" days are here again!—Daniel A. Poling.

* * *

A Siamese Definition

A certain Siamese teacher is remembered by a former missionary chiefly because of his unique definitions of English words. For instance, among his picturesque definitions was this: "Whisky—sin water." That's what whisky really is.—*Sunday School Times.*

* * *

Presumption Not Faith

"I'll loose my camel and commit him to Allah's care," said a man one day to the Prophet, who replied, "Tie up your camel and commit him to God." How many foolishly run into temptation, even though they know alcohol has a fatal attraction for them. The wise man or woman will, by God's help, "tie up" their besetting sin, and commit themselves moment by moment into God's care, to be kept by his grace.—*Christian Herald.*

* * *

A Mother Kneeling in the Snow

The story is told that John G. Woolley was in a saloon drinking when he saw his mother kneeling in the snow just outside the door. He was awfully ashamed of her and slipped out the back door. That day's work against the evil of drink cost his mother her life. The saloon went on with its nefarious business. The son staggered on downward for thirteen awful years of sottishness. But finally the snow-set prayers of his mother won. He was converted and proved to be one of America's bitterest foes to the saloon and most eloquent advocates of temperance and prohibition. It takes not only resolution to restrain, prohibition to prohibit, but God in answer to prayer to make and preserve a sober nation.—*Gospel Herald.*

* * *

Liquor's Dreaded Bedfellow

Has not Professor J. B. S. Haldane of Cambridge University told us that "a man is about five times as likely to get cancer if he drinks beer daily and no milk, as if he drinks milk daily and no beer"? Also that "the death rate in the alcoholic trades from cancer of the mouth, throat, etc., at ages under 65, is double the average." — *Sunday School Times.*

* * *

Alcohol's Color Scheme

"Beverage alcohol," said "the doctor who knew," as quoted in *Grit*, "gives you a red nose, a black eye, a white liver, a yellow streak, a green brain, a dark brown breath, and a blue outlook." A color scheme that wouldn't appeal to a truly artistic soul!—*Christian Union Herald.*

* * *

Why This Town Stays Dry

One town which has been, is, and will be dry, whatever happens to the Eighteenth Amendment, is Harriman, Tenn., with a population of eight thousand. A clause in every deed to land provides that liquor shall not be allowed to be manufactured, sold, or even stored on the property, or the lot will revert to the company which founded the town.—*The Union Signal.*

* * *

Said Sgt. York, "I Used to Drink Liquor"

Sgt. Alvin York said, "I used to drink liquor; drank it for ten years; drank it until I broke the hearts of those who loved me and prayed for me. And then, one night in 1914, I knelt at the altar in a little mountain church in East Tennessee, and confessed and repented of my sins. I arose from that altar a new man in Christ Jesus, and broke with liquor forever!" And he is the soldier who, in World War I, disarmed and brought 153 German prisoners into camp! — *The Chaplain.*

TEMPTATION — TESTING

Could Christ Have Sinned?

Dr. I. M. Haldeman tells of a scene in New York State among the mountains. A bridge had been thrown across a great chasm hundreds of feet deep. One day he heard the first train on the road approaching, and looking out saw two huge locomotives drawn up on the bridge. There was a sharp challenging whistle, then the brakes crashed down, and the two great machines came to a standstill. There they waited for fully half a day right in the center of the bridge, with their great tons of iron quivering and beating and the bridge beneath like a great spider's web supporting them. What did it mean? They were there to demonstrate the strength of the bridge, to show there was no weakness in it; but that it was able to bear up under the greatest test put on it, and so was worthy of the fullest trust on the part of man. "All the weight of temptation was crowded on our Lord Jesus Christ in that hour when the Devil met him on the mount. He was "tempted in all points as we are," from animal appetites and desires, to the highest reaches of ambition for self-gratification and power. He was tempted and tried and tested at every point to prove and demonstrate to angels and to men that he could not say, "Yes" to the temptation; that He could *not* have sinned; that it was no more possible for *Him* to have sinned than it was possible for God to lie. "That we might see Him as the majestic, unbreakable bridge across the deep chasm of sin and death; and so seeing fling ourselves without reserve, and in unhesitating confidence upon Him as the One and all supreme object of our unfaltering faith and profound adoration."—From pamphlet by Haldeman, *Could Our Lord Have Sinned?*

* * *

Always a Way of Escape

There is a place in the Hudson river where, as you sail, you seem to be entirely hemmed in with hills. The boat drives on toward a rocky wall, and it seems as if it must either stop or be dashed to pieces. But just as you come within the shadow of the mountain, an opening is suddenly discovered, and the boat passes out into one of the grandest bays on the river.

So it is with temptation. You are not to seek it, not to enter into it; God promises no way out in such a case. But if it meets you on your Heavenward journey, you are to go straight on though you see no way out. God does not promise "a way of escape" until the temptation actually comes. The way will reveal itself in due time if you only keep on, your way being the way of duty. And remember that as in the river the beautiful bay lies just around the frowning rock, so often your sweetest and best experience in life lies just behind your most threatening temptation.—Selected.

* * *

When Temptation Comes

I was talking with a young man some time ago, who had gotten into sin. He came from a lovely home and had fine training. He began to go out to night clubs, and it upset the whole family in a terrible way. He did not think. I had a talk with that young man about it, and I told him that he could not do that and be a Christian. The young man yielded to the Lord Jesus Christ, and he is all right today. One thing I said to him in our conversation was this: "Young man, when you are tempted to go this way, when you are tempted to go into this place, you simply stop where you are and say, 'Now, Lord Jesus, here I am, You lead me in.' Do you think you would go in very often if you did that?" He said, "No, I do not think I would." Of course he would not! Whenever temptation comes to you, all you need to do is to stop just where you are and say, "Now, Lord Jesus, You lead me in." And the Lord Jesus will turn you around and send you the other way just as fast as you can go. *There is victory in the conquest of self only in Jesus Christ.* Only trust Him!—*Christian Beacon.*

* * *

Don't You Know Where the Snags Are?

A Yankee applied for the vacant position of pilot of a Mississippi steamer. The boat was a New Orleans, and the Yankee said he thought he could give satisfaction, providing they were lookin' for a man about his size and build. The owner looked at the lank form and rugged face of the applicant with some amusement, and then said, "Your size and build will do well enough, but do you know about the river—where the snags are, and so on?" "Well, I'm pretty well acquainted with the river," drawled the Yankee, with eyes fixed on the stick he was whittling, "but when you come in talking' about snags, I don't know exactly where they are." "You don't know where the snags are!" said the captain in a tone of disgust, "then how do you expect to get a position as pilot on this boat?" "Well, sir," said the Yankee, raising a pair of keen eyes from his whittling, and meeting his questioner's gaze with a grin, "I may not know just where the snags are, but you can depend on me knowin' where they ain't, and that's where I calculate to do my sailin'."—*Sunday School Times.*

Tried and True

When a founder has cast his bell he does not at once put it into the steeple, but tries it with the hammer, and beats it on every side, to see if there is a flaw. So when Christ converts a man, He does not at once convey him to heaven, but suffers him to be beaten upon by many temptations and afflictions, and then exalts him to his crown. *As snow is of itself cold, yet warms and refreshes the earth, so afflictions, though in themselves grievous, keep the Christian's soul warm and make it fruitful.—Fellowship News.*

* * *

"Massa, Yo' Property Am in Danger"

A Negro who had accepted the Lord Jesus as his Saviour, and realized the truth, "Ye are not your own, ye are bought with a price" (I Cor. 6:19, 20) used to exclaim in moments of trial or temptation, "Massa, yo' property am in danger." Trusting alone to Him "that is able to keep" (Jude 1:24), he felt secure.—Mason.

* * *

It Never Even Shook

Years ago a terrific storm was sweeping from the Northwest coast. The people of the city said to one another, "The lighthouse has gone down." But three days afterward the keeper of the lighthouse was seen upon the streets of the city and one of his friends said to him, "We heard the lighthouse had gone down in the storm." The old keeper looked on him in amazement and said: "Gone down! It is true the storm was the fiercest I have ever known, but in all the time she never shook." This is also true of our foundation. Storms of temptation and trial may beset us, but the foundation standeth sure.—J. Wilbur Chapman.

Help for the Tempted

Frank W. Boreham passes on a story told by Handley Page, the airman. When Page landed at Kobar, in Arabia, a large rat managed to get into his airplane. When Page was in mid-air he discovered the rat's presence by the sound of gnawing behind him. Alarmed at the thought of the damage which those pitiless teeth might do, the aviator remembered that a rat is unable to survive in high altitudes. He determined to soar, and rose until he found difficulty in breathing. At length he ventured to descend to a lower level and upon landing he discovered that the rat was dead.

There is help for the tempted here. When we feel ourselves endangered by the pests that molest our souls, we need only to rise to a loftier level of Christian attainment.—*The Y. C. Companion.*

* * *

Garden Memories

In a garden Satan conquered, and in a garden he was conquered. Never walk in a garden without thinking of God our Saviour.—Graham Scroggie.

* * *

Not in the Direction of Home

Billy Bray, the Cornish miner and evangelist, says that one day when he was much discouraged, he found himself standing on the brink of a coal pit. Someone seemed to say to him, "Now, Billy, just throw yourself down there, and be rid of all your troubles." But he recognized the source of the temptation, and said, "Oh, no, Satan, you can just throw yourself down there. That is your way home. But I'm going to my Home in a different direction."—*Sunday Companion.*

* * *

How to Answer Satan

A famous preacher tells the story of a schoolboy who was brought to trust the Saviour through that wonderful verse, John 5:24. But when the boy got home, and was sitting on a sofa in a room by himself, Satan began to tempt him to think it was all a mistake, and that Jesus had not really saved him at all. At length the temptation became so fierce that the boy said it seemed as though Satan was actually under the sofa talking to him. For a while the young Christian did not know how to answer Satan; but then he thought of an idea. Opening his pocket Bible, he placed his finger at John 5:24, and reached it under the sofa, and said, *"There you are, Satan, read it for yourself!" The boy said it seemed as if at that moment the devil disappeared.*—Selected.

THANKSGIVING — PRAISE

Be on the Lookout

Be on the lookout for mercies. The more we look for them, the more of them will we see. Blessings brighten when we count them. Out of the determination of the heart the eyes see. If you want to be gloomy, there's gloom enough to keep you glum; if you want to be glad, there's gleam enough to keep you glad. Better lose count in enumerating your blessings than lose your blessings in telling over your troubles. "Be thankful unto Him, and bless His Name."—Maltbie D. Babcock.

* * *

Grace Before Meals

We are indebted to a pastor friend who has uncovered for us certain information concerning soldiers saying grace at meals. Perhaps the reading of this letter from Chaplain (L. Col.) John Williamson will encourage this custom in other organizations. It is a great and proper thing to acknowledge God as the bestower of all gifts.

"It is true that in Company K of the 800th Signal Training Regiment, grace is said before each meal, but it is also true that the 206th Arkansas Regiment, which has been in the Army of the United States for over three years, follows the same custom. I was chaplain of this regiment for more than nine years, and when it became a part of the Army of the United States in January, 1941, I had the extreme satisfaction of inaugurating this custom. Every company mess and the officers' mess had grace said before meals.

"Last November, I met my successor, who became chaplain of the regiment when I was transferred to this station, and he told me that this is still being done. As far as I know, this the only regiment in the United States where grace is said before meals at every mess."—Courtesy *Moody Monthly.*

* * *

Thanksgiving

For the days when nothing happens,
 For the cares that leave no trace,
For the love of little children,
 For each sunny dwelling-place,
For the altars of our fathers,
 And the closets where we pray,
Take, O gracious God and Father,
 Praises this Thanksgiving Day.

For our harvests safe ingathered,
 For our golden store of wheat,
For the bowers and the vinelands,
 For the flowers up-springing sweet,
For our coasts from want protected,
 For each inlet, river, bay,
By the bounty full and flowing,
 Take our praise this joyful day.

For the hours when Heaven is nearest
 And the earth-mood does not cling,
For the very gloom oft broken
 By our looking for the King,
By our thought that He is coming,
 For our courage on the way,
Take, O Friend, unseen, eternal,
 Praises this Thanksgiving Day.

—Margaret E. Sangster.

Why the Minister Was Thankful

A preacher going to a country church one Sunday morning, was overtaken by a deacon who remarked, "What a bitterly cold morning, sir. I am sorry the weather is so wintry." "Oh," replied the minister, "I was just thanking God for keeping His Word." The man stared at him. "What do you mean?" he asked. "Well, over three thousand years ago God promised that cold and heat should not cease, so I am strengthened by this weather to emphasize the sureness of His promises."—*Gospel Gleaners.*

* * *

Mountaintop Praise

When we get beyond the trials of this life we shall be filled more and more with thanksgiving. Ira D. Sankey used to tell a beautiful story. A child was on top of Mount Washington with her father, above the clouds, while a thunderstorm flashed and rumbled below. Where they stood was perfect calm and sunshine, though the eyes found nothing but the blue of heaven and a few rocks to rest upon. "Well, Lucy," said her father, "there is nothing to be seen here, is there?" But the child exclaimed: "Oh, Papa, I see the doxology! All around seems to say:

'Praise God from whom all blessings flow;
Praise Him, all creatures here below;
Praise Him above, ye heavenly host;
Praise Father, Son, and Holy Ghost.' "

—*Sunday School Times.*

* * *

Put on the Garment of Praise

"The only drawbacks to this lovely homestead," said a poetical auctioneer, "are the litter of the rose leaves and the noise of the nightingales." Many of you have no drawbacks worth mentioning but the lack of time to handle all the good things God has given you. Still you fail to sing. Put on the garment of praise and let it cover you from shoulder to ankles. Its graceful folds will hide many a native defect and deformity. A songful soul is Heaven's delight and an earthly joy.—*Gospel Herald.*

* * *

Let's Not Conceal It

A kind uncle who had just returned from Paris brought his little niece a fine French doll. "Did you thank Uncle for the beautiful present?" asked her mother, as the little girl rushed into the house all aglow with enthusiasm over the new toy. "Yes, Mamma, but I didn't tell him so." This is the way with much of our gratitude. If you are thankful to God, tell him so. If you are grateful for the kindness of a friend express it, that the friend and you may be the better for it.—*Record of Christian Work.*

* * *

The Ones Who Never Gave Thanks

An honest farmer was asked to dine with a gentleman, and there asked a blessing at table as he was accustomed to do at home. His host said jeeringly, "That is old-fashioned; it is not customary nowadays for well-educated people to pray at table." The farmer answered that with him it was customary, but that some of his household never prayed over their food. "Ah, then," said the gentleman, "they are sensible and enlightened. Who are they?" The farmer answered, "They are my pigs."—*Christian Herald.*

* * *

First Thanksgiving Proclamation

By George Washington, 1789

WHEREAS it is the duty of all nations to acknowledge the providence of Almighty God, to obey His will, to be grateful for His benefits, and humbly to implore His protection, aid and favors . . .

NOW, THEREFORE, I do recommend and assign Thursday, the 26th day of November next, to be devoted by the people of these States to the service of that great and glorious Being, who is the

Beneficent Author of all the good that was, that is, or that will be; that we may then all unite in rendering unto Him our sincere and humble thanks for His kind care and protection of the people of this country, and for all the great and various favors which He has been pleased to confer upon us.

* * *

After Saving Lives

Years ago, when the steamer *Lady Elgin* was sinking in Lake Michigan, a student in Evanston. Mr. Spencer, with great energy and exposure, saved seventeen lives. Broken in health from this effort, he was asked, when an old man, what returns of gratitude, if any, came. He answered, "Not one."—From accounts seen in the press at different dates.—*Sunday School Times.*

* * *

Thanksgiving Street

One night, at a prayer-and-praise meeting a good brother related a long, complaining strain of experiences about the trials and difficulties which are encountered on the way to Heaven. At the end of his talk, another brother arose and said, "I see that our brother who has just sat down, lives in Grumbling Street. I lived there myself for some time, but I never enjoyed good health. The air there is bad; the houses are bad, the water is bad; the birds never came and sang in the street, and I was gloomy and sad enough. But finally I moved. I moved to Thanksgiving Street, and ever since then I have had good health and so have my family. The air is pure, the water good, the houses are good; the sun shines in all day; the birds are always singing; and I am happy as I can be. Now, I would suggest to our brother, that he, too, move. There are plenty of houses 'to let' in Thanksgiving Street."

Which street are you living on: Grumbling Street, or Thanksgiving Street? Don't forget, there is plenty of room on Thanksgiving Street, and your health would be better, and your heart happier if you would move there.—*Gospel Herald.*

Complaining

Ben had fallen into the habit of grumbling about this and that. He complained about the weather; he found fault with his friends and with the members of his family. He wanted to stop it, but somehow, as soon as anything would not go his way, he found himself grumbling again. Then he came across this verse:

"When thou hast truly thanked thy God
For every blessing sent,
But little time will then remain
For murmur or lament."

"I see now what the trouble has been," he told himself. "I've been grumbling so much that I've almost forgotten to be thankful for the things I have. Every time I find myself starting to complain about something I don't have, I'm going to say 'Thank You' to God for something that He has given me."

Ben found that the idea worked. It was much easier to keep out the grouchy, grumbling thoughts when he filled his mind with thankful ones. There simply was no room for the trouble makers, and after a bit they disappeared.

Ben was surprised, too, to see how many things a plain, everyday boy had for which to be thankful. There are many things like the sunshine, the flowers, his friends, his home, which he had been taking for granted. As he began thanking God for these things, he had a better appreciation of them.

Let's all try his plan, for God is very displeased with a complaining spirit. He says, "Do all things without murmurings (complaining)" (Phil. 2:14). —*Junior Life.*

* * *

"Praise the Lord for He is glorious:
Never shall His promise fail;
God hath made His saints victorious;
Sin and death shall not prevail.

"Praise the God of our salvation!
Hosts on high His power proclaim;
Heaven and earth and all creation
Laud and magnify His name."

—*Gospel Herald.*

The Blessing from "Asking the Blessing"

I went into a restaurant one day and, after bowing my head and giving thanks for the food, a waitress came over to the table and said: "Pardon me, but you must be a Christian. I have looked for three months for a Christian to come in here, because I would like to be saved." I knew of at least fifteen professing Christians who were eating in that restaurant, but apparently not one of them had bowed his head, and I said, "Thank you, Lord." Here was this woman watching for a Christian and wanting to be saved, but seeing no one to help her.—From *A Sure Remedy.* by Dr. Walter L. Wilson.

* * *

Thinking and Thanking

Sir Moses Montefiore, the Hebrew philanthropist, had as the motto of his family, "Think and Thank." In the old Anglo-Saxon language thankfulness means "thinkfulness." Thinking of all God's goodnesses draws forth gratitude. —*The King's Business.*

* * *

Heavenly Father, kind and good,
Now we thank Thee for this food;
For Thy love and tender care,
For Thy blessings that we share.
Now to Thee our voices raise,
In a hymn of grateful praise."
—*Gospel Herald.*

* * *

Everything Not Lost

A man stood in the street and gazed at his bomb-wrecked home. Then he said to his wife: "This morning someone came into our dugout and told me that we had lost everything. It's a lie. Thank God, I've still got health and strength to carry on with my job. I still have you, my dear, and the children. Thank God, you're all safe. Hitler hasn't smashed my faith in the love and wisdom of God, or my faith in the ultimate victory of right. I still have hope for the future. I can still call my soul my own. I am still alive and ready for action again. So I reckon that you and I ought to thank God that we have saved far more than we have lost. Houses and buildings may be wrecked and ruined, but you and I can still hold on to things which can never be shaken or destroyed."—*Church Standard.*

* * *

His Last Words

Some years ago, in Germany, a young man lay upon the operating table of a hospital. A skilled surgeon stood near, a group of students round about. Presently, bending over the patient, the surgeon said: "My friend, if you wish to say anything, you now have the opportunity, but I must warn you that your words will be the last words that you will ever utter. (He had cancer of the tongue.) Think well, therefore, what you wish to say." You can readily imagine that such a statement at such a time would give pause to anyone. The young man therefore waited, apparently lost in deep thought. A deep solemnity settled over the faces of the onlookers. What words would he choose for such an occasion? The students bent eagerly forward. Some time passed, and then the lips at last parted, and at the sound of his voice you could have seen tears swim in the eyes of those present: "Thank God, Jesus Christ!"—*Evangelical Visitor.*

* * *

Be Thankful

One of the weekly duties of a young American girl in India was to visit a certain group of high-caste Hindu women—all younger than herself, mere girls, most of them, though already wives. She taught them the Life of Christ by telling them a new chapter in it each week, as they sat about their apartment, idly busy over their embroidery frames. She had come at last to the account of His death on the Cross, and was quietly relating the incidents of those six hours, when she caught the sound of sobbing—in the room, she thought. She paused, looked keenly about, saw nothing unusual, concluded the sound must have come in through the high lattice from the women's courtyard, and went on with her reading. Presently the sobs came again, unmistakably from a young girl whose back was almost turned toward the American girl. Quickly she knelt by her side, asking gently, "What is the trouble? Are you ill? In pain? What can I do to help you?" Through her raining tears the Hindu heathen girl answered, with sobs, "Oh, I cannot bear it—not another word! He suffered so—and you said it was for me! Oh, I cannot bear it—I love Him so!" Said the American girl when she told it afterward, "And I never knew till that minute how little I had loved my Saviour—I who had never shed a tear over His suffering for me."

Have you ever thanked Jesus for dying for you?—*Happy Hour.*

THOUGHTS

Our Thoughts

Our thoughts make us. They are the silent builders on the temple of character we are rearing. They give color and form to the whole building.

If we think truly, we are rearing a fabric whiter than Parian marble. If our thoughts are evil, the fabric that is rising within us is blemished.

The inner and the outer life will always correspond in the end. A bad heart will work through to the surface.

If a man's life is righteous you know his thoughts are just; unjust thoughts will never yield righteousness in conduct.

Thoughts seem mere nothings, flecks of cloud flying through the air, flocks of birds, flitting by, and gone. But they are the most real things about our life.

Our thoughts fly out like birds, and take their place in the world. Then our heart is still their home-nest, whither they will return at last to dwell.—*War Cry.*

* * *

"What Think Ye of Christ?"

Youth: Too happy to think—time yet.

Manhood: Too busy to think—more gold.

Prime: Too anxious to think—worry.

Declining years: Too aged to think—old hearts harder get.

Dying bed: Too ill to think—weak, suffering alone.

Death: 'Tis too late to think—the spirit has flown.

Eternity: Forever to think — God's mercy past. Into hell I am righteously cast. Forever to weep my doom!

Accept Christ today!

"Believe on the Lord Jesus Christ and thou shalt be saved."—Selected.

* * *

A Recipe for Health (Phil. 4:8)

"We do not advance upward unless we yearn upward,'" it has been said. Our thoughts shape our lives. We grow little or big by the ideals we cherish and the thoughts upon which we dwell.

"Avoid worry, anger, fear, hate, and all abnormal and depressing mental states," said an eminent authority on health. This victory over harmful thoughts cannot be achieved by suppressing these feelings, but by supplanting them with right thinking which is becoming to the followers of Jesus Christ, and which is the outgrowth of a close walk with the Lord.—*Gospel Herald.*

* * *

As We Think

The mind is like a crowded street
Where phantom thoughts, like people, meet:
Some hard at work, some idle are,
Some stay at home, some wander far.
Some thoughts wield power that ever lives—

A power that inspiration gives,
While others dwell with us awhile,
Then pass, as transient as a smile.

Thus come and go these thoughts of ours,
Some, perfume-laden as the flowers,
While others sear our lives with blight
And bring no pleasure or delight.
Our thinking lifts us to the stars,
Or seals our hearts with prison bars;
Confers on us both joy and strife,
For as we think we fashion life.
—Daniel Maurice Robins, in *War Cry*.

* * *

Thoughts Form Character

Every traveler should visit the mammoth caves of Kentucky and other parts of the South. Here one can see enormous pillars which have been formed by the steady dropping of water from the roof of the cavern. This masonry, formed of solid rock, made by the slow and silent process of nature, is truly marvelous. A single drop of water, finding its way from the surface down through the roof of the cave, deposits its sediment and another follows it and still another, each adding its imperceptible contribution, until the icicle of stone begins to grow, ultimately reaching the pillar which likewise has been forming on the bottom of the cave. It becomes a massive pillar which will stand until the end of the world.

There is a process just like that going on in each one of our hearts. Each thought that stirs for a moment sinks into the soul; as each little drop of water, with its limestone deposit, makes its contribution to the pillar in the cave. Other thoughts follow and yet others, until a habit of thought along a given line of reasoning, arousing similar emotions, is formed, erecting within our hearts monuments of purpose or pillars of ambition that have to do with our characters.

Character is the result of thought. Think high, and you will live high. Whether our lives shall be full and helpful, or cruel and hurtful, depends upon our thoughts. A good way to have clean, noble thoughts is to rise early each day and carefully read and study God's Holy Word, then wait before Him, letting the Word grip mind and heart.—*Pentecostal Testimony*.

TIME

"As thy days thy strength shall be.
This should be enough for thee;
He who knows thy frame will spare
Burdens more than thou canst bear!"
—Selected.

* * *

Lost, Two Golden Hours

Time — how precious it is, yet how much of this precious time is squandered. People have no time for the Lord, for their time is spent attending the movies, reading novels, and performing their social "duties."

Watch the second hand of a timepiece. It passes from one mark to the next, and that portion of time is gone forever. How short one moment is, and our lives are made up of moments. The present moment is the only one we can call our own; the last one has already gone into the past, and what has been done or left undone cannot be altered; the next moment has not come, and it may never come, for us. We have no promise of the morrow—no promise of the next moment. What does time mean to you, friend?

"Lost, between sunrise and sunset, two golden hours, each set with sixty diamond minutes. No reward is offered for they are gone forever." How about those wasted hours, wasted days and years of the past? It is true, they can never be recalled; they cannot be lived over; but our wasting them can be forgiven, time can be redeemed.

Do you take time to be holy? How easy to let the cares of this life rob you of the reward promised for time well spent. If you have done that, the best use you can now make of your time will be to regain that which you lost. "Time lost in mending nets is gained in catching fish." If your net is broken, do not let time go by without your mending it; for the Lord may come before your net is mended, and find that you have not been a "fisher of men."

If your time is the Lord's, you have no time for the pleasures of this world. How true that Satan finds work for idle hands to do.

"Redeeming the time, because the days are evil," is timely advice. Let us spend each moment in such a way that we shall never regret the manner in which it was spent. Time is yours, now—not yesterday, and not tomorrow, but now. Some day it will have slipped out of your grasp. Remember the testimony of the dying Queen Elizabeth: "All my possessions for one moment of time."—Margaret Broecker, in *Gospel Herald.*

* * *

Redeeming the Time (Col. 4:5)

Time is a pearl of great price, and the wise merchantman treasures it with great care, turns it to best advantage. Dr. Parker said to a student, "Do not gallop through the Scriptures, go slowly and look around." The speed of our travel today looks like an effort to redeem the time; but what does the swift traveler see of wayside flowers, what does he hear of the songs of birds, what does he do with the time he is supposed to have saved?

It means seeking the best things that may be available; take time to be holy, for holiness is more precious than rubies; take time to pray, the minutes are not lost that are taken from human engagements, and given to waiting upon God. Work exhausts our strength but waiting upon God renews it; this is an invaluable investment of time.

It means seizing opportunities to do good.—*The Christian* (London).

Redeeming the Time

The days are passing swiftly by,
  Let us redeem them, Lord, for Thee;
Not waste a moment as they fly,
Nay, e'en the seconds may we buy,
  Until Thy face we see.

May we spend well each hour, each day,
  In turning loss to perfect gain;
May this be ours; to point the way,
And bring to others Heaven's ray,
  Some sunshine 'mid their rain.

May we like sunbeams from the blue,
  Seek out each heaving, aching breast;
May we like sun-bursts, e'er break through
The clouds, to give to hearts, anew,
  The promise of sweet rest.

—R. E. Neighbour.

* * *

Begin Today

Dream not too much of what you'll do tomorrow,
  How well perhaps you'll do another year;
Tomorrow's chance you do not need to borrow.
  Today is here.

Boast not too much of mountains you will master;
  The time you linger in this world below;
To dream is well, but doing brings us faster
  To where we go.

Swear not some day to break some habit fetter
  When this old year is dead and passed away;
But if you really want to live much better,
  Begin today.

—Mrs. Carl W. Johnson, in *The Evangelical Beacon.*

* * *

Do It Now

If you have work to do—do it now.

If you have a witness to give—give it now.

If you have a soul to win—win him now.

If you have an obligation to discharge—discharge it now.

If you have a debt to pay—pay it now.

If you have a wrong to right—right it now.

If you have a confession to make—make it now.

If you have a preparation to make—make it now.

If you have children to train—train them now.

Remember, time is passing and you are passing out of time.

We are a procrastinating lot. It is always what we are going to do tomorrow that entices us, but it is only what we do today that counts.—*Gospel Herald.*

* * *

Tomorrow

Today is the tomorrow, that yesterday you feared,
You faced it with forebodings, and dreaded as it neared;
But, when it came a-smiling, all filled with sunshine bright,
You said: Why did I worry? God is, and all is right.

Remember your tomorrows are hidden in God's will,
So, fretting not, have faith in God, and patient be, and still;
Then when tomorrow is today, you'll find sufficient grace
To guide you through in victory and with a happy face.

Count up all the tomorrows, in yesterdays you knew,
You'll find as each became today, God led you safely through;
And He who led, will lead you on, till all of your todays,
Will stand behind you, all arrayed, as blessed yesterdays.
—R. E. Neighbour, in *Gospel Herald.*

* * *

Looking Forward

I've shut the door on Yesterday,
Its sorrows and mistakes;
I've locked within its gloomy walls
Past failures and heartaches.

And now I throw the key away
To seek another room,
And furnish it with hope and smiles,
And every springtime bloom.

No thought shall enter this abode
That has a hint of pain,
And every malice and distrust
Shall never therein reign.
I've shut the door on Yesterday,
And throw my key away—
Tomorrow holds no doubt for me,
Since I have found Today.
Anon.

* * *

Time Flies

When Raphael died at thirty-seven years of age, they carried his marvelous painting, "The Transfiguration," only half finished, in the funeral procession as a symbol of the incompleteness of life and the brevity of time. The wise and alert one girds up his loins to seize the present in doing and daring and enjoying.—A. C. Dixon.

* * *

Dealing with Eternity

When Sir William Russell was on the way to the scaffold, he took his watch out of his pocket and handed it to the physician who waited upon him, as he said, "Will you kindly take my timepiece and keep it? I have no use for it; I am now dealing with eternity!" With us, Time is slipping away; eternity is coming. And it is the presence of Christ which fits the Christian to deal with eternity.—A. C. Dixon.

* * *

Time

A moment is a little thing;
But moments make the day.
So crowd it with a worthy task
Before it slips away.

A minute is not with us long,
But oh, the joy or pain
That can be crowded into it,
With loss, or priceless gain.

An hour of precious time, a day
Will soon be slipping by,
A month, a year, the span of life—
Work; plan it well, and try.
—M. E. Detterline.

* * *

"Lord, for tomorrow and its needs
I do not pray;
Keep me, my God, from stains of sin
Just for today.
Help me to labor earnestly,
And duly pray;
Let me be kind in word and deed,
Father, today."
—*Gospel Herald.*

* * *

Do It Today

Wear today a cheerful face
In everything you do,
The sunshine that you radiate
Will shine right back at you.

Speak today a word of hope
To someone in distress,
When you lift another's load
You make your burden less.

Do today a gracious deed
And do it with a smile,
It is little acts like these
That make your life worth while.
—Grenville Kleiser.

Time is as much a trusteeship as money, and there are no capitalists. We cannot "invest" it to use in the future, but we can, by grace, use it fruitfully now and have the blessing and results in the future, to the glory of God. *Each day is a sacred trust, and never returns. Each hour is a privilege.* A wasted moment and a wasted coin are alike saddening to a believer.—*The Student of Scripture.*

* * *

"Redeeming the Time "

I have only just a minute,
Just sixty seconds in it;
Forced upon me—can't refuse it,
Didn't seek it, didn't choose it;
I must suffer if I lose it,
Give account if I abuse it;
Just a tiny little minute,
But eternity is in it.
—Selected.

* * *

The clock of life is wound but once,
And no man has the power
To tell just when the hands will stop—
At late or early hour.
Now is the only time you own;
So live, love, toil with a will;
Do not depend upon tomorrow, for
The clock may then be still.
—Rev. B. Meyer.

TITHING

When She Had No Testimony

Dr. Russell Conwell one night at a prayer meeting asked if there were any tithers present who had tithed through a series of years. Seven people stood up. He asked for a testimony from each one of them in emphasis of the fact of God's faithfulness in blessing them. Six gave radiant testimonies of blessings received. The seventh was a frail, gray-haired woman, who spoke with much reluctance: "I wish I could bear such testimony, but I cannot. I have skimped and saved and denied myself through the years to keep a vow made to tithe my income. But now I am old and I am losing my position. I have no means of support. I do not know what I shall do." She sat down, and the meeting was closed in the midst of a profound and distressing chill. Next day Dr. Conwell had an invitation from Mr. John Wanamaker to dine with him. At the table Mr. Wanamaker said: "I think you will be interested to know that we are about to inaugurate a pension system for our employees. The plan has been worked out, and we are to issue our first life pension today to a woman who has served us for twenty-five years." He mentioned her name, and it was that of the woman who had given the pessimistic testimony the night before!—*Herald of Holiness.*

Making $9 Go Farther Than $10

In recognizing the duty of tithe-giving, when one's income is limited and one's personal and family needs are great, it is essential to recognize the supernatural element in God's providential care of his children. If a Christian man has an income large enough to supply all his needs without difficulty, there is neither shadow of excuse nor show of decency in his failure to pay over one-tenth of it to the Lord. But when one feels the pinch of poverty every day of his life, then it is important that he should bear in mind that 9 cents will go farther than 10 cents would go and that $9 will go farther than $10 would go in providing for himself and his loved ones, when that other cent or that other dollar has been paid to the Lord, who claims it as His own. There is no mistake about this to him who has faith. Every child of God who has rested on this truth has found it to be a source of unfailing dependence. Only those disbelieve it who have never trusted God enough to try it even as an experiment. It is with individuals as it is with churches in this matter. Neither their troubles nor their doubts ever come from their giving too freely of their substance to the Lord.—The late Henry Clay Trumbull, founder of the *Sunday School Times.*

* * *

Tithing

A. A. Hyde, a millionaire manufacturer, said he began tithing when he was one hundred thousand dollars in debt. Many men have said they consider it dishonest to give God a tenth of their incomes when they were in debt. Mr. Hyde said he agreed with that thought until one day it flashed upon him that God was his first creditor. Then he began to pay God first and all the other creditors were eventually paid in full. *If a man owes you money, it would be wise business policy on your part to encourage him to pay his debt to God first.—Sunday School Times.*

God Gives Most

Some years ago I met a godly Baptist layman in South Carolina who was secretary and treasurer of a large cotton mill corporation. One day he told me: "Years ago when my children were small, my salary was too small for my actual needs. Strive as I would I could not keep out of debt. This became a heavy cross to me, and one night I was unable to sleep. I arose and went to my desk and spent a season in prayer to God for help and guidance. Then I took a pen and paper and wrote out a solemn contract with my heavenly Father. I promised Him that no matter what testings or trials came I would never turn back. Also that no matter how pressing were my obligations I would scrupulously tithe my income. Next I promised the Lord that if He would let me make a certain salary I would pay two-tenths, then if I made a certain larger salary I would pay three-tenths. Finally I named a larger salary, which was far beyond anything I had ever hoped to earn, and told the Lord that if I ever reached such a salary I would give Him one-half of my income." Then the old gentleman smiled, and tears came into his eyes as he said, "Brother Browning, for many years it has been my privilege to give one-half of my income to the Lord.' I do not know whether or not good stewards will get good salaries or a very meager living, but I do know there is a Bible prosperity and Bible success that every good steward can obtain.—*Sunday School Times.*

* * *

When They Tithed

The Belmont Presbyterian Church, South, at Roanoke, Va., with a membership of 425, ascertained through unsigned slips dropped in the collection plate, that 137 of its members had a definite income averaging $18 per week. The pastor challenged this group to tithe for a period of three months. One hundred and eighteen signed such an agreement. Immediately the weekly offering rose from $50 to $216 per week, amounting on one Sunday to $450. At the end of three months the people who said in good faith, "We cannot carry on," had contributed $2,626. Many said, "As long as God gives me any kind of income, I am going to pay Him the tenth." "Bring ye the tithe . . . prove Me . . . I will pour you out a blessing," saith the Lord. — From a Presbyterian Church financial suggestion.

* * *

William Colgate, The Soap Man

Many years ago a lad of sixteen years left home to seek his fortune. All his worldly possessions were tied in a bundle, which he carried in his hand. As he trudged along he met an old neighbor, the captain of a canal boat, and the following conversation took place, which changed the whole current of the boy's life:

"Well, William, where are you going?"

"I don't know," he answered, "Father is too poor to keep me at home any longer and says I must now make a living for myself."

"There's no trouble about that," said the captain. "Be sure you start right, and you'll get along finely."

William told his friend that the only trade he knew anything about was soap and candle making, at which he had helped his father while at home.

"Well," said the old man, "let me pray with you once more, and give you a little advice, and then I will let you go."

They both knelt down upon the towpath; the dear old man prayed earnestly for William and then gave this advice: "Someone soon will be the leading soapmaker in New York. It can be you as well as anyone. I hope it may. Be a good man; give your heart to Christ; pay the Lord all that belongs to Him of every dollar you earn; make an honest soap; give a full pound, and I am certain that you will be a prosperous and rich man."

When the boy arrived in the city, he found it hard to get work. Lonesome and far from home, he remembered his mother's words and the last words of the canal boat captain. He was then led to "seek first the Kingdom of God and His righteousness," and united with the church. He remembered his promise to the old captain, and the first dollar he earned brought up the question of the Lord's part. In the Bible he found that the Jews were commanded to give one-tenth; so he said, "If the Lord will take one-tenth, I will give that."

Having regular employment, he soon became a partner. After a few years his partner died, and William became the sole owner of the business.

He now resolved to keep his promise to the old captain; he made an honest soap gave a full pound, and instructed his bookkeeper to open an account with the Lord, and carry one-tenth of all his income to that account. He prospered; his business grew; his family was blessed; his soap sold, and he grew rich faster than he had ever hoped. He then gave two-tenths; prospered more than ever; then he gave three-tenths; then four-tenths; then five-tenths.

He educated his family; settled all his plans for life; and gave all his income to the Lord's work. He prospered more than ever. This is the story of Colgate, who has given millions of dollars to the Lord's cause, and left a name that will never die.—Wayne Wiman, in *Cumberland Presbyterian.*

* * *

"And Company"

"Can I put some money in this bank?" A fifteen-year-old boy in faded clothing stood before the teller's window of the bank in the little town of Barwick, Ga. His suit, badly worn, and his general appearance marked him as a tenant-farmer's son. Three layers of paste board thrust inside his ragged shoes kept his feet off the stone floor. "How much do you want to put in, John?" the banker asked. "Four dollars," the boy answered. "How do you want the account made out?" The man's voice was kindly, for he knew the boy as one of the regulars over at the Methodist Sunday School. "John W. Yates and Company," the youngster answered gravely. The banker peered through the grating with a quizzical look on his face. "Who's the Company?" he queried. "God," the boy replied very solemnly. "I got my first month's pay today, and I'm starting my tithe account. This is God's money." The life story of John Yates reads like that of a Horatio Alger hero. Bookkeeper, bank teller, cashier, army quartermaster whose checks for $10,000,000 were honored, insurance salesman, and finally general agent with a national reputation, this man has been described by two pastors of great churches as "one of the most valuable laymen in Methodism." His mother, Lillie Yates, entered into a new religious experience in a revival meeting, and out of deep poverty and struggle began to devote a tenth of all income to the Lord. Lillie Yates' old tithing account book lies in the lower drawer of her son's big walnut desk alongside of his New Testament. He has shown it to tens of thousands of people in audiences before whom he has preached the doctrine of stewardship. He says, "That book might not have the approval of a bigwig C.P.A., but I am sure our Heavenly Father calls it mighty good bookkeeping." This church and Sunday school worker says he owes it all to the fact that his mother was a tither; her devotion to that principle marked him for life.—*Herald of Light.*

* * *

How Much Shall We Keep?

A servant of God had a little girl whom he was eager should be brought up to serve Him. He wanted to teach her that we should give one-tenth of our possessions to God. One day he called her into his study, where he had arranged ten piles of money. And he said:

"You see, I have ten piles of money here. One, two, three, four, five, six, seven, eight, nine—they belong to me; but this tenth one belongs to God." The little girl said: *"Oh, Father, are you going to keep all the nine for yourself?"* —*The King's Business.*

Praying and Giving

I met at a small hotel and exchanged experiences with a certain lady who told me this: When she and her husband were married, they decided to tithe. Some years later her husband had raised some objections, saying now they had eight children to clothe, feed, and educate, and he thought they should not spare so much money. She suggested taking time to pray and think about the matter; and when it was mentioned again she told him she had made it a very special subject of prayer, and the more she prayed the more she thought of the promise they had claimed in the beginning (Mal. 3:10). They had brought the tithes and God had given the blessing. She feared that if they withheld the tithe, God would withhold the blessing. As far as she was concerned, she would prefer to go without some new clothes, and let the children go without some things they seemed to need, and to do without some things for the house, than to rob God of His tenth. Her husband's answer had been, "Oh, well, just as you say!" As the Christmas season approached she was thinking of a dinner for poor people to which for twenty years she had never missed making a contribution. Now business had been very bad for months, and their income small. As she washed dishes she talked to God about the matter, and then, like a flash, the question came, "Why not ask God to give it through someone else?" Drying her hands, she went into the little parlor and knelt down and talked with God again about it. She felt as sure of the money as though it were already in her hand. That evening her eldest daughter came in and said, "Mother, hold your hand." Placing there three coins, she said, "Mrs. So-and-so sent that to you for your poor people. She said you would know better where to send it than she would." Leading her daughter into the little parlor, she knelt once more, not to ask for anything, but to offer her thanks to God for lifting the burden and filling her soul with joy and peace.—*Serving and Waiting.*

A Peasant's Tithing

He came into the city one day after wheat harvest. Handing me fifty cents he said, "This is my tithe for the evangelistic team. I have just sold my wheat and received $5 for it." "But that means you have only $4.50 to live on until your crop of sweet potatoes is harvested!" "Yes, that is true, but you see this fifty cents is not mine. It belongs to my Heavenly Father, and I will not rob Him of that which is His." A week later he came in again and dropped twenty cents on my desk. "What is this?" I asked. "I have just sold my donkey for $2, and this twenty cents is not mine but the Lord's. I want it to go into the country evangelistic work."—C. R. Hills, in *China's Millions.*

* * *

Bonds or Tithes?

A poster caught my eye today;
"Give ten per cent of all your pay
To buy war bonds. Come, do your share
To let our boys know that you care."
I thought of folks this country o'er
Who give a tenth, and even more,
For bonds; and that's as it should be.
But then this thought occurred to me:

Did these same folks in days before
This awful tragedy of war,
When asked to tithe unto the Lord,
Say, "That's more than I can afford"?
—Courtesy *Moody Monthly.*

* * *

The Tithe

Abraham commenced it.
Jacob continued it.
Moses confirmed it.
Malachi commanded it.
Christ commended it.
—Selected.

TONGUE (See also: Gossip, 320)

The Crimes of the Tongue

There are pillows wet by sobs; there are noble hearts broken in the silence whence comes no cry of protest; there are gentle, sensitive natures seared and warped; there are old-time friends separated and walking their lonely way with hope dead and memory but a pang; there are cruel misunderstandings that make all life look dark—these are but few of the sorrows that come from the crimes of the tongue.—William George Jordan.

* * *

The Tongue

"A sharp tongue is the only edge-tool that grows sharper with constant use." —Washington Irving. "By examining the tongue of a patient, physicians find out the diseases of the body and philosophers the diseases of the mind."—Justin. "The most ferocious monster in the world has his den just behind the teeth."—Author Unknown. "Give not thy tongue too great liberty, lest it take thee prisoner."—Quaries. "Never throw mud. You may miss your mark, but you must have dirty hands."—Joseph Parker. "When men speak ill of you, live so that nobody will believe them."—Selected.

* * *

The Builder versus the Wrecker

I watched them tearing a building down—
A gang of men in a busy town;
With a "ho heave ho" and a lusty yell
They swung a beam and the side wall fell;
I asked the foreman, "Are these men skilled?
And the kind you would hire, if you were to build?"
He laughed and said, "Why, no indeed
Just common laborers is all I need;
They can easily wreck in a day or two
That which has taken builders years to do."

So I said to myself, as I went on my
way,
What part in the game of life do I play?
Am I shaping my deeds to a well-made
plan,
Carefully measuring with a rule and
square,
Patiently doing the very best I can,
Or am I a wrecker, who walks the
town,
Content with the labor of tearing down?
—Selected.

* * *

Blessed is the man who, having nothing to say, abstains from giving wordy evidence of it!—*War Cry.*

* * *

Mind that Tongue

John Wesley was preaching. He was wearing a new bow tie with two streamers hanging down from it. There was a sister in the meeting who didn't hear a word about Jesus, but sat with a long face and saw nothing but those two streamers. When the service was over she went up and said, "Pardon me, Mr. Wesley, will you suffer a little criticism?" "Yes," replied Mr. Wesley. "Well," she said, "Mr. Wesley, your bow tie is too long and it is an offense to me." He said, "Have you a pair of shears?" After receiving the shears he handed them to her saying that she would know how they would look best. She reached over and clipped off the streamers. Then he said, "Is that all right now?" "Yes, that is much better." He said, "Do you mind letting me have those shears? Would you mind a little criticism? Your tongue is a great offense to me—it is a little too long. Please stick it out while I take some off." Of course she resented the suggestion.

James said that if we could control the tongue we would be able to control the whole body.

Let us all seek God every morning to have Christ to possess us that our tongues will be under His control, speaking only words of kindness and wisdom. There will always be plenty of people to do the scolding, faultfinding, backbiting. A still tongue shows a wise head. If we must talk, let our words be measured words of wisdom, peace, and love.—*The Pentecostal Testimony.*

* * *

Only a Word

Only a word of anger,
But it wounded one sensitive heart;
Only a word of sharp reproach,
But it made the teardrops start;
Only a hasty, thoughtless word,
Sarcastic and unkind.
But it darkened the day before so
bright,
And left a sting behind.

Only a word of kindness,
But it lightened one heart of its
grief;
Only a word of sympathy,
But it brought one soul relief;
Only a word of gentle cheer.
But it flooded with radiant light
The pathway that seemed so dark before,
And it made the day more bright.
—*Our Pentecostal Boys and Girls.*

* * *

Unsaid—Undone

It is not always the thing that you say,
That brings the heavy heart;
But that which you have left unsaid
Oft brings the keenest smart.
For many a heart might lightened be
Through words which you might
speak;
And some poor soul new strength receive
That now is sad and weak.

It is not always the thing you do,
That brings the load of care;
But often things you leave undone
Bring souls nigh to despair.
The kindly deed, the pleasant smile,
The look you might have giv'n,
Perhaps had lifted fainting ones,
And brought them nearer Heav'n.

Not only for things said and done,
  Must we an answer make;
For things unsaid, and things undone
  Have caused full many an ache.
And many a load had never been,
  And many a care had flown,
Had you and I God's voice obeyed,
  Left naught unsaid, undone.
—Anna L. Dreyer, in *John Three Sixteeen.*

* * *

What Do with this Talent?

There are men who pride themselves on their candor, and it degenerates into brutality. One such man said to John Wesley once, "Mr. Wesley, I pride myself in speaking my mind; that is my talent." "Well," said John Wesley, "the Lord wouldn't mind if you buried that!" —Dr. Griffith Thomas.

* * *

Mean Tongues of Orthodox Christians

"If any man offend not in word, the same is a perfect man, and able also to bridle the whole body." That is what the Holy Spirit said through James in the third chapter of the book he wrote. This statement we should know to be true even if it were not in the Bible. All of us know, if we stop to think, that our most difficult task is to control our tongues. There is nothing today that is doing more to deaden the spiritual testimony of orthodox Christianity than the long, backbiting, mean tongues of some supposedly orthodox Christians. There are Christians that talk much about a separated life, and boast about what they do and do not do, and speak with great pride about their loyalty to orthodoxy, who spend their time dipping their tongues in the slime of slander and speaking the death warrant to the reputation of other orthodox Christians.

The Bible is filled with condemnation of people that slander other people. It condemns with great severity people who even take up a reproach about other people. It is just as bad to carry a rumor around after it starts as it is to start it.—Bob Jones, Sr., in *The Fellowship News.*

Be Silent

It is a great art in the Christian life to learn to be silent. Under oppositions, rebukes, injuries, still be silent. It is better to say nothing than to speak in an excited manner, even if the occasion should seem to justify a degree of anger. By remaining silent the mind is enabled to collect itself and call upon God in secret prayer. And thus you will speak to the honor of your holy profession, as well as to the good of those who have injured you when you speak from God. —Selected.

* * *

Spoken Words

Guard well thy lips; none, none can know (Prov. 13:3)
What evils from the tongue may flow (James 3:5, 6);
What guilt, what grief may be incurred (Judg. 11:35)
By one incautious word (Mark 6:22, 25, 26).
Be "slow to speak," look well within (Prov. 4:5),
To check what there may lead to sin (James 1:25),
And pray unceasingly for aid (Col. 4:2),
Lest unawares thou be betrayed (Luke 21:34).
"Condemn not, judge not"—not to man (I Cor. 4:3)
Is given his brother's faults to scan (Matt. 7:3).
The task is God's and His alone (Matt. 7:5),
To search out and subdue His own (1 Cor. 9:27).
Indulge no murmurings: oh, restrain (Phil. 2:14, 15)
Those lips so ready to complain (Job 27:4);
And if they can be numbered, count (Ps. 103:2, 3)
Of one day's mercies the amount (Lam. 3:23).
Shun vain discussions, trifling themes (Tit. 3:9);
Dwell not on earthly hopes and schemes (Deut. 6:4-7);
Let words of wisdom, meekness, love (James 3:13),

Thy heart's true renovation prove (Luke 6:45).
Set God before thee; every word (Gen. 17:1)
Thy lips pronounce by Him is heard (Ps. 139:4);
Oh, couldst thou realize this thought (Luke 12:2),
What care, what caution would be taught (Luke 12:3)!

—Anonymous.

TRACTS — PRINTED WORD

Does Tract Distribution Pay?

At a London "May Meeting," Rev. Dr. Len G. Broughton said: Some years ago one of the most brilliant young American actors that the stage had, was walking the streets of one of our Western cities one night, on his way to the theater, and as he turned a corner, near the theater, a humble woman, whose name has never been known, handed him a tract, and out of respect to the woman he put the tract in his overcoat pocket, never expecting to read it. He went to his hotel after he had performed in the theater, and somehow he got hold of the tract, and he said, "I believe I'll see what this tract is about," and he began to read it, and found it so interesting that he could not quit it. When he had finished the tract, he went to bed, and began to think along the lines of its teaching and somehow he found it impossible to sleep that night. All through the night the teaching of that tract kept wandering through his mind. Next morning he endeavored to dismiss it from his thoughts, and gave himself over to the rehearsal for the coming night, but he could not get it out of his mind, he could not sufficiently fix his mind on rehearsing his part, and presently it ended in his consulting a minister. He told him his experience, and the minister began, when he had done, to preach to him Jesus, and that brilliant young Western American actor then and there bowed his heart and yielded to Jesus. Five months after that he entered a theological seminary to prepare himself for the Christian ministry, and a few years ago George C. Lorimer, the pastor of Tremont Temple in Boston, went home to meet his God; and if he could stand on this platform tonight, he would say one of the greatest unused forces in the Christian Church today, is the tract.—*Evangelistic Echoes.*

* * *

Sister Abigail, while traveling on a ferry boat, put a Gospel tract in a bottle and threw it in the river. Some days later a shabbily dressed stranger with that very bottle in his hand stood at her door. He confided that he was about to commit suicide in the river when he saw the floating bottle. The Scripture verses found in the bottle so convicted him of his need of Christ that he came to see Sister Abigail, whose name appeared on the tract. Thus, this man who had been on the brink of eternal death passed into eternal life.—*Gospel Herald.*

* * *

Saved by a Tract

We feel strongly that there is a great need of causing all Bible-loving Christians to realize the importance of distributing the Gospel message in print, and thereby combatting the many errors that are propagated so largely by various religious cults and atheistic organizations, as well as arousing the careless and indifferent. One of the "weak things" which God is pleased to use is a Gospel tract—a little piece of paper on which is printed His Word—given in faith and love to the passer-by.

The following incident shows that God blesses such a ministry:

Recently a young Lithuanian was ordained to the Gospel ministry in Chicago. He had passed a creditable examination as to his salvation, his call to the ministry, and his knowledge of the Bible. This, in brief, is his story:

He was reared in the Roman Catholic faith in his native land. He came to this country when quite young. He became a confirmed gambler; one night in desperation he made a last plunge, and lost. After midnight he left the gambling hall intending to end it all in the lake. Walking down the street, someone handed him a tract entitled, "The Way of Life Made Plain." This tract has a diagram illustrating the two ways, the broad and the narrow—with the red Cross at the parting of the ways. It shows clearly the need of salvation, bringing the reader to the definite question, "Which way do you choose?"

The young Lithuanian stopped to look at the leaflet that had been given him. He read: "We must all meet God. Are you prepared? Are you saved? This is a very important question. Your happiness or misery for all eternity is involved in it." He was startled by the word "eternity" which seemed to stand out in bold letters. He was convicted of his lost condition and of his great need. He continued reading. He saw the way of life clearly pointed out. He called upon the Lord to save him, and God heard his cry. The work was begun in his heart, and soon he was rejoicing in the consciousness of sins forgiven and a new life imparted. He is now devoting all of his time in telling his fellow countrymen the good news of salvation by grace through faith in the Lord Jesus Christ.—Selected.

* * *

The Right to Distribute Tracts

Tract Distributors are sometimes hindered in their work by town and city officials. Sometimes they are forbidden to give out Christian literature from house to house. Many towns and cities have passed ordinances against such distribution. In the light of a Supreme Court decision, such ordinances are wrong, and any local official who stops tract distribution has not only gone beyond his power, but has interfered with the liberty of the distributor.

In an opinion rendered by Chief Justice, the Honorable Charles E. Hughes, on March 28, 1938, in the case of Lovell versus the City of Griffin, Ga. (see Volume 58, No. 12, April 15, 1938), the following was said:

"The liberty of the press is not confined to newspapers and periodicals. It necessarily embraces pamphlets and leaflets. Liberty of circulation is as essential to that freedom as liberty of publishing. Indeed, without the circulation, the publication would be of little value." —Courtesy *Moody Monthly.*

* * *

Only a Tract

It's only a tract! You may tear it,
And crumple it up in your hand;
The wind, as it passes, may bear it
And scatter it over the land.

It's only a tract! You may spurn it,
And deem it unworthy a thought;
May ridicule, trample, and burn it,
Despise it, and set it at naught.

It's only a tract! But it telleth
Of holiness, happiness, Heaven;
Where God in eternity dwelleth
With sinners His love has forgiven.

It speaks of a future in glory,
Of present enjoyment and bliss;
And will you neglect a message,
So loving, so joyous as this?

It whispers, "No matter how hardened,
No mater how vile you have been,
You may at this moment be pardoned
And saved from the bondage of sin."

It points to the Substitute dying,
The Sinless, for sinners like you.
Oh, soul, on His merits relying,
Come, prove that its message is true!

It is but a tract! Yet its warning
Is whispered in Jesus' own voice;
And at thy acceptance or scorning
Either Heaven or hell will rejoice!
—Selected.

Guided to Read

God's guidance, as with Israel, leads into spiritually enriching experience, rich fruitage and at times into miraculous God-honoring victories. Wilberforce was guided to read, *Rise and Progress of Religion in the Soul* by Doddridge. It led him to Christ, and through this came freedom to all slaves in the British Empire. Sir Walter Scott, guided to read Dr. Watts' *Hymn Book for Children,* was saved from suicide and a lost eternity. William Carey, guided to read, *Captain Cook's Voyages,* was led as a missionary to India where he gave the Bible to over 200,000,000 million people in different languages. Henry Martyn, guided to read *Carey's Published Letters,* went to India and Persia. Adoniram Judson, guided to read Buchanan's *Star in the East,* went to Burma. David Livingstone, being guided to read Dr. Dick's *Philosophy of a Future State,* went to his great work in Africa.

* * *

Objectors Silenced

There are those who object to tract work because they have seen tracts on the sidewalks which were discarded by the recipients. True, some of the tracts distributed may be wasted, but the work is abundantly worth while even making that allowance. (Luke 8:5-8).

When tracts are printed in very large quantities, an attractive two-page tract can often be produced at the rate of twenty-five for one cent, and a four-page tract at a dozen for a cent. At that rate one must see from a dozen to twenty-five tracts thrown away before the thought of wasting one cent could be entertained.

On the other hand, seeing a tract on the sidewalk by no means proves it wasted. A man wrote from Newark, N. J., saying he was walking to his work one rainy morning and noticed a piece of printed paper on the sidewalk which had been trampled upon. He was in a reading mood and although the paper was wet and dirty, he stooped, picked it up and perused it. He said: "The paper proved to be a tract entitled: '$35,000 Spurned For a Son.' As I read it, I thought of ten persons to whom I should like to give a copy. The tract bears your imprint, so would you please send me some extra copies of it?" The extra copies were cheerfully sent — so that discarded tract led to an increased circulation of itself.

Someone may say: "I have seen a tract taken from an envelope and hurled into the wastepaper basket." Granted. But even then you cannot be positive that it is wasted. A janitress in New York City wrote saying she had found a tract in a waste-paper basket and she liked it so well she was sending a dime for a quantity.

Another person may say: "I saw tracts torn to pieces and scattered to the winds." Maybe so — but if you concluded that that was wasted effort and material on the part of the tract worker, you may be mistaken! A person writing from a distance said he had found a piece of paper the title of which he didn't know for it was torn off. "But," said he, "there was sufficient left to show me my condition and my Saviour and to inform me where I could secure more such literature. So I am sending to you for a sample packet of all your literature as I should love to read the missing part of this paper!"—*Tracts and Their Use* by Olson.

* * *

Look to Jesus

An earnest city missionary in New York was passing through the tramcars going down to Fulton Ferry, distributing a little card, which read: "When tempted, when in despair, when sick, when dying, look to Jesus!" One of these cards fell into the hands of a passenger on the car, who read it. As the man who gave it to him started out of the car, the passenger followed him and said, "Friend, let me speak a word to you. I have just buried my wife and two children and I have been unfortunate in business. Life is a blank to me; it is as dark as midnight. I was on my way to Fulton Ferry, thinking I would end it all down there in the river, but the little card you gave me has given me hope!"—Dr. A. C. Dixon.

Tract Distribution Works

Ever since the invention of printing, God has been pleased to use the printed page as a means of getting His Word into the hands and hearts of men. John Wesley saw the importance of the printed page and wrote hundreds of tracts which he distributed in great quantities as he visited town after town on horseback. Think of the chain of blessing that has resulted through the conversion of Hudson Taylor who was brought to Christ as he read a tract that had been placed in one of his father's books.

I know that tract distribution works today because I have seen it work. In a New York subway, I watched a little girl of eleven pass through the cars and give tracts to 400 people. In a few minutes she reached more people with the Word of Life than some churches do in a whole week or month.

The other day a serviceman in a Calfornia hospital wrote telling of his conversion through a tract. In his letter he passed on a dollar and asked that we send more tracts of the same kind that he might give to his buddies as they lay in their beds with plenty of time to think.

Hitchhiking one day, a Canadian evangelist noticed a farmer plowing in his field. Upon seeing his lunch box by the fence post a little further down the road, the evangelist opened the bucket and placed a tract on top of the lunch. The farmer had been troubled about his soul. At noon when he saw the tract in his lunch bucket, he did not understand how it came to be there but its contents were a message from God, and the tract was the means of his conversion.

Tract distribution works... and every Christian should be a consistent distributor of the Word of Life in tract form. Our generation is hungry for the Word of Life. We must feed them. The tract is only a tiny morsel, but may be used by God in the salvation of a precious soul.

Someone has said, "The Pen is mightier than the sword." In the great challenging days ahead, we must be prepared to reach the great masses of people with the pen. In America, in our own Gospel enlightened country, there are 27,000,000 young people who do not darken the doors of any church. One way to reach this great number is by the printed page. I believe that printed page evangelism should be one of the means in God's hand in getting the Gospel to the uttermost parts of the world. Christian, He needs YOU. He needs your feet to go. He needs your hands to give out the Word of Life!—Clyde H. Dennis Director, *Tract club of America.*

* * *

Tracts Never Die

Just before a young man was about to embark from the United States as a marine, a woman put in his trunk a single tract. It lay in his trunk neglected for many months traveling thousands of miles in the world's waterways. Returning to this country years later, he was doing shore duty when he found the tract while rummaging through his trunk. To pass the time he read it. His conscience became aroused until he finally accepted Christ as Saviour.

Unlike a sermon, the message of a tract can be printed over and over again into millions of copies and the Word of Life can reach the far corners of the earth. When you give out a tract, you may never know how the Lord may use it. It may pass from hand to hand. It may go around the world. Its message may bring life to countless souls. Tracts never die... and every Christian has the privilege and responsibility of distributing them.

* * *

Tracts Bring Joy into Your Life

Doctor Sunshine is her name. She is a little old woman of 76 whom God saved. Handicapped, living alone, the Lord led her into tract work. She became known as Doctor Sunshine because of the joy in her own life and the sunshine which she brought into the hearts and homes of others. If you have never before given out tracts, we believe a new joy in the Christian life awaits you if you will start. By witnessing with tracts God can sweeten your day. Your fellowship with the Lord will be more precious and you will feel that you have tried to make Christ known by means of the printed page.

* * *

Every Christian Can Use Tracts

The housewife, the farmer, the business man, the factory worker... no matter what your position in life... there are multitudes of opportunities to give out tracts. Get in the habit of carrying tracts with you at all times. If you are a housewife, keep a tract box near the door. If you are a business man, always keep tracts in your letter folder. If you are a factory worker, keep a supply in your lunch box or in your jacket pockets. Look for opportunities to give out tracts. Give them on the elevator. Give them on the train, the bus, the street car. Put tracts in your letters. Send them with your checks and bills. Encourage the placing and the maintenance of a tract rack in your church. Encourage other Christians to use tracts. Show them titles that you have enjoyed using.—Clyde H. Dennis, Director, Tract Club of America.

* * *

Only a Tract

Yes, only a tract, but what wonders it can accomplish when it falls into the hands of a hungry heart. It is like the seed that falls upon good ground and takes root, springing up to bear much fruit. But the seed in itself is powerless and without value apart from the soil, and it can only be brought into contact with the soil through the sower. A marvelous illustration of this is the following experience.

In connection with her work among the Jewish people of St. Louis, Miss M. was visiting a friend in the hospital. While engaged in conversation, a woman patient across the room asked, "Do you carry your Bible with you to read to people who wish to hear?"

"Yes," was the answer.

Soon Miss M. was reading Psalm 27 to the woman, quoting also other Scriptures. Then she prayed with her.

The woman expressed deep appreciation for the interest shown her. After a heart-to-heart talk she realized her need of the Saviour, and then gave herself to Him. She was to be dismissed from the hospital that day and Miss M. desiring to help her find a church home where she might receive nourishment for her soul, handed her the tract, *Who Is He?* on which she wrote her name and telephone number.

Several days later, this friend called Miss M. and requested that she visit her. She had given that tract to a Jewish man, who had read it, and it had made a powerful impression on him. He asked if he might see Miss M. Of course she was glad of the opportunity, and the young Christian arranged the interview.

At the very outset of their visit, Miss M. asked the man, "What do you think of this Jesus of whom the tract speaks?"

His immediate reply was, "There must be something to it. I have never been more stirred in my life. How can it be false with so many indisputable proofs from prophecy and history that He is the true Messiah for whom my people have been looking so long."

Needless to say, this confession brought untold joy to the heart of the faithful worker. Several days later the man phoned her, requesting a prayer book. She gave him a copy of the New Testament instead, for which he was most grateful, and he promised to read it carefully. The worker took the occasion to help make the plan of salvation clearer, and he expressed his full intention to follow the Lord at any cost. A short time later he made a public profession of faith.

Here we have one of the most thrilling accounts of the marvelous leading of the Holy Spirit and the power of the silent witness. A follower of Christ visits in the hospital; a patient overhears and finds the Saviour. She in turn is immediately used to give an unbelieving Jew a little tract.

Only a tract, you say? Yes, but what marvels it can accomplish! In the hospitals, on the streets, in your office, in school, in the house next door — everywhere there are those who are waiting for someone to speak a word, or to hand them a tract which might start them on the upward road.—Rev. Jacob Gartenhaus; courtesy *Moody Monthly.*

* * *

His Head Was in a Noose

There went out a sower to sow (Mark 4:3). Mark J. Goodger, the "Highway Bible Evangelist," covers the United States every year on a bicycle, giving out tracts from door to door. At one two-story house in South Carolina he rang the bell six times because he heard sounds within. Finally a man opened the door, received the tract, and slammed the door violently in Mr. Goodger's face. A week later he was strangely led to ring the bell of the same house. This time, the man soon appeared. He led Mr. Goodger up to the attic. At the top, Mr. Goodger immediately saw a rope dangling from the rafters, a noose at the end, and a box below. The man said, "Sir, when you kept ringing my doorbell last week my head was in that noose. I was ready to jump. Because you were so persistent, I decided to go down and see who it was. After receiving your tract, I again returned to the garret, but I sat down because I was arrested by the title of your tract. I read the tract, and God spoke to me. Now I am trusting in the Lord." As the man sat on the box, Mr. Goodger seized his opportunity to show him clearly the way of salvation. But for a tract, the man would have been in eternity without Christ. — *Moody Church News.*

* * *

God's Use of an Oyster

A professional diver said he had in his house what would probably strike a visitor as a very strange chimney ornament. It was the shell of an oyster holding a piece of a printed paper. The possessor of this ornament was diving on the coast when he observed at the bottom of the sea this oyster on a rock with a piece of paper in its mouth, which he detached and commenced to read through the goggles of his headdress. It was a Gospel tract! Coming to him so strangely and unexpectedly it so impressed him that he said, "I can't hold out against God's mercy in Christ any longer, since it pursues me thus." And there in the ocean depths he became a repentant man, accepted Christ, and was assured that his sins were forgiven. "Saved at the bottom of the sea" is his testimony. Is it not wonderful that God can use even an oyster as His messenger? Perhaps God is forced to use oysters when men fail. Let's get busy for God.—*Christian Victory.*

TRUST

Madame Chiang Testifies

A missionary traveling inland writes the following:

We had the pleasure of meeting Madame Chiang Kai-shek during an air alarm. She is a charming woman, and her faith is triumphant. Madame Chiang said: "God has eyes, He can see, and He knows that our cause is righteous. The darkest hour comes before the dawn. It is easy to trust God when all goes smoothly, but when everything is dark, then it means faith."

Let us pray that she and the Generalissimo may continue to triumph. His favorite hymn is "Lead kindly light, amid the encircling gloom."—*China's Millions.*

* * *

Foolish Birds and People

One morning I wanted to feed the birds. It was gray and cold and the ground was covered with snow. I stepped out on the porch and flung them handfuls of crumbs and called to them. No, there they sat, cold and hungry and afraid. They did not trust me. As I sat and watched and waited, it seemed to me I could get God's viewpoint more clearly than ever before. He offers, plans, waits, hopes, longs for all things for our good. But He has to watch and wait as I did for my timid friends.—*Sunday School Times.*

* * *

"Careful and Troubled"

And Jesus answered and said...thou art careful and troubled about many things.—Luke 10:41.

By WINIFRED M. NIENHUIS,
Oak Park, Ill.

"Careful and troubled"—ah, weary one, rest;
Cease thy vain striving and lean on His breast;
He knows the dangers that lurk just ahead,
Knows, too, when heart fails and all hope has fled.

"Careful and troubled"—ah, burdened one, trust,
Why should you fear? God is faithful and just!
He has His covenant honored with you,
Surely the promises given are true.

"Careful and troubled"—so filled with unrest,
Dreading the dawn with its toil and its test,
Trust Him your courage and strength to renew,
He will give grace for each task you must do.

Nothing is hid from His all-seeing eye,
Never a teardrop, nor even a sigh;
"Careful and troubled" you never need be,
Trust Him completely and doubtings will flee.

—*Moody Monthly.*

* * *

A Great Compliment

One wet, foggy, muddy day, a little girl was standing on one side of a street in London waiting for an opportunity to cross over. Those who have seen London streets on such a day, with their wet and mud, and have watched the rush of cabs, hansoms, omnibuses, and carriages, will not wonder that a little girl should be afraid to try to make her way through such a Babel as that. So she walked up and down, and looked into the faces of those who passed by. some looked careless, some harsh, some were in haste, and she did not find the one she sought, until at length an aged man, rather tall and spare, and of grave yet kindly aspect, came walking down the street. Looking into his face, she seemed to see the one for whom she had been waiting, and she went up to him and whispered timidly:

"Please, sir, will you help me over?"

The old man saw the little girl safely across the street, and when he afterward told the story he said of the incident. "That little child's trust was the greatest compliment I ever had in my life."

That man was Lord Shaftesbury. He had received honors at the hands of a mighty nation; he was complimented with the freedom of the greatest city on the globe; he had received the honors conferred by royalty; but the greatest compliment he ever had in his life was when that little unknown girl singled him out in the jostling crowd of a London street and dared to trust him, stranger though he was, to protect and assist her.—Selected.

* * *

Where to Trust

Trust in yourself, and you are doomed to disappointment; trust in your friends, and they will die and leave you; trust in money, and you may have it taken from you; trust in reputation, and some slanderous tongue may blast it; but trust in God, and you are never to be confounded in time or eternity.—D. L. Moody.

Why Everyone but God?

How often we trust each other,
 And only doubt our Lord.
We take the word of mortals,
 And yet distrust His Word;

But oh, what light and glory
 Would shine o'er all our days,
If we always would remember
 God means just what He says.
 —A. B. Simpson.

* * *

A Million Testimonies

Shott's drug store in Galveston, Tex., was open continuously day and night for twenty-six years. At the close of this long period all their filled prescriptions were displayed, above them read this sign: "Trusted One Million Times." Daniel did not betray God's trust in him.—Courtesy *Moody Monthly.*

* * *

Can We Hold Out?

I met an old Negro and asked him how long he had been serving the Lord. "Fifty years," he replied. "Well, Uncle," I said, "after keeping the faith for so long, you must feel pretty confident of holding out to the end." "Ah, Massa," he replied, "it's only a question of whether de Lord can hold on, and I reckons I can trust Him."—*Sunday School Times.*

* * *

What though my life with wintry cares be vexed,
 On a kind Father's watchful love I rest,
He meets *this moment's need, I leave the rest:*
 And always trusting shall be always blest.

—Selected.

* * *

Without Any Props

A consecrated Christian worker writes in a personal letter to a friend; "The truth is, I have been pretty much worried by the financial situation, and yesterday the Lord sent peace into my heart, so that now I have that sweet assurance that He will provide in His own time... I have been learning that the kind of trust that God wants is when everything is gone and only God remains. It's no trick to trust the Lord when the props are still standing."—*Sunday School Times.*

* * *

Greatness of Faith

Two Christians were once speaking of their experiences, and one said, "It is terribly hard to trust God and realize His hand in the dark passages of life." "Well, brother," said the other, "if you cannot trust a man out of your sight, he is not worth much; and if you cannot *trust God* in the dark, it shows you do not trust Him at all."—Courtesy of *Moody Monthly.*

* * *

When the Check is Paid in Full

Only the one who went all the way received the blessing. Says Russell Sewall: "I carried a check halfway to the bank. Did the bank therefore pay me half the value of the check? Nay; the bank didn't pay me a cent till I went all the way to the paying teller's window. And then the check was paid in full. Half-trust in God is no trust at all, and gets no reward; and that is why so many Christians lead flabby lives."—*Christian Union Herald.*

* * *

Trusting the Doctor

A medical man under conviction of sin, was visiting a patient who was saved and happy in the Lord. "Now," said he addressing the sick one, "I want you just to tell me what is—this faith in Jesus, and all that sort of thing that brings peace." His patient replied, "Doctor, I felt that I could do nothing, and I have put my case in your hands—I am trusting in you! This is exactly what every poor sinner must do to be saved—

put implicit trust in the Lord Jesus." "Is that all," exclaimed the doctor, "simply trusting in the Lord Jesus? I see it as I never did before. He has done the work." "Yes, Jesus said on the Cross, 'It is finished' (John 19:30), and 'whosoever believeth in Him should not perish, but have everlasting life' (John 3:16)." From that sick bed the doctor went away rejoicing in Christ.—*Scattered Seed.*

* * *

Trust Illustrated

A bridge builder named Scott a few years ago superintended the erection of a railway bridge in Crawford, Ind. When that bridge was finished, he knew every joint in it and what it would stand. When the time came to put it into use the engineer asked Mr. Scott, before venturing to drive his train across, "Is the bridge all safe?" By way of reply the bridge builder laid his own body under the new bridge and signaled the train to come on.

When it is evident that a minister is trusting the same bridge into eternity that he recommends to others, it adds great weight to his testimony.—*New Century Leader.*

* * *

Resignation

A visitor was once walking along a high part of the shore of the Dead Sea when he lost his balance and fell into the water. He could not swim and, in desperation lest he should sink and be drowned, he began to fling his arms about. At last he was exhausted and felt he could do no more. Then he found something happen: the water bore him up. The water of the Dead Sea is so heavy with salt and other minerals that when he lay still in it he found he floated on the surface. He could not drown so long as he resigned himself to the power of the deep. So too with us. There is a power beneath us and around us waiting to bear us up. We should cease from all our flounderings and fruitless efforts and let the power of God undergird us. —R. H. W. Shepherd.

Joy in Trusting

"The Lord redeemeth the soul of His servants and none of them that trust in Him shall be desolate" (Ps. 34:22).

What a vast portion of our lives is spent in anxious and useless forebodings concerning the future, either our own or that of our dear ones! Present joys, present blessings, slip by, and we miss half their sweet flavor, and all for want of faith in Him who provides for the tiniest insect in the sunbeam. Oh, when shall we learn the sweet trust in God our little children teach us every day by their confiding faith in us? We, who are so mutable, so faulty, so irritable, so unjust: and He who is so watchful, so pitiful, so loving, so forgiving! Why cannot we, slipping our hand into His each day, walk trustingly over that day's appointed path, knowing that evening will bring us sleep, peace, and Home?—Phillips Brooks.

* * *

What Held Her Faith

"How did you feel, Auntie, while the horses were running down the hill?" "I trusted to Providence till the breeching gave way; then I shut my eyes and gave up for lost." The good woman in question was not the only Christian whose faith held only by a strap.—Dr. T. L. Cuyler.

* * *

Whom Do We Trust Most?

A mature Christian man who has served the Lord truly and effectively for many years writes to a friend about a new work and new experiences that he is having. He says: "What a change! I think, also, that I am going to enjoy resting wholly on the Lord for daily needs. I never did it before in my life. I do not know where the rent for next month is coming from, but I am not worried at all. I am wondering why I have always slept better when some big (financial) man underwrites me, and a bit nervous when only the Lord says He will supply all my needs! Aren't Christians funny?"—*Sunday School Times.*

Simply Trusting

There is an easy, practical way to have faith. A minister said to an evangelist who was holding services in his church: "I have no faith in this matter, but I see it is in the Word of God and I am going to act on God's Word, no matter how I feel." And the evangelist replied, "Why, that is faith!" The Word of God is the secret of faith. "Faith cometh by hearing, and hearing by the word of God." We do not attain or achieve faith, we simply receive it as we read God's Word...Many a child of God is failing to enjoy God's richest blessings in Christ because he fails to receive the gift of faith. He looks within himself for some quality that will enable him to believe, instead of "looking unto Jesus the author and finisher of our faith."—*Sunday School Times.*

I Stoop

Into a dark tremendous sea of cloud,
It is but for a time: I press God's lamp
Close to my breast: its splendours, soon
or late,
Will pierce the gloom: I shall emerge
ere long!"

—Browning.

* * *

He does not even watch the way.
His father's hand, he knows
Will guide his tiny feet along
The pathway as he goes.

A childlike faith! A perfect trust!
God grant to us today,
A faith that grasps Thy Father Hand
And trusts Thee all the way.

—*War Cry.*

VICTORY

More Than Conquerors

More than conquerors through Him who
loved us,
Read the promise o'er and o'er;
Not almost or very nearly,
But conquerors and more.
When the world to sin would lure me
Is there victory for me?
Can I stand against the pressure
And a conqueror truly be?
When the tempter like an angel
Garbs himself in robes of light,
Can I recognize his cunning
Be a victor in the fight?
And when passions rise within me,
Anger, jealousy and pride,
Can I still be more than conqueror
When by these I'm sorely tried?
By myself I'm weak and helpless,
And I'll fall in sore defeat,
As upon life's rugged highway
With temptation I shall meet.
But with CHRIST, oh blest assurance!
More than conqueror I shall be,
As I yield HIM full possession
And He lives and reigns in me.

—Lillian M. Weeks.

* * *

Either Give It Up or Get More

A very practical man has confessed: "I have too much religion or too little; I must either give up what I have, or get more. I have too much religion to let me enjoy a worldly life, and too much worldliness to let me enjoy religion." He ended the dilemma triumphantly. He solved the problem by the whole-hearted acceptance of Christ as his living Lord. He put an end to divided loyalty, to doubtful obedience.—Dr. C. C. Albertson.

* * *

Victory

If you can smile when things go wrong,
And everybody wears a frown;
If you can hum a little song,
When castles have all fallen down.

If you can smile when friends are few,
Or this world's treasures pass away;
If you can to yourself be true;
And keep on smiling all the day.

If you can smile when death has come,
Snatched someone dear to you away;
If you can keep your lips still dumb,
When others cruel things will say.

If you will sometimes play the clown,
Though aching is your heart the while;
If you can turn temptation down,
And with it always wear a smile.

Then you have fought the battle: won
A conquest greater far than wealth.
What others would—you've really done,
You've won a victory over self.
—Mary J. Theobald.

* * *

One Day at a Time

Learning to live only one day at a time is one of the most vital lessons of the Christian life. Yet how slow we often are to "learn it by heart"! A beautiful picture is given by William M. Strong in a recent bulletin of the Soldiers' and Gospel Mission of South America, of which he is founder and director: "Only those who have lived in a country where fruits and flowers are dependent on irrigation," writes Mr. Strong, "can fully comprehend the parable of God's provision which we see every hour of every day in the green fields that surround Coihueco during the summer months. Central Southern Chile is a land of great rains for about seven months in the year, and the balance of the time is one of almost utter dryness. It is in these dry months that we see one of the Lord's miracles at work. The snowcapped mountains in front of the house at Mission headquarters are the storehouses of one of God's inexhaustible blessings. That heavenly mechanism which controls all nature here lets down each day only just enough water to supply that day's need for the thirsty fields; so through these long, dry months of summer, every day in exactly the same quantity, comes flowing through the ditches that life-giving supply, without which an arid desert would form each year over the face of south-central Chile. What a striking picture this, to those of His children who have come to know Him well enough to walk with Him by faith, telling Him (*and Him alone*) of their need, and then seeing Him work with all His marvelous ways of supplying that need — many times from the most unexpected sources and, marvel of marvels, always quite enough!"—*Sunday School Times.*

* * *

Victory through the Blood of the Lamb

Dr. Sewall, an old Methodist, when dying, shouted aloud the praises of God. His friends said, "Dr. Sewall, do not exert yourself; whisper, doctor, whisper."

"Let angels whisper," said he, "but the soul cleansed from sin by the Blood of Christ, a soul redeemed from death and hell, just on the threshold of eternal glory—oh, if I had a voice that would reach from pole to pole, I would proclaim it to all the world: Victory! Victory! through the *Blood of the Lamb!*"

Perhaps we the saints, who are still alive and well, ought to shout out the glorious Gospel more!—*Christian Victory.*

* * *

Psalm 23 in Action

In the time of the Covenanters a group of children was ordered to be shot. A little girl of eight looked up into the face of one of the soldiers, and said: "Sodger man, will ye let me take my wee brither by the hand and die that way?" "Bonny Whigs ye are," cried Westerha, "to die without a prayer." "If it please ye, sir," said the little girl, "me and Alec canna pray, but we can sing 'The Lord's my shepherd.' My mother learned it us afore she gaed awa." Then all the bairns stood up, and from their lips rose the quavering strains, "The Lord's my shepherd; I'll not want." As they sang, trooper after trooper turned away. Man after man fell out, and the tears rained down their cheeks. At last even Westerha turned and rode away, *for the victory was to the bairns through the singing of the twenty-third Psalm.—Christian Union Herald.*

It's Worse in a Believer

A Christian woman who had found the secret of victory over sin through constant faith in Christ was waited on by a friend to persuade her that anything else than daily and hourly trespass was impossible in our present condition. As he left, he said, "Now, my friend, always remember that sin in a believer is a very different thing from sin in an unconverted person." "Yes," was the memorable reply, "it is a great deal worse." —*Times of Refreshing.*

* * *

Weighted Wings

Once when I was in Switzerland I saw an eagle, a splendid bird, but it was chained to a rock. It had some twenty or thirty feet of chain attached to its legs, and to an iron bolt in the rock. There was the king of birds, meant to soar into Heaven, chained to earth. That is the life of multitudes of believers. Are you allowing business, are you allowing the cares of the world, are you allowing the flesh to chain you down, so that you cannot rise?—Selected.

* * *

This Too Is Victory

To love Him more than all beside,
E'en more than life,
To serve Him on whate'er betide,
Through sin and strife;
To sing when shadows round you fall,
And know no grief;
To pray when dangers thick enthrall,
In all belief;
To faithful be where others stray,
And never fail;
To carry on when dark the way,
And never quail;
To stand aloof from ev'ry stain,
Keep pure and white;
To walk in solitude or pain,
Yet in the light;
To never swerve from all His will,
Whoe'er may call;
To onward press, all patient, still,
Whate'er befall;
This, too, is victory.
—R. E. Neighbour, D.D.

* * *

Not by Subtraction

"Put ye on the Lord Jesus Christ, and make not provision for the flesh, to fulfill the lusts thereof" (Romans 13:14).

A student, vile of mind, once filled the walls of his "den" at college with evil pictures. And one day when he did not expect her, his mother paid him a visit. She sat in his room and he knew she saw these evil things. Not a word of comment did she offer, but she went to a picture shop and bought the finest likeness she could get of Jesus Christ, and sent it to her son. When next she visited his room, there was not an evil picture in it, but on the wall in solitary grandeur was the big, fine picture of the Saviour. "You know, mother," he said in a shamefaced way, "I found the old, bad pictures would not go with this one, and so they had to come down and go out." She had solved his problem not by substraction, but by addition. And so Augustine found it fifteen hundred years ago. *"Thou didst cast out my sins,"* he said, *"by coming in Thyself, Thou greater sweetness."* — R. H. W. Shepherd.

* * *

A Living Hope

The saintly A. J. Gordon, as he lay in the chamber in West Brookline Street, Boston, looked up and with one radiant burst of joy, cried, "Victory! Victory!" and so he went Home.—*Gospel Herald.*

* * *

"Not I"

During the Welsh revival a man was converted who had been a notorious drunkard. His conversion made him a sober and respectable man. The publican was angry to lose such a good customer, and called out to him one day as he passed the public house: "What's gone wrong, Charlie? Why do you keep going past instead of coming in?" Charlie halted for a moment, then with a skyward glance and a grateful tear glistening in his eye, replied: "Sir, it is not just that *I* keep going past; *We* go past! Ah, yes, that is the secret! *We* go past—Jesus and I." Faith unites me to the living Christ, so that His life flows to me, and I can sing—

Moment by moment, I'm kept in His love;
Moment by moment, I've life from above.
—*Sunday School Times.*

VISION

"Living Above"

Over the door of a little cabinet-maker's shop in London there hangs this sign, "Living Above." It is a notification to his customers that he can be found above his shop if the door is locked. It is a great thing for a worker to be able to say he is living above his work; that his dreams and hopes and real life are above the level of his day's toil. He may have to work amid the clods and clutter, but at least he can live above. No matter how lowly a man's work, his life can be above.—Courtesy Moody Monthly.

* * *

What the Sculptor Saw in the Stone

In an article on "The World of the Unseen," in the *Presbyterian,* the Rev. Stuart Nye Hutchison, D.D., tells the following incident to illustrate the lure of the unseen. Out in the Black Hills of Dakota the distinguished sculptor, the late Gutzon Borglum, carved in the rocks of the mountainside one of the most stupendous memorials on earth. The greatest thing Borglum ever did, however, is the head of Lincoln in the capitol in Washington. He cut it from a block of marble which had long been in his studio. It is said that into that studio every morning came an old Negro woman to dust. She had become accustomed to seeing that marble block standing there, and for days had not noticed it. One morning she came in and saw to her astonishment and terror the unmistakable lineaments of Lincoln appearing in the stone. She ran to the sculptor's secretary and said, "Am dat Abraham Lincoln?" "Yes." said the secretary, "that is Abraham Lincoln." "Well," said the old woman, "how in de world did Massa Borglum know that Abraham Lincoln was in dat block of stone?" The vision of the unseen is what transforms and glorifies Christian work. The people for whom our missionaries labor are many of them so unattractive; that is what we see. But off in the unseen we see what Jesus saw in those men of Galilee, the men and women they may be and will be when touched by the Spirit of Christ.—*Alliance Weekly.*

* * *

Walking Straight

Some boys were once trying to see which could make the straightest track across a snowy field. One succeeded in making a perfectly straight track. When asked how he did it he said, "I kept my eyes fixed on the goal, while you fellows kept yours on your feet." If "mine eyes are ever toward the Lord," I will walk a straight way.—*Earnest Worker.*

* * *

They Looked Up

An article in *The Christian Advocate* not long ago told of a lesson which a London physician learned from his children in the early days of the present war. His children were playing outside the home one night when one of the sudden blackouts occurred. At first they were terrified by the sudden darkness, and *then they looked up.*

A short time later they made their way into their father's office, and with faces aglow with happiness, exclaimed: "Look, father, we can see the stars—stars right here in London!" The doctor had always associated those blackouts with the historic words of Sir Edward Grey, uttered August 3, 1914: "The lights are going out all over Europe tonight." To him those blackouts had been inexpressibly depressing, unrelieved by any gleam of grace or ray of hope. In relating the incident, the doctor says: "Now my heart tells me—taught by my children—that the lights of God are still shining. The very darkness makes them more visible, if we will but lift our downcast eyes."

Of course! "The lights of God are still shining." They remind us that the Saviour is still "upholding all things by the word of His power" (Heb. 1:3). They remind us that God has not abdicated in favor of any dictator or combination of dictators. Some time soon, probably when the night seems darkest, up there in the sky will appear "The Bright and Morning Star," to be seen only by His own, and "to be admired in all them that believe . . . in that day" (Rev. 22:16; II Thess. 1:10).—*The Ohio Independent Baptist.*

* * *

One with a vision of the Lord
Who walks beneath His shining face,
And never will his stand retrace,
And never sheathe his flaming sword.

One all endued with faith, who dares,
With iron in blood, tested nerves;
Who from his vision never swerves,
Whose torch shines steady, never flares.

—*Gospel Herald.*

* * *

A Lincoln Story

A good many years ago a young man living eight miles from the village of Charleston, Illinois was employed as a field laborer. When not hired out to neighboring farmers he would go into the forest on his father's homestead and cut cordwood.

In the fall of the year, before the autumn rains set in and made the roads impassable, he would yoke the oxen to an old cart and go to Charleston and sell wood to the residents of that town. Times were hard and quite often selling wood was far from being an easy task. On one occasion darkness came on before he was able to dispose of his wood.

At last the wood was unloaded and he started home. But before he had gone far, rain began to fall. Eight miles was a long journey with an ox team. At a farm house he asked permission to stay overnight. The request was granted.

The farmer was also the horse doctor and a man of influence in that section of the country. That night the farmer and the young man talked until long after midnight.

The next morning the farmer and his wife stood in their doorway and watched the youth and his oxen wind their way over the hill. The man turned to his wife and said, "Some day this country will hear of that fellow." He really meant the community would hear of that fellow. But it would have been correct if he had said, "Some day the world will hear of that fellow.' "

The name of that fellow was *Abraham Lincoln.*—Clinton M. Hicks.

* * *

Real Eyesight

Physical eyesight is one of God's best gifts to men—but there is something better. A devoted Christian woman has suffered from dimming sight, and recently a physician was examining her eyes. He did not find much encouragement in his first examination, and expressed his sympathy. She was not disturbed, but told him, in a true and radiant Christian testimony, how good the Lord had been to her and her husband. The physician made a reply that is worth remembering, "You have no eyesight," he said, "but you have vision." And he spoke the truth—for she sees and rejoices in eternal treasures that can never be taken from her.—*Sunday School Times.*

* * *

"I don't look back; God knows the fruitless efforts,
The wasted hours, the sinning, the regrets;
I leave them all with Him who blots the record,
And mercifully forgives, and then forgets.

"I don't look forward; *God sees all the future,*
The road that, short or long, will lead me Home,
And He will face with me its every trial
And bear for me the burdens that may come.

"*But I look up*—into the face of Jesus,
For there my heart can rest, my fears are stilled;
And there is joy, and love, and light for darkness,
And perfect peace and every hope fulfilled."

—Selected.

The Uplifted Eye

"I will lift up mine eyes unto the hills, from whence cometh my help. My help cometh from the Lord, which made heaven and earth" (Ps. 121:1, 2). We need to live the life of the upward look. If we keep our eyes constantly on the things of earth we live on a low plane and miss the best in life. We are like the man who found a gold coin on the streets and ever afterward kept looking downward in the hope of finding more of the treasures of earth. He missed the beauties of the flowers and the sky and kept his eyes fastened on the dust and mire of the street. We need the upward look in order to receive necessary help in the experiences of life. By keeping our faces turned Heavenward we are prepared to meet temptations and to care for the duties and responsibilities of life that come our way. "If ye then be risen with Christ, seek those things which are above, where Christ sitteth on the right hand of God."—*Christian Monitor.*

* * *

Gain or Loss

"A young man once found a five-dollar bill on the street," says William Feather, a well-known writer. "From that time on he never lifted his eyes when walking. In the course of years he accumulated 29,519 buttons, 54,172 pins, twelve cents, a bent back, and a miserly disposition. He lost the glory of the sunlight, the sheen of the stars, the smiles of friends, tree-blossoms in the spring, the blue skies, and the entire joy of living."—*San Francisco News.*

Seeing What Is Going to Be

A number of years ago a noted artist was working on a great mural. This was to be a great work of art which he intended to be the masterpiece of his life. He had erected a scaffold and was standing upon it, putting in the background of the picture. A friend suddenly came into the studio and stood quietly in the rear of the room, looking at the work. The artist was slapping on the gray tones and deep blues all across the canvas for the background. Then he wished to view his work from a better perspective so he descended the ladder and stepping back, with his eyes on the canvas, he backed right into his friend without seeing him. Enthusiastically he said, "This is going to be the masterpiece of my life! What do you think of it? Isn't it grand?" His friend replied, "All that I see is a great dull daub." Then said the artist, "Oh, I forgot. When you look at the picture you see only what is there. Now, whenever I look at it, I see what is going to be there."—H. A. Ironside.

* * *

The Lost Image

Michael Angelo lingered before a rough block of marble so long that his companion remonstrated. In reply, Michael Angelo said with enthusiasm, "There's an angel in that block and I'm going to liberate him!" Oh, what unbounding love would manifest itself in us towards the most unlovable—the most vile—if only we saw what they might become, and in our enthusiasm for souls we cried out, "There's the image of Christ—marred, scarred, well-nigh obliterated—in that dear fellow, and I'm going to make that man conscious of it." —A. E. Richardson.

Making a Dream Come True

A Scotch boy by the name of Alexander Duff had a dream in which, in a chariot of great glory, God drew near to him where he lay musing on a hillside, and calling to him said, "Come up, hither; I have work for thee to do."

That vision never faded from his memory. He went to grammar school and to St. Andrews University, where a missionary society was formed among the students, Duff becoming its first librarian.

In 1829 he went out to India as the first missionary from the Scottish church. He was a real pioneer. He opened a school in Calcutta, and later helped to establish a medical college there.

If you have a dream of doing great service for God, try to make it come true as Alexander Duff made his dream come true.—Selected.

* * *

The Faraway Look

A poor shoemaker, in his dreary little shop in a great city, one day found by accident that there was one little place in his dark room from which he could get a view, through a window, of green fields, blue skies, and faraway hills. He wisely set his bench at that point, so that at any moment he could lift his eyes from his dull work and have a glimpse of the great beautiful world outside. From the darkest sickroom, and from the midst of the keenest sufferings there is always a point from which we can see the face of Christ and have a glimpse of the glory of Heaven. If only we can find this place and get this vision, it will make it easy to endure even the greatest suffering.—*The King's Business.*

* * *

Not "What," But "Who"

We had rooms connecting: just a door between us, and it was open most of the time. Dr. Griffith Thomas was always engaged in work, and I am a man with enough to keep me employed. As we sat together in the hotel we could talk through the open door. I shall never forget the last season together, both ministering in a Southern city. Dr. Thomas looked up from his desk and said, "Oh, Tucker, we don't know what is in the future, do we?" "No, Dr. Thomas, thank God, we do not!" All was silent for a time; then again he cried, "Oh, Tucker, we know *who* is in the future, don't we?"—*The Wonderful Word.*

WAR

"Whence Come Wars"

There is something pathetic in the way humanity raises its wounded head after each war with a new determination to stop all war. Man repeats his age-old mistake of building without God. But there has been of late rather a widespread recognition that war is more than a material problem. Two outstanding military leaders have expressed this thought, as reported by *Time* (Sept. 10). Air Chief Marshal Sir Arthur Harris said: "If you couple the atomic bomb with the projected missile you have something with possibilities that hardly bear contemplation. . . . The whole world is now in the range of this weapon. . . .War will go on until there is a change in the human heart—and I see no signs of that." At the Japanese surrender General MacArthur said: "Military alliance, balances of power, League of Nations all in turn failed. . . . We have had our last chance. If we do not now devise some greater and more equitable system Armageddon will be at our door. The problem basically is theological and involves a spiritual recrudescence and improvement of human character that will synchronize with our almost matchless advance in science, art, literature, and all material and cultural developments of the past two thousand years. It must be of the spirit if we are to save the flesh." Sir Arthur Harris has got to the root of the trouble ("the human heart") and General MacArthur goes a step farther by pointing out that "the problem . . . involves a spiritual recrudescence." These statements approach two basic truths of Scripture, that the human heart is desperately wicked, and that man must be born again, and General MacArthur has indicated in a number of public utterances that he knows and believes the Bible. Scripture plainly teaches that the whole world will never be converted, and that wars will not cease until the return of Christ. But we may still hope and pray that men like Harris and MacArthur, and other leaders, may go still farther and recognize that even the human heart can be changed by the Gospel, which "is the power of God unto salvation to every one that believeth." —*Sunday School Times.*

* * *

Battlefield Yielding

William Howard Taft, of honored memory, with great optimism, once wrote, "The battlefield as a place of settlement of disputes is gradually yielding to arbitral courts of justice. The interests of great masses are not being sacrificed as in former times, to the selfishness, ambitions, and aggrandizement of sovereigns," etc. But Mr. Taft wrote this in 1911! However, the point is that many advocates of peace base their activities and expectation on the battlefields "gradually yielding." — *Gospel Herald.*

* * *

The Lord, a Man of War

Question: Is there a single precept or example in the New Testament justifying the use of carnal weapons for any cause?

Answer: Why restrict your question to the New Testament? Is not the God of the Old Testament the same as the God of the New Testament? Moses said of Him, "The Lord is a man of war: the Lord is his name" (Exod. 15:3). The record goes on to relate that He destroyed the hosts of Pharaoh in the Red Sea. There are righteous wars, such as wars waged in defense of one's country, or in defense of our civil and religious liberties, all of which necessitate the use of carnal weapons. Usually such wars are not wars of aggression, waged for the enlargement of territory. Again, righteous wars have been fought at the direct command of God for the punishment of national sins. For example, men, women, and children were ordered by God to be destroyed by the Israelites (Deut. 2:34). Concerning the New Testament teaching, has the questioner never read the book of Revelation? Of the rider upon the white horse, called faithful and true, that "in righteousness he doth judge and make war" (Rev. 19:11)? There are armies even in heaven (v. 14), and some day they will be victorious upon the earth (vv. 19, 20). We deplore wars, but sometimes they are righteous and necessary.— Courtesy *Moody Monthly.*

* * *

Wishful Thinking

"Who goes there
In the night,
Across the wind-swept plain?"

"We are the ghosts of a valiant war,
A million murdered men."

"Who goes there
At the dawn,
Across the sun-swept plain?"

"We are the ghosts of those who swear
It must never be again."

—Thomas C. Clark.

* * *

The "Spoils" of War

When, after many battles past,
Both, tired with blows, make peace at last,
What is it, after all, the people get?
Why! Taxes, widows, wooden legs and debt. —*Sunday School Times.*

Another Crop on Flanders Field

Yes, Flanders still produces them,
The blood-red poppies of the war.
In field, on hillside, they are seen,
The flame-red showing where they are.

The years have quickly sped along
Since cannon boomed above your head,
Since in amazement you looked on
And dropped your petals on the dead.

The spring and summer came around;
For men the seasons cannot stop.
And though your blossoms fall unseen,
You smile and bear another crop—

Another crop for Flanders fields?
Oh, not a crop of human life!
They fertilized your fields back there—
Those men who toppled in the strife.

Your soil is richer through their blood.
The world is poorer—poor, indeed,
Ignoring what at cost they taught,
And ever blind to human need.

The sheep now graze on Flanders field
A little lad to be their guide
Like other lads in other years,
Before, by cannon shot, they died.

The shepherd boy will soon be grown,
The poppies watch him through the years;
They bend and think of other boys—
You call it dew—but it is tears.

Oh, tell me, sin-mad world of men,
These wars of hatred, can they stop?
Don't drive these boys to battlefields,
And mow them down—another crop!
—Will H. Houghton.

* * *

What It Cost

The cost of killing a soldier increased from $50 in the time of Julius Caesar to between $50,000 and $75,000 in World War II, according to H. V. Churchill, an industrial chemist.

Churchill said the expense of war-time killing has risen steadily though the centuries, with a tremendously great advance occuring between World War I and World War II.

By the time of Napoleon, the cost had became $1,500 for each man killed, the chemist said, and during World War I the figure was about $2,500. He added that Napoleon's advisers and allies thought the cost far too high in their time.

Churchill cited as the reason for the huge increase in the cost the fact that war is now fought with machinery—which adds greatly to the cost—although manpower still is the backbone of war.

"The development of mechanical devices and improvement of machinery has lifted a great deal of hard physical labor from men's shoulders but military men are turning this machinery to war purposes instead of using it for peaceful pursuits," he declared.—*Chicago Daily News.*

* * *

Malice Toward None

"With malice toward none; with charity for all; with firmness in the right as God gives us to see the right, let us strive on to finish the work we are in; to bind up the nation's wounds, to care for him who shall have borne the battle, and for his widow and his orphan—to do all which may achieve and cherish a just and lasting peace among ourselves and with all nations."—From Second Inaugural Address by Abraham Lincoln.

WILL OF GOD

Dr. Gray's "Set Back"

Dr. James M. Gray says, "Once, when convalescing from a long illness, it was suggested that for the benefit of the change I visit the British provinces. The arrangements were all made when unexpectedly another malady threw me on my bed again. How disappointing! For what was I waiting longer in the sick room? Soon I received a satisfactory answer. Picking up a newspaper, I read that the steamer on which I should have sailed struck a reef on entering St. John harbor and almost instantly sank."—*Sunday School Times.*

* * *

Why God Changes Our Plans

Sudden changes in our plans may be hard to accept. But they may be forced upon us by some circumstance over which we may have no control. And God may be back of the circumstance. Yet the plans were very dear to us, and we had set our hearts upon carrying them through. Why should God have permitted them to be changed, or to be set aside completely?

Someone has written: "'Thou God seest me' is a precious thought. He sees us and our path beset with danger, and He plans our ways and guides us accordingly. That is why he often permits reverses and failure to come our way. *He changes our plans, for He sees the danger in them.*" What a blessing, then, that God does not always let us carry out our plans!

When a baby plans, with great interest and pleasure, to play with brightly burning fire, a loving parent is likely to change the baby's plans. Yet that brightly burning fire, dangerous as it is, may not be as grave a danger as would be the result of some plans that we are prevented by God's love from carrying through. As this writer reminds us: "knowing the end from the beginning, He cannot mistake." Our plans are sometimes mistaken; God's plans are always perfect.—*The Sunday School Times.*

* * *

One or the Other Must Go

At a meeting in Massachusetts, a speaker, who had just delivered an urgent appeal to a group of young people to accept Christ, was asked this startling question by a young girl, "Sir, I should like to know how we can be Christians, and have our own way." Perhaps many of us have either consciously or unconsciously asked this same question. We have sought, in a measure at least, to do God's will, but we have reserved the right to have our own way whenever it pleases us. This is not God's plan for Christian living and service, however, and it always brings conflict, and unrest, and lack of joy and power.—John W. Lane, Jr., in the *Sunday School Times* and *Christian Youth.*

* * *

Knowing and Doing God's Will

Why do we want to know God's will? Most Christians would feel that this was a strange question, for those whose lives are yielded to God have a real desire to know His plan for them in order that they may follow it in their lives. But is there not sometimes too great a lapse of time between knowledge and obedience? Dr. William L. Pettingill the well-known Bible teacher and author of many books, at a meeting of the Philadelphia Fundamentalists made a penetrating remark on this subject. "Most people," he said, "don't want to know the will of God in order to *do* it; they want to know it in order to *consider* it." It often takes time to learn just what God wants us to do in any particular matter, but once we know His purpose we ought not to delay in at least beginning to carry it out by His grace. And when obedience is prompt, "when we walk with the Lord in the light of His Word, what a glory He sheds on our way!"—*Sunday School Times.*

* * *

We Are His Workmanship

Behind our lives the Weaver stands,
And works His wondrous will;
We leave it in His all-wise hands,
And trust His perfect skill.
—Selected.

* * *

A Soft Pillow

Someone says, "The will of God which we sometimes think so hard, is, if we only knew it, just the softest pillow to rest upon." If we recognized that there was no choice but God's, no aim but such as had Him for its object, how it would take the worry and care from our lives! Have we learned that we are only safe, happy, right, when He chooses?—*Gospel Herald.*

* * *

God's Plan for Us

God has a plan for every life in Christ Jesus. What a wondrous truth is this! And yet how reasonable a one. Shall the architect draw the plans for his stately palace? Shall the artist sketch the outlines of his masterpiece? Shall the shipbuilder lay down the lines for his colossal ship? And yet shall God have no plan for the soul which He brings into being and puts "in Christ Jesus"? Surely He has.

Yea, for every cloud that floats across the summer sky: for every blade of grass that points its tiny spear Heavenward, God has a purpose and a plan. How much more then, for you who are His own in Christ Jesus, does God have a perfect life plan.—James H. McConkey.

* * *

Missing God's Plan

A gentleman captured two baby eagles and raised them with great care. They grew to be fine specimens of this noble bird, until one day the door of their cage was left open by accident and the birds escaped. One flew to a nearby tree, where it roosted on a low branch, for it could not use its wings, never having learned to fly except in the close confinement of its cage. It was not long until it met an untimely death by the gun of a hunter. The other eagle fell or was knocked into a swift flowing river and was drowned. Both of these eagles missed God's plan for their lives by being taken captive by man. They were created to live in high places and to soar aloft in the sky, but instead they were doomed to live on the ground and to meet an early death.

God created you and me to live on a high plane and to carry out the great plans He has for our life. May we have wisdom to yield our lives to Him so that the forces of sin may not take us captive, and cause us to miss His plan for our life.—*Gospel Herald.*

* * *

How to Know God's Will

When I was crossing the Irish Channel one dark starless night, I stood on the deck by the captain and asked him, "How do you know Holyhead Harbor on so dark a night as this?" He said, "You see those three lights? Those three must line up behind each other as one, and when we see them so united we know the exact position of the harbor's mouth." When we want to know God's will there are three things which always concur—the inward impulse, the Word of God, and the trend of circumstances! God in the heart, impelling you forward. God in His Book, corroborating whatever He says in the heart; and God in circumstances, which are always indicative of His will. Never start until these three things agree.—F. B. Meyer.

* * *

In the center of the circle
  Of the will of God I stand:
There can come no second causes,
  All must come from His dear hand.
All is well! For 'tis my Father
  Who my life hath planned.

Shall I pass through waves of sorrow?
  Then I know it will be best;
Though I cannot tell the reason,
  I can trust, and so am blest.
God is Love, and God is faithful,
  So in perfect Peace I rest.
—*Gospel Herald.*

* * *

When the Bird Stopped Struggling

Wordsworth, in one of his poems, tells about a bird that was carried from Norway by a storm. It fought hard against the gale in its effort to win its way back to Norway, but all in vain. At last it yielded to the wind, and instead of being carried to destruction it was borne to the warm shores of England, to the green meadows and forests. So when we try to fight against God's will we are making efforts which will come to naught, and are doing so to our own injury and loss. But if we willingly accept God's will, it will be for our good; we shall be borne on to blessedness and joy.—John T. Montgomery, M. A.

* * *

Go Slow

Be slow to take new steps in the Lord's service, or in your business, or in your families. Weigh everything well; weigh all in the light of the Holy Scriptures, and in the fear of God.

Seek to have no will of your own, in order to ascertain the mind of God, regarding any steps you propose to take; so that you can honestly say, you are willing to do the will of God, if He will only please to instruct you.

But when you have found out what the will of God is, seek for His help, and seek it earnestly, perseveringly, patiently, believingly, and expectantly: and you will surely, in His own time and way, obtain it.—Selected.

* * *

"My Jesus, As Thou Wilt"

The hymn, "My Jesus, as Thou Wilt" was written by Benjamin Schmolke, and is based on Mark 14:36. We can hear its heart-throbs in every line. Schmolke's home town was nearly destroyed by fire. Two of his own children were taken by flames. Later he himself was stricken with paralysis which eventually led to blindness. Yet he could sing his "Hymn of Trust":

My Jesus, as Thou wilt!
  Oh may Thy will be mine!
Into Thy hand of love
  I would my all resign.
Through sorrow or through joy,
  Conduct me as Thine own,
And help me still to say,
  "My Lord, Thy will be done."

—Ivan H. Hagedorn, S.T.D., in the *Sunday School Times.*

Misjudging God

A lady who had an only child said to Mrs. Pearsall Smith, "I do not dare to pray, 'Thy will be done,' because I am afraid God will take away my little boy or will send me some heavy trial." To which Mrs. Smith replied, "Suppose your child should come to you and say, 'I want to be and do just what you desire today,' would you say to yourself, 'Now is my opportunity to make this child do all the disagreeable duties I want done; I will take advantage of his willingness to please me by cutting off his pleasures today, and will keep him at hard discipline'?" "No, no," said the mother, "I would give him the best day I could possibly plan." "And can you think God is less just and loving than you?"—*Sunday School Times.*

* * *

God's Reason Always Perfect

To a severely afflicted man the question was put, "Do you see any special reason for this sore trial?" He answered immediately, "No, but I am as well satisfied as if I saw a thousand, for my Father's will is the perfection of reason.—G. H. Knight.

* * *

It Makes a Difference Who Is with You

What God calls a man to do, He will carry through. I would undertake to govern half a dozen worlds if God called me to do it; but if He did not call me to do it, I would not undertake to govern half a dozen sheep.—*Payson in Sabbath Reading.*

* * *

Seeing the Father's Hand

So long as we look at second causes, at men or things, as being the origin and source of our sorrows, we shall be filled completely with burning indignation and hopeless grief. But when we come to understand that nothing can happen to us except as our Father permits, and that, though our trials may originate in some lower source, yet they become

God's will for us as soon as they are permitted to reach us through the defense of His environing presence — then we smile through our tears and kiss the dear Hand that uses another as its rod, and our hearts are at rest.

Judas may seem to mix the cup and put it to our lips; but it is nevertheless the cup which our Father giveth us to drink—and shall we not drink it? Much of the anguish passes away from life's trials as soon as we discern our Father's hand. Then affliction becomes chastening. There is a great difference between the two. Affliction may come from a malignant and unfriendly source; but chastening is the work of the Father, yearning over His children, desiring to eliminate from their characters all that is unlovely and unholy, and to secure in them entire conformity to His character and will.—F. B. Meyer.

* * *

Sealed Orders

Sometime, I know not when or how,
All things will be revealed;
And until then content am I
To sail with orders sealed.
—Selected.

* * *

Of Which Will Are You Afraid?

In a prayer-meeting a good sister prayed, "Lord, we're afraid of our wills, we're afraid to do our wills for fear of the consequences; teach us Thy will!" There was something striking about that prayer. The majority of people, including some professed Christians, are afraid of God's will rather than their own.—*Spring Grove Ripplet.*

* * *

The Blueprints

An engineer was confined to his bed, his lower limbs being paralyzed, but because of his reputation for great skill he was asked to draw the blueprints for a great suspension bridge. The plans were at length completed and placed in the hands of those who were to do the work. Months passed by and the bridge was finished. Four men came to the engineer's room and carried him out on his cot to a place from whence he could view the bridge spanning a wide river, over which vehicles were rapidly passing. Tears filled his eyes, and looking down at the blueprints in his hands, he cried out, "It's just like the plan; its just like the plan." God has his blueprints. They are world plans; others are individual life plans. Have we found His plan for our lives, and are we obediently walking therein? There can be no greater reward, when looking back over our lives from eternity, than to hear Him say, "It's just like the plan; it's just like the plan."—*The Wonderful Word.*

* * *

Just to let the Father do,
What He will:
Just to know that He is true,
And be still.
Just to follow hour by hour
As He leadeth.
Just to draw the moment's power
As it needeth.
Just to trust Him, that is all,
Then the day will surely be
Peaceful, whatsoe'er befall,
Bright and blessed, calm and free.
—Selected.

* * *

God's Will Always Best

God's will is always the best; it is always divine love. A stricken wife, standing beside the coffin of her husband, said to a friend: "There lies my husband, my only earthly support, my most faithful human friend, one who has never once failed me; but I must not forget that there lies also the will of God, and that that will is perfect love." By faith she saw good and the blessing in what appeared to her the wreck of all her happiness. But truly the good and the blessing are in every dark providence which comes into the life of God's child. Our Father never means us harm in anything He does or permits. His word is, "I know the thoughts that I think toward you, thoughts of peace."—J. R. Miller.

Safely Having Our Own Way

One of my boys, when he was about eight or ten years of age, was what you would call a husky boy, and liked to have his own way. I said to him one day, "Philip, you ought not to want your own way." He dropped his head as if I had given him a problem to solve; after thinking awhile he said, "Father, if I choose the will of the Lord and go His way because I want to, don't I still have my own way?" If you learn that secret you have the whole secret of the Christian life. — *Sunday School Times.*

Better than Doing the Lord's Work

Miss Miriam Booth, daughter of the founder of the Salvation Army, a beautiful, brilliant, cultured woman, began her Christian work with great promise, and had unusual success. Very soon disease laid hold upon her and brought her down to the point of death. A friend visiting her one day told her that it seemed a pity that a woman so capable should be hindered by sickness from doing the Lord's work. She replied with gentle grace, "It is great to do the Lord's work, but it is greater to do the Lord's will."—*Northwestern Pilot.*

WITNESSING

Cured by Testimony

I have heard Dr. Fred Moffitt, who was born in Scotland, say that as a boy he stammered so terribly that he was the laughingstock of the neighbors. Soon after his conversion he attended a testimony meeting. He wanted to testify as to what the Lord had done for him, but the thought of his stammering tongue held him back. The call to testify became so insistent that he promised the Lord that if a girl sitting near him testified he would, too. Soon the girl arose and gave her testimony, and Fred Moffitt kept his promise. Not only did the Lord help him to give this testimony but his stammering tongue has given him no further trouble from that day to this. He is pastor of the great First Baptist Church of Frankfort, Ky.—*Sunday School Times.*

* * *

A Faithful Witness

Over seventy years ago, a United States naval cutter the *Colfax,* sailed under Captain Charles Jones. On board this ship was a little Chinese lad who very quickly won his way into the hearts of the captain and crew. Captain Jones became the hero of young Soong, and whatever he did was just right in the eyes of the lad.

One day the captain told Soong that Jesus Christ was the hero and guide of his life, and the Chinese boy, although he did not at first quite understand, began to get a new picture of God—a picture very different from the idols he had worshiped in the temple in China. Young Soong became a Christian and received his education in America. He went back to China with a wonderful message of what Christ had done in his life. He began to print the Gospel in the Chinese language.

Soong married a Chinese girl and they had six children. One girl is Mrs. Sun Yat Sen the wife of China's liberator; another girl is Mrs. H. H. Kung, wife of the minister of finance. Mei-ling Soong is Madam Chiang Kai-shek, a leader not only in China but throughout the world. A son, T. V. Soong, is a member of the cabinet. The generalissimo, his wife and all of her family, are Christians. And all because a sea captain was true to his calling as a Christian!

Because Captain Jones was a faithful witness, China today is showing the world what Christ can do in a nation that will give Him a chance. What glorious transformations we could behold in the hearts of individuals and in the life of nations, if more men remembered the words of the Risen Christ: "You are to be My witnesses both in

Jerusalem and in all Judea, and in Samaria, and to the very ends of the earth."—*Dallas "Reminder."*

* * *

His Answer Was God's Answer

A Hindu, who had become a Christian, on his way to church one Sabbath, passed some British soldiers who thought they would joke with him. "Hello, Sammy," they called. "How's Jesus this morning?" The Hindu stopped and looked at them. "You Sahibs come from a great country that has known Jesus a long time. It is your country that has given us this Book to teach us of Him," and he held up his Bible. "You ask how Jesus is this morning. Jesus Christ is the same yesterday, and today, and forever." Two of the soldiers could not sleep that night. The next day they went to the Hindu. They said, "We could not rest until we gave ourselves to Jesus. You brought us to him."—*The Presbyterian.*

* * *

While in Prison

A very earnest preacher of the Gospel was caught and put into prison in the south of Spain, and expected to die. There were Anarchists and Communists in the prison; they were desperate, and began to write curses on the wall against their captors, so the evangelist wrote on the wall, "Fear not them which kill the body, but are not able to kill the soul: but rather fear him which is able to destroy both soul and body in hell." Underneath he wrote John 3:16 in full. That attracted attention. One of the prisoners was a young schoolmaster, and the evangelist had the joy of leading him to Christ. One day the schoolmaster said to him. "My name is on the list today to be shot; I am so glad you wrote that text on the wall. Before, I should have been desperate, but now, although I do not want to die, I am not desperate, because I know I am going to be with Jesus, and I shall see you again one day." They embraced one another and he was taken out and shot, but one day we shall see him in Glory, brought to the Lord Jesus Christ by the faithful testimony given in prison.—From an address by P. J. Buffard to Women's Protestant Union.

* * *

Keep up Your Testimony

A Presbyterian youth from New Orleans was a naval "wireless" operator during the war. Early one morning, after a night on duty, he snatched a few minutes for his 'quiet hour" when no message was going over, and he was reading the Twenty-third Psalm. Suddenly the thought came to him to send the Psalm out over the water and see if any ship would take it up. He did, and as he sent the last word, sixteen ships answered a wireless "Amen."—The Elim Evangel.

* * *

Faithful Witnessing

Some years ago a commuter on the Long Island Railroad was known to every regular patron on the five o'clock local. He was a well-dressed, soft-spoken young man who lived at Jamaica. Every evening after the train left the subway he would rise and go to the front of the car. As he walked back he would speak to every passenger, saying, "Excuse me; but if any of your family or any of your friends are blind, tell them to consult Dr. Garl. He restored my sight." That is evangelism. He did not argue. He testified. Courteously, courageously, confidently he commended to each and all the one who had opened his eyes. He had good news and he told it. If we who are redeemed would do likewise!—United Presbyterian.

* * *

My Challenge to Laymen

My challenge to laymen is that when Christ said, "Go ye into all the world, and preach the Gospel," He did not mean only preachers but everyone who believed on Him as the Lord of Glory. The division between the clergy and the laity is a division of our own making, and was not instituted by Christ, nor was it evidenced in the early Church. They believed the word "Go" meant every man, and they obeyed the Lord's command. My challenge to you is for a return to this first century conception of Christianity where every believer is a witness to the grace of the Lord Jesus Christ.—R. G. Le Tourneau, Peoria, Ill.

* * *

In the Elevator

We have a marvelous opportunity to witness for the Lord Jesus Christ in a way preachers cannot witness. In business we meet multitudes of people who never go to church. Peter Stam comes into my office occasionally. He came one morning, and we had a delightful time of fellowship. When he was leaving, another gentleman, an executive in a large utility company, who had been calling on one of the members of our firm, was leaving also, and they took the same elevator. The only occupants of the car were Mr. Stam, the gentleman, and the lady who operates the elevator. Mr. Stam never misses an opportunity to witness. He said to the elevator operator, as he was getting off, "I hope when you make your last trip it will be up and not down." The girl was so startled she swallowed her gum. He said, "My dear girl, I am getting on in years. I am seventy, and one of these days I am going to meet my Lord and Saviour Jesus Christ. I hope I shall meet you there." She hasn't forgotten that.—Erling Olsen, in *Moody Monthly.*

* * *

Better Have a New One

Max I. Reich tells of a man who had a wonderful blessing in Christ. He wrote out the story of it and frequently used to read it to his friends. One day when a visitor came to his home he said to his wife: "Would you mind going upstairs and getting my blessed experience? I have not seen it for some time." When the wife returned she told him that the "blessed experience" had been chewed into small pieces by the mice. Do we not need to ask God to keep us fresh that our testimony may be ever new?—*The King's Business.*

* * *

Reluctant to Witness

A minister conversed with a man who professed conversion. "Have you united with the church?" he asked him. "No, the dying thief never united with the church and he went to heaven," was the answer. "Have you talked to your neighbors about Christ?" "No, the dying thief never did." "Have you given to missions?" "No, the dying thief did not." "Well, my friend," said the minister, "*the difference between you two seems to be that he was a dying thief, and you are a living one.*"—*Otterbein Teacher.*

* * *

Keep Witnessing

The Countess of Huntington was walking in her garden one day where a workman was repairing part of the garden wall. She spoke to the man about his soul, but the word seemed to have little effect. Years after, while speaking to another workman she said, "Thomas I fear you have not looked to Christ for salvation." "Your ladyship is mistaken," replied the workman, "I have looked and am saved." "How did it happen?" inquired the countess. "It was while you were speaking to James, my fellow workman, when we were repairing the garden wall." "How did you hear?" "I was on the other side, and heard your words through a hole in the wall." "Faith cometh by hearing, and hearing by the Word of God."—Selected.

* * *

Worship Witnesses

Genuine worship witnesses for Christ. Conversation on a Pullman was shockingly irreverent, and about gambling. A little fellow in wee pajamas, timidly kneeling at his berth, prayed with childish voice, "Now I Lay Me Down to Sleep." Profanity ceased. Gambling conversation died into silence. Eyes of hardened men became moist. One rough man said, "I would like to know what that little fellow (worshiper) has that I have lost."—*Gospel Herald.*

* * *

Nailing His Colors to the Pole

When Captain Hedley Vicars was converted he resolved at once to fly his colors. He bought a large Bible and laid it openly on his table. "It was to speak for me," he said, "before I was strong enough to speak for myself." It spoke with effect, and many of his old companions made sport of his religion, or cut him for it. He stood by his guns, but not without trembling. "Would that I felt as little fear of being called a Christian," he said, "as I used to feel in being enlisted against Christianity." Yet trembling was not retreating, and he went straight on with his duties alike as a Christian and as a soldier. "Enable me, Lord Jesus," he prayed, "to please my colonel and yet to please Thee"—*Sunday School Times.*

* * *

Does Persistence Pay?

One of his officers gave me the secret of this pastor's success when he told me his own experience. He found himself out of a position and decided he would call upon the minister and see if he knew of any opening. It was Monday morning. When he knocked at the minister's home, he was ushered in and asked to sit in the living room, and told that the pastor would be right down. As he sat waiting the thought occurred —now when the pastor enters he will say, "Good-morning Brother. Are you saved this morning?" This was his usual greeting to the milkman, the grocer, and every one he met. "Well," said the inner voice to the waiting man, "you might as well settle it now and be saved, so you can say 'yes' when he asks you." The man dropped on his knees, cried out in repentance, and was born of the Spirit. Soon the pastor came in and said, "Good-morning, Brother. Are you saved this morning?" "I am," said the visitor. The pastor knew the man and was surprised. "When did that happen?" "Two minutes ago," was the reply. "I knew you'd ask me, so I got it all settled before you came in."—Selected.

* * *

Why the Women Were Prominent

Some years ago, Dr. H. H. Snell, an English Bible teacher of repute, was walking along a busy street with a brother in the Lord, when their attention was attracted to two women who were conducting a street meeting, giving out the Gospel to a great throng of both sexes. The unnamed brother, a rigid stickler as to the letter of the Word, turned to the Doctor and said, "What a disgusting thing to see those women so forgetful of their place, as to be preaching in public!" The venerable Dr. Snell replied, "My brother, it is because you and I are not there that God is using them."—Dr. H. A. Ironside, in *Serving-and-Waiting.*

* * *

Ready Witnessing

An African slaveholder had in his employ a poor black boy who, having heard of the missionaries and their preaching, had a desire to go and hear about Christ. He crept away quietly one evening. But he had to pass by his master's window, and was seen by the slaveholder.

"Where are you going?" called the master.

The boy, trembling, answered, "Me go to hear the missionaries, Massa."

"To hear the missionaries indeed! If you ever go there, you shall have thirty-nine lashes and be put in irons."

The boy answered, "Me tell Massa —me tell the great Massa."

"What do you mean—tell the great Master?" asked the man angrily.

"Me tell the great Massa, Lord of Heaven, that Massa was angry with me because I wanted to go and hear His Word."

Greatly astonished, the master said, "Go along and hear them, then."

After the boy had gone, the master became restless and troubled. He had not thought that he himself had a Master in Heaven, who knew all that he was doing. He determined to follow the slave to the Christian service.

He stood in the rear of the little assembly and listened eagerly to the words of the missionary, who was preaching from the text, "Lovest thou Me?"

"Is there one poor slave here who loves Jesus Christ?" he asked. "One who dares to confess Him?"

The black boy sprang forward, and holding up both hands while tears coursed down his cheeks, cried out earnestly, "Yes, Massa, me do love Him! Me love Him with all my heart!"

The slaveholder went home still more astonished, but convinced of the power of the Gospel. As a result he gave his heart to God and lived a consistent Christian life.—*Gospel Herald.*

* * *

Putting in a Word for Jesus

Among others that came forward for special blessing at the close of a meeting for the deepening of spiritual life, in the north of London, was a lady who appeared to us to be far more concerned about her spiritual state than others did that had accompanied her. She was asked if it was pardon for sin she needed. "No," was the reply. "Then is it purity of heart that you are seeking?" "Oh! no," she sobbed again. "The reason that I have come forward is because I feel that I want power to put in a word for Jesus."—Dr. Thomas Payne.

* * *

How John Wanamaker Began the Christian Life

To Mr. Charles Alexander, Mr. Wanamaker told this story of his conversion: A salesman asked me if I wouldn't go to his church. I was at a prayer meeting there one night, where there were perhaps two hundred persons. It was a quiet, old-fashioned meeting. A handsome old man of about seventy years got up and, in the gravest way, said that he was just waiting for God to take him; that he had lived his life; that God had been good to him; and it was all summed up in the statement that religion was a good thing to DIE by. I sat back, and I always had a great fashion of talking to myself. I said: "Well, old man, you can't touch me; you have lived your life; you haven't any sympathy with a big boy; it has passed over my heart!" Soon after, a young man got up. He was perhaps thirty-five, and he said: "You have heard an old man tell you that religion was good to die by. I want to tell you it is good to LIVE by. I have just begun the Christian life. Two years ago I was converted. I had just begun business, and I had had a prejudice against religion. They told me that a man had to have a face a yard long and could not smile or do anything that would make him happy. You see, I was deceived about that. I am a great deal happier since I became a Christian because it settled things. I am a better business man; a great load has rolled off my heart, and I can give myself more to my work!" I listened to him, and I said to myself: "There you are; you want to be a business man, and he tells you how you can be a better business man. He tells you that religion is good to live by. Another man tells you that religion is good to die by!" I said; "Suppose you were in court and heard two statements like that, would you believe them?" "Yes," I replied to myself. "Well," I said, "do you intend ever to be a Christian?" "Yes," "Well, if it's a good thing, why don't you be it right away?" I said: "Yes, I WILL!" I waited in the meeting until everybody went out except the janitor and the old minister, and as he came down the aisle, he met a country boy coming up, and I was the boy. I simply said to him: "I have settled it tonight to give my heart to God." And he reached out his hand and said: "God bless you, my son; you will never regret it!" I didn't wait to get some feeling. I accepted the FACT that I was a sinner, and that there was a Saviour for sinners, and I came to Him simply on the proposition that the gift of God is eternal life!—Selected.

* * *

A Dumb Believer

"Well, I never knew before that you were a Christian," said one man to another in a Michigan logging camp, "though we've been on the job together here for two years. When the sky pilot was here last winter and talked with me about my soul, I told him if so clean a chap as you could get along without religion I believed I could take a chance on it myself." *The silent Christian felt that he had been disloyal to Christ.*—*New Century Leader.*

* * *

The Saved Bolshevist

A little Bolshevist girl had accepted Christ at a camp conference. A friend asked her what she would do when she got back to her Bolshevist home in Manitoba. "I'm afraid there isn't anything that I can do. The people would kill me if I tried to tell them about Jesus," she replied. "There are many who will spend their eternity in hell unless you show them the way to Heaven," explained her friend. She squared her shoulders, and with a look of determination said, "Yes, I am going back to tell them, no matter what it costs."—Courtesy *Moody Monthly.*

His Lesson on Swearing

Some time ago a client came to my office, a Southern gentleman who has approximately six million dollars of funds in our investments. During the course of the conversation he used my Lord's name in a way I didn't like, and I stopped him. "Please, sir, that name you just used is the most precious name I know anything about. I love it more than anything in this world, and I don't like to hear that name used in the fashion you did: I am a Christian." What do you think he said? "So am I. I teach a Sunday school class down South". "Well," I said, "you would not have guessed it in a thousand years," and something inside said to me, "Are you going to lose that contract?" Just recently I had in my office—the Southern gentleman, this time in company with his wife. He said, "This is the man who gave me such a thrashing when I was up here." She turned to me and said, "I am glad you did, because he deserved it. He has been a different man since."—Erling C. Olsen, in *Moody Monthly.*

* * *

A Word by the Wayside

An engineer on the Northwestern Railway, who is a true Christian, says: "I was one day waiting on the side track for the express to go by, when a tramp stepped into the cab and asked for something to eat. I took out my dinner pail and gave him a piece of pie and a sandwich. He thanked me, and in doing it swore an awful oath, in which he used the Name of our Lord Jesus Christ. I said, 'Brother, do you know who you are talking about?' He replied, 'No, sir,' I said, 'You have been speaking about the best Friend I have. He has done everything for me, and I wish you would not speak His Name again until you know Him.'

"He slowly climbed down and went towards the back of the train, with the sandwich in one hand and the piece of pie in the other, but he did not eat. He walked slowly and kept looking back toward the engine. Finally he went between two cars and ate his lunch. He met one of the train crew, near the back of the train, and said to him: 'What kind of an engineer have you got?' The brakeman replied: 'We have a good engineer. Didn't he treat you well?' 'Yes,' replied the tramp, 'but he said something to me that took me back to when I was a little fellow and said my prayers at my mother's knee.' That tramp went slowly around the curve and out of sight, and probably I will never see him again. But I do not think he will use the Name of the Lord Jesus Christ again as he did."—Selected.

Denying Christ

A boy in Sunday school unmercifully denounced Peter as a coward for denying his Lord and said that he knew he would have been faithful. Several weeks later his teacher noticed that he was much depressed and in a private interview asked the reason. Then he told how he was present when some boys talked against Christians and the Bible in a mean and irreverent way and he had not said a word in reply. He felt that by his silence he had denied his Lord and was as bad as Peter. How many older people have been guilty of similar denials!—Selected.

* * *

For Silent Christians

At a meeting in a city of Nankin a Chinaman rose and began to cry for mercy with groans and tears. When at length he found utterance he prayed, "O God, forgive me; I have been a dummy Christian. When I was converted the devil came to me and said, 'There are preachers to do the preaching; you need not bother about it.' I listened to the devil's lie, and all those years I have been a dummy Christian, living in ease while souls have been lost."—Selected.

* * *

Spreading the Joyful News

There was living in a fair-sized village in Tinnevelly a man who was sorely crippled by ulcers on both legs and feet. Someone persuaded him to go to the "White Doctor," who lived sixty miles away. The missionary put him to bed and washed and dressed those poor feet with tender care, day after day, week after week. And each day the patient listened to the Gospel message. One morning the doctor read John 1:12: "As many as received him, to them gave he power to become the sons of God." "Stop, sahib," cried the healed cripple. "Is it possible for *any* man to become a son of God?" What this "believing" and "receiving" meant was carefully explained. After a little prayer together, the native sprang up, and with a face radiant with joy, cried, "*Now I'm a son of God.* I must hurry back to my village and spread this joyful news." A few weeks afterward the patient returned with two of the leading men of the village with him, to say that everyone in his village desired to become "sons of God," and that he had taught them *how* to do so from the holy Book. The missionary was astonished. "How could you do that?" he asked. "You cannot read!" "No," said he, "but there was a man in the village who could read. He read and I explained." Then he begged the doctor to come to the village and teach the people more, and then baptize them.—Abridged from *The Unknown God*, by One Who Loves Him.

* * *

A Safe Rule to Follow

"Talk to God about your neighbors, and talk to your neighbors about God."

* * *

Miss Havergal's Brave Testimony

Frances Ridley Havergal was a devoted Christian as well as an accomplished singer. She was a guest at an occasion where many distinguished people, including the King himself, were present. A famous Italian prima donna had been engaged to furnish entertainment for the brilliant audience, and after a number of wonderful renditions, Miss Havergal was asked if she would sing. She paused a moment in uncertainty, then stepped to the piano and made a most exquisite rendering of a difficult aria from one of Handel's oratorios. Then even before the applause ceased she began to sing to her own accompaniment the words of one of her most deeply spiritual poems, for which her pen had become so noted:

Oh, Saviour, precious Saviour,
  Whom yet unseen we love,
Oh, Name of might and favor,
  All other names above.

Among the first to congratulate her was the renowned Italian artist who said to her, "You have something I do not have, and I want it."—*The Presbyterian.*

The Best Doctoring

There is an American medical missionary in a foreign field who is more interested in the spiritual health of his patients than in their physical health, while at the same time he is greatly used as a physician and surgeon. Difficult, even baffling, physical cases are brought to his hospital, and, by keeping in touch with the latest medical and surgical research in America, he has been able to restore health in a wonderful way. But the fact in which he rejoices is, as he wrote in a letter home last year, "The more the patients come in, the more the Gospel goes out."—*Sunday School Times.*

* * *

Subpoenaed

God hasn't retained many of us as lawyers, but He has subpoenaed all of us as witnesses.—*Heart and Life.*

WORK

Send Sombeody Else

The laziest man in the village was actually running. His hat was off, and his coat was flying in the wind. On and on he sped, till, crash, he collided with the portly vicar, and picked himself out of the roadway. "Why, what on earth has made you run— and so fast, Sam?" asked the vicar. "Can't wait," gasped Sam, "I heard of some work." The vicar caught him by the arm, "And did you get the job?" he asked. "I don't know," replied the man, struggling. "I only just heard of it. I'm going to find out." "Well, good success to you, Sam," said the vicar, releasing his grasp. "What kind of work is it?" "Some washing for me wife." Many people are like Sam; they say, "Here am I, Lord; send somebody else."—*Gospel Herald.*

* * *

Lost Taste

A woman in Philadelphia used to employ occasionally an old Negress known as Aunt Cecelia. For some time she lost sight of her. Meeting the washerwoman one morning, she said: "Good morning, Aunt Cecelia. Why aren't you washing nowadays?" "It's dis way, Miss Anne. I'se been out o' work so long, dat now, when I could work, I finds I'se done lost my taste for it." This is evidently the attitude of many nominal members of the church. They have become so accustomed to doing nothing for Christ, beyond occupying their pew once a week, that they have no inclination to Christian activity, even when the opportunities are right before them.—Courtesy *Moody Monthly.*

* * *

When God Wants Work Done

God never goes to the lazy or the idle when He needs men for His service. When God wants a worker He calls a worker. When He has work to be done, He goes to those already at work. When God wants a good servant, He calls a busy man. Scripture and history attest this truth.

Moses was busy with his flocks at Horeb.

Gideon was busy threshing wheat by the wine press.

Saul was busy searching for his father's lost beasts.

Elisha was busy plowing with twelve yoke of oxen.

David was busy caring for his father's sheep.

Nehemiah was busy bearing the king's wine-cup.

Amos was busy following the flock.

Peter and Andrew were busy casting a net into the sea.

James and John were busy mending their nets.

Matthew was busy collecting customs.

William Carey was busy mending and making shoes.—*Watchman-Examiner.*

Helping

Sam and Joe were two colored laborers. They were sent to the basement of the factory to work. The superintendent, on his regular morning round of inspection, failed to find the men. After searching a while he discovered Sam fast asleep. Looking for Joe the superintendent found him loafing about in the back part of the basement. "What have you been doing, Joe?" "Why, mister," said Joe, "I'se been a-helpin' Sam." There are too many of us helping Sam. It is now 1,900 years since Christ died, and half of the race does not know anything about it as yet. Important, worthwhile news of the world is flashed around the globe within twenty-four hours, but, selah! The greatest news ever to reach the ear of mortal man is yet unknown to half the race.—*Gospel Herald.*

* * *

The Hindered Christ

The Lord Christ wanted a tongue one day,
To speak a word of cheer
To a soul that was weary and worn and sad,
And freighted with doubt and fear.
He asked me for mine, but 'twas busy quite
With my own affairs from morn till night.

The Lord Christ wanted two hands one day,
To do a loving deed.
He wanted two feet on an errand for Him
To run with welcome speed.
But I had need of my own that day.
To His gentle pleading, I said Him nay.

So all that day I used my tongue,
My hands and feet I chose.
I said some bitter angry words
That hurt one heart God knows.
My hands I used in useless play
And my willing feet went a crooked way.

And the dear Lord's work, was it left undone,
For the lack of a willing heart?
It is through men that He speaks to men
And each must do his part—
I hope He used another that day
But I wish I'd let Him have His way.
The Pilot.

* * *

Prayer Plus

It is recorded of D. L. Moody that, upon one of his journeys across the Atlantic there was a fire in the hold of the ship. The crew and some volunteers stood in line to pass buckets of water. A friend said to Moody, "Mr. Moody, let us go to the other end of the ship, and engage in prayer." The common-sense evangelist replied, "Not so, sir; we stand right here and pass buckets and pray hard all the time." How like Moody this was! He believed that prayer and work were the two hands of the one person: that they should never be separated.—*Christian Herald* (London).

* * *

Thought for the Day

"Fronting my task, these things I ask:
To be true this whole day through;
To be content with honest work,
Fearing only lest I shirk;
To see and know and do what's right;
To come, unsullied, home at night."
—Selected.

* * *

"If faith produce no works, I see
That faith is not a living tree.
Thus faith and works together grow;
No separate life they e'er can know;
They're soul and body, hand and heart;
What God hath joined, let no man part."
—Hannah More.

* * *

Too Easily Pleased

A Japanese boy came to the home of a minister in Los Angeles and applied for a position. Now it happened that the household was already well supplied with servants; so the minister's wife said, "I am sorry, but we really haven't enough work to keep another boy busy."

"Madam," said the Oriental politely, "I am sure that you have. You may not know what a little bit of work it takes to keep me employed." One does not have to go to Japan to find such people; they can be found in most churches.—*Record of Christian Work.*

* * *

We are not here to play, to dream, to drift,
We have hard work to do, and loads to lift;
Shun not the struggle, face it; 'tis God's gift,
Be strong!!

It matters not how deep entrenched the wrong,
How hard the battle goes, the day how long,
Faint not, fight on, tomorrow comes the song,
Be strong!!

* * *

At the End of the Report

"It was my privilege to meet on one occasion with a little society in a small town," said the leader of a young people's organization. "But it was a little society with a large spirit. They required written reports at each business meeting. At the end of each report this sentence was added, 'This work done for Jesus Christ.' If nothing had been done, the report was written, 'Nothing done for Jesus Christ.' The president told me that that little sentence made a profound impression, and its effects were visible and audible in greatly improved work."—*Earnest Worker.*

* * *

The Italian Immigrant's Gratitude

When Mario Izzo, an Italian immigrant, was put on relief in a western Pennsylvania town, he looked at his first weekly check, seized a broom, and went out to sweep the streets six hours a day, six days a week. He explained: "I think this is a wonderful country. I decide I will be an honest man with this country. So I start to sweep. My bread it tastes sweet, and I feel like an honest man, because I work." A lesson for *you?* and for *me?—Readers' Digest.*

* * *

Why Trouble God?

Dr. Adam Clarke, the great commentator, was a slow worker, and he could only produce his wealth of literary treasures by long and patient toil. He therefore made it his custom to rise early every morning. A young preacher, anxious to emulate the distinguished doctor, asked him one day how he managed it. "Do you pray about it?" he inquired. "No," the doctor quietly answered, "I get up." Mr. Moody used to tell how once he came upon a group of wealthy American Christians praying for the removal of a debt of five hundred dollars on their church building. "Gentlemen," said Mr. Moody in his incisive way. "I don't think if I were you, I should trouble the Lord in this matter."—*Light.*

* * *

Don't Be a Wheelbarrow!

There is a sign at the entrance of a great manufacturing plant that reads: "If you are like a wheelbarrow—going no farther than you are pushed—you need not apply for work here." The real beauty of Christian living lies in "the second mile." Jesus talked at length to His followers that they were to be known by the beauty of going a little farther, and, consistent with His own teaching, He took the road to Calvary. —*Young People's Weekly.*

* * *

You Can Win

No matter how hard,
Your problem may be,
And rugged the hill to climb,
You can win the day
If you plug away
And make good use of your time.

The man who despairs
Before a hard task
And slumps in an easy chair,
Has nothing to win,
When he weakly gives in,
But vain disappointment and care.

Be up and alert,
Get on with your job.
Don't dream of the things you will do;
Push on toward the goal
With heart, mind and soul,
And prove the true mettle in you.
—Grenville Kleiser.

* * *

"Every Christian should be a workman for God, but no one can be a workman for God until he is the workmanship of God."—Selected.

* * *

A Question of Ownership

A Canadian Sunday school superintendent felt that he was not receiving sufficient co-operation from the parents, teachers, and officers of the school. In order to have the individual responsibility better realized, he assembled the entire school, and started his talk by asking, very emphatically, "Whose Sunday school is this?" For a moment there was silence, then a tiny blue mitten was raised. Leaning down to its wee owner in a front seat, the young superintendent said, smilingly, "All right, Penelope, you tell us." The child raised her blue eyes and in so soft a tone that he had difficulty in hearing her, said, "It's Jesus' Sunday school." The unexpected reply inspired the entire membership to a new spirit of consecration, as leader and classes alike recognized that they were indeed co-workers with God for the building up of His Kingdom.—Adapted from *Sunday School Times.*

* * *

A Safe Motto

When Temple Hall, London, was built, the Masters of the Bench ordered a handsome clock to be placed there, with an appropriate motto on the face of it. For many days the skillful mechanic waited for the motto, until, becoming impatient, he made his way to the Benchers' Chambers, and pressed them for the needed words. One of the Masters, becoming angry, rose up and said to the mechanic: "Go about your business." The latter, thinking this was the order, placed the words on the face of the clock, and there they were allowed to remain. If Christian workers would have for their motto, "Go about your Father's business," what mighty wonders would be accomplished!—*Sunday School Times.*

* * *

Emerson said:

"The human race is divided into two classes—those who go ahead and do something, and those who sit still and inquire why it was done in that way instead of another."

* * *

A Japanese Lad's Secret

The greatest defeat I ever had in my life was to take second place in an oratorical contest in college; to bow to a Japanese lad who had been in this country but five years. When he landed at Ellis Island in New York, having come through England, he could not speak twenty-five words of English; and yet he stood up there the master of English oratory. Why? I can give you the secret; I learned it; I wanted to know. The lad rose every morning at five o'clock and with his open Bible before him he spent the next hour in reading it and in prayer. And on Friday mornings, he, along with his fellow Japanese students, rose at four o'clock and spent two hours in prayer and went fasting without their breakfast to their classes in order that they might know the meaning of discipline and prayer. That is the power of religion in the life of youth. But how many of our colleges or great universities of today are teaching, are encouraging that sort of thing? —From address of Elmer Ward Cole at Christian Action Week, Lake James.

Not Ashamed

In the stone works a young man was suddenly set to do a piece of carving. The man on the job had been taken ill, and the task had to be finished on time. The young man did not know what the stone was for, but he went at the work in his accustomed painstaking way. He chiseled out a stem here, a leaf there, and flowers above. The master workman approved the job, and the stone left the works. Some months passed. Then one day the young man was walking through the great and beautiful building that the city had just completed and opened. He came to the most prominent pillar, a handsome column crowned with a piece of lily work. "Why," he exclaimed, "that's my bit of work!" And taking off his cap, he gazed at it and said reverently, "Thank God, I did that job well!" When I overhead the young man's remark, and saw the light in his eyes, and he told me about it, I knew, if I had never known before, that work is a holy thing. Right wages and just treatment for workmen are proper adjuncts, but above and beyond them your bit of work is holy to you.—*The Christian Life.*

* * *

Our Part in the Harvest

A famous evangelist was on one occasion trying to point out to a group of miners the care and bounty with which God had endowed the earth. "Look at your own occupation," he said. "Isn't it wonderful how God's foresight has enabled us to get fuel and power from the earth?" "That's quite right, sir," replied one of the men, "but I wish He had put it nearer the top." Is not this the spirit of many people today? They realize the goodness of God, no doubt; but wish He did not ask them to do so much. God gave the Israelites manna, but did not throw it into their tents; they had to gather it. He sends us the harvest year by year, but we must reap it.—*Christian Herald.*

* * *

"Unfolded" Legs

Samuel Johnson paid a high, though unintended, compliment to John Wesley: "His conversation is good, but he is never at leisure. He always has to go at a certain hour. This is very disagreeable to a man who loves to fold his legs and have his talk out as I do." John Wesley's legs were "unfolded" most of his ninety years. He had felt his Master's passion for souls, and sought to save the lost.—*Free Churchman.*

WORLDLINESS

Purity Dearer than Life

In the forests of northern Europe and Asia a little animal called the ermine lives. He is mostly known among us by his snow-white fur, a thing than which there is nothing more beautiful on the fur markets of the world. In some countries the state robes of judges are lined with it, the white being emblematic of purity and honor. The ermine has a peculiar pride in his white fur coat. At all hazards he protects it against anything that would spoil it.

It is said that the fur hunters take cruel advantage of the ermine's care to keep his coat clean. They do not set a snare to catch him at some unwary moment, but instead find his home, a cleft in the rock or the hollow of a decaying tree, and daub the entrance and interior with filth. Then their dogs start the chase. Frightened, the ermine flees toward his home, his only place of refuge. He finds it daubed with uncleanness, and he will not spoil his pure white coat. Rather than go into the unclean place, he faces the yelping dogs and preserves the purity of his fur at the price of his life. It is better that he be stained by blood than spoiled by uncleanness.

The ermine is right—purity is dearer than life.—Walking With God.

* * *

Whose Christ?

Christians who countenance places of worldly amusement give the world a false conception of Christianity, for they indicate by their presence in these places that Jesus Christ can save but He cannot satisfy; that there has to be some addition of the world to make the Christian happy. I met a girl in the city of Liverpool who listened one evening as I spoke about complete separation from the world. She went home, but was very unhappy. She came back in desperation to tell me that if the theater and movies and worldly amusements went out of her life, she would have nothing to live for. I said, "God help you." "But," she said, "I belong to the Oxford Group Movement." "Well," I said, "what has that to do with it?" "We are told to have our quiet time in the morning," she answered, "and then we can take Jesus into all these places." "Well," I said, "you may take *your* Jesus into those places, but you cannot take the One I know." —Herbert Lockyer, in *An Instrument of Ten Strings.*

* * *

Better than Good Mixers

We often hear someone say, when speaking of his pastor, "He's such a good mixer!" Commenting on this statement, an evangelist said: "You don't need a mixer; you need a separator!"—Selected.

* * *

When Blistering One's Feet

I have read somewhere of a minister sitting on a hotel plaza at Saratoga one morning. He was greeted by a young girl who said to him: "Good morning, Doctor." "Good morning," he replied. "Are you very well this morning?" She answered, "Oh, I am so tired! I blistered my feet dancing last night. By the way, Doctor, what do you think about dancing?" Very gravely he answered, "You are a professing Christian, are you not? Did you ever blister your feet for God?" The young girl felt the question deeply, and turned away. A few days afterward she spoke to the minister again and said: "Doctor, I have scarcely slept since you asked me that question, and I want to tell you I have never blistered my feet for the Lord, but from this time on I will work for him to the best of my ability."—*Watchman-Examiner.*

* * *

Dancing Christians

A young person once came to the venerable Daniel Witt, of Virginia, with the question, "Is there any harm in dancing?" The gentle and tender old man replied, thoughtfully, "Just how much harm there may be in dancing I cannot say, but of this much I am sure, I have been a Baptist minister for over forty years and I have never yet seen a dancing Baptist that was of any account as a church member."—*The Illustrator.*

* * *

Farewell, Vain World

David Brainerd, under the date of April 25, 1742, wrote in his journal:

"Farewell, vain world, my soul can bid adieu;
Your Saviour taught me to abandon you.
Your charms may gratify a sensual mind,
But cannot please a soul for God designed.
Forbear to entice, cease then my soul to call;
'Tis fixed through grace—my God shall be my all.
While He thus lets me Heavenly glories view,
Your beauties fade; my heart's no room for you."

—*Gospel Herald.*

Wishful Wishing

How often we wish that we had the ability of another! A devoted missionary who was at home on furlough had been called to speak in the neighborhood in which he spent his boyhood days. After a very interesting service, a boyhood friend of his stepped up to him and said, "Robert, you have an experience which I do not have. You have a character which will stand anything that can come to you. Really, I'd give the world to have such an experience and character as you have."

The missionary paused a moment, then he said, "John, that's exactly what my experience cost me. It cost me the world. I had my choice of the two. The world, with its perplexities, has nothing lasting, but if we give up the world for the Cross, we are not really giving up very much, and yet it is the hardest thing for people to give up."

"I never thought of that, but it's true that one has to choose between the world and life eternal and it is only by having a daily walk with God as you have had, that perfects character. Tonight I, too, want to give up the world with all its pleasures and follow Christ."

We say, "I'd give the world"—but would we?—*Gospel Herald.*

* * *

The Two Clocks

Traversing one night a city street, I was startled by a sharp clanging above my head. On looking up, I found myself directly beneath the tower wherein a huge clock was striking the midnight hour. I took my watch from my pocket, and lo, the slender overlying hands were pointing exactly to the hour of twelve.

It scarcely seemed possible that that tiny piece of mechanism in my hand could keep time with the huge machinery that filled a whole room of the tower; but the proof was before me, and as I gazed at the two pairs of hands of such diverse proportions, I understood as never before that *the most insignificant human being needed only to be clean, in running order, and divinely regulated to keep time with Divinity itself—to be perfect even as the Father is perfect.—Northern Christian Advocate.*

Reason for Alarm

Thomas Guthrie used to say: **If you** find yourself loving any pleasure better than your prayers, any book better than the Bible, any house better than the house of God, any table better than the Lord's table, any persons better than Christ, any indulgence better than the hope of Heaven—take alarm.—Selected.

* * *

A Young Man's Question

A young man of twenty wrote to the question and answer column of a newspaper as follows: "I'm puzzled about life, and I wonder if you could help me? Am I different from everyone else of my age? Or do they wear false masks as I do? I go to parties and dances and act as if I were enjoying myself like everyone else I know. But I am not enjoying myself at all. I always feel that there is *something missing,* and I don't know what it is. . . . Behind the laughing and the fun I think I look at life just a bit more seriously than most I know. I see more in life than just having a good time. Do you think this wrong at twenty? In a few years will I see things differently? Or should I take off the false face now, and act the way I feel?"

This young man was asking someone what was the matter with him, but got no help. He was not asking the right One. The Word of God would have put him on the right track.—*Young People's Delight.*

* * *

A Guide

Anything that dims my vision of Christ or takes away my taste for Bible study or cramps my prayer life or makes Christian work difficult is wrong for me, and I must, as a Christian, turn away from it. This simple rule may help you find a safe path for your feet along life's road.—J. Wilbur Chapman.

* * *

Not Loss, But Gain

A worldly, Christless young man went to visit his aunt, a Christian lady who had always been kind to him. During the visit she took every oportunity to impress upon her nephew the need of Christ. "Oh," he replied one day in answer to a remark from her, "Christianity and religion are all very good no doubt, when one comes to a certain time in life; but it is not the thing for a young fellow 22 years of age. How could I give up the pleasures of the world and wear a long face? When one is old it may be all very well then." "Why George!" gently asked his aunt, "who asked you to give up the pleasures of the world? I am sure I never did. I only asked you to *accept* Christ's gospel." "Oh, is that it?" he replied; "I always thought I had to give up a lot. Well, if I become a Christian, I would not be as tight-laced as some folk I know—for instance, I would go in for many jolly things you do not." "Never mind that," answered his aunt; "accept Jesus first, and see about all that in the future." Shortly afterwards the young man did accept Christ, and when next he saw his aunt, as they returned to their former conversation he remarked: "Do you know, aunt, I find I have given up far more than I ever dreamed I should be willing to; and yet I don't count it a loss but positive gain."—*Gospel Herald.*

* * *

Ask the Police About Dancing

Even the "nice" dances are dangerous. The mid-semester "prom" of the Central High School in St. Paul for several years had been regarded by the local police as "a bad one." To improve the situation, the Hi-Y clubs at Central, made up of Y.M.C.A. members, were asked to sponsor the dance; but this year the affair was worse than usual. Two police women who attended reported that they were repeatedly insulted and even threatened with slugging. Policemen had to be called to keep order, and the Hi-Y clubs were temporarily suspended. It is often said that the private high school and college dances are in an altogether different class from public affairs and are quite unobjectionable. Ask the police in your city about that!—*Walther League Messenger.*

But pleasures are like poppies spread;
You seize the flower, its bloom is shed;
Or like the snowflake in the river,
A moment white, then melts forever;
Or like the Borealis race,
That flit ere you can point their place;
Vanishing amid the storm.

These words are highly descriptive of the vanishing pleasures of time; but as Haldor Lillenas so clearly points out, we are:

Not made that our souls in sin should rust
And God's purpose forever miss;
Not made to be buried in the dust
But to rise to the heights of bliss.

Made to commune with God Himself,
And with Him ever be;
Not made for the trifling things of time,
But to live for eternity.

—*Gospel Herald.*

* * *

A. C. Dixon's Experience

The late A. C. Dixon, well-known American preacher, at one time pastor of the Moody Church in Chicago, and later of the Metropolitan Tabernacle, London, England, in one of his addresses tells of having been drawn into one of these orders with the understanding that he was joining a mutual insurance company.

In describing the initiation, he said: "When I got inside and found presiding over the idiotic orgies, my deacon, one of the most dignified of the church, and found him putting me through that sort of proceeding,—and some of the prominent church-members with him, I felt like a fool, and I had half a conviction that they felt a little the same way."

"Before the first meeting was over," said Pastor Dixon, "the Chairman of the Annual Ball Committee made a report, and informed us that the tickets for the public ball were for distribution, and each of us were expected to distribute so many, and urge his friends to attend. 'Well, well,' I thought, 'I am in it; I never thought I would get into a thing like this.' "

"So I didn't have any more sense than just to get up and say, 'I am not in the habit of attending public balls, and I don't know how to sell tickets to public balls. I believe your public ball is an abomination unto Heaven, and I cannot advise any of the members of my church to go.'"

"I went home," said the preacher, "feeling a little twinge of conscience, and I confess I did not go to sleep quite as early as usual that night. I had gotten mixed up with unbelievers, uneqally yoked. I could not manage them; they had all the yoke on their side, and they were just carrying me headlong like a blind ox yoked in with them. I could not do a thing but just kick and follow, and I did that."

Next came an invitation to a progressive euchre party, and some time later to a stag party. Pastor Dixon now wrote to the lodge secretary: "My dear Sir,— I don't believe in your balls, and I don't believe in your progressive euchre parties; and as I cannot influence this concern for good, I offer my resignation."— *The Christian Cynosure.*

* * *

A Colored Preacher's Sermon

In preaching on the text, "Adam, where art thou?" a negro preacher said: "I make three divisions to dis tex. Fustly, in de fust place, ebery man got to be somewhar. Secondly: Some men is whar dey ought not to be. Third, dey dat is whar they ought not to be, is gwine to find demselves whar dey don't want to be."

The man who walks in the counsel of the ungodly is where he ought not to be. And he is destined to find himself where he doesn't want to be.—Robert Greene Lee.

* * *

Going "Anywhere"

"I think a Christian can go anywhere," said a young woman who was defending her continued attendance at some very doubtful places of amusement.

"Certainly she can," rejoined her friend; "but I am reminded of a little incident which happened last summer, when I went with a party of friends to explore a coal mine. One of the young women appeared dressed in a dainty white gown. When her friends remonstrated with her, she appealed to the old miner who was to act as guide of the party.

"Can't I wear a white dress down into the mine?" she asked petulantly.

"Yes'm," returned the old man, "there's nothin' to keep you from wearin' a white frock down there, but there'll be considerable to keep you from wearin' one back."

There is nothing to prevent the Christian wearing his white garments when he seeks the fellowship of that which is unclean, but there is a great deal to prevent him from wearing white garments afterwards. — *Sunlight for the Young.*

* * *

How Many Legs Has a Dog?

Kapitango Kusita, an evangelist overseer of the Dondi Church, Portuguese Africa, was discoursing on following the "white" path, and the "white" path only. It was night, and the crowd of natives sat around the camp fire. A native dog passed between the fire and the listeners.

"Look at that dog! How many legs has it?" asked the preacher.

"Four," came the surprised reply.

"Yes, four indeed," retorted Kapitango, "but have you ever seen the four legs of a dog trying to follow more than one path at a time? No, no! The four all go together, but yet people with only two legs try to follow two paths, and even more at one time: Christ and the world, God and mammon!"—*Record of Christian Work.*

* * *

What Keeps the Eyes Clean?

Some years ago I ministered in the mountains of Pennsylvania to the miners in the soft coal region. The members of the little church were all miners. Between four and five o'clock in the evening they would come home from the mines, and I wouldn't recognize the men I knew very well, for they were just as black as the mines where they had been working. Working sometimes in veins only three feet in height, bending all day in that coal dust, they came out black as the coal. But there were two spots on each miner's face just as clean as when he went in in the morning—his eyes. The tear-glands of the eyes had kept their eyes just as clean and bright and shining, midst all the dirt, as when they went in. God said that He will keep us as the apple of His eye, and He does; He keeps us clean. It is the blood, the blood of Christ.—From the published lesson-sermons of Pastor Edward Drew, Paterson, N. J.

WORRY

Worry and Physical Ailments

"His commandments are not grievous," and they were given "for our good always (I John 5:3; Deut. 6:24). The blessings of obedience are very far reaching. In a recent article in the Philadelphia *Inquirer* Dr. James W. Barton writes that men returning from the war area are suffering from various ailments not caused by wounds, but by "the constant worry about the war itself." He says that civilians are even more easily upset by emotional disturbances than soldiers, "because soldiers, generally speaking, have more calmness of spirit and control of the emotions. . . . It is known that about one-half of patients consulting a physician have no organic disease and in about one-fourth of the cases seen by a consultant the cause of the symptoms is this tenseness or awareness, together with worry, strain, and fatigue. . . . Prolonged shock or fear (which is really worry) can affect the workings of all the organs of the body." Now it is perfectly *natural* for both soldiers and civilians to worry in these days of global warfare. But the Christian has within him a *supernatural* life. He is exhorted to "be careful for nothing," and at the same time he is told how to be rid of his care: "By prayer and supplication with thanksgiving let your requests be made known unto God. And the peace of God, which passeth all understanding, shall keep your hearts and minds through Christ Jesus" (Phil. 4:6, 7). And when this command is obeyed, through the strength that God gives, it brings with it physical as well as spiritual blessings.—*Sunday School Times.*

* * *

God Always Watches

An old lady in England had stood the bombings with amazing grit. When asked the secret of her fortitude amidst such frightful danger, she replied: "Well, every night I say my prayers and then I remember 'ow the parson told us God is always watching, so I go to sleep. After all, there's no need for two of us to lie awake."—*The Christian Century.*

* * *

Spiritual Sabotage

"Sabot" is the French word for a wooden shoe. Sabotage, then, was the practice of throwing a wooden shoe into the machinery to stop the work. It has come to mean any attempt to hinder production or spoil a product.

There is a wooden shoe that Satan would cast into our souls to hinder us in accomplishing the plan of God; that "sabot" is worry, which casts a cloud between the soul and God. It paralyzes the spirit, sours the disposition and hinders Christian service. Jesus was aware of this when He bade us "take . . . no thought for the morrow" (Matt. 6:34). He was not encouraging indifference or laziness, but exhorting us to trust our Father. Watch out for wooden shoes! Down with spiritual saboteurs. — Selected.

Anticipating Trouble

I have lived a long life and seen lots of trouble, but most of it didn't happen. Jacob prepared for a trouble that didn't happen.—A church bulletin board.

* * *

Why Worry?

Much has been written about the unique prayers of Edward Taylor, better known as "Father Taylor," the sailor preacher of Boston. One Sunday before he was to sail for Europe, he was entreating the Lord to care well for his church during his absence. All at once he stopped and ejaculated: "What have I done? Distrusted the providence of Heaven! A God that gives a whale a ton of herring for breakfast, will He not care for my children?"—*Finest of the Wheat.*

* * *

Worry and Stomach Trouble

Dr. W. C. Alvarez, the stomach specialist at the Mayo clinic says that 80 per cent of the stomach disorders that come to them are not organic, but functional. Wrong mental and spiritual attitudes throw functional disturbances into digestion. Most of our ills are caused by worry and fear and it is my experience that faith is more important than food in the cure of stomach ulcers.

In order to keep your commission clean you must be free from worry and fear. Worry is not merely weakness; it is wickedness. It is atheism. It says God has abdicated and that we have to hold the world together by our worrying. The opposite happens. Worriers wreck their world as well as their lives. Worry is sin against God and ourselves. Cast it on Christ and His Cross; then you will live by cheer, rather than by fear.

Keep your commission clean by refusing to indulge in unnecessary hate and restraint.—Selected.

* * *

Letting God Govern

When Bulstrode Whitelock was embarking as Cromwell's envoy to Sweden in 1653, he was much disturbed in mind as he rested in Harwich on the preceding night, while he reflected on the distracted state of the nation. It happens that a confidential servant slept in an adjacent bed, who, finding that his master could not sleep, at length said, "Pray, sir, will you give me leave to ask you a question?"

"Certainly."

"Pray, sir, do you not think that God governed the world very well before you came into it?"

"Undoubtedly."

"And pray, sir, do you not think that He will govern it quite as well when you are gone out of it?"

"Certainly."

"Then, sir, pray excuse me, but do not you think you may trust Him to govern it quite as well as long as you live?"

To the question Whitelock had nothing to reply, but, turning about, soon fell fast asleep.

Christian, don't you think God can govern the circumstances and steps of your life as He did for the Prophets and Apostles of old? "Consider the lilies of the field, how they grow. They toil not, neither do they spin; and yet I saw unto you, that even Solomon in all his glory was not arrayed like one of these" (Mat. 6:28, 29).—*Sunday School Times.*

* * *

Responsible for One End Only

The man sitting beside the stove in the little telegraph office dropped his newspaper as the person who had just handed in a message departed. "That's one of them little places way up Northwest, isn't it?" he asked. When the operator had assented he continued: "Well, according to the papers they've been having a terrible snowstorm up there lately—roads all blocked and everything. More than likely the message will never reach the man it's intended for after you've sent it." The operator looked up impatiently. "I'm not running both ends of the line," he said. "I'm only responsible for this end. Probably there's someone at the other end who knows his business without my trying to carry his worries for him." How many of our worries come from trying to take care of both ends of the line—our own and God's!—*Sunday School Times.*

* * *

Nothin' to Worry 'Bout

A Negro washerwoman who had a very happy disposition was a constant source of surprise to her employer. She was never in the dumps. She never had any despondent spells, but was always rejoicing in the Lord. She was a very poor woman. She lived in two small rooms with almost no furniture or comforts of any kind, yet at the age of fifty-nine she was quite happy and contented. One evening her master said, "Jack [here name was Mrs. Jackson], what makes you so happy all the time? I never see you in the dumps. I never see you crying over anything. What is the secret of your constant joy?" Her reply was wonderful. We may all learn a lesson from it. She said: "I have no money to lose, so I never worry 'bout losing nothin'. What little furniture I has at home has all been given to the Lord, so if it gets stole or burned up, the Lord done burned up His own stuff. He never burned up nothin' of mine. And then I has a big, healthy body, and if I gets sick and dies, I'se going right to be with Jesus, so I never worry 'bout that. I'd just as soon that would come. So, you see, I haven't nothin' to worry 'bout, so I just sings."—*Bible Expositor and Illuminator.*

* * *

Worry, a Denial of Faith

Prayer is an acknowledgment of faith; worry is a denial of faith. Prayer is putting my hand in God's, trusting to His loving guidance; worry is withdrawing my hand, and denying His power to lead me. Prayer leads through the door of faith into the presence of God; worry leads through the door of anxiety into the darkness of loneliness and discouragement. If prayer rules the life victory results.—Selected.

The Everlasting Arms

One dark night a man slipped and rolled down a steep place. He stopped the descent by grasping a bush on the hillside, which left him dangling in the air. His attempt to climb up the hill was in vain. Below was darkness. He strained every muscle as he kept a tight grip on the bush. Finally, his strength was exhausted. In despair he let go and dropped—just six inches! Many of us worry and struggle with our nerves at high tension when all the time we only need to let go and drop into the "everlasting arms" just beneath us.—Courtesy *Moody Monthly.*

* * *

"Be Anxious About Nothing"

"Modern science has brought to light the fact that *worry will kill,* and determines, from recent discoveries, how worry kills. Scores of deaths, set down to other causes, are due to worry alone. Anxiety and care, the fretting and chafing of habitual worry, injure beyond repair certain cells of the brain, which being the nutritive center of the body, cause other organs to become gradually injured; and when some disease of these organs, or ailments arise, death finally ensues. Insidiously, worry creeps upon the brain in the form of a single, constant, never-lost idea; and as the dropping of water over a period of years will wear a groove in a stone, so worry, gradually, imperceptibly, but no less surely, destroys the brain cells that are, so to speak, the commanding officers of mental power, health, and motion.

Worry is an irritant, at certain points, producing little harm if it comes at intervals or irregularly. But against the iteration and reiteration of one idea of a disquieting sort the cells of the brain are not proof. It is as if the skull were laid bare, and the surface of the brain struck lightly with a hammer every few seconds, with mechanical precision, with never a sign of a let-up or the failure of a stroke. Just in this way does the annoying idea, the maddening thought that will not be done away with, strike or fall upon certain nerve cells, never ceasing, and week by week, diminishing the vitality of these delicate organisms, so minute that they can only be seen under the microscope."

Do not worry. Do not hurry. *"Let your moderation be known to all men."* —Arthur T. Pierson.

WORSHIP

Why Did They Go to Church?

Lyman Beecher Stowe, in "Saints, Sinners, and Beechers," tells of one occasion when Thomas K. Beecher substituted for his famous brother, Henry Ward Beecher, at Plymouth Church, Brooklyn. Many curiosity seekers came to see and hear Henry Ward Beecher. Upon Thomas K. Beecher's appearance in the pulpit the sightseers started for the doors. Thomas K. raised his hand for attention, and made this announcement: "All those who came here this morning to worship Henry Ward Beecher may now withdraw from the church; all who came to worship God may remain."—*Christian Beacon.*

* * *

An Inopportune Moment

The moment seemed inopportune for worship. So many things needed prompt attention. No home for his wife and children. No shed for the cattle. So much required to be done that called for thought, plan, arrangement, effort, toil. If ever there lived a man who could plead that distracting necessities excluded the worship of God, that man was Noah. But not so with Noah. All shall be yielded to Him who is above all. He who is first shall be the first. He who is best shall have the best. The earth's first building after the judgment shall be an altar for the worship of Jehovah. Noah's first care is to bless the care which has so cared for him. His first posture is the bended knee and uplifted knife.—*"Christ Is All."*

Wesley's Open-Air Meetings

John Wesley conducted an open-air service in a little village in Cornwall two hundred years ago, and said concerning the same: "I preached Christ our 'wisdom, and righteousness, and sanctification, and redemption.' I could not conclude till it was so dark that we could scarce see one another. And there was on all sides the deepest attention: none speaking, stirring, or scarce looking aside. Surely here, though in a temple not made with hands, was God worshiped in the beauty of holiness."—*Methodist Recorder*, London.

* * *

Sunrise in a Tourist Camp

In the summer of 1927 we were driving from Seattle to Boston. Coming down the Black Hills Highway in South Dakota, we stopped late one afternoon at an isolated tourist camp. No other campers had arrived. At dusk, however, to our surprise, five carloads of Sioux Indians drove in. We learned that they were on their way to a Christian convocation service. At 4:30 next morning I looked out of our tent, and there about two hundred feet away, motionless as a bronze statue, silhouetted against the pale glow of the coming dawn, was an aged Indian kneeling. His hands were clasped, his face was up-turned, and his whole attitude was one of adoration and worship. Filled with wonder and awe, I quietly wakened the others in our party. Then as we looked out over the camp, we saw that in the lifted doorway of every tent, other Indians were kneeling. Silently our heads, and our hearts, too, bowed with those of our brothers in Christ.—*Secret Place.*

When One Partner Died

A traveler called his companion's attention to a firm's peculiar name. It was "Head & Hart." The companion remarked: "Poor Hart has died and left Head alone." This often occurs in Christian life, worship, and service—all head and no heart.—*Sunday School Superintendent.*

* * *

Roosevelt's Retort

Dr. L. S. Bauman, of Long Beach, recently used the illustration that Roosevelt was a church-goer. It is said that on one gloomy Sunday morning during the World War, he walked three miles in order to attend worship. One of his neighbors, noticing this, said to him: "I can worship in the fields or anywhere else." "Yes," replied Mr. Roosevelt, "but no one will ever suspect you of it!"—*The King's Business.*

* * *

What Is Worship?

Dictionaries tell us that worship is the act of paying Divine homage to God. Though manifestly external in varied ways, it remains definitely an internal experience—a matter of the spirit. Little Mary played blithely in the sunshine, catching at something with her hands. Obviously, the child was experiencing great joy. Her observing mother discovered from her words and movements that little Mary was "catching sunbeams." She reveled in the golden flood, loved it, adored it. Right now, she essentially worshiped in the sunshine, but not God.

A little later Mother joined her little girl. Comradely they called each other's attention to scenes burnished bright in the sunshine. Mother was careful to mention its warmth and beauty. "God is in the sunshine," she said reverently. "God—warming the world, making trees grow, birds sing, flowers bloom, and little girls healthy and happy. Thank You, God, for the good sunshine!"

That was all. Mother and child went their own way. Later in the afternoon, standing beside a bed of bright verbenas glowing in the sun, little Mary was heard to say, "Thank You, God, for the sunshine!" Mother smiled reverently. She knew that in the present sunshine her little girl had found and loved an ever-present God. Now the child had worshiped, not merely flowers and sunshine, but the Heavenly Father as the good Giver of them.

Every day is full of worship opportunities for the child. Now he is swept away by the beauty of a bird song; a half hour later he may stand amazed before a simple flower. He may reverently plant a seed which, in God's good ground, warmed by His sunshine, watered by His rain, attended to by the child himself leads through a series of experiences producing worshipful attitudes and bringing God into the life of the child. Even the awe of the storm can reveal the Heavenly Father.

To worship best, a child needs a reverent home environment. Father and mother, representing the governing power which the child knows, ought to make this seem good and in harmony with a higher Power to which they look and which they try to express. They should forget form and give attention to sincere experience. The child must find and interpret God through the things he knows and loves best.

A little song in the evening, a glittering star in the night, a word of prayer at bedtime, simple grace before meals, a deep appreciation for one another—such things as these can produce deep reverence in the child and associate God beautifully with his life. They should be an integral part of the home atmosphere and set up to best bless the children.

Worship is adoration, praise, respect, love coming from within and manifesting itself in numerous ways. We are not concerned greatly with outward demonstrations. Let them be what they will. The internal experience, the spontaneous Heavenward flight of the soul—that is what counts. It cannot happen amid irreverence or superficial routine in any home. Give the child a wholesome environment to grow in—and to find his God. — Herbert Wendell Austin, in *The Lighted Pathway.*

YOUTH

A Shabby Thing—Yet Not Hopeless

In my university days at Edinburgh there was a young medical student named Macfarlane. He was one of our finest athletes, and everybody liked him. One day he was stricken with typhoid, which proved fatal. Macfarlane in his days of boisterous health had neglected his Lord, and when one of his friends, visiting him in his sickness, led his thoughts to the Saviour, he turned and said: "But wouldn't it be a shabby thing to turn to Christ now?" "Yes," replied his friend, "it will be a shabby thing, but it will be shabbier not to turn to Him at all!" And I believe that poor Macfarlane turned his shame-filled soul to the Lord.

But it *is* shabby to offer our Lord the mere dregs of life's cup. It is shabby to offer Him the mere hull of the boat when the storms of passion have carried its serviceableness away.

Let me offer Him my best, my finest equipment, my youth! Let me offer Him the best, and give Him the helm when I am just setting sail and life abounds in golden promise! "Remember now thy Creator in the days of thy youth."—J. H. Jowett.

* * *

Give thou thy youth to God,
With all its budding love:
Send up thy opening heart to Him,
Fix it on One above.

Take thou the side of God,
In things or great or small,
So shall He ever take thy side,
And bear thee safe through all.

Quail not before the bad,
Be brave for truth and right,
Fear God alone, and ever walk
As in His holy sight.

Rev. Horatius Bonar.

* * *

Grown Cold

I once saw, lying side by side in a great workshop, two heads made of metal. The one was perfect,—all the features of a manly, noble face came out clear and distinct in their lines of strength and beauty; in the other scarcely a single feature could be recognized,—it was all marred and spoiled. "The metal had been allowed to grow a little too cool, sir," said the man who was showing it to me. I could not help thinking how true that was of many a form more precious than the metal. Many a young soul that might be stamped with the image and superscription of the King while it is warm with the love and glow of early youth, is allowed to grow too cold, and the image is marred.—*Sunday School Times.*

* * *

The Ideal Boy

The question was recently asked of young women students at the Moody Bible Institute, "What do you look for in a Christian young man?" Replied one of the first-term girls:

"I like to believe that the age of chivalry is not dead—that Christian mothers are raising their sons to love, honor and respect women.

"I'm glad I'm a Christian and can look forward to God's choice for my mate; and while I've never submitted this order to my Lord, here is my idea of the ideal boy:

"He loves the Lord with his whole heart, and is a servant of mankind for Jesus' sake. He is quiet and serious by nature, but possessed of a gratifying sense of humor. Nobility of character and gentleness of spirit mark him as a man of God.

"He is an aggressive person, not slothful in business; fervent in spirit, serving the Lord.

"Because he loves his fellow men he is always friendly and courteous. His manners, above reproach. His conversation, such as becomes a son of the King. He is patient, kind, and forgiving, willing to acknowledge his own shortcomings rather than to judge another's.

"I'll be a busy helpmate—when I find him—for I'll be everlastingly patching his clothes, especially the knees of his trousers!"—Courtesy *Moody Monthly.*

* * *

Give me, oh! give me back the days of my youth,
Poor, yet how rich!—my glad inheritance,
The inextinguishable love of truth,
While life's realities were all romance,
Give me, oh! give youth's passions unconfined,
The rush of joy that felt almost like pain,
Its hate, its love, its own tumultous pain,
Give me my youth again!
—Goethe.

* * *

The world winks at the sins of young men; and yet they are none so little after all: the bones of our youthful feastings at Satan's table will stick painfully in our throats when we are old men. He who presumes upon his youth is poisoning his old age. How large a tear may wet this page as some of us reflect upon the past! (Spurgeon). "O Lord, remember not my sins, but remember me!"—Selected.

* * *

Sunday Schools Instead of Jails

For five years Mayor E. H. Couch, of Guntersville, Alabama, has been sending minor offenders of all ages to Sunday School instead of levying fines or jail sentences. Only recently did the plan become known. Then it was found that not one over 100 so sentenced reappeared before Mayor Couch charged with any crime. About half of the culprits became regular attendants at Sunday School after their sentences expired. Most of them, before their sentences, had never been to Sunday School. When the plan was divulged, Mayor Couch made the following statement:

"I thought it was better to send offenders to a place where they would be in company with our best citizens rather than to the one place where in Guntersville they are sure to be thrown with our worst. For success of the idea I did not make public that they were being made to go to Sunday School. Then they would have been embarrassed."—*The Watchman-Examiner.*

* * *

The Ideal Girl

When young men were asked, "What do you look for in a Christian young woman?" one student replied:

"Assembling the following thoughts was not an easy job, but I believe that they cover almost everything anyway. I look for a girl who:

"1. Seeks God's will first.

"2. Has associates that I like.

"3. Is liked by my associates.

"4. Will give me the benefit of a doubt.

"5. Is neat and orderly in her appearance as well as in her work.

"6. Is practical.

"7. Is thoughtful about small things.

"8. Is a deep thinker, not just a silly talker.

"9. Manages her spare time wisely, such as in athletics.

"10. Is tactful.

"11. Is not agreeable at the expense of righteousness."

Wrote another boy student: "The worst predicament possible for me would be an unhappy marriage. Therefore, take away the nagging neurotic, the giggling no-account, the gossiping gadabout, the spendthrift socialite, or the painted plutocrat—a mixture of artificialities which leave me in doubt as to where the humbug ends and the woman begins.

"Give me a strong, sound, sociable, serious, sensible servant of our Saviour, burdened for souls and selected for the same field of service as I.

"Give me a champion cook, a child-cherishing, cheerful, chary, charming, capable, compassionate companion, and I'm certain of continual contentment." —*The Moody Student.*